COMMERCIAL BANK FINANCIAL MANAGEMENT

In the Financial Services Industry

THIRD EDITION

Joseph F. Sinkey, Jr.

Professor Of Finance and
The Georgia Bankers Association Chair of Banking
The University of Georgia

MACMILLAN PUBLISHING COMPANY

New York

COLLIER MACMILLAN PUBLISHERS

London

Copyright © 1989, Macmillan Publishing Company, a division of Macmillan, Inc.

Printed in the United States of America

Macmillan Publishing Company
866 Third Avenue, New York, New York 10022

Collier Macmillan Canada, Inc.

Library of Congress Cataloging in Publication Data

Sinkey, Joseph F.
     Commercial bank financial management in the financial service
  industry/Joseph F. Sinkey, Jr. -- 3rd ed.
        p.   cm.
     Includes bibliographies and indexes.
     ISBN 0-02-410591-0
     1. Bank management.   I. Title.
  HG1615.S57 1989
  332.1'2'068--dc19   88-28666
                                                 CIP

Printing: 1 2 3 4 5 6 7 8   Year: 9 0 1 2 3 4 5 6 7 8

This book is dedicated to the memory of my father
Joseph Francis Sinkey, Sr.
June 4, 1915—June 20, 1982 (Father's Day)

About the Author

Joseph F. Sinkey, Jr. is Professor of Banking and Finance and holds the Georgia Bankers Association Chair of Banking, College of Business Administration, The University of Georgia, Athens, Georgia. He received his Ph.D. in economics from Boston College in 1971 and his B.A. in economics from St. Vincent College, Latrobe, Pennsylvania in 1966. From 1971 to 1976, he was a financial economist with the Division of Research of the Federal Deposit Insurance Corporation, Washington, D.C. He joined the faculty of the University of Georgia in 1976 as an Associate professor and was promoted to Full Professor in 1983. In 1985, he received the GBA Chair.

Professor Sinkey has distinguished himself as a teacher, author, and researcher. He was recognized for superior teaching at The University of Georgia Honors Day in 1984 and 1985 and by the Georgia Finance Club in 1984. He is the author of five books: *Commercial Bank Financial Management*, published in 1983, 1986, 1989; *Application of Classification Techniques in Business, Banking, and Finance*, a coauthored research book published by JAI Press, Inc. in 1981; and *Problem and Failed Institutions in the Commercial Banking Industry*, a research book published by JAI Press, Inc. in 1979. Professor Sinkey has written numerous articles, chapters, and book reviews for various banking and finance publications. He is the Book Review Editor for the *Journal of Banking and Finance*, an Associate Editor of the *Journal of Financial Research*, and an ad hoc reviewer for major banking and finance journals.

In addition to his teaching and research duties, Professor Sinkey has served as a consultant to industry and government, testified before the United States Senate, and been an expert witness in cases involving banking and financial matters. Professor Sinkey teaches or has taught at various banking schools across the country including the School for Bank Administration, The Michigan Graduate School of Bank Management, The Management School of Bank Marketing, The School for Executive Development, and the Georgia Banking School.

Professor Sinkey has been married to Joanne M. Forsyth since 1970, and they have two daughters Alison, 14, and Jessica, 11. His nonacademic interests include golf, tennis, duplicate bridge, and long-distance running. A hole-in-one in 1986 and a completed marathon (26 miles 385 yards) in 1978 mark his accomplishments in these areas.

Preface

This book deals with the financial management of commercial banks in the rapidly changing financial-services industry. It describes the theory of commercial banking from a finance perspective and applies principles of financial management to banking. This approach is crucial today because of the dramatic changes occurring in the financial-services industry. The driving forces of change are captured by the acronym TRICK, which stands for

T = Technology,
R = Reregulation,
I = Interest-rate risk,
C = Customers (competition for), and
K = Kapital adequacy (with the German spelling of capital).

To be successful, bank managers must be able to respond rationally to these changes. Rules of thumb like the "3-6-3 rule" (i.e., money in at 3%, out at 6%, and be on the golf course by 3 p.m.) do not apply in today's dynamic environment. Although experience is great for handling routine problems, the theory of financial management provides the mechanism for understanding and coping with change.

Throughout this book, the process of financial innovation is described by the following model of change:

TRICK + Rational self-interest = Financial innovation.

Think of rational self-interest as driving managers to go after profitable opportunities. The combination of TRICK plus rational self-interest generates financial innovation. Understanding this process helps bank managers respond to change, and perhaps even to anticipate it.

Are commercial banks special or different from other business firms? To be a player in the financial-services industry, a company needs a different mix of assets compared to a nonfinancial corporation. Banks have very few real assets such as factories and machinery. Offices, furniture, computers, and software programs are the "hard" assets of banking. In contrast, banks use lots of intangible assets such as reputational capital, technical expertise, customer relationships, market presence, trade names, and deposit-insurance guarantees.

Banks use their real and intangible assets to produce financial products and services such as loans and checking accounts, items which appear on a bank's balance sheet. In addition, they produce items that do not appear on their balance sheets (e.g., loan commitments, letters of credit, and interest-rate swaps) that are known as off-balance-sheet activities. These activities generate "contingent claims" on a bank's balance sheet. The interest and fees paid for these products and services, whether on or off the balance sheet, are the "sales" of banking. Like any other business, banks expect to make a profit by having sales exceed costs. In addition, since business success is usually judged by value, banks strive to maximize their equity or net asset values by undertaking only positive net-present-value projects. Unlike most other businesses, however, banks are heavily regulated and have access to deposit insurance and the discount window. If anything makes banks special, regulation and deposit insurance do.

In the jargon of banking, the investment and financing decisions of financial firms are known as asset- and liability-management decisions. The coordinated management of these decisions is known as asset-liability management. Although bank dividend and capital decisions require no special terminology, they take on added significance because of regulatory pressure on banks to maintain adequate capital. This book focuses on how banks should make these decisions and the environment in which they make them.

Major Changes in the Third Edition

Although the size of the third edition is about the same as the second edition, the content and structure are substantially different. The 21 chapters and three cases of the second edition have been rearranged into 26 chapters in the third edition. The last chapter is unique in that it provides both an overview and summary of the book. Students should read it at the beginning and end of the course. Some of the new topics, issues, and questions addressed in the third edition include

1. The issue of bank specialness (or the lack of it) in Chapter 1.
2. A nontechnical discussion of the fundamentals of financial management in Chapter 3.
3. New material on banking and finance theory and models of the banking firms in Chapter 4, which is an expanded version of a similar chapter from the first edition but one that was dropped from the second edition.
4. Expanded emphasis on the role of financial innovation, especially in the five chapters in Part III but also throughout the book.
5. A new chapter, Chapter 11, on analysis of bank costs.
6. The management of bank portfolio risks brought together in the eight chapters of Part V.
7. Greater emphasis on futures, options, and swaps as tools for managing interest-rate risk and discussion of microhedges and macrohedges in Chapter 17.
8. Coverage of the management of credit risk in three chapters rather than two, including analysis of leveraged buyouts or LBOs.
9. A new chapter, Chapter 21, on the management of bank off-balance-sheet activities and securitization.
10. Discussion of risk-based capital requirements and a comparison of such requirements with a model for variable-rate deposit insurance in Chapter 22.
11. Greater emphasis on the process of market valuation for bank stocks in Chapter 23 and throughout the book.
12. Expanded coverage of the international debt crisis in Chapter 24 and introduction of the concepts of restructuring and corporate control in conjunction with the merger process described in Chapter 25.

Without sacrificing rigor, I have attempted to make the third edition more readable by reducing the amount of technical material and by trying to better control my penchant for using and creating acronyms. For those acronyms that remain, a glossary is provided at the end of the book. In addition, key acronyms are presented at the beginning of each chapter to guide the reader. Other pedagogical improvements include a list of key words and topics and a "matching" quiz at the end of each chapter. End-of-chapter questions and problems have been updated or revised in many cases. As in the previous two editions, both author and subject indices are provided and extensive references follow each chapter. The appendix to Chapter 2 contains a comprehensive list of various sources of banking information ranging from academic journals to bank computer simulations. The *Instructor's Manual* that accompanies this book has answers to all of the end-of-chapter quizzes, questions, and problems and a comprehensive test bank of objective questions.

This book is designed for both academic and practitioner markets and for anyone interested in the financial management of commercial banks in the financial-services industry. As a college textbook, upper undergraduates and graduate students are the intended audiences. In addition to bank management courses, the book can be used in courses dealing with the management of financial institutions.

Auxiliary Teaching Materials

In addition to the *Instructor's Manual and Test Bank* available with this text, Macmillan has a case book and a software package designed for use in banking courses. *Cases in Bank Management* by Benton E. Gup and Charles Meiburg is a book of 30 cases (plus a solutions manual). The software package developed by David Durst and Donald Conner is called *Bank Financial Decision Analysis*. It works in conjunction with LOTUS® 1-2-3® and has a book to go with the diskettes.*

Acknowledgments

Since I started teaching commercial banking at The University of Georgia in 1977, I recognized and thought about the need for a banking textbook based on the theory of finance. This vision was realized with the first edition of *Commercial Bank Financial Management*. The second and now the third edition of the book have kept that vision a reality.

For a person with a family, writing a book and revising it twice means fewer hours to spend with loved ones. I thank Joanne, my wife, and Alison and Jessica, my daughters, for their love, patience, encouragement, and understanding.

At The University of Georgia, I thank Albert W. Niemi, Dean of the College of Business Administration, and James A. Verbrugge, Head of the Department of Banking and Finance, for providing an environment conducive for research and writing. Elaine Dunbar was helpful in the preparation of the manuscript. John E. Earle and Joanne Sinkey provided valuable proofreading assistance. Last but certainly not least, I thank my support group of colleagues in the Department of Banking and Finance: Robert R. Dince (retired), David W. Blackwell, Mitchell C. Collins, Mary Dehner, and James J. Musumeci.

With Macmillan, various people (some no longer with the company) have contributed to this project. On the third edition, I have enjoyed working with Kenneth MacLeod, the college editor, and John Travis, the production supervisor, and thank them for their hard work and cooperation.

---

*Lotus and 1-2-3 are registered trademarks of Lotus Development Corporation.

Outside reviewers who provided valuable comments and suggestions on the manuscript for the third edition were:

Professor Theordore A. Andersen	*UCLA*
Professor James C. Baker	*Kent State University*
Professor Robert G. Beaves	*University of Iowa*
Professor Randall S. Billingsley	*Virginia Polytechnic Institute and State University*
Professor Charles W. Haley	*University of Washington*
Professor Gerald Hanweck	*George Mason University*
Professor James B. Kehr	*Miami University of Ohio*
Professor Samuel Penkar	*University of Houston*
Professor G. K. Rakes	*Ohio University*
Professor Alan K. Severn	*Wayne State University*

I thank you for taking the time to read and comment on the manuscript. Although the timing of some reviews was such that not all your suggestions could be included in the text, I sincerely appreciate your efforts.

Over the eight years that this book has evolved numerous people have contributed to its development. In this regard special thanks to (listed alphabetically) Harry Blythe, Lal Chugh, J. Kimball Dietrich, Adriani Fitzsimmons, Charles Haley, Fred Hays, Jimmy Hilliard, Paul Horvitz, Edward Kane, James Kehr, Morgan Lynge, William Marshall, Charles Maxwell, George McKinney, Hugh McLaughlin, James Miles, Verlyn Richards, Robert Rogowski, James Rosenfeld, Robert Schweitzer, James Seifert, Stephen Smith, Jack Verschuur, and Gary Wood.

If I have inadvertently omitted anyone from the acknowledgments, I apologize in advance.

Joseph F. Sinkey, Jr.
Athens, Georgia

Contents

CHAPTER 4

Banking and Finance Theory and Models of the Banking Firm   72

PART III
FINANCIAL INNOVATION AND THE ENVIRONMENT OF THE FINANCIAL-SERVICES INDUSTRY

CHAPTER 5

Financial Innovation and the Institutions, Markets, and Instruments of the Financial-Services Industry   97

CHAPTER 7
The Theory, Objectives, and Agencies of Bank Regulation   152

PART IV
THE BIG PICTURE: PERFORMANCE AND COST ANALYSES, STRATEGIC PLANNING, AND ASSET-LIABILITY MANAGEMENT

CHAPTER 10

The Return-on-Equity Model: Performance and Decomposition Analysis   263

CHAPTER 11

Bank Costs: Functions, Economies, Controls, and Analysis   308

CHAPTER 12

Bank Stragetic Planning in the Financial-Services Industry   328

CHAPTER 13
Asset-Liability Management (ALM)   360

PART V
MANAGEMENT OF BANK PORTFOLIO RISKS: LIQUIDITY, INTEREST RATE, CREDIT, AND OFF BALANCE SHEET

CHAPTER 14
An Overview of Bank Risk Management   391

CHAPTER 15
Management of Liquidity Risk: Stored Liquidity Versus Liability Management   412

CHAPTER 18

Management of Credit Risk I: Concepts, Models, and Credit Analysis   488

PART VI
BANK CAPITAL STRUCTURE, MARKET VALUATION, AND FINANCING ISSUES

CHAPTER 22
Bank Capital Structure: Theory and Regulation   603

CHAPTER 25

**Bank Mergers, Restructuring, and Corporate Control in the
    Financial-Services Industry   701**

PART VIII
EPILOGUE

CHAPTER 26
**Overview and Summary of Commercial Bank Financial Management in the
Financial-Services Industry   729**

PART I

INTRODUCTION TO BANKING AND THE FINANCIAL-SERVICES INDUSTRY

One of the major themes of this book is that banks operate in the financial-services industry and not in the more narrowly defined banking industry. The ongoing changes in the financial-services industry with respect to technology, reregulation, interest-rate risk, competition for customers, and capital adequacy guarantee that this dynamic process is not merely a cosmetic one but one of substance. Commercial banks were once big fish in a little pond. Today, they are smaller fish in a much bigger pond—the financial-services industry. Nevertheless, this book contends that commercial banks will reign as the kingpins of the financial-services industry, although their dominion will continue to shrink. In adapting to this new role, commercial banks are evolving into financial-services firms and vice versa. Banks that don't evolve probably won't be around for long. As Martin Mayer has written in *The Money Bazaars: Understanding the Banking Revolution Around Us,* "The bank is dead...long live the financial-services institution."

This part of the book introduces you to banking and the financial-services industry. In Chapter 1, the focus is on the environment of the financial-services industry and the issues facing banks in the industry. A model of change to highlight and explain the issues is presented. In addition, the major players in the worldwide financial-services industry are shown. In Chapter 2, we turn from the industry to look at the firm with emphasis on the banks of banking and alternative ways of viewing a bank. These concepts are related to the business and regulatory spectrums of the financial-services industry and a market strategy necessary for surviving in this dynamic environment.

CHAPTER 1

Banking in the Financial-Services Industry

ACRONYM GUIDE TO KEY TERMS AND CONCEPTS

FSF = financial-services firm
FSI = financial-services industry
DIDMCA = Depository Institutions Deregulation and
    Monetary Control Act of 1980
TRICK = Technology, Keregulation, Interest-rate risk,
    Customers, and Kapital adequacy

INTRODUCTION

Consider the following exchange.

Regulator: "Banks are special."

Banker: "How long can we afford to be special?"

Specialness, which is largely a Federal Reserve doctrine, is a line of thinking that says (commercial) banks play a unique (special) role in the economy and, therefore, they require extraordinary (special) regulatory treatment. Proponents of specialness and profit-motivated bankers, among others, are at odds on this issue.[1]

Careful thinking and analysis require objective investigators to consider both sides of an issue or argument. Since finance can be viewed as a way of thinking, its principles can be applied to the debate over the specialness issue. For example, looking at specialness from a risk-return perspective, clearly bankers, among other things, are concerned about return. Moreover, since regulators have a "safety-and-soundness" mandate (from Congress), they focus upon attempting to control bank risk exposure, among other objectives. Such single-mindedness, which of course is an oversimplification, serves to highlight the conflict between bankers and regulators regarding the issue of specialness. Finance theory and the art of political compromise suggest that the truth of the matter lies somewhere between the two extremes.

---

[1] See Corrigan [1982 and 1987] for the regulator's point of view and Aspinwall [1983], Barnard [1987], and Kane [1987] for the opposing arguments.

The Financial-Services Industry and the Financial-Services Firm

This chapter introduces you to two key concepts: (1) the financial-services industry (FSI) and (2) the financial-services firm (FSF). Beginning with the latter, the financial-services firm is a *conceptual* device to describe a business that supplies financial products and services. General categories of these products and services include transaction accounts (e.g., checking accounts), portfolio services (e.g., loans and deposits), insurance, investment banking (e.g., securities underwriting and broker/dealer transactions) fiduciary services (trust and estate management), financial planning, and information and data processing. Although commercial banks, which are the focus of this book, do not supply all of these products and services, they would like to supply them in the future. Analysis of the financial management of these activities is one of the tasks of this book.

The financial-services industry can be viewed as the aggregation of all firms that supply financial services and products. As such, the FSI is the amalgamation of such traditional and segmented industries as banking, thrift, securities, insurance, real estate, credit union, and finance. In addition, the FSI includes nonfinancial corporations such as General Motors, Ford Motor Co., Sears, and J. C. Penney that are engaged in the production and delivery of financial services and products.

We begin our study of banking in the FSI by presenting the Federal Reserve's position on specialness. By elaborating on the answer to the question about banks' specialness, you will better understand what a bank is and the changes taking place in the FSI. These changes are generating a fusion of previously segmented industries and markets.

THE FED'S POSITION: BANKS ARE SPECIAL

The Fed's view of banks' role in the FSI rests on the premise that commercial banks are special; see Corrigan [1982 and 1987]. This premise focuses on the interaction of three functions banks perform.

First, banks offer transaction accounts or services (e.g., checking accounts, automatic-transfer accounts, market-investment accounts, telephone bill paying, and wire transfers). These accounts or services are valuable to economic units (households, business firms, and governments) because they serve as (or facilitate) a means of payment or medium of exchange. Transaction services are distinguished from other financial services by their liquidity (i.e., by their cash or near-cash property). In the process of offering such services, banks operate or administer the nation's payments system. Specifically, they handle the clearing and settlement of financial claims among FSFs using such devices as checks or telephonic and electronic messages. Clearings are simply transfers of financial information, whereas settlements refer to the balancing of the particular accounts. The safety and reliability of any country's payments system is crucial to the smooth operation of its economy and financial system.

The second point in the Fed's specialness argument is that banks are the major source of backup liquidity for all economic units. Specifically, banks make loans and provide lines of credit to consumers, governments, and both financial and nonfinancial corporations. The process of allocating credit and providing reserve sources of funds affects the financial structures and spending-savings decisions of all economic units. During periods of economic prosperity, the credit expansion process serves to fuel real economic growth, or, if the process gets out of control, to fan the fires of inflation. However, during periods of economic hardships, financial stress, or credit restraint, the reserve or backup liquidity role becomes important. In this regard, banks are considered to be lenders of next-to-last resort. The operation of an efficient and equitable financial system requires lenders to allocate credit impartially and to provide reserve sources of funding during periods of financial stress.

The third and final point in the Fed's specialness doctrine is that banks are the focal or pivotal institutions in the transmission of monetary policy. The basic weapon of monetary policy is open-market operations (i.e., the buying and selling of government securities). These transactions put funds into the financial system when the Fed buys securities and takes them out of the system when the Fed sells securities. Buying is expansionary; selling is contractionary. Since these operations begin with dealers in government securities, who mainly but not exclusively are big New York City commercial banks, banks are seen as the key institutions in the transmission of monetary policy. The secondary weapons of monetary policy are reserve requirements and "discount-window" borrowing. The discount window is a vehicle whereby those FSFs subject to Federal reserve requirements may obtain funds for seasonal, temporary, or emergency needs. Providing emergency liquidity reflects the central bank's or Fed's role as *the* lender of last resort.

To summarize, the Federal Reserve's argument for specialness is based upon the *interaction* of three banking functions: (1) the provision of transactions services and the corresponding administration of the payments system, (2) the role as administrators of the credit decision-making process and providers of backup liquidity to the economy, and (3) the position as transmitters of monetary policy to the economy. Although the Fed acknowledges that banks are not the only FSFs to perform these functions, it argues that the interplay of the three together justifies the public policy of a safety net (in the form of deposit insurance and access to a lender of last resort) to support banks. In other words, banks have the benefit of a safety net because of the special functions they perform, and not vice versa. The specialness argument also leads to the position that the deposit-taking franchise must be kept competitively strong. To the Fed, keeping something strong usually means protecting and restricting it. However, since nonbank FSFs have made substantial inroads on the banking franchise, the Fed has had to deal with the reality of the financial marketplace, which means that it has had to balance expanded powers for banks with protecting the banking franchise.

THE OPPOSING VIEW: BANKS ARE NOT SPECIAL

The primary (published) spokesperson for the Fed's specialness doctrine has been Gerald Corrigan, President of the Federal Reserve Bank of New York. Next to being Chairman of the Board of Governors of the Federal Reserve System, the President of the New York Fed is the second most powerful position in the Federal Reserve System. In this section, we contrast Corrigan's view with those of an academic (Professor Edward J. Kane of The Ohio State University), a bank economist (Dr. Richard C. Aspinwall of the Chase Manhattan Bank of New York), and a politician (Representative Doug Barnard [D., GA], Chairman of the House Subcommittee on Commerce, Consumer and Monetary Affairs). The views of these individuals, which are summarized below, can be found in Kane [1987], Barnard [1987], and Aspinwall [1983]. In a nutshell, their opinion is that banks are not as special as the Fed would have us believe.

The View from Wall Street

Aspinwall [1983] argues against the specialness doctrine on two grounds. First, he contends that banks are not special by any criteria that merit the extent of current regulation. He points out that nonbanks, which are subject to substantially less regulation, provide essentially the same financial services as banks. Has the expansion of the banking franchise to nonbanks had any of the adverse consequences feared by bank regulators? To date, it has not; however, the experiment has yet to stand the test of time. Aspinwall's second point hinges upon the advantages of competition. He argues that fewer (not more) restrictions on pricing, service lines, and location will lead to improved financial services and to stronger FSFs. Thus, contrary to the Fed's position, Aspinwall does not see the need to protect the deposit-taking franchise.

The View from Academia: The Shifting Dimensions of Bank Specialness

Kane argues that the Fed's claim of specialness reduces to the lame assertion that banks exhibit a series of distinguishing characteristics (such as those described by Aspinwall [1983]). Drawing upon PBS's famed philosopher-poet, Fred Rogers,[2] Kane explains how pushing the Fed's argument to its logical extreme that we conclude, like Mr. Rogers, everyone and everything is special. Recall that Mr. Rogers teaches our children this with his song, "You Are Special." Continuing with this theme, Kane draws upon a second song by Mr. Rogers, "You Can Never Go Down the Drain," to reassure this "special you" that you are, indeed, too big to go down the drain. The latter, of course, refers to the safety net designed to reassure special FSFs (i.e., commercial banks) that they are, indeed, too big to go down the drain.

Kane lists five ways in which an FSF (e.g., a commercial bank or a savings-and-loan association, [S&L]) might be special. First, the institution might have a unique product line. For example, prior to deregulation of the FSI, commercial banks had monopoly power over checking accounts. Second, an FSF might have a distinctive strategy for managing its product line. For example, at one time, commercial banks specialized in making commercial-and-industrial (C&I) loans and S&Ls specialized in making residential mortgage loans, whereas they both drew mainly on the transaction or savings balances of their local communities to fund these loans. Today, however, both their sources and uses of funds are much more diversified. Third, an FSF might be run by a special breed of managers. To the extent that banking and the S&L businesses were once considered "clubs" run by "good old boys," this kind of managerial specialness may have existed in the good old days. Today, however, managers of FSFs must be as diverse as the products and services they sell.

Fourth, an FSF might serve a distinctive base of customers. Although the smallest FSFs still cater mainly to local customers, the traditional local customer base has given way to statewide, regional, national, and international banking. Finally, an FSF might be subject to special linkages with government agencies that control its activities in the form of entry and exit, expansion, deposit insurance, taxation, products, and prices. Although historic deregulation acts were passed in 1980 and 1982, the regulation and taxation of FSFs still remain a "jurisdictional tangle that boggles the mind." Moreover, the playing field is so uneven that even within the same class of institution, differential treatment exists (e.g., federal versus state regulations for insured banks

---

[2] Fred Rogers, Arnold Palmer, and yours truly claim Latrobe, PA as their birthplace. No fool, I challenge Fred to a game of golf and Arnie to a writing duel anytime.

or S&Ls). Across classes of firms such as banks, S&Ls, brokerage firms, and nonfinancial corporations (e.g., Sears, General Motors, and General Electric), the disparity in treatment is even greater.

The View from the Potomac

Since Congressman Barnard wrote an article for *The Wall Street Journal* entitled "Wrong-Way Corrigan," you know where he stands. Regarding Corrigan's [1987] hard-line position on the separation of banking and commerce, Barnard claims that it is a plan to protect inefficient banks. The Congressman goes on to argue that keeping commercial/industrial firms out of the banking "club" will simply force such firms to offer quasi-banking services in innovative ways outside the traditional financial system. If the Fed wants to control the financial system, and it does, then it is self-defeating to force an expansion of the uncontrolled segment. Barnard argues for a regulatory system based on fairness and equity in which qualifications for bank ownership are based on functional and operational guidelines such as sufficient capital and capable management, rather than the prospective owner's "parentage" (i.e., whether the FSFs is owned by U.S. Steel, Sears, Merrill Lynch, Citicorp, or the local land baron). The Congressman's objective is "... nothing less than a completely level playing field for open competition in all phases of our dynamic financial markets."

RECAPITULATION

In today's modern financial-services industry, the specialness of the past is in the process of giving way to a despecialization and homogenization or fusion of financial institutions and markets. Commercial banks and other federally insured financial institutions can be distinguished most easily from other FSFs on the basis of government guarantees (called deposit insurance) and government regulations. However, in today's deregulated environment of the FSI, commercial banks and thrift institutions may have difficulty competing with less-regulated players. Some New York bankers are so disturbed about the lack of a level playing field they have threatened to give up their commercial bank charters and operate as nonbank FSFs. Whether or not such threats are a bluff to gain additional powers (e.g., investment banking), only time will tell.

THE TRICK(Y) ENVIRONMENT OF THE FINANCIAL-SERVICES INDUSTRY

The financial-services industry, in which commercial banks operate, is in a state of dynamic change. Five critical factors in this process of change are captured by the acronym TRICK, which stands for

   T = Technology,
   R = Reregulation,
   I = Interest-rate risk,
   C = Customer, and
   K = Kapital adequacy (using the German spelling of capital)

Since the importance of TRICK for the FSI is a major theme of this book, it will be used frequently to describe and analyze various concepts and issues. At this juncture, each of the components of TRICK is described.

Technology

According to *Webster's*, one of the definitions of technology is "a technical method of achieving a practical purpose." From the banking customer's perspective, two of the practical purposes of banking are *convenience* and *accessibility* to both *funds* and account *information*. Technological advancements in financial-services delivery and production (e.g., automated teller machines or ATMs) have made it more convenient and efficient for customers to access funds and information.

The ongoing structural change in the FSI can be viewed, as Kane [1983] does, as a form of institutional metamorphosis. In technological terms, as depicted in Figure 1-1, depository institutions (and FSFs in general) can be viewed as evolving into electronic appliances with television-like features. Using a biological metaphor, Kane describes the process as "… the financial-industry equivalent of a laboratory photograph catching a caterpillar halfway through its transition to a butterfly." With the traditional brick-and-mortar bank building representing the cocoon, we see the modern financial-services firm bursting out of its shell with legs, antennae, cords, and

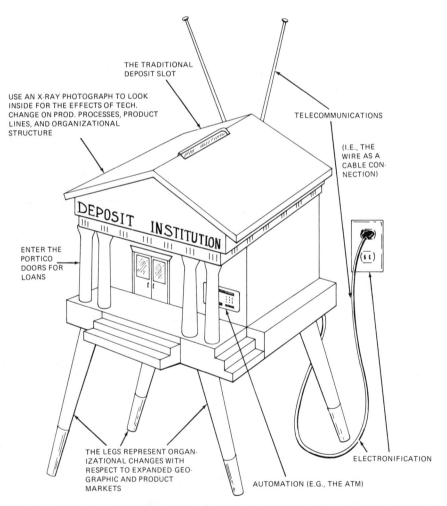

Figure 1-1   The Metamorphosis in Financial-Services Delivery and Production

Adapted from Kane [1983].

control devices that serve to wire the institution into the electronic age. These protrusions and graftings represent the technological (and organizational) changes taking place in a bank's customer-servicing systems.

Focusing on Figure 1-1, we see that three emerging technological forces are reshaping depository institutions: (1) electronics, symbolized by the plug and connecting wire, (2) automation, symbolized by the "hole-in-the-wall" or ATM, and (3) telecommunications, symbolized by the antenna and by interpreting the wire as a dual-purpose cable connection. The major implication of these technological changes is the displacement of paper transactions and human energy by electronic images and electrical power. As a result, some bank customers may view depository institutions as becoming more impersonal, as routine transactions are increasingly performed by computers. Alternatively, those customers singled out for special treatment as preferred clients (i.e., those with high net worths or wealth) may view the segmentation as long overdue.[3]

The legs or stilts of the evolving institution, which symbolize organizational changes, represent the expanded geographic and product markets open to modern FSFs. Although the importance of proximity and physical presence in a market has been reduced by technological developments (e.g., as demonstrated by the success of money-market mutual funds and mutual funds in general), organizational change still has a role to play in servicing new markets. For example, holding-company affiliates or direct ownership of subsidiary firms provide banks with vehicles to add a new function or expand into a new region. Charter conversions (mainly for thrift institutions), joint ventures (in ATM networks and in bank servicing of brokerage cash-management accounts), and customer sharing (via brokered deposits and discount brokerages) represent other methods of adaptive organizational change.

To complete the description of the metamorphosis in financial-services delivery and production, we need a special pair of X-ray glasses to look inside the brick-and-mortar façade shown in Figure 1-1. With these glasses, we could see how the three technologies of electronics, automation, and telecommunications are individually and jointly changing the internal production processes, product lines, and organizational structure of depository institutions.

Reregulation

The word *deregulation* suggests a movement away from regulation and, carried to its logical conclusion, it suggests an absence of regulation. Since a completely unregulated FSI is unlikely to occur in the United States, or in other developed countries, we use the term reregulation to describe the removal or relaxing of barriers to competition. The five primary barriers to banking competition are (1) price or interest-rate controls, (2) product restrictions, (3) organizational constraints, (4) geographic restrictions, and (5) taxes, both explicit (e.g., on income) and implicit (e.g., via reserve requirements and deposit-insurance fees). The complete removal of interest-rate ceilings on deposits in 1986 and the development of regional interstate banking in the 1980s mean that product and organizational changes will be the focus of the 1990s. And, unfortunately, like death, taxes are inevitable.

---

[3] One of the ways that banks achieve this market segmentation has been described by Fernand J. St Germain (who spells his last name without a period), chairman of the U.S. House Banking, Finance, and Urban Affairs Committee. Regarding banking changes since deregulation, he states: "The move to an affluent market and away from the blue collar, elderly, and less well-to-do is being accomplished through an elaborate fee system that effectively prices the 'undesirables' out of the bank." Quoted in *Fortune* [May 14, 1984,] p. 8. Credit unions, which are nonprofit cooperatives, and, to some extent thrifts and saving banks, tend to cater to less-affluent customers.

The reregulation of the 1980s was built around two important pieces of legislation. First, in 1980, the Depository Institutions Deregulation and Monetary Control Act (DIDMCA) was passed. The schizophrenic title of this act highlights the importance of the choice of "reregulation" as the operative word for the changes occurring in the regulatory arena. On the one hand, DIDMCA gives us *deregulation*; with the other, it imposes *control*. The second major piece of legislation was the Garn–St Germain Depository Institutions Act of 1982. Together these acts, among other things, enabled depository institutions to expand their investment powers, develop new products, and price deposit accounts without regulatory interference. The details of these acts are explained later in the book.

Interest-Rate Risk

The *I* component of TRICK stands for interest-rate risk. Since FSFs hold portfolios of financial assets and liabilities, their net asset values (i.e., net worth [NW] = assets [A]–liabilities [L]) are sensitive to *unanticipated* changes in interest rates. Since *actual* changes in interest rates (or any economic/financial variable) are equal to anticipated changes *plus* unanticipated changes, anticipated changes should be built into rational portfolio decisions. Accordingly, only unanticipated changes affect values.

Management of interest-rate risk is one of the key tasks of bank (or FSF) financial management. During the period of rising and volatile interest rates from 1966 to 1982, the critical importance of protecting a portfolio against interest-rate risk was highlighted. The plight of thrift institutions over this period shows what mismanagement of interest-rate risk can do to an industry and its deposit-insurance fund.

Customers

The *C* in TRICK stands for customers. In the modern FSI, the competition for customers has become fierce. When banks had "monopoly power," there was little need to go after customers by developing and marketing new products and services. However, in the competitive environment of the FSI, product development and marketing are critical factors in the degree of success experienced by FSFs.

Since the standard economic model of market structure implies survival of the lowest cost producers (holding product and service quality constant), customers should benefit from lower prices and a wider selection of financial products and services as competition increases. To the extent that suppliers of financial services were extracting economic rents (i.e., excess profits) from their monopoly positions, competition will reduce the surpluses with the benefits accruing to customers. To protect against this decline in profitability, FSFs will have to exploit alternative ways of increasing their efficiency (e.g., through economies of scale and/or economies of scope or joint production).

Kapital Adequacy

Using the German spelling of capital completes the TRICK acronym. From a finance perspective, capital adequacy can be interpreted as financial leverage, and thus as a measure of risk exposure. Regulators use capital-adequacy standards as important measures of "safety and soundness" for depository institutions because they tend to view capital as a buffer or cushion for absorbing losses. From a market perspective, the more adequate an FSF's capital position is, other things being equal, the more likely it is to be the acquirer as opposed to the acquiree when consolidations occur. "Be capitalized or beware" is an appropriate slogan for FSFs in the 1990s.

TRICK Summary

The managers of financial-services firms who can plan and control the risk–return trade-offs associated with the five critical components of TRICK—Technology, Reregulation, Interest-rate risk, Customers, and Kapital adequacy—are most likely to survive and prosper in the financial-services industry of the 1990s. Finally, the components of TRICK should not be viewed in isolation as they interact with each other. For example, technological and regulatory changes affect competition for customers; competition affects technological developments, reregulation, and capital adequacy; reregulation and interest-rate risk affect capital adequacy; and so on.

FINANCIAL INNOVATION AND A MODEL OF CHANGE IN THE FSI

The forces of TRICK in conjunction with rational self-interest can be viewed as a model of change in the FSI. In this framework, the interaction of TRICK and rational self-interest combine to produce financial innovation. Schematically, the model is

$$\text{TRICK} + \text{Rational Self-Interest} = \text{Financial Innovation} \qquad (1\text{-}1)$$

In this context, rational self-interest simply refers to the fact that the owners/managers of FSFs look out for themselves (in the case of closely held companies) or for the interests of their shareholders. This motivation in conjunction with the forces of change captured by TRICK lead to financial innovation. For example, consider the development of money-market mutual funds and how this model explains their phenomenal growth. During the 1970s with Regulation Q interest-rate ceilings still in force and with inflation leading to higher and higher interest rates, savers were looking for financial instruments whose returns would keep pace with inflation. With the technological help of the 800-telephone number, money-market funds were introduced in the early and mid-1970s. However, it was not until the double-digit inflation of the late 1970s and early 1980s that the rapid growth of these funds occurred. The managers of mutual funds recognized a need and were motivated enough to develop a financial innovation to meet the demand. Other innovations such as adjustable-rate mortgages, electronic funds transfer systems (e.g., automatic teller machines, ATMs), the holding-company movement, and regional interstate banking also can be explained within this framework.

THE "IZATION" OF THE FSI: INSTITUTIONALIZATION, GLOBALIZATION, AND SECURITIZATION

Three of the latest buzz words in the FSI are *institutionalization, globalization*, and *securitization*. You will not find any of these words in *Webster's*. They are creations of the modern FSI. Since all three of the terms have important implications for both commercial and investment banking, we use them, with literary reluctance, to explain the "ization" of the FSI.

For banks and other financial intermediaries, institutionalization refers to the full development and rapid growth of the channeling of savings into these organizations. Although the institutionalization of the savings process began shortly after the end of World War II, the phenomenon has experienced its most rapid growth over the past decade with the development of deferred-lifetime-compensation programs such as pension funds, Keogh plans, and IRA accounts. Much of this growth has been at the expense of traditional depository institutions (i.e., commercial banks, thrifts, and credit unions).

From an investment-banking perspective, institutionalization focuses on three dimensions: (1) investment bankers as dealers in large-scale trading, which requires size and agility, (2) investment bankers as market makers and seekers, and (3) the role of investment bankers in merger-related activities. Investment banking is a business that supplies two basic services: (1) the raising of cash through the issuance or "flotation" of new securities in the primary market and (2) the bringing together of buyers and sellers of existing securities in the secondary market by acting as brokers and/or dealers. Institutionalization of trading refers to the development of trading and risk-taking services on a large scale and at short notice.

Globalization refers to the internationalization of financial institutions and markets. A decade ago only the largest FSFs, mainly commercial and investment banking companies, ventured into this arena. Today, more and more FSFs of various kinds and sizes are doing deals in international markets, especially in the three major financial centers of the world: London, New York, and Tokyo. Hence, like ABC's "Wide World of Sports," FSFs are spanning the globe looking, not for the latest sports gimmick, but for lowest-cost sources of funds and/or for the most profitable investment opportunities. This fusion or linking of financial institutions and markets on a worldwide basis is called globalization.

Securitization simply refers to the selling of loans that are packaged as securities and sold to investors. Such pass-through securities, as they are called, are attractive to investors because they offer denomination, yield, liquidity, and risk considerations that are usually superior to holding the individual asset. Why would FSFs want to sell the loans that make up these securities? The key concepts in understanding the process of securitization are risk, liquidity, fees, and capital constraints. Consider the risk factor, either credit or interest-rate risk, or both. By selling loans, the originator passes the risk on to the investor, which might be another FSF. Regarding the liquidity factor, selling loans enables FSFs to generate liquidity. In the process of selling loans, FSFs generate fees because of their expertise and reputation as loan originators. In addition, if they service the loans and pass-through either the principal or interest, or both, they collect servicing fees. Finally, if regulated FSFs face balance-sheet constraints, in the form of minimum capital-to-asset ratios, they may be forced to get assets off their balance sheets. By securitizing loans, they can meet capital requirements and, by generating fees, attempt to maintain profit margins. To summarize, the phenomenon of securitization can be explained by the combination of risk, liquidity, fee, and capital-constraint factors.

Something is strange here, however. Securitization appears to be a win–win situation in which both the buyer and the seller benefit. To the extent that securitization increases the efficiency of financial markets, both parties do benefit. However, from a risk–return perspective, higher yields can come only from taking on additional risk. Transferring risk, whether interest-rate or credit risk, does not make it disappear. Someone must be the ultimate bearer of the risk. If third-party guarantees are involved, and they frequently are, then the third party bears some or all of the risk. If some form of recourse is permitted, then the risk-transfer process is an incomplete one. Both private and public institutions such as investment banks and government agencies frequently serve as third-party guarantors in the securitization process. To the extent that government guarantees are involved, taxpayers end up bearing the risk but without a share of the direct profits. Indirectly, however, taxpayers could benefit if the guarantees served to make the financial system or particular segments of it safer and/or more efficient.

The process of securitization has actually been around for over a decade, as exemplified by "Ginnie Mae" pass-through securities issued by the Government National Mortgage Association (GNMA) and by mortgage-backed bonds issued by thrift institutions. Today, the securitization process has been extended to other types of loans such as automobile loans and credit cards. Given the financial environment of the late 1980s, the ultimate "junk bond" of securitized credits would be a pass-through of agriculture, energy, and LDC (less-developed country) loans.

One view of the FSI of the future has traditional lending institutions such as banks and thrifts reduced to originators of credits with the real financial power residing with the securitizers of the assets, the investment banks. This scenario helps explain why commercial bankers are so eager to get into investment banking.

THE GLASS–STEAGALL ACT AND THE SEPARATION OF COMMERCIAL AND INVESTMENT BANKING

Two of the key segments of the FSI are commercial banking and investment banking. Prior to 1933, these two segments were united. However, following the financial collapse of the early 1930s, Congress deemed that commercial and investment banking were not compatible. The result was the Banking Act of 1933, commonly known as the Glass–Steagall Act. It requires, among other things, the separation of commercial and investment banking.

Good Intentions and Unintended Evils

Although the lawmakers of 1933 had good intentions, laws frequently have unintended evils that are unforeseen or ignored at the time of enactment. The good intentions of the lawmakers of 1933 are captured by the purpose of the Glass–Steagall Act: "... to provide for the safer and more effective use of the assets of banks, to regulate interbank control, to prevent undue diversion of funds into speculative operations, and for other purposes." To accomplish these objectives, the key provisions of the Act were (1) the creation of federal deposit insurance, (2) the prohibition of interest payments on checking accounts or demand deposits, (3) limitations on insider activities, (4) increased reporting and examination requirements, and (5) the separation of commercial and investment banking. This last provision was designed to promote the safer and more effective use of bank assets by prohibiting banks from engaging in speculative ventures through underwriting corporate securities and related activities.

Although the Banking Act of 1933 succeeded in restoring confidence in the banking system, at least in the short run (say, the 25-year period from the end of WW II to 1971), it did so at the expense of a competitively strong financial system. At its fiftieth anniversary in 1983, the unintended evils of Glass–Steagall were all too evident. By then, both legal (e.g., the deregulation acts of 1980 and 1982) and market forces were in the process of removing the shackles of the 1933 legislation. These forces were attempting to fuse or bring together the fragmented segments of the FSI.

The Stock Market Crash of 1987

On October 19, 1987, a Monday, the U.S. stock market crashed as the Dow Jones Industrial Average fell a record 508 points. This "Black Monday" was blacker than the "Black Tuesday" of October 28, 1929. The crash of 1929 was followed by a deep and prolonged depression as the Fed failed to provide liquidity to the economy. In contrast, immediately following the crash of 1987, the Fed announced its intention to supply the financial system, and hence the economy, with the liquidity necessary to prevent an economic collapse. In addition, President Reagan expressed his willingness to cooperate more fully with Congress to reduce the budget and trade deficits. The proper conduct of monetary and fiscal policy is the key to preventing wild fluctuations in economic activity.

Just as special interest groups used the economic disaster of the Great Depression to bring about the separation of commercial and investment banking, the proponents of the continued separation of commercial and investment banking used the stock market crash of 1987 as ammunition in their war to keep commercial bankers out of the securities business. For example, David Silver, president of the Investment Company Institute, the leading trade group for the mutual fund industry, said: "The events of last week bring into sharper focus the reason why the Glass–Steagall Act was enacted. We're not happy to have jammed telephones and see lines outside brokerage firms, but we'd all feel a lot worse about those kind of lines outside banks." From the commercial banker's perspective, the biggest event affecting the separation of commercial and investment banking in 1987 was not the stock market crash, but as Alan Greenspan, chairman of the Federal Reserve Board, has remarked: "the unexpected advocacy of Senator Proxmire for the repeal of Glass–Steagall" (*American Banker*, December 21, 1987, p. 1).

Until the dust settles, the longer-term effects of the stock market crash of 1987 remain to be seen. Although the basic issues discussed in this chapter have not changed as a result of the crash of 1987, the collapse, like the proverbial two-by-four, has gotten everyone's attention regarding the risks involved in the securities business, and in the FSI generally.

THE SEPARATION OF BANKING AND COMMERCE: THE FEAR OF THE CONCENTRATION OF ECONOMIC AND FINANCIAL POWER

Relative to, say, Japan, the United States is depicted as having a deep-seated distrust of overwhelming economic and financial concentration. This distrust is reflected in laws designed to prohibit the merging of financial and nonfinancial activities. For example, the Glass–Steagall Act calls for the separation of banking and commerce, and the Bank Holding Company Act (1956) prohibits nonbanking companies from owning banks. With the decline of industry and commerce and the rise of service and financial activities in the United States, many industrial and commercial concerns have refocused their businesses toward the FSI. The following excerpt from a 1987 *Wall Street Journal* advertisement reflects the trend: "Westinghouse is no longer making washing machines, but we're certainly turning out some sparkling financial packages for developers of residential real estate." In addition to real estate finance, Westinghouse Credit Corporation is engaged in corporate financing, acquisition financing, asset-based lending, leasing, and fixed-asset financing. Westinghouse is, of course, only one example of the many traditional nonfinancial corporations that have moved into the FSI. Others include U.S. Steel, National Steel, Sears, J.C. Penney, General Electric, General Motors, and Ford Motor Co. to mention a few. The basic issue is whether or not these companies should be permitted to own a commercial bank, that is, should banking and commerce (e.g., Westinghouse) be separate?

The debate about the separation of banking and commerce is a longstanding and ongoing one in the United States. Corrigan [1987] argues for the separation of banking from commerce in order to protect the soundness of the system and to avoid stifling regulation. Former Fed Chairman Paul Volcker favored the strict separation of banking and commerce to avoid conflicts of interest and self-dealing. In contrast, Barnard [1987] sees attempts to exclude commercial/industrial firms from the banking club as simply forcing these firms to offer quasi-banking services in innovative ways outside the traditional banking system. Our model of TRICK + rational self-interest can easily explain why the managers of these nonbanking firms would behave in such a manner. Barnard contends that it is preferable to have nonbanking firms with financial expertise and ambitions to operate within the system rather than outside it.

William Isaac, chairman of the FDIC from 1981 to 1985, views the separation of banking and commerce as "the tradition that never was." His position on the issue (Isaac [1987]) is reflected by the following excerpt from *The Wall Street Journal*:

> Neither American tradition nor modern-day reality requires the separation of banking and commerce to promote soundness and stability in banking. It is American tradition to fear, even loathe, concentration of economic and political power. We do not need a Bank Holding Company Act or a Glass–Steagall Act to avoid such concentrations. These laws are poor and inefficient substitutes for strong and effective antitrust enforcement (p. 30).

Another supporter of the merging of banking and commerce has been the Treasury Department of the Reagan administration. In 1987, Undersecretary of the Treasury George Gould was quoted as saying that the Treasury Department favored the creation of five or ten giant banks in combination with giant industrial companies. Not surprisingly the current chairman of the Federal Reserve, Alan Greenspan, a Reagan appointee, favors the merging of banking and commerce. He sees nothing wrong with such a combination, provided an effective "firewall" insulates the bank from the risks of the commercial enterprise. This firewall concept is known as the issue of corporate separateness, that is, can bank risk exposure be isolated or kept separate from the nonbanking risks?

The basic argument supporting the megabank concept is that these giant conglomerates would be better able to compete in world markets. Although the idea that big is better has been around for a long time, it came to the forefront in the United States in the 1980s when the largest banking companies were headquartered in Japan and Europe. As of 1987, Citibank and BankAmerica were the only two U.S. banks in the top 25 in the world. Thirty years ago, the United States had 15 banks in this group.

Opposition to the administration's once-secret plan for megabanks has been voiced by Sprague [1987]. He argues that American banks are large enough to compete in world markets and that the idea of megabanks is scary. He asks "... what does size itself mean?" Sprague's concern about megabanks in the United States is attributed to the "too-big-to-fail" doctrine (see Sprague [1986]). Regarding the concentration of power, Sprague [1987] concludes:

> Any concentration of power is oppressive; the concentration of economic power is frightening. Let us hope that Congress will have the guts or the wisdom to draw a line against the unbridled economic concentration that is implied in the Treasury's no-longer-secret plan (p. 28).

Finally, let's consider the views of Robert Strickland, chairman of the growing super regional, SunTrust Banks, Inc. He believes the lines between banking and commerce will blur and eventually disappear over time. However, regarding the megabank issue, he says, "...we want our bank to be the best, not necessarily the biggest in our business. Bigness is not necessarily beautiful. What is beautiful is the bottom line, or profitability" (Poulos [1987]).

THE SEPARATION OF BANKING AND COMMERCE: A RECAPITULATION

Three fundamental barriers are responsible for the separation of banking and commerce and the lack of megabanks or financial conglomerates in the United States: (1) the Glass–Steagall Act, which separates industry and commerce, and commercial and investment banking; (2) the Bank Holding Company (BHC) Act, which prohibits nonbanking companies from owning commercial banks; and (3) the distrust by many Americans (à la Sprague) against heavy concentrations of economic and financial power.

If banking and commerce are permitted to merge, the existence of megabanks or financial conglomerates presumably would follow. Although such organizations safely exist outside the United States, our present regulatory and insurance system is not equipped to handle such entities. A comprehensive reform package is a prerequisite for the fusion of banking and commerce in the TRICK(y) environment of the FSI.

THE BUSINESS AND REGULATORY SPECTRUMS OF THE FSI

As shown in Figure 1-2, the financial-services industry (FSI) can be perceived as consisting of a business spectrum and a regulatory spectrum. The business spectrum has four segments: (1) banking, (2) finance, (3) insurance, and (4) nonfinancial corporations (NFCs). These segments have both descriptive and functional content. For example, consider the banking segment. On the descriptive level, each of the segments—commercial, savings, investment, and mortgage—is associated with the word *banking*. On the functional level, each of the components share particular markets and are attempting to gain greater shares of each other's previously protected markets. Based on the discussion earlier in this chapter of the critical issues facing the FSI, note how the Glass–Steagall Act and the BHC Act create boundaries separating the business spectrum both within and across segments.

The Business Spectrum of the FSI

Banking	Finance	Insurance	NFC Segment
Commercial	Real estate	Life	Gasoline companies
Savings	Consumer	Property &	Retailers
Investment	Commercial	casualty	Captive finance
Mortgage	Factoring		Companies

The Regulatory Spectrum of the FSI

Regulated	Less-regulated	Unregulated
Commercial banking	Investment banking	Gasoline companies
Savings banking	Mortgage banking	Retailers
	Finance companies	Captive finance
	Insurance companies	companies

Notes: NFC = nonfinancial corporation. Savings banking is defined to include savings banks, savings-and-loan associations, and credit unions. In the regulatory spectrum, some businesses are collapsed into one regulatory listing, e.g., life insurance and P&C insurance into insurance companies.

Figure 1-2   The Financial-Services Industry and Its Components

TABLE 1-1   The Major Worldwide Players in the FSI December 31, 1986

Banks	Asset Growth	Deposit Growth	Net Income Growth	Primary Capital Growth	Total Employees
1 Dai-Ichi Kangyo (Japan)	13.5%	13.7%	20.2%	11.2%	20,000
2 Citicorp (U. S.)	10.5	9.7	14.8	16.1	88,500
3 Fuji Bank (Japan)	14.0	13.2	5.8	10.3	16,000
4 Sumitomo Bank (Japan)	13.4	13.0	20.6	12.3	14,000
5 Mitsubishi Bank (Japan)	11.0	10.7	15.4	8.0	13,000

Insurers	Asset Growth	Net Income Growth	Growth in Premiums	Investment Growth	Total Employees
1 Prudential (U. S.)	10.8%	N.A.	12.8%	8.5%	85,500
2 Metropolitan Life (U. S.)	9.5	−8.7	18.9	12.1	33,000
3 Nippon Life (Japan)	15.1	13.8[b]	13.1	14.9	80,000
4 Aetna (U. S.)	11.0	17.7	8.2	12.0	45,100
5 Equitable Life (U. S.)	8.2	−14.8	25.8	7.3	25,000

Financial-Services Firms	Capital Growth	Asset Growth	Revenue Growth	Net Income Growth	Total Employees
1 American Express (U. S.)	29.5%	31.7%	18.4%	19.3%	78,747
2 Salomon Inc. (U. S.)	16.4	68.3	23.2[a]	12.2	8,684
3 Merrill Lynch (U. S.)	35.7	24.6	18.9	17.5	45,000
4 Orient Leasing (Japan)	15.1	24.0	19.5	11.7	2,948
5 Nomura Securities (Japan)	19.7	28.0	25.3	34.4	9,445

[a] Four year growth rate.
[b] Mutual company, net change in capital reserves.
Note: Growth rates are five-year compound annual ones.
Source: Worldscope (Wrights Investors' Service, Bridgeport, Conn., and Center for International Financial Analysis and Research, Princeton, N. J.) as published in "A Special Report: Global Finance and Investing," *The Wall Street Journal* [September 18, 1987], Section 4, pp. 30D–32D.

Although London, New York, and Tokyo represent the financial capitals of the world, the biggest players in the globalized business spectrum of the FSI are found in the United States and Japan. Financial profiles of the five biggest banks, insurers, and financial-services firms, as of December 31, 1986, are shown in Table 1-1. Although Japan currently dominates the banking group, the United States has four of the five largest insurers and three of the five largest financial-services firms. Focusing on banks, the financial profile highlights the five-year compounded annual growth rates of assets, deposits, net income, and capital. For Citicorp, with 88,500 employees, its profile of these four growth rates is [10.5%, 9.7%, 14.8%, 16.1%]. As you study Table 1-1 note the frequency and size of the United States public companies not listed as banks, insurers, or diversified financial companies. Many of these companies (e.g., IBM, Exxon, General Electric, AT&T, Du Pont, Ford Motor, General Motors) are suppliers or would-be suppliers of financial services. The existence of these firms, which we call nonfinancial corporations (NFCs) because their basic businesses are not finance related, is an important descriptive and competitive aspect of the FSI.

The regulatory spectrum shown in Figure 1-2 is based on the existence and extent of regulation. For expositional purposes, let us think of the regulatory spectrum of the FSI in terms of three segments: (1) a regulated segment consisting of depository institutions and their holding companies, (2) a less-regulated segment consisting of investment, insurance, and finance companies, and (3) and an unregulated segment consisting of NFCs that supply financial services. The important point is that the degree and intensity of regulation varies considerably across the FSI. Moreover, even within segments, the playing fields are not level. For example, within the regulated segment, many state-chartered S&Ls, especially those in California, Florida, and Texas (dual banking, i.e., federal versus state regulation, is the culprit here), have greater latitude regarding their investment powers compared to other depository institutions. Here again, but in more dramatic fashion compared to the business spectrum, the Glass–Steagall Act and the BHC Act are the primary legal barriers defining the segments of the regulatory spectrum.

CHAPTER SUMMARY

The issues introduced in this chapter do not have easy answers; tough questions come that way. Perhaps the toughest one deals with the separation of banking and commerce. Nevertheless, each of the three key issues—the separation of banking and commerce and the issues of specialness and the separation of commercial and investment banking—to a large degree have been or are being determined in the marketplace, where the answers are: banks are not special, the separation of commercial and investment banking is not warranted, and the separation between banking and commerce will continue to blur.

The key analytical device for understanding the changes taking place in the financial-services industry (FSI) is our model of change:

$$\text{TRICK} + \text{Rational Self-Interest} = \text{Financial Innovation}$$

where TRICK stands for *T*echnology, *R*eregulation, *I*nterest-rate risk, *C*ustomers, and *K*apital adequacy and rational self-interest is best thought of as profitable opportunities. This model captures the dynamic forces of change that are reshaping the financial-services industry and generating the notion of a financial-services firm (FSF). By using this framework, we can better understand the critical issues facing banking in the FSI.

LIST OF KEY WORDS, CONCEPTS, AND ACRONYMS

Bank (commercial versus investment)
Bank Holding Company Act
Business spectrum of the FSI
DIDMCA
Fear (or distrust) of economic and
   financial concentration
Financial innovation
Financial-services firm (FSF)
Financial-services industry (FSI)

"Ization" of the FSI
Separation of banking and commerce
Separation of commercial and
   investment banking
Glass–Steagall Act
Regulatory spectrum of the FSI
Specialness doctrine
TRICK and the model of change

REVIEW/DISCUSSION QUESTIONS

1. Make a list of various financial innovations and see how well our model of change (TRICK + rational self-interest = financial innovation) can be used to explain the development of each one.

MATCHING QUIZ—II

Directions: At last count, there were 26 letters in the alphabet. Take the 11 unmatched items from the right-hand column of the above quiz and create left-hand column entries for them. In addition, identify the following individuals: Greenspan, Strickland, and Volcker.

SELECTED REFERENCES

Aspinwall, Richard C. [1983]. "On the Specialness of Banking," *Issues in Bank Regulation* (Autumn), pp. 16–22.

Barnard, Doug. [1987]. "Wrong-Way Corrigan," *The Wall Street Journal* (February 26), editorial page.

Corrigan, E. Gerald. [1987]. *Financial Market Structure: A Longer View*, New York: Federal Reserve Bank. (This essay also appears in the Bank's 1986 Annual Report, pp. 3–54.)

——— [1987a]. "A Perspective on the Globalization of Financial Markets and Institutions," *FRBNY Quarterly Review* (Spring), pp. 1–9.

———[1982]. "Are Banks Special?" *Annual Report*, Federal Reserve Bank of Minneapolis, pp. 2–24.

Isaac, William M. [1987]. "The Banking Tradition That Never Was," *The Wall Street Journal* (July 21), p. 30.

Kane, Edward J. [1987]. "How S&Ls and Ex-S&Ls Are Special," *Thrift Financial Performance and Capital Adequacy*, Proceedings of the Twelfth Annual Conference of the Federal Home Loan Bank of San Francisco, pp. 91–114.

———[1983]. "Metamorphosis in Financial-Services Delivery and Production," in *Strategic Planning for Economic and Technological Change in the Financial-Services Industry*. San Francisco: Federal Home Loan Bank of San Francisco, pp. 49–64.

Poulos, Nick. [1987]. "Megabank Idea Is Fraught with Many Problems," *The Atlanta Constitution* (July 23), p. 1D.

Sinkey, Joseph F. Jr. [1986]. "Can Regulation and Supervision Ensure Financial Stability?" *Financial Stability of the Thrift Industry*, Proceedings of the Eleventh Annual Conference of the Federal Home Loan Bank of San Francisco, pp. 133–148.

Sprague, Irvine. [1987]. "American Megabanks: Scary, Not Scarce," *The Wall Street Journal* (July 15), p. 28.

———[1986]. *Bailout: An Insider's Account of Bank Failures and Rescues*. New York: Basic Books.

The Banks of Banking: Consumer, Corporate, and Investment

ACRONYM GUIDE TO KEY TERMS AND CONCEPTS

BHC = bank holding company
DSU = deficit-spending unit
EM = equity multiplier
FDIC = Federal Deposit Insurance Corporation
FSF = financial-services firm
FSI = financial-services industry
OCC = Office of the Comptroller of the Currency
SSU = surplus-spending unit

INTRODUCTION

The word *bank* is quite prevalent in society today. In basketball, it's the *bank* shot. In Paris, there is the East *bank* and the West *bank*. The Red Cross has its blood *bank* and medical science its sperm *bank*. Financial collapse is known as *bank*ruptcy and underworld characters carry *bank* rolls rather than *bank* credit or debit cards. A high-rise building has a *bank* of elevators and advertising jingles say, "You can *bank* on us." Not to be outdone, the financial-services industry (FSI) has its share of *banks* in the form of *bank* holding companies, commercial *banks*, savings *banks*, investment *banks*, and even *nonbank* banks or consumer *banks*.

This chapter focuses on the various banks of the FSI and, in particular, on the banks of so-called commercial banking. The "banks of banking" refers to the primary business areas of *large* banking companies, which are consumer, corporate, and investment. For the most part, local or community banks, which number about 14,000, do not engage in the business of investment banking. They focus on the consumer and small-business segments of banking. Although the name "commercial bank" has always been a misnomer, it is particularly inappropriate for describing the modern banking institution. In the future, commercial bankers hope to (further) expand their "banks of banking" into real estate, securities, and insurance. Thus, in the 1990s, the banks of banking might read consumer, corporate, investment, real estate, securities, and insurance. Clearly, such a multiproduct/multiservice organization can best be described, as introduced in Chapter 1, as a financial-services firm (FSF).

We begin our study of the banks of banking by looking at the etymology of the word bank. From this linguistic beginning, we turn to four alternative ways of viewing a bank: (1) the notion of a bank as a department store of finance and a deliverer of financial services, (2) the notion of a bank as an information processor, (3) the notion of a bank as a balance sheet or portfolio, and (4) the notion of a bank as a regulated firm. In addition, we look at banks as financial intermediaries and as creators of money. The various classes and types of commercial banks are explained, including the notion of the *real* (versus *de jure*) dual banking system. The chapter concludes with a look at bank market strategy in the FSI.

THE ETYMOLOGY OF THE WORD *BANK*

Etymology refers to the linguistic history of a word. The etymology of the word *bank* can be traced to the French word *banque* and the Italian word *banca*. These words mean *chest* and *bench*, respectively. The connotations of these two words describe the two basic functions that banks perform. *Chest* suggests the *safekeeping* function, that is, a place where we keep valuables. Examples are a gold chest, a jewelry chest, a cedar chest, and a hope chest. Today, a bank's chest is its *portfolio* of earning assets. In concrete and steel, a bank's chest is its vault; however, the vault is only a hollow shell. The heart of a bank is its portfolio of earning assets. This portfolio provides a bank's lifeblood, namely earnings net of expenses and taxes. Depositors' checking-account balances and savings are stored for safekeeping in the bank's portfolio. If it helps you sleep better at night, think of the bank's portfolio as safely tucked away in its vault. However, if you want to understand banking, think of a bank's deposits as stored in financial assets representing claims on the earnings of households, business firms, and governments.

In twelfth-century Italy, *banca* (bench) referred to the table, counter, or place of business of a money-changer. This meaning suggests the *transactions* function, that is, the "changing of money" or more generally transacting business and hence paying for goods and services. Examples of places where such transactions occur today are the supermarket checkout counter, the window at a self-service gasoline station, and the counter at a fast-food restaurant. The usual means of payment at these establishments are cash, check, or credit card—means of payment supplied, but not inclusively, by commercial banks. In a bank itself, there are numerous "benches" such as the new-accounts desk, the teller's window, and the loan officer's desk. These benches provide customers with access to the safekeeping and transactions function that commercial banks perform.

To summarize, the two basic functions that commercial banks perform are (1) to provide a safe place to store savings, the safekeeping function; and (2) to furnish a means of payment for buying goods and services, the transactions function. Until December 31, 1980, but earlier for the northeastern part of the United States, commercial banks had a monopoly of the transactions function since they were the only institutions to have checking-accounting powers. Today, however, commercial banks share this power with other financial intermediaries such as "thrift institutions" (i.e., savings and loan associations, mutual savings banks, and credit unions), brokerage firms (such as Merrill Lynch), and money-market funds that offer check-writing services.

DEPARTMENT STORES OF FINANCE AND INFORMATION PROCESSORS

While it is true that the safekeeping and transaction functions are the two basic functions that commercial banks perform, they also provide numerous other financial services. Thus, one way to look at a commercial bank is from the perspective of the services it provides. The concept of a commercial bank as a "department store of finance" is expressed in industry slogans such as "one-stop banking" or "full-service banking." The idea is to convince customers that there is no need to shop anywhere else since commercial banks provide a complete menu of financial services. The notion of a commercial bank as a service organization or deliverer of financial services provides one perspective as to what a commercial bank is and what it does.

In the process of generating financial services, banks collect, analyze, store, retrieve, update, and monitor information about their customers, especially their borrowers. Commercial banks have developed a considerable reputation as information processors. In fact, one can view the existence of commercial banks to their ability to extract borrower-specific information efficiently.[1] The quality of these information flows, in terms of timeliness and accuracy, is a crucial factor determining a bank's asset quality. To illustrate, before funds flow between a would-be borrower and a lender, information flows. Only after these information flows have been collected and analyzed do careful lenders commit funds. If these information flows are faulty or lacking, bad lending decisions can be made. In the extreme, bad lending decisions cause banks to fail. The notion of a commercial bank as an information processor provides another perspective as to what a commercial bank is and what it does.

RECAPITULATION AND EXPANSION OF THE DEPARTMENT STORE

Up to this point, we have established commercial banks as providers of three basic financial services: (1) transactions services, (2) portfolio (or loan-and-deposit) services, and (3) information and data-processing services. Prior to the emergence of the new FSI (say in the mid-1970s), commercial banks did not experience the degree of competition for these basic services that they do today. As a result, banks are looking to expand their menu of financial services. In particular, they have their eyes on three fields: investment banking (e.g., securities underwriting), insurance, and real estate. Since commercial banks already have footholds in these markets, or in the case of multinational banks are already engaged in the activity overseas (e.g., investment banking), the prospects for the expansion of the department store appear to be bright.[2] In contrast, the specialness spotlight is growing dimmer and dimmer.

THE BALANCE-SHEET OR PORTFOLIO CONCEPT

An alternative way of looking at a commercial bank is the balance-sheet approach, the traditional way of examining a business firm. This approach is important because one of the major objectives of this book is to explain the composition of a typical

---

[1] Information-based theories dealing with the process of financial intermediation or lending activities can be found in Leland and Pyle [1977], Stiglitz and Weiss [1981], and Chan, Greenbaum, and Thakor [1986].

[2] Szego [1986] discusses the increasing interaction between banking and insurance and the complementarity that exists between the two fields.

commercial bank's balance sheet and the interrelationships among its balance-sheet accounts.

The basic balance-sheet identity is

$$\text{Assets } (A) = \text{Liabilities } (L) + \text{Net Worth } (NW) \tag{2-1}$$

Unlike nonfinancial firms, a bank's assets consist mainly of financial assets as opposed to physical assets. These financial assets are mainly in the form of loans to households, business firms, and governments.

To understand bank loans and the lending process, the concept of a *completed transaction* is needed. That is, with lending, unlike other businesses, bankers make loans (called sales in other businesses) and they must collect the loans at periodic intervals or in a lump sum at maturity. Thus, when a banker *makes* a loan, it is an *incomplete* transaction. Only after the loan has been *collected* without loss can the transaction be regarded as a *completed* one. Loan transactions that are never completed are called loan losses. Banks that go out of business (i.e., fail) frequently are plagued by heavy loan losses due to illegal insider transactions. The Number One rule of bank survival is: *Don't make too many bad loans*. To implement this rule, banks must conduct careful credit investigations of would-be borrowers, monitor the performance of existing borrowers, diversify their loan portfolios, and have a sound loan policy with adequate controls.

The typical commercial bank has only about 2 percent of its assets tied up in physical or fixed assets such as buildings, equipment, furniture, and fixtures. With so few fixed assets, commercial banks have a very low level of fixed operating expenses (e.g., depreciation, property taxes) in their cost structures. The presence of fixed operating expenses in a firm's cost structure is referred to as *operating leverage*. Nonfinancial firms such as producers of automobiles, steel, or aluminum have high degrees of operating leverage; financial firms such as commercial banks, life insurance companies, and savings and loan associations have very low degrees of operating leverage. Thus, one of the important characteristics of a bank's balance sheet is the absence of a substantial amount of fixed assets and hence a low degree of operating leverage.

Most of a commercial bank's liabilities are in the form of financial claims held by households, business firms, and governments. In banking jargon, these financial claims on a bank's assets are called *deposits*. Two important aspects of bank deposits are (1) the short-term nature of the claims and (2) the large volume of claims relative to the net worth or equity-capital base. These two characteristics of bank deposits are important because they have critical implications for the liquidity and risk exposure of a bank's assets. As a result, commercial banks need to have some optimal combination of relatively liquid and high-quality assets in their portfolios to offset their need for liquidity and their high degrees of financial leverage—the use of debt (deposit) financing by a firm (bank) is referred to as *financial leverage*.

The relationship between financial leverage and risk exposure in a bank can be explained as follows. One measure of financial leverage is the "equity multiplier," EM. Its definition is

$$EM = \frac{\text{Total Assets}}{\text{Total Equity Capital}} \tag{2-2}$$

EM measures the dollar amount of assets pyramided on a bank's equity base. In a commercial bank, equity capital serves as a cushion or buffer for absorbing potential losses, especially those arising from "bad" loans. Thus, the larger the EM, the greater is a bank's potential risk exposure, other things being equal. EMs tend to vary directly

TABLE 2-1   The Major Balance-Sheet Characteristics of Commercial Banks

Characteristic	Significance	Implications for Bank	
		Risk	Return
1. Few fixed or physical assets	Low Degree of operating leverage	Reduces risk	Reduces return
2. Substantial amounts of short-term liabilities (deposits)	Requires banks to be liquid	Reduces risk[a]	Reduces return[a]
3. Substantial amounts of assets relative to equity capital	High degree of financial leverage	Increases risk	Increases return

[a] Assumes that liquidity is acquired from the bank's balance sheet. For a bank that manages its liabilities (i.e., acquires liquidity in financial markets using federal funds, certificates of deposit. Eurodollars, etc.), the anticipated effect is to increase *both* risk *and* return. For example, consider the liquidity crisis faced by Continental Illinois from May 1984 until its bailout on July 26, 1984.

with bank size. The typical U.S. commercial bank has an EM of about 14, while the giant U.S. commercial banks have EMs in the range of 20 to 25.

The size and composition of a bank's balance sheet are important because of their effects on its risk (variability of return) and return (profitability). Throughout this book, emphasis is placed on the impact that managerial decisions and environmental changes (i.e., regulatory and competitive ones) have on a bank's risk–return position. To illustrate this kind of analysis, consider the three balance-sheet characteristics just established and their significance for a bank's risk–return framework. Such an analysis is summarized in Table 2-1.

The absence of a substantial amount of fixed assets in a commercial bank's balance sheet (item 1 in Table 2-1) is manifested in a low degree of operating leverage. This implies that a percentage change in output (loans) will have a relatively small impact upon the percentage change in operating profits before taxes. From an operating perspective, commercial banks have a small chance of *either* large *gains or losses* given a change in their output of earning assets. The ultimate effect, then, is a reduction in both potential risk and return.

Since most of a bank's liabilities are payable on demand—either by law or by practice—banks must possess liquidity to meet deposit withdrawals (item 2 in Table 2-1). Banks also want to be liquid to meet the loan demands of their best customers. These two factors force banks to attempt to hedge (i.e., maturity match) their balance sheets and thus to forgo more profitable but less liquid investment opportunities. The ultimate effect then is a reduction in both potential risk and return. (For a clarification regarding banks that manage their liabilities, see the footnote to Table 2-1).

The third balance-sheet characteristic in Table 2-1 implies that banks have a high degree of financial leverage. In banking circles, financial leverage is referred to as "capital adequacy" and is commonly measured by a bank's capital-to-asset ratio or the reciprocal of EM (see Equation 2-1). A bank with a high degree of financial leverage (i.e., a large EM) frequently is described as one with "inadequate capital." In a risk–return framework, financial leverage increases a bank's potential risk and return.

The results summarized in Table 2-1 are critically important for managerial and regulatory decision-making. To illustrate, suppose that a bank wants to increase its profitability. Three courses of action are evident from Table 2-1: (1) increase its operating leverage by acquiring more fixed assets, (2) reduce its liquidity and rely on purchased liquidity (i.e., manage its liabilities) or simply reduce its liquidity without attempting to manage its liabilities, and (3) increase its financial leverage by acquiring more assets and/or by reducing its capital base. Each of these actions will tend to increase the variability of bank profits, in other words, to increase bank risk. This trade-off, however, is consistent with the fundamental risk–return principle of the theory of finance, namely, the price of greater return is greater risk.

Consider now the regulatory policies of the banking authorities—the Federal Reserve, the Comptroller of the Currency, and the FDIC. They are primarily concerned about bank "safety and soundness" or in a loose sense, risk. As a result, they can be expected to continue doing what they have done in the past, that is, permitting banks to hold only a limited amount of fixed assets and requiring them to have both "adequate" liquidity and "adequate" capital. The regulated environment, then, is one of reduced risk and hence reduced return. It is one in which bank managers are forced to perform a risk–return balancing act to keep both their stockholders and regulators satisfied.

Representative balance sheets for a community bank, a regional bank, and a money-center bank are presented in Table 2-2. Each of the balance sheets is expressed as a percentage of total bank assets. Benchmark asset sizes for the three kinds of banks are $100 million, $5 billion, and $100 billion, respectively. Looking at the asset side of the balance sheet, all of the accounts show substantial differences across the three groups. On the liability side, the differences are just as pronounced and include the capital account. In spite of these differences, from a balance-sheet perspective, any commercial bank can be described as a highly leveraged organization that gathers deposits, mainly interest-bearing ones, and channels those funds into loans and other earning assets.

TABLE 2-2   Representative Balance Sheets for a Community Bank, a Regional Bank, and a Money-Center Bank

	% of Total Assets		
	Community Bank	Regional Bank	Money-center Bank
Assets			
Cash and due from banks	8.8	13.86	16.91
Total securities	29.4	15.36	5.83
Trading account securities	0.5	2.70	2.55
Federal funds sold and repos	6.1	5.55	2.84
Total loans, net	51.8	54.85	62.45
Customers' acceptance liability	0.0	4.25	4.67
Premises and equipment	2.0	1.25	1.06
Other assets	1.4	1.28	3.69
TOTAL	100.0	100.00	100.00
Liabilities	% of Total Liabilities and Capital		
Non interest-bearing domestic deposits	18.8	19.45	8.77
Interest-bearing domestic deposits	68.9	47.74	8.73
Foreign deposits	0.0	6.89	44.97
Federal funds purchased and other borrowings	2.1	13.43	19.60
Subordinated notes and debentures	0.2	0.50	5.25
Other liabilities	2.0	5.69	7.68
TOTAL	92.0	93.70	95.00
Total equity capital	8.0	6.30	5.00
TOTAL LIABILITIES AND CAPITAL	100.0	100.00	100.00

BALANCE-SHEET MANAGEMENT: A THREE-STAGE APPROACH

Figure 2-1 presents a general framework for analyzing the financial management of a commercial bank. The approach is in three stages and focuses on the management of a bank's balance sheet. The first stage is a *general* one that looks at the management of a bank's assets, liabilities, and capital. Stage 2, which is a more *specific* one, focuses on particular management areas within the three components of the general balance-sheet stage (including off-balance sheet activities). In stage 3, the balance sheet is viewed as *generating* the income-and-expense statement. Thus, the results observed in the profit-and-loss statement are *symptoms* of the bank's balance-sheet performance. Balance-sheet management should be directed toward maximizing the *value* of the bank. Policies that bank managers can focus on to achieve this objective are (1) spread and fee management, (2) control of overhead, (3) liquidity management, (4) capital management, (5) tax management, and (6) management of off-balance sheet activities.

In generating their profit-and-loss statements, banks earn some profits from the spread between loan and deposit rates. Other revenues and expenses are referred to as noninterest income (e.g., fees and service charges) and noninterest expenses (e.g., salaries and wages), respectively. Since noninterest expenses have exceeded noninterest income, the difference, which is sometimes called *burden*, has been covered by the positive spread on rates. Deregulation of deposit interest rates and greater competition from other financial-services firms (FSFs) have reduced the spread on bank earning assets. As a result, banks have tried to generate greater fee income and/or to reduce overhead expenses to maintain their profitability.

STAGE 1 (General)

Asset Management	Liability Management
	Capital Management

STAGE 2 (Specific)

Reserve-Position Management	Reserve-Position Liability Management
Liquidity Management	Generalized or Loan-Position Liability Management
Investment Management	Long-Term Debt Management
Loan Management	
Fixed-Asset Management	Capital Management

(Including Off-Balance Sheet Activities)

STAGE 3 (Balance Sheet Generates the Income-and-Expense Statement)

Profit = Revenue − Interest Cost − Overhead − Taxes

Policies to Achieve Objectives:

1. Spread and Fee Management
2. Control of Overhead
3. Liquidity Management
4. Capital Management
5. Tax Management
6. Management of Off-Balance Sheet Activities

Figure 2-1   Balance-Sheet Management: A Three-Stage Approach

A COMMERCIAL BANK'S INCOME–EXPENSE STATEMENT

Given the size of its balance sheet, a bank's profitability primarily is determined by the composition of its balance sheet and its operating efficiency. These two factors are reflected in the bank's income–expense statement. The typical format for this statement is shown in Table 2-3. A bank's bottom line profitability, called net income, is the sum of five components: (1) net interest income $(R - C)$, or the aggregate "spread" between lending and borrowing rates; (2) provision for loan losses (PLL); (3) net noninterest income $(F - O)$, which usually is negative and therefore called the bank's "burden"; (4) taxes (T); and (5) securities gains/losses (G). The symbols used are defined in Table 2-3.

Commercial banks have been described as surviving on "spread dope." That is, since a positive spread is needed to cover a bank's loan losses, "burden," taxes, and dividend, it is this "fix" that keeps them going. With the prospect of reduced spreads in the new FSI, banks have been trying to lighten their burdens. To do this, they need to increase noninterest revenues (i.e., fees and services charges) and/or to reduce their overhead expenses and thereby increase operating efficiency. The major noninterest expense for banks is salaries and wages.

Loans, which comprise the major part of a bank's portfolio of earning assets, are the major source of bank revenue. It is not surprising, therefore, that banks that experience financial difficulties have problems with their loan portfolios. These problems are manifested in the form of nonperforming assets (e.g., loans to less developed countries by the major banks) and loan losses (e.g., losses on energy-related loans by banks in the Southwest such as Penn Square, a 1982 bank failure). Banks that fail usually have such severe loan losses that their current earnings, loan-loss reserves, and capital are wiped out.

The source of a bank's dividend payment is its after-tax profits plus noncash outlays (e.g., depreciation). Since noncash outlays for banks are not substantial compared to nonfinancial firms, net income is a good approximation of the cash flow available for a bank's dividend payment. The earnings retained by a bank are its major source of capital. Moreover, for community banks with limited access to capital markets, retained earnings tend to be the only source of capital. Without external capital, if capital ratios are to be maintained, asset growth is constrained by profitability and dividend payout such that the internal capital generation rate (g) is equal to the product of the retention ratio (RR) and return on equity (ROE) (i.e., $g = RR \times ROE$).

TABLE 2-3   Typical Format for a Bank's Income–Expense Statement

(1)	Interest income (R)
(2)	Interest expense (C)
(3) = (1) − (2)	Net interest income ("spread," $R - C$)
(4)	Provision for loan losses (PLL)
(5) = (3) − (4)	Net interest income after provision for loan losses
(6)	Noninterest income (e.g., fees, F)
(7)	Noninterest expense ("overhead," O)
(8) = (6) − (7)	Net noninterest income ("burden," $F - O$)
(9) = (5) − (8)	Income before taxes and securities gains (losses) $(R - C) - \text{PLL} + (F - O)$
(10)	Income taxes (T)
(11) = (9) − (10)	Net operating income $[(R - C) - \text{PLL} + (F - O) - T]$
(12)	Securities gains/losses $(+/-G)$
(13) = (11) +/−(12)	Net income $(NI) = [(R - C) - \text{PLL} + (F - O) - T +/-G]$
(14)	Dividends (D)
(15) = (13) +/−(14)	Addition to retained earnings (RE) $= [(R - C) - \text{PLL} + (F - O) - T +/-G - D] = NI - D$

BANKS AS REGULATED FIRMS AND THE DEVELOPMENT OF NONBANK BANKS

In the 1970 Amendment to the Bank Holding Company Act of 1956, the U.S. Congress defines a commercial bank as an institution that "(1) accepts deposits that the depositor has a legal right to withdraw on demand, and (2) engages in the business of making commercial loans." This statutory definition is important because by not engaging in one of the specified activities a corporation can own and operate a bank without being subject to Federal Reserve regulation as a bank holding company (BHC). Banks that fit this mold have been referred to as "nonbank banks or limited-service banks." Moreover, since most of them have chosen to forgo commercial lending, these nonbank banks also have been called consumer banks. However, some banks have decided to forgo offering checking-account services (i.e., demand deposits). For example, Merrill Lynch has been granted a state bank charter in New Jersey. The new bank, called Merrill Lynch Bank & Trust Co., does not accept demand deposits but does make commercial loans and offers trust-related services, and also accepts *time* deposits. In addition to brokerage houses such as Merrill Lynch, insurance companies, retail chains, service conglomerates, and even industrial companies have taken advantage of the nonbank-bank loophole to buy their way into the banking business. Some of the companies that have started or attempted to start nonbank banks include Dreyfus and Fidelity Funds, Prudential-Bache, Commercial Credit Co., Parker Pen, Shearson/American Express, Household International, E. F. Hutton, Avco, Gulf + Western, J. C. Penney, and Dimension Financial Corp.

Are the commercial banks that meet the legal definition of a bank alarmed? No; at least not the giant BHCs, because they opened their own consumer banks across state lines. Using a legal loophole first discovered by U.S. Trust Corp., the giant BHCs (e.g., Mellon, First Interstate, Bank of New York, Chase Manhattan, Chemical, Citicorp) have seen the nonbank-bank loophole as a vehicle for moving to full interstate banking. The nonbank-bank movement, however, came to a halt with the passage of the Competitive Equity Banking Act of 1987, which bans further establishment of them. The 160 or so existing nonbank banks were grandfathered, but with restrictions on their activities (see Appendix C of Chapter 7).

Regarding the nonbank-bank controversy and the issue of a level playing field for banks, C. T. Conover, then Comptroller of the Currency, speaking before the North Carolina Bankers' Association 1984 annual convention, said:

> If I were in your shoes, I would consider trading in my commercial banking charter and becoming a unitary thrift holding company. Your holding company could include a savings and loan association, a full-service securities firm, an insurance company, and a commercial finance company. Your S&L could have a nationwide network of ATMs, and it could meet any portfolio test. If you started getting too many commercial loans you could sell them to your commercial finance company, buy them for your insurance company portfolio, or pool and sell them on the outside with your full-service securities firm. You certainly can't do any of that with the charter you have now. The prospects for further deregulation are not particularly bright right now.[3]

One financial institution that took the Comptroller's words seriously was the Old Stone Corporation of Rhode Island, the state's second largest financial institution and the parent organization of Old Stone Bank. Old Stone was chartered as a federal savings bank in 1819, converted to a commercial bank in 1973, and became

---

[3] *The American Banker* [May 1, 1984], p. 4.

a thrift holding company in 1984. The latest conversion will remove Old Stone from the Fed's control and make it easier for it to acquire the North Carolina S&L it wants, an acquisition prohibited by the Fed. At year-end 1983, Old Stone, which operates 95 offices in 22 states through its subsidiaries, had $2.3 billion in assets and profits of $16.6 million for a respectable return on assets (ROA) of 0.73 percent. Regarding Old Stone's conversion, Charles Hoffman, an economist with the American Bankers Association, said: "With the growing interest among commercial banks in converting to thrift charters, it seems proof we don't have the level playing field that we've been fighting for."[4] Old Stone officials candidly admitted that they had been looking for a more liberal regulator with respect to interstate banking and they found one at the Federal Home Loan Bank, the thrift regulator.

TYPES AND CLASSES OF COMMERCIAL BANKS

To gain further insight into the question of what is a commercial bank, it is useful to look at the various types and classes of banks that exist. To begin, consider how you would start a bank. The economic barriers to entry in banking are not that great: you need at least a million dollars in capital and at least a trailer with a telephone line and other accessories. And, of course, you would want an attractive name for your institution. In addition, and this is the important barrier to entry, you would need a *charter* from the Office of the Comptroller of the Currency (OCC) to start a *national bank* or from your state banking agency to start a *state bank*. This double mechanism for the chartering and regulating of commercial banks in the Unites States is referred to as *dual banking* or the *dual-banking system*. Thus, in the United States, a commercial bank is either a nationally chartered bank or a state-chartered bank.

To obtain a national charter, the founders of a bank are required to document a number of factors, the most important of which are[5]

1. the general character of the bank's management
2. the future earnings prospects of the bank
3. the adequacy of the bank's capital structure
4. The financial history and condition of the bank (relevant only for a bank that is switching from a state charter to a national one)
5. the convenience and needs of the area to be served by the bank.

Since it is highly unlikely that a state charter would be granted without federal deposit insurance (in fact some states make that a prerequisite for obtaining a charter) and since the standards for obtaining federal deposit insurance are similar to those for chartering a national bank, effective control over entry in banking is at the federal level.

A nationally chartered bank is required by law to join the Federal Reserve System (Fed) and all members of the Fed must have federal deposit insurance. In contrast, a state-chartered bank has the option of joining the Fed or not. If it joins the Fed, the bank must obtain federal deposit insurance. Thus, only a state bank can be a noninsured bank.

In addition to classification by type of charter and by federal regulation, banks can be identified by their structure, business orientation, and geographic presence. Regarding structure, there are unit banks, branch banks, and holding company banks.

---

[4] *The American Banker*, [September 21, 1984], pp. 1 and 54.

[5] The requirements are spelled out in the Banking Act of 1935.

TABLE 2-4   Various Commercial Bank Classifications or Categories

Charter

1. National Bank
2. State Bank

Federal regulation (agency)

1. National Bank (Office of the Comptroller of the Currency, OCC)
2. State Member Bank (Federal Reserve System, FRS)
3. State Insured Nonmember Bank (Federal Deposit Insurance Corporation, FDIC)
4. State Noninsured Bank (No Federal Regulation but Subject to State Regulation)
5. Banks or BHCs with 500 shareholders or more (Securities and Exchange Commission, SEC)

Structure or organizational form

1. Unit Bank
2. Branch Bank
3. Holding-Company Bank

Type of business

1. Wholesale Bank
2. Retail Bank
3. Wholesale/Retail Bank

Geographic market (business orientation)

1. Community or Local Bank (Retail)
2. Regional Bank (Wholesale/Retail)
3. Money-Center or Multinational Bank (Wholesale)

Real dual banking (number of banks)

1. Money-Center and Regional Banks (500)
2. The Rest of the Industry (14,500)

Moreover, within a holding company, banks may be either of the unit or branch type. A bank holding company (BHC) is simply an organization that owns or controls one or more banks; it is classified according to whether it controls one bank or more than one bank. The latter is referred to as a *multibank holding company* (MBHC) and the former is a *one-bank holding company* (OBHC). Today, BHCs are the most important organizational form in U. S. banking as they control roughly 80 percent of total bank deposits and assets. In addition to their banking business, BHCs are permitted to expand into certain closely related nonbanking areas. These permissible nonbanking activities are closely regulated by the Fed.

A bank also can be categorized according to its major business orientation. The three primary groupings are (1) wholesale banking, (2) retail banking, and (3) wholesale/retail banking. A wholesale bank is one with a commercial or corporate focus (e.g., Morgan Guaranty of New York). In contrast, a retail bank focuses on consumer business, with loan and deposit transactions characterized by much smaller size and higher activity than a wholesale bank would experience. A wholesale/retail bank is one with a more balanced mix of corporate and consumer accounts.

With respect to geographic presence or market coverage, commercial banks are described as community banks (operating in local markets), regional banks (operating in regional markets), or money-center or multinational banks (operating in national and international markets). The approximate linkage between geographic or market focus and business orientation is that community banks have a retail orientation (including small businesses); regional banks have a retail/wholesale orientation; and money-center banks have a wholesale orientation, although most of them still do some retail banking, especially for wealthy individuals. The catering of financial services to the rich is called "private banking." Take a stroll along Madison Avenue in midtown Manhattan and you will see the posh banking centers of the major New York City banks that provide private-banking services. Employees of these establishments literally are at the beck and call of these "preferred customers" to such an extent that some of them are required to carry beepers and be on call. Private banking, of course, is not restricted to New York City, but exists in all major metropolitan areas in the United States. If you don't meet the wealth requirements, please use the ATM, thank you. The various bank classifications and categories discussed in this section are summarized in Table 2-4.

THE REAL DUAL BANKING SYSTEM

The traditional notion of dual banking is a *de jure* one embodied in the dichotomy between federal and state regulation of banking. There is, however, a more important *de facto* definition of dual banking that describes the "real" dichotomy that exists in the banking industry. The *real dual banking* system is one that is divided along economic and political lines. In terms of numbers, we are talking about the 500 or so big banks (controlled by BHCs) versus the rest of the industry, made up of 14,000 or so community-type banks. The big banks have the economic and financial clout because they control the majority of bank assets and deposits. However, the rest of the industry historically has had the political clout (one bank one vote), as manifested in various state and independent banking associations made up of numerous small banks. While there is no doubt about which group has the economic power, in the political arena the battle for control has been an intense one. The large banks tend to be in favor of product and geographic deregulation, whereas the small banks tend to favor the status quo. The giant BHCs, which operate nationwide (through their nonbank subsidiaries) and internationally, consider it an absurdity that they cannot perform certain banking transactions (e.g., deposit gathering) across all state lines.

Recently, the banking industry, through such national organizations as the American Bankers Association (ABA) and the Bank Administration Institute (BAI), has been trying to present more of a united front on political issues. The rallying cry of a "level playing field" in the fight against nonbanking firms, such as thrift institutions and money-market mutual funds, has helped to close the political gap to some extent. Given the recent trend toward bank deregulation, it appears that the big banks are gaining political power to go with their economic power. The important point is that it is difficult to talk about "the commercial-banking industry" when, in effect, a *real* dual banking system exists.

COMMERCIAL BANKS AS FINANCIAL INTERMEDIARIES

A financial intermediary is an institution that channels funds from surplus-spending units (SSUs) to deficit-spending units (DSUs). Loosely, SSUs are "savers" and DSEs are "investors." The "units" described are the basic economic units in society, namely households, business firms, and governments (i.e., local, state, and federal). In the aggregate, households historically have been SSUs while business firms and

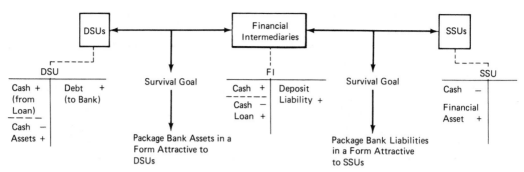

Figure 2-2   The Process of Financial Intermediation

governments have been DSUs. The movement of surplus funds to productive investment projects is an important economic function.

Commercial banks belong to a general class of financial intermediaries known as *depository financial institutions*. Other members of the group including savings-and-loan associations (SLAs or S&Ls), mutual savings banks (MSBs), and credit unions (CUs). The asset and liability structures of these institutions have been growing more similar over recent years. Nondepository financial institutions include such organizations as life insurance companies, property and casualty insurance companies, pension funds, finance companies, and investment companies.

The general process of financial intermediation is depicted in Figure 2-2. The diagram illustrates two fundamental goals that financial institutions must meet if they are to survive. First, they must package their liabilities in forms that are attractive to SSUs. And second, they must package their assets in forms that are attractive to DSUs. For commercial banks, this means that their loan and deposit services must be appropriately priced and conveniently available to customers relative to those of their competitors.

The process depicted in Figure 2-2 is sometimes referred to as *indirect finance*. It is indirect in the sense that DSUs and SSUs meet not directly but indirectly, through a financial intermediary. When DSUs and SSUs meet directly without the services of a financial intermediary, the process is referred to as *direct finance*. The process of securitization, discussed in Chapter 1, suggests a third type of finance, namely, *pass-through finance*.

The process of financial intermediation can be viewed in terms of the marginal T-accounts for the SSU, the DSU, and the financial intermediary (FI) as shown in Figure 2-2. For the SSU, the process is simply a transaction involving the swap of cash or savings for a financial asset in the form of a deposit account at the FI. For the FI, the deposit inflow means an increase on both sides of its balance sheet or T-account. When the FI lends, it swaps the cash inflow or excess reserves for a loan to the DSU. On the DSU's books, the loan transaction results in an increase in debt and a balancing increase in cash, which then is used to purchase the desired asset (e.g., a machine, an inventory, a house, a car, or a personal computer). The transactions represented below the dashed lines in the T-accounts in Figure 2-2 are second-stage activities for each economic entity.

In addition to the dollar flows that occur in the process of financial intermediation, important information flows occur. These flows are generated through the borrowing and lending activities transacted with the bank. Based upon these information flows, banks must develop sorting mechanisms to distinguish "good" customers from "bad" ones and price their products and services accordingly. Thus, the processing of information is an important part of the financial-intermediation business: banks send information signals to the marketplace about the creditworthiness of borrowers, whereas depositors and shareholders (who have contingent claims on banks' assets) signal information about the value of banks' assets.

Financial intermediaries exist because of the benefits or services they provide to their customers (i.e., the ultimate lenders—SSUs—and the ultimate borrowers—DSUs). The four basic services they provide are

1. liquidity intermediation
2. denomination intermediation
3. risk intermediation
4. maturity intermediation.

Liquidity intermediation is simply another name for the transactions function provided by financial institutions. It includes the liquidity needs of both borrowers (via loan demand) and lenders (via deposit withdrawals). The other three intermediation services represent a more sophisticated view of the safekeeping function provided by financial institutions. This intermediation trinity eliminates the need for a coincidence of wants on the basis of denomination (size), risk, or maturity. Thus, for example, a risk-averse SSU with $10,000 to lend for six months does not have to go through the costly process of finding a risk-averse DSU to borrow $10,000 for six months. As a result of financial intermediation, the preferences of SSUs and DSUs with respect to denomination, risk, and maturity do not have to match.

The intermediation services provided by financial institutions are suggestive of the managerial problems they face. Thus, to provide efficient liquidity intermediation, banks must be liquid so that they can meet loan demand and/or deposit withdrawals. Liquidity can be stored on the LHS of bank's balance sheet or obtained on the RHS of the balance sheet through liability management. "Denomination intermediation" suggests that longstanding customers with large deposit balances and regular borrowing patterns are preferred to those without such traits. This means that customer relationships are an important part of the business of banking.

Default risk and interest-rate risk arise from risk intermediation and maturity intermediation, respectively. A bank's success critically depends upon the efficient management of these two services. Moreover, the *mis*management of these two intermediation functions has been the major cause of failure in depository institutions. In today's environment, maturity intermediation with the accompanying interest-rate risk is the major financial-management problem that banks and other financial intermediaries face.

On balance, the efficient management of the four intermediation functions is the essence of intermediary financial management. Moreover, since denomination intermediation is not a critical management concern, the focus of this book (and of practical bank financial management) is on three key areas or risks: (1) liquidity risk, (2) credit risk, and (3) interest-rate risk. The management of these three risks is the heart of the intermediation business.

COMMERCIAL BANKS AS CREATORS OF MONEY

In a money-and-banking course, three preliminary questions can be asked:

1. What is money?
2. What is banking?
3. Why study money and banking together?

The answer to the second question is the focus of this chapter. To answer the first question in detail goes beyond the scope of this book. However, in brief, money is primarily a means of payment and can be measured by the instruments used for payment, namely currency and transactions balances (e.g., demand deposits, NOW accounts). On a broader basis, á la Milton Friedman, money can be viewed as a "temporary abode of purchasing power." Alternatively, a conceptually appealing framework is to view money as a weighted average of various means of payment, as Edward J. Kane has done.

To answer the third question, money and banking are studied together because commercial banks *create* the major component of the money supply, no matter how it is defined. How do depository institutions "create" money? It is a simple process, although the detailed mechanics of it and the related topics of monetary theory and policy go beyond the scope of this book. The creation of money goes like this. When a financial institution makes a loan, this usually results in the creation of a transactions-type account. In other words, a means of payment is generated and the money supply increases. Given the purpose of the loan, the new deposits will be spent and work their way through the economy as income to some other economic unit and perhaps into another (or the same) depository institution as reserves to generate more loans and so on. The result is the familiar deposit-expansion process or *multiplier* described in money-and-banking and principles-of-economics textbooks.

The money-supply process in the United States is shaped by three important factors or sectors:

1. the currency-holding public,
2. the financial-institutions sector, especially commercial banks, and
3. the Federal Reserve System (as the central bank).

Since commercial banks are the kingpins of the financial system, understanding their microeconomic foundations and behavior is important for comprehending the money-supply process.

THE BANKS OF BANKING

Table 2-3 summarizes the various classes of commercial banks. Within a particular bank, especially the largest ones, it is common to describe its businesses in terms of banks. Hence, we can talk about the "banks of banking." In general, the banks of banking include the consumer bank, the corporate bank, and the investment bank. Citicorp uses the "I formation" to describe its businesses, that is, Institutional Bank, Individual Bank, and Investment Bank. By adding information and insurance to Citicorp's classification scheme, we can talk about the five Is of banking. In terms of the retail/wholesale dichotomy shown in Table 2-3, the terms *consumer* and *individual* map into retail whereas the terms *corporate, institutional*, and *investment* map into wholesale.

The Corporate Bank

The corporate bank is the traditional bank of commercial banking. Typically, it offers the broadest range of corporate financial services (e.g., credit facilities [loans], cash-management services, and payment services) to corporations, financial institutions, and governments, both domestic and foreign. For a community bank, the corporate bank would be its "small-business bank." For a large bank holding company like Citicorp, and its main subsidiary Citibank, roughly one-half of its corporate (institutional) banking business is done overseas. In contrast, regional BHCs and the growing "super regionals" do substantially less, but a growing portion, of their corporate business overseas.

The Consumer Bank

Historically, commercial banks, as the name implies, did not cater to consumers or individuals. Moreover, a few of the largest commercial banks still regard themselves strictly as wholesale players (e.g., Morgan Guaranty). As such, they cater only to corporate customers and wealthy individuals. However, the overwhelming majority of commercial banks have a vital interest in providing consumers with financial services. These services include transaction accounts, savings acounts, loans, insurance (where permitted), investment (IRAs, discount brokerage, etc.), trust and estate management, and various electronic banking services in the form of ATMs, home banking, and wire transfers. A number of changes in the FSI such as the movement of thrift institutions and retail brokerage houses into consumer banking, the rapid growth and popularity of money-market funds, and the development of nonbank banks has made competition for the delivery of financial services to consumers an intense battle. Quality products and efficient and reliable service will determine the winners of this battle.

The Investment Bank

Although large U.S. BHCs engage in investment banking on a full scale overseas, their investment-banking activities are restricted within the United States. The development of investment banks within commercial banking organizations is a relatively new phenomenon. For example, Citicorp traces the origins of its investment bank to the late 1970s. The impetus for this development can be traced to fundamental shifts in the methods and techniques of corporation finance. To illustrate, as corporations turned increasingly to commercial paper, revolving underwriting facilities, and shelf registration of public-offered debt, commercial banks found their spreads in traditional bank lending narrowing and their share of the financial-services market dwindling. To combat these adverse changes (keep in mind the forces of TRICK here), commercial bankers began developing investment-banking products. They argue that their entry into this segment of the FSI will promote competition, lower costs, and strengthen the U.S. financial system. Securities firms, of course, oppose this encroachment on their turf (rational self-interest knows no bounds).

The typical menu of investment-banking products supplied by a large BHC includes fund raising, management of interest-rate and foreign-exchange risks, merger-and-acquisition services, securities products, liquidity for customer investments through trading activities, various economic and information products, management of investment portfolios by providing custodial and safekeeping services, and venture-capital activities.

BANK MARKET STRATEGY IN THE FINANCIAL-SERVICES INDUSTRY

Although this book has a financial-management focus, it also examines the environmental and marketing factors as fully as possible, especially in their technological and regulatory aspects. The great importance of the marketing function in banking is best illustrated by the acquisition in 1984 of the Bank Marketing Association by the American Bankers Association, the leading trade organization for commercial bankers. Let's look briefly at the importance of marketing to commercial banks.

Commercial banks operate in the financial-services industry (FSI) and not just in the banking industry. When the transportation revolution began in the United States, the managers of railroads failed to recognize that they were operating in the transportation industry and not just in the railroad industry. This strategic blunder was primarily responsible for the decline of the American railroads and for the dismal state of that industry in the United States today. To avoid the fate of the railroads, commercial banks must develop financial services and products that create a demand or meet a need, and they must be able to deliver these services in an efficient and effective manner to a highly competitive marketplace. Without market-oriented services and products, banks will follow the railroad tracks into oblivion. Most bank managers have recognized the strategic importance of seeing their business as the development and delivery of financial services and products, with information management as an important by-product. As financial intermediaries, banks collect and process tremendous amounts of information about their customers—both lenders and borrowers. These information flows must be processed, managed, and distributed efficiently and effectively within the banking organization to achieve optimal results. In addition, the information flows can be used to develop services (e.g., cash management) that banks can supply to their customers, including other banks.

Regarding myopic strategy, Walter B. Wriston, who retired as chairman of Citicorp/Citibank in 1984, stated in 1981:

> The philosophy of the divine rights of kings died hundreds of years ago, but not, it seems, the divine right of inherited markets. Some people still believe there's a divine dispensation that their markets are theirs—and no one else's—now and forevermore. It is an old dream that dies hard, yet no businessman in a free society can control a market when the customers decide to go somewhere else. All the king's horses and all the king's men are helpless in the face of a better product.
>
> Our commercial history is filled with examples of companies that failed to change with a changing world, and became tombstones in the corporate graveyard.[7]

Financial-services firms that fail to survive in the financial-services industry of today may be viewed tomorrow as having suffered from the railroad syndrome. Appreciation of this lesson is one of the keys to surviving in any business. The marketplace has a short memory and is more concerned with what a business can do for it now or in the future than with its past performance.

CHAPTER SUMMARY

From the etymology of the word *bank* to bank market strategy in the financial-services industry (FSI), this chapter has focused on the banks of banking (consumer, corporate, and investment) and alternative concepts of the banking firm. From the etymology, the two basic functions of banking are derived: transactions and safekeeping. The alternative conceptual devices include the notions of a bank as a department store of finance, as a balance sheet (or portfolio), as an information processor, and as

---

[7] Speech to the Securities Industry Association, New York, N.Y., January 21, 1981. Reprinted as *You Can't Tell the Players With a Scorecard*, New York: Citicorp Public Affairs Department [1981], p. 9.

a regulated firm. In addition, banks can be perceived as financial intermediaries and as creators of money. By linking these concepts with the issues addressed in Chapter 1, you should have a better understanding of those issues and be able to take a position regarding (1) specialness, (2) the separation of commercial and investment banking, and (3) the separation of banking and commerce.

LIST OF KEY WORDS, CONCEPT, AND ACRONYMS

Balance sheet (portfolio)
Balance-sheet management
Bank holding company (BHC)
Banks of banking (consumer,
   corporate, investment)
Deficit-spending unit (DSU)
Department store of finance
Dual banking (*de facto* or real versus
   de jure)
Equity multiplier (EM)
Etymology
Federal Deposit Insurance Corporation
   (FDIC)

Finance (direct versus indirect versus
   pass-through)
Financial intermediation
Market strategy
Nonbank bank or limited-service bank
Office of the Comptroller of the
   Currency (OCC)
Regulated firm
Surplus-spending unit (SSU)
Types and classes of commercial banks

REVIEW/DISCUSSION QUESTIONS

1. Trace the functional role of banks beginning with their etymology and ending with the notion of a department store of finance operating in the FSI.
2. Describe and discuss the importance of information processing to commercial banks and financial intermediaries in general.
3. Distinguish between a bank's physical vault and its "real vault." What is one approach to managing the latter?
4. Should a bank's balance sheet be measured in accounting terms or in real or market-value terms? Discuss.
5. Discuss the various types and classes of commercial banks. What is a nonbank bank?
6. What are the four basic services provided by financial intermediaries and how do they relate to the essence of intermediary financial management? Discuss the roles of commercial banks as financial intermediaries and as creators of money. What is the money supply and who controls it?
7. Discuss the concepts of "real dual banking" and the "banks of banking." How are they related, if at all?
8. What marketing lesson does the railroad industry have for the banking industry? Does the lesson apply to other financial-services firms such as insurance companies, thrift institutions, and brokerage houses? Discuss.
9. Go to your library and browse through some of the sources of banking information listed in the appendix of this chapter. *The American Banker* is the best source for keeping abreast of daily developments in banking and the financial-services industry.

MATCHING QUIZ

Directions: Select the letter from the right-hand column that best matches the item in the left-hand column.

___ 1. Safekeeping function

___ 2. Transaction function

___ 3. Information processing

___ 4. Nonbank bank

___ 5. Portfolio

___ 6. Bank holding company

___ 7. Equity multiplier

___ 8. Bank survival rule

___ 9. Real dual banking

___ 10. National bank regulator

___ 11. BHC regulator

___ 12. Retail bank

___ 13. Wholesale bank

___ 14. Deficit-spending unit

___ 15. Surplus-spending unit

___ 16. Fundamentals of financial intermediation

A. Don't make too many bad loans

B. Needs savings products

C. Needs loan products

D. *Banca* (bench)

E. *Banque* (chest)

F. Must precede lending decisions

G. Can't do DD *and* commercial
lending

H. A bank's real vault

I.   Dominant organizational form

J.   FDIC

K. OCC

L.   Federal Reserve

M. Big versus little economic clout

N. Consumer/small business bank

O. Corporate/investment bank

P. Inverted capital-adequacy measure

Q. Liquidity, denomination, risk, and
maturity

CHAPTER 2

APPENDIX
Sources of Banking Information

Newspapers
The American Banker
National Thrift News
Barron's (weekly)
The New York Times
The Wall Street Journal
Regional and local papers

Magazines
Business Week
Forbes
Fortune
The Money Manager

Trade publications (practitioner oriented)
ABA Banking Journal
Bank Credit Card Observer
The Bankers Magazine
Bankers Monthly
Bank Marketing
Bank Mergers and Acquisition
Financier, The Journal of Financial Affairs
The Independent Banker
Issues in Bank Regulation
Journal of Commercial Bank Lending
The Magazine of Bank Administration
The Mortgage Banker
Mutual Savings Banks Journal
Private Banking
Rate Percentgram
Real Estate Review
Savings Institutions
Secondary Mortgage Markets

Academic journals
The Banking Law Journal
Financial Management
The Financial Review
Journal of Accounting, Auditing, and Finance
Journal of Applied Corporate Finance
Journal of Banking and Finance
Journal of Bank Research (ceased publication
  in 1986)
Journal of Finance
Journal of Financial Economics

Journal of Financial and Quantitative Analysis
Journal of Financial Research
Journal of Financial Services Research
Journal of Money, Credit and Banking
Review of Financial Studies

Government publications
Annual Reports (FDIC, OCC, FRS, etc.)
Congressional Hearings, Reports, and Staff
  Studies usually may be obtained by writing
  the Chief Clerk of the Committee in question.
Bank Structure and Competition (Annual, FRB
  of Chicago)
Federal Home Loan Bank Board Journal.
Federal Reserve Bulletin and the Monthly/
  Quarterly Reviews of the District Federal
  Reserve Banks Treasury Bulletin

Cases
Intercollegiate Case Clearing House
Soldiers Field Post Office
Boston, MA 02163
Check bookstores and libraries for case books
  on commercial banking

Computer tapes (report of condition and report
  of income, i.e., balance-sheet and income-
  expense data, respectively, for commercial
  banks).
FDIC
FRS
OCC
Standard and Poor's Compustat Services, Inc.

Commercial-bank computer simulations
Stanford Bank Management Simulator,
  Stanford University
BankSim, American Bankers Association/FDIC
Asset/Liability Management: A Model for
  Commercial Banks, Olson Research
  Associates (Silver Spring, Maryland)

Miscellaneous
Bankers Desk Reference
Polk's Bank Directory

SELECTED REFERENCES

Chan, Yuk-Shee, Stuart I. Greenbaum, and Anjan V. Thakor. [1986]. "Information Reusability, Competition, and Bank Asset Quality," *Journal of Banking and Finance* (June), pp. 243–253.

Kane, Edward J. [1964]. "Money as a Weighted Aggregate," *Zeitschrift fur Nationalokonomie* XXIV, Heft 3, pp. 241–243.

Leland, Hayne, and David Pyle. [1977]. "Information Asymmetries, Financial Structure, and Financial Intermediation," *Journal of Finance* (May), pp. 371–387.

Martial, Alfred. [1969]. "Biological Analogies for Money: A Crucial Breakthrough," *Journal of Finance* (March), pp. 111–112.

Stiglitz, Joseph, and Andrew Weiss. [1981]. "Credit Rationing in Markets with Imperfect Information," *American Economic Review* (June), pp. 393–410.

Szego, Giorgio P. [1986]. "Bank Asset Management and Financial Insurance," *Journal of Banking and Finance* (June), pp. 295–307.

Tobin, James [1963]. "Commercial Banks as Creators of Money," in *Banking and Monetary Studies*, Deane Carson, ed. Homewood Hills, IL: Irwin, pp. 408–419.

PART II

BANKING THEORY AND FINANCIAL MANAGEMENT

This part of the book focuses on the theory of banking and finance and the fundamental building blocks of financial management. In Chapter 3, we look at the fundamentals of finance as applied to the real world with special emphasis on financial-services firms and in particular on commercial banks. In Chapter 4, we focus on banking in the theory of finance and on models of the banking firm. Although both chapters have a theoretical foundation, Chapter 3 has a more practical side to it and reflects one of the major themes of the book, namely, that for managers of financial-services firms, understanding and applying modern financial management is an important key, if not the key, to survival in the financial-services industry. In this context, management should see its objective as the maximization of shareholder value. In contrast, knowledge of banking theory and models of the banking firm plays a less critical role in the day-to-day operations of a bank. Nevertheless, the theories of the banking firm are interesting and important as an academic discipline and for generating insights about banking behavior. Moreover, a clearer understanding of the underpinnings of the banking system adds to our knowledge of the entire financial system and the overall economy. Finally, from a financial-management perspective, complete models of the banking firm provide for integrated views of both the real and financial aspects of bank behavior.

CHAPTER 3

The Fundamentals of Financial Management

ACRONYM GUIDE TO KEY TERMS AND CONCEPTS

CAPM = capital asset pricing model
EPS = earnings per share
EVA = economic value added
NPV = net present value
P/E = price-earnings ratio
ROE = return on equity
RR = retention ratio

INTRODUCTION

The essence of corporate finance is the acquisition of assets and the funding of those assets. The latter can be achieved through either direct finance or indirect finance. Direct finance involves the issuance of securities directly to surplus-spending units. Investment bankers provide financial services to enable companies to directly tap the debt and equity markets. In providing these services, investment bankers face underwriting risks; however, once these transactions are completed, the risks are removed. In contrast, commercial bankers serve as intermediaries by transferring claims against their firms (deposits) into earnings assets (loans), which are claims against borrowers. When bankers make loans, they make "incomplete transactions." Specifically, until the loans are repaid, the banker's job is not done—the transaction is incomplete. Over this time period, the lender is exposed to credit and liquidity risks, and, depending on how the loan is priced, possible interest rate risk.

As we have seen in the previous two chapters, a legal barrier or "Chinese wall," the Glass–Steagall Act, is attempting to keep commercial and investment bankers on separate sides of the financial-services fence. Whatever the outcome of this battle, commercial bankers need to know something about how the managers of borrowing companies select investment opportunities (in particular how they evaluate the riskiness of those projects) and how they finance those opportunities. By knowing more about how borrowers conduct the financial management of their businesses, lenders will be better able to assess their own risk exposure and better able to determine the products and services their customers need. In addition, this knowledge will better enable them to conduct the financial management of their own firms.

This chapter focuses on financial management for financial-services firms by high-lighting, in a nontechnical way, the fundamental building blocks of corporate finance.

MODERN FINANCE IN THE REAL WORLD

Joel Stern, a leading financial consultant and a person who understands and believes in the fundamental tenets of modern finance, says this about the acceptance of modern finance across the boardrooms of corporate America: "...the majority of our corporate directors and senior executives remain blissfully ignorant of, if not actively hostile toward, the central tenets of 'modern' finance."[1] According to Stern, this ignorance is best reflected in the adherence by corporate America to the "accounting model" of the firm, which says that stock prices are primarily determined by reported earnings, in particular earnings per share (EPS). In its most simplistic form, this approach relates value to a multiple of the firm's EPS such that

Stock Price = Price-Earnings Ratio × Earnings per Share

Or, in symbols,

$$P_0 = P/E \times EPS \tag{3-1}$$

where P_0 represents the current or period 0 stock price, P/E the industry price-earnings multiple, and EPS the firm's earnings per share. Given the firm's EPS, the accounting model says that industrywide P/E ratios determine its stock price. For example, a firm with an EPS of $5 in an industry with a P/E multiple of 10 would sell for $50. To maximize stock price, managers need only maximize EPS. The way some managers, stock analysts, and investors concentrate on a company's short-term earnings prospects suggests that Stern's claim is more fact than fiction.

THE ECONOMIC MODEL OF THE FIRM AND DISCOUNTED CASH FLOW

If the "accounting model" doesn't determine real value, then what does? In modern finance, discounted cash flow determines economic, real, or market value. Stern refers to this alternative to the accounting model as the "economic model." According to this view of valuation, the market value of a company's common stock (similar to the value of any other security or project that generates an earnings or cash flow stream) is equal to the present value of its expected future cash flow discounted at interest rates reflecting investors' required rates of return for investments of compara-ble risk.

When will the accounting model and the economic model give the same estimate of value? Two conditions are required: First, the firm's reported or accounting earnings would have to equal its cash flow, which in effect is the "return" requirement. And second, the firm would have to be a typical or average one in the industry such that the industrywide P/E ratio adequately captured its riskiness. The latter is the "risk" requirement. These two conditions or requirements highlight the fundamental deter-

---

[1] *Six Roundtable Discussions of Corporate Finance with Joel Stern* (edited by Donald H. Chew, Jr.). Westport, CT: Quorum Books [1986], p. 2. This section and the next three draw on these roundtable discussions.

minants of value: (1) risk and (2) return (i.e., cash flow). Holding other things constant, as return (cash flow) increases, value increases; as risk increases, value decreases. Since it is difficult to increase return without taking on additional risk, the terminology risk–return trade-off is common in finance.

When are these risk and return requirements likely to be equal across the two models? Hardly ever. Consider the return or cash flow requirement first. Differences in accounting and regulatory practices and managerial honesty suggest it is easy for managers to manipulate their reported earnings. Accordingly, the chances reported earnings will equal cash flow are remote. Certainly careful managers, investors, and lenders would not want to risk their money and/or their jobs on such an occurrence. Regarding risk, the accounting model implies "one risk fits all." Just as "one size fits all" seldom works in selecting clothing, it seldom works in evaluating risk. Each firm, in effect, has a unique P/E ratio tailored to the riskiness of its cash flows. Thus, only when the firm's cash flows are of average risk would the application of the industry-wide P/E be appropriate for capturing its riskiness. Again, careful analysts don't buy valuations from the "one-risk-fits-all" rack.

THE ECONOMIC MODEL, MARKET EFFICIENCY, AND "LEAD STEERS"

The cattle drive was an obligatory part of the Western movies of yesterday. Once the director made this commitment, the stampede scene was a must. The stampede usually was started by the bad guys, or by an approaching thunderstorm. To regain control of the herd, the good guys had to head off the lead steers, which they always did just before the thundering herd approached the proverbial cliff. Great drama when you are about ten years old. The good guys succeeded because they reached the lead steers, and because it was in the script.

In writing his finance script, Joel Stern has introduced the notion of "lead steers" as an important determinant of economic value, and as an important concept for understanding market efficiency. In Stern's parlance, "lead steers" are sophisticated investors who dominate financial markets. They have achieved this dominance because they have seen the "finance light" and thereby are able to distinguish between accounting illusion and economic reality in setting stock prices. As a result, they reward "value-maximizing behavior" by buying the stocks of companies whose managers read and practice the finance gospel, and by selling the stocks of the accounting-model heathens. By focusing on economic value, the lead steers ensure that companies' securities (whether debt or equity) are properly priced. In effect, lead steers do not select their risk evaluations from the "one-risk-fits-all" rack. They attempt to estimate future cash flows and discount those flows at interest rates reflecting the timing and riskiness of the future flows.

The three essential ingredients of finance are money (cash flow), time, and risk. Lead steers recognize the importance of these factors and act accordingly. In the marketplace, the lead steers are large institutional investors such as pension funds, insurance companies, and the trust departments of large banks. Although there is disagreement about how "dominant" the lead steers are, they do tend to lead the herd. According to Seely, the potential advantages of institutional ownership are (1) improved liquidity, (2) reduced volatility of stock prices, and (3) reduced likelihood of takeover.[2]

---

[2] *Ibid.*, p. 11.

CORPORATE FINANCIAL COMMUNICATION: REACHING THE LEAD STEERS

If lead steers exist and if they are as important as Stern and others would have us •believe, to whom should corporate financial communications be directed? Returning to our Western movie and the stampede scene, if the little investor is like a calf eating the dust of the thundering herd, then corporate financial communication directed at this investor will bite the dust also. Corporate road shows and glossy annual reports are the vehicles used to reach the little investor. According to Stewart and Glassman, "Clearly, the significance of the little investor has been exaggerated, and corporate financial communications may accordingly have been misdirected."[3]

Have corporate financial communications been misdirected? And, if they have been, how do lead steers get their information? What is the role of financial communication in an efficient market? Do the investor relations departments of publicly held companies perform useful services? Although the answers to these questions are neither easy nor obvious, we can suggest, with some degree of confidence, the following answers.

First, to the extent that financial communications say only where the company has been (i.e., provide historical information), they are not very useful. Lead steers certainly are not interested in such information. They want to know where the company is going and how it is going to get there in terms of future investment opportunities and how they will be financed (i.e., strategic planning see Chapter 12). To the extent that corporate road shows and glossy annual reports are directed at the small investor and to the extent that they contain only company history, then clearly they are misdirected. If this is the case, then how do lead steers get their information? Since company spokespersons are usually close-mouthed about future projects and their financing, lead steers will not get a jump on anyone else by waiting until the corporate "announcement date" to obtain information. Therefore, lead steers concentrate on suppliers, customers, and competitors as sources of new information for pricing securities. This scenario suggests that corporate financial communications inform only the "average investor" and not the one at the margin who actually determines value. Finally, the scenario also suggests that "effective corporate communication" treats all lead steers equally such that not one of them gets superior information.

Providing equal access to more and better information should be the goal of corporate financial communication. Although achieving this objective is unlikely to increase the firm's stock price, it may increase the stock's liquidity, defined as "...the ability to buy or sell large quantities of the stock without a discount from the prior trade."[4]

Now that we have looked at the role of modern finance in the real world, let's turn to a conceptualization of the role and objective of the financial manager by focusing on the key decisions of financial management, namely the investment, financing, dividend, and executive compensation decisions. Although the last decision is not made by the financial manager (it is made by the compensation committee of the board of directors), it is a critical decision because executive compensation and shareholder value are not independent. This area, which is a relatively new and exciting one in financial economics, is referred to as the economics of executive compensation.

[3] *Ibid.*, p. 57.

[4] *Ibid.*, p. 32.

THE ROLE AND OBJECTIVE OF THE FINANCIAL MANAGER

According to Stewart C. Myers of MIT, there is one unifying concept that occurs again and again in the field of financial management, that is, the idea that the financial manager is a person-in-the-middle between capital markets and the firm's operations. This person buys and sells real and financial assets with the goal of increasing the market value of the firm's equity. Any financial decision involves three important factors: (1) money, (2) time, and (3) risk. The theory of finance is concerned with the problem of evaluating alternative future monetary flows or values. Since the future is in general uncertain, the problem becomes one of evaluating risky monetary flows or values over time.

The financial manager has three important judgments to make[5]:

1. *The Investment Decision (I):* Decisions regarding how much to invest and in what specific assets. These decisions determine the *size* and *composition* of a firm's assets. Another name for the *I* decision is the *capital-budgeting* decision.
2. *The Financing Decision (F):* Decisions regarding how to raise the cash required for investment.
3. *The Dividend Decision (D):* Decisions regarding the firm's dividend-payout ratio, the ratio of dividends per share (DPS) to earnings per share (EPS): *DPS/EPS*.

These decisions determine whether or not shareholders' wealth or value (*V*) is maximized. At the margin, shareholders are made better off by any decision that increases the value of their investment in the firm. In symbols, the financial manager's objective function is:

$$Max\ V = f(I, F, D).$$

To the extent that some finance theorists regard the financing and dividend decisions to be "irrelevant," the investment decision becomes the critical one for maximizing value. Moreover, finance research has established that shareholder value is maximized when all investment opportunities with returns greater than the firm's cost of capital are undertaken.

Should the role and objective of the manager of a financial firm be any different from those of the financial manager of a nonfinancial firm? The answer is no. However, focusing on Figure 3-1, there are some minor adjustments to be made. First, to be more consistent with banking terminology, the *I, F,* and *D* decisions are renamed as *asset management, liability management*, and *capital/dividend manage-ment*, respectively. Second, at point 1, cash inflows from *deposit* and *money* markets are included, in addition to those from capital markets. At point 2 banks' *I* decisions (asset management) mainly involve transactions in *financial* assets and not *real* assets. Note that banks' asset and liability management (*I* and *F* decisions) are both domi-nated by transactions in *financial* assets. The descriptions at points 3 and 5 would be unchanged from those of the financial manager for the nonfinancial firm. The descrip-tion at point 4 is expanded to include cash (interest) returned to depositors. Note that the interest paid to depositors and creditors (i.e., holders of nondeposit debt such as capital notes and debentures), unlike the dividends paid to stockholders, is not subject to a payout decision; such interest payments are contractual obligations and must be made by law. However, since the owners are protected by *limited liability*, they do

---

[5] Professor James Van Horne of Stanford University emphasizes this approach. See Van Horne [1980], pp. 11–13.

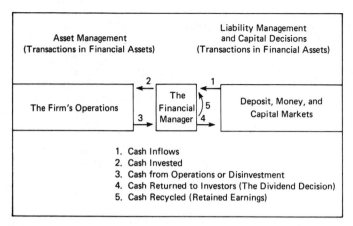

Figure 3-1   The Role of a Financial Manager of a Financial Services Firm

have the *option* of instructing the managers to default on the debt and turn the firm over to its creditors for liquidation. In the case of insured depository institutions, this would mean turning the firm over to the insurance agency to handle.

The Economics of Executive Compensation

Behavior can be conditioned by using either the "carrot" or the "stick," or some combination of the two. If you went to parochial school prior to the 1960s, you know about the stick as an incentive (or punitive) device. Since then, if you experienced the stick in your elementary, middle, or secondary education (in any school), you probably learned a lot about litigation. Give me a combination of the good old days of discipline in the educational systems *plus* a package of the right incentives for positive reinforcement.

Reaching adulthood does not free us from the carrot–stick method of conditioned behavior. For example, the behavior of corporate executives is shaped by the carrot of incentive compensation and by the stick of potential removal from office (i.e., being fired or asked to resign by the board of directors).[6] Executive compensation packages, including incentive clauses, are determined by negotiations between the executive (e.g., the chief executive officer, CEO, or the chief financial officer, CFO,) and the compensation committee of the board of directors.

According to Stewart, incentive compensation plans should be designed to (1) build morale, (2) retain good managers, and (3) promote decisions that will benefit shareholders.[7] The study of executive compensation, which is a relatively new and exciting area of financial management, has shown, contrary to the "conventional wisdom" of the financial press, that executive compensation is not independent of shareholder value.[8] The dilemma for shareholders is to ensure that their representatives on the board of directors understand the economics of executive compensation and provide the right kind of incentives to the management team.

[6] The executives of bank holding companies and insured commercial banks (and other federally insured depository institutions) face the additional threat of being removed from office by their regulators and/or deposit insurers.

[7] *Six Roundtable Discussions with Joel Stern, op. cit.,* p. 312.

[8] *Ibid.,* Chapter VI, pp. 265–320.

The economics of management compensation focuses such issues as the level of compensation, the relationship between executive compensation and shareholder annual returns, the design and effects of alternative management compensation contracts, barriers to adopting innovative compensation schemes in public companies, the role of stock options in executive compensation packages, adjusting performance standards for general economic or industry conditions, the relationship between mergers and acquisitions and management compensation plans, the costs to shareholders of "golden parachutes," the existence and effectiveness of discipline in the market for executive talent, and the independence of the corporate compensation committee from top management.[9] Although a discussion of these issues is beyond the scope of this book, let's look briefly at a measure that links incentive compensation to the goal of enhancing shareholder value.

Economic Value Added (EVA)[10]

To measure managerial performance, Stern Stewart & Co. has developed a joint measure of profitability and high-quality growth called "economic value added" (EVA). As a basis for incentive compensation, EVA focuses management's attention on the critical problem of allocating and managing capital, which is the fundamental task of modern finance. The notion of economic value added is important because it encourages management to seek profitable growth. Economic value added (EVA) is defined as:

$$EVA = [\text{Return on Capital} - \text{Cost of Capital}] \times \text{Average Total Capital}$$

Or, in symbols,

$$EVA = [r - k] \times K = rK - kK$$

where r is the return on capital, k is the cost of capital, and K is average total capital. By removing the brackets, EVA can be described as the level of earnings management generates, at the margin, minus the level of earnings investors require for bearing the risk associated with the investment (i.e., $rK - kK$). For positive values of K, the sign of EVA is determined by the sign of the bracketed term, the difference between the return and the cost of capital. Clearly, when the cost of capital exceeds the return to capital, management is not adding any economic value to the firm. Conversely, when the return is greater than the cost, economic value is added. When the return and cost of capital are equal, managers have maximized the value of the invested capital (the sum of the EVAs), and the economic value added is zero.

The intuitive appeal of this relationship, which gets at the commonsense benefit–cost foundation of modern finance, can be demonstrated by the following simple example. Consider a firm with a 10 percent cost of capital and the following schedule of returns associated with its investment opportunities: [.15, .12, .10, .08, .05]. Assuming each of the projects requires an equal investment of 100, the schedule of EVA is [5, 2, 0, −2, −5]. The value of invested capital is maximized when EVA is zero, at which point $r = k = .10$.

The linkages among EVA, profitable growth, and share price are straightforward and can be explained as follows. First, the use of EVA as a performance measure encourages management to expand the company, but not at the expense of profitability.

---

[9] See the previous footnote for an interesting and informative discussion of these issues.

[10] This section draws on Stewart, *op. cit.*, pp. 312–320.

Accordingly, the company should accept all profitable projects as long as they return more than the cost of capital. When EVA = 0, the company should stop growing until new profitable projects can be discovered. The linkage between EVA and share price also is a direct one. In an efficient market, the lead steers will ensure that market value, as reflected by share price, is equal to the present value of anticipated future EVA. Highly valued companies will be those whose managers have demonstrated to the market (i.e., to the lead steers) the ability to invest capital such that it earns a return greater than its opportunity cost. In contrast, companies unable to invest capital profitably will sell at discounts relative to the replacement values of their assets.

According to Stewart, EVA-based compensation plans are doubly desirable because they encourage a favorable allocation of capital and high stock prices for investors. Specifically, such plans provide incentives for managers (1) to increase the efficiency of assets in place, (2) to expand assets as long as the rate of return exceeds the cost of capital, and (3) to contract or redeploy underperforming assets.

KEEPING THE PRINCIPLE OF VALUE MAXIMIZATION IN PERSPECTIVE

In 1987, I had a conversation with an executive of Westinghouse Corporation about the notion of maximization of shareholder wealth as the objective of the firm. He argued that the idea has been carried to such an extreme that it is harming corporate America. Moreover, he laid the responsibility for this extremism on the business schools of the United States.

His argument goes like this. Since many managers and directors of corporate America are business school graduates, or products of their executive development programs, the principle gospel of corporate finance has reached the boardrooms of the United States. (Whether or not the gospel is understood [i.e., discounted cash flow versus EPS], as Stern claims, is another matter.) The practice of this gospel, with its emphasis on maximization of stock price, has led managers and directors to place less emphasis on employer–employee relationships, which has led to an inability to build company pride and loyalty among employees. As a result, some employees feel disenfranchised—like pawns in the game of stock price maximization. Moreover, the stock market crash of 1987 has served to increase this feeling of being manipulated, especially since workers (both blue and white collar) did not perceive any change in their productivity prior to the crash.

With employees perceiving their managers and directors as myopically concentrating on stock price, impersonal financial markets, and investor relations (and thereby ignoring employee relations), employee morale is low, absenteeism high, and productivity low. Such a work environment is not conducive to producing quality products. Since rational consumers, both at home and abroad, shop for quality products and services, imports tend to be favored at the expense of exports, which worsens the U.S. trade and budget deficits.

Can all of these problems be laid at the doorstep of the value-maximization principle? I don't think so (my business school defense mechanism at work here). Has the focus on stock price maximization contributed to some of these problems? Perhaps (my open-mindedness at work here). However, any manager or director who fails to recognize the linkage between such intangibles as company pride, loyalty, and morale and the tangible return on capital is not worthy of being a manager or director. Consider the following illustration. Two companies are considering identical investment projects. If all other things are equal, the *ceteris paribus* assumption common to finance and economics, the projects will yield the same return to both companies. However, assume one of the companies does a better job managing its employee relations, which leads to a higher sense of "belonging to the company." This overall higher *esprit de corps* will, through greater worker productivity associated with higher morale, lower absenteeism, greater company pride, and so on, reach the project's bottom line (i.e., its net cash flow). Other things equal, the company with the better employee relations will have the higher return on capital. Any manager or director who does not recognize this aspect of the business world is naive, at best.

One approach to instruction is to assume nothing. In adult education, this approach is captured by the acronym KISS, which stands for Keep It Simple Stupid. Perhaps with all of the technical complexities of modern finance, the profession has ignored, or failed to make explicit enough, the things being held constant (e.g., employee relations and other intangibles). Unless these other things are also optimized, managers and directors will not be successful in maximizing shareholder value. Although this directive may appear simple, making it explicit cannot hurt. Moreover, if shareholders want the values of their investments maximized, they should work to remove managers and directors who ignore this commonsense advice.

ALTERNATIVE MANAGERIAL MOTIVES

Most economic or financial models of managerial behavior are based on the optimization of some variable such as utility, wealth, or profit. To the extent managers have other objectives, these maximization models and their derivatives are open to challenge. Several studies have suggested that bankers may be concerned about motives other than simply maximizing profits.[11] These findings indicate, among other things, that (1) as bankers gain monopoly power (i.e., control over price), they tend to become more risk averse, (2) market concentration has a more significant impact on risk-adjusted profits than on unadjusted profits, (3) the greatest degree of risk-averse behavior is more likely to occur in banking markets that are monopolized rather than competitive, and (4) bankers with monopoly power tend to exhibit expense-preference behavior (i.e., they tend to hire more staff, pay higher wages, and be less conscious of costs in general).[12] The fourth point suggests that monopoly power may lead to higher expenses and less efficiency, a finding that may explain the lack of an observed strong correlation between concentration and profits in banking markets. All four of the above points fit neatly into Hicks' [1935] statement that "the best of all monopoly profits is a quiet life" (p. 8). It is easy to see how monopoly power could lead to attempts to achieve "a quiet life" by assuming a less risk-averse posture, surrounding oneself with more staff and paying them more, and the like. It will be interesting to see if the evidence on expense-preference behavior and other managerial motives persists in the reregulated and more competitive environment of the FSI in the 1990s and beyond. "A quiet life" is likely to be a thing of the past in today's banking markets.

[11] See Heggestad [1979], pp. 480–481 for a summary of these findings.

[12] In addition to Edwards' [1977] study, more recent evidence on the topic of expense-preference behavior includes Glassman and Rhoades [1980], Hannan and Mavinga [1980], Rhoades [1980], and for S&Ls Verbrugge and Jahera [1981] and Verbrugge and Goldstein [1981]. Also see Taggart [1978].

THE VALUE OF THE BANKING FIRM

Conceptually, the value of the banking firm can be viewed as consisting of three components as expressed in the following formula[13]:

$$
\begin{array}{c}
\text{Value of} \\
\text{Banking} \\
\text{Firm}
\end{array}
=
\begin{array}{c}
\text{Value of an} \\
\text{All-Equity} \\
\text{Bank}
\end{array}
+
\begin{array}{c}
\text{Present Value} \\
\text{of Tax Shield} \\
\text{from Debt}
\end{array}
-
\begin{array}{c}
\text{Present Value} \\
\text{of Costs of} \\
\text{Financial Distress}
\end{array}
\qquad (3\text{-}4)
$$

The objective of the financial manager is, of course, to maximize the value of the firm. In a pure-equity firm, the primary determinants of value would be market and production conditions (e.g., interest rates, resource costs, and the cost of capital). Once the firm becomes levered through the use of debt (deposits), liquidity and bankruptcy costs and the value of the tax shield associated with debt must be analyzed. The standard view of the components of Equation 3-4 is presented in Figure 3-2. The value of debt is equal to the sum of the present-value components of the tax-shield from debt and the costs of financial distress. Without the use of debt, the value of the firm is equal to the market value of its equity. Once the firm becomes levered, the tax benefits and the costs of financial distress interact to determine the bank's optimal capital structure. In banking, the costs of financial distress are a complex interaction of liquidity costs, bankruptcy costs, capital regulation, and deposit insurance. Moreover, if the costs of financial distress are absorbed by the government through deposit guarantees, then the way to maximize the value of the firm is to take on as much debt as possible, which leads to a *corner solution* in this model. See Buser, Chen, and Kane [1981]. To prevent the full use of this government subsidy or guarantee, the regulators of depository institutions require the firms to maintain "adequate capital" so as to

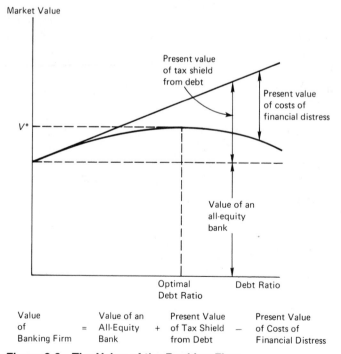

Figure 3-2   **The Value of the Banking Firm**

---

[13] See Brealey and Myers [1981], p. 384.

reduce the degree of financial leverage. Within the banking industry, this focus on capital adequacy has led some bankers to reinterpret the acronym FDIC as *Forever Demanding Increased Capital*.

IMPLEMENTING THE VALUE-MAXIMIZATION PRINCIPLE

A conceptual framework for implementing the value-maximization principle is presented in Figure 3-3. The bank's objective, which in theory should be the maximization of its equity value, is shaped by three basic forces: (1) owners' preferences, (2) management's attitudes and decisions, and (3) society, as manifested by its regulatory and economic environment. Alternatives to the wealth-maximization principle could include such goals as profit maximization, size maximization, "satisfying," or expense-preference behavior. Given the goal of maximizing the value of the bank's equity, there are six policy strategies that can be employed to achieve that objective. These policies are shaped by three factors: (1) the objective itself, (2) management's attitudes and decisions, and (3) society. The six policy strategies are[14]

1. spread management
2. control of "burden"
3. liquidity management
4. capital management
5. tax management
6. management of off–balance sheet activities

Recalling our bank profit equation from Chapter 2 [i.e., $P = (R - C) + (F - O) - PLL + T +/- G$], each of the policy strategies either directly or indirectly affects the bank's bottom line and its risk exposure, and hence affects its cash flow, cost of funds, and market value. For example, spread management affects the $(R - C)$ term. Control of "burden" and the management of off–balance sheet activities relate to the $(F - O)$ term and tax management to the T term. To maximize bank profit requires that the spread and fees be maximized while PLL, O, and T are minimized. Of course, all of the components of bank profitability are driven by the size and composition of the bank's balance sheet. The liquidity and capital management policies also are determined by the structure of a bank's balance sheet. Liquidity can be stored in assets

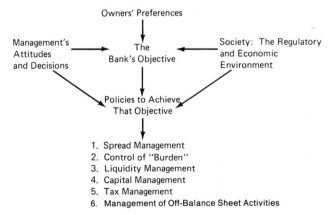

Figure 3-3   Implementation of the Value-Maximization Principle

[14] This framework is similar to the one suggested by Hempel and Yawitz [1977].

or acquired in the market place via liability management. Capital serves as a cushion or buffer to absorb potential losses. The riskier a bank's overall balance sheet is, the more liquidity and capital cushion it requires.

MARKET VALUE VERSUS BOOK VALUE

Financial managers should try to make decisions that make the firm's shareholders better off. Since success is usually judged by value, the best decisions are those that increase shareholders' value in the firm. The financial statements of most FSFs are stated in terms of *accounting* or *book* values. Financial managers, owners, and other interested parties must cut through the veil of book values and look at *market* values. Although determining market values for FSFs is not always easy, it is a task that must be done. For FSFs with actively traded securities in efficient markets, the task is, of course, a trivial one (i.e., simply check the financial press for the latest stock quote). To better understand the differences between book and market values, consider the following T-accounts, one expressed in book values and the other expressed in market values:

Book values		Market values	
A	L	A^*	L^*
	NW	I^*	NW^*

The asterisk (*) indicates market values and I^* indicates the market value of unidentifiable intangible assets, which for depository institutions includes such elements as the value of deposit-insurance guarantees, charter value, the value of customer relationships, and other unbooked assets. In general, these values account for the goodwill/going-concern value of the organization. The market-value equation for *real* net worth is:

$$NW^* = (A^* + I^*) - L^* = (A^* - L^*) + I^* \tag{3-5}$$

With Equation 3-5 it is easy to explain why firms with negative book net worth still trade in the marketplace at positive real values (e.g., "underwater" or insolvent thrift institutions). The reason, of course, is that the negative book net worth is more than offset by the value of intangible assets. In the case of insured institutions with negative book net worth, the unbooked insurance guarantee creates most of the real net worth. Of course, as any good accountant knows, an unbooked asset means that there is an unbooked liability floating around. This liability belongs on the T-account of the deposit insurer; the offsetting entry is a reduction in the insurer's net worth (i.e., in the real value of the deposit-insurance fund).

Looking at the difference between the book and market values of assets, we note that unrealized losses due to credit risk and interest-rate risk account for most of the differential. The market values of nonperforming loans relative to their book values are good examples of credit risk. However, without an active efficient secondary market for such loans, it is difficult to determine their true worth. Regarding interest-rate risk, the fixed-rate mortgage loans made by thrifts when interest rates were at historically low levels provide a good example. Unlike other loans, however, well-developed secondary markets exist for pricing mortgages.

Understanding how financial assets are valued is one of the objectives of capital-market theory. Divergences between book and market values are most pronounced and the role of intangible assets most critical when (1) financial institutions encounter difficulties due to credit and/or interest-rate risks and (2) purchase accounting mergers take place between going concerns (see Chapter 25).

THE STAR BUILDING BLOCKS OF FINANCE

A hexagon is a six-sided figure. In finance, six fundamental concepts or ideas provide the foundation of the discipline. For schematic purposes, the building blocks could be portrayed as the sides of a hexagon. However, since these six ideas are the guiding lights of financial management, they deserve more than just a flat edge. To make them "star," an equilateral triangle can be added externally on each side of a regular hexagon. The resulting figure is called a *hexagram*. It provides the appropriate shape for highlighting the six star building blocks of finance.

The Hexagram of Financial Management

Like the North Star, the six-point star or hexagram of financial management can guide you to the understanding of the financial management of financial-services firms. Since the core of the financial-services industry (FSI) is the commercial banking segment, the guiding light shines mainly on that sector. Other types of firms in the FSI are not left in total darkness; but since these other firms can be viewed as moving into the banking business, once the financial management of commercial banks is understood it is easy to apply the same approach to the imitating firms.

This brightest star in the financial firmament is depicted in Figure 3-4. Again like the North Star, the six-point star of financial management is the one toward which the axis of modern theory points. The major building blocks of the modern theory of financial management are:[15]

The Six Points Explained

1. *Valuation Rules:* Net Present Value and Value Additivity
   a. *Net present value* (NPV) is basically a simple idea. It says that financial managers must search for investments or projects that are worth more than they cost. The key, of course, is knowing how to determine the worth or *value* or proposed projects. NPV estimates are simply our "best guesses" as to what assets would trade for in efficient capital markets. The NPV technique is one of discounting future cash flows (CF_t) at the opportunity cost of capital (k), net of the cost of the project. The NPV formula in words and symbols is

   Net Present Value = [Present Value of Future Cash Flows] − [Cost]

   $$NPV = \sum_{t=1}^{N} \frac{CF_t}{(1 + k)^t} - Cost \qquad (3\text{-}6)$$

   The discount or opportunity-cost rate is the interest rate that reflects the expected rate of return on securities with similar risk to the project being evaluated. The NPV rule is to select only those projects that have positive NPVs—or equivalently, to select only those projects for which the expected return, call it $E(r)$, is greater than the opportunity cost, k.

---

[15] The six ideas are derived from Jensen and Smith's [1984] five fundamental building blocks of financial economics and Brealey and Myers' [1984] five most important ideas in finance. Weston [1981] provides a survey of developments in finance theory.

b. *Value additivity* conveys the basic notion that the value of the whole is equal to the sum of the parts. This principle is sometimes referred to as the *law of conservation of value*, which suggests that without changing the risk–return properties of projects the whole can never be greater than the sum of the parts. With *PV* representing present value, the principle of value additivity states

$$PV(A) + PV(B) = PV(AB). \tag{3-7}$$

where $PV(A)$ = the present value of project A, $PV(B)$ = the present value of project B, and $PV(AB)$ = the present value of the joint or combined project AB. Restating equation 3-7 in terms of cash flows, we have

$$PV(CF_A) + PV(CF_B) = PV(CF_{AB}) \tag{3.8}$$

Focusing on the first component, we note that

$$PV(CF_A) = \frac{CF_{A,1}}{1+k} + \frac{CF_{A,2}}{(1+k)^2} + \cdots + \frac{CF_{A,N}}{(1+k)^N} \tag{3-9}$$

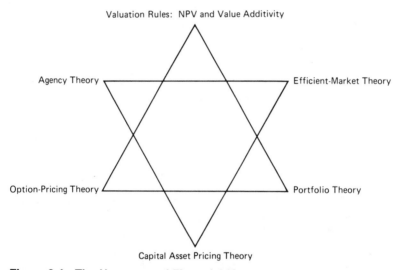

Figure 3-4   The Hexagram of Financial Management

The six-pointed star or hexagram of the modern theory of financial management is designed to guide you to a better understanding of the financial management of financial-services firms.

1. *Net present value* says that managers should invest in projects that are worth more than they cost; *value additivity* says that discounted cash flows are additive, but as long as the cash flows are unchanged the value of the whole is always equal to the sum of the parts.
2. *Efficient-market theory* says that in competitive markets there are no easy ways to make money because security prices quickly and accurately reflect available information.
3. *Portfolio theory* says that managers should evaluate securities and projects on the basis of their risk–return characteristics.
4. The *capital asset pricing model* provides an easy way of thinking about the required return on a risky asset by distinguishing between diversifiable and nondiversifiable risk.
5. *Option-pricing theory* provides a framework for determining the value of contingent claims or options, which are so common in finance.
6. *Agency theory* provides a framework for analyzing the control of conflicts in contractual relations that arise from different incentives and asymmetric information.

Thus, for any project that generates a stream of future cash flows, the present values are assumed to be additive. Moreover, since companies can be viewed as portfolios of assets or projects that generate future cash flows, value additivity (or subtraction) holds for companies as well as projects. Thus, value additivity implies that mergers, spin-offs, divestitures, and other tinkerings with component parts provide no benefits as long as cash flows are not affected.

The principle of value additivity also has important implications for the way projects or companies are financed. For example, if a company employs both equity and debt financing, then its market value, V, is simply the sum of the market value of equity, V_E, plus the market value of debt, V_D. That is,

$$V = V_E + V_D \qquad (3\text{-}10)$$

In words, financing decisions affect the *form* or packaging of the company's balance sheet but not the *substance* or value of it, unless they change the *total* cash flow generated by the company.

2. *Efficient capital markets* or efficient-market theory deals with the analysis of the equilibrium behavior of changes in security prices over time in speculative markets. The basic conclusion of the theory, which usually is stated as the *efficient-markets hypothesis*, is that security prices accurately and quickly reflect available information about security prices. The hypothesis suggests that in an efficient market it is impossible to make real or economic profits by trading on available information.

Depending upon the definition of "available information," there are three versions of the efficient-markets hypothesis. If security prices reflect only the information available in past prices, the market is said to be *weak-form efficient*. This version, which implies that changes in security prices are independent over time, also is known as the "random-walk theory." If security prices reflect *all* publicly available information, the market is said to be *semistrong-form efficient*. And if security prices reflect *all* available information, including "inside" information, the market is said to be *strong-form efficient*.

The fundamental idea of efficient-market theory is that in competitive markets there are no easy ways to make money because security prices reflect the real value of the underlying assets. Specifically, if investors act *rationally* and prices react only to *unanticipated* events, then all publicly available *information* is worthless because it is already embodied in current market values. The key concepts are rational behavior, unanticipated events, and the free flow of information associated with competitive markets. In the financial-services industry, and especially in banking, where book value accounting and other imperfections (e.g., regulation) restrict the flow of information or obscure its content, inefficiencies in capital markets may exist.

What does efficient-market theory have to say about the stock market crash of October 19, 1987? On that "Black Monday," the Dow Jones Industrial Average fell a record 508 points. In the words of Professor William Sharpe of Stanford University, "We're all totally perplexed. It's conceivable that a change in the well-informed forecast of future economic events moved the market as it did; you can't prove it one way or the other. On the other hand, it's pretty weird." (This quote and others in this section are from *The Wall Street Journal* [October 23, 1987], p. 7). Weird indeed. Fischer Black of Goldman, Sachs & Co. and coauthor of the standard option-pricing model said: "The only insight that market theory offers at this point is that stock prices are going to be more volatile

EXHIBIT 3-1
Three Reports on the Stock Market Crash of October 19, 1987

	President's Task Force on Market Mechanisms January 7, 1988	General Accounting Office report January 26, 1988	Securities and Exchange Commission report February 2, 1988
Possible causes of the crash			
Program trading and "portfolio insurance"	No market manipulation took place, but many buyers were scared off by huge gaps between stock and futures markets	Portfolio insurance could not work as intended in a rapid plunge, and resulting panic selling pushed prices even further down	Computer trading strategies did not cause the market decline, but did discourage other investors from buying in a hectic market
Lack of intermarket coordination	Traders tried to exploit price gaps between markets. As gaps grew, huge orders overwhelmed markets	Lack of timely, accurate information and uncertainty about what regulators would do led to panic selling	Index futures have been little understood in the markets and thus can be disruptive
Trading mechanics	Varying margin requirements and disconnected clearing systems among markets made chaotic conditions worse	Exchanges' computers were inadequate for the volatility and volume that occurred, clogging under pressure and causing more panic	A "disturbing number" of specialists on the NYSE and Amex floors did not do their job as buyers of last resort in a falling market
Bad economic news	Budget and trade deficits were just two factors leading to market pessimism	Ongoing market decline gained momentum from bad news the week before crash	Investor worries sent market down, triggering institutional selling that started crash
Possible remedies			
Changes in margin rules	**Yes.** Harmonize margin rules across markets	No recommendation	**Maybe.** Increased minimums should be studied
Limits on stock price swings	**Yes.** Recommended to limit volatility, especially between markets	**Maybe.** Effects should be studied before adopting any such limits	**No.** Limits on price swings would be "somewhat self-defeating"
Unified regulation of markets	**Yes.** Bring them under one regulator	**Yes.** Federal government must be responsible for ensuring orderly markets	No recommendation, but SEC chairman told Congress SEC wants a lead role

EXHIBIT 3-1 (*Continued*)

	President's Task Force on Market Mechanisms January 7, 1988	General Accounting Office report January 26, 1988	Securities and Exchange Commission report February 2, 1988
Possible remedies			
Put Federal Reserve in overall control	**Yes**. Fed is best placed to view whole market picture	**Maybe**. But if law passes to allow banks to trade stock, Fed's job in this role would be "complex and difficult"	No recommendation: SEC chairman said Fed lacks expertise on equity and futures markets
Changes in trading mechanics	**Yes**. Unity clearing systems and coordinate "circuit breakers" such as trading halts and price limits across markets	**Yes**. Overhaul exchanges' computers and clearing systems; take steps to give individual investors fairer treatment	**Yes**. Tighten rules covering trading of index futures; introduce standards for specialists' activities

Source: The Associated Press as reported in *The Atlanta Constitution* [February 4, 1988], pp. 1-E and 9-E.

than they have been." Peter Bernstein, another proponent of efficient-market theory and president of a pension-consulting firm bearing his name, stated, "There was no rational case for things being so far up there, only romantic reasons—things like new buyers such as the Japanese coming in because they saw value there."

Merton Miller, professor of finance at the University of Chicago, sought an explanation, in part, due to chaotic trading conditions and the restrictions imposed on futures trading and program trading. The latter employs a strategy of trading based on differences between futures prices and stock prices. He suggested: "Efficiency is affected by the cost of transactions, and the big overload in the system meant those costs became very high—not just the real cost of execution but in terms of uncertainty." For these reasons, Miller does not see the event as a "fair test" of market efficiency.

Although the crash put most efficient-market theorists on the defensive, the "behaviorists" were on the offensive. To illustrate, Robert Shiller, an investment behaviorist and professor of economics at Yale University, stated: "The efficient-market hypothesis is the most remarkable error in the history of economic theory. This is just another nail in its coffin." Investment behaviorists focus on the behavior of investors with respect to greed, fear, and panic and the role these emotions play in determining stock prices. Lawrence Summers, a professor of economics at Harvard University, adds: "If anyone did seriously believe that price movements are determined by changes in information about economic fundamentals, they've got to be disabused of that notion by Monday's 500-point movement."

Autopsies of the Stock Market Crash of 1987. When financial markets and their participants *act* too wildly, as they did on October 19, 1987, government regulators *react*. In the aftermath of the crash, the federal government generated three voluminous reports: (1) the Brady report prepared by the President's Task Force on Market Mechanisms (January 8, 1988), (2) the GAO report prepared by the General Accounting Office (January 26, 1988), and (3) the SEC report prepared by the Securities and Exchange Commission (February 2, 1988). These reports, which are summarized in the accompanying box, offered different views on the causes of and possible remedies for the stock market crash of 1987.

From a banking perspective, one of the more interesting conclusions came from the Brady report, which recommended that the Federal Reserve be the agency to jointly regulate the stock, futures, and commodities markets. The report argued that these three markets had become inextricably linked by computer technology and that they, in effect, functioned as one market. Accordingly, they should be subject to one regulator. Not surprisingly, the SEC report rejected this notion, claiming that the Fed lacked expertise in equity and futures markets. Federal Reserve Chairman Alan Greenspan, in effect, agreed with the SEC report. However, instead of saying the Fed lacked the expertise, he argued that the Fed's involvement in the securities market might be miscon-strued as an expansion of the bank regulatory safety net to brokerage firms.

3. *Portfolio theory* focuses on the selection of alternative groups of securities based upon their risk–return characteristics as reflected in the group's (portfolio's) expected return and the variability of that return (as measured by the variance of portfolio return). The theory leads to the notion of *efficient portfolios* (called *E–V* efficient with *E* for expected return and *V* for risk as measured by variance) and the concept of *dominance*. An efficient or dominant portfolio is one that provides the maximum return for a given level of risk (i.e., variance) or the minimum risk for a given level of return. Diversification is the *raison d'être* for portfolio theory, and mean-variance analysis provides a measure of the covaria-tion among securities. As long as the security added to a portfolio has a return that is less than perfectly correlated with the portfolio's return, diversification benefits are obtained. However, beyond a portfolio size of 10 or 12 securities, diversification benefits from added securities are limited.

Portfolio theory suggests that financial managers should evaluate projects on the basis of the project's risk–return contribution to the firm's portfolio of assets.

4. *Capital asset pricing theory* provides a method for determining asset prices based upon the asset's contribution to portfolio risk. The main idea underlying the capital asset pricing model or CAPM is the distinction between diversifiable and nondiversifiable risk. The former, also called unique, specific, residual, or unsystematic risk, can be diversified away; the latter, also known as market or systematic risk, cannot be eliminated. The CAPM provides a method for measuring the risk that cannot be eliminated and calls it β (*beta*). Statistically β, which can be viewed as an index of risk, is equal to

$$\beta_j = \frac{\text{Cov}(j,M)}{\text{Var}(M)} = \frac{\rho_{j,M}\sigma_j\sigma_M}{\sigma_M^2}, \tag{3-11}$$

where $\text{Cov}(j,M)$ is the covariance between the return on the *j*th security and the return on the market portfolio (e.g., the return on the S&P composite index). The covariance term in Equation 3-11 is equal to the product of the correlation coefficient, $\rho_{j,M}$, the standard deviation of returns on security *j*, σ_j, and the standard deviation of returns on the market portfolio, ρ_M. The square of the standard deviation produces the variance. The basic CAPM equation for estimating required rates of return or capitalization rates is

$$k_j = i + (k_M - i)\beta_j, \tag{3-12}$$

where k_j is the capitalization rate for the jth security, i is the riskless rate of return, k_M is the return on the market portfolio, and β_j is the index of risk for the jth security. The second component of Equation 3-12 is the *risk premium* and the term $(k_M - i)$ is the *market premium*. A security that moves exactly with the market (i.e., has the same sensitivity or volatility as the market) has a $\beta = 1$ and a risk premium equal to the market premium. Note what happens to Equation 3-11 if the jth stock moves exactly with the market portfolio. In this case, $\rho_{j,M} = 1$ and $\sigma_j = \sigma_M$. Therefore, $\beta_j = 1$, that is,

$$\beta_j = \frac{1 \sigma_M \sigma_M}{\sigma_M^2} = 1. \tag{3-13}$$

For stocks that are more volatile than the market portfolio, $\beta > 1$ and the risk premium is greater than the market premium. Such stocks ($\beta > 1$) are described as "aggressive" ones. For stocks that are less volatile than the market portfolio, $\beta < 1$ and the risk premium is less than the market premium. Such stocks ($\beta < 1$) are described as "defensive" ones. Bank stocks tend to have β's close to 1.

5. *Option-pricing theory* deals with the analysis of the determinants of the prices of contingent claims or options. In banking and finance, these claims and options are quite prevalent and financial managers need to know how to value them. Lenders are especially concerned about borrowers who exercise their option to default. In general, an option refers to the opportunity to trade in the future on terms that are fixed today. The basic determinants of the value of an option are the exercise or option price, the exercise or expiration date, the risk of the underlying asset, and the risk-free rate of interest. The pioneering work on valuing options was done by Black and Scholes in 1973. Their formula for pricing simple call options, which is one of the cornerstones of modern financial theory, is referred to as the Black–Scholes option-pricing model.

6. *Agency theory* deals with the contractual relationships between principals and agents. In this context, principal refers to a person who engages another person, the *agent*, to perform some service that involves decision-making authority. To protect their own interests or wealth, principals must monitor the activities of their agents. The surveillance costs incurred by principals in monitoring agents are called *agency costs*. The agency problem may arise because of (1) different goals and objectives, (2) asymmetric information, or (3) dishonesty (e.g., embezzlement). Examples of principal–agent relationships are

Principal	Agent
Owners	Managers
Landlords	Tenants
Employers	Employees
Lenders	Borrowers
Deposit Insurers	Insured Institutions
Uninsured Depositors	Depository Institutions

Understanding the agency problem and the costs associated with the last three examples is crucial to understanding the nature of the financial-services business, its regulation, and its market behavior. For now, think about these relationships; they will be discussed in detail later in the book. The relationship

EXHIBIT 3-2
The Saga of Herschel Walker: Agency Theory and Intercollegiate Athletics

An interesting example of the agency problem is the one between college coaches (principals) and star athletes (agents). At Georgia Football, Inc. from 1979 to 1983, the problem was a highly visible one. The principal was head football coach Vince Dooley; the agent was star football player Herschel Walker. During the recruiting year 1979–80, Assistant Coach Mike Cavan was successful in getting Walker to sign with Georgia, and the agency problem officially began. During Walker's tenure, the Georgia football program was the most successful in the country, with three straight Sugar Bowl appearances and a national championship in 1980. The revenues generated during this era far out-weighed the costs. The agency problem for Georgia was to keep Walker at Georgia for the full contract period, which is four years unless the "red-shirt clause" is invoked; then a fifth year can be added. Since the "dirty work flows downhill," Assistant Coach Cavan was assigned to hold Herschel's hand and try to keep him in the corporation. However, since the surveillance costs were only a very small percentage of the corporation's derived NPV in Walker, the costs were trivial in this case, which is not always the situation.

Now Herschel was his own man and he loved to play mental games with the press and anyone else who would listen. Therefore, at the end of each season, Herschel would say such things as (1) how much he loved track, (2) that football wasn't his favorite sport, (3) that he might sign with the Canadian Football League, (4) that he might challenge the NFL rule against drafting underclassmen, etc. Herschel's pronouncements, of course, caused great anxiety to Georgia's coaching staff and its football fans. Then, sometime during his tenure at Georgia, Herschel, the principal now, secured an agent, Jack Manton. Following Georgia's loss to Penn State in the 1983 Sugar Bowl, rumors started to fly that Herschel was going to sign with the new USFL. A late night meeting with a millionaire oil man in an Athens, Ga., motel room resulted in Herschel signing with the New Jersey Generals. Although some might argue (weakly) about the timing and style of the decision, no one could knock the rationality of it. Herschel, who had won the Heisman Trophy for his performance during the 1982 season, had secured his financial future. The next day Herschel denied that he had signed, a statement which he later regretted making. However, since Herschel was a *principal* now, he had to account for his own actions and those of *his* agent. Georgia football fans were shocked; the littlest fans said, "Say it ain't so, Herschel." It was so, however, and Georgia's opponents rejoiced, especially in Clemson, S.C.

EXHIBIT 3-2 (*Continued*)

The economic and financial implications of Herschel's signing were unambiguous. Wealth was transferred to its rightful owner, Herschel Walker. For Georgia, there was an opportunity-cost loss equal to the difference between what revenues would have been had Herschel stayed for his senior year (e.g., if there had been a fourth straight Sugar Bowl appearance, another Heisman trophy, or another national championship) and what they actually were (e.g., from the Cotton Bowl championship). Herschel's agent, of course, received his share (but not his "due" as far as some Georgia fans were concerned) and the Generals received, at a much higher price and for a longer term than Georgia had contracted for, the services of a great athlete. Finally, the implicit benefits accruing to the USFL for signing Herschel were minimal, at best, as the league is now defunct. The saga of Herschel Walker and Georgia's agency problem had ended.

between agency theory and intercollegiate athletics is described in "The Saga of Herschel Walker," Exhibit 3–2.

Recapitulation and Analysis

Now that our preliminary exploration of the star building blocks of financial management is complete, let's look at the importance of the six concepts to the understanding of financial management of financial-services firms (FSFs).

First, since FSFs engage primarily in lending and borrowing arrangements, they need to develop sorting mechanisms to distinguish good borrowers from bad ones and good lenders from bad ones (such as check kiters). This dilemma is simply an agency problem that arises from different incentives, asymmetric information, and/or dishonesty. The mastery of this problem is critical to the success of any lending institution.

Second, until the 1980s, markets for financial services, especially local banking markets, were more noted for their *lack of competitiveness* than for their competitiveness. Moreover, without well-developed secondary markets for most of the assets and liabilities held by FSFs, it is difficult to determine the true or market values of their net-worth positions. This problem may be exacerbated by any of three conditions: (1) many FSFs do not have equity and debt securities that are actively traded, (2) certain information flows are restricted in the name of the "safety and soundness" of the FSI, and (3) sometimes deposit-insurance guarantees, subsidies, and bail-outs are indiscriminately applied. The important point is that in noncompetitive markets inefficiencies and inequities can develop, as half-century of "cartel banking" (1933–1983) has demonstrated.

Third, lack of diversification with respect to credit risk (e.g., energy and foreign concentrations of credit) and interest-rate risks (e.g., S&L concentrations in fixed-rate mortgages) are the two major risks faced by FSFs. Modern portfolio theory preaches the benefits of diversification. Financial managers of FSFs would do well to listen to the sermon.

Fourth, if financial managers really understood the NPV rule and value additivity, would the rush to gobble up FSFs be as hectic as it has been? To create value, new cash flows must be generated; how the cash flows are divided is irrelevant.

Fifth, the use of contingent claims by FSFs (e.g., off-balance sheet activities) has increased over the past decade. To understand the full impact of such activities, financial managers need to know how to value such options.

And finally, the CAPM provides a way to think about the required return on risky assets in terms of systematic and unsystematic risks.[16] This concept probably is more important for the regulators and insurers of depository institutions than it is for the managers of such institutions. Bank regulators and deposit insurers can be viewed as "watchdogs" over portfolios consisting of their "turf" institutions. Moreover, only they can protect the financial system from individual failures due to unsystematic risk. It is the task of macroeconomic stabilization policy, through the judicious use of monetary and fiscal policy, to protect the system from systematic or nondiversifiable risk.

CHAPTER SUMMARY

This chapter has focused on the fundamentals of financial management as applied in the real world, with special emphasis on commercial banks. The heart of financial management is the allocation of capital across alternative investment opportunities and the financing of those opportunities. The economic model, as opposed to the accounting model, is the proper framework for analyzing financial decision-making. Money (cash flow), time, and risk, which are the key dimensions of this approach, are captured by the discounted-cash-flow method for analyzing investment opportunities. In an efficient market, sophisticated investors, known as "lead steers," ensure that securities are priced fairly. Corporate financial communications should be addressed to the lead steers in the market. Incentive compensation, based on the notion of economic value added, can be used to ensure that managers work to maximize shareholder wealth. Since managers may have alternative objectives and may fail to optimize nonfinancial variables, the objective of value maximization needs to be kept in perspective.

The fundamental building blocks of finance are captured by the hexagram of financial management. The highlights of this six-pointed star are (1) valuation rules: NPV and value additivity, (2) efficient capital markets, (3) portfolio theory, (4) capital asset pricing theory, (5) option-pricing theory, and (6) agency theory.

LIST OF KEY WORDS, CONCEPTS, AND ACRONYMS

Accounting model of the firm	Economic value added (EVA)
Agency theory	Economics of executive compensation
Book value	Efficient markets
Capital asset pricing model (CAPM)	Incentive compensation
Commercial bankers	Indirect finance
Corporate financial communication	Intangible assets
Direct finance	Investment bankers

[16] Arbitrage pricing theory (APT) represents a challenge to the CAPM, see Bower, Bower, and Logue [1984].

Discounted cash flow
Earnings per share (EPS)
Economic model of the firm
Market value
Money (cash flow), time, and risk
Net present value (NPV)
Portfolio theory
Price-earnings ratio (P/E)

Investment, financing, and dividend
  decisions
Lead steers
Option-pricing theory
Value additivity
Value maximization
Value of the banking firm

REVIEW/DISCUSSION QUESTIONS

1. In what sense is the financial manager a "person in the middle"?
2. Why are money, time, and risk important concepts in finance?
3. What are the major reasons why the agency problem exists? What are some examples of principal–agent relationships? Which ones are important in the FSI?
4. Explain how deposit insurance affects the value of insured institutions. *Hint:* What does the deposit guarantee encourage the managers of these institutions to do? Is the guarantee booked anywhere?
5. What is the essence of corporate finance? Distinguish between direct finance and indirect finance. What roles do investment and commercial bankers play in these alternative methods of finance?
6. Who are "lead steers" and what role do they play in financial markets? What are the potential advantages of lead steer ownership? Where do lead steers search for information?
7. Distinguish between the accounting and the economic models of the firm.
8. What should "effective corporate financial communication" accomplish? To whom should these communications be directed?
9. What is economic value added (EVA)? Is it an appropriate measure of managerial performance? What is the relationship between executive compensation and shareholder value? What should incentive compensation plans accomplish?
10. Is value maximization the only game in town? What are the alternatives? Can any financial objective function be maximized if nonfinancial variables such as employee morale, company pride, etc., are not optimized?
11. Briefly explain each of the components of the hexagram of financial management. How many of these ideas were covered in your introductory finance course? For the ones not covered, should they have been covered?
12. Equations and formulas are a language unto themselves. They represent a shorthand notation for expressing what would take many words; therefore, they are useful. Some students are "turned off" by formulas because they think that they have to *memorize* them; it is more important to *understand* them. Do you *understand* the equations on the formula sheet at the end of this chapter?

MATCHING QUIZ

Directions: Select the letter from the right-hand column that best matches the item in the left-hand column.

___ 1. Highlights building blocks	A. Set prices at the margin
___ 2. NPV rule	B. Discounted-cash-flow method
___ 3. Efficient markets	C. Accounting measure
___ 4. Portfolio theory	D. The acquisition and the financing of assets
___ 5. CAPM	
___ 6. Agency theory	E. Hexagram of finance
___ 7. Option-pricing theory	F. Benefits exceed costs
___ 8. Lead steers	G. Historical highlights
___ 9. Finance objective	H. Measures systematic risk
___ 10. Person between firms' operations and capital markets	I. Herschel Walker Saga
	J. Contingent-claims theory
___ 11. All-equity bank	K. Maximize value of firm
___ 12. Expense-preference behavior	L. Financial manager
___ 13. The best of all monopoly profits	M. No debt found here
___ 14. Economic model	N. Assist in indirect finance
___ 15. Accounting model	O. Alternative to value maximization
___ 16. Corporate financial communication	P. The quiet life
___ 17. Economic value added	Q. Average P/E ratio
___ 18. Bank/BHC betas (β)	R. Finance measure of value
___ 19. Book value	S. Assist in direct finance
___ 20. Investment bankers	T. $EPS \times P/E$
___ 21. Commercial bankers	U. Until loans are repaid
	V. Preaches diversification

___ 22. Essence of corporate finance

___ 23. Incomplete transaction

___ 24. Market value

___ 25. One-risk-fits-all concept

___ 26. Glossy annuals and road
shows

W. Values close to 1.0

X. Needs to reach lead steers

Y. Performance measure for CEO

Z. No money machines here

CHAPTER 3 FORMULA SHEET

Equation number	Formula
1	$P_0 = P/E \times EPS$
2	$\text{Max } V = f(I, F, D)$
3	$EVA = [r - k] \times K$
4	$\begin{array}{c}\textit{Value of} \\ \textit{Banking} = \\ \textit{Firm}\end{array} \begin{array}{c}\textit{Value of an} \\ \textit{All-Equity} + \\ \textit{Bank}\end{array} \begin{array}{c}\textit{Present Value} \\ \textit{of Tax Shield} - \\ \textit{from Debt}\end{array} \begin{array}{c}\textit{Present Value} \\ \textit{of Costs of} \\ \textit{Financial Distress}\end{array}$
5	$NW^* = (A^* + I^*) - L^* = (A^* - L^*) + I^*$
6	$NPV = \sum_{t=1}^{N} \dfrac{CF_t}{(1 + k)^t} - Cost$
7	$PV(A) + PV(B) = PV(AB)$
8	$PV(CF_A) + PV(CF_B) = PV(CF_{AB})$
9	$PV(CF_A) = \dfrac{CF_{A,1}}{1 + k} + \dfrac{CF_{A,2}}{(1 + k)^2} + \cdots + \dfrac{CF_{A,N}}{(1 + k)^N}$
10	$V = V_E + V_D$
11	$\beta_j = \dfrac{\text{Cov}(j, M)}{\text{Var}(M)} = \dfrac{\rho_{j,M} \sigma_j \sigma_M}{\sigma_M^2}$
12	$k_j = i + (k_M - i)\beta_j$
13	$\beta_j = \dfrac{1 \sigma_M \sigma_M}{\sigma_M^2} = 1$

SELECTED REFERENCES

Bower, Dorothy H., Richard S. Bower, and Dennis E. Logue. [1984]. "A Primer on Arbitrage Pricing Theory," *Midland Corporate Finance Journal* (Fall), pp. 31–40.

Brealey, Richard, and Stewart Myers. [1981, 1984]. *Principles of Corporate Finance*, 1st and 2nd eds. New York: McGraw-Hill.

Buser, Stephen A., Andrew H. Chen, and Edward J. Kane. [1981]. "Federal Deposit Insurance, Regulatory Policy, and Optimal Bank Capital." *Journal of Finance* (March), pp. 51–60.

Edwards, Franklin R., ed. [1979]. *Issues in Financial Regulation*. New York: McGraw-Hill.

Edwards, Franklin R. [1977]. "Managerial Objectives in Regulated Industries: Expense-Preference Behavior in Banking." *Journal of Political Economy* (February), pp. 147–162.

Fisher, Irving. [1896]. *Appreciation and Interest*. New York: Macmillan.

———. [1965]. *The Theory of Interest*. New York: Augustus M. Kelley, Bookseller. Original edition 1930.

Flannery, Mark J. [1981]. "Market Interest Rates and Commercial Bank Profitability: An Empirical Investigation." *Journal of Finance* (December), pp. 1085–1101.

——— and Christopher M. James. [1984]. "The Effect of Interest-Rate Changes on the Common Stock Returns of Financial Institutions." *Journal of Finance* (September), pp. 1141–1150.

Glassman, C. A., and S. Rhoades. [1980]. "Owner vs. Manager Control Effects on Bank Performances." *Review of Economics and Statistics* (Vol. 62), pp. 263–270.

Hannan, T. H., and F. Mavinga. [1980]. "Expense Preference and Managerial Control: The Case of the Banking Firm," *The Bell Journal of Economics* (Autumn), pp. 671–682.

Heggestd, Arnold A. [1977]. "Market Structure, Competition and Performance in Financial Industries: A Survey of Banking Studies." In Edwards [1977], *op. cit.*, pp 449–490.

Hempel, George II, and Jess B. Yawitz. [1977]. *Financial Management of Financial Institutions*. Englewood Cliffs, NJ: Prentice-Hall.

Hicks, J. R. [1935]. "Annual Survey of Economic Theory: The Theory of Monopoly." *Econometrica* (Vol. III), pp. 1–20.

Ibbotson, R. G., and R. A. Sinquefield. [1977]. *Stocks, Bonds, Bill, and Inflation: The Past (1926–1976) and the Future (1977–2000)*. Financial Analysts Research Foundation, Charlottesville, VA.

Jensen, Michael C., and Clifford W., Smith, Jr. [1984]. "The Theory of Corporate Finance: A Historical Overview." In *The Modern Theory of Corporate Finance*, Jensen and Smith, eds. New York: McGraw-Hill.

Kane, Edward J. [1968]. *Economic Statistics and Econometrics*. New York: Harper & Row.

———. [1977]. "Good Intentions and Unintended Evil." *Journal of Money, Credit and Banking* (February), pp. 55–69.

Markowitz, Harry M. [1952]. "Portfolio Selection." *Journal of Finance* (March), pp. 77–91.

Mason, John M. [1979]. *Financial Management of Commercial Banks*. Boston: Warren, Gorham, and Lamont.

Miller, M. H., and F. Modigliani. [1961]. "Dividend Policy, Growth, and the Valuation of Shares." *Journal of Business* (October), pp. 411–433.

Modigliani, F., and M. H. Miller. [1958]. "The Cost of Capital, Corporation Finance, and the Theory of Investment." *American Economic Review* (June), pp. 261–297.

Myers, Stewart C., ed. [1976]. *Modern Development in Financial Management*. New York: Praeger.

Rhoades, Stephen. [1980]. "Monopoly and Expense-Preference Behavior." *Southern Economic Journal* (October), pp. 419–432.

Rose, John T. [1978]. "The Effects of the BHC Movement on Bank Safety and Soundness." In *The BHC Movement to 1978: A Compendium*. Washington, D.C: Board of Governors of the Federal Reserve System.

———and Samuel H. Talley. [1984]. "Financial Transactions within Bank Holding Companies." *Journal of Financial Research* (Vol. VII, Number 3), pp. 209–217.

Rose, Sanford. [1984]. "Duration's Dual Payoff." *American Banker* (May 22), pp. 1, 4–6, 16.

Sinkey, Joseph F., Jr. [1985]. "Safety and Soundness, Suspensions, and Risk Elements of BHC." In *The Bank Holding Company 1956–1983: Developments, Regulation, and Performance* by Gerald C. Fischer, The Association of Bank Holding Companies.

Six Roundtable Discussions of Corporate Finance with Joel Stern. [1986]. Edited by Donald H. Chew, Jr. Westport, CT: Quorum Books.

Taggart, Robert A. Jr. [1978]. "Effects on Deposit Rate Ceilings: The Evidence from Massachusetts Savings Banks." *Journal of Money, Credit and Banking* (May), pp. 139–157.

Van Horne, James C. [1980]. *Financial Management and Policy*. Englewood Cliffs, NJ: Prentice-Hall.

Verbrugge, James A., and John J. Jahera. [1981]. "Expense-Preference Behavior in the Savings and Loan Industry." *Journal of Money, Credit and Banking* (November), pp. 465–476.

———**and Steven J. Goldstein.** [1981]. "Risk, Return, and Managerial Objectives: Some Evidence from the Savings and Loan Industry." *Journal of Financial Research* (Spring), pp. 45–58.

Vojta, George J. [1973]. *Bank Capital Adequacy.* New York: Citicorp.

Wallace, Anise. [1980] "Is Beta Dead?" *Institutional Investor* (July), pp. 23–30.

Weston, J. Fred. [1981]. "Developments in Finance Theory." *Financial Management* (Vol. 10, No. 2), pp. 5–22.

CHAPTER 4

Banking and Finance Theory and Models of the Banking Firm

ACRONYM GUIDE TO KEY TERMS AND CONCEPTS

DSU = deficit-spending unit
IOS = investment opportunity set
M&M = Modigliani–Miller
NPV = net present value
SSU = surplus-spending unit

INTRODUCTION

This chapter applies some theoretical propositions to financial institutions and capital markets. We begin with a look at the consumption–savings decision and how financial markets help to smooth spending patterns. In the process, we explore the foundations of the net-present-value (NPV) rule and investigate the effects of capital-market imperfections. Next, we use finance theory to analyze the main functions of banks. Assuming banking is competitive, this foundation enables us to show, as Fama [1980] has done, that bank portfolio activities (i.e., borrowing and lending) fall, in principle, under the Modigliani–Miller [1958] proposition of the irrelevance of pure financing decisions. This finding suggests that there is no need to control bank lending activities (i.e., deposit creation) to ensure a stable general equilibrium of prices and real economic activity. The chapter concludes with a look at alternative models of the banking firm.

THE CONSUMPTION–SAVINGS DECISION AND THE ROLE OF THE CAPITAL MARKET[1]

The notions of a surplus-spending unit (SSU) and a deficit-spending unit (DSU) were introduced in Chapter 2. A DSU can be viewed as one that trades future consumption for present consumption. In biblical terms, this unit can be called, at the extreme, the prodigal unit (for recklessly extravagant spending). In contrast, the SSU trades present consumption for future consumption. At the extreme end of this behavioral spectrum, we have the miserly unit that derives utility from hoarding its cash flow or wealth. The

---

[1] The material presented in this section closely follows that of Brealey and Myers [1984], pp. 15–21, which in turn is based on Fama and Miller [1972]. Since the original ideas trace to Fisher [1930] and Hirschleifer [1958], the analysis is frequently called the Fisher–Hirschleifer model.

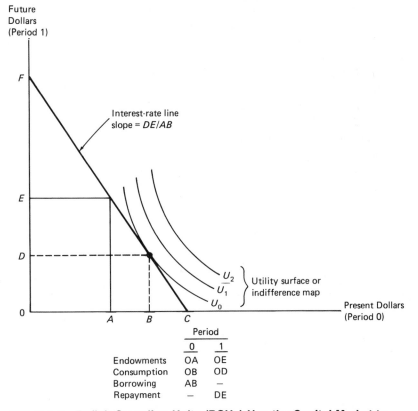

Figure 4-1   Deficit-Spending Units (DSUs) Use the Capital Market to Trade Future Dollars for Present Dollars to Increase Current Consumption

purpose of this section is to show how the capital market enables DSUs and SSUs to smooth their consumption patterns.

Suppose that you are a DSU. Depending upon the degree of your prodigal behavior, you might be willing to mortgage all of your future cash flow for present consumption. To illustrate how this process works, consider a two-period (perfect-certainty) model in which a DSU starts with two endowments or cash flows; one is available in the present period, call it period 0, and the other is available in the future, call it period 1. The available cash flows or initial endowments are illustrated by the line segments *OA* and *OE* in Figure 4-1. If the DSU wants to "live for today and the heck with tomorrow" (extreme prodigal behavior), it can trade all of its future cash flow (*OE*) for present consumption (*AC*). The unreasonableness of this kind of behavior, in a two-period model, is that in period 1 debt repayment is equal to the period's cash flow and nothing is available for period 1 consumption. Less extreme behavior is represented by trading *ED* of future consumption for *AB* of present consumption. In this case, the future cash flow (*OE*) is split between debt repayment (*DE*) and future consumption (*OD*). Where a particular economic unit falls on *FC* is determined by its tastes. Indifference curves or utility surfaces are used to reflect tastes or preferences. In Figure 4-1, a set of indifference curves is shown to correspond to the equilibrium coordinates *OB* and *OD*, where equilibrium is defined as the point of tangency between the interest-rate line (explained below) and the utility surface.

The smoothing of consumption to meet personal preferences, as illustrated in Figure 4-1, is accomplished by borrowing against future cash flow. This kind of transaction takes place in the capital market where economic units trade dollars today for dollars tomorrow and vice versa. Such transactions are not free, however. To trade tomorrow's dollars for today's (i.e., to borrow), the cost is $1 + r$ per dollar, where r denotes the one-period rate of interest. For lenders, r represents the rate of return. At this stage, borrowing and lending rates are assumed to be identical. In Figure 4-1, the line segment FC is called the interest-rate line. It shows how present dollars map into future dollars and vice versa. The rate at which this transformation takes place is represented by the slope of the line FC, which is equal to $1 + r$. (For convenience, we ignore the fact that FC is downward sloping. This negative slope reflects the fact that to gain future dollars one must give up present dollars and vice versa.) For the equilibrium depicted in Figure 4-1, the mapping of present dollars into future ones is represented by the following equation:

$$AB(1 + r) = ED$$

In words, for the opportunity to consume AB today, the DSU must pay in the future the amount borrowed (AB) plus an interest payment equal to $r(AB)$. Alternatively, the future value of AB at rate of interest r for one period is ED. Dividing both sides of the above formula by $(1 + r)$, we have

$$AB = ED/(1 + r)$$

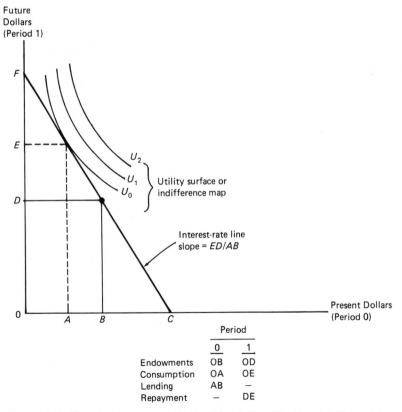

Figure 4-2 Surplus-Spending Units (SSUs) Use the Capital Market to Trade Present Dollars for Future Dollars to Increase Future Consumption

In words, the present value of the future amount *ED* at rate of interest *r* for one period is *AB*. In this case, *r* is called the discount rate and $1/(1 + r)$ is the discount factor or the present value interest factor. Alternatively, given the discount rate, *r*, the DSU knows that the future cash flow (*ED*) will map into *AB* of present consumption. The general present-value formula for an *N*-period cash flow is shown as Equation 3-9 in Chapter 3.

Let us now consider the case of an SSU and how the capital market enables it to save present dollars for future consumption. The case for the SSU is presented in Figure 4-2. The initial endowments or cash flows in this situation are *OB* and *OD*. At the extreme, the miserly SSU would consume nothing in period 0 and therefore have *OF* available for consumption in period 1, where $OF = OD + DF = OD + OB(1 + r)$. In a less extreme case, the SSU could consume *OA* and save *AB* for future consumption, which would be equal to $AB(1 + r)$ or *DE* in period 1. The total cash flow available for consumption in period 1 by the SSU would be $OE = OD + DE = OD + AB(1 + r)$. For the SSU in Figure 4-2, equilibrium corresponds to the coordinates *OA* and *OE*.

EXPANDING THE OPPORTUNITY SET: INVESTMENT IN REAL ASSETS

Economic units are not restricted to investing in financial assets; they may also invest in physical or real assets such as plant and equipment, fast-food franchises, golf courses, or health clubs. A schedule of these alternative investment projects is referred to as an investment opportunity set (IOS). A graph of this set is called an investment opportunity line, as illustrated in Figure 4-3. The IOS line has a negative slope to reflect the declining marginal productivity of capital. To illustrate this concept, consider an IOS in which projects are ranked according to their net present values (NPVs). Investors would choose to invest in the most profitable project first, the second most profitable project second, and so on down the line. If we plotted the IOS, we would trace out a locus of points such as the one shown in Figure 4-3. The graph of the IOS shows the cash flows available from investing in real assets; it maps present investment dollars into future cash flows and vice versa. The slope of the IOS line measures the marginal return on investment in physical or real assets. If we superimpose the interest-rate line from the capital market on the IOS (parallel interest-rate lines reflect the same rate of interest), the point of tangency between the two lines provides a rate-of-return decision rule: Invest up to the point at which the marginal returns (from physical and financial assets) are equal. In Figure 4-3, the optimal investment in real assets is *AB*, which has a future value of *OD*. The present value of *OD* is *AC* and the net present value (NPV) of the investment is $BC = AC - AB$ (see Equation 3-6 in Chapter 3).

The NPV measured by the line segment *BC* in Figure 4-3 is the maximum NPV available in this situation, which is not surprising because it coincides with the point of tangency between the IOS (measured by the curved line *BE*) and the capital-market line (measured by *CF*). To see this, take the interest-rate *CF* (either physically or in your mind's eye) and move it parallel such that it bisects *BE* at your desired investment in physical assets. As you conduct this experiment, your NPV will only get smaller. Thus, we have the NPV rule, which of course is equivalent to the rate-of-return rule: Invest in physical assets until NPV is maximized.

Let us now combine the notions of the capital market line and the IOS to see what this does for our DSU and SSU. The concepts are joined in Figure 4-4. Here we assume

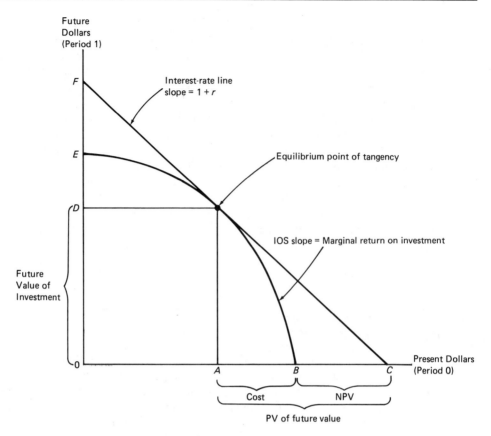

Optimal investment is *BA* which has a future value of *OD*. The present value of *OD* is *AC*. The NPV of the investment is *AC − AB = BC*.

Figure 4-3   The Investment Opportunity Set

an initial endowment of *OA* in period 0. Rational behavior requires that *AC* of the period 0 cash flow be invested in real assets. You could, of course, not choose to invest in real assets and trade consumption patterns along the line *AE*, where both the DSU and SSU attain utility levels of U_0. However, by investing in real assets at the optimal level of *AC*, you can obtain any point along *BG*. As shown in Figure 4-4, both the DSU and SSU are made better off ($U_5 > U_0$) by investing in real assets. The combination of capital-market and real investment opportunities parlays investment in real assets with borrowing and lending in the capital market such that any point along *GB* is obtainable. As a result, both DSUs and SSUs are made better off (i.e., able to reach higher utility levels). Where these economic units fall on *GB* depends on their particular tastes. The important points are that (1) tastes do not play a role in determining the optimal investment in real assets, and (2) the capital market is used to adjust spending patterns.

The Assumption of a Perfect Capital Market

The foregoing analysis is based upon the assumption of a perfectly competitive capital market. In general, perfect competition implies the absence of any frictions or impediments in the market and the absence of control over prices by any participants in the market. For the capital market to be perfectly competitive, the usual assumptions are that (1) all participants have free and equal access to the market and no one

Future Dollars (Period 1)

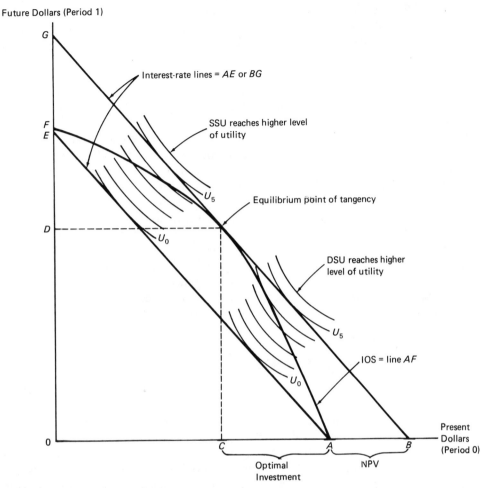

Figure 4-4 The Capital Market and the Opportunity to Invest in Real Assets Increases Economic Satisfaction

participant has control over any prices, (2) the relevant information flows about securities are freely and widely available to all participants in the market, (3) no impediments to the free trading of securities exist, and (4) no distorting taxes exist. If these conditions hold, then security prices accurately and quickly reflect available information about the securities, and capital markets are said to be efficient. The three versions of the efficient-markets hypothesis were discussed in Chapter 3.

Capital-Market Imperfections

Since financial markets in the United States are well developed, they are closer to perfection than imperfection. However, since perfection is in the eye of the beholder, one's perception of the degree of perfection will vary. Let's look at some of these perceptions of the imperfections in capital markets.

The insider-trading scandals that shocked Wall Street in 1986 and 1987 clearly attest to the fact that not all information flows are freely and widely available. Nevertheless, Security and Exchange Commission (SEC) regulation and industry self-regulation have moved to correct the problem, for the moment at least. Moreover, there is no evidence that these insider trades dominated the market by controlling prices. Regarding taxes, if you have seen one tax, you haven't seen them all. The moral: Taxes sometimes do cause distortions. Regarding transactions costs, the costs of trading financial assets are much less than the costs of trading real assets. Regarding the institutionalization of financial markets, although institutional trades frequently make financial news headlines, there still are numerous traders in financial markets. Moreover, even the largest traders control only a small portion of publicly traded stocks.

Finally, let's focus on the equal-access assumption, which was reflected in our analysis by the equality of borrowing and lending rates. If borrowing and lending rates were equal, financial intermediaries would have a hard time surviving. Commercial banks, for example, depend on this spread for their existence. Thus, the existence of financial intermediaries indicates that capital markets are not perfect. If borrowing and lending rates are not equal, then the notion of *the* interest-rate line for determining the level of investment in real assets is flawed, but only slightly. What's a financial manager to do? Take an average of the borrowing and lending rates, or have the staff do a simulation of all relevant rates. As long as the discount rate reflects the riskiness and timing of the future cash flows, shareholders should not be concerned. The important point is that managers who invest in projects with positive NPVs are acting in the best interests of the firm's shareholders.

BANKING IN THE THEORY OF FINANCE[2]

Fama [1980] has analyzed commercial banking from the viewpoint of the theory of finance. In his framework, he assumes that banks perform two main functions: (1) a transaction function and (2) a portfolio function. In performing the transaction function, banks provide an *accounting system of exchange* in which transfers of wealth are carried out with bookkeeping entries. The distinguishing characteristic of this accounting system, which works through bookkeeping entries (i.e., debits and credits, usually in the form of electronic impulses) is that it does not require a physical medium of exchange such as a currency. Although operating this accounting system of exchange does not require banks to hold the wealth being transferred, they do. As a result, banks also perform the function of portfolio management. That is, they gather deposits (i.e., issue liabilities) in order to make loans and buy securities. In focusing on the nature of banking, Fama assumes an unregulated banking environment as the ideal framework for demonstrating the characteristics of an accounting system of exchange and for showing that the concept of money plays no fundamental role in such a system.

Fama's basic point, however, is that when banking is competitive, the portfolio activities of banks fall under the type of pure financing decision covered by the Modigliani–Miller [1958] theorem. Thus, for the purpose of obtaining a stable general equilibrium in terms of prices and real economic activity, bank portfolio activities do not have to be controlled by the government.

An Unregulated Banking System

To highlight the microeconomic structure of an unregulated banking system, Fama begins by abstracting from the pricing process and by assuming the existence of a

[2] This section relies heavily on Fama [1980], who draws upon the works of Tobin [1963], Johnson [1968], and Black [1970].

numeraire in which the prices of goods and services are stated. What will banks pay for deposits in such a system? Or equivalently, what will be depositors' required rate of return? Since, by assumption, banking markets are unregulated and competitive, banks will pay competitive returns on deposits. Competitive with what? Competitive with the risk exposure of the portfolio assets held. Banks that funnel deposits into high-risk assets will have to pay returns commensurate with that risk exposure. Conversely, banks that hold safer assets will pay less for their deposits. The returns earned by depositors will be net of both a management fee for portfolio services and a transaction fee (service charge) for wealth-transfer services. Competition will ensure that these services are provided by the lowest-cost producers. In this unregulated system, depositors are free to choose the level of deposit risk they want. Banks, like the mutual funds of today, could label their deposit accounts as "speculative," "growth," or "conservative" to enable customers to select the level of risk (and return) suited to their preferences or tastes. Although none of the deposit returns would be "guaranteed," banks could offer risk-free accounts by holding the risk-free portfolio. The returns on risky accounts would vary with the market value of the assets held.

To summarize, in this unregulated banking system, we would observe financial-services firms, which we could call banks, offering deposit accounts that provide two basic services: (1) wealth-transfer services and (2) portfolio services. Since transaction services permit economic units to exchange wealth more efficiently than if such services were not available to society, banks play an important role in general equilibrium. (General equilibrium refers to a condition in which all markets in an economy are in equilibrium or a position of rest, i.e., there are no pressures on prices or quantities to change). Moreover, since banking services are not likely to be subject to special supply-and-demand conditions, they should be easy to price. Finally, regarding the portfolio-management services, since banks would provide accounts with varying degrees of risk, the net returns earned by depositors would depend on the riskiness of the corresponding portfolios and the competitively determined fees for services rendered.

Bank Financing Decisions and Policy Considerations

As portfolio managers, bankers play a critical role in the credit-allocation process, which means their decisions have important effects on the selection of real economic activities and how they are financed. (Recall that this is one of Corrigan's points about bank specialness; see Chapter 1.) However, from the perspective of the theory of finance, Fama [1980] shows that bank portfolio decisions are subject to the Modigliani–Miller [1958] theorem (i.e., bank portfolio decisions are of no consequence to investors because bank financing activities neither expand nor contract the investment opportunity set available to investors). Thus, as financial intermediaries, banks have no special control over the details of general equilibrium. To understand the importance of this conclusion, we need to focus on the Modigliani–Miller (M&M) theorem.[3]

In an abstract world without taxes and bankruptcy costs, M&M have shown that the market value of any firm is independent of its capital structure or financing decision. Recall that the objective of the financial manager is to find the combination of securities that maximizes the value of the firm. In M&M's world of perfect markets, the task is a trivial one as any combination of securities (i.e., debt and equity) is as good as

---

[3] The discussion of the M&M theorem here is based upon Fama [1980], which in turn builds upon Fama [1978] for the "equal-access" and "perfect-substitutes" versions of the theorem.

another. Accordingly, the value of the firm is unaffected by its financing decision or capital structure. For banks, the implication of M&M's theorem (referred to as Proposition I in the finance literature) is that their portfolio decisions are of no consequence to investors. Since Proposition I has both a strong-form and weak-form version, Fama [1980] considers how the application of each applies to bank portfolio management.

The Equal-Access Version of M&M

The strong form of M&M is based on the assumption of equal access to the capital market by all economic units. In this framework, since banks are just another economic unit, they have no special advantages vis-à-vis other participants in the capital market. As a result, the portfolios offered by banks to depositors can be restructured by depositors or other intermediaries to conform to depositors' risk preferences or tastes. In this world, banks hold portfolios primarily because it allows them to provide transaction services more efficiently. However, since portfolio opportunities are constrained by the *real* production-investment decisions of firms, bank portfolio activities in *financial* assets do not affect prices and real activity. In an equal-access market, a strong form of the M&M theorem prevails.

The Perfect-Substitutes Version of M&M

The equal-access assumption is an overly strong condition for arriving at the conclusion that the portfolio decisions of banks are of no consequence to investors and that the banking sector is at most a passive determinant of prices and real economic activity. Suppose that individuals are limited, relative to banks, in accessing the capital market. However, if among banks a competitive environment exists, then no individual bank can offer special products and services because potential perfect substitutes can be developed by other banks. As a result, banks are concerned with the fees they earn rather than with the type of portfolios they hold. Moreover, in a competitive environment, the management fees earned on each different type of portfolio, at the margin, are driven to equality. If a disequilibrium situation were to exist (i.e., inequality of management fees across similar portfolios), competitive forces (e.g., in the form of perfect substitutes) would eliminate the disparity and restore general equilibrium. Thus, no individual bank can affect the portfolio opportunities available to investors, and each one is subject to the M&M theorem.

Let us look at the policy considerations of this special environment in which banking is unregulated and the capital market is characterized by equal access or perfect substitutes. Is there anything in this kind of banking sector that makes it a special candidate for government control? Consider the economics of the situation. Since the banking sector is passive with no special control over prices or real economic activity, then, clearly, there is nothing in the economics of the banking sector to make it subject to government control.

Recapitulation

In a competitive world, banks are simply pure intermediaries that respond to the tastes and opportunities of ultimate borrowers and lenders. The role of a competitive banking system in a general equilibrium framework is passive. In contrast, the controlling factors are the tastes and endowments of individual economic units in conjunction with the economy's state of technology; these forces determine the economic activity that occurs, how such activity is financed, and the prices of securities, goods, and services. There is nothing in the economics of this artificial banking environment to suggest the need for government control.

MODELS OF THE BANKING FIRM

This section focuses on alternative approaches to the theory of the banking firm. The models (i.e., "mini-theories") in this area are evolving ones and the area is unsettled. As Sealey [1980] has written, "It is widely recognized that the theory of the depository financial intermediary is not well developed" (p. 1139). An earlier comment by Murphy [1972] suggests why the area is not well developed:

> Commercial banking is an interesting industry because, in my opinion, it is difficult to construct an integrated theory of the banking firm that treats liquidity management, portfolio selection, pricing policy, and physical production processes simultaneously (p. 614).

In looking at banking behavior from a theoretical perspective, the evolution of model development and the current state of the art will be noted. A clear understanding of the underpinnings of the banking system adds to our understanding of the entire financial system and the overall economy. From a financial-management perspective, complete models of the banking firm provide for integrated views of both the real and financial aspects of bank behavior.

Beginning with the Basics

In Chapter 2, we traced the etymology of the word *bank* and noted that *banca* and *banque* translated into the two basic functions that modern banks perform: transactions and safekeeping functions. The safekeeping function really is a portfolio-management function, that is, banks gather deposits and use the proceeds to purchase loans and securities. Regarding the transactions function, banks provide two basic transactions services. (1) They maintain a system of accounts in which transfers are carried out with bookkeeping entries. Cancelled checks and account statements are by-products of this recordkeeping service. (2) Banks provide for currency convertibility by exchanging deposits and other forms of wealth for currency. As we move toward a cashless society and home banking via personal computers, the currency-exchange service, already of secondary importance, will become even less important. The accounting system of exchange is the key transactions service provided by financial intermediaries.

The transactions services provided by banks require real resources in the forms of computers, key-punch operators, bookkeepers, tellers, brick-and-mortar branches, ATMs, and lots and lots of paper. The portfolio-management function also requires real resources but to a much smaller degree. Until recently, theoreticians have ignored the real-resource side of banking and thus models of the banking firm have been incomplete.

It is interesting to note the evolution that has occurred (and is continuing to occur) with respect to the transactions and portfolio functions. For years banks mainly were content to supply transactions services (i.e., demand deposits), until competition (induced by regulation and inflation) forced them to provide different portfolios of assets and liabilities. Meanwhile, sister financial institutions (e.g., mutual funds) began to supply transactions services previously monopolized by banks. Today, we are moving toward a system in which all financial institutions (and some nonfinancial corporations, such as Sears) will provide both transactions and portfolio-management services. In this kind of environment, understanding how "banks" behave takes on added significance, especially with respect to regulation and establishing a "level playing field" and with respect to monetary policy and controlling the money supply.

Two Approaches to Modeling the Banking Firm

To accurately model the behavior of the banking firm, both the transactions and portfolio-management functions must be incorporated into the theory. Until recently, this theoretical combination had not been achieved. Instead, two divergent approaches were followed.[4] First, some writers adopted a portfolio-theory approach.[5] The major advantage of this approach is the incorporation of uncertainty into the model. The portfolio framework, however, has two shortcomings: (1) real resource costs are excluded; and (2) rate-setting behavior on the liability side of the balance sheet is excluded. The latter results because the portfolio approach assumes that banks operate in perfectly competitive markets as quantity-setting price takers. While this assumption is not untenable as a description of bank asset markets, it breaks down in liability markets, where banks tend to set rates and face quantity uncertainty. Without deposit uncertainty, liquidity considerations are eliminated from the model.

The second approach employs the traditional theory of the firm as its basic foundation.[6] These models focus on market imperfections, resource costs, or deposit rate-setting to establish their analytical frameworks. Compared to the portfolio approach, the firm-theoretic models are limited because they are based upon certainty and/or linear risk preferences.

Sealey [1980] has attempted to combine the portfolio-management and theory-of-the-firm approaches. His model of financial-intermediary behavior integrates the risk considerations of the portfolio approach with the market conditions, cost factors, and deposit rate-setting behavior of the firm-theoretic approach. Comparative-statics experiments are conducted to determine the effect of risk aversion on optimal decision-making by financial intermediaries. Sealey's results, which are derived from some high-powered mathematical manipulations, are (for the most part) intuitively appealing. First, he shows how bank decision-making is jointly determined by cost, liquidity, and risks conditions. Second, he demonstrates that the effect of risk-averse behavior on optimal decision-making critically depend upon the liquidity and cost conditions facing the banking firm. Third, he shows that many of the results of the portfolio approaches (based upon quantity-setting behavior) cannot be generalized to complete models of the banking firm because they exclude real resource costs and deposit rate-setting behavior. And fourth, Sealey contends that his model provides an alternative explanation, based upon risk-averse behavior, to recent empirical evidence of expense-preference behavior in banking (e.g., Edwards [1977]).

The key elements of Sealey's model can be captured by the following summary statements:

1. Uncertainty is built into the model through random deposit supplies, which are the kernel of the bank liquidity problem (e.g., Continental's liquidity crisis in 1984), and random loan rates. Deposit supplies are viewed as being a function of the deposit rate and a random element. The loan market is assumed to be perfectly competitive.
2. The objective function of the model, which has a single-period planning horizon, is to maximize the expected utility of profit subject to the bank's balance-sheet constraint and deposit-supply function.

---

[4] See Sealey [1980] and Baltensperger [1980]. A third approach to modeling the banking firm is to focus on public confidence. This method is presented in Chapter 7, which deals with bank regulations. Government guarantees (a.k.a. deposit insurance) play a critical role in modeling the confidence function.

[5] Examples are Kane and Malkiel [1965] and Pyle [1971].

[6] See Klein [1971] and Sealey and Lindley [1977].

3. In terms of our basic profit equation (without taxes), $\pi = R - C - O$, Sealey's profit equation has the following components:

   a. *Revenues* (R) are divided into loan revenue and "liquidity" revenue. The latter may be positive, negative or zero depending upon the bank's position in the money market.[7] Negative liquidity revenue is, of course, a liquidity cost, in which case it would show up in C in our simpler formula.

   b. *Interest Costs* (C) consist of deposit interest costs and the aforementioned liquidity costs.

   c. *Overhead* (O) includes two components consisting of the resource costs of servicing loans and deposits. The resource costs of deposits are random whereas those of loans are not.

4. The solution of the model (in terms of first-order conditions) determines the optimal loan portfolio, the deposit rate and the bank's liquidity position.

5. The effects of risk aversion on optimal loan decisions by the bank can be summarized by the following propositions:

   a. The risk of bank profit is an increasing function of loan volume.

   b. Risk-averse bank managers hold smaller loan portfolios than risk-neutral ones. However, it is possible for the reverse to occur, especially in the Klein model.

6. The effects of risk aversion on optimal deposit-rate decisions are unclear unless certain restrictions are imposed, in which case the deposit rate set under risk-averse behavior is greater than the one set under risk neutrality.

7. The simultaneous effects of risk aversion on loan- and deposit-rate decisions are consistent with the nonsimultaneous effects discussed above. However, when the short-term borrowing and lending rates are not equal, the effects may not be consistent.

To summarize, Sealey's model makes an important contribution to the theory of the banking firm because it simultaneously incorporates deposit rate-setting behavior, liquidity considerations, resource costs, and (nonlinear) risk preferences into the analysis. If it disturbs you that the model ignores bank capital, think of the banking firm in his framework as a going concern. Bank capital becomes important mainly in crisis situations. Moreover, the adequacy of a bank's capital is determined primarily by its profitability and liquidity, which, in essence, are the substance of his model.

Partial Versus Complete Models of the Banking Firm

Baltensperger [1980] in his survey of the alternative approaches to the theory of the banking firm makes a distinction between "partial" and "complete" models. Partial models, or what Sealey calls portfolio-theoretic models, focus on either asset selection or liability management. They are partial models because they analyze only part of the banking firm's behavior. A complete model of the banking firm, according to Baltensperger (p. 18), must explain the bank's asset and liability decisions (and their interaction if any) and the size of the firm. The scale or size of the banking firm can be explained by market conditions, risk aversion, or real resource costs. Given this framework, Sealey's model is indeed a complete one.

---

[7] Sealey's balance-sheet constraint (p.1141) is $L = D + Z$, where L = loans, D = deposits, and Z = a *composite variable* measuring the difference between money-market borrowing and lending. Thus, the revenue associated with Z can be positive, negative, or zero depending upon the configuration of rates and quantities. Sealey makes no mention of bank capital in his model. (Let's hope that Senator Proxmire doesn't find out that the Last National Bank of Academia has zero capital.)

A brief description of the major developments in the theory of the banking firm is presented in Table 4-1. The studies are listed chronologically beginning with Edgeworth's [1888] mathematical theory of banking.

TABLE 4-1   The Evolution and Development of the Theory of the Banking Firm

Author	Year	Source[a]	Model Description/Comment
Edgeworth	1888	JRSS	First mathematical theory of banking
Hodgman	1961	RE&S	Analyzes deposit relationship and bank investment behavior
Porter	1961	Yale	Models bank portfolio selection
Hodgman	1963	Book	Focuses upon commercial bank loan and investment policy
Shull	1963	B&MS	A monopoly model of banks as multiple-product, price-discriminating firms
Kane & Malkiel	1965	QJE	A portfolio-management model with deposit variability
Cohen & Hammer	1967	JOF	Applied linear programming to optimal bank asset management
Poole	1968	JOF	Stochastic model of commercial bank reserve management
Brucker	1970	JOF	A microeconomic approach to banking
Pesek	1970	CJE	A real-resource model focusing on the role and behavior of banks and the financial system
Parkin	1970	RES	Models portfolio and debt selection of British discount houses
Klein	1971	JMCB	A monopoly model that determines bank size and portfolio structure
Pyle	1971	JOF	A model based on modern portfolio theory with hedging and quantity-setting behavior
Daly	1971	SEJ	Analyzes financial intermediation and S&L behavior
Pyle	1972	JFQA	Provides descriptive theories of financial institutions under uncertainty
Broaddus	1972	FRB Rich.	Linear programming model of bank portfolio management
Hart & Jaffee	1974	RES	A portfolio-theory approach in which the intermediary is a quantity-setter facing random deposit rates
Towey	1974	JMCB	A real-resource model in the traditional theory-of-the-firm framework
Pringle	1974	JMCB	An imperfect-markets and risk-aversion model focusing on bank capital decisions
Stillson	1974	JMCB	Analyzes information and transaction services in financial institutions
Wood	1975	Book	Analyzes commercial bank loan and investment behavior in the aggregate
Black	1975	JFE	Analyzes bank funds management in an efficient market
Havrilesky & Schweitzer	1975	JBR	Model of nonprice competition in banking
Benston & Smith	1976	JOF	A transactions-cost approach to the theory of financial intermediation
Ali & Greenbaum	1977	JOF	Presents a spatial model of the banking industry
Leland & Pyle	1977	JOF	Analyze information asymmetries in the financial-intermediation process
Edwards	1977	JPE	A model of expense-preference behavior applied to banking
Sealey & Lindley	1977	JOF	A neoclassical model based on production and cost theory

(continues)

TABLE 4-1 (*Continued*)

Author	Year	Source[a]	Model Description/Comment
Kane & Buser	1979	JOF	Focuses on portfolio diversification at commercial banks
Ratti	1979	JME	Models stochastic reserve losses and bank credit expansion
Santomero	1979	JME	Analyzes the role of transactions costs and rates of return on the demand deposit decision
Buser, Chen, & Kane	1980	JOF	Financial theory (M&M) used to explain deposit insurance, capital regulation, and optimal bank capital
Fama	1980	JME	A general equilibrium look at banking in the theory of finance
Baltensperger	1980	JME	A survey of alternative approaches to the theory of the banking firm with emphasis on "partial" versus "complete" models
Sealey	1980	JOF	A complete model with analysis of deposit rate-setting, risk aversion, market conditions, and resource costs
Campbell & Kracaw	1980	JOF	Focuses on information production and market signaling in a theory of financial intermediation
Stiglitz & Weiss	1981	AER	Focus on credit rationing in markets with imperfect information
Smith, Cargill, & Meyer	1981	JOF	Develop an economic theory of a union
Thakor, Greenbaum, and Hong	1981	JB&F	Analyze bank loan commitments and interest-rate volatility
Thakor	1982	JB&F	A theory of bank loan commitments
Smith & Brainard	1982	JOF	A disequilibrium model of S&Ls
Langohr	1982	JB&F	A note on alternative approaches to the theory of the banking firm
Sealey	1983	JOF	Focuses on valuation, capital structure, and shareholder unanimity for depository financial intermediaries
Diamond & Dybvig	1983	JPE	Focus on bank runs, deposit insurance, liquidity
O'Hara	1983	JOF	A dynamic theory of the banking firm
Chan	1983	JOF	Focuses on the positive role of financial intermediation in the allocation of venture capital in a market with imperfect information
Santomero	1984	JMCB	Latest survey on models of the banking firm; includes discussion comments by Taggart, Goldfeld, and Devany
Smith	1984	JOF	Presents a theoretical framework to analyze loan rates and savings deposits at credit unions
Diamond	1984	RES	Analyzes financial intermediation and delegated monitoring
Ramakrishnan & Thakor	1984	RES	Analyze information reliability and a theory of financial intermediation
Sealey	1985	JB&F	Model of portfolio separation for stockholder-owned deposit intermediaries
Chan, Greenbaum, & Thakor	1986	JB&F	Focus on information reusability, competition, and bank asset quality
Szego	1986	JB&F	Analyzes bank asset management and financial insurance
King	1986	JMCB	Models bank lending to test whether monetary policy is transmitted through bank loans or bank liabilities
Stanhouse	1986	JOF	Model of bank portfolio behavior with endogenous uncertainty
Devinney	1986	Book	Analyzes rationing in a theory of the banking firm

(*continues*)

TABLE 4-1 (*Continued*)

Author	Year	Source[a]	Model Description/Comment
Sealey	1987	Chicago Fed Confer.	Describes present state of the theory of financial intermediation and speculates as to why it has developed so slowly
Campbell	1987	*Ibid.*	A valuation-cost approach to the theory
Sprenkle	1987	JB&F	Model of bank behavior with both deposit and loan demand uncertainty
Chan & Thakor	1987	JOF	Analyzes equilibrium credit contracts and allocations with emphasis on moral hazard and private information of financial intermediation
James	1987	JFE	Presents some evidence on the existence of banks as delegated monitors
Blackwell, Collins, & Sinkey	1988	WP	Analyze investment opportunity set and corporate policy choices for financial-services firms

[a]A complete listing for each source can be found in the references at end of the chapter.

Portfolio-Management Models

Models in this category can be divided into asset-management or liability-management ones. In the asset-management area, most models focus on bank reserve and liquidity management. The idea is to find the optimal asset portfolio of reserves and loans, given the bank's deposits. The optimization process is one in which the marginal revenues and marginal costs of the choice variables are equated. Modifications of this basic framework usually take into account alternative loan demand schedules, reserve requirements, portfolio adjustment costs, information costs, asset diversifications, and determinants of the distribution of deposit changes. The latter, of course, is an important determinant of a bank's liquidity requirements.

Until recently, liability management was a neglected area for both model builders and bank portfolio managers. The liability side of the balance sheet simply was treated as being determined by outside factors and thus there was no need to model it explicitly. This passive approach was based upon the assumption that a bank simply *accepted* deposits and did not *purchase* funds. Even in this passive framework, it is reasonable to ask and attempt to model what the bank's optimal financial structure should be. This approach leads to questions regarding the impact of capital regulation and deposit insurance on the bank's financial structure.

Once the passive view of a bank as simply accepting deposits is abandoned, interesting questions regarding optimal deposit and liability structures, liquidity management, and capital adequacy can be addressed. On balance, when applying liability management it becomes necessary to consider the joint management of a bank's assets and liabilities or overall balance-sheet management.

A Complete Model

A complete model of the banking firm must provide for the simultaneous determination of asset structure, liability structure, and size. The basic models presented in the previous section began with bank size given and focused on asset allocation. Next, liability management was introduced as a means of permanently expanding the bank's balance sheet and its impact on asset selection was analyzed. Baltensperger [1980] considers a model in which real resource costs, liquidity costs, and insolvency (bankruptcy) costs are analyzed. His balance-sheet constraint can be stated as

$$R + E = D + K = A \tag{4-1}$$

where R = reserves, E = earning assets, D = deposits, K = capital, and A = assets. There are three choice variables in this model: (1) A, which determines the portfolio size of the bank, (2) the ratio E/A, which determines the asset structure of the bank, and (3) the ratio D/A, which determines the liability structure of the bank. Bank managers are to choose these three variables so as to maximize expected profit, $E(\pi)$. The profit function is rather complex but it can be explained as follows:

1. There is a spread management component defined as:

$$[ra - cd - (1 - d)k]A \qquad (4\text{-}2)$$

where

$$a = \frac{E}{A}$$

$$d = \frac{D}{A}$$

r = Expected Return on Assets

c = Interest Cost of Deposits

k = Opportunity Cost of Equity Capital

Let us look closely at each component of 4-2. The first term is

$$raA = r\left[\left(\frac{E}{A}\right)A\right] = rE$$

which is simply the revenue from earning assets. The second term is

$$cdA = c\left[\left(\frac{D}{A}\right)A\right] = cD$$

which is simply the interest cost of deposits. The third term is

$$(1 - d)kA = k\left[\left(\frac{1 - D}{A}\right)A\right] = kK$$

which is simply the opportunity cost of bank capital. In a simpler form, Equation 4-2 can be rewritten as

$$[rE - cD - kK] \qquad (4\text{-}3)$$

2. The second component focuses on real resources costs or "overhead" (O) and is

$$O(A, a, d) \qquad (4\text{-}4)$$

This equation should be read as "overhead is a function of the size and composition of the bank's balance sheet."

3. The third component measures liquidity costs (Q) and is expressed as

$$Q(A, a, d) \qquad (4\text{-}5)$$

Similar to 4-4 it says that liquidity costs are a function of a bank's balance-sheet characteristics.

4. The fourth component focuses on solvency costs (S) and is

$$S(A, a, d) \qquad (4\text{-}6)$$

As in 4-4 and 4-5, solvency costs are a function of a bank's size, asset structure, and capital structure.

Combining 4-2 and 4-4 to 4-6, expected profit becomes

$$E(\pi) = (ra - cd - (1 - d)k]A - O(A, a, d) - Q(A, a, d) - S(A, a, d) \qquad (4\text{-}7)$$

Substituting 4-3 for 4-2 and deleting the functional form notation on the cost expressions O, Q, and S, Equation 4-7 can be rewritten as

$$E(\pi) = rE - cD - kK - O - Q - S \qquad (4\text{-}8)$$

Although Equation 4-8 has a simpler notation, Equation 4-7 reflects the heart of the optimization process in this framework. To maximize expected profit, the bank must determine the optimal values of A, a, and d as an interdependent set (i.e., $[A^*, a^*, d^*]$) in terms of the parameters of the underlying return and cost functions[8]

A New Approach: Banks as Delegated Monitors[9]

How does a saver decide between an indirect-finance transaction (e.g., a bank deposit) and a direct-finance transaction (e.g., a marketable security, debt, or equity)? How does a business firm decide between a bank loan (indirect finance) and issuing debt through marketed securities (direct finance)? By engaging in indirect finance, the saver, as a depositor, does not have to *monitor* the financial condition and performance of the borrower; this task is *delegated* to the intermediary. For most savers, this choice is a rational one because, as *outsiders*, they do not have the time, inclination, money, or skill to evaluate the performance of *insiders*. Accordingly, they pass the agency problem and costs on to the intermediary, who acts as their *agent* (see the discussion of agency theory in the previous chapter). The bottom line is that outsiders are better off (in terms of costs saved) by delegating the task of monitoring insiders to those with human and reputational capital invested in the monitoring process (i.e., financial intermediaries such as banks and insurance companies).

Consider now the borrowing firm's dilemma. Should it seek out bank loans or marketable debt? The advantages with bank loans are their flexibility and the tendency for lenders to renegotiate loan contracts if the firm encounters financial difficulties. In contrast, bond contracts, although they generally have lower interest costs than bank loans, tend to be inflexible and constraining (e.g., restrictive convenants). Thus, flexibility does have its costs, or inflexibility its benefits. The fact that we observe firms with both bank loans and marketable securities suggests that firms derive benefits from both kinds of financing. Moreover, since banks serve as agents for depositors by monitoring the performance of borrowing firms, these firms may benefit in the marketplace by having some debt on their balance sheets that is "approved" by recognized players (monitors) in the financial system.

Of course, banks are not the only monitors in the financial system. As seen in the previous chapter, "lead steers" also play a crucial role by monitoring the performance of both financial and nonfinancial firms. In addition, insured depositors receive the additional benefit of monitoring by deposit insurers and bank regulators.

To summarize, we have the term *delegated monitors* and a theory dealing with financial intermediation and *delegated monitoring*. The theory focuses on the role of

---

[8] The optimization process involves finding $[A^*, a^*, d^*]$ such that the relevant marginal revenues and marginal costs are equal. See Baltensperger [1980].

[9] The seminal work on delegated monitoring is Diamond [1984]. For a nontechnical summary, see Berlin [1987]; for some empirical evidence on delegated monitoring, see James [1987].

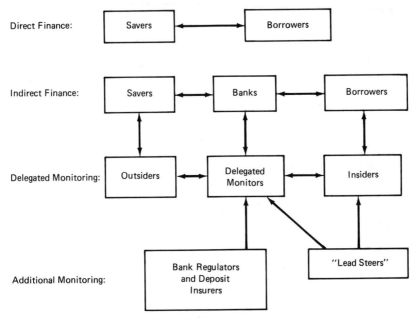

Figure 4-5 Banks as Delegated Monitors

banks in the financial system and the differences (and hence the choice) between bank loans and marketplace securities. The basic aspects of banks as delegated monitors are summarized in Figure 4-5.

CHAPTER SUMMARY

This chapter has focused on some fundamental theoretical propositions applied to financial institutions and capital markets. The capital market is a device that enables individuals to smooth their consumption patterns by trading dollars between current and future periods and vice versa. The introduction of the opportunity to invest-ment in real assets permits economic units to increase consumption either today or tomorrow because it expands their opportunity sets. Analysis of the Fisher–Hirschleifer model establishes the validity of the NPV rule for financial managers. In a competitive banking system, Fama has shown that banks are subject to the Modigliani–Miller proposition of the irrelevance of pure financing decisions. In this framework, nothing suggests that banks should be subject to government regulation. Finally, to model the banking firm completely, the simultaneous determination of a bank's asset and liability structures and its size is required.

LIST OF KEY WORDS, CONCEPTS, AND ACRONYMS

Accounting system of exchange
Bank portfolio management services
Bank wealth-transfer services
Capital market
Consumption patterns

Deficit-spending unit (DSU)
Delegated monitors
Equal-access assumption
General equilibrium
Indifference curve (utility surface)

Interest-rate line
Investment opportunity set (IOS)
Models of the banking firm (complete versus partial)
Marginal productivity of capital
Modigliani–Miller (M&M) Proposition I

Net-present-value (NPV) rule
Perfectly competitive market
Perfect-substitutes assumption
Rate-of-return rule
Surplus-spending unit (SSU)

REVIEW/DISCUSSION QUESTIONS

1. Explain in words and show in pictures (using graphs) how the capital market can be used by both prodigals and misers to smooth their consumption patterns.
2. Why are opportunities to invest in physical or real assets important? Use graphical analysis to demonstrate the advantages and show how the NPV and rate-of-return rules fall out of this analysis.
3. Using Figure 4-4, explain what would happen to the analysis if borrowing and lending rates were not equal. Should the financial manager determine the appropriate discount rate for projects based on shareholders' preferences or the riskiness of the projects' cash flows?
4. In a competitive banking system, how would deposit rates be set? Distinguish between gross and net rates. What types of deposit account would be likely to exist in such a system? How would the riskiness of these accounts be determined? Should the government guarantee any of these accounts? Why? Why not?
5. What is M&M's Proposition I? Under what conditions does it apply to banks? If banking is competitive, is there a need for the banking system to be regulated? Explain.
6. Under what conditions would financial markets be perfectly competitive? How close do U.S. financial markets come to meeting these conditions? Discuss.
7. What are the two basic transactions services provided by banks? Which one is the more important?
8. What evolution has been occurring in the financial system with respect to the provision of portfolio and transactions services?
9. What are the two basic approaches that have been used to model the banking firm?
10. What are the key elements and conclusions of Sealey's model?
11. Distinguish between "partial" and "complete" models of the banking firm. In which category does Sealey's model fall? Why? Update Table 4-1 by surveying the major banking and finance journals for new and important studies on the theory of the banking firm.
12. Carefully explain the components of Baltensperger's expected profit equation. Do you consider this model to be a "complete" one? If not, what is missing or misspecified?
13. What is delegated monitoring and how do banks serve as delegated monitors? Discuss fully.

MATCHING QUIZ

Directions: Select the letter from the right-hand column that best matches the term in the left-hand column.

___ 1. Capital market		A. Borrows to consume more now
___ 2. IOS		B. Lends to consume more later
___ 3. Equal access		C. Author of 1980 complete model
___ 4. Perfect substitutes		D. Trading place for dollars
___ 5. M&M Proposition I		E. Schedule of investment projects
___ 6. Sealey		F. Irrelevance of financing decisions
___ 7. Baltensperger		G. Overly strong assumption
___ 8. Santomero		H. Weaker assumption
___ 9. NPV rule		I. Author of 1980 survey
___ 10. Rate-of-return rule		J. Author of 1984 survey
___ 11. Fama		K. Assumes banking is competitive
___ 12. Fisher–Hirschleifer model		L. Describes Sealey's model
___ 13. Complete model		M. Maximizes value of firm
___ 14. Partial model		N. Describes bank portfolio model
___ 15. Slope of IOS		O. Negative sign is ignored
___ 16. Accounting system of exchange		P. Perfect-certainty framework
___ 17. Prodigal		Q. Established at tangency point
___ 18. Miser		R. Bookkeeping entries only

SELECTED REFERENCES

Ali, Mukhtar M., and Stuart I. Greenbaum. [1977]. "*A Spatial Model of the Banking Industry,* Journal of Finance (September), pp. 1283–1303.

Baltensperger, Ernst. [1980]. "Alternative Approaches to the Theory of the Banking Firm," *Journal of Monetary Economics* 6, pp. 1–37.

Benston, George J., and Clifford W. Smith, Jr. [1976]. "A Transaction Cost Approach to the Theory of Financial Intermediation," *Journal of Finance* (May), pp. 215–231.

Berlin, Mitchell. [1987]. "Bank Loans and Marketable Securities: How Do Financial Contracts Control Borrowing Firms?" *Business Review*, (July/August), Federal Reserve Bank of Philadelphia, pp. 9–18.

Black, Fischer. [1970]. "Banking and Interest Rates in a World Without Money," *Journal of Bank Research* (Autumn), pp. 9–20.

Blackwell, David W., Mitchell C. Collins, and Joseph F. Sinkey, Jr. [1988]. "The Investment Opportunity Set and Corporate Policy Choices for Financial-Services Firms," Working Paper, The University of Georgia.

Brealey, Richard, and Stewart Myers. [1984]. *Principles of Corporate Finance*. New York: McGraw-Hill.

Broaddus, Alfred. [1972]. "Linear Programming: A New Approach to Bank Portfolio Management," *Monthly Review*, Federal Reserve Bank of Richmond (November), pp. 3–11.

Brucker, Eric [1970]. "A Microeconomic Approach to Banking," *Journal of Finance* (March), pp. 1133–1141.

Buser, Stephen A., Andrew H. Chen, and Edward J. Kane. [1981]. "Federal Deposit Insurance, Regulatory Policy, and Optimal Bank Capital," *Journal of Finance* (March), pp. 51–60.

Campbell, Tim S. [1987]. "The Valuation-Cost Approach to the Theory of Financial Intermediation," Proceeding of the Conference on Bank Structure and Competition, Federal Reserve Bank of Chicago.

———— and William A. Kracaw. [1980]. "Information Production Market Signalling and the Theory of Financial Intermediation: A Reply," *Journal of Finance* 37 (September), pp. 1097–1099.

Chan, Yuk-Shee. [1982]. "Information Production, Market Signalling, and the Theory of Financial Intermediation: A Comment," *Journal of Finance* (September), pp. 1095–1096.

————and Stuart I. Greenbaum. [1987]. "Collateral and Competitive Equilibrium with Moral Hazard and Private Information," *Journal of Finance* (June), pp. 345–363.

————Stuart I. Greenbaum, and Anjan V. Thakor. [1986]. "Information Reusability, Competition, and Bank Asset Quality," *Journal of Banking and Finance* (June), pp. 243–254.

Cohen, Kalman J., and Fredrick S. Hammer, [1967]. "Linear Programming and Optimal Bank Asset Management Decisions," *Journal of Finance* 22 (May), pp. 147–168.

Daly, George G. [1971]. "Financial Intermediation and the Theory of the Firm: An Analysis of Savings and Loan Association Behavior," *Southern Economic Journal* 37 (January), pp. 283–294.

Devinney, Timothy M. [1986]. *Rationing in a Theory of the Banking Firm*. Berlin-Heidelberg-New York-Tokyo: Springer-Verlag.

Diamond, Douglas W. [1984]. "Financial Intermediation and Delegated Monitoring," *Review of Economic Studies* (July), pp. 393–414.

————and Phillip H. Dybvig. [1982]. "Bank Runs, Deposit Insurance, and Liquidity," *Journal of Political Economy* (December), pp. 340–371.

Edgeworth, Francis Y. [1888]. "The Mathematical Theory of Banking," *Journal of Royal Statistical Society* 51 (March), pp. 113–127.

Edwards, Franklin R. [1977]. "Managerial Objectives in Regulated Industries: Expense-Preference Behavior in Banking," *Journal of Political Economy* (February), pp. 147–161.

Fama, Eugene F. [1980]. "Banking in the Theory of Finance," *Journal of Monetary Economics* 6, pp. 39–57.

————and Merton H. Miller. [1972]. *The Theory of Finance*. New York: Holt, Rinehart, and Winston.

Fellows, James A. [1978]. "A Theory of the Banking Firm," *The American Economist* (Spring), pp. 22–25.

Fisher, Irving. [1930]. *The Theory of Interest*. New York: Augustus M. Kelley, Bookseller, 1965 reprint of original edition.

Hart, Oliver D., and Dwight M. Jaffee. [1974]. "On the Application of Portfolio Theory to Depository Financial Intermediaries," *Review of Economic Studies* 41 (January), pp. 129–147.

Havrilesky, Thomas M. [1985]. "Theory-of-the-Firm Models of Bank Behavior," in Havrilesky et al., eds., *Dynamics of Banking*. Arlington Heights, IL: Harlan Davidson, Inc., pp. 5–26.

———— and Robert L. Schweitzer. [1975]. "A Model of Non-Price Competition in Banking," *Journal of Bank Research* 6 (Summer), pp. 113–121.

Hirschleifer, Jack. [1958]. "On the Theory of Optimal Investment Decision," *Journal of Political Economy* 66 (August), pp. 329–352.

Hodgeman, Donald R. [1961]. "The Deposit Relationship and Commercial Bank Investment Behavior," *Review of Economics and Statistics* 42 (August), pp. 257–268.

———. [1963]. "Commercial Bank Loan and Investment Policy," Bureau of Business and Economic Research, University of Illinois.

James, Christopher. [1987]. "Some Evidence on the Uniqueness of Bank Loans," *Journal of Financial Economics* (December), pp. 217–235.

Johnson, Harry G. [1968]. "Problems of Efficiency in Monetary Management," *Journal of Political Economy* 76 (September/October), pp. 971–990.

Kane, Edward J., and Burton G. Malkiel. [1965]. "Bank Portfolio Allocation. Deposit Variability, and the Availability Doctrine." *Quarterly Journal of Economics* (February), pp. 113–134.

———and Stephen A. Buser. [1979]. "Portfolio Diversification at Commercial Banks," *Journal of Finance* 34 (March), pp. 19–34.

King, Stephen R. [1986]. "Monetary Transmission: Through Bank Loans or Bank Liabilities," *Journal of Money, Credit and Banking* (August), pp. 290–303.

Klein, Michael A. [1971]. "A Theory of the Banking Firm," *Journal of Money, Credit and Banking* (May), pp. .205–218.

Langohr, Herwig. [1982]. "Alternative Approaches of the Theory of the Banking Firm," *Journal of Banking and Finance* (June), pp. 297–304.

Leland, Hayne E., and David H. Pyle. [1977]. "Information Asymmetries, Financial Structure, and Financial Intermediation," *Journal of Finance* (May), pp. 371–387.

Modigliani, Franco, and Merton H. Miller. [1958]. "The Cost of Capital, Corporation Finance, and the Theory of Investment," *American Economic Review* 48 (June), pp. 261–297.

Murphy, Neil B. [1972]. "Costs of Banking Activities: Interactions Between Risk and Operating Costs, A Comment," *Journal of Money, Credit and Banking* (August), pp. 614–615.

O'Hara, Maureen J. [1983]. "A Dynamic Theory of the Banking Firm," *Journal of Finance* 38 (March), pp. 127–140.

Parkin, M. [1970]. "Discount House Portfolio and Debt Selection," *Review of Economic Studies* 37 (October), pp. 469–497.

Pesek, Boris P. [1970]. "Banks' Supply Function and the Equilibrium Quantity of Money," *The Canadian Journal of Economics* (August), pp. 357–385.

Poole, William. [1968]. "Commercial Bank Reserve Management in a Stochastic Model: Implications for Monetary Policy," *Journal of Finance* 23 (December), pp. 769–791.

Porter, Richard C. [1961]. "A Model of Bank Portfolio Selection," *Yale Economic Essays* 1 (Fall), 323–359.

Pyle, David H. "On the Theory of Financial Intermediation," *Journal of Finance* (June), pp. 734–747.

———. [1972]. "Descriptive Theories of Financial Institutions Under Uncertainty," *Journal of Financial and Quantitative Analysis* 26 (December), pp. 2009–2031.

Pringle, John J. [1973]. "A Theory of the Banking Firm: Comment," Journal of Money, Credit and Banking (November), pp. 990–996.

———. [1974]. "The Imperfect Market Model of Commercial Bank Financial Management," *Journal of Financial Quantitative Analysis* (January), pp. 69–87.

Ratti, Ronald A. [1979]. "Stochastic Reserve Losses and Bank Credit Expansion," *Journal of Monetary Economics* 5 (April), pp. 283–94.

Santomero, Anthony M. [1979]. "The Role of Transaction Costs and Rates of Return on the Demand Deposit Decision," *Journal of Monetary Economics* 5 (July), pp. 343–364.

Sealey, C.W. [1980]. "Deposit Rate-Setting, Risk Aversion, and the Theory of Depository Financial Intermediates," *Journal of Finance* (December), pp. 1139–1154.

———. [1983]. "Valuation, Capital Structure, and Shareholder Unanimity for Depository Financial Intermediaries," *Journal of Finance* (June), pp. 857–871.

———. [1985]. "Portfolio Separation for Stockholder Owned Depository Financial Intermediaries," *Journal of Banking and Finance* (December), pp 477–490.

———. [1987]. "Finance Theory and Financial Intermediation," *Proceedings of the Conference on Bank Structure and Competition*, Federal Reserve Bank of Chicago.

——— and J. T. Lindley. [1977]. "Inputs, Outputs, and a Theory of Production and Cost at Depository Financial Institutions," *Journal of Finance* (September), pp. 1251–1266.

Snull, Bernard. [1963]. "Commercial Banks as Multiple-Product Price-Discriminating Firms," *Banking and Monetary Studies*, Homewood, II: Irwin.

Smith, Donald J. [1984]. "A Theoretical Framework for the Analysis of Credit Union Decision Making," *Journal of Finance* (September), pp. 1155–1168.

Smith, Donald, Thomas Cargill, and Robert Meyer. [1981]. "An Economic Theory of a Credit Union," *Journal of Finance* (May), pp. 519–528.

Smith, Gary, and William Brainard. [1982]. "A Disequilibrium Model of Savings and Loan Associations," *Journal of Finance* (December), pp. 1277–1293.

Sprenkle, Case M. [1987]. "Liability and Asset Uncertainty for Banks," *Journal of Banking and Finance* (Vol. 11, No. 1, March), pp. 147–159.

Stanhouse, Bryan. [1986]. "Commercial Bank Portfolio Behavior and Endogenous Uncertainty," *Journal of Finance* (December), pp. 1103–1114.

Stiglitz, Joseph E., and Andrew Weiss. [1981]. "Credit Rationing in Markets with Imperfect Information," *American Economic Review* (June), pp. 393–410.

Stillson, Richard T. [1974]. "An Analysis of Information and Transaction Services in Financial Institutions," *Journal of Money, Credit and Banking* 6 (November), pp. 517–535.

Szego, Giorgio P. [1986] "Bank Asset Management and Financial Insurance," *Journal of Banking and Finance* (June), pp. 295–307.

Thakor, Anjan V. [1982]. "Toward a Theory of Bank Loan Commitments," *Journal of Banking and Finance* 6 (March), pp. 55–83.

——— Stuart I. Greenbaum and Hai Hong. [1981]. "Bank Loan Commitments and Interest Rate Volatility," *Journal of Banking and Finance* 5 (December), pp. 471–510.

Tobin, James. "Commercial Banks as Creators of Money," in Dean Carson, ed., *Banking and Monetary Studies*. Homewood Hills, IL: Irwin, pp. 408–419.

Towey, Richard E. [1974]. "Money Creation and the Theory of the Banking Firm," *Journal of Finance* (March), pp. 57–72.

Wood, John. [1975]. "Commercial Bank Loan and Investment Behavior," New York: Wiley.

Wood, John H. [1981]. "Financial Intermediaries and Monetary Control," *Journal of Monetary Economics* 8, pp. 145–163.

PART III

FINANCIAL INNOVATION AND THE ENVIRONMENT OF THE FINANCIAL-SERVICES INDUSTRY

This part of the book contains five chapters focusing on the environment of the financial-services industry. The key stimuli for change in this environment are technology, reregulation, interest-rate movements, and competition for customers. These four factors are captured by the T, R, I, and C components of TRICK. Recalling our model of change (from Chapter 1),

TRICK + Rational Self-Interest = Financial Innovation

we highlight how the environmental factors (T, R, I, and C), in conjunction with rational self-interest, serve to stimulate financial innovation.

In Chapter 5, the focus is twofold: (1) the process of financial innovation is defined and described and (2) the institutions, markets, and instruments of the FSI are highlighted. The roles of technology and the development of electronic funds transfer systems are stressed in Chapter 6. The next two chapters focus on various aspects of the regulatory and deposit-insurance systems and alternative ways of reforming them. Finally, in Chapter 9, we focus on the theories, conventions, and innovations associated with interest rates and asset prices, and look at the interest-rate environment of the financial-services industry.

Over these five chapters (and throughout the book), you should think about how the dynamic forces of change as captured by technology, reregulation, interest-rate volatility, and competition for customers serve to stimulate financial innovation, and in the process shape the financial-services industry and its components.

Financial Innovation and the Institutions, Markets, and Instruments of the Financial-Services Industry

---

ACRONYM GUIDE TO KEY TERMS AND CONCEPTS

FSF = financial-services firm
FSI = financial-services industry
LHS = left-hand side (of balance sheet)
RHS = right-hand side (of balance sheet)
TRICK = Technology, Reregulation, Interest-rate risk,
  Customers, and Kapital adequacy

INTRODUCTION

Innovation means the introduction of something new, such as a new idea, method, or device. From the end of World War II until the early 1960s, nothing new *seemed* to happen in banking—no new ideas, methods, or devices. Moreover, except for the Korean War, the economic, political, and social climate of this period was one of relative calm and stability; it was the period of the "generals"—General Motors, General Electric, and General Eisenhower. The saving graces of the 1950s were rock and roll and '57 Chevy convertibles.

By February of 1961, a key banking innovation had occurred—the introduction of the first *effective* negotiable certificate of deposit (CD). This instrument, which was introduced by First National City Bank of New York (now Citibank), was important because it permitted banks to purchase funds and thereby manage their liabilities, hence the term *liability management.* Since then, numerous innovations have kept on coming. Relative to the 1960s and the 1970s, the greatest rush of financial innovations and other changes (e.g., mergers, consolidations, and failures) has occurred in the 1980s.

This chapter focuses on the process of financial innovation and how it has affected the institutions, markets, and instruments of the financial-services industry (FSI). Special emphasis is placed on the role of depository institutions and the increased competition they have received from nonbank institutions. We begin by reviewing our model of change (introduced in Chapter 1) and then proceed with a detailed look at the process of financial innovation and the various innovations that have occurred in financial institutions, markets, and instruments.

A DYNAMIC MODEL OF CHANGE AND THE PROCESS OF FINANCIAL INNOVATION

The components of TRICK are Technology, Reregulation, Interest-rate risk, Customers, and Kapital adequacy (see Chapter 1 if you need a review of the importance of each of these factors to the FSI). TRICK is a comprehensive conceptual device that captures the major forces of change operating in the FSI. For comparison, Van Horne [1985] lists six stimuli that prompt financial innovation: (1) volatile inflation rates and interest rates, the *I* component of TRICK; (2) regulatory changes and circumvention of regulations, the *R* component of TRICK; (3) tax changes—the notion of "regulation as a tax" implies the *R* component of TRICK; (4) technological advances, the *T* component of TRICK; (5) the level of economic activity, the *I* component of TRICK (the interest-rate cycle) as a proxy for this measure; and (6) academic work on market efficiency and inefficiencies. Although the last point is missing from TRICK, how many practitioners would list it as an important stimulus for change in the FSI? Prior to the market crash, however, a number of high-powered academics were lured from their ivory towers to Wall Street, which gives some credence to Van Horne's point. Nevertheless, as a stimulus for change, academic research pales in relationship to the forces of change captured by the components of TRICK.

The combination of TRICK and rational self-interest generates our model of change, or a framework for analyzing the process of financial innovation, that is,

$$\text{TRICK} + \text{Rational Self-interest} = \text{Financial Innovation} \qquad (5\text{-}1)$$

To make the notion of rational self-interest more palatable, think of it as profitable opportunities. When such opportunities exist, rational businesspersons go after them. What explains the existence of profitable opportunities? Given our paradigm of perfect competition and efficient markets (see the previous chapter), we can look for market imperfections and inefficiencies as potential sources of profitable opportunities. Of course, if markets are competitive, then the mere existence of such opportunities would eventually eliminate them as other innovators (or followers) would compete away the profits. Assuming efficient, lowest-cost producers, the competitive process works such that the consumers of financial services *eventually* reap the benefits of the process of financial innovation through lower prices and/or better quality products and services. At this stage in the process, the innovators, waiting for the next exploitable opportunity, turn to writing books about how to make money with their innovations—a sure sign their profits are exhausted.

THE DIFFUSION OF FINANCIAL INNOVATIONS: SOME PRELIMINARY DISTINCTIONS

To make the diffusion of financial innovations more intelligible, let's consider the three preliminary distinctions made by Kane [1983] with respect to (1) invention versus innovation, (2) autonomous innovation versus induced innovation, (3) and market-induced innovation versus regulation-induced innovation. These distinctions are summarized in Figure 5-1, which includes a glossary of the relevant terms.

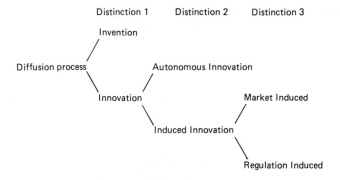

Glossary: Invention is an unfolding technological opportunity.
Innovation is a profitable application of an invention.
Autonomous innovation is one not induced by outside forces; it just happens. Psychologists
might look at toilet training (or the lack of it) as the catalyst.
Induced innovation is one generated by outside forces.
Market-induced innovation is one generated by market forces such as price or interest-rate
movements.
Regulation-induced innovation is one stimulated by regulatory constraints such as geographic,
price, c˜ product restrictions.

Figure 5-1   The Diffusion of Financial Innovations: Three Important Distinctions
Source: Adapted from Kane [1983].

The first distinction is one in which an invention refers to an unfolding technological opportunity, whereas innovation refers to the profitable application of an invention. The lag between an invention and its embodiment in an innovation is called the innovation lag. For example, although personal or home computers have been available for several years now, the profitable application of these devices to home banking has not materialized yet. In the financial-services industry, technology tends to be downstreamed, after a delay, from wholesale applications to retail ones. This lag reflects the time it takes to reduce the operating costs of the new technology to a level that permits profitable application to retail customers. Thus, one way to attempt to forecast future products and delivery services at the retail level is to look at the state-of-the-art technology on the wholesale level.

The second distinction separates innovations into those that are induced by market or regulatory forces and those that are autonomous (i.e., not caused by market or regulatory forces). Think of autonomous innovations as just happening. For example, in the birth process, labor can occur naturally (say autonomously) or it can be induced chemically. Regarding autonomous innovation, psychologists might look for the catalyst in the innovator's toilet training, or lack of it. With financial innovations, however, it is much easier to explain them as being induced by either market or regulatory factors, which is Kane's third distinction. Of course, in some instances, market and regulatory forces work jointly to induce financial innovations. For example, new savings products in the late 1970s and early 1980s were induced jointly by Regulation Q (interest-rate ceilings) and inflation-generated high interest rates.

Since few financial institutions operate on the cutting edge of technology, most of their innovations are induced by regulatory or market forces. The major environmental factors driving the process of financial innovation are, of course, captured by TRICK. During the 1970s and the early 1980s, Kane argues, financial adaptation responded primarily to the T, R, and I components of TRICK. With the disinflation, increased competition, loan-quality problems, and record bank failures of the mid and late 1980s, reregulation (R), competition for customers (C), and capital adequacy or safety (K) have been the critical factors.

CLASSES OF FINANCIAL SERVICES AND RECENT INNOVATIONS

From the perspective of the customer, banks or financial-services firms can be viewed as providing six classes of services or products: (1) transaction services, (2) savings or investment instruments, (3) financing or credit arrangements, (4) securities underwriting and distribution, (5) insurance, and (6) fiduciary. Using this framework, let's look at some of the innovations in each of these areas over the past decade or so.

Transaction Services

Transaction services are designed to transfer funds. Technological developments in the area of electronic funds transfer systems (EFTS) have been the key innovations in this area. The three primary technological innovations have been automated teller machines (ATMs), point-of-sale systems (POSs), and automated clearinghouses (ACHs). In addition, wire-transfer systems, debit cards, automatic-transfer accounts, share-draft accounts, home banking (via personal computers), limited-service or nonbank banks offering demand deposits, electronic security trading, and advances in credit-card processing have developed. (The next chapter is devoted to the exciting area of "electronic banking.") Finally, in the wholesale area, sophisticated cash-management systems for corporate clients have been developed.

Savings Products

The formal removal of all interest-rate ceiling on savings (or deposit) instruments in 1986 gave managers of depository institutions considerable discretion to develop new products to compete with less-regulated players. For almost a decade prior to 1986, the piecemeal removal of interest-rate restrictions on savings products had been occurring. Two highly successful innovations that were taking deposits away from banks were the money-market mutual fund and the cash-management account developed by brokerage firms. In the aftermath, bankers responded with such innovations as money-market certificates, all-savers certificates, NOW accounts, super NOW accounts, brokered CDs, and money-market investment accounts. In addition, various retirement plans in the form of IRAs and Keogh plans have been developed. In the area of "wholesale" savings products, which predate the consumer savings products described above, the innovations have included negotiable CDs, options to purchase federal funds, repurchase agreements (RPs or repos), subordinated debentures, and numerous other debt-financing arrangements such as zero-coupon bonds, coupon stripping, bonds with put options, and so-called junk bonds.

Credit or Financing Arrangements

This area refers to making loans. In wholesale commercial lending, "either–or facilities" have developed such that borrowers may secure funds at the prime rate (plus or minus) in the domestic market or from the Eurodollar market at LIBOR + some risk premium, where LIBOR stands for the London Interbank Offer Rate. In addition, the development of limited-service or nonbank banks specializing in commercial lending were established. In consumer lending, many earlier developments used in wholesale lending have filtered down to the consumer level in the form of variable-rate loans, home-equity loans (often based on prime rate-plus pricing), and various innovations in the pricing and servicing of credit-card accounts.

Insurance

Historically, insurance was a one-product industry, then a two-product industry. First, it was wholelife insurance, then it was wholelife versus term insurance. Today, it is those two products plus various forms of "universal-life" policies, annuities, financial planning, and other products and services. Many bankers have wooed insurers into their lobbies by leasing them space in their buildings. Moreover, if permitted by state law, banks have been selling various kinds of insurance products.

Securities Underwriting and Distribution

More broadly, this area covers investment banking. The numerous profitable innovations in this area help explain why commercial bankers are so eager to enter this field. Some of the innovations in this area are shelf registration, adjustable-rate preferred stock, securitization of mortgages and other financial assets, interest-rate and currency swaps, interest-rate futures, options, options on futures contracts, the development of various specialized mutual funds, and the explosion of innovative deals in mergers and acquisitions.

Fiduciary or Trust Services

Traditional fiduciary services include investment management, pension, trust, agency, safekeeping, and advice. Although this area has, for the most part, not seen much in the way of direct innovation, several of the innovative products and services described above have had indirect effects on the investment-management and pension areas. One innovation in the trust area has been the ability to commingle funds.

Two important innovations to be discussed later in this part of the book are (1) alternative modes for delivering financial services with emphasis on electronic banking (Chapter 6) and (2) alternative organizational structures with emphasis on the bank-holding-company (BHC) movement (Chapter 8).

FINANCIAL INNOVATION: THE LAST TWENTY YEARS AND THE NEXT

This section bears the same title as an article by Miller [1986], who, by the way, is the Miller of Modigliani and Miller (M&M) from Chapter 3. Miller sees the past and future of financial innovation this way:

> The word revolution is entirely appropriate for describing the changes in financial institutions and instruments that have occurred in the past twenty years. The major impulses to successful financial innovations have come from regulations and taxes. The outlook for the future is for a slowing down of the rate of financial innovation, but much growth and improvement are still in prospect (p. 459).

In his article, Miller establishes criteria for a "successful innovation" and attempts to judge the most significant successful innovation of the past 20 years. First, he defines innovation as the counterpart to the unanticipated change observed in statistical time series (p. 460). Such series consist of two components: anticipated changes and unanticipated changes. The latter refers to the "surprises" or "unanticipated, unforecastable changes." Thus, for Miller, financial innovations are surprises, not due to chance, but generated primarily by regulation and taxes.

Continuing with the statistical framework, Miller next defines a successful or truly significant innovation as one that is "permanent" as opposed to "transitory." More specifically, a successful innovation is one that not only survives, but continues to grow, "sometimes very substantially, even after the initiating force has been removed" (p. 462). In the process of becoming "permanent," a successful innovation "reduces dead-weight transaction costs and expands the reach of the market" (p. 463).

Finally, Miller goes about the task of selecting "the" most significant financial innovation of the past 20 years. His nominees include such innovations as zero-coupon bonds, the Eurobond market, interest-rate swaps, options trading, and financial futures. His choice for the most significant financial innovation of the last twenty years is *financial futures*. Miller reasons that financial futures have been important in and of themselves, but in addition they have stimulated important further innovations (p. 463). He views them as having set off a chain reaction in the process of financial innovation. If you are eager to know what financial futures are, please hold on, as they are explained later in the chapter and also in Chapter 17.

FINANCIAL MARKETS AND INSTRUMENTS

The buying and selling of financial claims by financial institutions takes place in financial markets. For the purposes of this book, the most important markets are the *money* and *capital markets*. These two markets are distinguished according to the maturity of the instruments traded. Short-term instruments, defined as maturities of one year or less, are traded in the *money market*. Instruments with maturities greater than one year are traded in the *capital market*. The major instruments of the capital and money markets are presented in Tables 5-1 and 5-2, respectively.

The Markets for Financial Futures and Options

In the new FSI there are three relevant financial markets: (1) the cash market, (2) the options market, and (3) the futures market. Since most FSFs operate only in the cash

TABLE 5-1　Instruments of the Capital Market (March 31, 1987)

Instruments	Amount Outstanding ($ billions)	Percent of Total[a]
1. Corporate stocks	4,135	35.6
2. Residential mortgages	1,693	14.6
3. U.S. government securities (marketable, long term)	1,372	11.8
4. Corporate bonds	1,035	8.9
5. State and local government bonds	566	4.9
6. Bank business loans	552	4.7
7. Consumer installment loans	725	6.2
8. Commercial mortgages	566	4.9
9. Mortgage pools	573	4.9
10. U.S. government agency securities	307	3.2
11. Farm mortgages	96	0.8
TOTAL	11,620	100.0

[a]Total subject to rounding error.
Sources: Federal Reserve Flow of Funds and Federal Reserve Bulletin.

TABLE 5-2   Instruments of the Money Market (May 31 1987)

Instruments	Amount Outstanding ($ billions)	Percent of Total
1. Large denomination time deposits[a]	460	44.9
2. U.S. treasury bills[b]	268	26.2
3. Commercial paper	254	24.8
4. Bankers' acceptances	42	4.1
TOTAL	1,024	100.0

[a] $100,000 or more.
[b] Includes coupons with remaining maturities of less than 12 months.
Source: Statistical Release, Federal Reserve, [July 23]

market, the futures and options markets are the frontier areas. The noncash markets are important because they offer participants in the cash market the opportunity to transfer risk. The options and futures markets are new to the financial arena: they began in 1973 and 1975, respectively. Since then, these markets have experienced phenomenal growth. In fact, the Chicago Board Options Exchange (CBOE) currently ranks as the world's second largest securities market in terms of the dollar value of securities traded. Since options and futures trading are specialized businesses with languages of their own, the limited objective of this section is to introduce the basic concepts and to show how the managers of FSFs can use these markets to hedge interest-rate risk.

Financial Futures[1]

The *I* in TRICK has been responsible for the rapid growth of financial futures, which also are known as *interest-rate futures*. More specifically, the catalyst has been the increasing volatility of interest rates since 1966. Trading in financial futures began in 1975. The first full year of trading produced about 129,000 contracts. During the 1980s, millions of contracts were traded each year (40 million in 1984).

The linkage between the volatility of interest rates and the growth of financial futures is a straightforward one. That is, widely fluctuating interest rates result in widely fluctuating prices for rate-sensitive financial instruments such as mortgages and bonds. This price volatility creates serious risk for the holders of rate-sensitive instruments and potentially profitable opportunities for speculators. Since the managers of FSFs tend to be risk averse, they are interested in transferring interest-rate risk to speculators. The marriage of these hedgers and speculators in the financial futures market was a natural.

A futures contract is simply an agreement to buy or sell something in the future. Until the mid-1970s, the something that was bought or sold mainly was in the form of an agricultural commodity or a precious metal. For the managers of FSFs, the something is in the form of financial futures. The major contracts in interest-rate futures and various specifications of the agreements are presented in Table 5-3. Futures contracts have four distinguishing features: (1) they are binding agreements (options are not); (2) they are standardized with respect to quality, grade, date, and place; (3) they are highly liquid; and (4) they are agreements with the clearing corporation (e.g., the CBOE). The latter is a feature unique to futures contracts; the

[1] This section and the following one on options draw on the work of Melton and Pukula [1984], especially Chapters 6 and 7. See Miller [1986] for an interesting description of the origins and development of financial futures. The use of futures to manage interest-rate risk is discussed in Chapters 9 and 11.

TABLE 5-3 Contract Specifications for Interest-Rate Futures[a]

Futures Contract	Exchange Traded	Contract Size	Trading Month	Minimum Fluctuation in price (Tick Size)	Dollar Value of Minimum Fluctuation in Price (Tick Size)	Price[b] Limit	Last Trading Day
Ninety day T-bill	IMM	$1,000,000	MAR, JUNE, SEPT, DEC	.01 of 1% (1 basis pt)	$25.00	$1,500	Wednesday after third Monday of contract month
Domestic certificate of deposit	IMM	$1,000,000	MAR, JUNE, SEPT, DEC	.01 of 1% (1 basis pt)	$25.00	$2,000	Second to last day of contract month
Eurodollar time deposit	IMM	$1,000,000	MAR, JUNE, SEPT, DEC	.01 of 1% (1 basis pt)	$25.00	$25.00	Second London business day before third Wednesday of contract month
GNMA CDR 8%	CBT	$ 100,000	MAR, JUNE, SEPT, DEC	$\frac{1}{32}$ of 1 pt	$31.25	$2,000	Second to last day of contract month
GNMA II	CBT	$ 100,000	MAR, JUNE, SEPT, DEC	$\frac{1}{32}$ of 1 pt	$31.25	$2,000	Seven business days prior to last business day of contract month
Ten-year U.S. treasury note	CBT	$ 100,000	MAR, JUNE, SEPT, DEC	$\frac{1}{32}$ of 1 pt	$31.25	$2,000	Seven business days prior to last business day of contract month
Thirty-year U.S. T-bond	CBT	$ 100,000	MAR, JUNE, SEPT, DEC	$\frac{1}{32}$ of 1 pt	$31.25	$2,000	Seven business days prior to last business day of contract month

[a] Specifications subject to change at discretion of the exchanges.
[b] Limit is above or below previous day's settlement price.
Notes: The initial margin and the maintenance margin on all of the contracts are $2,000 and $1,500, respectively. Trading hours are 8:00 A.M. to 2:00 P.M. Chicago time, except for the CD and Eurodollar contracts which trade from 7:30 A.M. to 2:00 P.M. Chicago time. CBT = Chicago Board of Trade, IMM = International Monetary Market, and CDR = Collateralized Depository Receipt.
Source: Shearson Lehman/American Express, 1984.

other party in the contract is always the clearing corporation, which provides safety, liquidity, and ease of negotiation.

Since futures contracts are simply agreements made before delivery, the price for the future delivery is established at the time the contract is signed. Orders for immediate delivery occur in the spot or cash market. Futures markets perform a risk-transfer function by transferring risk from risk averters to risk takers (called speculators). Risk averters desire to hedge their positions, whereas risk takers are willing to speculate—to take on high risk for the chance of a high return. A perfect or effective hedge results in a futures gain to offset a loss in the cash market or a futures loss to offset a gain in the cash market. By adopting a hedging strategy, the risk averter forgoes the *opportunity* to benefit from favorable price (interest-rate) movements but at the same time is protected from adverse price movements. When the hedger gains by avoiding a loss, the speculator loses; however, when the hedger forgoes the opportunity gain, the speculator wins.

Financial Options

Suppose that an FSF manager has used interest-rate futures to hedge a portfolio of long-term assets against an increase in interest rates. If interest rates decline instead, the gain in the cash market is offset by the loss in the futures market. Isn't there some way that FSF managers can have their cake and eat it too? The answer is yes, in part at least. To understand this possibility, the most recent addition to the FSF manager's arsenal of weapons to fight interest-rate risk, financial options, must be considered. Option pricing theory (OPT), one of the stars of the financial-management hexagram, is the topic of this section. However, before we get into OPT, let's look at what exactly an option is.

An option is simply a right to buy (called a *call* option) or sell (called a *put* option) something at a predetermined price prior to the expiration date of the option. As with financial futures, the something that FSF managers want is an option to buy or sell financial instruments, including interest-rate futures. At present, options exist on actual securities and on financial futures. Moreover, since options, unlike futures, are not binding agreements, they can be permitted to expire unexercised. Returning to the simple example at the beginning of the previous paragraph, the FSF manager can buy futures options instead of buying the futures contracts themselves. If interest rates move against the portfolio, the futures options are exercised. However, if interest rates take a favorable turn, then the options are permitted to expire unexercised. Since options, of course, are not costless, the cash outflow in either case is the price or premium paid for the option. In the unexercised case, FSF managers get to have their cake (less a small piece representing the cost of the option) and eat it too. Since the topic of futures options is more relevant for FSF managers than stock options, the discussion in this section focuses on futures options.

Futures Options

A futures option is the right (not the obligation) to buy or sell a specific futures contract at a predetermined price (called the exercise or *strike price*) at any time (an *American* option)[2] prior to the expiration date of the option. To obtain this right the investor pays a fee known as the premium or price of the option. When FSF managers exercise *call* options, they trade their call positions for *long* futures positions. In

---

[2] An option that can be exercised only at maturity (i.e., on the expiration date) is called a European option. The use of futures and options as tools for managing, interest-rate risk is explained in Chapter 17.

contrast, when they exercise put options, they trade their put positions for *short* futures positions. The buyer of an option, whether a call or a put, is called the "holder" of the option; the seller is called the "writer" of the option.

One of the songs from the great musical *Cabaret* is "Money, Money (makes the world go around)." To understand options, you must learn a different song about money. The key lyrics are "in-the-money," "at-the-money," and "out-of-the-money." Please follow the bouncing ball, as we go through the OPT version of "Money, Money."

Common sense suggests that in-the-money is the place to be in just about anything, and options are no exception. The "locational" words in the options-money jargon (i.e., *in*, at, and out) are distance measures of the option's exercise or strike price relative to the current market price of the underlying futures contract. More important, however, the distance measures translate into whether or not the option has *intrinsic* value. For call options, if the futures price exceeds the strike price, the option has intrinsic value and is said to be in-the-money. In the opposite case, the option has no intrinsic value and is out-of-the-money. In the case of equality, the option is at-the-money. For put options (which are similar to selling short), if the strike price exceeds the futures price, the put has intrinsic value and is said to be in-the-money. Statements parallel to the description of calls give the "out" and "at" position for puts.

To illustrate the valuation and money concepts, consider the following examples for T-bond futures trading at 76–00.[3] Except for the at-the-money position, note that for a given strike price calls and puts have opposite results with respect to their valuations and money descriptions.

Call Options			Put Options		
Strike Price	Money Term	Intrinsic Value	Strike Price	Money Term	Intrinsic Value
70	In	Yes	70	Out	No
76	At	—	76	At	—
80	Out	No	80	In	Yes

Option-pricing theory (OPT) focuses on the valuation process for options, which is a complex phenomenon[4]. Following the previous discussion of intrinsic value, the value of a futures option is basically determined by five variables: (1) the value of the underlying futures contract, (2) the variability or riskiness of the underlying futures contract, (3) the exercise price, (4) the maturity of the option, and (5) the risk-free rate of interest. Factors 1 and 2 describe the financial characteristics or risk–return parameters of the underlying futures contract (or security in the case of a stock option). Factors 3 and 4 are parameters of the option contract and factor 5 is a market parameter. Note that factors 1 and 3 were used above to define intrinsic value. In a nutshell, the value of an option can be viewed as the sum of its intrinsic value and its time value. The latter measures the amount of the option value that would be lost if the option were held to maturity with the underlying price of the futures contract not changing. The time-value component of an option is, in effect, a wasting or decaying

---

[3] Option prices on T-bond futures are quoted in 64ths, whereas futures prices on T-bonds are quoted in 32nds.

[4] The Black-Scholes [1973] valuation model is described and applied in the appendix of Chapter 8, based on a study by Sinkey and Miles [1982].

TABLE 5-4   Contract Specifications for Options on U.S. Treasury Bond Futures [a]

Exchange traded	Chicago Board of Trade
Contract Size	$100,000
Trading Month	March, June, September, December
Trading hours	8:00 A.M.–2:00 P.M., Chicago time
Last day of trading and expiration	Options stop trading in the month prior to the futures-contract delivery month at noon on the first Friday preceding, by at least five business days, the first notice for the corresponding T-bond futures contract. Unexercised options expire at 10:00 A.M. on the first Saturday following the last day of trading.
Deliverable grade and method	The holder of a call receives a long position of CBT U.S. T-bond futures. The holder of a put receives a short position.
Strike price	Two-point (integral) multiples per T-bond futures contract (e.g., 70, 72, 74, etc.).
Premium Payment	Due in full at the time of the option purchase.
Price quotation and minimum fluctuation	1/64th of 1% of a T-bond futures contract or $15.625.
Price limit	$2,000 above or below the previous day's settlement price. Limits do not apply during the option's expiration month.
Exercise	The buyer or holder may exercise the option on any business day prior to expiration by giving notice to the clearing corporation by 8:00 P.M. that day. The notice is assigned to a seller and the clearing corporation established a futures position for the buyer and an opposite position for the seller at the strike price before the opening of trading on the following business day.

[a] Subject to change.
Source: Chicago Board of Trade.

asset that approaches zero as the option approaches its expiration date. For an option without any intrinsic value (i.e., one that is out-of-the-money), its premium or value is equal to its time value.

As of this writing, the only futures option available for trading is on T-bond futures. Thus, the opportunity to use futures options to hedge interest-rate risk is limited at present. However, the Commodity Futures Trading Commission (CFTC) is expected to expand futures options to other financial instruments in the future. The specifications for the options on T-bond futures are presented in Table 5-4.

Futures Versus Options

Should the manager of an FSF use futures or options, or both, to hedge interest-rate risk? With the limited availability of futures options, the question is somewhat moot at present, although it is expected to be more relevant in the future. Nevertheless, we can examine the advantages and disadvantages of the two techniques. Since both futures and options trading are complex frontier techniques that require skilled personnel, they both start off with a disadvantage because FSFs, at present, frequently lack specialists in these areas. On the plus side, options are not subject to margin requirements, have low transactions costs, and are an attractive hedging tool. On the negative side, options can be more expensive to use than futures because they provide greater relative safety from price fluctuations and because of the absence of margin requirements. For futures, the main advantage is in the form of a well-developed and relatively inexpensive market; margin requirements are their main disadvantage. On balance, managers of financial-services firms should be prepared to use mixed strategies of futures, options, and/or duration matching to cope with the tasks of value maximization, risk management, and strategic planning. The use of these various techniques for managing interest-rate risk is explained in Chapter 17.

TABLE 5-5 The U.S. Financial-Services Industry: Assets Owned by Various Sectors ($ billions)

	1946		1977		1980		1984 [b]		1986	
	$B	%	$B	%	$B	%	$B	%	$B	%
Savings and loan associations	10.2	4.4	459.2	17.1	630	16.1	912	16.9	1,158	14.7
Mutual savings banks	18.7	8.0	146.7	5.5	171	4.4	199	3.7	239	3.0
Credit unions	0.4	0.2	51.5	1.9	69	1.8	113	2.1	166	2.1
Life insurance companies	47.5	20.3	337.6	12.6	470	12.0	656	12.2	880	11.1
Private pension funds	3.6	1.5	189.4	7.0	287	7.3	584	10.8	826	10.4
State & local gov't retirement funds	2.9	1.2	132.2	4.9	198	5.0	326	6.1	503	6.4
Other insurance companies	7.1	3.0	100.1	3.7	180	4.6	229	4.2	330	4.2
Finance companies	4.9	2.1	124.8	4.6	199	5.1	272	5.1	412	5.2
Open-end investment companies	1.3	0.6	42.8	1.6	64	1.6	137	2.5	488	6.2
Security brokers and dealers	3.4	1.5	28.5	1.1	33	0.8	49	0.9	79	1.0
Real estate investment trusts	—	—	7.6	0.3	6	0.1	5	0.1	9	0.1
Money market funds	—	—	3.5	0.1	74	1.9	178	3.3	228	2.9
Total private nonbank financial institutions	100.0	42.7	1,623.9	60.3	2,381	60.7	3,660	67.9	5,318	67.3
Commercial banking	134.2	57.3	1,068.2	39.7	1,539	39.3	1,733	32.1	2,580	32.7
Total private financial institutions	234.2 [a]	100.0%	2,692.1	100.0%	3,920	100.0%	5,393	100.0%	7,898	100.0%

[a] Totals may not sum exactly due to rounding.
[b] June 30, other years are December 31.
Sources: Sparks [1978], Table 1, pp. 16–17 for 1946 and 1977, and Federal Reserve for 1980, 1984, and 1986.

COMPETITION FROM LESS-REGULATED INSTITUTIONS

One of the leading defenders of the "invasion of the banking market" has been Citicorp, the parent company of Citibank. Citicorp/Citibank has been arguing for the past decade that commercial banks are at an increasing disadvantage vis-a-vis manufacturers and retailers in providing financial services to consumers. Citicorp's position has been documented in staff papers by Sparks [1978] and Christophe [1974] and in several speeches given by former Chairman Walter B. Wriston[5]. Citicorp's basic argument is that nonfinancial corporations are not subject to the same degree of regulation that commercial banks are, and therefore these nonbank institutions have a competitive advantage over banks. Some of the regulations that nonfinancial corporations are *not* subject to include reserve requirements, geographic restrictions, and limitations on the business activities that they can include under their corporate umbrella. (The nonbank activities that BHCs are permitted to engage in are determined by the Fed; see Chapter 8) Citicorp's recommendation to end what it sees as a competitive disadvantage for banks is not regulation of the financial services of nonfinancial corporations, but continued deregulation of the banking industry. With the battle for interest-rate deregulation won, geographic and new services deregulation are the current battlefronts.

One indication of the competition in the financial-services industry is provided by the data presented in Table 5-5. From 1946 to 1977, commercial banks' share of the financial-assets pie declined by 17.6 percentage points. As of year-end 1977, only $4 out of every $10 of financial assets held by private financial institutions were owned by commercial banks compared with roughly $6 out of every $10 in 1946. From 1977 to 1980, commercial banks held their own, losing only 0.4 of a percentage point in market share. Over the next 3.5 years, they lost 7.2 percentage point and as of mid-year 1984 they controlled only $3.2 for every $10 of assets in the FSI. However, over the next 2.5 years, this downward trend was reversed as bank market share increased slightly (+0.6). Since 1977 retirement funds (private and public) and money-market funds primarily have been responsible for reducing commercial banking's share of FSI total assets.

DEPOSITORY INSTITUTIONS

Depository institutions (defined to include banks, thrifts, and credit unions) are the most important *group* of firms in the FSI. They control roughly $5.3 out of every $10 of total financial sector assets. The name "depository institutions" is of course an incomplete description of what these intermediaries do, because it ignores the LHS of their balance sheets. They are, in effect, deposit-*and*-lending institutions. In addition, commercial banks, especially the large ones, make extensive use of *non-deposit* sources of funds.

The central role of commercial banks in the financial-intermediation process reflects their position as the *least specialized* of the depository institutions. They borrow from and lend to all of the basic economic units—households, firms, and governments. The competitive advantage provided by their diversity of financial services is being eroded, however, as other depository institutions move from a highly specialized financial-intermediation role toward greater product *de*specialization.

[5] For a critique of Christophe's paper see Greer and Rhoades [1975]. Citicorp's rebuttal is by Christophe [1975].

Nonbank depositories traditionally have relied on household time and savings deposits for their major source of funds. Thrift institutions intermediated these deposits mainly into mortgage loans, whereas credit unions shifted the funds primarily into consumer loans. The despecialization that has been permitted for these institutions is occuring on *both* sides of their balance sheets. On the RHS, they have been permitted to offer interest-bearing checking accounts and, on the LHS, they have been permitted a limited degree of asset diversification.

Depository institutions in the U.S. are characterized by two important traits: overabundance and growing similarity. The crowded condition is demonstrated by the following benchmark figures:

Industry	Number of Firms
Commercial banking	14,500
Savings and loan	3,000
Mutual savings bank	2,000
Credit union	22,000
TOTAL	41,500

Using a population figure of 225 million, we have a depository institution for every 5,422 people. Excluding credit unions, the ratio is one to 11,538; for commercial banks only, the ratio is one to 15,517.[6] To put the last ratio in perspective, the corresponding numbers for West Germany, Japan, and Canada are one to 975,000, 1.5 million, and 2.6 million, respectively. Indeed, the U.S. has an overabundance of commercial banks.

NONDEPOSITORY FINANCIAL INSTITUTIONS

The nondepository financial institutions included in Table 5-6 can be grouped under the four headings shown below. Just as depository institutions are noted for selling particular products, namely financial services, the nondepository intermediaries listed here also have products to sell. Their major product lines are protection, retirement benefits (a form of protection), credit services, and investment services. It is important in understanding the management policies of commercial banks to understand, in turn, how the management policies of nondepository institutions are affected by their specialized sources of financing and their specialized portfolio investment policies.

| Category | Total Assets (Billions of Dollars) | |
	December 31, 1980	December 31, 1986
Pension/retirement funds	485	1,329
Insurance companies	650	1,210
Investment companies	177	804
Finance companies	199	412
TOTAL	1,511	3,755

[6] A more meaningful figure would be based upon the number of banking offices, because these indicate the availability of banking facilities to the public. As of December 31, 1984, there were roughly 55,000 insured commercial-banking offices in the U.S. or one office for every 4.091 people. Since other developed countries have fewer banking offices then the U.S., using office data strengthens the over-abundance argument.

Insurance Companies

Insurance companies sell protection in the form of life, property, and casualty insurance. The major source of funds for these companies is the premiums paid by holders of the insurance contracts.[7] Over time the accumulation of premiums (net of expenses) constitutes a relatively stable flow of savings into insurance-company "reserves," the major item on the RHS of their balance sheets. The intermediation function for insurance companies occurs when they transfer reserves (premiums) into earning assets. The assets held by these companies are closely tied to the degree of uncertainty (risk) associated with the potential claims against them. For example, life insurance companies (LICs) have a considerable amount of confidence regarding future claims against them because of stability in the mortality rate. Thus, they can *hedge* their long-term claims (liabilities) by holding long-term assets. In particular, they hold mainly fixed-income securities in the form of nonresidential mortgages and corporate bonds. Low interest-rate policy loans have created an increasing "disintermediation" problem for LICs.

In contrast to LICs, property and casualty insurance companies have greater uncertainty about the future claims against them. Because of this greater business risk, they are forced to (1) reach out for higher earning assets and (2) maintain a supply of "hurricane money" (liquidity) for emergency purposes. In terms of the LHS of their balance sheets, property and casualty insurance companies must hold some short-term (liquid) assets and tend to prefer variable-rate instruments as opposed to (taxable) fixed-rate investments. Like commercial banks, property and casualty insurance companies are subject to taxation on their earnings. Thus, they attempt to shelter some of their earnings from taxes by holding a substantial amount of tax-free state and local securities and by taking advantage of the fact that 85 percent of the dividends received from other corporations can be excluded from taxable income, an incentive to hold stock and equity investments.

Pension and Retirement Funds

Pension and retirement funds, as well as life insurance companies, sell pension and retirement benefits, that is, they sell protection against living too long. These institutions obtain funds from contributions made by the participants; all of their liabilities are pension/retirement claims. Private pension funds intermediate members' contributions mainly into corporate equities and secondarily into corporate bonds. In contrast, the more conservative investment policy of *public* pension funds leads to a concentration in fixed-income instruments. While corporate bond investments still predominate, public pension funds have made a major shift in investments from municipal securities to corporate stock. The more aggressive investment approach of private funds is designed to minimize company contributions by earning a higher yield on the asset portfolio. The fundamental financial-management lesson provided for commercial banks and other depository institutions by the contractual intermediaries is that a viable policy of long-term portfolio investments requires an accompanying availability of long-term financing sources.

Finance Companies

Finance companies are a major competitor of commercial banks in providing credit services (loans) to households and business firms. The major sources of funds for

---

[7] Premiums from pension and retirement programs offered by LICs are growing much more rapidly than insurance premiums.

finance companies are bank loans, commercial paper, long-term debt (bonds), and equity capital (internal and external). These funds are intermediated into consumer and business loans. With the exception of captive finance companies (e.g., GMAC), modern finance companies are diversified into the consumer, sales, and commercial-lending areas. In fact, it is increasingly difficult to distinguish the lending policies of noncaptive finance companies.

Investment Companies

Investment companies provide investment services to their customers. Excluding brokers and dealers,[8] who provide transactions rather than intermediation services and who receive commissions for their services, investment companies secure funds through the sale of equity rather than debt securities and channel these pooled funds into diversified portfolios of securities that are shared pro rata by the investors. The primary function of investment companies is simply investment. If investment companies meet certain qualifications and if they distribute at least 90 percent of their income to their shareholders, income from their investments usually is exempt from corporate income tax.

The two basic types of investment companies are (1) open-end investment companies (i.e., "mutual funds") and (2) closed-end investment companies. The only liability of open-end investment companies is the ownership shares they issue. The so-called mutual funds agree to buy or sell their shares at the current (pro rata) asset value at any time. In contrast, closed-end investment companies, which operate as ordinary corporations, simply sell shares to the public like any other corporation. The prices of these shares are determined in securities markets by the forces of supply and demand. Real estate investment trusts (REITs), which specialize in real estate investments, mortgages, and construction loans, are similar to closed-end investment companies.[9]

Mutual funds are distinguished on the basis of whether or not they charge a selling *commission. Load* mutual funds charge a commission, whereas *no-load* mutual funds do not. The commission on a load fund is equal to the difference between the net asset value of the fund's shares and the price at which these shares are sold to the public. Mutual funds also are described according to their investment objective. Typical investment objectives for mutual funds include aggressive growth, growth and income, balanced income, bond, municipal bond, and option income.

The primary mutual fund growth area in the late 1970s and early 1980s has been the money-market mutual fund. As indicated in Table 5-5, these funds had total assets of $178 billion as of mid-year 1984. As the name indicates, the funds invest in money-market instruments. Money-market funds have achieved a rapid rate of growth in recent years. As of year-end 1977, their total assets were only $3.9 billion. Growing at a compound annual rate of roughly 167 percent, they reached $74 billion by the end of 1980. Over the previous three-year period (1974 to 1977), the growth rate was approximately 18 percent per year. What is even more phenomenal is that from December 31, 1980, to December 1, 1981, money-market funds more than tripled as they reached their all-time peak of $242.5 billion! However, by the end of the month, they had fallen to $215.3 billion as depository institutions were able to compete with

---

[8] Strictly speaking, brokers and dealers are not investment companies. They provide transactions rather than intermediation services. They were included in the category to simplify the presentation. Merrill Lynch is the most prominent retail brokerage house. Brokers have been moving into the banking area by developing services that perform checking-and-savings functions (e.g., Merrill Lynch's "Cash Management Account"). Brokers and dealers also are known as investment bankers.

[9] See Sinkey [1979], pp. 237–255, for a description of the commercial bank–REIT relationship of the 1970s.

the funds via their newly acquired money-market deposit accounts (MMDAs). By November 30, 1984, MMDAs had grown to $397 billion, with $256 billion on deposit at commercial banks and the balance of $141 billion at thrift institutions. Since the flow of funds into MMDAs was not matched by an equal outflow from MMFs, most of the influx was due to internal funds rolling up into the higher-yielding MMDAs. As of June 30, 1987, bank MMDAs were $368 billion compared to $186 billion at thrift institutions, and $211 billion at MMFs.

There are roughly 150 money-market funds in existence; the average fund size is about $1.2 billion. The managers of these funds have been innovative and aggressive as they recognized opportunities provided by the *R* and *I* components of TRICK to supply "small savers" with market rates of return. The two latest MMF innovations have been tax-free funds and funds that invest solely in U.S. government securities. The development and success of the latter can be traced to concerns about the safety of banks and thrifts; the former can be traced to increasing sophistication among investors.

YOU CAN'T TELL THE PLAYERS *WITH* A SCORECARD

This is the catchy title of a speech by Walter Wriston given at a luncheon of the Securities Industry Association held in New York City January 21, 1981. The players in Wriston's story are businesses; the scorecards are their annual reports. The challenge is to identify the industry to which each of the companies belongs, or, if you are really good, to identify the firm. Here are Wriston's descriptions. See how well you can do.

Company A is a major lender to both businesses and individuals. In 1979, they bought a large "industrial loan company," which offers commercial and residential real estate loans, equipment leasing, and passbook thrift accounts. They also formed "a joint venture corporation in Japan to offer selected consumer loan services." Their normal, everyday financial activities include writing insurance policies and the financing of everything from furniture to pianos, cars, other companies, aircraft, computers, telecommunications and medical equipment.

Company B also makes loans and takes deposits. It holds shares in a number of financial institutions and widely diverse business concerns. Its 1979 annual report states that "new closed-end property funds met with strong interest among customers . . . In June, the building of the First National Bank of Atlanta was purchased for one closed-end property fund."

Company C owns "the seventh-largest publicly held savings and loan holding company" in the United States. They, too, take deposits, make loans, give mortgages and engage in the real estate development business. They are looking, the company states in its annual report, for "further possible ventures into related (financial) fields."

Company D serves "eight out of ten families in the U.S. every year." They take deposits and do commercial and consumer financing, mortgages and insurance. But that's not all they do. Company D retails its merchandise in over a thousand stores and in more than thirty-five hundred franchised outlets. They sell shirts, ties, suits, dresses, blouses, coats, apples, oranges, milk, meat, hammers, power saws, and nails. They manufacture industrial and consumer products. They have a controlling interest in an airline, and run "one of the largest car rental companies in the world."

To broaden its range of services, *Company E* recently applied for and got a state bank charter. It now operates a full-service bank, which like any other bank manages pooled accounts for pension plans. This gives them the opportunity to go after a $255 billion market in employee-benefit plans.

Company F is in the financial services business. It "provides a full line of banking and investment banking services." In its annual report, Company F states that it is the country's leading corporate investment banker." In October of 1979, they "handled 67 percent of U.S.

corporate financings." And they're not resting on their laurels either: "We expect that our company," their annual report states, "will be even more innovative and reach new heights in the financial services industry in the 1980s."

At this point, you may need a hint, so here it is. Wriston was quoting from the annual reports issued by a bank, a manufacturer, a brokerage house, a mutual fund, a finance company, and a steel corporation. His point is that it is hard to tell them apart even with a scorecard. The names of the companies are:

Company	Name
A	General Electric
B	Deutsche Bank
C	National Steel Corporation
D	Household Finance Corporation
E	Fidelity Group
F	Merrill Lynch

According to Wriston, the reason it is so hard to identify the players is that "... yesterday's image of a financial-services business bears little relationship to today's reality" (p. 6). What is today's reality in the financial-services industry? The reality is that EFTS, computers, satellites, microcircuitry, and high-speed optical telephone lines make constraints on the time, geography, and volume of financial transactions obsolete. In a nutshell, nonfinancial corporations can marshal substantial resources in the financial marketplace to compete against commercial banks. In contrast, commercial banks legally are not permitted to engage in activities that are not "closely related" to banking. This is another example, from the perspective of the giant banks, of the so-called uneven playing field.

THE EMERGENCE OF FINANCIAL CONGLOMERATES

The new merger wave that began in 1981 brought about the emergence of financial conglomerates headed by such companies as Sears, American Express, and Prudential. For example, in 1981 Sears acquired Coldwell Banker & Co., the nation's largest real-estate brokerage company, and Dean Witter Reynolds Organization Inc., the fifth-largest brokerage house. Sears (technically Sears, Roebuck & Co.) has a four-dimensional line of commerce that includes merchandise, insurance, real estate, and financial services. The last three areas make up the Sears financial conglomeration and include such companies as Allstate Insurance Co., Sears U.S. Government Money Market Trust, Allstate Savings and Loan Association, and the aforementioned Coldwell Banker and Dean Witter. The potential for Sears to tap the financial market is exemplified by the following facts:[10] (1) in their merchandise business Sears has almost 1,000 retail department stores (845 domestic and 172 foreign), 2,778 U.S. catalog outlets and limited-merchandise stores, and, most important, 25 *million active credit accounts*; (2) in the insurance business they have 20 million policies outstanding and 10,800 agents to service them. The additions of Coldwell Banker and Dean Witter (with 4,000 brokers) further increases this potential. The important point is that Sears has an unparalleled system for delivering financial services.

Walter Wriston claims that Citicorp's major competition in the future won't be another bank but Sears, Roebuck & Co. "I said it ten years ago," he claims. "Nobody

[10] These data are from Dentzer et al. [1981].

LIST OF KEY WORDS, CONCEPTS, AND ACRONYMS

Capital market
Depository institutions
Financial futures
Financial innovation
Financial intermediation (liquidity,
    denomination, risk, maturity)
Financial options
Financial services (classes)
Financial-services firms (FSFs)
Financial-services industry (FSI)
LHS = left-hand side (of balance sheet)

Money market
Money-market (mutual) fund (MMF)
Nondepository financial institution
Rational self-interest (and profitable
    opportunities)
RHS = right-hand side (of balance
    sheet)
TRICK = *T*echnology, *R*eregulation,
    *I*nterest-rate risk, *C*ustomers, and
    *K*apital adequacy

REVIEW/DISCUSSION QUESTIONS

1. After explaining our model of change and Kane's distinctions for understanding the process of financial innovation, use these frameworks to analyze the following innovations: money-market funds, cash-management accounts,, MMDAs, financial futures, options trading, and electronic funds transfer systems. Finally, contrast and compare Kane's notion of innovation with that of Miller's.
2. Are the components of TRICK independent? Explain and discuss.
3. What are the major groups of financial institutions and the particular members of each category? Is the United States overpopulated with depository institutions?
4. Distinguish between the money and capital markets and identify the major instruments of each market.
5. What are the major sources and uses of funds (in terms of money- and capital-market instruments) for the various financial institutions?
6. What are the four basic services provided by financial intermediaries? Explain how the provision of these services is suggestive of the financial-management problems faced by banks.
7. What are the four distinguishing features of futures contracts?
8. Should the manager of a financial-services firm use futures or options to hedge interest-rate risk? Discuss the advantages and disadvantages of each.
9. Explain the product despecialization that is occurring among financial institutions. How specialized are commercial banks?
10. What is the fundamental financial-management lesson provided for depository institutions by the contractual intermediaries?
11. What are some of the financial services that "nonfinancial" corporations provide? Use the financial conglomeration controlled by Sears, Roebuck & Co. to illustrate your answer. What potential does Sears have for tapping financial markets and delivering financial services? Can polyester, plastic, and stocks really be sold together? What "image" does Sears portray and how important is the image to its financial forays? America really doesn't bank at Sears today. What are the chances that we will bank there in the future? High? Low? Discuss.
12. Do you think that Citicorp is a real champion of the free marketplace? To what extent, if at all, are Citicorp's pronouncements self-serving?

MATCHING QUIZ

Directions: Select the letter from the right-hand column that best matches the item in the left-hand column.

___ 1. Focus of rational self-interest

___ 2. Miller's notion of innovation

___ 3. Invention

___ 4. Sees academics as FSI catalysts

___ 5. TRICK

___ 6. Innovation lag

___ 7. Transaction service

___ 8. Savings product

___ 9. New insurance product

___ 10. Credit arrangement

___ 11. Securitization

___ 12. Fiduciary service

___ 13. Opposite of money market

___ 14. Miller's "the" innovation

___ 15. "Recognized players"

___ 16. "Disadvantaged players"

___ 17. "Trickle-down effect"

___ 18. A money-market instrument

___ 19. A capital-market instrument

___ 20. A binding agreement

___ 21. A depository institution

___ 22. Author of "scorecard test"

___ 23. Proponent of specialization

A. Adam Smith

B. Walter Wriston

C. Few banks per capita

D. Profitable opportunities

E. Unanticipated change

F. Unfolding technology

G. James Van Horne

H. Negotiable CDs

I. Time from invention to innovation

J. Capital market

K. Wholesale to retail

L. "Boob-tube" phenomenon

M. Credit union

N. Futures contract

O. Universal life

P. Local institutions

Q Captures forces of change

R. Automatic billing paying

S. MMDA

T. Either–or facility

U. Investment-company service

V. Many banks per capita

W. Bank business loans

___ 24. U.S. banking system

___ 25. European/Japanese banking systems

___ 26. Futures price > strike price

X. Financial futures

Y. Trust/estate management

Z. In the money

SELECTED REFERENCES

Abken, Peter A. [1981]. "Commercial Paper." *Economic Review*, Federal Reserve Bank of Richmond (March/April), pp. 11–21.

Aspinwall, Richard. [1985]. "Shifting Institutional Frontiers in Financial Markets in the United States," Chase Manhattan Bank (January 15).

Baker, James V., Jr. [1982]. "Statistical Relationships Are the Key to Banks' Use of Interest-Rate Futures." *ABA Banking Journal* (May), pp. 88–92.

Black, Fischer, and Myron Scholes. [1973]. "The Pricing of Options and Corporate Liabilities." *Journal of Political Economy* (Vol. 81), pp. 637–654.

Christophe, Cleveland A. [1974]. *Competition in Financial Services.* New York: Citicorp.

Christophe, Cleveland A. [1975]. "Evaluation of Competition in Financial Services: A Reply." *Journal of Bank Research* (Spring), pp. 66–69.

Cook, Timothy A., and Bruce J. Summers. [1981]. *Instruments of the Money Market*, 5th ed. Federal Reserve Bank of Richmond.

Dentzer, Susan, et al. [1981]. "Where America Will Bank." *Newsweek* (October 19), pp. 80 and 85.

Ford, William F. [1982]. "Banking's New Competition: Myths and Realities." *Economic Review*, Federal Reserve Bank of Atlanta (January), pp. 4–11.

Gigot, Paul A. and Thomas J. Lueck. [1981]. "Financial Forays: Sears Expansion Brings Increased Competition to Bankers and Brokers." *The Wall Street Journal* (October 12), pp. 1 and 24.

Greer, D. F., and S. A. Rhoades. [1975]. "Evaluation of a Study on Competition in Financial Services." *Journal of Bank Research* (Spring), pp. 61–65.

Hilder, David B., Tim Mertz. [1984]. "A Spate of Acquisitions Puts American Express in a Management Bind." *The Wall Street Journal* (August 15), pp. 1 and 18.

How Consumer America Views the Changing Financial-Services Industry." [1984]. *The American Banker*, reprinted from October 20, 1984, to October 29, 1984.

Jarrow, Robert A., and Andrew Rudd. [1983]. *Option Pricing.* Homewood Hills, IL: Dow Jones-Irwin.

Kane, Edward J. [1983]. "The Metamorphosis in Financial-Services Delivery and Production," in *Strategic Planning for Economic and Technological Change in the Financial-Services Industry.* San Francisco: Federal Home Loan Bank of San Francisco, pp. 49–64.

Kaufman, George C. [1980]. *The U.S. Financial System: Money, Markets, and Institutions.* Englewood Cliff, NJ: Prentice-Hall.

Kidwell, David S., and Richard L. Peterson. [1984]. *Financial Institutions, Markets, and Money.* Hinsdale, IL: The Dryden Press.

LeMaistre, George A. [1978]. Statement on the "International Banking Act of 1978." Washington, DC: FDIC, Press Release 65–78.

McMurray, Scott. [1984]. "Prudential-Bache Had Nine-Month Loss of $104.8 Million; Sale Rumors May Grow." *The Wall Street Journal* (December 7), p. 3.

Melton, Carroll R., and Terry V. Pukula. [1984]. *Financial Futures: Practical Applications for Financial Institutions.* Reston, VA: Reston Publishing Company.

Miller, Merton H. [1986]. "Financial Innovation: The Last Twenty Years and the Next." *Journal of Financial and Quantitative Analysis* (Vol. 21, No. 4, December), pp. 459–471.

Picou, Glen. [1981]. "Managing Interest-Rate Risk with Interest-Rate Futures." *The Bankers Magazine* (May–June), pp. 76–81.

Sametz, Arnold W., ed. [1984]. *The Emerging Financial Industry: Implications for Insurance Products, Portfolios, and Planning.* Lexington, MA: D.C. Heath.

Sinkey, Joseph F. Jr. [1979]. *Problem and Failed Institutions in the Commercial Banking Industry.* Greenwich, CT: JAI Press.

Sinkey, Joseph F. Jr., and James A. Miles. [1982]. "The Use of Warrants in the Bailout of First Pennsylvania Bank." *Financial Management* (Autumn), pp. 27–32.

Sparks, Will R. [1978]. *Financial Competition and the Public Interest.* New York: Citicorp.

Statistical Information on the Financial-Services Industry. [1983]. Washington, DC: American Bankers Association, February.

Van Horne, James. [1985]. "Of Financial Innovations and Excesses." *Journal of Finance* (July), pp. 621–631.

Volcker, Paul A. [1979]. "Treatment of Foreign Banks in the United States: Dilemmas and Opportunities." FRBNY *Quarterly Review* (Summer), pp. 1–5.

Wriston, Walter B. [1984]. "You Can't Tell the Players *with* a Scorecard." New York: Public Affairs Department, Citicorp.

CHAPTER 6

Bank Technological Innovation, the Payments System, and Information Processing

ACRONYM GUIDE TO KEY TERMS AND CONCEPTS

ACH = automated clearinghouse
ATM = automated teller machine
EFTS = electronic funds transfer system
POS = point of sale

INTRODUCTION: TECHNOLOGY IN BANKING

How important is technology to banking? According to John B. McCoy, the chairman of Banc One of Columbus, Ohio, "With deregulation, technology is how we're going to be able to beat the other guys."[1] As we saw in the last chapter, banks—especially local ones—are not on the leading edge of technology. To document this statement, consider the results of a special report, "Technology in the Workplace," conducted by *The Wall Street Journal* (Section 4, June 12, 1987). This report attempted to grade the technological prowess of nine industries. In alphabetical order, the industries, their grades, and brief industry profiles are:

		Profile		
		Revenue or Operating Income		
Industry	Grade	1986 ($ bls)	% Change Since 1980	Employment
Airlines	B	$ 50	+47%	583,800
Autos	C	$ 197	+83%	833,200
Banking	C–	$ 191	+43%	1,509,000
Computers	B+	$ 87	+199%	400,500
Money management	A–	$3,565 (assets)	+264%	178,200
Petroleum	A	$ 231	–33%	155,300
Pharmaceuticals	B	$ 38	+69%	207,700
Publishing	B–	$ 109	+65%	1,504,100
Telecommunications	C–	$ 125	N.A.	1,352,300

---

[1] See Apcar [1987], p. 42D.

The grades in this report were based on the following, admittedly subjective, criteria: Has the industry in question made use of technological advances in a timely manner? Did it participate in or encourage the development of new technologies? And in its use of new technology, has the industry improved its competitive standing, efficiency, or profitability?

As any lady or gentleman student knows, a C- is not a very good grade. Combine this with a tie for last in the class and you get the idea: Banking is not doing well in the area of technology on the basis of this report card. Why? Two reasons: paper and people. Banking has too much of both. Moreover, it has had too much of both for a long time. The paper comes in the form of processed checks, deposit slips, credit-card receipts, customer statements, and the like. Regarding people, as shown in the industry profiles above, the banking industry comes in first across the nine industries with 1,509,000 employees. Clearly, banking is a labor-intensive industry with paper as a major by-product. (Although it is appropriate to refer to banks as paper factories, we will refrain from calling their employees "paper pushers.") Combine these facts with the inertia of an historically "conservative" industry and you can see why banking has been slow moving into the technological age. In addition, since many customers, especially older ones, have grown accustomed to the faces, and the paper, they are reluctant to change their banking habits.

This chapter focuses on describing and analyzing the economic and financial implications of technological innovation in banking, especially with respect to paper (e.g., in the payments system) and people. Technological innovation in banking has appeared mainly in the form of electronic funds transfer systems (EFTS or EFT systems). The basic components of EFTS are automated teller machines (ATMs), point-of-sale (POS) terminals, and automated clearinghouses (ACHs). Less visible than EFT, but more important to bank operating efficiency is the state of the art of a bank's "backroom technology" (i.e., its computer operating systems). A typical example of backroom inefficiency in banking is the failure to link separate computer systems to provide a complete profile of customers and their needs. A common symptom of this problem is the inability of a bank to provide a single financial statement covering various customer accounts. In contrast, the brokerage industry, a primary bank competitor with its cash management accounts, has been supplying such statements for several years.

The state of technology in banking has been aptly described by Fisher [1979]: "Right now, EFT is not the grand and glorious future—it's another hole in the wall for the ATM" (p. 22). As documented by *The Wall Street Journal's* special report above, Fisher's statement, made in 1979, is not far from the truth even today. Our first step in analyzing electronic banking is to look at the process of technological innovation and its diffusion. From this foundation, we will focus on the various components and functions of electronic funds transfer systems.

NEW TECHNOLOGY, THE PROCESS OF INNOVATION, AND THE DIFFUSION OF ELECTRONIC BANKING

This chapter focuses on the technology or T component of TRICK. The driving force of technology combined with rational self-interest (i.e., the quest for profitable opportunities) generates innovation. In the financial-services industry, the technological focus is on electronic banking. Since it is important to understand the interrelationships among new technology, the process of innovation, and the process of diffusion, we first focus on Exhibit 6-1, which describes how a new technology spreads. Please read it before proceeding.

EXHIBIT 6-1
How a New Technology Spreads

Adoption of check substitutes represents an example of the technological innovation process. We expect that the adoption of check alternatives will follow the same pattern as the adoption of other technologies ranging from hybrid corn to color television.

Consumer acceptance or rejection clearly determines any product's success—or failure. Technology itself is virtually never the primary determinant. We feel that the adoption process of technology, regardless of product, involves a similar set of consumer responses. Collectively, individual consumer decisions produce a diffusion process that research has shown to be consistent.[a]

An *innovation* is an idea perceived as new by an individual.[b] The "newness" of the discovery underlying the innovation is not crucial; its "newness" to the individual is the critical consideration. Thus, when we look at innovations such as electronic payment products, we must look beyond the products themselves to the perceptions that individuals hold about them. The definition suggests that the product alone cannot be the innovation.

According to marketing expert Everett M. Rogers, who took a broad look at the implications of diffusion, "the essence of the diffusion process is the human interaction in which one person communicates a new idea to another person."[c] The product itself is not the critical factor. Communication of the idea is the significant element in analyzing the diffusion of innovations.

The adoption or rejection of electronic payment products probably will begin with individual opinion leaders. Many people will defer their adoption of an electronic product until enough others are also willing to accept it.

Rogers makes an important distinction between adoption and diffusion, saying:

> ...the adoption process deals with adoption of a new idea by one individual while the diffusion process deals with the spread of new ideas in a social system, or with the spread of innovations between social systems or societies.[d]

Throughout this special issue, we intend to maintain the distinction between the diffusion process and the five classes in the adoption process.

In the adoption process an individual passes through five stages: "awareness, interest, evaluation, trial, and adoption."[e] Many people may hear of an idea at about the same time. However, some will complete the adoption process sooner than others. Five "adopter categories" classify individuals according to the length of time it takes them to adopt

EXHIBIT 6-1 (*Continued*)

an innovation: innovators, early adopters, early majority, late majority, and laggards.[f]

Of course, not everyone who hears of a new idea adopts it. People may reject it at the conceptual level if they never try it, or they may reject it after a trial.[g] Similarly, we can anticipate that some peoople will reject electronic payment alternatives at various stages within and after the adoption process.

One practical application of the diffusion process, the product life cycle concept, has evolved for use in marketing. Market researchers identify five stages through which a product typically passes: pioneering, market acceptance, turbulence, saturation, and obsolescence.[h] Those five stages in the product life cycle parallel the five classes in the adoption process.

Rogers also emphasizes a distinction between the invention and the innovation, saying that economists have stressed the distinction on the grounds that an invention has little or no economic significance until it is applied.[i] An innovation, then, represents application of an invention.

Usually there is a distinct time lag between invention and innovation. According to Rogers, the lag "seems to vary considerably and is commonly 10 years or more for major inventions."[j]

In reality, a gray area exists between invention and wide-scale innovation because most inventions are very crude and inefficient at the date when they are recognized as constituting a new invention. They are, of necessity, badly adapted to many of the ultimate uses to which they will eventually be put; therefore, they may offer only very small advantages, or perhaps none at all, over previously existing techniques.[k]

By trying to identify a specific time lag between a "crude" invention and its diffusion as an innovation, we sometimes engage in a sort of conceptual foreshortening which distorts our view of later events. We are led to treat the period after the conventional dating of an invention as one where a fairly well-established technique is awaiting adoption when, in fact, major adaptations typically are waiting to be made. It is this same foreshortening of perspective that greatly increases our general impression of the slowness of diffusion.[l]

Where, then, do we draw the line between invention and innovation? We will proceed on the assumption that invention status continues beyond the initial "discovery" while a product evolves a marketable configuration. We will start referring to the product as an innovation when it becomes available, beyond test marketing.

Implicit in the distinction is some degree of consumer acceptance, a pivotal concept in our personal check displacement model. An invention does not seek or does not win consumer acceptance. An innovation has some consumer acceptance. We expect that each of our

EXHIBIT 6-1 (*Continued*)

check-displacement phases will be preceded by an extensive period of "tinkering" with the invention leading to the requisite innovation.

[a] Everett M. Rogers, *Diffusion of Innovations* (The Free Press, 1962), pp. 12–13. This discussion relies on Rogers' description of the diffusion of innovations. For a more traditional "economics-based" treatment, see "How the Economic System Generates Evolution," in Joseph Schumpeter's *Business Cycles*, Vol. 1.
[b] Rogers, p. 13.
[c] Rogers, p. 13.
[d] Rogers, pp. 17–18.
[e] Rogers, p. 17.
[f] Rogers, p. 19.
[g] Rogers, pp. 18–19.
[h] Thomas A. Staudt and Donald A. Taylor, *A Managerial Introduction to Marketing* (Prentice-Hall, Inc., 1965), p. 144.
[i] Edwin Mansfield, *Microeconomics Theory and Application* (W. W. Norton and Company, Inc., 1970), pp. 456–57.
[j] Mansfield, p. 457.
[k] Nathan Rosenberg, "Factors Affecting Diffusion of Technology," *Explorations in Economic History* (Academic Press, 1972), p. 10.
[l] Rosenberg, p. 9.
Source: Federal Reserve Bank of Atlanta *Economic Review* (August 1983), p. 10.

Now that you have some idea of how technology spreads, let's take a look at *how long* it takes for a product to spread throughout society. In Figure 6-1 the focus is on the speed of diffusion of major consumer products. This chart shows how long it has

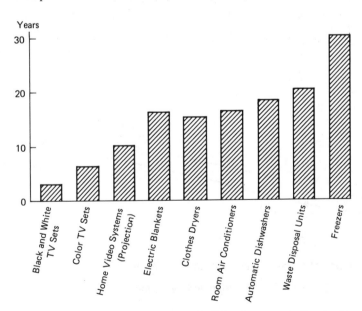

Figure 6-1   Speed of Diffusion of Major Consumer Products

Graph shows number of years required for penetration to increase from 10% to 50%.
Source: Video: A New Era, Research Report 621. Menlo Park, CA: SRI International [November 1979], p. 10.

taken for these products to increase their penetration from 10 percent of U.S. households to 50 percent. For example, the fastest one was black-and-white TV sets at less than three years; the slowest one was freezers at almost 30 years. The important point is that product diffusion takes time and, if you have seen one product diffusion, you have not seen them all. Moreover, tracing the entire process from technological invention to innovation to marketing of the product, the process of diffusion takes many years.

Although the diffusion of electronic banking may not require the patience of Job (as in *The Book of Job*), it will take considerable time because payment habits, especially consumer ones, are slow to change. As a result, electronic banking tends first to make inroads in wholesale banking transactions and then diffuse down to the retail level. Overnight technological breakthroughs are the stuff of science fiction.

THE EVOLUTION OF MONEY AND THE DEVELOPMENT OF PAYMENTS SYSTEMS

Money has evolved from the concrete (e.g., animals, hides, trinkets, etc.) to the ethereal (i.e., electronic impulses). Economic units in the United States employ three generations of money: (1) currency, (2) checks, and (3) electronic funds. Of these three transaction vehicles, checks are by far the dominant means of payment. During 1979, the number of commercial-bank checks written was estimated to be 32 *billion* (see Figure 6-2).[2] If the annual growth rate in check volume of 5.6 percent continues, the volume will reach roughly 84 billion by 1991. It is unlikely, however, that check volume will continue to grow at the 5.6 percent pace. The product life cycle of the check should reach its peak sometime within the next decade. The speed with which that peak is reached critically depends upon how banks price electronic transactions relative to paper transactions. Households have been reluctant to accept electronic transfers mainly because they had no economic incentives to offset the loss of float provided by credit cards or checks. If paper transactions (e.g., credit-card and

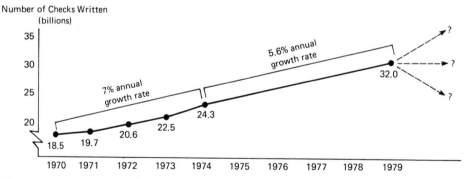

Figure 6-2   Number of Commercial-Bank Checks Written, 1970–1979

Source: Metzker [1982], Fig. 2, p. 35. Reprinted by permission.

---

[2] In 1979, the Federal Reserve processed 15.1 billion checks with a value of $8.5 trillion. See Mitchell and Hodgdon [1981], p. 112. They estimate the number of checks written in 1979 to total between 33 billion and 35 billion. McHenry [1981] claims that 38 billion checks were processed in 1980. Whatever the exact number is, the U.S. financial system is a paper-dominated one.

check services) are priced at their full delivery costs, the reluctant consumer will be enticed into using electronic banking more quickly.

The Federal Reserve Bank of Atlanta (*Economic Review*, August 1983), in a study that generated quite a bit of controversy on Wall Street for the check-printing industry, estimated that the volume of personal-check "equivalents" (estimated to be 18 billion of the 1979 total volume of 32 billion checks) would slow to a 4 percent annual growth and stand at 32.4 billion by 1994. If nominal check volume grew at the same rate, it would reach 57.6 billion by 1994. Based upon a complicated estimation procedure, the study estimated that personal-check volume would reach a peak sometime between 1987 and 1989. The concept of the volume of personal-check equivalents is based upon the estimation of personal checks, assuming that there had been no access to preauthorized drafts, ACH debits, or ATMs in 1979.

Except for ATMs, which basically are convenience devices that permit 24-hour banking, consumers have not embraced electronic banking with open arms.[3] In contrast, large nonfinancial corporations, financial institutions, and governments have been more eager to accept and adopt EFT systems. For example, Humphrey [1981] reports that in 1979 84 percent of ACH volume was due to transfer of funds from the federal government to the private sector. About 75 percent of government-originated ACH volume is due to Social Security payments. In the private sector, large corporations such as oil and airline companies have set up ACHs for reducing and clearing intercorporate transactions.[4] In Houston, Bank of the Southwest developed a system called Petro-Clear for handling the intra-industry debits and credits of oil companies In New York, Chase Manhattan Bank handles net settlements for the major airlines and, using a check-transaction program, processes roughly half of all the credit-union share drafts in the U.S.

Between the retail market and wholesale market for large corporations lies a vast middle market of business electronic financial services. As shown in Figure 6-3, this market segment has tremendous potential for the use of electronic financial services. The proliferation of low-cost technology in the form of the personal computer (PC) has opened up regional markets for electronic business banking. In 1984, there were roughly 50 million keyboard-terminals and computers in use by business firms. This volume of equipment implies one electronic keyboard for each white-collar employee. Moreover, it is estimated that 80 percent of this equipment can access financial data. The message is that computer-based financial products are not limited to large corporations. To meet this challenge, banks must apply mass marketing to the middle-market and small-business segments of the wholesale market.

Banks have developed EFT systems for three main reasons:[5] (1) to protect and increase market share, (2) to reduce operating costs by substituting physical capital and technology for labor, and (3) to generate new revenues. The first reason frequently is associated with keeping up with the competition, whereas the last two are profit-motivated reasons. We would be remiss if we didn't mention the inefficient U.S.. mail service as also contributing to the development of EFTS. "The check is in the mail" is not always a false statement.

---

[3] For example, Vickrey writes "...there are all sorts of people who say that they do not want this kind of (EFT) system. They want the results but none of the fancy mysterious electronic stuff" (insertion mine). See Edwards [1979], p. 309. To illustrate, until recently West Virginia had a law requiring payments to be made either in cash or by check, thereby prohibiting electronic fund transfers.

[4] See Rose [1977], pp. 212, 216, 218.

[5] See Hosemann [1979].

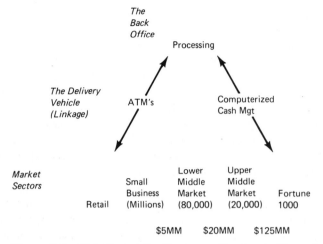

Figure 6-3   The Market for Business Electronic Financial Services

Source: Cohen [1985], Fig. 2, p. 20.

The Basic Components and Functions of EFTS

EFTS is a generic term referring to various computer-based technologies for delivering banking services. The basic EFT components are ATMs, ACHs, and POS systems. In addition, such services as cash management, telephone bill payment, automatic transfers, check verification, check truncation, and home banking are part of the total EFT picture. These EFT components are the catalysts that are slowly driving the U.S. and world financial systems from a paper base to an electronic foundation. In this transition, the processing of information, as both an input and an output has become more and more important to the business of banking. As Walter Wriston, the chairman of Citicorp from 1970 to 1984, has remarked: "The information standard has replaced the gold standard as the basis of world finance" (Hamilton [1986], p. 30).

As a new way of collecting and processing transaction-related data, EFT systems perform three functions: (1) funds transfer, (2) authorization, and (3) generation of information for recordkeeping. Compared to paper-based transactions, EFT, in its *most* efficient form, offers instantaneous verification and transfer and reduces the flow of costly paper in the recordkeeping process. To assess the benefits and costs of EFT is a complex task. Kane [1977] likens it to the fable of the blind men trying to describe an elephant, because it is difficult to analyze more than a small segment of the complex EFT matrix at one time. The multidimensional analyses of the sectoral benefits and costs of EFT have focused on such issues as privacy, ownership, competitive effects, antitrust implications, the impact on monetary policy, and the development and sharing of systems.

The Payments System: Some Preliminary Distinctions and Concepts

A payments system is a fundamental component of any modern society. It links the real or economic sector with the financial sector. Users of the payments system demand two services: efficiency and safety. Such traits instill user confidence in the payments system. Because of the lag between issuance of payment and the debiting of the payer's account (what we call "float" or "clearing time"), any payments system is by its nature a credit system. These extensions of credit can vary from a few hours to several days or weeks. On average, two or three clearing days are representative. Whatever the length of time, confidence in receiving funds is critical to the smooth operation of the payments mechanism because in many transactions the parties involved have little or no knowledge of the payer's creditworthiness. Such systems work because of users' confidence in the institutional arrangements provided by financial-services firms and government agencies to ensure credit checks and quality controls.

In economically developed countries such as the United States, England, West Germany, or Japan, the payments system can be viewed as having the following pairwise components: (1) wholesale (meaning large) versus retail (meaning small), (2) electronic versus paper, and (3) domestic versus foreign or international. Moreover, across these pairs, we tend to observe the following linkages; international transactions tend to be wholesale and electronic-based; wholesale transactions, whether domestic or foreign, tend to be electronic; and retail transactions tend to be small and paper-based.

Payment and Settlement Risks

Although any disturbance to the payments system is disconcerting, especially for the parties involved, the large-dollar payments mechanisms entail the greatest risk for the system as a whole. In the United States, large-dollar electronic payments are primarily handled by the Federal Reserve System and the New York Clearing House Association. In conjunction with other clearing and settlement systems, the major financial institutions of the world are linked together. Corrigan [1987] contends that the payment and settlement risks in these associations have increased sharply in recent years. The specific risks involved are the operational, liquidity, and credit interdependencies shared by these systems. Similar to modern-day athletes, it is the size *and* speed of the transactions (players) that make the difference. Corrigan puts it this way: "Because they are so large, so fast and so interdependent, even temporary computer or mechanical failures can be highly disruptive beyond the institution where the breakdown originates" (p. 10).

To put these concerns about the large-dollar payments systems into perspective, let's consider some of the characteristics of these systems. In the United States these mechanisms handle transactions in excess of one trillion dollars *daily*. The bulk of the transactions are purely financial ones involving the buying and selling of funds, securities, and foreign currencies. Although the number of financial institutions with access to the payments system is in the thousands, the large commercial and investment banking firms dominate the system (another manifestation of *real* dual banking).

The key technological innovation in payments systems has been the development of automated clearinghouses (ACHs). Let's now turn to a description and analysis of this important area.

AUTOMATED CLEARINGHOUSES (ACHs)

A clearinghouse is a system used by banks for clearing or exchanging checks drawn on each other. In a traditional clearinghouse, bundles of paper checks are exchanged; in an ACH, computer images or tapes are exchanged. ACHs are very efficient at handling recurring transactions such as preauthorized deposits or payments. The ACH processing mechanism for a direct payroll deposit and a preauthorized insurance premium is illustrated in Figure 6–4.

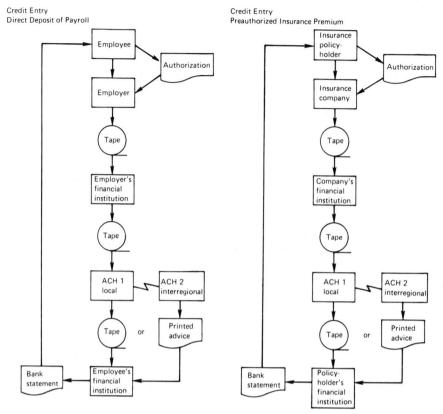

Figure 6-4   The ACH Processing Mechanism

Source: Hamilton [1979], p. 526.

The ACH Players

As Figure 6–4 indicates, an ACH system involves several "players" or participants. To reap the full benefits of an ACH system, all the basic economic units in society (i.e., households, firms, and governments) must participate. At present, ACH volume is dominated by transfers from governments to the private sector, with about 75 percent of that volume due to Social Security payments. Moreover, of the 15 billion or so checks cleared by the Fed, only about 1 percent of them are ACH transactions. At present, the checkless society is a long way from reality.

The major suppliers of ACH services include:[6]

1. The Fedwire and 38 regional ACH associations, 37 of which (excluding the New York City ACH)[7] are subsidized by the Fed;
2. Bank Wire, a system owned cooperatively by 190 commercial banks;
3. CHIPS (Clearing House Interbank Payment System), a system owned by the New York Clearing House Association (NYCHA), which clears respondent transactions through NYCHA members' reserve accounts;

---

[6] See Kane [1981], p. 35, and Mitchell and Hodgdon [1981] p. 114.

[7] The New York ACH uses the Fed's delivery and settlement facilities.

4. SWIFT (Society of Worldwide Interbank Financial Telecommunications), a network oriented toward international payments that includes both foreign and United States banks.

The Fedwire and the ACH system are Federal Reserve facilities for electronic deposit transfers. Bank Wire, CHIPS, and SWIFT are privately owned and operated transfer systems that compete with the Fedwire and the ACH system. The Fedwire is used mainly for large-denomination transfers between financial institutions.[8] In contrast, check volume is dominated by a large number of small transactions. Fedwire transfers can be originated by paper or electronically by telephone, terminal, or computer. The Fedwire operates nationwide and transfers are made on reserve accounts instantaneously.

The ACH network supported by the Fed consists of 38 regional ACHs representing 10,500 commercial banks and 2,700 thrift institutions.[9] The regional ACHs have been organized by the member institutions in that region. Members agree to abide by the rules and procedures for the initiation and delivery of electronic transfers. The Fed's ACH facilities process millions of debit and credit transfers annually. Typical deposit transfers are illustrated in Figure 6-5.

To upgrade its electronic capabilities for the 1980s, the Fed undertook a project known as FRCS-80 (Federal Reserve Communications System for the Eighties). The system is designed to be a general-purpose data communications network through which the Fed can provide services to financial institutions, the Treasury, and other government agencies. Under FRCS-80, the functions of the Fed's existing separate communications networks were consolidated into a monolithic system. According to Mitchell and Hodgdon [1981], the benefits of the new network are expected to

1. improve the reliability, efficiency, and availability of communications services to financial institutions
2. accommodate significant volume increases in the 1980s and beyond
3. reduce the total cost of System communications

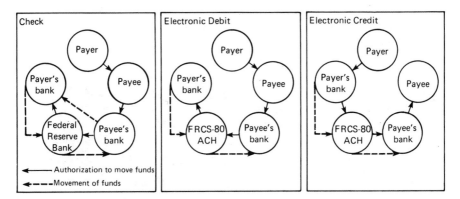

Figure 6-5   Typical Deposit Transfers

Source: Mitchell and Hodgdon [1981], chart 2, p. 112.

---

[8] Data in this paragraph and the next one are from Mitchell and Hodgdon [1981], p. 114. The average Fedwire transaction was about $1.8 million in 1979.

[9] All of these institutions receive payments but only about 500 of them initiate payments for business and government customers. The regional ACHs are organized nationwide through the National Automated Clearing House Association (NACHA).

4. provide a standard that will be recognized by the industry for connecting financial institutions to FRCS-80
5. offer increased security of data moving within the Federal Reserve System
6. facilitate check truncation or the conversion of checks into electronic debits by forwarding essential payment information needed for collection
7. offer financial institutions greater overall flexibility through terminal resource sharing
8. minimize disruption from converting to the new network by using transition aids, which will allow current software to be compatible with the new network.

The FRCS-80 district-office spine network is pictured in Figure 6-6. In this network, no single central-switching site is required so the "Culpeper switch" is eliminated. The FRCS plan calls for the computer power to be distributed among the 12 Federal Reserve Banks, the Treasury Department in Washington, and the Culpeper operations center, which will be called the Network Management Centre (NMC). The important implication of FRCS-80 is that the Fed has positioned itself to operate a national ACH network. One of the important EFT issues, addressed later, is whether such a network should be privately or publicly owned and operated.

ACH Scale Economies

Evidence exists to indicate that substantial economies of scale exist at most of the ACH processing centers in the United States. For example, Humphrey [1981] found that from 1977 to 1979 total ACH production costs rose on average by only 6 to 7 percent for each 10 percent rise in volume. Since a picture supposedly is worth a thousand words, consider the ones in Figure 6-7. These pictures summarize Humphrey's scale-economy findings. In Fig. 6-7(a), average cost curves for 36 ACH offices are presented. Although the various offices show varying degrees of economies of scale (for example, compare the Memphis office, labeled 2, with the New York office, labeled 40), the obvious conclusion is that average cost declines as volume increases. For 1979, Humphrey estimated that average ACH production costs were 4.7 cents per

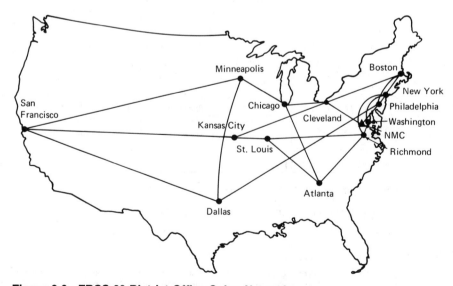

Figure 6-6   FRCS-80 District-Office Spine Network.

Source: Mitchell and Hodgdon [1981], pp. 110–111.

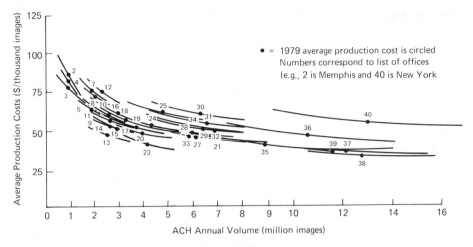

(a)   Average Cost Curves for 36 ACH Offices (1979).

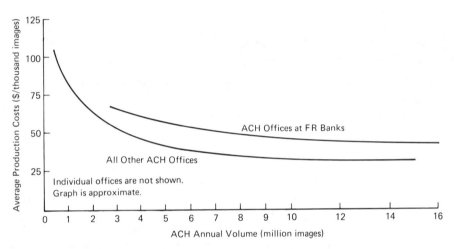

(b)   Average Cost Curves for Two Groups of ACH

Figure 6-7   ACH Scale Economies

Source: Humphrey [1981], Figs. 3 and 4, pp. 77–78. Reprinted by permission.

image. The 1978 estimate of average cost was 4.2 cents per image. The increased average cost from 1978 to 1979 indicates a decreased potential for scale economies as volume expands.

In Fig. 6-7(b), the graphical representations of the scale-economy estimates for ACH offices located at Federal Reserve banks are compared with those for ACH offices located at FRB branches and regional check processing centers (RCPCs). Although the findings indicate substantial economies of scale in both types of offices, ACH operations at FRB branches and RCPCs have greater scale-economy potential.[10]

Understanding the cost characteristics of EFT equipment is important. Most EFT systems have large start-up costs and hence high total cost. However, the *marginal*

[10] Humphrey's scale-economy estimates are 7.2% (banks) versus 6.1% (other) for a 10% increase in volume. Walker [1978] estimates scale economies for ATMs to be in the range of 2.5% to 5% for a 10% increase in ATM volume. Thus, the long-run average cost curve for ATMs declines more sharply than the one for ACHs.

cost of processing an additional image is very small. Thus, as volume expands, average cost declines (i.e., scale economies exist). The basic problem is generating sufficient volume to make the EFT system cost-effective. For example, in 1979 the Fed's average cost of processing a check was only .9 cents compared to 4.7 cents for an EFT image. To be cost-effective ACH volume would have to rise to about 200 million images annually per office.[11] With the average Fed office processing 314 million checks in 1979, this volume is a feasible target. The key to generating the required volume is to institute pricing policies that provide economic incentives for users to shift from paper to EFT images.

To summarize, the ACH scale-economy evidence suggests three important conclusions:[12] (1) ACH operations present a viable and potentially cost-effective alternative to the traditional processing of paper checks; (2) ACH operations have the potential to become a "natural monopoly"; therefore, like a public utility, a single supplier of ACH services would be the lowest-cost producer (The development of FRCS-80 strongly suggests that the Fed would like to have that natural monopoly.); and (3) to induce the volume required for ACH cost efficiency, ACH services need to be priced on a marginal-cost basis.

The Price and Quality of ACH Services:
The Private Sector Versus the Fed

Although pricing is the key factor in generating the volume necessary to make ACHs cost-effective, the quality of service in terms of speed and reliability probably will determine *who* does the ACH processing (i.e., the private sector or the Fed), assuming, of course, that the Fed operates on a fully costed basis. Kane [1981] sees the Fed's long-run problem as its ability to compete on a *quality* basis. George White, formerly of Chase Manhattan Bank and a vocal critic of the Fed's role in the ACH process, would like to see the Fed relegated to a "clearer of last resort."[13] White thinks that it is "outrageous" that the Fed uses banks' reserves and then offers services that compete with (correspondent) banks. Moreover, he claims that the Fed preempted the private sector by establishing the ACH system. Since Chase Manhattan currently handles about 10 percent of the nation's private-sector ACH volume, it would be in the best interests of the bank if the Fed was a provider of last resort and not a competitor. If the Fed is the clearer of last resort, then, as Kane [1981] colorfully puts it, the private correspondent networks must see themselves as playing United Parcel Service to the Fed's U.S. Postal System.

As the functional equivalent of the federal postal system, the Fed has subsidized unprofitable services (e.g., remote collection and distribution) to provide a truly national payments system. In the process of trying to do this, overall Fed service has suffered and the private sector has entered to skim off certain lucrative services. The battle between the private sector and the Fed for a share of the ACH market (and for correspondent-banking services in general) will hinge upon five critical factors: (1) the Fed's explicit fees, which are required by DIDMCA to be fully costed, (2) the quality of service, (3) competition from respondent banks that form local clearinghouses, (4) the Fed's efforts to reduce float and the subsequent reduction in the due-to balances of correspondent banks, and (5) the success of FRCS-80, and the Fed's grand design for capturing the national system of electronic payment.

---

[11] Humphrey [1981], pp. 79.

[12] Ibid., p. 71.

[13] See "Special Report: Operations and Automation" [May, 1980], p. 84, and White and Nadler [1981], pp. 38–40.

AUTOMATED TELLER MACHINES (ATMs)

Although ATMs are not as ubiquitous as the vending machines that dispense soft drinks, they are by far the most popular form of EFT service. By 1990, some analysts foresee 100,000 ATMs in place as the banking system moves toward a self-service delivery mode in the retail area. In terms of a delivery-system life cycle, the ATM was expected to enter its rapid-growth stage during the 1980s. Alternative delivery systems and their approximate life-cycle stages include:

Delivery System	Life-cycle Stage (% of Transactions)
Home office	Declining
Brick-and-mortar branches	Declining
Drive-in branches	Peak/declining
ATMs	Rapid growth
Telephone/home banking	Developmental

These alternative delivery systems give customers the option of deciding how they want to bank. The last two delivery systems represent self-service modes; they are the delivery systems of the future in the retail banking area.

First-generation ATMs were nothing more than cash-dispensing machines. Next, off-line units were developed, followed by on-line units with direct access to information on customer accounts. The basic services usually available through the third-generation ATMs include cash dispensing (against transactions-type accounts or preauthorized lines of credit), making deposits, loan repayments, bill paying (e.g., utility), transfer of funds between accounts, and account-balance inquiries. In addition, some ATMs dispense travelers' checks and are linked to other ATMs in a local shared network.[14] In addition, shared systems have been established on regional and national bases.

Why Establish ATMs?

Market share, cost reduction, and revenue generation are the key concepts for evaluating the existence of ATMs. In new ATM systems, maintenance of customer base and potential cost reductions are the prime considerations. At this stage of the delivery system, ATMs are seen as "defensive" alternatives to keeping branches open evenings and weekends, as well as a means of reducing teller lines, maintaining market share, and, most important perhaps, stabilizing and ultimately reducing teller staffing requirements and costs. In more mature systems, off-premise ATMs located in high-traffic areas are employed as "offensive" weapons to increase market share and thereby to generate revenue.

Whether or not ATMs provide transaction-displacement benefits depends on whether or not ATM users substitute multiple electronic transactions for teller-assisted ones. Based on a recent survey, Zimmer [1981] found that 45 percent of the survey participants (bankers) regarded multiple ATM transactions as a substitute for teller visits.[15] Moreover, the participants estimated the "substitution" ratio to be 2 to 1 (that

---

[14] See Nadler [1982] for a discussion of the decision of whether or not a bank should join an ATM network. In 1980, ATM networks were established in New York City by 21 savings banks and in Chicago by 17 commercial banks. The basic strategy in both networks was to establish off-premise ATMs in key high-traffic areas. See the *American Banker* [June 24, 1980], p. 2.

[15] The other responses were 21 percent for no substitution, 28 percent "don't know," and 5 percent no answer. See Zimmer [1981], Figure 1, p. 32.

is, two ATM transactions replaced one teller visit). This finding suggests that a teller handling 5,000 routine transactions a month can be replaced by an ATM handling 10,000 transactions per month.

Pricing ATM Services

The fundamental reason for the slow growth of EFT systems has been the lack of appropriate economic incentives by the suppliers of the services. With the advent of Fed pricing and a general economic concern for cost effectiveness, explicit pricing is playing a more important role in the financial-services industry. This structural shift away from implicit pricing and subsidization and toward explicit pricing, accountability, and cost effectiveness will promote greater economic efficiency.

One strategy to promote the use of EFTS is to employ a two-tiered pricing schedule that favors electronic or machine transactions over teller-assisted or paper-generating transactions. The essence of such a strategy is to entice customers to maintain high account balances and to use self-service banking facilities.

A Burning Desire for ATMs: The Norwest Experience[16]

When it comes to getting customers to use ATMs, bankers throughout the country seem to have stumbled against a so-called "33 percent barrier," meaning that only about one-third of cardholders will use ATMs during a given year. But there is no reason to consider the barrier insurmountable. *Near the close of 1983, Norwest Bank, Minneapolis, MN, had 75 percent of its demand deposit account base holding ATM cards and a usage rate of 55 percent. By the end of 1984, its usage rate was 72 percent.*

In 1982, Norwest was struggling with the 33 percent barrier. Then a major fire destroyed the bank's physical plant and made reliance on electronic delivery a necessity. Norwest AVP William Brewer says, "Our need changed from having an EFT program to needing an EFT program ... to having to rely completely on that network to do the routine banking for our customers." The fire caused Norwest to emphasize its off-premise ATMs and to position them as electronic branches. *Repositioning required promotion, and in the first 10 months of 1983 the bank initiated 12 separate communications with the public.* The messages ranged from information on locations to publicity campaigns, to sweepstakes, to reminders of exactly how to use the machines, all complemented by demonstrations and by recording devices for after-hour services. "We had so many messages going out to our public last year," says Brewer, "that when we finally got into sharing arrangements, it was no surprise to them when Cirrus[17] became alive and cards could be used nationwide. The customers embraced it, used it and *transactions are flowing regularly to us through the Cirrus system.*"

Brewer stresses that *it is important to know demographics and understand the people to whom you are communicating.* The median population age in the Minneapolis area is in the mid-40s. In an "older" environment, repetitive consistency in communications is necessary. This is the reason for the numerous customer communications. There is a tremendous difference in the demographics or environment characteristics in different areas of the country. In Atlanta and Phoenix, for example, the median age is the mid-20s. This produces a much different learning curve.

---

[16] This section is excerpted from the sample issue of *Banking Issues & Innovations*, The Bank Administration Institute [1985], pp. 4–5.

[17] Cirrus is a nationwide ATM network. ATM networks are discussed in the next section.

Activation of cards, according to Brewer, is "limited only by your own thinking about it. The 33 percent barrier is only in the mind of the financial institution. *The challenge is to find the reasons and to create the needs in each of your customers for them to want and use the card.*"

ATM Networks

In general, an EFT network is a system of many separate suppliers of financial services interconnected in some way for a mutual benefit. The latter usually takes the form of cost reductions through sharing. Thus, a network is simply a shared system or any interchange between shared systems. Networks may exist at the state, regional, or national level. An ATM network is a shared system of ATMs. Merrill [1985] reports that in 1984 there were 16,000 ATMs on line to regional networks with over 50 percent of United States commercial banks involved. Over 50 million cards are said to be outstanding. The network industry is not heavily concentrated, as the top five firms account for only 28 percent of the transactions; the top 10 have 43 percent; the top 50 have 70 percent; and the top 100 have 80 percent. In essence, the network industry is fragmented much like the banking industry. Elliott [1984] reports the following distribution of regional networks within a state by state:

Number of Regional Networks within a State	Number of States
0	6
1	7
2	12
3	13
4	7
5	1
6	2
7	2

From a pure marketing sense, Elliott thinks that eventually there is going to be a shake-out in the number of networks because there are simply too many for the financial system to support. A look at the number of ATMs per network further supports his claim. That is,

Number of ATMs per Network	Percentage of ATMs
1–10	33
11–20	17
21–30	12
31–40	10
41–60	10
61–100	8
101–150	6
201–300	2
Over 300	2
	100

The fact that 33 percent of the networks are systems with only one to 10 ATMs explains why there were almost 500 networks in the United States in 1984. To achieve the cost effectiveness necessary to continue in operation (from a data-processing perspective), Elliott contends, a network needs at least 200 ATMs.

Merrill [1985] identifies four policy dimensions that managers of networks must consider. The first dimension is the type of network *owner* or *sponsor*. Elliott [1985] provides the following market-share data by type of network:

Type of Network	ATM Market Share
Proprietary	55%
Shared lead bank	26
Shared co-op/third-party processor	15
Shared co-op	2
Proprietary/card issuers	1
Fee access/site owners	1
TOTAL	100%

The second dimension is *exclusivity*, that is, who gets to join the network. The third dimension is a *geographic* one that focuses on the market breadth of the network (ie., state, regional, or national). The fourth dimension focuses on the *economic* and *financial* aspects of the network. This factor is simply the pricing dimension: How is the service priced and who pays whom for what? In this regard, it is important to note, as Merrill does, that the ATM is not a product but a communications device through which some sort of content must be carried. In this framework, Merrill views the evolution of the ATM as now moving into the "content wave" or stage, which is one of product differentiation. Currently, if you have seen one ATM network, you have seen them all. That is, the cards are the same, the machines are the same, and the networks are the same. In other words, there is no *content* or product differentiation. It is in this sense that Merrill sees the next stage in the development of ATM networks as the content wave. The *T* and *R* components of TRICK are the environmental factors that will constrain this next stage of development (i.e., technology, geographic reregulation, and product reregulation).

One of the leading national ATM networks is Cirrus System Inc. In 1984, Cirrus decided to expand its system to also support POS transactions. Cirrus, a nonbank vendor, depends on banks to do its switching and processing. Mellon Bank of Pittsburgh provides the "switch" for Cirrus's 5,300 ATMs; see Table 6-1. A switch is the computer used in shared networks that routes transactions to the appropriate financial institution when cardholders use another institution's terminal. A switch is used for both ATM and POS transactions. (A diagram of an ATM/POS switch is shown in Figure 6-8.) Mellon, which has devoted considerable resources to developing a sophisticated

TABLE 6-1   The National ATM Networks, 1987

Network	Financial Institutions	States	Projected Terminals
Nationet Inc.	3,408	26	5,967
Plus System Inc.	1,000	47	3,000
The Exchange/Banking USA	564	33	3,000
Cirrus System Inc.	900	41	5,300
MasterTeller/MasterCard	167	19	760
Visa International	57	30	1,000

Note: By the year 1995, *The Nilson Report* projects the number of ATM cards outstanding will be 250 million.

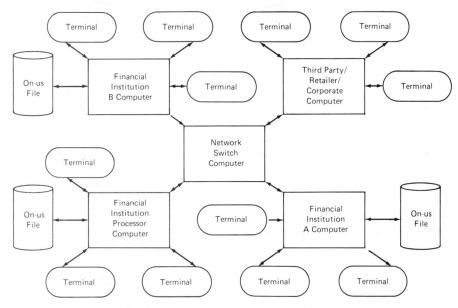

Figure 6-8   An ATM/POS Network Computer Switch

data processing operation, came in with a bid of 3 or 4 cents per transaction to win the Cirrus contract. Since the industry benchmark is "a dime a time" (i.e., 10¢ per transaction), some of the other bidders described Mellon's bid as a "sweetheart deal."[18]

The number of financial institutions, states, and projected terminals of the six national ATM networks is shown in Table 6-1. By 1995, the Nilson Report projects this number of ATM cards outstanding will be 250 million.

POINT-OF-SALE (POS) SYSTEMS

A point-of-sale system is an on-line system that allows customers to transfer funds instantaneously from their bank accounts to merchants' accounts when making purchases. To date, POS systems have been the least successful of the three basic EFT components. An example of a POS system is depicted in Figure 6-8.

A true POS system uses a debit card to activate the EFT process. The problem with the debit card is that there is no economic incentive for customers to use it. Moreover, as long as credit cards are priced with an effective interest-free period of 30 to 40 days or more, the problem will persist. Without the cards out there to generate the volume, POS systems will be ineffective EFT devices.[19]

On the other side of the (would-be) POS terminal, the merchant has focused on the electronic cash register with inventory-control features. Until the technology at the cash register is interfaced with POS technology, POS development will be slow and

---

[18] The details in this paragraph are from Smith [1984].

[19] One bank president predicted (in 1980): "Larger numbers of cards will take us another five years, as I see it. That's when POS is going to evolve, and when it happens, it's going to explode." More conservative analysts predicted 1985 to 1990 as the takeoff stage for POS systems. See "Special Report, Part II" [June, 1980], pp. 98 and 100.

uneven. The lack of cards and terminals easily explains why POS systems are dead last in the EFT race.

Secondary POS Services

The primary POS service is to move funds electronically. This function has been frustrated by the lack of economic incentives to both customers and merchants. Secondary POS services available to merchants are credit-card authorization and check verification or guarantee. The former is more important to the merchant than the latter and it has been more successful. The use of the card-authorization service is valuable to merchants because it streamlines cashiering operations by eliminating the need to check a "hot-card list" or make a telephone verification for a credit-card purchase. The key breakthrough in this area was the direct interconnection of bank-authorization networks with merchant technology in the form of microcomputers at the store level.[20] Visa is pushing this type of system and had electronic authorization of at least 80 percent of its transactions in 1985.[21] As of 1982, Visa merchants in retail locations had more than 17,000 POS terminals.

Electronic authorization via POS terminals is designed to reduce the chronic problem of bank-card fraud and credit losses and to eliminate much of the manual, paper-based recovery system. Based upon loss-control tests, Visa found that electronic authorization reduced its losses by 80 percent. To encourage merchant participation in its program, Visa has adopted a two-tier interchange rate. Under this pricing scheme, there is an incentive (in the form of a lower discount rate) for a merchant to obtain "zero-floor-limit" authorization (i.e., authorization for every noncash purchase). Visa offers a guaranteed response time with its electronic-authorization program. J. C. Penny was the first major retailer to push for direct interconnection for bank credit-card authorization. The number of cardholders for major credit cards is shown in Table 6-2.

To summarize, the environment is becoming more favorable for POS systems. The direct interconnection, two-tier pricing, guaranteed response time, and other factors are moving merchant credit-card operations to a zero-floor-limit authorization. Once this foundation has been laid, two-tiered pricing on the consumer level can be employed to induce the use of debit cards and complete the transition to a true POS system.

TABLE 6-2   Estimated Number of Cardholders for Major Credit Cards, 1986

Card	Number of Cardholders
VISA	67,000,000
Sears	53,000,000
MasterCard[a]	51,000,000
J.C. Penney	34,000,000
Montgomery Ward	28,000,000
American Express	15,000,000
Diners Club and Carte Blanche	1,400,000

[a] Includes both credit and debit cards.

[20] *Ibid.*, p. 100.
[21] See Trigaux [1982].

ATMs AND POSs: THE HEART OF THE ISSUE

ATMs and POSs are the driving forces in the revolution in retail payments. Exhibit 6-2 presents a summary by Peter Merrill, a leading bank consultant, on the heart of the issue. The focus is on how communications technology in the form of ATMs and POSs is displacing established payments methods. The key question in this area is whether or not banks are being disenfranchised. Merrill (see Exhibit 6-2) sees the net franchise shift as being away from banks and toward nonbanks. The trend is for nonbanks to develop bank-like relationships with banking clients. To buck this trend, banks need quality management, marketing, strategy, implementation, and some luck. The challenge is to be in the right place at the right time, to anticipate the financial services and products that consumers want, and to have the organizational structure to respond quickly to those needs.

TELEPHONE/HOME BANKING AND VIDEOTEX

Telephone banking offers customers the capability of performing certain routine banking functions via telephone (e.g., bill paying). In 1980, there were about 300 telephone-bill-payment organizations in the country. However, as White points out, only seven of them could generate a magnetic tape to be delivered through the ACH network.[22] To use the telephone bill payment/ACH mechanism, companies receiving payments have to designate an account where funds are to be sent. One company that has shown some leadership in this area is Equitable Life Assurance Society, which now provides such routing information on its bills. White contends that the slow growth of telephone banking is a corporation/bank problem and not a consumer problem.

The development of full-blown home banking requires that the customers have a computer to communicate with the bank's computer. With the recent development of personal computers, the technology is available for this. John Fisher of Banc One in Columbus, Ohio, sees this "gee-whiz" era of home banking and "videotex" taking off by the end of the 1980s.[23] The year 2000 or later seems like a more realistic prediction, because customers will have to buy their own terminals. More fundamentally, however, home terminals cannot dispense cash or accept deposits. In a society that is far from being cashless, this aspect of home banking is a major drawback. Nevertheless, home banking can easily handle such standard banking activities as balance inquiry, bill payment, stop payment, money transfer, and other special services. Such services, however, also can be conducted via telephone without investment in a home terminal. Some of the organizations involved in home-banking projects are shown in Table 6-3.

Fisher and others view home banking as the potential entry application of videotex into the household sector. *Videotex* is the generic term to describe home information retrieval systems. In addition to home banking, videotex is expected to offer

---

[22] See "Special Report, Part II" [1980], p. 102. White concludes that the financial-services industry really is not geared up for telephone transactions. The seven institutions with magnetic tape capabilities are Arizona Telco Credit Union, Chase Manhattan Bank, The Greater New York Savings Bank, Hollywood (Florida Federal Savings and Loan, Rainier Bank (Seattle), Rhode Island Hospital Trust National Bank (Providence), and Union Trust Co. (New Haven, CT).

[23] "A Futuristic View of Banking" remarks by John Fisher at the 1981 annual meeting of the Financial Management Association. Banc One conducted a home-banking experiment, called Channel 2000, in 1981 in Columbus, Ohio.

EXHIBIT 6-2
The Heart of the Issue
by Peter Merrill[a]

One major conclusion from this morning's discussion is that bankers are not particularly optimistic about justifying the ATM or POS product on the basis of cost or even market share. This leads some to ask why a bank would want to leap into these products at an early stage. Should they not wait and let the "guerrillas" make the investment, allow unit costs to decline, and then enter on some kind of shared basis? No argument has been forwarded that convinces me that this would not be the most profitable course of action.

A second major conclusion is that deregulation is leading us all to more explicit pricing, which is creating a cost-allocation conflict between the banks and the nonbanks discussing various joint venture arrangements. If it is agreed that the consumer ultimately will bear the cost of innovation, we should now be asking how the costs during the product introduction phase will be allocated between joint venture partners—between banks and retailers, for instance.

The third major point that emerged was that, in this entire EFT/POS/home banking area, we are not speaking about either a pure banking product or a pure retailing product. What we are talking about is a whole new kind of business. The potential service provider—be it a bank, a retailer, or an intermediary—must decide whether it wants to get into this business or not.

Where do these three conclusions finally lead us? Are banks getting "disenfranchised"? If I were to answer that question in a word, I would have to say "yes." The trend increasingly is for nonbanks to develop bank-like relationships with banking clients.

What do banks do about that? Most banks will move more toward service or segment niches to try to differentiate themselves; and many of them will undertake joint ventures with nonbanks. We should note that the entry of nonbanks onto the "turf" of banking results, at least in part, from most banks' inability to bear the cost of introducing the new systems, particularly in the absence of clearly demonstrated customer demand. The retailer, who clearly stands to benefit from the availability of POS services, should reasonably share the costs. Despite the current standoff between bank and retailer over the cost issue, I would predict that we will see more and more viable cost-sharing arrangements because the benefits are shared.

I question whether "disenfranchisement" is an appropriate term. The topic under discussion is rooted in expanding the availability and convenience of banking services. To do this, we are moving outside of

EXHIBIT 6-2 (*Continued*)

the traditional service delivery location—the bank building. While still the intermediary, the bank is no longer meeting the customer in the old brick-and-mortar environment. Since one of the trends is toward a "shared" environment (with either a competitor, or a retailer, or both), cost sharing is inevitable, and so new ways of calculating shared costs based on shared benefits must be found.

The dissociation of services from the brick-and-mortar setting has another major implication for banks. At least for transaction services, banks will be much less able than in the past to differentiate themselves competitively. Differentiation was based to a great extent on either head office or branch location and amenities, or on the personality and attention of employees. Since transaction services are being moved "off-site" in this way, *differentiation must focus on non-transaction services*. This ultimately may redefine the term "primary banking relationship."

Finally, I would think that one noteworthy implication of today's workshop is that heavy pressure will be placed on the Federal Reserve System, other regulators, the Congress, and the courts, because retailers will begin to resemble banks. Is the bank looking more like a retailer? Not really, unless you count all the toasters and teddy bears in the give-away inventories, or unless bank services are liberalized to a far more significant degree than is now considered possible.

In my opinion, therefore, the net franchise shift is toward the nonbanks. Whether this implies that the bank charter will be less meaningful over time will depend on the ultimate uniqueness of the bank account. The determinants of bank power will be banks' ability to invest in new systems, their willingness to share in systems development and usage with other banks, and the time horizon for payback that banks will find feasible. The largest institutions will have the deepest pockets; the rest will have to share or make other bets.

[a] The author is president of Peter Merrill Associates, Inc., a Boston consulting firm specializing in strategic planning for the financial services and communications industries.
Source: Economic Review, Federal Reserve Bank of Atlanta [July/August, 1984], p. 48.

electronic versions of both the Yellow and White Pages, sports, news, weather, classified ads, retailers' catalogs, a community bulletin board, and a host of other services. A critical step in the marketing of videotex is to determine the services that users will pay for. AT&T has been conducting tests in this area to decide how and when it will offer videotex services commercially. Regarding market potential, AT&T estimates that by 1990 some 8 million household (7 percent of the total) will have videotex terminals. At the other end of the forecast spectrum, Strategic Inc., a California consulting firm, predicts that one-third of all U.S. households (45 million) will

TABLE 6-3   Organizations Involved in Home Banking Projects

Organization	Project	Who Operates Switch
Banks		
Chase Manhattan Bank	Home Banking	Proprietary
Chemical Bank	Pronto	Proprietary
Citibank	Homebase	Proprietary
First Interstate Bank of California	Day & Night Video Banking	Tymshare
Horizon Bancorp	Horizon Home Banking and Information System	CompuServe
Hunting Bank	Banc Share	CompuServe
Madison National Bank	Hometeller	Proprietary
National Bank of Detroit	Video Information Provider	Proprietary
Shawmut Bank of Boston	Home Banking	CompuServe
Toledo Trust	Vistabanc	Proprietary
Retailers		
J. C. Penney	First Hand	Tymnet
Sears[a]	Trintex	N. A.
Communications companies		
CBS	Venture One	The Treasurer, Inc.
Continental Telecommunications	Contelvision	Proprietary
Cox Communications	Indax	Chase Manhattan
Times Mirror Videotex	Times Mirror Videotex	VideoFinancial Services
Viewdata Corporation (subsidiary of Knight-Ridder Newspapers)	Viewtron	VideoFinancial Services
Other organizations		
ADP	Home Banking Interchange	Proprietary
Keycom Electronic Publishing	Masterkey	VideoFinancial Services
Financial Interstate Services	Bank-at-Home	CompuServe
Macrotel	Macrotel	Metroteller
Shuttle Corporation	Shuttle	Proprietary

[a]Newly formed joint venture with CBS and IBM. *Source*: Federal Reserve Bank of Atlanta [April 1984].

have videotex services of some kind by 1990.[24] Since the electronic transformation has been more evolutionary than revolutionary, the "smart money" is riding on AT&T's forecast.

Benchmark prices that many observers think are required for the mass marketing of videotex are (1) $500 or less for the computer terminal or the specially equipped TV set and (2) a monthly service charge of less than $50 for a package of videotex services ranging from banking and shopping to news and information retrieval. Regarding the latter, Fisher states: "If videotex is not good enough to lure customers at that price, it is not going to change habits." He summarizes the videotex situation this way: "We're absolutely convinced that the technology is sound and that the consumer will be able to utilize these systems—the consumer will accept them greedily."[25]

To summarize, home banking and videotex are the frontier areas in the financial-services/telecommunications field. The developments in this field over the next two decades promise to be dynamic and exciting ones. While the market for (home) videotex is just emerging, major U.S. corporations have been leading the way in

[24] See *Business Week* [June 29, 1981], p. 76.

[25] *Ibid.*, p. 83. All figures and quotations in the paragraph are from this source.

electronic data retrieval, a development that has important implications for corporate EFT and the bank-customer relationship. The business of banking will indeed be different by the year 2000.

THE FINANCIAL-MANAGEMENT IMPLICATIONS OF ELECTRONIC BANKING AND INFORMATION PROCESSING

When we cut through all the electronic wizardry, the acronyms (EFT, ATM, ACH, POS, etc.), and the jargon (videotex), what are the financial-management implications of electronic banking for commercial banks? The key point is that the bank delivery systems of the future are going to be *electronic*, both in the wholesale and retail areas. These systems will be most efficient and generate the lowest costs. With explicit pricing and most, if not all, services required to carry their own weight, cost efficiency will be imperative. In addition, fee income from electronic and information services will be an important source of bank revenue, especially since interest margins can be expected to remain thin because of competitive pressures. In terms of the return-on-equity (ROE) model,[26]

$$ROE = PM \times AU \times EM$$

electronic banking needs to support the bank's threatened profit margin (PM) by holding costs down, and to pump up the bank's asset utilization (AU) by generating additional fee and service-charge income. To the extent that a bank can use electronic banking as an aggressive weapon to expand its asset base safely, it can increase its equity multiplier (EM), given a fixed capital base. With a constant return on assets ($ROA = PM \times AU$), this greater leverage will mean a higher return on equity (ROE). If this higher ROE can be achieved without changing the market's perception of the bank's risk exposure, the bank's market value should rise. In terms of the constant-growth model,

$$P_0 = D_1/(k - g)$$

electronic banking needs to manipulate the cash flow, risk, and growth parameters of the valuation process to increase the bank's stock price. How well a bank is able to manage the risk-return trade-offs of the new EFT environment will be an important determinant of its financial success.

THE EFT ENVIRONMENT OF THE FUTURE

A schematic representation of a potential EFT environment of the future is depicted in Figure 6-9. In this situation, the bank has direct interconnects via POSs, ACHs, ATMs, and home-banking equipment with all its major customers and service providers. It is an environment in which electronic funds and mail can be transferred instantaneously. When will this Orwellian view of banking materialize? Clearly, it wasn't "1984" in 1984 and we probably have at least another decade or two to go. The following exchange between the bank analyst Paul Nadler and EFT expert George White is prescient:[27]

---

[26] See Chapter 10 for a complete explanation of the ROE model.

[27] White and Nadler [1981], p. 42.

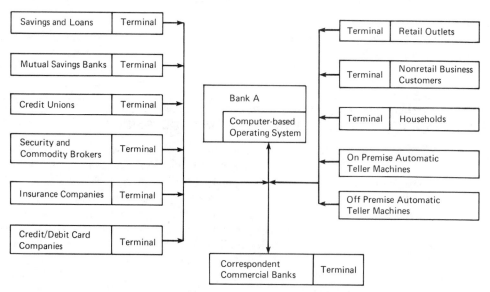

Figure 6-9   A Single Commercial Bank in an EFT Environment

Source: Phillips [1979], Fig. 6-1, p. 276. Reprinted by permission.

Paul Nadler: Can we sum up by saying that banking without paper is feasible, that if the volume gets up there it can truly be a cost-saver for banks of all sizes, and the key to getting public acceptance is knowledge and incentive pricing?

George White: Yes. But it is the banks which also must accept the premise. Sometimes we are our worst enemy in not looking at the opportunities that we have ahead. I am concerned that competitors are getting ahead of us because we in banking are not looking sufficiently at the opportunity that we have. The ACHs are just a good example of this. In our bank, the ACH effort is already profitable, and I encourage others to look aggressively at the potential of the automated clearinghouse.

CHAPTER SUMMARY

Electronic impulses will be the dominant transfer messengers of the future. They will emanate from a vast array of electronic hardware known only by strange acronyms and covered by the super acronym EFTS. In conjunction with structural changes in the components of TRICK, the changing technology of electronic banking will add another dimension to the dynamic and complex world of the financial-services industry. The interaction of new technology and the processes of financial innovation and product diffusion will shape the FSI of the future, one in whch financial-services firms also will be known for their processing of information flows and communications.

LIST OF KEY WORDS, CONCEPTS, AND ACRONYMS

ACH = automated clearinghouse
ATM = automated teller machine
ATM network

CHIPS = Clearing House Interbank
   Payment System
Diffusion

Domestic versus international (transactions)	Home banking
Electronic versus paper (transactions)	Innovation
EFTS = electronic funds transfer system	Payments system (large-dollar)
FedWire	Scale economies
FRCS − 80 = Federal Reserve Communications System for the Eighties	Videotex
	Wholesale versus retail (transactions)

Domestic versus international
  (transactions)
Electronic versus paper (transactions)
EFTS = electronic funds transfer
  system
FedWire
FRCS − 80 = Federal Reserve
  Communications System for the
  Eighties

Home banking
Innovation
Payments system (large-dollar)
Scale economies
Videotex
Wholesale versus retail (transactions)

REVIEW/DISCUSSION QUESTIONS

1. What are the interrelationships among new technology, the process of innovation, and product diffusion? What evidence exists regarding the speed of diffusion of consumer products?

2. Describe the market for electronic business financial services and the major service it needs. Where and why have substantial opportunities opened up recently?

3. Are banks being disenfranchised in the competition for retail payments? If they are, what can they do about it?

4. What are the major drawbacks to home banking? At present, is it any better than banking by phone?

5. Distinguish briefly but carefully among the following EFT components: ATM, ACH, and POS.

6. What basic functions do ATMs perform? What is an ATM network?

7. What is a two-tiered pricing strategy and how can it be used to get customers to use ATMs?

8. Describe the ACH processing mechanism for a direct payroll deposit and a preauthorized insurance payment.

9. Who are the ACH players? What is FRCS-80?

10. Explain the terms economies of scale, diseconomies of scale, and constant returns to scale. What do the graphs of the average cost curves associated with these alternative economies look like? Discuss the scale-economy evidence for ACHs and ATMs. What can you say about the cost characteristics of EFT systems? How important is volume to EFTS?

11. Should the Fed own and operate a national ACH? Discuss. What role should the private sector play?. Is George White overcritical of the Fed? Should the Fed be relegated to a "clearer of last resort"? Describe Kane's postal-system analogy of the ACH system.

12. Why are POS systems currently running last in the EFT big-three conference? What is the future outlook for such systems? What are "secondary" POS services? Are they valuable?

13. What are Visa's electronic-authorization plans? What is a "zero-floor-limit" authorization?

14. What is videotex? What is home banking? How are the two related? Who are the players in this game? What would *you* be willing to pay for a comprehensive videotex service? What services would you want?

15. What are the financial-management implications of electronic banking for commercial banks?

16. Describe what a bank's EFT environment might be in the future.

17. Researchers at Stanford University have found that the impact of technological change usually is underestimated, whereas the time it takes for technological change to have an impact usually is overestimated. In other words, the "boom" is louder and sooner than expected. Discuss this finding with respect to EFTS.
18. What does "a dime a time" refer to? How does Mellon's bid for the Cirrus switch relate to this rhyme? Refer to your answer to Question 10 as you answer this one.
19. According to Walter Wriston, retired Citicorp chairman, "The information standard has replaced the gold standard as the basis for world finance." Explain and discuss.
20. John Reed, Walter Wriston's protégé and his successor as Citicorp's chairman, said, "Bricks and mortar didn't interest me, communications did." How does such a revealed preference fit in with the future of banking?

MATCHING QUIZ

Directions: Select the letter from the right-hand column that best matches the term in the left-hand column. A letter may be used more than once.

___ 1. Most credit cards outstanding	A. Banking industry
___ 2. ATM network covering most states	B. 250 million
___ 3. Scale economies	C. Money management
___ 4. Paper and people intensive	D. Most widely used EFT
___ 5. Rates high in use of technology	E. Little incentive to use
___ 6. As labor intensive as banking	F. ACH operations
___ 7. "Backroom technology"	G. Checking characteristic
___ 8. ATM	H. Freezers
___ 9. POS	I. Federal Reserve System
___ 10. ACH	J. Electronic payments
___ 11. Application of an invention	K. Funds transfer
___ 12. Fast diffusion time	L. Corrigan
___ 13. Slow diffusion time	M. Fisher
___ 14. EFT function	N. McCoy
___ 15. High volume + low average value	O. White
	P. VISA

___ 16. Low volume + high average value

___ 17. Concerned about payments risks

___ 18. FRCS-80

___ 19. Potential for natural monopoly

___ 20. "Clearer of last resort"

___ 21. ATM pricing strategy

___ 22. Number of ATM cards in 1995

___ 23. Secondary POS service

___ 24. Can't deliver cash

___ 25. Innovative bank

___ 26. Low grade for technology

Q. Sears

R. Computer operating systems

S. Plus System Inc.

T. Average cost declines

U. Telecommunications

V. Check verifications

W. Home banking

X. Banc One

Y. Cirrus System

Z. Innovation

AA. Two-tiered pricing

BB. Color TVs

CC. Competitor of private ACHs

DD. Home information retrieval

EE. Handles recurring transactions efficiently

SELECTED REFERENCES

Apcar, Leonard M. [1987]. "A Special Report Technology in the Workplace: Banking," *The Wall Street Journal* (June 12), Section 4.

Bank Cards. Washington, D.C.: American Bankers Association, 1983.

Cohen, Allen M. [1985]. "Electronic Financial Services: A Battleground for Survival." *The Magazine of Bank Administration* (January 1985), pp. 18–21.

Compton, Eric N. [1987]. *The New World of Commercial Banking*. Lexington, MA: Lexington Books.

Corrigan, E. Gerald. [1987]. "Financial Market Structure: A Longer View," *Annual Report* Federal Reserve Bank of New York, pp. 3–54.

Edwards, Franklin R. [1979]. *Issues in Financial Regulation*. New York: McGraw-Hill.

EFT in the United States: Policy Recommendations and the Public Interest. [1977], Washington, D.C.: National Commission on Electronic Transfers, October 28.

"Electronic Banking: A Retreat from the Cashless Society." [1977]. *Business Week* (April 18), pp. 80–90.

Elliott, John C. [1984]. "Nonbanks." In *Payments in the Financial-Services Industry of the 1980s, Conference Proceedings* (sponsored by the Federal Reserve Bank of Atlanta). Westport, CT: Quorum Books, pp. 81–90.

Fisher, John. [1981]. "A Futuristic View of Banking." Remarks at the 1981 Annual Meeting of the Financial Management Association, Cincinnati, October 22.

———. [1979]. "New Concepts for the World of Banking." *The Bankers Magazine* (March–April), pp. 21–22.

Gart, Alan. [1985]. *Banks, Thrifts, and Insurance Companies.* Lexington, Ma: Lexington Books.

Hamilton, Adrian. [1986]. *The Financial Revolution.* New York: The Free Press.

Hamilton, Earl G. [1979]. "An Update on the Automated Clearinghouse." *Federal Reserve Bulletin* (July), pp. 525–531.

Hosemann, Michael J. [1979]. *The Rationale for Electronic Banking.* Washington, DC: American Bankers Association.

Humphrey, David B. [1987]. "Cost Dispersion and the Measurement of Economies in Banking," *Economic Review* Federal Reserve Bank of Richmond (May/June, Volume 73/3), pp. 24–38.

———. [1981]. "Scale Economies at Automated Clearinghouses." *Journal of Bank Research* (Summer), pp. 71–81.

Kane, Edward J. 1981. "Changes in the Provision of Correspondent-Banking Services and the Role of Federal Reserve Banks under the DIDMC Act." Columbus: The Ohio State University, College of Administrative Science, Working Paper Series 81–55 (July).

Kirkman, Patrick. *Electronic Funds Transfer Systems: The Revolution in Cashless Banking & Payment Methods.* Oxford: Basil Blackwell.

Little, Arthur D., Inc. [1975]. *The Bankers' EFT Handbook.* Washington DC: American Bankers Association.

McHenry, Wendell, Jr. [1981]. "EFT in the 1980s." *The Bankers Magazine* (May–June), pp. 30–33.

Merrill, Peter. [1984]. "Winners and Losers in the Network Race." In *Payments in the FSI, op. cit.,* pp. 93–99.

Metzker, Paul F. [1982]. "Strategic Planning for the Check-Collection System and its Alternatives." *The Magazine of Bank Administration* (January), pp. 33–35.

Mitchell, George W. and Raymond F. Hodgdon. [1981]. "Federal Reserve and the Payments System: Upgrading Electronic Capabilities for the 1980s." *Federal Reserve Bulletin* (February), pp. 109–116.

Nadler, Paul S. [1982]. "Choice of an ATM Network Is a Major Decision." *American Banker* (February 1), pp. 1 and 6.

Niblack, William C. [1976]. "Development of Electronic Funds Transfer Systems." Federal Reserve Bank of St. Louis *Review* (September), pp. 10–18.

"Norwest Smashes '33% Barrier' on ATM Usage." [1984]. *Banking Issues and Innovations* (Sample Issue), pp. 4–5.

Payments in the Financial-Services Industry of the 1980s, Conference Proceedings. [1984]. Westport, CT: Quorum Books.

Phillips, Almarin. [1985]. "Changing Technology and Future Financial Activity," in *Handbook for Banking Strategy,* R. C. Aspinwall and R. A. Eisenbeis, eds. New York: Wiley, pp. 125–150.

———.[1979]. "Implications of the New Payments Technology for Monetary Policy." In *Issues in Financial Regulation,* ed. Franklin R. Edwards, New York: McGraw-Hill, pp. 269–286.

Power, William. [1987]. "A 'Magician' Makes $86,000 Disappear from Cash Machines," *The Wall Street Journal* (May 18), pp. 1 and 23.

"Revolution in Retail Payments." [1984]. Federal Reserve Bank of Atlanta *Economic Review* (special issue, July/August).

Rose, Sanford. [1977]. "More Bang for the Buck: The Magic of Electronic Banking." *Fortune,* (May), pp. 202–226.

Smith, David M. [1980]. "Electronic Mail in Banking." *The Magazine of Bank Administration* (October), pp. 49–54.

Smith, Terence M. [1984]. "Mellon Bank is Cirrus' Choice." *American Banker* (September 26), pp. 1 and 14.

Solomon, Elinor H. [1979]. "EFT and Bank Sharing: Some Competitive Questions." In *Issues in Financial Regulation* Franklin R. Edwards, ed. New York: McGraw-Hill, pp. 287–299.

"Special Issue: Displacing the Check." [1983]. Federal Reserve Bank of Atlanta *Economic Review* (August).

"Special Report: Operations and Automation, After a Decade, Where is EFT Headed?" [1980]. *ABA Banking Journal* (May), pp. 82–91.

"Special Report Part II, Where is EFT Going?" [1980]. *ABA Banking Journal* (June), pp. 97–103.

Trigaux, Robert. [1982]. "Visa Will Go 80% Electronic by 1985." *American Banker* (January), pp. 1 and 3.

Walker, David A. [1978]. "Economies of Scale in Electronic Funds Transfer Systems." *Journal of Banking and Finance* (August), pp. 65–78.

"Window on the World: The Home Information Revolution." [1981]. *Business Week* (June 29), pp. 74–83.

White, George C. Jr., and Paul S. Nadler. [1981]. "Banking Without Paper." *The Bankers Magazine* (May–June), pp. 34–42.

Zimmer, Linda Fenner. [1981]. "ATM Acceptance Grows." *The Magazine of Bank Administration* (May), pp. 31–35.

The Theory, Objectives, and Agencies of Bank Regulation

ACRONYM GUIDE TO KEY TERMS AND CONCEPTS

BHC = bank holding company

DIDMCA = Depository Institutions Deregulation and Monetary Control Act

CSBS = Conference of State Bank Supervisors

FDIC = Federal Deposit Insurance Corporation

FSI = financial-services industry

FSLIC = Federal Savings and Loan Insurance Corporation

OCC = Office of the Comptroller of the Currency

NBSS = National Bank Surveillance System

SEC = Securities and Exchange Commission

INTRODUCTION

To start a bank, you need a charter from either the federal or state government. Since it is highly unlikely that you could start an uninsured bank or even a state-insured bank (because of the Ohio and Maryland insurance crises of the mid-1980s), federal deposit insurance is a must. Thus, before your bank even opens its doors, the regulators and deposit insurers have made their surveillance known and will continue their watchdog function as long as the bank exists. Why do we have bank regulation and deposit insurance? What are the objectives of bank regulation? Who are the regulators? The answers to these questions form the foundation of this chapter. In the next chapter, we focus on the role of regulatory restrictions in stimulating innovations such as the bank holding company movement and the payment of implicit interest.

Since trying to keep up with the reregulation of the banking system requires (almost) daily attention to the financial news, the most recent developments in banking legislation appear in the appendix of this chapter. There you will find summaries of three key banking laws: (1) the Depository Institutions Deregulation and Monetary Control Act (DIDMCA) of 1980, (2) the Garn–St Germain Act of 1982, and (3) the Competitive Equality Banking Act of 1987. Please stay tuned to the financial news for the latest developments in banking legislation.

A BRIEF HISTORY OF BANK REGULATION

In the early days of the United States, Thomas Paine wrote[1]:

> The whole community derives benefit from the operation of the bank: It facilitates the commerce of the country. It quickens the means of purchasing and paying for country produce and hastens on the exportation of it. The emolument, therefore, being to the community, it is the office and duty of government to give protection to the bank.

Clearly, the idea that U.S. banks should be protected has deep historical roots. Moreover, for the most part, there was agreement that banking required some form of regulation because it was a public trust. However, there was considerable disagreement over the particular form that the regulation should take. Should banks be chartered and who should charter them? What should banks do and where should they be permitted to do it? Over 200 years have passed since these questions and others were first asked, and they have stood the test of time because the answers still are in dispute. Today, some of the most pressing questions of regulation are quite similar to those earlier ones, for example: What is a bank? What products and services can banks produce? Where and in what form should banks be permitted to operate? And a question that is only about half a century old: How should deposit insurance be priced and administered?

THE OBJECTIVES OF BANK REGULATION

Bank regulators traditionally have attempted to serve three masters: (1) safety, (2) stability, and (3) structure. These three objectives refer, respectively, to (1) the protection of depositors and the deposit-insurance fund, (2) the protection of the economy from the vicissitudes of the financial system, and (3) the protection of bank customers from the monopoly power of banks.

Prior to the introduction of deposit insurance in 1933, the *safety* objective was cast in terms protecting the risk associated with bank liabilities (i.e., protecting banks from deposit runs and hence from failure). Although the latter still is effectively the safety objective today, it is under the guise (and subsidy) of deposit insurance. The bank *stability* objective is closely linked with the goal of macroeconomic stabilization of the economy. The "domino theory" of bank failure tends to dominate thinking in this area. According to this theory, bank failures are contagious and therefore they must be contained to prevent the system from collapsing. A modern-day example of this kind of regulatory thinking was the handling of the collapse of Continental Illinois National Bank in 1984. Rather than close the bank and give *de jure* recognition to its *de facto* failure, the regulators argued that "hundreds" of banks would have been adversely affected by its closing and therefore the bank had to be bailed out—at taxpayers' expense, by the way.

The stability and safety objectives can be viewed in terms of some fundamental microeconomic and macroeconomic motives. First, on the macroeconomic level, the money supply is an important determinant of total economic activity—monetarists would say the most important. Alternative views of the macroeconomic transmission mechanism focus on interest rates (the Keynesian approach) or the supply of bank

---

[1] From Hammond [1957], p. 60, in reference to the Bank of North America, which Hammond describes as "The first real bank, in the modern sense, on the North American continent" (p. 50). The Bank of North America was founded by Robert Morris and incorporated on December 31, 1781.

credit as the critical linkage. Although in today's economy commercial banks are only one of the creators of money, they still are the most important component of the money-supply process. Thus, to protect the money supply and give the central bank some leverage to attempt to control bank reserves, interest rates, or credit, banks are regulated. The MC (= *Monetary Control*) of DIDMCA is an example of this kind of *control* regulation. Ironically, however, as Milton Friedman [1962] has pointed out, a fractional-reserve banking system is "inherently unstable." To counteract this tendency to self-destruct, a central bank (the Federal Reserve System) with lender-of-last-resort powers was created in 1913. One of the tasks of macroeconomic stabilization policy is to protect the money supply from rapid shrinkage via open-market operations and access to the discount window, a task that was not accomplished in the 1930s. Because the Fed failed to prevent the financial crisis of the early 1930s, the U.S. Congress established the Federal Deposit Insurance Corporation in 1933 and imposed various restrictions on commercial banks (e.g., prohibition of interest payments on demand deposits and rate ceilings on savings and time deposits) to attempt to control "ruinous competition." By 1959, Friedman [1959] was saying that deposit insurance had made the banking system " panic-proof." By 1980, after a decade and a half of increasingly severe disintermediation, savers were saying that deposit-rate ceilings had to go, and the thrifts were dying because of the ceilings *and* product restrictions. As a result, the banking acts of 1980 and 1982 aimed directly at dismantling the interest-rate and product-specialization restrictions imposed by the legislation of the 1930s and subsequent amendments. Geographic restrictions, the other major class of bank regulation, are due to the McFadden Act of 1927 and the Douglas Amendment (1970) to the 1957 BHC Act. A major development in this area occurred in 1985 when the U.S. Supreme Court rejected Citicorp's challenge to regional interstate banking. Citicorp was protesting state legislation that excluded it, and other money-city banks, from participating in regional interstate banking.

The overall goal of bank regulation and deposit insurance is to maintain public confidence in the banking system. On the microeconomic level, the focus is upon limiting the risk exposure of *individual* banks and isolating bank failures to avoid a "domino effect" within the system. To do this, the banking authorities try to see that each individual bank is operated in a "safe and sound" manner. The main tool for the prompt detection of potential bank insolvency is the on-site bank examination. This kind of failure-prevention regulation is manifested in such factors as capital and liquidity requirements, asset-quality standards, and compliance with laws and regulations. The banking authorities use regulatory interference (e.g., cease-and-desist orders, removal of officers, required capital injections.) to channel bank behavior in the desired direction. By pursuing the microeconomic goal of limited failure prevention, the banking authorities expect to maintain public confidence in the banking system.

The *structure* objective is best viewed in terms of the degree of competitiveness and efficiency in the banking industry. The linkage between structure and competition is provided by the IO model, where IO stands for industrial organization. Since this model links structure with conduct and then with performance, it is also referred to as the structure-conduct-performance model. Given the basic conditions of supply and demand, the IO model postulates the following linkages:

Structure → Conduct → Performance

where *structure* refers to the number of firms in the market, *conduct* to the behavior of the firms in the market, and *performance* to the quantity and quality of products and services produced by the firms in the market. The fundamental conclusion of the model is that the more firms that are in the market, the smaller the chances of anticompetitive behavior, and the greater the chances of high-quality products and services provided at competitive prices. In the FSI, competitive prices for customers mean low loan rates and high deposit rates. If monopoly profits exist in an industry, firms are encouraged to enter, if permitted, and compete away the excess profits.

Conflicting Objectives

Since the structure or competition objective conflicts with the safety and stability objectives, regulators and legislators must weigh the trade-offs between them. The other players in this struggle with a vested interest in the outcome are the financial-services firms (e.g., banks) and their customers. Both of these groups make their wishes known to Congress and the regulators via lobbying efforts. Since the regulatory environment is not a static one, various regimes have existed in U.S. banking over the past 200 years. These regimes can be classified as follows[2]:

Regime Description	Period	Dominant Objective
Chartered banking	1776–1837	Anticompetitive structure (as manifested by prohibition against nationwide banking)
Free banking	1838–1932	Competitive structure and efficiency
Cartel banking	1933–1978	Safety and stability
Competitive (but safe) banking	1979–	A better balance between competition and efficiency versus safety and stability

The current regulatory regime is attempting to strike a better balance among the conflicting objectives of safety, stability, and structure. Its focus is on competitive but safe banking, or what might be called "balanced" banking. This latest regime was born on a Saturday night, October 6, 1979. On this night, a dramatic event, sometimes called the "Saturday night special," took place in Fed monetary policy. Paul Volcker, then Chairman of the Fed, initiated a shift in monetary policy from an interest-rate target to a monetary-aggregates target. This shift, which would permit greater interest-rate volatility (keep the I in TRICK in mind), marked a willingness on the part of the Fed to accept greater instability in the financial system. If regulated firms were to survive in such an environment, some of the shackles of cartel banking would have to be removed. The deregulation or reregulation acts of 1980, 1982, and 1987 were *reactions* to the economic and technological changes operating in the financial system. As a result of these legislative actions *and* other inactions, interest-rate and product controls were relaxed and "windows" to greater geographic freedom were opened. Under the current regime, the promotion of competition and the efficiency of the financial marketplace are being highlighted. This focus has, in turn, created concern about the ability of the current deposit-insurance and regulatory structures to function in the new FSI. To date, bailouts (e.g., Continental) and other stop-gap measures (especially for thrifts) have been used to camouflage the structural weaknesses in the system.

The SEC Effect, Disclosure, and Market Discipline

Since the banking authorities are concerned with avoiding "deposit runs" and promoting the safety and soundness of the banking system, they have a tendency to paint a rosier picture of a troubled bank's financial condition than reality might dictate.

---

[2] The first three regimes are described by Huertas [1983].

In contrast, the Securities and Exchange Commission (SEC) is concerned that stock-holders and would-be investors have full information (via disclosure) for making in-vestment decisions. The failure of several large banks over the past decade and the international debt crisis have heightened the call for greater bank disclosure. The clash between "secrecy" and "disclosure" was inevitable. The fact that there is something called the "SEC effect" indicates who is winning some of the battles. At present, the banking agencies must adopt disclosure requirements "substantially similar" to the corresponding SEC regulations, or publish reasons for the differences.[3] Moreover, the Fed, FDIC, and OCC have established Securities-Disclosure Units (in effect "mini-SECs") within their own agencies. A bank or BHC with 500 or more shareholders is subject to SEC disclosure standards.

The basic bank-disclosure issue relates to the amount of detail that should be supplied regarding the loan-loss reserves and nonearning (or nonperforming) assets of troubled banks. Litigation in some of these cases has focused on this issue; the shareholders claimed that they did not have enough information to judge the quality of the bank's loan portfolio.

The fact that bank regulators have become more "user oriented" in terms of financial disclosure is a manifestation of the SEC effect and of their recognition that market discipline has an important role to play in constraining the risk exposure of major banks. If the marketplace is to perform this function effectively, it must have adequate and reliable information via disclosure. In its deposit-insurance study, the FDIC (1983) considered disclosure proposals dealing with the measurement of a bank's interest-rate risk, a narrative analysis of a bank's operating results and financial position, and the publication in the *Federal Register* of final statutory enforcement actions taken against that bank.

THREE LAYERS OF FINANCIAL-SERVICES COMPETITION[4]

As developed in Chapter 4, models of the banking firm have emphasized two primary dimensions of competition: explicit price and user convenience. Prior to the deregula-tion of the 1980s, the post-Depression era of banking was characterized by lack of explicit pricing and reliance on implicit pricing through convenience devices such as more branches and longer banking hours. In 1973, the U.S. banking system was rocked by its first billion-dollar bank failure in FDIC history when the United States National Bank of San Diego was closed. Since then numerous banks and thrift institutions have failed. The burden of the thrift failures has been so great that its federal insurance agency, the Federal Savings and Loan Insurance Corporation (FSLIC), went belly-up and had to be bailed out by the federal government in 1987 (see Appendix C). In addition, several state or private deposit-insurance agencies were forced to close, most notably in Ohio and Maryland.

Since volatile interest rates and numerous failures of financial institutions have started to shake the public's confidence in the U.S. financial-services industry, it is appropriate, as Kane [1984, 1986] has suggested, to introduce a third dimension of financial-services competition: public confidence. Thus, the three layers or dimen-sions of financial-services competition are (1) explicit price, (2) user convenience, and (3) public confidence. Because these three components have important effects on

---

[3] See Dince [1979].

[4] This section, including the various subsections, relies heavily on the work of Kane [1986]. Regarding the importance of public confidence to the financial system, see Apcar [1987]. His article "Frightened Money" deals with depositor worries over troubled banks and S&Ls in Texas.

the demand for borrowing and lending arrangements, they can be regarded as intermediate services produced *jointly* by financial-services firms and their regulators. Since various aspects of pricing behavior are discussed elsewhere in this book, our focus here is on modeling the convenience and confidence elements with emphasis on the regulatory effects.

Modeling the Confidence Function

The *K* in TRICK stands for capital adequacy (using the German spelling of capital). For a financial institution, a strong capital base relative to its risk exposures is a sign of financial strength. Using accounting or finance language, we can refer to this capital base as the institution's net worth (NW) or equity. For banks, the primary source of capital is generated internally through retained earnings. (The internal capital generation rate, g, equals $ROE \times RR$, where ROE = return on equity and RR = retention ratio.) Positive and stable earnings, thus, are desirable traits for a bank to have because they permit "safe-and-sound" growth (i.e., growth in which capital adequacy is maintained).

Drawing on a key concept from Chapter 3, we know that one of the primary sources for agency problems is asymmetric information. If users of the banking system are to have confidence in it, they must have easy access to reliable and low-cost information—in particular, information about an institution's real net worth and variability of earnings. As discussed above, the role of the SEC and disclosure are important here.

To summarize (and for the moment assume an unregulated banking system), our model of the public's confidence in the system can be expressed as:

Confidence = f(net worth, stability of earnings, information quality)

where $f(\ldots)$ is read as a function of. The functional relationships are all direct ones, that is, as net worth, stability, or quality of information increases, other things equal, confidence increases.

Let's let the government enter the picture and consider what effect this has on our analysis. In particular, let's introduce deposit insurance. Since deposit insurance in the United States is not insurance, per se, but a system of government guarantees, we refer to these arrangements as external guarantees. Our concern is with the market value of these guarantees to insured institutions. Using G to represent the market value of government guarantees and obvious mnemonics from the previous function, we have

Confidence = $f(NW, SOE, IQ, G)$

As with the other three "independent" variables, as G increases, confidence increases. The market value of G depends, among other things, on the explicit and implicit promises made by the government and its willingness to back them up. In the United States the explicit promise by the government is deposit insurance up to a maximum of $100,000 per account. In practice, except for the smallest banks, the implicit promise is one of 100 percent deposit insurance. And if that's not good enough, then if the bank/BHC is a multibillion dollar organization, the FDIC will bail it out (e.g., Continental Illinois in 1984 and First Pennsylvania in 1980). The latter is known as the "too-big-to-fail doctrine." Of course, as Lockheed and Chrysler bear witness, this government policy does not apply only to financial institutions.

The role and importance of government guarantees is most easily demonstrated in the case of distressed institutions. Given our confidence function, a distressed institution is simply one with low or negative net worth, unstable earnings, and unreliable and costly information (i.e., low quality information). In an unregulated environment, such institutions would be prime candidates for failure. However, if government guarantees are perceived by the marketplace as genuine, they can offset or even exceed the adverse operating characteristics of the insured firm. The best real-world examples of this phenomenon are the numerous insolvent thrift institutions that existed in the 1980s, the ones Kane [1986] calls "zombie" S&Ls, whose equity shares traded in the marketplace at positive values. These positive values were due to the values associated with G, the government guarantees. Since the FSLIC was *de facto* bankrupt over most of these years, clearly, it was the government's promise to make good on the FSLIC's liabilities that created this value and not deposit insurance.

Modeling the Convenience Function

When you shop for anything, what attracts you? Most of us look for convenience and service or quality. Shopping for financial services is no different than shopping for nonfinancial services. Regulations in the form of geographic and product restrictions make it inconvenient for customers to use institutions subject to such constraints. Absent such restrictions, the firm's capital base is the primary determinant of the breadth and depth of its product and geographic markets. Given these parameters, the cost of services and the quality of products and services can be viewed as important arguments of the convenience function. In the FSI, quality can be measured by the speed and reliability of the services the institution provides.

This discussion suggests the following model of the convenience function for a particular financial-services firm:

$$\text{Convenience} = f(\text{geog, prod, cost, qual})$$

where "geog" stands for the firm's geographic reach in terms of owned and shared facilities (e.g., ATM networks), "prod" stands for the vector of products and services supplied by the firm, "cost" stands for the average cost of accessing the firm's facilities, and "qual" stands for the quality or speed and reliability of the services generated by the firm. Except for the cost factor, user convenience is positively related to the arguments of this function. Specifically, as a firm's geographic reach, products, and quality of service expands, user convenience is enhanced. Conversely, as the average cost of using a firm's facilities increases, user convenience is reduced.

The Role of Regulation in Shaping the Confidence and Convenience Functions

Let's think of regulators as producing regulatory services. As such, they should have profit, revenue, and cost functions. Why would regulatees (e.g., insured banks) pay for regulatory services? The answers are found in our expressions for confidence and convenience. Regulatees pay for such services because by doing so they expect to improve their confidence and/or convenience functions vis-à-vis their competitors. With respect to confidence, regulatory services can help improve the quality of information and the market value of government guarantees. Regarding convenience, regulatory services (think of the absence of restrictions as valuable services) can have a direct effect on all of the arguments of the convenience function.

To understand the notion of regulatory services, recall the objectives of bank regulation discussed at the beginning of this chapter. They are safety, stability, and structure. To achieve these objectives, bank regulation attempts to monitor, correct (e.g., via market discipline), and coordinate the behavior of supervised firms. The benefits of regulatory services may accrue directly to the firm in the form of greater *safety*, to their customers due to a more favorable financial *structure* (i.e., the benefits of a more competitive environment), or to society as a whole in the form of a more *stable* financial system.

Since the production of regulatory services entails costs, a regulator's profit (or loss) is simply the difference between its regulatory revenues and its costs. As government or quasi-government entities, regulatory agencies may be required, perhaps under political duress, to transfer their profits to the national Treasury. Obviously, the inability to transfer funds may be a source of political discontent. Even more disquieting to politicians would be to force them to live up to their implied deposit-insurance guarantees, as in the case of the $10.8 billion bail out of the FSLIC in 1987 (see Appendix C).

The Competition for Regulatory Services

The C component in TRICK stands for competition for customers among the financial-services firms of the FSI. Kane [1986] argues that "running parallel to this competition ... is a less-visible layer of competition for rights to produce and deliver regulatory services to these institutions" (p. 10). To model this behavior, Kane proposes a contestable-markets view of regulation. According to Baumol [1982], the contestable-markets model is a generalization of the concept of a perfectly competitive market. Although both frameworks imply optimal behavior, the contestable-markets version is more general because it applies to the full range of market structures, including monopoly and oligopoly. Baumol, Panzar, and Willig [1986] define a contestable market as one in which entry and exit costs are zero such that the possibility of hit-and-run entry (i.e., the threat of potential competition) by outside competitors serves to constrain industry profits.

Since regulators must have client firms to sell their regulatory services to, it makes sense to talk about market share for regulators. Like other participants in contestable markets, regulators want to protect their market shares, which generate the regulatory revenues and profits discussed above. Regulatory quests for market share are sometimes referred to as "turf battles." In this context, reregulation (i.e., the relaxing of one or more regulatory restrictions) can be seen as complex behavior driven by the desire to increase or maintain market share and preserve regulatory revenues and profits. The multidimensional nature of this rational behavior requires regulators to keep their clients satisfied and the financial system safe and sound while they maintain market share. Like other forms of competition, competition for regulatory services should be healthy for the FSI. However, Kane [1986] warns that "... many of the benefits of regulatory competition can be undone by explicit and implicit government subsidies to risk-bearing" (p. 2).

Recapitulation

This section, drawing on the work of Kane [1986], has offered an explanation of regulatory behavior based on the notions of customer confidence and convenience. Regulators are viewed as producers of regulatory services designed to enhance the safety, stability, and competitive structure of the financial system. Financial-services firms "purchase" regulatory services because they view them as enhancing their abilities to provide greater customer confidence and convenience. In a contestable market, regulatory competition should produce the lowest-cost production of customer confidence and convenience.

THE REGULATORY DIALECTIC OR STRUGGLE MODEL[5]

The battle between regulators and regulatees (i.e., managers of FSFs) can be viewed as a "struggle model." The foundation of the theory is based on the philosopher Hegel's[6] concept of the *dialectic*. The Hegelian process of change consists of three stages: (1) *thesis*, (2) *antithesis*, and (3) *synthesis*. In this process, the thesis and antithesis clash and through an ongoing struggle evolve into a synthesis. The synthesis then becomes a new thesis and the process of change or struggle goes on and on. Cast in a regulatory framework, the regulatory dialectic pits the regulators against the regulatees in an ongoing struggle. The regulators attempt to impose constraints on the financial system (e.g., interest-rate, product, or geographic controls). The regulatees, who tend to be driven by profit- or wealth-maximization motives, attempt to circumvent the restrictions because they act as taxes on their profits. If the circumvention is successful, which it usually is because profit-motivated individuals tend to move faster and more efficiently than bureaucrats, then the regulators attempt to close the "window" or "loophole" and the struggle becomes an ongoing one. One positive aspect of the struggle process is that it tends to spur financial innovation by regulated firms and to encourage less-regulated firms to infringe upon the more-regulated firms. Thus, the regulatory dialectic also can be viewed as a theory of financial innovation.

Economies of Scope and Structural Arbitrage

The process of change in the FSI can be viewed as occurring autonomously or as being induced either by market forces (e.g., technology) or regulatory ones, or both. To ignore any of these components presents a less than complete picture of the process of change in the FSI. To focus on the interaction of technological and regulatory forces in the developing fusion of FSI competition, the concepts of structural arbitrage and economies of scope are needed.

Structural arbitrage (Kane [1984]) refers to adaptive changes in a firm's organizational form designed to lighten its tax and regulatory burdens. The process creates costs and benefits for government officials that require reactive adjustments in operative tax codes and regulations. The contemporary realignment of federal and state regulatory frameworks is largely a process of competitive reregulation. Thus, just as financial arbitrage moves funds across markets in search of profitable opportunities, structural arbitrage moves FSFs across laws and regulatory bodies in search of profitable opportunities.

An important component of the reregulation process is the contestability theory of multimarket competition.[7] Contestability theory maintains that market structure adapts through entry and exit to permit customer demand to be served at minimum cost. The desegmentation or fusion of financial markets involves the expansion of low-cost producers at the expense of high-cost ones. Regulatory interference slows the rate of adaptation by imposing entry restrictions and corresponding avoidance costs on particular firms. But in a free society in which multiple legislatures and regulatory agencies compete for regulatees, tax receipts, and/or budgeted funds, authorities cannot induce either great or long-lasting divergences between the actual and the cost-minimizing market structure. To focus on these product restrictions and the costs of exclusionary rules, the notion of *economies of scope* (or scope economies) is required.

---

[5] This section is based on the work of Kane [1977, 1981, 1983, and 1984].

[6] Georg Wilhelm Friedrich Hegel (1770–1831), German philosopher.

[7] See Baumol, Panzar, and Willig [1983] and Kane [1984].

Consider two goods, X_1 and X_2. Economies of scope exist when the total costs of producing the two goods jointly is less than the combined cost of producing the same amounts of each good separately. That is,

$$C(X_1,X_2) < C_1(X_1) + C_2(X_2) \rightarrow Scope\ Economies \tag{7-1}$$

Alternatively, condition 7-1 can be rearranged to define scope economies as

$$C_1(X_1) + C_2(X_2) - C(X_1,X_2) > 0 \tag{7-2}$$

In essence, economies of scope are economies of joint production. They come into play when two outputs share one or more capital or labor inputs in the production process. Examples are

1. A multipurpose dam that produces electricity, flood control, and recreational services cheaper than could be produced on a stand-alone basis.
2. A financial-services firm that uses its computer, communications network, and branch-office system to jointly produce standardized deposit, loan, brokerage, and insurance services cheaper than specialized producers.

Product Restrictions and the Costs of Exclusionary Rules

Exclusionary rules promote attempts to circumvent such restrictions. These attempts are, of course, not costless. Let's designate the minimum cost of perfectly circumventing or avoiding a given set of restrictions against multiproduct operation as C_A. These avoidance costs are the incremental costs of creating an unregulated substitute product of institutional arrangement. As long as the reduced costs of joint production exceeds the costs of avoidance, joint production is favored. That is,

$$C_1(X_1) + C_2(X_2) - C(X_1,X_2) > C_A \tag{7-3}$$

In other words, if the benefits of joint production (i.e., the economies of scope) exceed the avoidance costs, avoidance activities are encouraged. The social cost of a regulatory exclusion is the sum of (1) the administrative costs of promulgating and enforcing the restriction, C_R, and (2) the smaller of the forfeited economies of scope and avoidance costs. Consider the following numerical example from Kane [1984]:

Technology	Economies of Scope	Avoidance Costs	Regulatory Costs
State I	10 − 8 = 2	3	3
State II	10 − 7 = 3	2	3

In State II, although the costs of the specialized production are unaffected, innovation drives the costs of joint production to 7 and avoidance costs to 2. As a result, the exclusionary rule is unenforceable in State II because scope economies at 3 exceed the avoidance costs of 2. In State I, the reverse holds and the rule is enforceable. The social costs of regulatory exclusion are the same in both states as $5 = 3 + 2 = C_R + min\ [C_A,\ scope\ economies]$.

Recapitulation

This section has built extensively on Kane's ideas of the regulatory dialectic, structural arbitrage, and various cost concepts. These ideas provide important insights into how the technological and regulatory components of TRICK are serving to integrate

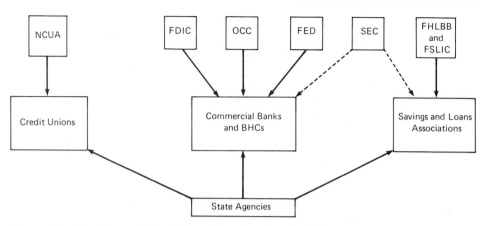

Figure 7-1   The Current Regulatory Structure for Depository Institutions

diverse financial institutions in the new and competitive FSI. The next section focuses on the traditional forms of bank regulation, which innovative managers have been trying to circumvent for the past 50 years.

REGULATION OF DEPOSITORY INSTITUTIONS

The current regulatory structure for depository institutions is depicted in Figure 7-1. Recall that depository institutions consist of three groups of firms: commercial banks, savings-and-loan associations, and credit unions. The primary federal regulators for these three groups are (1) the Fed, the FDIC, and the Office of the Comptroller of the Currency (OCC) for commercial banks; (2) the Federal Home Loan Bank Board (FHLBB) and the Federal Savings and Loan Insurance Corporation for S&Ls; and (3) the National Credit Union Administration (NCUA) for credit unions. Three other dimensions of the current regulatory structure include the dual system of federal and state chartering and supervision, SEC monitoring of banks and thrifts with actively traded shares of equity, and regulation of bank and thrift holding companies by the Fed and the FHLBB, respectively. The remainder of this chapter focuses on the agencies of commercial bank regulation and deposit insurance and their functions. The functions performed by nonbank regulatory agencies are similar, only the names are different. We begin with a look at deposit insurance and the FDIC.

DEPOSIT INSURANCE

From 1971 to 1976, I was employed as a research economist at the Federal Deposit Insurance Corporation (FDIC). During those years, whenever I told someone where I worked, there was almost instant recognition of the acronym FDIC. Rarely did I have to say what the initials meant. Most of the recognition was in one of two casual forms: (1) the familiar FDIC logo at the bank or (2) the radio or television commercial that ends with "member FDIC." People understand and take for granted that their deposits are insured (as of 1982 to $100,000). As a result, there is confidence in the banking system. However, while people know their deposits are insured and recognize the FDIC logo, they know very little about deposit insurance and the operations of the FDIC. The purpose of this section and material in the next chapter is to reduce that informational void.

Judging a Book by Its Cover[8]

The words behind the FDIC's initials describe only part of its formal operations. In addition to selling deposit insurance (at bargain *explicit* rates, incidentally), the FDIC performs four regulatory functions: (1) entry regulation, (2) examination, (3) regulation of deposit rates, and (4) disposition of failed and failing banks.

Entry Regulation

Since it is just about impossible to get a bank charter without deposit insurance, the entry of new firms into the industry is, in effect, controlled by the FDIC. This power enables the FDIC to protect the value of existing bank charters, which is the first line of defense for the deposit-insurance fund. The FDIC also rules on merger and branch proposals for nonmember banks.

Examination

Two-thirds of the FDIC's employees are associated with the bank-examination function. By inspecting and monitoring a bank's records, operations, policies, and management, the FDIC is able to extract *implicit* fees for deposit insurance. The combination of explicit and implicit fees gives the FDIC, in effect, a variable-rate deposit-insurance scheme. High-risk banks encounter regulatory interference and disincentives to such behavior. The overall purpose of the bank-examination process is to preserve a bank's capital so that its chapter value is maintained and the insurance fund protected.

Regulation of Deposit Rates

As explained above, this technique has been used to restrict a bank's ability to compete on a price basis so that its growth opportunities are reduced. The FDIC, prior to DIDMCA, set deposit-rate ceilings for insured nonmember banks and insured mutual savings banks (MSBs). These policies were coordinated with the Federal Reserve so that all commercial banks faced the same rate constraints. As required by DIDMCA, interest-rate ceilings were eliminated in 1986.

Disposition of Failed and Failing Banks

When an insured bank fails, the FDIC is responsible for disposing of the bank's assets and liabilities (and net worth, if there is any). Prior to failure, the FDIC has the power, under special circumstances, to provide financial assistance to *failing* banks. The techniques used in handling failed and failing banks are discussed in detail in Chapter 8.

Recapitulation

Deposit insurance has been the most important factor in establishing confidence in individual banks. As a result, there has been confidence in the banking system as a whole since the threat of a "domino failure effect" due to widespread deposit withdrawals is mitigated. In addition to its insurance function, the FDIC performs four regulatory functions: (1) entry regulation, (2) examination, (3) regulation of deposit rates, and (4) disposition of failed and failing banks. These regulations attempt to preserve banks' charter values, which are the front-line defense of the deposit-insurance fund.

---

[8] See Buser, Chen, and Kane [1981]. Deposit-insurance reforms are discussed in the next chapter.

THE OFFICE OF THE COMPTROLLER OF THE CURRENCY

If we can't judge the FDIC by its initials, what can we say about the OCC? Not much. The name of the agency is an historical relic dating back to the Civil War years when its function was to provide the nation with a safe and uniform currency system. Today, the OCC is simply the chartering and regulatory agency for national banks. The agency performs two regulatory functions: (1) entry-and-exit regulation and (2) examination.

The Comptroller's Strength-in-Banking Equation

At the 1984 ABA National Convention in New York City, C. T. Conover, then Comptroller of the Currency, proposed the following strength-in-banking equation:

Strength = New powers + Firm supervision

New powers refers to reregulation on the geographic and product frontiers, with the latter focused on insurance, securities, and real estate. Firm supervision is likely to be manifested in the form of (1) a modernized legal structure to accompany the new regulatory and competitive environment, (2) tougher enforcement for either violations of the law or imprudent banking practices, and (3) higher capital standards at the primary level. To encourage the process of change, the Comptroller urged bankers to do three things: (1) to send a consistent message regarding legislative changes through a united front with consideration given to other segments of the marketplace; (2) to garner the support of consumers and small businesses; and (3) to continue to be prudent bankers and honest custodians of depositors' money so that the public trust is maintained.

THE FEDERAL RESERVE SYSTEM

The Federal Reserve System is indeed a "system" because it is a decentralized organization with 50 offices spread throughout the United States.[9] The "glamorous" part of the system is the Fed's headquarters, the Board of Governors, in Washington, D.C. The "Board's" supporting cast includes (1) 12 district Federal Reserve Banks located in Boston, New York, Philadelphia, Cleveland, Richmond, Atlanta, Chicago, St. Louis, Minneapolis, Kansas City, Dallas, and San Francisco, (2) 25 branches of the district banks, (3) 11 regional check-processing centers,[10] and (4) a communications center called the Network Management Center located in Culpeper, Virginia.

As the central bank of the United States, the Fed mainly is concerned with the formulation and implementation of monetary policy. Since the Fed's role as central bank is covered extensively in money-and-banking courses, it will not be discussed here. As a bank regulator, the Fed's main responsibility is in the BHC area, a topic discussed in detail in the next chapter. In addition, the Fed is charged with examining the 1,000 or so state member banks, a task which could easily be handled by the FDIC and state banking agencies. Until 1986, deposit-rate ceilings for all member banks were set by the Fed.

[9] Kane [1981a] contends that the political rationale for the Fed's decentralized structure—i.e., quieting populist fears that the U.S. central bank would come to be dominated either by Wall Street (i.e., financial interests) or by Washington, D.C. (i.e., by elected federal politicians)—has become inoperative because fear of centralized government has long since been taken over by concern for accountability and cost-effectiveness in government activities. Kane provides an excellent discussion of the role of Federal Reserve Banks under DIDMCA.

[10] The subject of competition between the Fed and private suppliers to provide correspondent services to depository institutions was discussed in Chapter 6.

TABLE 7-1 Federal Reserve Regulations

Regulation	Subject Matter
A	Loans by the Fed to depository institutions
B	Equal credit opportunity
C	Home mortgage disclosure
D	Reserve requirements
E	Electronic funds transfers
F	Registration and filing of securities statements by state-chartered member banks
G	Extensions of credit to finance securities transactions
H	Membership requirements
I	Member stock in federal reserve banks
J	Check collection and funds transfer
K	International banking operations
L	Interlocking bank relationships
M	Consumer leasing
N	Relationships with foreign banks
O	Loans to executive officers of member banks
P	Member bank protection standards
Q[a]	Interest on deposits
R	Interlocking relationships between securities dealers and member banks
S	Reimbursement for providing financial records
T	Margin credit extended by brokers and dealers
U	Margin credit extended by banks
V	Guarantee of loans for national defense work
X[b]	Borrowers who obtain margin credit
Y	Bank holding companies
Z	Truth in Lending
AA	Consumer complaint procedures
BB	Community reinvestment

[a] As of 1986, the only remaining restriction was on the payment of interest on commerical demand deposits.
[b] Regulation W, which was revoked in 1952, pertained to extensions of consumer credit.
Source: "A Guide to Federal Reserve Regulations," Board of Governors of the Federal Reserve System [September, 1981].

The extent of the Fed's involvement in the regulation of the banking system is captured by its list of regulations shown in Table 7-1. As you can see, the Fed is on its second pass through the alphabet. Of course, without an expansive and elaborate turf to regulate, the Fed's role would be diminished vis-à-vis other regulatory agencies.

The Fed, as central bank, provides the lender-of-last-resort function to the economy. This function is an important one to bank managers because it means that when an emergency arises liquidity usually will be available from the discount window. The Fed, however, regards such borrowing as a privilege and conducts surveillance of the discount window to guard against abuses. For normal liquidity needs that can be anticipated (e.g., seasonal needs), the Fed is sympathetic and permits banks to arrange for such borrowing in advance. Attempts to arbitrage the discount window are considered an abuse of the borrowing privilege.

CONFERENCE OF STATE BANK SUPERVISORS (CSBS)

Just as the Fed, OCC, and FDIC attempt to cooperate on matters of bank regulation and supervision (through an interagency task force), the 50 state banking departments (plus three territorial departments) have a central organization called the Conference of State Bank Supervisors (CSBS).[11] Although each state agency concentrates on

[11] See Kreider [1978] for a detailed description of the CSBS.

regulatory matters in its own state, the CSBS provides a vehicle for cooperation among the various states. State banking departments perform two main functions (identical to the OCC): (1) entry-and-exit regulation and (2) examination. Regarding on-site examinations, state departments are handicapped by a lack of resources. Greater cooperation between the state agencies and the FDIC has resulted in a more efficient allocation of both federal and state resources. Regarding entry regulation, the FDIC plays an important *de facto* role at the state level because it would be highly unusual for a state charter to be granted without deposit insurance. Regarding the failure of state banks, only the chartering agency can declare a state bank insolvent. Then the FDIC usually is appointed receiver of the closed bank. Of the 1,000 or so insured commercial banks that failed from 1934 to 1986, roughly 80 percent have been state banks. The deposit size of the average failed state bank has been about $10 million, compared to $40 million for the average failed national bank. Because of their smaller size and greater tendency to be located in unit-banking states, failed state banks are more likely to be handled by the FDIC with the deposit-payoff method (e.g., 54 percent compared to 34 percent for failed national banks).

According to Kreider [1978], the CSBS has two major objectives: (1) to achieve and maintain strong and effective state banking departments nationwide and (2) to achieve and maintain a banking and bank regulatory structure with adequate state/federal checks and balances so as to minimize government monopoly in bank regulation. The latter can be interpreted as a mandate to preserve the dual-banking system.

Given this stance, it is not surprising that many members of the CSBS view the universal reserve requirements imposed by DIDMCA as an attempt by the Fed to undermine state banking authority. To counteract this federal power play and to avoid a potential "state membership problem," some banking commissioners (e.g., in California, Delaware, Georgia, Missouri, New York, and Pennsylvania) have eliminated or reduced reserve requirements for nonmember banks in their states. This federal–state regulatory competition for turf manifests the concepts of competition in laxity and structural arbitrage. State legislatures (e.g., in Delaware and South Dakota) are fostering such opportunities when they attempt to lure out-of-state affiliates of BHCs to their states. The demand for such opportunities can be traced to banks' efforts to reduce the burden of state tax and usury laws. Although DIDMCA has succeeded in diffusing the Fed's membership problem, it has not succeeded in diffusing the competition between federal and state regulators, which now has shifted to the issue of what banking services may be provided legally by nonbanking companies.

With the large number of small independent state banks, the CSBS can be viewed as having a large secondary constituency. In the past, the political clout of these banks has far exceeded their economic power. If a substantial consolidation of the banking industry occurs over the next decade, this political power will decline. On balance, the reregulation of the industry is viewed more kindly by larger banks.

THE NEED FOR REGULATORY AND INSURANCE REFORM

There will be a need for bank regulation as long as the banking authorities continue to provide the deposit-insurance and lender-of-last-resort functions. These functions, as they are currently administered, encourage a bank to hold as risky a portfolio as regulations permit, which creates the wrong kinds of incentives. Risk-based pricing of the insurance and lender functions would be a step in the right direction. Thus, a major problem of today's financial system, but one that is being addressed (albeit slowly), is the need for *structural* reform of the regulatory and insurance systems. Although these frameworks have worked effectively in the past, they have not kept pace with the revolution that has occurred in the financial-services industry over the past few years. An environment characterized by price and interest-rate volatility, major deregulation, intense competition, and extensive international financial activity requires a modern, fair, and flexible regulatory and insurance apparatus. Since the current system is antiquated, inequitable, and at times less than flexible, a major overhaul is needed.

CHAPTER SUMMARY

This chapter has focused on the theories, objectives, and agencies of U.S. banking regulation. Bank regulators usually have good intentions but in a dynamic system unintended evils and induced innovations frequently develop. The traditional forms of bank regulation have attempted to place constraints on a bank's ability to grow and diversify. These constraints have taken the form of interest-rate, geographic, and product-specialization restrictions. The U.S. system of bank regulation is a "jurisdictional tangle" comprised of four federal agencies (FDIC, OCC, Fed, and SEC) and 50 state banking departments. The regulatory dialectic provides a useful framework for studying the ongoing struggle between regulators and regulatees. In addition, such concepts as economies of scope, structural arbitrage, contestable markets, and customer confidence and convenience add richness to the analysis of TRICK and its effect on the new FSI.

LIST OF KEY WORDS, CONCEPTS, AND ACRONYMS

Bank holding company (BHC)
Banking eras (e.g., "free")
Competitive Equality Banking Act of 1987
Conference of State Bank Supervisors (CSBS)
Confidence and convenience functions
Contestable markets
Deposit insurance (FDIC and FSLIC)
Depository Institutions Deregulation and Monetary Control Act (DIDMCA)
Dual banking
Federal Deposit Insurance Corporation (FDIC)
Federal Home Loan Bank Board (FHLBB)
Federal Reserve System ("the Fed")
Federal Savings and Loan Insurance Corporation (FSLIC)

Financial-services industry (FSI)
Garn–St Germain Act of 1982
Government guarantees (role of)
Industrial organization (IO) model (structure-conduct-performance model)
National Bank Surveillance System (NBSS)
National Credit Union Administration (NCUA)
Objectives of bank regulation (safety, stability, and structure)
Office of the Comptroller of the Currency (OCC)
Regulatory dialectic ("struggle model")
Scope economies (economies of scope or joint production)
Securities and Exchange Commission (SEC)
Structural arbitrage

REVIEW/DISCUSSION QUESTIONS

1. What are the objectives of bank regulation? Discuss these objectives in terms of their economic foundations. How do the objectives conflict? Describe the varying degrees of emphasis that have been placed on the objectives over time. What trade-offs are currently taking place with respect to the objectives?

2. Regarding the SEC effect, disclosure, and market discipline, what differences, if any, are likely to exist within the *real* dual-banking system?

3. What is the relationship between competition and economic efficiency? How does the IO model aid in explaining the relationship? What is a "contestable market"?

4. What is the philosophical foundation of the regulatory dialectic? How well does the theory serve as an explanation of the regulatory process? Explain how the regulatory dialectic can be viewed as a theory of financial innovation.

5. What is the contestability theory of multimarket competition? How well does it explain (1) the process of change in the FSI and (2) regulatory behavior? Regarding the latter, explain the role of the confidence and convenience functions in the FSI. What are the three layers of financial-services competition?

6. How has bank regulation been used to frustrate asset growth and diversification strategies? What frustrations are bankers likely to face in the future?

7. "St. Paul Volcker Guns Down Billy the Kid Isaac." Chairman Issac of the FDIC proposed (in 1984) a new regulatory structure, unlike the one shown in Figure 7-1. St. Paul didn't like Billy's proposed gospel and when push came to shove he nailed the kid. Was Paul behaving unsaintly? Design a new regulatory structure that even the Fed can live with. With all of the concern about "turf," what are the chances for consolidation or major restructuring of the federal banking agencies?

8. Explain why you can't judge the FDIC by its cover (i.e., acronym). What about the OCC?

9. What are the important factors that regulators look at before they grant a bank charter? What role, if any, does the FDIC play in entry regulation?

10. During 1984, some bankers described OCC examiners as behaving in a "red-neck fashion" with respect to problem loans. How do these stories jibe with the Comptroller's strength-in-banking equation? What role, if any, do you think the OCC's embarrassments (e.g., Penn Square, Continental) have played in the development of the equation?

11. Federal Reserve Regulations A, D, Q, Y, and Z are more commonly known than the other members of the alphabet-soup gang. What are these five regulations?

12. Why are state banking agencies at a disadvantage vis-à-vis the federal ones? What are the chances that there will always be a (*de jure*) dual-banking system? Will there always be a *real* dual-banking system?

13. Analyze each of the major components of DIDMCA, the Garn–St Germain Act, and the Competitive Equality Banking Act in terms of its effect upon banking and the FSI with respect to:
    a. each of the components of TRICK
    b. the profit formula: $\pi = R - C - O - T$,
    c. the constant growth model: $P_0 = D_1/(k - g)$

MATCHING QUIZ

Directions: Select the letter from the right-hand column that best matches the item in the left-hand column.

___ 1. Deposit insurance	A. 1980 banking law
___ 2. Charters national banks	B. 1982 banking law
___ 3. Bankrupt insurer	C. 1979–
___ 4. Regulator objectives	D. Goes hand in hand with charter
___ 5. Supervises BHCs	E. Safety, stability, and structure
___ 6. DIDMCA	F. FHLBB
___ 7. Garn–St Germain Act	G. FSLIC
___ 8. Competitive Equality Act	H. OCC
___ 9. Regulatory dialectic	I. Early Warning System
___ 10. Contestable markets	J. NCUA
___ 11. Scope economies	K. structure-conduct-performance
___ 12. Structural arbitrage	L. Contains FSLIC rescue package
___ 13. IO model	M. Economies of joint production
___ 14. Chartered banking era	N. Struggle model
___ 15. Free banking era	O. Changes in organizational form
___ 16. Cartel banking era	P. Government guarantees critical
___ 17. Competitive banking era	Q. f(geog, prod, cost, qual)
___ 18. Confidence function	R. Hit-and-run tactics observed
___ 19. Convenience function	S. Federal Reserve
___ 20. Regulates thrifts	T. Federal and state jurisdiction
___ 21. SEC focus	U. 1933–1978
___ 22. "Jurisdictional tangle"	V. 1838–1932
___ 23. Regulates credit unions	W. 1776–1837
___ 24. Coordinates state agencies	X. Disclosure of information
___ 25. Dual banking	Y Description of U.S. bank regulation
___ 26. Detection of problem banks	Z. CSBS

PROBLEMS

1. Given the following information:

Technology	Economies of Scope	Avoidance Costs	Regulatory Costs
State I	20 – 16=	6	6
State II	20 – 14=	4	6

   Determine for each State the following:
   a. the costs of joint production
   b. scope economies
   c. scale economies
   d. the social costs of regulatory exclusion
   e. the enforceability of the exclusionary rule

2. Given a nominal deposit rate of 12 percent, calculate the effective cost of deposits for the following reserve requirements: 100%, 50%, 12%, 3%, and 0%.

APPENDIX A
The Depository Institutions Deregulation and Monetary Control Act of 1980 (DIDMCA)

If the schizophrenic title of this historic piece of legislation has you puzzled, remember that Big Brother has the power to give *and* to take away. Thus, in DIDMCA, Big Brother giveth deregulation, but not complete deregulation (i.e., reregulation), of major constraints on the behavior of depository institutions. Regulations always seem to die in a piecemeal fashion and the DID of DIDMCA was no exception as it was relaxed in a partial, gradual, and discretionary way. To oversee this phase-out, there was of course a Depository Institutions Deregulation Committee (DIDC).[1] The MC of DIDMCA is its restrictive part, the part where Big Brother taketh away. The control feature of DIDMCA slaps Federal reserve requirements for the first time on approximately 36,000 depository institutions consisting of roughly 9,000 nonmember commercial banks, 5,000 savings and loan associations, 500 mutual savings banks, and 22,000 credit unions. The law's nine titles and major points are summarized in Table 7-A1.

TABLE 7-A1   The Depository Institution Deregulation and Monetary Control Act of 1980 (Public Law 96–221)

Title I.	The Monetary Control Act
Title II.	Depository Institutions Deregulation Act
Title III.	Consumer Checking Account Equity Act
Title IV.	Powers of Thrift Institutions and Miscellaneous Provisions
Title V.	State Usury Laws
Title VI.	Truth-in-Lending Simplification and Reform Act
Title VII.	Amendments to the National Banking Laws
Title VIII.	Financial Regulation Simplification Act
Title IX.	Foreign Control of United States Financial Institutions

DIDMCA's Major points are:

1. Permits nationwide NOW accounts after December 31, 1980 (Title III).
2. Phases out deposit interest-rate ceilings over a six-year period (Title II).
3. Eliminates usury ceilings (Title V).
4. Increases level of federally insured deposits to $100,000 (Title III).
5. Requires reserves on all transactions accounts at depository institutions (Title I).
6. Permits the Federal Reserve Board to impose supplemental reserve requirements (Title I).
7. Provides access to the discount window (Title I).
8. Establishes fees for Fed services (e.g., check clearing and collection) (Title I).
9. Expands power of thrift institutions (Title IV).
10. Simplifies truth in lending disclosures and financial regulations (Titles VI and VIII).

Source: Capital [1980] and McCord [1980].

APPENDIX B
The Garn–St Germain Depository Institutions Act of 1982

The key provisions of the Depository Institutions Act of 1982 are summarized in Table 7-B1. In a nutshell, authorization for the money-market deposit account (MMDA) and provisions for saving the thrift industry were the highlights of the Act. The main features of the Act are summarized in this Appendix, which is excerpted from *Leveling the Playing Field* (pp. 31–33) published by the Federal Reserve Bank of Chicago in its series *Readings in Economics and Finance*, December, 1983.

The Main Features of the Act

The 1982 act is complex, containing eight titles dealing in detail with different areas of financial reform. To emphasize those aspects considered most important, details are passed over in the following summary. The discussion is divided into three sections: provisions permanently widening the sources of depository institution funds, and contributing toward the removal of interest-rate ceilings; provisions permanently expanding the uses of funds and other powers; and provisions that temporarily grant regulators emergency powers to deal with the current depository institution crises.

The Sources of Funds

The act makes four contributions to broadening the catchment area for funds.

1. The best known provision of the Garn–St Germain Act is its authorization (in Title III) for the new money market deposit account (MMDA). The Congress, impressed by the recent rapid growth of MMMFs, amended DIDMCA to authorize depository institutions to offer an account "directly equivalent to and competitive with money market mutual funds." This account, which has been widely available since December 14, 1982, is federally insured, pays an interest rate restricted only by the discretion of the institution (on initial and average

TABLE 7-B1 Key Provisions of the Garn–St Germain Depository Institutions Act of 1982

1. Federally chartered savings associations and savings banks gain new investment powers and restructuring changes.
2. FSLIC-insured institutions can tap new capital assistance program to boost net worth.
3. Federal preemption is extended to those state laws restricting due on sale and alternative mortgage instruments.
4. Broader authority is granted to the FSLIC and FDIC to aid troubled financial institutions.

maintained balances of $2,500 or more),[1] and has limited transaction features (six transfers per month: preauthorized, automatic, or by telephone, of which no more than three may be by check, but unlimited personal withdrawals). On personal accounts it carries no required reserves; a 3 percent reserve requirement is imposed on nonpersonal accounts. If the average balance falls below $2,500, the NOW account ceiling is applicable.

This authorization is regarded as a major breach of the regulatory barriers that restrict competition for funds by depository institutions. It came as a surprise, therefore, that the DIDC acted quickly to authorize another new account, available beginning January 5, 1983. This Super NOW account is restricted to the NOW account clientele (see below), has a minimum initial and maintained average balance of $2,250[2], has unlimited transaction features, and unregulated interest rates (it pays a NOW rate on balances below the $2,500 level). But it carries a reserve requirement as a transactions account—presently 12 percent.

2. Besides this major permission for market-interest-paying accounts, the act makes three other provisions to broaden depository institutions' ability to obtain funds. Title VII of the act permits federal, state, and local governments to hold NOW accounts. Previously these accounts had been limited to persons and to nongovernment, nonprofit organizations.

3. Federally chartered savings and loan associations are permitted to offer demand deposits to persons or organizations that have a business loan relationship with the association or that wish to receive payment due from nonbusiness customers (Title III). Previously, only commercial and mutual savings banks had been able to accept demand deposits.

4. The DIDC was required to remove by the beginning of 1984 any existing differential in the Regulation Q rate permitted to banks and thrifts (Title III). Previously, thrifts were typically permitted to offer a rate $\frac{1}{4}$ percent above that of commercial banks on most types of deposits subject to ceiling regulation.

The Uses of Funds and Other Powers

Both thrift and bank institutions benefit to some degree from the act's provisions for expanded powers. However, the powers of federal savings and loan associations and savings banks (SBs) are enhanced most by the act. Five sets of provisions are discussed below.

1. Title III authorizes federally chartered S&Ls and SBs for the first time to make overdraft loans; to invest in the accounts of other insured institutions; and most important, to make commercial loans. The act also enhances their powers to invest in state and local government obligations; to make residential and nonresidential real estate loans; to make consumer and educational loans.[3]

2. The existing state-imposed restrictions on the execution of the due-on-sale provisions of mortgage contracts are preempted in Title II for both federal and state institutions. The preemption is delayed for certain seriously affected ("window period") loans, and is prohibited in the case of within-family property transfers.

---

[1] On January 1, 1985, minimum balances were reduced to $1,000 and removed on January 1, 1986.

[2] *Ibid.*

[3] S&Ls now have powers to take demand deposits and to make commercial loans. These are the critical elements necessary to meet the Federal Reserve's definition of a bank. Therefore, in order for S&Ls to avoid the restrictions incumbent on that classification, the definition of a bank has been amended to exclude institutions insured by the FSLIC or chartered by the FHLBB.

3. Thrifts are given wide powers in Title III to alter their charters. They can convert from state to federal charter and conversely, where state law permits. They may switch between mutual and stock form and between savings and loan association and savings bank charters.

4. State banks and thrifts are empowered in Title VIII to offer the alternative, variable-rate, mortgage instruments that are permitted to their federal counterparts.

5. National banks receive some relatively minor adjustment of their powers. For example, the "safety and soundness" limitations on the size of loans made to a single borrower are relaxed. Previously, a bank could lend no more than 10 percent of its capital and surplus to any individual borrower. Now, that percentage is raised to 15 percent plus an additional 10 percent for loans secured by readily marketable collateral. However, these limitations will henceforth be applied to loans made to foreign governments and their agencies. Also, restrictions on bank real estate lending and on "insider" loans are relaxed. Banks are also permitted to charter "bankers' banks" and the scope of bank service corporation activities is broadened. However, new restrictions are placed on the large bank holding companies.

Emergency Powers

Titles I and II of the act enhance, for three years, the powers of the Federal Deposit Insurance Corporation (FDIC) and Federal Savings and Loan Insurance Corporation (FSLIC) to aid troubled banks and thrifts.[4] The agencies can aid institutions which are closed, insolvent, in default or so endangered; or where severe financial conditions exist that threaten the stability of the financial system; or in order to reduce the corporations' exposure to loss. They are empowered to take six types of action. They can issue guarantees; purchase or assume an insured institution's assets or liabilities (but, to preclude nationalization, not its common stock); make loans and contributions to and deposits in a troubled insured institution or company that will acquire it; organize charter conversions; arrange extraordinary mergers and acquisitions; and issue net worth certificates to banks and thrifts with substantial residential real estate loans.

The act provides a framework for both the FDIC and FSLIC to arrange emergency acquisitions of failing institutions across geographic and institutional barriers. While many opposed these powers on the grounds that they would blur the distinction between banks and thrifts and open the door to interstate banking, the regulators argued successfully that they need these provisions to avert potential crises. In some particularly hard-hit regions, it had become increasingly difficult to find merger partners that fit the old rules. In fact, during 1982, the Federal Reserve Board (FRB) and the FHLBB had already authorized both interstate and interindustry mergers, including Citicorp's controversial acquisition of Fidelity Federal Savings and Loan Association of Oakland, Calif.

Under the new rules the FDIC can authorize the acquisition of a large, closed commercial bank, or a closed or endangered mutual savings bank (assets over $500 million) by another federally insured institution, in-state or out-of-state. The FSLIC may exercise such powers regardless of the size of the failing thrift. Further, any qualified purchaser, including out-of-state banks, holding companies, other insured institutions, or *any* other acceptable company may submit bids for the failed thrift. Any

---

[4] The act gives similar powers to the National Credit Union Administration (NCUA) to aid troubled credit unions.

federally insured depository institution can bid for a failed large bank. If the lowest bid comes not from an in-state, similar-type institution, all within-the-ball-park bidders may bid again. Then the corporation must attempt to minimize its risk of loss subject to the following priorities:

   i.   like, in-state institutions
   ii.   like, out-of-state institutions
   iii.   different, in-state institutions
   iv.   different, out-of-state institutions
   v.   among out-of-state bidders, priority is to be given to adjacent state institutions
   vi.   the FSLIC, but not the FDIC, is to give priority to minority-controlled bidders when a minority-controlled thrift fails.

Provisions are made for consultation with state regulators where appropriate.

CHAPTER 7

APPENDIX C
The Competitive Equality Banking Act of 1987

The passage of this Act marked the first major banking legislation since 1982. Two key aspects of the bill were the grandfathering of more than 160 nonbank banks, including those owned by Sears and American Express, and a $10.8 billion rescue package for the FSLIC. The primary architect of the legislation, Senator William Proxmire (D-Wis) predicted the law would mark the demise of nonbank banks. In contrast, the reaction from Sears' executives was that the legislation would not stop them from expanding in the FSI. The key provisions of the Competitive Equality Banking Act are summarized below.[1]

Key Banking Bill Provisions

Nonbank Banks

The bill closes the loophole that has permitted Sears, Roebuck and Co. and other commercial enterprises to own limited-service banks. It grandfathers the 160 or so existing nonbank banks, but with restrictions on their activities. Among other things, the nonbank banks cannot cross-market products and services with their parents. One year after the bill becomes law, the limited-service institutions will be held to growth of 7% annually.

In addition, the bill contains exemptions for bona fide trust companies and credit card banks, and permits owners of nonbank banks to bid for failing thrifts of $500 million or more in assets.

Restraints on Commercial Banks

Several moratoria on new services are contained in the bill. First, it prohibits federal regulators from permitting banks to engage in new insurance, real estate, or securities activities. The moratoria are generally retroactive to March 6 of this year and would expire after March 1, 1988.

A section aimed at the Office of the Comptroller of the Currency forbids the agency from permitting banks, "by action, inaction or otherwise," to engage in any securities activity not legally authorized in writing prior to March 5, 1987. This section would prevent Marine Midland Banks, for example, from serving with Salomon Brothers again as comanager of an underwriting of securities backed by auto receivables.

The bill also prohibits regulators from permitting banks to operate a nondealer marketplace in options, a section aimed specifically at Security Pacific National Bank,

---

[1] The summary presented here is from the *American Banker* [August 7, 1987], p. 2.

Los Angeles, which applied to the Fed for approval to provide back-office support for options trading.

State-chartered banks that are not members of the Federal Reserve System would be covered by sections of the Glass–Steagall Act, which prohibit banks from affiliations with companies principally engaged in securities activities. Previously, state-chartered non-member banks were exempt from Glass–Steagall.

The bill does not affect the authority of states to grant new insurance powers to state-chartered institutions.

Rescuing the Federal Savings and Loan Insurance Corp.

The FSLIC, technically insolvent, would be authorized to raise $10.8 billion over three years through a newly chartered financing corporation, which will be headed by the director of the office of finance of the Federal Home Loan Banks and two district home loan bank presidents. No more than $3.75 billion can be raised in any one year. The recapitalization includes $825 million specifically to permit replenishment of the secondary reserve, which was depleted earlier this year when the General Accounting Office declared FSLIC insolvent. The reserve had been carried as an asset on the books of thrifts.

The financing corporation will be required to purchase zero coupon bonds from the U.S. Treasury in sufficient volume to assure repayment of the principal amount of its borrowings. Interest will be paid from FSLIC's regular income, including assessments on deposits. Bonds issued by the financing company will be subject to federal, but not state, taxes.

For one year following enactment of the bill, FSLIC-insured institutions will be prohibited from leaving the insurance fund. After that, they may apply for membership in the Federal Deposit Insurance Corp., if they meet requirements of the bank industry insurance fund. But they must pay an "exit fee" to the FSLIC equal to two times the annual and special FSLIC assessments they pay on deposits. Institutions that applied to leave FSLIC on or before March 31 are exempt from exit fees.

The FSLIC is required to phase out by 1991 the special assessment it now charges member institutions, unless the Federal Home Loan Bank Board determines that "severe pressures" warrant a continuation of the assessment.

Supervisory Forbearance

The bill requires that the Federal Home Loan Bank Board give troubled thrifts time to work out their problems. The forbearance program is intended to apply to well-managed thrifts in depressed regions of the country—particularly the energy and farm belts. Institutions must apply to the Bank Board for permission to participate. The section expires when FSLIC has exhausted its borrowing authority.

Thrifts with net worth as low as 0.5%, well below what is required by either bank or thrift regulators, must be granted capital forbearance. Savings and loans with even lower net worth are eligible for forbearance if the Bank Board determines that the institution has a reasonable chance of recovery. Regulators are also required to encourage institutions to restructure problem loans and to permit thrifts to use accounting rules, which would avoid writing down restructured loans. Thrifts are required to move toward generally accepted accounting principles.

The law also requires the Federal Asset Disposition Association, which was created to dispose of assets acquired from failing thrifts, to submit to annual audits by the General Accounting Office, an arm of Congress.

Regulatory Authority

The Federal Deposit Insurance Corp. is authorized to arrange interstate takeovers of failing institutions with assets of more than $500 million, so long as the agency provides financial assistance in the transaction. The FDIC is required to give priority in the bidding process to banks from states with interstate banking laws. In the case of failing minority-owned banks, the FDIC is required to give preference to other minority institutions. The bill also permits the FDIC to establish bridge banks to operate failed banks until purchasers can be found.

The bill takes bank, thrift, and credit union regulators out from under the authority of the Office of Management and Budget and exempts them from the Gramm–Rudman–Hollings budget balancing act.

Check Clearing

By September 1, 1990, the Federal Reserve must have in place regulations requiring banks, thrifts, and credit unions to clear local checks within one intervening business day, and other items within four intervening business days. A temporary schedule takes effect September 1, 1988, giving institutions two intervening business days to make available funds from local checks and six days for other items. The bill also requires disclosure of check hold policies.

Credit Union Amendments

The National Credit Union Administration is authorized to permit credit unions to offer mortgage loans of more than 15 years—the current maturity limit—and to appoint conservators for troubled institutions.

Farm Loans

Agricultural banks are permitted to write down farm loans over a seven-year period, rather than immediately deducting loan losses from capital.

SELECTED REFERENCES

Annual Report, FDIC. Washington, D.C. (various issues).

Apcar, Leonard. [1987]. "Frightened Money," *The Wall Street Journal* (September 1), pp. 1 and 14.

Baumol, William J. [1982]. "Contestable Markets: An Uprising in the Theory of Industry Structure," *The American Economic Review* (March), pp. 1–15.

Baumol, W. J., J. C. Panzar, R. D. Willig. [1983]. "On the Theory of Perfectly Contestable Markets." Bell Laboratories, Economic Discussion Paper #268 (June).

Benston, George J. [1973]. *Bank Examination*. Rochester, NY: University of Rochester, Center for Research in Government Policy and Business, Reprint Series No. C-16.

Bowden, Elbert V. [1980]. *Revolution in Banking*. Richmond, VA: Robert F. Dame, Inc.

Bremer, C. D. [1935]. *American Bank Failures*. New York: Columbia University Press.

Burns, A. F. [1974]. "Maintaining the Soundness of Our Banking System." Federal Reserve Bank of New York, *Monthly Review* (November), pp. 263–267.

Buser, Stephen A., Andrew H. Chen, and Edward J. Kane. [1981]. "Federal Deposit Insurance, Regulatory Policy, and Optimal Bank Capital." *Journal of Finance* (March), pp. 51–60.

Regulatory Restrictions, Financial Innovation, and Deposit Insurance

---

ACRONYM GUIDE TO KEY TERMS AND CONCEPTS

BHC = bank holding company
BOPEC = the Fed's BHC rating system
CAMEL = the federal banking agencies' bank rating system
MBHC = multibank holding company
OBHC = one-bank holding company

INTRODUCTION

The bank-holding-company (BHC) movement, the payment of implicit interest (i.e., nonprice competition), and the exploitation of deposit-insurance subsidies have been three important innovations in commercial banking over the past three decades. These phenomena were encouraged by government regulations: the BHC movement by geographic and product restrictions, implicit interest by interest-rate restrictions, and deposit-insurance subsidies by the mispricing of deposit insurance. This chapter focuses on explaining why and how such innovations occur and their implications for the management, regulation, and structure of commercial banking. The major theme of the chapter is that regulatory forces (in conjunction with market forces, e.g., technological change) induce financial innovations—which in turn, because the regulators are slow to act and react, necessitates the need for regulatory and insurance reforms. The process can be viewed in the framework of the regulatory dialectic with the interaction among the components of TRICK as the core of the process of change. The chapter focuses on an analysis of the BHC movement followed by and analysis of the payment of implicit interest. Next, a detailed review of the deposit insurance system is presented. The chapter concludes with a look at the need for reform of the regulatory and insurance structures.

THE EFFECTS OF REGULATION: GOOD INTENTIONS AND UNINTENDED EVILS

In general, the process of regulation can be viewed as trying to control the shape of an inflated balloon. When one part of the balloon is squeezed, the air rushes to another part. Squeeze it somewhere else and a similar result is achieved. Place too many hands on the balloon or squeeze with too much force and the balloon will burst. In this analogy, the squeezing hand represents bank regulation, the rushing air is bankers' attempts to innovate or circumvent the heavy hand of regulation, and the balloon represents the banking system. The bursting balloon represents, at the extreme, what heavy-handed regulation will do to any system if that system is controlled too tightly.

Two of the most important innovations in commercial banking, the negotiable CD and the holding-company movement, were developed (in part at least) to circumvent interest-rate and geographic restrictions, respectively. A more recent example is Citicorp's decision to move its credit-card operations to South Dakota, a state without usury laws. Citicorp found a provision (in the federal law that prohibits interstate branching) that allows banks to set up brand-new banks in other states, if they are invited to do so by the state's legislature. You can guess what happened from there. Hans Angermueller, Citicorp's regulatory expert, symbolizes the "rushing-air" attitude with these words: "We're willing to go to bat either by pushing forward with innovation until stopped or by trying to persuade legislators to drop restrictions or modify them."[1] In this view of the regulatory world, innovations are seen as being induced by regulation.

GEOGRAPHIC RESTRICTIONS: THE McFADDEN ACT OF 1927

One way to impose uniformity on the dual-banking system is to have both national and state banks subject to the same laws. This could be achieved, for example, by having a federal law simply state that for certain activities national banks are subject to the banking laws of the state in which their main or head office is located. This is exactly what the McFadden Act of 1927 does with respect to the branching authority of national banks. The Act, which was intended as an antibranching law, originally was very restrictive in that banks were permitted to establish branches *only* in the same community as their main office. Scott [1979] refers to these facilities as "inside branches." In 1933, the McFadden Act was amended to permit national banks to establish branches *elsewhere* in their home-office state (i.e., "outside branches"), provided that state law granted such authority to state banks, and under the same locational restrictions as applied to state banks.[2] Thus, on a state-by-state basis, the McFadden Act produces fairly uniform criteria for branching by both national and state banks. However, there is no statutory uniformity *across* states with respect to branching. There are three broad categories of geographic restrictions by state, referred to as unit-banking states (U), *limited*-branching states (L), and *statewide*-branching states (S).

It is interesting to note that the McFadden Act per se does not forbid interstate branching; it only prohibits interstate branching by national banks. Thus, interstate branching could develop either by repeal of the McFadden Act or by relaxation of state laws. The latter already has occurred in most regions of the country as states (e.g., Georgia and Florida) have entered into reciprocal interstate branching agreements. The hallmark of these early compacts has been the exclusion of states in which money-center banks are located from participation in the agreements. The intended effect of these exclusionary clauses is to give regional BHCs time to grow, through mergers with other regionals, to some unspecified size at which they can successfully

---

[1] Quoted by Julie Salamon in "Challenges Lie Ahead for Dynamic Citicorp …," *The Wall Street Journal* [December 18, 1980], pp. 1 and 24.

[2] The Amendment was part of the Banking Act of 1933 (also referred to as the Glass–Steagall Act). One of the major provisions of the 1933 Act was the separation of commercial and investment banking.

ward off any takeover attempts by money-center banks. Of course, once state branching laws are changed, then, according to the McFadden Act, national banks in those states have the same branching privileges.

In 1956, a loophole in the McFadden Act, which would have permitted the interstate *acquisition* of banks, was closed by the Douglas Amendment to the Act.[3] The Amendment stated that a bank or BHC in one state could not acquire a bank in another state. Prior to 1956, some BHCs had acquired banks in states outside their home state. However, because the United States Constitution forbids for passage of *ex post facto* laws, these organizations were permitted to keep their interstate banks. Such banks are said to be "grandfathered" and are referred to as "grandfather banks" (meaning that they were established prior to the law that forbade the activity). Just as interstate branching could come about as a result of a reciprocal agreement between two state legislatures, interstate acquisitions by BHCs could be authorized by similar agreements. As will be discussed later in this chapter, BHCs are permitted to have *nonbank* subsidiaries located in states outside of the one in which they are headquartered.

What have been the implications of the McFadden Act and its amendments for the management, regulation, and structure of commercial banking? The regulatory reflex of 1927, cushioned by a secondary reflex in 1933 and tightened by a tertiary reflex in 1956, has set in motion a dialectic process of confrontation over geographic restrictions between banks and the banking agencies. The major vehicle in this process has been the BHC movement, a phenomenon that has had a significant effect on the banking structure. Today, BHCs are the dominant form of organizational structure in commercial banking as they control the majority of banking assets. In achieving this dominance, the exploiting of loopholes in BHC regulations and the subsequent closing of those gaps by the banking authorities have been a common occurrence. The OBHC loophole permitted by the BHC Act of 1956 and its subsequent closing by the 1970 Amendment to the Act is a prime example of this dialectic process.[4] The unintended evils of the McFadden Act have evolved as a result of developments that were unforeseen by the makers of the law. They include such phenomena as technological developments in banking, the entry and growth of thrifts in banking markets, and the provision of financial services by non-financial corporations—in general, structural changes in the components of TRICK.

WHAT IS A BHC?

A bank holding company or BHC is simply any organization (e.g., corporation, partnership, or association) that *controls* one or more banks in the United States. What constitutes control is an important issue in this definition. Under present BHC laws, direct *or* indirect control of more than 25 percent of a bank's voting shares requires an organization or company to register with the Fed as a BHC. If the company owns less than 5 percent of the voting shares, the law assumes an absence of control. Ownership between 5 percent and 25 percent is defined as a "gray area" in which the Fed has discretionary power to determine whether such ownership constitutes control.

There are two major forms of BHCs: (1) those that control only one bank or one-bank holding companies (OBHCs) and (2) those that control two or more banks

---

[3] Loopholes for foreign banks in the McFadden Act and the Glass–Steagall Act were closed by the International Banking Act of 1978.

[4] The loophole was that the BHC Act of 1956 did not apply to OBHCs. The Act and the loophole are discussed in detail later in this chapter.

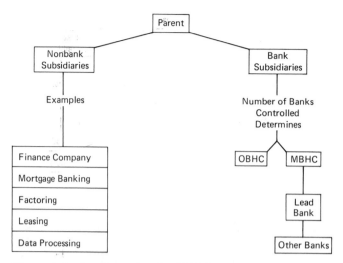

Figure 8-1   An Example of a BHC Structure

or multibank holding companies (MBHCs). BHCs developed for three primary reasons: (1) to circumvent geographic restrictions regarding branching, (2) to provide a broader menu of financial services (i.e., to circumvent product restrictions), and (3) to reap potential tax benefits from the BHC organizational form. According to Eisenbeis [1983], tax considerations probably have been the single most important factor in the formation of BHCs. The fact that most BHCs are single-subsidiary companies, which cannot benefit from diversification in terms of products or geography, strongly supports his claim. Focusing on the nontax considerations, OBHCs that engage in nonbanking activities primarily are motivated by the second reason, whereas MBHCs without nonbanking activities primarily are motivated by the first reason. The broadening the menu of financial services also has a geographic flavor to it, since the nonbanking activities of BHCs are not subject to geographic restrictions. Finally, MBHCs with nonbanking activities see both reasons as being important in motivating their development.[5]

A BHC's subsidiaries or affiliates can be divided into those engaged in banking and nonbanking activities. An example of a BHC organizational structure is presented in Figure 8-1. Nonbanking subsidiaries may include such activities as a finance company, a mortgage-banking company, or a service corporation. Frequently, there is confusion about the cash flows associated with a BHC. Figure 8-2 attempts to eliminate that possibility. Four important groups are depicted in this cash-flow diagram: (1) the public investors or owners, (2) the parent holding company, (3) subsidiaries, and (4) external creditors. The two-party cash flows illustrated in the diagram are fairly self-explanatory. However, one three-party transaction that is not self-evident occurs when parent debt is invested in subsidiaries as equity. Such a condition is referred to as "double leverage."[6] If the parent-issued debt simply is downstreamed to subsidiaries as debt, it is called "simple leverage."

Focusing upon Figures 8-1 and 8-2, let's consider the major tax advantages of a BHC (see Eisenbeis [1983], pp. 141–143). Since the major source, and frequently the only

---

[5] See Searle [1978] for a detailed look at the potential advantages and disadvantages of the BHC form of organization.

[6] For a more detailed discussion of double leverage see DeBussey [1978] and Boczar and Talley [1978]. The concept of double leverage is covered in detail in Chapter 14.

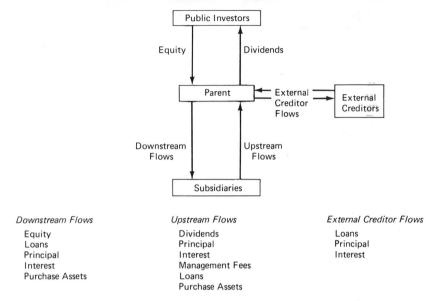

Figure 8-2   The Cash Flows Associated with a Bank Holding Company

Source: Eisemann and Budda [1980], exhibit 1, page 5. Reprinted by permission.

source,[7] of income for the BHC parent is *tax-deductible* dividends from its subsidiaries, the parent company usually starts with a zero or a very small *taxable* cash inflow. Thus, after interest and other expenses are paid, the parent company usually has negative taxable income. Consequently, since a consolidated tax return may be filed for the entire organization, the negative tax flow is used to reduce—or offset completely—positive taxable income in other parts of the company. Two additional tax considerations have encouraged the expansion of BHCs: (1) the opportunity to avoid *local* taxes by establishing subsidiaries in states or municipalities other than where the institution is headquartered and (2) the opportunity to avoid *federal* income taxes by conducting foreign operations through separately chartered subsidiaries rather than through foreign branches (i.e., in so-called tax havens, especially in the Caribbean islands). Regarding the second incentive, under present tax law, only repatriated income from *subsidiaries* is subject to United States tax; in contrast, all income from foreign *branches* is subject to full taxation. Thus, the tax incentive is to establish subsidiaries in low-tax countries and to repatriate, in the form of dividends, as little income as possible to the United States parent.

The Dominance and Growth of BHCs

As of December 31, 1985, there were roughly 6,000 BHCs in the United States. These organizations controlled nine out of every ten dollars in the (domestic) banking system, whether measured by total deposits or total assets. Using foreign data, the concentrations are only slightly higher at 92 percent for assets and 91 percent for deposits. Clearly, BHCs are the dominant organizational form in the banking system.

The most common type of BHC is the OBHC, as 85 percent of companies fit this description. However, the average OBHC only has about $80 million of deposits. In contrast, the average MBHC has about $1.4 billion of deposits across an average of five

[7] If the parent company is an operating company (i.e., if it is something other than just a "shell"), then it potentially has other sources of income.

TABLE 8-1   The Growth of Bank Holding Companies

(A) The Growth of BHCs

Year	Registered BHCs[a]	BHC Subsidiary Banks		BHC Deposits Relative to Total Deposits
		Number	Deposits ($ billions)	
1956	53	428	14.8	7.5%
1960	47	426	18.2	8.0%
1965	53	468	27.5	8.3%
1968	71	629	57.6	13.2%
1970	11	895	78.1	16.2%
1971	1,567	2,420	297.0	55.1%
1973	1,667	3,097	446.6	65.4%
1975	1,821	3,674	527.5	67.1%
1977	1,948	3,908	814.3	72.0%
1982	4,289	6,719	1,080.8	80.0%
1985	5,946	9,256	1,595.2	89.3%

(B) The Growth of OBHCs

Year	OBHCs	Total Deposits ($ billions)	OBHC Deposits Relative to Total Deposits
1965	548	13.9	4.5%
1968	783	108.2	27.5%
1970[b]	1,116	138.8	32.6%
1973	1,449	224.7	32.9%
1977	1,607	403.5	35.7%
1982	3,802	469.4	33.9%
1985	5,077	395.2	22.2%

(C) The Growth of MBHCs

Year	MBHCs	MBHC Banks	Total Deposits ($ billions)	MBHC Deposits Relative to Total Deposits
1965	53	468	27.6	8.3%
1968	74	629	57.6	13.2%
1970	111	895	78.1	16.2%
1973	218	1,726	233.3	34.2%
1977	341	2,301	410.8	36.3%
1982	487	2,917	639.1	46.1%
1985	869	3,981	1,199.9	67.8%

[a] Until 1971 only MBHCs were required to register with the Fed. Thus, in Panel A, for the years 1956 to 1970, OBHCs are not included, but they are listed separately in Panel B.
[b] As of April, all other figures are as of December 31.
Source: Board of Governors of the Federal Reserve System.

banks. Of the 14,367 commercial banks in the United States in 1985, 9,256 (64 percent) were owned by BHCs. The growth of BHCs in terms of numbers of companies and total deposits for the period 1956 to 1985 is shown in Table 8-1.

The BHC as a Vehicle for Circumventing Geographic Restrictions

To the extent that geographic restrictions encourage the development of BHCs, they should be more prevalent in states that restrict branching. This hypothesis is supported by the data shown in Table 8-2. As of year-end 1985, there were 5,522 BHCs

TABLE 8-2 BHCs and Branching Restrictions December 31, 1985

Branching Restrictions[a]	Number of States + D.C.	BHCs		State Deposits	
		Number	Percent	$ Billions	Percent
U	8	2,338	35	308.7	19
L	18	3,184	48	491.6	31
S	25	1,140	17	800.7	50
TOTAL	51	6,662	100	1,601.0	100

[a] Code: U = Unit banking
  L = Limited branching
  S = Statewide branching
  Source: American Statistical Digest [1986], Table 80, p. 199. Since companies that are subsidiaries of BHCs are included here, the totals are different from those in Table 8-2.

(83 percent of all BHCs) located in states with either unit or limited-branching restrictions. Earlier data were even more supportive of this hypothesis. For example, in 1982, when there were 11 unit-banking states, 53 percent of BHCs were found in those states. As more and more states liberalize their branching laws, this hypothesis becomes more and more obsolete. For example, in 1977, the unit, limited-branching, and statewide-branching numbers (U,L,S) were [12,16,22]; in 1982, they were [11,16,23]; and in 1985, they were [8,18,24].

Table 8-3 shows further support for the hypothesis that branching restrictions encourage the development of BHCs. The three states with the greatest number of BHCs in either 1982 or 1985 were the unit-banking states of Illinois, Texas, and Kansas. There were 1,552 BHCs in these three states in 1985 compared to 1,184 in 1982. In 1977, there were only 463 BHCs in Kansas (194), Illinois (181), and Texas (88). Again, the 1982 data are more supportive of the hypothesis than the 1985 data. For example, in 1982, there were only three limited-branching states and no statewide-branching states in the top ten. In contrast, in 1985, there were five limited-branching states and one statewide-branching state in the top ten. Although the top ten states ranked by number of BHCs have over one-half the number of BHCs and banks, they have only 35.6 percent of the deposits in the domestic banking system.

Turning to Table 8-4, except for Colorado, the top ten states ranked by degree of deposit control are all statewide-branching states. Tiny Rhode Island leads the way with 98.6 percent of their deposits controlled by BHC banks. However, BHC control of deposits is also evident in such states as New York and California where the percentages are 97.9 and 93.5, respectively. Comparing Table 8-3 with Table 8-4, the percentage of deposits controlled by the two groups in 1985 is about the same, but the concentrated group does it with only 721 BHCs and 1,831 banks compared to 3,583 BHCs and 7,845 banks for the other group.

Finally, let's turn to Table 8-5, which shows the top ten states ranked by BHC total deposits. With the large number of money-center banks located in the "Big Apple," it is not surprising that New York with only 88 BHCs, about 1.3 percent of the total number of BHCs, controls almost 13 percent of BHC total deposits. In addition to New York with $230 billion, the other states with more than $100 billion in total deposits are California with $193 billion, Texas with $156 billion, and Illinois with $103 billion. It is not surprising that the states shown in Table 8-4 correlate strongly with the population, industrial, and economic centers of the United States. Counting New York and California as centers unto themselves, the sun, oil, and rust belts are all represented in Table 8-5.

TABLE 8-3   The Top Ten States Ranked by Number of BHCs Domestic Data Only

Panel A. December 31, 1985

State	Number of BHCs	Subsidiary Banks		State Percentages	
		Number	Total Deposits (Millions of $)	Offices	Deposits
1. Texas (U)	602	1,936	155,986	69.2	86.4
2. Illinois (U)	525	1,235	102,923	69.8	85.4
3. Kansas (U)	425	623	20,658	76.9	83.1
4. Minnesota (L)	400	735	36,771	80.4	90.5
5. Iowa (L)	346	622	24,864	81.7	82.5
6. Oklahoma (L)	322	534	27,287	72.9	84.1
7. Nebraska (L)	293	453	13,750	75.2	85.5
8. Missouri (U)	247	673	39,565	81.2	89.6
9. California (S)	218	460	193,466	81.1	93.5
10. Wisconsin (L)	205	574	31,329	73.7	80.2
Ten state totals	3,583	7,845	636,599	28.9	35.6
All states + D.C.	5,985	14,367	1,786,340	NA	NA
Top ten/all states	59.9%	54.6%	35.6%	NA	NA

Panel B. December 31, 1982

State	Number of BHCs	Subsidiary Banks		State Percentages	
		Number	Total Deposits (Billions of $)	Banks	Deposits
1. Illinois (U)	417	476	65.9	38.0	71.8
2. Texas (U)	395	845	94.9	52.8	78.8
3. Kansas (U)	372	380	12.2	61.3	73.8
4. Minnesota (L)	325	463	23.3	61.0	83.1
5. Oklahoma (U)	292	292	19.7	57.1	78.5
6. Iowa (L)	288	382	14.8	59.2	68.9
7. Nebraska (U)	286	292	9.1	62.9	79.9
8. Missouri (U)	209	467	26.0	63.6	82.5
9. Colorado (U)	141	281	14.5	66.6	89.1
10. Wisconsin (L)	141	281	15.0	44.7	61.7
TOTALS	2,866	4,159	295.4	28.7	26.6

Notes: The letter in parentheses in the state column indicates the branching code for the state: (U) = unit banking, (L) = limited branching, and (S) = statewide branching. The figure given in the offices column of state percentages for 1985 is for banks *and* branches as a percentage of total commercial banking offices in the state. The total banking offices in these ten states in 1985 were 16,920, more than double the number of banks. NA indicates not applicable.

Sources: American Statistical Digest [1986], Table 80 and Board of Governor of the Federal Reserve System.

Recapitulation

The data presented in Tables 8-1 to 8-5 clearly demonstrate the rapid growth and dominance of BHCs as the leading organizational structure in the United States banking system. Although the current configuration of BHCs supports the conjecture that they were developed, in part, to circumvent branching restrictions, earlier data are even more convincing. As more and more states remove branching restrictions, as regional banking grows and grows, and as technology spans the globe with electronic funds transfer systems, the idea of restricting a bank to a single location (or two) becomes more and more obsolete. Cast in terms of our model of change (i.e., TRICK + rational self-interest) and the regulatory dialectic, the evolution and rapid growth of BHCs is easily explained. Specifically, with taxes and geographic and product controls restricting bankers (the thesis), they found an innovative form of organizational structure, the BHC (the antithesis), to circumvent the constraints. The

TABLE 8-4 The Top Ten States Ranked by Degree of Deposit Control by BHCs December 31, 1985

State	Percent of State Deposits	BHCs	Subsidiary Banks	
			Number	Deposits ($millions)
1. Rhode Island (S)	98.6	12	16	6,502
2. New York (S)	97.9	88	194	229,914
3. Arizona (S)	95.7	26	52	20,865
4. Massachusetts (S)	95.1	43	115	45,637
5. Florida (S)	94.4	163	424	73,366
6. North Carolina (S)	94.2	20	63	32,642
7. California (S)	93.5	182	460	193,466
8. Colorado (U)	92.4	168	459	21,007
9. Hawaii (S)	91.4	7	22	7,959
10. Idaho (S)	90.6	12	26	5,966
Ten state totals	35.7	721	1,831	637,324
All states + D.C.	100.0	5,985	14,367	1,786,340
Top ten/all states	35.7%	12.0%	12.7%	35.7%

Notes: (U) = unit banking, (L) = limited branching, and (S) = statewide branching. Deposits are domestic data only.
Source: American Statistical Digest [1986], Table 80.

TABLE 8-5 The Top Ten States Ranked by BHC Total Deposits December 31, 1985

State[a]	Deposits ($Millions)	BHCs	Number of Offices	
			Banks	Branches
1. New York (S)	229,914	88	194	3,402
2. California (S)	193,466	182	460	4,882
3. Taxes (U)	155,986	602	1,936	391
4. Illinois (U)	102,923	525	1,235	778
5. Pennsylvania (L)	92,760	102	312	2,808
6. Florida (S)	73,366	163	424	2,224
7. Ohio (L)	63,247	72	320	2,571
8. Michigan (S)	57,764	58	458	2,187
9. New Jersey (S)	50,004	43	126	1,800
10. Massachusetts (S)	45,637	43	115	1,087
Ten state totals	1,065,067	1,878	5,580	23,299
All states + D.C.	1,786,340	5,985	14,367	44,227
Top ten/all states	59.6%	31.4%	38.8%	52.7%

Notes: (U) = unit banking, (L) = limited branching, and (S) = statewide branching. Deposit data are domestic only.
Source: American Statistical Digest [1986], Table 80.

synthesis is the ongoing struggle between the regulator and the regulatees. Of course, the development of the BHC movement created the opportunity for a regulatory reflex in the form of BHC regulation, the topic of the next section.

THE REGULATION OF BHCs

Federal regulation of BHCs began with the Banking Act of 1933, which was the reflex action of the United States Congress to the banking difficulties of the late 1920s and early 1930s. Today, however, BHC regulation is based on the BHC Act of 1956 and its subsequent amendments.

The BHC Act of 1956[8]

Since the BHC Act of 1956 applied only to BHCs that controlled two or more banks, it was custom-made for Kane's regulatory dialectic. The Act gave primary authority and responsibility for the administration of the law to the Board of Governors of the Federal Reserve System. Granting the Fed substantial control over the activities of BHCs was a significant break away from the regulatory trinity of OCC-FRS-FDIC. Under the BHC Act and its amendments, the Board has responsibility for[9]

1. granting prior approval for BHC formations
2. granting prior approval for bank acquisitions by BHCs
3. determination of permissible nonbanking activities for BHCs
4. granting prior approval for nonbank acquisitions by BHCs
5. granting prior approval and regulation of foreign bank and nonbank affiliates of BHCs as well as joint ventures (minority interests) abroad
6. general supervision of holding companies and their subsidiaries, including the power to examine each affiliate and to obtain examination reports from the OCC, the FDIC, and state bank supervisors.
7. restricting unlawful tie-ins between banking and nonbanking affiliates; in addition, the Board exercises authority with respect to interaffiliates' financial transactions under Section 23A of the Federal Reserve Act.

From 1956 to 1965 (see Table 8-2A), the number of registered BHCs remained fairly constant, although there was some growth in the number of subsidiary banks and deposits they controlled. Over the same time period, the number of OBHCs was increasing but by 1965 they still controlled less than 5 percent of total bank deposits. However, from 1965 to 1970, OBHC activities exploded (see Table 8-2B). In particular, large banks became interested in forming OBHCs. This is illustrated by the fact that the average OBHC increased in size from roughly $25 million in 1965 to approximately $125 million in 1970 (again see Table 8-2B).

Since OBHCs do not circumvent branching restrictions, how does the OBHC movement fit into the regulatory dialectic? Four important developments in other banking areas were occurring that fit nicely into the regulatory-dialectic model of the OBHC movement. First, the Bank Merger Act was passed in 1960, and the first important "antimerger" decision under the Act came down in 1963, in the Philadelphia National Bank case. As a result, big banks became cautious about expanding via the merger route. Second, the Fed was applying the BHC Act fairly strictly, making it difficult to expand via the MBHC avenue. Third, over at the OCC, "the Saxon era" was coming to an end. This period, November 16, 1961 to November 16, 1966, marked the reign of James J. Saxon as Comptroller of the Currency. He was a firm believer in competition. His philosophy involved relaxing chartering and branching restrictions for *national* banks and permitting them to engage in other related activities (e.g., data processing) on the grounds that macroeconomic stabilization policy was effective enough to permit freer competition in banking. Unfortunately, the bank competition was not welcomed in some nonbanking circles and some banks became involved in costly litigations. As a result, a reluctance to expand along the Saxon-nonbank route existed. Fourth, the negotiable CD, which had been introduced in the early 1960s as a tool of liability management, had its effectiveness as an expansionary device reduced by Reg Q interest-rate ceilings. Thus, in our continuing saga of the regulatory

[8] For a description of the events leading up to the passage of the Act see Upshaw [1968].
[9] See Shull [1980], p. 281.

dialectic, these four factors pushed the OBHC as the means of expansion, especially for large banks. Since the OBHC was exempt from the BHC Act of 1956, it became the vehicle for expansion into nonbanking activities and for circumventing Reg Q (e.g., by parent company issues of commercial paper, notes and debentures, etc.; see Figure 8-2). And fifth, but most important, as mentioned earlier, OBHCs were a vehicle for tax avoidance.

The End of the OBHC Loophole

The 1970 Amendments to the BHC Act of 1956, which were the result of a two-year legislative battle, were signed into law by President Nixon on December 31, 1970.[10] The main provisions of the 1970 amendments are (1) the OBHC loophole is closed by adopting a broader definition of a BHC; (2) permissible BHC nonbanking activities have to be "closely related to banking" with specific permissions or denials to be determined by the Board of Governors of the FRS; and (3) specification of a "grandfather clause" in which the Board had the power to determine whether a BHC with subsidiaries engaged in subsequently denied activities (on or before June 30, 1968) would be permitted to continue in the activities.[11] A summary of Fed rulings on activities that have been permitted or denied to BHCs is presented in Table 8-6.

The Nonbank-Bank Loophole

The 1970 Amendment to the BHC Act of 1956 defines a commercial bank as an institution that both accepts demand deposits and makes commercial loans. By engaging in only one of these activities, an institution is not legally a commercial bank. Thus, it is easy to see how innovative FSFs would exploit this loophole by engaging in one of the activities but not both. It is important to understand that once the particular activity is selected the organization is not limited solely to that activity. For example, if an institution wants to be a "consumer bank," it accepts demand deposits and offers a host of other financial services and products, except for commercial loans. In 1987, the United States Congress closed the nonbank-bank loophole, although it grandfathered some 160 or so existing nonbank banks (see appendix C of Chapter 7).

TEN Cs OF HOLDING-COMPANY REGULATION

In a 1976 speech before the Association of BHCs, Philip E. Coldwell, then a member of the Fed's Board of Governors, spelled out a framework for analyzing the regulation of BHCs. He calls his framework the "Ten Cs of Holding-Company Regulation" and regards BHC regulatory concerns as reflective of broader financial concerns for the entire United States. Coldwell's ten Cs are

1. Convenience and needs
2. Competition
3. Compromise of small banks
4. Concentration
5. Conflicts of ownership and control
6. Concern of classified assets, capital adequacy, and management

---

[10] See Jessee and Seelig [1977], pp. 19–32, for a summary of the amendments and their legislative history.

[11] A ten-year divestiture period was allowed for any activity that the Board decided was not in the public interest.

TABLE 8-6 Permissible Nonbanking Activities for Bank Holding Companies—Under Section 4(c)8 of Regulation Y (May 1, 1982)

Activities Permitted by Regulation	Activities Permitted by Order	Activities Denied by the Board

1. Extension of credit [b]
  Mortgage banking
  Finance companies,
    consumer sales,
    and commercial
  Credit cards
  Factoring
3. Servicing loans and other
  extensions of credit [b]
4. Trust company [b]
5. Investment and financial
  advising [b]
6. Full-payout leasing of personal
  or real property [b]
7. Investment in community
  welfare projects [b]
8. Providing bookkeeping or data
  processing services [b]
9. Acting as insurance agent or
  broker primarily in connection
  with credit extensions [b]
10. Underwriting credit life,
  accident, and health insurance
11. Providing courier services [b]
12. Management consulting for
  unaffiliated banks [a,b]
13. Sale at retail of money orders
  with a face value of not more
  than $1,000, travelers checks
  and savings bonds [ab]
14. Performing appraisals of real
  estate [a]
15. Audit services for unaffiliated
  banks
16. Issuance and sale of travelers
  checks
17. Management consulting to
  nonbanking depository
  institutions
	1. Issuance and sale of
	  travelers checks [b,f]
	2. Buying and selling gold and
	  silver bullion and silver
	  coin [b,d]
	3. Issuing money orders and
	  general purpose variable
	  denominated payment
	  instruments [a,b,d]
	4. Futures commission
	  merchant to cover gold and
	  silver bullion and coins [a,b]
	5. Underwriting certain federal,
	  state, and municipal
	  securities [a,b]
	6. Check verification [a,b,d]
	7. Financial advice to
	  consumers [a,b]
	8. Issuance of small
	  denomination debt
	  instruments [a]
	9. Arranging for equity financing
	  of real estate
	10. Acting as futures
	  commissions merchant
	11. Discount brokerage
	12. Operating a distressed
	  savings and loan association
	13. Operating an Article XII
	  investment company
	14. Executing foreign banking
	  unsolicited purchases and
	  sales of securities
	15. Engaging in commercial
	  banking activities abroad
	  through a limited purpose
	  Delaware bank
	16. Performing appraisal of real
	  estate and real estate advisor
	  and real estate brokerage on
	  nonresidential properties
	17. Operating a Pool Reserve
	  Plan for loss reserves of
	  banks for loans to small
	  businesses
	18. Operating a thrift institution in
	  Rhode Island
	19. Operating a guarantee
	  savings bank in New
	  Hampshire
	20. Offering informational advice
	  and transactional services for
	  foreign exchange services
		1. Insurance premium funding
		  (combined sales of mutual funds
		  and insurance)
		2. Underwriting life insurance not
		  related to credit extension
		3. Real estate brokerage [b]
		4. Land development
		5. Real estate syndication
		6. General management consulting
		7. Property management
		8. Computer output microfilm
		  services
		9. Underwriting mortgage guaranty
		  insurance [c]
		10. Operating a savings and loan
		  association [a,e]
		11. Operating a travel agency [a,b]
		12. Underwriting property and casualty
		  insurance [a]
		13. Underwriting home loan life
		  mortgage insurance
		14. Orbanco: Investment role issue
		  with transactional characteristics
		15. Real estate advisory services

[a] Added to list since January 1, 1975.
[b] Activities permissible to national banks.
[c] Board orders found these activities closely related to banking and denied proposed acquisitions as part of its "go slow" policy.
[d] To be decided on a case-by-case basis.
[e] Operating a thrift institution has been permitted by order in Rhode Island, California, and New Hampshire only.
[f] Subsequently permitted by regulation.
Source: Economic Review, Federal Reserve Bank of Atlanta [April 1983].

7. Compliance with prior agreements, conditions of acquisition, and divestiture
8. Capacity to handle and control impact of nonbank activities
9. Contributions of MBHCs
10. Congressional limitations

Of these ten factors, the four most important are convenience and needs (or service); competition; concern of classified assets, capital adequacy, and management; and capacity to handle and control nonbank activities. Since the last two items reflect concerns about safety and soundness, the priority areas of BHC regulation are service, competition, and safety. As with the three objectives of overall bank regulation (i.e., safety, stability, and structure), the objectives of service, competition, and safety are conflicting ones. Recall that in the IO model of structure-conduct-performance linkage, competitive structure produces high-performance service. The four major factors of Coldwell's ten Cs are highlighted in this section.

Convenience and Needs

This factor focuses on the so-called public-benefits test. In all BHC applications, the Fed is charged with looking out for the public interest. Public benefits are associated with such factors as increased competition, improved services, lower prices, greater efficiency, or rescue of a failing institution. Most proposed BHC applications are likely to result in at least some public benefits. However, only when this convenience-and-need factor substantially outweighs the competitive and banking factors will the acquisition be approved. Thus, convenience and needs seldom carry enough weight to overcome significantly adverse findings with respect to competitive, financial, and managerial considerations.

Competition

Analysis of this factor is similar to the analysis conducted in bank merger cases. Thus, the Fed must investigate the competitive implications of the proposed acquisition by determining the relevant market and the applicant's position in the market. In horizontal acquisitions, three important factors are considered: (1) the resulting change in market share; (2) the extent of overlap of the deposit or loan patterns between the parties in the proposed acquisition; and (3) analysis of the potential loss of a means of market entry for another BHC. If the firms are in different markets, the key elements in the analysis are (1) the market share of the firm to be acquired; (2) the likelihood that the acquiring organization will be a future *de novo* entrant into the market if the acquisition is denied; (3) the number of other potential entrants, and (4) the existing level of concentration in the market.

The importance of a structure-conduct-performance model in Fed analysis of proposed acquisitions is highlighted by the following quote from Coldwell's [1976] speech:

> The Board has traditionally taken a rather "hard" stand on competitive issues. The position is based on the view that the bank market *structure* importantly affects bank *conduct*, which in turn affects market *performance* (p. 4, italics mine).

To further illustrate the Fed's "hard" stand on the competitive factor, consider the following order disapproving the acquisition of a BHC. On April 3, 1987, the Board of Governors of the Federal Reserve System (see *Federal Reserve Bulletin* [June 1987], pp. 463–469) did not approve the application of Sunwest Financial Services, Inc. of Albuquerque, New Mexico, to acquire Rio Grande Bancshares, Inc. of Las Cruces, New Mexico. Chairman Volcker and Governor Angell stated that "... consummation of the proposed acquisition ... would substantially lessen competition in two of the three relevant banking markets." In contrast, Governors Johnson and Heller, who did not object to the approval, stated:

> We believe that consummation of the proposal would not substantially reduce competition in any market. We believe that the concentration ratio and other statistics set out in the statement of the other Board members do not reflect the true state of competition in the Las Cruces and Silver City markets. While these statistics give consideration to the competition afforded by savings-and-loan institutions, they ignore the substantial competition banks face from a broad array of products and services provided by other financial institutions in these markets.

Although the analysis of competitive factors at the Fed includes some "softer" views, the majority opinion still favors a relatively narrow definition of product markets.

Concerns of Classified Assets, Capital Adequacy, and Management

This factor reflects the traditional bank regulatory concern about "safety and soundness" as manifested in asset quality, leverage, and managerial ratings. This kind of regulatory concern was illustrated dramatically during the 1974 interest-rate crunch and recession, when the Fed issued its famous "go-slow policy." The purpose of the directive was to encourage BHCs to get their own financial houses in order, especially their banking operations, before they considered any additional acquisitions.

In 1987, an interesting series of events took place regarding concerns about the asset quality and capital adequacy of major banks/BHCs. The interesting twist is that the concern came from the BHCs and not from the Fed, or other banking agencies. During May of 1987, Citicorp announced that it was adding $3 billion to its loan-loss reserve to cover potential loan defaults by third-world countries (e.g., Brazil, Mexico). This dramatic move forced other BHCs with similar (relative) exposures to follow Citicorp's reserve leadership, which resulted in a massive second quarter loss for the industry (see Musumeci and Sinkey [1988]). Citicorp continued its leadership role by announcing in August of 1987 its intention to raise slightly over $1 billion in equity to bolster its capital position. From a financial-management perspective, the decision to raise equity seemed to be a wise one. Although some short-sighted analysts talked about earnings dilution, the insightful ones saw the move as strengthening Citicorp's balance sheet. Following Citicorp's lead, Manufacturers Hanover and several other BHCs adopted similar plans to raise equity capital. The failure of bank regulators to act on this aspect of the international debt crisis suggests that regulators are slow to react.

Capacity to Handle and Control Impact of Nonbank Activities

This factor focuses on the capacity of BHCs to handle and control the impact of permissible nonbank activities. Nonbank subsidiaries may create financial problems for a BHC because of either internal (e.g., poor judgment on the part of management) or external (e.g., recession) factors. The financial difficulties that REITs and mortgage-banking subsidiaries created for certain BHCs during the mid-1970s are good examples of such difficulties.[12] The Fed is concerned about protecting subsidiary banks from potential problems that might be created by nonbank subsidiaries or

---

[12] For a description and analysis of the commercial bank-REIT crisis see Chapter 8 of my 1979 book, *Problem and Failed Institutions in the Commercial Banking Industry*.

the parent company (i.e., the issue of corporate separateness). Three subsidiary banks that got into financial trouble in the 1970s because of BHC-related difficulties included Beverly Hills National Bank (California, 1974), Hamilton National Bank (Tennessee, 1976), and Palmer National Bank (Florida, 1976). By monitoring BHC financial statements and through the use of on-site examination of subsidiary banks, the Fed hopes to be able to identify future BHC problems before they become serious.

The Ten Cs: A Recapitulation

Coldwell's notion of the "Ten Cs of BHC Regulation" provides a convenient framework for analyzing Fed and Congressional concerns about the regulation of BHCs. The key concepts of the approach are (1) service, (2) competition, and (3) safety and control. Increased service is important in meeting the convenience and needs of the public, greater competition promotes economic efficiency, and safety and control help insure against excessive concentration, potential abuses, and unsound banking practices. Of course, emphasis on the safety-and-control factor tends to restrict the service and competition elements. Thus, the Fed needs to balance these risk-return trade-offs to achieve the greatest degree of public benefit.

THE FEDERAL RESERVE'S BHC RATING SYSTEM[13]

To evaluate the "safety and soundness" of BHCs, the Fed employs a rating system that is grounded in the on-site bank examination process. The system is a management information and supervisory tool designed to assess the condition of BHCs in a systematic way. It uses a "component approach" consisting of (1) evaluating the financial condition and risk characteristics of each major component of the BHC, (2) assessing the important interrelationships among the components, and (3) analyzing the strength and significance of key consolidated financial and operating performance characteristics. This approach is particularly appropriate since holding companies are supposed to be a source of financial and managerial strength to their bank subsidiaries.

To arrive at an overall assessment of financial condition, the following elements of the BHC are evaluated and rated on a scale of 1 (excellent) to 5 (lousy) in descending order of performance quality:

1. Bank subsidiaries (B)
2. Other (nonbank) subsidiaries (O)
3. Parent company (P)
4. Earnings—consolidated (E)
5. Capital adequacy—consolidated (C)

The acronym for the rating system is BOPEC. The ideal rating is the golfer's fantasy of five aces (i.e., B = 1, O = 1, P = 1, E = 1, C = 1). BHCs that are "out of bounds" score 5s on the BOPEC course.

The first three elements of the BOPEC rating, that is, bank subsidiaries, other subsidiaries, and parent company, reflect the contribution of each component to the fundamental financial soundness of the holding company. The ratings of consolidated earnings and consolidated capital recognize the importance that regulators place on these factors and their crucial roles in maintaining the financial strength and supporting the risk characteristics of the entire organization. Since the ability and competence

---

[13] Condensed from "BHC Rating System," Federal Reserve Press Release [February 7, 1979].

of holding-company management bear importantly on every aspect of holding-company operations, the quality of management is a major factor in the evaluation of each of the five principal elements of the rating, as well as in the assignment of an overall holding-company rating.

In addition to the individual elements described above, each company is assigned an overall or composite rating in both the financial and managerial areas. The financial composite score is based upon an overall evaluation of the ratings of each of the five principal elements of BOPEC. The financial composite rating is also based upon a scale of 1 to 5 in descending order of performance quality. The managerial composite is predicated upon a comprehensive evaluation of holding-company management, as reflected in the conduct of the affairs of the bank and nonbank subsidiaries and the parent company. The managerial composite is indicated by the assignment of S, F, or U for, respectively, management that is found to be satisfactory, fair, or unsatisfactory.

The complete rating represents a summary evaluation of the BHC in the form of a rating "fraction." The "numerator" reflects the condition of the major components of the holding company, and assessments of certain key consolidated financial and operating factors. The "denominator" represents the composite rating including both its financial and managerial components. While the elements in the "numerator" represent the essential foundation on which the composite rating is based, the Fed insists that the composite need not reflect a simple arithmetic mean of the individual performance dimensions. Since any kind of formula could be misleading and inappropriate, the composite should reflect the rater's judgment of the overall condition of the BHC based upon his/her knowledge and experience with the company. The complete BHC rating is displayed as follows:

$$\frac{[B,O,P,E,C]}{[F,M]}$$

The BHC rating system, to some degree, parallels the Uniform Interagency Bank Rating System by utilizing similar rating scales and performance definitions to evaluate both the individual elements and the summary or overall condition of the holding company. The bank rating system is based upon a financial profile called CAMEL, which stands for Capital, Asset quality, Management, Earnings, and Liquidity. Since the bank-condition component of the BHC rating system is a CAMEL-driven rating and since banks account for most of BHC revenues and assets, BOPEC is driven by CAMEL, which in turn is driven by bank examiners' perceptions of asset quality and bank capital adequacy (Sinkey, [1978]). The Fed's BHC rating system is summarized in Figure 8-3.

Both BOPEC and CAMEL scores are treated as confidential information by the banking agencies. Attempts by this author, under the Freedom of Information Act, to obtain such ratings for troubled BHCs/banks of the 1980s were denied. However, based upon my research at the FDIC from 1971 to 1976 and upon information disclosed at Congressional hearings since then, it is clear that the banking agencies have been highly successful over the past 15 years in *identifying* almost all problem situations at least one year prior to failure. Thus, the "regulatory problem" appears to be one of *enforcement* rather than *identification*. For example, in the congressional hearings regarding the collapse of Continental Illinois, the OCC was charged by the chairman of the House Banking Committee with "timid regulation." The apparent regulatory policy of "benign neglect" is desirable, however, because high-risk institutions *should* fail. Unfortunately, the regulators, in the name of financial stability, have bailed out, at taxpayers' expense, some of the nation's largest high-risk banks/BHCs (e.g., Continental Illinois, First Pennsylvania, and Bank of the Commonwealth). As a result, the marketplace has come to expect a 100 percent government guarantee

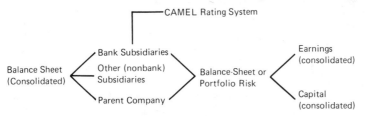

Figure 8-3   The Fed's BHC Rating System

The overall BHC rating is summarized as $[B,O,P,E,C]/[F,M]$, where F and M are financial and managerial composite ratings. The financial composite is some examiner-determined weighted average of the elements of BOPEC whereas the managerial composite is a comprehensive evaluation of overall holding-company management (i.e., banks, nonbank subsidiaries, and parent company). The bank-condition component (B) of BOPEC is a CAMEL-driven rating derived as a weighted average (based upon asset size) of the subsidiary banks' composite CAMEL scores. Two sample ratings are

Best Possible Rating	*Worst Possible Rating*
CAMEL = [1,1,1,1,1]	CAMEL = [5,5,5,5,5]
BOPEC = [1,1,1,1,1]	BOPEC = [5,5,5,5,5]
FM = [1,S]	FM = [5,U]

behind the debt of large banks/BHCs. To illustrate, regarding the bank-LDC problems Moody's Investor Service stated, "Major banks are too important to the economy, too interconnected, and too confidence-sensitive to run the risk of permitting default" (*The Wall Street Journal* [September 7, 1984], p. 7).

To summarize, although bank (and therefore BHC) examination data are available only every year or two and involve some subjective judgments by examiners, the data have been successful in providing early-warning signals of most problem situations at least one full year in advance of failure. Of course, about 90 percent of the BHCs/banks with problems don't fail, but those seldom make the financial news. Regarding the ones that do fail, the objective of bank regulation and examination is not, and should not be, a zero failure rate. The ultimate goal is to preserve *confidence* in the supply of money and credit and to provide a stable or safe-and-sound financial system for the U.S. and world economies.

THE PAYMENT OF IMPLICIT INTEREST AND NONPRICE COMPETITION

The payment of implicit interest on deposits was a way (albeit an inefficient one) of circumventing Reg Q interest-rate restrictions. Thus, like the BHC movement, the notion of implicit interest fits compactly into the regulatory-dialectic mold. The purpose of this section is to define, describe, and analyze the concept of implicit interest. Even though interest-rate ceilings were formally removed in 1986, depository institutions have continued to pay implicit interest.

Explicit Versus Implicit Interest[14]

Prior to the removal of Reg Q interest-rate ceilings, banks were forced to tease their customers and disguise their interest payments with a camouflage of merchandise

[14] See Kane [1979], pp. 157–168.

premiums (luggage, crystal, etc.), longer banking hours, superfluous branches, and free checking. More subtle forms of nonprice competition include discriminatory price and service concessions for valued customers. Thus, bankers tended to leave a lot to their customers' imagination regarding their total return (i.e., explicit interest plus implicit interest). Of course, these nonprice innovations were induced by a combination of market and regulatory forces. Even without Reg Q, some depository institutions find it difficult to break away from their old habits and insist on paying implicit interest to attract deposits (e.g., merchandise premiums). Of course, some forms of implicit interest, such as excess brick-and-mortar branches, are not easily eliminated.

Depository institutions pay explicit interest in what Kane [1979] calls "coin of the realm." In the United States the "coins" are dollars, in England pounds, and in Japan yen, for example. From 1933 to 1980, the payment of interest on checking accounts (or demand deposits) by most commercial banks was prohibited by law. However, this restriction did not stop banks from attempting to compete for profitable commercial accounts or what Kane and Malkiel [1965] call L^* *customers*.[15] These valued customers receive a variety of accounting and financial services from U.S. banks for fees that are less than the true marginal costs. In addition, L^* customers expect to be accommodated with loans at preferential interest rates (e.g., the "discount" prime rate) even when money and credit are tight.

What's Wrong with Implicit Interest?

Nonprice competition (implicit interest) is less efficient than price competition (explicit interest). In terms of the evolution of efficient markets, it is a step backward toward barter. Subverting the price mechanism tends to produce inefficiencies and disincentives. A prime example is checking-account services provided by commercial banks. Since such services tend to be underpriced or given away, there is no incentive to use them economically. Thus, in writing checks, for example, bank customers have no incentive to economize and freely substitute checks for coin of the realm even for the smallest transactions. A study by Selby [1980] found that roughly 30 percent of the

TABLE 8-7   Distribution of the Dollar Value of Checks Written

Dollar Range of Checks	Survey of a Small Bank's Accounts[a]		Survey of Checks Clearing One Federal Reserve Bank[b]	
	Percentage Distribution of Checks Written	Cumulative Percentage	Percentage Distribution of Checks Written	Cumulative Percentage
.01–2.00	2.5	2.5	1.7	1.7
2.01–4.00	7.8	10.3	2.5	4.2
4.01–8.00	19.8	30.1	7.6	11.8
8.01–16.00	23.7	53.8	16.1	27.9
16.01–32.00	19.9	73.7	18.8	46.7
32.01–64.00	13.7	87.4	15.6	62.3
64.01–128.00	7.1	94.5	12.7	75.0
128.01–256.00	3.8	98.3	11.0	86.0
256.01–512.00	1.0	99.3	6.9	92.9
512.00 and over	0.7	100.0	7.1	100.0
TOTAL	100.0		100.0	

[a] Based on a survey of all checks written during a one-month period by 10 percent of the demand deposit customers (randomly selected) of a small bank.
[b] Based on a survey of all checks clearing through the Federal Reserve System within one Federal Reserve District during a one-week period.
Source: Selby [1980], Table 1, p. 93. Reprinted by permission.

[15] The concept of the customer relationship and L^* customers are discussed further in Chapters 14 and 18.

checks written in one small bank were for $8.00 or less (see Table 8-7). However, on a broader basis, the percentage was only about 12 percent using Federal Reserve data. The important point is that a lot of costly paper (about 30¢ per check) has to be handled by individual banks and the banking system. As banking markets become more competitive and coin-of-the-realm interest replaces implicit interest, marginal costs and benefits will show less disparity.

The total interest paid (or received) on a deposit account consists of the explicit interest *plus* the implicit interest. Since implicit interest is difficult to police, the opportunity for abuses arises. Thus, from the customer's perspective, implicit interest is desirable as a form of tax-exempt income that escapes the jaws of the IRS. From the bank's perspective, implicit interest presents the opportunity to practice a subtle form of price discrimination, especially against small or unsophisticated savers. By being able to segment deposit markets (basically into an interest-sensitive component and an interest-insensitive component), bankers are able to hold down interest costs and, other things equal, earn higher profits. Price discrimination also may be achieved by banks through special terms and services provided to valued customers. In terms of equity and efficiency, Kane [1979] painted a bleak picture of Reg Q and implicit interest.

> From the point of view of society, deposit-rate regulation is defective in that it promotes tax avoidance and makes discrimination more respectable and less likely to alienate disfavored customers. This subtle and systematic discrimination against owners of interest-insensitive funds (predominantly the old and the poor) is the ugliest face of liability management (p. 158).

DEPOSIT INSURANCE: BACKGROUND, ISSUES, AND REFORMS

In *The Gathering Crisis in Federal Deposit Insurance*, Kane [1985] employs a metaphor in which an old and undermaintained automobile is used to highlight the shortcomings of the system of federal deposit insurance, which was adopted during the 1930s and essentially has remained unchanged since then. Kane sees the deposit-insurance jalopy as not having many more interest-rate mountains left in it. Moreover, it is unlikely that it will be able to negotiate the TRICK(y) curves found in the new FSI. Kane's objective is to change the way people think about deposit insurance by having them look at it from the point of view of a taxpayer. Grab someone by the pocketbook and it usually gets his or her attention. With the full faith and credit of the U.S. government now explicitly standing behind the deposit-insurance system, "we, the people"—in one way or another—are the ultimate guarantors of the system. For example in 1987, the U.S. Congress Authorized a $10.8 billion bailout of the FSLIC.

The purpose of this section is to examine the background, critical issues, and suggested reforms regarding deposit insurance. Although the analysis focuses on the FDIC, for the most part, similar remarks apply to the FSLIC. The FDIC insures commercial banks and mutual savings banks whereas the FSLIC insures savings-and-loan associations.

The Federal Deposit Insurance Act

The so-called deposit-guaranty section of the Banking Act of 1933 provided for the establishment of a federal deposit insurance corporation. On June 16, 1934, the Federal Deposit Insurance (FDI) Act was passed and later amended by the Banking Act of 1935. The purpose of the FDIC was to provide for the speedy liquidation of failed banks and to protect the deposits of small savers against losses due to bank failures. Originally, a "small" saver was one with a deposit equal to or less than $2,500; today $100,000 is the definition of "small." Obviously, if a bank does not fail, its depositors do not incur losses. Thus, from the beginning, failure prevention was one of the FDIC's major goals. By preventing bank failures, the FDIC protects its insurance fund.[16]

Who Pays for Deposit Insurance?

Deposit insurance is an atypical insurance contract, since the depositor does not explicitly pay the insurance premium; nominally the bank does. Insured banks pay a *fixed* annual premium or assessment of 1/12 of 1 percent (.000825) of their total assessable deposits for FDIC insurance. Prior to the 1980s, because of the small amount of claims on the deposit-insurance fund, the effective insurance premium had been about half the nominal rate or roughly 1/24 of 1 percent (.0004125). The difference came in the form of an assessment credit for next year. Thus, a bank with $100 million in assessable deposits, regardless of how risky it is, would pay an insurance premium of $82,500 and, under normal circumstances, would receive a credit toward next year's assessment equal to about half the nominal fee or, in this example, $41,250. Because of the large number of bank failures in the 1980s, assessment credits have been smaller or nonresistent over this decade.

To the extent that banks pass on the costs of deposit insurance to their customers or owners, the latter share indirectly in this expense. For example, depositors may pay by receiving lower deposit rates of interest, borrowers by paying higher loan rates, or stockholders by receiving lower rates of return on their investment. To the extent that all of the members of these groups benefit from a stable financial environment, it is not unfair that they should share in the cost burden of deposit insurance. What is unfair is that high-risk institutions are subsidized by low-risk firms and the mismanaged companies (e.g., Continental Illinois) are bailed out at taxpayers' expense.

Handling Problem Banks and Failed Banks

When an insured bank is closed (i.e., declared insolvent by its chartering agency), the FDIC usually functions as the receiver or liquidator. (The FDIC receivership appointment is a statutory requirement for all national banks but optional for state banks.) To protect depositors, the FDIC usually arranges either a deposit payoff or a deposit assumption. A *deposit payoff* simply involves paying off the insured depositors, whereas a *deposit assumption* involves the purchase and assumption (usually with the FDIC's financial assistance) of the failed bank's total deposits by a viable insured bank.

In the case of a deposit payoff, payments to insured depositors historically have been made within five to seven days after the bank's closing. In an assumption transaction, *all* the deposits of the failed bank (including the uninsured ones) are absorbed by the assuming bank, usually on the next business day after the closing.[17]

---

[16] Since the FDIC bears most of the risk of bank failure, Benston [1973] contends that "Examinations should now be directed only towards protecting the insurance fund" (p. 57). Moreover, as Horvitz [1980] points out, "Protection of the insurance fund does not require *prevention* of failure; all it requires is *prompt detection* of bank insolvency, a task that can be performed through bank examination" (p. 655).

[17] Since an assumption saves the FDIC the administrative cost of actually paying off insured depositors, an absorption is, other things equal, less costly than a payoff to the FDIC. The administrative expenses, which in a large failed bank are quite substantial, involve such things as verifying deposits and offsetting assets, writing checks, and making the payoffs.

Thus, a deposit assumption provides 100 percent deposit insurance (i.e., uninsured depositors receive the same protection as insured depositors). A deposit assumption is not costless to depositors, however, since established bank–customer relationships are severed.

The payment of the financial assistance in a deposit assumption (also called a purchase-and-assumption transaction), until 1981 was in the form of cash to the acquiring bank. However, since then, FDIC assistance, especially for troubled mutual savings banks, has taken the form of "income-maintenance agreements" whereby the FDIC promises to make a stream of future payments such that the resulting institution or "phoenix" would remain financially sound, with the ability to compete effectively in its market. In this kind of transaction, the FDIC holds a contingent liability that depends upon the future performance of the acquired assets, which for a portfolio of fixed-rate mortgages may subject the insurance fund to substantial amounts of interest-rate risk. To determine the true or market value of the insurance fund, these contingent claims must be evaluated. To do this evaluation, one of the fundamental building blocks of financial management, option-pricing theory (OPT) is required. Since OPT procedures are quite complex, it is difficult to determine the market value of the contingent claims on the insurance fund. As a result, the true value of the fund itself remains somewhat of a mystery.

In addition to fraud-type cases, the FDIC may encounter circumstances in which, because of size or legal (branching, holding company, antitrust, etc.) restrictions, the *effective* purchase premium is zero. In other words, there are simply no eligible buyers for the failed bank. In such cases, the FDIC has four alternatives: (1) to pay off the failing bank, (2) to appeal to Congress for statutory exemption to handle the case, (3) to provide financial assistance to keep the bank from failing, or (4) to establish a Deposit Insurance National Bank. These last two alternatives are discussed next.

Under Section 13(c) of the FDI Act, the FDIC can financially assist an insured bank to remain in operation if it can establish that (1) but for the assistance, the bank is in danger of closing *and* (2) the bank is essential in providing adequate banking service to the community. The key to meeting the statutory test is, of course, the second requirement, since enough bailout money can prolong any ailing bank's life. Although the FDIC has provided financial assistance to failing banks only infrequently, in 1984 and 1980 it provided massive aid to bail out two billion-dollar banks, Continental Illinois and First Pennsylvania. Continental's rescue package was worth $4.5 billion whereas First Pennsylvania's aid was *only* $325 million. In providing financial assistance to insured institutions on an "open-bank basis," the FDIC has argued that its cost has been substantially lower than the *estimated* cost of either a deposit assumption or a deposit payoff. In addition, the FDIC avoids exposure to any contingent liabilities and the administrative expenses of a failed-bank receivership. Unlike the cases of Continental and First Pennsylvania, financial assistance also is provided to facilitate acquisition of a distressed bank by a healthy one (e.g., the acquisition of Abilene National Bank by the Mercantile Texas Corporation in 1982). In deposit-insurance transactions, "financial assistance" is simply a euphemism for payment required to close the deal.

A fourth alternative available to protect depositors is for the FDIC to organize (charter) and operate a Deposit Insurance National Bank (DINB) to take care of the emergency banking needs of a community (Section 11 of the FDI Act). A DINB, which provides only limited banking services, is permitted to operate for only two years before it must be closed or taken over by another bank or by new owners. It is designed to bridge the gap between the closed bank and what is hoped to be a new bank established and capitalized by the local community. The FDIC disposes of a DINB either by offering capital stock in the bank for sale or by transferring its business to an insured bank within the community. Former stockholders of the failed bank have the first opportunity to purchase such stock. The most famous DINB was the one established after the deposit payoff of Penn Square Bank in 1982. Penn Square was the largest deposit payoff in FDIC history with total deposits of $465 million, more than half of which were uninsured. The DINB, which was terminated on August 18, 1983, with Charter National Bank of Oklahoma City assuming the insured deposits of the DINB, served as a vehicle for paying depositors. From a practical standpoint, a prospective DINB can be unattractive either financially or legally, or both. In the case of Penn Square, the largest DINB in FDIC history, it was unattractive on both counts.

Modified Payoffs and Market Discipline

In 1983 (1982 for the FSLIC), the FDIC began experimenting with a hybrid method for handling failed banks called a "deposit transfer." The impetus for the experimentation was an attempt to get uninsured depositors and creditors to pay more attention to an institution's financial condition and thereby exert "market discipline" on high-risk institutions. The reason that the technique gets the attention of uninsured creditors is because it provides less than 100 percent deposit insurance (i.e., it puts uninsured creditors at risk). Since a deposit assumption provides 100 percent insurance, the term "modified assumption" is an accurate description of the technique. In a deposit transfer, all of the insured deposits and some part of the uninsured deposits are transferred to the assuming bank. The latter is determined by the FDIC based upon its estimated recoveries from liquidating the failed bank. The remaining uninsured liabilities are held by the FDIC in receivership along with the assets of the failed bank. Thus, potential acquiring banks bid *en masse* only for the two blocks of deposits. The winning acquiring bank acts as an agent for the FDIC and assumes the liability for administering the transferred deposits. The uninsured creditors, who are effectively subordinated to the insured depositors, are given "receiver's certificates" valued by the FDIC at some percentage of the face value of their deposits. For example, if the FDIC expects to collect 75¢ on the dollar for the failed bank's assets, uninsured liabilities would be valued at the same ratio.

The value of a technique that reduces the perception of a 100 percent deposit-insurance guarantee behind *all* bank liabilities is that it forces uninsured creditors to investigate the financial condition of their banks. If high-risk institutions find it difficult to attract funds, they may be inclined to seek less risk exposure. Such a change in behavior would reduce both the subsidy provided by low-risk institutions and that provided by the insurance fund (i.e., taxpayer). A slight variation of the deposit-transfer technique was used in the Penn Square DINB as uninsured depositors were issued receiver's certificates. In 1987, the FDIC arranged 40 deposit transfers out of the 184 banks failing that year. The other 144 failures consisted of 132 purchase and assumptions, 11 deposit payoffs, and one "bridge bank." In addition, 19 banks were given financial assistance to prevent them from failing. Thus, in 1987, there were 203 *de facto* bank failures.

During the summer of 1987, Congress gave the FDIC the power to take over a failed bank and operate it, for up to two years, as if it was a private bank. Under this procedure, the interim organization is known as a *bridge bank*, which is in effect an unrestricted form of DINB. The purpose of establishing a bridge bank is to improve the failed bank's condition such that it will be attractive for another buyer. With the bridge-bank technique, the FDIC buys time with the objective of reducing its costs of handling bank failures. The FDIC first used the bridge-bank technique in the case of the $372 million Capital Bank of Baton Rouge, LA, which was closed on October 30, 1987 and required an initial FDIC outlay of $103.5 million. The FDIC operated the bridge bank under the name of Capital Bank & Trust Company, National Association until May 1988 when it was purchased (as a whole-bank transaction because the FDIC did not keep any of the bank's bad assets as it does in a P&A) by Grenada Sunburst Systems Corporation, a Mississippi bank holding company.

An Insider's Account of Bank Failures and Rescues

This section heading is the subtitle of a book by Irvine Sprague [1986] called *Bailout*. The first sentence of Sprague's book says, "Bailout is a bad word." This word is so bad that he suggests that "It sounds almost un-American." Of course, if the bailout is in your own self-interest, it can be "un-anything" as long as you are protected.

Bailed out organizations are the offspring of a national policy that does not permit *large* enterprises to fail when market forces have dictated their demise. Capital infusions and/or loans from the government or its agencies are the financial methods for bailing out troubled firms. Both banks and nonbanks in the United States have been the beneficiaries of such financial-assistance packages.

As in personal life, it is important not to confuse the means with the end. Just as illegitimate children can turn out to be good citizens, "illegitimate businesses" can turn out to be Chryslers—with the right adoptive Iacocca-type parents, of course. To my mind, it is the means that raises the ire of the critics of this national policy, especially when the managers have been high-flying risk-seekers. It is much easier to empathize with legitimate energy and farm lenders, who faced severe hardships in the 1980s, than it is with managers and directors who bet the bank. A bailout policy sends the wrong kind of signal to the marketplace.

Sprague's book is accurately described by its subtitle: *An Insider's Account of Bank Failures and Rescues*. There is no doubting Sprague's credentials for telling this story. As Chairman and Director of the FDIC, Sprague handled more bank failures than anyone else in FDIC history. More important, however, he was directly involved in crafting the four bailouts which are the focus of his book. These bailouts were (1) Unity Bank (Roxbury, Mass) in 1971, (2) Bank of the Commonwealth (Detroit) in 1972, (3) First Pennsylvania Bank (Philadelphia) in 1980, and (4) Continental Illinois (Chicago) in 1984. At the time of their bailouts, these institutions had total assets of $11.4 million, $1.26 billion, $8.4 billion, and $41 billion, respectively. As you can see, the bailouts have gotten bigger and bigger with more and more of a drain and contingent claim on the FDIC's insurance fund. However, unless one considers the mutual-savings-bank crisis and the bailouts in that industry (e.g., Bowery Savings Bank [New York] in 1985 with total assets of $5.3 billion), the total claims on the insurance fund are underestimated. Since Sprague does not tell us the "phoenix story" about the thrift failures and rescues, there is a need for *Bailout, Part II*. Only then will taxpayers know the full story, and perhaps the full effect, of a policy that threatens to nationalize the banking industry.

The first part of Sprague's book focuses on describing what a bailout is and the legal framework for its implementation. The key concept here is the "essentiality doctrine." It simply means (as interpreted by the FDIC) that if a bank or its holding company can be found to be "essential" to its community, then the FDIC may provide financial assistance to prevent the organization from failing. Since the FDIC insures banks and not bank holding companies (BHCs), the bailout of BHCs shows the breadth of the FDIC's interpretation. Both social and financial considerations have been important in establishing the essentiality doctrine. The definition of community (market) has been as narrow as ghettos in metropolitan areas to as wide as the international financial market. Early on Sprague (p. 10) tells us the "real reason" for doing the four bank bailouts: "Simply put, we were afraid not to." Even recognizing that fear is a great motivating factor, should not we expect something more from our highest policymakers? Although Sprague and his colleagues spent hours agonizing about these bailout decisions and additional hours justifying their actions, they appear to have made the "easy" decision. The "hard" decision (and perhaps the wrong one) would have been to apply the Darwinian rule of survival of the fittest. However, unlike the physical sciences where controlled experiments can be conducted, "social scientists," such as regulators, do not have the luxury of an experimental laboratory. In an industry characterized by "conservative" players and regulators, it is unrealistic to expect "radical" free-market solutions.

What were bank regulators "afraid of" in these cases? The prospects for social unrest and ghetto violence played a major role in the decisions to bail out Unity and Commonwealth. The bailout of First Pennsylvania is noteworthy because it provided the prototype for bailing out distressed megabanks. Nevertheless, it is not clear why First Pennsylvania should have been bailed out in the first place. Regarding First Pennsy's bailout, Sprague tells the amusing story of trying to get a check for $325 million from the U.S. Treasury and how he personally carried it to Philadelphia to close the deal. In Continental's case, once the potential for a financial panic had abated and the possibility of limited contagion had been assured, what were the regulators fearing?

Sprague also gives us an insider's account about two potential bailouts that never occurred: Penn Square and Seafirst. Penn Square, as discussed above, was unique because uninsured depositors and other creditors were not protected by the FDIC's safety net of 100 percent insurance, which for a bank with $517 million in assets was unusual FDIC treatment. Presumably, the handling of Penn Square in this way was intended to be a signal to the marketplace that the regulators were serious about market discipline. However, with Continental on the horizon, the signal was a short-lived one. Seafirst, which was absorbed by BankAmerica Corporation in 1983, was the first major casualty from Penn Square. Without the appearance of the white knight, Sprague suggests that Seafirst would have been a serious bailout candidate.

Sprague devotes five chapters to a description and analysis of Continental's crisis. The FDIC's battles with the U.S. Treasury and the FDIC's selection of the management team make for interesting and intriguing reading. More mundane matters such as the bank's liquidity crisis, the search for a permanent solution, and the liquidation of Continental's bad assets occupy the balance of this longest part of the book.

Sprague concludes with two chapters focusing upon the lessons learned and the public policy debate regarding bailouts. Regarding the lessons, Sprague sees two major ones. First, since certain bank managers do not learn from past mistakes, those mistakes will be committed again in the future. The main culprit here, according to Sprague, is greed in the form of growth at any cost, myopic profit maximization without regard to risk, insider transactions, and betting on interest rate. The second lesson focuses on the jurisdictional tangle of bank regulation. Sprague recommends consolidating the agencies, as former Senator Proxmire (D-Wis) did in the mid-1970s. Sprague's monolithic agency would have responsibility for regulating and supervising all banks and their holding companies, regardless of their chartering authority or

Federal Reserve membership. To keep the agency insulated from political influence, it would be headed by a seven-person board whose chairperson would be named by the President, and whose members would be balanced to ensure that all competing interests are represented. Since the details of Sprague's restructuring are sketchy, especially with respect to the role of the FDIC, his reform ideas require more thought.

Given Sprague's role as an architect in a national policy of bailing out large banks/BHCs, we would be shocked if his answer to the public policy debate was not in favor of such a policy. His answer is "... megabanks must and will continue to be bailed out if they are failing..." (p. 262). That is the bad news. The goods news is "... but they should pay a price for this protection, and they should be handled so that management and stockholders suffer, as nearly as possible, the same fate as an outright failure" (p. 262). To equalize the cost of deposit insurance, Sprague suggests that FDIC assessments be levied on all deposits, foreign and domestic. Since the current assessment applies only to domestic deposits, the megabanks, which have (on average) about a one-to-one ratio of foreign-to-domestic deposits, receive a "free lunch" ultimately at taxpayers' expense. The megabanks like the too-big-to-fail doctrine as long as they can continue booking it in the too-smart-to-pay-for-it account.

As a devotee of problem and failed banks and bank regulatory policy, I poured through Sprague's book quickly but carefully. It is interesting and easy reading. Sprague tells an insider's story that has never before been told. His account is both personal and factual. The stress of making bailout decisions is revealed by the fact that on separate occasions Sprague and William Isaac (FDIC Chairman when Sprague was Director), both suffering from exhaustion, thought that they were having heart attacks. Only after hospitalization did they learn the truth. It is much easier on us academics to simply say that no bank is too big to fail.

The Ten Biggest Commercial Bank Collapses

As of September 9, 1987, the second largest bailout in FDIC history occurred when First City Bancorporation of Houston was given $970 million in financial assistance. This bailout was one that Sprague did not have to worry about, since he was no longer with the FDIC. That was the good news; the bad news was that he did not have a chance to include this one in his insider's account of bank failures and rescues. With $12.2 billion in assets, First City also become the second largest *de facto* failure in FDIC history. A *de facto* failure is one that is an economic failure but because it is bailed out it never enters the official failure record.

The ten largest commercial bank collapses handled by the FDIC (as of January 18, 1988) are shown in Table 8-8. This list includes both *de jure* and *de facto* failures. In this "big ten conference," four of the members are of the *de facto* variety. The fact that the three largest collapses were bailouts reflects the too-big-to-fail doctrine. The fourth largest bailout and seventh in the failure list is BancTexas Group Inc., another rescue that occurred after Sprague's departure. It is interesting to note that five of the ten collapses in Table 8-8 were associated with the energy crisis in the southwest. The Texas and Oklahoma banks are the four obvious ones. The fifth one is Continental Illinois, whose demise began in 1982 with its linkage to the Penn Square Bank of Oklahoma City.

In addition to problems associated with energy lenders (e.g., in 1987, 95 banks were closed in the energy states of Texas [50], Oklahoma [31], and Louisiana [14]), the FDIC has also been plagued in the 1980s with numerous problem and failed banks in

TABLE 8-8   Ten Biggest Commercial Bank Collapses

	Assets (in billions)	FDIC Outlay (in millions)	Expected FDIC Cost[a] (in millions)
Continental Illinois Corp. (FDIC assistance 7/26/84)	$33.6	$4,500[b]	$1,700
First City Bancorporation (FDIC assistance 9/9/87)	12.2	970	$800–900
First Pennsylvania Bank (FDIC assistance 4/28/80)	5.5	325[c]	0
Franklin National Bank (failed 10/8/74)	3.6	1,800[c]	0
First National Bank & Trust Co. of Oklahoma City (failed 7/14/86)	1.4	635	347
First National Bank of Midland, Texas (failed 10/14/83)	1.4	1,200	615
Banc Texas Group Inc. (FDIC assistance 7/17/87)	1.3	150[d]	150
U.S. National Bank, San Diego (failed 10/18/78)	1.3	222	67
United American Bank, Knoxville, Tenn. (failed 2/5/78)	0.8	466	392
Banco Credito y Ahorro Ponceno, Ponce, Puerto Rico (failed 3/31/78)	0.7	98[c]	0

[a] Expected FDIC cost is the amount of the agency's reserve for losses on each bank as of 12/31/86.
[b] Includes $3.5 billion in borrowings by the FDIC from the Federal Reserve Bank of Chicago, due 9/26/89.
[c] Since repaid.
[d] Capital infusion.
Source: FDIC.

agricultural areas. For example, in 1987, 54 so-called ag banks failed. The majority of the banks failing in the 1980s have been energy or ag banks. The saving grace from the FDIC's perspective is that these many failures have been small, resulting in small claims and contingent liabilities on the insurance fund.

Structural Weaknesses in the Deposit-Insurance System

The failure of deposit insurers to recognize the serious problem facing the deposit-insurance system calls to mind a scene from the movie *Young Frankenstein*. As the young Dr. Frankenstein arrives at the Transylvania railroad station and hands his baggage to the faithful humpbacked assistant, Igor, he says, "I am a great doctor." Dr. Frankenstein leans forward to peer at the mountainous hump rising from poor Igor's shoulder and adds, "I can fix that hump for you, Igor." From his perpetual crouch, Igor casts a baleful eye up to the doctor and says, "Vot hoomp?"

The willful suspension of belief in the obvious must be great comfort to deposit insurers as they inquire "Vot problem?" The deposit-insurance system is in need of major surgery. There is no disputing that the present system has worked well for half a century; even such antagonists as Milton Friedman and John Kenneth Galbraith agree on that point. To understand the problem, let's focus on the distinction between regulated and unregulated risks.

Prior to the 1960s structural changes in the components of TRICK were not the major systematic forces that they have become over the past quarter century. Only recently have bank regulators begun to measure and to attempt to control three heretofore *unregulated* risks: interest-rate risk, foreign risk, and technological risk. In the rapidly changing environment of the financial-services industry, some unregulated (i.e., not yet administratively penalized) risks are likely to exist. Kane [1983] explains the existence of unregulated risks as due to the fact that avoidance lags are shorter than regulatory lags. The differential lags reflect differences in the adaptive capacities of the regulated institutions (faster) and the regulators (slower) in response to changes in the components of TRICK. In effect, the regulators always seem to come up "a day late and a dollar short." In addition to the unregulated risks mentioned above, many of the risks associated with off-balance-sheet activities are largely unregulated or just now coming under regulatory purview (e.g., loan commitments).

Since the major function of any insurer is risk management, the existence of unregulated risks creates a special problem for deposit insurers, known as "adverse selection." An insurance arrangement in which the insuree has more information about risk than the insurer leads to adverse-selection behavior. Critical information gaps currently exist with respect to interstate-rate risk, foreign risk,[18] and the risks associated with off-balance-sheet activities. To manage risk effectively (i.e., to control risk exposure), deposit insurers must have information systems that measure all relevant forms of risk.

The adverse-selection problem can be contrasted with another problem that insurers face, namely "moral hazard." This term refers to changes in behavior when insurance is introduced. Moral-hazard and adverse-selection problems are exacerbated by uniform or flat-rate insurance policies. Thus, most rationally priced insurance contracts are not uniform; they contain deductibles, coinsurance, and other special features. Such tailor-made contracts provide preferred premiums for low-risk customers. This process of self-selection permits insurees to choose from a menu of insurance contracts. The track record indicates that "good risks" select low coverage and "bad risks" select high coverage. When there is no choice, the deposit-insurance record indicates that the "high rollers" take on excessive risk; as a result, they are subsidized by the more risk-averse managers.

Agency Theory

The best framework for analyzing deposit insurance is in terms of *agency theory* (see Chapter 3). Recall that the agency problem may arise from (1) different goals and objectives, (2) asymmetric information, or (3) dishonesty. In this context, the principal–agent relationship is between deposit insurers and insured institutions. To protect the deposit-insurance fund (and the taxpayers, since the government stands behind the fund), the insurers must monitor the activities of the insurees. The costs incurred in the surveillance activities are called *agency costs*. The primary source of the agency problem for deposit insurers is asymmetric information. The asymmetry exists in two forms: (1) managers know more about their risk exposure than deposit insurers can be expected to know and (2) some risks, the unregulated ones, are not yet under regulatory scrutiny. As a result, managers of insured institutions have the opportunity to exploit the insurance fund by passing some portion of their risk-taking onto the fund. This opportunity encourages some managers, among other things, to hold riskier assets, to engage in more aggressive forms of liability management, and to use greater leverage than they might otherwise choose. Moreover, as bank risk-taking expands, in both its regulated and unregulated forms, the lags associated with regulatory inertia further exacerbate the problem.

---

[18] The additions to loan-loss reserves by large BHCs in 1987 may have contained critical information about the quality of loans to less-developed countries. Musumeci and Sinkey [1988] analyze the information content of these disclosures.

In its present form, the system of deposit insurance creates the wrong kinds of incentives. A subsidy for risk-bearing encourages the kind of behavior that regulators are trying to control. To manage such adverse behavior, regulators must monitor risk-taking and enforce administrative penalities (cease-and-desist orders, removal of bank officers, etc.) on high-risk or so-called problem institutions. Since deposit-insurance subsidies and guarantees are not free, they come at the expense of the general taxpayer and institutions that maintain low-risk profiles.

THE PROSPECTS FOR INSURANCE AND REGULATORY REFORM

To dramatize the prospects for insurance and regulatory reform, let's take refuge in a (slightly altered) apocryphal story.[19] In this story, the President of the American Bankers Association, the President of the United States League of Savings Associations, and an academic economist are ushered into the presence of God and each allowed to ask Him a single question. The ABA president goes to God and inquires, "Tell me, Father, how long until my membership is strong again?" God replies: "Half a decade." The ABA President weeps and leaves. The President of the U.S. League of Savings Associations steps up next and asks: "Tell me, Father, how long will my membership have to worry about their survival?" "Two decades," answers God. The U.S. League President weeps and leaves. Finally, the academic economist goes to God and asks the deeper question, "How long will it be until federal deposit insurance is fairly and rationally priced and bank regulation is no longer a jurisdictional tangle that boggles the mind?" This time, *God* weeps and leaves.

CHAPTER SUMMARY

This chapter has focused upon the *R* or reregulation component of TRICK with emphasis on three areas: (1) regulatory restrictions, (2) financial innovation, and (3) the need for regulatory and deposit-insurance reforms. The notions of the regulatory dialectic and the regulatory reflex provided the theoretical foundations for connecting the three areas. The BHC movement, the payment of implicit interest, and subsidized risk-taking at the expense of the deposit-insurance fund have been three of the key faces of innovative bank management. These three phenomena fit into the regulatory-dialectic framework as responses to geographic and interest-rate restrictions and the mispricing of deposit insurance. The BHC movement was discussed in terms of fundamental definitions and relationships with emphasis placed upon the growth, regulation (Ten Cs), and public benefits of BHCs. In addition, BHC managerial perspectives and strategies in both the banking and nonbanking areas were analyzed. Analysis of the payment of implicit interest was based on the fundamental distinction between explicit and implicit interest. Regarding deposit insurance, background, issues, and reforms were discussed. As long as the banking authorities provide the deposit-insurance and lender-of-last-resort functions, there will be a need for bank regulation. The major problem with the existing insurance and regulatory structure is that it encourages risk-taking at the expense of more risk-averse individuals and institutions. Although the structure has worked effectively for five decades, it has not kept pace with the recent revolution in the financial-services industry.

---

[19] This story appeared in an earlier version of Kane's [1985] deposit-insurance study.

LIST OF KEY WORDS AND CONCEPTS

Bailouts and "too-big-to-fail" doctrine
Bank failures
Bank holding company (BHC,
    concepts, legislation, and regulation)
Bank Merger Act of 1960
Banking restrictions (interest rate,
    geographic, and product)
BOPEC (the Fed's BHC rating system)
CAMEL (federal regulator's bank rating
    system)
Competitive Equality Act of 1987
Convenience and needs
Deposit assumption (or purchase and
    assumption, P&A)
Deposit Insurance National Bank
    (DINB)

Deposit-insurance premium
Deposit payoff
Deposit transfer
Explicit interest
Federal deposit insurance (concepts,
    legislation, and practices)
Loan loss reserves
Implicit interest
McFadden Act (1927)
Modified payoffs
Multibank holding company (MBHC)
Nonprice competition
One-bank holding company (OBHC)
Problem banks (in general and of the
    1980s)
Regulatory dialectic

REVIEW/DISCUSSION QUESTIONS

1. Explain how the McFadden Act imposes uniformity on the dual-banking system.
2. What did the Douglas Amendment to the McFadden Act accomplish?
3. Explain what the term "grandfather" means in banking and give an example.
4. Carefully explain both the structure and related cash flows of a BHC.
5. Write a brief essay about the growth of BHCs using the data from Table 8.2
6. What is the strongest evidence in this chapter to support the conjecture that the BHC movement was designed primarily to circumvent geographic restrictions?
7. What are the major provisions of the 1970 amendments to the BHC Act?
8. Why should BHCs be restricted to nonbanking activities that have to be "closely related to banking"?
9. List and explain what appear to be the four most important Cs of the ten Cs of BHC regulation.
10. What would you suggest as a remedy for reducing the large number of small denomination checks that are written?
11. Make a list of the merchandise premiums that you (or your family) have received as implicit interest.
12. Define the notion of an L^* customer. How do they tend to receive their implicit interest?
13. Why is it advantageous for banks to be able to segment their deposit markets? Is it fair?
14. Why should taxpayers be concerned about the gathering crisis in federal deposit insurance?
15. Describe, contrast, and compare the various procedures that the FDIC has available for handling problem and failed banks.
16. Use agency theory to explain the dilemma facing deposit insurers and explain the terms *adverse selection* and *moral hazard* in this context.
17. Professor George Kaufman of Loyola University of Chicago contends that "Evaluating the riskiness of banks is more difficult than evaluating that of, say,

automobile drivers." Do you agree or disagree? Why? Why doesn't the FDIC have a variable-rate deposit-insurance premium? Wouldn't a risk-based pricing mechanism make more sense? How would you implement such a mechanism? In what sense does the FDIC already have a variable-rate scheme?

18. What was the "real reason" Sprague gave for doing the four bailouts described in his book? Discuss and evaluate this reason and the stress that bank regulators were under during the 1980s.

19. Discuss and evaluate the following statement made by former Federal Reserve Governor Jackson in 1978.

I think the industry as a whole has become overregulated by the way its supervisors set standards for a bank's capital and assets. We need to stop treating banks like public utilities and allow the marketplace by its own risk analysis to make a determination between the successful and the unsuccessful bank. No government official, regardless of how competent or well intentioned, can manage an individual bank or the industry as a whole as well as the collective efforts of bank stockholders, directors and officers.

20. In a 1963 speech dedicating the FDIC's headquarters building, Wright Patman, then Chairman of the House Banking and Currency Committee said:

... I think we should have more bank failures. The record of the last several years of almost no bank failures and, finally last year, no bank failure at all, is to me a danger signal that we have gone too far in the direction of bank safety.

Discuss what Patman's reaction might be to the bank failures of the 1980s.

21. Using Table 8-8 and the appendix to this chapter, discuss the cost effectiveness and role of incentives when the FDIC has used warrants in bailout situations.

MATCHING QUIZ

Directions: Select the letter from the right-hand column that best matches the item in the left-hand column.

___	1. Effects of regulation	A. $\frac{1}{12}$ of one percent
___	2. The McFadden Act of	B. Implicit interest
___	3. BHC	C. Bank rating system
___	4. OBHC	D. BHC rating system
___	5. MBHC	E. Way of viewing BHC reg
___	6. BHC downstream cash flow	F. Citicorp
___	7. BHC upstream cash flow	G. 1970 BHC amendment
___	8. Double leverage	H. Comp. Equality Act of 1987
___	9. State with most BHCs in 1985	I. 1927
___	10. Applied to only MBHCs	J. 1960

___ 11. Year Bank Merger Act passed	K. Public-benefits test
___ 12. Closed the nonbank-bank loophole	L. Good intentions and unintended evils
___ 13. Closed the OBHC loophole	M. Debt downstreamed as equity
___ 14. Convenience and needs	N. BHC Act of 1956
___ 15. Loan-loss reserve leader	O. Federal Reserve System
___ 16. Ten Cs	P. Dominant organizational form
___ 17. Regulator of BHCs	Q. Texas
___ 18. BOPEC	R. Dividends
___ 19. CAMEL	S. Equity
___ 20. Form of nonprice competition	T. Numerous but small
___ 21. FDIC premium	U. Permits FDIC bail outs
___ 22. Section 13(c)	V. Control bulk of BHC deposits
___ 23. Deposit assumption	W. 1984 bail out
___ 24. Penn Square Bank	X. 1982 bank failure
___ 25. Continental Illinois	Y. Purchase and assumption

CHAPTER 8

APPENDIX

The FDIC's Use of Warrants in the Bailouts of First Pennsylvania Bank and First City Bancorporation

Introduction

This appendix serves the triple purpose of introducing you to (1) the details of the Black–Scholes [1973] option-pricing model, which you will recall is one of the fundamental building blocks of financial management; (2) an application of this model to the FDIC's bailout of First Pennsylvania Bank; and (3) the incentive plans used to attract management teams and investment bankers to turnaround situations as illustrated by the case of First City Bancorporation of Houston.

The Case of First Pennsylvania Bank[1]

On April 28, 1980, First Pennsylvania Corporation, the parent holding company of First Pennsylvania Bank, was required to issue to the FDIC and 27 assisting banks (pro rata on the basis of $500 million loan) warrants to purchase 20 million shares of its common stock at $3 per share. In present-value terms, the issuance of the warrants was responsible for these effects:

1. substantially diluting shareholders' equity (there are only 15.6 million shares of First Pennsylvania's common stock outstanding)
2. strengthening the bank's capital position (the exercise money of $60 million must be invested by the holding company as equity in the bank)
3. compensating the FDIC and the assisting banks for the bailout.

Regarding the dilution and compensation issues, a class-action suit on behalf of First Pennsylvania's 25,000 shareholders challenged the FDIC's action. The unsuccessful suit contended that the exercising of the warrants by the participants in the bailout "take(s) the property of the shareholders without just compensation or due process."[2] One important aspect of this appendix is to determine whether or not the warrants represent "just" compensation for the agreed-upon loan package.

Since a warrant is similar to a call option, the analysis is couched in terms of the BlackScholes [1973] option-pricing model. The following material combines (1) a fundamental concept of financial management—warrants, (2) an application of the

---

[1] This part of the appendix is based on a study by Sinkey and Miles [1982]. The verbatim parts are reprinted by permission.

[2] See Scheibla [1980], p. 24.

option-pricing model, and (3) a real-world example. The concept-model-example feature shows the application of option-pricing theory to practical problems in financial management.

Warrants and the Option-Pricing Model

Warrants are one of those items that usually appear in the special-topics section of a financial-management textbook. Since such sections rarely are covered in a basic finance course, the concept of a *warrant* as a financial term, as opposed to a legal one, frequently is unknown. Moreover, the relationship between a warrant and a call option is even less familiar. This section clarifies the concept of a warrant and defines the relationship between a warrant and a call option.

A *warrant* is a security that provides its owner with the right (or option) to buy common stock of the issuing company at a fixed price called the *exercise price*. Warrants typically expire anywhere between a few months and several years.[3] When a warrant is exercised the holder surrenders it to the issuing company in exchange for common stock. As an instrument of corporate finance, warrants usually are attached to new bond or preferred-stock issues. If the warrants are "detachable," they can be traded separately from the original bond or preferred stock. In this context, the warrants are used as compensation or a "sweetener" to the original issue. That is, the investor receives not only the interest rate on the debt or preferred stock but also an option to purchase common stock at the exercise price. As the market price of the stock rises, the warrants become more valuable. Under normal circumstances, a borrower should be able to obtain a lower rate of interest through the use of warrants. For high-risk companies such as First Pennsylvania, the use of warrants may be critical in obtaining debt financing. In addition to their "sweetener" role in debt financing, warrants also are used as compensation to underwriters and venture capitalists in starting new firms.

A call option also gives the owner the right to buy common stock at a fixed price called the *exercise price*. The most important difference between a call option and a warrant is that a warrant is a liability of the issuing corporation, whereas the call option is a liability of the option seller. If a call option is exercised, the writer of the call option must deliver the required number of shares. Upon delivery, the writer receives the exercise price. If a warrant is exercised, the firm must issue a new share and deliver it to the owner of the warrant. The firm then receives the exercise price.

Galai and Schneller [1978] have shown that the relationship between the value of a warrant and the value of a call option can be expressed as

$$W = S/(1 + q), \tag{8-A1}$$

where W is the value of a warrant, S is the value of the call option, and q (the dilution factor) is the ratio of the number of warrants issued to the number of shares of common stock outstanding. It is assumed that W and S have the same exercise price and expiration data. S is the value of a call option in a firm that does not have warrants outstanding; W is the value of the corresponding warrants of the same firm.

Black and Scholes [1973] have shown that under certain conditions the value of a call option can be specified as

$$S = VN(d_1) - Ce^{-r_fT}N(d_2) \tag{8-A2}$$

---

[3] To illustrate, the owners are the participating banks and the FDIC, the issuing company is First Pennsylvania Corporation, the exercise price is $3, and the time-to-expiration is seven years.

where

S = *market value of the call option* (it is assumed that the call option is on 1 share of common stock)

V = *market value of 1 share of the underlying common stock*

C = *exercise price*

r_f = *riskless interest rate*

T = *time to expiration*

$N(x)$ = *area under the normal curve and to the left of x*. For example, if $(x) = 0$, $N(x) = .5$.

Letting σ^2 represent the instantaneous variance of percentage returns on V, d_1 and d_2 are defined as

$$d_1 = \frac{\ln \dfrac{V}{C} + \left(r_f + \dfrac{1}{2}\sigma^2 \right) T}{\sigma \sqrt{T}}$$

$$d_2 = d_1 - \sigma \sqrt{T}.$$

Given Equations 8-A1 and 8-A2, the valuation of warrants appears, on the surface, to be a straightforward procedure. That is, compute S using Equation 8-A2 and then adjust for dilution as indicated in Equation 8-A1. There are some complications, however. First, Equation 8-A1 requires that the value of S be computed for the firm without warrants already outstanding. Thus, the inputs to Equation 8-A2, such as market price per share and variance, must be the values that would prevail in the absence of outstanding warrants.[4] If a firm already has warrants outstanding, it is difficult to measure these variables. However, we are concerned with estimating the value of the warrants *before* the decision is made to issue them. Of course, if the market anticipates the warrant issue, the observed values of share price and variance are contaminated. Since the FDIC had never used warrants in conjunction with a Section 13(c) action before, it is unlikely that the market would have anticipated the warrant issue.[5] Thus, for the purpose of estimating warrant value before the warrants are issued, Equation 8-A2 should provide a reasonable first approximation.

A second complication is that Black and Scholes, in their derivation of Equation 8-A2, assumed no dividend payments. This is a reasonable assumption for any call option that expires before the next dividend payment. Since a "typical" warrant has a life of several years, the assumption of no dividend payment is a restrictive one for valuing the warrants of dividend-paying firms. In the First Pennsylvania case, however, the assumption is less restrictive because the parent company was not paying a dividend at the time the warrants were issued. Under the terms of the assistance package, no dividends could be paid by the bank or the holding company without the FDIC's approval.

[4] At the time of the bailout, First Pennsylvania did have 2.2 million warrants outstanding with an expiration date of May 8, 1983, and an exercise price of $20. For the two months preceding the bailout, the warrants traded in the range of $\frac{3}{4}$ to $1\frac{3}{8}$. Assuming an average warrant value of 1, the total value of the outstanding warrants was only $2.2 million, or less than 3 percent of First Pennsylvania's equity at a market value of $93.6 million. Because of the relatively small value of the warrants compared to First Pennsylvania's equity base, our working assumption is that the outstanding warrants will not substantially distort our calculations using Equation 8-A2.

[5] Section 13(c) of the FDI Act authorizes the FDIC to assist an operating insured bank if the bank is in danger of closing and its continued operation is essential to maintain adequate banking service in the community. See Chapter 8, pp. 201–202.

The Financial-Assistance Package

On April 28, 1980, a $500-million assistance package[6] was provided jointly by the FDIC and a group of banks to First Pennsylvania Bank (see Table 8-A1 for the list of banks and the aid they provided). The assistance package, which was in the form of five-year subordinated debt, had the components shown below.

Lender	Amount	Interest Rate
FDIC	$325 million	125% of the FDIC portfolio yield for the next 4 years (no interest the first year)
Banks outside	$150 million	Reserve-adjusted one-year CD rate (established annually)
Philadelphia banks	$ 25 million	Reserve-adjusted one-year CD rate (established annually)

TABLE 8-A1   List of Private Lending Institutions

Banks[a]	Loan ($ thousands)	Percentage $175 million	Percentage $500 million	Pro Rata Share of 20 Million Warrants (Thousands of Warrants)
1. Citibank	23,895	13.66%	4.78%	956
2. Chase Manhattan Bank	18,159	10.39	3.63	726
3. Manufacturers Hanover. Trust Co.	16,726	9.57	3.35	670
4. First National Bank of Chicago	14,336	819	2.87	574
5. Bankers Trust Company	11,469	6.55	2.29	458
6. Chemical Bank	11,469	6.55	2.29	458
7. Marine Midland Bank	11,469	6.55	2.29	458
8. Crocker National Bank	7,646	4.37	1.53	306
9. Morgan Guaranty Trust Co.	7,646	4.37	1.53	306
10. Security Pacific National Bank	7,646	4.37	1.53	306
11. Wells Fargo Bank	7,646	4.37	1.53	306
12. Girard Bank	7,168	4.10	1.43	286
13. Philadelphia National Bank	7,168	4.10	1.43	286
14. Bank of America	3,823	2.18	0.76	152
15. Continental Illinois National Bank	3,823	2.18	0.76	152
16. Philadelphia Savings Fund Society	2,867	1.64	0.57	114
17. Provident National Bank	2,389	1.36	0.48	96
18. AmeriTrust Company, Cleveland	1,912	1.09	0.38	76
19. Fidelity Bank	1,912	1.09	0.38	76
20. Republic National Bank of Dallas	1,529	0.87	0.31	62
21. Continental Bank	956	0.55	0.19	38
22. North Carolina National Bank	956	0.55	0.19	38
23. Beneficial Savings Bank	478	0.27	0.10	20
24. Central Penn National Bank	478	0.27	0.10	20
25. Germantown Savings Bank	478	0.27	0.10	20
26. Industrial Valley Bank & Trust Co.	478	0.27	0.10	20
27. Western Savings Bank	478	0.27	0.10	20
Bank Total	175,000	100.00%	35.00%	7,000
FDIC	325,000	185.71%	65.00%	13,000
Grand Total	500,000	285.71%	100.00%	20,000

[a]Eleven of the listed banks are located in the Philadelphia area, including 12, 13, 16, 17, 19, 21, and 23 through 27. Their loans total $24.85 million.
Source: Federal Deposit Insurance Corporation.

[6] The details of the financial-assistance package are described in *Joint News Release* [1980].

At the time of the loan, the yield on the FDIC's portfolio was 8.54 percent. Even with the 125 percent markup (i.e., 10.675%), the FDIC loan rate involved a subsidy. For example, to borrow from the Federal Reserve discount window at the "special circumstances" rate, it would have cost 12 percent at the time of the loan. For the participating banks, the reserve-adjusted one-year CD rate represents an effective opportunity cost. However, this rate also included a subsidy, since it was unlikely that First Pennsylvania could have borrowed in the open market at this rate. The FDIC loan was subordinate to the credit provided by the participating banks, but senior to First Pennsylvania's outstanding subordinated debt. The loans from the assisting banks were subordinate to deposit debt and other general credits but senior to other subordinated debt. Principal on the loan was due at the end of five years (April 28, 1985) and could be prepaid. All loan repayments were to be shared *pro rata* by the participating banks and the FDIC.

In addition to the five-year subordinated loan, the assistance package included (1) a commitment of $1 billion in lines of credit from various banks, (2) access to the Federal Reserve discount window as appropriate, and (3) the use of warrants.

As part of the assistance package, First Pennsylvania Corporation, the parent company, was required to issue *pro rata* to the FDIC and the assisting banks warrants to purchase 20 million shares of its common stock at $3 per share. The exercise price was 50 percent of the average daily closing prices of the holding company's common stock from March 17, 1980, to April 15, 1980. This period represents the 30 days immediately preceding initiation of discussions between the FDIC and the bank. The warrants had a seven-year life and any proceeds from their exercise had to be invested by the holding company as equity in the bank.

As of March 11, 1980, First Pennsylvania Corporation had 15,605,996 shares outstanding, plus certain other warrants and options. If the 20 million warrants were exercised, the number of shares outstanding would more than double. At the same time, however, the bank would receive a $60-million infusion of equity capital (i.e., 20 million warrants times the $3 exercise price).[7] As of March 31, 1980, First Pennsylvania Bank had total equity capital (book value) of roughly $307 million with a market value of $113 million.

The Value of the Warrants

The Mechanics of the Valuation

The Black–Scholes equation can be used to approximate the value of the warrants issued as part of the First Pennsylvania bailout. The value of the warrants is the amount of compensation paid by First Pennsylvania in exchange for the assistance package. The warrants were not marketable at the time of the bailout, but they were clearly a liability of First Pennsylvania. Consequently, some effort should have been made to estimate their value. Equation 8-A2 can be used to obtain an estimate for the value of these warrants. The inputs for the equation include the market value of a share of First Pennsylvania's common stock, the exercise price, the time to expiration of the warrant, an estimate of the "riskless" interest rate, and an estimate of the instantaneous variance of percentage returns on the underlying common stock. The most difficult input to obtain is an estimate of the variance.

One way to estimate variance is to look at past stock returns; this method is

---

[7] These funds are referred to as the exercise money. When warrants are exercised, the value of equity increases by the exercise money, that is, *new equity = old equity + exercise money*.

acceptable if past variance is the same as investors' perceptions of future variance. Another method, and the one employed here, is to use the variance implied by the market value of First Pennsylvania's existing warrants.[8] At the time of the bailout, First Pennsylvania had 2.2 million warrants outstanding with an expiration date of May 8, 1983, and an exercise price of $20. Various values for σ^2 can be plugged into the right-hand side of Equation 8-A2. Next, the value of σ^2 that produces a price equal to the actual market value of one of these warrants can be used as an estimate of variance. An advantage of this approach is that this estimate of σ^2 is based on investors' estimates for variance of future returns rather than historical returns.

The time period consisting of March and April of 1980 was used to estimate σ^2. While this was a volatile period for First Pennsylvania (because of the adverse publicity it was receiving), it was the relevant time period for estimating the variance. Daily values for both the warrants and common stock were plugged into Equation 8-A2 and corresponding values of σ^2 were computed using the prevailing three-year government bond rate of 14 percent. The low value of the standard deviation over the two-month time interval was .65 and the high was .80. The next step was to use this range of standard deviations to establish a range of warrant prices.

For these warrants, an exercise price of $3 was chosen by the FDIC, which was (by design) one-half the average common stock price for the period March 17–April 15, 1980. This calculation implies that $6 is the "representative" share price for First Pennsylvania's common stock prior to the start of negotiations for the bailout.[9] The share price of $6 when inserted into Equation 8-A2, along with the range of standard-deviation estimates obtained previously, leads to the values shown in Table 8-A2. The Black–Scholes equation yields values for an "equivalent" call option, that is, a call option with an exercise price of $3 and a life of seven years. However, due to the effects of dilution a warrant will be worth less than an "equivalent" call option. Thus, the value of the call option must be divided by $(1 + q)$ to get the warrant value, where q is the number of warrants divided by the number of shares outstanding. Here, q is 20 million/15.6 million or 1.28. Since the seven-year government bond rate had fallen to 10 percent by May 1980, it was the rate used to develop the figures in Table 8-A2.

It is important to note that the estimated warrant values in Table 8-A2 reflect the price First Pennsylvania's shareholders already have paid for the bailout. In an efficient market, once the warrant agreement was announced, its dilutive effects would have been reflected in the market value of First Pennsylvania's common stock. At that time, the shareholders paid for the bailout. If the warrants happen to expire unexercised, the shareholders' ownership in the firm will not be diluted.[10]

A Comparison of Warrant and Subsidy Values

The question of whether or not the required issuance of warrants by First Pennsylvania represented "unfair" treatment of that firm's shareholders is a difficult question to answer. So far, we have *estimated* the value of the warrants but now must compare those values with *estimates* for the value of the loan subsidies provided to First Pennsylvania. Our strategy is to make assumptions that will favor the "unfair treatment" contention and compute an upper bound to the wealth transferred from First

---

[8] Latane and Rendleman [1976] use this method. If a firm does not have outstanding warrants, the only alternative is to measure the variance using historical returns on its common stock.

[9] The notion of a "representative" price is not consistent with the efficient-markets concept. In efficient markets, the "representative" price at any instant is the prevailing market price.

[10] According to Scheibla [1980], "FDIC plans either to sell its warrants or to exercise them to buy First Penn stock and then sell its holdings" (p. 32).

TABLE 8-A2   Estimated Value of the Warrants Held by the FDIC and the Consortium of Banks

Common Stock Price	Standard Deviation Used	Interest Rate Used[a]	Estimated Option Value	Corresponding Estimated Warrant Value[b]
$6.00	.650	9.53%	$4.97	$2.18
$6.00	.725	9.53%	$5.09	$2.23
$6.00	.800	9.53%	$5.20	$2.28

These calculations assume:
Stock price	$6.00
Exercise price	$3.00
Time to maturity	7 years
Dividends	0

[a] When the discrete time rate is 10% per year, the continuously compounded rate of return is 9.53% (i.e., log 1.10 = .0953).

[b] Using the estimated standard deviation of .13 from historical stock returns, the corresponding estimated warrant value is $1.95. If we used this warrant value in our analysis, our argument that the stockholders were not treated unfairly would be strengthened. We do not use it for two reasons. First, our strategy is to make assumptions and use estimated values that will favor the claim of unfair treatment by the shareholders. And second, we believe that the standard deviations implied by the outstanding warrant prices are better estimates of investors' perceptions of future return variance.

Source: Sinkey and Miles [1982], Table 1. Reprinted by permission.

Pennsylvania to the participants in the bailout. The assumptions are as follows:

1. The warrants were worth $2.28 each; this was the upper bound to our range.
2. The FDIC loan at 125% of the FDIC portfolio yield contained no subsidy other than the forgivement of the first year's interest payment. At the time of the bailout, the FDIC portfolio yield was 8.54% so the interest rate for the first year on the FDIC's portion of the loan was 10.675%.
3. The loan of $175 million by the consortium of banks at the reserve-adjusted CD rate contained no subsidy.
4. The $1 billion in lines of credit made available to First Pennsylvania was of no value.
5. Tax write-offs are of no value to First Pennsylvania. In the following analysis the tax deductibility of certain expenses is ignored as the bank is not expected to pay taxes before 1987. Since the bank can carry its losses forward, this assumption only approximates reality and a more detailed analysis is possible.

The analysis to follow is separated into two parts. We first analyze the FDIC's transactions and then look at the consortium of banks. The FDIC received $325 million/$500 million or 65 percent of the 20 million newly issued warrants. This represents $2.28 times 13 million warrants, or $29,640,000 in market value. In exchange for the warrants, the FDIC forgave the first annual interest payment of 10.675% × $325 million, or $34,693,750. The present value of this interest payment at 10.675% is $31,347,414. Under these *extreme* assumptions, the FDIC almost broke even. More realistic assumptions would show that the warrants did not adequately compensate the FDIC for its role in the bailout.

Our assumption that the bank loans contain no subsidies implies that the 7 million warrants issued to the consortium represented a $15,960,000 overcompensation (7 million warrants × $2.28 per warrant). However, by relaxing the assumptions of no interest-rate subsidy and a free $1 billion line of credit, the $16 million dollars of overcompensation can be transformed easily and realistically into a situation of undercompensation. To illustrate, assuming *prime-rate terms* of (1) a 300 basis-points subsidy on the loan and (2) a .5 percent annual commitment fee (paid up front) on the line of credit, the relevant cash flows are shown below.[11] A conservative estimate of the subsidy provided by the consortium of banks is $36.88 million, more than double the value of the warrants held by the banks.

Period	Cash Flow (Millions)	Present Value (15%) (Millions)
0	5.00	5.00
1	10.25	8.92
2	10.25	7.75
3	10.25	6.74
4	10.25	5.86
5	5.25	2.61
TOTAL	51.25	36.88

Setting the Terms of Future Bailout Warrants

Any time warrants are used as part of a Section 13(c) action, the FDIC can control the value of the warrants in a number of ways (i.e., they can specify time to expiration, exercise price, and number of warrants to be issued). Viewing the First Pennsylvania case retrospectively, one can see how this might proceed. First, the FDIC decides on the size of the capital injection (i.e., the exercise money), say $60 million. Next, the exercise price should be set, wherein lies the "art" of the analysis. If the price is too high, the warrants could go unexercised. The FDIC technique (described above) resulted in an exercise price of $3. Thus, 20 million warrants had to be issued to generate the desired injection of capital. Finally, the time to expiration has to be determined. The longer this period is, the greater are the chances that the warrants will be exercised. Setting the time to expiration longer than the maturity of the bailout loan appears to be a reasonable rule.

After the FDIC has set values for the terms of the warrants, Equations 8-A1 and 8-A2 can be used to compute the value of warrants. If this value seems unreasonable in relation to the estimated value of the loan subsidy, some or all of the control variables can be changed. Increasing any of these variables will increase the value of the warrants. The trial-and-error procedure suggested here is necessary since it is difficult (if not impossible) to solve algebraically for any of the variables appearing on the right-hand side of Equation 8-A2. However, it is an easy matter to write a computer routine to produce warrant values for any set of input variables.

Implications for Compensation, Dilution, and Capital Regulation

The FDIC's decision to use warrants in the First Pennsylvania case was a novel one. When the warrants were used, three important events occurred: (1) the FDIC and the 27 assisting banks received compensation for their role in the assistance package, (2) the shareholders' positions were diluted (i.e., they paid for the bailout), and (3) when the warrants are exercised, the bank receives a $60-million injection of capital.

The major point is that the shareholders are forced to pay for the bank's mismanagement and the subsequent bailout.

[11] At the time of the bailout, the reserve-adjusted one-year CD rate was roughly 11.98 percent, assuming an unadjusted CD rate of 10 percent and a $16\frac{1}{2}$ reserve requirement. The "quoted" prime rate was at 19 percent and the "discount" prime rate was around 15 percent.

Compensation

Although the FDIC is not in the investment-banking business, it deserves to be compensated for the services it provides. The use of warrants provides the FDIC with a tool that can be used for compensatory purposes. The use of the warrants as a compensatory device in the First Pennsylvania case is supported by the following statement by the FDIC's General Counsel regarding the seven-year term of the warrants versus the five-year maturity of the loans: "The longer the warrants, the better chance we have to get more for them."[12] In contrast to the FDIC's position, the 27 assisting banks appeared to be somewhat embarrassed by the fact that they were holding warrants on a sister institution. In a telephone interview, a spokesperson for Citibank stated: "We did not ask for the warrants."

Dilution

The fact that the dilution factor q in Equation 8-A1 has a value greater than unity indicates the substantial amount of dilution involved with the warrants. Shareholders have been upset about the dilution and a lawsuit was filed against the FDIC to block the use of the warrants.[13] From a financial perspective, our estimates of the value of the warrants indicate that the FDIC's compensation was not unreasonable, implying, of course, that the dilution effects were not excessive given the riskiness of the situation.

Capital Regulation

Normally, firms issue warrants to raise equity capital. Banks with "thin" capital positions frequently are "jawboned" by the banking authorities into improving their "capital adequacy."[14] Since First Pennsylvania's top management and its owners opposed the use of the warrants, it is safe to say that jawboning was instrumental in their issuance. As a component of the FDIC's arsenal, warrants are a double-barreled weapon with capital-adequacy and control elements. By transferring its warrants to the desired control group, the FDIC generates an injection of capital for the bank and at the same time can insure removal of the management team. Thus, the warrants provide the FDIC with leverage to determine control of the holding company and hence control of the bank. If the current managers do not improve the bank's performance, the FDIC can transfer control of the bank to a new group of owners. Regardless of the control motives, the exercise of the warrants provides for an injection of capital into a problem bank. Finally, since it is underpriced deposit insurance that permits weak financial institutions to remain open, warrants provide a means of extracting additional deposit-insurance premiums from such high-risk firms.[15]

Warrants as Incentives for Bailout Management Teams and Investment Bankers: The Case of First City Bancorporation

As shown in Table 8-8 in the text of this chapter, the second largest bailout in FDIC history (as of this writing) occurred on September 9, 1987. When a problem bank

[12] Scheibla [1980], p. 32.

[13] *Philip Zinman* vs. *FDIC* (1980), U.S. District Court for the Eastern District of Pennsylvania, Philadelphia, Pennsylvania. Another suit, against the SEC and others, charged the defendants with failure to make full disclosure of First Pennsylvania's financial condition as required by the securities' law and the SEC.

[14] See Sinkey [1979], pp. 42–66.

[15] Capital regulation can be viewed as an implicit premium paid for deposit insurance. See Buser, Chen, and Kane [1981] and Kane [1981]. Sinkey [1979] shows how capital regulation determines the FDIC's "problem-bank" list. These concepts are discussed in Chapter 22.

is bailed out, its existing management team is jettisoned. To attract capable managers to turnaround situations, which are high-risk ventures, financial incentives are needed. When the use of warrants provides the potential for a $16.6 million bonus, would-be managers are attracted. This potential windfall was the key ingredient in attracting a new management team to the defunct First City Bancorporation of Houston. In closing this appendix, let's look briefly at the details of the warrants used by the FDIC in the capital restructuring plan for First City (see Apcar [1987]).

A. Robert Abboud, a former Chicago banker, is the head of First City's new management team. He and four other top executives could *earn* stock warrants to purchase as many as 667,000 shares of First City's common stock over the next five to ten years as stipulated in the terms of the agreement. Note the emphasis on the word "earn." If the warrants (options) are to be "in the money," First City must be profitable in the future (i.e., it must be turned around). To test for the existence of any FDIC subsidy involved in the First City bailout, an analysis similar to the one conducted by Sinkey and Miles [1982] for First Pennsylvania is required. This exercise is recommended as a graduate research project.

The FDIC-approved plan calls for an exercise price of 7.5¢ per share, which means the warrants will cost the management team only $50,025 (= .075 × 667,000) and an exercise period of ten years. Since First City's attempt to raise new capital following the bailout has an offering price of $25 per share, a little arithmetic, $25 × 667,000 = $16,675,000, shows the potential net benefits of the deal to be $16,624,975 (= 16,675,000 − 50,025). This windfall, of course, would be split five ways among the management team with Abboud reaping the largest percentage. L. William Seidman, chairman of the FDIC, said: "It's a very significant carrot for coming into a difficult turnaround situation. We reviewed the package and thought it was fair." The details of the incentive plan were not disclosed by the FDIC.

The management teams in bailout situations are not the only parties given incentives to participate. Consider the role of investment bankers in these situations. The lead investment banker in the First City deal is Donaldson, Lufkin & Jenrette Securities Corp. of New York. This company is the lead underwriter for the public offering of First City's common and preferred shares expected to total $500 million. Along with cash fees of $25 million, the FDIC allowed Donaldson Lufkin to purchase one million warrants for 7.5¢ per share on the first day of the public offering. If the new common stock offering would go at $25 per share, the immediate net gain to the investment banker would be $25 million less the cost of the warrants of $75,000 (= .075 × 1,000,000). The word on the street was that Donaldson Lufkin planned to hold the First City warrants as an investment.

In closing, by comparing the potential dollars gains across the two parties discussed here—the bailout management team versus the investment bankers—$17 million versus $50 million, respectively, it should be clear why commercial bankers want to remove the "Chinese Wall" separating commercial and investment banking, and why investment bankers want to keep them on the other side of the wall.

SELECTED REFERENCES

(*The*) *Bank Holding Company Movement to 1978*: A Compendium. [1978]. Washington, DC, A Study by the Staff of the Board of Governors of the Federal Reserve System (September).

Baughn, William H., ed. [1975]. *Advanced Bank Holding Company Management Problems*. Dallas: SMN Press.

Benston, George J. [1973]. *Bank Examination*. Rochester, NY: University of Rochester, Center for Research in Government Policy and Business, Reprint Series No. C-16.

"BHC Rating System." [1978]. *Federal Reserve Press Release* (February 7).

Boczar, Gregory E. [1980]. "The External Growth of Multibank Holding Companies." *Journal of Bank Research* (Autumn), pp. 147–158.

Boczar, G. E. and Samuel H. Talley. [1978]. "Bank Holding Company Double Leverage," Washington, DC: Board of Governors of the Federal Reserve System.

Chase, Samuel B., Jr., and John J. Mingo. [1975]. "The Regulation of Bank Holding Companies," *Journal of Finance* (May), pp. 281–292.

Coldwell, Philip E. [1976]. "Ten C's of Holding Company Regulation." Washington, DC: Board of Governors of the Federal Reserve System (November 12).

Debussey, Fred W. [1978]. "Double Leverage in Bank Holding Companies." *Bankers Magazine* (March–April), pp. 86–90.

"Deposit Insurance in a Changing Environment." [1983]. Washington, DC: Federal Deposit Insurance Corporation (April 15).

Eisenbeis, Robert A. [1983]. "Bank Holding Companies and Public Policy." In *Financial Services*, George J. Benston, ed. Englewood Cliffs, NJ: Prentice-Hall, pp. 127–155.

Eisemann, Peter C. and George A. Budd. [1980]. *An Approach of Capital Planning at Bank Holding Company Parents*. Atlanta: Georgia State University.

Francis, Darryl R. [1975]. "Public Policy for a Free Economy." *Review*, Federal Reserve Bank of St. Louis (May), pp. 2–5.

Federal Deposit Insurance Corporation: The First Fifty Years. [1984]. Washington, DC: Federal Deposit Insurance Corporation.

Fischer, Gerald C. [1985]. *The Bank Holding Company 1956–1983: Development, Regulation, and Performance*. Washington, DC: The Association of Bank Holding Companies.

Graddy, Duane B., ed. [1979]. *The Bank Holding Company Performance Controversy*, Washington, DC: University Press of America.

Heggestad, Arnold A. [1975]. "Riskiness of Investments in Nonbank Activities by Bank Holding Companies." *Journal of Economics & Business* (Spring), pp. 219–223.

Horvitz, Paul M. [1980]. "A Reconsideration of the Role of Bank Examination." *Journal of Money, Credit and Banking* (November), pp. 654–659.

Jackson, P. C. [1978]. Address Before the Alabama Bankers Association, Mobile, Alabama, May 11. Board of Governors, Federal Reserve System, Washington, DC.

Jessee, Michael A., and Steven A. Seelig. [1977]. *Bank Holding Companies and the Public Interest*. Lexington, MA: Lexington Books, D.C. Heath.

Johnson, Richard B., ed. [1973]. *The Bank Holding Company 1973*. Dallas: SMU Press.

Kane, Edward J. [1985]. *The Gathering Crisis in Federal Deposit Insurance: Origins, Evolution, and Possible Reforms*. Cambridge, MA: MIT Press.

———. [1983]. "Metamorphosis in Financial Services Delivery and Production," Columbus: The Ohio State University, WPS 83-6.

———. [1981]. "Accelerating Inflation, Technological Innovation, and the Decreasing Effectiveness of Banking Regulation." *Journal of Finance* (June), pp. 355–367.

———. [1979]. "The Three Faces of Commercial Bank Liability Management." In *The Political Economy of Policy-Making*, M. P. Dooley, et al., eds. Beverly Hills: Sage, pp. 149–174.

———. [1978]. "Getting Along Without Regulation Q: Testing the Standard View of Deposit-Rate Competition During the 'Wild-Card Experience'." *Journal of Finance* (June), pp. 921–932.

———. [1977]. "Good Intentions and Unintended Evil," *Journal of Money Credit, and Banking* (February), pp. 55–69.

———. [1970]. "Short-Changing the Small Saver: Federal Government Discrimination Against Small Savers During the Vietnam War." *Journal of Money, Credit, & Banking* (November), pp. 513–522.

———, and B. G. Malkiel. [1965]. "Bank Portfolio Allocation, Deposit Variability, and the Availability Doctrine." *Quarterly Journal of Economics* (February), pp. 113–134.

Mason, John J. [1979]. *Financial Management of Commercial Banks*. Boston: Warren, Gorham, & Lamont.

Mayne, Lucille S. [1980]. "Funds Transfer Between Bank Holdiing Companies and Their Affiliates." *Journal of Bank Research* (Spring), pp. 20–27.

Musumeci, James J., and Joseph F. Sinkey, Jr. [1988]. "The International Debt Crisis, Loan-Loss Reserves, and Bank Security Returns in 1987," Working Paper, The University of Georgia.

Nathan, Harold C. [1980]. "Nonbank Organizations and the McFadden Act." *Journal of Bank Research* (Summer), pp. 80–86.

Nowesnick, Mary. [1980]. "The FSLIC at 50: Time to Unwrap a New Plan," *Savings Institutions* (December), pp. 44–60.

Partee, J. Charles. [1979]. Statement before the Commerce, Consumer and Monetary Affairs Subcommittee of the Committee on Government Operations, House of Representatives, March 22.

Pyle, D. H. [1974]. "The Losses on Savings Deposits from Interest-Rate Regulation." *Bell Journal of Economics and Management Science* (Autumn), pp. 614–622.

Scott, Kenneth E. [1979]. "The Dual Banking System: A Model of Competition in Regulation." In *Issues in Financial Regulation*, Franklin R. Edwards, ed. New York: McGraw-Hill.

Searle, Philip F. [1978]. "Alternative Organizational Structures." In *The Bankers' Handbook*, W. H. Baughn and C. E. Walker, eds. Homewood Hills, IL: Dow Jones-Irwin, pp. 26–47.

Selby, Edward B. Jr. [1980]. "Needless Checking Account Costs." *Bankers Magazine* (March–April), pp. 92–94.

Shull, Bernard. [1980]. "Federal and State Supervision of Bank Holding Companies." In *State and Federal Regulation of Commercial Banks*. Washington, DC: Federal Deposit Insurance Corporation, pp. 271–374.

Sinkey, Joseph F., Jr. [1985]. "Safety and Soundness, Suspensions, and Risk Elements of BHCs." In *The Bank Holding Company 1956–1983: Development, Regulation, and Performance*, Gerald C. Fisher, ed. Washington, DC: The Association of Bank Holding Companies.

———. [1985]. "Regulatory Attitudes Toward Risk." In *The Banking Handbook*, Richard A. Aspinwall and Robert A. Eisenbeis, eds. New York: Wiley, pp. 347–380.

———. [1984]. "Risk Regulation in Banking." In *Banking Structure and Competition*. Chicago: Federal Reserve Bank, pp. 432–460.

———. [1979]. *Problem and Failed Institutions in the Commercial Banking Industry*. Greenwich, CT: JAI Press.

Sprague, Irvine H. [1986]. *Bailout: An Insider's Account of Bank Failures and Rescues*. New York: Basic Books.

Stover, Roger D. [1980]. "The Single-Subsidiary Bank Holding Company." *Journal of Bank Research* (Spring), pp. 43–50.

Taggart, Robert A. Jr. [1978]. "Effects of Deposit-Rate Ceilings: The Evidence from Massachusetts Savings Banks." *Journal of Money, Credit and Banking* (May), pp. 139–157.

Varvel, Walter A. [1979]. "Nonbank Activities of Fifth District Bank Holding Companies." *Economic Review*, FRB of Richmond (Nov./Dec.), pp. 2–9.

Volcker, Paul A. [1984]. Statement before the Committee on Banking, Housing, and Urban Affairs. Washington, DC: U.S. Senate, July 25.

SELECTED REFERENCES (APPENDIX)

Apcar, Leonard M. [1987]. "Abboud Team Wins $16.6 Million Bonus as Part of Rescue of First City Bancorp." *The Wall Street Journal* (September 15), p. 3.

Black, Fisher, and Myron Scholes. [1973]. "The Pricing of Options and Corporate Liabilities." *Journal of Political Economy* (81, May–June), pp. 637–654.

Buser, Stephen A., Andrew H. Chen, and Edward J. Kane. [1981]. "Federal Deposit Insurance, Regulatory Policy, and Optimal Bank Capital." *Journal of Finance* (XXXV, No. 1), pp. 51–60.

Galai, Dan, and Mier I. Schneller. [1978]. "Pricing of Warrants and the Value of the Firm," *Journal of Finance* (XXXIII No. 5), pp. 1333–1342.

Joint News Release. [1980]. "Regulators Announce Joint Bank-FDIC Assistance to First Pennsylvania Bank," PR-42-80, April 28, Comptroller of the Currency, Federal Deposit Insurance Corporation, and Federal Reserve Board.

Kane, Edward J. [1981]. "S&Ls and Interest-Rate Re-Regulation: The FSLIC As An Industry Bail-Out Program," The Ohio State University, Working Paper Series 81-57 (July).

Latane, Henry, and R. J. Rendleman, Jr. [1976]. "Standard Deviation of Stock Price Ratios Implied in Option Prices." *Journal of Finance* (XXXI, No. 2), pp. 369–382.

Pettway, Richard H., and Joseph F. Sinkey, Jr. [1980]. "Establishing On-Site Bank Examination Priorities: An Early-Warning System Using Accounting and Market Information." *Journal of Finance* (Vol. XXXV, No. 1), pp. 137–150.

Scheibla, Shirley Hobbs. [1980]. "Untold Philadelphia Story—First Pennsylvania: No Bottom Line." *Barron's* (October 13), p. 11 ff.

Sinkey, Joseph F., Jr. [1979]. *Problem and Failed Institutions in the Commercial Banking Industry*. Greenwich, CT: JAI Press.

———. [1981]. "The Performance of First Pennsylvania Bank Prior to Its Bail-Out." Working Paper, University of Georgia, 1981.

——— and James A. Miles. [1982]. "The Use of Warrants in the Bail-Out of First Pennsylvania Bank." *Financial Management* (Autumn), pp. 27–32.

Interest Rates, Asset Prices, and the Interest-Rate Environment: Theories, Conventions, and Innovations

---

ACRONYM GUIDE TO KEY TERMS AND CONCEPTS

CD = certificate of deposit
FSF = financial-services firm
IO = interest only
PET = pure-expectations theory
PO = principal only

INTRODUCTION

A critical distinction between financial corporations and nonfinancial corporations is the greater interest-rate sensitivity of the assets and liabilities of financial-services firms (FSFs). If a firm's assets and liabilities are interest-rate sensitive, then, clearly, its net worth (assets minus liabilities) is subject to such sensitivity. In finance, this vulnerability is called interest-rate risk; in this book, interest-rate risk is represented by the I component of TRICK. Along with changes in the technological, regulatory, and competitive environments (the T, R, and C components of TRICK), the interest-rate environment is one of the key determinants of how well a financial-services firm performs. The plight of thrift institutions throughout the 1970s and 1980s attests to the problems associated with interest-rate risk. If managers of FSFs want to maximize their net-worth positions, they need to understand interest-rate risk and how to manage it. This chapter focuses on the relationships between interest rates and asset prices, between interest rates and inflation, and among interest rates. These theoretical developments are complemented by descriptions of the conventions and innovations surrounding interest rates and asset prices. The "how to" part of managing interest-rate risk is covered in Chapter 17.

THE VALUATION OF FIXED-INCOME SECURITIES

Chapter 3 presented the mechanics of the discounted-cash-flow method of valuation. For the most part, the focus there was on variable-income securities or common stocks. In this chapter, we focus on fixed-income securities or bonds, both short-term and long-term ones. With the development of floating-rate debt, various kinds of "stripping" have been made available through the process of securitization (e.g., interest-only obligations, called IOs, principal-only obligations, called, you guessed it, POs) and other financial innovations. As a result, the study of fixed-income securities is becoming more and more complex. Nevertheless, don't let all of the bells and whistles confuse you because the basic valuation properties are still the same. The most basic principle still holds: the value of an interest-bearing obligation (defined to include the special case of a zero-coupon bond) is equal to the present discounted value of its future cash flows, where the discount rate is the going rate of interest on obligations of similar risk and maturity.

The Basic Bond-Valuation Formula

Using the following symbols, C_t = coupon or interest-payment in period t, F = face or maturity value of the obligation, N = the maturity of the obligation, and i = the discount rate or the going rate of interest on similar obligations, the present value or price, P_0, of the security (also called obligation, instrument, or asset) is

$$P_0 = \sum_{t=1}^{N} [C_t/(1 + i)^t] + F/(1 + i)^N \tag{9-1}$$

In words, the value an investor receives from this instrument consists of two components: (1) the present value of the interest payments (the first term on the RHS of Equation 9-1) and (2) the present value of the lump-sum payment at maturity (the second term on the RHS of Equation 9-1). When the coupon interest payment is fixed, we have the "plain vanilla" or standard debt instrument or bond. Viewed in this framework, it is easy to illustrate the various innovations (e.g., derivative securities) that have occurred in debt financing over recent years.

First, let's focus on the interest-payments term of Equation 9-1. If coupon payments are variable and not fixed, then we have a floating-rate bond. In this case, the stream of interest payments cannot be treated as an annuity (i.e., a stream of constant payments over some time period). In the mechanics of valuation, since each interest payment is different, it must be treated as an individual lump-sum payment. Floating-rate obligations usually have interest payments linked to some highly visible interest rate such as a Treasury rate or the prime rate. A recent banking innovation has been the linking of deposit returns, not to market interest rates on debt obligations, but to the performance of indices or prices in equity markets. These market-index deposits (called MIDs) usually offer a specified portion of any gain in the index (e.g., the S&P 500) and guarantee some minimum return (see King and Remolona [1987]).

Next, let's consider the case in which the investor receives only a lump sum at maturity. Since the coupon-interest payment is zero, this case is a variation in the stream of interest payments. Such a situation may arise under two different circumstances. The first occurs when the obligation is issued as a zero-coupon bond. Under this condition, the bond sells at a discount and the investor's return is solely in the form of a capital gain, equal to the difference between the face value of the bond and its selling price. The other circumstance arises through the process of "stripping" a debt instrument in the secondary market. If the interest payments are stripped away from an obligation, it is called a "principal-only" instrument or PO. A PO is, in effect, a zero-coupon obligation issued in the secondary market. Although mortgages are the primary financial instrument used for stripping, the process of securitization has extended to all kinds of assets from credit-card receivables to automobile loans.

Let's now consider variations in the face value of the standard debt instrument represented in Equation 9-1. If the face value has been stripped away then we have an "interest-only" obligation or IO. If the interest payment is fixed, the IO is simply an annuity. If the annuity goes on forever, it is a perpetual annuity or a perpetuity; in England, such instruments are called "consols." If the stripped interest payments are variable, then we have a variable annuity.

To summarize, valuation of financial assets, whether debt or equity instruments, is a two-step process: (1) project or estimate the future cash flows (i.e., the annuities and/or lump-sum payments) and (2) calculate the present values of the future cash flows. Table 9-1 presents a recapitulation of the instruments discussed above and

---

TABLE 9.1   The Valuation of Bonds and Bond Derivatives

Basic valuation formula: $P_0 = \sum_{t=1}^{N} [C_t/(1+i)^t] + F/(1+i)^N$

where P_0 = price or present value
          C_t = coupon-interest payment in period t
          F = face, principal, or maturity value
          i = discount rate or going rate of interest
          N = maturity
          Σ = sigma or summation sign over $t = 1$ to N.

Case 1: "Plain vanilla". A five-year bond with a 10% annual coupon and a $1,000 face value. If the going rate of interest on similar obligations is 8%, the bond will sell at a *premium* price of $1,080. The cash flows at 10% are more valuable because other similar instruments are paying only 8%. If the going rate of interest is 12%, the bond will sell at a discount price of $927. Its cash flows at 10% are less valuable than those at 12%.

Case 2: Zero-Coupon Bond. The same bond as above except without any interest payments. As long as the going rate of interest is positive, the instrument must sell at a discount. At i = 10 percent, its value is $620.92. By the way, the IRS requires the investor to prorate the discount ($379.08) over the maturity of the obligation and to pay taxes on that portion even though no income is received. The valuation approaches for a PO and a zero-coupon bond are the same.

Case 3: Interest Only. The same bond as in case 1 but stripped of its principal payment. The instrument is simply an annuity. At i = 10 percent, the annuity has a present value of $379.08. Note that the addition of the IO and PO values at 10 percent are, of course, equal to the present value of the plain vanilla bond at 10 percent. The whole is equal to the sum of the parts.

Case 4: Perpetual Bond or Consol. The same bond as in case 3, except the interest payments never cease. If the coupon payment is fixed, the valuation is the same as a zero-growth model. Specifically, simply divide the payment by the going rate of interest. For example, at i = 10 percent, the value is $100/.10 = $1,000; at 8 percent, it's $1,250; and at 12 percent, it's $833.

Case 5: Floating-Rate Instruments. In this situation, there is uncertainty about the size of the interest payments. For example, if the coupon rate floats at 200 basis points over the prime rate, then coupon payments will vary with the prime rate. Assume the bond in case 1 has its coupon rate so defined and the prime rate (on an annual basis) is 8%, 8.5%, 9%, 9.5%, and 10% over the maturity of the bond. Given this interest-rate scenario, the coupon rate in each of the five years will be 10%, 10.5%, 11%, 11.5%, and 12%. If the bond's discount rate moves in proportion to its coupon rate, assuming it sells at par, the present value of the interest-payments stream will not change. Of course, as interest rates rise, the present value of the principal payment will decline. The promised payment of $1,000 at maturity, however, does not vary.

Note: It is assumed you know how to use a hand-held calculator or present-value tables to verify the figures presented in this table.

numerical examples of the valuation process for each case. Now that you have been introduced to the basics of bond valuation, let's focus on some refinements and more advanced concepts.

PURE-DISCOUNT (ZERO-COUPON) SECURITIES AND DURATION

Treasury bills are the key instrument of the money market. Since they have no intermediate cash flows, they belong to a class of financial instruments called *pure-discount* (or *zero-coupon*) *securities*. Zero-coupon securities have only one cash flow, a lump-sum payment at the maturity of the obligation. The return comes in the form of price appreciation. Any nonamortizing financial asset is, in effect, a zero-coupon security. For example, a loan that is not amortized and is simply paid off at maturity with a single payment of principal plus interest is a zero-coupon instrument. Such securities *always* trade at *discounts* from their face or maturity values because they promise no intermediate cash flows. In banking, zero-coupon instruments sometimes are called "bullet loans" if they are assets and "bullet deposits" if they are liabilities. The single-payment loan described above is an example of a bullet loan; a zero-coupon CD is an example of a bullet deposit.

The distinguishing characteristic of a zero-coupon security is that its maturity and its duration are equal. Any security with an intermediate cash flow (e.g., a coupon bond) has a duration that is *always* less than its maturity. Duration is the *average* life of a security or *effective* time until maturity or repricing. Maturity simply measures the *nominal* term or life of an instrument. Duration also can be viewed as the average amount of time that it takes to recoup the cost of an investment. Consider a Treasury bill as an example. Since there are no intermediate cash flows, the average time it takes to recoup the cost of the investment is simply the term to maturity of the bill. Thus, duration and maturity are the same in this case.

Duration When Securities Have Intermediate Cash Flows

Consider now a financial instrument that has some intermediate cash flows. How do we measure its duration? The traditional measure of duration as established by Macaulay [1938] is

$$D = \frac{\sum_{t=1}^{N}\left[\frac{C_t}{(1+i)^t}\right]t + \left[\frac{F}{(1+i)^N}\right]N}{P_0} \tag{9-2}$$

where P_0 is the (unweighted) present value of the instrument and the numerator is a weighted cash-flow term. Thus, mechanically duration is simply a ratio of a weighted present value to an unweighted present value. In the numerator of Equation 9-2, C_t represents the cash flow or coupon interest paid in period t, F is the face value of the instrument to be paid at maturity in period N, and i, the discount rate, is the going rate of interest on obligations of similar risk. Thus, the numerator of Equation 9-2 is the sum of the present value of the coupon payments weighted by the respective time elements t plus the present value of the face value weighted by the term to maturity.

To illustrate the calculation of D, consider a five-year bond with a 10 percent coupon and a $1,000 face value. If the going rate of interest is 10 percent, the price of the bond is $1,000. Thus, in Equation 9-2 for this example, $P_0 = $1,000. The numerator of 9-2 is calculated as follows:

t	Cash Flow	Present Value of Cash Flow at 10%	Weighted Present Value (column 1 × column 3)
1	$100	$90.91	$90.91
2	$100	$82.64	$165.28
3	$100	$75.13	$225.39
4	$100	$68.30	$273.20
5	$1,100	$683.01	$3,415.05
		$999.99	$4,169.83

Thus, the bond's duration is

$$D = \frac{4,169.83}{1,000} = 4.16983 \text{ or } 4.17$$

What does a duration of 4.17 mean and does duration have any significance? A duration of 4.17 *years* represents the *average* time until the initial cash investment in a bond is recovered. For a coupon-paying bond, its duration is always less than its term to maturity (e.g., 4.17 < 5). Duration is a significant concept because it is a measure of a bond's interest-rate risk,[1] a fact that is explained more fully below.

Price Elasticity

Elasticity is a measure of responsiveness or sensitivity to change. With respect to a financial asset, price elasticity (E) measures the percentage change in price with respect to a percentage change in rate, that is,

$$\text{Price Elasticity} = \frac{\text{Percentage Change in Price}}{\text{Percentage Change in Rate}}$$

Or, in symbols,

$$E = \frac{\dfrac{\Delta P_0}{P_0}}{\dfrac{\Delta i}{i}} < 0 \tag{9-3}$$

Price elasticity always is negative because asset prices and interest rates are inversely related. Using the five-year, 10 percent coupon bond from the previous example, an illustration is

i	P_0	E
8%	$1080 ⎫	−.4015
10%	$1000 ⎬	
12%	$ 927 ⎭	−.3625

Note that both elasticities are calculated on the basis of movements away from the coupon rate of 10 percent. The greater price elasticity for downward movements in rates explains why capital gains exceed capital losses for a given yield change. Since

[1] See Hopewell and Kaufman [1973] and Yawitz, Hempel, and Marshall [1975].

Equation 9-3 can be rearranged as $\Delta P/P = E(\Delta i/i)$, it shows the impact that E has on $\Delta P/P$ for a given $\Delta i/i$. Thus, the greater an asset's E is, the greater its price fluctuations will be for a given change in interest rates.

The Relationship Between Duration and Elasticity

The relationship between price elasticity and duration has been shown to be:[2]

$$E = D\left(\frac{i}{1+i}\right) \tag{9-4}$$

Since D and i are strictly positive and E is negative, Equation 9-4 refers to the equality of the absolute value of the LHS with the RHS of the formula. It is clear from the relationship that E and D vary directly. In general functional notation, D can be expressed as

$$D = D(\overset{+}{N}, \overset{-}{c}), \tag{9-5}$$

that is, duration increases as term to maturity (N) increases and as the coupon rate (c) decreases. Thus, the longer the term to maturity and/or the lower the coupon rate, the greater duration, price elasticity, and price fluctuations will be, other things equal.

To gain further insight into the relationship between duraion and changes in the values of financial assets, we can solve Equation 9-3 for the percentage change in price; substituting Equation 9-4 for E, the percentage change in price at the margin is

$$\frac{\Delta P}{P} = -D\left(\frac{i}{1+i}\right)\frac{\Delta i}{i} = -D\frac{\Delta i}{1+i} \tag{9-6}$$

Thus, price fluctuations mainly are a function of D, i, and Δi, with D primarily a function of N and c. Alternatively, the change in price can be expressed as

$$\Delta P = -D(\Delta i/(1+i))P_0 \tag{9-7}$$

In words, the change in price or value is equal to the *negative of the duration* times the *percentage change* in interest rate times the initial or present value of the security. Continuing with the example of the five-year bond, its duration was 4.17 years. Therefore, given a change in the interest rate of 100 basis points or .01, the change in price using Equation 9-7 is $\Delta P = -4.17(.01/1.1)1000 = 37.91$. If the rate rises, the change in price is $-\$37.91$; if the rate declines, the price change is $\$37.91$. Using Equation 9-6, we can say that a 1 percent relative change in rates produces a -4.17 percent relative change in price. That is, $\Delta P/P = -4.17(1\%) = -4.17\%$. For small changes in interest rate, Equation 9-6 or 9-7 gives the same results as Equation 9-4. Moreover, for large changes in rates (say 100 basis points), the approximation error is relatively small (i.e., typically less than 1%).

RECAPITULATION OF THE VALUATION PROPERTIES OF FIXED-INCOME SECURITIES

Eight asset-valuation properties have been introduced in this chapter. The first four are simple while the last four are more complex. However, by introducing the concepts of duration and elasticity, the complex properties become more understandable. If financial managers have a firm understanding of the basic concepts of asset

---

[2] See Haugen and Wichern [1974] and Hicks [1965].

valuation, their investment portfolios are more likely to be managed efficiently. To summarize, the eight properties are

1. If $i = c$, the asset sells at *par*.
2. If $i > c$, the asset sells at a *discount*.
3. If $i < c$, the asset sells at a *premium*.
4. Asset prices and yields are inversely related.

Four additional properties of fixed-income securities, which focus on fluctuations in their prices,[3] are:

5. The longer is an asset's term to maturity (or duration), the more sensitive is its price to a change in the rate of interest or yield.
6. As the term to maturity increases, the percentage price changes described in (5) increase at a diminishing rate for any given change in yield.
7. For a given maturity and a given change in yield, the capital gain from the decrease in yield exceeds the capital loss from the increase in the yield.
8. Except for one-year and perpetual assets, the higher an asset's coupon rate, the less sensitive is its price to a change in yield.

For a speculator, the greatest opportunity for making a profit in the bond market would come from buying (that is, taking a long position in) long-term bonds with low coupon rates at a time when interest rates are expected to fall. However, since most managers of FSFs tend to be risk-averse, especially those of depository institutions, tools for hedging interest-rate risk are more important than knowing how to bet the bank on interest rates. This penchant for risk aversion is reinforced by bank examiners, who frown upon speculative trading by bank managers. Duration matching (see Chapter 17) is the key to effective repricing and the immunization of value due to unexpected changes in interest rates.

PRICING CONVENTIONS AND THE YIELDS ON TREASURY BILLS

Treasury bills, which are short-term U.S. Treasury IOUs, have maturities of 13, 26, and 52 weeks. The 13- and 26-week T-bill auctions occur every Monday (or the next business day, when financial markets are closed on Monday) throughout the year. The auction for one-year bills takes place on the same day, but only every four weeks. T-bills, which are an important source of corporate liquidity, are sold at a discount through a competitive-bidding process. The return (i.e., the discount) to the investor is the difference between the face value and the purchase price. Since T-bills do not pay an intermediate cash flow (e.g., a coupon-interest payment), they are called a *pure-discount* (or *zero-coupon*) security or bond. Other examples of money-market instruments that trade as discount securities are *commercial paper* and *bankers' acceptances*. Until the early 1980s, most certificates of deposit (CDs) were issued as interest-bearing securities; although they still dominate the CD market, zero-coupon CDs are increasing in popularity.

Three alternative conventions are used to express the return or yield on a Treasury bill. Market participants use the *bank-discount* method when they are buying and selling bills and the *coupon-* or *bond-equivalent* method when they are measuring rates of return. When comparing rates of return on alternative investments (e.g.,

[3] See Francis [1980], p. 202.

bills with different maturities), financial managers and analysts usually calculate an *effective* yield assuming continuous compounding. The yields associated with these three price conventions are called the bank-discount yield, the coupon-equivalent yield, and the effective yield.

In banking, finance, economics, and society in general, there are various conventions that develop over time and that frequently defy logical explanation. When we encounter such conventions, we can attempt to change them but usually we must learn to cope with them. The alternative price conventions for Treasury bills represent one of those challenges. See how well you cope with the challenge.

The bank-discount method[4] for calculating the yield on a Treasury bill is

$$\text{Bank-Discount Yield} = \frac{F - P}{F} \times \frac{360}{N} \tag{9-8}$$

where F and P are the face value due at maturity and the current market price, respectively, and N is the maturity (in days) of the bill. To illustrate, on August 31, 1987, the 182-day T-bill sold at an average price of $6.795 (see Table 9-2). Using formula 9-8, the yield is

$$\frac{100 - 96.795}{100} \times \frac{360}{182} = \frac{3.205}{100} \times 1.978 = 6.34\%$$

With a minimum transactions unit of $10,000, the cost of one six-month T-bill was $9,679.50, a discount of $320.50. On March 3, 1988, the investor received the face-value payment of $10,000. Thus, the investor received a return of $320.50 for an investment of $9,679.50 for a 182-day yield of 6.34 percent. This return, of course, is not the true yield but simply the one dictated by convention. The effective annual yield (y) on the six-month bill is

$$y = \left(1 + \frac{320.5}{9679.5}\right)^{365/182} - 1$$

$$= 6.53\%$$

Note that in this case, the effective yield is 19 basis points higher than the yield indicated by the bank-discount method. The general formula for calculating the

TABLE 9-2   Results of the August 31, 1987, Treasury-Bill Auction

	13 week[a]	26 week[a]
Applications	$29,296,265,000	$24,600,955,000
Accepted bids	$6,604,080,000	$6,605,580
Accepted at low price	37%	27%
Accepted noncompetitively	$1,014,500,000	$974,800,000
Average price (rate)	98.435(6.19%)	96.795(6.34%)
High price (rate)	98.443(6.16%)	96.815(6.30%)
Low price (rate)	98.433(6.20%)	96.785(6.36%)
Coupon equivalent	6.393%	6.66%

[a] Both issues were dated September 3. The 13-week bills matured December 3, 1987, and the 26-week bills matured March 3, 1988.
Source: The Wall Street Journal [September 1, 1987], p. 43.

---

[4] See Monhollon [1977] and Robichek, Coleman, and Hempel [1976].

TABLE 9-3   Alternative Methods of Calculating Yields on Treasury Bills

Method	Formula	Example: Six-month T-Bill of August 31, 1987
Bank discount	$\dfrac{F-P}{F} \times \dfrac{360}{N}$	$\dfrac{100-96.795}{100} \times \dfrac{360}{182} = 6.34\%$
Coupon equivalent	$\dfrac{F-P}{P} \times \dfrac{365}{N}$	$\dfrac{100-96.795}{96.795} \times \dfrac{365}{182} = 6.64\%$
Effective yield	$\left(1+\dfrac{F-P}{P}\right)^{365/N} - 1$	$\left(1+\dfrac{100-96.795}{96.795}\right)^{365/182} - 1 = 6.53\%$

Sources: Monhollon [1977], p. 158 and Robichek, et al. [1976], pp. 39–41.

effective yield on a Treasury bill is[5]

$$\text{Effective Yield} = \left(1+\frac{F-P}{P}\right)^{365/N} - 1. \tag{9-9}$$

The three basic differences between Equations 9-8 and 9-9 are

1. compound interest rather than simple interest
2. dividing the discount by the price rather than the face value
3. the 365-day year rather than the 360-day year.

The coupon-equivalent method for calculating T-bill yields employs points 2 and 3 above but not point 1. The formula is

$$\text{Coupon-Equivalent Yield} = \frac{F-P}{P} \times \frac{365}{N} \tag{9-10}$$

For the six-month T-bill of August 31, 1987, the coupon-equivalent yield is

$$\frac{1000 - 96.795}{96.795} \times \frac{365}{182} = 6.64\%$$

Reported T-bill rates are calculated using the bank-discount method described above. Under this technique, higher bidding narrows the investor's return while lower bidding widens it. Treasury bills are allocated according to the following scheme: All noncompetitive bids (tenders) are filled; they have a maximum of $500,000 per bidder. The total face value of these bids is subtracted from the total face value of the Treasury's offering. The balance is sold to the competitive bidders, with orders from the highest bidders filled first, until the total issue is sold. The lowest competitive bid accepted is called the "stop-out" price. The average accepted competitive bid is the price paid by the noncompetitive bidders. Money-center banks, securities dealers, and other institutional investors are the major competitive bidders in T-bill auctions. The alternative methods for determining the yields on Treasury bills are summarized in Table 9-3.

TREASURY BILLS AND MONEY-MARKET RISK PREMIUMS

Treasury bills, which are the cornerstone of the money market, are attractive short-term investments because (1) they provide a competitive return set by the forces of supply and demand, (2) they are highly liquid due to the active secondary market provided by the dealers in government securities, (3) they are considered to be free of

[5] See Robichek, et al., [1976]. Equation 9-9 also can be written as $y = (365/N) \ln (F/P)$, where ln stands for natural logarithm. See Garbade [1982].

default risk and (4) they are exempt from state and local income taxes. In a nutshell, T-bills provided a safe and liquid investment vehicle for storing short-term funds at a competitive return. Although T-bills generate the lowest *explicit* return of the major money-market instruments, they pay *implicit* returns in the form of safety and liquidity. As of November 19, 1984, and August 31, 1987, the yields and risk premiums on the major money-market instruments listed in *The Wall Street Journal* (p. 49 and p. 43, respectively) were

Money-Market Instrument	November 19, 1984		August 31, 1987	
	Yield (%)	Risk Premium (%) Relative to T-Bill	Yield (%)	Risk Premium (%) Relative to T-Bill
Treasury Bill (13-week, bank discount)	8.59	—	6.19	—
GMAC commercial paper (60–89 only)	9.00	0.41	6.68	0.49
Bankers' acceptances (90 days)	9.10	0.51	6.91	0.72
Dealer-placed commercial paper (90 days)	9.20	0.61	6.85	0.66
Certificates of deposit (3-month)	9.35	0.76	7.00	0.81
Federal funds (average of closing bid + asked)	9.47	0.88	6.84	0.65
London late Eurodollars (average of range)	9.69	1.10	6.91	0.72

Relative to the rate on the 13-week T-bill, which is the anchor rate in the money market, the risk premium, defined as the difference between the rate on the non-Treasury instrument and the T-bill rate, ranged from 41 to 110 basis points on the 1984 date and 49 to 81 basis points on the 1987 date. Risk premiums tend to vary directly with the level of interest rates in the economy and the market's perception of the issuer's credit-worthiness. For example, going back to February 23, 1981, when the bank-discount yield on the 13-week T-bill was 14.10 percent, the risk premium ranged from only 15 basis points on GMAC paper to 224 basis points on Eurodollars. Two weeks earlier, when the T-bill rate was 15.40 percent, the corresponding risk premiums were 35 and 260 basis points. Over these four test dates, most of the money-market risk premiums were higher when the 13-week T-bill rate was higher.

T-Bill Transactions in the Secondary Market

Government securities dealers, known simply as "dealers," provide an active secondary market in all U.S. Government securities, but especially in U.S. Treasury securities. The primary dealers in U.S. Treasury securities are presented in Table 9-4 and listed according to whether they are bank or nonbank dealers. The prices at which dealers are willing to buy (called *bid*) and sell (called *asked*) are quoted in terms of the bank-discount formula, Equation 9-8. Using y_{bid} to represent the discount yield *bid* and y_{asked} to represent the discount yield *asked*, we can solve Equation 9-8 for the dealer's bid and asked prices. That is,

$$P_{bid} = F - y_{bid}F \times \frac{N}{360} \qquad (9\text{-}11)$$

$$P_{asked} = F - y_{asked}F \times \frac{N}{300} \qquad (9\text{-}12)$$

The dealer's spread is the difference between the asked price and the bid price. "Buy low, sell high," is the dealer's profit axiom. In terms of yields, the axiom translates into: "Buy at high yields (low prices), sell at low yields (high prices)." For example,

TABLE 9-4   Government Securities Dealers Reporting to the Federal Reserve Bank of New York (as of September 12, 1984)

* Bank of America NT & SA
* Bankers Trust Company
Bear, Stearns & Co.
Briggs, Schaedle & Co., Inc.
Carroll McEntee & McGinley Incorporated
Chase Manhattan Government Securities, Inc.
* Chemical Bank
* Citibank, N.A.
* Continental Illinois National Bank and Trust Company of Chicago
* Crocker Natioinal Bank
Discount Corporation of New York
Donaldson, Lufkin & Jenrette Securities Corporation
Drexel Burnham Lambert Government Securities Inc.
The First Boston Corporation
* First Interstate Bank of California
* First National Bank of Chicago
Goldman, Sachs & Co.
Greenwich Capital Markets, Inc.
* Harris Trust and Savings Bank
E. F. Hutton & Company, Inc.
Kidder, Peabody & Co., Incorporated
Kleinwort Benson Government Securities, Inc.
Aubrey G. Lanston & Co., Inc.
Lehman Government Securities, Inc.
* Manufacturers Hanover Trust Company
Merrill Lynch Government Securities Inc.
* Morgan Guaranty Trust Company of New York
Morgan Stanley & Co. Incorporated
* The Northern Trust Company
Paine Webber Incorporated
Wm. E. Pollock Government Securities, Inc.
Prudential-Bache Securities, Inc.
Refco Partners
Salomon Brothers Inc
Smith Barney Government Securities, Inc.
Dean Witter Reynolds Inc.

Note: This list has been compiled and made available with statistical purposes only and has no significance with respect to other relationships between dealers and the Federal Reserve Bank of New York. Qualification for the reporting list is based on the achievement and maintenance of reasonable standards of activity.
* Indicates bank dealer.
Source: Market Reports Division, Federal Reserve Bank of New York.

using the 13-week bill from the auction of August 31, 1987, the bank-discount yield was 6.19 precent. If 31 days later $(91 - 31 = 60)$ the bid and asked discounts are 6.30 and 6.10 percent, respectively, then the corresponding bid and asked prices are

$$P_{bid} = 100 - (.0630)100 \times \frac{60}{360}$$

$$= 100 - 1.05 = 98.95$$

$$P_{asked} = 100 - (.0610)100 \times \frac{60}{360}$$

$$= 100 - 1.02 = 98.98$$

In this example, the dealer's spread is $.03 or 3¢ per $100, which seems a mere pittance. However, since average trades in the dealer market are in millions of dollars, the actual dollar flows are much larger. To illustrate, the dollars flows on trades of $1 million, $10 million, and $100 million are $300, $3,000, and $30,000, respectively. The formula for the cash flow on a spread trade is ($ *amount of trade*) × (*spread*/100), which for the $1,000,000 trade is: $1,000,000 × .03/100 = $300. In the financial press, bid and asked discounts usually are reported along with the coupon-equivalent yield corresponding to the asked price. Thus, in the previous example, the quoted yield would be $(1.02/98.98) \times \left(\dfrac{365}{60}\right) = (.0103) \times (6.0833) = 6.27$ percent.

CD YIELDS AND PRICES

A negotiable certificate of deposit (CD) is a money-market instrument that can be traded in the secondary CD market. Although negotiable CDs have a minimum face value of $100,000, most trades are in the millions of dollars. Unlike T-bills, bankers' acceptances, and commercial paper, most CDs are *interest-bearing securities*. Until recently, the operative word was "all" CDs; however, beginning in the early 1980s some banks and thrifts began to offer zero-coupon CDs. This section looks at the price-and-yield mechanics of interest-bearing securities, using the negotiable CD as an example.

To find the *maturity value* of a CD (or any interest-bearing security), the simple formula for future value is used. Using c to represent the coupon or stated rate of interest on the CD and MV to represent the maturity value, the formula for the CD's future value per $100 is

$$MV = 100 \left(1 + c\frac{N}{360}\right) \qquad (9\text{-}13)$$

As before, N represents the term to maturity of the obligation. To determine the market price or present value of the CD, we simply discount the future value at the going rate of interest, i. That is,

$$P = \frac{MV}{1 + (N/360)i} \qquad (9\text{-}14)$$

Like other interest-bearing instruments, if $c = i$ at the time of issue, the CD trades at its maturity value.

To illustrate Equations 9-13 and 9-14, let's consider a 90-day CD with a stated rate of interest of 10 percent. Using Equation 9-13, the CD has a maturity value of $102.5; a million-dollar block would have a maturity value of $1,025,000. If 45 days later the going rate of interest on comparable CDs has risen to 12 percent, then the CD would have a market value of $1,009,852.20. That is, using Equation 9-14, the value is

$$P = (1,025,000)/(1 + (45/360).12)$$
$$= 1,025,000/1.015 = 1,009,852.20$$

If the going rate had stayed at 10 percent, the price of the CD would be $1,012,345.60. Thus, the increase in the market rate from 10 to 12 percent reduced the value of the CD by $2,493.40 or $12.467 per basis-point increase. In contrast, if the going rate had decreased to 8 percent, the CD, with 45 days remaining until maturity, would be worth $1,041,851.40. In this case, the decrease in the market rate increased the value of the

CD by \$2,505.80 or \$12.529 per basis-point decrease. The asymmetry in value changes is due to the greater price elasticity for downward movements in rates relative to upward movements, as explained earlier in the chapter.

Like Treasury bills, CDs trade in the secondary market on the basis of bid and asked yields. To find the prices corresponding to these yields, simply plug the appropriate yield into Equation 9-14 and solve for the price. The difference between the asked price and the bid price is the CD dealer's profit or spread.

ASSET PRICES AND YIELDS: A RECAPITULATION

The numerous formulas on the preceding pages of this chapter attest to the technical nature of determining asset prices and yields and measuring the sensitivity of assets prices (e.g., duration). The formulas come with the territory. Thankfully, however, we have computers and powerful calculators to take care of the manipulations. Nevertheless, unless you understand the formulas and can interpret the output, the old computer adage "garbage in, garbage out" will apply. The remainder of this chapter focuses on the theories and structures of interest rates.

THE FISHER EFFECT

As indicated in Chapter 3, the nominal riskless rate of interest, i, can be approximated by the sum of the real rate of interest, r, plus a premium for anticipated inflation, x^*, that is,

$$i \approx r + x^* \tag{9-15}$$

Equation 9-15 is referred to as the *Fisher effect* and is more exactly specified as[6]

$$i = r + x^* + rx^* \tag{9-16}$$

The Fisher equation specifies the relationship between the nominal rate of interest, i, the real rate of interest, r, and anticipated inflation, x^*. To illustrate, with $r = 4$ percent and $x^* = 6$ percent, $i = 10$ percent using Equation 9-15 and $i = 10.24$ percent using Equation 9-16. If anticipated inflation doubles, then $i = 16$ percent and $i = 16.48$ percent respectively. The larger the anticipated inflation, the more inexact Equation 9-15.[7] Note that r and x^* are not directly observable pieces of information.[8] However, i and x, actual inflation, are observable. Thus, two important concepts are *unanticipated inflation* $(x - x^*)$ and the *historical real rate of interest* $(i - x)$. Unanticipated inflation is important because as long as it is zero $(x^* = x)$, neither the borrower nor the lender gains (or loses) from inflation. For example, if $x^* = 10$ percent but $x = 15$ percent, then there is unanticipated inflation and borrowers benefit at the expense of lenders because borrowers repay with *cheaper* dollars. Unanticipated inflation results in redistributional effects from lenders to borrowers or vice versa.

---

[6] Irving Fisher, *Appreciation and Interest*, New York: Macmillan Publishing Co., Inc., 1896. Note that Equation 9-16 also can be expressed as $(1 + i)/(1 + x^*) = 1 + r$.

[7] For computational ease, unless otherwise indicated, the approximation of the Fisher effect (equation 9-15) is used in this book.

[8] Anticipated inflation, x^*, can be measured indirectly via surveys of financial managers or by mechanical forecasting models.

An alternative way of looking at unanticipated inflation is to observe the historical relationship between i and x, that is, $r \approx i - x$. Irving Fisher[9] reports:

> The real rate of interest in the United States from March to April, 1917, fell below minus 70 percent! In Germany at the height of inflation, August to September, 1923, the real rate of interest fell to the absurd level of minus 99.9 percent, which means that lenders lost all interest and nearly all their capital as well; and then suddenly prices were deflated and the real interest rate jumped to plus 100 percent.

For a more recent example, consider the U.S. economy in the period 1979–1980. With long-term Treasury bonds yielding roughly 10 percent over this period and with a inflation of approximately 13 percent, the real rate of interest was roughly minus 3 percent. Certainly an unacceptable performance, but relative to 1917 or 1923 a fantastic job. Assuming an anticipated real rate of interest of 4 percent, if Treasury bonds had been "correctly priced," they would have returned 17 percent. In other words, there was unanticipated inflation of 7 percent. The critical points are (1) nominal rates of interest contain a premium for anticipated inflation and (2) in an uncertain inflationary environment this premium may prove to be inadequate. In contrast, during 1984 long-term Treasury rates were around 12.5 percent with inflation down around 4.5 percent. In this case, the real rate was 8 percent and there was *unanticipated deflation* of 3.5 percent. As a result, lenders were repaid dollars that were worth more than those they lent out. More recently, in 1987, long-term Treasuries were around 9.0 percent and inflation in the range of 3 to 4 percent, implying an *ex post* real rate of 5 to 6 percent.

AN OVERALL THEORY OF INTEREST-RATE DETERMINATION

The three determinants of market rates of interest are

$$k = r + x^* + p \tag{9-17}$$

In words, the observed market rate of interest (k) is equal to the sum of the real rate of interest (r), the expected rate of inflation (x^*), and a default-risk premium (p). The real rate of interest or marginal productivity of capital represents the investor's reward for forgoing consumption. The real rate of interest is determined by the forces of supply and demand as reflected by (1) individuals' time preferences or impatience for consumption now versus saving for future consumption and (2) the investment opportunities available for productive use of capital. The inflation premium is supposed to protect the investor against loss of purchasing power due to anticipated inflation. Together the real rate of interest and the inflation premium form the nominal risk-free rate of interest (i.e., $i = r + x^*$). Given i, the third determinant of market interest rates is the default-risk premium, the reward for bearing default risk.

Introducing the concept of maturity intermediation, Equation 9-17 can be expanded to

$$k = r + x^* + p + m \tag{9-18}$$

The term m in this case represents the premium for bearing maturity or interest-rate risk. Since the risk-free rate of interest is the same for all financial assets, the market rate of interest for the jth financial asset can be viewed as being determined by the default risk and maturity of the underlying obligation. That is,

$$k_j = i + p_j + m_j \tag{9-19}$$

---

[9] *The Theory of Interest*, New York: Augustus M. Kelley, Bookseller [1965], p. 44. Original edition 1930.

To illustrate, a long-term rate of interest of 15 percent could have the components shown below.

Symbol	Value	Description
r	4%	Reward for foregoing consumption
x^*	5%	Premium for anticipated inflation
p	3%	Premium for bearing default risk
m	3%	Premium for bearing interest-rate risk
$\overline{k}$	15%	MARKET RATE OF INTEREST

Applying this framework to the deposit and loan rates of depository institutions provides some insight into the nature of their financial-intermediation business. Because of deposit insurance and capital regulation, depository institutions rarely default on their liabilities (i.e., for depositors p ≈ 0). An alternative interpretation of the zero default-risk premium is that retail depositors are willing to pay for the portfolio diversification and professional risk-evaluation capabilities attributed to banks. In other words, the bank's reward for its risk-intermediation service is a reduced cost of funds. In addition, because most of a bank's liabilities are of a short-term nature, depositors do not have to bear a substantial amount of interest-rate risk (i.e., m ≈ 0). Finally, banks may be able to pay lower real rates of return because of the convenience of banking with a local institution and because of the provision of ancillary services such as checking accounts and safe-deposit boxes. Thus, depository institutions may be able to attract funds simply by paying a rate of interest that will compensate for anticipated inflation or purchasing-power risk. However, as noted earlier in the chapter, large CDs, depending on the level of interest rates, tend to have risk premiums in the range of 50 to 250 basis points compared to the 13-week T-bill rate. For the purposes of this example, let's assume that the bank pays 10 percent for funds, a risk premium of 100 basis points or 1 percent.

Now consider the depository institution's loan rate and assume that it is the 15 percent rate discussed above. The pricing of the loan will be a function of the bank's cost of funds, the default risk of the borrower, the maturity of the loan, and the strength of the bank-customer relationship (i.e., "good" or prime-rate customers usually receive preferential treatment). The difference between the loan and deposit rates, which is 5 percent (15%-10%) in this case, is the spread that the bank has to cover its operating expenses, taxes, and profit margin. (Recall our profit equation $(\pi = R - C - O - T)$ and see how this example fits that framework). Thus, the essence of bank financial intermediation is to borrow "short" at the cost of funds and to lend "long" at a rate sufficiently above the cost of funds to cover expenses and taxes, and generate a profit. The difference between these rates represents the reward that banks receive for providing financial-intermediation services, that is, for pooling funds and thereby reducing transactions costs, for providing diversification benefits and thereby reducing default risk, and for bearing interest-rate risk.

YIELD CURVES AND THE TERM STRUCTURE OF INTEREST RATES

A yield curve shows the relationship between the yield to maturity and the term to maturity of similar securities (e.g., U.S. Treasury obligations or corporate bonds of the same quality). The curve itself is simply a two-dimensional picture of the following function:

$$i = f(N) \tag{9-20}$$

The idea is to observe what happens to i as N changes, other things equal. Another name for the yield-curve relationship is the term structure of interest rates. Yield curves typically are described in terms of their *shape* (slope) and *position*. As depicted in Figure 9-1, there are four basic shapes of yield curves:

1. ascending (positively sloped)
2. descending (negatively sloped)
3. flat (zero slope)
4. humped (slope changes).

The position of the yield curve refers to the *level* of interest rates and can be described as being high, low, or in transition. There is a link between the position of the yield curve and its shape. When rates are low, yield curves tend to be positively sloped; when rates are high, they tend to be negatively sloped or humped. When rates are in transition from low to high or vice versa, yield curves tend to be flat.

The fact that short-term rates fluctuate more than long-term rates and the fact that yield curves flatten out as term to maturity increases (see Figure 9-1) can be explained by the valuation properties established earlier in this chapter. For example, rearranging Equation 9-3, the percentage change in yield ($\Delta i/i$) can be expressed as $(\Delta P_0/P_0)/E$. For a given $\Delta P/P$, yield changes depend upon E, which is smallest for short-term bonds and increases at a diminishing rate as N increases.

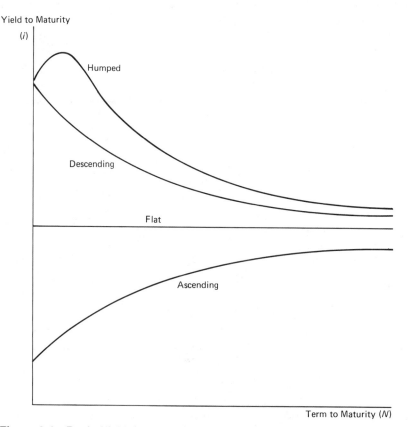

Figure 9-1   Basic Yield-Curve Shapes

Yield-Curve Construction

The construction of the Treasury yield curve for September 28, 1984 is pictured in Figure 9-2. As indicated in the legend, alternative coupon issues are plotted in i and N space. Note that the coupon-equivalent method is used for determining the yields of the Treasury bills. Based only on the most actively traded issues, the curve is fitted by eye. The Treasury's approach to yield-curve construction is to exclude yields on coupon issues due in less than three months and to avoid using "outlier" yields in fitting the curve. Outlier issues have yields that are significantly affected by special features (e.g., callability).

On September 28, 1984, the Treasury yield curve was positively sloped with short-term rates in the range of 10.50 to 11.50 percent and long-term rates in the range of 12.25 to 12.5 percent. The insert in Figure 9-2 indicates the tendency of yield curves to flatten out as term to maturity increases. For a positively sloped yield curve, its position was a high one by historical standards. For example, on September 29, 1972, the Treasury yield curve also was positively sloped but in the range of 4.6 to 6.5 percent. Why was the 1984 position of the yield curve so much higher? Part of the answer is inflation. Comparing the long-term rates and assuming the long-term *real* rate to be stable, the difference would be an inflation premium that is roughly six hundred basis points higher.

Why Construct a Yield Curve?

Why should a financial manager or any other investor construct a yield curve? The purpose of constructing a yield curve is to identify issues whose yields are not comparable with bonds of similar term to maturity. These issues are the so-called "outliers." Since their yields are different, then, of course, their prices will be different from those issues that lie on or near the yield curve. Those issues lying above the yield curve can be described as being "underpriced" and those lying below it are said to be "overpriced." If bond markets were perfect, all securities would be priced correctly. However, because of taxes (e.g., capital-gains tax) and market imperfections (e.g., transactions costs and getting a large new issue into the market), profitable investment opportunities may exist, although only temporarily. From this perspective, the yield curve is a tool to assist the investment manager in identifying such opportunities.

Yield Curves and the Interest-Rate Cycle

The interest-rate cycle is a concept designed to capture the movement of interest rates over the business cycle by focusing on the notion of some *average* rate of interest over time. A typical interest-rate cycle is depicted in Figure 9-3. It consists of four stages or phases. In Stage I, interest rates are low, the demand for credit is small, and banks have maximum *stored* liquidity. In State II, interest rates are in transition moving from low to high, the demand for credit is rising, and bank liquidity is declining. In Stage III, interest rates peak, the demand for credit is strong, and bank liquidity is squeezed. With stored liquidity practically exhausted, banks must depend on liability-management liquidity to meet credit demands or else turn down requests for funds. In Stage IV, the credit crunch breaks and rates are in transition from high to low, the demand for credit eases, and bank liquidity begins to improve. As indicated by the trend line, the new cycle begins at a higher level of rates because of the secular increase in inflation, a characteristic of U.S. interest-rate cycles for the past two decades. Matching the yield-curve shapes with the stages of the interest-rate cycle, note that in Stages II and IV the yield curve tends to be flat; in Stage I it is positively sloped; and in Stage III it tends to be negatively sloped or humped.

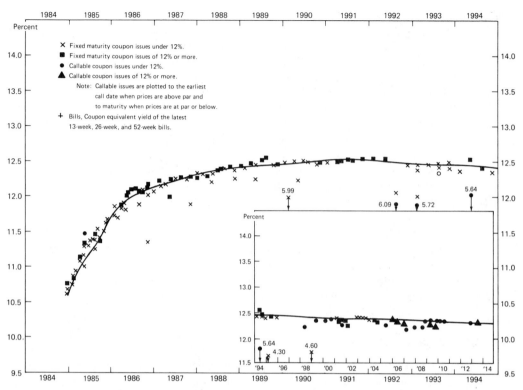

Figure 9-2   Yields of Treasury Securities, September 28, 1984 (Based on Closing Bid Quotations)

Source: *Treasury Bulletin* [Fall, 1984], p. 35.

Yield-Curve Movements and Recent Credit Crunches

From 1966 to 1988, the U.S. financial system has experienced five "credit crunches" with each successive one being more severe than the previous one. The dates of the credit crunches were 1966, 1969–1970, 1974, 1979–1980, and 1980–1981. The volatility of rates can be demonstrated by the fact that from 1966 to 1981 both short- and long-term rates roughly tripled. The dramatic movement of the Treasury yield curves around the 1979–1980 credit crunch are shown in Figure 9-4. The scenario goes like this: From February 28, 1975, to July 31, 1978, the yield curve gradually moves upward over this stagflation era with short-term rates up over 125 basis points and long-term rates up about 75 basis points. At midyear 1979, the yield curve is relatively flat at 9 percent with a hump in the early maturities. By the end of the year, the yield curve is negatively sloped, with short-term rates around 12.5 percent and long-term ones slightly above 10 percent. The crunch comes in March 1980. At the end of the month, short-term rates are between 15 and 16 percent, with long-term rates around 12.5 percent. However, by the end of April, the yield curve is relatively flat, with rates between 10.5 and 11.5 percent. By May 30, 1980, the yield curve is positively sloped, with short-term rates between 8 and 8.5 percent and long-term rates slightly below 10.5 percent, roughly 275 basis points above the beginning of the cycle. The 1979–1980 ride on the yield curve roller coaster is over, but the 1980–1981 version is waiting in the wings.

TABLE 9-5   Alternative Explanations of the Term Structure of Interest Rates

Descriptive Category	Theory		
	Pure Expectations	Modified Expectations	Market Segmentation
Key determinant	Expectations	Modified expectations	Institutional behavior
Conceptualization of the key determinant	Forecasts of short-term interest rates	Forecasts of short-term interest rates plus compensating premiums (e.g., liquidity premiums)	Demand and supply curves for securities
Equilibrating mechanism	Profit-maximizing behavior over the investor's holding period	Profit-maximizing behavior plus some nonexpectational element (such as maturity preferences) induced by uncertainty	Forces of supply and demand in segmented markets (i.e., hedging pressure)
Relationship between long- and short-term interest rates	Linkage by formula using expected rates	Linkage by formula using forward rates (i.e., expected rates plus compensating premiums)	No linkage by formula, markets are segmented
Description of forward rates	Pure expected rates	Expected rates plus compensating premiums	None given
Restrictiveness of assumptions	Very restrictive	Less restrictive than PET (e.g., admits uncertainty)	Not restrictive
Intuitive appeal	Expectations are important although difficult to measure	Nonexpectational elements such as maturity preferences, uncertainty, or transactions costs	Institutional structures and behavior; supply-and-demand forces
Importance of relative supplies of securities	Unimportant unless they affect expectations	Relatively important because they determine the size of compensating premiums	Critically important
Important contributors	Lutz, Meiselman	Hicks, Kessel, Modigliani & Sutch, Kane & Malkiel, Kane, Malkiel	Culbertson, Homer & Johannesen

For expositional purposes, let us refer to those explanations adopting an expectations approach, but stopping short of the pure-expectations approach, as modified-expectations theories. In this framework, the liquidity-preference theory is a modified-expectations approach; its modifier is the notion of a liquidity premium. The pure-expectations theory and the market-segmentation theory represent diametrically opposed explanations of the term structure; the modified theories stand between these two extremes. The major theories of the term structure are summarized in Table 9-5 and explained below.

The Pure-Expectations Theory (PET)

The PET approach contends that investors' expectations of future short-term interest rates determine the slope of the yield curve. Since expectations and expectations alone are said to explain the term structure, the theory is referred to as the *pure-expectations theory*. PET makes a number of simplifying assumptions, the most important of which are

1. investors are profit maximizers, whose expectations are firm, uniform, and endless.
2. perfect certainty, including accurate forecasts.
3. zero transactions costs.

Given these assumptions and the investor's holding period, each investor selects the portfolio that maximizes the holding-period return. The PET equilibrium condition is

$$(1 + {}_tR_N) = [(1 + {}_tR_1)(1 + {}_{t+1}r_1)...(1 + {}_{t+N-1}r_1)]^{1/N} \tag{9-21}$$

where uppercase R indicates an observed rate and lowercase r an expected rate. The presubscript indicates *time* and the postsubscript *maturity*.

Equation 9-24 describes the PET linkage by formula between long-term rates and short-term ones. It specifically states that in equilibrium the actual long-term yield equals the compound yields based on a series of short-term investments. Consider the case for $N = 2$. The equilibrium condition is

$$(1 + {}_tR_2) = [(1 + {}_tR_1)(1 + {}_{t+1}r_1)]^{1/2}$$

or

$$(1 + {}_tR_2)^2 = (1 + {}_tR_1)(1 + {}_{t+1}r_1)$$

A numerical example will help to clarify the equilibrium process. To simplify the calculations, arithmetic averaging is employed. Suppose that the current yield on a one-year security $({}_tR_1)$ is 14 percent, the current yield on a two-year security $({}_tR_2)$ is 12 percent, and the yield anticipated next year for reinvestment in a one-year security $({}_{t+1}r_1)$ is 10 percent. This configuration of rates is an equilibrium one, since $.12 = (.14 + .10)/2$. Thus, an investor with a two-year holding period would be indifferent between holding a two-year bond at 12 percent versus holding a series of one-year bonds at successive yields of 14 percent and 10 percent. Suppose, however, that the two-year rate was 14 percent, a disequilibrium situation. Investors would prefer to go long and they would drive the price of the two-year bond up and its yield down until the expected holding-period return was 12 percent. Note that the one-year holding-period return (HPR) is defined as

$$HPR = \frac{C + \Delta P}{P_0} \tag{9-22}$$

where C = coupon payment and P = purchase price. The HPR for the two-year bond, assuming $C = \$14$, would be[10]

$$HPR = \frac{14 - 1.785}{101.785} = \frac{12.215}{101.785} = .12$$

Consider now a positively sloped yield curve with ${}_tR_1 = 12$ percent, ${}_tR_2 = 12.5$ percent, and ${}_{t+1}r_1 = 13$ percent and an investor with a one-year holding period. Will the investor be indifferent as between the one-year bond and the two-year bond held for one year? The answer is "yes," because the term structure is an equilibrium one [$.125 = (.12 + .13)/2$]. The one-year bond will return 12 percent. At the end of the

---

[10] This is the *period* 2 HPR assuming the security has been forced to an equilibrium price by the end of period 1, where 101.785 is the present value of $114 at 12%.

first year the price of the two-year bond will be

$$P = \frac{12.5 + 100}{1.13} = 99.557 \approx 99.5$$

and its HPR will be

$$HPR = \frac{12.5 - .5}{100} = .12$$

Thus, the two-year bond held for one year also will return 12 percent.

To emphasize how future short-term interest rates determine the term structure, consider the following schematic:

$$\begin{bmatrix} _tR_1 \\ _{t+1}r_1 \\ _{t+2}r_1 \\ \vdots \\ _{t+N-1}r_1 \end{bmatrix} \xrightarrow{\text{Determines}} \begin{bmatrix} _tR_2 \\ _tR_3 \\ \vdots \\ \vdots \\ _tR_N \end{bmatrix}$$

Given the one-year rate $(_tR_1)$, it is the vector of future short-term rates that determines the term-structure vector.

It is important to note that the PET linkage-by-formula mechanism involves a simple "average variable–marginal variable" relationship. Since long-term rates are an average of future short-term rates, the following relationships hold:

1. If $_{t+N}r_1 > {}_tR_N$, $N \geq 2$, the yield curve will be positively sloped (i.e., as long as the marginal contribution is greater than the average, the average will rise).
2. If $_{t+N}r_t < {}_tR_N$, $N \geq 2$, the yield curve will be negatively sloped (i.e., as long as the marginal contribution is less than the average, the average will fall).
3. If $_{t+N}r_1 = {}_tR_N$, $N \geq 2$, the yield curve will be flat (i.e., as long as the marginal contribution equals the average, the average will remain constant).

Given these basic relationships, the PET can explain any shape of yield curve. When these relationships are turned around, they indicate that (1) a positively sloped yield curve implies that investors expect short-term rates to rise, (2) a negatively sloped yield curve implies that investors expect short-term rates to fall, and (3) a flat yield curve implies that investors expect short-term rates to remain unchanged.

Although expected rates cannot be observed directly, the PET equilibrium condition can be used to generate such rates, which are called *forward* rates and denoted by *F*. According to the PET, there is a one-to-one correspondence between forward rates and expected rates. Schematically, the process is

$$\begin{bmatrix} R_1 \\ R_2 \\ \vdots \\ R_N \end{bmatrix} \xrightarrow{\text{Generates}} \begin{bmatrix} _{t+1}F_1 \\ _{t+2}F_2 \\ \vdots \\ _{t+N-1}F_1 \end{bmatrix} = \begin{bmatrix} _{t+1}r_1 \\ _{t+2}r_1 \\ \vdots \\ _{t+N-1}r_1 \end{bmatrix}$$

To illustrate, consider the following Treasury-bill term structure with $_tR_1 = 16$ percent, $_tR_2 = 17$ percent, $_tR_3 = 15.5$ percent, and $_tR_4 = 15$ percent, where the maturity postsubscript is a quarterly one. Thus, $_tR_1$ represents the coupon-equivalent yield on three-month T-bills, $_tR_2$ the yield on six-month T-bills, and so on. What are the forward (expected) rates implied by this bill-rate structure? According to the PET, the expected three-month bill rates, using arithmetic averaging are

$$_{t+1}r_1 = 2(.17) - .16 = .18.$$

$$_{t+2}r_1 = 3(.155) - .16 - .18 = .125$$

$$_{t+3}r_1 = 4(15) - .16 - .18 - .125 = .135$$

In other words, to generate the observed hump in the yield curve, the expected three-month bill rates three, six and nine months in the future must be 18 percent, 12.5 percent, and 13.5 percent, respectively. That is, the three-month bill rates must be expected to rise, fall, and then rise to generate the hump.

Modified-Expectations Theories

The most famous expositor of the modified-expectations approach is J. R. Hicks [1946], the father of the Hicksian liquidity-premium theory. Hicks argued that, because of uncertainty about future interest rates and bond prices, investors had to be paid a liquidity premium for bearing the interest-rate or maturity risk of going long. This "constitutional weakness" in the bond market is why, even if future short-term rates are expected to remain unchanged, the normal yield-curve relationship is a positive one. Hicks was searching for an explanation of why, on average, long-term rates were greater than short-term ones. His theory focused upon the notion of liquidity premiums (L) as compensation for bearing interest-rate risk. The equilibrium condition for the Hicksian LPT is

$$(1 + _tR_N) = [(1 + _tR_1)(1 + _{t+1}r_1 + L_2)...(1 + _{t+N-1}r_1 + L_N)]^{1/N} \qquad (9\text{-}23)$$

where $L_N > L_{N-1} > 0$, $N \geq 2$ (i.e., the liquidity premiums are strictly positive and increase monotonically). Under this approach, the one-to-one correspondence between forward rates and expected rates disappears, that is,

$$_{t+N-1}F_1 = _{t+N-1}r_1 + L_N \qquad (9\text{-}24)$$

To illustrate, suppose that $_tR_1 = 10$ percent and that expected one-year rates for the next three years are 9.5 percent, 9.25 percent, and 9.00 percent. Furthermore, assume that the following liquidity premia exist: $L_2 = .75$ percent, $L_3 = 1.20$ percent, and $l_4 = 1.40$ percent. Using arithmetic averaging, the equilibrium term structure implied by these conditions is

$$R_2 = \frac{.10 + (.095 + .0075)}{2} = .1025$$

$$R_3 = \frac{.10 + (.095 + .0075) + (.0925 + .012)}{3} = .1032$$

$$R_4 = \frac{.10 + (.095 + .0075) + (.0925 + .012) + (.09 + .014)}{4} = .1034$$

The existence of the liquidity premiums results in a positively sloped yield curve. If $L_N = 0$, the implied term structure is a negatively sloped one (i.e., .10, .0975, .0958, .0944). In the Hicksian view of the term structure, the shape of the yield curve is explained by expectations of future short-term interest rates *plus* liquidity premiums.

A more general modified-expectations approach is the *preferred-habitat theory* associated with Modigliani and Sutch (1966).[11] According to this approach, either

---

[11] The preferred-habitat theory also could be viewed as a modified market-segmentation theory.

policy-determined or regulatory-imposed *risk aversion* leads investors to *hedge* their balance sheets by staying in their preferred (maturity) habitat. Unless the rates on other maturities offer an expected premium sufficient to compensate for the risk and cost of moving out of one's habitat, investors are content to stay with their preferred maturities. The concepts of segmented markets and hedging behavior, which the preferred-habitat theory builds upon, are explained more fully in the next section.

The equilibrium condition for the preferred-habitat theory is similar to Equation 9-23, except that no restrictions are placed on the *compensating* premiums, a_N (i.e., $a_N \gtrless 0$). In other words, in Equations 9-23 and 9-24 replace L_N with a_N and note that a_N is unconstrained. Along each segment of the yield curve, the compensating premiums are pegged by the forces of demand and supply. Through the forces of speculation or arbitrage, it is possible that such premiums (or discounts, i.e., $a_N < 0$) could bring about shifts in the flows of funds among different maturity segments. Thus, it is possible for nonexpectational elements to affect the term structure of interest rates.

The Market-Segmentation Theory

The market-segmentation theory adopts an institutional approach focusing on the hedging behavior of market participants. According to this explanation, the forces of supply and demand in *segmented* markets determine the yields in those markets. Since markets are segmented on the basis of maturity preferences tied to hedging behavior, there is no linkage by formula between short- and long-term interest rates as in expectations-based theories. Using the traditional trichotomy of short-, intermediate-, and long-term markets, the concept of segmented markets is illustrated in Figure 9-5. In each of these segments, the rates are determined by the forces of supply and demand as manifested by hedging-pressure behavior. The short-term segment is dominated by companies that require liquidity such as commercial banks, nonfinancial corporations, and money-market funds. Their maturity needs (or habitat preferences) lead them to attempt to hedge their balance sheets by investing in short-term assets. For example, at the beginning of the interest-rate cycle, when loan and product demand is slack, these institutions bid the prices of short-term securities up; hence low yields are observed. At the peak of the cycle, when liquidity is scarce, the opposite occurs. In general, investors in the short-term segment of the market are more concerned about *certainty of principal* than *certainty of income*.

The long-term segment of the market is dominated by institutions with long-term liabilities such as life insurance companies and pension funds. Hedging behavior leads these institutions to prefer to operate in the long-term segment of the market, where they tend to generate a fairly uniform demand for long-term assets such as bonds, stocks, and mortgages. In this segment of the market, investors are more concerned about *certainty of income* than *certainty of principal*. Thus, over the long

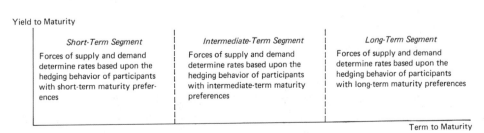

Figure 9-5   The Market-Segmentation Theory

run, risk-averse behavior prompts them to prefer long-term securities over short-term ones.

The intuitive appeal of market segmentation is diminished somewhat when analyzing the intermediate-term segment of the market. Unlike the short- and long-term markets, there are no easily identified institutions that prefer to operate solely in the intermediate-term maturity range. This absence of a dominating participant explains why the intermediate-term market frequently is described as thin and inactive compared to the short- and long-term segments. Some of the institutions that overlap into the intermediate-term range are commercial banks, property and casualty insurance companies, life insurance companies, and pension funds. Commercial banks also operate to a limited degree in the long-term U.S. government bond market while property and casualty insurance companies store their "hurricane money" in the short-term segment of the market. These overlapping markets argue against the polar version of market segmentation, which calls for completely segmented markets and no substitutability across maturities.

The concept of market segmentation has intuitive appeal because of the observed preference of certain institutions to operate in particular maturity segments. It is diametrically opposed to the PET and argues that, within a particular maturity segment, rates are determined by the forces of supply and demand, to the exclusion of future expected rates and alternative current yields. The preferred-habitat theory of Modigliani and Sutch, which adopts an eclectic approach, uses three building blocks: (1) maturity preferences, (2) expectations of future short-term rates, and (3) the notion of compensating premiums. Under this approach, investors can be coaxed out of their preferred habitats (think of the combined effect of small shifts by many transactors) if the compensating premiums are attractive. In contrast, the market segmentation theory denies such substitutability.

THE DEFAULT-RISK STRUCTURE OF INTEREST RATES

The risk premiums between corporate and Treasury bonds are referred to as *yield spreads*. They measure the additional return that risky bonds must pay to induce investors to hold them instead of riskless bonds. The risk premium is, of course, a payment for the greater default risk of the risky bond. The relationship between bond yields and default risk is referred to as the *default-risk structure of interest rates*. In general, yield spreads or risk premiums are the differences between the yields of any two bonds of equal term to maturity. For example, given the bond ratings in Table 9-6, we can talk about the risk premium or yield spread between AAA and A-rated bonds or between any other pair of bonds. The standard benchmark, however, is to compare the yield on a risky bond with a Treasury bond yield. Thus, the usual definition is

$$\text{Yield Spread} = (\text{Yield on Risky Bond}) - (\text{Yield on U.S. Treasury Bond}) \quad (9\text{-}25)$$

Default risk can be measured using bond ratings. The relationship between bond ratings and yields is depicted in Figure 9-6. The usual relationship is a nonlinear one with an increase in yield that is more than proportional to the decline in the quality rating. As noted earlier, yield spreads vary over time; for the U.S. bond market they have increased substantially over the past decade. Within a particular risk class (i.e., bond rating), a range of yields usually is observed, and this range increases as the quality of the rating declines. At the extreme end of the risk spectrum, the yields (and prices of defaulted bonds) are negotiable within wide ranges. With higher yields required for lower-quality bonds, high-quality bonds are valued dearly by investors.

TABLE 9-6   Bond Ratings

Descriptive Category	Yield to Maturity	Ratings	
		Standard & Poor's[a]	Moody's[a]
High quality	Lowest	AAA	Aaa
		AA	Aa
		A	A
Medium quality	Low intermediate	BBB	Baa
		BB	Ba
		B	B
Speculative	High intermediate	CCC	Caa
		CC	Ca
		C	C
Bonds in default	Highest	DDD,DD,D	—
Bonds of bankrupts	Highest	E	—

[a] Ratings refinements include the use of "p" by S&P to indicate a provisional rating and the use by Moody's of "1" to indicate a bond in the upper end of its category, "2" for the middle of a category, "3" for the lower end of a category, and "Con" to indicate a conditional rating. The triple-B rating (BBB or Baa) is regarded as the cutoff point for "investment-grade quality."

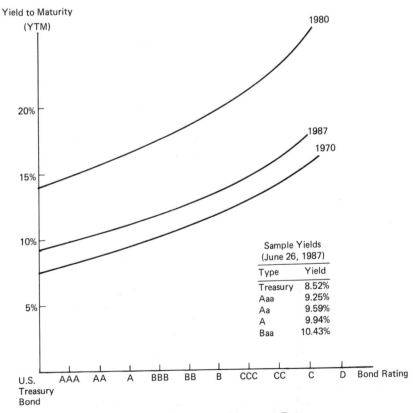

Figure 9-6   The Default-Risk Structure of Interest Rates

The Determinants of Risk Premiums on Corporate Bonds

Focusing on the sample yields shown in Figure 9-6, the risk premiums over the composite Treasury bond yield were 73, 107, 142, and 191 basis points for the Aaa, Aa, A, and Baa bonds, respectively, for the week ending June 26, 1987. What are the determinants of these risk premiums? In 1959, Fisher answered this question in an article published in *The Journal of Political Economy*. Although lots of refinements have been added to this area of research since 1959, Fisher's study still is regarded as the classic one on the determinants of risk premiums on corporate bonds.

Fisher's basic hypothesis has four components. First, he postulated the average risk premium on a firm's bonds to be a function of the firms's probability of defaulting on its bonds (i.e., its risk of default) and the marketability of its bonds. Second, he argued that the risk of default was a function of three variables: (1) the variability of the firm's earnings, (2) the length of time the firm has been operating without exposing creditors to losses, and (3) the ratio of the market value of the firm's equity to the par value of its debt. Third, he contended marketability could be measured by the market value of all the firm's publicly traded debt. And fourth, he specified a multiplicative relationship among the variables, which was estimated in a log-linear regression. Using data from selected years 1927 to 1953, Fisher accepted his basic hypothesis. Overall, his model explained about 75 percent of the variation in the (common logarithm) of the average risk premium, and he concluded that the elasticities were reasonably stable over his test period.

As noted in our discussion of money-market risk premiums, risk premiums on long-term corporate debt also show cyclical variation. Jaffee [1975] considered three theories of cyclical variation analogous with term-structure theory: (1) a pure-expectations or perfect-substitutes approach, (2) a modified-expectations approach based on preferred habitats, and (3) a market-segmentation approach. Under the perfect-substitutes theory, risk spreads should be constant and independent of the forces of supply and demand. Opposite this approach is the segmentation theory, which postulates that the market for each premium is determined in isolation by its own exogenous forces of supply and demand. As in term-structure theory, the preferred-habitat approach adopts an eclectic position in which elements of substitutability and segmentation play a role in explaining the cyclical variation in the risk structure of interest rates. Based on his empirical tests, Jaffee concluded in favor of the perfect-substitutes explanation for risk categories.

CHAPTER SUMMARY

This chapter has focused on the theories, conventions, and innovations surrounding interest rates and asset prices. Specifically, the notions of valuation of fixed-income securities, securitization (and derivative securities), duration, pricing conventions for Treasury bills, the Fisher effect, interest-rate theory, yield curves, term-structure theory, and default risk were introduced. These concepts are crucial for understanding interest rates and the pricing of debt instruments. The volatility of interest rates over the past quarter century has increased the need for managers of financial-services firms to understand these ideas. Since betting on interest rates can be risky business, risk-averse managers should welcome the recent innovations in the management of interest-rate risk. For example, the process of securitization leads to the derivative securities discussed in this chapter (e.g., interest-only and principal-only obligations). In Chapter 17, the groundwork established here will be useful in understanding the application of the various techniques (e.g., duration) for managing interest-rate risk.

LIST OF KEY WORDS, CONCEPTS, AND ACRONYMS

Bond valuation
Bank-discount yield
Certificate of deposit (CD)
Coupon-equivalent yield
Default-risk structure
Duration
Effective rate of interest
Financial-services firm (FSF)
Interest-rate cycle
Interest only (IO)
Liquidity premium and theory

Market-segmentation theory
Modified-expectations theory
Preferred habitat
Pure-expectations theory (PET)
Principal only (PO)
Risk premium
Term structure
Treasury bill
Yield curve and shapes
Zero-coupon (pure-discount) security

REVIEW/DISCUSSION QUESTIONS

1. Why is maturity intermediation a problem for depository institutions? Is the problem more or less severe for thrift institutions compared to other depository institutions?

2. Describe in words the alternative conventions for calculating yields on Treasury bills and explain how the bids for Treasury bills are allocated.

3. Carefully define each of the following terms:
   a. Face (par or maturity) value
   b. Coupon payment
   c. Coupon rate
   d. Yield to maturity
   e. Market price
   f. Duration
   g. Elasticity
   h. Term to maturity

4. What is a yield curve? What shape of yield curve is most likely to be observed at the various stages of the interest-rate cycle? What shape of yield curve exists *today* and at what stage of the current interest-rate cycle do you think the economy is?

5. Carefully distinguish between the default-risk structure of interest rates and the term structure of interest rates.

6. What is the Fisher effect?

7. Contrast and compare the following terms: interest-rate risk, default risk, and purchasing-power risk.

8. Explain how the following equation represents an overall theory of interest-rate determination:

$$k = r + x^* + p + m$$

9. Use the previous equation to explain how the bank financial-intermediation process works to determine loan and deposit rates. How does the interest-rate equation for k relate to the bank profit equation ($\pi = R - C - O - T$)?

10. Discuss the relationship between the dependent and the independent variables in Fisher's study of the determinants of risk premiums. How does Jaffee link his explanation of the cyclical variation in risk premiums with the term structure?

What do the following bond-rating refinements indicate: "*p*", "1", "2", "3", and "Con." Which agency uses which ones?

11. You are the proud owner of a 30-year, mortgage-backed security which has been stripped into interest-only (IO) and principal-only (PO) components. Originally issued in a fixed-rate market, rates suddenly and unexpectedly jump up by 200 basis points. What would you expect the price movements on each component to be and why? [*Hint:* Think about what is likely to happen to prepayments under this scenario.]

12. Do you *understand* the equations on the formula sheet for this chapter?

13. What are the alternative explanations of the term structure of interest rates? How does a forward rate differ from an expected rate according to the alternative theories?

14. Figure 9-7, page 256, shows the Treasury yield curve as of September 30, 1987. Figure 9-2 shows the yield curve as of September 28, 1984. Using these two point estimates, describe what has happened to rates over this three-year period.

MATCHING QUIZ

Directions: Select the letter from the right-hand column that best matches the item in the left-hand column.

___ 1. Classic risk-structure study

___ 2. Linked term and risk structures

___ 3. Stripped of interest payments

___ 4. Stripped of principal payments

___ 5. The *I* component of TRICK

___ 6. Effective time until repricing

___ 7. Basic bond-valuation formula

___ 8. Zero-coupon security

___ 9. Perpetual bond

___ 10. Floating-rate debt

___ 11. Bond price elasticity

___ 12. Immunization condition

___ 13. If $i = c$,

___ 14. If i greater than c,

A. J. R. Hicks

B. PV of future cash flows

C. Duration

D. Negatively sloped/humped

E. Fisher effect

F. Duration match

G. Expected interest rate

H. Inversely related

I. $(F - P)/F \times 360/N$

J. $(F - P)/P \times 365/N$

K. $365/N \times \ln(F/P)$

L. CD

M. Treasury bill

N. Fisher

___ 15. If i less than c,

___ 16. Asset price and yields are

___ 17. Bank-discount yield

___ 18. Coupon-equivalent yield

___ 19. Effective yield

___ 20. Interest-bearing security

___ 21. Includes anticipated inflation

___ 22. Explains nominal yields

___ 23. When rates are high, yield curve is

___ 24. Under PET, forward rates are

___ 25. Supply and demand important

___ 26. Liquidity-premium theorist

O. Jaffee

P. IO

Q. PO

R. Interest-rate risk

S. Market segmentation

T. Pure expected rates

U. Asset sells at par

V. Asset sells at discount

W. Asset sells at premium

X. Consol

Y. Ratio of % changes

Z. Inflation innovation

PROBLEMS

1. At the close of business on the day before Christmas Eve of 1987, the 13-week and 26-week T-bill rates were 5.73% and 6.32%, respectively. What is the forward rate embodied in this abbreviated term structure? Under what conditions is this forward rate a pure expected rate? If there is a 15 basis point liquidity premium embodied in the 26-week rate, what are the forward and expected rates under this condition?

2. On the same date as the information for the previous problem, the following structure of LIBOR (London Interbank Offered Rates) was observed:

Three months	7.44%
Six months	7.50%
Twelve months	7.87%

What forward (expected) rates are contained in this LIBOR structure? If you believe the LIBOR market is rigidly segmented, how are the rates in this market connected?

3. A consol is a perpetual bond (i.e., its maturity extends indefinitely). If the going rate of interest is 10 percent, determine the value of the following consols with coupon interest rates of
   a. 5 percent
   b. 10 percent
   c. 15 percent

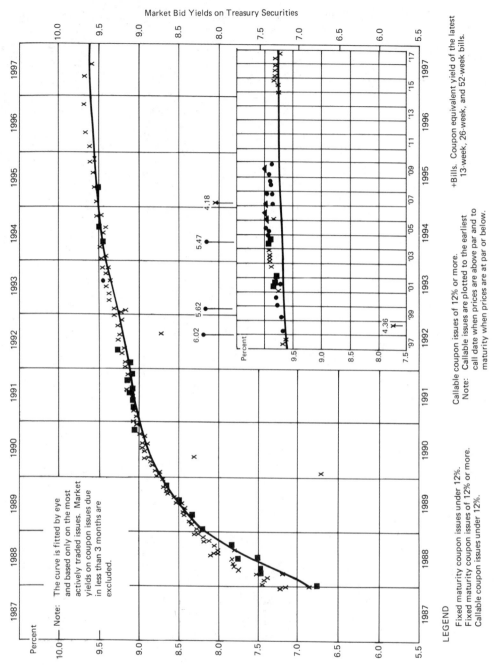

Figure 9-7   Exhibit to Accompany Review Question 14

Source: Treasury Bulletin, [December 1987], p. 47.

4. Find the value of the following bond:

   Par value = $1000

   Semiannual coupon payment = $60 ($120 per year)

   Maturity = 20 years

   Real rate of interest = 4 percent

   Anticipated inflation rate = 10 percent

5. Determine the bank-discount yield and the coupon-equivalent yield on a six-month T-bill that sells for $92.00.

6. Using arithmetic averaging, find the expected rates embodied in the following abbreviated term structure:

   $R_1 = 14$ percent

   $R_2 = 15$ percent

   $R_3 = 13$ percent

   $R_4 = 12$ percent

   How would your answer change if the following liquidity premia existed: $L_2 = 1$ percent, $L_3 = 1.5$ percent, $L_4 = 2$ percent?

CHAPTER 9 FORMULA SHEET

Equation number	Formula
1	$P_0 = \sum_{t=1}^{N} C_t/(1+i)^t + F/(1+t)^N$
2	$D = \dfrac{\sum_{t=1}^{N} \left[\dfrac{C_t}{(1+i)^t} \right] t + \left[\dfrac{F}{(1+i)^N} \right] N}{P_0}$
3	$E = (\Delta P_0/P_0)/(\Delta i/i)$
4	$E = D(i/(1+i))$
5	$D = D(N,c)$
6	$\Delta P/P = -D(\Delta i/(1+i))$
7	$\Delta P = -D(\Delta i/(1+i))P_0$
8	Bank-Discount Yield $= \dfrac{F-P}{F} \times \dfrac{360}{N}$
9	Effective Yield $= \left(1 + \dfrac{F-P}{P}\right)^{365/N} - 1$
10	Coupon-Equivalent Yield $= \dfrac{F-P}{P} \times \dfrac{365}{N}$
11	$P_{bid} = F - Y_{bid}F \times N/360$

12      $P_{asked} = F - Y_{asked}F \times N/360$

13      $MV = 100(1 + cN/360)$

14      $P = MV/(1 + (N/360)i)$

15      $i \approx r + x^*$

16      $i = r + x^* + rx^*$

17      $k = r + x^* \, p$

18      $k = r + x^* + p + m$

19      $k_j = i + p_j + m_j$

20      $i = f(N)$

21      $(1 + {}_tR_N) = [(1 + {}_tR_1)(1 + {}_{t+1}r_1)\ldots(1 + {}_{t+N-1}r_1)]^{1/N}$

22      $HPR = (C + \Delta P)/P_0$

23      $(1 + {}_tR_N) = [(1 + {}_tR_1)(1 + {}_{t+1}r_1 + L_2)\ldots(1 + {}_{t+N-1}r_1 + L_N)]^{1/N}$

24      ${}_{t+N-1}F_1 = {}_{t+N-1}r_1 + L_N$

25   Yield Spread = (Yield on Risky Bond) $-$ (Yield on T-Bond)

SELECTED REFERENCES

Cramer, Robert H., and James A. Seifert. [1976]. "Measuring the Impact of Maturity on Expected Return and Risk." *Journal of Bank Research* (Autumn), pp. 229–235.

Culbertson, John M. [1957]. "The Term Structure of Interest Rates." *Quarterly Journal of Economics* (November), pp. 485–517.

Epperson, James F., James B. Kau, Donald C. Keenan, and Walter J. Muller, III. [1984]. "Pricing Default Risk in Mortgages." Athens: The University of Georgia.

Federal Reserve Bulletin. Board of Governors of the Federal Reserve System, Washington, DC (various issues).

Fisher, Lawrence. [1959]. "Determinants of Risk Premiums on Corporate Bonds," *The Journal of Political Economy* (June), pp. 217–237.

Francis, Jack Clark. [1980]. *Investments: Analysis and Management*. New York: McGraw-Hill.

Garbade, Kenneth D. [1982]. *Securities Markets*. New York: McGraw-Hill.

Haugen, Robert A., and Dean W. Wichern. [1974]. "The Elasticity of Financial Assets." *Journal of Finance* (September), pp. 1229–1240.

Hicks, J. R. [1946]. *Value and Capital*. London: Oxford University Press.

Hilliard, Jimmy E. [1984]. "Duration as the Effective Time to Repricing." Athens: The University of Georgia.

Homer, Sidney, and Richard L. Johannesen. [1969]. *The Price of Money, 1946 to 1969*. Rutgers University Press.

Hopewell, M. H., and G. C. Kaufman. [1973]. "Bond-Price Volatility and Term to Maturity: A Generalized Respecification." *American Economic Review* (September), pp. 749–753.

Jaffee, Dwight M. [1975]. "Cyclical Variation in the Risk Structure of Interest Rates," *Journal of Monetary Economics* (I), pp. 309–325.

Kane, Edward J. [1970]. "The Term Structure of Interest Rates: An Attempt to Reconcile Teaching with Practice." *Journal of Finance* (May), pp. 361–374.

Kane, Edward J. and Burton G. Malkiel. [1967]. "The Term Structure of Interest Rates: An Analysis of a Survey of Interest-Rate Expectations." *Review of Economics and Statistics* (August), pp. 343–355.

———. [1970]. "Expectations Versus Habitats: Some Survey Evidence." Boston: Boston College, Working Paper Number 1.

Kessel, Reuben A. [1965]. *The Cyclical Behavior of the Term Structure of Interest Rates.* Occasional Paper 91, National Bureau of Economic Research.

King, Stephen R., and Eli M. Remolona. [1987]. "The Pricing and Hedging of Market Index Deposits," *Quarterly Review*, Federal Reserve Bank of New York (Fall), pp. 9–20.

Lutz, F. A. [1940]. "The Structure of Interest Rates." *Quarterly Journal of Economics* (November), pp. 36–63.

Maisel, Sherman J. [1973]. *Managing the Dollar.* New York: W. W. Norton.

Malkiel, Burton G. [1966]. *The Term Structure of Interest Rates: Expectations and Behavior Patterns.* Princeton, NJ: Princeton University Press.

Meiselman, David. [1962]. *The Term Structure of Interest Rates.* Englewood Cliffs, NJ: Prentice-Hall.

Modigliani, Franco and Richard Sutch. [1966]. "Innovations in Interest-Rate Policy." *American Economic Review*: Papers and Proceedings (May), pp. 178–197.

———. [1967]. "Debt Management and the Term Structure of Interest Rates: An Empirical Analysis." *Journal of Political Economy* (August), pp. 569–589.

———. [1969]. "The Term Structure of Interest Rates: A Reexamination of the Evidence." *Journal of Money, Credit, and Banking* (February), pp. 112–120.

Monhollon, Jimmie R. [1977]. "Treasury Bills." In *Instruments of the Money Market*, Timothy Q. Cook, ed. Federal Reserve Bank of Richmond, pp. 13–20.

Mullineaux, Donald. [1973]. "Deposit-Rate Ceilings and Noncompetitive Bidding for U.S. Treasury Bills." *Journal of Money, Credit and Banking* (February), pp. 200–212.

Nelson, Charles R. [1972]. *The Term Structure of Interest Rates.* New York: Basic Books.

Robichek, Alexander, et al. [1976]. *Management of Financial Institutions.* Hinsdale, IL: Dryden Press.

Roll, Richard. [1970]. *The Behavior of Interest Rates.* New York: Basic Books.

Sinkey, Joseph F., Jr. [1979]. *Problem and Failed Institutions in the Commercial Banking Industry.* Greenwich, CT: JAI Press.

———. [1973]. The Term Structure of Interest Rates: A Time-Series Test of The Kane Expected-Change Model of Interest-Rate Forecasting." *Journal of Money, Credit and Banking* (February), pp. 192–200.

———. [1971]. "The Term Structure of Interest Rates: Theory, Models of Interest-Rate Forecasting, and Empirical Evidence." Doctoral Dissertation, Boston College.

Toevs, Alden, and William Haney. [1984]. *Guide to Asset-Liability Models.* New York: Morgan Stanley.

Treasury Bulletin, United States Treasury Department. Washington, DC (various issues).

Yawitz, J. B., et al. [1975]. "The Use of Average Maturity as a Risk Proxy in Investment Port-folios." *Journal of Finance* (May), pp. 235–335.

THE BIG PICTURE: PERFORMANCE AND COST ANALYSES, STRATEGIC PLANNING, AND ASSET-LIABILITY MANAGEMENT

Where is the bank today? Where is it going? How is it going to get there? To see the big picture, top management must ask and answer these three questions; they are the basic thrust of strategic management. In Chapters 10 and 11, we focus on where the bank is today in terms of its financial performance. Chapter 10 concentrates on the return-on-equity (ROE) model and decomposition analysis; Chapter 11 focuses on the cost characteristics of banks with special emphasis on the notions of economies of scale and economies of scope, and the empirical evidence about their existence. These two chapters are designed to tell us where the bank is today in terms of its profit and cost performances. From there, we go on to look at where the bank is going in Chapter 12 with the focus on strategic planning and management. In Chapter 13, the technique of asset-liability management (ALM), which is the coordinated management of the bank's balance sheet in the short run, is explained and illustrated. Since ALM has a short-run focus, it can be viewed as the first step in moving the bank in its desired (or target) direction as determined by strategic management.

The Return-on-Equity Model: Performance and Decomposition Analysis

---

ACRONYM GUIDE TO KEY TERMS AND CONCEPTS

AU = asset utilization
EM = equity multiplier
FSI = financial-services industry
P/E = price-earnings ratio
PM = profit margin
ROA = return on assets = $PM \times AU$
ROE = return on equity = $ROA \times EM = PM \times AU \times EM$

INTRODUCTION

Finance theorists would argue that in an efficient market (see Chapter 3) there is little need for performance analysis based on accounting data (except perhaps for filler in glossy annual reports) because the firm's best gauge of its performance is its stock price. On a relative basis for comparisons across firms or industries, price-earnings (P/E) ratios could be employed, where the P/E ratio is simply the ratio of the firm's market value to its earnings per share. In other words, the P/E ratio shows what value the firm's current earnings command in the marketplace. However, even P/E ratios are flawed since real value is based on the present value of the firm's future cash flows, and not on some multiple of current accounting earnings. Moreover, P/E ratios sometimes get way out of line, as they did prior to the stock market crashes of 1929, when the average P/E was approximately 21.5, and 1987, when the average P/E was roughly 23. Since the early 1900s, the average P/E has been about 13. Nevertheless, the more closely reported earnings track expected future cash flows, the more accurate P/E ratios are as measures of true value.[1]

Although most finance theorists acknowledge some form of market efficiency, most practitioners, whose livelihoods depend on keeping their customers in the dark about the notion of efficient capital markets, engage in analyzing and keeping performance scores using accounting data. Moreover, about 95 percent of the firms in the banking

---

[1] See Verbrugge [1987] for an interesting discussion of the lessons of modern finance for financial-services firms and Chew [1986] for a roundtable discussion of some practical aspects of corporate finance.

industry do not have their shares publicly traded. Thus, except for the largest bank holding companies and other large players in the financial-services industry, many financial-services firms are not subject to the discipline of efficient capital markets. In this regard, keeping score on the basis of accounting data can be regarded as the only game in town. Unfortunately, accounting models of performance such as the ones considered in this chapter (e.g., the ROE model) represent only an imperfect second-best solution. Although the efficient-market model is the best gauge of performance, accounting models, adjusted for quality of earnings and assets, are useful second-best tools for analyzing financial performance. With these caveats in mind, let's begin our study of performance analysis and the return-on-equity (ROE) model.

READING A BANK'S BALANCE SHEET

Shortly after the failure of Franklin National Bank of New York in 1974, Harry Keefe, a well-known analyst of bank stocks, remarked that "People who can read a balance sheet were out of there long ago." Of course, he was talking about Franklin National Bank. For a person who heads a firm that analyzes bank stocks, it was a very judicious statement to make. Obviously, in such a business, you want to convince your customers and would-be customers that your firm really does know how to analyze bank financial statements. Thus, some of those who are keenly interested in the analysis of bank balance-sheet and income-expense reports are bank-stock analysts. For obvious reasons, bank owners, directors, managers, and regulators also are interested in this topic.

Given a modicum of intelligence combined with the time, the inclination, and some basic tools, you can learn to analyze any firm's financial statements. The purpose of this chapter is to provide the basic tools for analyzing the financial statements of a bank. Whether or not you develop proficiency in this technique depends mostly on the time and inclination you devote to the topic. The chapter begins with a definition of ratio analysis and a look at its strengths and weaknesses. The return-on-equity (ROE) model and the technique of decomposition analysis are presented next. The chapter contains numerous examples of ROE analysis and the decomposition process.

RATIO ANALYSIS

Ratio analysis is a technique or tool for evaluating the financial condition and performance of a firm. The basic component of ratio analysis is a single ratio, constructed by dividing one balance-sheet and/or income-expense item by another. The denominator of such a ratio may be conceived as a "base" or "scale" factor. For example, the profitability ratios, ROE and ROA, use equity capital and total assets, respectively, as the scale factors. ROE and ROA provide yardsticks for measuring a bank's profit performance. ROE measures a bank's profits per dollar of equity capital whereas ROA measures profits per dollar of total assets. Suppose that a bank's ROE is 12 percent. By itself, this piece of information does not reveal much about the financial condition of the bank, although it does tell us that the bank's profits were positive. While this is better than negative profits (i.e., losses), we need a standard or norm against which to judge such figures. To provide a meaningful basis for evaluating a bank's financial statements, we make comparisons with *similar* firms and/or with its own performance over time. The important point is that by themselves ratios are relatively useless. To be useful, ratios must be (1) analyzed over time (trend analysis), (2) compared with those of a control group of *similar* firms (cross-section or peer-group analysis), or (3) combined in a peer-group/trend analysis (i.e., time-series/cross-section analysis).

STRENGTHS AND WEAKNESSES OF RATIO ANALYSIS

Ratio analysis is a useful tool. As when using any tool, however, the user must be familiar with the capabilities and limitations of the mechanism. Ratio analysis mainly is conducted using historical accounting data. In this context, it only gives information about a bank's past history and its current financial position. In this sense, ratio analysis is a static tool. However, it can be made into a dynamic technique through the use of pro forma or forecasted data that permit pro forma financial ratios to be constructed. In addition, ratios can be used in conjunction with alternative statistical techniques to attempt to predict corporate bankruptcy or in early-warning systems for distressed financial institutions.

Regarding the use of accounting data, such information is subject to different interpretations and to manipulation or "window dressing." Moreover, earnings are especially subject to manipulation. Three techniques for managing earnings are

1. changing accounting methods
2. fiddling with managers' estimates of costs
3. shifting the period when expenses and revenues are included in results.

The third technique is dominated by one particularly malleable element: *judgment.* The opportunity for judgment in accounting matters to affect earnings is most potent in two industries: (1) banking and (2) property and casualty (P&C) insurance. Banks must make a provision to cover loans that will ultimately go bad and P&C companies establish reserves to cover claims to be paid out on current policies. Prior to the Tax Reform Act of 1986, large banks (over $500 million in assets) could deduct provision for loan losses from profits in the year they were added to reserves, rather than in the year the loan was charged off.[2] Under current tax laws (see the Appendix to Chapter 11 for the provisions and effects of this law on banks), large commercial banks are permitted to take deductions for bad debts (i.e., loan losses) only when the loans become partially or wholly worthless. Regardless of the tax treatment, a judgment call on the "worthlessness" of the loan is still required. In addition to earnings manipulation, bank accounting data also are subject to "window dressing" (e.g., with respect to end-of-period liquidity positions via federal funds and/or other securities transactions).

Since ratio analysis can be no better than the inputs upon which it is based, the computer adage, "garbage in, garbage out," must be kept in mind. A simple but often overlooked fact is that any ratio contains two pieces of information, one in the numerator and the other in the denominator (as in ROE = After-Tax-Profits/Equity). Thus, for example, ROE may be large because profits are large or because the equity base is small or both. It is important not to lose sight of the fact that a ratio is simply a way of collapsing two pieces of information into one. In the process, some information is gained and some is obscured. It also is important to keep in mind that ratios

---

[2] See Greenawalt and Sinkey [1988] and Scheiner [1981] for evidence regarding the income-smoothing behavior of large banks/BHCs.

only reflect symptoms of good or bad performance and not causes. The decomposition analysis, discussed later in this chapter, attempts to pinpoint the causes of good or bad performance that are identified through ratio analysis.

OVERALL BANK PERFORMANCE: A RISK–RETURN FRAMEWORK

Consistent with the financial-management goal of stock-price maximization, overall bank performance can be couched in a risk–return framework as depicted in Figure 10-1. From this viewpoint, overall bank performance is divided into a risk component as measured by the variability of ROE and a return component as measured by ROE. In turn, the ROE component can be split into the familiar leverage (EM) and return-on-assets (ROA) elements. Next, the ROA figure can be further split into factors that are controllable and noncontrollable by the bank. In this context, however, control does not imply absolute control but simply a degree of control. Noncontrollable environmental factors would include most of the elements of TRICK and others. In general, the basic supply and demand conditions that a bank faces are noncontrollable factors. Controllable factors would include such elements as the bank's business mix, income production (the ability to generate revenue from the chosen business mix), loan quality (the riskiness of the loan portfolio as reflected in loan losses), expense control (the ability to hold down overhead costs), and tax management (the ability to reduce taxable income). Note that these controllable factors fit nicely into the bank profit equation ($\Pi = R - C - O - T$) and the value-maximization framework depicted in Figure 10-2. The first three controllable factors in Figure 10-1 are just alternative ways of describing the spread-, liquidity-, and capital-management elements of Figure 10-2, topics that are discussed in detail in later parts of this book.

The concept of risk is a critical part of Figure 10-1. It can be summarized via the frameworks for analyzing BHC and bank risk presented in Chapter 14; see Figures 14-2 and 14-4 on pages 396 and 399. In addition, recall the Fed's BHC rating system discussed in Chapter 8 (pages 195–197). Summarizing from these materials, BHCs/banks face six generic risks: (1) portfolio or balance-sheet risk, (2) regulatory risk, (3)

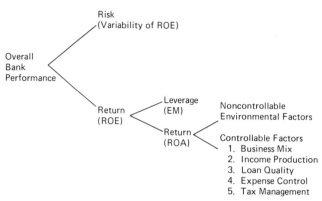

Figure 10-1   Overall Bank Performance: A Risk-Return Framework

The first four controllable factors are those suggested by Gillis, Lumry, and Oswold [1980], pp. 70–71.

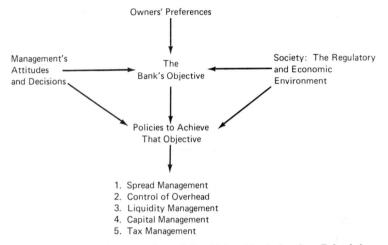

Figure 10-2   Implementation of the Value-Maximization Principle

technological risk, (4) affiliation risk, (5) operating-efficiency risk, and (6) market-strategy risk. From a practical rather than a conceptual standpoint, portfolio and operating-efficiency risks have the most direct effect on the variability of earnings. The critical portfolio risks in banking are credit risk, interest-rate risk, liquidity risk, leverage risk (with respect to debt servicing), and capital-adequacy risk. The I and K components of TRICK reflect two of these key risk factors.

In general, risks are important because they give rise to variability of earnings. In banking, the effects of some of these risks are more obvious (e.g., loan losses arising from bad credit risks) than others. With respect to the components of TRICK, the I and K elements are the obvious ones. However, the T, R, and C components, which work more subtly, can be just as devastating over the long run. Note that the C or customers factor can be measured in terms of market-strategy risk. Although the T, R, and C components are not as conspicuous in terms of their effects on short-run profits, financial-services firms that fail to adapt with respect to technology, reregulation, and customers face the ultimate risk—extinction. To avoid extinction, FSFs must engage in strategic planning, the topic of Chapter 12. In this chapter, the focus is on identifying indicators of financial strength or weakness by analyzing a firm's balance sheet and income-expense statement.

THE RETURN-ON-EQUITY MODEL[3]

The starting point for ROE analysis is a bank's return on equity. ROE can be calculated in a number of ways depending upon how the numerator and denominator of the ratio are specified. In general, ROE measures profits per dollar of bank capital. Since there are several definitions of profits and capital, ROE figures may be constructed in alternative ways. For example, three common measures of bank profits are

1. income before taxes and securities gains or losses
2. income after taxes but before securities gains or losses
3. net income (after taxes and securities gains or losses).

[3] See Cole [1974].

Three common measures of bank capital include

1. total equity capital (consisting of common stock, surplus, and undivided profits)
2. total equity capital plus reserves for losses
3. total equity capital plus reserves plus debt capital.

The definition of ROE used in this book employs net income in the numerator and total equity capital in the denominator. Net income is used because it reflects the "bottom line" or total operations of the bank; total equity capital is employed because of the emphasis on shareholders' return as a short-run proxy for long-run value maximization. Since some bank analysts and banks continue to report profitability measures using income after taxes but before securities gains or losses, be sure to check the definitions used before making comparative analyses.

The First and Second Stages of ROE Decomposition Analysis

The basic return-on-equity model is presented in Table 10-1. The first stage of ROE decomposition analysis splits ROE into its ROA and EM components. In the example in Table 10-1, $ROE = .1386$, consisting of $ROA = .009$ and $EM = 15.4$. Note that $ROE = ROA \times EM = .1368 = .009 \times 15.4$. The leverage component (EM) enables a bank with an ROA of less than 1 percent to return almost 14 percent on equity.

The second stage of the decomposition analysis splits ROA into a profit-margin component (PM) and an asset-utilization component (AU).[4] In the example, the ROA of .009 consists of a PM of .081 and an AU of .1111. Note that $ROA = PM \times AU = .009 = .081 \times .1111$. PM measures profits per dollar of revenue or total operating

TABLE 10-1   The Return-on-Equity Model

Return on Equity = Return on Assets × Equity Multiplier

$$= ROA \times EM$$

= Profit Margin × Asset Utilization × Equity Multiplier

$$= PM \times AU \times EM$$

$$\frac{\text{Net Income}}{\text{Average Equity}} = \frac{\text{Net Income}}{\text{Operating Income}} \times \frac{\text{Operating Income}}{\text{Average Assets}} \times \frac{\text{Average Assets}}{\text{Average Equity}}$$

$$= \frac{\text{Net Income}}{\text{Average Assets}} \times \frac{\text{Average Assets}}{\text{Average Equity}}$$

$$= \frac{\text{Net Income}}{\text{Average Equity}}$$

Example: $.1386 = .0810 \times .1111 \times 15.40$

$$= .0090 \times 15.40$$

$$= .1386$$

Note that the inverse of the equity multiplier is the familiar capital-asset ratio. For the previous example:

Capital-Asset Ratio = Average Equity/Average Assets

$$= (15.40)^{-1} = .0649$$

$$= 6.49\%$$

---

[4] In the world of corporation finance this stage is called the du Pont system of financial analysis and AU is described as an "activity" or "turnover" ratio, measured by the ratio of sales to assets. Of course, a bank's "sales" are measured by its total operating income. Given a bank's tax rate, the PM and AU figures can be expressed on a tax-equivalent basis by computing tax-free income as taxable revenue.

income, AU measures revenue per dollar of assets, and ROA measures profits or net income per dollar of assets. In the example, the bank can be described as generating (1) $8.10 of net income per $100 of total operating income, (2) $11.11 of total operating income per $100 of assets, and, as a result, (3) $.90 of net income per $100 of assets. With $15.40 in assets for every dollar of equity capital, the bank generates $13.86 of net income for every $100 of equity capital. To summarize, $ROE = PM \times AU \times EM = ROA \times EM = .1386 = .081 \times .1111 \times 15.4 = .009 \times 15.4$.

Four Pieces of Accounting Information

Four pieces of accounting information are required to start ROE analysis:

1. net income
2. total operating income
3. average assets
4. average equity.

The first two pieces of information are *flow* variables that come from a bank's income statement, while the last two are *stock* variables that come from the balance sheet. To make the stock and flow variables more compatible, average balance-sheet figures should be used. To illustrate, consider a bank that starts the year with $95 million in total assets and $6.17 million in total equity capital. If the corresponding mid-year and end-of-year figures are $100 million and $6.49 million, and $105 million and $6.82 million, respectively, how should the asset and equity components of the ROE model be measured? Assuming that net income for the year was $900,000 and total operating income was $11.1 million, three ROE calculations can be made on the basis of beginning-of-year equity ($6.17 million), year-end equity ($6.82 million), and average equity ($6.49 million) = (6.17 + 6.49 + 6.82/3). The corresponding ROE figures are 14.58 percent, 13.20 percent, and 13.86 percent, respectively. Thus, for a bank with a growing equity-capital base, ROE can be "window dressed" to overstate or understate the "true" ROE of 13.86 percent. In the case of a bank with a shrinking equity-capital base, the opposite would be true. Note that the example is constructed so that the average figures correspond with the ROE analysis in Table 10-1.

The important point in ROE analysis is to be *consistent*, so that you are not attempting to compare apples with oranges. As a practical matter, most analysts tend to use year-end balance-sheet data because they do not require calculation of the average figures. As long as the comparative peer-group or trend data are constructed in the same manner, you will be analyzing similar data.

DECOMPOSITION ANALYSIS: THE THIRD STAGE

To review, the first and second stages of ROE decomposition analysis are

Stage One: $ROE = ROA \times EM$

and

Stage Two: $ROA = PM \times AU$.

Stage three involves a detailed examination of both PM and AU. Note that the numerators of the PM and AU ratios are the variables π and R, respectively, from the profit equation, $\pi = R - C - O - T$. Thus, another way of looking at stage three of

ROE analysis is as an investigation of the profit equation on a relative or ratio basis. Stage three of ROE decomposition analysis is summarized in Figure 10-3, which resembles a decision-tree diagram. In the top branch of the diagram, net income or the profit equation ($\pi = R - C - O - T$) is analyzed. The interest-expense branch can be broken into deposit and nondeposit (e.g., federal funds) interest costs. The

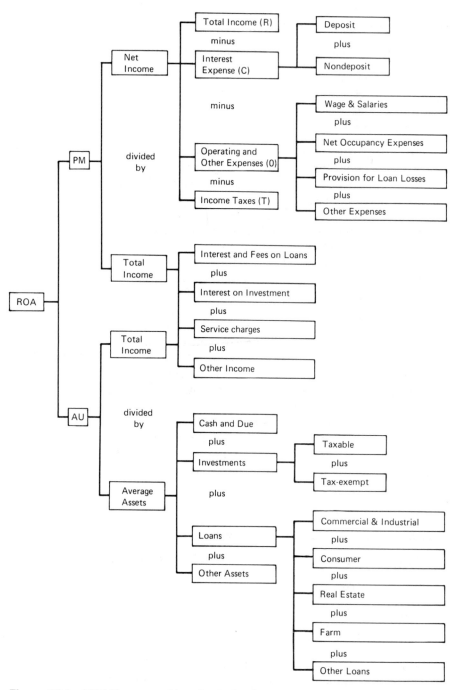

Figure 10-3   ROE Decomposition Analysis: Stage Three

operating-expense branch can be analyzed in terms of four components:

1. wages and salaries
2. net occupancy expenses
3. provision for loan losses
4. other expenses.

The total-income branch can be viewed in terms of four sources of revenue:

1. interest and fees on loans
2. interest on investments
3. service charges
4. other income.

The final branch is the asset one, consisting of cash and due, investments, loans, and other assets. Investments can be analyzed in terms of their tax status and loans in terms of the four basic categories: commercial and industrial, consumer, real estate, and farm.

The individual components of the third stage of the ROE decomposition framework usually are analyzed with respect to a bank's total income or total assets. Thus, for example, it is possible to look at wages and salaries per dollar of income or assets. The objective of this stage of the analysis is to identify symptoms of good or bad performance by pinpointing trends and significant peer-group differences. From a troubleshooting perspective, adverse trends and differences can be traced to the *cause* of the malperformance so that remedial attention can be applied to the sore spot. Since bank policies and those individuals who make and carry out the policies are the ultimate causes of good or bad performance, the identification of adverse symptoms calls for a review of the policies and personnel in the troubled area. To illustrate, suppose that a bank finds that its interest expense for federal funds is substantially higher than that of its peers. At first glance, this symptom suggests a short-run reserve management problem. Thus, the bank's policy regarding federal-funds borrowing should be reviewed and the person in charge of managing the bank's reserve position evaluated. This investigation may reveal the cause of the problem or it may suggest a longer-run cause due to the bank's strategy of asset/liability management (e.g., of placing an undue burden on federal funds for financing loans and investments).

ROE ANALYSIS AND DECISION-MAKING

Throughout this discussion, keep in mind our familiar profit equation, $\pi = R - C - O - T$. Given environmental and regulatory constraints, it is not unreasonable to expect bank managers to attempt to

1. maximize revenues including interest and fees
2. minimize costs including interest and overhead
3. avoid taxes (i.e., shelter income).

Obviously, if these three steps are achieved, managers will be successful in maximizing profits.

ROE analysis involves the calculation of three measures of profitability (i.e., ROE, ROA, and PM). Other things equal (i.e., AU and EM), you can improve both ROE and ROA by improving PM. The relevant question is: How can a bank improve its profit margin? As an exercise, answer this question. You must be specific! All of your specific recommendations should fall under the following umbrella of general concepts:

1. spread management
2. control of loan quality

3. control of overhead
4. generation of fee and service-charge income
5. tax avoidance (as opposed to tax evasion, which is, of course, illegal).

Do you have a recommendation that doesn't fit any of the general categories?

An alternative way of attempting to improve both ROE and ROA is to focus upon AU. If PM and EM remain unchanged, then better AU will mean higher ROE and ROA. One way to improve AU is through portfolio management. In particular, a shift from lower-yielding assets (usually securities) to higher-yielding assets (usually loans) is required. How does this portfolio shift affect a bank's risk exposure? What can a bank manager do to increase the size of his/her loan portfolio? How can this expansion be financed? These questions are anticipatory ones, so don't be discouraged if you feel at a loss for the answer. They will be answered later in the book.

Since ROA = PM × AU, the way to improve ROA is to improve either PM or AU or both. However, an improvement in AU may result in a deterioration in PM or vice versa. Can you explain how these situations might arise? Moreover, since $ROE = ROA \times EM$, the way to improve ROE is to improve ROA or EM or both. Again however, an improvement in ROA may result in a deterioration in EM or vice versa. Can you explain how these situations might arise?

Regarding *EM*, recall that its reciprocal is the familiar capital-to-asset ratio. If bank managers attempt to increase *ROE* by using greater leverage (i.e., a larger EM, which implies a lower capital-to-asset ratio), they may incur the wrath of the bank regulator. As you know, bank regulators regard a bank's capital-to-asset ratio as an important indicator of its risk exposure. That's why the acronym for the FDIC has been redefined by the banking community as *Forever Demanding Increased Capital*. Thus, bank managers are faced with a dilemma regarding EM. They must earn a return high enough to keep stockholders satisfied, and one way to try to do this is through greater financial leverage. However, if at some point the leverage becomes too great (i.e., the capital-to-asset ratio becomes too low), the regulators usually attempt to restrict a bank's growth and/or call for an infusion of capital.

Juggling the demands of stockholders and regulators to try to keep both groups satisfied is only one of the balancing acts that bank managers must perform. In general, these kinds of decisions involve fundamental trade-offs between risk and return. Thus, a key to sound decision making is to be able to identify and measure the relevant risks and returns associated with a particular decision.

ROE ANALYSIS FOR THE U.S. BANKING SYSTEM, 1981–1986

Appendix A of this chapter presents detailed financial information for the U.S. banking system (defined as all insured commercial banks) for the years 1981 through 1986. The first four tables in the appendix show portfolio composition, interest rates, and income and expenses for four classes of banks: (1) banks with assets less than $100 million, (2) banks with assets between $100 million and $1 billion, (3) money-center banks, and (4) large banks other than money-center banks. (The last two groups include all banks with assets over $1 billion.) As of December 31, 1986, the number of banks in each of these groups were 11,011; 2,398; 9; and 321; respectively, for a total 13,739. Although there are about 1,000 more banks in the U.S., these were the banks included in Federal Reserve's analysis conducted by Danker and McLaughlin [1987]. The last two tables in the appendix show reports of income for all insured commercial banks from 1981 to 1986 and various ratios and data for the second quarter of 1987 for all insured commercial banks.

Let's begin our ROE analysis with a look at Table 10-2, where ROE and ROA for the groups described above are shown for the years 1981 through 1986. For this six-year period, the average ROE and ROA for all banks were 11.43 percent and .69 percent, respectively. The equity multiplier (EM) implied by these figures is .1143/.0069 = 16.56. The reciprocal of EM, 6.04 percent, is the ratio of equity capital to assets for all insured commercial banks.

It is interesting to note how the forces of change as captured by TRICK have affected ROE and its components. Let's begin with the implied equity multipliers for all insured commercial banks. Beginning with 1981, these figures are 17.22, 17.04, 16.78, 16.56, 16.17, and 15.98. To get these figures, you simply divide ROE by ROA for each year (e.g., for 1986 15.98 = .1023/.0064). Market and regulatory pressures for greater "capital adequacy" serve to explain the downward trend in EM. Conversely, the capital ratio for all insured banks has risen from 5.81 percent ($=17.22^{-1} \times 100$) to 6.27 percent ($15.98^{-1} \times 100$).

Since the ROE data for all banks tend to camouflage the diversity of performance within the banking system, let's focus on the size groups shown in Table 10-2. Although the system trends have been downward for both ROE and ROA, small banks (i.e., those with assets under $100 million) have been hit the hardest by the forces of change, especially by interest-rate deregulation and changes in deposit composition. (An analysis of bank cost characteristics is presented in Chapter 11, also see Appendix A of this chapter.) The ROE and ROA data clearly demonstrate the adverse effects on the profitability of small banks. Specifically, in 1981 ROA was a healthy 1.14 percent for the average bank in this group of 12,353; in contrast, in 1986 the figure was cut by more than one-half to 0.53 percent for the 11,011 banks in the group. Over the same time period, ROE fell by more than ROA but was cushioned by a slight increase in

TABLE 10-2   Return on Equity and Return on Assets for All Insured Commercial Banks by Year and Size of Bank, 1981–1986 [a]

Percent

Type of Return and Size of Bank [b]	1981	1982	1983	1984	1985	1986
Return on assets [c]						
All banks	.76	.71	.67	.64	.70	.64
Less than $100 million	1.14	1.07	.96	.81	.70	.53
$100 million to $1 billion	.91	.84	.84	.88	.84	.71
$1 billion or more						
Money-center banks	.53	.53	.54	.52	.45	.46
Others	.66	.60	.54	.53	.78	.75
Return on equity [d]						
All banks	13.09	12.10	11.24	10.60	11.32	10.23
Less than $100 million	13.39	12.45	11.12	9.50	8.18	6.24
$100 million to $1 billion	12.78	11.74	11.86	12.41	11.69	9.87
$1 billion or more						
Money-center banks	13.57	13.27	12.57	11.42	9.60	9.50
Others	12.80	11.42	10.15	9.66	13.69	12.61

[a] Before 1984, data are based on averages for call dates in December of the preceding year and in June and December of the current year. In 1984, data are based on averages for call dates at the beginning and end of the year only. After 1984, data are based on averages of the call date in December of the preceding year and all four call dates in the current year.
[b] Size categories are based on year-end fully consolidated assets.
[c] Net income as a percentage of average fully consolidated assets net of loss reserves.
[d] Net income as a percentage of average equity capital.
Source: Danker and McLaughlin [1987], Table 2, p. 539.

leverage for the group. For example, in 1981 ROE was 13.39 percent with a leverage factor (or equity multiplier) of 11.75; by 1986 the figures were 6.24 percent and 11.77, respectively.

For banks with assets greater than $100 million up to $1 billion, the pressure on profitability has been less severe. Specifically, in 1981 the average bank in this group of 1,651 had an ROA of 0.91 percent; by 1986, when the number of banks in the group had grown to 2,398, ROA had fallen to 0.71 percent. The corresponding ROE and EM figures for this group were 12.78 percent and 14.04 ($= .1278/.0091$) for 1981 and 9.87 percent and 13.90 ($ = .0987/.0071$) in 1986.

Let's now focus on the banks with over $1 billion in assets. The banks in this group are further segmented into money-center and nonmoney-center ones. Calling the latter group "regional banks," we consider their profitability first. In 1981 the average ROA was 0.66 percent for the 195 banks in the group; in 1986 with 321 banks in the group ROA was 0.75. The regional banks were the only group of the four analyzed here to experience an increase in ROA over the years 1981 to 1986. However, because of a decline in leverage from 19.39 in 1981 to 16.81 in 1986, the average ROE for this group did not increase, but fell from 12.80 percent in 1981 to 12.61 percent in 1986. When analyzing ROE, always remember it has two components: (1) a pure profitability measure in the form of ROA and (2) a leverage factor in the form of the equity multiplier, EM, such that ROE $=$ ROA $\times$ EM.

Finally, let's focus on the nine banks in the money-center group. The number of banks in this group did not change over the years 1981 to 1986. In 1981 ROA was 0.53 percent; in 1986 it was 0.46 percent. The corresponding figures for ROE and EM were 13.57 percent and 25.6 in 1981 and 9.50 percent and 20.65 in 1986. If money-center banks had been permitted to maintain their 1981 leverage positions (a counterfactual proposition), the groups average ROE would have fallen only to 11.78 percent ($= .0046 \times 25.6 \times 100$) rather than 9.50 percent.

Geographic Variation in ROA

ROA not only varies by bank size, but also by region of the country. Figure 10-4 shows ROA for the years 1980, 1985, and 1986 by Federal Reserve District. For reference, the boundaries of the Federal Reserve Districts are also shown in Figure 10-4. The bar graphs in Figure 10-4 warrant the following conclusions. First, the only areas with average ROAs above 1.0 percent in 1986 were the Philadelphia and Richmond districts. Second, the rebound in profitability in New England and the "rust belt" is evident. Third, the sectoral problems in energy and agriculture in the 1980s are evident by the sharp declines in ROA in the Kansas City and Dallas districts. And fourth, the figures for the San Francisco district are biased downward by the financial difficulties experienced by BankAmerica, the second largest bank in the United States behind Citibank.

Cyclical Variation in ROE and ROA

The cyclical variation in ROE and ROA over the period 1970 through 1986 for all insured commercial banks is shown in Figure 10-5. The left-hand scale measures ROA and the right-hand scale measures ROE. The decade of the 1970s started off with an industry ROA slightly less than 1 percent and an ROE slightly above 12 percent, implying an equity multiplier of 13 or so. In the early 1970s, increasing leverage was used to offset the decline in ROA, and even increase it in 1973. However, with the credit crunch of 1974 and the following recession, both ROE and ROA declined over the next two years. With both regulators and the marketplace calling for more bank capital, bank growth slowed as capital positions were rebuilt, especially by the large

cial banks is depicted for the years 1980 through 1986. It is obvious that the dispersion has more than doubled over this time period, a clear indication of greater risk for the banking system. In addition, the distribution has become skewed toward negative ROA values as reflected by the mean ROA of .64 percent in 1986 versus the median ROA (i.e., the 50th percentile or middle value shown in Figure 10-6) of roughly .80 percent. Recall from your study of statistics that when the distribution is skewed to the left, the median is greater than the mean, as extremely low values pull the mean below the median. Since the ROA distribution is skewed to the left, the median ROA is a better measure of the overall performance of the system. Finally, note what has happened to the dispersion between the 5th and 50th percentiles and the 50th and 95th percentiles. The latter has remained fairly stable whereas the former has accounted for all of the increase in the ROA dispersion. What this indicates is that one-half of the banks in the system (and not always the same half) have been able to perform very well with respect to ROA; however, the ROA performance of the lower half has become more and more dispersed as its performance has deteriorated.

Getting to a Bank's Bottom Line

Although the mechanics of a bank's income-expense statement were presented in Chapter 2, it is useful to review those details here. To assist in this process, consider the data presented in Table 10-3, which are income and expense items as a percentage

TABLE 10-3   Income and Expense Items as a Percentage of Average Assets for All Insured Commercial Banks, 1981–1986 [a, b]

Item	1981	1982	1983	1984	1985	1986[c]
Gross interest income	11.93	11.36	9.63	10.23	9.44	8.38
Gross interest expense	8.77	8.07	6.38	6.97	6.06	5.10
Net interest margin	3.17	3.28	3.25	3.26	3.38	3.28
Noninterest income	.90	.96	1.03	1.19	1.32	1.40
Loss provision	.26	.40	.47	.57	.67	.77
Other noninterest expense	2.77	2.93	2.96	3.05	3.19	3.22
Securities gains (losses)	−.08	−.06	.00	−.01	.06	.14
Income before tax	.96	.85	.85	.83	.90	.82
Taxes[d]	.20	.14	.18	.19	.21	.19
Extraordinary items	.00	.00	.00	.01	.01	.01
Net income	.76	.71	.67	.64	.70	.64
Cash dividends declared	.30	.31	.33	.32	.33	.33
Net retained earnings	.46	.40	.34	.33	.37	.31
MEMO						
Net interest margin, taxable equivalent [a]	3.53	3.66	3.60	3.73	3.77	3.68

[a] See Table 10-2 note a.
[b] Assets are fully consolidated and net of loss reserves.
[c] Some of the income and expense items in this table appear to be understated a bit in 1986 because of the increased importance of merger activity within the banking industry that year. In the most common type of merger, the income statement for the consolidated bank at the end of the year would not include the income and expenses of the acquired bank in the period before the merger. Thus the income and expense figures presented in this table apparently are biased downward slightly. In the case of interest income and interest expense as a share of assets, we have estimated this bias to be roughly 10 basis points. Over the income statement as a whole, the omitted data appear to be just offsetting and would not affect the net income figure.
[d] Includes all taxes estimated to be due on income, extraordinary gains, and securities gains.
[e] For each bank with profits before tax greater than zero, income from state and local obligations was increased by $[t/(1 - t)]$ times the lesser of profits before tax or interest earned on state and local obligations (t is the marginal federal income tax rate). This adjustment approximates the equivalent pretax return on state and local obligations.
Source: Danker and McLaughlin [1987], Table 1, p. 538.

of average net assets for all insured banks for the years 1981 through 1986. Since we are concerned with the details of a bank's income-expense statement, don't worry about subgroup (e.g., money-center banks) characteristics. If you are interested, those details can be gleaned from the data available in Appendix A.

Let's focus on the year 1986 and see how we get to a bank's bottom line. Keep in mind the following figures are expressed as a percentage of average net assets (or dollars and cents per $100 dollars). In 1986, the average bank generated $8.38 of interest income per $100 of assets. With interest expenses of $5.10, net interest margin was $3.28. Since noninterest income was $1.40 per $100 of assets, the average bank's asset utilization was $9.78 per $100 of assets (i.e., the sum of $8.38 and $1.40). Combining noninterest expense with noninterest income shows the average bank's "burden" to be −$1.82 (= $1.40 − $3.22). Recall that burden is simply the difference between a bank's noninterest income and its noninterest expense. Since this difference is negative, it is in effect the bank's "burden."

Net interest margin must cover a bank's "burden," its loan losses (or provision for such losses), its taxes, its dividends, and other items such as security losses and extraordinary charges, if the bank is to have a positive addition to retained earnings. In 1986 net interest margin was up to this task as the drains against it totaled only $3.11, consisting of $1.82 for burden, $.77 for loan losses, $.19 for taxes, and $.33 for dividends, which net to only $.17. However, with capital gains from the sale of securities of $.14 and an extraordinary item of $.01, the net addition to retained earnings was $.31 per $100 of assets. (The fact that .17 + .14 + .01 is not equal to .31 is due to rounding errors.)

Focusing on the trends from 1981 through 1986, some interesting observations can be made about the data in Table 10-3. First, the average bank has been able to maintain its net interest margin despite the "growing concerns" about declining spreads in banking. For example, the average spread is up 11 basis points over 1981, but down 10 basis points from 1985. (As noted in the memo to Table 10-3, tax-equivalent net interest margin increased by 15 basis points over the same period.) Second, the emphasis on increasing noninterest income in banking is evident by the movement of this figure from $.90 in 1981 to $1.40 (per $100 of assets) in 1986. Moreover, and third, since the increase in noninterest income outstripped the increase in noninterest expense, the average bank's burden declined from $1.87 in 1981 ($1.97 in 1982) to $1.82 in 1986. The latter is a joint reflection of attempts by bankers to increase fees and service charges and to hold down increases in operating expenses (i.e., salaries and benefits, occupancy expenses, and equipment costs). Fourth, the steady deterioration in the average bank's loan quality is reflected by the upward trend in provision for loan losses, which moved from $.26 in 1981 to $.77 in 1986. If loan quality in 1986 could have warranted the same provision expense as incurred in 1981, other things equal, the average bank's ROA would have been $1.15 per $100 of assets, instead of $.64! Fifth, the capital losses incurred on security sales in the early 1980s have been swapped for securities gains in 1985 and 1986, helping to offset losses in the loan portfolio. And sixth, additions to retained earnings have declined from $.46 to $.31 over the six-year period. The latter is an indication that the banking system's strengthened capital position has come from the ability of the largest banks to tap external sources of capital.

Money-Center Banks Bite the LDC Bullet in 1987

Following Citicorp/Citibank's leadership, the banks with major lending exposures to less-developed countries (LDCs), especially with loans to Brazil, allocated roughly

$20 billion for loan-loss provisions during the second quarter of 1987. (FDIC data for the first half of 1987 are presented in an appendix of this chapter). This unprecedented quarterly provision resulted in a $10.6 billion aggregate second-quarter loss for the commercial banking industry. Combined with the record first-quarter earnings of $5.3 billion, the industry recorded an aggregate loss of $5.3 billion (= $5.3 − $10.6) for the first half of 1987. The huge second-quarter provision was preceded (in the first quarter of 1987) by decisions by bank LDC lenders to place most of their $23.6 billion in loans to Brazil on nonaccrual status, which means interest income is not recorded until it is received. Because of the second-quarter loss, industry ROA for 1987 fell to 0.12%, the lowest level since 1934. However, the median ROA was about the same as its 1986 value of 0.8 percent.

BANK PROFITABILITY IN THE FINANCIAL-SERVICES INDUSTRY

Within the financial-services industry (FSI) how profitable are commercial banks? More important, given commercial banks are the most heavily regulated players in the FSI, what are our expectations for their relative profitability? If the effects of regulation are to restrict the profitable opportunities available to regulated players, then we should expect heavily regulated firms to be less profitable than less regulated or unregulated firms. In addition to commercial banks (and other insured depository institutions), insurance companies (both life and property and casualty) are subject to extensive regulation. Of course, any stockholder-owned firm with actively traded

TABLE 10-4   Bank Profitability and Valuation in the Financial-Services Industry

Industry	Average After-Tax Return on Equity 1980–84	Average Price/Earnings Ratio 1977–84
Commercial banking	12.2%	6.3
17 multinational BHCs	12.9	6.1
Finance companies	12.6	6.2
Mortgage companies	13.1	n.a.
Securities	18.7	7.9
Investment banks	26.0	n.a.
Other securities	15.8	n.a.
Life insurance	13.4	n.a.
Stockholder-owned	15.2	6.4
Mutual	10.5	n.a.
Property and casualty		
Insurance	7.4	n.a.
Stockholder-owned	7.7	7.1
Mutual	7.4	n.a.
Insurance brokerage		
Large firms	18.3	12.8
Small firms	9.2	n.a.
Diversified financial firms	13.1	8.3
Nonfinancial firms (S&P 400)	13.7	9.6

Source: Federal Reserve Bank of New York [1986], Table 1, p. 372.

shares of stock is subject to some form of regulation (e.g., SEC disclosure requirements). Thus, the relevant question is the degree of regulation (see Chapter 1 and the
regulatory spectrum). On balance, banks and insurance companies are subject to a
greater degree of regulation than other players in the FSI.

Table 10-4 presents profitability and valuation measures for nine segments of the
FSI. The profitability measure is average after-tax ROE for the years 1980 through
1984; the valuation measure is the average price-earnings (P/E) ratio for the period
1977 through 1984. The figures for commercial banks, which rank near the bottom for
both measures, are 12.2 percent ROE and 6.3 P/E for all banks with market data, and
12.9 percent and 6.1 P/E for the group of 17 multinational BHCs. In contrast, consider
the figures for securities firms with an ROE of 18.7 percent and a P/E ration of 7.9. The
investment banking component of the latter had an average ROE of 26.0 percent. For
the period 1977 through 1984, large insurance brokers, who are not the (more
regulated) "straight" insurance players, had the highest P/E ratio at 12.8. Nonfinancial
firms, as measured by the S&P 400, had an average ROE of 13.7 percent and an average
P/E ratio of 9.6 over the respective time periods. As noted in the introduction of this
chapter, the average P/E ratio since the early 1900s has been about 13, and the P/E
ratios prior to the stock market crashes of 1929 and 1987 were in the low 20s.

HIGH-PERFORMANCE BANKS

In today's highly competitive banking environment, high-performance banks are
those organizations that consistently return slightly over one percent on assets and
between 16 and 20 percent on equity. In the less competitive days of the 1970s,
high-performance banks had an average ROA of 1.49 percent and an average ROE of
20.8 (see Ford and Olson [1978]). Since then, however, market and regulatory forces
have served to restrict bank profit rates, with ROE ($= ROA \times EM$) taking a double hit
as both ROA and EM have been forced down. Nevertheless, most high-performance
banks derive their strong ROEs not from the use of greater financial leverage (i.e.,
high EMs) but from more efficient use of assets as reflected by higher ROAs.

How do high-performance banks consistently achieve more efficient asset usage?
Although the banking environment of the 1980s is different from that of the 1970s,
the keys characteristics of high-performance banks have not changed. These characteristics, as determined by Ford and Olson [1978], are shown in Table 10-5. The
three general traits of high-performance banks are (1) maximization of revenues,
(2) control of expenses, and (3) consistently good management. The details of Ford
and Olson's findings are summarized in Table 10-5. Although the conclusions under
the first two points are self-explanatory, a brief interpretation of the third point is
required. The larger, less-controllable factors refer to such big-ticket items as wages
and salaries and interest on deposits. In contrast, the smaller, controllable factors refer
to such items as provision for loan losses and net occupancy expenses. On balance,
Ford and Olson conclude that the various factors distinguishing high-performance
banks from other organizations can be classified into three functional areas: planning,
organizing, and controlling.

High-Performance Banks of the 1980s

A dozen high-performance banks for the years 1984 through 1986 are shown in Table 10-6. The group includes one multinational bank holding company, J. P. Morgan,
and 11 regional BHCs. The 12 BHCs were selected from the 46 banking organizations
covered by Goldman Sach's investment research on the basis of an ROA above

TABLE 10-5   Key Characteristics of High-performance Banks

1. Maximization of Revenues

   High loan income attained through appropriate pricing and avoidance of non-accruing loans, rather than relatively high volume
   Maximization of income from tax-exempt securities
   Maintenance of sufficient flexibility in asset structure to take advantage of changes in interest rates

2. Expense Control

   Low investment in fixed assets, lower occupancy expense
   Proper control of overhead and discretionary costs such as "other operating expense"
   Minimization of loan losses through proper credit analysis
   Control of personnel expense through efficient use of fewer employees, rather than through low salaries

3. Consistenly Good Management

   Large comparative advantages in the management of smaller, controllable factors
   Smaller comparative—but large absolute—advantages in management of larger, less controllable factors

Source: Food and Olson [1978], Table 1, p. 37. Reprinted by permission.

TABLE 10-6   High-Performance Banks of the Mid-1980s

	Return on Average Assets (percent)					
				2nd Q	Averages	
Banking Organization	1984	1985	1986	1987	1984–86	1984–87
Multinational Group						
J. P. Morgan	0.87	1.06	1.19	−2.90	1.04	nm
Regional Group						
Banc one	1.13	1.37	1.23	0.44	1.24	1.04
First Union	1.11	1.19	1.21	0.94	1.17	1.11
First Wachovia	1.11	1.18	1.15	0.67	1.15	1.03
Fleet Financial	1.24	1.33	1.37	1.03	1.31	1.24
Hartford National	1.08	1.12	1.11	0.72	1.10	1.01
Norstar Bancorp.	1.16	1.12	1.07	0.85	1.12	1.05
PNC Financial Corp.	1.12	1.12	1.20	0.25	1.15	0.92
Signet Banking	1.01	1.06	1.04	−1.64	1.04	nm
Sovran	1.11	1.07	1.08	1.03	1.09	1.07
State Street Bank	1.18	1.12	1.08	1.15	1.13	1.13
SunTrust Banks	1.04	1.03	1.03	1.12	1.03	1.05
Averages						
Multinational (10)	0.57	0.67	0.72	nm	0.65	nm
Regional (36)	0.83	0.88	0.90	nm	0.87	nm
Combined (46)	0.77	0.83	0.87	nm	0.82	nm

Notes: Return on assets is defined as net income less preferred dividends divided by average total assets. Figures for the second quarter of 1987 are annualized ones. Because of the heavy provision for loan losses taken by many banks in the second quarter of 1987, averages including that quarter are considered "not meaningful" (nm). Figures in parentheses for the group averages are the number of banks in each group.
Source: Investment Research, Goldman Sachs [Second Quarter, 1987], pp. 6–7.

1 percent for each of the three years 1984 to 1986, except for the member of the multinational group which was selected on the basis of the highest average ROA for the three-year period. On this basis, "the" high-performance regional bank of the mid-1980s was Fleet Financial Group of Providence, Rhode Island, with an average ROA of 1.31 percent. Fleet's average ROE for this period was 18.7 percent, implying an

equity multiplier of 14.3 (= .187/.0131) or an equity-to-asset ratio of 7 percent. To illustrate the differences across banks with respect to asset efficiency and leverage, consider the ROE profile for Barnett Banks of Florida (not shown in Table 10-6). Barnett's average ROE for the three years 1984 through 1986 was 17.2 percent, consisting of an average ROA of 0.91 percent and an average equity multiplier of 18.9. The combination of Fleet's asset efficiency and Barnett's leverage would have produced an ROE of 24.7 percent (= 1.31% × 18.9).

To demonstrate how fleeting financial performance can be in the volatile 1980s, the annualized ROA for the second quarter of 1987 is also shown in Table 10-6. Using our ROA standard of at least 1 percent, only four of the 12 BHCs met this criterion. Averaging the projected 1987 ROA with the other three years, Fleet Financial Group is still on top with an average ROA of 1.24 percent; its financial performance was not fleeting. In second place is State Street Bank of Boston with an average ROA of 1.15 percent followed by First Union Corporation of Charlotte, North Carolina, with an average ROA of 1.11 percent. The decline in J. P. Morgan's ROA in the second quarter of 1987 was due to its "biting the LDC loan bullet," as explained earlier in the chapter.

CITICORP'S "COMPETITOR ANALYSIS"

In 1980, Citicorp's earnings dropped 6 percent from its 1979 level. On the same day that the 1980 earnings were reported, Citicorp's president, William Spenser, announced there would be no incentive raises for "Citipeople" in 1981.[5] These raises in past years had ranged between 10 and 15 percent. Naturally, some Citipeople were upset. However, one Citiperson with a philosophical bent remarked, "Anybody who was disappointed hasn't been reading the tea leaves." The purpose of this section is to look at the way a major BHC, Citicorp, "reads the tea leaves"—that is, analyzes its own performance and that of its major competitors. The formal Citicorp document is called "Competitor Analysis." It is a 20- to 30-page document generated quarterly. The package is an excellent example of trend and peer-group applications of ratio analysis.

Reading the Tea Leaves at Citicorp

Since Citicorp's "Competitor Analysis" is an extensive document, space limitations do not permit a review of the entire package. The contents of a typical Citicorp "Competitor Analysis" are listed in Table 10-7. A convenient starting point is the first stage of ROE decomposition analysis (i.e., $ROA \times EM = ROE$), which is presented in Table 10-8. For the purpose of its "Competitor Analysis," Citicorp defines its peer group to consist of eight competitors:

1. BankAmerica
2. Chase Manhattan
3. Manufacturers Hanover
4. Morgan Guaranty
5. Chemical
6. Continental Illinois
7. Bankers Trust
8. First Chicago

[5] As reported in *The Wall Street Journal* [January 22, 1981], Section 2, p. 27. By the way, this was just the third time in 30 years that Citicorp's year-to-year earnings had dropped.

TABLE 10-7   Contents of Citicorp's Competitive Analysis First Quarter 1984

Comments (i.e., narrative summary)
Net income
Earnings per share
Return on assets
Profitability/return on equity
Pretax earnings
Effective tax rate
Net interest revenue (T/E basis)
Net interest revenue (book basis)
Non-interest expenses
Bond trading income
Foreign exchange income
Nonperfoming loans
Reserve for loan losses
Provision for loan losses
Net loan losses
Selected balance sheet items
Primary capital

The ROE analysis in Table 10-8 provides Citicorp with two relative measures of its profitability. First, it reveals the change in ROE (and its components) relative to last year's ROE; and second, it indicates the level of ROE relative to its competitors both this year and last year. The decomposition of ROE into ROA and EM is interesting for the insight that it provides about the ROE performance of the giant BHCs. Relative to regional BHCs and community banks, it is clear that Citicorp and its competitors use greater leverage to attempt to offset their lower ROA. Prior to the early 1980s, they were more successful in doing this. For example, if we apply Citicorp's 1983 EM of 25.5 to its 1985 ROA of .62 percent, its ROE is 15.8 percent. Since then, however, market and regulatory demands for increased capital have restricted bank equity multipliers.

The most important asset function that commercial banks perform is making loans. Thus, the quality of a bank's loan portfolio is an important measure of its risk exposure. A traditional measure of a bank's loan quality is the ratio of net loan losses to loans, with losses recorded as gross charge-offs minus recoveries. Net loan losses

TABLE 10-8   Return-on-Equity Analysis: Citicorp and Its Competitors

	Return on Assets		Equity Multiplier		Return on Equity	
	1985	1986	1985	1986	1985	1986
Citicorp	0.62%	0.58%	24.3	23.8	15.1%	13.8%
BankAmerica	nm	nm	nm	nm	nm	nm
Chase Manhattan	0.65	0.65	20.9	20.3	13.6	13.2
Manufacturers	0.54	0.54	22.7	22.4	12.3	12.1
Morgan	1.06	1.19	17.1	16.0	18.1	19.0
Chemical	0.70	0.70	20.8	19.4	14.6	13.6
Continental	0.53	0.59	15.7	14.4	8.3	8.5
Bankers Trust	0.79	0.79	21.0	20.6	16.6	16.3
First Chicago	0.43	0.71	19.5	18.7	8.4	13.3
COMPETITOR AVERAGE	0.67%	0.74%	19.7	18.8	11.7%	13.7%

Source: "Bank Ratios and Rankings," *Investment Research*, Goldman, Sachs & Co. [Second Quarter, 1987], pp. 6–9.

TABLE 10-9   Net Loan Losses: Citicorp and Its Competitors

Net Loan Losses/Average Loans			
	1984[a]	1983[a]	1982[a]
Citicorp	0.30%	0.51%	0.33%
BankAmerica	0.60	0.39	0.35
Chase Manhattan	0.37	0.48	0.36
Manufacturers Hanover	0.38	0.48	0.23
Morgan Guaranty	0.16	0.49	0.16
Chemical	0.24	0.37	0.15
Continental Illinois	1.59	1.24	0.28
Bankers Trust	0.37	0.18	0.19
First Chicago	0.83	0.55	0.41
COMPETITOR AVERAGE	0.57%	0.52%	0.27%

[a] Data are as first quarter of the year.
Source: Competitor Analysis, Citicorp [First Quarter 1984], p. 25 and [Second Quarter, 1982], p. 23.

for Citicorp and its competitors are shown in Table 10-9. Focusing on some additional details of Citicorp's write-off experience, we see the breakdown of its loan losses between commercial and consumer loans depicted by the following data:

Year/Quarter	Commercial Loan Losses		Consumer Loan Losses	
	$ Millions	% of Loans	$ Millions	% of Loans
1984-1	9.0	.06	60.0	.74
1983-4	108.0	.72	53.0	.75
1983-3	43.0	.28	47.0	.75
1983-2	35.0	.23	46.0	.78
1983-1	56.0	.37	50.0	.88

Focusing on the experience for the full year 1983, we see that Citicorp had total loan losses of $438 million, consisting of $242 million in commercial loans (.40 percent of total commercial loans) plus $196 million in consumer loans (.79 percent of total consumer loans). Based on 1983 loss experience, Citicorp's consumer loans on a relative basis were twice as risky as its commercial loans; however, in terms of absolute dollar costs, commercial losses were more expensive.

Another important dimension of loan quality is captured by the notion of *nonperforming* loans. A nonperforming loan is one where the contractual payment is more than 90 days past due. Such loans are also described as nonaccruals. Data on nonperforming loans for Citicorp and its competitors for the years 1984 to 1986, and as of the second quarter of 1987, are shown in Table 10-10. Three interesting aspects of these data are (1) the substantial increase in nonperforming loans in 1987, due to a more realistic appraisal of the international debt situation; (2) the ongoing deterioration of BankAmerica's loan portfolio, which was exacerbated by its acquisition of Seafirst Corporation on July 1, 1983; and (3) the steady improvement (until 1987) of Continental's loan portfolio under the close supervision of bank regulators following its bailout (i.e., "nationalization") during the summer of 1984.

TABLE 10-10   Nonperforming Loans: Citicorp and Its Competitors

| | Nonperforming Assets as a % of Period End Loans | | | |
	1984	1985	1986	Second Quarter 1987
Citicorp	2.33	1.93	1.95	4.80
BankAmerica[a]	4.99	4.59	5.84	8.84
Chase Manhattan	3.50	3.29	2.87	6.72
Manufacturers Hanover	2.94	2.62	3.79	6.29
Morgan Guaranty	2.45	2.06	1.82	5.27
Chemical	3.20	3.03	3.42	5.90
Continental Illinois	4.18	4.08	3.07	4.64
Bankers Trust	3.00	3.20	3.01	5.03
First Chicago	2.74	2.72	3.42	4.95
COMPETITOR AVERAGE	3.37	3.20	3.65	5.95

[a] On July 1, 1983, BankAmerica acquired Seafirst.
Source: "Bank Ratios and Rankings," Investment Research, Goldman, Sachs & Co. [Second Quarter, 1987], p. 24.

Since the equation $g = RR \times ROE$ expresses a firm's capital-generation rate as the product of its retention rate (i.e., RR = one minus the dividend payout ratio) times its ROE, this rate is a measure of g in the capitalization-rate formula $k = D_1/P_0 + g$. Estimates of this internal capital-generation rate for Citicorp and its competitors are presented in Table 10-11. Although these data are no longer included in the latest version of Citicorp's "Competitor Analysis," they are useful to look at for insights regarding the internal capital generation rate. During 1980 and 1979, the benchmark generation rate g for money-center banks was about 10 percent. The importance of this rate is that it sets a ceiling on the rate at which assets may grow if the bank's capital-to-asset ratio is not to deteriorate. Of course, with external capital to supplement internal capital, the bank may grow at a rate faster than g and maintain or even improve its capital adequacy. For the year 1986, Citicorp's g was 9.0 percent, consisting of an ROE of 13.8 percent and an RR of 65.55 percent (i.e., $.0904 = .1380 \times .6555$).

TABLE 10-11   Internal Capital Generation Rate: Citicorp and Its Competitors

| | Return on Equity[a] × | | Earnings Retention Rate = | | Capital Generation Rate | | |
	1980	1979	1980	1979	1980	1979	Change
Citicorp	14.4%	15.4%	66.6%	68.2%	9.6%	10.5%	−0.9%
BankAmerica	17.3	17.8	67.1	68.3	11.6	12.1	−0.5
Chase Manhattan	16.3	14.5	71.1	68.2	11.6	9.9	1.7
Manufacturers Hanover	14.1	14.5	62.8	63.9	8.9	9.3	−0.4
Morgan Guaranty	17.3	15.6	68.6	65.3	11.9	10.2	1.7
Chemical	13.2	12.2	62.4	59.7	8.2	7.3	0.9
Continental Illinois	16.3	14.9	72.3	69.7	11.8	10.4	1.4
Bankers Trust	22.1	12.7	76.7	58.5	16.9	7.5	9.4
First Chicago	7.4	12.0	45.9	67.8	3.4	8.1	−4.7
COMPETITOR AVERAGE	15.5%	14.3%	65.9%	65.2%	10.5%	9.4%	1.1%

[a] Based on Operating Earnings. Data are as of the second quarter of the year.
Source: Competitive Analysis, Citicorp [Second Quarter 1980], p. 15.

CHAPTER SUMMARY

This chapter has focused upon a systematic way of analyzing bank financial statements using the return-on-equity model. The idea is to identify *symptoms* of good or bad performance and to track those symptoms, through decomposition analysis, to the *causes*. The fundamental aspects of the technique and the various stages of the analysis were emphasized. The ROE model was illustrated using the performance of various groups of banks over the recent past. Cases of both high-performance and low-performance banks were analyzed and the competitive-analysis system of Citicorp was considered. The appendices to this chapter present an opportunity for you to apply the concepts and techniques developed in this chapter.

LIST OF KEY WORDS, CONCEPTS, AND ACRONYMS

Asset utilization (AU)

"Burden"

Decomposition analysis

Equity multiplier (EM)

Internal capital generation rate
  $(g = ROE \times RR)$

Net interest margin

Peer group (and analysis)

Price-earnings ratio (P/E)

Profit margin (PM)

Provision for loan losses

Ratio analysis

Retention ratio (RR)

Return on assets $(ROA = PM \times AU)$

Return on equity
  $(ROE = ROA \times EM = PM \times AU \times EM)$

ROE model

Trend analysis

REVIEW/DISCUSSION QUESTIONS

1. In an efficient market, what is the best measure of a firm's performance? How efficient are bank equity markets?
2. How can ratio analysis be used to read a bank's balance sheet (and its income-expense statement)? What are the important dimensions of ratio analysis? What are the strengths and weaknesses of ratio analysis?
3. What are the six generic risks facing banks/BHCs? What are the critical portfolio risks in banking?
4. What four pieces of accounting information are required to start ROE analysis? Discuss the first, second, and third stages of ROE decomposition analysis. How can ROE analysis be related to bank decision making?
5. Focusing on ROE analysis for the U.S. banking system for the years 1981 to 1986, describe and discuss the following items:
   a. alternative size groups
   b. ROE and ROA across alternative size groups
   c. geographic variation in ROA
   d. cyclical variation in ROA
   e. the dispersion of bank earnings
   f. getting to a bank's bottom line.
6. What happened to money-center banks in the second quarter of 1987?
7. How profitable are banks in the financial-services industry?

(*continued on page 288*)

MATCHING QUIZ

Directions: Select the letter from the right-hand column that best matches the item in the left-hand column.

___ 1. Capital generation rate

___ 2. Asset utilization

___ 3. Return on assets

___ 4. Return on equity

___ 5. Profit margin

___ 6. Financial early-warning systems

___ 7. Provision for loan losses

___ 8. Peer group analysis

___ 9. Trend analysis

___ 10. "Burden"

___ 11. Equity multiplier

___ 12. Price-earnings multiple

___ 13. High-performance bank

___ 14. 2nd quarter of 1987

___ 15. Removal of Reg Q ceilings

___ 16. ROA down in these "belts"

___ 17. Dispersion of bank earnings

___ 18. Left-skewed distribution

___ 19. Net interest margin

___ 20. Low-performance bank

___ 21. Main source of bank capital

___ 22. 50th percentile

___ 23. Rank of bank profitability in FSI

___ 24. P/E ratio prior to "crashes"

___ 25. Major noninterest expense

___ 26. Noninterest income

A. Can't detect bank fraud

B. Net income/total income

C. *ROE/ROA*

D. Difference between noninterest income & expense

E. *ROE × RR*

F. Stock price/*EPS*

G. Values in the low 20s

H. BHCs bite the LDC bullet

I. Hurt community banks most

J. Total income/assets

K. Median

L. Mean below median

M. Increasing since 1980

N. Includes leverage factor

O. "Pure" asset performance

P. Reflection of loan quality

Q. Retained earnings

R. Wages and salaries

S. Near bottom

T. Fees and services charges

U. Bank's "bread and butter"

V. Energy and agricultural

W. BankAmerica

X. Comparisons across similar firms

Y. Time-series comparisons

Z. Fleet Financial Group

8. Define and describe the term "high-performance bank."
9. Who are Citicorp's competitors? Who are the strongest and the weakest ones? Describe the content of Citicorp's "Competitor Analysis." If Citicorp is so worried about Sears as a competitor, why isn't it part of the competitor-analysis package?
10. What are some of the ways of measuring bank loan quality? How can *future* loan quality be determined? Based upon Citicorp's experience, how do commercial and consumer loans compare in terms of degree of risk exposure? How has BankAmerica's acquisition of Seafirst affected it?
11. As a major project, write a 15-page ROE report based upon a bank's five most recent years of data. (This is a routine assignment for my summer-internship and cooperative-education students. Moreover, the project can be assigned to students who work in any type of organization and not just banks.)

PROBLEMS

1. Given: Interest income $395,532
            Interest expense   216,505
            Provision for loan losses   38,033
            Noninterest income   72,621
            Noninterest expense   154,921
            Taxes   9,450
            Dividends   19,110

   Find: a. Net interest income
             b. Burden
             c. Total income
             d. Total expenses
             e. Net income
             f. Addition to retained earnings
             g. Dividend payout ratio

2. The data in the previous problem were for the period from January 1, 1987, to June 30, 1987. Given total assets of $10,935,356 and total equity capital of $739,305, as of June 30,1987, conduct the first two stages of ROE decomposition analysis. Assuming this bank has been a consistent performer, would you conclude that it is a 'high-performance bank"? By the way, since all the bank's data are in thousands (000), you are analyzing a $10.9 billion bank. Does this fact affect your decision about its performance?

   The remaining problems require the use of data from Appendix A, page 290.

3. For the four size classes shown in Table 10-A1, contrast and compare the composition of deposit liabilities and the effective interest rates paid for interest-bearing deposits over the years 1981 through 1986. Be sure to note the extent of money-market liabilities across the various balance sheets.

4. Using the same groups as in the previous problem, contrast and compare the percentage of interest-bearing assets and net interest margins over the years 1981 through 1986.

5. Using the report of income shown in Table 10-A2, find the following dollar figures or ratios for the years 1981 through 1986, and analyze the trends:
   a. net interest income
   b. "burden"

    c. profit margin (PM)

    d. dividend payout ratio.

6. Table 10-A3 groups information into four categories: (a) group characteristics such as number of banks, (b) performance ratios such as ROA and ROE, (c) condition ratios such as capital and nonperforming assets ratios, and (d) growth rates applied to such variables as net income, capital, and assets. These four categories are segmented across asset size classes and geographic areas. Highlight what you think are the major differences across the size classes and geographic areas.

CHAPTER 10

APPENDIX A
Financial Data for Insured
Commercial Banks, 1981–1987

This appendix contains balance sheet and income-expense data collected and tabulated either by the Federal Reserve or the FDIC for all insured commercial banks for the years 1981 through 1986 and the first half of 1987. The contents of the appendix are:

Table	Description
10-A1	Portfolio composition, interest rates, and income and expenses for all insured commercial banks, 1981 to 1986.
	Panel A. Banks with less than $100 million in assets
	Panel B. Banks with assets greater than $100 million but less than $1 billion
	Panel C. Money-center banks
	Panel D. Large banks (assets greater than $1 billion) other than money-center banks.
10-A2	Report of income for all insured commercial banks, 1981 to 1986
10-A3	The FDIC's Data Bank for the Second Quarter of 1987 (contains portfolio composition, performance ratios, condition ratios, and growth rates for all banks and banks by size and location)

TABLE 10-A1   Portfolio Composition, Interest Rates, and Income and Expenses, Insured Commercial Banks, 1981–86 [a]

A. Banks with Less Than $100 Million in Assets

Item	1981	1982	1983	1984	1985	1986
	Balance-Sheet Items as a Percentage of Average Consolidated Assets					
Interest-earning assets	90.84	91.10	91.02	90.77	91.00	90.91
Loans	53.72	52.55	51.49	52.26	53.15	51.51
Commercial and industrial	12.26	12.91	12.88	12.90	13.53	12.67
Real estate	19.60	18.37	17.98	18.88	19.83	20.77
Consumer	13.97	12.91	12.28	12.36	12.50	11.73
Securities	29.35	29.61	31.00	30.39	29.32	28.90
U.S. government	17.38	18.25	20.52	20.85	20.17	19.65
State and local government	11.50	10.94	10.01	9.01	8.55	8.27
Other bonds and stocks	.46	.41	.46	.54	.60	.98
Gross federal funds sold and reverse repurchase agreements	5.87	6.35	5.96	5.53	5.78	7.22
Interest-bearing deposits	1.90	2.60	2.57	2.59	2.75	3.28

[a] See notes to Tables 10-2 and 10-3 in the text.
Source: Danker and McLaughlin [1987], p. 547.

(*continues*)

TABLE 10-A1 (*Continued*)

A. Banks with Less Than $100 Million in Assets

Item	1981	1982	1983	1984	1985	1986
	Balance-Sheet Items as a Percentage of Average Consolidated Assets					
Deposit liabilities	87.56	87.17	87.83	88.18	88.23	88.54
Demand deposits	22.52	19.04	17.01	16.10	14.62	14.10
Other checkable deposits	4.01	6.14	7.55	8.14	8.53	9.49
Large time deposits	10.03	10.67	9.80	10.23	10.98	10.96
Other deposits	51.00	51.32	53.46	53.71	54.10	53.95
Gross federal funds purchased and repurchase agreements	1.41	1.68	1.21	1.01	.85	.73
Other borrowings	.52	.48	.41	.35	.34	.29
MEMO						
Money market liabilities	11.96	12.83	11.42	11.59	12.18	12.02
Loss reserves	.51	.51	.52	.58	.67	.76
	Effective Interest Rate (percent)					
Rates earned						
Securities	9.69	10.82	10.58	10.66	9.83	8.86
State and local government	6.45	7.24	7.47	7.84	7.87	7.70
Loans, gross	14.91	15.34	13.70	14.16	12.71	11.73
Net of loss provision	14.27	14.39	12.55	12.80	11.06	9.92
Taxable equivalent						
Securities	11.70	12.95	12.53	12.23	11.42	10.38
Securities and gross loans	13.75	14.46	13.24	13.45	12.25	11.24
Rates paid						
Interest-bearing deposits	11.21	10.96	9.15	9.54	7.99	6.96
Large certificates of deposit	15.14	13.74	9.20	10.84	8.74	7.39
Other deposits	10.56	10.51	9.15	9.34	7.86	6.88
All interest-bearing liabilities	11.31	11.01	9.11	9.54	8.00	6.96
	Income and Expenses as a Percentage of Average Net Consolidated Assets					
Gross interest income	11.55	11.75	10.60	10.89	10.33	9.32
Gross interest expense	7.15	7.35	6.32	6.73	6.06	5.28
Net interest margin	4.39	4.40	4.28	4.17	4.28	4.04
Taxable equivalent	4.93	4.96	4.82	4.66	4.75	4.48
Noninterest income	.68	.67	.69	.74	.77	.77
Loss provision	.29	.42	.51	.63	.87	.92
Other noninterest expense	3.24	3.31	3.29	3.28	3.38	3.39
Securities gains or losses (−)	−.10	−.02	.01	−.01	.08	.16
Income before tax	1.45	1.31	1.18	.99	.88	.66
Taxes	.31	.24	.23	.19	.19	.15
Extraordinary items	.00	.00	.00	.01	.01	.02
Net income	1.14	1.07	.96	.81	.70	.53
Cash dividends declared	.35	.39	.38	.39	.41	.38
Net retained earnings	.79	.67	.58	.41	.29	.16
MEMO						
Average assets (billions of dollars)	352	365	373	383	385	384
Number of banks	12,353	12,081	11,811	11,554	11,332	11,011

(*continues*)

TABLE 10-A1 (*Continued*)

B. Banks with $100 Million to $1 Billion in Assets

Item	1981	1982	1983	1984	1985	1986
	Balance-Sheet Items as a Percentage of Average Consolidated Assets					
Interest-earning assets	88.37	89.34	89.65	89.58	90.02	89.88
Loans	54.40	53.71	52.98	54.41	56.26	55.94
Commercial and industrial	16.34	16.88	16.84	17.51	17.96	16.76
Real estate	20.02	19.38	18.89	19.61	21.07	22.34
Consumer	14.00	13.16	12.86	13.14	13.54	13.61
Securities	25.68	25.30	26.51	26.18	25.60	25.05
U.S. government	13.15	13.48	15.34	15.46	14.76	13.60
State and local government	11.88	11.16	10.29	9.77	9.86	10.09
Other bonds and stocks	.65	.66	.87	.95	.98	1.36
Gross federal funds sold and reverse repurchase agreements	5.46	5.91	5.59	5.41	5.33	6.37
Interest-bearing deposits	2.84	4.42	4.58	3.58	2.84	2.51
Deposit liabilities	83.18	82.89	84.34	85.14	85.51	85.74
In foreign offices	.24	.24	.22	.27	.28	.39
In domestic offices	82.94	82.66	84.12	84.87	85.23	85.35
Demand deposits	24.97	21.31	19.51	18.71	17.31	16.94
Other checkable deposits	3.62	5.21	6.10	6.44	6.80	7.73
Large time deposits	14.98	15.35	12.94	12.95	13.22	12.53
Other deposits	39.37	40.79	45.57	46.76	47.89	48.15
Gross federal funds purchased and repurchase agreements	6.08	6.47	5.21	4.59	4.13	3.70
Other borrowings	1.28	1.15	1.21	1.04	1.01	1.28
MEMO						
Money market liabilities	22.58	23.20	19.57	18.86	18.65	17.90
Loss reserves	.58	.59	.61	.65	.72	.81
	Effective Interest Rate (percent)					
Rates earned						
Securities	9.15	9.96	9.89	9.97	9.22	8.34
U.S. government	11.55	12.41	11.86	10.35	10.40	9.17
State and local government	6.52	7.03	7.03	7.43	7.44	7.32
Other bonds and stocks	10.15	10.52	11.31	10.39	9.39	7.95
Loans, gross	15.23	14.70	12.78	13.61	12.16	11.20
Net of loss provision	14.56	13.71	11.81	12.65	11.04	9.82
Taxable equivalent						
Securities	11.37	12.27	12.08	12.15	11.33	10.43
Securities and gross loans	13.90	13.84	12.50	13.13	11.90	10.96
Rates paid						
Interest-bearing deposits	11.47	10.67	8.83	9.33	7.80	6.81
Large certificates of deposit	16.05	13.91	8.90	10.88	8.56	7.20
Deposits in foreign offices	15.84	14.48	9.23	15.80	8.45	7.76
Other deposits	9.99	9.71	8.82	8.95	7.63	6.72
All interest-bearing liabilities	11.98	10.98	8.80	9.39	7.79	6.80

Source: Danker and McLaughlin [1987], p. 548.

TABLE 10-A1 (*Continued*)

B. Banks with $100 Million to $1 Billion in Assets

Item	1981	1982	1983	1984	1985	1986
	Income and Expenses as a Percentage of Average Net Consolidated Assets					
Gross interest income	11.37	11.18	9.92	10.39	9.81	8.91
Gross interest expense	7.44	7.19	6.02	6.50	5.79	5.04
Net interest margin	3.94	4.00	3.90	3.89	4.02	3.87
Taxable equivalent	4.46	4.53	4.42	4.42	4.57	4.40
Noninterest income	.83	.86	.90	.97	.98	1.02
Loss provision	.27	.42	.43	.46	.61	.76
Other noninterest expense	3.37	3.45	3.39	3.33	3.42	3.41
Securities gains or losses (−)	−.10	−.07	−.01	−.01	.06	.14
Income before tax	1.03	.92	.98	1.06	1.03	.86
Taxes	.13	.09	.14	.19	.20	.17
Extraordinary items	.01	.00	.00	.01	.01	.01
Net income	.91	.84	.84	.88	.84	.71
Cash dividends declared	.39	.40	.42	.43	.45	.43
Net retained earnings	.52	.44	.42	.44	.39	.27
MEMO						
Average assets (billions of dollars)	382	413	454	488	508	539
Number of banks	1,651	1,813	2,012	2,135	2,259	2,398

C. Money-Center Banks

Item	1981	1982	1983	1984	1985	1986
	Balance Sheet Items as a Percentage of Average Consolidated Assets					
Interest-earning assets	80.63	82.19	81.56	81.14	80.56	80.09
Loans	59.14	62.27	62.93	63.66	61.91	60.07
Commercial and industrial	30.21	32.34	32.31	31.78	29.46	26.49
Real estate	8.62	9.16	9.22	9.82	10.49	11.45
Consumer	4.50	4.61	4.72	5.28	5.78	6.13
Securities	6.48	5.96	6.39	6.68	7.15	8.49
U.S. government	2.77	2.37	2.60	2.33	2.31	2.28
State and local government	2.39	2.37	2.49	2.90	3.02	3.48
Other bonds and stocks	1.32	1.23	1.30	1.45	1.82	2.73
Gross federal funds sold and reverse repurchase agreements	2.11	2.50	2.52	2.51	3.54	3.62
Interest-bearing deposits	12.90	11.43	9.72	8.29	7.95	7.91
Deposit liabilities	75.37	73.69	72.18	72.08	70.74	69.92
In foreign offices	39.86	39.99	37.93	35.21	35.86	34.64
In domestic offices	35.51	33.70	34.25	36.88	34.88	35.28
Demand deposits	15.06	11.28	11.43	11.83	11.51	12.46
Other checkable deposits	.83	1.06	1.19	1.24	1.30	1.63
Large time deposits	12.95	13.75	10.55	10.62	8.18	7.30
Other deposits	6.68	7.61	11.08	13.20	13.89	13.88
Gross federal funds purchased and repurchase agreements	7.23	7.27	7.86	7.42	7.66	8.17
Other borrowings	4.54	4.75	5.12	5.34	6.51	7.95
MEMO						
Money market liabilities	64.58	65.76	61.46	58.58	58.21	58.07
Loss reserves	.49	.54	.59	.69	.83	1.02

Source: Danker and McLaughlin [1987], p. 549.

(continues)

TABLE 10-A1 (*Continued*)

C. Money-Center Banks

Item	1981	1982	1983	1984	1985	1986
	Effective Interest Rate (percent)					
Rates earned						
Securities	9.89	9.73	9.56	9.72	9.41	8.51
U.S. government	10.97	10.81	11.92	11.58	10.51	9.07
State and local government	7.55	7.46	6.33	7.61	7.24	7.09
Other bonds and stocks	11.99	11.93	11.46	11.10	11.45	9.79
Loans, gross	17.32	15.47	12.64	13.85	12.08	10.53
Net of loss provision	16.62	14.63	11.75	12.97	10.85	9.18
Taxable equivalent						
Securities	12.46	12.36	11.86	12.58	11.75	10.89
Securities and gross loans	16.56	14.94	12.32	13.73	12.05	10.58
Rates paid						
Interest-bearing deposits	15.94	13.95	10.23	11.06	8.91	7.41
Large certificates of deposit	16.64	14.47	8.96	10.70	9.07	7.45
Deposits in foreign offices	17.12	14.89	10.77	12.90	9.59	7.88
Other deposits	9.97	10.15	10.02	7.83	7.43	6.47
All interest-bearing liabilities	16.06	13.84	10.56	11.53	9.16	7.57
	Income and Expenses as a Percentage of Average Net Consolidated Assets					
Gross interest income	12.55	11.63	9.40	10.22	9.10	7.85
Gross interest expense	10.45	9.29	7.00	7.84	6.74	5.57
Net interest margin	2.10	2.34	2.40	2.38	2.36	2.28
Taxable equivalent	2.25	2.49	2.53	2.83	2.53	2.49
Noninterest income	.98	1.05	1.12	1.42	1.75	2.02
Loss provision	.21	.30	.36	.50	.75	.79
Other noninterest expense	1.99	2.25	2.34	2.54	2.71	2.96
Securities gains or losses (−)	−.05	−.06	.01	.02	.06	.13
Income before tax	.83	.77	.84	.78	.71	.68
Taxes	.30	.24	.30	.26	.26	.22
Extraordinary items	.00	.01	.00	.00	.00	.00
Net income	.53	.53	.54	.52	.45	.46
Cash dividends declared	.22	.23	.27	.24	.25	.21
Net retained earnings	.31	.30	.26	.29	.21	.25
MEMO						
Average assets (billions of dollars)	538	564	582	594	623	652
Number of banks	9	9	9	9	9	9

D. Large Banks Other Than Money-Center Banks

Item	1981	1982	1983	1984	1985	1986
	Balance-Sheet Items as a Percentage of Average Consolidated Assets					
Interest-earning assets	82.33	84.19	84.77	84.62	85.45	85.95
Loans	55.33	56.52	56.07	57.78	59.23	59.56
Commercial and industrial	22.42	23.70	23.15	23.19	23.17	22.47
Real estate	13.02	13.25	13.25	13.74	14.74	15.73
Consumer	9.02	8.68	8.88	10.31	11.58	12.43
Securities	14.00	13.43	14.28	14.81	15.72	17.19
U.S. government	6.14	5.91	7.04	7.35	7.38	7.76
State and local government	7.35	6.97	6.58	6.71	7.46	8.25
Other bonds and stocks	.51	.54	.66	.75	.89	1.18
Gross federal funds sold and reverse repurchase agreements	3.68	4.09	4.20	4.01	4.04	3.78
Interest-bearing deposits	9.32	10.15	10.21	8.02	6.45	5.42

Source: Danker and McLaughlin [1987], p. 550.

TABLE 10-A1 (*Continued*)

D. Large Banks Other Than Money-Center Banks

Item	1981	1982	1983	1984	1985	1986
		Balance-Sheet Items as a Percentage of Average Consolidated Assets				
Deposit liabilities		73.89	73.07	73.43	73.77	73.63	72.59
In foreign offices		14.01	13.85	13.03	10.77	9.49	7.85
In domestic offices		59.89	59.22	60.40	62.99	64.14	64.74
Demand deposits		22.02	18.89	18.21	18.37	17.79	18.18
Other checkable deposits		2.21	2.92	3.33	3.68	4.00	4.64
Large time deposits		16.75	16.75	13.84	13.65	12.63	11.75
Other deposits		18.90	20.66	25.02	27.29	29.73	30.17
Gross federal funds purchased and repurchase agreements		11.84	12.39	12.05	11.68	11.79	12.74
Other borrowings		2.94	2.92	3.23	3.29	3.66	4.27
MEMO							
Money market liabilities		45.53	45.91	42.16	39.39	37.56	36.61
Loss reserves		.60	.65	.70	.78	.86	.97
		Effective Interest Rate (percent)				
Rates earned							
Securities		8.74	9.17	9.16	9.42	8.89	8.01
U.S. government		10.64	11.12	11.18	11.13	10.27	9.01
State and local government		6.96	7.24	6.95	7.36	7.28	6.99
Other bonds and stocks		12.11	12.66	10.84	11.46	10.49	8.79
Loans, gross		16.80	15.08	12.29	13.37	11.78	10.61
Net of loss provision		15.98	13.92	10.99	12.11	10.80	9.37
Taxable equivalent							
Securities		11.60	12.09	11.66	12.06	11.51	10.58
Securities and gross loans		15.55	14.31	12.00	13.10	11.73	10.61
Rates paid							
Interest-bearing deposits		13.92	12.20	9.09	9.73	8.12	6.84
Large certificates of deposit		16.88	14.17	8.83	10.52	8.71	7.30
Deposits in foreign offices		17.98	14.84	9.48	12.04	9.25	7.54
Other deposits		9.54	9.66	9.08	8.71	7.62	6.56
All interest-bearing liabilities		14.55	12.28	9.24	10.04	8.13	6.82
		Income and Expenses as a Percentage of Average Net Consolidated Assets				
Gross interest income		11.95	11.06	9.19	9.89	9.13	8.13
Gross interest expense		9.02	8.00	6.17	6.76	5.79	4.82
Net interest margin		2.94	3.06	3.02	3.13	3.34	3.31
Taxable equivalent		3.31	3.42	3.35	3.56	3.75	3.76
Noninterest income		1.00	1.09	1.19	1.34	1.43	1.44
Loss provision		.29	.46	.56	.64	.57	.71
Other noninterest expense		2.79	2.97	3.01	3.14	3.29	3.23
Securities gains or losses ($-$)		$-.10$	$-.07$	$-.01$	$-.02$	.05	.13
Income before tax		.76	.65	.63	.67	.96	.94
Taxes		.10	.05	.10	.16	.20	.20
Extraordinary items		.00	.00	.00	.01	.02	.01
Net income		.66	.60	.54	.53	.78	.75
Cash dividends declared		.30	.29	.29	.27	.29	.34
Net retained earnings		.37	.31	.25	.25	.49	.41
MEMO							
Average assets (billions of dollars)		668	759	850	953	1,047	1,204
Number of banks		195	220	243	263	290	321

TABLE 10-A2   Report of Income, All Insured Commercial Banks, 1981–86

Millions of dollars

Item	1981	1982	1983	1984	1985	1986
Operating income, total	247,577	257,293	239,264	274,273	273,461	269,292
Interest, total	230,148	237,193	216,059	245,640	239,952	230,702
Loans	164,715	168,619	153,323	181,873	175,679	168,429
Balances with banks	23,905	23,867	16,739	16,557	13,590	11,132
Gross federal funds sold and reverse repurchase agreements	12,183	11,309	9,198	10,464	9,352	8,922
Securities (excluding trading accounts)	29,345	33,398	36,799	36,746	41,331	42,219
State and local government	9,704	10,648	10,620	11,817	12,820	14,956
Other	19,641	22,749	26,179	24,929	28,511	27,263
Service charges on deposits	3,892	4,584	5,399	6,512	7,280	7,902
Other operating income[a]	13,538	15,517	17,806	22,121	26,229	30,689
Operating expense, total	227,490	238,274	220,236	254,273	252,057	250,399
Interest, total	169,078	168,651	143,215	167,335	154,094	140,467
Deposits	138,830	141,185	119,843	139,331	128,837	115,889
Large certificates of deposit	38,896	37,366	22,523	25,761	22,472	19,257
Deposits in foreign offices	46,696	41,754	29,021	35,781	30,013	24,440
Other deposits	53,238	62,065	68,299	77,789	76,352	72,192
Gross federal funds purchased and repurchase agreements	23,752	20,628	16,438	19,323	16,236	15,766
Other borrowed money[b]	6,496	6,838	6,934	8,682	9,020	8,812
Salaries, wages, and employee benefits	27,901	31,244	33,637	36,463	39,338	42,258
Occupancy expense[c]	8,558	9,975	11,101	12,092	13,407	14,551
Loss provision	5,080	8,429	10,621	13,690	16,965	21,194
Other operating expense	16,873	19,975	21,662	24,694	28,254	31,929
Securities gains or losses (−1)	−1,595	−1,282	−30	−142	1,504	3,773
Income before tax	18,491	17,737	18,998	19,858	22,908	22,665
Taxes	3,859	2,976	4,076	4,665	5,369	5,261
Extraordinary items	57	64	70	217	318	271
Net income	14,689	14,826	14,992	15,409	17,858	17,674
Cash dividends declared	5,841	6,542	7,338	7,585	8,402	9,135

[a] Includes income from assets held in trading accounts.
[b] Includes interest paid on U.S. Treasury tax and loan account balances and on subordinated notes and debentures.
[c] Occupancy expense for bank premises net of any rental income plus furniture and equipment expenses.
Source: Danker and McLaughlin [1987], p. 551.

TABLE 10-A3   Second Quarter 1987 Bank Data (Dollar figures in billions, ratios in %)

		Asset Size Distribution						Geographic Distribution					
								EAST			WEST		
	All banks	Less than $100 Million	$100–300 Million	$300–1,000 Million	$1–5 Billion	Greater than $5 Billion	Ten Largest Banks	Northeast Region	Southeast Region	Central Region	Midwest Region	Southwest Region	West Region
Number of banks reporting	13,937	11,212	1,864	523	255	73	10	1,081	1,929	3,078	3,288	3,010	1,551
Total assets	$2,912.0	$399.3	$300.7	$264.9	$548.5	$715.8	$683.3	$1,138.1	$381.4	$462.8	$202.1	$286.2	$441.7
Total deposits	2,264.3	355.4	263.4	219.2	427.7	501.4	497.2	832.1	306.1	372.6	157.5	233.7	362.2
% total banks	100.0%	80.4%	13.4%	3.8%	1.8%	0.5%	0.1%	7.8%	13.8%	22.1%	23.6%	21.6%	11.1%
Asset share (%)	100.0	13.7	10.3	9.1	18.8	24.6	23.5	39.1	13.1	15.9	6.9	9.8	15.2
Deposit share (%)	100.0	15.7	11.6	9.7	18.9	22.1	22.0	36.7	13.5	16.5	7.0	10.3	16.0
Number of unprofitable banks	2,354	2,000	209	58	41	36	10	98	185	249	459	951	412
Number of failed banks	45 %	43	2	0	0	0	0	0	2	2	12	20	9
Performance Ratios (annualized)													
Yield on earning assets	9.59%	9.60%	9.51%	9.61%	9.35%	9.51%	10.09%	9.87%	9.78%	9.24%	9.67%	8.88%	9.81%
Cost of funding earning assets	5.67	5.16	5.11	5.12	5.10	5.75	6.97	6.36	5.21	5.35	5.46	5.45	5.07
Net interest margin	3.92	4.442	4.40	4.50	4.24	3.77	3.12	3.52	4.57	3.89	4.20	3.42	4.75
Net noninterest expense to earning assets	2.25	2.80	2.69	2.69	2.38	2.08	1.64	1.95	2.56	2.20	1.91	2.39	2.97
Net operating income to assets	-1.50	0.57	0.67	0.32	0.33	-1.61	-5.67	-2.94	0.83	-0.56	0.10	-1.08	-0.82
Return on assets	-1.46	0.61	0.71	0.36	0.35	-1.58	-5.60	-2.84	0.88	-0.55	0.13	-1.17	-1.79
Return on equity	-23.43	7.04	9.33	5.04	5.39	-28.97	-123.51	-50.30	12.70	-8.06	1.77	-17.85	-31.36
Net charge-offs to loans and leases	0.85	1.11	0.82	0.99	0.77	0.78	0.82	0.60	0.57	0.54	1.42	2.05	1.08
Condition Ratios													
Loss allowance to loans and leases	2.66%	1.63%	1.53%	1.70%	1.68%	2.84%	4.60%	3.14%	1.43%	2.17%	2.38%	2.81%	3.00%
Nonperforming assets to assets	2.57	2.29	1.94	2.04	1.60	2.38	4.19	2.58	1.12	1.48	2.16	4.97	3.62

(continues)

TABLE 10-A3 (Continued)   **Second Quarter 1987 Bank Data** (*Dollar figures in billions, ratios in %*)

| | | Asset Size Distribution | | | | | | Geographic Distribution | | | | | |
| | | | | | | | | EAST | | | WEST | | |
	All banks	Less than $100 Million	$100–300 Million	$300–1,000 Million	$1–5 Billion	Greater than $5 Billion	Ten Largest Banks	Northeast Region	Southeast Region	Central Region	Midwest Region	Southwest Region	West Region
Equity capital ratio	6.01	8.69	7.60	7.12	6.40	5.20	3.87	5.30	6.94	6.69	7.46	6.41	5.47
Primary capital ratio	7.48	9.51	8.39	8.01	7.22	6.77	6.63	7.07	7.57	7.85	8.69	7.84	7.27
Net loans and leases to assets	59.08	51.26	56.34	61.45	62.43	61.20	59.03	59.10	60.34	57.47	53.30	54.56	65.20
Net assets repriceable in one year or less to assets	6.39	−9.82	−8.35	−7.24	−5.96	−6.17	−3.76	−4.79	−9.81	−5.32	−14.53	−8.75	−3.43
Growth Rates (from year-ago quarter)													
Assets	5.0%	5.1%	7.5%	10.1%	13.6%	12.2%	−0.1%	7.8%	9.0%	6.0%	4.4%	−2.8%	−0.5%
Earning Assets	5.6%	5.7%	8.3%	10.7	14.5	12.9	0.3	8.7	10.1	6.6	5.2	−3.2	−0.3
Loans and leases	5.6	5.7	8.3	10.7	14.8	12.9	−0.3	8.7	10.1	6.6	5.2	−3.2	−0.3
Loss reserve	79.6	16.7	25.0	34.0	42.2	93.3	165.2	140.1	25.5	64.0	33.7	27.6	66.2
Net charge-offs	7.5	−17.8	0.4	29.6	32.7	−2.0	−19.0	3.1	16.8	−12.5	−28.7	−3.7	−14.1
Nonperforming assets	33.2	3.7	10.1	28.0	29.5	52.6	63.6	74.5	19.1	3.0	−7.4	35.4	14.1
Deposits	5.4	5.3	7.5	9.2	13.0	13.2	2.5	10.0	8.9	6.1	2.9	−3.3	−0.5
Equity capital	−0.2	3.6	7.9	6.3	13.6	3.6	−19.5	−2.0	11.3	0.9	3.5	−9.9	−2.4
Interest income	1.6	−2.8	−0.1	2.3	7.0	9.2	2.9	9.5	3.2	−1.0	−2.9	−13.3	−6.8
Interest expense	0.7	−8.6	−6.2	−3.8	0.9	7.2	7.0	11.5	−3.0	−5.8	−8.1	−15.1	−13.4
Net interest income	5.1	5.0	8.0	10.5	15.4	12.3	−5.2	6.1	11.4	6.3	4.9	−10.2	−1.4
Loan loss expense	397.0	−14.0	6.4	69.7	116.1	473.1	580.2	903.6	89.1	450.5	44.6	27.8	247.5
Noninterest income	13.4	10.7	9.4	10.0	10.6	16.0	20.8	18.8	13.3	7.1	5.2	10.7	7.6
Noninterest expense	8.5	6.9	8.1	10.5	11.4	19.8	7.1	12.7	8.3	6.2	5.1	−0.4	5.2
Net operating income	N/M	24.9	−5.4	−51.5	−49.6	N/M	N/M	N/M	−4.3	N/M	−81.1	N/M	N/M
Net income	N/M	−3.0	−10.2	−55.0	−52.8	N/M	N/M	N/M	−12.0	N/M	−81.8	N/M	N/M

REGIONS: Northeast—Connecticut, Delaware, District of Columbia, Maine, Maryland, Massachusetts, New Hampshire, New Jersey, New York, Pennsylvania, Puerto Rico, Rhode Island, Vermont.
Southeast—Alabama, Florida, Georgia, Mississippi, North Carolina, South Carolina, Tennessee, Virginia, West Virginia
Central—Illinois, Indiana, Kentucky, Michigan, Ohio, Wisconsin
Midwest—Iowa, Kansas, Minnesota, Missouri, Nebraska, North Dakota, South Dakota
Southwest—Arkansas, Louisiana, New Mexico, Oklahoma, Texas
West—Alaska, Arizona, California, Colorado, Hawaii, Idaho, Montana, Nevada, Oregon, Pacific Islands, Utah, Washington, Wyoming

N/M—Not meaningful, due to negative earnings in 1987.
Source: FDIC Quarterly Banking Profile [Second Quarter, 1987], Table 3, p. 4.

APPENDIX B

Continental Illinois Corporation: How Did it Become "Not Worth A Continental"?

Introduction

On October 15, 1981, the front page of *The Wall Street Journal* described the lead bank of Continental Illinois Corporation as, "On the Offensive: Behind Homely Image of Continental Illinois Is an Aggressive Bank." The subheadline read: "Its Risks Sometimes Backfire, But Its Cut-Rate Lending Has Yielded Major Gains." The risks that Continental Illinois National Bank & Trust Co. was taking were in lending and on interest rates. Stuart Greenbaum of Northwestern University described the bank's managers as "... extraordinarily aggressive. They've sold the hell out of the corporate market by taking more than average risks in well selected areas." Sanford Rose of the American Banker said, "Continental has been a bigger dice thrower than most."

Regarding Continental's perceived gambler's posture, Chairman Roger E. Anderson said, "I think we're conservative but aggressive." How does an organization serve both of these masters? In banking and finance, what is a "conservative but aggressive" investment? One interpretation is low risk and high return. Which, of course, is nonsense because it violates the fundamental principle of a risk–return trade-off. Another interpretation is more basic and focuses upon the possible deception of self-perception or self-evaluation. What we think or perceive about ourselves or our organizations may not be what objective outsiders see. Alternatively, and more plausibly, Continental's managers knew exactly what they were doing; they were not misguided village idiots who thought high return could be generated by a low-risk portfolio. As Paul Gigot, a staff reporter for the WSJ, wrote, "Behind that homely, country-boy self-image stand some of the nation's slickest, most aggressive bankers."

And Now For The Rest Of The Story: The Dice Came Up Snake Eyes

Radio and television commentator Paul Harvey is famous for his line, "And now, the rest of the story." In the Continental story, the gambling bank rolled snake eyes at the Penn Square table in, of all places, Oklahoma City. The good old boys from Chicago were roped in by some real country bumpkins at the shopping-center bank.

By December 31, 1981, Continental Illinois appeared to be in sound financial condition and performing well. Its assets totaled $47 billion with $33 billion in loans, $30 billion in deposits, and $1.7 billion in equity capital. On the earnings side, net interest icome (TE) was $910 million and net income was $255 million. On a per share basis, EPS was $6.44 with a DPS of $1.90. The Corporation's ROE was 15.8 percent, consisting of an ROA of 0.58 percent and an EM of 27.3, figures which were about average for its peer group of money-center banks. On December 31, 1981, Continental Illinois' common stock closed on the NYSE at $33.125 or 77 percent of its book value of $43.19. (Discounts from book values were not uncommon for the stocks of financial institutions at this time.)

Continental's Achilles' Heel: Penn Square Bank

On July 5, 1982, Penn Square Bank was declared insolvent by the OCC. The FDIC, as receiver, established a Deposit Insurance National Bank (DINB) to pay off the insured deposits of the failed institution. How does the failure of a $465 million bank in Oklahoma City affect a $47 billion, multinational bank headquartered in Chicago? When the Chicago bank has purchased more than $1 billion in loans from the fly-by-night bank, it has a severe effect, especially when substantial amounts of the participations are bad credits. Mainly as a result of the failure of Penn Square, Continental's 1982 net income dropped to $78 million as net credit losses rose to $393 million (from $71 million in 1981) with $191 million of the charge-offs due to participations purchased from Penn Square. In addition, Continental's provision for credit losses increased to $492 million in 1982 from $120 million the year before.

The 1984 Liquidity Crisis and Bailout

On Thursday, May 10, 1984, Continental began experiencing liquidity problems as "rumors" about the bank's financial condition spread throughout both national and international financial markets. The following week, as described in Exhibit 1, p. 301, was one of turmoil at Continental Illinois. The week culminated with the announcement of an unprecedented bailout arranged by the FDIC, the OCC, the Fed, and a group of 24 major banks. (See pp. 302–303.) The financial-assistance program provided Continental with the liquidity, capital, and time to resolve its problems in an orderly and permanent fashion. However, by July 1, 1984, even the $7.5 billion safety net was proving inadequate, as Continental was forced to sell almost $5 billion of its assets over the months of May and June. The shrinkage trimmed Continental's asset base to roughly $37 billion, down $10 billion from year-end 1981.

Throughout July regulatory attempts to find a "private solution" to Continental's problems continued to be futile. Because no investor was willing to come to Continental's rescue without government financial assistance, the regulators did it themselves on July 26, 1984. The rescue package, which nonregulators called a "nationalization" and the regulators denied, was, in effect, a blank check that provided whatever financial aid needed to ensure Continental's survival. The details of the rescue, which are complex, are summarized in Exhibit 2. In a nutshell, the plan gave the FDIC 80 percent ownership of Continental for buying up to $4.5 billion of its problem loans. The ownership structures of Continental before and after its nationalization are shown in Figure 10-B1.

One of the interesting aspects of Continental's *de facto* failure was that it began as a liquidity crisis. At the time, Continental had book net worth, including reserves, of roughly $2.3 billion. However, the market value of its shareholders' equity was dropping rapidly as the stock price fell from $13.125 at the close on May 9 to $10.25 on May 17. The low price on the day of the May bailout was $8.625 and the volume was 2,659,500 shares traded. With about 40 million shares outstanding, Continental's total market value was roughly $400 million. On February 1, 1984, Continental's stock price was $21.25; by March 30, it had dropped to $17.875. During Independence week, the price had plummeted to $4.125, down $1.375. During this same week, Continental's

---

EXHIBIT 1
Week of Turmoil at Continental Illinois

Thursday, May 10: Continental's stock falls $1\frac{1}{8}$ points in heavy trading on rumors the bank's financial condition has worsened. Continental issues denial.

Friday, May 11: Continental's stock rebounds as rumors of deteriorating financial condition appear to die down. Illinois commissioner of banks and trust companies assures state-chartered banks Continental can meet its obligations.

Monday, May 14: Banking industry, in plan backed by Federal Reserve Board, arranges $4.5 billion safety net for Continental in attempt to halt an outflow of deposits. Fund to be provided by 16-bank group led by Morgan Guaranty Trust Co. of New York. Standard & Poor's lowers the bank's debt ratings.

Tuesday, May 15: Continental draws on safety net. Money markets appear to have been calmed.

Wednesday, May 16: Safety net appears to calm commercial depositors as trading in Continental's certificates of deposit stabilizes some.

Thursday, May 17: Continental says it is seeking a merger as federal regulators arrange $2 billion of financial assistance and group of 24 major United States banks agrees to provide more than $5.3 billion in funding. This package replaces $4.5 billion, 16-bank safety net. Continental also omits common stock dividend and says nonperforming loans in second quarter to be above first-quarter level of $2.3 billion.

Continental's average daily overnight funding needs during the last week: $2.25 billion from the 16-bank group, $4 billion from the Federal Reserve Board, $1.75 billion from other sources. Total: $8 billion.

Source: Bailey and Hill [1984].

---

preferred stock (1,788,000 shares outstanding) dropped $1.25 to $13.625. Over the previous 52-week period, its high price was $51.25, with a new low established on July 6, 1984 at $13.50.

Financial Information

Tables 10-B1 to 10-B3 on pages 304–305 provide financial data on Continental Illinois Corporation for the period 1979 through 1983. In Table 10-B1, selected balance-sheet and income-expense figures are presented. Information to conduct an analysis of Continental's interest-rate sensitivity is shown in Table 10-B2. In Table 10-B3, selected loan data are provided. As of year-end 1983, the assets of Continental Illinois National Bank accounted for 96.54 percent of the assets of Continental Illinois Corporation. Thus, for all practical purposes, the bank is the holding company.

EXHIBIT 2

Office of the Comptroller of the Currency

July 26, 1984   Federal Deposit Insurance Corporation

Federal Reserve Board

FOR RELEASE
9:00 a.m. e.d.t., 7-26-84

PERMANENT ASSISTANCE PROGRAM FOR
CONTINENTAL ILLINOIS NATIONAL BANK AND TRUST COMPANY
CHICAGO, ILLINOIS

SUMMARY STATEMENT

A multi-billion dollar program to rehabilitate the Continental Illinois National Bank and Trust Company and restore it to financial health was announced today by the Federal Deposit Insurance Corporation, the Comptroller of the Currency and the Federal Reserve Board.

Major components of the plan include installation of a proven, internationally recognized management team, the removal from the bank of $4.5 billion in problem loans, the infusion of $1 billion in new capital, and ongoing lines of credit from the Federal Reserve and a group of major U.S. banks. The resulting institution will be smaller, but immeasurably stronger and positioned to profitably serve the full range of banking needs of its customers.

Key management appointments are John E. Swearingen as Chairman of the Board and Chief Executive Officer of Continental Illinois Corporation and William S. Ogden as Chairman of the Board and Chief Executive Officer of Continental Illinois National Bank.

Mr. Swearingen, 65, widely acclaimed throughout international business circles, recently retired as Chief Executive Officer of the Standard Oil Company (Indiana), headquartered in Chicago. In addition to his extensive background in the energy business, where a significant amount of Continental Illinois' loans reside, he is a director of The Chase Manhattan Bank (a position he will resign).

On May 17, 1984, the Federal Deposit Insurance Corporation, the Federal Reserve Board and the Comptroller of the Currency announced an interim financial assistance package for the Continental Illinois National Bank and Trust Company. The program was designed to alleviate the liquidity pressures facing the bank in order to provide the time needed to resolve the bank's problems in an orderly and permanent way and to avoid general instability in the financial system.

EXHIBIT 2 (*Continued*)

Since the announcement the agencies have conducted an examination of the bank and have held extensive discussions with prospective merger partners and potential investors. A number of proposals from various sources have been reviewed.

After careful evaluation of all of the alternatives, the agencies have decided that the best solution is to provide sufficient permanent capital and other direct assistance to enable the bank to restore its position as a viable, self-financing entity. Factors considered in reaching this determination included the cost to the FDIC, competitive consequences and the banking needs of the public.

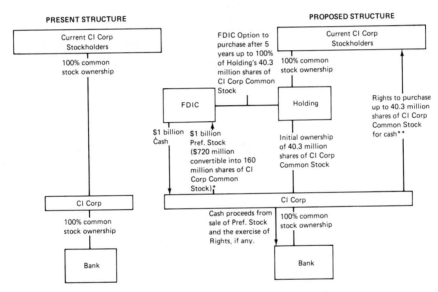

Figure 10-B1   Ownership Structure of Continental Illinois

TABLE 10-B1 Continental Illinois Corporation Selected Financial Data, 1979–1983

Average Balance Sheet Items	1983	1982	1981	1980	1979
Earning assets	$36,167[a]	$40,254	$37,113	$32,979	$27,427
Total assets	40,268	45,662	44,004	39,565	33,252
Deposits	26,747	28,225	27,428	24,953	22,370
Long-term debt	1,273	1,088	722	600	521
Common stockholders' equity	1,722	1,721	1,616	1,443	1,294
Income-Expense Items					
Total operating income	$ 4,381	$5,889	$6,286	$4,715	$3,376
Total interest income	3,977	5,579	5,964	4,472	3,168
Total interest expense	3,146	4,688	5,158	3,742	2,594
Net interest income	831	891	806	730	574
Total other operating exp.	721	673	624	558	464
Net income	108	78	255	226	196
Interest income (TE) adjust.	81	105	105	107	103
Per-Share Items					
EPS	$2.63	$1.95	$6.44	$5.75	$4.99
DPS	2.00	2.00	1.90	1.70	1.52
Book value	43.13	42.80	43.19	38.76	34.75
Market value	21.87	20.37	33.12	31.25	31.12

[a] All figures are millions, except per share data.
Source: Continental Illinois Corporation, Annual Reports and Form 10-K [1979–1983].

**TABLE 10-B2 Continental Illinois Corporation
Interest-Rate Sensitivity, 1980–1983**

Earning assets	1983	1982	1981	1980
0–30 days	$22,099[a]	$21.394	$17.850	$14,073
31–90 days	5,371	5,413	9,568	7,626
91–180 days	2,069	2,442	4,233	3,524
181–365 days	815	1,603	1,148	1,920
Over 1 year	7,072	7.939	7,907	7,832
TOTAL	37,426	38,791	40,706	34,975
Interest-Bearing liabilities				
0–30 days	$20,908	$21,434	$20,107	$14,770
31–90 days	7,781	7,289	8,085	6,833
91–180 days	1,984	3,448	5,227	5,280
181–365 days	821	825	1,235	2,152
Over 1 year	2,209	1,947	1,447	2,477
TOTAL	33,703	34,943	36,131	31,512
Interest-Sensitive Gap				
0–30 days	$ 1,191	$ (40)	$(2,257)	$ (697)
31–90 days	(2,410)	(1,876)	1,483	793
91–180 days	85	(1,006)	(994)	(1,756)
181–365 days	(6)	778	(87)	(232)
Over 1 year	4,863	5,992	6,430	5,355
TOTAL	3,723	3,848	4,575	3,463

[a] All figures are millions.
Source: Continental Illinois Corporation, Annual Reports and Form 10-K [1980–1983].

(1) the borrowing and lending or pure intermediation part and (2) the production part, which involves the "backroom" operations of the bank. As established in the previous chapter, bank accounting separates interest income and expense from noninterest income and expense, and the differences between these respective items are called net interest revenue or income and net noninterest income or "burden." Furthermore, after netting out loan loss expense, we have net interest revenue after loan loss expense. Thus, in bank cost accounting, we have three components of total costs (called total operating expenses by bank regulators): (1) interest expense, (2) provision for loan losses or loan loss expense and (3) (other) operating or noninterest expense. Total interest expense includes the interest costs of all sources of funding from insured savings accounts to capital notes and debentures (i.e., long-term nondeposit and uninsured debt). Although actual loan loss expense is simply an ex post reflection of credit or default risk, provision for loan losses should contain an expectational element designed to capture some portion of future loan-loss experience.

Bank noninterest or (other) operating expense consists of five items: (1) salaries, (2) employee or staff benefits, (3) net premises expense, (4) equipment expense, and (5) other expense. This chapter focuses primarily on the behavior and characteristics of these five items together (i.e., on bank operating expenses). Of these five components, salaries are the major noninterest expense incurred by banks. Together salaries and employee benefits drain off anywhere from 10 to 25 percent of a bank's total income. The figure for total operating expenses (the sum of the five items above) tends to range between 20 and 40 percent of bank income. A representive cost profile is 15 percent for salaries and benefits, 5 percent for occupancy and equipment expense, and 10 percent for other expense for a total of 30 percent. Such a configuration leaves 70 percent of bank income to cover interest expense, loan losses, taxes, and the targeted level of profits. Since bank managers (or the consultants they may hire) cannot do much about interest expense or loan losses, they typically resort to (or recommend) tax planning or loopholes, closing branches, and/or cutting staff as cost-cutting measures. The first strategy may incur increased surveillance from the IRS, whereas the last two tactics tend to be unpopular with either bank employees, who may lose their jobs, or bank customers, who may lose their local branch, or both.

In production terminology, the banking industry can be viewed as consisting of plants and firms, where a firm is simply an aggregation of plants. In unit banking states, where banks are restricted to having only one plant, the firm and the plant are one and the same. In contrast, in branch banking states, the firm is equal to the sum or aggregation of the various plants or branch banks, or banking offices. In this context, a bank holding company can be viewed as an aggregation of firms.

PRODUCTION AND COST FUNCTIONS

Given the existing state of technology, a production function shows the relationship between inputs (factors of production) and outputs. Like other firms, the primary inputs for banks are labor, L, and capital, K. The total respective costs of these inputs are the salaries and benefits, and the occupancy and equipment expenses referred to above. Banks combine labor and capital to produce products and services in the form of loans, deposits, and other services (lock-box services, safety deposit boxes, etc.). Although banks are clearly multiproduct firms, for simplicity we begin by assuming only one homogeneous output, Q.

Important Properties of Production Functions

Taking the state of technological progress as being constant at any point in time, our simplified production function can be represented as

$$Q = f(L,K) \tag{11-1}$$

Managers should be concerned about how output changes when inputs are changed. Does output increase by the same percentage as the percentage change in inputs, by more, or by less? Economists have specific names for each of these relationships, which are constant returns to scale, increasing returns to scale, and decreasing returns to scale, respectively. Algebraically, these relationships can be represented in terms of the following formula:

$$f(aL,aK) = a^n f(L,K) = a^n Q, \tag{11-2}$$

where the letter a represents some constant by which inputs are increased and the exponent n denotes what is called the "degree of homogeneity of the production function." Now if $n = 1$, the production function exhibits constant returns to scale and it is called a linear homogeneous production function (i.e., if inputs increase by 10 percent, output increases by 10 percent). If $n > 1$, the production function exhibits increasing returns to scale because when inputs increase, say, by 10 percent, output increases by more than 10 percent. If $n < 1$, the production function exhibits decreasing returns to scale because when inputs increase, say, by 10 percent, output increases by less than 10 percent. In general, a production function is said to be homogeneous of degree n, if when inputs increase by the constant a, output increases by the factor a^n. It follows then, if $n = 1$, $a = a^n$; if $n > 1$, $a < a^n$; and if $n < 1$, then $a > a^n$.

The Mapping from Production Space to Cost Space

Given the firm's production function and its input prices, we can move from the notion of a production function to the idea of a cost function. Specifically, the total cost, TC, of producing output $Q = F(L,K)$ is simply $TC = P_L L + P_K K$, where P_L and P_K are the input prices for labor and capital, respectively. Dividing TC by Q, we have the concept of average total cost (ATC). Thus TC can be represented by

$$TC = ATC \times Q = [P_L L + P_Q K]/Q \times f(L,K) \tag{11-3}$$

This formula says total costs are a function of inputs (L and K), input prices (P_L and P_K), and how the inputs are combined $[f(L,K)]$ to produce the output, Q. Holding input prices constant, the properties of the producton function will be reflected by the cost function. Thus we can talk about constant costs when the production function exhibits constant returns to scale, economies of scale when the production function exhibits increasing returns to scale, and diseconomies of scale when the production function exhibits decreasing returns to scale.

Economies of Scale

Behind all the economic verbiage of the previous section, we are simply concerned with the potential benefits of size or scale. In other words, is there an advantage, in terms of cost, to being big? This advantage to bigness is what economists call economies of scale or scale economies. Thus, when we talk about economies of scale, as we did in Chapter 6 with our discussion of electronic funds transfer systems (EFTS), we are referring to a condition in which the average cost of production, in the long

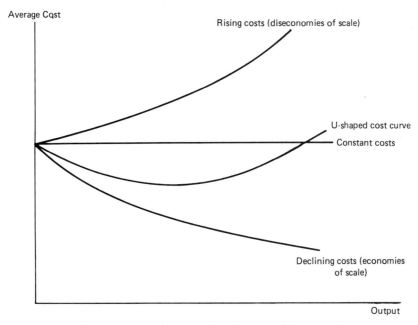

Figure 11-1   Scale Economies and the Shapes of Average Cost Curves

run, declines as output increases. Scale economies are measured by the ratio of the percentage change in costs relative to the percentage change in output. When the scale economies ratio is less than one, scale economies exist as average cost is falling. When the ratio is one, no scale economies (or diseconomies) exist as average cost is constant. And when the ratio is greater than one, scale diseconomies exist as average cost is rising.

Four alternative relationships between average cost and output are illustrated in Figure 11-1. The shallow U-shaped cost curve indicates a cost function exhibiting all three of the cost characteristics shown in the other three curves.

Economies of Scope Revisited

Recall from Chapter 7 that economies of scope refer to economies of joint production. Since banks are multiproduct firms with a desire to expand their product offerings, the possibility of scope economies is real. For example, bank computer operations are such that adding new products and services might be achieved at relatively low cost. Scope economies exist when joint production costs are less than stand-alone production costs. Consider two products Q_1 and Q_2 and their stand-alone costs functions $C(Q_1)$ and $C(Q_2)$. If the joint costs of producing the two products is represented by $C(Q_1, Q_2)$, then economies of scope exist when

$$C(Q_1, Q_2) < C(Q_1) + C(Q_2) \tag{11-4}$$

The existence of economies of scope is attributed to interproduct or cost complementarities (see Willig [1979] and Gilligan, Smirlock, and Marshall [1984]). For a multiproduct banking firm, cost complementarities refer to the extent to which the costs of producing a particular financial service or product (e.g., deposits) may vary with the output levels of other products or services (e.g., loans). In other words, when inputs such as labor (e.g., bank calling officers) and capital (e.g., bank computer equipment) are shared, the joint production of various outputs may generate cost savings compared to separate production of the outputs.

The Notion of Ray Average Cost

For multiproduct firms, the concept of average cost is complicated because average cost is defined only for single-product firms. Thus, we cannot simply look for the most efficient size firm at the minimum point of the average cost curve. Recall that $ATC = TC/Q$. The problem is how to measure output or Q for the multiproduct firm. One solution would be to devise some aggregate output index for multiproduct firms. Baumol [1977] has proposed an alternative solution based on the behavior of total costs as all of the firm's outputs are increased by the same proportion. This relationship is referred to as "ray average cost." The notion is most easily explained with the help of a three-dimensional diagram such as the one in Figure 11-2. The "floor" of the diagram is the output space for loan and deposit services, which are produced in the proportion given by the vector or ray labeled OR. The term "ray" explains why the production costs are called ray average costs. Think of any point along the ray, OR, as representing "output bundles" having fixed proportions of loans and deposits. Since a loan-to-deposit ratio of 0.70 is not unusual, think of it as being a representative proportion. The firm's choice of output proportions will determine the location of the ray along which it will operate. This choice depends on the degree of cost complementarity in the production of outputs (e.g., loans and deposits).

The locus of points corresponding to the output bundles and the ray average costs trace out the ray average cost (RAC) curve shown in Figure 11-2. The height of the diagram measures the ray average cost associated with each output bundle. Since along any such ray the behavior of average cost is definable, the point of minimum RAC represents the most efficient scale (size) for the firm producing loans and deposits in the proportion defined by the ray OR. The output bundle Q^* corresponds to the RAC minimum. The degree of scale economies at Q^* can be measured by the ratio of $1/(1 + e)$, where e is the elasticity of the RAC curve. The ratio is greater than,

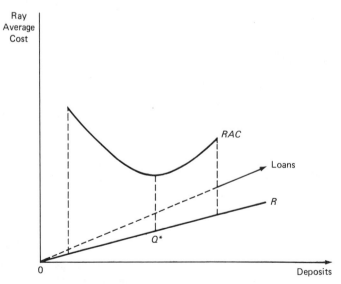

Figure 11-2   Economies of Scale for Multiproduct Firms: The Concept of Ray Average Cost

Source: Adapted from Baumol [1982].

less than, or equal to one as the slope (derivative) of the *RAC* curve is less than, greater than, or equal to zero. In words, declining *RAC* corresponds to the notion of scale economies for the single-product firm. In this case, the ratio $1/(1 + e)$ is greater than one. The elasticity of ray average cost with respect to output is captured by $1 + e$.

Scale and Scope Economies: A Recapitulation

Suppose a bank has only one output called Q_1. If output of Q_1 is expanded, either by expansion of existing operations or by merging with another producer of Q_1 and the average cost of producing Q_1 falls, then scale economies exist. Now suppose that the bank adds a new product Q_2, either through product development or acquisition of a producer of Q_2. If the bank can produce the two products more cheaply than they were produced separately, then economies of scope exist. If the resulting two-product bank now makes a proportionate increase in its outputs, Q_1 and Q_2, and its ray average cost declines, economies of scale exist for the multiproduct firm. In a nutshell, if economies of scale and scope exist, then banks will be able to reduce costs by expanding the scale (size) and scope (number of products) of their operations.

EXPIRICAL EVIDENCE ON THE EXISTENCE OF ECONOMIES OF SCALE AND SCOPE

Since empirical studies of cost characteristics of banks (and other financial institutions) face complicated problems of methodology and data, the findings presented in this section need to be interpreted with care. As methodological and empirical advances are made, previous findings may be overturned. Moreover, keep in mind the cynic's retort against "statistics": "There are lies, damn lies, and statistics!" Given this caveat, let's begin.

Focusing first on the issue of scale economies, Humphrey [1985], in a survey article covering both banks and thrift institutions, concludes (pp. 778–779):

1. Scale economies exist in banking but apparently are limited to smaller institutions, where average costs first decline then start to rise around a deposit size of $50 million. When the measure of scale economies for a branch banking firm is properly specified, large institutions appear to encounter diseconomies of scale.
2. The average cost curve for the production of the main products of banking (i.e., loans and deposits) is U-shaped. Moreover, this shape of cost curve (a) exists for banks in both unit and branch banking states, (b) is consistent across different measures of bank output (e.g., number of accounts versus dollars), and (c) holds even when interest expenses are added to operating costs.

In a study finished after Humphrey's survey, Berger, Hanweck, and Humphrey [1986] add the following qualification. Using some advanced cost concepts (such as expansion path product mix and expansion path subadditivity) and methodological developments, they found banks in branching states to be competitively viable at all scales of operation and existing product mixes; however, large unit state banks were not viable because of scale diseconomies. They concluded that large unit state banks "... probably will have to alter their output configurations to survive interstate banking. Presumably, this will involve replacement of large banking offices and reliance on purchased funds with branching networks" (p. 58). It is interesting to note how this prediction (on an ex post basis) fits a description of the problems faced by Continental Illinois in 1984.

What are the policy implications of these findings? First, for bank managers, simply being big will not, on average, generate cost savings or advantages, especially for large unit banks. Two qualifications here are noted by Kolari and Zardkoohi [1987], who found that demand deposits and credit cards have cost characteristics conforming to those of a natural monopoly (i.e., declining average cost over all output ranges). Their managerial prescription is for small banks to purchase such services from large banks rather than produce them in-house. Second, for shareholders, beware of bankers who argue for mergers because of potential economies of scale. The evidence suggests such economies do not exist. And third, for regulators, the movement toward nation-wide banking should not lead to consolidation of the banking industry (i.e., to natural monopoly) on the basis of cost and scale economies alone. However, regulators do need to be concerned about the viability of large unit state banks in an environment characterized by interstate banking.

Let's now look at the evidence regarding economies of scope. Gilligan, Smirlock, and Marshall [1984] find evidence that bank cost functions are characterized by economies of scope. This finding means cost savings are available from joint production of financial services. Alternatively, it implies the existence of cost complementarities across a bank's balance sheet, which means the costs of producing any one service (e.g., loans) varies with the level of output of other services (e.g., deposits). However, Berger, Hanweck, and Humphrey contend these findings are incorrect because of methodological difficulties. Their findings, which are consistent with those for savings and loans, do not show the existence of scope economies in banking. They argue that the slight mix and scope diseconomies found for both unit and branch banks are consistent with customers' demands for jointly produced financial services and with regulatory pressures for diversified portfolios to reduce interest-rate and credit risks.

Regarding specific cost complementarities available in banking, Kolari and Zard-koohi [1987] report scope economies for the joint production of loans and deposits, but not for demand and time deposits or securities and loans. They interpret their findings (p. 123) as indicative of (1) the substantial economies of "vertical integration" in the intermediation process and (2) the lack of cost savings to be gained in the acquisition of deposits (what they call stage one of the bank production process) or in the administration of bank assets (their stage two). For banks in both unit and branching states, Kolari and Zardkoohi claim banks can reduce, on average. "...the cost of expansion by about 30 to 50 percent by increasing outputs at the same time, as opposed to increasing each output separately, one at a time" (p. 123). They also find that small banks are not at a disadvantage relative to large banks in the joint expansion of outputs.

What are the policy implications of the empirical evidence with respect to economies of scope? Since the empirical evidence is mixed, only tentative conclusions can be drawn. For bank managers, since not all output combinations may exhibit cost complementarities, they need to find the output mix or bundle that minimizes their costs, and serves their markets. Whatever that mix is, by jointly expanding output, banks presumably will not encounter substantial cost increases. Because of the potential cost interactions among banking products, regulators must weigh the consequences of product and price restrictions carefully. The imposition of such restrictions may prevent banks from attaining a cost-efficient output bundle. The combination of scope and scale evidence suggests that regulators (and bank customers) have nothing to fear regarding the development of a natural monopoly in banking. However, the viability of large state banks in a competitive environment is open to question.

Finally, for bank shareholders, since cost efficiency is a prerequisite for maximization of shareholder wealth, they should encourage managers to be cost conscious and beware of managers who make too much use of cost arguments due to economies of scale and/or scope to justify their actions.

COST DISPERSION AND THE MEASUREMENT OF ECONOMIES IN BANKING: A NEW TWIST

Humphrey [1987] has added a new twist to the study of bank costs. He notes that the observed variation in cost among banks can be divided into two components: (1) scale or cost economies across different-sized banks and (2) cost differences between similar-sized banks. His new twist is to focus on the second component, as the first one already has been studied extensively. He finds that estimated cost economies (when they occur) are dominated by differences in average cost levels. Specifically, Humphrey found the difference in average cost between banks with the highest costs and banks with the lowest costs was two-to-four times greater than the observed

Average Cost ($)
(Operating and interest cost per dollar of assets)

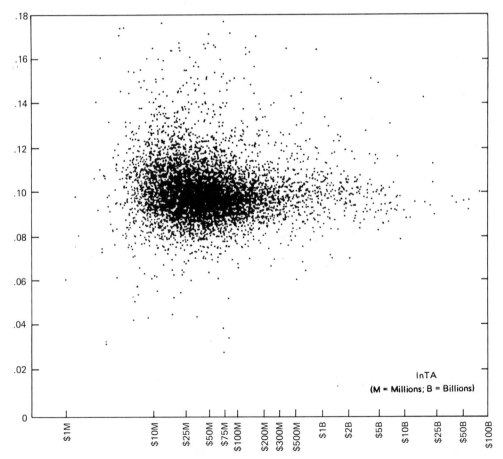

Figure 11-3   Scatter Diagram: Average Cost of Branch State Banks (1984; 7,611 Banks)

Source: Humphrey [1987], Figure 1a, p. 26.

variation in average costs across bank size classes. On the basis of these findings, he concludes: "... the existence of bank scale economies (or diseconomies) should have little competitive impact relative to those competitive effects which already exist as a result of large differences in cost levels" (p. 24).

Since a picture supposedly is worth a thousand words, let's consider the two pictures (scatter diagrams) in Figures 11-3 and 11-4 to highlight Humphrey's findings. On the vertical axis in both pictures, average cost is measured, defined as total costs (operating and interest expenses) divided by total assets. Thus, we are measuring total costs per dollar of assets. In both scatter diagrams, the average costs range from about 3 cents per dollar of assets to 18 cents per dollar of assets. On the horizontal axis, the logarithm of total assets is measured, ranging from $1 million to $100 billion. If we fit a regression line to the scatters in Figures 11-3 and 11-4, we would find them to decline initially (scale economies) and then to be relatively flat (constant costs) or perhaps to rise slightly (diseconomies of scale) beyond an asset size of about $25 million. This point, however, is not the one Humphrey wants to emphasize because it is old news. What he wants us to focus on is the dispersion of costs about this line for different size classes. You do not have to be a statistician to see the considerable dispersion that exists, especially for the smaller banks. As size increases, this dispersion is reduced but not eliminated. The important point is that banks of similar size have substantially different average cost per dollar of total assets. This conclusion

Average Cost ($)
(Operating and interest costs per dollar of assets)

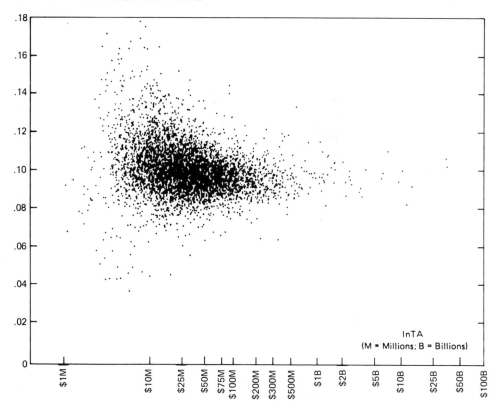

Figure 11-4   Scatter Diagram: Average Cost of Unit State Banks (1984; 6,298 Banks)

Source: Humphrey [1987], Figure 1b, p. 27.

holds for both scatter diagrams. The difference between the two diagrams is simply that Figure 11-3 is for banks in branch banking states (which he calls branch state banks) whereas Figure 11-4 is for banks in unit banking states (which he calls unit state banks).

Humphrey analyzed data for 13 different size classes for each of the years 1980, 1982, and 1984. He found banks do not lie on the same cost curve over time and, at any point in time, only sometimes do they lie on the same curve across size classes.

Let's consider some of Humphrey's specific cost figures. The most populous size group for branch banks in 1984 was the $25 million to $50 million range. There were 2,054 banks in this group (26.8 percent of his sample). Focusing on average cost quartiles and moving from lowest cost to highest, the cost figures (in cents per dollar of assets) are 8.8, 9.7, 10.2, and 11.5. (The corresponding figures for unit state banks are quite similar at 8.8, 9.6, 10.1, and 11.2.) The spread from most efficient to least efficient is 2.7 cents per dollar of assets. To illustrate the importance of these cost differences, consider the following experiment. Suppose that a bank with zero ROA had a cost ratio of 11.5 percent. If it had had a cost ratio of 8.8 percent, its ROA would have been 2.7 percent! Clearly, cost efficiency is important.

Next let's consider the largest banks in the system, those with more than $10 billion in assets. In 1984, there were 18 branch banks in Humphrey's sample. The average cost quartiles for this group are 9.0, 9.6, 9.9, and 11.7 for a differential of 2.7. For the five big unit banks in the sample, all of the quartile costs are lower at 8.2, 9.2, 10.0, and 10.4 for an efficiency spread of 2.2.

Asset Cost Elasticities

To measure the responsiveness of total cost to asset size, Humphrey calculated asset cost elasticities (ACE) for each of his 13 size groups for each of the years 1980, 1982, and 1984. If ACE is less than one, cost economies exist. If ACE equals one, costs are constant. And, if ACE is greater than one, cost diseconomies exist. To determine the elasticities, Humphrey estimated the following quadratic regression equation;

$$\ln TC = a + b(\ln TA) + c[.5(\ln TA)^2] \tag{11-5}$$

where $\ln TC$ indicates the logarithm of total cost, $\ln TA$ is the logarithm of total assets, and a, b, and c are the parameters of the regression equation. Since the variables are expressed as logs, the estimated slope coefficient, b, measures the asset cost elasticity, which can vary with bank size according to $ACE = b + c(\ln TA)$. Given Equation 11-5, Humphrey is asking the question: How do total costs vary at the firm level when output and *all other things change*? This question is different from the typical economies of scale question which asks: How do operating costs vary with output when *all other things are held constant*?

On the basis of 1984 data, Humphrey finds cost economies in banking but only for higher cost and/or smaller banks. As a result, he concludes that these cost economies do not confer competitive advantages for large banks over small ones for at least two reasons. First, most of the ACE estimates are not significantly different from unity, indicating constant costs. And second, because of the differences in costs within size groups, the magnitudes of the ACEs would have to be on the order of .49 to .66 to make up for the differences.

Average Costs Over Time

In closing our discussion of Humphrey's study, let's focus on his results for the movement of average costs over time. His findings are shown in Figure 11-5, panel A

Average Cost ($)

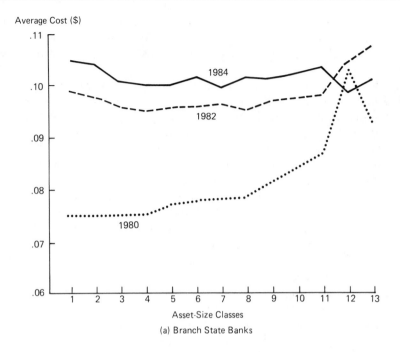

(a) Branch State Banks

Average Cost ($)

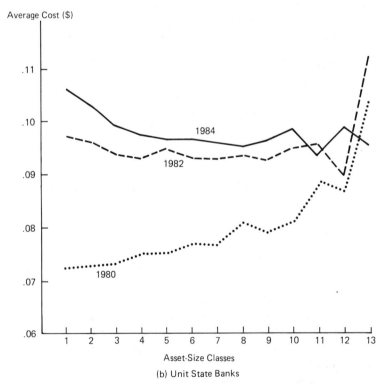

(b) Unit State Banks

Figure 11-5   The Movement of Bank Average Costs Over Time

Source: Humphrey [1987], Figures 4a and 4b, p. 34.

for branch state banks and panel B for unit state banks. Each panel shows average cost across the three years 1980, 1982 and 1984 according to his 13 size classes. The obvious conclusion is that the curves became flatter from 1980 to 1984. Interest-rate movements explain the volatility of the large bank portion of the curve, whereas the removal of Regulation Q interest-rate ceilings is the primary reason why the small bank portion of the curve whipped upward. For example, interest rates were at record levels in 1980 and 1982, driving the cost of purchased funds for large banks above the interest cost for small ones, which in 1980 relied more heavily on less costly core deposits. However, with the DIDMCA-mandated removal of rate ceilings occurring over the years 1980 to 1984, small banks were forced to pay market rates for interest-bearing core deposits over these years. As a result, their interest costs rose dramatically. Finally, Humphrey points out a less obvious reason contributing to the flattening of the curves, namely, the lagged effects of inflation on operating expenses (i.e., employee and premises/equipment costs) at smaller institutions. Since these expenses are a larger portion of total costs at small banks, inflation has a greater proportional effect on them.

TECHNICAL CHANGE AND ECONOMIES OF SCALE

Production and cost functions typically are analyzed and estimated under the assumption of no changes in technology. When we compare firms against each other at one point in time, this assumption is acceptable. However, in a dynamic and changing environment, if firms are compared over time, the assumption is an untenable one (i.e., technological change should be incorporated into the analysis).

Technical change occurs when a given set of inputs is capable of producing a larger maximum output. Such progress occurs over time and can be attributed to such factors as increased managerial expertise and/or more efficient capital equipment. The latter may be due to new innovations or better production techniques; the former to greater experience or knowledge. In terms of capital equipment, technical change in banking has appeared on two fronts: (1) the development of electronic funds transfer systems and (2) advances in "backroom" computer operations. On the labor front, the development of continuing education programs in banking and the greater willingness of banks to compete for skilled labor (e.g., MBAs) should mean a more qualified and better trained labor pool. In this context, technical change can be viewed as being embodied in more efficient inputs. Moreover, since technical change implies more efficient production, it should be highly correlated with scale economies.

Until recently the effects of technical change on bank production and costs have been ignored. Hunter and Timme [1986] eliminated this oversight by analyzing the effects of "embodied technical change" on scale economies. Using a simple, but clever, test based on a trend variable to capture technical change over time, they estimated scale economies for a sample of 91 bank holding companies for the years 1972 to 1982 using data from *Bank Computstat*. Their study was the first one to use either BHCs or the Compustat data base to analyze scale economies. Since these large banking organizations are the ones most likely to adapt to technical change, the use of the BHC sample seems most appropriate for their experiment.

Without going into the complexities of their estimation procedures, we highlight their findings in Figure 11-6, which illustrates the effects of technical change on the relationship between BHC output and total cost. Although they employed various output and cost definitions, the ones shown in Figure 11-6 are for output defined as

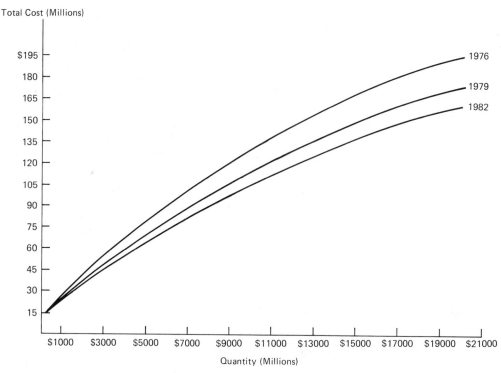

Total Cost (Millions)

Quantity (Millions)

Figure 11-6   The Effects of Technical Change on BHC Operating Costs

Source: Hunter and Timme [1986], Figure 1, p. 160, reprinted with permission of the authors and the *Journal of Money, Credit and Banking.*

the sum of all loans plus total investment securities plus total deposits, less reserves for losses on loan and securities; and for total operating costs defined as the sum of physical capital and labor expenses. Given these definitions, Figure 11-6 shows the relationship between output and total cost for the years 1976, 1979, and 1982. Although Figure 11-6 involves only three dimensions (i.e., output, cost, and technical change), it was derived from a multidimensional framework. Thus, a number of factors behind the scenes are held constant; they include BHC organizational form (MBHC vs. OBHC), changes in the number of offices, and factor input prices through time.

In a nutshell, Hunter and Timme's findings illustrate what happens to the BHC output–cost relationship or cost curve when technical change is incorporated into their model. Figure 11-6 clearly shows the downward shift in the BHC cost curve over time. To the extent their model was effective in holding all other things constant, the downward shifts in the cost curve can be attributed to the technical change embodied in the factors of production (i.e., physical capital and labor).

FUNCTIONAL COST ANALYSIS

Functional cost analysis (FCA) reports are collected (via annual survey) by the Federal Reserve System. FCA data represent the most detailed data available on bank operating costs and income. Although these cost accounting data are collected for only about 600 banks (roughly 4 percent of the population), they provide a representative sample of the commercial bank population, except for the largest banks, which are underrepresented. According to Humphrey [1985], one of the leading researchers in this area, the underrepresentation of the largest banks is not a major problem because their cost data are consistent with those available for large banks in the FCA sample.

Until the mid-1980s, most researchers used FCA data to study scale economies and other bank cost issues. Three studies noted earlier in this chapter, Humphrey [1987], Kolari and Zardkoohi [1987], and Hunter and Timme [1986], are exceptions. Since FCA data have detailed information on number of accounts and the costs and income of those accounts, researchers who wanted to define bank output in terms of number of accounts were restricted to using FCA data, or left with the impossible task of trying to collect their own data. FCA data will be used in later chapters of this book, where specific bank products or accounts such as loan and deposit categories are analyzed.

CHAPTER SUMMARY

This chapter has focused on the characteristics of bank costs by analyzing the functions, economies, and controls of the expense process. As noted in the previous chapter, one of the key characteristics of high-performance banks is "expense control." Such control is a prerequisite for achieving the goal of maximization of shareholder wealth. Moreover, in the dynamic environment of the financial-services industry, the forces of change (as captured by TRICK) dictate that more and more emphasis be placed on cost control as a key ingredient in bank success, if not survival.

By understanding the mechanics of the production and cost processes, you should have keener insight into the concepts and issues involved in cost analysis. The key concepts are production and cost functions, economies of scale and scope, average cost and ray average cost, the role of technical change, and the various bells and whistles that can be added to these notions. Since the complexity of the methodological and empirical issues makes existing evidence subject to change, this area is a fruitful one for future research.

The key policy issues for managers, shareholders, and regulators revolve around the issues of scale and scope economies, which have important implications for managerial strategies and regulatory restrictions regarding geographic and product expansion. Regarding public policy, the existing evidence suggests that the removal of geographic restrictions will not lead to a natural monopoly in banking, but that the viability of large unit state banks will be tested. In addition, although the evidence is mixed, certain product restrictions could prevent banks from achieving cost efficiency (i.e., reaping the benefits of economies of scope). For bank managers, the evidence suggests focusing on the scope and efficiency of production processes and cost functions, rather than myopic focus on the size of the organization. If shareholders want to maximize their returns, they should look for managers who have such a focus.

KEY WORDS, CONCEPTS, AND ACRONYMS

ATC = average total cost
Cost complementarities
Cost dispersion
Cost function

Economies of scale (or scale economies)
Economies of scope (or scope economies)

Factors of production
FCA = functional cost analysis
Input prices
Operating expenses
Production function

RAC = ray average cost
Returns to scale
Technical change
Total cost
U-shaped cost curve

REVIEW/DISCUSSION QUESTIONS

1. In bank cost accounting, total costs can be viewed as consisting of three components. What are they and what are their relative magnitudes?
2. What is a production function? Explain the concepts of returns to scale and the "degree of homogeneity of the production function. What is a linear homogeneous production function?
3. Explain the mapping from production space to cost space and discuss the notion of economies of scale. What is a natural monopoly?
4. Define economies of scope and explain what accounts for their existence.
5. Baumol has proposed a solution to deal with the problem of average cost for the multiproduct firm. What is it? Use a graph in your explanation.
6. Briefly summarize the empirical evidence on the existence of economies of scale and scope. What are the policy implications of these findings?
7. Discuss Humphrey's [1987] new twist on bank cost dispersion and his measurement of economies in banking. Use Figures 11-3 and 11-4 in your discussion.
8. Using Figure 11-5, explain what happened to bank average costs over the years 1980 to 1984.
9. What is technical change and how does it become "embodied" in factor inputs? How did Hunter and Timme test for the effect of technical change on bank scale economies and what did they find?
10. Explain what FCA data are. Who collects the data, who reports, and what is unique about the database?

MATCHING QUIZ

Directions: Select the letter from the right-hand column that best matches the item in the left-hand column.

___ 1. Natural monopoly

___ 2. Scale economies

___ 3. Scope economies

___ 4. Production function

___ 5. Ray average cost

___ 6. Technical change

A. Contain account information

B. Responsiveness of change in cost to change in assets

C. Labor and physical capital

D. Undefined for multiproduct firm

E. Concept developed by Baumol

G. New twist on bank cost studies

___ 7. Hunter and Timme

___ 8. Humphrey

___ 9. HPB characteristic

___ 10. "Burden"

___ 11. Salaries

___ 12. Primary inputs

___ 13. Cost complementarities

___ 14. Gilligan, Smirlock, & Marshall

___ 15. FCA reports

___ 16. Asset cost elasticities

___ 17. Average total cost

___ 18. Cost minimization

___ 19. Bank operating expenses

___ 20. The production plants of
     banking

H. Expense control

I. Noninterest income minus
   noninterest expense

J. Major noninterest expense

K. Tested for scope economies

L. Give rise to scope economies

M. ATC declines for all outputs

N. Exhausted early in banking

O. Economies of joint production

P. $f(L,K)$

Q. Tested for embodied technical
   change

R. Held constant in most bank cost
   studies

S. Prerequisite for maximization of
   shareholder wealth

T. Drains off 20 to 40 percent of bank
   income

U. Branch banks or offices

CHAPTER 11

APPENDIX

The Tax Reform Act of 1986 and Its Effects on Commercial Banks[1]

The Tax Reform Act of 1986 (the "Act") is, by all accounts, the most significant piece of tax legislation to be enacted in 30 years. The Act is doubly significant for banks because it changes the tax law environment in which they operate. Major changes are made in the tax treatment of the interest paid and received by their customers, among other things. This appendix focuses on the changes directly affecting banks' tax treatment.

Reserve for Bad Debts

Under current law, a bank can deduct bad debts using the specific charge-off method or a reserve method (experience or percentage of eligible loans method). After 1987, the only acceptable reserve method (under current law) is the experience method. Banks using the specific charge-off method deduct bad debts in the year that specific loans are identified as worthless. Banks using the reserve method deduct the addition to their bad debt reserve (determined based on average loan losses over the last six years).

The Act eliminates any deduction under the reserve method for "large" banks, thereby forcing use of the specific charge-off method. A bank is considered a "large" bank if its assets (and those of any other members of a parent–subsidiary controlled group, in the aggregate) have an average basis in excess of $500 million for any taxable year beginning after December 31, 1986. If a bank is ever considered a large bank, it is always thereafter subject to the prohibition on use on the reserve method. Banks with assets having an average adjusted basis of up to $500 million are not subject to this change in the law and may continue to use the reserve method (experience or percentage method until the first taxable year beginning in 1988, experience method only thereafter) or the specific charge-off method.

Large banks forced onto the specific charge-off method by the Act must either (a) recapture the reserve by taking it into income over a period of up to four years, or (b) elect the cut-off method. If the bank recaptures the reserve, it does so by taking it into income 10 percent in the taxable year beginning in 1987, 20 percent in the taxable year beginning in 1988, 30 percent in the taxable year beginning in 1989, and 40 percent in the taxable year beginning in 1990. A bank may take more than 10 percent into income in the first year (as, for example, where it has a net operating

---

[1] The text of this appendix is a slightly edited-version of an article by Caproni [1987]. It is reprinted with his permission. The secondary source for Table 11-A1 is Buynak [1987].

TABLE 11-A1   New Federal Income Tax Rules Affecting Commercial Banks

Title	Old Tax Provision	New Tax Provision
Effective date		General Effective Date: Jan. 1, 1987
		Corporate Rate Cuts: July 1, 1987
Corporate tax rate	46% top rate, 4 lower rates on income up to $100,000	34% top rate, 2 lower rates on income up to $75,000
Corporate minimum tax	15% of the amount of which the sum of tax preference items exceeds the greater of $10,000 or the regular tax liability	20% alternative minimum tax; $40,000 income exemption
Bad-debt reserve	Deductible	Eliminates bad-debt tax reserve for banks with more than $500 million in assets
Tax-exempt securities	80% of municipal bond interest expense is exempt from federal taxation	100% of municipal bond interest expense is taxed
Net operating loss carryover	Losses carried back 10 years and forward 5 years	Losses carried back only 3 years, but forward 15 years
401(K)s and IRAs	401(K):$30,000 maximum IRAs: $2,000/$250 for nonworking spouse	401(K):$7,000 maximum IRAs: Limits imposed on high-income workers with pensions
Foreign tax credit	Credit determined on aggregated foreign income	Less liberal foreign tax credits, with transition provisions
Depreciation	Accelerated	Less generous write-offs, particularly for real estate
Investment tax credit	6% to 10%	Repealed

Source: Ernst & Whinney. Tax Reform—1986, An Analysis of Provisions Relating to the Financial Services Industry, E&W No. X58055; and Tax Reform—1986, An Analysis of the Internal Revenue Code of 1986, E&W No. 66196.

loss that would otherwise expire). In such case, 2/9, 1/3, and 4/9 of the balance of the reserve is recaptured in each of the succeeding taxable years. The recapture provisions are, however, suspended for any year that a bank is a "financially troubled bank," as defined in the Internal Revenue Code.

The cut-off method, if elected by the bank, requires the bank to charge any losses from (and credit any recoveries on) existing loans against the reserve (with no deduction, since the deduction was claimed when the reserve was created) until the reserve is exhausted. Any losses on existing loans in excess of the reserve will be deductible as those loans are determined to be worthless.

Interest Expense

Taxpayers are generally prohibited from deducting interest expense incurred to acquire or carry tax-exempt obligations. Under existing law, financial institutions, including banks, are not subject to this disallowance of interest expense except to the extent of 20 percent of their otherwise deductible interest expense attributable to tax-exempt obligations acquired on or after January 1, 1983.

The Act continues the 20 percent disallowance for tax-exempt obligations acquired after January 1, 1983, and on or before August 7, 1986. Obligations acquired after August 7, 1986 (unless acquired pursuant to a contract dated before September 25, 1985, or one of certain specifically identified projects, which are deemed acquired before August 8, 1986), will be subject to a 100 percent disallowance beginning with the bank's first taxable year ending after 1986. If the bank's year ends on or before

December 31, 1986, the 20 percent rule will continue to apply for that year even to obligations acquired after August 8, 1986.

The disallowed deduction is computed by allocating the bank's interest expense. The portion of the otherwise allowable interest for which no deduction is allowed is determined by multiplying the total interest by the ratio of the average adjusted bases of the tax-exempt obligations acquired after August 7, 1986, to the average bases of all assets.

There is an exception to the 100 percent disallowance rule for "qualified tax-exempt obligations," which remain subject to the 20 percent disallowance rule. A qualified tax-exempt obligation (QTEO) cannot be a private activity bond and must be designated by the issuer as a QTEO. The issuer of a QTEO cannot reasonably anticipate issuing more than $10 million in QTEOs in a calendar year and cannot designate more than $10 million in obligations as QTEOs in any calendar year.

Accounting Methods

The cash method of accounting (for income tax purposes) has been eliminated by the Act for all corporations (other than S corporations) having average annual gross receipts of more than $5 million for the three preceding taxable years. Any adjustment to taxable income caused by the change to the accrual method will be taken into account over a period of not more than 4 years.

Net Operating Loss Rules

Under present law a bank can carry a net operating loss (NOL) back to the 10 preceding taxable years and forward to the 5 taxable years following the loss year. For taxable years beginning January 1, 1987 or thereafter, all financial institutions are limited to carrying NOLs back only 3 years, but may carry NOLs forward for 15 years.

There is a limited exception to this change in the law for commercial banks. The exception permits the portion of any NOL incurred for any taxable year beginning before January 1, 1994, which is attributable to the bad debt deduction to be carried back 10 years and forward 5 years as under current law.

Alternative Minimum Tax

The new alternative minimum tax created by the Act provides that corporations must pay the greater of their regular tax or the AMT (at 20%). The AMT tax base has been expanded to include one-half of the difference between financial statement income and AMT income. In addition, accelerated depreciation on any depreciable property placed in service after 1986 is a preference item. Also included as a preference item is the amount by which the bad debt using the reserve method exceeds what the deduction would have been using the bank's actual experience. Further, tax-exempt interest on private-use bonds issued after August 1, 1986 is, considered a preference item.

Rate Reduction

The maximum federal corporate income tax rate under current law is 46 percent. The Act provides that the first $50,000 of taxable income will be subject to tax at 15 percent, the next $25,000 at 25 percent and all taxable income in excess of $75,000 subject to tax at the maximum rate of 34 percent.

Investment Tax Credit Repeal

The investment tax credit ("ITC") is repealed for any property placed in service after December 31, **1985**, unless acquired pursuant to a binding contract that was binding on the taxpayer prior to December 31, 1985, and at all times thereafter. Further, ITC carried forward into years beginning after June 30, 1987, is reduced by 35 percent. There is no modification of this reduction for years that straddle June 30, 1987. For example, a calendar year bank will have any ITC carried forward into 1987 reduced by $17\frac{1}{2}$ percent.

Other Matters

The Act has reduced the deduction for certain travel and entertainment expenses to 80 percent of the expenses incurred. Further, a meal expense is deductible only if directly related to business and the meal followed or preceded a substantial business discussion.

Conclusion

The changes made by the Tax Reform Act of 1986 will have far-reaching implications for banks. Certain favorable treatment available under existing law ceases to exist and numerous tax advantages have been eliminated.

SELECTED REFERENCES

Baumol, William J. [1982]. "Contestable Markets: An Uprising in the Theory of Industry Structure," *The American Economic Review* (March), pp. 1–15.

Berger, Allen N., Gerald Hanweck, and David B. Humphrey. [1986]. "Competitive Viability in Banking: Scale, Scope, and Product Mix Economies," Research Papers in Banking and Financial Economics (January), Board of Governors of the Federal Reserve System.

Buynak, Thomas, M. [1987]. "How Will Tax Reform Affect Commercial Banks?" *Economic Review* Federal Reserve Bank of Cleveland (Quarter 2).

Caproni, Albert III. [1987]. "Tax Reform Act of 1986: Its Impact on Commercial Banks," *Georgia Bankers Association Newsletter* (January), pp. 6–7.

Gilligan, Thomas, Michael Smirlock, and William Marshall. [1984]. "Scale and Scope Economies in the Multiproduct Banking Firm," *Journal of Monetary Economics* (13), pp. 393–405.

Humphrey, David B. [1987]. "Cost Dispersion and the Measurement of Economies in Banking," *Economic Review* (May/June), pp. 24–38, Federal Reserve Bank of Richmond.

Humphrey, David B. [1985]. "Cost and Scale Economies in Bank Intermediation" in *Handbook for Banking Strategy*, Richard C Aspinwall and Robert A. Eisenbeis, eds. New York: Wiley, pp. 745–782.

Hunter, William C., and Stephen G. Timme, "Technical Change, Organizational Form, and the Structure of Bank Production," *Journal of Money, Credit and Banking* (May), pp. 152–166.

Kolari, James, and Asghar Zardkoohi. [1987]. *Bank Costs, Structure, and Performance*. Lexington, MA: Lexington Books.

Mester, Loretta. [1987]. "Efficient Production of Financial Services: Scale and Scope Economies," *Business Review*, Federal Reserve Bank of Philadelphia, (January/February), pp. 15–25.

Willig, Robert. [1979]. "Multiproduct Technology and Market Structure," *The American Economic Review* (May), pp. 346–351.

Bank Strategic Planning in the Financial-Services Industry

ACRONYM GUIDE TO KEY WORDS AND CONCEPTS

ABA = American Bankers Association
BHC = bank holding company
CEO = chief executive officer
FSI = financial-services industry
MBHC = multi bank holding company
OBHC = one-bank holding company
ROA = return on assets
ROE = return on equity
SWOT = *S*trengths, *W*eaknesses, *O*pportunities, and *T*hreats
TRICK = *T*echnology, *R*eregulation, *I*nterest-rate risk, *C*ustomers, and *K*apital adequacy

---

JUSTICE HOLMES AND WHERE AM I GOING?

Strategic planners must ask and answer at least three important questions. One of these questions is presented in the following apocryphal story concerning one-time Supreme Court Justice Oliver Wendell Holmes. Justice Holmes, as the story goes, was riding on the (then great) Pennsylvania Railroad. The conductor, a young man, was collecting tickets. As he approached the Justice, Mr. Holmes began searching for his ticket among the various pockets of his three-piece suit. The conductor, sensing the man's frustration and recognizing him as "the" Justice Holmes, said: "Sir, I am sure that the great Pennsylvania Railroad will be glad to transport you to your destination, where you may purchase another ticket." Justice Holmes looked up at the conductor in exasperation and said: "The problem, my young man, is not where is my ticket, but where am I going?"

For strategic planners in the financial-services industry, the punch line of this story translates into: Where is the financial institution going? As a trinity, the three important questions are:

1. Where is the organization today?
2. Where is the organization going?
3. How is the organization going to get there?

The first question is a factual or audit query whereas the second and third questions involve corporate vision and corporate execution, respectively. The mere fact that these questions are being asked suggests that top management is thinking about the organization's future. Moreover, the need to "plan to plan" must come from the top of the organization; without the commitment of top management, the planning process is doomed. This chapter explores the critical issues, approaches, and techniques of strategic planning in the financial-services industry. Let us begin by looking at what strategic planning is and why it is important.

WHAT IS STRATEGIC PLANNING?

The essence of strategic planning is contained in the three questions listed above. To capture this essence and thereby define strategic planning, let us consider each question individually. First, where is the organization today? To answer this question an information system that provides relevant data for analyses of past, present, and future situations is required. Strategic planners need to know where they are before they can decide where to go and how to get there. What they need to know consists of both internal and external information. Internally, planners must know the organization's strengths and weaknesses with respect to both its financial and marketing performance. The ROE decomposition and cost analyses (introduced in the previous two chapters) provide frameworks for evaluating financial performance. Externally, managers must be aware of the opportunities and threats contained in the environment, which requires knowledge about customers, markets, regulations, and economic conditions. In addition, planners must be aware of the expectations of major outside interests (e.g., stockholders, depositors, uninsured creditors, borrowers) and inside interests (e.g., directors, top managers, middle managers, staff).

In the jargon of strategic planners, the overall process of determining where the organization is today is sometimes called "the situation audit." It is, of course, a prerequisite for planning. The cornerstone of the situation audit is SWOT analysis, where SWOT is the acronym for Strengths, Weaknesses, Opportunities, and Threats. The elements of SWOT (together let's call them the SWOT team) underlie the planning process. The situation audit and the SWOT analysis assist managers in identifying alternative courses of action and in evaluating them. The idea is to build upon or exploit strengths and opportunities and to correct or eliminate weaknesses and threats; strengths and weaknesses typically are perceived as internal factors whereas opportunities and threats are external factors.

Once the managers know where their institution is, they can decide where it should be going. In effect, a target for the organization is established. Typically, this target has a five-year time horizon and in some instances it may extend to seven or ten years. In the financial-services industry, because of increased uncertainty, a three- or four-year planning horizon probably is more realistic. Whatever the time horizon is, the strategic plan is not a one-shot deal that is to be put on the shelf to gather dust. In strategic planning, the long-run target or objective is an elusive one because it is subject to annual readjustments. Thus, strategic plans should not be rigid and static; they should be flexible so they can adapt to changing SWOT conditions and other dynamic factors.

In establishing where a financial institution is going, an articulated corporate vision is essential. In essence, this vision is an image of what the organization should look like, say, five years hence. It should contain more than platitudes about quality, pieties about competitiveness, and lengthy digressions into forecasts and projections. Instead, the corporate vision or master strategy should identify customers and services representing the bank's priorities and how the bank wishes to be positioned in those markets identified as having high priority. In short, the statement of vision is the blueprint for two of the issues in the trinity, namely, where is the organization going and how will it get there? The articulation of a master strategy or vision statement should be the responsibility of the chief executive officer (CEO) of the corporation. Since nothing is more counterproductive than to start a strategic (or short-run) planning program without the whole-hearted *involvement* of *top* management, the CEO must establish the importance of the planning process and the need to "plan to plan."

To illustrate the notion of corporate vision, consider the role played by John G. McCoy in establishing a master strategy for Banc One Corp. in Columbus, Ohio. When he took over in 1959, he envisioned building a high-quality, "Tiffany" bank, not a merely big "Woolworth" bank, out of an also-ran with $140 million in assets (see Wysocki [1984]). McCoy's approach to planning was to thrust "zealot"-style executives together with "implementer" and "control" executives. These groups engaged in "gentle confrontation" to establish Banc One's corporate vision and execution plan. One of the leading zealots at Banc One is John F. Fisher, senior vice president, who, along with other zealots, is seen as an elephant clearing new paths in consumer banking. McCoy, who retired as CEO in 1984, had a philosophical tactic of trying to hire people who are exceptional at something and giving them some room to operate. Banc One, one of the high-performance banks listed in Chapter 10, is considered a pioneer in consumer banking. As an innovator, Banc One was not afraid to break with tradition as it played an important role in the establishment of Merrill Lynch's cash management account.

Given a bank's long-run strategic target, which should be viewed as multidimensional, the next step is to focus on the alternative strategies that will best exploit its unique SWOT conditions. In brief, how is the bank going to move in the direction of its desired target? At this stage, what-if analysis, scenario planning, computer models and simulations, and other planning tools and techniques can be used to evaluate alternative strategies. Once an overall plan and specific strategy have been developed, they must be implemented *and* monitored. The monitoring part is important because the dynamic nature of the planning process requires annual revisions of most strategic plans.

By focusing on how to answer the three basic questions of strategic planning, we get a clearer idea about the *process* of strategic planning. Strategic planning is, in effect, a thought process or way of thinking about the future of one's business. To put it more formally, consider Drucker's [1974] definition of the strategic-planning process (p. 611):

> ...the task of thinking through the mission of the business, that is, of asking the question "what is our business and what should it be?" This leads to the setting of objectives, the development of strategies and plans, and the making of today's decisions for tomorrow's results. This clearly can be done only by an organ of the business that can see the entire business; that can make decisions that affect the entire business; that can balance objectives and the needs of today against the needs of tomorrow; and that can allocate resources of men and money to key results.

More succinctly, Kane [1984] says, "Allowing for alternative futures is the stuff of strategic planning." Although the "stuff" of strategic planning is indeed complex and requires detailed information flows, managers must avoid getting bogged down in picayune details. They must look at the overall "forest" and not at the individual "trees" and certainly not at the myriad of "leaves." Accordingly, strategic planners should foresee the overall effect of their financing and investment decisions. In addition, by exploring alternative futures, they are better prepared for "surprises" and how to react to them. Without strategic planning, the decision-making process becomes a black box; with strategic planning, the black box is replaced by the strategic plan.

For a large bank or BHC, the completed strategic plan should be a substantial document. A medium-sized institution should have a plan with similar content but less detail and documentation. And, for a small community bank, the strategic plan may only be an implicit one that exists in the mind of the bank's president. Nevertheless, it is important to put the plan down on paper so that it can be reviewed later. Whatever the size of the bank or BHC, the basic elements for answering the three fundamental questions of strategic planning should be similar. The extent of the planning effort will, of course, depend upon the resources committed to it.

WHY IS STRATEGIC PLANNING IMPORTANT?

Survival is the most fundamental reason for undertaking the process of strategic planning. However, since most managers want to do more than just survive (e.g., maximize some variable like stock price profits or market share, be an industry leader, be innovative), there are higher reasons for planning than just mere existence. The concept of long-range or strategic planning has been around since the early 1960s and some banks, including Irving Trust and First Chicago, started formal planning then. However, most banks have adopted the process only since the mid-1970s. In a study for the Bank Administration Institute (BAI), Binder and Lindquist [1982], concluded (p. 13):

> Finally, there is a distinct increase in long-range planning. The development is real but, overall, the results are unimpressive. Planning efforts have been poorly organized and concentrated. It may be argued that the uncertainty faced by the industry discourages and inhibits planning. However, it is precisely during periods of uncertainty that planners will be winners. That view appears to be making headway, and while it may never achieve prominence throughout the industry, it will mark the efforts of larger banks that achieve dominance and of the smaller banks that survive.

The message is a clear one: bankers who plan will have a better chance of being "winners," achieving "dominance," and, at the very least, surviving. In the rapidly changing environment of the financial-services industry of the 1980s, a banker without a strategic plan is like a chef without a recipe, a home builder without a blueprint, or a coach without a game plan. Except for blind luck, we wouldn't expect such individuals to survive in their professions, let alone be winners or achieve dominance.

WHO ARE THE STRATEGIC PLANNERS AND WHAT DO THEY PRODUCE?

Managers plan, not planners. Since the CEO is the head of the management team, he or she is the *de facto* chief of planning. As stated above, the CEO should be responsible for articulating the organization's corporate vision or master strategy. For our purposes then, managers are the *real* strategic planners and the management team is the *real* planning team. Once the primary role of annointed planners is seen as one of custody of the formal planning apparatus (i.e., of the timing, content, performance tracking, accountability, internal consistency, and environmental assumptions of the plan), it is easier to see that managers plan, not planners.

There is ample evidence that excessive and complex planning arrangements make planning an *end* instead of a *means*. The heart of the planning process should be the expression of alternatives. When planning becomes an end instead of a means, the expression process usually is strangled. Once planning is seen as a *means* and not an *end* in itself, managers are apt to be less concerned about what is the *output* of the strategic-planning process. In a competitive marketplace, the continued existence of a viable organization is *prima facie* evidence of a corporate vision that sees the business as it is today and foresees what it will be tomorrow.

THE STRUCTURE OF THE PLANNING PROCESS

One view of the structure of the planning process is depicted in Figure 12-1. Similar diagrams can be found in Steiner [1979, p. 17] and Yalif [1982, p. 26]. Figure 12-1 presents in schematic form the major points discussed in answering the three basic questions of strategic planning. To illustrate, in answering the first question (Where is the organization today?), the situation audit provides the foundation. There are three key building blocks in this first step. First, the expectations of major interests, both internal and external to the bank, must be identified. External interests include such groups as regulators, stockholders, customers, and the community or service area. Internally, the expectations of directors, managers, and staff and line employees are important. The second building block is an analysis of the environment, which also involves both external and internal considerations. The key element in this step is the SWOT analysis of the bank's strengths, weaknesses, opportunities, and threats. The third building block of the situation audit involves the compilation and analysis of the internal and external data bases. Past, present, and future marketing and financial information flows are the key elements in this step. In addition, strategic decisions require adequate information about human resources and operations.

After the situation audit is completed, the financial institution should know where it stands today *and* where it can go in the future. The next step in the planning process is to decide where to go and how to get there. By setting the master and program strategies, the organization is provided with direction and alternative routes toward its desired destination. The medium- and short-range plans and programs are the vehicles that start the organization moving on its desired strategic path. After the plan is implemented, it needs to be monitored on the basis of the decision and evaluation rules established as part of the overall plan. Finally, the plan needs to be reviewed and evaluated on an annual basis for major changes in direction. "Reviewing the plan" means much more than a cursory once-over of the hallowed document that represents a one-shot attempt to freeze in long-term objectives. Instead, it means reassessing progress toward stated goals, trying to figure out why certain targets (e.g., ROA) weren't hit, and figuring out whether that was good or bad. In addition, reviewers need to ask themselves whether external or internal changes have created a need to change the objectives or the route by which they are to be attained.

As illustrated in Figure 12-1, the planning process is preceded by the bank's plan to plan or its planning guide. In larger institutions, the plan to plan usually is set out in a document called the planning manual, which provides the basic guidelines for the bank's planning process. A bank's planning manual and the conceptualization of the planning process presented in Figure 12-1 both provide more form than substance because they provide only the structure or skeleton of the strategic-planning process.

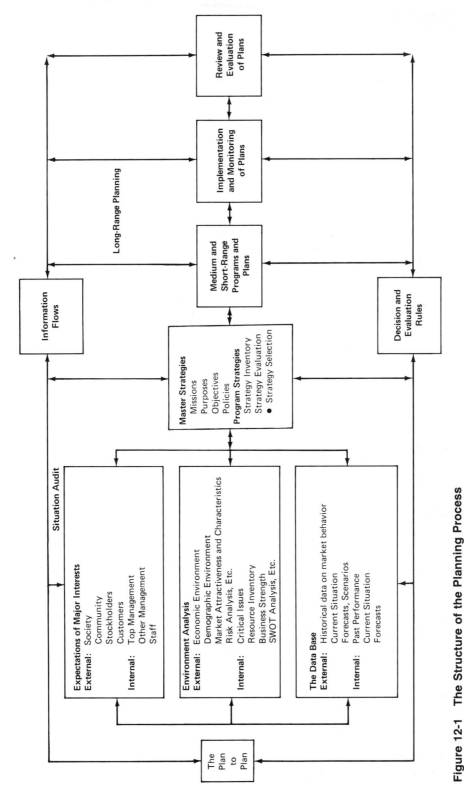

Figure 12-1   The Structure of the Planning Process

Source: Adapted from Steiner [1979], p. 17 and Yalif [1982], p. 26.

THE TRICK TO STRATEGIC PLANNING IN
THE FINANCIAL-SERVICES INDUSTRY

Since allowing for alternative futures is the "stuff" of strategic planning, how should managers go about analyzing future scenarios? Five key factors that must be considered in financial-services planning are embodied in the acronym TRICK, which stands for

T = Technology

R = Reregulation

I = Interest-rate risk

C = Customers

K = Kapital adequacy

In making timely reappraisals of evolving business options, the elements of TRICK represent five of the key factors shaping the future of the financial-services industry. The purpose of the reassessments is to make sure that market opportunities and problems opened up by changes in TRICK are explored in timely fashion. Since each of the components of TRICK is discussed in detail in other parts of the book, only a brief restatement of their importance to strategic planning is presented here.

Technology

Technology in the form of electronics, automation, and telecommunications is reshaping financial-services delivery and production. Figure 12-2, which was first shown in Chapter 1, details the changes in these processes. This metamorphosis in financial-services delivery and production is a technological representation of the evolution of money and banking from the concrete to the ethereal. The details of electronic banking are provided in Chapter 6.

Reregulation

Since the U.S. banking system is one of the most heavily regulated industries in the world, planning for the ebb and flow of the regulatory tides is imperative. In this regard, strategic planners need to search continuously for loopholes in the fabric of regulation (e.g., the nonbank-bank loophole) and to evaluate their potential profitability. Since the components of TRICK are by no means independent of each other, planners should look for ways in which, for example, new technologies could be used to circumvent burdensome federal or state regulations. To exploit such opportunities, managers must have the power and flexibility to move quickly before the "window" closes.

Interest-Rate Risk

In the area of asset-liability management (ALM), one of the key concerns is with interest-rate risk. Although strategic planners should not be concerned with the details of ALM, they need to consider the bank's overall approach to ALM and how alternative interest-rate scenarios will affect that approach. In addition, managers should plan for the use of financial futures, options, and swaps and consider duration matching to improve their techniques of portfolio management.

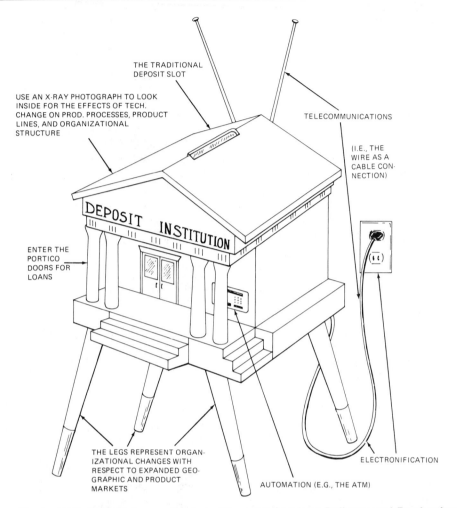

USE AN X-RAY PHOTOGRAPH TO LOOK INSIDE FOR THE EFFECTS OF TECH. CHANGE ON PROD. PROCESSES, PRODUCT LINES, AND ORGANIZATIONAL STRUCTURE

THE TRADITIONAL DEPOSIT SLOT

TELECOMMUNICATIONS

(I.E., THE WIRE AS A CABLE CON-NECTION)

ENTER THE PORTICO DOORS FOR LOANS

DEPOSIT INSTITUTION

THE LEGS REPRESENT ORGAN-IZATIONAL CHANGES WITH RESPECT TO EXPANDED GEO-GRAPHIC AND PRODUCT MARKETS

ELECTRONIFICATION

AUTOMATION (E.G., THE ATM)

Figure 12-2   The Metamorphosis in Financial-Services Delivery and Production

Source: Adapted from Kane [1983].

Customers

The competition for customers in the FSI is keen. Businesses with the best products and delivery systems are likely to win most of the battles for customers. These battles can be viewed as competitive struggle models. According to Porter [1980], the key structural features of industries that determine the strength of the competitive forces and hence industry profitability are (1) threat of entry, (2) intensity of rivalry among existing competitors, (3) pressure from substitute products, (4) bargaining power of buyers, and (5) bargaining power of suppliers. The first three factors have changed substantially in the financial-services industry over the recent past and they are expected to remain in a state of flux in the future. Managers must continually reassess the effects of these structural changes on customers and products. For example, emerging technologies might facilitate the entry of new competition into the bank's traditional markets and threaten market share. Items (4) and (5) in the list can be interpreted as the bargaining power of borrowers (buyers) and the bargaining power of depositors and creditors (suppliers)—in general, the bargaining power of customers. Strategic planners should be concerned about the long-run effects of borrowers with alternatives such as commercial paper, and uninsured depositors and creditors who seek high rates of return together with low risk (e.g., the run on Continental Illinois in 1984).

Kapital Adequacy

To expand and grow both the regulators and financial markets require that banks have "adequate" capital. Since a bank's internal capital generation is limited (i.e., $g = RR \times ROE$), access to financial markets for external capital is a prerequisite for rapid growth and expansion. Managers need to be concerned with how expansion into new markets and products will be financed. For example, if economies of scope can be found in new technologies, then new and existing products can be produced jointly with lower investment and operating costs.

DEVELOPING REASONABLE ASSUMPTIONS FOR TRICK

Managers must develop a set of reasonable assumptions for TRICK. As of this writing, except for interest-rate risk, the operative adjective would appear to be "more." That is, managers should plan for *more* innovative technology, *more* reregulation (e.g., product and geographic), *more* competition for customers, and *more* capital-adequacy supervision in the form of higher mandatory capital ratios and tougher examination of problem loans. Regarding interest-rate risk and inflation, managers must focus on "when" (not "if") the next upswing will occur. However, since the course of future interest rates is so difficult to predict, hedging and immunization plans provide important sources of protection for financial institutions.

The reasonable assumption of "more" could shift to "less" in the face of a crisis in the financial system (e.g., another Continental, a collapse of the thrift industry, or contagion from the stock market crash of 1987). A severe crisis would likely bring a call for the return to cartel banking and the imposition of 1930s-type rules without reason. The element of TRICK that is most insulated from economic and political vicissitudes is the big *T*—Technology. Innovative technology will be the driving force of TRICK for many years to come.

The purpose of developing a set of reasonable assumptions regarding TRICK is to assist top management with the task of scenario building and forecasting, which serves to highlight some of the uncertainty and strategic challenges/choices facing banks. At the minimum, important issues and uncertain paths can be identified. More specifically and completely, scenarios and forecasts regarding interstate banking, new product offerings, reregulation prospects, technological developments, financial innovations, customer bases, and competitors (among others) can be developed. By considering alternative futures, top management is better prepared to construct or choose a set of strategies for dealing with the future course of its business.

HOW TO SWOT TRICK

Strategic planners must know their institutions' strengths, weaknesses, opportunities, and threats (SWOT) with respect to the technology, reregulation, interest-rate risk, customers, and capital adequacy. Since planning is primarily concerned with determining business matters (i.e., what the business is and what it should be), customers can be viewed as the key factor in how to SWOT TRICK. In other words, SWOT needs to be tied specifically to customers, products, and delivery systems. To illustrate, money-market funds have exploited technological and regulatory opportunities (e.g., the 800 telephone number and less regulated production processes, respectively) to become viable competitors for the consumer savings dollar. In the financial-services industry, great rewards will be available to those players who make certain that market opportunities opened up by technology and competitive reregulation are exploited in a timely fashion to deliver innovative products to customers.

Financial Innovation: One Way to SWOT TRICK

To make the diffusion of financial innovations more intelligible, consider the three preliminary distinctions made by Kane [1983] with respect to (1) invention versus innovation, (2) autonomous innovation versus induced innovation, and (3) market-induced innovation versus regulation-induced innovation. Although these concepts were introduced in Chapter 5, it is worthwhile to review them briefly here.

The first distinction is one in which an invention refers to an unfolding technological opportunity whereas an innovation is a profitable application of an invention. The lag between an invention and its embodiment in an innovation is called the *innovation lag*. In the financial-services industry, technology tends to be downstreamed, after a delay, from wholesale applications to retail ones. This lag reflects the time it takes to reduce the operating costs of the new technology to a level that permits profitable application to retail customers. Thus, one way that planners can forecast future products and delivery systems at the retail level is to look at the state-of-the-art technology on the wholesale level.

The second distinction separates innovations into those that are induced by market or regulatory constraints and those that are autonomous (i.e., not caused by prior shifts in market or regulatory constraints). The third distinction classifies induced innovations into those caused by market forces and those caused by regulatory forces. Since few financial institutions operate on the cutting edge of technology, most of their innovations are induced by regulatory or market forces. The major environmental developments that drive the process of financial innovation are expressed by TRICK. During the 1970s and early 1980s, Kane argues, financial adaptation responded primarily to the T, R, and I components of TRICK. With the disinflation and increased competition of the mid-1980s, the T, R, and C components should be of primary concern to bank strategic planners.

Kane's approach provides an interesting framework for analyzing the diffusion of financial innovations. Taking his approach one step further, let's focus on some of the characteristics associated with excellent, innovative companies.[1] Looking at organizational form, innovative companies tend to have "simultaneous loose–tight properties" (i.e., they are *both* centralized and decentralized). Regarding personnel, they combine "simple form" with "lean staff" and emphasize autonomy, entrepreneurship, and productivity through people. Innovative companies recognize the importance of being "close to the customer" and "sticking to the knitting" (i.e., they never acquire a business they don't know how to run). Finally, innovative companies tend to have "a bias for action, for getting on with it," and they tend to be "hands-on, value-driven."

The really important question, which to my knowledge no one has answered yet, is:[2] How does an organization develop the "chemistry" or "corporate culture" that

---

[1] For a complete discussion of these attributes, see Peters and Waterman [1982].

[2] For an attempt, see Peters and Waterman's 1982 book, *In Search of Excellence*.

generates the excellence, innovativeness, and synergy found in the best corporations? This book doesn't have *the* answer either. Given the basic ingredients of skilled people and efficient organizational form, it is probably the pride and leadership of top management to provide quality products and service that make the difference. Kanter [1983] describes such people as *The Change Masters* (the title of her book) and defines them as "those people and organizations adept at the art of anticipating the need for, and of leading productive change" (p. 13).

Citicorp/Citibank as Innovator

On September 1, 1984, John S. Reed, at the age of 45, became Chairman of Citicorp. He succeeded Walter B. Wriston. Both of these men have been described as having "wide, expansive, and visionary minds," which no doubt is one of the reasons why Citicorp has been a leader of banking changes on the technological, regulatory, and competitive fronts. Innovative and adaptive managers and planners are key ingredients in the strategic-planning process and in getting companies to change. On his rise to the top, Reed, a technocrat with an MIT engineering degree, was responsible for cleaning up Citibank's bank-office mess and developing a systems approach to the operations of its proposed national consumer and electronic banking network. Like Wriston, Reed is expected to continue Citicorp's innovative and expansionary ways, which includes a plan to make the organization a world-wide force in investment banking, insurance, and information processing, in addition to its traditional banking activities. One of Citicorp's strategies has been to challenge or circumvent regulations that impede its progress (i.e., to SWOT the *R* in TRICK). Citicorp's approach to potential opportunities is reflected in the following statement by Wriston regarding the possibility of Citicorp acquiring Continental Illinois during the Chicago bank's 1984 liquidity crisis. "We're always interested in anything. We've had people studying all the possible scenarios" (*American Banker* [April 29, 1984], p. 22).

An Alternative View of Citibank's Innovativeness

On August 30, 1984, the editorial page of *The Wall Street Journal* carried a story (see Stabler [1984]) that lauded the stewardship of Walter Wriston as the innovative leader of Citicorp/Citibank. The article, which appeared three days before Wriston's retirement, compared the innovative changes introduced by Citibank (described as an "avalanche") to the glacier-like movements of the industry as a whole.

On September 26, 1984, Clark Bass, Chairman of the First National Bank of McAlester, Oklahoma, had the following letter to the editor of *The Wall Street Journal* published under the heading of "Performance Audit."

> Only time will determine the accuracy of your glowing article concerning the stewardship of Walter Wriston in the banking industry ... Negotiable certificates of deposit and variable-rate loans are no big deal. We even have these out here in the boondocks and have had for years. However, third world loans we don't have. The only reason the "Great Crisis" Mr. Wriston mentioned has not already occurred is that the taxpayers put up billions of dollars in order for banks like Mr. Wriston's to avoid a great crisis. One of these days the taxpayers are going to rebel against such practices, and then and only then will the true value of his leadership be determined.

As you can see, Chairman Bass has a different view of Wriston's stewardship. Most community bankers *probably* would support the view from 235 E. Choctaw rather than the one from Wall Street. In my opinion Citicorp/Citibank has been an innovator. However, when Mr. Bass raises the question of taxpayer subsidies to bail out third-world lenders (which is a different issue), he is right on target.

Citicorp's View of Winning the Financial-Services Battle

What will it take to be competitive in the financial-services industry? One view of a potential winning game plan is presented in Table 12-1. The strategy was formulated by George Vojta, a Citicorp executive. His nine-point program can be grouped into two broad categories focusing on (1) financial management and (2) customers, products, and markets. Items 1, 2, 3, 4, and 8 are financial-management factors that fit nicely into the basic income-expense statement presented in Chapter 2. These five points emphasize the importance of consistent earnings and a portfolio of earning assets that is maturity- (or duration-) balanced or hedged; flexibility to permit portfolio restructuring; maintaining ROE in the face of lower spreads by increasing asset utilization; and increasing productivity by controlling overhead costs and rewarding productivity in people. Items 5, 6, 7, and 9 focus on customers, products, and markets. The key elements in these areas stress the importance of segmentation and positioning in markets; complete and competitive products; and development of integrated businesses for the financial-services industry.

In looking at the battle for financial services, it is interesting and instructive to focus on some specific bank strategies in this area, such as: National Bank of Detroit's winning bid to be the switch for Cirrus; efforts by southern regional banks (e.g., SunTrust) to use interstate reciprocity to avoid being gobbled up; home banking experiments (Banc One of Columbus, Ohio, had one of the first); major banks selling their headquarters building and leasing it back (e.g., BankAmerica); Bankers Trust selling off branches and credit cards; and First Chicago buying credit cards from Bankers Trust. Since each of these examples fits neatly into one (or more) of the components of TRICK, the list also serves to illustrate the validity of TRICK.

TABLE 12-1   What It Will Take to Win the Financial Services Battle [a]

1. **Profitability.** A winner will be able to make a reasonable profit during any phase of the business cycle. Earning assets should be funded on a matched or hedged basis.

2. **Liquifying and Repositioning Assets.** A winner will be able to liquidate assets when they no longer suit the book or risk profile of the institution. Winners will not be acquiring assets to hold to maturity.

3. **Positive Margin.** A winner will be able to earn an adequate return on capital even with lower spreads. Losers are likely to have too much capital earning unacceptable returns.

4. **Increased Productivity.** A winner will be committed to lower nonfinancial costs, to develop new, less costly modes of distribution and to achieve higher productivity. Lower margins will necessitate low costs.

5. **Market Segmentation.** A winner will be able to identify, organize, and manage discrete market segments effectively. Winners will look to organizing discrete businesses to serve particular sets of customers.

6. **Complete and Competitive Product Lines.** A winner will be able to achieve product superiority in whatever market segments they compete. The consumer will ultimately select the best product on the market, regardless of who offers it.

7. **Structuring Integrated Businesses.** A winner will be able to organize and effectively use subsidiary businesses as an integrated unit. The key to effective management will be to know what business you are in.

8. **Restructuring Compensation Policies.** A winner will be able to pay people who get successful results. Hierarchical compensation structures will be a thing of the past for the winners.

9. **Market Position.** A winner will be able to select a market niche they can defend against all comers. This will be especially important for smaller institutions as major competitors move in.

[a] Formulated by George Vojta
Source: The Magazine of Bank Administration [July 1983].

BANK TRUST DEPARTMENTS: PLANNING A NEW IMAGE FOR THE PRODUCTS AND MARKETS OF THE FINANCIAL-SERVICES INDUSTRY

Bank trust departments have been criticized for their "marketing myopia" (see Levitt and Cunningham [1979]). By not recognizing that they belong to the financial-services industry instead of the trust industry, trust departments have been compared to the U.S. railroads of years ago, which failed to recognize that they belonged to the transportation industry instead of the railroad industry. As a result, as Heiss [1981] puts it: "The trust department of the bank doesn't enjoy an image that makes an investor want to seek the service that is available and is usually as good as he or she can get anywhere else" (p. 21).

Levitt and Cunningham [1979] have criticized trust departments for defining their business in terms of what they do as opposed to what customers need and want. Like the railroads of yesterday, they try to do a better job of what they already do instead of *also* doing what they should be doing. What they should be doing is expanding into other segments of the financial-services industry.

Figures 12-3 and 12-4 are presented to provide some insight into the markets and products available to trust departments in the financial-services industry. In Figure 12-3, the overlapping niches in the financial-services industry are depicted. The evolutionary process shown is a multistage one in which firms diversify into more and

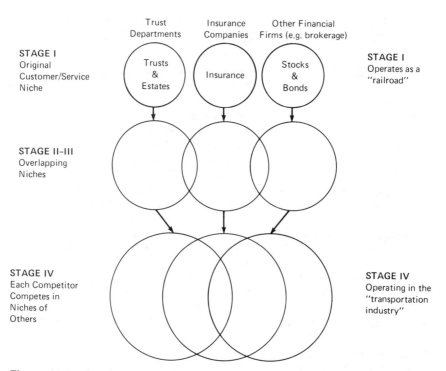

Figure 12-3   Overlapping Niches in the Financial Services Industry

Source: Levitt and Cunningham [1979], Chart 1, p. 18. Reprinted by permission.

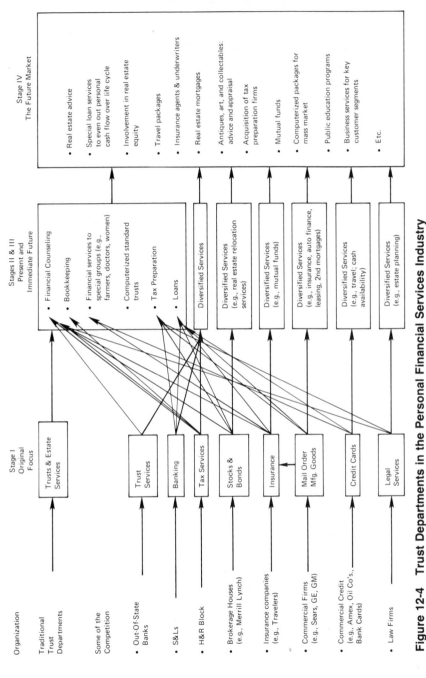

Figure 12-4 Trust Departments in the Personal Financial Services Industry

Source: Levitt and Cunningham [1979], Chart 2, p. 20. Reprinted by permission.

more products and eventually develop niches in competing markets. In a dynamic environment, firms with marketing myopia (e.g., railroads) are reluctant to change and diversify. They remain in their original customer/service niche and stagnate. In contrast, companies without the "railroad syndrome" develop new products and explore new markets.

Figure 12-4 shows some of the activities that trust departments could develop as they expand into the financial-services industry. The evolutionary process again is pictured as a multistage one in which firms expand from (railroad) tunnel vision to a cosmos view of products and markets. According to Levitt and Cunningham, the main danger for trust departments is that competitors will exclude them from product/ market niches that they should have included in their own strategies.

To pursue a process of systematic development, Levitt and Cunningham have suggested a general framework that a trust department might follow in attempting to establish itself in the financial-services industry. The strategic approach consists of four stages[3]:

1. marketing present services to present customers
2. moving to new services and new customers
3. expanding new services and new customers
4. ongoing adjustments to customers and services.

For this strategy to be successful and move the trust business into its own "transportation industry," the key factors are (1) the development of a specific strategy, (2) an understanding of the consumer, (3) interdepartmental cooperation within the bank, (4) the establishment of a "profit" tradition and culture with the trust department, (5) the removal of legislative barriers and the avoidance of requests for regulatory protection, and (6) the interest and support of the bank's CEO.[4]

In 1982, the Management Committee of the ABA's Trust Division recommended three courses of action for trust departments.[5] (1) They could basically maintain the status quo and focus on fine-tuning their specialized skills, while remaining independent of commercial banking. (2) They could plan an aggressive and innovative expansion into the financial-services industry through a mutually beneficial integration of trust and commercial banking. Or (3) they could go out of business. Regarding the last option, marketing myopia and salary issues have led some banks to spin off their trust departments.

For trust departments that want to develop the second course of action, the ABA has suggested the arrangement of banks' products and services into a four-level hierarchy (see Table 12-2). The concept behind this approach is that the whole bank is involved in a continuous flow of services from the basic ones (Level I) to the most sophisticated ones (Level IV). As customers move to the various levels of sophistication in bank products and services, they encounter and demand different skills, delivery systems, and service support from the bank.

SUCCESS FACTORS IN STRATEGIC PLANNING

In a recent BAI-Arthur Andersen & Co. study entitled *New Dimensions in Banking: Managing the Strategic Position*, strategic success factors for banks were grouped into four categories: (1) general management, (2) marketing, (3) technology/operations,

---

[3] See Levitt and Cunningham [1979], pp. 23–27.

[4] Ibid., pp. 28–33.

[5] See "Special Report: Trust" [1982], p. 38.

TABLE 12-2   Four Levels of Sophistication in Bank Products and Services

Level and Description	Products and Services	Marketing Implications
Level IV: Products and services that require detailed knowledge of the customer's family or personal situation sound judgment, and good technical knowledge.	Complex estate planning ←——— Complex financial planning Complex tax planning consulting Fiduciary services	Customer contact staff add value through detailed knowledge of the customer, sound judgment, and good technical knowledge. ↑
Level III: Products and services that require detailed technical knowledge or access to superior judgmental advice.	Full service broker-dealer ←——— services (equities, bonds, options, government/government agencies, commodities, financial futures, currency futures, tangibles) Commingled asset management Simple financial planning Simple personalized insurance planning Simple tax plan Packaged tax shelters Other limited-partnership investments Lending as part of a financial plan Complex tax-return preparation Real estate brokerage Real estate management Personal services (bill payment, completion of Medicare forms, arrangement of health-care services, etc.)	Customer contact staff add value through personal contact and input of judgment into decisions. ↑ Comprehensive customer information to support customer contact staff and free them up for personal contact and for decision making.
Level II: Products and services that require a low level of judgment or that can be delivered on an impersonal packaged basis.	Money market funds Other mutual funds Directed insurance products Annuity products Discount brokerage services Variable rate mortgages Standard tax return preparation Comparative shopping services	Opportunity to combine individual products and services into integrated modularized packages to establish a systems-based customer relationship. Services can be delivered electronically, and comprehensive statements can be prepared.
Level I: Commodity products and services that can be understood and evaluated on an unaided basis by most consumers.	Checking/NOW accounts Savings accounts Auto and home insurance Term life insurance Auto loans Fix-rate mortgages Credit/debit cards Revolving credit facilities Second mortgages	

Source: ABA Banking Journal [February, 1982], p. 39. Reprinted by permission.

TABLE 12-3   Strategic Success Factors for Banks

General Management

  Management quality
  Management evaluation and motivation
  Risk management
  Responsiveness to change

Marketing

  Product offerings
  Customer service
  Segmentation
  Marketing skills

Technology/Operations

  Technological readiness
  Distribution

Finance

  Capital Access
  Pricing
  Asset and liability management

Source: Arthur Andersen & Co. [1983], Exhibit 1, p. 5.

and (4) finance. These categories and their major subheadings are listed in Table 12-3. Under the category of general management, the importance of quality, evaluation and motivation skills, and responsiveness to change have been stressed. In the area of risk management, the risks associated with the elements of TRICK make for a convenient and relevant risk-analysis framework. The risk–return preferences of managers and planners with respect to diversified portfolios of traditional and nontraditional banking services are important here.

To some observers, the financial-services industry is becoming increasingly a market- and customer-driven business. For these managers, marketing, with its emphasis on product offerings, customer service, segmentation, and market-research skills, has increased in importance. In fact, some banks (e.g., Mellon National) regard their strategic-planning process as being a marketing-driven one. The five *P*s of marketing in a strategic-planning framework are

1. product,
2. place,
3. price,
4. promotion, and
5. people.

Given the organization's people, a bank may pursue a marketing strategy based upon one or more of the other factors. For example, of the ten largest U.S. banks, Chemical Bank has stressed the product approach, especially its cash management; Citibank and BOA have emphasized place; Bankers Trust has bet on price (underselling); and Manny Hanny has concentrated on advertising and promotion. Since the above characterizations of certain banks are at best incomplete, they are presented only for illustrative purposes. Needless to say, some large banks have no focus, whereas others benefit from well-articulated visions in which strategies in all five areas are pursued.

The third and fourth success factors, technology/operations and finance, respectively, are embodied in the *T*, *I*, and *K* elements of TRICK. Moreover, the four strategic success factors in Table 12-3, like the components of TRICK, are not independent; they interact and must be coordinated for the strategic-planning process to be successful.

IMPORTANT QUESTIONS FOR STRATEGIC PLANNERS

In a 1984 issue of the *American Banker* [April 25, 1984, pp. 4, 6], Jack W. Whittle, a leading consultant to financial-services firms, discussed some criteria for judging a bank's preparedness for the future. In the area of strategic planning, his firm focuses on the following questions:

1. Has the bank conducted market research to determine the demographic makeup of its market, the financial products and services consumers want, and its image in the marketplace vis-à-vis other banks and competitors?
2. Has the bank developed marketing strategies for segmenting its retail customers and determining the appropriate mix of products for each segment?
3. Does the bank have a mechanism in place for keeping abreast of relevant legal and regulatory developments?
4. Has the bank developed, or is it in the process of developing, a central information file to maintain greater control over retail banking relationships?
5. Does the bank have a cohesive long-range strategy for surviving in a geographically deregulated marketplace? Is the bank going to be a local, regional, or nationwide organization?
6. Has the bank developed strategies to maintain or improve its stock price to ward off unwanted takeovers?
7. If the bank is not a subsidiary of a holding company, has management examined the advantages and disadvantages of the holding-company structure?

Whittle's approach to strategic planning focuses on four elements for shaping a bank's future under deregulation:

1. internal staff, with its strengths, weaknesses, and potential
2. the marketplace
3. the uniqueness of the customer base
4. most important, the battle plans set by all of the bank's different competitors.

A PLANNING APPROACH FOR SMALL BANKS

Managers of small banks may feel overwhelmed by the task of developing a strategic plan. However, once they start *thinking*, rather than *feeling*, about the project, the task will appear more manageable. Dunahee [1983] has suggested an approach and framework for small banks to follow to get the planning process started. The first step is to organize the planning process by appointing an officer to shepherd staff and data through (1) the planning schedule and (2) the thinking through of the plan. These last two points are illustrated in Figure 12-5. In Figure 12-5A, a sample planning schedule is presented with steps, deadlines, and responsibilities specified. In Figure 12-5B, the process of thinking through a brief sample plan is summarized. Dunahee [1983] suggests (like Whittle) organizing the logical flow of the plan into a series of questions about the bank's performance and its future. Only when the answer to the questions

Panel A
The planning schedule

Step	Deadline	Responsibility
(1) Preparation for planning day	August	Planning officer (manager of product development)
(2) Planning day	September	All senior vice-presidents, the CEO, and the president
(3) First draft of plan	October	Planning officer
(4) Middle-management input	October	Sampling of line and staff officers
(5) Final draft of plan	November	Planning officer
(6) Communicate plan Officer dinner meeting Branch, dept. meetings	November	Everybody
(7) Develop action plans	December	Branch managers and department heads
(8) Develop budgets	December	Branch managers and department heads
(9) Follow-up action plans and budgets	Quarterly	CEO

ORGANIZE PLANNING by appointing an officer to shepherd staff and data through a process like this— then think it through as below, says the author.

Panel B
Thinking planning through

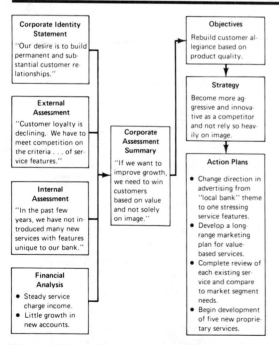

Figure 12-5   A Planning Approach for Small Banks

Source: Dunahee [1983], p. 189, reprinted by permission.

are in dispute are research and analysis (which are scarce resources in small banks) needed. This approach emphasizes thinking, which is what the planning process is all about, and urges smaller banks to match their desire for data with their resources.

Presidents of community banks need to put their plans (i.e., their thoughts about the future of their organizations and their businesses) down on paper so they can review them later. The plan, in this case, could be as simple as a short list of objectives. Top managers will be better off if they do some formal communicating among themselves regarding their objectives at least once a year.

A SURVEY OF STRATEGIC PLANNING: WHO, WHAT, WHEN, AND HOW?

In December 1983, the Federal Reserve Bank of Atlanta published in its *Economic Review* the results of a nationwide survey on strategic planning in financial institutions (Gup and Whitehead, [1983]). The findings of this survey are summarized in Tables 12-4 to 12-7. A total of 449 financial institutions participated in the survey, consisting of 217 commercial banks, 114 S&Ls, 68 MBHCs, and 50 OBHCs. Although the banks in the sample were representative of the general population and included banks from each of the 50 states, the S&L sample was not representative, with only four S&Ls having over $500 million in assets. Thus, the survey provides only limited information on planning by large thrifts.

The institutions with no formal planning process (i.e., without a written plan) were 78 banks (36 percent), 51 S&Ls (45 percent), three MBHCs (4 percent), and one OBHC (2 percent). Together these nonformal planners were 25 percent of the sample. Conversely, 75 percent, or three out of four of the institutions surveyed had a formal (written) planning process. As shown in Table 12-4, planning is positively related to asset size for banks and S&Ls. Almost all BHCs had a formal planning process and only

TABLE 12-4 Percentage of Respondents with a Formal Planning Process[a]

Asset Size	Banks	S&Ls	BHCs	OBHCs	Total
$0–$50m	54%	38%	—	100%	48%
50–100	60	38	—	80	57
100–500	58	70	100	100	68
500–1B	74	100	100	100	82
1B and over	90	100	95	100	95
TOTALS for all sizes	64%	55%	96%	98%	70%

[a] This table reflects all 449 respondents.
Source: Federal Reserve Bank of Atlanta.

TABLE 12-5 Objectives of Strategic Planning

Objectives	Past	Future
Provide a competitive return on assets and equity	1	1
Growth of market share	2	3
Survive in a more competitive environment	3	2
Improve prestige in financial community	4	8
Reduce portfolio risk	5	6
Achieve a competitive advantage	6	5
New technology for customer use	7	4
New technology for internal use	8	7

Source: Federal Reserve Bank of Atlanta.

TABLE 12-6   Techniques of Strategic Planning

Techniques	Rank
Portfolio analysis	1
Brainstorming	2
Corporate financial simulation models	3
Cash flow	4
Market research	5
Conferences	6
Risk and decision analysis	7
Futuristic projections	8
Panel consensus	9
Product Information Market System (P.I.M.S.)	10
External on-line data banks	11
Product life cycle	12
Leading indicator analysis	13
Time series analysis	14
Econometric analysis	15
Regression analysis	16

Source: Federal Reserve Bank of Atlanta.

TABLE 12-7   Critical Issues of the 1980s

1. Deregulation
2. Potential interstate banking
3. Government regulation
4. Productivity
5. Innovation and creativity
6. Trend toward market segmentation
7. Changes in communication technology
8. Growth in the use of strategic planning concepts
9. Inflation
10. Slow economic growth in most industrialized countries
11. Growth of entrepreneurial management
12. Focus on cash flow

Source: Federal Reserve Bank of Atlanta.

four of them (3.4 percent) had no written plan. Quite surprisingly, three of the four organizations without a written plan were MBHCs with assets over $1 billion. Although the findings show that 75 percent of the institutions surveyed are now planning, only 20 percent of them have been doing it for more than five years. Evidently the TRICK(y) competitive environment of the 1980s has promoted the planning process.

The objectives of strategic planning as seen by the survey respondents are presented in Table 12-5. The Number One objective is a competitive ROA and ROE. Survival, market share, and new technology for internal use are other important future objectives. Who sets these objectives and operating targets? The survey findings indicate that the boards of directors and CEOs are mainly responsible for setting corporate objectives, with directors playing a greater role in the smaller institutions and CEOs being more important in the larger organizations. Not surprisingly, the responsibility for planning rests with a team consisting of senior officers, or some combination of top management and the planning department. When only one individual is the planner, it is usually the president. Most plans are revised on an annual basis (45.6 percent of the respondents), although 24.2 percent indicate they revise "continuously."

The techniques of strategic planning used by the survey respondents are presented in Table 12-6. Of the 16 techniques reported, the top five were (1) portfolio analysis (i.e., evaluating the composition and value of assets in current or would-be portfolios), (2) brainstorming, (3) simulation models, (4) cash-flow analysis, and (5) market research. The more sophisticated the statistical technique is, the *less* important it tends to be as a planning tool. Since planning is a way of thinking, it is not surprising that it requires more "brain time" than "CPU time."

To illustrate, when Irving Trust, one of the first banks to undertake the planning process in the mid-1960s, started planning, its focus was on a numbers-oriented, bottom-up line format. Later, the bank shifted its focus to a combination of brainstorming and research under the aegis of its Executive Committee.

Regarding future trends, the survey respondents were asked to rank the critical issues of the 1980s. The findings are presented in Table 12-7. The first three items are really only variations on one issue—regulation. Using some liberal interpretations, these issues can be mapped into the TRICK framework as follows:

Element of TRICK	Critical Issue (from Table 12-7)
Technology (T)	4, 5, 7
Reregulation (R)	1, 2, 3
Interest-rate risk (I)	1, 9, 12
Customers (C)	1, 2, 4, 5, 6, 7, 8, 11
Kapital adequacy (K)	3, 12

The mappings here are either a "cause" or "effect" relationship. To illustrate, using the customers or *C* element, customer competition is stimulated by deregulation (1) and potential interstate banking (2); to maintain customers in a competitive environment requires, among other things, productivity (4), innovation and creativity (5), market segmentation (6), technology (7), strategic planning (8), and entrepreneurial management (11).

What is the bottom line on strategic planning? The overwhelming majority of planners find it beneficial in terms of three objectives: (1) establishing implementing, and attaining missions and objectives, (2) improving decision-making, and (3) assessing the competitive environment. Financial institutions with effective strategic-planning processes are more likely to develop the characteristics of successful firms. In this regard, four common traits shared by major American corporations with a history of success are the following.

1. They emphasize innovation, particularly in the area of technology.
2. They feature an entrepreneurial managerial style that keeps their organizational structures lean and flexible for prompt action.
3. They view employees as associates, their most valued long-term asset, rather than as management's adversaries.
4. They share an ongoing, sharply defined attention to marketing strategy that focuses on their comparative advantages.[6]

These four characteristics tend to be grounded in a corporate culture or identity that makes the company—for consumers, employees, and management—more than the

---

[6]*Economic Review*, Federal Reserve Bank of Atlanta [June, 1984], p. 11.

sum of its products. "This identity reflects a widespread pride in belonging not just to a winning team but to a socially significant and useful institution, seeking to make a profit in the long run."[7]

TEN FORCES RESHAPING AMERICA

Strategic planners need to think about the future. The March 19, 1984, issue of *U.S. News & World Report* provided some food for thought in the article, "Ten Forces Reshaping America." According to the report, the ten critical factors are

1. a maturing society
2. lure of the Sun Belt
3. the computer revolution
4. foreign competition
5. women on the move
6. the rise of minorities
7. the decline of the superpowers
8. government under fire
9. the education boom
10. medical miracles.

The forces having the greatest effect on the reshaping of the financial-services industry are 3, 4, and 8. By broadening the interpretation of "foreign competition" to include "foreigners" who have invaded the banking industry (e.g., Merrill Lynch, Sears) in search of customers, and interpreting "government under fire" as the process of reregulation, the three critical factors are simply the *T*, *R*, and *C* components of TRICK. In addition, from a marketing perspective, which is an important part of the strategic-planning process, the importance of a maturing society, lure of the Sun Belt, women on the move, rise of minorities, the education boom, and medical miracles cannot be overlooked when a financial institution decides what products to produce and how to market and deliver them.

ANOTHER VIEW ON STRATEGIC PLANNING: BOBBY KNIGHT ON GENERAL PATTON

Bobby Knight and General George Patton are two renowned strategic planners in two vastly different games. Knight is the highly successful basketball coach at Indiana University (successful both because his teams win *and* his players tend to graduate and become productive citizens). Patton was a highly successful general in the Big One, World War II. Knight, who coached at West Point from 1965 to 1971 (six seasons with a record of 102–50 and three National Invitational Tournament bids), also is a student of military history. In a 1984 interview, Knight had these words on Patton the military strategist:

> Patton had an incredible ability to see what to do and how to do it.... I admire him because of his ability to grasp what he was confronted with and then beat it.... he recognized opportunities and developed strategies—we'll use this road because it takes us here and that one *can't*—and the way he was willing to get down in the mud and direct tanks.[8]

[7] *Ibid.*

[8] *Playboy* [August 1984], p. 62. In other parts of the interview, Knight has some less flattering words to say about Patton.

Patton knew how to SWOT the enemy long before some B-school whiz coined the term. To some managers, the competitive nature of the financial-services industry of the 1980s may look like "the Big One" all over again and they may wish to retire. To others the battle cry will be, "We have not yet begun to fight!"

CHAPTER SUMMARY

Since this chapter began with a "railroad story," it is appropriate to end it with one also. The popular analogy today is to compare today's banks (and other financial-services firms) with the transportation revolution faced by the railroads following World War II. The ill fate of the railroads was established when they failed to recognize (i.e., have the vision to see) that they were operating in the *transportation industry* and not in the *railroad industry*. Bankers who fail to recognize that they are operating in the *financial-services industry* (FSI) and not in the *banking industry* will eventually receive the same fate as the railroads, or at best wind up as the caboose on the FSI express. To put it more elegantly, consider John Naisbitt's statement from his book, *Megatrends* [1982, p. 92]:

> Unless banks reconceptualize what business they are in, they will be out of business. In the next few years, we will witness many bank mergers and bank failures. When I was a young person growing up with the memories of the Depression all around me, bank failures meant the end of the World. Today bank failures only mean that, like the railroaders, some bankers are just waiting around for their virtue to be rewarded. There will still be abundant banking services available from many kinds of institutions.

Five key factors that are important for strategic planners to think about are captured by the acronym TRICK, which stands for *T*echnology, *Re*regulation, *In*terest-rate risk, *C*ustomers, and *K*apital adequacy. Managers of financial-services firms need to develop reasonable assumptions regarding the future of each of the elements of TRICK.

LIST OF KEY WORDS, CONCEPTS, AND ACRONYMS

American Bankers Association (ABA)	One-bank holding company (OBHC)
Bank holding company (BHC)	Railroad syndrome
Chief executive officer (CEO)	Return on assets (ROA)
Financial-services industry (FSI)	Return on equity (ROE)
How is the bank going to get there?	Strategic planning
Innovation	SWOT
Invention	TRICK
Major forces shaping America	Where is the bank going?
Multibank holding company (MBHC)	Where is the bank today?
Planning (for community banks)	

REVIEW/DISCUSSION QUESTIONS

1. What is strategic planning? Discuss the who, when, and how of the planning process. What is the plan to plan and how important is it?
2. How would you attempt to SWOT TRICK?

3. Contrast and compare the following pairs of terms:
   a. *invention* versus *innovation*
   b. *induced innovation* versus *autonomous innovation*
   c. *market-induced innovation* versus *regulation-induced innovation*
4. Is John Reed likely to carry on the "Wriston tradition" at Citicorp/Citibank? Explain. Evaluate Wriston's stewardship as Citicorp's chief.
5. Should a strategic plan be considered an exact forecast of future interest rates, earnings, and other financial variables? Why or why not?
6. Discuss the major findings of the Federal Reserve Bank of Atlanta's survey of strategic planning by financial institutions. What's wrong with its S&L sample?
7. What is the railroad–banking analogy?
8. What are the three important questions of strategic planning? Discuss the ten forces reshaping America in this context.
9. Discuss the "marketing myopia" of bank trust departments. What do they have to do to avoid the "railroad syndrome"?
10. One of the strategic success factors for banks is "finance." Explain and discuss the critical elements of this success factor.
11. What business are banks in? What are the megatrends in banking?

MATCHING QUIZ

Directions: Selet the letter from the right-hand column that best matches the item in the left-hand column.

___ 1. Justice Holmes	A. Former West Point coach
___ 2. John Reed	B. Battlefield planner
___ 3. Walter Wriston	C. CEO of Citicorp at age 45
___ 4. John McCoy	D. Allowing for alternative futures
___ 5. John Fisher	E. Where now, where going, how to
___ 6. Clark Bass	F. Retired innovator
___ 7. Planning trinity	G. Competitive ROA and ROE
___ 8. SWOT team member	H. Marketing
___ 9. Banc One	I. Financial innovation
___ 10. Stuff of strategic planning	J. Savings account
___ 11. Planners	K. Money market fund
___ 12. Internal capital generation	L. Full service broker-dealer
___ 13. One way to SWOT TRICK	M. Fiduciary service

___ 14. Bank trust departments

___ 15. Level I product

___ 16. Level II product

___ 17. Level III product

___ 18. Level IV product

___ 19. The five Ps of

___ 20. Primary objective of planning

___ 21. Leading technique of planning

___ 22. A critical issue of the 1980s

___ 23. Major force shaping America

___ 24. Bobby Knight

___ 25. George Patton

___ 26. John Naisbitt

N. High performance innovator

O. Where am I going?

P. Former chairman Banc One

Q. Banc One zealot

R. Resides at 235 E. Choctaw

S. Opportunities

T. $ROE \times RR$

U. Government under fire

V. Managers

W. Marketing myopia

X. Portfolio analysis

Y. Megatrends

Z. Deregulation

APPENDIX

A Banker's Profile: First Union Corp's "Mr. Fix-It" Turns His Attention to Georgia Operation[1]

Harald Hansen was dining in Ireland in the summer of 1986 when he got a call from Edward Crutchfield, Jr.

It was Hansen's fifth career-changing call in 15 years from the chairman of First Union Corp. of Charlotte, N.C.

This time, Crutchfield, deep into merger talks with executives of First Railroad and Banking Company of Georgia, needed to know in a hurry if Hansen would be willing to move to Atlanta.

Crutchfield wanted a battle-tested point man to coordinate the complex task of consolidating First Railroad into First Union. He'd already picked Hansen in the 1970s and early 1980s to run First Union's credit card division, its trust division, its branches in the Charlotte region and finally the corporation's world banking division.

"My pattern has been to work in two- to five-year periods to get some part of the bank humming," Hansen, First Union's chief executive in Georgia, said last week. "This may be my last project."

Hansen, 56, the son of a founder of Duke University Medical School and a former U.S. Marine Corps officer, entered banking by accident. Then 25 years ago he quit the business, only to be lured back by people like Crutchfield.

"I once hated the banking business. I thought it was the pits," Hansen said. "I couldn't do anything without asking someone else. In the Marine Corps you did what you could and stood accountable for it. I didn't think banking let you spread your wings."

There is little in Hansen's family background to suggest that he'd wind up a banker.

In the early 1900s, his grandfather was Denmark's ambassador to Peru. His father left Peru in 1918 with $25,000 and a desire to go to the best medical school in the world.

Without much knowledge of English, Oscar Hansen enrolled in Johns Hopkins University. After graduation he practiced medicine and taught at the school. In 1926, he and nine other doctors left Johns Hopkins to start Duke University Medical School and Duke Medical Center. His later career focused on leukemia research.

For a while, the doctor's son was enrolled in a pre-med program at Duke, but he switched to psychology and political science. When the younger Hansen was unable to

---

[1] This appendix was written by Peter Mantius, a staff writer for *The Atlanta Journal and Constitution*. The article appeared in the paper on December 7, 1987 (pp. 1E and 10E) and is reprinted with the author's permission.

get a draft deferment to go to graduate school, he decided to become an officer in the Marines.

But it was 1955, the aftermath of the Korean War, and the next Marine officers' school was full. Concerned that he might be drafted before the next class started, Hansen dodged to Iceland for four months. He met his wife, Betsy, there before returning to enter the next Marine class.

After leaving the Marines in 1959, Hansen took a job with a High Point, N.C., company that bought receivables of other companies at a discount. Hansen was a sophisticated collections agent.

When an executive of Central Carolina Bank in Durham, N.C., home of Duke University, asked him to start a commercial credit department, Hansen agreed. That's when he decided that banking wasn't challenging enough.

He moved to Raleigh, N.C., to work for a company that bought credit card receivables from high-fashion retailers. He hooked up with Crutchfield when First Union bought the firm in the late 1960s.

First he was called to Charlotte to help steady First Union's weak credit card business. He began by charging off $3 million of a $30 million portfolio.

Three years later, Crutchfield asked him to take over the corporation's sleepy trust department. Hansen brought in talent to the investment management division and then turned to improve sales.

In 1976, Hansen moved into the bank's headquarters office in Charlotte, which was struggling at the time amid fierce competition from Wachovia Bank and NCNB National Bank. Eventually he ran the retail branches in a region that included Charlotte.

In 1983, Crutchfield asked Hansen to head First Union's world banking unit. The company stopped lending to foreign companies and began beefing up loan production offices in Richmond, Baltimore, Atlanta, Tampa and Nashville—cities that could become important once interstate banking became legal.

"Ed has watched Harald over the years manage a lot of different groups and be successful," said Sid Tate, First Union's chief executive officer in South Carolina and the former head of its Atlanta bank.

Crutchfield's willingness to delegate big decisions apparently helped Hansen grow out of his sour opinion about the banking business.

Less than two months before Crutchfield called him in Ireland, Hansen had volunteered to move from North Carolina if an interstate acquisition required his high-powered management expertise.

Hansen arrived at the Georgia bank—now named First Union Corp. of Georgia—as an executive vice president. While Walton K. Nussbaum was chief executive officer and Charles Presley was chairman, few doubted that Hansen was Crutchfield's man on the scene.

Recently, the company announced that Presley would retire, Nussbaum would step up to chairman and Hansen would take over as chief executive officer. The changes occurred with a minimum of corporate infighting.

But that doesn't mean all aspects of the merger have gone smoothly.

Hansen said the biggest surprise has been the questionable quality of the Atlanta loan portfolio.

Many of loans were made to thinly capitalized companies, and at times clients were allowed to borrow to pay their interest payments, he said.

But the most challenging part of Hansen's project so far has been merging 17 separate banks into one nationally chartered bank based in Atlanta.

When it was acquired, First Railroad had assets of $3.6 billion—making it the fourth-largest in Georgia—and the most extensive statewide banking franchise outside Atlanta.

However, the merger of the 17 banks has caused unwanted waves in several communities and First Union has lost its No. 4 spot to Bank South Corp.

"First Union's style of management is so radically different than First Railroad's was that sometimes the banking public sees it as a negative," one banking industry official said. "They're so centralized while First Railroad was so decentralized. That's one reason we've had so many groups looking for new charters."

Former First Railroad officers or local directors have applied for new bank charters in Roswell, Norcross, and Pine Mountain. They plan to compete head-to-head with First Union branches in their towns.

First Union is in the process of phasing out between 500 and 1,000 jobs in cities and towns outside Atlanta. In Columbus, for example, about 80 of 250 First Union jobs will go. Many of those positions are in loan collections.

But First Union is growing in Atlanta as fast as it cuts back elsewhere. It is building a new processing center in south Atlanta and its downtown headquarters is nearly overflowing.

Looking forward, Hansen said First Union would like to build a "signature building" in Atlanta. He also foresees a time when more than half of the Georgia bank's assets will be from Atlanta, compared with less than one-third today.

That kind of growth in Atlanta will require a sophisticated corporate lending effort. To build that, the company assigned Benjamin P. Jenkins III, 43, former chief executive of the company's South Carolina bank, to be president of First Union National Bank of Georgia, reporting to Hansen.

"I put in an order for Ben," Hansen said. "He's the best commercial banker I've ever been associated with. He wanted to come to Atlanta."

SELECTED REFERENCES

Allen, Pat. [1984]. "Managers Build Many-Hued Strategies for Success." *Savings Institutions* (January), pp. 42–47.

Arthur Andersen & Co. [1983]. *New Dimensions in Banking: Managing the Strategic Position.* Chicago: Bank Administration Institute.

Aspinwall, Richard C. [1982]. "Prospects for Competition in Markets for Consumer Financial Services." In *Strategic Planning for Economic and Technological Change in the Financial Services Industry.* Federal Home Loan Bank of San Francisco.

Austin, Douglas V., and Thomas J. Scampini. [1984]. "Long-Term Strategic Planning." *The Bankers Magazine* (January–February), pp. 61–66.

———. [1983]. "A Guide to Short-Term Strategic Planning." *The Bankers Magazine* (November–December), pp. 62–68.

Bedwell, Donald, and Melinda Dingler. [1984]. "High Performance: How Do We Achieve It?" Federal Reserve Bank of Atlanta *Economic Review* (June), pp. 10–17.

Benston, George J., ed. [1983]. *Financial Services: The Changing Institutions and Government Policy.* Englewood Cliffs, NJ: Prentice-Hall.

Bierman, Harold, Jr. [1980]. *Strategic Financial Planning.* New York: The Free Press.

Binder, Barrett F., and Thomas W. F. Lindquist. [1982]. *Asset/Liability Management at U.S. Commercial Banks.* Chicago: Bank Administration Institute.

Byars, Lloyd L. [1984]. "The Strategic Management Process: A Model and Terminology." *Managerial Planning* (May–June), pp. 38–44.

Cocheo, Steve. [1983]. "Which New Services Are for Your Bank?" *ABA Banking Journal* (May), pp. 228, 232.

"Consumer Goods Marketing and Banking Strategies." *Bankers Monthly Magazine* (April 15), pp. 16, 22.

Cravens, David. [1984]. "Developing Market-Driven Strategies for Financial Institutions." *The Bankers Magazine* (March–April), pp. 32–38.

Drucker, Peter F. [1974]. *Management: Tasks, Responsibilities, Practices.* New York: Harper & Row.

Dunahee, Michael H. [1983]. "Small Banks Can Have Better Plans Without Big-Bank Staffs." *ABA Banking Journal* (October), pp. 187–189.

Fannin, William, and Carol B. Gilmore. [1984]. "Managing with Deregulation: Management's New Challenge." *Managerial Planning* (July–August), pp. 28–31.

Flax, Steven. [1984]. "The Toughest Bosses in America." *Fortune* (August 6), pp. 18–23.

Frieder, Larry A. [1983]. "Banking's New Peer Group." *Bankers Magazine* (September–October), pp. 76–82.

Gregor, William T. [1984]. "Strategic Planning of Consumer Financial Services." In *The Emerging Financial Industry: Implications for Insurance Products, Portfolios, and Planning,* Arnold W. Sametz, ed. Lexington, MA: Lexington Books.

Gup, Benton E. [1979]. "Begin Strategic Planning by Asking Three Questions." *Managerial Planning* (November/December), pp. 28–31, 35.

Gup, Benton E., and David D. Whitehead. [1983]. "Shifting the Game Plan: Strategic Planning in in Financial Institutions." Federal Reserve Bank of Atlanta *Economic Review* (December), pp. 22–33.

Hart, N. Berne. [1984]. "Strategic Planning: Responsibility of the CEO." *The Magazine of Bank Administration* (March), pp. 74–78.

Holmberg, Stevan R., and H. Kent Baker. [1982]. "The CEO's Role in Strategic Planning." *Journal of Bank Research* (Winter), pp. 218–227.

Hubler, Myron J., Jr. [1983]. "Financial Planning: A Case Study." *Managerial Planning* (July/August), pp. 41–46.

Johnson, Keith D. [1981]. "Interest Margin Variance: An Aid for Fund Managers." *Managerial Planning* (November/December) pp. 26–29.

Kane, Edward J. [1984]. "Strategic Planning in a World of Reregulation and Rapid Technological Change." In *The Banking Handbook,* Richard C. Aspinwall and Robert A. Eisenbeis, eds. New York: Wiley.

——. [1984a]. "Technological and Regulatory Forces in the Developing Fusion of Financial-Services Competition." *Journal of Finance* (July), pp. 759–772.

——. [1983]. "Metamorphosis in Financial-Services Delivery and Production." in *Strategic Planning for Economic and Technological Change in the Financial-Services Industry.* San Francisco: Federal Home Loan Bank of San Francisco, pp. 49–64.

Kanter, Rosabeth Moss. [1983]. *The Change Masters: Innovation for Productivity in the American Corporation.* New York: Simon & Schuster.

Karkut, Carol T. [1983]. "The Growing Importance of Fee Income in Strategic Planning." *The Magazine of Bank Administration* (January), pp. 20–24.

Kauss, James C. [1987]. "A Guide to Strategic Planning for Banks," *Bank Administration* (August), pp. 18–19.

Kilzer, James R., and Timothy A. Kurtz. [1984]. "Strategic Plans Enable Managers to Tackle Change, Meet New Goals." *Savings Institutions* (July), pp. 97–103.

Klein, Hans N. [1982]. "How Well Does Your Banker Plan for the Future?" *Managerial Planning* (January/February), pp. 17–20.

Krane, Robert A. [1983]. "Let's Plan Our Future, Not Stumble Into It." *ABA Banking Journal* (July), pp. 43–48.

Lee, David R. [1981]. "Interest-Rate-Sensitivity Analysis (IRSA): A Bank Planning Approach to the Interest-Rate Cycle." *Managerial Planning* (March/April), pp. 16–22, 37.

Leveson, Irving. [1982]. *The Future of the Financial Services Industry.* New York: Hudson Institute.

Levitt, Theodore, and Scott Cunningham. [1979]. *Marketing Myopia in the Trust Business.* Washington, DC: American Bankers Association.

Metzger, Robert O., and Susan E. Rau. [1982]. "Strategic Planning for Future Bank Growth." *The Bankers Magazine* (July–August), pp. 57–65.

Nadler, Paul S. [1984]. "Banking's Next 100 Years." *Bankers Monthly Magazine* (January 15), pp. 13–15.

Naisbitt, John. [1982]. *Megatrends.* New York: Warner Books.

"New Breed of Strategic Planner." [1984]. *Business Week* (September 17), pp. 62–68. (A) *New Decade in Banking.* [1981]. Toronto: The Canadian Bankers Association.

Olson Research Associates. [1984]. *The Community Bank Financial Performance Guide.* Washington, DC: American Bankers Association.

Peters, Thomas J., and Robert H. Waterman, Jr. [1982]. *In Search of Excellence.* New York: Harper & Row.

Porter, Michael E. [1980]. *Competitive Strategy: Techniques for Analyzing Industries and Companies.* New York: The Free Press.

Prasad, S. Benjamin. [1984]. "The Paradox of Planning in Banks." *The Bankers Magazine* (May–June), pp. 77–81.

Reilly, Robert F. [1982]. "Planning for an Acquisition Strategy." *Managerial Planning* (March/April), pp. 36–42.

Revell, Jack, and Paul. Barnes, [1984]. "The New Technology and Financial Institutions." *Managerial Finance* (Vol. 10, No. 1), pp. 1–5.

Salem, George M. [1984]. "Ten Ideas to Help You Cope, Adapt, and Prosper." *ABA Banking Journal* (February), pp. 28.

Sapp, Richard W. [1980]. "Banks Look Ahead: A Survey of Bank Planning." *The Magazine of Bank Administration* (July), pp. 33–40.

Sapp, Richard W., and Robert E. Seiler, [1981]. "The Relationship Between Long-Range Planning and Financial Performance of U.S. Commercial Banks." *Managerial Planning* (September/October), pp. 32–36.

Scherer, F. M. [1984]. *Innovation and Growth: Schumpeterian Perspectives.* Cambridge, MA: The MIT Press.

Soter, Arthur P. [1984]. "What Will It Take for Banks to Succeed in a Free Market? A Security Analyst's View." *The Magazine of Bank Administration* (January), pp. 37–40.

"Special Report: Trust." [1982]. *ABA Banking Journal* (February), pp. 38–43.

Stabler, Charles N. [1984]. "Wriston Set Off an Avalanche in a Glacier-like Industry." *The Wall Street Journal* (August 30), p. 18.

Steiner, George A. [1979]. *Strategic Planning: What Every Manager Must Know.* New York: The Free Press.

Synergy in Banking in the 1980s. [1982]. Washintgon, DC: American Bankers Association.

Vilardi, Vivienne E. [1981]. "Planning in the Financial Services Environment." *Managerial Planning* (May/June), pp. 6–8.

Wallerich. Peter K., and Gail H. Wham. [1983]. "Strategic Planning Isn't Just for the Giants." *ABA Banking Journal* (October), pp. 184–185.

"Want to Win? Then Adapt to New Competitive Ties." *Savings Institutions* (July), pp. 156–157.

Wark, David. [1982]. "Strategic Balance Sheet Management: Simulation Versus Optimization." *The Magazine of Bank Administration* (July), pp. 38–40.

Weisler, James B. [1986]. "Planning for Success: Back to Basics," *The Magazine of Bank Administration* (July), pp. 19–21.

Whittle, Jack W. [1984]. "Criteria for Judging Your Bank's Preparedness for the Future." *American Banker* (April 25), pp. 4, 6.

Williamson, Mick. [1984]. "Information Technology and Financial Institutions." *Managerial Finance* (Vol. 10, No. 1), pp. 6–10.

Wood, D. Robley, and R. Lawrence La Forge. [1980]. "The Evolution and Current State of Profit Planning Systems in Large U.S. Banks." *Managerial Planning* (May/June), pp. 28–31.

———. [1979]. "The Impact of Comprehensive Planning on Financial Performance." *Academy of Management Journal* (September), pp. 516–526.

Wright, Bruce J. [1983]. *Total Financial Planning*. New York: American Management Association.

Wright, Don. [1981]. *Banking: A Dynamic Business*. Richmond, VA: Robert F. Dame.

Wysocki, Bernard, Jr. [1984]. "Executive Style." *The Wall Street Journal* (September 11), pp. 1, 12. First of a five-part series.

Yalif, Anat. [1982]. "Strategic Planning Techniques." *The Magazine of Bank Administration* (April), pp. 22–26.

———. [1982]. "The Process of Strategic Planning in Banking." *Managerial Planning* (May/June), pp. 19–24.

CHAPTER 13

Asset-Liability Management (ALM)

ACRONYM GUIDE TO KEY WORDS

ALCO = asset-liability-management committee
ALM = asset-liability management
GAP = dollar or funds gap = $RSA - RSL$
NII = net interest income
NIM = net interest margin
ROA = return on assets
ROE = return on equity = $ROA \times EM$
RSA = rate-sensitive asset
RSL = rate-sensitive liability

INTRODUCTION

In the novel *Firefox* (and the subsequent movie starring Clint Eastwood), Americans hijack a Soviet jet fighter. The plane is unique because its guns can be fired by the pilot's thoughts. That is, the pilot sees a target, thinks that it should be destroyed and, bang, it is. The linkage between the thought and the action is in the minicomputer in the pilot's helmet where the mere thought of shooting the target is transmitted through it to the trigger mechanism in the plane's weapons. Instant destruction. A foxy machine, indeed.

To succeed in today's TRICK(y) environment of the financial-services industry, bank managers need Firefox-type helmets that can make instantaneous duration adjustments in their portfolios the second that changes in interest rates are perceived—a bit of hyperbole, but you get the idea. Since the Fed's "Saturday Night Massacre" of stable interest rates on October 6, 1979, portfolio rebalancing has required asset-liability managers to be gymnasts. As a result bank managers don't have to exercise after work because they spend their days doing "gapnastics" (i.e., vigorous gap management).

Jane Fonda, and lots of other celebrities, have exercise books, records, and tapes designed primarily to make them money and as a by-product to keep faithful practitioners in shape. This chapter describes the "gapnastics" that ALM managers must learn to keep their portfolios in shape. ALM can be viewed as the first step in implementing the bank's strategic plan. Now that you are warmed up, we can get into the rigors of gapnastics.

THE ROLE AND OBJECTIVE OF ALM

From the previous chapter, we know that allowing for alternative futures over the horizon of two to five years is the stuff of strategic planning. Allowing for alternative liquidity and interest-rate scenarios over the next 12 months is the stuff of asset-liability management (ALM). Viewed in the context of strategic planning, ALM is the *first step* in moving the organization in the direction of its long-run target. The importance of ALM is highlighted by Binder and Lindquist's [1982] study conducted for the Bank Administration Institute in which they focused on a detailed analysis of the asset-liability and funds-management strategies of 60 U.S. commercial banks, consisting of 25 regional banks and 35 smaller banks. They report that there is strong agreement among bankers that the asset-liability management committee (ALCO) "... is the single most important management group and function in the bank."[1] The importance and function of asset-liability management is captured by the three-stage approach to balance-sheet management introduced in Chapter 1.

Focusing on Table 13-1, we can see that asset-liability management involves a global or general approach (Stage I) that requires coordination of the various specific

**TABLE 13-1   Balance-sheet Management:
A Three-Stage Approach**

Stage I (General)	
Asset management	Liability management
	Capital management
Stage II (Specific)	
Reserve-position management	Reserve-position liability management
Liquidity management	Generalized or loan-position liability management
Investment management	Long-term debt management
Loan management	
Fixed-asset management	Capital management

Stage III (Balance sheet generates the income-and-expense statement

   Profit = Revenue − Interest Cost − Overhead − Taxes

Policies to Achieve Objectives:
1. Spread management
2. Control of "burden"
3. Liquidity management
4. Capital management
5. Tax management
6. Management of off-balance-sheet activities

Definition: Balance-sheet or asset-liability management involves a global or general approach (Stage I) that requires coordination of the various specific functions (Stage II) to achieve the bank's desired policy objectives. The essence of the process is the planning, directing, and controlling of the levels, changes, and mixes of the various balance-sheet accounts. Although the focal variables of ALM are NIM and its variability, the overall objectives are to maximize ROE and to minimize fluctuations in ROE.

---

[1] Rose [1982], p. 1. Although the term asset-liability management connotes a slightly narrower focus than overall balance-sheet management, the terms are used interchangeably in this text.

functions (Stage II) to achieve the bank's desired policy objectives (Stage III). The tools of asset-liability management include information systems, planning models, simulation or "scenario" analysis, monthly reviews, and special reports. In essence, asset-liability management can be viewed as an "intermediate-term" planning function (3 to 12 months) designed to move the bank in the direction of its long-run plan (2 to 5 years) while maintaining the flexibility to adapt to short-run (monthly) changes. In addition to the *planning* aspect of asset-liability management, *direction* and *control* of the levels, changes (flows), and mixes of assets, liabilities, and capital are integral parts of overall balance-sheet management.

The gospel according to finance theory is that managers should maximize the value of the firm. The two key commandments in this religion are simple directives: (1) maximize return and (2) minimize risk as measured by the variability of return or profitability. For ALM managers or the ALCO, these directives translate into maximize net interest margin (NIM) and minimize its potential variability. These focal variables are, of course, only symptoms of the bank's underlying balance-sheet structure. The planning, directing, and controlling of balance-sheet structure and gaps represent the heart of ALM. Although NIM is the immediate focal variable of ALM, managers must not lose sight of ROE, ROA, and EM. In this broader view, capital, noninterest income and expense, tax strategies, and strategic choices regarding products, markets, and bank structure all must be linked to ALM. Moreover, since $ROE = ROA \times EM$, the overall objectives of ALM should be to maximize ROE and to minimize its variability. As shown in Table 13-1, six policies to achieve these objectives are (1) spread or NIM management, (2) control of burden, (3) liquidity management, (4) capital management, (5) tax management, and (6) management of off-balance sheet activities (e.g., loan commitments and lines of credit).

With respect to the elements of TRICK, ALM managers are most concerned about *I* or interest-rate risk, as it has a direct link to NIM. Since NIM is the major source of bank profits and since profits are the major source of bank capital, the *K* component of TRICK (recall that we use the German spelling of *Kapital* to complete the TRICK acronym) ranks second in order of concern to ALM managers. Finally, since ALM must be coordinated with the bank's strategic plan, ALM managers must keep abreast of developments with respect to the *T*, *R*, and *C* components of TRICK (i.e., with respect to technology, reregulation, and customers).

RETHINKING ALM STRATEGIES IN THE AFTERMATH OF CONTINENTAL

The first nine months of 1984 were not good ones for banking firms, especially the money-center BHCs. This period witnessed the *de facto* failure and subsequent government bailout of Continental Illinois, regulatory crackdowns on First Chicago and BankAmerica, and widespread concern about the international-debt situation. Confidence in the banking system reached its nadir during the summer with the rescue of Continental on July 26, 1984. However, by the end of the fourth quarter of 1984 the system appeared healthy and bouncing with life. What happened during the fourth quarter of 1984 is that the big banks (and other banks too) had strong earnings that enabled them to build up their capital positions. James McDermott, a bank-stock analyst with Keefe, Bruyette & Woods, stated: "I'm not saying that we're out of the woods completely. But," he added, "the strong profitability in the fourth quarter has enabled banks to build up their balance sheets, and this has diminished the degree of concern with the safety-and-soundness issue. It puts the banks on a firmer footing."[2]

Behind the symptoms of the distressed banks of the 1980s, one sees bad loans, large bets on interest rates, rapid growth, aggressive liability management, lack of controls and checks and balances, errors in judgment, and (in some cases) dishonesty. Continental's situation, because of its prominence as a bank in the top ten, is the most intriguing. In testimony before the Senate banking committee, Volcker [1984] described the situation as follows (p. 11):

> The problems of Continental Bank essentially reflected serious weaknesses in the domestic loan portfolio of a bank that had engaged in aggressive growth and lending practices for some time, including heavy involvement in participations in energy loans of the Penn Square Bank that failed two years ago. As other credit losses surfaced and earnings pressures continued, market sources of funding were reduced and the bank became heavily dependent on discount window borrowings during the spring. As the atmosphere surrounding the bank deteriorated and threatened to disturb markets more generally, the supervisory authorities, together with a group of other major banks, provided a massive financial assistance program pending a more permanent solution.

One day after Volcker's statement, a more permanent solution, in the form of a $4.5 billion nationalization of Continental, was arranged.

The two major portfolio risks that banks face are credit risk and interest-rate risk. Regarding the interaction of these risks, Volcker went on to say (p. 12):

> In a period of rapid economic and credit expansion, there can be temptations to relax prudent credit standards in an effort to maximize growth. With deposit markets deregulated, there may be a perception by individual banks that added funds can be raised as needed in domestic or foreign markets by bidding rates higher to fund larger and larger loan portfolios—and that loan rates can be raised as fast as deposit rates. But the aggregate supply of funds is ultimately not really inexhaustible; confidence must be maintained, and high and volatile interest rates can undermine the creditworthiness of weaker borrowers.

As a result of Continental's debacle, other big banks began to rethink their ALM strategies, especially with respect to the aggressiveness of their liability management. In this regard, the chief economist of Republic Bank in Dallas stated: "We are going back to the drawing board now. Our strategic plans have always assumed that marginal growth could be funded effortlessly abroad ... Now we see that money may not always be tappable."[3]

AN OVERVIEW AND HISTORICAL PERSPECTIVE OF ALM

To understand the importance of efficient ALM for modern commercial banks, a brief historical perspective is useful. During the 1940s and 1950s, banks had lots of low-cost funds available in the form of demand deposits and saving deposits. The basic managerial problem was what to do with these funds. Hence, the emphasis during this period was on asset management. During the 1960s funds started to become less plentiful as corporate treasurers began economizing on cash balances. At the same time, the economy was prospering due to the Kennedy tax cut and then the Johnson Administration's attempt to fund both social programs and the war in Vietnam. As a result, loan demand was strong. To finance the growth of loans, banks turned to

[2] As quoted by Daniel Hertzberg in *The Wall Street Journal* [January 17, 1985], p. 10.
[3] As quoted in *The Wall Street Journal* [August 7, 1984], p. 35.

managing their liabilities. Thus, during the 1960s and early 1970s, liability management was the dominant approach to bank balance-sheet management. *Liability management* simply refers to the practice of buying money through CDs (both domestic and foreign, i.e., Eurodollar CDs), fed funds, and commercial paper to fund profitable loan opportunities. Since banks were described as taking these purchased funds and lending them out at profitable spreads, the term *spread management* also became popular around this time. During the 1970s, inflation, volatile interest rates, and a severe recession in the middle of the decade caused banks to concentrate more on the management of both sides of their balance sheets. The technique of managing both assets and liabilities together became known as *asset-liability management* (ALM). An insightful view of ALM is that it simply combines the portfolio management techniques of the previous three decades (i.e., asset, liability, and spread management) into a *coordinated* process. Thus, the central theme of ALM is the coordinated management of the bank's entire balance sheet, rather than a piecemeal approach.

During the 1980s, the dynamic process of change with respect to the components of TRICK has accelerated even faster. As a result, ALM is becoming even more important and harder and harder to do successfully. Although ALM is a relatively new short-run planning tool, it is evolving from the simple idea of maturity-matching assets and liabilities across various time horizons to include more sophisticated concepts such as duration matching, variable-rate pricing, and the use of interest-rate futures, options, and swaps. Despite these technical developments, ALM still is an art and not a science. Since there are no black boxes or easy solutions to ALM, banks are attempting to develop systematic approaches to the process. Moreover, given the diversity of the banking industry with respect to money-center banks, regional banks, and community banks and the uniqueness of local banking markets, the ALM process is somewhat different for each bank.

HOW MUCH REPRICING CONTROL DO ALM MANAGERS ACTUALLY HAVE?

In the risk–return framework for overall bank performance presented in Chapter 10, the notion of controllable and noncontrollable factors was first introduced. Because of regulations, customer relationships, and market conditions, there are certain balance-sheet items that are subject to some degree of discretionary control, at least in the short run, and others that are beyond such control. In the context of ALM, "control" refers to the ability to reprice. The major problem faced by the ALM managers of depository institutions, and especially by the managers of thrifts, is *l*iabilities *r*epriced *b*efore *a*ssets (LRBA). If an asset or liability can be repriced, then it is subject to ALM control.

Because they typically have very short maturities (i.e., 24–72 hours), federal-funds transactions and repurchase agreements are subject to considerable discretionary control and can be used either to dispose of or to generate funds. For large banks, the most important source of discretionary funds is, of course, large negotiable CDs. In general, the easier a bank's access to money-market sources of funds, the more discretion it will have in the management of its funds. For example, such items as Eurodollar borrowings or issues of commercial paper are available only to the largest banks or BHCs. However, as Continental's liquidity crisis clearly demonstrated, without the confidence of the impersonal marketplace, there is no guarantee that purchased funds always will be available.

On the asset side of the balance sheet, in addition to Fed funds and repos, discretionary assets would include unpledged government securities, trading account securities (i.e., securities held solely for market-making activities), and those variable-rate loans that can be repriced. Keep in mind, however, that customer relationships and the practice of making loan commitments have taken much of the discretion and flexibility out of bank's loan portfolios, especially in the short run. One exception to this is loans to brokers and dealers for the purpose of carrying securities; these are call loans, payable on demand and subject to short-run control. Keep in mind that reducing an asset is just as much a source of funds as increasing a liability.

To summarize, only those assets and liabilities that are under the bank's short-run control can be the instruments of asset-liability management. In general, managers in large banks have more instruments with greater control and flexibility than those in small banks. In addition, small banks are less likely to have access to off-balance-sheet activities such as interest-rate futures to use as hedging tools. Thus, the real dual-banking system puts small banks at a disadvantage when it comes to managing their assets and liabilities.

NET INTEREST MARGIN AND ITS DECOMPOSITION

The immediate performance focus of asset-liability management is interest-rate risk and return as measured by a bank's net interest margin. On a tax equivalent basis,[4] net interest margin is defined as

$$NIM = \frac{\text{(Tax-Equivalent Interest Revenue} - \text{Interest Expense)}}{\text{Earning Assets}} \qquad (13\text{-}1)$$

Since the numerator of Equation 13-1 is simply net interest revenue, the formula can be rewritten as shown in Equation 13-2.

$$NIM = \frac{\text{Net Interest Revenue}}{\text{Earning Assets}} \qquad (13\text{-}2)$$

Alternatively, by removing the parentheses in Equation 13-1, rearranging, and letting EA = earning assets, we have:

$$NIM = [\text{Interest Yield on } EA) - [\text{Interest Cost of } EA] \qquad (13\text{-}3)$$

Since Equation 13-1 is expressed on a tax-equivalent basis, formulas 13-2 and 13-3 should be interpreted similarly. Using 1987 FDIC data for all insured commercial banks, the "spread" shown in Equation 13-3 was 3.92 percent (= 9.59% − 5.67%).

The conceptual effects of NIM on overall bank performance are depicted in Figure 13-1. The level and variability of a bank's NIM are the primary determinants of its overall risk–return position. A bank's NIM in turn is a function of the interest-rate sensitivity, volume, and mix of its earning assets and liabilities. That is,

$$NIM = f(\text{Rate, Volume, Mix}) \qquad (13\text{-}4)$$

The variability of net interest margin (or risk of ALM) is determined by the rate, volume, and mix variances of interest revenue and interest expense.

---

[4] To convert tax-exempt interest revenue to a tax-equivalent basis simply divide the dollar amount by $(1 - t)$, where t is the bank's marginal tax rate, and add it to the taxable interest revenue. For example, if a bank has total interest revenue of $1,000 consisting of $800 of taxable revenue and $200 of nontaxable revenue with $t = .40$, then tax-equivalent interest revenue is $800 + $333 = $1,133, where $333 = $200/(1 - .4)$.

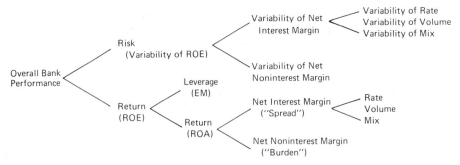

Figure 13-1   The Performance Focus of Asset-Liability Management: Net Interest Margin

Definitions: Net interest margin ("spread") = net interest revenue/earning assets, where net interest revenue = tax-equivalent interest revenue − interest expense. Net noninterest margin (net overhead or "burden") = (noninterest revenue − noninterest expense)/earning assets. Earning assets = total assets − cash and due − fixed assets − other assets.

Within the banking industry, NIMs vary considerably, as illustrated by the following FDIC data for insured commercial banks for the second quarter of 1987:

Total Assets ($ millions)	Average Net Interest Margin	Number of Banks
Under 100	4.44%	11,212
100 to 300	4.40	1,864
300 to 1,000	4.50	523
1,000 to 5,000	4.24	255
5,000 or more	3.77	73
Ten largest banks	3.12	10
ALL BANKS	3.92	13,937

Since the largest banks operate in loan and deposit markets substantially more competitive than the local ones in which community banks compete, large banks have lower net interest margins. This phenomenon is reflected by the dramatic drop-off in NIM beyond the $1 billion size class, and is most noticeable for the ten largest banks.

To get a better picture of net interest margins for the largest banks/BHCs, consider the data presented in Tables 13-2 and 13-3. Using data from Citicorp's Competitor Analysis, Table 13-2 shows net interest revenue (or income) and net interest margins for Citicorp and its competitors for the third quarters of 1983 and 1984. For the latter date, and excluding Continental, the NIMs ranged from 2.68 to 4.11 with a competitor mean of 3.20, up four basis points from the previous third quarter.

In Table 13-3, the focus is on the composition of Citicorp's net interest revenue and its "burden." The last column shows that Citicorp's burden as a percent of its net interest revenue (before provision for loan losses) declined from 48.94 in 1981 to 35.51 in 1987. Such a trend is a favorable one, of course, as all banks need to reduce the burden placed on net interest revenue, and hence on NIM, ROA, and ROE. However, if loan quality, as reflected by provision for loan losses, is included in net interest revenue (see note *b* in Table 13-3), the picture is quite different. In this case, the ratio of burden to net interest revenue rose from 54.94 percent in 1981 to 60.49 percent in 1986. Moreover, given Citicorp's $3 billion provision for loan loss in the

TABLE 13-2   Citicorp's Competitor Analys
Net Interest Revenue and Net Interest Mar

	Net Interest Revenue ($ Mi Taxable Equivalent Bas		
	3rd Qtr 1984	3rd Qtr 1983	Perc chal
Citicorp	$1,109	$979.0	13.3
BankAmerica	1,071	937.0	14.3
Chase Manhattan	652.0	606.0	7.6
Manufacturers	504.9	433.0	16.6
Morgan	368.9	353.8	4.3
Chemical	427.5	375.9	13.7
Continental Ill.	—	212.1	—
Bankers Trust	253.8	218.4	16.2
First Chicago	257.4	193.2	33.2
COMPETITOR AVERAGE			15.1%

[a] Net interest revenue (taxable equivalent basis) annualize
Source: Competitor Analysis Third Quarter 1984. Citicorp.

368   Part IV   Asset Management

TABLE 13-4   Analysis of Chang
Interest Revenue (Taxable Eq

In Millions
Loans—com
Loans—c
Federa

TABLE 13-3   Citicorp's Net Interest Revenue and "Burden," 1981–1987

Year	(1) Interest Revenue	(2) Interest Expense	(3) = (1) − (2) Net Interest Revenue[b]	(4) Noninterest Revenue	(5) Noninterest Expense	(6) = (5) − (4) Burden	(7) = (6)/(4) Burden/NIR
1981	$16,658[a]	$14,179	$2,783	$1,574	$2,936	$1,362	48.94%
1982	16,173	12,647	3,999	1,595	3,398	1,803	45.09
1983	15,197	11,154	4,543	1,840	3,757	1,917	42.20
1984	18,194	13,875	4,319	2,300	4,456	2,156	49.92
1985	19,474	14,028	5,446	3,030	5,517	2,487	46.67
1986	19,224	13,096	6,128	4,272	6,875	2,603	42.48
1987	21,994	15,528	6,466	5,994	8,290	2,296	35.51

[a] All figures in millions except the last column.
[b] Before provision for loan losses. For the years 1981 through 1987, the loan-loss provision ($millions) were 305, 473, 500, 619, 1,243, 1,825 and 4,410 respectively.
Source: Citicorp Annual Report and Form 10-K [1983 and 1987].

second quarter of 1987 and $4.4 billion for all of 1987, the ratio skyrocketed to 103.7 percent, a reflection of the cost of the LDC crisis.

THE EFFECTS OF RATE, VOLUME, AND MIX ON NET INTEREST MARGIN AND REVENUE

The combined effects of rate, volume, and mix determine a bank's net interest margin. Given the interest-rate volatility of the 20-year period 1965 to 1985, banks have shown that they can live with volatile rates, if they position their portfolios correctly with respect to the volume and mix of their resources. Focusing on the net-interest-revenue part of NIM, let's examine the various accounts that make up this key element. The analysis is illustrated using changes in Citicorp's net interest revenue for the years 1981 to 1983 as shown in Table 13-4. Assuming that each of the accounts (e.g., commercial loans) is homogeneous, the net change in the account revenue can be decomposed into a change due to change in volume and a change due to change in rate. Thus, for example, in 1983 revenue from commercial loans decreased by $1,268

...es in Citicorp's Net
...uivalent Basis)

	1983 vs. 1982			1982 vs. 1981		
	Increase (Decrease) due to Change in:			Increase (Decrease) due to Change in:		
	Average Volume	Average Rate	Net Change[a]	Average Volume	Average Rate	Net Change[a]
...mercial	$ 297	$(1,565)	$(1,268)	$ 859	$(1,446)	$ (587)
...onsumer	776	(82)	694	481	23	504
...funds sold & resale	197	40	237	114	(35)	79
...reements						
...vestment securities	(17)	(30)	(47)	(221)	43	(178)
Trading account securities	(3)	(56)	(59)	(54)	16	(38)
Lease financing	(4)	(4)	(8)	(11)	41	30
Interest-bearing deposits	(157)	(388)	(545)	(91)	(196)	(287)
Total interest revenue	$1,089	$(2,085)	$ (996)	$1,077	$(1,554)	$ (477)
Deposits	$ 556	$(2,167)	$(1,611)	$ 591	$(1,677)	$(1,086)
Funds borrowed	251			96	(542)	(446)
Total interest expense	$ 807	$(2,300)	$(1,493)	$ 687	$(2,219)	$(1,532)
NET INTEREST REVENUE	$ 282	$ 215	$ 497	$ 390	$ 665	$ 1,055

[a] Rate/volume variance is allocated based on the percentage relationship of changes in volume and changes in rate to the total "Net Change."
Source: Citicorp Annual Report and Form 10-K [1983], p. 56.

million, consisting of $297 million due to volume variance and $1,565 million due to rate variance. Note that most of the rate variance in net interest revenue is due to two accounts: commercial loans and deposits. For Citicorp, most of the funds in these accounts are floating- or variable-rate instruments.

To illustrate the calculations performed in Table 13-4, consider the following example. Suppose that account revenue, volume, and rate are defined as R, V, and r, respectively, and that they have initial values of $1000, $10,000, and .10, respectively. Since $R = V \times R$, the one-period change in revenue[5] (ΔR) is

$$\Delta R = V\Delta r + r\Delta V + g_v g_r Vr \qquad (13\text{-}5)$$

where g_v is the growth rate of V and g_r is the growth rate of r. Alternatively, using average values for V and r (i.e., $\overline{V}$ and $\overline{r}$), the change in revenue[6] also can be written as

$$\Delta R = \overline{V}\Delta r = \overline{r}\Delta V \qquad (13\text{-}6)$$

The first term on the RHS of 13-6 represents one way to calculate the average-volume figure in Table 13-4 and the second term represents the average-rate figure. If next period's account parameters are $V = $15,000$ and $r = .12$, then, using 13-6, the change in revenue is

$$\Delta R = .02(12,500) + .11(5,000)$$
$$= 250 + 550$$
$$= 800$$

[5] Equation 13-5 is simply the difference between $[(1 + g_v)V(1 + g_r)r]$ and Vr, where the bracketed term is next period's revenue. Note that $\Delta r = g_r r$ and $\Delta V = g_v V$.

[6] If you are mathematically inclined, show that Equations (13-5) and (13-6) are identical; otherwise, accept it on faith.

where 250 is the average-volume component of the net change (31.25) and 550 is the average-rate component (68.75). Note that $V = (10{,}000 + 15{,}000)/2$ and $r = (.10 + .12)/2$. Alternatively, using 13.5, the change in revenue is

$$\Delta R = .02(10{,}000) + .10(5{,}000) + .5(.2)(10{,}000) .10$$
$$= 200 + 500 + 100$$
$$= 800$$

In this case a decision must be made regarding the allocation of the cross-product term (i.e., what the note in Table 13-4 calls the rate/volume variance) of 100 between volume variance and rate variance. Using 13.6, the rate/volume variance was divided equally due to the averaging effect. Based on the percentages implied by using 13-6, the allocation would be 30 to average volume (or rate variance) and 70 to average rate (or volume variance) for totals of 230 and 570, respectively.

INTEREST-RATE SENSITIVITY AND GAP MANAGEMENT

Net interest revenue and net interest margin are symptoms of asset-liability management. Consistent with our analysis throughout this book, we want to get behind the symptoms to the causes of the good or bad performance. Our analysis so far has indicated that rate, volume, and mix are the key determinants of net interest revenue and net interest margin.

The actual management of a bank's assets and liabilities focuses on controlling the "gap" between its rate-sensitive assets (RSA) and its rate-sensitive liabilities (RSL), where a rate-sensitive instrument is one which Binder [1980a] says "...can mature or be priced upward or downward within the next 90 days or fewer" (p. 44). A bank's rate-sensitive instruments are the discretionary ones discussed above (i.e., Fed funds, repos, CDs over $100,000, variable-rate loans, etc.); they are the instruments of ALM. Some terminology used in ALM is summarized in Table 13-5.

Gap Terminology and Definitions

A bank's dollar or funds gap is measured by

$$GAP = RSA - RSL \tag{13-7}$$

TABLE 13-5 Asset-Liability Management Terminology

GAP[a]	Book	Funding	Price
Negative GAP ($RSA < RSL$)	Short book	Short funded	Liabilities repricing before assets (LRBA)
Zero GAP ($RSA = RSL$)	Matched book	Match funded	Neutral position
Positive GAP ($PSA > RSL$)	Long book	Long funded	Assets repricing before liabilities (ARBL)

Multinational banks/BHCs have global or worldwide books consisting of a domestic book and a foreign or Euro book. Clearly, the coordinated management of a global book makes the task of ALM much more complicated for multinational organizations.

[a] Although the GAP may be measured on the basis of maturity, the preferred measure is duration. See Chapter 17 for the details of duration analysis.

If a bank has a zero gap (i.e., $RSA = RSL$), then it has matched the maturity of its assets and liabilities. Thus, one approach to asset-liability management is a maturity-matching strategy.[7] The objective of this strategy is to maintain a zero gap or a gap ratio of 1, where the gap ratio is defined as RSA/RSL. This ratio is important so let's give it a formula number:

$$\text{Gap Ratio} = RSA/RSL \qquad (13\text{-}8)$$

Binder and Lindquist [1982] report that community and small regional banks attempt, in theory at least, to achieve maturity balance. In practice, however, these banks tend to have negative gaps (i.e., more rate-sensitive liabilities than rate-sensitive assets).

A zero-gap position does not eliminate completely the risk of interest-rate movements (i.e., such a position is not a perfect hedge). The problem is that the movements of asset rates (e.g., the prime rate) and liabilities rates (e.g., the CD rate) are not synchronized perfectly. Changes in loan rates, because of their administered nature, tend to lag behind changes in market rates, especially around turning points in the interest-rate cycle. This phenomenon holds back the growth of bank earnings during upswings but cushions the decline in earnings during downswings. In addition to this lag problem, there are volume and mix changes that occur over the interest-rate cycle that make a zero-gap position difficult to obtain and, if obtainable, a less than perfect hedge.

A second gap-management position is one in which RSA exceeds RSL. The dollar and ratio definitions for this position, which is described as a positive gap or asset-sensitive position, are

$$RSA - RSL > 0 \qquad (13\text{-}9)$$

$$\frac{RSA}{RSL} > 1 \qquad (13\text{-}10)$$

For example, a bank with RSA of $100 million and RSL of $50 million has a dollar gap of $50 million and a gap or sensitivity ratio of 2. A positive gap is desirable when the yield curve is shifting from a flat position to a negative or humped shape.

A third gap-management position is one in which RSL exceeds RSA. Traditionally, this negative-gap position has been the normal one for depository institutions because they borrow short and lend long. Given an upward-sloping yield curve, such as characterized most of the 1950s and 1960s, a negative gap is a profitable (arbitrage) position because banks borrow in a low-cost, short-term market and lend in a higher-yielding, longer-term market. A negative gap or liability-sensitive position has the following dollar and ratio definitions:

$$RSA - RSL < 0 \qquad (13\text{-}11)$$

$$\frac{RSA}{RSL} < 1 \qquad (13\text{-}12)$$

When interest rates are rising, a negative gap involves considerable amounts of liquidity risk and interest-rate risk. The classic example of how damaging a negative gap can be during periods of high and volatile interest rates is reflected by the plight

---

[7] The technique of duration matching is discussed in Chapter 17.

TABLE 13-7   The Time Horizon of Gap Management

Maturity[a]	Assets ($ Millions)	Liabilities ($ Millions)	Gap Position ($ Millions)	Cumulative Gap Position ($ Millions)
1 day	5	40	−35	−35
30 days	10	30	−20	−55
60 days	15	20	− 5	−60
91 days	20	10	10	−50
182 days	25	10	15	−35
365 days	30	5	25	−10
TOTAL SHORT TERM	105	115	−10	
Over one year	95	70		
Capital	—	15		
TOTAL	200	200		

[a] The dollar amounts (in millions) can be viewed as being spread out within the various maturities rather than the total amount maturing on a particular day.

widely understood nor widely used by practitioners, especially by the myriad of community bankers. When we use the term *maturity*, let it be understood that we mean *effective* maturity, that is, duration.

The measurement of a bank's gap position critically depends upon the time horizon over which the gap is measured. A range of three to six months or shorter probably captures the relevant time frame for asset-liability management. In terms of coordination with a bank's annual budget, a one-year horizon is appropriate. To illustrate both of these planning horizons, consider the hypothetical balance sheet presented in Table 13-7. Within the one-year horizon, a maturity composition of both assets and liabilities is determined and the gap and the cumulative-gap positions are measured at each maturity. Using a one-year horizon, the bank appears to be relatively balanced with a negative gap of $10 million. However, over the 30- to 182-day horizon, the bank's cumulative gap ranges from $35 million to $55 million. The one-day gap of $35 million is a money-desk or reserve-position problem. The asset-liability management committee should focus its immediate attention on the $55 million negative gap that occurs within the next 30 days. This gap represents the potential cumulative net outflow or liquidity risk that the bank is subject to within the next month, because the maturing liabilities may be withdrawn even if they are variable-rate instruments.

Interest-Rate Forecasting by Time Frame

The interest rates at which dollar flows will be repriced must be determined. Since spread management is an integral part of ALM, this step permits banks to monitor their spreads by time frame. The idea is to spot potential margin problems early so that knee-jerk ALM reactions can be avoided. Long-term rewards (versus short-term results) require that assets and liabilities be matched profitably.

Projection of Future Income

The quantities (i.e., dollar volumes) and prices (i.e., interest rates) generated by the previous two blocks provide the foundation for the third building block—the projection of future income. The purpose of this step is to allow ALM managers to look into the future. Since the idea is to measure the bank's vulnerability to alternative interest-rate scenarios, simulation models are useful in this step. At the minimum, a best case, worst case, and most likely case should be generated.

Testing Different Strategies

This block is the fun part because it is where the "art" of ALM is practiced. The previous three blocks are more "scientific" or mechanical in nature (i.e., grub the data and run it through the simulator). Of course, without the science of ALM, there would be no ALM art to practice. Thus, the previous blocks must be constructed and constructed solidly. From this foundation, alternative ALM strategies are reviewed and checked for consistency with the bank's strategic plans. Recall that ALM is the first step in implementing the bank's strategic plan. Different ALM strategies must be analyzed with respect to their effects on the bank's bottom line. Unlike decomposition analysis, which works from symptoms to causes, ALM strategy sessions focus upon how the arrangement of the basic building blocks affects the performance symptoms (e.g., NIM, ROA, and ROE). The critical decision variables in the arrangement process are pricing strategies; product mix; the size, growth, and composition of the balance sheet; and the extent of off-balance-sheet activities. To be an effective management tool, ALM models should generate two products: (1) the optimum short-run portfolio of assets and liabilities in terms of the risk–return parameters of NIM, and (2) information for top management to evaluate the short-run direction of its strategic plan so that any necessary adjustments can be made.

An Important ALM Caveat: Don't Bet the Bank

The conventional wisdom about ALM places a heavy burden on superior interest-rate forecasting. In today's environment of volatile interest rates, attempts to forecast interest rates beyond three to six months is a tricky business. Keep in mind the quip attributed to Sanford Rose of the *American Banker*: "He who lives by the crystal ball is doomed to eat shattered glass." Since superior forecasting ("beating the market") is a high-risk (speculative) strategy, banks need to consider carefully the cost of being wrong. The key factor here is the size of the bet on interest rates. The nature of banking is such that all banks bet on interest rates to some extent. Win or lose, however, big bets make for unstable earnings (i.e., risk). Foolish gamblers, whether at the craps table or the money desk, have tunnel vision—they see only the big payoff. The cost of being wrong seldom enters their thinking. First Pennsylvania and First Chicago are two examples of ALM where the large size of the interest-rate bets caused them to finish last rather than *first*.[11] Regarding the size of the interest-rate bet, the objective should be to "protect the bank" and not to "bet the bank."

Cyclical Gap Management

The key to gap management is to maintain balance-sheet flexibility. The task is easier said than done, however, because banks do not have complete discretionary control over all their assets and liabilities. The deregulation of the liability side of the balance sheet will put most of the burden of maintaining flexibility on the asset side of the balance sheet (i.e., on the numerator of the sensitivity ratio RSA/RSL). The *ideal*

[11] In 1980, First Pennsylvania was bailed out by the FDIC and a consortium of big banks. During 1984 and 1985, First Chicago was under regulatory and market pressure to increase its capital. Alternative strategies for risk control and profit in ALM (mainly for big banks) can be found in Stigum and Branch [1983].

strategy over a typical interest-rate cycle would be to establish the following target dollar gaps:

Slope of Yield Curve	Strategy	Target Dollar Gap
Positive	Borrow short/lend long	Negative
Flat (low-to-high transition)	Maturity match	Zero
Negative	Borrow long/lend short	Positive
Flat (high-to-low transition)	Maturity match	Zero

To flipflop from a positive gap to a negative one as the yield curve is in transition would require a flexible balance sheet indeed. A more realistic objective is simply to be somewhat flexible and in position to take advantage of rate changes. David Cates [1978], a bank-management consultant, puts it this way:

> To be potentially imbalanced but deliberately and significantly off-balance according to interest-rate trends is an ideal posture. But it is one which (1) is probably available only to larger banks, and (2) depends on proper forecasting and intelligent implementation, with corresponding penalties for poor planning and execution. (p. 25)

Paul Nadler [1980], another noted bank analyst, uses the following analogy to stress the importance of flexibility, and a balanced position, especially for small banks: "When I cross the ocean, I don't care how deep it is as long as I am on the top" (p. 16). The point is that banks shouldn't care what happens to rates as long as both their assets and liabilities have floating rates that move together. This is especially true for small banks with limited resources to play the gap-management game. Thus, for small banks a low-risk strategy of attempting to maintain a zero gap by maturity-matching their balance sheets is a reasonable second-best approach.

The relationship between a bank's net interest margin and movements in short-term interest rates depends on its gap position or sensitivity ratio. The three general situations that banks may face are depicted in Figure 13-2. (The federal-funds rate is used to capture the movement of short-term rates.) In (a), the sensitivity ratio is 1 (i.e., a zero-gap position) and thus the bank's net interest margin remains constant (i.e., it is invariant to changes in the federal-funds rate). In (b), the sensitivity ratio is greater than 1 (i.e., a positive-gap position) and net interest margin varies directly with the level of short-term rates. In (c), the sensitivity ratio is less than 1 (i.e., a negative-gap position) and net interest margin varies inversely with the level of short-term rates.

GAP MANAGEMENT AND THE EFFECTS OF INTEREST-RATE SENSITIVITY ON BANK PERFORMANCE

To demonstrate the effects of interest-rate sensitivity on bank performance, consider the situation depicted in Table 13-8. Given the initial conditions for the bank, we trace through a 200 basis point or 2 percent increase in short-term interest rates, which affects only rate-sensitive assets and liabilities. Since the bank has a negative GAP of −100, the increase in rates will worsen bank performance. However, we can expect rational ALM managers to attempt to offset these adverse effects. Nevertheless, market forces may prevent a complete adjustment.

This comparative-statics experiment consists of four stages of analysis: (1) initial conditions, (2) interest-rate shock, (3) portfolio readjustment, and (4) counterbalancing market forces. The bank performance measures analyzed are the dollar or funding

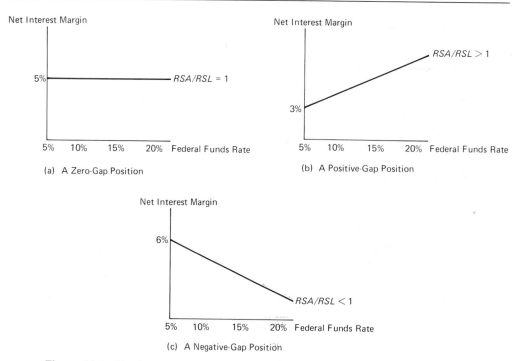

(a) A Zero-Gap Position

(b) A Positive-Gap Position

(c) A Negative-Gap Position

Figure 13-2   Net Interest Margin, Movements in Short-Term Interest Rates, and the Sensitivity Ratio

gap, net interest income (NII), net interest margin (NIM), net income, addition to retained earnings, and return on equity ($ROE = ROA \times EM$). The experiment can be summarized as follows:

	Stage of Analysis			
Performance Measure	Initial Position	Interest-Rate Shock	Portfolio Adjustment	Counterbalancing Market Forces
Dollar gap	−100	−100	0	−70
Net interest income	41.2	39.2	45.2	40
Net interest margin	4.58%	4.36%	4.76%	4.2%
Net income	10	8	14	8.8
Addition to retained earnings	6	4.8	8.4	5.28
Return on equity	12.5%	10%	17.5%	11%
Return on assets	1%	.8%	1.4%	.88%
Equity multiplier	12.5	12.5	12.5	12.5

The analysis presented in Table 13-8 contains several important points. First, when interest rates rise, the existence of a negative gap worsens bank performance. Second, if the change in rates had been anticipated and if the bank had the portfolio flexibility to adjust, the rate increase could have been used to the bank's advantage, as shown in the portfolio-adjustment stage. Third, market forces (e.g., customers' quests for interest-bearing balances and market rates of return) serve to restrict bank profits as they benefit bank customers. And fourth, although the immediate focus of ALM is net interest margin (and its variability), ALM has a much broader reach because it affects a bank's bottom line and its capital adequacy. The latter reinforces the global or general approach to ALM shown in Table 13-1.

TABLE 13-8 The Effects of Interest-Rate Sensitivity on Bank Performance

Initial Conditions for Balance Sheet Items

Item	Volume	Rate	Mix (% of Assets)
Rate-sensitive assets	$ 600	11%	.60
Fixed-rate assets	300	14	.30
Nonearning assets	100	0	.10
Total or averages	$1000	10.8%[a]	1.00
Rate-sensitive liabilities	$ 700	8%	.70
Fixed-rate liabilities	120	9	.12
Noninterest-bearing liab.	100	0	.10
Equity capital	80	15[b]	.08
Totals or averages	$1000	7.88%[a]	1.00

Initial Performance Measures
Net interest income = .11(600) + .14(300) − .08(700) − .09(120)
$$= 66 + 42 − 56 − 10.8 = 41.2$$
Net interest margin = 41.2/900 = 4.58%
$GAP = RSA − RSL = 600 − 700 = −100$
Assuming provision for loan losses, burden, securities gains/losses, and taxes total 31.2. Net income is 10 = 41.2 − 31.2. If the bank's payout ratio is .4, the addition to retained earnings is 6. Thus, $ROE = ROA \times EM = .01 \times 12.5 = .125$ or 12.5%

Comparative Statics Experiment

System shock: Interest rates on rate-sensitive assets and liabilities increase by 200 basis points or 2 percent.
Balance-sheet adjustments: None, volumes and mix remain constant.

New Performance Measures
NII = .13(600) + .14(300) − .10(700) − .09(120)
$$= 78 + 42 − 70 − 10.8 = 39.2$$
$NIM = 39.2/900 = 4.36\%$
Net Income = 39.2 − 31.2 = 8 and Addition to Retained Earnings = 4.8
$ROE = .008 \times 12.5 = .10$ or 10%

Portfolio Adjustments to Rate Changes

RSA Increases to 700 as nonearnings assets decline to 50 and fixed-rate assets decline to 250.
New $GAP = 700 − 700 = 0$.

Performance Measures after Portfolio Rebalancing
NII = .13(700) + .14(250) − .10(700) − .09(120)
$$= 91 + 35 − 70 − 10.8 = 45.2$$
$NIM = 45.2/950 = 4.76\%$
Net Income = 45.2 − 31.2 = 14 and Additions to Retained Earnings = 8.4
$ROE = .014 \times 12.5 = .175$ or 17.5%

Market Forces Counterbalance

Market forces drive RSL to 770 as noninterest-bearing liabilities decline to 50 and fixed-rate liabilities decline to 100. $GAP = −70$.

Counterbalanced Performance Measures
NII = .13(700) + .14(250) − .10(770) − .09(100)
$$= 91 + 35 − 77 − 9 = 40$$
$NIM = 40/950 = .042$ or 4.2%
Net Income 40 − 31.2 = 8.8 and Addition to Retained Earnings = 5.28
$ROE = .0088 \times 12.5 = .11$ or 11%

[a] Weighted average cost or return.
[b] Shareholders required return.

Formula Linkages

A couple of simple formulas can be used to link changes in interest rates to changes in two of our key performance measures: net interest income (NII) and net interest margin (NIM). The formula for the change in NII is

$$\Delta NII = \Delta r \times GAP \qquad (13\text{-}13)$$

To illustrate, given the dollar gap of -100 and the 200 basis point increase in rates, the change in NII is simply $.02 \times -100 = -2$, which is equal to $41.2 - 39.2$ as shown in Table 13-8. The formula for the percentage change in NIM is[12]

$$\Delta NIM/NIM = [GAP/EA] \times [\Delta r/NIM], \qquad (13\text{-}14)$$

where EA stands for earning assets. Using the data for the interest-rate shock as shown in Table 13-8, we have $[-100/900] \times [.02/.0458] = -.1111 \times .4367 = -.0485$. Since the change in NIM is equal to $-.0458 \times 4.58\% = .22\%$, the new level of NIM is $4.58\% - .22\% = 4.36\%$, as shown in Table 13-8.

Figure 13-2 and Formulas 13-13 and 13-14 clearly show the keys to cyclical GAP management. Focusing on Equation 13-13, we see that if rates are expected to rise, a negative GAP will reduce NII. Conversely, if the bank can arrange a positive GAP, then if rates do increase, NII will increase. If rates are expected to decline, then a negative GAP will lead to an increase in NII. To illustrate, let's use the data from the final stage of Table 13-8 and assume a rate decline of 200 basis points or 2 percent. Since $GAP = -70$, the change in NII is simply $-.02 \times -70 = 1.4$, and the new level of NII is $40 + 1.4 = 41.4$. The percentage change in NIM is given by Formula 13-14 as $[-70/950] \times [-0.2/.042] = -.0737 \times -.4762 = .0351$. Hence, the change in NIM is $.0351 \times 4.2\% = .15\%$, and the new level of NIM is 4.35%.

METHODS OF ASSET-LIABILITY MANAGEMENT

In the actual management of their assets and liabilities, bank managers usually employ a combination of techniques. Baker [1978d] has suggested a "system method" of asset-liability management that combines several component parts.[13] He defines the approach as follows:

> The system method of asset/liability management fosters a frame of mind, a way of thinking if you will, that can help bank managers dissolve some of the complexity and at the same time assist them in today's constantly changing environment. In an age of accelerating change banks cannot expect to accomplish today's objectives with yesterday's tools and techniques. (p. 114)

Since financial management frequently is described as a "way of thinking," Baker's approach is all the more relevant for a book on commercial bank financial management.

The value of using a systematic method that stresses a way of thinking is that it forces managers to think about such things as objectives, forecasted financial statements, and

---

[12] See Rose [January 5, 1982] and Hayes [1980], p. 52. The GAP in Formula (13-13) and (13-14) can be interpreted as an average. Moreover, both of these formulas are simplifications of more complex relationships. To see the complexity, set up an equation for NII and derive the change in NII, and note the assumptions needed to arrive at Equation (13-13).

[13] Baker considers the system method to include various features of the experience, asset-allocation, conversion-of-funds, and liability-management methods.

analysis. Under the system approach, Baker recommends that a target ROE be established, say 15 percent. Given the ROE objective, there are various combinations of net interest margins and burden ratios that can meet the objective. The cornerstone of the system method is to generate the pro forma financial statements that permit the bank's net interest margin and burden to be calculated. In addition to the ROE objective, the system approach stresses the importance of managing earnings stability (risk). Thus, the rate-sensitivity analysis discussed in the previous section is a critical component of the system method. In fact, Baker [1978d] says, "Rate-sensitivity management has become possibly the single most important tool in asset/liability management" (p. 124). He recommends that a 90-day horizon be used to define rate-sensitive assets and liabilities but that a "layered" technique also be employed (as depicted in Table 13-5, for example). The focal point of rate-sensitivity management is the sensitivity of gap ratio, RSA/RSL. Baker regards the RSA/RSL ratio as the "common thread" of the system method with applicability to all banks. However, Binder and Lindquist [1982] report that ALCOs are devoting greater attention to the dollar gap rather than the sensitivity ratio. Moreover, they are relating this gap to earnings, assets, and capital to arrive at some assessment of the bank's overall interest-rate risk. The measurement problem notwithstanding, in today's environment efficient gap management is one of the keys to consistent earnings performance.

The component parts of Baker's system method are similar to the four basic building blocks of ALM described earlier in this chapter. Regarding ALM analysis, Baker recommends that a table of key ratios be calculated based upon the projected data. The important areas that need to be covered in the summary table are (1) earning assets and their profitability, (2) capital adequacy, (3) net operating income, (4) net income, and (5) rate sensitivity. Because of the importance of rate-sensitivity analysis to asset-liability management, Baker suggests a special summary for this area. To illustrate, assume that the data in Table 13-6 are three-month projections. Using a 91-day measure for rate sensitivity, the summary information would be

Rate-Sensitivity Summary	
Total assets	= $200,000,000
Total capital	= $ 15,000,000
RSA/RSL	= 0.50
RSA − RSL = GAP	= −$50,000,000
Gap/Total Assets	= −0.25
Gap/Total Capital	= −3.33

The relative measures of gap (with respect to total assets and total capital) give an indication of the bank's vulnerability to alternative interest-rate scenarios. For example, over the next three months this bank is well positioned for a decline in rates but vulnerable to a rise in rates. If the bank anticipates a rise in rates, it should attempt to reduce its vulnerability. By conducting a sensitivity analysis (or at least considering best case, worse case, and most-likely case scenarios), the bank can further pinpoint its vulnerability to particular interest-rate movements and attempt to adjust its gap strategy accordingly.

ALM in Practice and Current Issues

The following excerpt from the 1981 Annual Report of Barnett Banks of Florida (p. 27) provides a good example of how a major regional BHC uses ALM and reports its ALM position to its shareholders:

> Approximately 33 percent and 32 percent, respectively, of Barnett's consolidated assets and liabilities were sensitive to short-term interest rate fluctuations at the end of 1981. The term "rate-sensitive" generally refers to any asset or liability maturing within one year. At year-end 1981, Barnett was slightly liability-sensitive on a one-year basis. However, the Company is asset-sensitive on a 30- to 60-day basis because of the amount of commercial and construction loans which are tied to the prime rate. The consumer loan portfolios is not tied to prime and will not fluctuate as much as the yields on commercial loans.
>
> The entire balance sheet is carefully monitored through use of an asset/liability management model. Management reviews trends in interest rates and in the volume and mix of assets and liabilities on a regular basis. Based on these trends, a variety of projections are made using different interest-rate scenarios. Management then reviews the various analyses and implements strategies that will position the Company to continue its earnings momentum— by protecting its margins while pricing liabilities to ensure continuing growth.

Regarding current issues in ALM, Houghton [1983] focuses on the following six areas: (1) market share versus profitability, (2) utilization of funds, (3) current strategies for coping with disinflation, (4) to gap or not to gap, (5) hedging gaps with interest-rate futures, and (6) the future of ALM. We conclude this chapter with a brief look at each one of these issues.

Market Share Versus Profitability

This issue is an ongoing battle in most ALCO meetings. The ideal, of course, is profitable growth. In some instances, however, gaining market share may reduce current profitability but enhance it in the future. Short-term pain for long-term gain usually is worthwhile. The Atlanta experience with money-market deposit accounts (MMDAs) during December 1982 is illustrative. Most Atlanta banks went aggressively after market share at the expense of current profits by paying 18 to 21 percent for 30-day money, which was about double the going rate.[14] The strategy was to recoup funds lost to the money-market funds in previous years. By November 30, 1984, MMDAs totaled $256.1 billion at commercial banks and $141.3 billion at thrift institutions. Of course, some of these funds simply were rolled up from lower-yielding accounts and did not represent new market share. In the aftermath of Continental's liquidity crisis, a related market-share issue has been the question of wholesale versus retail sources of funds. Structural changes in the components of TRICK, which appear to be permanent rather than temporary, suggest that banks may be faced with both reduced market share and reduced profitability in the future.

Utilization of Funds

Since funds matching is an important part of ALM, let's examine some specific matching policies that a bank may employ. First, jumbo CDs of $100,000 or more and other "hot money" should be matched with floating-rate commercial loans (i.e., loans that float with the prime rate or that are repriced at regular intervals, e.g., every 90 days).

---

[14] My colleagues and I welcomed the arbitrage opportunity by leveraging ourselves to the hilt for 30 days to invest in an insured account. A local savings bank, which wasn't participating in the rate war, lent us and others a total of $10 million (at a handsome spread over its opportunity cost) to finance the arbitrage scheme. Reg Q retribution is fun; we should have more of it.

This technique matches an RSL with an RSA or vice versa. Second, six-month consumer CDs can be used to finance commercial or consumer loans that mature in six months or to finance secured term loans that are repriced every six months. Third, two and a half-year certificates can be matched with consumer installment loans. Fourth, longer-term consumer CDs and IRAs with intermediate terms can be matched with term loans of similar duration. IRAs that are repriced every year or sooner should be laid off against similarly priced assets. Finally, long-term, fixed rate capital notes and debentures can be used to finance long-term fixed-rate assets (e.g., mortgages). Variable-rate, long-term debt can be matched with variable-rate mortgages.

Regarding the MMDAs mentioned above, what should banks do with this money? Should MMDAs be treated as core deposits (i.e., as stable deposits from local markets)? Based upon their limited track record, it appears that MMDAs can be treated as core deposits. However, they are a new breed of core deposit because they reprice regularly. Therefore, they should be matched with an asset with similar repricing. The latter may call for the marketing of new loan products such as variable-rate installment loans.

For banks/BHCs that operate in major wholesale markets, bankers' acceptances, Eurodollar CDs, Euro placements, and other instruments can be used both for sources and uses of funds.

Strategies for Coping with Disinflation

Disinflation refers to the slowing down of the rate of inflation. The disinflation of 1982–1986 was a welcome relief from the prior years of rapid inflation. As a result, interest rates have dropped substantially and the yield curve has been upward or positively sloped. Such a yield curve rewards institutions with negative gaps. Since the interest-rate cycle has yet to be declared dead, banks and especially thrifts must avoid the temptation to get locked in to long-term assets. Recall that according to the expectations theory of the term structure, a positively sloped yield curve implies that future short-term rates are expected to rise. Unfortunately, the theory doesn't tell us *when* they will rise. The name of the game for profitable investing over the interest-rate cycle is timing or guessing the turning points. Uncertainty dictates that prudent ALM managers restrict the size of their interest-rate bets. Since strategies should be different for different stages of the rate cycle, managers must know where they are in the rate cycle. Ideally, any gap should be kept manageable and easily reversible.

To Gap or Not to Gap

Shakespeare's soliloquy for Hamlet as recited by an ALM manager would begin with these words. The dilemma, however, may not be that great because in today's TRICK(y) environment it would appear that banks have to do some gapping to maintain profit margins. A zero gap means forgoing funding profits (i.e., the spread across maturities) and, of course, it means forgoing the potential for funding losses due to an adverse movement in the yield curve. Increased pressure on bank margins may force ALM managers to take on larger funding or gap risks than in the past. Since it is usually easier to reduce a positive gap than to cure a negative one (e.g., witness the plight of thrifts), ALM managers need to be extra cautious about their negative gaps. Once again, the ALM objective should be to maximize NIM and then to protect it from unexpected changes in rates. In addition, prudent banking practice requires that liquidity and capital standards be maintained.

Hedging Gaps with Interest-Rate Futures

Interest-rate futures provide a tool for bridging the basic conflict between banks' ALM needs and customers' preferences (i.e., many customers prefer fixed-rate loans but the bank is saddled with variable-rate liabilities). Rather than fight this basic conflict banks can use it to their advantage if they employ financial-instrument futures to hedge their gap risks. However, like the technique of duration matching, hedging gaps with interest-rate futures is widely talked about but not that widely practiced. Three problems that act to restrict the use of futures are (1) "basis risk" makes perfect hedges difficult to construct, (2) "marking to market" tends to destabilize earnings and present accounting problems, and (3) hedged positions must be monitored and adjusted to market changes. In addition, there is the more fundamental problem of a lack of skilled personnel, especially in community banks, to manage the hedging function. Finally, disinflation and reduced interest-rate volatility have, temporarily at least, reduced the need for hedging with financial futures. Various techniques for managing interest-rate risk are discussed in Chapter 17.

The Future of ALM

ALM is, of course, here to stay. Moreover, in the TRICK(y) environment of the FSI its importance as the leading step in implementing the bank's strategic plan is likely to increase. The fact that bank management is becoming less inbred is fortunate because there is a need for managerial talent beyond the traditional lending area. Bank ALM and strategic planning require individuals who can blend common sense and practical managerial skills with new entrepreneurial, marketing, and financial techniques.

CHAPTER SUMMARY

This chapter has focused on the important topic of asset-liability management. In today's environment the coordinated management of a bank's assets and liabilities is a must. The focal variable of this analysis is a bank's net interest margin, which is a function of the bank's interest-rate sensitivity, volume, and mix. Net interest margin is, of course, a reflection of a bank's underlying balance-sheet structure. The interest-rate sensitivity of a bank's balance sheet depends upon the relationship between its rate-sensitive assets (RSA) and its rate-sensitive liabilities (RSL). This important relationship can be expressed in dollar form or as a ratio. The dollar gap is defined as $RSA - RSL$ and the gap or sensitivity ratio is defined as RSA/RSL. The dollar gap can be zero, positive, or negative; the ratio can be $\gtreqless 1$. The balanced portfolio position is defined as a zero gap or a ratio of 1. The cyclical management of a bank's gap position is the key to high-performance banking, given the bank's "burden" (i.e., the difference between its noninterest revenue and noninterest expense).

A modern approach to ALM involves a system method in conjunction with a bank's strategic plan. The building blocks of ALM are the reporting, forecasting, analyzing, and testing of different strategies dealing with asset and liabilities that are repriced over different time frames. Two important ongoing issues in ALM focus on (1) market share versus profitability and (2) utilization of funds. The use of duration matching and interest-rate futures as tools of ALM has received more printer's ink than actual practice. In the TRICK(y) environment of the FSI, ALM, which is the first step in implementing the bank's strategic plan, is the heart and soul of bank financial management. The ALM caveat is: Don't bet the bank.

LIST OF KEY WORDS, CONCEPTS, AND ACRONYMS

Asset-liability management (ALM)
Asset-liability-management committee
 (ALCO)
ALM performance measures (GAP, NII,
 NIM, ROA, ROE)
ALM terminology (gap, funding, book,
 and price)
Assets repricing before liabilities
 (ARBL)
Balance-sheet management (a
 three-stage approach)
Betting on yield-curve movements
Betting the bank
"Burden"
Continental Illinois' liquidity crisis
Dollar or funds gap ($GAP = RSA - RSL$)
Duration
Earning assets (EA)
Equity multiplier (EM)

Funding profits (losses)
GAP (see dollar or funds gap)
Gap management
Interest cost of earning asset
Interest-rate forecasting
Interest-rate futures
Liabilities repricing before assets
 (LRBA)
Net interest income (NII)
Net interest margin (NIM)
Return on assets (ROA)
Return on equity ($ROE = ROA \times EM$)
Rate-sensitive asset (RSA)
Rate sensitive liability (RSL)
Rate, volume, and mix
Savings bank/thrift crisis
Spread
Yield on earning assets

REVIEW/DISCUSSION QUESTIONS

1. Trace the evolution of asset-liability management over the last four decades. How does ALM fit to a bank's strategic plan?
2. How much control do bank managers actually have over their assets and liabilities? What are the key instruments of asset-liability management and what is the relevant time horizon?
3. What is net interest margin and why is it important? What is "burden" and its relationship to NIM? What is the future outlook for margin and burden in the TRICK(y) FSI?
4. What are the building blocks of ALM and what are the current issues in ALM?
5. In 1984, Continental Illinois experienced a silent (electronic) run. How was the run on the bank stopped, and what happened to ALM strategies after this event?
6. Describe the plight of thrifts in terms of gap-management terminology. Distinguish between liquidity risk and interest-rate risk in this situation.
7. What would be an ideal cyclical gap-management policy? How practical would such a policy be?
8. Explain how a bank can have a gap of -10 and a -60 depending upon the time horizon over which the gap is measured.
9. What is the implication of Cates' quote for the asset-liability-management strategy to be pursued by small banks?
10. Label and explain each of the following graphs in terms of net interest margin, movements of short-term interest rates, and the sensitivity ratio.

MATCHING QUIZ

Directions: Select the letter from the right-hand column that best matches the term in the left-hand column.

__ 1. "Spread"		A.	"Saturday night massacre"
__ 2. To gap or not to gap		B.	Clint Eastwood
__ 3. Large negotiable CDs		C.	Due to severe negative gap
__ 4. Savings bank crisis		D.	The ALM committee
__ 5. Negative gap		E.	Measures effective maturity
__ 6. Positive gap		F.	Domestic + Euro book
__ 7. Zero gap		G.	ALM caveat
__ 8. RSA and RSL		H.	ALM focal variable
__ 9. Duration		I.	Demonstrates formula linkage
__ 10. $NII = r \times GAP$		J.	Broad view of ALM
__ 11. Net interest margin		K.	Control NIM risk and return
__ 12. ALCO		L.	Upward sloping
__ 13. Balance-sheet management		M.	Victim of EFT run
__ 14. Objective of ALM		N.	Difficult since the "massacre"
__ 15. Continental Illinois		O.	Recommended by Baker
__ 16. Global or worldwide book		P.	Used to hedge gaps
__ 17. Interest-rate forecasting		Q.	Sensitivity ratio
__ 18. Common shape yield curve		R.	Due to spread across maturities
__ 19. System method of ALM		S.	NIM yield differential
__ 20. Interest-rate futures		T.	LRBA
__ 21. *RSA/RSL*		U.	ARBL
__ 22. Don't bet the bank		V.	Matched book
__ 23. Funding profits		W.	Reported demise is premature
__ 24. Interest-rate cycle		X.	Rate-sensitive items
__ 25. Wore *Firefox* helmet		Y.	Big bank ALM instrument
__ 26. October 6, 1979		Z.	ALM manager's soliloquy

PROBLEMS

1. Given the initial conditions in Table 13.8 in the text, assume an interest-rate shock of a 200 basis point decrease in interest rates and rework the analysis for the comparative-statics experiment. As in the analysis in the text, assume that only rate-sensitive assets and liabilities are affected by the interest-rate shock. Furthermore, assume that the same portfolio adjustments and counterbalancing market forces described in Table 13-8 exist in this case. Use Formulas 13-13 and 13-14 to check your answers for NII and NIM.

2. Referring to the notes in Table 13-8, define and/or demonstrate the calculation of (a) the weighted average cost, (b) the weighted average return and (c) shareholders required return.

3. The Gap Bank faces the following abbreviated yield curve $(R_S, R_L) = (.07, .10)$, where R_S = short-term rate and R_L = long-term rate. The bank's ALCO expects the following yield structure to exist in the near future $(.15, .12)$. Assuming that the ALCO's expectations are realized, what will the bank's funding profits be under each of the following gap strategies?
   a. negative gap
   b. positive gap
   c. current negative gap but immediate switch to a positive one
   d. zero gap
   If the ALCOs expectations are not realized and the actual yield curve turns out to be flat at 11 percent, how will your answers change? Exchange the actual and realized yield curves and rework the problem. In your analysis incorporate the concepts of a liquidity premium in the term structure and prediction error by the market.

4. Calculate net margin and net interest revenue given the following information:

Taxable interest revenue =	$ 100.00
Tax-free interest revenue =	10.00
Marginal tax rate =	.34
Interest expense =	60.00
Earning assets	= $1200.00

5. Determine the volume and rate variances for the following data:

	Period	
	t	$t + 1$
Volume ($)	90	100
Rate (%)	12	15

6. Conduct a rate-sensitivity summary and an analysis for the following bank:

Total assets =	$1000
Total capital =	$ 60
RSA =	$ 300
RSL =	$ 200

7. Assuming a one-year horizon, project the change in NIM for each of the following banks:

Bank	GAP	Earning Assets	Δ Interest Rate (Basis Points)	NIM
A	−100	100	400	4%
B	− 20	100	400	4%
C	0	100	400	4%
D	20	100	400	4%
E	−100	100	400	4%

SELECTED REFERENCES

Ahlers, David M. [1980]. "Increasing Asset-Liability Management Committee Effectiveness." *The Bankers Magazine* (July–August), pp. 18–22.

Angotti, Arthur A., and Morris L. Maurer. 1980. "Slope and Spread." *The Magazine of Bank Administration* (August), pp. 28–34.

Baker, James V., Jr. [1982]. "Statistical Relationships Are the Key to Banks' Use of Interest-Rate Futures." *ABA Banking Journal* (May), pp. 88–92.

———. [1981]. *Asset/Liability Management.* Washington, DC.: American Bankers Association.

———. [1978a]. "Why You Need a Formal Asset-Liability Management Policy." *Banking* (June); p. 33 and *passim.*

———. [1978b]. "Asset-Liability Management II." *Banking* (July), p. 78 and *passim.*

———. [1978c]. "Asset-Liability Management III." *Banking* (August), p. 74 and *passim.*

———. [1978d]. "Asset-Liability Management IV." *Banking* (September), p. 114 and *passim.*

———. [1978e]. "Asset-Liability Management V." *Banking* (October), p. 82 and *passim.*

Bench, Joseph. [1980]. *"The Case for Financial Futures." Bankers Monthly Magazine* (May 15), pp. 10 and 12.

Binder, Barrett F. [1980a]. "Asset-Liability Management, Part I." *The Magazine of Bank Administration* (November), pp. 42–48.

———. [1980b]. "Asset-Liability Management, Part II." *The Magazine of Bank Administration* (December), pp. 31–35.

———. [1981a]. "Asset-Liability Management, Part III." *The Magazine of Bank Administration* (January), pp. 42–50.

———. [1981b]. "New Initiatives in Asset-Liability Management. *The Magazine of Bank Administration* (June), pp. 56–64.

———, and Thomas Lindquist. [1982]. *Asset-Liability Handbook.* Rolling Meadows, IL: Bank Administration Institute.

Black, Fischer. [1975]. "Bank Funds Management in an Efficient Market." *Journal of Financial Economics* (December), pp. 323–339.

Brewer, Elijah. [1980]. "Bank Funds Management Comes of Age—A Balance-Sheet Analysis." *Economic Perspectives*, Federal Reserve Bank of Chicago, (May/June), pp. 13–18.

Broaddus, Alfred. [1972]. "Linear Programming: A New Approach to Bank Portfolio Management." Federal Reserve Bank of Richmond *Monthly Review*, (November), pp. 3–11.

Cates, David C. [1978]. "Interest Sensitivity in Banking." *The Bankers Magazine* (January–February), pp. 23–27.

Chance, Don., and William R. Lane. [1980]. "A Re-examination of Interest-Rate Sensitivity in the Common Stocks of Financial Institutions." *The Journal of Financial Research* (Spring), pp. 49–55.

Cohen, Kalman J., Steven F. J., and James H. Vander Weide. [1981]. "Recent Developments in Management Science in Banking." *Management Science* (October), pp. 1097–1119.

Cordell, David M. [1981]. "Commercial Bank Spread Management: A Duration Approach." Baton Rouge: LSU Working Paper Series (September).

Flannery, Mark J. [1981]. "Market Interest Rates and Commercial Bank Profitability: An Empirical Investigation." *The Journal of Finance* (December), pp. 1085–1101.

Francis, Jack Clark. [1978]. "Portfolio Analysis of Asset and Liability Management in Small-, Medium-, and Large-Sized Banks." *Journal of Monetary Economics* (4), pp. 459–480.

Glavin, William M. [1982]. *Asset/Liability Management: A Handbook for Commercial Banks.* Rolling Meadows, IL: Bank Administration Institute.

Hayes, Douglas A. [1980]. *Bank Funds Management.* Ann Arbor: University of Michigan.

Hempel, George H. [1981]. *Funds Management under Deregulation.* Washington, DC: American Bankers Association.

Hilliard, Jimmy E. [1984]. "Duration as the Effective Time to Repricing." Athens: Working Paper, University of Georgia.

Houghton, Kenneth R. [1983]. "Asset & Liability Management: A Practical Approach." Atlanta: Trust Company of Georgia, Course Outline (April 20).

Howard, Donald S., and Gail M. Hoffman. [1980]. *Evolving Concepts of Bank Capital Management.* New York: Citicorp.

Kane, Edward J. [1985]. *The Gathering Crisis in Federal Deposit Insurance.* Cambridge, MA: MIT Press.

———. [1983]. "The Role of Government in the Thrift Industry's Net-Worth Crisis." In *Financial Services* George J. Benston, ed. Englewood Cliffs, NJ: Prentice-Hall, pp. 156–184.

Kung, S. W. [1981]. "Asset-Liability Management for Smaller Banks." *The Bankers Magazine* (January–February), pp. 78–81.

Land, Rufus F. [1978]. "Evolution and Overview of Asset-Liability Management." In *The Bankers' Handbook*, W. H. Baughn and C. E. Walker, eds. Homewood, IL: Dow Jones-Irwin, pp. 433–444.

Levison, Paul. [1980]. "The Case for Interest-Rate Futures." *Bankers Monthly Magazine* (May 15), pp. 28–33.

Maisel, S. J., and R. Jacobson. [1978]. "Interest-Rate Changes and Commercial-Bank Revenues and Costs." *Journal of Financial and Quantitative Analysis* (November), pp. 687–700.

McKinney, George W., Jr. [1977]. "A Perspective on the Use of Models in the Management of Bank Funds." *Journal of Bank Research* (Summer), pp. 122–127.

McCabe, George M., and James M. Blackwell. [1981]. "The Hedging Strategy: A New Approach to Spread Management Banking and Commercial Lending." *Journal of Bank Research* (Summer), pp. 114–118.

McLeod, Robert W., and George M. McCabe. [1980]. "Hedging for Better Spread Management." *The Bankers Magazine* (July–August), pp. 47–52.

Morris, John. [1982]. "First Chicago Stops Playing the Rate Game." *American Banker* (February 12), pp. 1 and 14.

Nadler, Paul S. [1980]. "Managing the Spread." *Bankers Monthly Magazine* (June 15), p. 13 and *passim.*

Olson, Ronald L., and Harold M. Sollenberger. [1978]. "Interest Margin Variance Analysis: A Tool of Current Times." *The Magazine of Bank Administration* (May), pp. 45–51.

Olson, Ronald L., et al [1980]. The Management of Bank Interest Margins in the 1980s, Parts 1, 2, 3 and 4." *The Magazine of Bank Administration* (March, April, May, and June).

Picou, Glen. [1981]. "Managing Interest-Rate Risk with Interest-Rate Futures." *The Bankers Magazine* (May–June), pp. 76–81.

Powers, Mark, and David Vogel. [1981]. *Inside the Financial Futures Markets.* New York: Wiley.

Rose, Sanford. [1984]. "Duration's Dual Payoff." *American Banker* (May 22), pp. 1, 4–6, 16.

———. [1982a]. "The Spread, the Margin and the Need for Fees." *American Banker* (February 25), pp. 1 and 4.

———. [1982b]. "Gleanings from a Major Study." *American Banker* (January 5), pp. 1 and 4.

Roussakis, Emmanuel N. [1977]. *Management Commercial Bank Funds.* New York: Praeger.

Samuelson, Paul A. [1945]. "The Effect of Interest-Rate Increases on the Banking System." *American Economics Review* (March), pp. 16–27.

Santoni, G. J. [1984]. "Interest-Rate Risk and the Stock Prices of Financial Institutions." Federal Reserve Bank of St. Louis *Review* (August/September), pp. 12–20.

Sibler, William L. [1977]. *Commercial Bank Liability Management.* Chicago: Association of Reserve City Bankers.

Sprague, Ralph H., Jr., and Ronald L. Olson. [1979]. "The Financial Planning System of Louisiana National Bank." *Management Information Systems* Quarterly (Vol. 3, No. 3), pp. 35–46.

Stigum, Marcia L., and Rene O. Branch. [1983]. *Managing Bank Assets and Liabilities.* Homewood Hills, IL: Dow Jones-Irwin.

Toevs, Alden, and William Haney. [1984]. *Guide to Asset-Liability Models.* New York: Morgan Stanley.

MANAGEMENT OF BANK PORTFOLIO RISKS: LIQUIDITY, INTEREST RATE, CREDIT, AND OFF-BALANCE SHEET

Risk management is the heart of bank financial management. The critical portfolio risks of banking are liquidity risk, interest-rate risk, and credit risk. In addition, because of the surge in bank off-balance-sheet activities in recent years, risk management of these activities has taken on added importance. This part of the book focuses on the management of the portfolio risks of banking, whether they are on or off the balance sheet.

Chapter 14 presents an overview of the risks of banking. Building on the alternative notions of what is a bank (see Chapter 2), a comprehensive framework for analyzing the risks of banking is developed. This framework serves as the foundation for the analysis covered in the following seven chapters. The management of liquidity and its risks are the focus of Chapter 15. In Chapter 16, the characteristics and risk management of the investment portfolio are analyzed. The management of interest-rate risk using duration, financial futures and options, and interest-rate swaps is the focus of Chapter 17. Management of credit risk and the lending function highlight Chapters 18, 19, and 20. In Chapter 21, an analysis of off-balance-sheet activities and their financial management, including securitization, is presented.

CHAPTER 14

An Overview of Bank Risk Management

ACRONYM GUIDE TO KEY WORDS AND CONCEPTS

BHC = Bank holding company
MBHC = Multibank holding company
OBHC = One-bank holding company
OBSA = Off-balance-sheet activity
SLC = Standby letter of credit

INTRODUCTION

The heart of bank financial management is the ability to manage the portfolio risks of banking, whether these risks are on or off the bank's balance sheet. This chapter presents overviews of the risks of banking and the management of these risks. We begin with a look at two key concepts: risk and portfolio. From this foundation, we move to a comprehensive framework that catalogs the critical risks faced by bank holding companies (BHCs) and their subsidiary banks, a framework that applies to any firm in the financial-services industry. The highlights of this framework are the three key portfolio risks faced by commercial banks: (1) liquidity risks, (2) interest-rate risk, and (3) credit or default risk. The traditional portfolio risks of banking have been liquidity and credit exposures. However, since the increased interest-rate volatility dating from 1979 when the Federal Reserve shifted to a monetary aggregates target, interest-rate risk, which always has been present, has taken on added significance.

As regulatory and market pressures have forced banks to strengthen their capital positions, bankers have responded by moving assets off the balance sheet, either through securitization or off-balance-sheet activities, or both. Thus, the 1980s have witnessed the "birth" of two additional portfolio risks for banks: the risks of securitization and of off-balance-sheet activities. Although these activities are new, their risks are manifested in the traditional measures of bank risk exposure as reflected by liquidity, interest-rate, and credit considerations. These new sources of risk are important because of the contingent claims they generate against bank earnings and capital.

To highlight the key concepts of this chapter, a simple model of bank portfolio allocation is employed. Using graphical and numerical presentations, risk management aspects of liquidity and pricing are demonstrated and related to the risks associated with deposit structure, liquidity and reserve requirements, and off-balance-sheet activities.

THE ETYMOLOGIES OF THE WORDS RISK AND PORTFOLIO

From a finance point of view, risk is best understood in a portfolio context. A useful starting point is with the etymologies of the words *risk* and *portfolio*. *Portfolio* has its origins in the Italian word *portafoglio*. The component derivatives are from the Latin words *portare* meaning to carry and *foglio* meaning "leaf" or "sheet." In the days of the Holy Roman Empire, portfolios were used to carry important documents of state. Today, we think of *portfolio* in an investment context, as in "a portfolio of financial assets." However, any business firm can be conceived of as a portfolio of assets. As noted in Chapter 2, a commercial bank can be thought of as a portfolio of earning assets consisting mainly of loans. The owners of those portfolios consider the contents to be very important papers, even more important than documents of state. Do you know any portfolio owners who are not concerned about the *safety* (risk) and *value* of their portfolios? In this context, doesn't the goal of value or wealth maximization seem eminently sensible? The basic valuation formula is one that discounts the cash flow from a *risky* (portfolio) asset using an appropriate capitalization rate with a premium for risk. It is critically important to understand how risk enters and affects the valuation process (see Chapter 3).

The etymology of the word *risk* can be traced to the Vulgar Latin (popular or "street" Latin as opposed to classical Latin or Late Latin) word *rescum* meaning "risk at sea," "danger," or "that which cuts." The passengers of the *Titanic*, motorists on the New Jersey Turnpike, and Vietnam veterans can all tell you about the respective meanings of *rescum*. Common sense suggests that risk is something to be avoided; uncommon sense suggests that 'risk sweetens the reward" or gives the feeling of having "pulled it off." In finance, risk is something that requires compensation for bearing it, hence, the terminology, *risk–return tradeoff*.

Since risk is associated with uncertainty, where does uncertainty originate? Uncertainty is reflected by unanticipated changes in events. For bankers, and lenders in general, portfolio uncertainty arises from changes in interest rates, in deposit flows and in the ability of borrowers to repay loans. These unknowns generate the three basic portfolio risks faced by banks: interest-rate risk, liquidity risk, and credit risk. If bank managers control their portfolio risks and operate their firms efficiently, they do not have to worry about insolvency or failure. We can attempt to measure the latter (insolvency or failure risk) by focusing on the adequacy of a bank's capital, which is the buffer for absorbing losses due to portfolio and/or operational deficiencies. Thus, the greater a bank's potential risk exposure, the more capital a bank/BHC should have. Since a bank's main source of capital is its internal earnings stream, we can think of risk in banking as any unanticipated portfolio and/or operational change which creates an unanticipated claim on bank earnings and capital.

Anticipated Versus Unanticipated Changes

In a nutshell, think of risk as arising from the uncertainty associated with future events. Since rational managers incorporate *anticipated* changes in their decision making, risks arise only from *unanticipated* changes. Although anticipated changes are not directly observable, we can attempt to measure them through surveys or through use of the following relationship:

$$\text{Actual Change} = \text{Anticipated Change} + \text{Unanticipated Change} \qquad (14\text{-}1)$$

Thus, after the fact, historical or actual change can be decomposed into an anticipated component and an unanticipated component. In the case of perfect certainty or foresight, the unanticipated change disappears, and the actual and anticipated changes are equal. This special case clearly shows unanticipated change as the source of risk. Morever, since change and variability mean, in effect, the same thing, we have a linkage back to our theoretical/statistical concept of variability as the financial-management measure of risk. As a practical matter, highly variable earnings and depleted capital positions are signs of poor risk management. Risk management is made easier by a better understanding of how to form accurate expectations and by better identification of the sources of unexpected change.

To better understand these ideas about risk, consider the credit or default risk associated with a bank's loan portfolio. After the fact, we can observe the bank's performance in this area by using Equation 14-1. Specifically, we have:

$$\text{Actual Loan Losses} = \text{Anticipated Losses} + \text{Unanticipated Losses} \qquad (14\text{-}2)$$

If actual and anticipated loan losses are equal, then the bank had no (unpleasant) "surprises" in its loan portfolio. Such a situation would be the exception rather than the rule in the business of lending because (1) lenders are human and they sometimes make mistakes in their judgments about creditworthiness (Of course, if lenders make too many mistakes, they can expect to lose their jobs.), and (2) external events such as movements in the business cycle and natural disasters cannot be predicted with 100 percent accuracy (e.g., the severe economic downturns in the energy and agricultural sectors in the 1980s). These "internal" and "external" sources of risk are, of course, interrelated as lenders have to make judgments about borrowers' vulnerability to economic conditions.

The "bottom line" is that borrowers' cash flows, the primary source of loan repayment, are uncertain. Thus, lenders need to know something about the level and variability (risk) of borrowers' cash flows. Invoking Equation 14-1, the change in a borrower's or would-be borrower's cash flow can be analyzed as

$$\text{Change in Cash Flow} = \text{Anticipated Change} + \text{Unanticipated Change} \qquad (14\text{-}3)$$

Given the honesty factor (i.e., borrower willingness to repay), analysis of a borrower's cash flow is the critical part of testing for and ensuring creditworthiness. To analyze cash flow on the commercial level requires detailed knowlege of a borrower's business, financial statements, management, and industry, among other things. These factors form the heart of credit analysis, which is covered in Chapters 18, 19, and 20.

Proper risk analysis enables bankers to price products and services such that they receive fair compensation for the risks they bear. Let's turn now to this notion of compensation for bearing risk.

VARIABILITY AS THE FINANCIAL-MANAGEMENT MEASURE OF RISK

In finance, *risk* can be defined as the uncertainty associated with some event or outcome (e.g., a portfolio return). The relationship between the events and the *probability* of their occurrence is called a *probability distribution*. A basic statistical measure of such uncertainty is the *standard deviation* or its square the *variance*. The standard deviation or variance of a probability distribution is a measure of *dispersion*; the more the dispersion the greater the risk or uncertainty. It is a measure of *variability*. For example, portfolio variance or standard deviation is a measure of a portfolio's variability or riskiness. The market portfolio, as measured by the S&P composite index, has had a standard deviation of about 20 percent a year. Although most individual stocks have higher standard deviations than the market portfolio, their unique or unsystematic risk can be eliminated through diversification. However, diversification cannot eliminate market or systematic risk. As shown in Chapter 3, the capital asset pricing model provides a way of estimating market or β risk.

RISK–RETURN TRADE-OFFS IN BANKING

The notion of a risk–return trade-off is a fundamental concept of financial management: to obtain a higher rate of return an investor must be willing to take on more risk. This idea is, of course, applicable to bank managers. Bankers, however, are legally restricted in the extent to which they can reach out for higher returns (i.e., take on more risk). The restrictions are numerous. For example, they are restricted from holding various kinds of assets (e.g., common stocks); they are *forced* to diversify their loan portfolios by avoiding concentrations of credit to individual borrowers, and they are discouraged, via the bank-examination process, from making "high-risk" loans. Thus, regulated financial-services firms, such as commercial banks, face geographic and product restrictions that limit their investment opportunities. However within their restricted investment environment, risk-return trade-offs still are available.

Risk–Return Trade-Offs and Diversification

Unless diversification has a positive effect on risk-adjusted cash flow, it does not affect a firm's value. For asset returns that are less than perfectly correlated, portfolio or asset diversification does reduce risk. In banking, the dominant organizational form is the bank holding company (BHC). Since BHCs are permitted to engage only in nonbanking activities that are "closely related to banking" (see Chapter 1 and the discussion of the separation of banking and commerce and the separation of commercial and investment banking), expected diversification benefits will depend on how closely related the activities are. In the case of savings and loan associations, Benston [1986] has argued that asset restrictions have inhibited the ability of thrifts to recover from the ravages of their realized interest-rate risk.

Many bankers and analysts contend that commercial banks and their holding companies must be granted expanded investment opportunities if they are to be able to compete effectively in the financial-services industry. Since BHCs and banks are highly regulated firms, the opportunity to expand into new activities may serve to reduce risk (through diversification) and at the same time to increase expected return. This apparent contradiction is explained by the expanded opportunity set (or efficiency frontier) available to the BHC and is illustrated in Figure 14-1. The curve RR represents the BHC's more restricted opportunity set. It is an efficient frontier in the sense that any point on the line (e.g., point A) gives the maximum expected return for a given level of risk or the minimum risk for a given level of return. However, if the opportunity set is shifted outward, say because of deregulation, then the BHCs risk–return position can be improved unambiguously by moving from point A to points B, C, or D. Relative to point A, point B produces the same return with less risk, point C produces a higher return and less risk, and point D produces a higher return for the same risk. The particular point on the opportunity set where the BHC resides will depend on top management's risk–return preferences or utility function. Assuming a movement from point A to point D, an attempt to reach out from point D to a higher expected return (i.e., point E) can be achieved only by taking on more risk. To

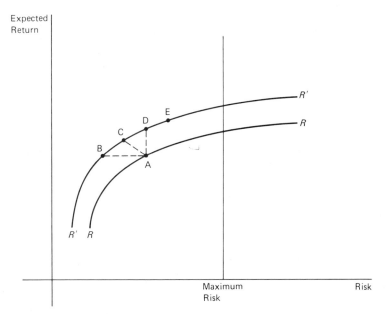

Figure 14-1 BHC Opportunity Set or Efficiency Frontier

the extent that regulatory constraints induce innovative behavior (designed to circumvent such restrictions), BHCs engage in an ongoing struggle with the regulator. Thus, innovative players are capable of creating expanded opportunity sets (beyond $R'R'$) and taking on unregulated risks that may even challenge the regulatory-perceived maximum risk.

A FRAMEWORK FOR ANALYZING BHC RISK[1]

A bank holding company, similar to a bank, can be conceptualized as a consolidated balance sheet, a regulated firm, or deliverer of financial services. These three notions provide a convenient and logical foundation for constructing a framework for analyzing BHC risk. See Figure 14-2. Viewing a BHC as a consolidated balance sheet, the notion of a portfolio and hence *portfolio risk* comes to mind. The consolidated portfolio consists of three components or subportfolios. The major component is the bank subsidiary (in the case of a one-bank holding company, OBHC) or subsidiaries (in the case of a multibank holding company, MBHC). In the case of an MBHC, a lead bank usually is identified as the major institution in the organization. The other two components of the BHC portfolio are the nonbank subsidiaries and the parent company. The parent company, of course, owns the subsidiaries, either partially or wholly.

The three basic portfolio risks that a BHC faces are associated with the simple balance-sheet identity of Assets = Liabilities + Net Worth or Capital and are described as *asset-management risk, liability-management risk*, and *capital-management risk*. In this context, another name for portfolio risk is *asset-liability-management risk* or simply *ALM risk*, which includes the capital component.

[1] This section draws on my four articles listed in the references.

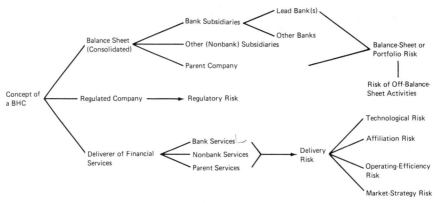

Figure 14-2   A Framework for Analyzing BHC Risk

Viewing a BHC as a regulated company, the concept of regulatory risk is high-lighted. This term refers to the risk that unforeseen regulatory action will impair the BHC's profitability. Since regulatory actions or inactions affect how BHCs manage their portfolios and how they deliver their services, the three basic concepts and their associated risks form an interactive system. These interactions can be analyzed in terms of Kane's [1977] notion of the regulatory dialectic (i.e., a "struggle model"). That is, a particular regulation, designed to restrict a certain activity and its associated risk, may lead BHCs and their banks to attempt to circumvent the restriction, thereby moving into unrestricted activities and taking on unregulated risks. As a result, an ongoing struggle exists as regulators and regulatees battle over permissible and nonpermissible activities and regulated and unregulated risks.

Focusing on the lower third of Figure 14-2, the notion of a BHC as a "deliverer of financial services" suggests the concept of "delivery risk." This risk can be separated into four components: (1) technological risk, (2) affiliation risk, (3) operating-efficiency risk, and (4) market-strategy risk.

The metamorphosis in financial-services delivery and production, as explained in Chapter 1, is most evident in the technological area where the forces of electronics, automation, and telecommunications are reshaping depository institutions. These changes present technological risks that need to be managed and monitored. BHCs with excessive amounts of "brick-and-mortar" subsidiaries are especially prone to technological obsolescence and greater risk exposure.

The dominant organizational form in United States banking is the bank holding company. With the growth of BHCs and subsidiary activities, affiliation risk has become a major component of delivery risk. The inclusion of this element in the risk framework implies that it is not feasible to separate such risk-taking from the overall riskiness of the bank or the BHC. Within the holding-company movement, areas of fundamental organizational change include (1) geographic expansion, (2) product expansion, (3) charter conversions (mainly for thrifts), and (4) joint ventures (with both depository and nondepository firms).

The operating-efficiency component focuses on cost minimization or, more col-orfully, on the "run-'em-cheap" theory. The risk of inefficient BHC operations is, of course, a reduced stream of earnings. BHC operating risks are becoming more complex and potentially more dangerous. For example, with the growth of franchis-ing, networking, and purchased processing, the risks associated with the collapse of vendors and suppliers of services are increasing.

Regarding market-strategy risk, BHCs and their subsidiaries operate in the financial-services industry (FSI) and not in the banking industry. Thus, as discussed in Chapter 12, to avoid the fate of the railroads, BHCs (and their subsidiaries) must develop financial services and products that create a demand or meet a need.

The Risk Exposure of Subsidiary Banks

According to Rose [1978], the organizational and financial flexibility of the BHC structure offers four ways of affecting the risk exposure of subsidiary banks: (1) expansion of banking activities via nonbank affiliates, (2) BHC expansion into new activities, (3) multibank expansion, and (4) parent-company leveraging. Focusing on Figure 14-3 and assuming that the BHC's regulatory and delivery systems are given or fixed, we see that the four ways of affecting bank risk exposure can be analyzed in terms of how they affect both bank portfolio risk and the consolidated portfolio risk of the BHC. Given the parent, bank, and other (nonbank) components of the BHC, let's analyze the riskiness of this triangular relationship. Is it, like the classic love triangle, a very volatile reltionship or is it of a more subdued nature? To focus on this question, consider the schematic diagram presented in Figure 14-3. The four ways of affecting the risk exposure of subsidiary banks (listed above) are included in the diagram. From an analytical perspective, the major concern is with the cash-flow effects in terms of both the level of cash flow (i.e., return) and the variability of cash flow (i.e., risk).

BHC cash flows can be described in terms of upstream, downstream, or lateral movements of funds. Upstream cash flows move from subsidiaries to the parent and include such payments as dividends, principal, interest, management fees, loans, and purchased assets. Downstream flows move from the parent to the subsidiaries and include such payments as equity, loans, principal, interest, and purchased assets Lateral flows occur between subsidiaries and include such items as fees for services (e.g., data processing), principal and interest payments, loans, and asset purchases. The major concerns from a bank safety-and-soundness standpoint are whether or not (1) the bank subsidiaries may be exposed to cash-flow drains, (2) troubled assets may be moved into the bank subsidiaries from nonbank affiliates (e.g., the failure of Hamilton National Bank in 1976), and (3) adverse publicity from troubled situations involving the parent or nonbank subsidiaries may spill over onto the bank subsidiaries (e.g., the REIT crisis of the mid-1970s). More specifically, cash outflows from the bank may reduce its earnings, impair its capital position, and lead to a liquidity crisis.

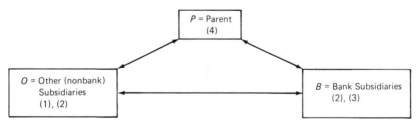

Figure 14-3   The BHC structure offers four ways of affecting the risk exposure of subsidiary banks (Rose [1978])

1. Expansion of banking activities via nonbank affiliates
    a. Spinning off banking activities
    b. Acquiring companies engaged in activities permissible to banks
2. BHC expansion into new activities
3. Multibank expansion
4. Parent-company leveraging

Alternatively, if troubled situations develop in other parts of the holding company, the bank subsidiaries may be deemed guilty by association and face liquidity crises. The ultimate foundation of the banking system is confidence; and when that confidence is eroded, for whatever reason, banks face financial difficulty. Thus, although from a structural perspective the parent company is the head of the holding company (as shown in Figure 14-3), from a safety and soundness perspective, bank subsidiaries are the focal point.

The potential benefits of multibank expansion arise from geographic diversification, whereas the potential costs are associated with "more aggressive management," increased demand for upstream cash flow, and adverse spillover effects.

The final activity in Figure 14-3 is parent-company leveraging. Other things equal and assuming an existing parent financial structure that is optimal, greater leverage (i.e., a higher ratio of debt to equity) means greater risk exposure. Since bank dividends are the major source of parent income, subsidiary banks may be under greater pressure to provide the upstream flow to service the parent's debt. However, since parent-company leveraging usually is in the form of "double leverage" (i.e., parent-company debt downstream as equity to the bank), there is a direct benefit to the bank in the form of an injection of capital. The net benefit, of course, depends upon the balance between the greater risk of the earnings drain from the bank and the benefit of the capital influx.

The net benefits of the above activities on bank risk exposure are empirical questions. Unfortunately, the existing evidence is mixed and incomplete (see Rose [1978]). The major drawback is the inability to measure the indirect costs and benefits, especially those associated with geographic and product diversification. To echo the words of Rose [1978., p. 178], until these areas are more fully explored, the net effect of the BHC movement on bank risk exposure will be unknown.

A Framework for Analyzing Bank Risk Exposure

Since the bank subsidiaries of a BHC form the kernel of the overall organization (e.g., for most BHCs well over 90 percent of consolidated assets and revenues are due to the bank subsidiaries), the words *bank* and *BHC* are, for the most part, interchangeable. In this context, then, a framework for analyzing bank risk exposure is a prerequisite for analyzing BHC safety and soundness. By substituting the word *bank* for *BHC* in Figure 14-4, an overview of the major generic risks faced by banks is obtained. Given the regulatory environment and the bank's delivery system, a bank's portfolio of assets, liabilities, and capital determines its risk exposure. The management of these accounts produces the specific portfolio risks shown in Figure 14-4.

The critical portfolio risks in banking are credit risk, liquidity risk, and interest-rate risk. Credit risk, which is mainly a function of the quality of the bank's loan portfolio, can be associated with three factors: (1) fraud risk (e.g., insider transactions), (2) foreign risk, and (3) nonfraud/nonforeign or "normal domestic" risk. Fraud-type risk has been an important cause of current and past bank failure.[2] This kind of risk

---

[2] Three of the larger *de jure* bank failures in United States history, Franklin National Bank of New York in 1974 with $1.45 billion in deposits, United States National Bank of San Diego in 1973 with $932 million in deposits, and United American Bank of Knoxville in 1983 with $794 million in deposits, all were plagued to varying degrees by some kind of insider or fraud-type transactions. These activities, of course, tend to be deliberately masked and therefore more difficult to uncover. For example, to avoid the scrutiny of bank examiners, C. Arnholt Smith kept some of USNB's records at his personal residence, whereas Jake Butcher allegedly shuffled adversely classified loans back and forth between UAB and other banks that he controlled. By the way, of these three banks only Franklin was a BHC bank. A 1984 Congressional report indicated that criminal misconduct by insiders of financial institutions has been a major contributing factor in half of all commercial bank failures and one quarter of all S&L failures between 1980 and 1983.

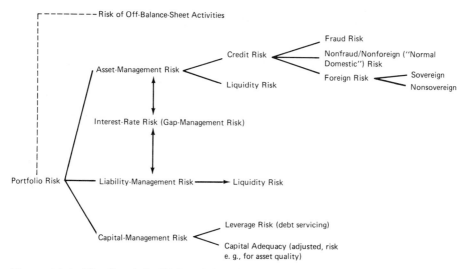

Figure 14-4   The Portfolio Risks of Banking

frequently takes the form of concentration of credit to friends, relatives, and/or business associates of the bank's top managers, United States National Bank of San Diego (1973) and United American Bank of Knoxville (1983). In addition, fraud-type risk usually is associated with bank directors who tend to function merely as "rubber-stamp bodies" and do not exercise proper oversight of the bank's activities. When these irregularities are discovered by bank examiners, they usually are so pervasive that they eventually lead to the bank's insolvency.

Because of the difficulties that large banks have been having with their loans to less developed countries (LDCs) and because most banks (at least 14,000 of them) have no foreign credit exposure at all, a separate category of foreign credit risk is shown in Figure 14-4. Foreign credit risk is further broken down into sovereign or governmental credit risk and nonsovereign (or private) credit risk. The latter represents a particularly thorny problem because of the absence of an international bankruptcy law similar to the United States domestic law. As a result, United States banks have limited recourse in the case of a default by a nonsovereign borrower. Regarding sovereign debt, an IMF safety net exists to protect against widespread defaults and "market discipline" serves to keep individual countries from repudiating their debts (i.e., because if they did they would become outcasts in international financial markets). Given that most bankers are honest and have no foreign loans, the major credit risk they face is nonfraud, nonforeign, or "normal domestic" risk. To control this risk, the *raison d'être* of portfolio theory, *diversification*, should be followed.

As an historical tribute to the days when banks stored liquidity in their balance sheets and to the fact that the degree of access to liability and capital markets varies according to bank size and quality, liquidity risk is presented as a component of both the asset and liabilities management factors in Figure 14-4. For community-type banks, liquidity, which such banks still store in their balance sheets to some extent, is provided by liquid assets, stable deposit relationships (i.e., few uninsured depositors), and reliable correspondent relationships. In contrast, money-center and regional banks that aggressively manage their liabilities, and therefore cannot afford to store expensive liquidity in their balance sheets, must depend on their good names and current performance records for continued access to financial markets. Once the "hot money" suspects trouble, a liquidity crisis occurs and the Federal Reserve, as lender of last resort, must be tapped (as it was by Continental, First Pennsylvania, and Franklin). If the so-called crisis is based upon unfounded rumors (e.g., Manny Hanny in May 1984), it usually fizzles out. The point is that true liquidity crises are not spontaneous events; they tend to be grounded in excessive risk exposure associated with portfolio mismanagement, usually in the form of bad loans.

In today's environment of interest-rate deregulation and volatility, interest-rate risk has become a vital concern. The focus is on gap management of rate-sensitive assets (RSAs) and rate-sensitive liabilities (RSLs), where rate sensitivity is defined as maturity or repricing within some specified time period (e.g., one month).[3] Rose [1984] claims that Continental Illinois's aggressive gap management eventually produced losses that "... emboldened the bank to recoup by taking additional loan-underwriting risks" (p. 1). Continental's problem situation was the reserve of First Pennsylvania's, where imprudent credit policies led to aggressive interest-rate gambles. The nexus between credit risk and interest-rate risk is one that deserves careful managerial and regulatory scrutiny, especially for large banks that have the flexibility to change their portfolio positions quickly and aggressively.

The final component of portfolio risk in Figure 14-4 is capital-management risk. It can be viewed in terms of leverage risk (debt-servicing ability) and the regulatory notion of capital adequacy, which requires adjustment for various risks, e.g., asset quality. Although bank regulators have always attempted to adjust bank capital for classified assets (mainly bad loans), only recently have they attempted more comprehensive risk-based capital requirements.

Real Dual Banking and the Risks Facing Large Banks/BHCs

Given the concept of real dual banking (i.e., big banks versus little banks), let's focus on the risks that are unique to big banks and therefore to the major BHCs. For convenience, consider the 300 largest banks/BHCs, a group that includes roughly all banks with assets over $1 billion and captures most of the major problem/failed situations since the FDIC was established (e.g., Continental, First Pennsylvania, Franklin, Security, USNB, Midland, Commonwealth, UAB, and Penn Square). The portfolio risks that are unique to this group include foreign credit risk and the liquidity and interest-rate risks associated with money-market liability management. For example, although bad energy-related domestic credits were Continental's major problem, excessive foreign-credit, liquidity, and interest-rate risks also were present. Regarding delivery risk, large banks and BHCs, because of the size and extent of their operations and holding-company activities, may be more vulnerable to structural changes in technology, innovative operations, and BHC regulations than smaller organizations.

Since the end of World War II, the banking system and individual banks have become more risky. But, at the same time, the quantity and quality of financial services provided by banks has increased. Thus, definite benefits have accrued to the users of financial services. A fundamental risk–return or cost–benefit trade-off has accrued. Figures 14-2 through 14-4 provide an analytical framework for understanding the risks faced by BHCs and their subsidiaries. Moreover, this framework can easily be applied to other financial-services firms, especially other depository institutions.

---

[3] Flannery [1981] reports that for the period 1959–1978 fifteen money-center banks had effectively hedged their balance sheets against changes in interest rates. Contrary to "conventional wisdom" he found that the average large bank had an an average liability maturity of 1.81 years compared to an average asset maturity of 1.26 years. Because of their maturity imbalance, interest-rate risk is more relevant for thrift institutions than commercial banks. Flannery and James [1984] have shown that the stock returns of large banks and S&Ls are inversely related to their maturity balances.

Banking Risks Viewed Through TRICK-Colored Glasses

Since TRICK captures the major forces of change taking place in the financial-services industry (FSI), it should also be relevant for analyzing the major risks faced by financial-services firms. The mapping from TRICK to risk space produces the following categories and definitions of risk for the FSI and its players.

1. *Technological risk.* The risk that technological change will render existing production and delivery systems obsolete, and thereby impair a firm's earnings potential and capital.
2. *Regulatory risk.* The risk that unforeseen regulatory actions or inactions will impair a firm's earnings potential and capital.
3. *Interest-rate risk.* The risk that unforeseen changes in interest rates will adversely affect a firm's net interest income, and thereby impair its earnings potential and capital.
4. *Customer risk.* The risk that competing players will capture a firm's customers and markets, and thereby impair its earnings potential and capital. Customer risk can also be referred to as "business" or "competition" risk.
5. *Kapital-adequacy risk.* Assuming a comprehensive risk-based capital measure, this risk can be viewed as the probability that the firm will have its capital impaired (i.e., become insolvent). Specifically, if all the risks faced by the firm impair its earnings potential, then eventually, other things equal, the firm's capital will be exhausted.

The risk aspects of TRICK are, of course, an integral part of our model of change, that is,

TRICK + Rational Self-Interest = Financial Innovation

Thus, when managers of financial-services firms go about their business of risk management, they may generate financial innovations (e.g., interest-rate futures to manage interest-rate risk). Moreover, structural innovations in organizational form are part of this process too. Thus, when a financial-services firm restructures its organization (i.e., structural arbitrage), say, to circumvent regulatory restrictions, it behaves in a rational and innovative way. As shown in Figures 14-2 and 14-4, the risk aspects of TRICK are captured by the comprehensive frameworks for analyzing BHC/bank risks, frameworks that apply equally well to other financial-services firms.

THE RISK OF OFF-BALANCE-SHEET ACTIVITIES AND SECURITIZATION

Why do off-balance-sheets activities (OBSAs) exist? The first stage of return-on-equity analysis provides a framework for explaining the existence of these activities or businesses. Specifically, since $ROE = ROA \times EM$, off-balance-sheet activities provide a way for banks to increase ROA, and hence ROE, without taking on any additional financial or capital leverage. Two aspects are at work here. First, off-balance-sheet activities generate fees, which help to reduce a bank's "burden" (i.e., the difference between its noninterest income and its noninterest expenses), which in turn boosts ROA and ROE, other things equal. And second, since these activities are "off the balance sheet" or "unbooked," they do not affect the ratio of assets to equity (the equity multiplier). However, even though these activities are not booked on the balance sheet, they are still risky. An activity that was all return (fee income here) and no risk would fly in the face of our financial intuition.

TABLE 14-1   Categories of Off-Balance-Sheet Activities

A. Traditional bill and trade finance activities

    1. Documentary credits or commercial letters of credit
    2. Acceptance participations[a]
    3. Endorsements

B. Financial guarantees

    1. Loan guarantees
    2. Asset sales with recourse
    3. Irrevocable letters of credit such as standby letters of credit
    4. Revolving-underwriting or note-issuance facilities[b]

C. Investment-related activities

    1. Forward foreign-exchange transactions
    2. Interest-rate swaps
    3. Currency swaps and options
    4. Interest-rate futures

[a] Participations in bankers acceptances. Acceptance participations are unbooked contingent liabilities.
[b] These are credit facilities to fund long-term commitments if the borrower cannot successfully market short-term Euronotes at or below a predetermined spread above LIBOR.
Source: Derived from Chessen [1987], pp. 11–15.

The primary risk of off-balance-sheet activities comes in the form of contingent claims placed on the firm's balance sheet, and hence on its equity capital. To illustrate, most bank off-balance-sheet activities involve credit-related businesses such as loan commitments, lines of credit, and letters of credit. These guarantee arrangements are simply off-balance-sheet underwritings. The distinguishing feature of these credit facilities is that the bank initially lends (or rents) its "reputational capital" rather than its financial capital or money. Bank customers buy these credit facilities in order to substitute the bank's name and reputation for their own in the marketplace. In the process, banks and their customers become intertwined in financial markets (e.g., consider the role of backup lines of credit for commercial paper).

Unlike booked or balance-sheet assets, unbooked or off-balance-sheet assets do not require immediate funding. Only if these credit facilities are drawn down does financial capital flow and funding become necessary. When this occurs, bookable assets are created, which will affect the bank's exposure to liquidity risk, interest-rate risk, and credit risk. In this sense, off-balance-sheet activities generate contingent claims on a bank's earnings and its capital position.

As shown in Table 14-1, Chessen [1987] has classified off-balance-sheet activities into three categories. However, since these categories are often overlapping, they are not mutually exclusive. Nevertheless, since our primary concern here is with the risk characteristics of the various off-balance sheet categories, Table 14-1 is useful for describing general classes of off-balance-sheet activities.[4]

Recapitulation

The motivation for bankers to engage in off-balance-sheet activities is clear: By generating fee income, they can increase earnings without taking on any additional

---

[4] A detailed analysis of off-balance-sheet activities and their risk management is presented in Chapter 20 of this book.

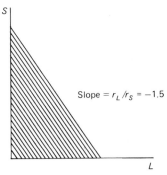

Slope = r_L/r_S = −1.5

The Family of Objective Functions

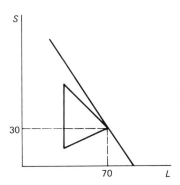

30

70 L

The Optimal Asset Portfolio

Solution Set (S^*, L^*) = (30, 70)

Figure 14-6 The Family of Objective Functions and the Solution to a Bank LP Problem

Adapted from Broaddus [1972].

Given r_L = .15 and r_S = .10, a family of objective functions can be derived with a slope equal to the ratio of r_L to r_S or −1.5.[7] The family of objective functions is depicted in Figure 14-6. The problem is to reach the highest objective function possible given the bank's feasible region. Combining the objective function and opportunity set in one graph, as shown in Figure 14-6, the solution set [S^*, L^*] is seen to be [30, 70]. The optimal income, I^*, is

$$I^* = r_L L^* + r_S S^* \qquad (14\text{-}9)$$

Thus,

$$I^* = .15(70) + .10(30) = 13.5$$

Given the constraints faced by the bank, $13.5 million is the maximum income the bank can obtain. Note that as long as $r_L > r_S$, the effective solution set will be determined by the liquidity constraint. That is, to maximize income, place the smallest amount possible in the lower-yielding asset without violating the liquidity constraint (i.e., 30[100] = 30). If $r_L < r_S$, then the new solution set [65, 35] would be dominated by the loan constraint.

---

[7] Taking the total derivative of the income function, $I = r_L L + r_S S$, it can be shown that the slope ds/dL is equal to $-r_L/r_S$

Portfolio Restrictions: The Tax Effect of Reserve Requirements

The tax effect of reserve requirements can easily be demonstrated with a continuation of this example. Suppose that the bank's financial structure is given by $[D + T + C] = [50 + 42 + 8]$ and that reserve requirements on D and T are 10 percent and 5 percent, respectively. The new balance-sheet constraint is

$$R + S + L \leq 100 \tag{14-10}$$

or

$$S + L \geq 100 - R$$

where $R = .10(50) + .05(42) = 7.1$ or 7.0 for convenience. In this situation, the solution set is $[28, 65]$ and $I^* = 12.5$. The decline in I^* from 13.5 to 12.5 represents the implicit tax paid by the bank. With required reserves, the bank should be able to relax its liquidity constraint and shift some funds into the higher-yielding asset to offset the tax burden of reserve requirements. For example, if the liquidity constraint was relaxed to $.20(S + L)$, the revised solution set would be $[19, 74]$ with $I^* = 13$, reducing the tax burden by 0.5.

Liability Management and Liquidity Requirements

The comparison of one equilibrium solution with another after a change or shock has been introduced is called a comparative-statics experiment. Such mental gymnastics can provide useful insights regarding the analytical use of a model. The introduction of reserve requirements and the subsequent relaxation of the liquidity constraint discussed above are examples of such experiments.

Let's go back to our original solution of $[30, 70]$ and $I^* = 13.5$ and consider another experiment. Suppose that through liability management the bank is able to acquire an additional \$20 million in time deposits subject to a 5 percent reserve requirement. What effect will this change have on the solution to the model and what insights can be gained about how much the bank should be willing to pay for the funds?

With the reserve requirement on the additional funds, the effective constraint on earning assets is $S + L \leq 119$ and the solution set is $[35.7, 83.3]$, where $35.7 = .3(119)$. Since the corresponding value of I^* is 16.1, the newly acquired funds generate additional income of $2.6 (= 16.1 - 13.5)$ for a gross return of 13 percent $(= 2.6/20)$ on total assets at the margin. (The return on earning assets is 13.68 percent $[= 2.6/19]$). If the bank has a target profit margin of 1.0 percent and real resource costs of 1.0 percent, then it should pay no more than 10.45 percent for the funds, which is net of the .55 percent cost allocation for the 5 percent reserve requirement. The effective cost of funds subject to a reserve requirement is the nominal cost divided by one minus the reserve requirement. In this case, 11 percent $= 10.45\%/(1 - .05)$. To summarize, the gross return of 13 percent would have to cover the following costs:

Interest cost of funds	10.45%
Allocation for a 5% reserve requirement	.55%
Overhead (real resource cost)	1.00%
Profit allocation	1.00%
Gross return	13.00%

Let us now view the liquidity constraint as being a function of the ratio of core (i.e., stable) deposits to total deposits and consider the newly acquired funds to be core deposits. With the ratio of core deposits to total deposits now higher, assume the liquidity manager is comfortable with relaxing the liquidity constraint to .25 from .30. Therefore, $S \geq .25(S + L)$. The new solution set is [29.75, 89.25] and I^* equals 16.4. With the relaxed liquidity constraint, the gross return on the newly acquired funds is 14.5 percent ($= 2.9/20$). Under these circumstances, the bank could pay 11.87 percent for the funds, other things equal. In this case, the components of the gross return are

Interest cost of funds	11.87%
Allocation for a 5% reserve requirement	.63%
Overhead (real resource cost)	1.00%
Profit allocation	1.00%
Gross return	14.50%

Liquidity Risk: Core Deposits Versus Purchased Funds

In the previous example, the relaxation of the liquidity constraint implied that the funds acquired through liability management had sufficient stability to reduce the bank's liquidity risk. Deposits gathered in local markets and characterized as being *less* sensitive to "hot-money influences" (e.g., higher interest rates and lack of explicit deposit-insurance coverage) are referred to as *core deposits*. In the face of hot-money influences, core deposits are expected to remain in the bank. In contrast to this "warm money," which makes bankers feel comfortable, there is "hot money," which makes bankers a bit nervous, especially after Continental Illinois's liquidity crisis in 1984. Purchased funds such as large negotiable CDs, Eurodollars, and federal funds are examples of "hot money" items that are sensitive to changes in interest rates and creditworthiness.

Suppose that the balance sheet expansion to 120 described above is financed with hot money rather than with core deposits. In this case, the liquidity constraint is not likely to be relaxed and might even be raised because of the greater potential for deposit variability. To illustrate, assume the liquidity constraint is raised to $S \geq .32(S + L)$. The solution set in this hot-money situation (i.e., one with a tighter liquidity constraint) is $S^* = 38$ and $L^* = 81$ (using rounded numbers), which generates $I^* = 15.9$. The marginal return on the additional funds is only 12 percent ($= 2.4/20$). With similar cost and profit allocations, the bank could pay only 9.50 percent for the funds.

This example clearly illustrates the inverse relationship between liquidity and return, as well as the importance of linking liquidity requirements to deposit structure. However, as core deposits have diminished and deposit variability increased, many bankers have not opted for higher liquidity standards. As a result, the liquidity risk of individual banks and the banking system have increased. The deposit-insurance system for banks and thrifts, backed by the "full faith and credit" of the U.S. government, have become the ultimate bearers of this greater liquidity risk.

Analysis of Off-Balance-Sheet Activities

Let's return to our original solution set of [30, 70] and I^* of 13.5. Suppose now that rather than expanding its balance sheet, the bank engages in off-balance-sheet activities (OBSAs) generating 1.5 of fee income and raising its gross revenue to 15. As discussed earlier in this chapter, bank OBSAs frequently take the form of letters of credit, lines of credit, and loan commitments. If these activities are to be something other than a "free lunch" (i.e., all return and no risk), the risk of OBSAs needs to be priced. In the context of our simple model, the pricing could take the form of a higher liquidity requirement. Suppose that the level of OBSAs needed to generate the fee income of 1.5 necessitates a liquidity coefficient of .33 on booked assets (i.e., $S \geq .33(S + L)$). Under this new constraint, the optimal solution set becomes $[33, 67]$ with income from booked assets reduced to 13.35 from 13.5. With the fee income of 1.5 unchanged, the new gross revenue is 14.85 down from 15. In this example, the risk of OBSAs is priced (indirectly by the higher liquidity constraint) at 10 percent of the fee income generated by the activities, where $.10 = .15/1.5$. The portfolio or balance-sheet effect of the constraint on OBSAs is manifested on the balance sheet by forcing the bank to hold a safer and more liquid set of assets. The compensation for the risk of the off-balance-sheet activities is the reduced return on booked assets. However, the bank is still better off than it was without the OBSAs; it simply has been made to acknowledge that OBSAs are not a "free lunch."

CHAPTER SUMMARY

Risk management is the heart of bank financial management. This chapter has presented overviews of the key risks of banking and the process of risk management. The critical portfolio (or asset-liability management) risks of banking are liquidity risk, interest-rate risk, and credit risk. In addition banks and their holding companies face other risks such as technological risk, market-strategy risk, regulatory risk, operating risk, and subsidiary/affiliation risk. The total effect of these various risks can be viewed as being captured by the bank's risk of insolvency or failure, and measured by its capital adequacy (i.e., the ability to absorb the unanticipated losses associated with the various risks of banking). To the extent that banks move activities and risks off their balance sheets, these activities and risks need to be monitored and priced properly. As a practical matter, realized risks are manifested in the variability of bank earnings and the level of bank capital.

The key concepts of this chapter are (1) the alternative ways of viewing a bank/BHC (i.e., as a consolidated balance sheet or portfolio, as a regulated company, and as a deliverer of financial services) and the risks associated with each of these perspectives, including their interaction; (2) the decomposition of a change in any variable into an anticipated change and an unanticipated change; (3) the idea of risk as arising from unanticipated changes in key variables; and (4) the contingent claims associated with off-balance-sheet activities. Using a simple model of bank portfolio allocation, the chapter concluded with an analysis of the interrelationships among liquidity, liability management, deposit structure, off-balance-sheet activities, deposit pricing, and cost allocation.

LIST OF KEY WORDS, CONCEPTS, AND ACRONYMS

Actual Change = Anticipated Change + Unanticipated Change

Asset-liability management (ALM) and ALM risks
Bank holding company (BHC)

Banking/BHC risks

> Key: credit, interest rate, and
> liquidity
> Other: regulatory,
> off-balance-sheet,
> technological, market
> strategy, operating, and
> subsidiary/affiliation
> Composite: insolvency or failure

Capital adequacy and risk-based capital
requirements
Comparative-statics experiment
Contingent claim
Core deposits and deposite structure
Fee income and financial leverage in
terms of $ROE = ROA \times EM$
Money: "hot" versus "warm"

Multibank holding company (MBHC)
Off-balance-sheet activities (OBSAs)
One-bank holding company (OBHC)
Portfolio and portfolio-allocation
models
Purchased funds
Real dual banking
Risk and risk management
Securitization
Standby line of credit (SLC)
Variability (of earnings and in
statistics)
Ways of viewing a bank/BHC

> Consolidated balance sheet or
> portfolio
> Deliverer of financial services
> Regulated company

REVIEW/DISCUSSION QUESTIONS

1. Trace the etymologies of the words *portfolio* and *risk*. How far back in financial history does modern portfolio theory go? What is the basic financial-management measure of risk? What is the difference between systematic and unsystematic risk?
2. Describe how regulatory restrictions may injure regulated firms. How can the removal of regulatory restrictions increase return without increasing risk?
3. The actual change in any variable consists of two components. What are they? Explain how this simple but powerful relationship relates to such ideas as risk, perfect certainty, and uncertainty. Use this relationship to illustrate and analyze the basic portfolio risk faced by banks.
4. What are the alternative ways of viewing a bank or bank holding company and what are the risks associated with each of these views? To catalog the various risks of banking, complete the following risk classification scheme,

> Banking risks: Key:
> > Other:
> > Composite:

5. If banking and commerce are permitted to merge and/or if commercial and investment banking are permitted to merge, how can the risk exposure of sub-sidiary banks be protected?
6. How do banking risks differ across the real dual-banking system? How easy or difficult is it for community banks to diversify?
7. What are off-balance-sheet activities (OBSAs) and why do banks find these busi-nesses so attractive? What are the most common types of OBSAs and what are the primary risks associated with these activities?
8. What are core deposits and how can a bank's deposit structure be linked to its liquidity requirements? Distinguish between "warm" and "hot" money.
9. What did the Federal Reserve System do in October 1979 and how has this event affected bank risk exposure? Was the Fed's decision more important for banks or thrift institutions? Why?

10. Evaluate and discuss the following statement[8]:

> Avoiding risk is sometimes an error. Failing to consider risk is always a mistake. ... the object is ... to determine whether the promised or the actual returns are sufficient to compensate for the risks incurred. The problem is that measuring risk is not a simple matter.

MATCHING QUIZ

Direction: Select the letter from the right-hand column that best matches the item in the left-hand column.

___ 1. Unanticipated change	A. Standby line of credit
___ 2. Perfect certainty	B. Experienced area of OBSA
___ 3. Actual change	C. Large CDs and Eurodollars
___ 4. OBSAs	D. Sale of assets
___ 5. Implication of $r_L > r_S$	E. Dates only from mid-1950s
___ 6. Backups for commercial paper	F. Source of all risk
___ 7. Modern portfolio theory	G. Actual = Anticipated
___ 8. Risk management	H. Liquidity, credit, and rate
___ 9. Securitization	I. Deposit insurance and taxpayer
___ 10. ALM risks	J. Bank dividends
___ 11. Liquidity	K. Highest credit risk of OBSAs
___ 12. Reserve requirements	L. Difficult for community banks
___ 13. Regulatory restrictions	M. Risk of obsolete equipment
___ 14. Technological risk	N. Attempt to price OBSAs
___ 15. Corporate separateness	O. Source of fee income
___ 16. Major source of parent income	P. Act as a tax
___ 17. Diversification	Q. Limit profit opportunities
___ 18. Continental Illinois	R. Hold minimum amount of S
___ 19. Purchased funds	S. Heart of bank financial management
___ 20. Bill and trade finance	
___ 21. Financial guarantees	T. Can be stored or purchased
___ 22. Ultimate bearer of banking risks	U. Would protect bank from nonbank subsidiaries
	V. Had liquidity crisis in 1984
___ 23. Risk-based capital requirements	W. Focus on cash flow

[8] See Bowers, Bowers, and Logue [1984], p. 31.

___ 24. Commercial credit analysis

___ 25. Interest-rate risk

___ 26. Liquidity risk

X. Investment-related OBSA risk

Y. Depends on deposit structure

Z. Anticipated + Unanticipated

PROBLEMS

1. If the nominal interest cost of deposits is 10 percent and the acquired funds are subject to a 10 percent reserve requirement, what is the effective cost of the funds?
2. Find the solution to the original linear-programming problem if $r_S = .20$ and $r_L = .15$. Could such a configuration of rates ever exist?
3. Prove that the slope of the objective function, $I = r_S S + r_L L$, is equal to $-r_L/r_S$.
4. What is a comparative-statics experiment? Describe the portfolio-allocation model used in the text and some of the comparative-statics experiments used to illustrate the model. Using this model, construct a comparative-statics experiment to illustrate a pricing or risk-management problem.

SELECTED REFERENCES

Benston, George. (1986). *An Analysis of the Causes of Savings and Loan Association Failures*, Monograph 1985-4/5. New York: Salomon Brothers/NYU.

Bower, Dorothy H., Richard S. Bower and Dennis E. Logue. [1984]. "A Primer on Arbitrage Pricing Theory," *Midland Corporate Finance Journal* (Fall), pp. 31–40.

Broaddus, Alfred. [1972]. "Linear Programming: A New Approach to Bank Portfolio Management," *Monthly Review*, Federal Reserve Bank of Richmond, (November), pp. 3–11.

Chessen, James. [1987]. "Feeling the Heat of Risk-Based Capital: The Case of Off-Balance Sheet Activity," *Regulatory Review*, Office of Research and Strategic Planning, FDIC, (August), pp. 1–18.

Flannery, Mark J. [1981]. "Market Interest Rates and Commercial Bank Profitability: An Empirical Investigation," *Journal of Finance* (December), pp. 1085–1011.

Flannery, Mark J. and Christopher M. James. [1984]. "The Effects of Interest Rate Changes on the Stock Returns of Financial Institutions," *Journal of Finance* (September), pp. 1141–1150.

Kane, Edward J. [1977]. "Good Intentions and Unintended Evil: The Case Against Selective Credit Allocation," *Journal of Money, Credit and Banking* (February), pp. 55–69.

Rose, John T. [1978]. "The Effects of the BHC Movement on Bank Safety and Soundness," In *The BHC Movement to 1978: A Compendium*. Washington, D.C.: Board of Governors of the Federal Reserve System.

Rose, Sanford. [1984]. "Duration's Dual Payoff," *The American Banker* (May 22) pp. 1, 4–6, 16.

Sinkey, Joseph F., Jr. [1986]. "Can Regulation and Supervision Ensure Financial Stability," *Proceedings of the Eleventh Annual Conference* Federal Home Loan Bank of San Francisco, pp. 133–148.

Sinkey, Joseph F., Jr. [1986a]. "Bank Safety and Soundness: The Interrelationship Between the BHC Movement and Financial Stability," *Issues in Bank Regulation* (Autumn), pp. 6–19.

Sinkey, Joseph F., Jr. [1986b]. "Bank Holding Company Safety and Soundness," In *Bank Holding Companies 1956–1983: Development, Regulation, and Performance* by Gerald C. Fischer, BHC Association, pp. 200–220.

Sinkey, Joseph F., Jr. [1985]. "Regulatory Attitudes Toward Risk," In *Handbook for Banking Strategy* edited by Richard C. Aspinwall and Robert A. Eisenbeis. New York: Wiley-Interscience, pp. 347–380.

CHAPTER 15

Management of Liquidity Risk: Stored Liquidity Versus Liability Management

---

ACRONYM GUIDE TO KEY WORDS AND CONCEPTS

DIDMCA = Depository Institutions Deregulation and
  Monetary Control Act
LLD = Large-liability dependence
LM = Liability management

BANK LIQUIDITY AND THE STOCK MARKET CRASH OF 1987

On October 20, 1987, the day after the stock market crash ("Black Monday"), Citibank increased its loans outstanding to 20 securities firms to $1.4 billion from its normal range of $200 to $400 million. E. Gerald Corrigan, the president of the Federal Reserve Bank of New York, had called John Reed, the chairman of Citicorp, and asked him to provide liquidity to securities firms. Since the Federal Reserve had announced that the discount window was open, Reed knew the central bank was standing behind Citicorp/Citibank, and the banking system. However, Reed did not throw caution to the wind. He summed up the situation this way:[1]

> We were providing as much liquidity as we could. Quite a few of the firms went right up to their loan limits. We didn't take physical possession of securities, but we were damn close to our customers. You have a tremendous conflict there. On one hand, there's a need for liquidity in the system. On the other hand, when you're dealing in $100 million lot sizes, you can't afford to be wrong. We can't take a $100 million write-off to save a broker. The stockholders would lynch me and with good reason.

This event dramatically illustrates the vital role bank liquidity plays in the financial system, and the economy in general, and the potential conflict between meeting that macroeconomic need and the bank's objective of maximizing shareholder wealth. Although the shareholders of Citicorp, or any other financial-services firm, would certainly benefit from a stable financial system, they should not be expected to use

---

[1] The information in this paragraph and the quotation are from Guenther [1987]. Also see Ricks [1987].

their wealth to provide such stability, which explains why Citibank stayed close to its customers in the aftermath of the stock market crash.

The ability of a bank, or any financial-services firm, to provide liquidity requires the existence of a highly liquid *and* readily transferable stock of financial assets. Liquidity and transferability are the key ingredients for such transactions. The liquidity requirement means that financial assets must be available to owners on short notice (a day or less) at par. The transferability requirement means that ownership rights in financial assets must be portable, at par, to other economic agents, and in a form acceptable to the other party. Checkable deposits and wire transfers (for large transactions) are the primary instruments of liquidity and transferability.

This chapter focuses on bank liquidity and its risk management. Since banks can either store liquidity in their balance sheets or purchase it in the marketplace, or do both, we highlight these two aspects of bank liquidity management.

INTERNAL VERSUS EXTERNAL SOURCES OF BANK LIQUIDITY: AN HISTORICAL PERSPECTIVE

Stored liquidity is an "internal" source of funds in the sense that it is in (or "stored" in) certain assets on the bank's balance sheet. Such liquidity is realized or generated when assets are converted into cash. This process, which is known as the *asset conversion* or *shiftability* approach to liquidity management, was popular following World War II. Asset conversions can be either discretionary or nondiscretionary in nature. Nondiscretionary conversions are those that occur without any explicit decision by the bank to raise funds. They, in effect, occur "naturally" as loans and securities mature and principal and interest payments flow into the bank. When nondiscretionary conversions are planned to meet the borrower's expected cash inflows, the strategy is known as the *anticipated income theory*. This approach is valuable because of its focus on the cash flow characteristics of both the bank and the borrower. From the bank's perspective, the theory led to the development in the 1950s of amortized loans and staggered or spaced investment maturities.

In contrast to this natural or anticipated inflow of funds, banks can attempt to speed up the inflow of funds by selling or lending their assets. These discretionary conversions take place when assets are sold or lent (e.g., repurchase agreements) prior to maturity. The primary risk of a "premature" conversion is the possibility of capital losses if assets are converted (sold) at prices below their purchase values (because interest rates rose after assets were purchased).

Beginning in the 1960s with the full development of the federal funds market and the effective introduction of the negotiable certificate of deposit (NCD or CD), banks began to focus on liabilities for both liquidity and for profitable expansion of their balance sheets. This development is known as *liability management*. Under this approach, banks acquire debt in the marketplace to generate liquidity. In contrast to internal or stored liquidity, this liquidity is, in effect, an "external" source of funds. The practice of liability management, which in its purest form is not available to all banks, critically depends on a bank's creditworthiness and reputation.

The major contribution of the theory of liability management has been to give bankers greater flexibility in managing their balance sheets, and to force them to think about both sides of the balance sheet as potential instruments of liquidity management. Even more broadly, it has forced bankers to think about the coordinated management of their entire balance sheets, which is the focus of this book.

Why Banks Need Liquidity and How They Generate It

Banks need liquidity to meet their customers' liquidity requirements (e.g, the case of the securities firms following the stock market crash of 1987). Bank customers can meet their liquidity needs by withdrawing funds they have on deposit with the bank or by borrowing from the bank. For example, because of the severity of the stock market crash, securities firms did not have enough funds on deposit to draw down; therefore, they had to borrow.

Since deposit withdrawals and borrowing activities occur on a regular basis (e.g., daily for funds using activities such as check writing and wire transfers but usually less frequently for borrowing, except for daily federal funds sales, overdraft accounts, and active lines of credit), banks must be prepared to meet these needs on a daily, and sometimes hourly, basis (e.g, daylight overdrafts). To do this, banks need sources of funds. From sources-and-uses-of-funds analysis, we know that decreases in assets and increases in liabilities or net worth are sources of funds. Accordingly, banks can obtain liquidity by selling assets or by acquiring additional liabilities. (Since liquidity is a short-term concept and net worth is a long-term source of funds, we ignore net worth [and long-term debt] in our discussion of liquidity.)

The primary assets held by banks are various kinds of loans. From a liquidity perspective, loans, especially short-term ones, are attractive because of their "self-liquidating nature." Specifically, they generate cash inflows via loan repayments (principal plus interest if the loan is amortized) on a regular (nondiscretionary) basis, usually monthly for a particular loan. Moreover, across a bank's loan portfolio such inflows occur on a daily basis. Thus, loans and other maturing bank investments (e.g., government securities) provide a "natural" and steady flow of funds to meet liquidity needs. In addition, because of the existence of secondary markets for securities and loans (e.g., mortgages) and the increasing development of securitization, bank assets also can be sold (converted) to generate liquidity. The strategy that banks should concentrate on making short-term, self-liquidating loans, which was popular prior to the 1930s, is known as the *commercial loan theory* or *real-bills doctrine*.

On the liability side of the balance sheet and assuming the bank's market area is growing, deposit growth also provides another "natural" source of funds. If the *expected* inflow from loans and deposits are not adequate enough to cover *expected* uses of funds (i.e., primarily new loans and deposit withdrawals), then the bank has a liquidity need. The severity of the problem is defined by the size of the discrepancy between the sources and uses of funds. To augment the shortfall in sources of funds, banks must either draw down their inventories of stored liquidity at a rate faster than their "natural" one and/or purchase the liquidity in the marketplace.

THE RISKS OF LIQUIDITY MANAGEMENT

The risks of liquidity management have a price element and a quantity element. The price or interest-rate-risk factor focuses on the price at which assets can be sold and the rate at which liabilities can be acquired. The quantity factor focuses on whether or not assets exist that can be sold and whether or not funds can be acquired in the marketplace at any cost. If assets can be sold at par or without price concessions, then the pricing risks associated with stored liquidity are negated. However, if assets must be sold at a loss, then the pricing risk will depend on the size of the price concession, which in turn will depend upon how much interest rates have risen relative to when the assets were purchased.

On the liability-management side, if banks have to "pay up" for funds (i.e., pay an additional risk premium) or if funds are not available, then these are the potential risks. In contrast, if funds are readily available at the bank's "normal" cost of funds, then the risks of liability management are negated. The latter requires the borrowing bank to maintain its creditworthiness and its reputation in the money market.

RECAPITULATION

To summarize, banks need a cushion of liquidity to meet *unexpected* deposit withdrawals and/or *unexpected* loan demand. Since banks can plan for expected withdrawals and expected borrowings, it is the unexpected changes in these variables that produce liquidity risk. If the unexpected changes are adverse, but small, the bank should be able to meet its liquidity needs without costly disruptions. However, if the changes are large and the bank is vulnerable, a liquidity crisis could develop (e.g., Continental Illinois, see the appendix to Chapter 10).

When expected sources and expected uses of bank funds are equal (i.e., without any "surprises"), liquidity problems are nonexistent. In the real world, such perfect synchronization does not exist. In other words, expected and actual changes are rarely equal because of the existence of *unexpected* changes. Accordingly, bank liquidity risk arises from unexpected changes in the sources and uses of bank funds. These unexpected changes can be caused by factors either internal to the bank (such as poor liquidity planning and management) or external to it (such as unexpected economic or financial collapse, e.g., the problems in the energy and agricultural sectors during the 1980s, the stock market crashes of October 29, 1929 and October 19, 1987).

SOURCES OF UNEXPECTED CHANGE

Liquidity problems can range from being nothing more than a minor embarrassment to a crisis so severe it requires a federal bailout, as in the case of Continental Illinois in 1984. At the embarrassment end of the spectrum, consider the experience of Robert Bacon, President of the First National Bank of Browning, Montana. On Wednesday, March 5, 1980, his bank virtually ran out of cash. Next to your bank being declared insolvent, can you think of a more embarrassing situation for a banker? According to the OCC and the FDIC, there was no record that this had ever happened to a U.S. bank since the FDIC was established. There was, of course, a federal investigation. It revealed that the "cause" of the bank's "liquidity crisis" was the local high school's success in a state basketball tournament. As a result of that victory, weekly paychecks were issued early to government employees on the nearby Blackfeet Indian Reservation and to many of the town's 1,700 residents. Since most of them were planning to watch the "Browning Indians" play 200 miles south in Missoula, they wanted to cash their checks. As a result, it did not take long for the only bank and two local check-cashing stores to run out of cash. By 2:10 P.M., First National's tellers were left with only small change in their drawers. Not only was the bank caught cash-out, the town was without liquidity too. One merchant reported, "Business was way down because nobody in town had money until the bank put out a sign at 11:00 the next morning saying they would cash checks." Another merchant said, "The whole town left for the game and they took the money."

President Bacon's reaction to the incident was:

> We can't always plan ahead because the money comes from the Federal Reserve branch office in Helena, and that's 400 miles away. They won't come here more than once a week. We've run low a couple of times before, but never out.[2]

The lesson here is that small banks, especially those in one- or two-bank towns in isolated areas, need to keep in close contact with major employers in their towns so they can be informed about changes in payroll schedules. Normally, banks can receive funds quickly through the Fed or correspondent banks, but Browning's isolated location prevented such a remedy. First National, a $10 million bank, was able to begin cashing checks at 11:00 the next morning only after Mr. Bacon had driven 130 miles to Great Falls for some cash. As of Friday morning, Mr. Bacon noted that the bank had received a few calls from worried depositors but no accounts had been closed. The OCC's regional administrator in Portland, Oregon, indicated that, "If this happens again, we can conduct an examination to suggest changes in the planning process." Alternatively, since First National now is paying for Fed services, perhaps they can obtain more frequent deliveries of cash to Browning. While First National's "green-out" was indeed an isolated incident, it clearly points out the importance of planning for liquidity needs. Thus, the success of the high-school basketball team was not the true cause of the liquidity crisis; the real cause was the bank's failure to maintain an information flow with the town's major employer. With such communication, First National could have averted its "liquidity crisis."

And Now For the Rest of the Story

In 1983, 48 FDIC-insured banks experienced the ultimate cash-out—insolvency. One of those banks was, you guessed it, First National Bank of Browning. On November 10, 1983, the OCC declared the bank insolvent and the FDIC arranged a deposit payoff for the bank's 4,000 depositors. Since the FDIC's disbursement of $9,675,000 was about $2,000,000 shy of the bank's total deposits of $11,602,000, some uninsured depositors got burned. A comparison with the treatment of uninsured depositors in Continental Illinois and other big banks points out one of the ugly aspects of the FDIC's handling of failed banks.

Since there wasn't a state basketball tournament in Montana on the day First National bit the dust, what could have caused its demise? Perhaps the Browning Indians had an important football game on that Friday in November. The FDIC's news release on the failure did not mention anything about the cause of the bank's demise. However, it did mention that the FDIC did not receive any acceptable bids for a purchase-and-assumption transaction and therefore the bank had to be handled as a deposit payoff. Based on a sample of one, we can conclude that three years and eight months after a bank has a cash-out experience it can be expected to fail.

Continental's Liquidity Crisis: An Electronic Cash-Out

During the banking collapse of the 1930s, deposit runs were characterized by long lines of bank customers waiting and hoping to recover their funds. A half century later in the 1980s, the thrift crises associated with state-insured S&Ls in Maryland and Ohio generated similar scenes. Photographs of deposit runs tend to make the evening news and the front pages of newspapers and magazines. In contrast, silent or electronic

---

[2] As reported by *The New York Times* in *The Atlanta Constitution*, March 21, 1980.

runs, which are invisible, still make news headlines but without the pictures of long lines of depositors. During the spring and summer of 1984, the liquidity crisis and subsequent bailout of Continental Illinois National Bank and its holding company, Continental Illinois Corporation, dominated the financial news (see the appendix to Chapter 10 for details). The run on Continental was a silent but deadly one—an electronic one in which billions of dollars of hot money "impulsed" out of the bank. For the seven-day period ended May 17, 1984, which was the height of the crisis, Continental required a massive infusion of $8 billion to stop its electronic hemorrhaging. Continental's liquidity crisis represents, at the extreme, the risks of aggressive liability management. Without a substantial foundation of core deposits (i.e., stable local deposits), Continental was vulnerable to an electronic or silent run. Once the marketplace, in the form of uninsured creditors, lost confidence in Continental's creditworthiness, the stage was set for the run to begin.

The term *anno Domini* (AD) is used to indicate the time division that falls within the Christian era. In banking, *anno Continental* (in the year of the Continental) may go down in history as a watershed year for liability management. As a result, the eras before and after 1984 may be marked by BC for *Before Continental* and AC for *After Continental.* The liquidity crisis, collapse, and bailout of Continental in 1984 have caused liability managers to rethink their assumptions regarding the availability of purchased funds. Prior to Continental's problems, the working assumption was that funds would always be available, especially in the international arena. Even a guarantee by the FDIC of all of Continental's liabilities could not stop the run on the bank. In the AC era, bankers, uninsured creditors, and regulators all are likely to be more cautious.

THE TRADE-OFF BETWEEN LIQUIDITY AND PROFITABILITY

To meet their day-to-day liquidity requirements banks must hold some nonearning assets in the form of cash or cash equivalents. By their very nature, these assets reduce a bank's profitability (i.e., they are nonearning or low yielding). Therefore, banks want to hold a minimum amount of such assets and still be able to meet their operational requirements for cash. The increased competition in the financial-services industry and the removal of deposit interest-rate ceilings have reinforced the need for banks to minimize their stocks of nonearning (and low yielding) assets.

The Characteristics of Liquid Assets

The "normal" shape of the yield curve is upward sloping with short-term rates lower than long-term ones. Moreover, since the market values of short-term investments are less sensitive to changes in interest rates, their interest-rate risks are less. Focusing on the default-risk structure of interest rates, we know that safe or low-risk assets return less than higher-risk ones. These three notions lead us to two desirable characteristics of liquid assets and a "fact of financial life." Specifically, liquid assets have minimal amounts of interest-rate risk and credit risk, which, of course, limits the reward they generate for risk bearing.. The one exception to this situation occurs when the yield curve is "abnormally" shaped as indicated by a negative slope or a humped configuration. When this occurs, short-term investors get the best of both worlds in the form of low risk and high return. Historically, since the normal slope of the yield curve has been positive, this phenomenon has been a short-lived one.

The final requirement for a liquid asset is a well-established market in which it can be traded. Given the low-risk profile of such assets, their market and face or nominal values show little divergence. In other words, buyers do not expect discounts, which means little or no capital loss (price depreciation) to the seller.

To summarize, the traits described above produce the standard definition of a liquid asset as one that is easily coverted into cash with little or no capital loss (price depreciation). By their nature, such assets generate low returns, which accounts for the notion of the trade-off between liquidity and profitability.

THE FUNCTIONS OF BANK LIQUIDITY

Let's define *bank liquidity management* as *the process of generating funds to meet contractual or relationship obligations at reasonable prices at all times.* In general, the obligations are to meet loan demand and/or deposit withdrawals, which are the two basic functions of liquidity. More specifically, liquidity serves

1. to demonstrate to the marketplace, which tends to be risk-averse dominated, that the bank is "safe" and therefore capable of repaying its borrowings
2. to enable the bank to meet its prior loan commitments, whether formal (i.e., legally binding) or informal
3. to enable the bank to avoid the unprofitable sale of assets
4. to restrain the size of the default-risk premium the bank must pay for funds
5. to avoid abuse of the privilege of borrowing at the Fed's discount window.

The first function can be called the "confidence" factor. As the experience of Continental Illinois has demonstrated, the confidence of the marketplace is critical for banks engaged in aggressive liability management. A strong balance sheet and the existence of government guarantees via federal deposit insurance and the lender of last resort are the primary determinants of such confidence. However, since an explicit guarantee by the federal government for both Continental bank and its holding company was not enough to stop its run, the ultimate guarantor is a strong balance sheet and capable management.

The second function is an integral part of the bank customer relationship, call it the "relationship" factor. Since commercial banks provide credit or backup liquidity facilities for their customers, they play a vital role in the credit decision-making process. The strength of these relationships determine, in part, the extent to which banks will "go to bat" for the customer in providing liquidity. Since a bank does not want to harm existing strong relationships nor inhibit the growth of promising new ones, it wants to provide for the liquidity needs of these customers. By the same token, it can send a signal to customers with weak relationships by not providing for their liquidity needs, assuming the bank does not have a legally binding commitment. The experience of Citibank following the stock market crash of 1987 (described in the first section of this chapter) illustrates the role of banks in providing "relationship" liquidity.

The third function of liquidity enables the bank to avoid having a "fire sale" of assets to generate funds. Such sales are unprofitable because the assets must be sold at fire-sale prices (i.e., deep discounts), as opposed to "reasonable prices."

The fourth function, like the previous one, focuses on the "reasonable prices" aspect of our definition of bank liquidity management. Banks with strong balance sheets will be perceived by the marketplace as being "liquid" or safe. Such banks will be able to buy funds at risk premiums reflecting their perceived creditworthiness. For example, think of the market for negotiable CDs as being tiered on the basis of strong, average, or weak balance sheets with corresponding CD rates below, equal to, or above the going market rate.

The fifth function relates to how frequently and extensively the bank uses the lender of last resort (i.e., the Fed's discount window). Since the discount rate is an administered rate set below market rates, banks could arbitrage the discount window without Fed surveillance. Sound liquidity management enables banks to avoid abusing their privilege of borrowing at the discount window. Excessive use of such borrowings could lead to increased Fed surveillance and/or reduced confidence in the marketplace.

LIQUIDITY STORED IN THE BALANCE SHEET

A traditional approach to bank liquidity management is to store liquidity in bank investments or to use federal funds as a temporary source of funds until a more permanent adjustment can be made. This technique can be described as the "shiftability" or "asset-conversion" theory. The idea is to *shift* or *convert* liquid assets into cash to meet the needs of the bank (e.g., increased loan demand). The focus of this approach is liquidity or safety at the expense of profitability. Because of the squeeze on bank profit margins, the practice of storing costly liquidity has become less popular but it still exists. It is common to describe the warehousing of liquidity in terms of a reserve-classification system with four components:[3]

1. a primary reserve
2. a secondary reserve
3. a tertiary reserve
4. an investment reserve.

The primary reserve is simply that part of a bank's cash or reserve account over and above its required legal reserve. This excess can be viewed as the bank's working reserve. The objective should be to minimize this sterile asset but at the same time keep enough of it to avoid embarrassing cash shortages.

The secondary reserve consists of federal funds sold and short-term U.S. government securities (e.g., Treasury bills). To be included in this classification, a security must have high quality (very low default risk), short maturity (less than one year until maturity to mitigate interest-rate risk), and marketability (the ability to be sold on short notice). Assets in this category form the kernel of the liquidity-reserve approach because they epitomize the definition of a liquid asset. Over the planning horizon covered by the secondary reserve (say, up to two years), federal funds sold (24-hour maturity) can be used for immediate liquidity requirements, Treasury bills with 2 to 182 days remaining until maturity can be used for intermediate requirements, and Treasury notes with six months to one year until maturity can be used for the more distant requirements. The function of the secondary reserve is to provide liquidity for (1) seasonal demands for funds, (2) unanticipated short-term increases in loan demand, and (3) other minor unforeseen developments.

The tertiary reserve is designed to provide liquidity protection against longer-term changes such as increased loan demand or reduced deposit inflows. Government securities with maturities of one to two years usually are included in this category. The

---

[3] For example, see Watson [1972]. In today's environment, the maturity ranges of the various components are shorter than those described by Watson.

investment reserve typically consists of securities with maturities longer than two years. This account is designed primarily to produce income. To the extent that it performs a reserve or liquidity function, it is used only as a last resort.

The reserve classification system provides a bank with a spaced-maturity investment portfolio. The spacing, however, is uneven because of the emphasis placed on short-term securities so that capital losses can be avoided. The central idea is to store various degrees of liquidity in the alternative reserve categories. Since the system does not have to be as rigid as the one described here, some flexibility can be built into the approach. Like any tool, however, the reserve classification system should be used to set guidelines for liquidity management and not as a straitjacket. On balance, the approach tends to be a conservative one that results in a suboptimal investment portfolio.[4]

LIQUIDITY PURCHASED IN THE MARKETPLACE

As an alternative to storing liquidity in balance-sheet items, a bank may attempt to generate liquidity by managing its liabilities. This approach, which began in the early 1960s with the development of the certificate of deposit (CD), is referred to as *liability management* and labelled *LM*. The idea behind LM is to acquire funds and use them profitably, especially to meet loan demand. What is unique about LM is that nontraditional borrowing arrangements are used to acquire the funds. The uniqueness is manifested in interest, maturity, and service characteristics that differ in important ways from traditional deposits or nonmanaged liabilities. The technique of LM focuses on a permanent expansion of a bank's asset base as opposed to the compositional change in assets that the liquidity-reserve approach adopts. The tools of LM include such instruments as federal funds, CDs, notes and debentures, Eurodollars, repurchase agreements, and brokered deposits. By adopting a strategy of LM, a bank does not have to store as much liquidity in its assets and thus it frees funds for more profitable loan and investment opportunities. Managerial preferences regarding risk–return trade-offs will govern the aggressiveness of a bank's LM position and the extent to which it stores liquidity.

The Composition and Cost of Bank Liabilities

Selected liabilities (as a percentage of total assets) for all insured commercial banks for the years 1981 to 1986 are shown in Table 15-1. Over this five-year period (i.e., year-end 1981 to year-end 1986), total deposit liabilities as a percentage of total assets have declined slightly from 78.6 percent to 76.7 percent. Regarding the composition of bank liabilities, a number of important trends have emerged for the industry. First, demand deposits continued to decline, although they turned up slightly from their 1985 figure of 15.7 percent to 16.0 percent in 1986. Second, the decline in demand deposits was partially offset by the increase in other checkable deposits (e.g., NOW accounts), which increased from 2.4 percent of total assets in 1981 to 5.2 percent in 1986. Third, the decline in the extent of "aggressive" LM is indicated by two variables: (1) the decline in deposit liabilities in foreign offices from 15.9 percent of total assets in 1981 to 11.6 percent in 1986 and (2) the decline in large time deposits from 14.1 percent of total assets in 1981 to 10.7 percent in 1986. These two trends can be explained, respectively, by the international debt crisis, which has caused multinational

---

[4] Suboptimal in the sense that there are other portfolios with risk-return parameters that dominate it. The topic of bank investment management is discussed in detail in Chapter 16.

TABLE 15-1   Selected Liabilities as a Percentage of Total Assets, All Insured Commercial Banks, 1981–86 [a]

Item	1981	1982	1983	1984	1985	1986
Deposit liabilities	78.61	77.61	77.68	77.93	77.47	76.72
In foreign offices	15.93	15.79	14.71	12.94	12.65	11.61
In domestic offices	62.68	61.82	62.97	64.99	64.83	65.11
Demand deposits	20.76	17.35	16.53	16.47	15.69	16.04
Other checkable deposits	2.43	3.43	4.03	4.34	4.58	5.21
Large time deposits [b]	14.12	14.61	12.15	12.22	11.42	10.75
Other deposits [c]	25.37	26.44	30.26	31.95	33.14	33.12
Gross federal funds purchased and repurchase agreements	7.54	7.99	7.81	7.51	7.62	8.26
Other borrowings	2.62	2.64	2.84	2.87	3.33	4.00
MEMO						
Money market liabilities [d]	40.21	41.03	37.51	35.55	35.01	34.61
Average assets (billions of dollars)	1,940	2,101	2,259	2,418	2,562	2,779

[a] Before 1984, data are based on averages for call dates in December of the preceding year and in June and December of the current year. In 1984, data are based on averages for call dates at the beginning and end of the year only. After 1984, data are based on averages of the call date in December of the preceding year and all four call dates in the current year.
[b] Deposits of $100,000 and over.
[c] Including savings, small time deposits, and MMDAs.
[d] Large time deposits issued by domestic offices, deposits issued by foreign offices, repurchase agreements, gross federal funds purchased, and other borrowings.

banks to rethink their overseas strategies, and by the high interest rates of the early 1980s, which forced banks to seek out lower-cost sources of funds. Both of these aspects are captured by the memo item in Table 15-1, which shows money market liabilities declining from 40.2 percent of total assets in 1981 to 34.6 percent in 1986.

In addition to other checkable deposits, three categories of bank liabilities have shown upward trends: (1) other deposits, which include savings deposits, small time deposits, and money market demand accounts (MMDAs), increased from 25.4 percent of total assets in 1981 to 33.1 percent in 1986; (2) federal funds purchases and repurchase agreements increased from 7.5 percent of total assets in 1981 to 8.3 percent in 1986; and (3) other borrowings increased from 2.6 percent of total assets in 1981 to 4.0 percent in 1986. Finally, average industry assets, which serve as the deflator for the percentages in Table 15-1, grew from $1.9 trillion in 1981 to $2.8 trillion in 1986, a compound annual growth rate of 7.45 percent.

The rates paid for fully consolidated liabilities for all insured commercial banks for the years 1981 to 1986 are shown in Table 15-2. Most of the rates at year-end 1986 are roughly one-half the level they were at year-end 1981. This dramatic decline in rates is due to the substantial reduction in inflation over the five-year period. Recall that nominal rates of interest equal real rates plus a premium for expected inflation. Two other interesting aspects of the data in Table 15-2 are (1) the lower cost of core deposits (as measured by other deposits) relative to large CDs (i.e., in 1986 6.67 percent versus 7.31 percent, respectively) and (2) the higher cost of deposits in foreign offices relative to domestic ones, either core or large deposits.

THE THREE FACES OF LIABILITY MANAGEMENT

Liability management refers to the process by which bankers attempt to develop nontraditional borrowing arrangements (i.e., purchased funds) and to use them

TABLE 15-2   Rates Paid for Fully Consolidated Liabilities, All Insured Commercial Banks, 1981–86 [a] **(Percent)**

Item	1981	1982	1983	1984	1985	1986
Interest-bearing deposits	13.42	12.10	9.32	9.92	8.21	6.98
Large certificates of deposit	16.42	14.13	8.90	10.67	8.73	7.31
Deposits in foreign offices[b]	17.37	14.87	10.32	12.62	9.48	7.78
Other deposits	10.07	9.99	9.11	8.84	7.67	6.67
Gross federal funds purchased and repurchase agreements	17.53	12.84	9.69	11.23	7.97	6.78
Other liabilities for borrowed money	13.84	12.81	11.88	13.38	10.67	8.01
TOTAL	13.89	12.21	9.46	10.19	8.29	7.01

[a] Calculated as described in the "Technical Note," *Federal Reserve Bulletin*, vol. 65 [September 1979], p. 704, for years through 1984. For more recent years, rates are derived from expense items and quarterly average balance sheet data.
[b] Series break after 1983. Reporting instructions classified international banking facilities as domestic offices until the end of 1983 and as foreign offices thereafter. Income data are not sufficiently detailed to allow construction of a consistent series on the new basis for rates of return as has been done for balance sheet data in other tables in this chapter.
[c] Including subordinated notes and debentures.

profitably, especially to meet loan demand. Given the profit motive, Kane's[5] explanation of the phenomenon of liability management focuses on three relatively unchanging aspects of the business of U.S. commercial banking:[6]

1. banks' desire to minimize deposit interest costs by varying applicable deposit rates with the interest sensitivity of specific pools of customer funds
2. banks' written and unwritten commitment to meeting spurts in loan demand even when the Federal Reserve seeks in monetarist fashion to restrain aggregate deposit growth
3. banks' desire to offset regulatory burdens imposed on them by reserve requirements and deposit-insurance fees.[7]

In a nutshell, this explanation of liability management hinges on three basic concepts: (1) the minimization of bank interest expenses, (2) the importance of customer relationships, and (3) the circumvention of regulatory restrictions (see Figure 15-1). In the following analysis, these components are scrutinized individually. However, keep in mind that it is the interaction of the components that has been and is the driving force behind liability management.

Minimizing Deposit Interest Costs

The ability to minimize deposit interest costs depends upon the responsiveness of particular deposit groups to changes in deposit rates. The more interest sensitive specific pools of customer funds are, the more difficult it is to minimize deposit interest expenses. As illustrated in Figure 15-2, transactions-type balances are less sensitive to rate changes than purchased funds. In Figure 15-2a, the supply curve SS represents a pool of funds that is perfectly inelastic. In this case, there is no incentive for the bank to pay more than some nominal rate of interest. If the supply schedule becomes sensitive to rate changes (as indicated by the clockwise rotation of SS to S'S'), it takes a higher rate of interest to generate an equivalent amount of deposits. In

[5] This section draws on an article by Kane [1979].

[6] *Ibid.*, pp. 149–150.

[7] Prior to DIDMCA, deposit-rate ceilings played a major role in the development of liability management.

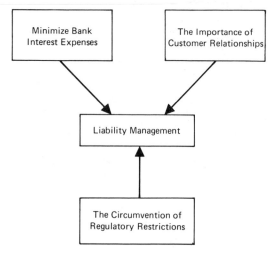

Figure 15-1   The Three Faces of Commercial Bank Liability Management

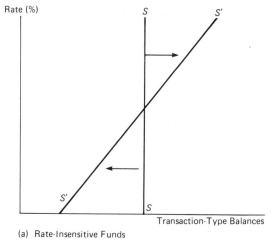

(a) Rate-Insensitive Funds

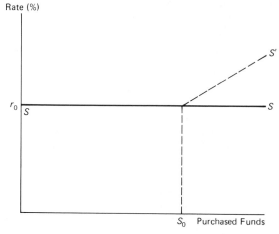

(b) Rate-Sensitive Funds

Figure 15-2   The Interest-Rate Sensitivity of Alternative Sources of Funds

addition to transactions-type balances, specific pools of customer funds may be rate insensitive because of ignorance, lack of competition, minimum purchase requirements (e.g., a $10,000 T-bill investment), transaction cost, or other factors. In Figure 15-2b, the case of purchased funds that are supplied perfectly elastically is depicted. At rate r_0, the prevailing market rate, a bank may obtain all the purchased funds it wants given the supply curve SS. However, beyond some level of deposits, S_0, the supply curve may be less than perfectly elastic (as indicated by the dashed line segment labeled S') and higher rates may be necessary to generate additional funds.

The important point in this analysis is the ability of banks to *segment* their deposit customers or markets on the basis of rate sensitivity. By varying deposit rates across these segments (compare the market for passbook savings with the market for negotiable CDs, for example), banks are able to reduce their deposit costs. Why do banks go after these higher-cost sources of funds? They want such funds primarily to meet the loan demand of their best customers.

Customer Relationships

The second face of liability management explains why banks go after high-cost purchased funds. Bankers enter into formal and informal agreements with their best customers to accommodate requests for credit. Failure to meet these loan demands will not enhance customer relationships and may have an adverse effect upon a bank's long-run profitability. Thus, to ensure that such events do not occur, banks attempt to manage their liabilities even when the Fed is seeking to restrict the growth of the supply of money and credit.

The important point is that customer relationships play an important role in commercial bank loan decisions.[8] Such relationships are valuable because of the broad-based foundation they establish with borrowers, especially corporate ones. Beyond the attractive net rate of interest business loans earn, such loans are important because they are associated with valuable deposit balances and the use of ancillary services that generate fee income. Banks' attempt to get existing customers to use more bank services is referred to as *cross-selling*. Cross-selling is important because it generates fee income that is used to offset declining profit margins.

The customer-relationship aspect of liability management involves a combination of deposit balances, customer service, and loans. Corporate deposit balances receive implicit interest payments in the form of services provided by the bank at a price below their true costs. As the account size increases relative to account activity, these deposit balances become more valuable to the extent that the implicit interest payments result in a declining cost per dollar of deposit balance. Because of the prime-rate and compensating-balance conventions, some corporate customers may be given concessions on interest rates charged for credit extensions. The existence of the "discount" prime rate supports this notion. Moreover, to protect the long-term availability of low-cost, corporate balances, the bank even may be willing during periods of credit restraint to grant loans at a rate very close to its marginal cost of purchased funds. On balance, the net rate of interest on such business loans provides an attractive return to the bank in terms of its joint deposit-loan pricing strategy.

---

[8] The notion of the customer relationship also is discussed in Chapters 18 and 19. See Hodgman [1963] and Kane and Malkiel [1965] for more complete discussions of the role of customer relationships. Budzeika [1976] has shown that the desire to satisfy loan demand has been the major focus of liability management by New York City banks.

Circumventing Regulatory Restrictions

Reserve requirements, deposit-insurance fees, and other regulatory burdens (e.g., Reg Q prior to DIDMCA) impose costs on firms subject to such restrictions. In the quest for long-run profits, commercial banks have attempted to circumvent these restrictions. Bankers' desires to offset these regulatory burdens constitute the third face of liability management.

Deposit-Rate Ceilings

Although deposit-rate ceilings no longer exist today, they played a major role in the development of liability management. Prior to their removal, Reg Q ceilings restricted the ability of banks (and thrifts) to attract funds and made them especially vulnerable to disintermediation during periods of high interest rates (e.g., the credit crunches of 1966, 1969, 1974, and the early 1980s). Like other forms of price controls, deposit-rate ceilings cause distortions and inefficiencies. The distinction between *explicit* and *implicit* interest is important here. Deposit-rate ceilings restrict the amount of *explicit* interest (i.e., coin of the realm) that banks can pay. However, banks can attempt to make the supply of rate-restricted or small-denomination deposits more interest-rate sensitive by resorting to the payment of *implicit* interest in the form of more branches, longer hours, merchandise premiums, and the like. The effects of deposit-rate ceilings and implicit interest on such deposits are pictured and described in Figure 15-3. In addition to the payment of implicit interest, banks attempted to develop sources of funds that were not subject to deposit-rate ceilings. On balance, rate ceilings forced banks to invest time and resources developing and testing implicit-interest and liability-management schemes. Such plans lead to distortions and inefficiencies compared to unrestricted markets. In addition, such arrangements are relatively inflexible both to put into place and to dismantle (e.g., a branch) compared to explicit interest.

Reserve Requirements

Reserve requirements are a form of implicit taxation. Prior to DIDMCA and universal reserve requirements, banks could reduce their reserve-requirements tax by choosing not to be a member of the Federal Reserve System.[9] Moreover, since all bank liabilities are not taxed the same (some liabilities even have a zero reserve requirement), banks are encouraged to develop sources of funds that are less heavily taxed.

The Structure of Deposit Insurance

The fundamentals of deposit insurance were established in Chapters 7 and 8. The explicit deposit-insurance fee is 1/12 of one percent of a bank's *total domestic* deposits in return for $100,000 coverage per account. However, because of the dominant use of the deposit-assumption technique in handling bank failures, especially the larger ones, and because of the use of federal bailouts (e.g., Continental Illinois and First Pennsylvania Bank), the FDIC implicitly provides 100 percent deposit insurance for most banks. However, as the case of Penn Square Bank demonstrates, 100 percent deposit insurance is not guaranteed in all situations. Since the FDIC's insurance premium is a flat fee, it is not a function of a bank's riskiness. Thus, deposit insurance is a bargain that banks try to take advantage of by increasing their risk exposure. They can accomplish this task by taking on additional asset risk and/or by shifting large

[9] Membership in the Federal Reserve System still is optional today but all depository institutions are subject to Federal Reserve requirements based upon type of deposit and deposit interval.

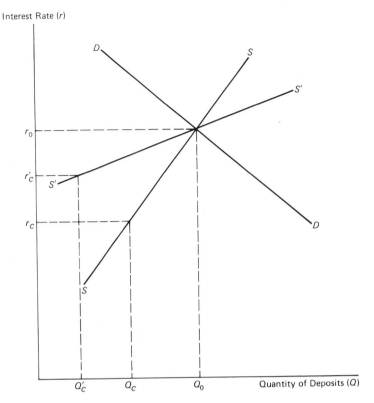

Analysis of Figure 15-3:

1. Unconstrained solution: The equilibrium market-clearing solution is (r_0, Q_0).
2. The impact effect of deposit-rate ceilings: The constrained solution is (r_c, Q_c). Disintermediation is equal to the distance Q_0 minus Q_c and the interest loss to savers (or expense saved from the bank's perspective) per dollar of deposits is equal to the distance r_0 minus r_c.
3. The imposition of deposit-rate ceilings leads banks to develop schemes for paying implicit interest, leading to a higher effective ceiling rate at r'_c. With the original supply curve *SS*, the implicit interest would recoup some of the disintermediated funds. However, because of competition from unregulated intermediaries, the supply curve for small-denomination balances becomes more elastic, rotating clockwise to *S'S'*. As a result, disintermediation increases to a total distance of Q_0 minus Q'_c and the benefits that depository institutions derive from rate ceilings are squeezed.

Figure 15-3   A Geometric Analysis of the Effects of Deposit-Rate Ceilings and Implicit Interest on the Market for Small-Denomination Deposits.

funds (over $100,000) from deposit to nondeposit categories. To protect the deposit-insurance fund, all the federal banking agencies impose implicit insurance premiums on excessive bank risk-taking. Such implicit fees are imposed via the examination and regulatory processes of the banking authorities. Thus, the effective total deposit-insurance premium consists of an explicit fee *plus* an implicit one, the latter being a unique function of each bank's risk exposure as determined by its annual (or more frequent) on-site inspection.

Regulatory Recapitulation

Prior to DIDMCA, the ultimate accomplishment for a bank liability manager was to find a liability instrument that was not subject to deposit-rate ceilings, reserve requirements, or deposit-insurance fees. Such achievements usually were short-lived, however, because the instruments frequently were restricted in some way by the banking authorities. This cat-and-mouse game played in the liability-management arena was another manifestation of the regulatory dialectic. Today, although competitive reregulation has eliminated some restrictions, the game goes on.

TWO DISTINCT ASPECTS OF LIABILITY MANAGEMENT: LM-1 AND LM-2

Kane [1979] considers *liability management* to cover two distinct phenomena, which he labels LM-1 and LM-2. LM-1 is defined as the process of supplementing asset management with very short-term borrowing. It is referred to as money-desk or reserve-position liability management. In contrast, LM-2, which is called generalized or loan-position liability management, refers to the process of closely managing *all* liabilities, whatever their maturity. Thus, LM-1 is a subset of LM-2.

Reserve-Position Liability Management (LM-1)

The primary ground for distinguishing between LM-1 and LM-2 is the time domain. Money-desk or reserve-position liability management is a technique used to systematically supply a bank with liquidity by issuing new short-term liabilities. The strategy is to purchase funds as needed to complement liquidity stored in the balance sheet. Since this approach permits a bank to hold a higher-yielding, less-liquid portfolio, its major benefit is a *compositional* one. The principal instrument of LM-1 is one-day purchases of federal funds.[10] Thus, when a bank *temporarily* loses reserves because of deposit withdrawals or net additions to earning assets, it bids for one-day federal funds; in the opposite case of temporary excess reserves, it sells federal funds. Viewed in this light, LM-1 increases the efficiency of the financial-intermediation process and probably cushions the vulnerability of the banking system to downward shocks. In particular instances, however, certain banks (e.g., Continental, Franklin National, and First Pennsylvania) have attempted to use federal funds as a *permanent* source of funding. This strategy worked fine as long as the banks were able to roll over the federal funds (that is, as long as the supply was perfectly elastic—see Figure 15-2a). However, once these banks' performances dropped off and their financial difficulties became public knowledge, they could not obtain financing from the federal-funds market. As a result, all three banks required immediate financial assistance to prevent them from failing, although Franklin eventually was closed in October of 1974. Continental and First Pennsylvania were bailed out by the FDIC.

Of course, there is nothing new about LM-1, because banks have been lending funds to each other for decades. The interbank system of bank lending was encouraged by the establishment of the Federal Reserve System in 1913. According to Kane, the Fed helped to develop the federal-funds market by (1) reducing the cost of regional check clearing, (2) introducing an additional source of short-term credit, and (3) creating a new reason for borrowing—to meet reserve requirements.

---

[10] Or the use of repurchase agreements (RPs or repos), i.e., the sale of a security with agreement to repurchase at a specified price.

**TABLE 15-3   Some Evidence on
the Extent of LM-1, 1974–1985**

	Federal Funds ($ millions)[a]			
Year	Purchased	Sold	Net Purchases[b]	Purchased to Total Assets
1974	$ 51,217	$ 38,944	$12,273	5.70%
1975	52,190	37,361	14,829	5.56%
1976	70,299	45,855	24,444	6.95%
1977	82,952	49,881	33,071	7.29%
1978	91,292	48,756	42,536	7.17%
1979	112,149	61,065	51,084	7.98%
1980	132,461	70,135	62,326	8.61%
1981	163,501	90,664	72,837	9.68%
1982	179,494	103,213	76,281	9.57%
1983	177,769	92,712	85,057	8.77%
1984	188,760	110,701	78,059	7.52%
1985	221,987	133,091	88,896	8.13%

[a]Data are for all insured commercial banks and include repurchase agreements.

[b]"Net Purchases," which are equal to "Purchased" minus "Sold," indicate the use of noncommercial bank sources of funds and include the following lenders: S&Ls, mutual savings bank, MSBs, Federal Home Loan Banks and Board, U.S. government agencies, and securities dealers. Member banks are not permitted to buy "regular" federal funds from business corporations, state and local governments, foreign banks, and foreign official institutions.

Source: FDIC, *Annual Report* [1979], Table 109, pp. 170–171 and FDIC, *Statistics on Banking* [1983], Table 109, pp. 43–45 and [1985], Table RC-9, p. 42.

Recent activity in the federal-funds market is summarized by the data presented in Table 15-3. Since these data are dominated by the customary one-day interbank transactions, they are a good indication of the use of LM-1 by the banking system. To the extent that longer-term transactions exist in the data, the series also contains an LM-2 component. The net purchases figure in Table 15-3 measures the use of nonbank sources of short-term borrowings (see the notes to Table 15-3). As of year-end 1985, federal-funds purchases (including repos) amounted to roughly 8 percent of total bank assets. Moreover, the majority of these purchases are made by the largest banks, resulting in a flow of funds from community banks to the giants of the industry.

Generalized or Loan-Position Liability Management (LM-2)

In explaining the evolution of LM-2, Kane [1979] emphasizes two important distinctions previously established in this book: (1) the concept of *anticipated* versus *unanticipated* inflation and (2) the concept of *explicit* versus *implicit* interest. Given these distinctions and the three faces of liability management, Kane sees unanticipated inflation and regulatory restraints (in the form of Reg Q, reserve requirements, and deposit-insurance fees) as causes of LM-2. The helter-skelter development of both LM-1 and LM-2 in the 1960s and 1970s can be traced to periods of tight money (characterized by high interest rates, disintermediation, and unanticipated inflation) and to the tightening and relaxing of regulatory restrictions related to liability management.

Generalized liability management is designed to expand *permanently* the size of a bank's balance sheet. Viewed as a series of regulation-induced innovations, LM-2 involves primarily the expansion of a bank's loan portfolio through the use of discriminatory interest-rate competition with respect to nontraditional liabilities. In addition, to the extent that LM-2 reduces deposit volatility by increasing the average maturity of a bank's liabilities, the reduction in uncertainty becomes another aspect of LM-2 strategy. The prime instrument of LM-2 is the negotiable certificate of deposit (CD).

LM-2 can be viewed as consisting of a *planned* component and a *reactive* component.[11] The planned component represents the systematic effort by bank management to expand its balance sheet profitably. The reactive component is an explicit counterweight used by managers to offset exogenous disturbances elsewhere in the balance sheet. The reactive element, which is a conditional random variable, is a function of the uncertain changes in deposit supplies and loan demands. It is in this sense that managed liabilities are a random variable possessing a standard deviation. This distinction is a refinement of Kane's concept of LM-2.

LM-1 and LM-2: A Recapitulation

Both types of liability management involve an active rather than a passive approach toward attracting funds. The notion of the bank's funds constraint as given or determined by outside forces is outdated both in theory and in practice. Liability-management bankers are constantly looking for new ways to profitably package their liabilities in a form attractive to surplus-spending units. The driving forces behind both LM-1 and LM-2 have been unanticipated inflation and regulatory constraints.

Kane [1979] contends that the regulation-induced innovations of LM-2 activity by large banks have built up a panic potential in the U.S. financial system. His argument goes like this: The LM-2 activity of large U.S. banks has focused on relatively inflexible and cost-increasing ways for paying implicit interest (e.g., branching) and on attracting pools of "hot money" (e.g., Eurodollars). This strategy increases the volatility of large-bank liabilities. In addition, bank contingent liabilities, such as guarantees of customers' commercial-paper issues, have increased and to some extent become more risky too.

In conjunction with their use of costly liability management, large U.S. banks have reached out for higher-returning assets. As a result, they have tended to accept greater default risk, as evidenced by their holdings of low-rated municipal securities, loans to REITs, and credits to financially weak and politically unstable foreign countries While bank asset risk has been increasing, the capital cushion held by banks has been declining.

Kane sees banks that adopt these "modern" portfolio practices as increasing their exposure to liquidity crises and becoming more dependent upon the Fed and the FDIC to bail them out in the event of adverse market developments. The cases of Continental and First Pennsylvania fit Kane's scenario perfectly. What has the banking authorities worried (and presumably Kane too) is the possibility that a chain of bank failures could trigger a nationwide financial panic. While the probability of such an event occurring is small, it is difficult to argue that it has not increased recently because of the more aggressive asset-liability management strategies employed by large banks.

To summarize, Kane finds an instructive parallel in the TV commercial that encourages consumers to change their automobile oil filters regularly. His "You-can-pay-me-now-or-pay-me-later" punch line for the financial system is

> Sooner or later, pressures generated by regulatory efforts to plaster over depository institutions' festering solvency problems are going to find release. We can only pray that the valves and rods of our national economic engine are not damaged in the process [1979], p. 173).

---

[11] See Sinkey and Jahera [1981] and Kane and Malkiel [1965].

MEASURING BANK LIQUIDITY

Since liquidity can be either stored in a bank's balance sheet or purchased in the marketplace, or both, we need at least two alternative measures of liquidity. It is somewhat easier to measure stored liquidity than it is to gauge the confidence money and deposit markets have in a particular borrower. However, we can get a handle on the potential liquidity available in the marketplace (through liability management) by focusing on the concept of excess or unused debt capacity. The idea is a straightforward one. If a bank has the potential to be a liability-management organization (i.e., if it has the size, reputation, and creditworthiness), we can measure the extent to which it has actually tapped these markets for funds. Banks that have been very aggressive in acquiring funds may have little excess capacity compared to banks that have been more cautious. Again, however, everything rests on the confidence factor because whether a bank has excess debt capacity or not, if the market lacks confidence in the borrower, the funds will be withdrawn or not available.

The other side of the excess-capacity coin is that aggressive LM banks can be described as having a "large-liability dependence" (LLD).[12] At the extreme, this dependence means a vulnerability to a Continental-type deposit run. Although there are various ways to measure LLD, Cates Consulting Analysts, Inc., have suggested the following formula:

$$LLD = \frac{\text{Large Liabilities} - \text{Temporary Investments}}{\text{Earning Assets} - \text{Temporary Investments}} \tag{15-1}$$

The ratio is a measure of the extent to which hot money supports the bank's basic earning assets. Since the numerator of formula 15-1 represents short-term, interest-sensitive funds that are largely supplied by institutions, a positive and high ratio implies some risk of illiquidity. How high is high? Peer-group analysis is used to set some norm or standard upon which "high" can be based. For the largest banks, an LLD ratio of 50 percent is not unusual. Note that LLD is not a meaningful ratio for the thousands of community banks in the United States because they simply do not have many large liabilities. Moreover, since they carry large amounts of temporary investments, their LLD ratios are negative. Thus, LLD is a relevant measure of liquidity risk only for banks that practice liability management.

To determine whether a given LLD ratio is "manageable" within a particular peer group, Cates has proposed comparing it with the bank's BHC's net interest margin (NIM).[13] The crucial part of the test is the movement of the bank's NIM over the course of the interest-rate cycle. If NIM is stable or moving with the cycle, then the bank is viewed as being better able to handle the level of interest sensitivity implied by LLD. The worst of both worlds is to have a high LLD combined with a volatile NIM. The gauge or benchmark for the NIM movements or shifts are provided by the bank's peer group.

Eight alternative measures of bank liquidity are presented in Table 15-4. The data, which are as of December 31, 1985, cover nine size classes ranging from less than $25 million in assets to over $10 billion. Each of the ratios and how they vary with bank size are described below.

---

[12] *The Cates Bank Financial Analysis Course, Book I.* New York: Cates Consulting Analysts, Inc. [1984], pp. 80–82.

[13] *Ibid.*, pp. 82–84.

TABLE 15-4   Alternative Measures of Bank Liquidity (Median Values as of December 31, 1985)

	All Banks	Banks With Domestic and Foreign Consolidated Assets of—								
		Less than $25M	$25M to $50M	$50 M to $100M	$100M to $300M	$300M to $500M	$500M to $1B	$1B to $3B	$3B to $10B	$10B or more
Liquidity										
Core deposits to assets	79.63	80.12	80.70	79.89	78.04	74.77	71.85	65.83	57.72	29.03
Loans & leases to assets	53.81	51.66	53.37	53.59	57.23	58.77	59.28	60.07	61.32	63.16
Temporary investments to assets	17.34	19.45	17.09	16.42	15.48	14.47	14.17	14.56	14.22	15.12
Temporary investments to volatile liabilities	176.87	236.73	201.65	162.46	122.17	82.63	71.41	58.74	39.47	28.18
Brokered deposits to total deposits	0.00	0.00	0.00	0.00	0.00	0.00	0.00	0.00	0.70	1.40
Investment securities, market to book:										
Taxable securities	100.00	100.00	100.00	99.73	98.99	99.02	98.38	98.28	98.05	97.25
Nontaxable securities	101.87	101.77	102.04	101.96	101.85	101.55	101.48	101.61	101.22	102.31
Pledged securities to total securities	24.39	18.62	22.19	25.84	36.03	44.54	46.87	56.06	52.61	63.30
Miscellaneous										
Total number of banks	14,406	5,327	3,729	2,788	1,762	295	204	192	83	26
Total number of employees (Full-time equivalent, year-end)	1,525,564	68,613	100,419	142,202	198,182	72,671	107,938	218,196	249,326	368,017
Number of bank failures[a]	118	77	30	7	4	0	0	0	0	0

[a] Does not include two Savings Bank Failures
Source: FDIC, *Statistics on Banking* [1985], Table RT-1, p. 160.

Core Deposits to Assets

This ratio measures a bank's stable or core deposit base relative to its total assets. Core deposits are funds expected to remain in the bank, regardless of the economic environment. As such, core deposits tend to have two distinguishing features: (1) collection in local markets, referred to as the bank's service area, and (2) account size less than $100,000, which means the funds are insured. In Table 15-4, core deposits are defined as average total deposits less average time deposits over $100,000 and, if applicable, less deposits in foreign offices. Community-type banks should have high values for this ratio, whereas LM banks should have low values. As shown in Table 15-4, banks with total assets less than $25 million have a ratio of core deposits to assets of 80 percent, whereas banks with assets greater than $10 billion have a ratio of 29 percent. The ratio declines monotonically as bank size increases. If we subtract the core deposits-to-asset ratio from one, we get the ratio of noncore deposits to assets. In this form, the emphasis is on liability management as we get a measure of large-liability dependence, and, of course, the ratio is higher for LM banks (e.g., 71 percent for banks with assets greater than $10 billion).

Loans and Leases to Assets

Until the process of securitization is fully developed, most loans and leases do not have the benefit of well-established secondary markets. To this extent, they are the least liquid of bank earning assets. Accordingly, the ratio of loans and leases to assets is a measure of bank liquidity. A high ratio is indicative of a bank that is "loaned up" or relatively illiquid, whereas a low ratio indicates a liquid bank with excess lending capacity. The loan-to-asset ratio tends to vary directly with bank size. As shown in Table 15-4, the ratio increases monotonically, ranging from 52 percent for the smallest size group to 63 percent for the 26 largest banks.

Loans and Leases to Core Deposits

The loan-to-deposit ratio is a traditional measure of bank liquidity, indicating the extent to which deposits are used to meet loan requests. A variation on this theme is the ratio of loans and leases to core deposits. Although this ratio is not shown in Table 15-2, it is easily obtained by dividing the second ratio in the table (loans and leases to assets) by the first one (core deposits to assets). The lower this ratio is the more *stored* liquidity a bank has, other things equal. Given our analysis of the components of this ratio, we would expect the ratio of loans and leases to core deposits to vary directly with bank size. To illustrate, for banks with assets less than $25 million, the ratio is 64 percent (= 51.66%/80.12%); however, for the largest banks, the ratio is greater than one (e.g., 1.06 and 2.17 for the two largest size categories, respectively).

The point at which the ratio of loans and leases to core deposits switches from less than one to greater than one can be regarded as a benchmark separating stored-liquidity banks from liability-management banks. For the data shown in Table 15-2, this crossover point occurs at an asset size of $3 billion. For banks with assets between $1 billion and $3 billion, the ratio is 91 percent (= 60.07%/65.83%); for banks with assets between $3 billion and $10 billion, the ratio is 109 percent (= 61.32%/57.72%). The components of the ratio of loans and leases to core deposits reveal the reasons for the switching point. First, liability-management banks have fewer core deposits per dollar of assets. And second, they make more loans per dollar of assets. As bank size increases, the interaction of these two components results in a growing relative volume of loans and leases supported by a shrinking relative volume of core deposits.

Temporary Investments to Assets

This ratio measures a bank's most liquid assets as a percentage of total assets. In Table 15-2, temporary investments are defined as the sum of three items: (1) interest-bearing balances due from depository institutions, (2) federal funds sold and securities purchased under agreements to resell (reverse repos), and (3) trading-account assets and investment securities with maturities of one year or less. These items represent funds "temporarily" stored in the balance sheet, funds which can be easily, quickly, and safely converted into cash. Across these accounts, community-type banks are more likely to have relatively larger amounts of federal funds sold and investments. In contrast, because of their correspondent activities, larger banks are more likely to have relatively larger amounts of balances due and trading-account assets. On balance, the ratio should decline as bank size increases, with the decline cushioned by the effect of greater correspondent activity at larger banks. For all insured banks, temporary investments were 17 percent of total assets in 1985. The ratio shows only limited variability across the various size groups ranging from 19 percent for the smallest banks to 15 percent for the largest ones. For banks with assets greater than $300 million but less than $10 billion, the ratio is relatively flat at 14 percent.

Temporary Investments to Volatile Liabilities

Compared to the previous ratio, this one substitutes volatile liabilities for total assets in the denominator. Volatile liabilities are defined as the sum of five items: (1) all time deposits of $100,000 or more, (2) deposits in foreign offices, (3) federal funds purchased and securities sold under agreements to repurchase, (4) interest-bearing demand notes (note balances) issued to the U.S. Treasury, and (5) other liabilities for borrowed money. Since smaller sized banks have few, if any, volatile liabilities, the ratio will decrease as bank size increases. As shown in Table 15-2, banks with assets less than $25 million had temporary investments equal to 237 percent of volatile liabilities compared to 28 percent for banks with assets greater than $10 billion.

Volatile Liabilities to Assets

The quotient of the previous two ratios generates the ratio of volatile liabilities to assets. It measures the extent to which a bank's balance sheet is funded with volatile liabilities. Banks engaged in aggressive liability management will have higher ratios than those with limited money-market opportunities and/or more cautious funding strategies. For all insured commercial banks, the ratio is only 10 percent, but it ranges from 8 percent for banks with assets less than $25 million to 54 percent for banks with assets greater than $10 billion.

Brokered Deposits to Total Deposits

A liability management technique of the 1980s that has enabled aggressive banks and thrifts, of any size, to tap national markets for funds has been brokered deposits. Investment bankers, such as Salomon Brothers, Merrill Lynch, and First Boston Corporation, act as money brokers in these transactions. As such, they provide a third party to the normal two-party transaction. The services of deposit brokers are especially helpful to depository institutions lacking the reputation and size to market their CDs on a national basis. For these banks, the funds are typically parceled out in blocks of $100,000 or less, so they are covered by deposit insurance; however, this size constraint is not binding for creditworthy borrowers. Brokered deposits are another example of financial innovation adapting to market and regulatory forces.

In January 1984, the FDIC and the FHLBB attempted a power play that would have stripped deposit insurance protection from brokered deposits. The measure was defeated, however, and several studies have shown that "... there is no evidence that brokered deposits are more likely to be misused or to contribute to institutions' losses than other kinds of rate-sensitive purchased liabilities."[14]

In Table 15-2, the ratio of brokered deposits to total deposits is shown. However, the use of median values does not provide much insight regarding the use of brokered deposits because, except for the two largest size classes, the figures are zero (i.e., 0.7% and 1.4%, respectively). More meaningful data are provided by Benston [1985], who found that in 1985, 22 failed S&Ls had a mean ratio of brokered deposits to earnings assets of 20 percent compared to 7 percent for a group of nonfailed S&Ls (Table 1, p. 28). The mean difference of 13 percent had a standard deviation of 5.4 percent.

Investment Securities: Market to Book Value

When market-to-book value ratios are less than one, bankers are sometimes described as being "locked-in" to their investment portfolios because of fears about taking capital losses. Of course, in an efficient market for the bank's equity, discrepancies between market and book values of bank assets will automatically be reflected in the market value of the bank's equity. If market values are substantially below book values and if bankers are reluctant to take capital losses, then a market-to-book ratio less than one would indicate a lack of liquidity until interest rates drop enough to raise market values. During periods of declining interest rates, bank investment portfolios are most likely to have a market-to-book ratio greater than one.

Bank investment portfolios are typically segregated on the basis of taxability. In Table 15-2, market-to-book ratios for both taxable and nontaxable securities are shown. The tendency of banks to hold longer-term nontaxable securities than taxable ones is reflected by these two ratios. This investment preference, combined with the movements of interest rates since the securities were purchased, accounts for the gains in the nontaxable portfolio and the losses in the taxable one.

Pledged Securities to Total Securities

Just as banks require some of their customers to pledge collateral for certain transactions, some bank creditors require banks to supply collateral for certain transactions. Such "pledging requirements" are typically met by supplying U.S. Treasury securities or municipal obligations as collateral to be held by a third-party trustee. To encourage banks to purchase municipal obligations, such securities frequently are valued at 110 percent of par to meet the pledging requirements of state and local governments. Bank investment securities pledged as collateral are not available for liquidity needs until the claims against them have been removed, or other collateral is made available. Accordingly, measures of stored liquidity should be net of any pledged securities. Bank liabilities that require collateral are (1) borrowings at the "discount window" of the various Federal Reserve banks, (2) securities sold under agreements to repurchase, and (3) the "public deposits" of various governmental units including the U.S. Treasury and state and local governments.

---

[14] Committee on Government Operations. [1984]. *Federal Regulation of Brokered Deposits in Problem Banks and Savings Institutions,* House Report 98-1112, 98th Congress, 2nd Session, p. 9. Also see Benston [1985].

In Table 15-2, the ratio of pledged securities to total securities is shown. For all insured banks, the 1985 ratio was 24 percent. However, across the various size classes, it increased steadily and ranged from a low of 19 percent for banks with assets less than $25 million to 63 percent for banks with assets greater than $10 billion. Since as bank size increases both the use of repos increases and the ability to serve larger governmental units increases (i.e., the ability to attract public deposits increases), it is not surprising that the ratio of pledged securities to total securities increases with bank size.

Measuring Bank Liquidity: A Recapitulation

The miscellaneous information at the bottom of Table 15-2 includes the number of banks in each size class. In 1985, there were 13,606 insured commercial banks (94 percent of the population) with assets less than $300 million. Across the various measures of liquidity, there is little evidence these banks manage their liabilities in the sense discusssed in this chapter. In fact, it is only in the two largest size classes (109 banks or 0.8 percent of the population) that banks really manage their liabilities, and therefore depend on the marketplace for liquidity. The 691 banks in the "middle" between $300 million and $3 billion (5 percent of the population) may be having an identity crisis when it comes to liquidity management. Should they attempt to store it in their balance sheets or purchase it in the marketplace? Since the banks in this group are likely takeover targets in the game of interstate banking, they may have outsiders solve their dilemma for them.

LIQUIDITY MANAGEMENT IN PRACTICE

For the hundred or so largest banks in the United States, liquidity management is, for the most part, synonymous with liability management. For the rest of the industry of over 14,000 banks, liquidity management involves the management of liquidity stored in the balance sheet. Of course, large banks still need cash balances and other highly liquid assets to conduct their day-to-day operations. Thus, as we have seen in Table 15-2, although all banks store liquidity in their balance sheets, only the largest banks have the ability to use large amounts of purchased funds to manage their portfolios of earning assets. This greater flexibility enjoyed by large banks has its costs, however, as reflected by the need to maintain a trouble-free balance sheet and reputation. The case of Continental Illinois dramatically illustrates the costs of not maintaining such an image.

CHAPTER SUMMARY

Discussing liquidity and the availability of capital with the House Banking Committee's Subcommittee on Financial Institutions Supervision following the stock market crash of October 1987, David Ruder, the Chairman of the Securities and Exchange Commission, said: "I personally regard that question as probably the most important to come out of the market decline."[15] As the major supplier of liquidity to the economy and financial markets, commercial banks must have access to liquidity. Bank liquidity can be either stored in a bank's balance sheet or purchased in the marketplace, or both. However, since only the largest banks have true access to financial markets, both international and national, they are the only banking organizations to really practice

[15] Ricks [1987], p. 2.

liability management, in the sense of being able to purchase funds in the marketplace. In contrast, all banking organizations have to store a certain degree of liquidity in their balance sheets. The smaller the bank is, the greater is its dependency on stored liquidity. This chapter has focused on these two alternative approaches to liquidity management.

LIST OF KEY WORDS, CONCEPTS, AND ACRONYMS

Asset-conversion theory
Brokered deposits
Continental Illinois versus First
  National Bank of Browning, Montana
Core deposits
Depository Institutions Deregulation
  and Monetary Control Act
  (DIDMCA)
Deposit rate ceilings (effects of)
Unexpected Change = Actual
  Change − Expected Change
External versus internal sources of
  liquidity
Functions of bank liquidity
Implicit interest
Interest-rate sensitivity of bank funds
Large-liability dependence (LLD)
Liability management (LM, LM-1, and
  LM-2)

Liquidity versus transferability
Loans and leases
Pledging requirements
Risks of liquidity management
Securities (book value, market value,
  and pledged)
Self-liquidating assets
Sources and uses of bank funds
Stock market crash of October 1987
  (bank liquidity implications)
Stored liquidity
Temporary investments
Three faces of liability management
Trade-off between liquidity and
  profitability
Too-big-to-fail doctrine
Volatile liabilities

REVIEW/DISCUSSION QUESTIONS

1. Unexpected changes such as the stock market crash of 1987 create liquidity needs for bank customers such as securities firms. Describe the roles played by the Fed and money-center banks in averting a liquidity crisis following the crash.

2. The commercial loan theory, the asset conversion theory, the anticipated income theory, and the theory of liability management are alternative ways of viewing the dilemma of liquidity management. What are the basic ideas of each of these approaches and when were they popular? Which methods are used by banks today?

3. Distinguish between internal and external sources of liquidity. How do pledging requirements and predilections against taking capital losses alter a bank's liquidity position?

4. What are the functions of liquidity and the risks of liquidity management? What are some unexpected changes that could affect a bank's liquidity? Can you (or your instructor) explain why Continental's liquidity crisis occurred in May 1984 and not in July 1982? The earlier date is when it was disclosed that Continental had purchashed about $1 billion in bad loans from Penn Square Bank.

(continued on page 438)

How important is it that this bank maintain the confidence of the marketplace? Suppose that this bank has 50 percent of both its temporary investments and its securities pledged and that the market-to-book ratio of its securities portfolio is .75. If the bank experiences a run on its volatile liabilities, what will be the size of the bank's liquidity cushion?

SELECTED REFERENCES

Aigner, Dennis J. [1973]. "On Estimation of an Econometric Model of Short-Run Bank Behavior." *Journal of Econometrics* (September), pp. 201–228.

Baker, James V. [1978]. "The Liability-Management Method Demonstrates Six Principles." *Banking* (August), pp. 74–78.

Benston, George J. [1985]. *An Analysis of the Causes of Savings and Loan Failures.* New York: Salomon Brothers Center for the Study of Financial Institutions and Graduate School of Business Administration New York University, Monograph Series in Finance and Economics, Monograph 1985-4/5.

Budzeika, George. [1978]. "A Study of Liability Management by New York City Banks." Federal Reserve Bank of New York Research Paper (January).

Buser, Stephen A., Andrew H. Chen, and Edward J. Kane. [1981]. "Federal Deposit Insurance, Regulatory Policy, and Optimal Bank Capital." *Journal of Finance* (March), pp. 51–60.

Cates Bank Financial Analysis Course, Book I. [1984]. New York: Cates Consulting Analysts, (January).

Crosse, Howard and George H. Hempell. [1980]. *Management Policies for Commercial Banks.* Englewood Cliffs, NJ: Prentice-Hall.

Diller, Stanley. [1971]. "The Expectations Component of the Term Structure." In *Essays on Interest Rates* (Vol. II), Jack M. Guttentag, ed. New York: NBER, pp. 413–433.

Friedman, Milton. [1953]. "The Effect of Full-Employment Policy on Economic Stability: A Formal Analysis." In *Essays in Positive Economics.* Chicago: University of Chicago Press, pp. 117–132.

Garino, David P. [1979]. "Loans Are Hard to Get in Many Small Towns as Banks Lack Funds." *The Wall Street Journal* (April 4), pp. 1ff.

Gilbert, Alton. [1980]. "Lagged Reserve Requirements: Implications for Monetary Control and Bank Reserve Management." *Review*, Federal Reserve Bank of St Louis (May), pp. 7–20.

Giroux, Gary. [1980]. "A Survey of Forecasting Techniques Used by Commercial Banks." *Journal of Bank Research* (Spring), pp. 51–53.

Guenther, Robert. [1987]. "Reed to Tighten Citicorp Investment Bank," *The Wall Street Journal* (December 7), p. 2.

Harris, John M., Jr., James R. Scott, and Joseph F. Sinkey, Jr. [1986]. "The Wealth Effects of Regulatory Intervention Surrounding the Bailout of Continental Illinois," *Proceedings: Bank Structure and Competition*, Federal Reserve Bank of Chicago, pp. 104–126.

Hayes, Douglas A. [1980]. *Bank Funds Management: Issues and Practices.* Ann Arbor: The University of Michigan.

Heimann, John G. [1981] Statement Before the Committee on Banking, Housing, and Urban Affairs, United States Senate (April 28).

Hendershott, Patric H., and James P. Winder. [1979]. "Commercial Bank Asset Portfolio Behavior in the United States." *Journal of Banking and Finance* (July), pp. 113–131.

Hester, Donald D. [1978]. "Dynamic Portfolio Behavior and Market Clearing by Weekly Reporting Banks." Special Studies Paper, Number 99 (June 13), Division of Research and Statistics, Federal Reserve Board, Washington, D.C.

Ho, Thomas, and Anthony Saunders. [1980]. "A Catastrophe Model of Bank Failure." *Journal of Finance* (December), pp. 1189–1208.

Hodgman, D. R. [1963]. *Commercial Bank Loan and Investment Policy.* Champaign: University of Illinois Press.

Jackson, P. C. [1978]. Address Before the Alabama Bankers Association, Mobile, Alabama, May 11. Washington, DC: Board of Governors, Federal Reserve System.

Kane, Edward J. [1981]. "Reregulation, Savings-and-Loan Diversification and the Flow of Housing Finance." Working Paper Series 81-1, The Ohio State University (January).

———. [1979]. "The Three Faces of Commercial Bank Liability Management." In *The Political Economy of Policy-Making*, M. P. Dooley, et al., eds. Beverly Hills/London: Sage Publications, pp. 149–174.

———. [1970]. "The Term Structure of Interest Rates: An Attempt to Reconcile Teaching with Practice." *Journal of Finance* (May), pp. 361–374.

———, and Burton G. Malkiel. [1965]. "Bank Portfolio Allocation, Deposit Variability, and the Availability Doctrine." *Quarterly Journal of Economics* (February), pp. 113–134.

Knight, Robert E. [1977]. "Guidelines for Efficient Reserve Management." Federal Reserve Bank of Kansas City, *Monthly Review* (November), pp. 11–23.

Lucas, Charles M., et al. [1977]. "Federal Funds and Repurchase Agreements." Federal Reserve Bank of New York, *Quarterly Review* (Summer), pp. 33–48.

McCord, Thomas. [1980]. "The Depository Institutions Deregulation and Monetary Control Act of 1980." *Issues in Bank Regulation* (Spring), pp. 3–7.

McKinney, George W., Jr. [1977]. "A Perspective on the Use of Models in the Management of Bank Funds." *Journal of Bank Research* (Summer), pp. 122–127.

Pettway, Richard H., and Joseph F. Sinkey, Jr. [1980]. "Establishing On-Site Bank Examination Priorities: An Early-Warning System Using Accounting and Market Information." *Journal of Finance* (March), pp. 137–150.

Ricks, Thomas E. [1987]. "Liquidity Seen Main Concern in Market Crash," *The Wall Street Journal* (December 10), p. 2.

Schweitzer, Stuart A. [1976]. "Bank Liability Management for Better or Worse." In *Current Perspectives in Banking*, T. M. Havrilesky and J. T. Boorman, eds. Arlington Heights, IL: AHM Publishing Corporation, pp. 113–124. Originally published in *Business Review*, Federal Reserve Bank of Philadelphia [December 1974], pp. 3–12.

Sinkey, Joseph F. [1979]. *Problem and Failed Institutions in the Commercial Banking Industry*, Greenwich, Connecticut: JAI Press.

Sinkey, Joseph F., Jr. [1973]. "The Term Structure of Interest Rates: A Time-Series Test of the Kane Expected Change Model of Interest-Rate Forecasting." *Journal of Money, Credit and Banking* (February), pp. 92–200.

———, and John J. Jahera. [1981]. "Bank Liability Management and Portfolio Allocation." Working Paper, University of Georgia.

Stigum, Marcia L., and Reno O. Branch, Jr. [1983]. *Managing Bank Assets and Liabilities*. Homewood Hills, IL: Dow Jones-Irwin.

Watson, Ronald D. [1972]. "Bank Bond Management: The Maturity Dilemma." Federal Reserve Bank of Philadelphia, *Business Review* (March), pp. 23–29.

Willis, Parker B. [1978]. *Federal Funds Market*. Boston: Federal Reserve Bank of Boston.

CHAPTER 16

Characteristics and Risk Management of the Investment Portfolio

INTRODUCTION

A bank's "investment portfolio" consists of various debt securities issued by federal, state, and local governments. Like other bank customers, these governmental units need a strategic combination of financial services. One of these services is credit. When banks buy securities issued by these units, they supply governments with funds. The securities are, of course, earning assets held by the banks. The role of a bank's investment portfolio is to generate income (in the form of interest revenue, capital gains, and fees from the provision of investment services) and to provide a liquidity reserve. In addition, prior to the Tax Reform Act of 1986, the municipal bond component of bank investment portfolios provided an important vehicle for tax sheltering income, especially for smaller banks. However, except for special circumstances (described later), this tax shelter has been lost for future investments but "grandfathered" for existing holdings.

A bank's investment portfolio has credit, interest-rate, and liquidity risks like any other bank asset. Although the credit risk is minimal for securities issued by the federal government (in theory we call them risk-free), state and local obligations (also called municipal obligations or "munis") have various degrees of default risk. Nevertheless, since the default rates have been low, liquidity and interest-rate risk are the more important considerations. A bank's investment portfolio plays a crucial balancing role in the structure of its earning assets and risk exposure. This chapter focuses on describing and analyzing this role.

ACTIVE VERSUS PASSIVE INVESTMENT MANAGEMENT

Given the residual nature of bank investment management, one might expect the management of such a portfolio to be quite passive. However, this residual nature only partially explains the dominance of the passive approach (in terms of the small number of banks engaged in active management). Additional factors are the lack of experienced investment personnel in many banks, regulatory pressure not to engage in speculative investment trading, and efficient securities markets. As a result, for the

441

thousands of community-type banks in the United States, passive investment management is the *modus operandi*. In contrast, money-center and regional banks engage in active investment management. Nevertheless, the increased competition in the financial-services industry has put greater pressure on *all* bank investment managers to attempt to generate more income (per unit of investment risk) from their investment portfolios.

In distinguishing between "active" and "passive" investment policies, Radcliffe's definitions [1982, p. 253] are insightful. He uses the term *passive* simply to distinguish investment policies from the more active trading associated with speculators. Although bank examiners frown on speculative trading, portfolio managers at the larger banks have been known to make an occasional bet on the future course of interest rates. Since the financial press, like its nonfinancial counterpart, thrives on publicizing adversity, we know more about the interest-rate bets that went wrong (e.g., First Pennsylvania and First Chicago) than we do about the ones that went right.

For the purposes of this chapter, we define *active investment managers* as the set of investment managers who engage *jointly* in the ongoing practice of betting (speculating) on future interest rates and providing dealer and market making services. Most of the members of this set will be found in regional, superregional, and money-center banks. Speculating on interest-rate movements is manifested in the active trading of securities as opposed to a buy-and-hold strategy. Although passive investment management is relatively inactive, it does permit "rebalancing" to adjust to changing market conditions. Accordingly, if market conditions result in portfolio positions inconsistent with the bank's investment objectives, the portfolio should be realigned whether it is actively or passively managed. On balance, passive investment management can be viewed as active management sans speculation and dealer activity.

EVIDENCE OF ACTIVE INVESTMENT MANAGEMENT

Table 16-1 provides evidence of the existence of active investment management in insured commercial banks. The data are for the balance sheet item "assets held in trading accounts." Insured banks with total assets of $1 billion or more are required to itemize this account into eight categories: (1) U.S. Treasury securities; (2) U.S. Government agency and corporation obligations; (3) securities issued by states and political subdivisions in the United States; (4) other notes, bonds, and debentures; (5) certificates of deposit; (6) commercial paper; (7) banker's acceptances; and (8) other. The sum of these items is known as "trading-account securities." Since these securities are held for "trading" purposes, as opposed to "nontrading" ones, they are an indicator of "active" investment management.

Although banks are free to decide what part of their securities portfolio is held in the trading account, there are two accounting differences in the treatment of trading-account securities versus nontrading-account securities. First, securities held in the trading account must be valued on the bank's balance sheet at market value or cost, whichever is lower. This treatment is, in effect, an asymmetrical mark-to-market rule which requires capital losses to be taken immediately but ignores capital gains. In contrast, all nontrading-account securities are carried at cost. The second difference has to do with the treatment of capital gains and losses. Gains (losses) on securities held in the trading account are included as part of noninterest income and therefore affect net operating income or income before securities gains (losses). In contrast, gains (losses) on nontrading-account securities are treated as an extraordinary item (net of taxes) and affect only a bank's bottom line or net income. For banks that do not

TABLE 16-1   Evidence of Active Investment Management in Insured Commercial Banks: Assets Held in Trading Accounts December 31, 1985

Bank Class (Number of Banks)	Dollar Amount (Millions)	As a percent of	
		Securities	Assets
Without foreign offices			
Assets less than $100 million (12,093)	151	0.12	0.03
$100 million to $300 million (1,542)	96	0.14	0.03
$300 million or more (497)	860	1.03	0.21
Total (14,132)	1,107	0.04	0.09
With foreign offices			
Domestic offices only	27,767	18.91	2.33
Foreign offices only	11,732	69.64	2.89
Total, consolidated offices (272)	39,499	24.13	2.47
TOTAL, all banks (14,404)	40,606	9.24	1.49

Notes: Assets held in trading accounts may include U.S. Treasury securities; U.S. government agency and corporation obligations; securities issued by states and political subdivisions in the United States; other bonds, notes, and debentures; certificates of deposit; commercial paper; banker's acceptances; and other investments. For the banks without foreign offices, the interest income on trading-account securities was $77 million in 1985 for a gross return of 6.95 percent. In contrast, banks with foreign offices generated $3,268 million in 1985 for a gross return of 8.27 percent.

Source: FDIC, *Statistics on Banking* [1985], Table RC-2, p. 33 for the balance sheet data and Table RI-2, p. 48 for the revenue figures in the notes.

like to take capital losses and that focus on a steadily growing income before securities gains (losses) as a key performance measure, the two accounting conventions would encourage them to deemphasize trading-account securities. Since banks traditionally have shown a preference for both of these practices, they help explain the data in Table 16-1.

As shown in Table 16-1, except for the 272 banks with foreign offices (in 1985), assets held in trading accounts are miniscule parts of either total bank securities or total bank assets. For example, the 13,635 banks without foreign offices and with total assets less than $300 million (per bank) held only $247 million in trading-account securities, a figure amounting to only 0.13 percent of their total securities and 0.03 percent of their total assets. In contrast, the 272 banks with foreign offices, which accounted for 58 percent of total industry assets in 1985, held $39.5 billion in their trading accounts, for 24 percent of their total securities and 2.5 percent of their total assets. Clearly, trading-account activities are dominated by banks with foreign offices, which are, of course, the largest ones in the U.S. banking system.

Regarding revenue generating from trading-account activities (see the notes to Table 16-1), banks with foreign offices are more efficient than banks without foreign offices. For example, banks without foreign offices generated $77 million in gross revenue on invested funds of $1,107 million for a gross return of 6.95 percent. In contrast, the 272 banks with foreign offices generated $3,268 million on invested funds of $39,499 million for a gross return of 8.27 percent.

The Market Structures of Active Investment Management

Securities are traded in three different market structures described as brokered trading, dealer trading, and market making.[1] The trading activities of commercial

---

[1] See Bloch [1986], pp. 50–55 for a complete description of these market structures. This section draws, in part, on his work.

banks focus on dealer trading and market making.[2] Under 1988 banking laws and regulations, commercial banks are prohibited from trading equity securities (for income purposes as opposed to providing discount-brokerage services to bank customers) and encouraged to trade only investment-grade debt or comparable instruments (i.e., those with a Baa rating or better). Although banks are permitted to make loans with equity securities taken as collateral, they must liquidate the securities within a reasonable time if they are acquired through borrower default. On balance, banks may hold and trade certain debt securities but not equities (e.g., common stock). Nevertheless, the risks of active investment management are real. According to Bloch [1987], the trading of debt securities implies "... over-the-counter market making on a large scale with large amounts of risky inventories being positioned by dealers such as investment bankers and commercial banks ..." (p. 54).

Regarding dealer trading, a dozen or so of the largest U.S. banks (plus nonbank dealers) operate with the Federal Reserve Bank of New York as primary dealers in government securities (see Table 9-4 in Chapter 9 for the list of bank and nonbank dealers). When the Federal Reserve is conducting open market operations, it deals only with these primary dealers. Under an expansionary monetary policy, the central bank buys securities and bank dealers become more liquid (i.e., securities decrease, reserves increase). Since bank reserves are nonearning assets, banks seek earning assets—including loans that will stimulate the economy. Under a contractionary policy, the central bank sells securities and bank dealers become less liquid (i.e., securities increase, reserves decrease). To meet reserve requirements, bank dealers sell securities to other banks, who in turn sell securities, and so on. Since selling securities drives prices down and interest rates up, the Fed ultimately hopes higher interest rates will restrict the creation of money and credit, and thereby slow down the growth of the economy. By trading with other financial institutions, the primary dealers transmit the effects of monetary policy throughout the financial system.

Dealer markets operate on a bid-ask basis. The spread between the ask or selling price and the bid or buying price represents the dealer's dollar profit. For example, if a dealer bids 98 for a security and sells it for 100, the spread is 2 per unit. Dealers set bid-ask spreads for each security they trade. Compared to brokers, who are price takers, dealers are price makers. Moreover, unlike brokers, dealers hold inventories of securities. To reduce their inventories, dealers reduce both bid and ask prices. Inventory reductions serve to lower both carrying costs and exposures to interest-rate and credit risks. However, if inventories become too thin, dealers run the risk of being unable to meet customers' needs at reasonable prices. The problem of maintaining adequate inventory and managing portfolio risks can be balanced through the use of synthetic contracts such as financial futures and options. For example, the risks of a larger securities inventory can be hedged with interest-rate futures. In this case, the risk is laid off, for a fee, in another market. Dealers recoup the higher cost of a larger and safer inventory by raising the spread. The ability to trade in volume is one of the major distinctions between dealers and brokers.

---

[2] Brokered trading involves agents (the brokers) acting for buyers and sellers by bringing them together for transactions with the commission paid by the initiator of the transaction, or shared by both parties. Since brokered trading usually takes place on an organized exchange, it is supported by the operations, bureaucracy, and regulations of the exchange. Brokers do not bear any of the risk associated with carrying securities because they do not hold inventories of securities. Brokers operate in financial markets as price takers.

As of this writing, the securities eligible for underwriting and dealing by commercial banks fall under three broad categories:[3] (1) U.S. Treasury obligations; (2) obligations of U.S. government agencies such as Federal Farm Credit Banks, Federal Home Loan Banks, Student Loan Marketing Association, Tennessee Valley Authority, and U.S. Postal Service; and (3) obligations of states and political subdivisions including general obligations, revenue obligations, and agencies for housing, university, or dormitory purposes.

An underwriter is a dealer who purchases securities from an issuer and distributes them to investors. Since it is common for the underwriter to "make a market" for the issue after the underwriting is closed, the dealer is said to be engaged in "market making." Market making, however, is not restricted to the underwriting firms as other dealers may be willing to engage in such activity. As market makers, commercial banks primarily trade U.S. government securities (both Treasuries and agencies), selected state and local obligations, and selected foreign issues.

To summarize, the three market structures or trading systems used for securities transactions are brokered trading, dealer trading, and market making. Commercial banks are active in dealer trading and market making for debt securities of federal, state, and local governments and certain foreign issues. They engage in these trading activities for several reasons: (1) to generate income, (2) to provide investment services to their customers (e.g., respondent banks), (3) to maintain a flow of information for pricing securities, and (4) to establish trading relationships in institutional markets, both domestic and foreign. As documented above with the data on trading-account activities, these activities are for larger banks: 300 out of about 14,500.

The Investment Portfolio of Insured Commercial Banks

The investment portfolio composition (as a percentage of total assets) for insured commercial banks for the years 1981 to 1986 is shown in Table 16-2. On average, for the period 1981 to 1986, the typical commercial bank held about 17 percent of its assets in securities, with slightly more than one-half of that amount held in U.S. governments. The yields on bank investments vary, of course, with the interest-rate cycle, and, as shown in the lower half of Table 16-2, these returns declined from 1984 through 1986, following a period of high and volatile interest rates.

The Effect of Bank Size on Portfolio Composition

A more detailed breakdown of the composition of bank investments is shown in Table 16-3. These data, which are for December 31, 1985, use the same size classes and foreign-domestic scheme as shown in Table 16-1. A percentage comparison of the investment portfolios of banks without and those with foreign offices is enlightening:

	Without Foreign Offices	With Foreign Offices
U.S. governments	62.2%	45.2%
State and local	34.2	40.4
Other domestic	3.4	4.0
Foreign	0.2	10.4
Total	100.0%	100.0%
Pledged	36.0%	52.5%
Trading accounts	0.0%	24.1%

[3] The securities activities of commercial banks are described in Kaufman [1985].

**TABLE 16-2   The Investment Portfolio of Insured
Commercial Banks 1981–1986**

	As a Percentage of Total Assets			
Year	U.S. Government	State and Local	Other	Total
1981	8.63	7.62	0.75	17.00
1982	8.59	7.25	0.73	16.56
1983	9.79	6.84	0.83	17.47
1984	9.89	6.76	0.93	17.58
1985	9.53	7.02	1.09	17.64
1986	9.25	7.49	1.55	18.29

	Rates of Return			
	Nominal		Tax equivalent	
Year	Total Securities	State & Local	Total Securities	State & Local
1981	9.28	6.74	11.65	11.96
1982	9.96	7.20	12.43	12.81
1983	9.83	7.04	12.06	12.58
1984	9.95	7.51	12.18	13.45
1985	9.27	7.43	11.46	13.08
1986	8.34	7.20	10.53	12.53

Notes: Before 1984, data are based on averages for call dates in December of the preceding year and in June and December of the current year. In 1984, data are based on averages for call dates at the beginning and end of the year only. After 1984, data are based on averages of the call date in December of the preceding years and all four call dates in the current year. Rates of return are calculated as described in the "Technical Note," *Federal Reserve Bulletin*, Vol. 65 [September 1979.] p. 704, for years through 1984. For more recent years, rates of return are derived from income items and quarterly average balance sheet data. Tax equivalent yields include all taxes estimated to be due on income, extraordinary gains, and securities gains.
Source: *Federal Reserve Bulletin*, Vol. 73 [July 1987], Table 5, p. 542 and Table 6, p. 543.

This comparison, which is simply one of "little bank" versus "big one," shows that little banks hold almost twice as many U.S. government securities as they do state and local obligations, and that their holdings of foreign securities are miniscule. In contrast, big banks hold nearly equal amounts of U.S. government and state and local securities, but with 10 percent of their portfolios in foreign securities. Regarding pledged securities, big banks pledge slightly more than one-half of their portfolios compared to about one-third for community-type banks. And finally, from Table 16.1, we know that banks without foreign offices hold less than 0.1 percent of their securities in trading accounts compared to 24 percent for banks with foreign offices.

THE RISK–RETURN CHARACTERISTICS OF INVESTMENT SECURITIES

Whether bank earning assets are in the form of loans or investment securities, the critical portfolio considerations are interest-rate, liquidity, and credit risks. As with other financial portfolios, the objective of investment management is to obtain the maximum return for a given level of risk, or the minimum risk for a given level of return. The ultimate goal is, of course, to increase the value of shareholder interest in the bank, other things equal. Returns on the investment portfolio come in the form of interest income, capital gains, fees generated by providing investment services, and bid-ask spreads on dealer and market making activities. Rates of return on the investment portfolios of insured commercial banks for the years 1981 to 1986 are shown in the lower half of Table 16-2.

TABLE 16-3   The Effect of Bank Size on the Composition of Bank Investments All Insured Commercial Banks, December 31, 1985

		Banks without Foreign Offices				Banks with Foreign Offices		
	Total	Total	Less than $100 Million[a]	$100 Million to $300 Million	$300 Million or More	Consolidated Total	Domestic Offices	Foreign Offices
U.S. Treasury securities and U.S. government agency and corporation obligations	245,546	171,493	83,562	40,085	47,846	74,053	73,881	172
U.S. Treasury securities	118,262	61,836	N/A	26,962	38,874	56,426	56,264	162
U.S. govt. insured certificates of participation	24,059	12,502	6,240	2,890	3,372	11,557	11,557	0
All other U.S. government securities	103,226	97,156	77,322	10,233	9,601	6,070	6,060	10
Securities issued by states and political subdivisions	160,555	94,417	37,410	25,506	31,501	66,138	65,535	603
Other domestic securities	15,871	9,312	2,749	2,584	3,979	6,559	6,056	503
Private certificates of participation	538	281	136	66	79	257	254	3
All other domestic securities	15,334	9,032	2,613	2,519	3,900	6,302	5,803	499
Foreign securities	17,366	420	N/A	125	295	16,946	1,377	15,569
Total securities (debt & equity)	439,340	275,644	123,721	68,301	83,622	163,696	146,849	16,847
Memo: Pledged securities	185,126	99,139	33,039	26,123	39,977	85,987	N/A	N/A

[a] For banks with total assets of less than $100 million, the amount for U.S. Treasury securities is not separately available. Therefore, all such amounts are included in the category of "All other U.S. government securities." Also, for banks with less than $100 million in total assets, the dollar amount for foreign securities is not separately available. Therefore, for these banks, any foreign securities are included in the category for "All other domestic securities."

N/A-not available

Source: FDIC, Statistics on Banking [1985], Table RC-4, p. 36.

To see the contribution of the investment portfolio to bank interest income, the following data for the year 1985 are informative[4]:

Source	Banks without Foreign Offices		Banks with Foreign Offices	
	$ Millions	% of Income	$ Millions	% of Income
Investments	24,888	23.1	12,851	9.1
Trading accounts	77	0.0	3,258	2.3
Total	24,965	23.1	16,109	11.4
Nontrading gains	661	0.6	905	0.6
Overall	25,626	23.7	17,014	12.0

These findings are consistent with the other characteristics of the bank investment portfolio described in this chapter. Note that securities gains (or losses) are not reported as part of interest income, but treated as a separate line item in the income-expense statement.

To understand the risk–return aspects of bank investment securities, we need to draw on four key finance concepts established in previous chapters: (1) the Fisher effect or how inflationary expectations get built into nominal interest rates, (2) the term structure of interest rates or the relationship between yield to maturity and term to maturity of similar securities, (3) the default-risk structure of interest rates or the relationship between return and default risk, and (4) the notion of liquidity. The risks of bank investment management are manifested in the deviation of actual returns from expected ones. As in our previous analyses of risk, the culprit, once again, comes in the form of unexpected changes. For investment securities, these sources of unexpected change are unanticipated inflation and unanticipated defaults. Given the quality of bank investments (Baa or better as recommended by bank regulators), default risk is not a major concern for bank investment managers. Accordingly, the primary source of investment risk are unanticipated inflation and interest-rate risk.

Unanticipated Inflation and the Interaction between Interest-Rate Risk and Liquidity Risk

Suppose a bank's investment manager anticipates a long-term, risk-free bond rate of 9 percent consisting of a 4 percent real rate and a 5 percent premium for expected inflation. (Ignore the cross-product term of the Fisher effect of 0.20% in this case.) What happens if unexpected inflation of 3 percent occurs such that actual inflation is 8 percent? If the inflation is expected to persist, then the long-term rate will move to 12 percent and the value of fixed-rate debt will decline. If some of the long-term (fixed-rate) bonds were purchased at par, the bank now has "paper losses" in these securities, which represent a liquidity risk because the market-to-book ratio for the investment is less than one. Moreover, if the bank is reluctant to take capital losses for fear of reducing reported profits, the bank will be "locked-in" to the investment. On the positive side, the interest payments can be reinvested at the higher going rates of interest. However, assuming identical inflationary expectations, the higher cost of bank liabilities will offset this apparent advantage.. To avoid such a predicament, the manager could have purchased a variable-rate bond or laid off the interest-rate risk of the fixed-rate bond in the futures market.

[4] FDIC, *Statistics on Banking* [1985], Table RI-2, p. 48.

If actual inflation turned out to be 2 percent instead of the expected 5 percent and if the 2 percent level became the new expectation, then the long-term rate would drop to 6 percent. In this case, the bank would have a "paper gain" in the securities but a reinvestment problem because the coupon payments cannot be reinvested at the same yield. To reinvest at the same rate, the manager would have to accept a lower quality obligation. This apparent disadvantage, however, is offset by the lower cost of liabilities.

To summarize, unanticipated inflation means unexpected changes in interest rates, which produces interest-rate risk. Interest-rate risk has a price risk and a reinvestment risk. When interest rates rise, prices of fixed-rate instruments fall but reinvestment rates rise. When interest rates decline, prices rise but reinvestment rates fall.

Liquidity Risk: Size and Quality Considerations

Some bank securities are not traded because of the reluctance of managers to take capital losses after interest rates have risen. In other instances, the markets for particular securities may be "thin," which means the securities cannot be easily traded. When this situation occurs, the security is not very marketable and hence not very liquid. Typically, an illiquid security is a nonrated issue of small size. Accordingly, a security tends to be more liquid the larger the issue size and the higher the bond rating. On balance, there is safety (liquidity) in quality and size.

Regarding trading in thin markets, the old adage about everything (and everyone) having a price applies. It is not that the security cannot be sold, but the size of the discount the owner is willing to take. If a very deep discount must be taken to sell a security, the investment manager may be unwilling to take the hit. The existence of thin markets and/or rising interest rates may have the effect of eliminating or substantially reducing the liquidity reserve function of the investment portfolio. However, for banks that do not depend on liquidity stored in their balance sheets (i.e., liability management banks), such a change is not crucial.

The notions of "thin" and "thick" markets can be captured by the supply curves shown in Figure 16-1.[5] Figure 16-1a shows the supply curve of U.S. government securities. Because the market for these securities is so extensive, no single buyer (e.g., bank) can influence the yield (price) at which a particular issue trades. This lack of control over price results in a perfectly elastic supply curve. In contrast, consider the "thin market" depicted in Figure 16-1b, which represents an imperfect market for a relatively small issue of municipal obligations. Because the market for this issue is thin, if the bank wishes to expand its holdings of the issue (from A to B), it must bid a higher price and accept a lower yield. In contrast, if it wishes to reduce its holding (from B to A), the bank must discount the security. Since a supply curve with a negative slope is somewhat counterintuitive, think of the relationship as reflecting the demand for bank funds from the municipality. In this context, the lower the yield is, the more funds municipalities will demand from the bank (i.e., the more securities they will supply).

Credit Risk

Credit risk is simply the risk that the borrower will not pay interest and/or principal on time. Realized credit risk takes the form of deviations of actual payments from expected ones. Moreover, since borrowers never pay back more than the amount

[5] This paragraph draws on Mason [1979], pp. 42–44.

Yield to Maturity

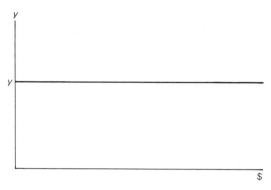

(a) U.S. Government Securities

Yield to Maturity

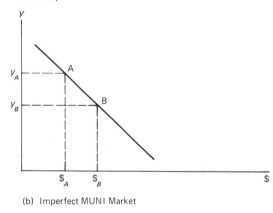

(b) Imperfect MUNI Market

Figure 16-1   Representative Supply Curves for Bank Investments

Adapted from Mason [1979], Fig. 2-1, p. 43.

promised, we are talking about an asymmetric distribution of expected returns. This downside risk is usually associated with deteriorating economic conditions at the national, regional, or local level.[6]

Given the characteristics of the typical bank's investment portfolio and the Baa-or-better regulatory guideline, it is not surrprising that credit risk in bank investments has not been a major problem for commercial banks. Since U.S. Treasury securities are considered free of default risk and since federal agency securities carry at least an implicit government guaranty, a large portion of bank investments are effectively free of default risk. Kaufman [1987] documents the history and scope of federal guarantees and raises an important policy issue of whether or not the federal government should engage in insurance activities of any kind.

Since the largest banks purchase some corporate and foreign bonds, the greatest potential for credit risk in bank investments rests with these securities, some of which do not have the benefit of the U.S. government safety net. However, since these large banks/BHCs also have investment departments or holding-company subsidiaries of

---

[6] Internal factors also play a role in determining default risk. For example, see Fisher's model of the determinants of risk premiums on corporate bonds in Chapter 9. The securities ratings shown in Table 16-5 (and Table 9-6 of chapter 9) are measures of credit risk.

considerable size and expertise, they should be able to handle the challenge. In the case of debt securities that are not rated, the investment manager has the responsibility to conduct a credit investigation similar to a commercial loan request. The borrower's credit file provides documentation of the credit analysis and enables bank examiners to exercise oversight judgment on the bank's loan decision.

Call Risk

A call feature is simply an "acceleration-of-maturity" clause at the issuer's option. Since the exercise of the call eliminates intermediate cash flows beyond the call date, the holder is compensated with a "sweetener" called the *call premium*. Since the existence of a call provision adds uncertainty, callable bonds promise higher yields. Given the bank's investment horizon, callable bonds, with call dates beyond the horizon, can be used to increase the return on the portfolio.

THE PORTFOLIO OF MUNICIPAL SECURITIES

The distinguishing feature of municipal securities is that their *coupon interest* is exempt from federal income taxes and most state taxes. However, capital gains or "discount returns" from municipal securities are fully taxable when realized. (The tax treatment is symmetrical as realized losses are fully deductible from taxable income). Regarding tax-exempt securities,[7] it is important to understand the following riddle: Question: How are tax-exempt securities like a free lunch? Answer: When you look closely, there is no such thing. Although *explicit* taxes are zero, holders of municipal bonds (e.g., banks) pay implicit taxes in two ways. First, they accepted, prior to 1987, lower yields than were available on equivalent taxable securities. The difference in interest receivable may be regarded as federal tax payments collected and redirected to the state and local governments that issued the bonds. Second, many holders of municipal bonds give up additional implicit interest by accepting lesser liquidity or greater portfolio risk than they would prefer (see Figure 16-1 for a reflection of this). These implicit taxes may be called the *costs of tax avoidance*. They include lower yields, illiquidity, and greater risk. The effective yield is, of course, higher, but it is not free; it comes at the expense of greater risk. A corollary to the adage "There is no such thing as a free lunch" is that "Greater return can be gained only by taking on more risk." Risk-adjusted returns determine if real gains exist.

Banks have two basic ways of acquiring municipal securities, with different policy criteria applicable for each strategy.[8] First, they may acquire *local* obligations through competitive bidding or private negotiation. Bank activity in this area mainly focuses on maintaining or establishing customer relationships with local governments. The idea is to have revenue from other banking services (e.g., data processing) to offset the costs of tax avoidance. The second method involves strictly an investment motive without the customer-relationship linkage. In this situation, securities should be chosen on the basis of an objective evaluation of the risk–return parameters. The primary motives for holding these securities are mixed: (1) to provide an outlet for core deposits that are not required for liquidity or loan purposes, (2) to generate income, especially when used as part of an aggressive liability-management program,

[7] See Kane [1980] for an energetic exposition of some basic tax concepts.
[8] See Hayes [1980], pp. 85–100.

and (3) to serve as a tertiary reserve account. Given their access to alternative tax shelters, large banks mainly are driven by the second reason.

Quality Considerations

The financial difficulties of cities like New York and Cleveland have caused investors to look more closely at the quality of municipal obligations (i.e., at the creditworthiness of the issuer). These developments suggest that a bank should review its minimum quality standards for such holdings, if it has not done so already. Hayes [1980] found that the larger the bank, the lower the minimum quality standard tends to be (e.g., Baa versus A). In addition, large banks have a greater tendency to accept nonrated obligations; this can be traced to their ability to do in-house research on the creditworthiness of municipalities. Hayes recommends that banks should adopt a policy requiring at least an A rating on municipal credits (or the equivalent on nonrated obligations). Given the greater perceived risk of municipal bonds, the portfolio should, of course, be a well-diversified one.

The Tax Reform Act of 1986

Although investment banks have been the leading underwriters of municipal securities, commercial banks have been the leading institutional holders of these obligations. The Tax Reform Act of 1986, however, has caused a major shakeout in the municipal bond market. The biggest shock to the market occurred on October 12, 1987, when Salomon Brothers announced it was withdrawing from the slumping municipal bond business. As the leading underwriter of municipal obligations, Salomon Brothers had such valued clients as New York's Municipal Assistance Corporation, the state of Massachusetts, and the New York State Transit Authority. The firm also played a crucial role in providing liquidity to the municipal bond market.

Although many observers regarded Salomon's decision to withdraw from the market as "proof" that the municipal bond business will not rebound from its tax-reform slump, at least one analyst saw the move as shortsighted. He stated: "There is between $2 trillion and $3 trillion of municipal financing that will inevitably be financed with some form of municipal securities over the next 20 years. For Salomon Brothers to abandon the field leads me to believe they haven't thought through the long-term strategy for the firm as a whole."[9]

The slump in the municipal bond market is directly attributable to tax-reform-induced changes in both the supply of and demand for municipal securities. On the supply side, the law imposes a state-by-state volume cap on municipal bond issuance, thereby reducing new business. To illustrate the effect, during the first nine months of 1987 Salomon was the lead manager on 77 issues totaling $7.5 billion compared to 97 issues totaling $9.9 million for the comparable 1986 period. This reduction in new business combined with the longer-term decline (since 1981) in underwriting fees (e.g., from 2.9% in 1982 to 1.9% in the first quarter of 1987) has made the municipal bond business less profitable.

On the demand side, the Tax Reform Act of 1986 has reduced the tax advantage of purchasing municipal obligations. On the institutional side of the market, commercial banks and insurance companies have been the largest holders of municipal bonds. (As a group, individual investors are the largest holders of municipal bonds.) To illustrate the cutback in institutional demand, MONY Financial Services Inc., the parent com-

---

[9] The quotation and other details in this section (e.g., Salomon Brothers' decision) are from Peers [1987], p. 3.

pany of Mutual Life Insurance Company of New York and a former municipal client of Salomon Brothers, held about $330 million in municipal obligations in its $11 billion portfolio of 1984 compared to only a few issues in its $20 billion portfolio of 1987.

The reduced demand for municipal securities by institutional investors is due to the denial under the 1986 tax law of any deduction for interest expense to purchase or carry tax-exempt securities. The one exception to the repeal of carrying costs applies to small municipalities (but not states) with annual sales of tax-exempt obligations to financial institutions of $10 million or less. In this case, the financial institution can deduct 80 percent of the interest expense associated with the purchase of these "small" issues.

Calculating Tax-Equivalent Yields

The easier way to see how changes in the tax codes have affected the demand for municipal securities is to employ the formula for calculating tax-equivalent yields. Letting $r(te)$ represent the tax-equivalent yield on a tax-exempt security, the relevant formula is

$$r(te) = [r - (d \times c \times t)]/[1 - t], \tag{16-1}$$

where r is the nominal yield on the tax-exempt security, d is the percentage disallowance on the interest carrying cost due to TEFRA, c is the average interest cost of funds for carrying the security, and t is the institution's marginal tax rate.[10] Four regimes will be used to demonstrate how changes in the tax laws have affected the calculation of $r(te)$, which, since it is the effective rate of return on tax-exempt securities, will govern the demand for the securities.

The Pre-1983 Era

In this era, financial institutions could deduct the full cost of purchasing and carrying municipal and state obligations. In terms of Equation 16-1, the disallowance, d, was zero, which simplified the formula to $r(te) = r/(1 - t)$. Using a marginal tax rate of .46, the benchmark rule was to double the tax-exempt yield to get an approximation of the tax-equivalent yield. The exact multiplier was $1.85185\ldots = 1/(1 - .46)$.

Let's consider the following example, which we will carry through into the other three regimes. Suppose we want to compare a tax-exempt security with a 5.75 percent yield to a taxable one with a 7 percent yield. Our first approximation of doubling the yield gives a tax-equivalent return of 11.5 percent. More exactly, we get 10.65 percent $= 5.75/(1 - .46)$, assuming a marginal tax rate of 46 percent. If the spread of 365 basis points ($= 10.65\% - 7\%$) over the taxable security is enough to offset nonrate factors such as greater credit risk and lack of liquidity, the tax-exempt security is the preferred investment.

The 1983 to 1986 Era

During this era, TEFRA specified the disallowance to be 20 percent, which means we must use Equation 16-1 to calculate the tax-equivalent yield. Continuing with the previous example and assuming an average cost of funds of 4.5 percent, we get $r(te) = 9.88$ percent $(= [5.75 - (.2 \times 4.5 \times .46)]/[1 - .46])$. In this case, the tax-equivalent yield has fallen 77 basis points from what it was under the earlier tax

---

[10] TEFRA stands for the Tax Equity and Fiscal Reform Act of 1982. Formula 16-1 is from the *ABA Banking Journal* [February 1987], p. 35.

regime, resulting in a lower spread over the taxable security (i.e., 2.88% = 9.88% − 7% versus 3.65% = 10.65% − 7%).

The Transition Year: 1987

In this regime, the disallowance rises to 100 percent ($d = 1$) and the marginal tax rate (in transition between 46% and 34%) is approximated by 40 percent. With $d = 1$, the municipal bond market (from an institutional perspective) is devastated because $r(te) = 6.58$ percent ($= [5.75 − (1 \times 4.5 \times .40]/[1 − .4])$). With the taxable yield equal to 7 percent, there is no reason to hold a riskier security that has a lower yield, and probably has less liquidity.

The Post-1987 Era

The only change to bring in here is the lower marginal tax rate of 34 percent, which only serves to push the tax-equivalent yield even lower relative to the taxable one. Specifically, $r(te) = 6.39$ percent $= 5.75 − (1 \times 4.5 \times .34)/(1 − .34)$. In this case, the tax-exempt security has a 61 basis point disadvantage compared to the taxable yield of 7 percent.

Tax-Reform Recap and Implications for Bank Investment Portolios

The previous four examples clearly illustrate why the demand for municipal securities has decreased. Formula 16-1 represents an easy method for calculating the tax-equivalent yields associated with the various tax regimes. The reduced demand for municipal securities combined with the supply restrictions on new issues explains the slump in the municipal bond market.

What are the implications of tax reform for bank investment portfolios? As of this writing, the full effects are unclear. However, one thing *is* clear: Commercial banks will be holding fewer tax-exempt securities in their portfolios, other things equal. Given the existing opportunity set of earning assets, what replacement assets will banks seek? Assuming banks will be looking for the best risk-adjusted yields, only two options currently exist: (1) expand the loan portfolio and/or (2) reach out for longer-term taxable securities. The *ABA Banking Journal* summarized the municipal bond situation this way: "Banks' municipal bond portfolios will in time be just a memory under tax reform. Other instruments may come into their own." And as one banker put it: "It's a whole new ball game."[11]

ESTABLISHING A BANK INVESTMENT POLICY

Just as they are responsible for establishing compensation, loan, and asset-liability management policies, top management and the board of directors are responsible for establishing a bank's investment policy. Every business organization should attempt to establish in writing what its various policies are. From an asset management perspective, commercial banks need to have written loan and investment policies. The components of a model investment policy, as developed by Hoffland (1978), are shown in Table 16-4.

[11] *Ibid.*

TABLE 16-4 A Model Investment Policy

1. Basic Policy Objectives
2. Responsibility
3. Composition of Investments
4. Acceptable Securities
5. Maturities
6. Quality and Diversification
7. Making Portfolio Adjustments
8. Pledging
9. Safekeeping
10. Deliveries
11. Computer Program
12. Gains and Losses on Securities Sales
13. Swapping Securities
14. Trading Activity
15. Credit Files
16. Exceptions to This Policy

Source: Hoffland [1978].

To summarize, Hoffland views his investment policy as a model to be used by other banks in writing their own investment policies. He classifies it as a conservative approach and feels that banks with deposits under $300 million might use the policy as is. Since there are roughly 14,000 banks with deposits less than $300 million, Hoffland considers his policy to be appropriate for all but the largest banks.

FDIC AND OCC GUIDELINES

According to the FDIC's *Manual of Examination Policies* (Section H, p. 5), a sound investment policy for a bank should establish standards for the selection of securities with respect to

1. credit quality (default risk—see Table 16-5)[12]
2. maturity
3. diversification
4. marketability
5. income

In evaluating a bank's investment policy, the FDIC's *Manual* (Section H, p. 6) suggests the following factors as a guide for the examiner:

1. The *general character* of the bank's business as manifested in the characteristics of its loan and deposit accounts and its general economic environment.
2. *Analysis* of the bank's deposit structure in terms of the number, types, and size of accounts and in terms of deposit trends, composition, and stability.
3. *Capital funds.* In general, the smaller a bank's capital cushion, the more conservative its investment policy should be because it has fewer funds to absorb potential losses.

[12] The FDIC's *Manual of Examination Policies* states: "That securities should be purchased and held for income and not in anticipation of speculative profits is axiomatic" (Section H, page 8, revised, December 1, 1962). The OCC's Handbook for Examiners (sec. 203.1) states: "Speculation in marginal securities to generate more favorable yields is an unsound banking practice."

TABLE 16-5 Acceptable Rating Classifications as Determined by the OCC

Standard & Poor's	Moody's	Description
Bank quality investments		
AAA	Aaa	Highest grade obligations
AA	Aa	High grade obligations
A	A-1, A	Upper medium grade
BBB	Baa-1, Baa	Medium grade, on the borderline between definitely sound obligations and those containing predominantly speculative elements. Generally, the lowest quality bond that may qualify for bank investment
Speculative and defaulted issues		
BB	Ba	Lower medium grade with only minor investment characteristics
B	B	Low grade, default probable
D	Ca, c	Lowest rated class, defaulted, extremely poor prospects
Provisional or conditional rating		
Rating—P	Con. (Rating)	Debt service requirements are largely dependent on reliable estimates as to future events

Source: Comptroller of the Currency, Administrator for National Banks [1979]. *Comptroller's Handbook for National Bank Examiners*. Englewood Cliffs, NJ: Prentice-Hall, sec. 203.1,5.

4. *Economic and monetary factors.* It is suggested that intelligent portfolio management should consider basic economic and monetary factors in formulating and executing investment policies. However, the *Manual* cautions that preoccupation with such analysis may be indicative of "speculative tendencies which are unwholesome in banking."

CHAPTER SUMMARY

This chapter has focused on the characteristics and risk management of the bank investment portfolio. Since servicing loan customers and managing the bank's liquidity position takes precedence over investment securities, bank investment management has a "residual" nature. As a result, except for the largest banks, most banks have adopted a relatively passive approach to investment management. The volume of trading-account securities held by the largest banks is an indicator of their more active approach to investment management. Given the nature of bank investments, credit risk is not a major concern for investment managers. The primary focus is on interest-rate risk with a secondary focus on liquidity risk. In the wake of the Tax Reform Act of 1986, commercial banks are scrambling to realign their investment portfolios. By establishing investment policies, banks should be better able to manage, control, and monitor their investment activities.

LIST OF KEY WORDS, CONCEPTS, AND ACRONYMS

Active management
Bond ratings and agencies
Brokered trading
Credit risk

Dealer trading
Default-risk structure
Fisher effect
Institutional investor

Interest-rate risk

Investment-grade securities

Investment policy

Liquidity risk

Market making

Passive management

Taxable securities

Tax-equivalent yield

Tax-exempt securities

Tax Equality and Fiscal Reform
Act of 1982 (TEFRA)

Tax Reform Act of 1986

Term structure of interest rates

Trading-account securities

Unanticipated inflation

REVIEW/DISCUSSION QUESTIONS

1. Describe the bank investment function and the risks associated with it. How has the Tax Reform Act of 1986 affected this function?
2. Distinguish between "active" and "passive" bank investment management. Why is this distinction essentially along the lines of big banks versus little ones?
3. What are trading account securities and how are they an indicator of active investment management?
4. Describe the various market structures for trading securities. Which ones are commercial banks active in? Why aren't they active in all three? Distinguish between a price taker and a price maker.
5. Describe the investment portfolio of the typical insured commercial bank. How does bank size affect this portfolio? How much do banks depend on their investments for revenue?
6. Credit risk, interest-rate risk, and liquidity risk are the key portfolio risks of banking. How prevalent is each of these risks in bank investment portfolios? What role does unanticipated inflation play in driving these risks? How do these risks vary with bank size, if at all?
7. What is the linkage between the supply curves of bank securities and "thin" and "thick" markets? Explain in terms of liquidity and elasticity considerations.
8. Prior to the Tax Reform Act of 1986, how real was the "free lunch" aspect of tax-exempt securities? Describe the tax changes that have been responsible for restructuring the municipal bond market. How have some market participants such as investment banks, commercial banks, and insurance companies reacted?

PROBLEMS

1. The formula for calculating tax-equivalent yields is

$$r(te) = [r - (d \times c \times t)]/[1 - t]$$

Explain each of the components of the formula. Given the various tax regimes described in the text, how has this formula changed over time?
2. Given the various tax regimes from the previous problem, compare a five-year, 5 percent municipal bond with a five-year treasury note yielding 6.60 percent. Assume a cost of bank funds of 4.5 percent and use the d and c parameters that apply to the corresponding tax regimes. Explain why the spread, if any, between the tax-equivalent yield for the tax-exempt security and the taxable yield may not be large enough to convince some institutional investors to buy the tax-exempt issue. Are the calculated yields merely representative or can they be applied to any bank? Discuss.

MATCHING QUIZ

Directions: Select the letter from the right-hand column that best matches the item in the left-hand column.

___ 1. Trading-account securities

___ 2. Credit risk

___ 3. Liquidity risk

___ 4. Interest-rate risk

___ 5. Fisher effect

___ 6. Active management

___ 7. Passive management

___ 8. TEFRA

___ 9. Tax Reform Act of 1986

___ 10. Salomon Brothers

___ 11. MONY

___ 12. Tax-equivalent yield

___ 13. Pre-1983 $r(te)$

___ 14. Unanticipated inflation

___ 15. Bank dealers

___ 16. Market making

___ 17. Brokered trading

___ 18. Dealer trading

___ 19. David Hoffland

___ 20. The 1983 to 1986 era

A. $d = .20$

B. Agents bring buyers and sellers together

C. Price maker sets bid-ask spread

D. Indicator of active management

E. Permits portfolio rebalancing

F. $r/[1 - t]$

G. Muni market dropout

H. Model investment policy

I. $[r - (d \times c \times t)]/[1 - t]$

J. Report to New York Fed

K. 1982 law

L. Drives interest-rate risk

M. Found in thin markets

N. Rarity in bank investments

O. Primary concern for bank investment managers

P. Builds inflationary expectations into interest rates

Q. Financial services holding company

R. Killed the municipal bond market

S. Role of correspondent bank

T. Province of large banks

SELECTED REFERENCES

Bloch, Ernest. [1986]. *Inside Investment Banking*. Homewood Hills, IL: Dow Jones-Irwin.

Bradley, Stephen P., and Dwight B. Crane., [1975]. *Management of Bank Portfolio*. New York: Wiley.

Comptroller's Handbook for National Bank Examiners. [1979]. Englewood Cliffs, NJ: Prentice-Hall.

Cramer, Robert H., and James A. Seifert. [1976]. "Measuring the Impact of Maturity on Expected Return and Risk." *Journal of Bank Research* (Autumn 6), pp. 229–235.

"Farewell to Municipals and Other Tax Effects" [1987]. *ABA Banking Journal* (February), pp. 35–36.

Federal Reserve Bulletin, Washington, DC: Board of Governors of the Federal Reserve System (various issues).

Garbade, Kenneth D. [1982]. *Securities Markets*. New York: McGraw-Hill.

Granito, Michael R. [1984]. *Bond Portfolio Immunization*. Lexington, MA: Lexington Books.

Hayes, Douglas A. [1980]. *Bank Funds Management: Issues and Practices*. Ann Arbor: University of Michigan.

Hoffland, David L. [1978]. "A Model Bank Investment Policy," *Financial Analysts Journal* (May/June), pp. 64–67.

Kane, Edward J. [1980]. "Tax Exemption, Economic Efficiency, and Relative Interest Rates." Prepared for Conference on Efficiency in the Municipal Bond Market.

Kaufman, George G. [1987]. "The Federal Safety Net: Not for Banks Only," *Economic Perspectives*, Federal Reserve Bank of Chicago (November/December), pp. 19–28.

Kaufman, George G. [1985]. "The Securities Activities of Commercial Banks." In *Handbook for Banking Strategy*, Richard C. Aspinwall and Robert A. Eisenbeis, eds. New York: Wiley, pp. 661–702.

———. "Measuring and Managing Interest-Rate Risk: A Primer." *Economic Perspectives,* Federal Reserve Bank of Chicago (January/February), pp. 16–29.

Mason, John M. [1979]. *Financial Management of Commercial Banks*. Boston: Warren, Gorham, and Lamont.

Manual of Examination Policies, FDIC, Washington, DC (various revision dates).

McKinney, George W., Jr. [1977], "A Perspective on the Use of Models in the Management of Bank Funds." *Journal of Bank Research* (Summer), pp. 122–127.

Municipal Bond Handbook, Vols. I and II. [1983]. Fabozzi, et al. eds., and Feldstein, et al., eds., respectively. Homewood Hills, IL: Dow Jones-Irwin.

Peers, Alexandra. [1987]. "Public Finance Shakeout Is Signaled by Salomon's Municipal Bond Decision," *The Wall Street Journal* (October 13), p. 3.

Radcliffe, Robert C. [1982]. *Investment: Concepts, Analysis, and Strategy*. Glenview, IL: Scott, Foresman.

Robinson, Roland I. [1962]. *The Management of Bank Funds*. New York: McGraw Hill.

Sinkey, Joseph F., Jr. [1979]. *Problem and Failed Institutions in the Commercial Banking Industry*. Greenwich, CT: JAI Press.

Statistics on Banking, FDIC, Washington, DC (various issues).

Stigum, Marcia L., and Rene O. Branch. [1982]. *Managing Bank Assets and Liabilities*. Homewood Hills, IL: Dow Jones-Irwin.

Watson, Ronald D. [1972] "Bank Bond Management: The Maturity Dilemma." Federal Reserve Bank of Philadelphia *Business Review* (March), pp. 23–29.

Wolkowitz, Benjamin. [1985]. "Managing Interest-Rate Risk." In *Handbook for Banking Strategy*, Richard C. Aspinwall and Robert A. Eisenbeis, eds. New York: Wiley, pp. 407–456.

Woodworth, G. Walter. [1967]. *The Management of Cyclical Liquidity of Commercial Banks*. Boston: The Bankers Publishing Company, pp. 116–119.

Managing Interest-Rate Risk: Duration, Futures, Swaps, and Options

INTRODUCTION

Financial-services firms, such as commercial banks, savings-and-loan associations, credit unions, and insurance companies, have portfolios of assets and liabilities with varying degrees of interest-rate sensitivity. Since 1966, and especially since 1979, interest rates have been volatile (see Table 17-1). The combination of interest-rate sensitivity and volatility makes life difficult for the managers of financial-services firms, especially for those who borrow short (at variable rates) and lend long (at fixed rates). These difficulties often cause adverse changes in net cash flows and net-worth positions. Unanticipated changes in interest rates cause these difficulties. Since perfect foresight to predict future changes in interest rates is a bit too much to expect, managers of financial-services firms must look for other means to attempt to manage interest-rate risk. This chapter focuses on four techniques for managing interest-rate risk: (1) duration analysis, (2) interest-rate swaps, (3) interest-rate or financial futures, and (4) financial options. Although interest rates have been relatively stable since 1982, the interest-rate cycle is not dead and managers must know how to cope with interest-rate risk.

BETTING ON INTEREST RATES AND UNEXPECTED CHANGES IN INTEREST RATES

By its nature, the business of banking involves "betting" on interest-rate movements. For example, a banker making a fixed-rate loan with a duration longer than the duration on a variable-rate funding source is betting that interest rates will not rise more than his or her expectation. Since the *expected* rise in rates is built into the banker's spread, it is the *unexpected* change in rates that causes interest-rate risk. Adverse unexpected changes reduce interest-rate spreads and thereby lower bank profits, which slows the growth of internal equity capital, other things equal.

By not betting on interest rates or by gaining perfect foresight on the future course of interest rates, banks could avoid interest-rate risk altogether. However, since the

TABLE 17-1 The Volatility of Interest Rates, 1975–1987

Panel A. The Volatility of Interest Rates as Measured by the Standard Deviation of Daily Changes

Period	Treasury Bills (Three-Month)	Certificates of Deposit (Three-Month)	Treasury Bonds (Thirty-Year)
1975–1979[a]	7.1	6.0	2.7
1979–1982[b]	28.9	32.4	14.4
1982–1987[c]	8.1	8.9	8.0

Panel B. Change in Mortgage Rate in Week After Change in Ten-Year Treasury Yield

Period	Change in Mortgage Rate[d] (Basis Points)
1975–1979	2.0
1980–1982	3.2
1983–1985	4.0
1986–1987	8.2

[a] September 1975 through August 1979 for three-month bills and CDs; for the 30-year bond, September 1977 through August 1979.
[b] October 1979 through September 1982.
[c] October 1982 through September 1987.
[d] The mortgage rate is the commitment rate on fixed-rate home loans. Both rates are weekly averages. The 1987 observations are through mid-November.
Source: Federal Reserve Bulletin [Januarry, 1988], Table 3, p. 5, for Panel A and Table 5, p. 12, for Panel B.

former would forgo funding profits and the latter would be a nice money machine, neither approach is plausible. Nevertheless, banks can restrict the size of the bets made on the future course of interest rates by being prudent. In doing so, they limit their exposure to interest-rate risk. In contrast, banks and S&Ls that have been on the verge of failure have taken big gambles on interest rates and/or credits (the nothing-to-lose syndrome), letting the FDIC or FSLIC pick up the pieces if the bets went wrong.

On balance, the *modus operandi* of financial intermediaries is to bet on interest rates. The larger the bet, the more imperative it is to protect the firm's balance sheet from adverse unexpected changes in interest rates. The various techniques for obtaining such protection are the foci of this chapter. We begin by looking at the concept of hedging.

THE CONCEPT OF HEDGING

In my *Webster's* the third definition of "hedge" (vt) is "to protect oneself from losing by a counterbalancing transaction." Given the interest-rate environment of the past quarter century, managers of financial-services firms should have been looking for lots of counterbalancing transactions to minimize the risks of their interest-rate bets. Four ways to construct such counterbalancing transactions are (1) to duration match assets and liabilities, (2) to swap debt in accordance with the balance-sheet character-istics of the institution, (3) to buy or sell interest-rate futures, (4) to buy or sell debt options. Assuming the existence of the relevant financial instruments and markets, a duration match does not require a second or third party, whereas interest-rate swaps, futures, and options do. Duration and swap activities occur in the cash market, whereas futures and options transactions occur in the futures and options market. All of these transactions are designed to protect (hedge) against loss due to adverse price movements in the cash market.

For our purposes, a hedger is an individual who is unwilling to risk a serious interest-rate loss in his or her cash position and therefore takes a counterbalancing position to attempt to offset the loss. If the adverse event occurs, the institution still earns a profit if it has used duration or swapping; in the case of a futures (options) transaction, the profit in the futures (options) market reduces the loss in the cash market. On balance, hedging is a type of financial insurance. The cost of the insurance or hedge is the forgone profitable opportunities from a favorable movement in interest rates.

The Role of the Speculator

External hedging transactions require at least two parties[1]: a hedger and a speculator. The hedger is unwilling to bear risk, whereas the speculator is willing to bear risk. In effect, the hedger is buying insurance; the speculator is selling it. As seen in the previous chapter, bank regulators do not like banks to engage in speculative activities. It is not surprising, therefore, that commercial banks, except those with dealer operations (which as we have seen are the big banks) are restricted from using options and futures for speculative purposes. Thus, perforce most commercial bankers are hedgers looking for insurance to protect their balance sheets from interest-rate risk. But the most important commercial banks (in terms of economic and financial power and in terms of risk to the financial system) can use their dealer operations and trading-account activities to speculate on the future course of interest rates in cash, futures, or options.

Micro Versus Macro Hedges

Managers of financial-services firms may attempt to hedge specific assets, liabilities, or off-balance-sheet activities (e.g., loan commitments) or they may attempt to hedge the firm's overall interest-rate risk or "gap position." Transactions designed to hedge individual components of the balance sheet are referred to as *microhedges*, whereas strategies designed to protect the overall balance sheet are called *macrohedges*. As of this writing, bank accounting treatment requires recognition of futures transactions on a micro basis, which means connecting futures transactions with specific cash items. This treatment may explain the inability of some financial institutions to actually reduce total portfolio risk through futures hedging programs. On balance, accounting and regulatory restrictions may limit the ability of bank managers to reap the full potential of futures transactions. In contrast, the duration and swap approaches are not subject to accounting or regulatory restrictions, and options (as off-balance-sheet activities) are just beginning to receive greater regulatory scrutiny.

Examples of microhedges include the following: (1) the duration match of a particular asset with a particular liability (e.g., a five-year term loan with a balloon payment at maturity [a "bullet loan"] funded with a five-year zero-coupon CD); (2) a fixed-rate lender swapping its variable-rate debt for fixed-rate debt; and (3) the hedging of a fixed-rate loan commitment using the options market. By aggregating the previous examples to cover the entire balance sheet, rather than particular components of it, we have examples of macrohedges. This chapter presents detailed illustrations of the application of these various hedging techniques.

---

[1] In the case of interest-rate swaps, third-party intermediaries (e.g., large commercial or investment banks) frequently arrange and guarantee the transactions. In the case of financial futures (see Chapter 5), a clearing corporation serves as *the* second party. In contrast, a duration match is an internal hedge that does not require outside parties.

DURATION ANALYSIS: A TOOL FOR MANAGING INTEREST-RATE RISK AND PREDICTING INTEREST-SENSITIVE CASH FLOWS[2]

Although the idea of duration was first introduced by Macaulay in 1938, it took about three decades before the concept began to receive widespread attention in both academic and practitioner-oriented journals. It is not surprising that this increased interest in the topic coincided with the beginning of a period of greater interest-rate volatility marked by the credit crunch of 1966. As the severity of the interest-rate crunches increased (e.g., in 1969, 1974, and the early 1980s), the spotlight on duration grew brighter and brighter. As an important tool for the management of interest-rate risk, the focus on duration analysis was natural because the technique can be used to analyze changes in a firm's financial position due to unanticipated changes in interest rates.

Duration is usually defined as a measure of the effective (or average) time to maturity of a series of fixed cash flows. When viewed in a financial/economic context, the key insight provided by this notion is that rate-induced changes in a security's market value are directly proportional to the security's duration. In depository institutions, financial assets generally have longer durations than liabilities so that an unexpected increase (decrease) in rates causes the market value of assets to decrease (increase) more than the market value of liabilities. Thus, an increase (decrease) in rates leads to a decrease (increase) in the net market value of the firm. This relationship explains why the common stocks of financial-services firms (with negative gaps) tend to increase in value during periods of disinflation or deflation.

The financial concept of duration is closely related to a pro-forma sources-and-uses statement. When financial assets are bought by issuing debt, which must be "rolled over," changes in net market value result from changes in the magnitude and sign of future net cash flows. This problem is intimately tied to the concept of duration. To illustrate, consider the bank (or thrift) manager's typical repricing problem—the purchase of a long-term asset (e.g., a mortgage) funded by short-term liabilities (e.g., deposits). The manager faces forecasting problems because interest-rate fluctuations may cause the deposit liabilities to "reprice" several times before the asset matures, a phenomenon which Stigum and Branch [1983] have called "LRBA" for *L*iabilities *R*epricing *B*efore *A*ssets. If interest rates do not change, the institution receives the anticipated net cash surplus at maturity, generated by a positive yield spread. However, if rates rise, liabilities must promise larger than anticipated cash outflows each time they reprice. When the asset finally matures, the net cash surplus will be less than anticipated and perhaps even negative. This section focuses on the relationship between this repricing risk, as measured by duration, and the sources-and-uses of funds approach.

Duration as the Effective Time to Repricing

Although duration and repricing concepts are consistent and complementary, financial managers and accountants have failed to exploit the operational advantages of the duration approach. Since the standard definition of duration as the "average time to maturity" (Bierwag [1978]) does not adequately convey its risk-proxying characteristics, duration is better defined as "the effective time to repricing," which should be more intuitive for managers, regulators, accountants, and shareholders (not to

---

[2] This section draws on the works of Hilliard [1987] and Hilliard and Sinkey [1987]. See Chapter 9 for additional information on duration.

mention students). To show the equivalence of the duration and cash-flow concepts requires some restructuring of the traditional duration formula and the development of a plausible scenario for modeling the response of asset and liability values to interest-rate changes. The remainder of this section sets forth the appropriate duration formulas and demonstrates the similarity between duration analysis and an item-by-item repricing, or cash-flow analysis based on the traditional sources-and-uses accounting statement.

Duration as a Measure of Cash-Flow Sensitivity

To compare duration models to cash-flow models, the following technical concepts and definitions are used:

V_A = value of an asset

V_L = value of a liability

C_A = cash inflow from an asset

C_L = cash inflow from a liability

r_A = interest rate on an asset

r_L = interest cost of a liability

In addition, we use a presubscript t (e.g., $_tV_A$) to denote (1) the time period in which the asset or liability is valued, (2) the period in which the cash flow occurs (e.g., $_tC_A$), and (3) the period in which the interest rate is observed (e.g., $_tr_A$). The time periods run from 1 to N (i.e., $1,2,3,\ldots,N$) and $t = 0$ is used to indicate the present. Using these symbols, the relevant financial concepts we want to establish are

1. present value or market value
2. future value
3. duration
4. changes in market value.

Beginning with present value, consider a single-payment asset of $1,000 (or "bullet loan") that promises a cash inflow of $1,100 one year from today consisting of $1,000 in principal and $100 in interest. If the going rate of interest on assets of similar risk is 15 percent, what is the value of this asset in the marketplace? First, note that the future or maturity value of the loan is

$$_1V_A = \$1,000(1.10) = \$1,100$$

The present value of the loan, discounted at 15 percent, is

$$_0V_A = \$1,100/1.15 = \$956.52$$

In this case, the loan has a paper capital loss of $43.48 due to the fact that the relevant rate of interest is 500 basis points above the stated rate on the loan.

Suppose that this loan was financed with a one-year "bullet deposit" or zero-coupon certificate of deposit (CD) at 9 percent, giving the lender a one percent spread. The future value of the CD is

$$\$1,090 = \$1,000(1.09)$$

If the CD rate instantaneously increases by 500 basis points, as the loan rate did, then the CD has a present value of

$$_0V_L = \$1,090/1.14 = \$956.14$$

However, because there is no repricing risk associated with either the asset or the liability, the spread is locked in and the net asset value, defined as $V_A - V_L$, is preserved, that is, the change in market value, $dV = dV_A - dV_L$, is zero. In this example, the change in interest rates, r, was assumed to be the same for both the asset and the liability, that is, $dr = dr_A = dr_L$, where d denotes an incremental change.

The duration analysis for this example is extremely simple because zero-coupon or bullet assets (or liabilities) have durations equal to their maturities. (This correspondence was shown in Chapter 9.) Moreover, duration matching of assets and liabilities immunizes a balance sheet against changes in interest rates. Thus, when a one-year bullet asset in financed with a one-year bullet liability, the interest-rate spread is locked in and the net asset value is preserved or immunized.

More Complex Repricing Examples

When assets and liabilities have unequal durations, net cash flows are not perfectly predictable. The examples given in this section quantify risk exposure by comparing the detailed cash-flow approach with duration analysis. Although the methods give equivalent results, the duration approach is easier to compute and to generalize to different scenarios. Accordingly, it provides both new insights into the problem of forecasting interest-sensitive cash flows and offers possible solutions to the dilemma.

Pure Discount Assets and Liabilities

The following example depicts, in essential ways, the cash-flow problems due to interest-rate risk. Suppose a $1,000,000 asset with a one-year maturity is to be financed by a portfolio of short-term liabilities, consisting of a three-month CD and a six-month CD, each selling initially for $500,000. The three-month CD will be repriced after three, six, and nine months, while the six-month CD will be repriced after six months. The asset rate of return is 14 percent, while the three- and six-month CDs cost 10 and 11 percent, respectively. At maturity, the asset will return cash flows of $1,000,000 \times 1.14 = \$1,140,000$. If rates do not change, and identical liabilities are issued to fund the maturing CDs, the three-month liability will require a final outflow of $500,000 \times 1.10 = \$550,000$, while the six-month CD will require a final outflow of $500,000 \times 1.11 = \$555,000$ (see the sources-and-uses statement in Table 17-2). Ignoring transactions costs, the net cash flow anticipated at the end of the year is, therefore, $\$1,140,000 - (\$550,000 + \$555,000) = \$35,000$.

Now consider the effect of a one-time, one percent increase in rates immediately after the positions are taken. Although the cash inflows produced by the asset will be unaffected, increased outflows will be required to fund the maturing liabilities (see Table 17-3 for details). At initial maturity, the three-month CD requires a cash outflow of $500,000 \times (1 + .10)^{.25} = \$512,056.84$. This CD and successive three-month CDs are paid off by issuing CDs at the higher yield of 11 percent. At the end of the year, the cash outflow required to discharge the final three-month CD is $\$512,056.84 \times (1 + .11)^{.75} = \$553,745.75$. The six-month CD reprices only once. After six months, it matures at the fixed value (prior to the rate change) of $\$500,000 \times (1 + .11)^{.5} = \$526,782.69$. Since it must be repriced at 12 percent, the six-month CD requires a cash outflow at the end of the year of $\$526,782.69 \times (1 + .12)^{.5} = \$557,494.40$. The actual net cash flow at the end of the year is, therefore, $\$1,140,000 - (\$553,745.75 + \$557,494.40) = \$28,759.85$. The cost of repricing under this scenario is the anticipated net cash flow minus the actual net cash flow = $\$35,000 - \$28,759.85 = \$6,240.15$.

TABLE 17-2   Statement of Sources and Uses of Funds under a Scenario of No Change in Rates[a]

Action	Elapsed Time (Months)				
	0	3	6	9	12
Source of Funds					
Issue 3-month CD	500,000	512,057	524,404	537,050	
(percent)	(10)	(10)	(10)	(10)	
Issue 6-month CD	500,000		526,783		
(percent)	(11)		(11)		
One-year note					1,140,000
Use of Funds					
Buy 1-year note	1,000,000				
(percent)	(14)				
Pay off 3-month CD		512,057	524,404	537,050	550,000
Pay off 6-month CD			526,783		555,000
Net flow of cash	0	0	0	0	+35,000

[a] Entries rounded to nearest dollar.
Source: Hilliard and Sinkey [1987], Table 1.

TABLE 17-3   Statement of Sources and Uses of Funds under a Scenario of an Immediate One Percent Increase in Rates[a]

Action	Elapsed Time (Months)				
	0	3	6	9	12
Source of Funds					
Issue 3-month CD	500,000	512,057	525,592	539,485	
(percent)	(10)	(11)	(11)	(11)	
Issue 6-month CD	500,000		526,783		
(percent)	(11)		(12)		
One-year note					1,140,000
Use of Funds					
Buy 1-year note	1,000,000				
(percent)	(14)				
Pay off 3-month CD		512,057	525,592	539,485	553,746
Pay off 6-month CD			526,783		557,494
Net flow of cash	0	0	0	0	+28,760

[a] Entries rounded to nearest dollar.
Source: Hilliard and Sinkey [1987], Table 2.

Duration Analysis

When a security has a single cash-flow promised at maturity, duration is identical to maturity. For example, a CD that matures in three years has a duration equal to three years. However, duration is less than maturity for all securities promising cash flows prior to maturity. Consider, for example, a note promising $1,000 dollars in one year and $2,000 in two years. If both one- and two-year interest rates are 10 percent, the present value of the cash flow in year one is $1,000/1.10 = $909.09 while the present value of the cash flow occurring in year two is $2,000/(1.10)» = $1,652.89. The present value of the security is $V = $909.09 + $1,652.89 = $2,561.98$. Now, consider a portfolio of two securities identical to this single security. The portfolio contains one security with a $1,000 maturity value in one year and a second security with a $2,000 maturity value in two years. Clearly, this portfolio is identical to the single security. Now, what is the weighted average maturity of the portfolio? Letting $PV(1)$ be the present value of security one and $PV(2)$ be the present value of security two, the weighted-average maturity of the portfolio is

$$1 \text{ year} \times PV(1)/V + 2 \text{ years} \times PV(2)/V = [1 \times PV(1) + 2 \times PV(2)]/V$$

Plugging in the present values, the duration calculation is

$$1 \text{ year} \times .355 + 2 \text{ years} \times .645 = 1.645 \text{ years}$$

The weighted-average maturity of the portfolio is precisely the duration of the original security. Thus, the duration of a security with intermediate cash flows may be defined as the weighted-average maturity of an equivalent portfolio of pure discount securities. To illustrate the general duration formula, consider a security with present value promising n intermediate cash flows, each with present value $PV(i)$, $i = 1, 2, \ldots n$. Let $W(i)$ be the fraction of present value contributed by the cash flow in period i so that $W(i) = PV(i)/V$. The duration, D, of the security is

$$D = 1 \times W(1) + 2 \times W(2) + 3 \times W(3) + \cdots + n \times W(n) \tag{17-1}$$

Sources and Uses Revisited: A Duration Approach

A duration analysis of the previous example gives the same results as the traditional sources-and-uses method. The duration approach however, is more concise and extends easily to different sets of assumptions about the direction and magnitude of interest-rate changes. These computational efficiencies and insights regarding interest-rate risk are especially important when the portfolio of assets and liabilities is large. The first step in the analysis is to establish an appropriate formula for simultaneous analysis of assets and liabilities. Since the change in net value at time t ($_t dV$) is the change in the value of assets minus the change in the value of liabilities, the relevant formula is

$$_t dV = {}_t dV_A - {}_t dV_L \tag{17-2}$$

where (as defined above) subscripts A and L denote assets and liabilities, respectively. Using calculus, it can be shown, as demonstrated in the appendix of this chapter, that the change in security value at time T, the planning horizon, due to an incremental change in rate, dr, is

$$[V_A \cdot (1 + r_A)^{T-1} \cdot (T - D_A) - V_L \cdot (1 + r_L)^{T-1} \cdot (T - D_L)] dr \tag{17-3}$$

In words, Equation 17-3 says that the change in net asset value over the planning horizon, T, is equal to the difference between the duration-adjusted future values of assets and liabilities times the change in interest rates. Note that if the portfolio is duration matched such that $D_A = D_L = T$, then it is immunized against any change in interest rates even if asset and liability rates do not move in the same direction and by the same magnitude. The duration matching of a *portfolio* (or balance sheet) of assets and liabilities creates a *macrohedge*. In contrast, the duration matching of an *individual* asset and liability creates a *microhedge*.

Returning to the repricing example, the parameters of Equation 17-3 are

$$V_A = \text{initial value of assets} = \$1,000,000$$

$$V_L = \text{initial value of liabilities} = \$1,000,000$$

$$T = \text{planning horizon} = 1 \text{ year}$$

r_A = initial rate on assets = .14

r_L = initial rate on liabilities

= .10($500,000/$1,000,000) + .11($500,000/$1,000,000)

= .105

D_A = duration of asset = 1 year

D_L = duration of liabilities

= .25($500,000/$1,000,000) + .50($500,000/$1,000,000)

= .375

Note that the interest rate on liabilities and liability duration are weighted averages. The latter is derived directly from Equation 17-1, where the period 1 and 2 weights are equal to the maturities of the liabilities (i.e., .25 and .50) and $W(1) = W(2) = \$500,000/1,000,000$. Thus, D_L = .375.

The change in net cash flow at the end of the year (T, the planning horizon is one year) can be computed directly from Equation 17-3 as

$$_1dV = [\$1,000,000(1.14)^0(1 - 1) - \$1,000,000(1.105)^{1-1}(1 - .375)]dr$$
$$= -\$1,000,000(.625)dr = -\$625,000dr$$

For a 1 percent increase in rates ($dr = .01$), the net change in value is $_1dV = -\$6,250$. This figure closely approximates the $6,240.15 change in net cash outflow obtained by the sources-and-uses approach (see Tables 17-2 and 17-3). Since the duration formulas contain a slight approximation error, which approaches zero as the change in interest rates becomes smaller, the two approaches do not produce identical results. In this particular example, a 100 basis point change results in an error of less than 1 percent in computing the net change in value ($6,250 - $6,240)/$6,240 = .0016 = .16%.

This example points out interesting features of the duration model. First, since asset duration is equal to the planning horizon, that is, $T = D_A = 1$, the asset contributed nothing to repricing cost. This finding is not at all surprising since there is no repricing risk on the asset. And second, the CDs, which are repriced before the end of the year (their maturities generate the weights .25 and .50 in calculating the weighted-average duration of .375), are the source of repricing risk. This risk is manifested by the inequality between the liability duration of .375 years versus the planning horizon of one year.

In summary, for plausible scenarios such as the one analyzed here, the duration formulas accurately reflect the detailed sources-and-uses statement.

Securities with Intermediate Cash Flows

The previous example used duration analysis for the case of securities with no intermediate cash flows. Since maturity always equals duration for securities without intermediate cash flows, it was essentially a careful *maturity* analysis. In the next example, the same $1,000,000 asset is employed; however, it is to be financed by a six-month CD (as before) *and* a four-month note which promises cash flows after two months and at maturity. The specifics of the example are: The four-month liability has an initial rate of 10 percent, while the six-month liability starts at a rate of 11 percent. The four-month note is issued for $500,000 and pays $254,002.97 in two months and $258,070.03 at maturity. The intermediate payment is financed by issuing two-month notes at 10 percent; at maturity, all payouts are financed by a new four-month note. The six-month CD is issued for $500,000 and pays $500,000 × $(1 + .11)^{.5}$ = $526,782.69 at maturity.

If rates do not change, the net cash flow at the end of one year is as before. The cash flow from the asset at maturity is $1,140,000, whereas the six-month CD and four-month note require an outflow of $555,000 + $550,000 at maturity. Thus, the net cash flow at the end of the year is $1,140,000 − ($555,000 + $550,000) = $35,000.

Suppose now that rates increase by one percent immediately after the portfolio is issued. The six-month CD will require a year-end cash outflow of $557,497.40 as before. The sources-and-uses analysis in Table 17-4 shows the calculation of the cash outflows for the four-month note to be more complex. At the end of two months, the intermediate interest payment of $254,002.97 will be financed by a two-month note written at the new rate of 11 percent. At the end of four months the cash outflow components are $254.002.97 × $(1 + .11)^{1/6}$ = $258,459.57 due on the two-month note plus $258.070.03 due on the maturity value of the original four-month note. The total outflow is $516,529.60. Funding this outflow by similar four- and two-month notes until maturity requires a year-end cash outflow of $516,529.60 × $(1 + .11)^{2/3}$ = $553,745.92. Together with the six-month note, total cash outflows at year end are $557,494.40 + $553,745.92 = $1,111,240.32. The *net* cash flow is therefore $1,140,000 − $1,111,240.32 = $28,759.68. The cost of repricing is the anticipated cash flow minus the actual cash flows or $35,000 − $28,759.68 = $6,240.32 (see Table 17-4).

To illustrate the efficiency of the duration approach, the previous (tedious) example can be solved quickly by using Equation 17-3. Since the parameters are exactly the same as in the first example, the duration model gives the net change in cash flow to be −$6,250., which is very close to the −$6,240 obtained by the sources-and-uses analysis.

TABLE 17-4   Statement of Sources and Uses of Funds Analyzing Notes with Intermediate Cash Flows [a]

Action	\	\	\	Elapsed Time (Months)	\	\	\
	0	2	4	6	8	10	12
Source of Funds							
Issue 2-month CD		254,003		262,796		272,099	
(percent)		(11)		(11)		(11)	
Issue 4-month note	500,000		516,530		534,814		
(percent)	(10)		(11)		(11)		
Issue 6-month CD	500,000			526,783			
(percent)	(11)			(12)			
One-year note							1,140,000
Use of Funds							
Buy 1-year note	1,000,000						
(percent)	(14)						
Outflows 2-month CD			258,460		267,407		276,873
Outflows 4-month note		254,003	258,070	262,796	267,407	272,099	276,873
Pay off 6-month CD				526,783			557,494
Net flow of cash	0	0	0	0	0	0	+28,760

[a] Entries rounded to nearest dollar.
Source: Hilliard and Sinkey [1987], Table 3.

For the first example (no intermediate cash flows), the repricing cost was $6,240.15; here it is $6,240.32. The duration analysis supplies important insights, absent in the accounting approach, as to why the costs are almost identical. The duration model shows that there is less repricing risk in the second example, where assets are being supported by longer-term liabilities. Specifically, a four-month CD with intermediate cash flows financed half of the price of the asset in the second case, whereas a three-month note financed half of the price of the asset in the first case. Using Equation 17-1, a quick duration calculation provides a critical insight. The three-month CD clearly has a three-month duration. However, the four-month note, because of its intermediate cash flows, also has a three-month duration, that is,

$$D = \{[2 \text{ months} \times \$254,000.97/(1.10)^{1/6} +$$
$$[4 \text{ months} \times \$258,070.03/(1.10)^{1/3}]\}/\$500,000$$
$$= 2 \text{ months} \times .5 + 4 \text{ months} \times .5 = 3 \text{ months}$$

Since the two present-value calculations inside the brackets both equal $250,000, both weights are .5. Clearly, since both instruments have the same duration, they possess the same interest-rate risk. Two important points are illustrated: (1) duration analysis is consistent with straightforward cash-flow calculations, and (2) duration, not maturity, is the appropriate proxy for pricing interest-rate risk.

Recapitulations and Extensions

The approach to duration analysis presented here is based on two foundations: First, we defined duration as the effective time until a financial asset (or liability) reprices. And second, we have shown that the duration model closely approximates the more tedious, longhand version of cash-flow analysis based on a sources-and-uses financial statement. Clearly, since the duration approach is computationally more efficient and provides economic insight about cash-flow volatility, it is an attractive alternative to the traditional accounting approach for analyzing interest-sensitive cash flows. By simplifying the description and application of duration analysis, both the concept and the technique are made more palatable.

Since the duration differences in our examples were relatively short (e.g., $D_A - D_L = 1 - .375 = .625$ years = 7.5 months), they are most relevant for commercial banks. However, the analysis can easily be extended to other financial institutions. For example, consider the case of an eight-year duration mismatch for an institution with assets and liabilities equal to $50 million. A 2 percent change in rates will lead to an immediate change in market value of $7,142,857 (= $50,000,000 × 8 × .02/1.12) for such an institution (use Equation 17-3 with $V_A = V_L$, $r_A = r_L = .12$, and $T = 0$).

To summarize, by duration matching their *portfolios* of assets and liabilities (i.e., their entire balance sheets), asset-liability managers can obtain a *macrohedge*. The matching of *individual* assets and liabilities generates a *microhedge*.

SWAP FINANCE AND THE MARKET FOR INTEREST-RATE SWAPS[3]

In general, swap finance refers to various specialized financial transactions in which two or more parties exchange or swap instruments in the same currency, or in two or more different currencies, at predetermined prices and maturities. Swap transactions,

[3] For everything you wanted to know about swap finance (but were afraid to ask), see *Swap Finance* (vols. 1 and 2) edited by Boris Antl [1986]. This section draws on these two volumes, especially the chapters by Gray, Kurz, and Strupp; Lindberg, Weston, and Wheat; Beckstrom; Peters; and Leibowitz.

which are negotiated agreements, can be arranged for various money and capital market instruments. Currency and interest-rate swaps are the cornerstones of swap finance, and they have contributed greatly to the globalization and efficiency of world and domestic financial markets. The market for swaps, which began with currency transactions in the early 1970s, is estimated to be between $100 billion and $200 billion. For the purposes of this chapter, we are concerned with interest-rate swaps as a tool for managing interest-rate risk. Interest-rate swaps, which developed in the early 1980s, were a direct outgrowth of the currency swaps of the early 1970s.

According to Beckstrom [1986], the first interest-rate swaps were arranged in the Euromarket in 1981, while the first swap in the United States was completed by the Student Loan Marketing Association (Sallie Mae) in 1982. These initial swaps were fixed- versus floating-rate transactions, which still are the most common form of interest-rate swap. Today, the U.S. dollar market for interest-rate swaps is the largest in the world, with New York City as the hub and important spokes in London and Tokyo. The market for interest-rate swaps has both primary and secondary segments with the primary sector subdivided along Eurodollar and Eurobond lines. Activity in the primary market can be distinguished according to maturity (duration) and type of player. In the short-term segment of the market (three-years or less), the major players are commercial and investment banks both U.S. domestic and foreign. Since the transactions in this interbank market are motivated by funding and hedging activities, it is a volatile one (as measured by interest-rate spreads against U.S. Treasury bills or six-month LIBOR, the London Interbank Offer Rate), and therefore quite risky. However, the expansion of the secondary market for swaps has served to reduce some of the risk in the short-term primary market.[4]

In the longer-term segment of the market for interest-rate swaps, U.S. thrift and nonfinancial institutions are the major players, with the Eurobond market the central focus. This segment of the market prices off U.S. Treasury securities, and the spreads are relatively stable compared to the spreads in the short-term segment of the swap market.

Why Swap Finance Exists

The development of swap markets and products can be explained by risk, return (cost), and regulatory considerations. Regarding risk, volatile exchange and interest rates have taken their toll on the profits and equity positions of various classes of financial (and nonfinancial) institutions. Swaps offer a way to combat these adverse external conditions. With respect to return (cost), by exploiting profitable arbitrage opportunities in worldwide money and capital markets, financial institutions can lower their cost of funds, and thereby increase their returns, other things equal. And third, regulatory constraints make certain financial transactions difficult or impossible to obtain. Swaps permit the circumvention of such restrictions. Nevertheless, since regulatory restrictions vary across countries, the driving forces in the development of swap transactions have been the financial ones of risk and return.

The Use of Interest-Rate Swaps to Manage Interest-Rate Risk

The old adage "You scratch my back and I'll scratch yours" can be used to get at the heart of what an interest-rate swap is. Specifically, "You make my interest

---

[4] During a week in the spring of 1985, Bankers Trust unwound about $1 billion in swaps, which demonstrated the depth of the secondary market for interest-rate swaps. According to Lindberg, et al. [1986], the swap transactions involved 23 separate components with sizes ranging from $5 million to $75 million (p. 62).

payments and I'll make yours." Since that covers what an interest-rate swap is, we only need to know two more things: (1) Why they exist? and (2) How they work? The following example will answer both of these questions.

The most common type of interest-rate swap is the one in which floating-rate payments and fixed-rate payments are swapped. Although the general motivating force for the swap is to hedge interest-rate risk, the existence of potential arbitrage opportunities drives swap transactions. Since these opportunities permit both of the swapping parties to be made better off, swaps are mutually beneficial. Therefore, rational self-interest dictates that swaps happen.[5]

The arbitrage opportunities of interest-rate swaps are most easily seen by appealing to the "theory of comparative advantage," one of the cornerstones of international trade theory. Consider two companies: a AAA-rated bank and a BBB-rated conglomerate, a nonfinancial corporation. Because of its higher creditworthiness, the AAA bank will have an absolute advantage over the BBB corporation in issuing any kind of debt. To illustrate consider the following parameters:[6]

	BBB Corp.	AAA Bank	Advantage
Funding objective	Fixed-rate funds	Floating-rate funds	
Fixed rate	14%	11.625%	2.375%
Floating rate	LIBOR + .5%	LIBOR + .25%	.250%
Arbitrage potential			2.125%

The BBB corporation prefers to fund its long-term assets with fixed-rate debt, whereas the AAA bank wants to hedge its variable-rate assets with floating-rate debt. Because the bank has a AAA credit rating, it has an absolute advantage in both short- and long-term financial markets over the conglomerate with its BBB rating. This advantage is reflected by the default-risk premiums of 2.375 percent in the fixed-rate market and .25 percent in the short-term or LIBOR market. However, if we focus on the notion of comparative advantage, the corporation is at a lesser disadvantage in the LIBOR market. Alternatively, the bank has its greater comparative advantage in issuing long-term debt. In the language of international trade, the bank should "specialize in the production" of fixed-rate debt and the corporation should "specialize in the production" of floating-rate debt. In the language of swap finance, the bank should raise the fixed-rate debt and let the corporation service it, whereas the corporation should raise LIBOR funds (where it has a comparative advantage) and let the bank service this short-term debt.

The arbitrage potential in a swap transaction is reflected by the spread between the absolute advantage figures, that is, 2.625 percent = 0.25 percent = 2.125 percent. The interest-rate arbitrage represents the total financial benefits to be shared by the parties entering a swap transaction. The benefits take the form of lower borrowing costs to both parties. Since interest-rate swaps are negotiated transactions, the contract negotiations determine how the benefits are shared. Figure 17-1 illustrates one way in which the AAA and BBB conglomerate might structure a specific swap.

The transaction depicted in Figure 17-1 involved the exchange or swap of $50 million of the bank's fixed-rate, five-year debt for $50 million of the corporation's floating-rate debt. The swap contract calls for 10 semiannual interest payments to be

---

[5] Viewing interest-rate swaps as a financial innovation, their development fits nicely into our model of change, that is, TRICK + rational self-interest = financial innovation (see Chapters 1 and 5).

[6] The numbers in this example are the same ones used by Peters [1986], pp. 201–204.

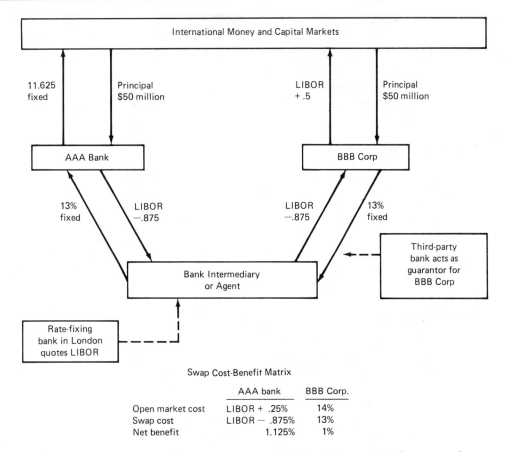

Swap Cost-Benefit Matrix

	AAA bank	BBB Corp.
Open market cost	LIBOR + .25%	14%
Swap cost	LIBOR − .875%	13%
Net benefit	1.125%	1%

Notes: The sum of the net benefits is 2.125% which is equal to the arbitrage potential. The swap cost for the corporation of 13% consists of the bank's 11.652% fixed cost plus the .875% it must add to its floating rate cost plus a .5% margin to the lender. The total all-in cost to the corporation, which is somewhat complicated, is shown by Peters [1986, p. 204] to be 14.25%, which is .72% lower than its direct fixed-rate cost of 14.97%. The swap contract called for 10 semiannual interest payments.

Figure 17-1   The Structure of a Fixed-to-Floating Interest-Rate Swap

Source: The numbers used to illustrate this swap transaction are from Peters [1986], pp. 201–204.

made by both parties. The swap enabled each of the participants to meet their funding objectives at lower costs than they could have achieved without the swap. The net benefit to the AAA bank is 1.125 percent and the net benefit to the BBB conglomerate is one percent. The sum of the net benefits is equal to the arbitrage potential discussed above.

As shown in Figure 17-1, in addition to the AAA bank and BBB corporation, several other parties were either directly or indirectly involved in the swap transaction. First, a bank intermediary served as the agent for the swap agreement (an eight-page document in this case) and handled both the receipts and payments to and from both parties. Payments were escrowed and not disbursed until both parties had paid the agent bank. Second, another bank with a branch in London served as the rate-fixing bank for LIBOR. The agent bank was responsible for obtaining the LIBOR rate from the rate-fixing bank and calculating the floating-rate payments. The floating rate was defined as the arithmetic mean of three-month LIBOR for two consecutive periods beginning at the start of the contract minus .875 percent. The semiannual fixed-rate payment was $3,250,000 (= [$50,000,000 × .13]/2). And third, since the AAA bank was unwilling to accept the credit risk of the BBB corporation, the conglomerate had to secure a third-party guarantor. One of the corporation's banks agreed to provide this service in the form of an irrevocable letter of credit for $32,500,000, which was the total interest payment due to the bank (i.e., $50,000,000 × .13 × 5). The guarantor received a commission of .125 percent of the line of credit per year for a first year fee of $40,625.

The Rest of the Story

It's Paul Harvey time again! Peters [1986, p. 204] reports that two years after the interest-rate swap shown in Figure 17-1 was arranged, the BBB-rated corporation was acquired by a AA-rated firm. In addition, because of third-world debt problems, the AAA-rated bank was effectively downgraded to AA. As a result, the original credit-risk differences between the two parties were now effectively eliminated. To compensate for this reduced risk to the bank, the requirement of a third-party guarantor was cancelled, which eliminated the cost of the letter of credit to the corporation and thereby reduced its swap costs.

Swap Recapitulation

Having gone through the "trees" of an interest-rate swap, let's not lose sight of the "forest." The purpose of an interest-rate swap is to hedge interest-rate risk. By arranging for another party to assume your interest payments such a hedge can be put in place. The arbitrage potential associated with different comparative financing advantages (spreads) enables both parties to benefit through lower borrowing costs. In addition to the parties entering the swap agreement, other financial institutions by acting as agents and guarantors generate fees by providing agency and guarantee services to the contracting parties.

USING FINANCIAL FUTURES TO HEDGE INTEREST-RATE RISK

Interest-rate futures are another tool for managing interest-rate risk. The distinguishing features of futures contracts were introduced in Chapter 5. The objective of this section is to show how these contracts can be used to create either micro or macro hedges to protect against interest-rate risk. A hedge is put in place when a financial manager takes a position in the futures market that is equal and opposite to an existing, expected, or committed position in the cash market. The futures transaction is a temporary one to be replaced by the cash transaction at a later date. In the ideal situation of a perfect hedge, which is a rarity, a loss in one market is completely offset by a gain in the other market.

The two common hedging positions faced by bank asset-liability managers are

Objective	Spot Market	Futures Market
Guarantee future lending rate	Short	Long
Guarantee future borrowing rate	Long	Short

Since the position taken in the futures market provides the verbiage for describing the futures transaction, we have the terms "long hedge" and "short hedge." "Long" indicates an ownership or buying position, whereas "short" indicates a funding need or selling position.

Examples of Microhedges

A microhedge is one applied to an individual asset or transaction. If successful, the hedge immunizes only that particular transaction; it does not protect the firm's entire balance sheet. Let's consider the two basic situations in which an asset-liability manager might want to establish a microhedge.

First, consider a *long hedge*, which is defined as the *purchase* of a futures contract designed to lock in a yield on an anticipated future *cash inflow*. Maturing securities, balloon loan repayments, and deposit inflows are examples of cash inflows that asset-liability managers might want to hedge. In this situation, managers have two choices: (1) wait for the inflow to occur and accept the risk that rates may decline or (2) hedge the risk now by buying futures contracts. The manager's or ALM committee's expectation regarding the direction of future interest rates should influence the choice. If rates are expected to decline, then a long hedge will be put in place. A long hedge is also known as a buy hedge. By buying a futures contract, the hedger owns a financial instrument that can be sold at a specified price and date in the future. Owners of anything, including futures contracts, hope for increases in the values of their possessions. If interest rates actually do decline, then the future cash inflow will be invested at a lower yield. However, this opportunity loss will be offset (exactly if the hedge is perfect), by the gain on the futures contracts.

To illustrate a long hedge, consider an asset-liability manager who has funds to invest for six months at a time when the yield curve is inverted (i.e., the three-month T-bill is yielding more than the six-month bill). The manager would like to "strip" two three-month bills to cover the six-month investment horizon. However, if rates decline, the rollover into the second bill will be at a lower rate. To protect against this rate/price risk, a long hedge in T-bill futures can be used. Accordingly, the manager should buy the nearest T-bill futures contract to hedge the risk. If rates do decline, then the opportunity loss on the rollover will be cushioned by the gain on the lifting of the hedge. In contrast, if rates increase, then the higher yield on the rollover will be reduced by the loss on the lifting of the futures contract.

Let's put some numbers on this example. Suppose the three-month T-bill yield is 10 percent, the six-month yield 9.5 percent, the yield on the three-month T-bill future is 9.0 percent, and the manager has $1,000,000 to invest. To hedge the planned strip, the manager buys T-bills in the cash market *and* in the futures market. After three months, assume the T-bill rates are 9 percent in the cash market and 8.5 percent in the futures market. The bank's average return on the strip is 9.5 percent (what the pure expectations theory suggests, i.e., $9.5 = [10 + 9]/2$). However, this does not include the profit on the futures contract which was bought at 9.0 percent (or $91 = 100 - 9$) and sold at 8.5 percent (or $91.5 = 100 - 8.5$). At $25 a basis point, the 50 basis point decline translates into $1,250. On a million dollar investment for 90 days, this transaction adds 50 basis points to the 9.5 percent yield to make the total return 10 percent, which is what the manager set out to do (i.e., to lock in the 10 percent return for six months).

The second general situation of bank microhedging involves an expected cash outflow. Expected draws on loan commitments and maturing debt that must be rolled over (e.g., CDs and repurchase agreements) are common examples of cash outflows faced by asset-liability managers. In the case of expected cash outflows, funds are needed in the future to meet these events. Again, the expected future course of

TABLE 17-5   A "Perfect" Short Hedge by a Bank Portfolio Manager

	Cash Market	Futures Market
Today:	Manager decides to hedge anticipated sale of $10 million of 20-year 8% U.S. Treasury bonds currently priced at 100-00 (Yield 8.00%)	Sells 100 Treasury bond futures contracts at 99-08 to generate $9,925,000
Three months later:	Manager sells $10 million of 20-year 8% U.S. Treasury bonds at market price of 96-00 (Yield of 8.42%) Loss on cash market sale: $400,000	Lifts hedge by purchasing 100 Treasury bond futures contracts at 95-08 at cost of $9,525,000 Gain on futures hedge: $400,000

Source: Picou [1981], p. 77. Reprinted by permission.

interest rates is critical in deciding what to do. If rates are expected to decline, then the outflows can be funded by lower-cost money in the future. However, if rates are expected to rise, then funds will be more expensive in the future. To hedge against this risk, the manager can undertake a *short hedge*, defined as the *sale* of a futures contract designed, in this case, to lock in the cost at which an expected *cash outflow* can be funded. If expectations are realized, then the higher cost of the future cash funds is offset (exactly if the hedge is perfect) by the gain on the futures contract. A short hedge is also known as a sell hedge. By selling a futures contract, hedgers are in a "short" position, which means they could be forced to deliver assets they do not own. Accordingly, they hope that rates will rise and prices of assets fall, including futures.

Let's illustrate the case of a short hedge with some numbers. Suppose a bank loan officer knows that a $10 million loan commitment will be drawn down in three months. Further assume the bank has some long-term bonds that it wishes to liquidate. The proceeds from the sale of the bonds will be used to fund the future loan commitment. To hedge against a decline in the price of the bonds, the portfolio manager plans to sell U.S. T-bond futures on the Chicago Board of Trade. He contracts for 100 futures contracts at $100,000 per contract for the needed $10 million. The bank's contracts are bought by a bond speculator for a price of 99-08 (i.e., 99 and $8/32$ or $99.25). The speculator is betting that long-term interest rates will drop before the futures contracts expire.

If cash and futures prices move together (i.e., if the hedge is "perfect"),[7] the result of the transaction, assuming that the bond price falls by four points (i.e., rates rise), is presented in Table 17-5. The four-dollar drop in the price of the bond means that the market value of the $10 million in bonds has fallen by $400,000. However, since the hedge is perfect, the $400,000 loss on the sale of the bonds in the cash market is offset by the $400,000 gain in the futures market. In other words, the four-point loss in the cash market is offset by the four-point gain in the futures market and the bank has effectively hedged its $10 million cash requirement.

In contrast, suppose that interest rates fall such that the price of the bond rose by four points. In this case, the bank would have a $400,000 gain in the cash market

---

[7] The term *basis* refers to the difference between the price of the interest-bearing instrument and the price of the futures instrument. The tendency of these prices to move together is the economic foundation of hedging. The instability of these movements is called *basis risk*. In practice, there is always some basis risk because the price movements are not perfectly synchronized. As a result, "perfect" hedges are rare in the real world.

but a $400,000 loss in the futures market. The bank still has a perfect hedge but it has forgone the opportunity to make $400,000 on the sale of the bonds. This lost opportunity is the speculator's profit.[8] Thus, hedging is not a riskless practice but simply a way of reducing risk.

As an alternative to liquidating the bond, the asset-liability manager could purchase the funds to meet the loan commitment in the CD market. Accordingly, if rates are expected to rise, the bank can hedge its cost of funds by buying CD futures contracts now. In this case, when the CDs are issued in the cash market three months hence, their higher cost, assuming rates actually rise, will be offset by the gain from lifting the CD futures contract. However, if rates decline, the bank has a loss in the futures market and no offsetting gain in the cash market. As a result, loan commitments cannot be hedged by using futures contracts alone. Loan commitments (and fixed-rate loans without prepayment penalties) must be hedged using options or a combination of futures and options. (The use of options to hedge interest-rate risk is discussed later in this chapter.)

To further illustrate a short hedge at the micro level, consider the case of an asset-liabililty manager who has funds to invest for three months. If the yield curve is positively sloped, the six-month T-bill held for three months will generate a higher yield, a technique called "riding the yield curve." However, if interest rates rise, the six-month bill when it is sold in three months will incur a capital loss. To protect against such a loss, the manager can buy the nearest T-bill futures contract at the time the six-month bill is purchased in the cash market. Accordingly, if rates do rise, then the loss in the cash market will be cushioned by the gain in the futures maket. In contrast, if rates fall, the gain in the cash market will be reduced by the loss in the futures market. On balance, fund managers who want to ride the yield curve can buy "rate-volatility insurance" in the T-bills futures market. Since perfect hedges are rare, the effectiveness of the "insurance" will depend on (1) the correspondence between the length of time to be hedged and the maturity of the futures contract and (2) whether or not the instrument to be hedged has an exact counterpart in the futures market.

The Macrohedge: Protecting the Entire Balance Sheet

Recall that a firm's equity can be immunized through duration matching (i.e., by setting the duration of its assets equal to the duration of its liabilities). In this case, the bank's entire balance sheet is hedged rather then specific components of the balance sheet. Suppose, however, that the duration matching of the entire balance sheet is not feasible because of incomplete financial markets (i.e., all the instruments and markets needed to obtain the duration match are not available). Can a macrohedge still be put in place? Yes, it can and let's see how.

Chapter 13 has focused on overall balance sheet management and, in particular, on asset-liability management (ALM). We know that the focus of ALM is gap (or duration) management. A bank with a zero gap or a duration match has immunized its balance sheet. We want to consider the situation in which the zero gap is not obtainable. To hedge maturity mismatches of rate-sensitive assets (RSA) and rate-sensitive liabilities (RSL), the Treasury-bill futures market can be used. To hedge a negative gap (because rates might rise), T-bill futures contracts can be sold. The number of contracts to be

---

[8] Futures positions are established on a daily basis on what is called "mark-to-market." Thus, if losses result in a drop in the futures margin below the prescribed maintenance level, the account is subject to a margin call (i.e., an injection of cash up to the maintenance level). The margin convention means that losses on a hedge usually are realized before the hedge is lifted.

sold (bought) can be obtained from the following formula:[9]

$$\text{Number of Contracts} = \left(\frac{\$GAP}{2}\right) \times \left(\frac{N}{M}\right) \tag{17-4}$$

where division by 2 averages the impact of the *dollar gap*, N = number of months the gap is to be hedged, and M = the maturity in months of the instrument used to hedge the gap. To illustrate, if a bank wanted to hedge a $24 million negative gap over the next month using three-month T-bills, the number of futures contracts to be *sold* would be four—that is, $(-24/2) \times (1/3) = -4$; the negative sign means "to sell short." Since interest rates may rise, the idea is to make a profit on the short sale of the T-bill futures to offset the decline in bank earnings due to the negative gap. What if rates decline? The hedge still works because the loss in the futures market is offset by the increase in bank earnings.

To hedge a positive gap (because rates might decline), T-bill futures contracts should be *bought*. Using the same figures as above but changing the sign of the gap, the bank would buy four T-bill futures contracts. One month later, it sells the four contracts at a profit (loss) if rates have declined (increased). The profit in the futures market offsets the decline in bank earnings due to the positive gap in the face of falling rates. If interest rates rise, the loss in the futures market is offset by the increase in the bank's earnings.

Interest-rate futures offer banks the opportunity to protect their earnings from interest-rate risk when they get locked into an undesirable gap position. Banks that lack the expertise to use the futures market obviously need to monitor their gap positions more carefully. However, the mere existence of the futures market should not lead banks to become careless about gap management; they should regard the futures market as a safety net.

To implement a hedging program in a bank, Picou [1981] suggests five steps: (1) the backing of top management be obtained; (2) a hedging plan be developed that includes an in-depth study of the technical and strategic aspects of the futures market; (3) a working relationship with a broker be established to assist in the planning process; (4) regulatory, legal, and accounting matters be investigated; (5) and finally, trading be begun. The best advice, according to Picou, is to begin small. On balance, he concludes: "Both in their own activities, and on behalf of their customers, commercial banks are coming to the conclusions that interest-rate futures are an important financial management tool that is here to stay" (p. 81).

USING FINANCIAL (DEBT) OPTIONS TO MANAGE INTEREST-RATE RISK[10]

Financial options (see Chapter 5 and the appendix to Chapter 8) can be used as the basis for a hedging program, income generation, or to create various *synthetic* positions for managing risk. Options are available on organized exchanges for both

---

[9] See Baker [1982], p. 91. Formula 17-4, which is also known as the "hedge ratio," assumes that the expected change in interest rates on the (cash) gap and the futures contract are the same. If they differ, then the number of contracts needs to be adjusted by the ratio of the change in the spot rate to the change in the futures rate. However, for all practical purposes, the ratio of rates can be assumed to be 1. Each T-bill contract is $1 million. A negative gap is defined as $RSA - RSL < 0$.

[10] This section draws, in part, on the works of Goodman [1986] and *Characteristics and Risks of Standardized Options*, The Options Clearing Corporation [1987].

debt and equity (stock) instruments, and informally on just about anything that trades (e.g., an option to buy a house). Debt options offer financial institutions another tool for managing interest-rate risk. As of this writing, debt options are traded on U.S. Treasury securities requiring delivery of the underlying security on exercise of the option. The exercise values of these price-based options are expressed in terms of the values of the underlying securities. When the value of the underlying debt instrument increases (because interest rates fell), the option to buy that security (called a call option) becomes more valuable. In contrast, the opinion to sell it (called a put option) becomes less valuable. When interest rates rise, puts become more valuable and calls less valuable.

As the basis for a hedging or income program, there are four basic option strategies: buying or selling (writing) calls and buying or selling (writing) puts. Consider the case of a financial institution with a negative gap. If interest rates rise, the firm is adversely affected; if they fall, it is favorably affected. To hedge its position, the firm could buy put (debt) options. If rates rise (bank earnings down), debt prices decline and the puts become more valuable. When the option to sell (the put) is exercised, the profit on the sale is used to cushion the decline in bank earnings. If rates decline (bank earnings up), the put option is allowed to expire and bank earnings are reduced slightly by the premium paid for the put. The further out-of-the-money an option is, the cheaper (and riskier) it is.

What about the bank with a positive gap? If rates rise, it gains; if they fall, it loses. The appropriate strategy here is to buy a call option. If rates rise (bank earnings up), the call will be-out-of-money and permitted to expire. The cost of the calls will act as a drag on the increase in bank earnings. However, if rates decline (bank earnings down), the call will be in-the-money and generate profits to cushion the decline in bank earnings.

The other two basic option strategies are writing puts and writing calls. The potential gain in either of these strategies is associated with premium income from selling the options. In the case of call writing, consider a bank with a negative gap. If it writes call options on the securities in its portfolio, the bank, in effect, reduces its interest sensitivity. Specifically, if rates rise (bank earnings down), the buyer of the option will not exercise the call and the premium income will cushion the decline in bank earnings. In contrast, if rates fall (bank earnings up), the bank still receives the premium income but it forgoes the potential for greater price appreciation on the securities because the call option will be exercised by the holder, which removes the security from the bank's investment portfolio.

Consider the case of writing puts. The buyer of the put owns the option to sell the security at the strike price over the exercise period. The bank, as the writer (seller), receives the premium. If rates decline, the buyer of the put will not exercise the option and the bank benefits. However, if rates rise, the option to sell will be exercised and the bank must buy the security at a price below its market value.

The Asymmetric Risk of Loan Commitments

When bankers make loan commitments at specified fixed rates, they, in effect, have written put options. The fee income on the commitment is the premium on the borrower's option to take down a loan. If interest rates rise (far enough), borrowers usually will exercise their options and take the commitments. If rates decline (far enough), they will let the options expire. The bank faces a situation of asymmetric risk: If rates rise, it loses; if rates fall, the game is called off. Since the bank has written (sold) a put option in the form of the commitment, it can offset or hedge it by purchasing a put option. If rates rise (the case were the bank loses), the bank can exercise the put to reduce the opportunity loss.[11]

To summarize, in the case of loan commitments, banks are adversely affected by rising interest rates. To hedge this asymmetric risk, they can buy put options. In situations of asymmetric risk where they are adversely affected by *falling* rates, banks need to *buy call options*. When a bank makes a loan commitment, it says, in effect, "Heads, you win; tails, I lose."

Creating Synthetic Futures by Combining Puts and Calls

Synthetic long and short futures can be created by combining puts and calls as follows:

Synthetic Long Futures = Long (Buy) Call + Short (Write) Put

and

Synthetic Short Futures = Long (Buy) Put + Short (Write) Call

The underlying principle in these synthetic positions is that values of the puts and calls will move in opposite directions. By canceling each other, they create the desired hedge in the synthetic position. In practice, differences in options prices and futures margin requirements may result in differences between the values of synthetic futures and the nonsynthetic ones.

Synthetic futures, which apply to situations of symmetric risk, are used to set bounds on gains and losses. A bank with a negative gap will be adversely affected by rising rates but benefit from falling rates.. By buying puts and writing calls, the bank can hedge the symmetric risk of its negative gap. In the case of a positive gap, the bank is adversely affected by falling rates but benefits from rising rates. By buying calls and writing puts, the bank can hedge the symmetric risk of its positive gap.

EPILOGUE: THE BELLS AND WHISTLES OF MANAGING INTEREST-RATE RISK

Although duration analysis, swaps, futures, and options are the basic tools for managing interest-rate risk, there are other techniques, mainly combinations of the existing ones, that can be used for the same purpose. For example, options on financial futures (e.g., calls and puts on Eurodollar futures) can be used to manage interest-rate risk.[12] As with futures, the asset-liability manager can focus on hedging specific assets or liabilities to develop microhedges, or attempt a macrohedge by focusing on the entire balance sheet from a gap or duration perspective. Options on futures are attractive because they permit greater profitability from favorable price changes. However, to beat stand-alone futures, the price changes must be substantial.

The markets for futures and options are known as *speculative markets*. These markets, along with the market for interest-rate swaps, have been and will continue to be the innovative markets of the United States and international financial systems. In the aftermath of the stock market crash of October 19, 1987, the heavy hand of regulation may slow developments in these markets. On the other hand, in the context

---

[11] Another case of asymmetric risk, described by Goodman [1986, p. 579] is when long-term, fixed-rate loans (without prepayment penalties) are funded with floating-rate liabilities.

[12] Options on futures are regulated by the Commodity Futures Trading Commission (CFTC) and options on cash instruments (i.e., debt options) by the Securities and Exchange Commission (SEC).

of a struggle model (the regulatory dialectic), attempts to regulate speculative markets may serve to stimulate innovative practices. Whatever course regulation may take, these markets will continue to evolve. As they do, refinements in the techniques for managing interest-rate risk will follow.

CHAPTER SUMMARY

Banks (and financial intermediaries in general) increasingly make bets on the future course of interest rates. Given the size of the bet and attitudes toward risk, managers may want to hedge their interest-rate bets. When asset-liability managers attempt to hedge their entire balance sheets, they engage in macrohedges. In contrast, when they attempt to hedge individual assets and liabilities, they practice microhedging. This chapter has analyzed four techniques that can be used by financial institutions in their hedging operations: (1) issuing instruments with more suitable durations (duration matching), (2) interest-rate swaps, (3) interest-rate futures, and (4) debt options. Other techniques also are available. For example, as discussed elsewhere in this book, the phenomenon of securitization offers banks and other intermediaries an opportunity to remove interest-rate risk (and credit risk) from their balance sheets through the sale of assets. Although securitization has mainly been restricted to long-term credits such as mortgages, it has recently spread to short-term credits in the form of automobile loans and credit-card receivables.

A fundamental principle of risk management is that risk should be shifted to other markets in the most economical way. For example, the risk in fixed-rate mortgages may be shifted, in part, to consumers via adjustable-rate mortgages (ARMs). However, since this segment of the market charges a high premium for bearing risk (i.e., an institution may have to initially sacrifice 100 to 300 basis points on an ARM), this approach is an expensive one. Conversely, although some investors in the futures, options, and swaps markets may be willing to accept risk at low cost, participation in these markets by institutions may entail significant information and human-capital costs, especially to small banks. Although duration analysis offers an alternative, it is a more complex concept than maturity and faces operational difficulties. However, by defining duration as the effective time until repricing and linking it to sources-and-uses of funds analysis, the technique becomes less mysterious, but still faces operational problems.

On balance, various financial-management techniques are available to attempt to cope with unanticipated changes in interest rates. As future managers, regulators, accountants, and shareholders, the more familiar you become with these various techniques, the better prepared you will be to understand the importance of interest-rate risk and its effects.

LIST OF KEY WORDS AND CONCEPTS

Agent	Duration
Betting on interest rates	Effective time to repricing
Bullet loan (deposit)	Financial futures (interest rate)
Debt options (puts, calls)	Gap positions (negative, positive, zero)

Guarantor (third party)
Hedge (long, short)
Interest-rate risk
Interest-rate volatility
Liabilities repriced before assets
  (LRBA)
Loan commitment
London Interbank Offer Rate (LIBOR)
Mark-to-market
Macrohedge

Microhedge
Riding the yield curve
Speculative markets
Speculator
Standby letter of credit
Statement of sources and uses of funds
Swap finance (interest-rate swap)
Synthetic futures
Unexpected changes in interest rates
Zero-coupon security

REVIEW/DISCUSSION QUESTIONS

1. Using the information in Table 17-1, discuss the volatility of interest rates since 1975 and the implications of this volatility for the financial management of financial-services firms, especially commercial banks.
2. Is it possible for a depository player in the financial-services industry to avoid betting on interest rates? What does "betting on interest rates mean" and how important is the size of the bet? What kinds of firms have made large bets? When large bets go wrong, who picks up the pieces?
3. What is *the* source of interest-rate risk? What is hedging? Distinguish between a short hedge and a long hedge and between a microhedge and a macrohedge. What role do speculators play in hedging?
4. What is duration and how does it differ from other techniques for managing interest-rate risk? How does duration relate to source and uses of funds analysis?
5. What is swap finance and why does it exist? What are interest-rate swaps and how can they be used to manage interest-rate risk? What does "arbitrage potential" refer to and how does it relate to the benefits derived from a swap? Who are supporting players typically found in a swap transaction?
6. What is a debt option? On what securities are debt options traded? Distinguish between a put and a call option. What are the relationships among the prices, yields, and option values of debt securities? What are the four basic option strategies for hedging interest-rate risk? How can synthetic futures be created using options?
7. Explain the asymmetric risk of loan commitments. How can such commitments be hedged?
8. As a tool for risk management, how does securitization differ from the techniques described in this chapter? How likely are any of these techniques to be found in community-type banks? Regional banking companies? Money-center/multinational banking companies?
9. What are speculative markets and how do the various innovations in these markets fit into our model of change, i.e., TRICK + rational self-interest = financial innovation?

months. Because of loan commitments, the bank will have to roll over the CDs at maturity for another six months. If the ALM manager expects CD rates to rise to 10 percent, how can the upcoming CD transaction be hedged?

6. Harriet Kaufman, the manager for The Sisters Bank of Saloman, expects a downturn in interest rates plus slack loan demand in the bank's local economy. The bank has loan repayments of $5 million due in three months. Since the loans are not expected to be renewed and the deposits behind them do not mature until three months after the loans are repaid, how can Ms. Kaufman use T-bill futures to hedge her portfolio's interest-rate risk? The loans were made at 12 percent and the current T-bill rate is 10 percent, but she expects it to fall to 8 percent. The CDs were issued at 11 percent.

CHAPTER 17

APPENDIX A
Demonstration of the Duration Linkage between a Change in Value and a Change in Rate

The anticipated value at time T of a fixed-payment security with present value, V, is $_TV = V \cdot (1 + r)^T$. Using the product rule, the total derivative of this relationship is

$$T^{dV} = [V \cdot T \cdot (1 + r)^{T-1} \cdot dr + (1 + r)^T dV] \qquad (17\text{-A1})$$

However, we can substitute the familiar duration result

$$dV = -D \cdot V \cdot dr / (1 + r) \qquad (17\text{-A2})$$

for dV in Equation 17-A1, giving

$$T_{dV} = V \cdot (1 + r)^{T-1} \cdot (T - D) \cdot dr \qquad (17\text{-A3})$$

Since the change in net asset value, dV, is defined as the change in the value of assets (subscript A) minus the change in the value of liabilities (subscript L), Equation 17-3 in the text is simply the difference between the right-hand side of Equation 17-A3 defined for A and for L. Letting T represent the planning horizon, the change in value at time T due to an incremental change in rate, dr, is given by

$$[V_A \cdot (1 + r_A)^{T-1} \cdot (T - D_A) - V_L \cdot (1 + r_L)^{T-1} \cdot (T - D_L)]dr \qquad (17\text{-A4})$$

This is Equation 17-3 in the text.[1]

SELECTED REFERENCES

Antl, Boris, ed. [1986]. *Swap Finance*, Vols. 1 and 2. London: Euromoney Publications.

Baker, James V., Jr. [1982]. "Statistical Relationships are the Key to Banks' Use of Interest-Rate Futures." *ABA Banking Journal* (May), pp. 88–92.

Bierwag, G. O. [1978]. "Measures of Duration," *Economic Inquiry* (Vol. XVI, October), pp. 497–507.

Characteristics and Risks of Standardized Options. [1987]. Chicago: The Options Clearing Corporation.

Hilliard, Jimmy E. [1987]. "Duration as the Effective Time to Repricing," University of Georgia Working Paper (April).

Hilliard, Jimmy E., and Joseph F. Sinkey, Jr. [1987]. "Duration Analysis as a Tool for Predicting Interest-Sensitive Cash Flows," University of Georgia Working Paper.

---

[1] This proof is from Hilliard and Sinkey [1987].

Fabozzi, Frank J. [1986]. "Hedging with Financial Futures," in *Handbook of Financial Markets*, Frank J. Fabozzi and Frank G. Zarb, eds., Homewood Hills, IL: Dow Jones-Irwin, pp. 665–701.

Goodman, Laurie S. [1986]. "Hedging with Debt Options," in *Handbook of Financial Markets* Frank J. Fabozzi and Frank G. Zarb, eds., Homewood Hills, IL: Dow Jones-Irwin, pp. 572–585.

Hopewell, M. H., and G. G. Kaufman. [1973]. "Bond-Price Volatility and Term to Maturity: A Generalized Respecification," *American Economic Review* (September), pp. 749–753.

Kaufman, George G. [1984]. "Measuring and Managing Interest-Rate Risk: A Primer," *Economic Perspectives* (January/February), Federal Reserve Bank of Chicago, pp. 16–29.

Macaulay, Frederick R. [1938]. *The Movement of Interest Rates, Bonds, Yields, and Stock Prices in the United States Since 1865*. New York: Columbia University Press, pp. 44–53.

Peters, L. R. [1986]. "Fixed-to-Floating Interest-Rate Swap," in *Swap Finance*, Vol. 2, Boris Antl, ed. London: Euromoney Publications, pp. 201–204.

Schwarz, Richard, Joanne M. Hill, and Thomas Schneeweis. [1987]. *Financial Futures: Fundamentals, Strategies, and Applications*. Homewood Hills, IL: Dow Jones-Irwin.

Stigum, Marcia L., and Rene O. Branch, Jr. [1983]. *Managing Bank Assets and Liabilities*. Homewood Hills, IL: Dow Jones-Irwin.

Wolkowitz, Benjamin. [1985]. "Managing Interest-Rate Risk," in *Handbook for Banking Strategy*, Richard C. Aspinwall and Robert A. Eisenbeis, eds. New York: Wiley-Interscience, pp. 407–456.

CHAPTER 18

Management of Credit Risk I: Concepts, Models, and Credit Analysis

ARE BANK LOANS SPECIAL?

In Chapter 1, we began with the question: Are banks special? Here we narrow the question down to the major component on the left-hand side of a bank's balance sheet and ask: Are bank loans special? In particular, are bank *business* loans special? Why ask this question? One of the things that makes banks special is reserve requirements (along with deposit insurance, access to the discount window, bank examination, etc.). Reserve requirements are, of course, an implicit tax imposed on banks. An important question is: Who pays this tax? Is it depositors or borrowers, or a combination of the two? This issue is known as the incidence of the reserve-requirement tax.

Fama [1985] and James [1987] present evidence that bank borrowers (and not CD holders) bear the burden of the implicit tax due to reserve requirements. Unless bank loans are special (unique), why would bank borrowers bear this burden? Suppose the use of bank loans by nonfinancial corporations increases shareholder wealth. This proposition is exactly the one tested by James. Moreover, he accepted it. His tests and findings can be summarized briefly as follows. James looked at public announcements of three classes of debt: (1) new bank credit agreements, (2) privately placed debt agreements (mainly with insurance companies), and (3) public straight debt offering for cash (i.e., bonds). His sample consisted of 207 financing announcements including 80 bank loan agreements, 37 private placements, and 90 straight debt offerings covering the period 1974 through 1983.

Using the market model, James tested for the announcement effects of the alternative debt financings. Such tests are designed to determine the "wealth effects" or "excess returns" associated with particular events and are commonly known in finance as "event studies." James measured the "average prediction error" (APE) across the three types of debt to look for abnormal stock returns. His findings were that (1) positive (and statistically significant) stock price responses to the announcement of new bank credit agreements, (2) negative abnormal returns accruing to stockholders of firms announcing private placements, and (3) negative abnormal returns associated with the announcement of private placements and straight debt issues used to retire bank debt. James performed a series of additional tests to determine if the differences in abnormal performance were due to differences in the characteristics of the loan (e.g., maturity) or the characteristics of the borrower (e.g., size and default risk). Controlling for these factors did *not* explain the abnormal returns.

To summarize, the package of James's results are (1) the incidence of the reserve-requirements tax falls on borrowers, (2) the announcement of new bank loan agreements generates positive abnormal returns, and (3) controlling for other factors does not explain the abnormal returns. On the basis of these findings, James concludes: "…banks provide some special service not available from other lenders. Further research is needed to identify that unique service or unique attribute of bank loans and to explain its relation to the market value of the firm" (p. 234).

DELEGATED MONITORING AND THE BANK–CUSTOMER RELATIONSHIP AS EXPLANATIONS FOR WHY BANK BUSINESS LOANS ARE SPECIAL[1]

Chapter 4 presented the notion of banks as delegated monitors. To review, this idea simply says that savers (in this case bank depositors) do not have the time, inclination, or expertise to monitor borrowers for default risk. Therefore, they engage in indirect finance rather than direct finance. Bank depositors believe in a Greyhound bus-type motto: "Save in the bank and leave the monitoring to us." Commercial banks have developed substantial amounts of reputational capital as monitors of credit risk. If the marketplace values such monitoring highly, this phenomenon could explain the excess returns found by James. Since I have no "hard evidence" on this matter, it is simply my conjecture, or interpretation if you like. Moreover, although James references the key article on the theory of delegated monitoring, Diamond [1984], James never explicitly claims delegated monitoring as a potential explanation.

When it comes to monitoring, are all financial firms equal? If you have seen one monitor, have you seen them all? In particular, do insurance companies have the same reputational capital, as monitors, as commercial banks do? My conjecture is that insurance companies, in part since they are not depository institutions (disregarding the "dumb savers" who buy forced savings plans disguised as "whole-life insurance"), have less reputational capital than the kingpins of the financial system—commercial banks. Accordingly, when a borrowing firm switches from "the" monitor in the system to a second-rate monitor, the marketplace may view this negatively and penalize shareholder returns. This explanation raises a question, which James calls a "curious" one: Why do managers switch from bank financing to private placements or straight debt, given the adverse price reaction? James finds that differences in maturity between bank loans and either private placements or public debt offerings do not explain this curiosity.

In Chapter 1, we concluded that if banks are special, deposit insurance, regulatory privileges (e.g., access to the discount window), and regulatory restrictions (e.g., reserve requirements) are the stuff of this specialness. In addition, the largest banks have a safety net in the form of the "too-big-to-fail" doctrine. Finance theory and empirical evidence suggest these trappings enhance the wealth of bank shareholders (e.g., Buser, Chen, and Kane [1981] and Harris, Scott, and Sinkey [1986]). In a similar fashion, the deposit insurance and regulatory trappings of banks should enhance their reputational capital as delegated monitors. Confidence in the banking system is closely tied to the phenomena of deposit insurance and bank regulation. Since

[1] This section draws on Sinkey [1988].

insurance companies do not have the same extent and degree of regulation and supervision as commercial banks, the marketplace may not look at them with the same respect as it does banks. Thus, savers (bank depositors) and equity investors look to banks, and have confidence in banks, as delegated monitors because of two phenomena: (1) the reputational capital of banks and (2) the reputational capital of the systems of deposit insurance and bank regulation, as delegated monitors (for taxpayers) of the "safety and soundness" of the banking industry. Moreover, the interaction between these two phenomena may create a synergy which makes the whole greater than the sum of the parts.

On balance, insurance companies may pale in relationship to banks as delegated monitors. On these grounds, it seems reasonable for the marketplace to penalize firms for shifting from bank debt to debt placed with insurance companies. It is more difficult to explain why the market penalizes borrowers who shift from bank debt to public debt. If the "lead steers" (see Chapter 3) are doing their job, why should their monitoring differ from bank monitoring, or be perceived by the marketplace as different?

Relationship Banking

As a famous song goes, "Is that all there is?" Does delegated monitoring tell it all? An alternative explanation focuses on the notion of the "bank–customer relationship" (Hodgmen [1961] and Kane and Malkiel [1965]). Although James refers to Kane and Malkiel, he is reluctant to attach much weight to the bank–customer relationship as an explanation for his findings. What is the customer relationship? It is a concept (and a recognized practice) representing a strategic combination of deposits, loans, and other financial services that gives commercial banking its unique institutional character. Under current laws, such combinations or bundles are not available to business firms from insurance companies or investment banks. The bank–customer relationship is that "special service not available from other lenders" that James needs to enrich the interpretation of his results. In this context, it makes sense that bank borrowers would accept the incidence of reserve-requirements taxation in exchange for a bundle of services not available from any other player in the financial-services industry.

Is there a "hook" in this strategic combination of financial services that draws business firms into the bank? The logical choice is transaction accounts and access to the large dollar payments system. Perhaps this is the "unique service" to complete James's puzzle. To test this conjecture would seem to require the transaction-account balances of individual firms, which are not publicly available.

To summarize, although the bank–customer relationship offers a reasonable explanation for why bank borrowers would submit to the reserve-requirements tax, it does not add any insight into the abnormal returns uncovered by James. However, as explained above, the notion of banks as delegated monitors seems to complete that part of James's puzzle.

Recapitulation

James has presented some evidence to suggest that bank loans are unique. By drawing on the notions of delegated monitoring and the bank–customer relationship, we have attempted to add richness and depth to the interpretation of his results. These additional insights should in no way be interpreted as taking away from his research efforts, nor as proof of my conjectures.

THE CREDIT DECISION-MAKING PROCESS

At its heart, the financial system is a credit system in which financial institutions make decisions about the creditworthiness of borrowers. This chapter focuses on the credit decision-making process of commercial banks by emphasizing the various concepts and analytics at the center of the process.

For openers, let's establish the importance of the process. As Corrigan [1987] has emphasized, traditional bank intermediation plays an important role in the financial system. First, it supplies the process (and profits) whereby credit is granted and monitored over time. Second, the credit process, in the form of lines of credit and banking relationships, provides backup liquidity before the lender of last resort, the central bank, may be forced to enter the picture. And third, because banking relationships are different from the impersonal financing of the marketplace, the bank credit process permits liquidity problems to be solved in an orderly fashion when they arise. For example, witness the role of the banking system in supplying investment bankers with liquidity following the stock market crash of October 19, 1987 (see Chapter 15).

The Delegated-Monitoring Functions of the Bank Credit Process

As delegated monitors for their depositors and other creditors, banks perform the following functions. First, they exercise control and judgment over who gets credit. The granting or denying of credit must be objective, fair, and rigorous. Second, after credit is granted, lenders must monitor the performance of borrowers to ensure the repayment of funds. And third, when borrowers get into trouble, as some of them inevitably do, relationship banking requires (without sacrificing shareholder wealth) monitoring workout situations, or, in the case of loan defaults, monitoring the process of attempting to recover charged-off credits.

As delegated monitors for their depositors and other creditors, banks act as "agents." However, in transforming these liabilities into earning assets (loans), banks become "principals" and must monitor the performance of "agent" borrowers. In this context, the notion of agency theory (see Chapter 3) as an analytical device is important.

AGENCY THEORY AND THE LENDING PROCESS

The loan contract is the legal document that binds lenders and borrowers. It may be in the appearance of a formal agreement such as a term loan contract or an informal one such as a verbal commitment to supply funds via a line of credit. Agency theory provides a framework for analyzing and controlling conflicts in contractual relations that arise from different incentives and asymmetric information. In agency-theory jargon, the lender is referred to as the *principal* and the borrower as the *agent*. To protect the interests of the lending firm, lenders must monitor the activities of the borrower agents because they have the opportunity (through default) to abscond with shareholders' wealth. The surveillance costs incurred by principals in monitoring agents are called *agency costs*. The agency problem may arise because of (1) different goals and objectives, (2) asymmetric information, or (3) dishonesty. In the lending process, the last two factors are the important ones for understanding loan pricing and risk management.

The Problem of Asymmetric Information

Since borrowers know more about their true financial condition than lenders can expect to know, lenders face the problem of *asymmetric information*. Given this set of imperfect information, lenders must sort potential borrowers into "accept" and "reject" categories and then further sort the acceptables on the basis of risk (i.e., loan pricing). A situation in which the borrower has more information about risk than the lender can lead to *adverse selection*. In other words, the lender may accept too many of the "wrong" borrowers and/or misprice the risk of the accepted ones. Lenders who habitually make such mistakes don't remain in the lending business for long. To control their risk exposure, lenders must have information systems and lending officers capable of measuring and analyzing all relevant forms of risk, including the interaction between interest-rate risk and credit risk.

As the name *commercial bank* suggests, the heart of the bank lending business, especially for large banks, is commercial lending. Information difficulties and sorting procedures for middle-level companies and small businesses are more complex than those for Fortune 500 companies. With greater emphasis in banking on the production of fee income, commercial lending, where the big fees are generated, faces the special problem of conflicts between adverse selection and incentives for fee income. As a result, lending officers may be motivated to let too many high-risk borrowers through the sorting mechanism simply to generate high front-end fees. Such fee-induced adverse selection raises the specter of high-risk exposure for future earnings. The conflict involved here is due to differing objectives within the organization (i.e., current earnings versus long-term value maximization) rather than asymmetric information. It is the responsibility of top management and the board of directors to monitor such internal agency problems.

The agency costs incurred by lenders are due to their sorting and surveillance mechanisms. The sorting procedures were described above. The surveillance procedures are designed to monitor the performance of *existing* borrowers to ensure compliance with the terms of their loan agreements. The conceptual techniques and analytics of sorting and surveillance mechanisms are described later in the chapter.

The Problem of Dishonesty

The agency problem in loan contracts also can arise because of dishonesty on the part of borrowers. Although most borrowers are honest, some are not. The character part of credit analysis is designed to sort scrupulous borrowers from unscrupulous ones. To the extent that unscrupulous borrowers supply misinformation deliberately, the dishonesty and asymmetric-information problems are intertwined.

The character problem faced by lenders can be summarized by the following adage: "You can't do good business with bad people." However, because bad things do happen to good people, you can do bad business with good people. The flexibility of relationship banking permits bankers to attempt to go that extra yard when bad things happen to good people.

MODELING THE CREDIT RISK FUNCTION

The credit risk (or quality) of a bank's loan portfolio depends on two sets of factors: (1) those factors exogenously determined, such as the state of the economy, natural disasters, etc; and (2) those factors subject to managerial discretion.[2] Although the first

---

[2] This section builds, in part, on Greenawalt and Sinkey [1988].

category of factors is exogenously determined, bank managers can influence the effects of these forces on bank performance (e.g., earnings, loan losses, nonperforming loans) through safe-and-sound banking practices and/or their attitudes toward risk-taking (by holding a diversified loan portfolio, by doing careful credit analysis and underwriting, etc.). Nevertheless, geographic barriers to nationwide expansion and the lack of a well-developed secondary market for nonmortgage loans make banks vulnerable to adverse external events.

To illustrate the interaction between the exogenous and endogenous factors, consider the banks that first encountered financial difficulties due to the energy and agricultural crises of the 1980s. They were the banks with the weakest internal controls, ones permitting excessive growth, poor underwriting practices and procedures, and other lending shortcomings, and/or those with the greatest penchant for risk-taking. Eventually, however, because the downturns in the energy and farm sectors were so severe, even banks with stronger managers and internal controls were hurt. Thus, although bank managers have direct control over the endogenous factors that determine credit risk and hence loan quality and earnings, only the strongest managers can be expected to survive the vicissitudes of the business and interest-rate cycles.

The second set of factors affecting the quality or riskiness of a bank's loan portfolio attempts to capture management's philosophy or attitude toward risk-taking. Keeton and Morris [1987] find that differences in loan quality, as measured by loan losses, can be attributed, in part, to differences in attitudes toward risk-taking. For example, their findings suggest that "...some banks with a high propensity to take risk deliberately made loans with a high probability of default" (p. 12). By treating their fiduciary responsibility to their depositors and other creditors lightly, such bankers fail in their roles as delegated monitors.

Lenders' attitudes toward loan portfolio risk-taking, which are not directly observable, are reflected in, among other things, bank loan policy, the quality of bank credit analysis and loan surveillance, and the expertise of bank loan officers. The expertise of loan officers can be expressed in terms of their skill, training, and experience.

Within this general framework for modeling credit risk or loan quality, our function is

$$\text{Credit Risk} = f(\text{Internal Factors}, \text{External Factors}) \qquad (18\text{-}1)$$

Our task now is to specify proxy variables for the components of the function. To proxy credit risk, suppose we consider a bank's net loan losses (NLL). In the jargon of modeling, this variable is called the "dependent variable." It is the one we want to explain or model. The explanatory or "independent variables" are the internal and external factors. Our next task is to develop proxies for these factors.

For the external factors, we want to capture the state of the economy and, in particular, specific measures that are likely to be associated with loan defaults in the bank's market area. Suppose we consider some composite measure of economic performance in the bank's relevant geographic market, such as personal income adjusted for inflation. (For multinational banks, we might consider real GNP.) Label this variable ECY and note that the relationship between NLL and ECY should be an inverse one. That is, as economic activity increases, borrowers should have an easier time repaying their loans, and net loan losses should be low. Conversely, when economic activity is down, borrowers should have greater difficulty repaying their loans, and net loan losses should be high. Of course, borrowers whose cash flows vary inversely with the state of the economy would show the opposite relationship and would provide diversification benefits to the bank's loan portfolio.

As alternative external proxies, we might consider more specific measures of economic activity associated with credit risk such as the number or the dollar value of current liabilities of business failures. Either of these variables should be positively correlated with net loan losses. Let's assume we measure this variable in dollar amounts and label it FAIL.

Consider now proxies for the internal factors, the ones bankers can control. These variables should reflect bankers' attitudes toward loan portfolio risk-taking. The key internal determinants of credit risk should be such measures as loan volume, loan policy, and loan mix. As loan volume increases, credit risk should increase. In other words, the more loans a bank makes, the more losses it is likely to have, other things equal. To capture the bank's overall loan policy, we could use the ratio of total loans to total assets. The more aggressive a bank's loan policy is, the higher this ratio should be. Such banks should, of course, have higher loan losses. To capture loan mix or composition, we could use the ratio of commercial and industrial loans to total loans. The higher this concentration is, the greater should be the bank's loan losses. This expectation is based on the fact that commercial and industrial (C&I) loans are the least marketable and most heterogeneous of bank earning assets.[3] Finally, suppose that a bank's loan losses are also related to its level of operating income such that when income is up loan losses will be taken. Under this scenario, banks follow an "income-smoothing hypothesis"[4] (i.e., they take "hits" when they are most capable of being hit).

To summarize the internal determinants of credit risk, let VOL represent loan volume, LAR represent the loan-to-asset ratio, C&I represent the ratio of C&I loans to total loans, and INC represent bank income. Given these symbols, our bank credit risk function can be written as

$$NLL = (\overset{+}{VOL}, \overset{+}{LAR}, \overset{+}{C\&I}, \overset{+}{INC}, \overset{-}{ECY}, \overset{+}{FAIL}). \tag{18-2}$$

The signs above the independent variables indicate the expected relationship between each independent variable and the dependent variable.

Since bankers do not have direct control over the external factors affecting credit risk, the focus of the management of credit risk is on the internal factors. However, by holding diversified loan portfolios, bankers can be better prepared to handle the downside vulnerability associated with adverse external conditions. To the extent that geographic barriers restrict the ability of (smaller) banks to diversify, such restrictions can be potentially destabilizing. Of course, these smaller organizations are in a "Catch 22" because even if they were permitted to expand, they lack the dollar and/or human capital to do so. To attempt to offset these disadvantages, such banks must have strong control over the internal factors of their credit risk functions.

Given a bank's policies with respect to the volume and composition of its loan portfolio, the credit analysis done by individual loan officers ultimately determines credit risk. Accordingly, the training, experience, judgment, and supervision of lending officers is crucial to the management of the credit risk function. The credit analysis function can be represented by what is called the "five Cs" of creditworthiness, which we turn to now.

---

[3] Several bank failure studies have shown C&I loans to be an important discriminator between failed and nonfailed banks. See Sinkey [1979] and Altman, Avery, Eisenbeis, and Sinkey [1981] for a description of these bank failure studies.

[4] For tests of the income-smoothing hypothesis, see Scheiner [1981] and Greenawalt and Sinkey [1988].

CREDIT RISKS AND DETERMINING CREDITWORTHINESS

The five Cs of credit management make nice reading. They are

1. Character (good citizen)
2. Capacity (cash flow)
3. Capital (wealth)
4. Collateral (security)
5. Conditions (economic, especially downside vulnerability).

The banker's problem is to attempt to *quantify* these five Cs so that meaningful and consistent decisions can be made regarding borrowers' creditworthiness. This procedure is called *credit analysis*. Its purpose is to determine a borrower's credit risk. Credit analysis determines whether or not a loan should be made and provides critical input regarding the pricing of the loan and the setting of nonprice terms. Bankers must attempt to discriminate on the basis of credit risk. It is, of course, illegal for them to discriminate on the basis of sex, race, religion, and so on. Thus, there are business reasons and jurisprudence reasons for bankers to attempt to develop uniform and objective standards for evaluating borrower credit risk.

In a risk–return setting, borrowers with "weak" financial positions and hence "high" credit risk should pay more for credit than borrowers with "strong" financial profiles and hence "low" credit risk. It is imperative not to confuse *risk–return pricing*, which is a fundamental tenet of financial management, with *unequal credit opportunity*, which is an aberration in a free society. If society decides through a majority vote of its taxpayers (as opposed to the actions of a select group of do-gooders) to subsidize certain segments of the economy (e.g., small businesses), such programs should be established to interface with the market mechanism and not to subvert it.

To be meaningful for credit-analysis purposes, the verbal vagueness of "strong versus weak" financial positions and "high versus low" credit risk needs to be quantified. To achieve this objective, each of the five Cs is analyzed in terms of its potential to be quantified. Next, some classification techniques dealing with bank-ruptcy-prediction and credit-scoring models are explored. One factor that is quantified quite easily is the symptom of poor credit risk as manifested in a bank's loan-loss experience. Thus, it is easy to identify banks that have made bad credit-risk decisions in the past (coupled perhaps with some bad luck) by observing the quality of their loan portfolios. The important point, however, is how to determine creditworthiness before the fact, keeping in mind that a bank is expected to incur some loan losses in the normal course of doing business.

Character

Good citizens, including individuals and corporate entities, stand ready to pay their debts. In this context, character suggests a borrower's willingness to pay. How can this trait be identified? Three sources of information are (1) past credit history (a potential indicator of willingness to pay), (2) character references, and (3) a loan officer's judgment of the borrower's character based upon a face-to-face interview. Since past credit history combines willingness and ability to pay, it becomes difficult to separate the two items in cases involving poor credit records. Thus, character references may provide important information in situations where a borrower's willingness to pay is in doubt. In the final analysis, willingness to pay is difficult to quantify and judge. To the extent that experienced bank loan officers qualify as quasi-psychologists, they may be good judges of a borrower's character based upon personal contact. In small rural markets (e.g., one- or two-bank towns) where bankers tend to get to know their customers personally, it probably is easier to judge character than it is in a sprawling urban market. On balance, to judge character, bankers must get to know their customers. In cases where character is unknown and not easily discernible, credit analysis hinges on a borrower's economic and financial profile.

Economic and Financial Characteristics

Ability to pay can be established by analyzing a borrower's capacity (cash flow), capital (wealth), and collateral (security). These characteristics can be measured from the borrower's financial statements, preferably audited ones. Since financial statements are subject to "window dressing" or "puffing," it is important to know that they are accurate and reliable. Given this information, a borrower's capacity can be measured by take-home pay, after-tax profits, or cash flow; capital can be measured by the borrower's net-worth position; and collateral can be evaluated by the quality of the assets the borrower is willing to place as security for a loan. Other things equal, a borrower's creditworthiness is directly related to these three financial characteristics. The fifth C, which refers to economic conditions, is designed to measure a borrower's vulnerability to an economic downturn or credit crunch. The conditions factor can be viewed as involving a worst-case scenario of a borrower's ability to pay.

A good historical example of the failure of large BHCs to carefully evaluate the conditions factor occurred in the early 1970s when these institutions extended large amounts of credit to REITs.[5] When the 1974 credit crunch and subsequent recession hit, the REIT industry was on the verge of collapsing. As a result, the lending banks incurred substantial losses and became involved in work-outs (reduced interest rates, forgiving interest and sometimes principal payments, etc.) to attempt to save their original investments. Samuel Lefrak, the nation's largest builder and owner of apartment houses, summed up the REIT-bank situation of the mid-1970s as follows[6]:

> Why didn't those usurers [the bankers] call me before? Now they're asking me questions about the guys they lent money to two years ago. Their properties are in trouble, so now they beg, "Sam, bail me out."

The REIT-bank episode clearly illustrates the importance of evaluating economic conditions *and* the importance of street or shop talk. When loans are priced on a variable-rate basis, the conditions factor takes on added significance because the lender must determine the borrower's ability to pay in the face of higher interest rates.

SOURCES OF LOAN REPAYMENT: CASH FLOW IS THE NAME OF THE GAME

A borrower has only three sources of loan repayment: (1) cash flow, (2) asset liquidation, or (3) another source of financing. Commercial bankers traditionally have been cash-flow lenders, which explains the banker's penchant for watching cash flow. Over the long haul, accrued profits, adjusted for dividends and capital investments, tend to equal net cash flow. However, over the short run, say one year, accounting profits and cash flow are rarely equal. Accordingly, bankers, as cash-flow lenders, need to know something about the concept and measurement of cash flow, especially since cash-flow problems are the most common cause of business failures. Beaver [1967], in

---

[5] See Sinkey [1979], Chapter 8.

[6] *The Bankers Magazine* [Spring 1975], p. 30.

his classic study of bankruptcy, found the ratio of cash flow to total debt was his best predictor of impending failure.

The Concept of Cash Flow

Because of accounting conventions, the concept of cash flow can become obscured. It shouldn't. Cash flow (net) is the difference between cash inflow or dollars received and cash outflow or dollars paid out. This flow process forms the heart of the valuation process because the net present value rule is stated in terms of cash flow (see Chapter 3). In particular, we are interested in incremental (after-tax) cash flows and economic value added (see Chapter 3). Although profits are a company's major source of cash flow, cash flow, of course, is not equal to accounting profits.

Most introductory finance textbooks define cash flow in an "add-back" fashion as profits plus noncash outlays with depreciation as the major noncash outlay, or item to be added back. However, since there is no uniformly accepted way of calculating cash flow, the methods used by lenders do vary. According to Kelly [1986], some analysts define cash flow as

> Net profit
>
> + Depreciation
>
> − Increase in Accounts Receivable
>
> − Increase in Inventories
>
> + Increase in Accounts Payable
>
> = Cash Flow   (18-3)

Since many analysts (e.g., O'Glove [1987]) regard management of accounts receivable and inventories as critical to a firm's success, this definition of cash flow has some merit. Clearly, large increases in these accounts reduce a firm's cash flow. Accordingly, the composition of a firm's cash flow is important. To further illustrate, a cash flow dominated by an increase in accounts payable (say because of slow bill paying) is not a desirable situation.

When Formula 18-3 is expanded to cover all the items on a firm's balance sheet, the familiar sources and uses of funds statement is generated. On a cash basis, the *uses* of cash are (1) increases (or investments) in noncash assets (e.g., the accounts receivable and inventories of Formula 18-3) and (2) decreases in liabilities or equities. The *sources* of cash are (1) decreases in noncash assets and (2) increases in liabilities or equities. These changes combined with the cash flow from a firm's operations (derived from the profit-loss or income-expense statement) permit analysts to see where a firm's cash comes from and where it goes.

In the commercial lending or credit school segments of bank training programs, accounting and analysis of financial statements are emphasized. There you will learn the methods, techniques, and software packages employed by the bank. In this regard, courses in accounting and working capital management provide desirable backgrounds for would-be commercial lenders.

Potential Signals about Cash-Flow Problems

As in any other endeavor, experience plays an important role in the credit decision-making and monitoring process. Bennett [1987] discusses some warning signals he looks for as an experienced lender. These factors, which sometimes go beyond financial statements, are described by Bennett from the borrower's perspective.

1. *You show up on the wrong lists.* The lists a borrower does not want to show up on include checks drawn on uncollected funds, overdraft accounts, large transactions, past-due loans, loans with incomplete collateral, and late financial statements.
2. *You act as if you are hungry for cash.* Bennett regards frequent requests for small loans as a potential indicator your company is not generating enough cash. By the same token, if your company maintains high credit card balances, he wonders why you are not paying off the balance. In addition, debt servicing may be a problem for companies with large net worth positions but small cash flows.
3. *You make one change too many.* Frequent changes in loan requests suggest the company can be out of control or not know what it is doing. Bennett applies this adage to both changes in personnel and loan requests. Since frequent changes can suggest underlying problems, too many changes are unsettling to most bankers.
4. *You look a little rough around the edges.* Since the character factor is difficult to monitor, changes in physical appearance may indicate changes in behavior related to alcoholism, drug abuse, gambling, abrupt changes in marital status, or problems with the business. In addition, if the company and its surroundings are not adequately maintained, this may signal lack of concern for details and/or inadequate cash for basic maintenance.

From the borrower's perspective, if you see any of these things happening to your company, Bennett suggests it is time to call or see your banker and explain what is going on.

Estimating and monitoring future cash flows is a critical part of credit analysis and risk evaluation. In addition to the cash flows derived from financial statements, ratio analysis offers another tool for use by loan officers. These inputs (ratios and cash flows) provide the nuts and bolts of credit analysis, as well as potential variables for classification models designed to identify risky borrowers.

The Usefulness of Accounting Ratios to Loan Officers

This section describes an experiment by Libby [1975] designed to determine whether accounting ratios provide useful information to loan offices trying to predict business failures. Using a set of five variables, commercial bank loan officers were asked to analyze the ratios and then to predict either "failure" or "nonfailure." Libby judged the usefulness of the accounting information on the basis of the accuracy of the loan officers' predictions.

Libby's sample consisted of 60 firms, divided equally between failed and non-failed firms. He began the experiment with 14 ratios computed for *one* of the three years prior to failure (chosen at random), resulting in an equal number of firms for each of the three years before failure (10 failed and 10 nonfailed). Using a statistical technique called principal components, Libby identified five independent sources of variation within the 14 variable set. The five dimensions and the five ratios are

Dimension	Ratio
1. Profitability	Net Income/Total Assets
2. Activity	Current Assets/Sales
3. Liquidity	Current Assets/Current Liabilities
4. Asset balance	Current Assets/Total Assets
5. Cash position	Cash/Total Assets

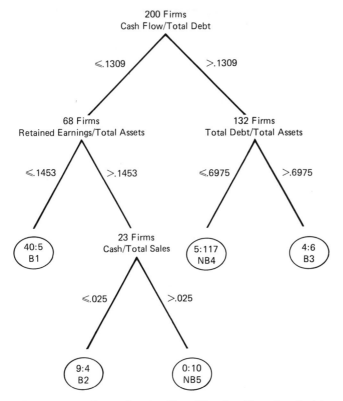

Figure 18-1   Example of a Classification Tree Applied to the Identification of Bankrupt Firms

Source: Frydman, Altman, and Kao [1985], Figure 1, p. 272.

the colon are the nonbankrupt firms identified as bankrupt ones (i.e., 15 = 5 + 4 + 6). The classification accuracy rate for the bankrupt firms is 53/58 = 91.4 percent; for the nonbankrupts, it is 127/142 = 89.4 percent. We get the same results if we look at the two NB nodes. Try it. The overall accuracy rate is 180/200 or 90 percent, which is quite good.

What makes CART or recursive partitioning attractive is its combination of multivariate analysis in conjunction with simple splits based on a single variable. Although the statistics behind the tree are quite complex, but no more complex than those behind parametric techniques, the use of the tree procedure has great intuitive appeal.

The application of CART by Marais, Patell, and Wolfson focused on a loan classification model. Bank examiners and most bank internal review committees classify loans into one of five categories based on the degree of *perceived* default risk. The procedure is a subjective one that is difficult to quantify or make objective. The usual risk categories are as follows:

1. *Current.* If a loan is "current," it is being paid back on schedule and perceived to be an acceptable banking risk.
2. *Especially mentioned.* A loan in this category usually has some minor problem (e.g., incomplete documentation) requiring it to be "criticized." However, the problem is not severe enough to warrant the loan being "adversely classified"
3. *Substandard.* A loan in this category has weaknesses presenting some chance of

default. The weaknesses, however, usually are correctable. The bank regulatory weight attached to the category implies a 20 percent chance of default.

4. *Doubtful*. A loan in this category has considerable weakness and the bank is likely, say 50 percent chance, of sustaining a loss.

5. *Loss*. A loan in this category is deemed to be uncollectible. Such loans are usually written or charged off.

Marais, Patell, and Wolfson analyzed 921 loans consisting of 839 current loans, 37 especially mentioned loans, 32 substandard loans, and 13 doubtful loans. They had no loss loans in their sample, which consisted of 716 loans to private firms and 205 loans to public firms. The substandard, doubtful, and loss categories are considered to be adversely classified assets. Marais, Pattell, and Wolfson used 13 standard financial ratios and 13 other variables to construct their models. Although they used the CART methodology, they did not present a tree diagram of their results. Accordingly, it is difficult to summarize their findings compactly. From the perspective of bank loan officers and the credit decision-making process, their most important finding is in line with Libby's conclusion. Namely, financial statements provide useful information for credit decisions, although the statements of private firms are not quite as accurate for classification purposes as those of public firms.

Zeta Analysis

Zeta analysis is a term coined by Altman, Haldeman, and Narayanan [1977] to describe their model for identifying the bankruptcy risk of corporations. They find the following seven variables to be good discriminators between failed and nonfailed business firms:

1. *return on assets*, measured by EBIT/total assets
2. *stability of earnings*, measured by the inverse of the standard error of estimate around a 10-year trend in return on assets
3. *debt service*, measured by EBIT/total interest payments
4. *cumulative profitability*, measured by retained earnings (BS)/total assets
5. *liquidity*, measured by current assets/current liabilities
6. *capitalization*, measured by a five-year average market value of the firm's common stock/total long-term capital
7. *size*, measured by the firm's total assets.

EBIT stands for *earnings before interest and taxes and retained earnings* (BS) means that the retained earnings are taken from the firm's balance sheet. These seven variables are designed to measure the following dimensions: (1) current profitability, (2) risk or variability of return, (3) interest coverage, (4) long-run profitability, (5) liquidity, (6) leverage, and (7) size. Since the coefficients of the Zeta model are not publicly available, we use Altman's [1968] model to illustrate the use of this kind of bankruptcy-prediction model. Altman's 1968 model has five variables:

X_1 = Working Capital/Total Assets

X_2 = Retained Earnings/Total Assets

X_3 = EBIT/Total Assets

X_4 = Market Value of Equity/Book Value of Total Debt

X_5 = Sales/Total Assets

By the way, both the 1968 model and the Zeta model employ a statistical technique called *multiple discriminant analysis* (MDA). The objective of MDA is to find the set of variables that best discriminates between the two groups, in Altman's case failed and nonfailed firms. Altman's linear MDA or Z-score equation is

$$Z = 1.2X_1 + 1.4X_2 + 3.3X_3 + 0.6X_4 + 1.0X_5 \qquad (18\text{-}4)$$

The classification rule for Equation 12-7 is

1. If $Z < 2.675$, assign to the bankrupt group.
2. If $Z \geq 2.675$, assign to the nonbankrupt group.

Since Altman found that misclassifications occurred in the Z-score range of 1.81 to 2.99, he referred to this overlap area as the "zone of ignorance."

Application of Altman's Z-Score Model[7]

Altman [1968] contends that his model could be used to complement (1) business-loan evaluations, (2) accounts-receivable management, (3) internal-control procedures, and (4) investment strategies. Regarding business-loan evaluations, Altman suggests using his "quantitative" model to complement the "more qualitative and intuitive" approach of loan officers. However, he is careful to point out that the model is not a credit-scoring mechanism nor a substitute for the evaluations of loan officers. He argues that the model and its generated Z-scores could be a valuable tool for determining the overall creditworthiness of business customers.

One of the most important tasks that a bank loan officer performs is the evaluation of a firm's policies and managerial skills, factors that ultimately determine how well a company performs. Direct measurement of the effectiveness of managerial skills and policies is a difficult task. Consequently, indirect measurement frequently is employed using comparative ratio analysis. Ratios, of course, reflect symptoms, not causes. However, by identifying atypical or abnormal ratios, problem areas can be identified and the cause(s) of the difficulty investigated. Altman's model can be used to rate a company's overall performance (via its Z-score) and to pinpoint problem areas (via individual ratios). To illustrate this type of application, consider the following example derived from the article, "How To Figure Who's Going Bankrupt," *Dun's Review* [October 1975]. In this article Z-scores for some 1,200 publicly-owned companies were computed. The companies with the 14 highest and 14 lowest Z-scores were listed. In this example, the 4 companies with the following Z-scores are analyzed: (1) highest (2) lowest, (3) highest of the 14 lowest, and (4) lowest of the 14 highest. The Z-scores and ratios for these 4 companies (Taylor Wine, Memorex, Telex, and Data General) are presented in Table 18-2.

According to Altman's classification rule, Memorex and Telex were headed for bankruptcy, whereas Data General and especially Taylor Wine were performing very well. The managers of Memorex and Telex should have been concerned about their low Z-scores—and their jobs. Moreover, bank managers should have been concerned about making loans to these companies. Looking at Memorex's profile of five variables, it is clear that as of year-end 1974 the company had serious profitability (both current and cumulative), liquidity, and solvency problems.

Since the Z-score to Telex (1.78) is quite close to Altman's "zone of ignorance" (i.e., 1.81–2.99), one has less confidence in its prediction of insolvency. However, relative

---

[7] This section draws on Chapter 7 of my 1981 book (with Altman, Avery, and Eisenbeis) entitled *Application of Classification Techniques in Business, Banking and Finance*.

TABLE 18-2   Z-Scores: Best and Worst Performers

Company	Z-score	Ratios				
		X_1	X_2	X_3	X_4	X_5
Taylor Wine (6/74)[a]	304.09[b]	0.52	0.61	0.24	501.45	0.97
Data General (9/74)	36.32	0.47	0.31	0.27	55.45	1.17
Telex (3/75)	1.78	0.22	−0.19	0.13	0.35	1.12
Memorex (12/74)	0.74	0.19	−0.49	0.04	0.25	0.92

[a] Figure in parentheses beside company name indicate date of data, except for the X_4 data, which are as of year-end 1974.

[b] The Z-scores are calculated using Equation 18-2. Going across the table, the discriminant coefficients are 1.2, 1.4, 3.3, 0.6, and 1.0, respectively.

Source: Dun's Review [October, 1975], p. 65. Reprinted by permission.

to Memorex's ratios, Telex's five-variable profile is superior. In terms of contribution to Z-score, the cumulative-profitability variable (X_2) accounts for the greatest difference in the Memorex–Telex Z-score spread. For example, if Memorex had Telex's X_2 ratio and vice versa, the Z-score would be Memorex 1.16 and Telex 1.36. As indicated in Table 18-3, Memorex and Telex did *not* go bankrupt. In fact both companies turned their operations around. It is interesting to note that Telex received substantial financial assistance from Bank of America in its recovery. One of the problems with statistical models is their inability to take into account the customer relationship that is so important in commercial banking.

It is important to understand in what sense Altman's Z-scores are predictions or forecasts. A prediction or forecast usually involves a statement at time *t* about some future event, at time *t + k* (e.g., predictions about tomorrow's weather, future interest rates, or next year's GNP). Such forecasts usually incorporate *expectational* variables such as anticipated movements of weather systems, expected rates of inflation, and anticipated consumer and investment expenditures. Since Z-scores are not calculated using expectational variables, in what sense are they predictive? They are predictive because the coefficients of the discriminant function are estimated *prior* to actual past bankruptcies. In effect, the coefficients provide the expectational content, *provided they are stable*. For example, Memorex's Z-score of 0.74 (see Table 18-2) indicated that as of December 31, 1974, Memorex's five-variable profile was more similar to Altman's average bankrupt firm one year before failure than to his average nonbankrupt firm. The predictive implication was that if Memorex's financial condition *continued* to deteriorate, in the manner of the average bankrupt firm, then one year hence Memorex probably would be bankrupt. It is obvious (after the fact) the Memorex's managers and their bankers were aware of their financial difficulties and took the necessary steps to prevent the company's further deterioration. In the final analysis, a Z-score is simply an early-warning signal.

TABLE 18-3   Stock Prices: Best and Worst Z-Scores

Company (Exchange)	Closing Prices			
	12/31/74	10/12/76	4/7/81	1/28/88
Taylor Wine (OTC)	$10\frac{3}{8}$	$17\frac{3}{8}$	a	a
Data General (NYSE)	$12\frac{7}{8}$	$44\frac{1}{8}$	$55\frac{3}{4}$	$26\frac{1}{2}$
Telex (NYSE)	$2\frac{1}{4}$	$2\frac{1}{2}$	$8\frac{1}{8}$	48
Memorex (OTC/PSE/NYSE)	3^b	$21\frac{1}{4}$	12	NA

[a] In July 1977, Taylor Wine was acquired by Coca-Cola Company.

[b] Indicates average of high ($4\frac{3}{4}$) and low ($1\frac{3}{8}$) prices for the year 1974. Telex's 1975 high was $\frac{3}{4}$; its low was $\frac{1}{4}$.

Source: The Wall Street Journal and *Moody's Industrial Manual.*

The Libby and Altman experiments are important because they indicate the usefulness of accounting data and show how to package such information for analytical purposes. From the loan officer's perspective, classification models can be used to complement the loan-evaluation process. They provide a technique for quantifying the capacity and capital components of the five Cs.

Credit-Scoring Models

This section presents examples of actual credit-scoring models for both consumer and business loans.[8] Regarding the use of credit-scoring models by banks, the words of David Durand [1941], *the* pioneer in credit-scoring research, should be kept in mind:

> A credit formula is ordinarily regarded as a supplement to, rather than a substitute for, judgment and experience. It may enable a loan officer to appraise an ordinary applicant fairly quickly and easily; and in large operations, it may be of service in standardizing procedure, thus enabling most of the routine work of investigation to be handled by rather inexperienced and relatively low-salaried personnel. A credit formula may not be satisfactory, however, in the investigation of extraordinary cases. (p. 84)

Business Loans

To illustrate the technique of credit scoring for a commercial loan customer, a model developed by Chesser [1974] is presented. The purpose of the model is to predict noncompliance with the customer's original loan agreement, where noncompliance is defined to include not only default but any work-out that may have been arranged resulting in a settlement of the loan less favorable to the lender than the original agreement (e.g., the REIT work-outs described earlier in this chapter). Chesser used data from four commercial banks in three states over the years 1962 to 1971. His observations consisted of a paired sample of 37 satisfactory loans and 37 unsatisfactory (noncompliance) loans one year before noncompliance. Two years before noncompliance, he had only 21 pairs.

Chesser's model, which was based on a technique called logit analysis (a method similar to MDA), consisted of the following six variables;

$X_1 =$ (Cash + Marketable Securities)/Total Assets

$X_2 =$ Net Sales/(Cash + Marketable Securities)

$X_3 =$ EBIT/Total Assets

$X_4 =$ Total Debt/Total Assets

$X_5 =$ Fixed Assets/Net Worth

$X_6 =$ Working Capital/Net Sales

The estimated coefficients, including an intercept term, are

$$y = -2.0434 + -5.24X_1 + .0053X_2 - 6.6507X_3 + 4.4009X_4$$
$$-.0791X_5 - .1020X_6 \tag{18-5}$$

---

[8] For a technical analysis of these and other credit-scoring models, see Altman, Avery, Eisenbeis, and Sinkey [1981].

The variable y, which is a linear combination of the independent variables; is used in the following formula to determine the *probability* of noncompliance, P.

$$P = \frac{1}{1 + e^{-y}} \tag{18-6}$$

where $e = 2.71828$. The estimated y value can be viewed as an index of a borrower's propensity for noncompliance; the higher the value of y, the higher the probability of noncompliance for a particular borrower. Chesser's classification rule for Equation 18-6 is

1. If $P > .50$, assign to the noncompliance group.
2. If $P \leq .50$, assign to the compliance group.

Using both original and holdout samples, Chesser's model was able to classify correctly roughly three out of every four loans one year before noncompliance. Two years before, the accuracy rate was only 57 percent.

To illustrate the use of Equations 18-5 and 18-6, consider the following ratios calculated from the 1980 Annual Report of General Motors:

$X_1 = 0.1074$

$X_2 = 15.5400$

$X_3 = -0.0343$

$X_4 = 0.4094$

$X_5 = 0.8412$

$X_6 = 0.0545$

Plugging these values into equaton 18-5, $y = -.5661$. Plugging this value into Equation 18-6, the probability figure is .3621, indicating membership in the compliance group. Even though 1980 was not a good year for General Motors, which is reflected by its X_3 value of $-.0343$, GM still was predicted to be a member of the compliance group on the strength of its balance sheet. If GM's 1978 EBIT figure of $6.485 billion had been earned in 1980, the value of X_3 would have been .1875. In this counterfactual situation, the new y and P values would have been -1.585 and .1701, respectively. This example illustrates the importance of looking at more than one ratio to judge performance and the sensitivity of the logit function to a change in a particular variable.

Chesser's "credit-scoring" model is in effect a loan-review model. However, his approach is typical of the framework used to build either credit-scoring or loan-review models. Credit-scoring models usually are associated with the decision whether or not to grant credit. Once a loan is made, loan-review models can be used to monitor loan compliance.

Consumer Loans

The classic work in the area of consumer credit scoring is a 1941 study by David Durand. Based on an analysis of good and bad loans made by commercial banks, one of the credit-scoring models he developed is based on the following nine factors:

1. *Age:* a score of .01 for each year of age over 20, with a maximum score of .30.
2. *Sex:* a score of .40 for a female, 0 otherwise.

3. *Stability of residence*: a score of .042 for each year at present residence, with a maximum score of .42.
4. *Occupation*: a score of .55 for either of two good-risk occupations, 0 for either of two bad-risk occupations, a score of .16 for all others.[9]
5. *Industry*: a score of .21 for those employed in utility industries, government service, and banking or brokerage business.
6. *Stability of employment*: a score of .059 for each year at present employment, with a maximum score of .59.

7–9. *Three asset items*: a score of .45 for a bank account, .35 for real estate, and .19 for life insurance.

Let's see how I would rate as of April 11, 1988, using Durand's formula:

Factor	Professor Sinkey	Customer X
Age	.24	.24
Sex	.00	.40
Stability of residence	.42	.42
Occupation	.55	.16
Industry	.21	.21
Stability of employment	.59	.59
Bank account	.45	.45
Real estate	.35	.35
Life insurance	.19	.19
SCORE	3.00	3.01

My score is 3.00. Consider now Customer X, who is a female, age 44, and employed as a departmental secretary at the University of Georgia for the past 15 years. She has a bank account, real estate, and life insurance. Her score is 3.01.

On the basis of his formula, Durand found a marked separation between good and bad loans. The cutoff score that best separated the groups was 1.25. A score greater than 1.25 indicates a profile more characteristic of the good-loan group, whereas a score equal to or less than 1.25 indicates a profile more characteristic of the bad-loan group.

Large retailers such as J. C. Penney, Montgomery Ward, and Sears, Roebuck & Co. make extensive use of credit-scoring models. However, because of the proprietary nature of these systems, information about their specific content and structure is relatively scarce. Sexton [1977] reports that the following variables have been common to the credit-scoring systems of the three large retailers mentioned above:

1. good credit record
2. married
3. single
4. divorced or separated
5. number of dependents
6. age
7. primary monthly income
8. presence of extra income

---

[9] See Durand [1941], Table 13, p. 70, for the list of these occupations. Because of the difficulties in making occupational classifications, it would be misleading to present the occupations here. The interested reader should see Durand's p. 69–74.

9. home owner
10. home renter
11. home telephone
12. credit investigation made.

An additional 24 variables were shared by the various pairs of retailers, including sex, months at present job, presence of savings account, number of derogatories, and occupation.

The passage of the Equal Credit Opportunity Act in 1974, its amendments in 1976, and its implementation through the Fed's Regulation B have placed the burden of proof on any institution using credit-scoring mechanisms to see that their models are methodologically and statistically sound.[10] Whether a lending institution uses a credit-scoring system or not, what all of this legislation and regulation means is that lenders have a very difficult time figuring out what information they can and cannot use in the credit-granting decision; and, if they can use it, how it can be used legally. Moreover, once the decision has been made to grant a loan, the lender must be careful not to violate any rules regarding truth-in-lending disclosures, some of which have been simplified by DIDMCA.

Recapitulation and Credit Analysis in Practice

This section primarily has focused on quantitative techniques of risk analysis. In practice, most bank lending decisions are not made using these methods. The important point, however, is that the financial-statement information available for making such decisions is the same whether quantitative or nonquantitative techniques are employed. Thus the differences are more a matter of form than substance. In either case, the objective is to package the available information into a form that is useful to loan officers for making lending decisions and for monitoring the performance of outstanding loans. This packaging can be in the form of a computer printout or the handwritten notes of an experienced loan officer. Given this information, a judgment must be made regarding the borrower's ability to repay (i.e., creditworthiness). Given this judgment and the customer's relationship with the bank, a loan package can be put together to meet the customer's needs and, just as important, to attempt to control the bank's risk exposure. Since loan packaging has a multidimensional nature, there are various control devices (such as interest rate, loan amount, maturity, collateral, restrictive convenants, etc.) that can be used. The greater a borrower's credit risk is perceived to be, the more specialized the loan agreement tends to be. In contrast, prime borrowers receive more standardized loan contracts.

CHAPTER SUMMARY

If bank business loans are indeed special, we can look at the concepts of delegated monitoring and the bank–customer relationship for explaining this uniqueness. The bank–customer relationship is grounded in the strategic combination of deposits,

---

[10] The 1974 Act prohibits discrimination in the granting of credit on the basis of sex or marital status. The 1976 amendment added the following factors: race, color, religion, national origin, age, receipt of public assistance benefits, and good faith exercise of rights under the Consumer Credit Protection Act. Regulation B describes the statistical criteria credit-scoring models must satisfy before they legally would qualify to use the prohibited age variable.

loans, and other financial services that give commercial banking its unique institutional character. As delegated monitors, banks have developed reputational capital in the credit decision-making process. The heart of this process is the evaluation and monitoring of risk, a process which is complicated because of dishonesty and asymmetric information. A bank's credit-risk function (or loan quality) is determined by a combination of internal and external factors such as attitudes toward risk-taking, loan policies, and economic conditions. Credit analysis is designed to quantify the five Cs of creditworthiness. The ratios and cash flows derived from financial statements provide the nuts and bolts for credit analysis and the potential inputs for classification models designed to identify risky borrowers.

LIST OF KEY WORDS AND CONCEPTS

Accounting profits
Accounting ratios (usefulness to loan officers)
Agency theory
Announcement effects (event studies)
Asymmetric information
Bank business loans
Bank–customer relationship
Bankruptcy-prediction models
Cash flow (concept and measurement)
Classification and Regression Trees (CART)
Credit-risk model (internal versus external factors)

Credit-scoring models
Creditworthiness (five Cs)
Delegated monitoring
Insurance companies
Parametric techniques and tests (versus nonparametric ones)
Private placements
Reserve requirements (incidence of tax)
Straight debt
Wealth effects (excess returns or average prediction errors)
Zeta analysis and Z-score model

REVIEW/DISCUSSION QUESTIONS

1. What evidence exists to suggest that bank loans are unique? What roles do the notions of delegated monitoring and bank–customer relationships play in explaining this uniqueness? Discuss fully.
2. On whom does the incidence of the tax on reserve requirements fall? Does the finding make sense?
3. How do bank business loans, private placements, and straight debt compare with respect to flexibility and in terms of a strategic combination of financial services?
4. In what sense is the financial system a credit system? What role does traditional bank intermediation play in this credit system?
5. What functions do banks perform as delegated monitors in the credit process? In this role, what agency problems do banks face? What is the relationship between asymmetric information and adverse selection?
6. What are the five Cs of creditworthiness and how can they be quantified?
7. Describe the experiment Libby conducted to determine the usefulness of accounting ratios to loan officers. What did he prove, if anything?

8. Classification models such as credit-scoring and bankruptcy-prediction models (and IRS audit models) are designed to look for "statistical outliers." In other words, if you are in the middle of the pack, you are unlikely to get flagged. Describe what these basic models look like and how they can be useful to bank lenders. How can they be abused? Also distinguish between parametric and nonparametric techniques.

9. Get some credit card applications from banks and major retailers and try to figure out what information they are using in their credit-scoring models. What is a binary variable? Why and how does the fact that a credit-card applicant does or does not have a telephone enter such a model?

10. What is cash flow, how important is it to bank lenders, and how can cash flow be measured? What roles do accounts receivable, inventories, and accounts payable play in cash-flow analysis? What are some potential early warning signals of impending cash-flow problems?

MATCHING QUIZ

Directions: Select the letter from the right-hand column that best matches the item in the left-hand column.

___ 1. Beaver's best predictor

___ 2. Agency theory

___ 3. Asymmetric information

___ 4. Cash flow lenders

___ 5. Cash flow

___ 6. Zeta analysis

___ 7. Average prediction errors

___ 8. Insurance companies

___ 9. Delegated monitoring

___ 10. Dishonesty

___ 11. Five Cs

___ 12. Announcement effects

___ 13. Private placements

___ 14. Bank–customer relationship

A. "Second-rate" monitors

B. Borrowers have superior knowledge compared to lenders

C. Need to be quantified for credit analysis

D. Commercial banks have "the" stock of reputational capital

E. Difficult to monitor

F. Statistical measure of excess returns

G. Focus of event studies

H. Strategic combination of deposits, loans, and other services

I. Useful tool for bank lenders

J. f(Internal and External Factors)

K. Nonparametric technique

____ 15. Incidence of reserve tax   L. Bank business loans are unique

____ 16. Accounting ratios   M. Alternative source of finance

____ 17. Accounting profits   N. Not equal to cash flow

____ 18. James's finding   O. Does not fall on holders of CDs

____ 19. Credit-risk model   P. Cash flow-to-debt ratio

____ 20. Source of loan repayment   Q. Principal–agent relationships

____ 21. CART   R. Commercial banks

____ 22. Probit and logit   S. Insurance companies important here

T. Key to credit analysis

U. Bankruptcy-prediction model

V. Parametric classification models

PROBLEMS

1. Use Altman's 1968 bankruptcy-prediction model to calculate GM's Z-score for 1980, given the following information:

Item	Amount ($ Millions)
Current assets	15,421
Current liabilities	12,273
Total debt	14,159
Total assets	34,581
Retained earnings	15,737
Sales	57,728
EBIT (loss)	(1,186)
Market value of equity	13,412

How does Altman's Z-score for GM compare with Chesser's credit-rating score for GM?

2. Czinki State Bank prices its commercial loans on a cost (of funds) plus basis. In a world without reserve requirements, its cost of funds is 10 percent. What will the bank's cost of funds be if reserve requirements of 3 percent, 5 percent, and 10 percent are imposed on the bank? What happens to the bank's effective lending and borrowing rates if the incidence of the tax is borne fully by depositors? By borrowers? Shared equally? Why would either group willingly accept the incidence of the tax?

3. Using Formula 18-3, calculate and analyze the cash flows of QRS Corporation for the years t, $t - 1$, $t - 2$, and $t - 3$, given the following information (millions of dollars).

	t	$t - 1$	$t - 2$	$t - 3$
Net profit	(370)	2369	420	475
Depreciation	130	127	124	121
Accounts receivable (change)	(169)	114	110	100
Inventories (change)	(11)	450	400	375
Accounts payable (change)	(41)	(334)	250	150

4. Using the classification tree in Figure 18-1, indicate whether the following firms would be classified as bankrupt or nonbankrupt.

	Firm A	Firm B	Firm C	Firm D	Firm E
Cash Flow/Total Debt	.10	.13	.15	.16	.12
Total Debt/Total Assets	.60	.75	.80	.55	.70
Retained Earnings/Total Assets	.12	.15	.14	.17	.16
Cash/Total Assets	.01	.03	.02	.04	.00

SELECTED REFERENCES

Altman, Edward I. [1968]. "Financial Ratios, Discriminant Analysis, and the Prediction of Corporate Bankruptcy," *Journal of Finance* (September), pp. 589–609.

——, Robert B, Avery, Robert A. Eisenbeis, and Joseph F. Sinkey, Jr. [1981]. *Application of Classification Techniques in Business, Banking and Finance.* Greenwich, CT: JAI Press.

——, G. G. Haldeman, and P. Narayanan. [1977]. "ZETA Analysis: A New Model to Identify the Bankruptcy Risk of Corporations," *Journal of Banking and Finance* (1), pp. 29–54.

Beaver, William H. [1967]. "Financial Ratios as Predictors of Failure," *Empirical Research in Accounting: Selected Studies 1966, Journal of Accounting Research* (Supplement to Vol. 4), pp. 71–111.

Bennett, Thomas E., Jr. [1987]. "Mixed Signals," *INC.* (October), p. 153.

Buser, Stephen A., Andrew H. Chen, and Edward J. Kane. [1981]. "Federal Deposit Insurance, Regulatory Policy, and Optimal Bank Capital," *Journal of Finance* (36), pp. 51–60.

Chessen, Delton L. [1974]. "Predicting Loan Noncompliance," *Journal of Commercial Bank Lending* (August) pp. 2–15.

Corrigan, E. Gerald. [1982]. "Are Banks Special?" *Annual Report*, Federal Reserve Bank of Minneapolis, pp. 2–24.

——. [1987]. *Financial Market Structure: A Longer View.* New York: Federal Reserve Bank.

Diamond, Douglas W. [1984]. "Financial Intermediation and Delegated Monitoring," *Review of Economic Studies* (51), pp. 393–414.

Durand, David. [1941]. *Risk Elements in Consumer Installment Lending.* New York: National Bureau of Economic Research.

Fama, Eugene F. [1985]. "What's Different About Banks? *Journal of Monetary Economics* (15), pp. 29–36.

Frydman, Halina, Edward I. Altman, and Duen-Li Kao. [1985]. "Introducing Recursive Partitioning for Financial Classification: The Case of Financial Distress," *Journal of Finance* (March), pp. 269–291.

Harris, John M. Jr., James R. Scott, and Joseph F. Sinkey, Jr. [1986]. "The Wealth Effects of Regulatory Intervention Surrounding the Bailout of Continental Illinois," *Proceedings of a Conference on Bank Structure and Competition*, Federal Reserve Bank of Chicago, pp. 104–126.

Greenawalt, Mary Brady, and Joseph F. Sinkey, Jr. [1988]. "Bank Loan-Loss Provisions and the Income-Smoothing Hypothesis: An Empirical Analysis, 1976–1984," Working Paper, The University of Georgia, forthcoming *Journal of Financial Services Research.*

Hodgman, Donald R. [1961]. "The Deposit Relationship and Commercial Bank Investment Behavior," *Review of Economics and Statistics* (42), pp. 257–268.

James, Christopher. [1987]. "Some Evidence on the Uniqueness of Bank Loans," *Journal of Financial Economics* (December), pp. 217–235

Kane, Edward J., and Burton G. Malkiel. [1965]. "Bank Portfolio Allocation, Deposit Variability, and the Availability Doctrine," *Quarterly Journal of Economics* (79), pp. 113–134.

Keeton, William R., and Charles S. Morris. [1987]. "Why Do Banks' Loan Losses Differ," *Economic Review*, Federal Reserve Bank of Kansas City (May), pp. 3–21.

Kelly, John M. [1986]. *Managing Cash Flow.* New York: Franklin Watts.

Libby, Robert E. [1975]. "Accounting Ratios and the Prediction of Failure: Some Behavioral Evidence," *Journal of Accounting Research* (Spring), pp. 150–161.

Marais, M. Laurentius, James M. Pattell, and Mark A. Wolfson. [1985]. "The Experimental Design of Classification Models: An Application of Recursive Partitioning and Bootstrapping to Commercial Bank Loan Classification," *Journal of Accounting Research* (Vol. 22 Supplement 1984), pp. 87–114.

O'Glove, Thorton L. [1987]. *Quality of Earnings.* New York: The Free Press.

Scheiner, J. H. [1981]. "Income Smoothing: An Analysis in the Banking Industry," *Journal of Bank Research* (Summer), pp. 119–123.

Sexton, Donald E., Jr. [1977]. Determining Good and Bad Credit Risks Among High and Low Income Families," *Journal of Business* (April), pp. 236–239.

Sinkey, Joseph F., Jr. [1979]. *Problem and Failed Institutions in the Commercial Banking Industry.* Greenwich, CT: JAI Press.

———. [1985]. "Regulatory Attitudes Toward Risk," in *Handbook for Banking Strategy*, R. Aspinwall and R. Eisenbeis, eds. New York: Wiley, pp. 347–380.

———. [1988]. "Delegated Monitoring and Bank–Customer Relationships as Explanations for Why Bank Business Loans Are Unique," Working Paper, The University of Georgia.

CHAPTER 19

Management of Credit Risk II: The Diversification and Pricing of Risk

CORPORATE PHILOSOPHIES WITHOUT ROOM FOR ANALYSIS OF RISK

In August of 1984 I attended a symposium on issues and options dealing with the problems and failures of large banks, sponsored by The Bank Administration Institute (BAI) at Dartmouth College in Hanover, N.H. The back nine of Dartmouth's golf course, which was designed by a mountain goat, is treacherous and frustrating. But my *second* most frustrating experience at the conference was a statement made by a representative of Continental Illinois. During a discussion of corporate philosophy and strategic planning, this person expressed the opinion that you didn't get to the top of a major corporation if you worried about risk. I was flabbergasted by the remark. Surely, the financial-management concepts of risk management and risk–return trade-offs weren't that far removed from the real world. It was obvious that no one who worried about risk had gotten to the top at Continental, and look what happened to it.

Corporate philosophies without room for risk tend to be common in problem and failed banks. Another "war story" is illuminating. In 1985 and 1986, I did some work as an "expert witness" involving a failed energy bank in Texas. Such cases generate hundreds of documents for review by attorneys and witnesses. For the purposes of this chapter, the most interesting documents were the "minutes" of the loan committee, the "minutes" of the Board of Directors meetings, and the bank's strategic plan (prepared by an outside consultant). Conspicuous by its absence in these documents was the mention of risk and evidence that anyone in the organization was concerned about it, until it was too late. To be fair, the consultant did recommend the bank form a holding company and begin a program of geographic diversification. The recommendation was ignored by the bank's managers and directors.

The minutes of the various meetings made fascinating reading. For example, at one point in a meeting, the agenda called for discussion of some problem loans. However, because some new loans also had to be considered, the discussion was postponed until the next meeting. Although this shuffling of the agenda might be construed as a minor point, it, in effect, captured the bank's philosophy, which, in my opinion, was one of growth for growth's sake. Diversification be damned. Man the loan desks and full speed ahead. On balance, the bank *appeared* to be more concerned about loan growth than loan quality. The bank's rapid growth in the 1970s and early 1980s resulted in a concentrated loan portfolio, one that was extremely vulnerable to a downturn in energy prices. When the downturn came, the bank was one of the first energy-related failures. It was closed in 1983.

DILEMMA: HOW CAN UNIT BANKS OR BANKS WITH LIMITED RESOURCES DIVERSIFY?

Hindsight is usually perfect and being a "Monday morning" quarterback is no great shakes. Continental Illinois and the failed energy bank described above both were unit banks, that is, in essence, one-office banks. Continental obviously had more resources at its disposal than the energy bank, which was only a $1 billion institution. How can such banks diversify? The energy bank had a concentrated loan portfolio *and* concentrated funding from "hot money." Although Continental had a diversified loan portfolio, it had the same kind of problem with its liabilities, only its money was even hotter. In addition, Continental had its embarrassing Penn Square "hair shirt" to wear. When concerns about the quality of these banks' loan portfolios surfaced, the hot money left both banks in a hurry. Banks with aggressive liability management strategies must be doubly cautious about the quality of their loan portfolios (i.e., they must be willing to sacrifice growth for loan quality). Both Continental and the energy bank threw caution to the wind and opted for the high-growth strategy. The results speak for themselves.

The Lesson

Do you see the lesson of corporate philosophies without the room for risk? The combination of rapid growth and concentrated asset and liability portfolios is a volatile mixture, one easily ignited by adverse external conditions. Moreover, the growth and concentration decisions are discretionary choices made by managers and directors. Although the words of a bank officer calling for careful analysis of risk, quality growth, and diversification may not be appreciated in the short run, in the long run, they are important words to hear in corporate boardrooms and to see in the minutes of such meetings. You never know when some "hired gun" will be looking for the "smoking gun."

When things go wrong a good retrenchment rule is to get back to basics. For basketball players, it's defense, rebounding, and shot selection. For tennis players, it's quick feet, early racket preparation, and a smooth swing. For golfers, it's grip, aim, posture, and position. For bridge players, it's analyze the lead, review the bidding, count your winners (and losers), and decide how to play the hand. For people, it's family, friends, and religion. And for bankers, it's borrowing and lending. Three important aspects of the financial management of lending are credit analysis, portfolio diversification, and loan pricing. Given our investigation of credit analysis in the previous chapter, this chapter focuses on the diversification and pricing of credit risk. These concepts are basic tools bankers must have in their diversification and pricing bags.

LOAN-PRICING MODELS AND CONTAGION EFFECTS[1]

Loan-pricing models are mechanisms for evaluating (pricing) risk. Contagion effects (think of contagious diseases) can be analyzed between bank portfolios or within a bank portfolio. The latter is more commonly referred to as a concentrated portfolio or one lacking in diversification, which can lead to contagion. For example, the problem/failed energy and farm banks of the 1980s had undiversified loan port-folios. As a result, they were vulnerable to contagion because the loans in their portfolios were so highly correlated. Since the decline in energy and farm prices was systematic, it adversely affected their concentrated loan portfolios.

The problem of contagion across banks focuses on the potential for one bank's financial difficulties (e.g., Continental Illinois in 1984, First Pennsylvania in 1980, and Franklin National in 1974) to spread to others, resulting in a financial crisis. This form of contagion is a macroeconomic concern at both national and international levels because of the potential social costs/externalities associated with the lack of confi-dence in a country's (or the international) financial system. Some good news in this regard, according to Saunders [1987], is that "…the degree of contagion appears to have fallen since the early 1970s (the oil shock–Franklin National–Herstatt period)" (p. 226). One possible explanation for this reduced contagion is the "too-big-to-fail doctrine," or what Saunders calls the "more interventionist" role of bank regulators since 1974 (in all developed countries but especially in the United States).

Loan pricing models and the effects of contagion (i.e., the lack of diversification) typically are analyzed using three different approaches. The first approach focuses on default-risk premiums or spreads in the deposit-loan markets. The second approach is a supply-side one commonly referred to as credit rationing. And the third approach focuses on bank equity returns in the capital market. These three approaches are analyzed in this chapter. To my knowledge, an eclectic model attempting to combine these alternative frameworks has not been attempted. In this regard, banking practice may be ahead of the finance theory.

PORTFOLIO THEORY, RISK PREMIUMS, AND BANK LENDING

Portfolio theory suggests that financial managers of lending organizations should evaluate loans on the basis of the loan's risk–return contribution to the loan port-folio.[2] Diversification is, of course, the *raison d'être* for portfolio theory. To de-velop the implications of modern portfolio theory for bank lending, we begin with a look at how the riskiness of an individual loan differs from the riskiness of a portfolio of loans. The objective of the analysis is to gain insight into the process of loan pricing and risk management.

Pricing Default Risk

Abstracting from real resource costs (overhead, loan processing, etc.), a profitable loan contract rate, call it i^*, must compensate the lender for the time value of money as reflected by the nominal rate of interest, i, and for the risk of default. Letting d

---

[1] This section and the one below on credit rationing follow Saunders [1987], especially pp. 206–213. He has applied the approach in a study dealing with contagion effects in the international banking market.

[2] Flannery [1985] provides a conceptual guide to portfolio issues in bank lending. This section draws, in part, upon his analysis. Also see Saunders [1981].

represent the probability of default, the loan contract rate can be expressed as:

$$i^* = (1 + i)/(1 - d) - 1 \tag{19-1}$$

Rearranging Equation 19-1 in dollar terms (i.e., by adding 1 to both sides), the new expression shows that the contract calls for the repayment of $(1 + i)/(1 - d)$ dollars for every dollar lent. That is,

$$1 + i^* = (1 + i)/(1 - d) \tag{19-2}$$

To illustrate, consider a short-term loan, say for one year. If the one-year T-bill rate is .10 and the expected probability of default is .01, then the loan contract rate should be $(1.1/.99) - 1 = .1111$ or 11.11%. In dollar terms, the lender should receive $1.11 for every $1 lent. Suppose that the borrower subjects the lender to greater risk exposure as reflected by an expected probability of default of .05. In this case, the contract rate should be 15.79 percent and the lender should receive $1.16 for every $1 lent. If the default rates and the loans in the previous two examples were for three months rather than one year, then, assuming a flat yield curve, the annualized loan rates would be 14.58 percent for the low-risk borrower $[.1458 = (1.1/96) - 1]$ and 37.5% for the high-risk borrower [i.e., $.375 = (1.1/.8) - 1$]. The annualized default rate is simply expressed as $4 \times d$, when d is a quarterly rate.

The Default-Risk Premium

In the previous examples for the one-year loan, the default-risk premium (let's label it *DRP*) was 1.11 percent for the low-risk borrower and 5.79 percent for the high-risk borrower. There is a *loose* one-to-one correspondence between d and *DRP*. More exactly, $DRP = i^* - i$. The default-risk premium compensates the lender for the expected loss on the loan. The typical credit analysis performed by a bank is directed at assessing the default risk of individual borrowers. Morever, the DRP usually is established based solely upon the borrower's profile of creditworthiness and relationship with the bank, without consideration of the marginal effect of the loan on the overall loan portfolio. The contribution of modern portfolio theory to understanding loan pricing and risk management enters at this point.

The Portfolio-Risk Premium

The diversification principle suggests that portfolio managers cannot assess the riskiness of an individual asset in isolation; rather, it must be evaluated in terms of its relationship to other assets in the portfolio. In a similar way, loan portfolio managers must evaluate individual loans with respect to the *covariation* with their loan portfolios. To correctly price loan risk, lenders must receive compensation for the portfolio risks they assume. This portfolio-risk premium (let's label it *PRP*) also will depend upon the lender's degree of risk aversion. The more risk averse a lender is, the higher the premium will have to be. Overall, the PRP compensates the lender for the *uncertainty* about the probability of default or how much of the loan will be repaid.

To incorporate the concept of the PRP into the formula for i^*, the profitable loan contract rate, let's denote it, for compactness, by p and rewrite Equation 19-1 as

$$i^* = (1 + i)/(1 - d - p) - 1 \tag{19-3}$$

In dollar terms, the counterpart to Equation 19-2 is

$$1 + i^* = (1 + i)/(1 - d - p) \tag{19-4}$$

Historical interest rates do not permit us to observe the individual risk premiums, but only their sum in the form $(i^* - i)$. Conceptually, however, we can think of the contract loan rate as consisting of the following components:

$$i^* = i + d + p = i + DRP + PRP \tag{19-5}$$

In words, lenders require compensation for the time value of money, default risk, and portfolio risk.

To illustrate the concept of portfolio risk in bank lending, consider the following example derived from Flannery [1985, pp. 460–461]. A lender has a choice of making two risky loans, A and B. The expected cash flows from the loans are state-dependent as shown in the following matrix:

Loan	State 1	State 2
A	$4	$2
B	$0	$3

If each of the states is equally likely to occur and if the lender holds a portfolio consisting of 60 percent of loan A and 40 percent of loan B, then the expected cash inflow is $2.40 regardless of which state prevails. That is, in state 1, the outcome is .6($4) + .4($0) = $2.40; in state 2, it is .6($2) + .4($3) = $2.40. The undiversified portfolios have expected outcomes of $3 for loan A and $1.50 for loan B. However, when the loans are combined in the 60/40 portfolio, they generate the same return (i.e., the portfolio return is state independent), resulting in a riskless portfolio. The magic ingredient in this portfolio is the negative correlation between the outcomes for A and B. That is, in state 1, the return on loan A is high whereas the return on loan B is low; in state 2, the opposite occurs. In a portfolio, negative correlations, which are rare in the real world, are desirable because they provide a cushion when earnings (values) turn down. The important point is that loan pricing and risk management require knowledge of a loan's riskiness in conjunction with the lender's holdings of other loans.

Diversification and Loan Losses

Energy-lending banks (e.g., Penn Square), loan-participation banks (e.g., Continental Illinois), LDC-lending banks (e.g., the money-center banks), and farm-lending banks are prime examples from the 1980s of lenders who have failed to diversify their loan portfolios. Loan contracts do not generate "windfall gains" because borrowers never repay more than the promised amounts. However, they sometimes pay less than the contract amount. It is these "incomplete transactions" that generate loan losses. The possibility of default is the source of credit risk in lending, but the variability of actual loan losses can be reduced by spreading a dollar volume of loans over a large number of independent borrowers. The banks mentioned above were not lending to independent borrowers and therefore they were not really diversifying. Volatile loan losses mean volatile profits, which mean reduced equity values.

Diversification Versus Specialized Lending

The gospel of portfolio theory is that portfolios should be diversified. In contrast, institutional lenders develop expertise by specializing in specific industries or sectors of the economy. For example, loan officers may be trained to specialize in such areas as gas and oil, minerals, chemicals, transportation, or services. Banks that develop a reputation and lending skills in a particular area have a vested interest in perpetuating that expertise. The lesson from portfolio theory however, is that this specialization with its accompanying loan concentration can mean greater credit risk in the loan portfolio. To compensate for this increased risk exposure, lenders must construct loan contract rates with portfolio-risk premiums as shown in Equations 19-3 to 19-5. Loan pricing is, of course, only one way of attempting to control risk exposure. In addition, the nonprice terms of loan agreements should be structured to reflect the borrower's effect on the lender's overall risk exposure.

THE CREDIT-RATIONING APPROACH

An alternative to increasing risk premiums or spreads to control the allocation of credit is to ration credit to risky borrowers. According to this model, banks have (flexible) lending constraints or credit ceilings for borrowers, and beyond those constraints they will not lend at any rate (price). The credit-rationing approach is grounded in the perceived weaknesses of the risk-premium model. Specifically, beyond some point, higher interest rates are said to create adverse selection and incentive effects for borrowers, which may reduce the expected return on the loan. To see this, let's label the expected return on the loan $E(r)$, and compare it with the loan contract rate, i^* from Equation 19-5. The relationship is shown in Figure 19-1 (see Stiglitz and Weiss [1981]). The inverted U-shaped curve assumes the existence of an equilibrium contract rate that maximizes the bank's expected return. As a bank increases its loan contract rate (i^*), its expected return [$E(r)$] first rises. However, beyond some point, defined as the equilibrium rate i_e^*, the expected return declines. The explanation for why the expected return declines is based on the notions of adverse selection and default or risk-taking incentives.

Adverse Selection

The problem of adverse selection is the lender's dilemma of picking creditworthy borrowers (i.e., ones who will repay on time). This task is complicated by the fact that

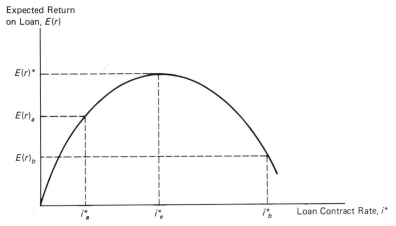

Figure 19-1   The Relationship between the Expected Return and the Loan Contract Rate

Source: Adapted from Saunders [1987], Figure 6.7, p. 209.

when interest rates are relatively high the best-quality borrowers tend to stay out of the market. If this occurs, the bank will be lending to a pool of borrowers whose marginal credit risk is higher than when rates are low. As a result, expected returns will be lower. In contrast, when rates are relatively low, the most creditworthy borrowers are in the market, and the chances of lender adverse selection are reduced as the marginal credit risk is improved.

Risk-Taking Incentives

At relatively low rates of interest, the ability of borrowers to repay loans is high, other things equal. Accordingly, there is little need for them to take on high-risk projects to ensure interest coverage. In contrast, when interest rates are high (and the quality of the pool of would-be borrowers is already reduced by adverse selection), existing borrowers are more likely to take on high-risk projects to prevent default.

The Equilibrium Expected Rate

In the credit-rationing model, the expected return, at the margin, can be viewed as consisting of (1) the increase in expected return due to a higher interest rate on the loan, (2) the reduction in expected return due to the increase in risk associated with adverse selection, and (3) the reduction in expected return due to the increase in risk associated with default incentives. As long as the increase in rate outweighs the rate-reducing effects of greater risk, the expected return rises. In equilibrium, which is defined by the coordinates $[E(r)^*, i_e^*]$ in Figure 19-1, these effects are equal. To the left of the equilibrium point, expected return rises as the loan rate is increased. However, to the right of the equilibrium point, the expected return declines with further increases in the loan rate. The downturn occurs because the increased risk associated with adverse selection and default incentives outweighs the positive effect of the increase in the loan rate.

The Credit-Rationing Process

To see how the credit-rationing process might work, let's focus on Figure 19-2 and consider the following scenario. Suppose the bank faces three groups of borrowers: Group AAA (for strong creditworthiness), Group BBB (for intermediate creditworthiness), and Group CCC (for weak creditworthiness). Although the groups are partially identifiable by their perceived creditworthiness, they are not completely separate, as indicated by the group overlaps. The group overlaps cause adverse-selection risk for the bank. For example, a BBB borrower may pass for a AAA one or a CCC for a BBB. Asset size, leverage, and the number of years the borrowing firm has been in business can be thought of as risk-sorting characteristics. As creditworthiness decreases, the equilibrium group contract rate increases, but the expected return declines as shown in Figure 19-2. The locus of points for each of the borrowing groups shown in Figure 19-2 depicts the same relationship shown in Figure 19-1. Specifically, each curve shows how expected return varies as the loan rate changes.

Given the lender's perceptions of credit quality, the bank's risk-free cost of funds will determine which groups receive (are rationed) credit. If the risk-free rate indicated by the straight horizontal line in Figure 19-2 applies, then the bank will lend to any members of groups AAA and BBB (and BBB's overlap with CCC). However, if the risk-free rate rises above its point of tangency with the locus of points for Group BBB, then all CCC-type borrowers will be rationed out of the market. Thus, movements in the level of the risk-free rate are one of the determinants of who gets

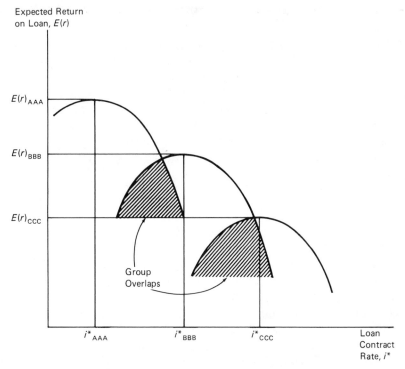

Figure 19-2   The Credit-Rationing Process

Source: Adapted from Saunders [1987], Figures 6.8 and 6.9, pp. 210–211.

credit in this model. The other determinant of credit rationing in this framework is the lender's perceptions of borrowers' creditworthiness. Shifts in these perceptions will move the group curves up and to the left for improved perceptions of credit quality, and down and to the right for deteriorated perceptions. Moreover, to the extent the risk-free rate affects lenders' perceptions, there will be an interaction effect between the two.

To summarize, when the risk-free rate is relatively low and lenders' perceptions of the credit environment are favorable, it is easier to get credit, and little rationing occurs. However, when the risk-free rate is relatively high and the credit environment is perceived to be unfavorable, it is difficult to get credit, and rationing is more prevalent.

Contagion and Credit Rationing

A contagion effect on the supply of bank loans can be analyzed using Figure 19-2. Suppose Group BBB borrowers are perceived as being less creditworthy (i.e., more risky). In this case, the BBB curve would shift down and to the right such that the group's equilibrium loan contract rate is now higher and its equilibrium expected return lower. As an exercise, draw this new curve in and label it BBB'. In the absence of contagion, this shift would not affect any other group of borrowers. However, if contagion is present, it would. To see this, imagine (or draw in on Figure 19-2) the AAA curve also shifting down and to the right such that its equilibrium contract loan rate is now higher and its equilibrium expected return lower. In this case, AAA-type borrowers have been "contaminated" by the perceived decline in Group BBB's creditworthiness and, assuming the risk-free rate has not changed, been penalized by having to pay a higher spread over the risk-free rate.

On balance, contagion tends to lead to increased credit rationing, characterized by a declining volume of loans to all borrowers and to higher contract rates and spreads for those borrowers able to get funds. From the lender's perspective, the higher loan contract rates mean lower expected returns, assuming movement from one equilibrium to another. Finally, although contagion is typically couched in terms of adverse effects, there is no reason for its effects to be one-sided or asymmetrical. Accordingly, the improved risk perception of one group of borrowers could spread to other groups, a riding-the-coattails effect.

CAPITAL-MARKET MODELS

The capital-asset-pricing model (CAPM) provides a framework for determining asset prices based on the asset's contribution to portfolio risk. Conceptually, the application of this kind of framework to loan pricing has great intuitive appeal; operationally, its implementation would be difficult. However, both the theory and the empirics are complicated by the fact that bank loans do not trade in markets where prices are easily observed. Hence, no easy way to construct the loan-market equivalent of the market portfolio exists. The institutional equivalent of asset pricing in the lending area is provided by bank credit analysis. The latter, which is more "art" than "science," is an experience-oriented task in which loan officers not only price loans (i.e., evaluate creditworthiness), but also attempt to construct deals that keep both the bank and its customer satisfied.

A loan-pricing model, similar to CAPM, would be one capable of generating "loan betas" and pricing loans relative to the "market loan portfolio." A loan or portfolio of loans with the same volatility as the market loan portfolio would have a beta of 1. Aggressive loans would have betas greater than 1 and defensive loans would have betas less than 1. Loans would be priced on the basis of their volatility relative to the market loan portfolio and marked up relative to the risk-free rate. The critical factors in the calculation of a loan beta would be the covariance between the return on the loan and the return on the market loan portfolio, and the variance of the market loan portfolio itself. The focal variable in the covariance term is the correlation between the loan and the market portfolio. Unless a lender knows the covariation of a loan's return (default) with its portfolio of other loans, it cannot price the loan properly. To illustrate, consider two loans with the same expected returns and probabilities of default. However, if one of the loans is negatively correlated with the other loans in the portfolio, it is more valuable to the lender's portfolio than the other one. As a result, the borrower with the desirable negative loan correlation should receive a lower contract rate than the one with the assumed positive correlation. In our hypothetical framework, this desirability would show up as a negative loan beta.

Contagion in Capital Markets

Contagion is present in capital markets whenever an event or information flow (whether positive or negative) with respect to one firm (bank) affects the equity values (stock prices) of other firms (banks). The approach used by James [1987] (as described in the previous chapter) of examining residual returns from the market model is one way to check for "announcement effects." Such tests are designed to check for covariation across bank equity returns adjusted for expected returns. The residual or abnormal return is the difference between actual and expected returns. If such returns are nonzero and statistically significant for a particular stock or portfolio of stocks, the event or announcement is said to account for the abnormal return. Contagion is present across stocks, when the event or announcement is "contagious" and spreads to the returns of "nonevent" companies (i.e., those without the particular announcement being investigated).

Regarding the event-study methodology, which is so widely used in finance research, Kane and Unal [1988] investigated the variability in the risk components of bank and savings and loan equity returns over the period 1975 through 1985. They found significant variability in three risk measures: (1) market betas, (2) interest-rate factors, and (3) residual risk. Kane and Unal employed an estimation technique called the Goldfeld and Quandt [1976] "switching regression method." They concluded that "...event-study methods tend to overreach their data."

VARIABLE-RATE PRICING AND THE INTERACTION BETWEEN INTEREST-RATE RISK AND CREDIT RISK

Regarding variable-rate pricing, to paraphrase Matthew 16:26, "What does it profit lenders, if they price the loan on a variable-rate basis, but suffer the loss of the loan?" The lesson from the financial-management scriptures is that lenders must consider the interaction between interest-rate risk and credit risk. Lenders who pass interest-rate risk on to borrowers who can't handle it (i.e., who end up defaulting) are jumping from the interest-rate frying pan into the proverbial fires of default.[3]

The critical point is that the pricing mechanism used in lending agreements must be consistent with the borrower's ability to pay. To use variable-rate pricing in a contract with a borrower who is extremely vulnerable to interest-rate risk increases the chances of default and defeats the fundamental objective of lending (i.e., to have the transaction completed and get repaid). Banks, of course, face a dilemma in this area because, if they do not use variable-rate pricing during periods of volatile interest rates, they are forced to accept both the credit risk and the interest-rate risk in one contract. Under these circumstances, it is even more imperative that fixed-rate loans be priced properly. On balance, the shifting of interest-rate risk from the lender to the borrower cannot be viewed as a *ceteris paribus* action—the other factors *won't* stay the same. That is, a borrower's expected cash flows are likely to be sensitive to the pricing mechanism used in the loan contract, and the greater uncertainty associated with variable-rate pricing may destabilize the borrower's earnings stream such that default occurs. Lenders who make variable-rate loans have an obligation (to their shareholders) to consider how such a pricing mechanism will affect the probability of the borrower's default and the risk exposure of the overall loan portfolio. The bottom line is that loan pricing needs to mesh with the borrower's ability to pay. "What does it profit a lender, if ..."

Portfolio Composition and Variable-Rate Pricing

Institutional descriptions of the loan portfolio in terms of commercial and industrial, consumer, real estate, and agriculture make for nice reading, but the terms lack

---

[3] Additional chapter and verse on this subject can be found in Santomero [1985].

financial content. A more meaningful breakdown of the loan portfolio is in terms of variable-rate loans and fixed-rate loans. In addition to deciding how to price individual loans, depository institutions must decide what *portion* of their loan portfolios should be priced on a variable-rate basis. As we have seen in Chapter 13, the focal variable of gap management is the relationship of rate-sensitive assets (RSA) to rate-sensitive liabilities (RSL). Moreover, the decision on how to price individual loans and what is the appropriate portion of them in the loan portfolio are the major determinants of RSA. A bank's underlying balance-sheet structure in terms of its dollar gap ($RSA - RSL$) or ratio (RSA/RSL) determines its interest-rate exposure. An analysis of the costs and benefits of interest rate risk is important because, as shown above, interest-rate risk affects the lender's degree of credit risk and willingness to bear it.

The important point is that asset-liability management involves more than the management of interest-rate risk; it involves the management of all relevant balance-sheet risks, with the interaction of interest rate risk and credit risk being the critical concern. The pricing and risk management of the loan portfolio are the two primary determinants of this interaction.

THE PRIME RATE: MYTH AND REALITY[4]

In banking jargon, the most appropriate dictionary definition of *prime* (from *Webster's*) is the adjective form of the word, as "first in excellence, quality, or value." You must understand that the term *prime rate* is simply a *symptom* of a borrower's underlying creditworthiness or potential riskiness to the lender. Thus, a prime-rate customer is one who is first in excellence, quality, or value with respect to credit-worthiness. In a risk-based pricing scheme, with other relevant factors held constant, such customers deserve the lowest rate of interest as borrowers. This *concept* represents the *reality* of the prime rate. As such, it simply represents a "benchmark" rate off which rates for other borrowers can be set. The actual rate for an individual borrower could be *above* or *below* the benchmark rate (recall our discussion of the importance of negative correlations) depending on the nature and quality of the borrower's set of other factors. In other words, the loan-pricing decision is not driven solely by the prime rate; it is a complex decision that depends on a number of factors.

The *myth* of the prime rate has come from its *misinterpretation* as the *lowest* rate of interest available to a bank's best corporate customers. Some banks made the mistake of perpetuating this myth and as a result became involved in costly litigation in the early 1980s. The path-breaking case was a class-action suit brought against the First National Bank of Atlanta. The foundation for the case was the contention that the bank overcharged prime-based borrowers by pegging their interest rate to the bank's *announced* prime rate, rather than to the "discount" prime rate its *overall* best corporate customers received. First Atlanta compounded its error when it permitted bank officers to engage in an "abusive" telephone campaign to attempt to coerce class members to drop out of the case.[5] In March 1984, First Atlanta agreed to a nonmythical out-of-court settlement amounting to as much as $13.5 million. As a result, any lender

---

[4] This section bears a title similar to Fischer's [1982] study of the prime rate.

[5] The 11th Circuit Court of Appeals ruled in January 1985 to uphold a lower court's ruling that the bank's law firm and general counsel had committed an "ethical violation" in approving the phone campaign.

who values his/her job today *never* refers to the prime rate as the *lowest* rate of interest charged by the bank. It is a benchmark rate. Depending on the borrower's overall relationship with the bank, the actual rate charged may be above or below the stated or announced prime rate.

Below-Prime Lending Is not a New Phenomenon

Banks have been lending at rates below the level of the announced prime for a number of decades. In contrast, the "discovery" and publicity of the "discount" prime has been a more recent phenomenon. For example, the results of a Federal Reserve study of the discount prime rate are shown in Table 19-1. During the survey week of May 5–10, 1980, the posted prime rate ranged between 17.5 and 18.5 percent. However, during this week, 53.0 percent of the short-term business loans made at 48 large banks were below the prime rate. The average discount was 413 basis points. In other words, the discount prime rate was roughly 14 percent compared to the posted prime rate of 18 perent. At medium and smaller banks for this same week, the figures were 26.8 percent of the loans at an average discount of 247 basis points. It is interesting to note that for the week ending May 10, 1980, the three-month commercial paper rate was roughly 10 percent. Thus, a corporation with access to the commercial-paper market would have had bargaining power to get a discount from the posted prime rate of 18 percent.

The strategy of undercutting the prime rate has its advantages and disadvantages. On the plus side, the bank can keep its prime-rate customers happy by giving them discounts and still make a profit. For example, during the week that ended May 10, 1980, the three-month CD rate in the secondary market was 10.26 percent. With the discount prime rate at 14 percent, there was a 374-point spread to cover noninterest expenses and profit, assuming the CD rate is the appropriate marginal cost of funds. On the minus side, the strategy runs the risk of alienating nonprime customers, whose loans are tied to the *posted* prime rate, and of incurring greater scrutiny about pricing practices from the banking authorities and the United States Congress. In addition, the practice of undercutting the prime rate can erode the effectiveness of the competitive restraints imposed by the coordinated use of the prime-rate and compensating-balance conventions. On balance, it is in the bank's interest to move the posted prime rate up quickly and down slowly. Moreover, if nonprime customers do not have alternative sources of funds and if the political risks are not costly, it makes economic sense to establish a discounted prime rate for good customers. Preferential treatment of good customers is a common practice in any business and banking is no exception.

TABLE 19-1   The "Discount" Prime Rate[a]

Class of Bank	Percent of Business Loans Made at Rates below Prime				Spread Between Prime Rate and "Discount" Prime Rate (Basis Points)			
	1977	1978	1979	1980	1977	1978	1979	1980
48 large banks	8.8	16.1	32.6	45.3	79	62	92	177
Medium and smaller banks	3.0	10.5	33.4	18.6	87	82	162	189

[a] Data are annual averages for the four survey weeks in each year. Short-term loans have a maturity of one year or less. The prevailing prime rate is that posted at a majority of 31 large banks.
Source: Board of Governors of the Federal Reserve System.

Customer Relationships, Compensating Balances, and the Prime Rate

The customer-relationship, compensating-balance, and prime-rate conventions are integral parts of the bank loan-pricing function.[6] The fact that bank loan (and investment) policies have been strategically subordinated to the customer-service aspects of banking has been stressed by Hodgman [1963]. Hodgman contends that these practices have evolved for the purpose of restricting interbank competition for prime depositor-borrower customers. Since banks like customers who have large deposit balances, borrow regularly, and have been with the bank for a long time, these customers receive preferential treatment, especially when credit is tight. Such characteristics usually are associated with commercial or corporate customers; they are the bank's prime depositor-borrower customers. Kane and Malkiel [1965] refer to these customers as a bank's L* (read L-star) customers. They are those depositor-borrowers whose relationships play an important and favorable role in calculations of the bank's expected profits and aggregate risk exposure, which explains why they receive preferential treatment.

According to Hodgman, the coordinated use of the compensating-balance and prime-rate conventions may serve as an effective device to restrain interbank competition for L* customers. With a national prime rate and generally accepted minimum compensating-balance requirements, the extension of credit, especially when money is tight, and the provision of customer service are the key instruments in interbank competition for L* customers. Kane and Malkiel stress the point that to turn down L* requests for loan accommodation is to introduce explicit and ascertainable risks of customer alienation that could endanger deposit relationships. On balance, the concept of the *customer relationship* represents the strategic combination of customer service, loans, and deposits that gives commercial banking its unique institutional character.

The Options Available to Lenders and Borrowers

Let's look, in a nontechnical way, at the options available to lenders and borrowers. Beginning with the lenders, they have the option (1) to lend or not to lend, (2) to price on a fixed- or variable-rate basis, (3) to tailor the nonrate provisions of the loan agreement to suit the needs of the borrower and to protect the interests of the bank, and (4) to call the loan. In contrast, borrowers have the option (1) to take their business elsewhere, (2) to default, (3) to pay slowly, and (4) to prepay with or without refinancing. Recognition of these options serves to highlight the importance of the overall customer relationship to the lending process. For example, consider the potential ramifications on the customer relationship of the lender's decision to refuse a loan request, to price a loan too high, to make nonrate provisions too restrictive, or to call a loan at an inopportune time for the borrower. Moreover, since the customer relationship is a two-way street, the borrower must be aware of the consequences of defaulting, paying slowly, or prepaying.

Option-pricing theory (OPT) focuses upon the analysis of the determinants of the prices of contingent claims or options. Since options on loan contracts are common, lenders need to know how to value them. Lenders are especially concerned about borrowers who exercise their option to default, since loan losses affect both the level

---

[6] A compensating balance refers to the percentage of the borrower's loan that must be kept on deposit with the bank as additional compensation for the loan. If the balance requirement is effective, then it increases the real cost of the loan.

and the variability of bank earnings. The pricing of loan contracts may create adverse incentives that encourage borrowers to exercise their options to default. Obviously, lenders want to avoid such pricing schemes. Another borrower option that affects bank earnings is the prepayment option. Prepayments are a refinancing phenomenon whereby borrowers attempt to reduce interest expenses during periods of declining interest rates. Reduced interest expenses for borrowers mean reduced interest revenues for lenders. To discourage prepayments, lenders frequently build prepayment penalties into loan agreements. One of the interesting areas of OPT research has been the application of the theory to the valuation of the complex options involved in loan agreements (e.g., the evaluation of the default and prepayment options in the mortgage contract).

In the securities market, an *option* refers to the opportunity to trade in the future on terms that are fixed today. The basis determinants of the value of an option are (1) the exercise price, (2) the exercise date, (3) the risk of the underlying asset, and (4) the risk-free rate of interest. Developing analogous concepts and measures for the options contained in loan contracts is the key to bridging the gap between OPT and institutional banking. Lenders need to understand when and how borrowers will be tempted to trade against them in loan agreements. (See the appendix to Chapter 8 for an application of OPT.)

Prime-Plus Pricing Versus Prime-Times Pricing

A common banking practice is to price credit on the basis of markups on the prime rate. The standard procedure is an additive one such that borrowers are quoted something like "prime + 2," which means the prime rate plus 200 basis points or 2 percent. Given the existence of the discount prime rate, certain L^* customers might be quoted "prime − 2."

An alternative to prime-plus pricing is prime-times pricing, which is a multiplicative formula rather than an additive one. In general, this pricing procedure can be expressed as:

Quoted Rate = Multiplicative Adjustment Factor × Prime Rate

To illustrate, if the prime rate is 10 percent and the adjustment factor is 1.1, then the borrower is quoted a rate of 11 percent = 1.1 × 10 percent. Suppose that the spread between the quoted rate and the prime rate accurately compensates the bank for the borrower's greater default risk relative to that of a prime borrower. In this case, the prime-plus formula would be "prime + 1." However, notice what happens if rates change. Suppose the prime increases by 100 basis points to 11 percent. If the borrower has a variable-rate loan outstanding, it would reprice to 12 percent under the additive rule. However, under the multiplicative formula, the loan would reprice to 12.1 percent (= 1.1 × 11 percent). In contrast, if the prime rate falls by 100 basis points (from 10 percent to 9 percent), the loan would reprice at 10 percent under the "plus" scheme and at 9.9 percent under the "times" approach.

Assuming the loan is priced correctly when the multiplicative factor is set and assuming the prime rate is at some historic norm (i.e., it is neither too high nor too low), the prime-times approach has an adjustment procedure implying that as interest rates increase, the borrower is more likely to default. Accordingly, the bank is entitled to greater compensation because it is bearing more risk. Moreover, the prime-times approach is symmetrical because it implies that when rates are declining, borrowers are more likely to be able to repay their loans. Accordingly, it permits them to share this reduced risk with lenders by receiving a lower loan rate. To attempt to maximize loan revenue, the lender's strategy should be to use prime-times pricing when interest rates are expected to rise and to use prime-plus pricing when rates are expected to fall. In contrast, however, borrowers should negotiate for the opposite configuration of pricing formulas.

A RISK-MANAGEMENT APPROACH TO LOAN PRICING

Once the decision to grant credit has been made, the terms of the loan must be set, including the price of the loan or its rate of interest. Nonprice terms include such items as compensating-balance requirements, size of the loan, maturity, and collateral requirements. The concept of loan pricing within a risk–return framework is presented in Figure 19-3. Using the credit-scoring concept to capture the risk element in lending, both the decision to grant credit and a risk-based pricing scheme are illustrated. Given the bank's cutoff score, all customers with scores below it are eligible for credit. Within this group, the less risky a customer is (i.e., the more creditworthy he or she is), the lower the loan price will be, other things equal. For example, as depicted in Figure 19-3, Customer A has a better credit score than Customer B and therefore A is charged a lower price than B. Customers C and D, who are denied credit by the bank, are not excluded from the credit market; they are

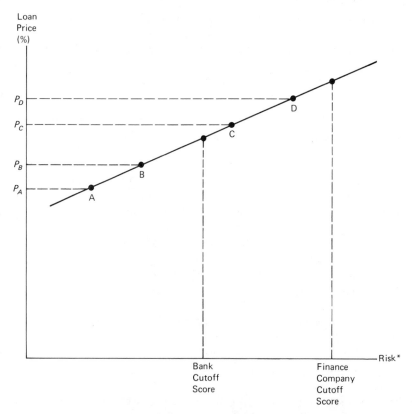

Figure 19-3   Loan Pricing. "Risk" indicates that the risk factor is captured by a credit score, with a low score being good and a high score bad

acceptable risks for the finance company. Since Customer C is more creditworthy than Customer D, C is charged a lower price than D by the finance company. In practice, bank loan losses on consumer installment loans are relatively low, reflecting the high credit standards imposed by banks on borrowers. In contrast, loss rates on loans at consumer finance companies are roughly four times higher, reflecting their lower credit standards. As a result, they have to charge higher rates of interest.

Loan pricing usually involves some combination of target ROE and markup pricing. Buck [1979] has suggested a risk-management approach to pricing loans that employs these concepts. The basic idea in his framework is to develop a unique target price for each loan, including adjustments for identifiable risks and costs. He defines the profit element as a margin over the cost and risk factors. Thus, the target price equals the cost factor plus the risk factor plus the profit margin. To illustrate, consider the following example:[7]

Profit Margin	.86%
Costs:	
Funds	12.00%
Overhead	.75%
Risks:	
Credit	1.25%
Maturity	.65%
Collateral Value	.10%
TARGET VALUE	15.61%

Let's consider the components of the target price. To calculate the target profit margin, the bank is required to establish a desired ROE. Given the bank's leverage (L) and its tax rate (t), Buck shows that the margin (M) is:

$$M = \frac{ROE \times L}{1 - t} - L \times C \tag{19-6}$$

where C is the bank's cost of funds and L is measured by the bank's capital-to-asset ratio, $L = EM^{-1}$. Given target ROE = 15%, L = 8%, t = 34%, and C = 12%, the value of M is 0.86 percent, that is,

$$M = \frac{.15 \times .08}{.66} - .08 \times .12 = .0086.$$

To determine the costs associated with a loan, the bank needs to know its cost of funds and its overhead or administrative expenses for the loan function. The cost of funds should reflect the marginal cost of all funds used to support the loan. The administrative costs of the loan function usually are based on functional-cost data, cost-accounting figures allocated to average assets, or the bank's best estimates of the costs. According to Buck, the particular method is not important as long as management is satisfied that the costs of the loan function are covered. Total costs (12.75%) are the sum of the money (12%) and overhead expenses (.75%) and enter the target-price calculation.

---

[7] The cost of funds in this example can be viewed as the weighted-average marginal cost of capital. The target price, then, is a risk-adjusted discount rate, if the profit margin is excluded.

Regarding the risk components, credit, maturity, and collateral-value risks are considered in the example. The credit-risk premium could be provided by a credit-scoring model or by a markup scheme based upon Moody's ratings. For example, the latter might be expressed as follows:

Rating	Credit-Risk Premium
Aaa	.10%
Aa	.40%
A	.75%
Baa	1.25%
Ba	2.00%
B or below	No credit granted

The borrower in this example is assumed to have a Baa rating and therefore a risk premium of 1.25 percent is assigned. The longer the maturity of a loan, the greater is the interest-rate risk and the risk that the borrower's creditworthiness might deteriorate. As a result, the longer the maturity of a loan, the larger the maturity-risk premium should be. The use of variable-rate loans can be used to offset interest-rate risk. However, a maturity-risk premium still might be required to compensate for potential deterioration in the borrower's credit strength. *Collateral-value risk* refers to potential decreases in collateral value relative to the loan balance for a secured loan. Collateral that is expected to hold its value over the term of the loan (e.g., corporate aircraft) will have little collateral-value risk, whereas collateral that depreciates more rapidly (e.g., restaurant equipment) has greater collateral-value risk. A simple way to classify collateral-value risk is to use *good, average,* and *poor* categories. In the above example, the maturity-risk factor is .65 percent (indicating an intermediate-term loan) and the collateral-value factor is .10 percent (indicating average risk). The sum of these components equals the target price of 15.61 percent.

The target price of 15.61 percent can be translated into our prime-plus or price-times formulas as follows. Let's assume the prime rate is 13.10 percent (= 12% cost of money, .75% overhead, and .10% credit risk). The target price of 15.61 percent translates into a prime-plus formula of "prime + 2.51" and a prime-times formula of "1.192 × prime." For practical purposes, the borrower could be quoted "prime + 2.5" or "1.2 × prime."

The loan-pricing framework discussed in this section is a practical one that builds on the fundamental concepts of a risk–return trade-off and a target ROE. Although the determination and implementation of the loan-pricing mechanism require some subjective judgments about the cost and risk components of the target price, the establishment of such a framework provides a foundation for consistent decision making by loan officers. Another factor that should be incorporated into the analysis is the portfolio-risk premium discussed earlier. A loan that promises "diversification benefits" is more valuable to the bank's loan portfolio than one that lacks the potential. The former deserves a discount, whereas the latter might even be assessed a surcharge. Both of these objectives could be achieved by employing the following strategy: Borrowers with diversification potential could be priced on a prime-plus basis if rates were expected to rise and on a prime-times basis if rates were expected to fall. This strategy would reward them relative to other variable-rate borrowers who were priced differently In contrast to "milk" profits from less desirable borrowers, they should be priced at prime-times if rates are expected to rise and prime-plus if rates are expected to fall.

CHAPTER SUMMARY

This chapter has focused on the management of credit risk in terms of its diversification and pricing. The key conceptual devices employed were (1) a risk-premium or spread model, including the notion of a portfolio risk premium; (2) a credit-rationing model; (3) the relationships between diversification and contagion, and contagion and credit rationing; (4) a loan-pricing model à la the CAPM; (5) the interaction between interest-rate risk and credit risk, (6) the prime-rate convention in conjunction with the notions of compensating balances, the customer relationship, and prime rate-pricing formulas; and (7) a risk-management approach to loan pricing. These concepts, along with the foundations of credit analysis established in the previous chapter, provide an overall analytical framework for understanding bank credit risk and its management. In the next chapter, we turn to some operational aspects of bank lending and loan administration.

LIST OF KEY WORDS AND CONCEPTS

Adverse selection
Bank–customer relationship
Compensating balances
Contagion
Continental Illinois
Contract loan rate
Corporate philosophies (without room for analysis of risk)
Cost of funds
Credit rationing
Default-risk premium (DRP or d)
Diversification

Energy and farm banks (of the 1980s)
Expected return
Incentive effects
Interest-rate risk (interaction with credit risk)
Overhead costs (of making loans)
Prime rate and prime-rate pricing (plus versus times)
Portfolio-risk premium (PRP or p)
Risk-free rate
Target ROE and markup loan pricing
Variable-rate pricing

REVIEW/DISCUSSION QUESTIONS

1. When (not "if") you make it to the corporate board rooms of America, how will you be (not "Will you be?") a champion of sound risk management and a spokesperson for "quality growth"? Are these concepts you should be proud to recommend? Why aren't these principles found in all managers, directors, and their corporate documents? Are "hired guns" (i.e., "expert witnesses") "mental prostitutes"? Ask your instructor (a) if he/she has ever been "used" in this fashion and (b) for some "war stories."
2. Carefully distinguish between the default-risk premium and the portfolio-risk premium.
3. What are the interrelationships, if any, among portfolio diversification, specialized bank lending, and bank loan losses?
4. What are the interrelationships, if any, among variable-rate pricing, interstate-rate risk, and credit risk?

5. Figure 19-1 shows the relationship between the expected return on a loan and the loan contract rate. Why does this locus of points have an inverted U-shape? What is the difference between adverse selection and incentive effects, and what role do they play in this relationship?

6. Credit rationing offers a supply-side approach to loan pricing. Explain what this means. Using Figure 19-2, show your ability to do some mental gymnastics by conducting the following comparative-statics experiments: Describe and draw pictures to illustrate (a) an increase (decrease) in the risk-free rate and (b) an increase (decrease) in perceived riskiness for each of the three groups. How does contagion or the lack of it affect your analyses and your pictures?

7. To what extent are the conventions of the prime rate, compensating balance, and customer relationship integral parts of the bank-loan pricing function? Distinguish between the myth and realities of the prime rate. Why would a bank be willing to lend at below the prime rate? What is the bank-customer relationship of a borrower who receives discounts from the prime rate likely to be like?

8. What are the basic ingredients in a risk-management approach to loan pricing?

MATCHING QUIZ

Directions: Select the letter from the right-hand column that best matches the item in the left-hand column.

___ 1. Incentive effects	A. Favors bank when rates are rising
___ 2. Interest-rate risk	B. Favors bank when rates are falling
___ 3. Overhead costs	C. Part of risk management approach
___ 4. Prime rate	D. Protects against interest-rate risk
___ 5. Portfolio-risk premium	E. Major cost of making loans
___ 6. Adverse selection	F. Encourage risk-taking
___ 7. Bank–customer relationship	G. May interact with credit risk
___ 8. Compensating balances	H. Form of implicit pricing
___ 9. Contagion	I. Benchmark rate subject to discounting
___ 10. Continental Illinois	
___ 11. Contract loan rate	J. Mainly people and paper costs
___ 12. Default-risk premium	K. Covariation important here
___ 13. Diversification	L. Kane and Malkiel's L* customer
___ 14. Energy and farm banks	M. Bailed out in 1984
	N. Many closed in the 1980s

___ 15. Expected return

___ 16. Risk-free rate

___ 17. Corporate philosophies

___ 18. Cost of funds

___ 19. Credit rationing

___ 20. Target ROE

___ 21. Variable-rate pricing

___ 22. Prime plus

___ 23. Prime times

___ 24. Too-big-to-fail doctrine

___ 25. CAPM and market model

O. Default-risk anchor rate

P. Supply-side approach

Q. Must consider risk

R. Begins to decline at some point

S. Reward for bearing default risk

T. Reflection of greater intervention

U. Macroeconomic concern among big banks

V. Lowers expected return

W. $(i + 1)/(1 - p - d)$

X. Test for announcement effects

Y. Gospel of portfolio theory

PROBLEMS

1. Given a prime rate of 8.5 percent (February 4, 1988) and a perceived default-risk premium of 200 basis points for Latigid Manufacturing Company, determine the interest rate on its variable-rate, three-year term loan under the following interest-rate and pricing scenarios.

Year	Prime Rate	Prime Plus	Prime Times
1	8.5		
2	10.0		
3	9.5		

If the bank had perfect information regarding the future course of interest rates and complete flexibility in structuring the loan pricing scheme for Latigid, what should the bank do if (a) it wants to cultivate the customer relationship versus (b) it wants to maximize interest revenue?

2. Given the following information, determine the bank's target prices for customers A, B, and C and describe their relative risk profiles.

Bank Information	
Target ROE	= .20
Total capital	= $1 billion
Total assets	= $20 billion
Cost of funds	= .15
Tax rate	= .46
Loan overhead	= .0075

Customer information:

Risks	A	B	C
Credit	0.0	.0150	.0200
Maturity	0.0	.0025	.0075
Collateral value	0.0	.0000	.0025

3. Determine the loan contract rates and the dollar amounts that the lender should receive back for each dollar lent for each of the following would-be borrowers. Assume that the risk-free rate is 10 percent and that the loans are for one year. Which borrowers are the most attractive ones? Why?

Customer	Expected Default Rate	Portfolio-Risk Premium
A	.01	.01
B	.03	.03
C	.05	.05
D	.05	−.05

SELECTED REFERENCES

Buck, Walter H. [1979]. "Risk-Management Approach to Pricing Loans and Leases." *Journal of Commercial Bank Lending* (April), pp. 2–15.

Clark, Lindley H., Jr. [1981]. "Lending at Less Than Prime Rates Produces a PR Problem for Banks." *The Wall Street Journal* (February 27), Section 2.

Fischer, Gerald C. [1982]. *The Prime: Myth and Reality*. Philadelphia: Temple University.

Flannery, Mark J. [1985]. "A Portfolio View of Loan Selection and Pricing," in *Handbook for Banking Strategy*, R. C. Aspinwall and R. A. Eisenbeis, eds. New York: Wiley, pp. 457–472.

Goldfeld, Stephen M., and Richard E. Quandt. [1976]. "Techniques for Estimating Switching Regressions," in *Studies in Nonlinear Estimation*, Goldfeld and Quandt (eds.) Cambridge, MA: Ballinger Publisher.

Hale, Roger H. [1983]. *Credit Analysis: A Complete Guide*. New York: Wiley.

Hodgman, Donald R. [1963]. *Commercial Bank Loan and Investment Policy*. Champaign, IL: University of Illinois, Bureau of Economic and Business Research.

Kane, Edward J., and Burton G. Malkiel., [1965]. Bank Portfolio Allocation, Deposit Variability, and the Availability Doctrine." *Quarterly Journal of Economics* (February), pp. 113–134.

Kane, Edward J., and Haluk Unal. [1988]. "Change in Market Assessments of Deposit-Institution Riskiness." *Journal of Financial Services Research* (forthcoming).

Prochnow, Herbert V. [1981]. *Bank Credit*. New York: Harper & Row.

Santomero, Anthony M. [1985]. "Pricing Business Credit," in *Handbook for Banking Strategy*, R. C. Aspinwall and R. A. Eisenbeis, eds. New York: Wiley, pp. 589–606.

Saunders, Anthony. [1987]. "The Interbank Market, Contagion Effects, and International Financial Crises," in *Threats to International Financial Stability*, Richard Portes and Alexander K. Swoboda, eds. Cambridge: Cambridge University Press.

Scott, George C. [1972]. "How To Price A Loan." *New York State Banker* (November 6), pp. 2, 6–7.

Sihler, William W. [1981]. *Classics in Commercial Bank Lending*. Philadelphia: Robert Morris Associates.

Simonson, Donald G., and Edmond E. Pace. [1977]. "Loan Pricing (A Training Feature)." *Journal of Commercial Bank Lending* (September), pp. 813–822.

Sinkey, Joseph F., Jr. [1985]. "Regulatory Attitudes Toward Risk," in *Handbook for Banking Strategy*, R. C. Aspinwall and R. A. Eisenbeis, eds. New York: Wiley, pp. 347–380.

———— 1979. *Problem and Failed Institutions in the Commercial Banking Industry*. Greenwich, CT: JAI Press.

Stiglitz, J. E., and A. Weiss. [1981]. "Credit Rationing in Markets with Imperfect Information," *American Economic Review*, (June), pp. 373–409.

CHAPTER 20

Management of Credit Risk III: Lending Practice and Loan Administration

---

ACRONYM GUIDE TO KEY WORDS

C&I = Commercial and industrial (loans)
FCA = Functional cost analysis
LBO = Leveraged buyout
LDC = Less-developed country
REIT = Real estate investment trust

LOAN QUALITY IS THE NAME OF THE GAME

J. Richard Fredericks is a bank security analyst for Montgomery Securities in San Francisco. On February 12, 1988, he appeared on the television show *Wall Street Week* (with Louis Rukeyser on PBS). The scriptwriter's "hook" for the show was the "number one threat to the U.S. and international banking system: third world debt, or bank loans to less-developed countries (LDCs)." After Fredericks said he thought the banking system was "safe," the Q&A discussion turned to the criteria he used to pick bank stocks. What does a bank stock analyst, like Fredericks, look at to separate the "winners" from the "losers"? His two main criteria are capital and earnings, or what he calls "fortressed balance sheets." Beyond earnings and capital, he looks for "discipline" with respect to costs, loan losses, and loan growth.

Let's consider the importance of the loan portfolio in Fredericks's analytical framework, as interpreted by yours truly. It goes like this. Bank capital is important. A bank's main source of capital is its earnings. Its main source of earnings is revenue from loans. "Discipline" of the loan portfolio means controlling its operating costs, losses, and growth. Next to its cost of money, a bank's major operating cost is the one associated with the administration of its loan portfolio (e.g., salaries and other overhead expenses). Banks whose earnings and capital become impaired typically have lost control (discipline) over the growth and quality of their loan portfolios. When this occurs in conjunction with adverse external conditions (i.e., the fifth C of creditworthiness), banks are in financial trouble. Particular areas of financial difficulty for banks in the 1980s have been energy, agricultural, and real estate loans, mainly in the Southwestern part of the United States. Regarding the latter, acquisition, development, and construction (ADC) loans, especially by thrift institutions in Houston and

Dallas, were problem areas. The LDC debt problem has mainly been confined to the money-center banks (e.g., Manufacturers Hanover with 352 percent of its year-end 1987 capital in loans to such countries and BankAmerica with 349 percent). In the early to mid 1970s, real estate lending and bank associations with real estate investment trusts (REITs) were a sore spot. Regarding the future, some analysts and bankers see leveraged buyouts (LBOs) as a potential dark cloud on the banking horizon. On balance, loan quality problems in the banking and thrift industries can be traced to overaggressive lending practices and disregard for the principle of diversification.

DELEGATED MONITORING AND THE KEYS TO SUCCESSFUL MANAGEMENT OF THE LOAN PORTFOLIO

Banks serve as delegated monitors for their depositors and creditors. As opposed to the theoretical approach of the previous two chapters, this chapter focuses on some practical aspects of the business of lending and the administration of the loan function. On balance, the essence of these two tasks can be captured by the notion of "monitoring." If the inability of a bank to monitor and control ("discipline") the costs, loan losses, and growth of its loan portfolio is *the* source of downfall for a bank, then the flip side of this record should be *the* key to bank success in the area of loan management. Accordingly, this chapter focuses on how banks monitor the costs, quality, and growth of their loans. Careful monitoring of these three areas provides the "discipline" a bank needs to successfully manage its loan portfolio. Specifically, we focus on the kinds of loans banks make, the terms of lending, the costs of making loans and the profitability of individual customer accounts, the various techniques banks use to monitor their loan portfolios, various measures of loan quality, and the actual loan policy used by a major regional bank.

A LOOK AT A BANK'S LOAN PORTFOLIO

Wachovia Bank and Trust Company (WB&T), National Association, of Winston-Salem, N.C., is a major commercial bank in the Southeast. WB&T and the First National Bank of Atlanta are the lead banks of First Wachovia, a bank holding company formed by the "merger of equals" between the two parent companies. First Wachovia is a "superregional" bank/BHC, and by the way was on Fredericks's recommended buy list on February 12, 1988. (As an exercise and assuming your investment period extended from the first business day after February 12 until the time you read this, determine the holding period return on an investment in First Wachovia, which trades on the New York Stock Exchange). We will use data from WB&T's balance sheet (or "Report of Condition," to use regulatory jargon) to illustrate various aspects of a bank's loan portfolio.

The Kinds of Loans Banks Make

Bank annual reports contain different amounts of "gloss" and information (see Chapter 3 for our discussion of "lead steers" and the information content of such reports). To provide a uniform framework for analyzing the various kinds of loans banks make, we use "Schedule RC-C—Loans and Lease Financing Receivables" from WB&T's Report of Condition filed with the Office of the Comptroller of the Currency at the close of business December 31, 1987. The label "RC-C" stands for Schedule C of the bank's Report of Condition (RC). The schedule, which is shown in Table 20-1,

TABLE 20-1 Schedule RC-C: Loans and Lease Financing Receivables
Wachovia Bank and Trust Company, National Association
December 31, 1987

	(Column A) Consolidated Bank	(Column B) Domestic Offices	Item Number
	$ Thousands	$ Thousands	
1. Loans secured by real estate	1,917,965		1.
a. Construction and land development		343,390	1.a.
b. Secured by farmland (including farm residential and other improvements)		51,817	1.b.
c. Secured by 1–4 family residential properties			
(1) Revolving, open-end loans secured by 1–4 family residential properties and extended under lines of credit		200,821	1.c.(1)
(2) All other loans secured by 1–4 family residential properties		570,758	1.c.(2)
d. Secured by multifamily (5 or more) residential properties		61,563	1.d.
e. Secured by nonfarm nonresidential properties		689,616	1.e.
2. Loans to depository institutions:			
a. To commercial banks in the U.S.		9,737	2.a.
(1) To U.S. branches and agencies of foreign banks	69		2.a.(1)
(2) To other commercial banks in the U.S.	9,668		2.a.(2)
b. To other depository institutions in the U.S.	20,057	20,057	2.b.
c. To banks in foreign countries		1,998	2.c.
(1) To foreign branches of other U.S. banks	None		2.c.(1)
(2) To other banks in foreign countries	1,998		2.c.(2)
3. Loans to finance agricultural production and other loans to farmers	32,805	32,805	3.
4. Commercial and industrial loans:			
a. To U.S. addressees (domicile)	2,376,158	2,376,158	4.a.
b. To non-U.S. addressees (domicile)	97,816	33,286	4.b.
5. Acceptances of other banks:			
a. Of U.S. banks	None	None	5.a.
b. Of foreign banks	None	None	5.b.
6. Loans to individuals for household, family, and other personal expenditures (i.e., consumer loans) (includes purchased paper)		1,978,762	6.
a. Credit cards and related plans (includes check credit and other revolving credit plans)	305,442		6.a.
b. Other (includes single payment, installment, and all student loans)	1,673,320		6.b.
7. Loans to foreign governments and official institutions (including foreign central banks)	37,388	33,375	7.
8. Obligations (other than securities and leases) of states and political subdivisions in the U.S. (includes nonrated industrial development obligations):			
a. Taxable obligations	None	None	8.a.
b. Tax-exempt obligations	494,458	494,458	8.b.
9. Other loans	311,387		9.
a. Loans for purchasing or carrying securities (secured and unsecured)		16,859	9.a.
b. All other loans (exclude consumer loans)		294,528	9.b.
10. Lease financing receivables (net of unearned income)		37,270	10.
a. Of U.S. addressees (domicile)	37,270		10.a.
b. Of non-U.S. addressees (domicile)	None		10.b.
11. LESS: Any unearned income on loans reflected in items 1–9 above	8,061	8,061	11.
12. Total loans and leases, net of unearned income (sum of items 1 through 10 minus item 11) (total of column A must equal Schedule RC. item 4.a)	7,307,740	7,239,197	12.

has two columns: column A is for the "Consolidated Bank," which means domestic plus foreign operations, and column B is for "Domestic Offices" only. Looking at line 12, total loans and leases, we can see that WB&T does little foreign lending, as the difference between columns A and B is only $68.5 million, less than 1 percent of its loan portfolio. Also note that the name of the schedule gives too much weight to "lease financing receivables," as they account for only $37.3 million of lending activity, or .5 percent of the total portfolio.

Let's look at the composition of WB&T's $7.3 billion loan portfolio. Three categories of loans dominate it:

	$ Billions	Percent
Commercial and Industrial loans (line 4a + 4b)	2.473	33.8
Loans to individuals (line 6)	1.978	27.1
Loans secured by real estate (line 1)	1.917	26.2
Subtotal	6.368	87.1
Other loans (all other lines)	.940	12.9
TOTAL (line 12)	7.308	100.0

For WB&T, the major component of "other loans" is in the form of "obligations" to state and local governments, as shown in line 8b. These tax-exempt loans (e.g., for industrial development) totaled $494.4 million, 52.5 percent of the other category. Since WB&T's markets are primarily non-agricultural, its farm loans (line 3) amount to only $32.8 million, less than .5 percent.

To put WB&T's loan portfolio in perspective, let's compare it to some of its other financial characteristics. Relative to its total assets of $11.7 billion and its equity capital of $793 million, WB&T's ratio of loans to assets is 62.4 percent and its multiple of loans to equity capital is 9.2, compared to its equity multiplier of 14.75. The portfolio of loans and leases generated income and fees of almost $620 million during 1987 for a gross portfolio yield of 8.48 based on year-end loan balances. For the three main components of WB&T's loan portfolio, the revenue and yield for 1987 were

	$ Millions	Yield (%)
C&I loans	189.5	7.66
Loans to individuals	215.0	10.87
Real estate loans	157.9	8.24
TOTAL/AVERAGE	562.4	8.83

Since the yield figures do not take account of loan losses, they are preloan loss (and pretax) returns. Given the loan revenue of $620 million, these three categories of loans accounted for 90 percent of loan income and fees. Compared to WB&T's total interest income of $834 million in 1987 (from loans, securities, and other activities), they generated 67 percent of the bank's revenue.

A complete schedule of interest income corresponding to the balance sheet items shown in Table 20-1 is shown in Table 20-2. Item 1.a.(2) in the table represents the interest income generated by WB&T's foreign loans. The revenue of $7.4 million on an investment of $68.5 million represents a gross return of 10.79 percent.

Now that you have some idea of the kinds of loans banks make and the revenues they generate from them, let's turn to some measures of loan quality.

TABLE 20-2   Total Interest Income for the Period January 1, 1987, to December 31, 1987, Wachovia Bank and Trust Company, National Association

	$ Thousands	Item
1. Interest income:		
a. Interest and fee Income on loans:		
(1) In domestic offices:		
(a) Loans secured by real estate	157,865	1.a.(1)(a)
(b) Loans to depository institutions	2,117	1.a.(1)(b)
(c) Loans to finance agricultural production and other loans to farmers	3,614	1.a.(1)(c)
(d) Commercial and industrial loans	189,472	1.a.(1)(d)
(e) Acceptances of other banks	None	1.a.(1)(e)
(f) Loans to individuals for household, family, and other personal expenditures:		
(1) Credit cards and related plans	37,746	1.a.(1)(f)(1)
(2) Other	177,300	1.a.(1)(f)(2)
(g) Loans to foreign governments and official institutions	1,775	1.a.(1)(g)
(h) Obligations (other than securities and leases) of states and political subdivisions in the U.S.:		
(1) Taxable obligations	None	1.a.(1)(h)(1)
(2) Tax-exempt obligations	34,308	1.a.(1)(h)(2).
(i) All other loans in domestic offices	5,559	1.a.(1)(i)
(2) In foreign offices, Edge and Agreement subsidiaries, and IBFs	7,391	1.a.(2)
b. Income from lease financing receivables:		
(1) Taxable leases	2,828	1.b.(1)
(2) Tax-exempt leases	None	1.b.(2)
c. Interest income on balances due from depository institutions:[a]		
(1) In domestic offices	None	1.c.(1)
(2) In foreign offices, Edge and Agreement subsidiaries, and IBFs	28,311	1.c.(2)
d. Interest and divided income on securities:		
(1) U.S. Treasury securities and U.S. Government agency and corporation obligations	93,885	1.d.(1)
(2) Securities issued by states and political subdivisions in the U.S.		
(a) Taxable securities	None	1.d.(2)(a)
(b) Tax-exempt securities	51,254	1.d.(2)(b)
(3) Other domestic securities (debt and equity)	4,156	1.d.(3)
(4) Foreign securities (debt and equity)	4	1.d.(4)
e. Interest income from assets held in trading accounts	13,469	1.e.
f. Interest income on federal funds sold and securities purchased under agreements to resell in domestic offices of the bank and of its Edge and Agreement subsidiaries, and in IBFs	23,115	1.f.
g. Total interest income (sum of items 1.a through 1.f)	834,169	1.g.

[a] Includes interest income on time certificates of deposit not held in trading accounts.
Source: Consolidated Report of Income, December 31, 1987. Wachovia Bank and Trust Company, National Association.

MEASURES OF BANK LOAN QUALITY

Net loan losses, provision for loan losses, allowance for loan losses, past due loans, nonperforming loans, and nonaccruing loans are measures of bank loan quality. Tables 20-3 and 20-4 present data for each of these measures for WB&T for the year 1987. Let's look at these data and discuss each of the measures.

TABLE 20-3   Schedule RI-B: Charge-Offs and Recoveries and Changes in Allowance for Loan and Lease Losses
Wachovia Bank and Trust Company, National Association December 31, 1987

Part I. Charge-Offs and Recoveries on Loans and Leases
Part I excludes charge-offs and recoveries through the allocated transfer risk reserve.

	(Column A) Charge-Offs	(Column B) Recoveries	
	Calendar Year-to-Date		
	$ Thousands	$ Thousands	Item
1. Loans secured by real estate:			
a. To U.S. addressees (domicile)	197	43	1.a.
b. To non-U.S. addressees (domicile)	None	None	I.b.
2. Loans to depository institutions and acceptances of other banks:			
a. To U.S. banks and other U.S. depository institutions	None	None	2.a.
b. To foreign banks	None	340	2.b.
3. Loans to finance agricultural production and other loans to farmers	310	99	3.
4. Commercial and industrial loans:			
a. To U.S. addressees (domicile)	5,933	752	4.a.
b. To non-U.S. addressees (domicile)	14,454	141	4.b.
5. Loans to individuals for household, family, and other personal expenditures:			
a. Credit cards and related plans	2,456	641	5.a.
b. Other	2,154	452	5.b.
6. Loans to foreign governments and official institutions	14,416	27	6.
7. All other loans	49	16	7.
8. Lease financing receivables:			
a. Of U.S. addressees (domicile)	None	None	8.a.
b. Of non-U.S. addressees (domicile)	None	None	8.b.
9. Total (sum of items 1 through 8)	39,969	2,511	9.

Memorandum
To be completed by national banks only.

	Cumulative Amounts from January 1, 1986, to date		
1. Charge-offs and recoveries of Special-Category Loans, as defined for this Call Report by the Comptroller of the Currency	None	None	M.1.

Part II. Changes in Allowance for Loan and Lease Losses and in Allocated Transfer Risk Reserve

	(Column A) Allowance for Loan and Lease Losses	(Column B) Allocated Transfer Risk Reserve	
	$ Thousands	$ Thousands	Item
1. Balance originally reported in the December 31, 1986, Reports of Condition and Income	78,580	None	1.
2. Recoveries (column A must equal part 1, item 9, column B above)	2,511	None	2.
3. LESS: Charge-offs (column A must equal part 1, item 9, column A above)	39,969	None	3.
4. Provision (column A must equal Schedule R1, item 4.a; column B must equal Schedule R1, item 4.b)	57,147	None	4.
5. Adjustments (see instructions for this schedule)	None	None	5.
6. Balance end of current period (sum of items 1 through 5) (column A must equal Schedule RC, item 4.b; column B must equal Schedule RC, item 4.c)	98,269	None	6.

Source: Consolidated Report of Income, December 31, 1987. Wachovia Bank and Trust Company, National Association.

TABLE 20-4 Schedule RC-N: Past Due and Nonaccrual Loans and Leases Wachovia Bank and Trust Company, National Association December 31, 1987

	(Column A) Past Due 30 through 89 Days and Still Accruing	(Column B) Past Due 90 Days or More and Still Accruing	(Column C) Nonaccrual	Item
	$ Thousands	$ Thousands	$ Thousands	
1. Loans secured by real estate:				
a. To U.S. addressees (domicile)	30,132	1,190	2,459	1.a.
b. To non-U.S. addressees (domicile)	None	None	None	1.b.
2. Loans to finance agricultural production and other loans to farmers	360	117	206	2.
3. Commercial and industrial loans:				
a. To U.S. addressees (domicile)	18,597	4,249	2,290	3.a.
b. To non-U.S. addressees (domicile)	1,200	None	9,202	3.b.
4. Loans to individuals for household, family, and other personal expenditures	42,231	1,975	693	4.
5. All other loans	17,688	1,571	14,267	5.
6. Lease financing receivables:				
a. Of U.S. addressees (domicile)	None	None	None	6.a.
b. Of non-U.S. addressees (domicile)	None	None	None	6.b.
7. Total (sum of items 1 through 6)	110,208	9,102	29,117	7.
Memorandum				
1. Restructured loans and leases included in item 7 above	None	None	None	M.1.

Note: The information reported in column A and in all of Memorandum item 1 is regarded by the Federal Financial Institutions Examination Council (FFIEC) as confidential.

Source: Consolidated Report of Condition, December 31, 1987. Wachovia Bank and Trust Company, National Association. Association.

Net Loan Losses

Net loan losses are equal to loan charge-offs minus recoveries. This measure is an ex post or after-the-fact indicator of loan quality. For the year 1987, WB&T charged off $40 million in loans and recovered $2.5 million for a net loss of $37.5. Relative to its year-end loan balance of $7.3 billion, the loan-loss rate for 1987 was 0.51 percent. One would assume this is the kind of loan-loss "discipline" bank stock analyst Fredericks has in mind when he picks his "winners." Moreover, the composition of the charge-offs is interesting and insightful. In Table 20-3, lines 4b and 6 amount to $28.8 million of the $40 million in charge-offs. Both of these lines are related to foreign lending activities, line 4b is charge-offs for C&I loans to non-U.S. addressees and line 6 is charge-offs for loans to foreign governments and official institutions. Given the "retreat" regional banks have made from foreign lending (a retreat based on 50 cents on the dollar), such charge-offs should soon be exhausted, which, other things equal, should mean lower loan losses in the future.

Provision for Loan Losses and Allowance for Loan Losses

Provision for loan losses is an expense item which flows through a bank's income-expense statement to a reserve account on the balance sheet called "allowance for loan and lease losses." The provision is, in effect, an estimate designed to keep the bank's ratio of loan-loss allowances to total loans equal to the bank's target ratio, which might be some peer group average or industry norm. Part II of Schedule RI-B in Table 20-3 shows how charge-offs and the provision estimate affect the reserve balance. WB&T started 1987 with a balance in its reserve account of $78.6 million. As shown above, its net charge-offs for 1987 were $37.5 million. Without a provision for 1987, the reserve account would have been diminished by $37.5 million. However, WB&T expensed through the provision account (on a quarterly basis throughout 1987) $57 million to its reserve account. As a result, the balance in the account increased to $98.3 million as of December 31, 1987, a figure which is 1.34 percent of total outstanding loans and leases.

The provision and allowance accounts represent the first line of defense against loan losses. Since some loan losses are a necessary part of the business of lending, most banks like to keep a reserve balance that provides some cushion against *unexpected* loan losses. Of course, as we have emphasized throughout this book, unexpected changes are the source of all risk, whether it is credit, interest-rate, or liquidity risk. In today's banking environment, most banks like, and competitive pressures demand, a ratio of allowance to loans in the range of 1.25 percent to 1.5 percent. A bank's second and third lines of defense against loan losses are its current earnings and its retained earnings. At the extreme, when a bank's "discipline" over its loan portfolio breaks down, loan losses will eat up its allowance account, its current earnings, and its retained earnings; without an infusion of external equity, insolvency and failure result.

Past Due, Nonperforming, and Nonaccrual Loans

Schedule RC-N in Table 20-4 shows how past due and nonaccrual loans are reported by banks to their regulators. Since banks use accrual accounting, as opposed to cash accounting, they record interest and principal payments as being made even if they do not receive the payments. As shown in Table 20-4 columns A, B, and C represent three categories of nonperforming loans: (1) loans past due 30 through 89 days and still accruing (column A), (2) loans past due 90 days or more and still accruing (column B), and (3) nonaccruals (column C). Loans past due 90 days or more usually are described as "nonperforming loans." Nonaccrual loans are ones switched to a cash basis, which means unless payments are actually received they are not recorded. Since bankers and their regulators allow a 29-day grace period before a loan is required to be classified as past due, past dues are recorded beginning with the 30th day. However, most lenders charge a late penalty before the 29th day (e.g., the Sinkeys' mortgage has a 15-day grace period with a late-penalty fee of 5 percent.)

Focusing on Table 20-4, we see that WB&T had past due and nonaccrual loans and leases of $110 million, $9 million, and $29 million across the three categories described above, (i.e., across columns A, B, and C, respectively). If we lump all three of these categories together ($148 million), they amount to roughly 2 percent of outstanding loans and leases, or 2.2 percent using a quarterly average of loans outstanding (i.e., $6.7 billion). Clearly, however, the last two categories are the more serious classifications, and they amount to only .5 percent of WB&T's loan volume.

On an absolute basis, WB&T's loan quality appears to be exceptional. However, to put it in perspective, we need some yardstick for comparison. Such a yardstick is provided by the data in Table 20-5, which shows delinquency rates at large insured commercial banks by type of loan, and in the aggregate for all banks. Since the delinquency rate in Table 20-5 is defined as the ratio of nonaccruals and past due 30 days or more to average loans outstanding, the relevant figure for WB&T is 2.2 percent. Although Table 20-5 does not have data for year-end 1987 (because of reporting lags for industry data), it is clear that WB&T has outstanding loan quality compared to both other large banks ($300 million or more in assets) and to all banks.

TABLE 20-5   Delinquency Rates at Large Insured Commercial Banks, by Type of Loan[a]

Delinquent Loans as a Percent of Average Amount Outstanding, Annual Rate

Type of Loan	1983[b]	1984[b]	1985[b]	1986				1987[c]	
				Q1	Q2	Q3	Q4	Q1	Q2
Real estate loans	6.61	5.79	5.25	5.46	5.30	5.02	5.19	5.44	5.08
Commercial and industrial loans	7.39	6.18	5.59	5.55	5.72	5.79	5.52	6.45	6.33
Consumer loans	2.65	2.59	3.01	3.38	3.20	3.17	3.33	3.44	3.29
Farm loans	10.85	11.14	9.39	12.60	12.52	10.58	10.36	13.87	12.66
Other loans in domestic offices[d]	3.78	2.64	2.47	2.22	2.10	2.04	2.03	7.14	6.77
Loans in foreign offices	4.95	5.76	5.50	4.62	4.55	4.39	4.52	n.a.	n.a.
Total	5.74	5.11	4.73	4.59	4.55	4.44	4.46	5.83	5.57
MEMO									
Total for all banks	5.54	5.01	4.78	4.84	4.79	4.62	4.61	5.72	5.45

[a] Delinquent loans include nonaccrual loans, as well as those past due 30 days or more and still accruing. These data are for banks with at least $300 million in assets, except the last row, which is calculated for all insured U.S.-chartered commercial banks.
[b] Figures for 1983, 1984, and 1985 are averages of quarterly data.
[c] Series break: Beginning in March 1987, banks report delinquent loans in domestic offices and foreign offices on a consolidated basis. Thus, loans previously reported for foreign offices are now included in loans by type. Also, in contrast to earlier data, which are averages of quarter ends, first-quarter data for 1987 are calculated on an end-of-quarter basis.
[d] Beginning in 1987, includes other loans booked in foreign offices.
n.a. Not available.
Source: Federal Reserve Bulletin [January 1988], Table 2, p. 4. Simpson [1988] prepared the article in which this table appeared.

In general, most banks had delinquency rates ranging from 4.5 percent to 5.8 percent over the period 1984 to second quarter 1987. Clearly, when it comes to disciplining the quality of its loan portfolio, WB&T has got it.

Examiner Classified Assets: Substandard, Doubtful, and Loss

The major output of the bank examination process is examiner judgments or perceptions about the quality of a bank's loan portfolio. The process of classifying assets, mainly loans, is more of an "art" than a "science." The objective of the process is to estimate the probability of default for a sample of the bank's loan portfolio. In terms of increasing risk of default, examiner adverse classifications are described as "substandard," "doubtful," and "loss." In addition, examiners have a category called "special mention" for loans that have minor problems such as incomplete documentation. In the CAMEL rating system, described in Chapter 8, the A stands for asset quality, and to refresh your memory C is for capital adequacy, M for management/administration, E for earnings, and L for liquidity. The asset-quality rating is based on the examiner-determined classified assets of substandard, doubtful, and loss. Weights of 20 percent, 50 percent, and 100 percent are applied to these classes, respectively. This weighted dollar amount is then compared to the sum of a bank's loan-loss reserve and equity capital to judge the bank's ability to absorb the implied potential losses associated with the adversely classified assets. A bank's assets are judged for adversity by bank examiners from its supervising agency, federal or state, or both. For a national bank such as WB&T, it's examiners from the OCC. For insured state nonmember banks, it's FDIC examiners, and for state member banks, it's Federal Reserve examiners. In some cases, state-chartered banks are examined by both federal and state regulators.

Since the CAMEL ratings and dollar amounts of a bank's classified assets are considered confidential information by the banking agencies, one needs a "deep throat" to get such data on individual banks (see Sinkey [1979], pp. xxv–xxviii). However, if we take a mapping from WB&T's past due and nonaccrual data in Table 20-4 to the examiner adverse classifications, which seems a reasonable transformation to make, we get a proxy weighted dollar amount of .2($110 million) + .5($9 million) + 1.0($39 million) = $65.5 million. With equity capital of $793 million and a loan-loss reserve of $98 million, WB&T has a substantial cushion to absorb any losses arising from its past due and nonaccrual loans.

The Repricing Risk of a Bank's Loan Portfolio

Schedule RC-J of the Report of Condition, which has been available only since the mid-1980s, is entitled "Repricing Opportunities for Selected Balance Sheet Categories." Our concern here is with the repricing risk of WB&T's loan portfolio and its dollar gap relative to interest-bearing deposits, as another measure of loan quality. WB&T's loan-deposit gaps as of December 31, 1987 were

Repricing Within	Dollar Amounts (Thousands)		
	Loans (L)	Deposits (D)	GAP = L – D
Immediately or 1 day	3,023,015	1,464,484	1,558,531
3 months or less	1,764,311	2,138,620	–374,309
3 to 6 months	165,833	675,251	–509,418
6 to 12 months	282,165	505,729	–223,564
1 to 5 years	1,149,963	365,641	784,322
Over 5 years	901,397	19,886	881,511
TOTAL	7,286,684	5,169,611	2,117,073

The dollar gaps reported above should not be misinterpreted. First, the gaps are not cumulative; and second, they do not cover the entire balance sheet, only loans and interest-bearing deposits. Since WB&T had total assets of $11.7 billion on December 31, 1987, the major rate-sensitive groups excluded are securities ($1.9 billion) and federal funds purchased and repos ($1.45 billion). WB&T's $2.4 billion in noninterest-bearing deposits accounts for the big difference between its interest-bearing assets and liabilities. Finally, because of certain exclusions in the repricing schedule, the total loans from Schedule J above do not match exactly the figure from Schedule C of $7,307,740.

With these caveats in mind, let's look at the pricing of WB&T's loan portfolio. With 41.5 percent of its loans repricing immediately or within one day, the bank is vulnerable to a decline in interest rates but protected against a rise in rates. Moreover, since the volume of immediately repricing deposits is only about one-half of the volume of immediately-repricing assets, WB&T has a positive gap over this interval, which does not change the interpretation of vulnerability to a decline in rates. Over the next year, however, viewed in intervals of 3 months, 3 months, and 6 months, WB&T has (noncumulative) negative gaps within each of the intervals. Nevertheless, on a cumulative basis, WB&T has a positive gap of $452 million on a 12-month horizon. As the horizon is extended beyond one year, the size of the positive gap gets larger. The cumulative gap for all rate-sensitive loans and deposits is $2.1 billion.

On balance, WB&T's loan–deposit gap can be described as one positioned to take advantage of an increase in interest rates. By the same token, however, it is vulnerable to a decline in rates. Nevertheless, given the volume of its loans repricing immediately, WB&T appears to have the flexibility to handle any future course of interest rates.

Recent data (not shown) indicate that the C&I portfolio of weekly-reporting banks is well diversified. Except for the construction category at less than 5 percent of the portfolio, the other classifications typically contain between 10 and 20 percent of the loan basket. One of the reasons why large banks are less risky than small banks is their ability to diversify their loan portfolios on an industry and geographic basis. A *small* bank in a one-industry town has limited opportunities to diversify its C&I portfolio. In contrast, roughly one-half of a *large* bank's loan portfolio tends to be in a diversified C&I portfolio, with about one-half of the portfolio in the form of term loans (i.e. original maturity more than one year). Penn Square Bank, which was closed on July 5, 1982, suffered from a lack of diversification. Its loan portfolio had a heavy concentration of C&I loans (e.g., 71.91 percent as of December 31, 1980), mainly in energy-related areas.

"HUNTERS" VERSUS "SKINNERS": THE PROBLEMS OF INCENTIVES, DISCIPLINE, MONITORING, AND CONCENTRATIONS OF CREDITS

If you talk to bankers who work as "calling officers," they will tell you they are salespersons. Their job is to sell banking products and services. The basic product they sell is credit. However, since the credit end of the business has become so competitive, bankers who cannot "cross-sell" are finding their bottom lines (and their bonuses) shrinking. Nevertheless, selling credit and credit-related products is the name of the game. Bankers who specialize in selling can be viewed as "hunters." Their job is to go out and "hunt down" customers, bringing the "carcasses" (i.e., financial statements and other customer information) back to the bank for "skinning." The job of the "skinners" (sometimes referred to as "credit gurus" or "green eye-shades") is to spread the financials and determine the creditworthiness of the customers. If the hunters are paid up-front fees for bringing in new business, then it is imperative that a system of checks and balances be in place to ensure they do not give away the shop. One can also see the potential for conflict when the hunters and skinners are at odds regarding a customers' creditworthiness. However, consider the incentive problems that could arise if the hunter also did the skinning. One way to discipline this potential problem, when the hunter/skinner is combined, is to make the hunter/skinner responsible for the ultimate outcome of the credit (e.g., up-front fees may be reduced by back-end penalties). Economic incentives and disincentives, in the form of bonuses, fees, and penalties, and accountability (i.e., responsibility for one's actions) are the keys to motivating and disciplining people.

Monitoring Credit Concentrations

A well-diversified loan portfolio is the best internal safety net a bank can provide its shareholders and uninsured creditors. To achieve this diversification, especially for small banks in restricted geographic markets, is not an easy task. Even if a bank can diversify, it requires internal controls in the form of monitoring mechanisms to ensure the diversification is maintained. In this regard, banks have numerous internal codes or methods for classifying loans designed to monitor concentrations of credits. In addition to the loan classifications shown in Table 20-1, some other common ways bankers like to classify loans are the following:

Purpose (type) of loan: seasonal, working capital, mortgage, construction, development, small business, personal, education, home improvement, mobile home, auto, RV, boat, credit card, refinancing, lease, etc.

Collateral type: land, buildings, equipment, manufactured goods, assignments (e.g., government contracts), receivables, investment securities and savings, livestock (Lenders quip: "Don't take anything as collateral that eats"), farm crops, etc.

Rate: floating versus fixed.

SIC code: The Standard Industrial Classification (SIC) System provides a numerical scheme, developed by the U.S. Bureau of the Budget, to classify businesses by type of activity. Since loans to businesses engaged in the same activity present a concentration risk, monitoring by SIC code provides valuable information.

Credit rating: AAA, AA, A, etc. (if available).

Domestic versus foreign: To monitor country risk exposure, foreign loans are classified by country. "MBA loans" (i.e., Mexico, Brazil, and Argentina) have been a problem for the money-center banks. Regarding country risk, Coca-Cola Company (a nonbanking company as of 1988) has an interesting philosophy: Its top management does not worry about nor does it attempt to measure or monitor country risk. Why? Whatever happens in a country, they firmly believe people will always be drinking Coke. Therefore, why worry about country risk and spend resources trying to monitor it? Could a money-center bank adopt the same philosophical approach?

To summarize, as one of my former students who is now a banker has told me, we (meaning his bank) have "tons of codes" for classifying credits. The purpose of these codes is to enable lenders to have some systematic way of monitoring concentrations of credits. Avoiding such concentrations provides a bank with an internal safety net based on the principle of portfolio diversification.

A Look at Leveraged Buyouts (LBOs)

Certain acronyms associated with particular kinds of banking credits have not been too kind to bankers in the past. In the 1970s, it was loans to REITs (real estate investment trusts). In the 1980s, it has been loans to LDCs (less-developed countries). Will the 1990s be remembered (badly as in the REIT/LDC sense) as the decade when the LBO bird came home to roost, and laid an unwanted egg? Some bankers are optimistic and others are not. Let's take a look at the LBO situation and the role of banks in financing these deals.

First, in terms of background, LBOs are a form of activity under the general heading of "corporate restructuring." Other forms of corporate restructuring include mergers and acquisitions, divestitures, going private, and spin-offs.[1] A merger usually is arranged on a friendly basis, whereas an acquisition (e.g., "hostile takeover") is not. A divestiture simply is a sale of assets for cash, whereas a spin-off is a corporate transaction whereby a separate company with its own shares is established. The owners of the company conducting the spin-off receive shares of the newly created or spun-off firm. Finally, "going private" refers to the repurchasing of all outstanding shares from the market at once. It is, in effect, the opposite of "going public." Except for corporate restructurings that imply a change in the value of assets (i.e., merger, acquisitions, and divestitures), all other corporate restructurings imply no change in the value of assets. These "nonvalue-changing transactions" (including LBOs) claim a benefit from the restructuring of the right-hand side of the balance sheet. For example, in a going-private deal, the lack of separation between owners and managers is said to reduce monitoring incentives or agency costs.

Corporate restructurings have been at the center of the wave of investment-banking

---

[1] See Bloch [1986], pp. 91–115.

activity that has dominated the 1980s, until October 19, 1987. The presumed profitability of these transactions explains, in part, why commercial bankers have been so eager to enter investment banking. However, with a longer-run perspective on the market crash, this eagerness may wane. Given this brief background on corporate restructuring, let's take a look at LBOs.

A leveraged buyout is a deal or transaction in which a group of investors (or a wealthy single investor) uses leverage (debt) to buy out the existing owners of a company. Since the cash for the buyout might come from a commercial bank, banks get involved in LBOs. LBOs usually involve companies with substantial amounts of unused or excess debt capacity. Using A for assets, D for debt, E for equity, L for loans, and T for time deposits, the following simple T-accounts are illustrative of an LBO:

Pre-LBO Firm		Post-LBO Firm		Lending Bank	
$A = 100$	$D = 10$	$A = 100$	$D = 90$	$L = 90$	$T = 90$
	$E = 90$		$E = 10$		

Note that the LBO has affected only the right-hand side of the firm's balance sheet. However, in the process, the deal probably has used up the firm's excess debt capacity as its debt-to-asset ratio has increased from 10 percent to 90 percent. The financing for the LBO is shown as being provided by a bank and indicated by the bank's *marginal* T-account. The risk to the bank depends on the firm's ability to service its new larger debt, and on the diversification benefits (costs) of adding the new larger credit to the bank's loan portfolio. The latter depends on the firm's credit rating and its SIC code. The returns to the lending bank come in the form of a higher interest rate (i.e., a firm with a debt-to-asset ratio of 90% has to pay more for credit than one with a 10% ratio). Moreover, if the borrowers have had a longstanding relationship with the bank, the potential for cross-selling and implicit returns may create additional incentives for the bank to participate in the deal.

Both commercial and investment bankers act as agents or packagers in arranging LBOs, receiving fees for their services. For commercial banks, constrained by capital requirements, such activities offer a way to generate fee income without expanding their balance sheets. Nevertheless, because of the high expected profitability of LBOs, both commercial and investment bankers usually want and take a piece of the action. In contrast, in the case of the largest deals (say $100 million or more), prudence dictates spreading the risk through participations.

The Case against LBOs

Miller [1987] has made a case against LBOs. His argument is not that banks should not do such deals, just that they should be cautious; otherwise they might have another REIT crisis on their hands. He thinks many banks have been, and still are, too eager to do LBOs. Miller makes a distinction between the megabuck Wall Street LBOs and what he calls the "reality of asset-based lending." He is mainly concerned about the latter, which he views as the kind of deals likely to be found in the secured lending departments of regional banks.

By way of backgound, Miller contends LBOs are not new, but just an old transaction with a new name. In the 1960s LBO-type deals were called "bootstrap financing"; in the 1970s, they were called "acquisition financing." Whatever the name, the deals are a form of asset-based lending. The basis of such lending is the ability of the borrower to repay the debt by liquidating the assets pledged to secure the loan. Excluding the megabuck deals, Miller sees asset-based lending topping out at a ceiling of $100 million because of the difficulty in collecting or liquidating assets (e.g., receivables, inventory, and machinery) over that amount. Since LBOs are asset-based loans, it is imperative they be backed by "hard" assets and not "soft" ones such as goodwill. In addition, Miller warns against structuring LBOs *solely* on the basis of cash flow without any regard for collateral values.

According to Miller, six potential problems and pitfalls to be considered in investigating and structuring LBOs focus on the following areas: (1) legal considerations, (2) finding out why the company is being sold, (3) thorough investigation of the new management, (4) careful analysis of cash-flow projections, (5) getting the reactions of trade creditors to the deal, and (6) checking to see if all key employees have a stake in the new company's future. Since all but the first point are self-explanatory, let's focus on it.

One of the key legal considerations in LBOs is the possibility of "fraudulent conveyance." To avoid this potential pitfall, the lender needs to be able to show that the company was both solvent and viable at the time of the financing. If the new company fails shortly after the buyout is completed, such documentation is vital because the bank's security lines could be challenged by a bankruptcy court as a fraudulent conveyance. The greater riskiness of LBOs, compared to more traditional forms of bank lending, increases the need for lending officers to have the assistance of competent attorneys, appraisers, and accountants in structuring LBOs. In less complicated and safer deals, some slack in these areas can be tolerated; in LBOs, such slack could be fatal to the success of the deal.

The Case for LBOs

In the bankers' debate about LBOs, Fox [1987] contends banks are *not* too eager about LBOs. According to him, the deciding factor in LBO financing decisions should be the capacity of the bank to handle the deal. This capacity can be viewed as a function of four factors: (1) the existence of a policy specifying the limits of key parameters (e.g., geographic and industry constraints) for LBO transactions, (2) diversification guidelines for the LBO portfolio and the maximum exposure for any deal, (3) an analytical framework for investigating and presenting LBO transactions, and (4) recognition that certain nonquantifiable factors, such as the evaluation of management, may be critically important in LBOs. The last point suggests that "soft analysis" may be just as vital to effective evaluation of proposed LBOs as "hard analysis."

In evaluating LBOs, Fox suggests specific attention to the following details: (1) A careful analysis of the trade-off between adequate cash-flow coverage and adequate coverage through asset value to compensate for the high balance-sheet risk of LBOs should be made. (2) Since LBOs have not been tested through either a recession or an environment of high interest rates, they must be structured and priced to withstand such adverse conditions i.e., by doing "worst-case scenarios" and by pressing the new managers for their contingency plans under such conditions. (3) If the deal is considered to be a short-term one, then the projected cash flow must be able to carry the project until it is flipped. And (4) given the competitive environment of reduced spreads and higher write-offs of all kinds of loans, banks cannot ignore the higher spreads offered by LBOs.

Fox concludes by providing a "litmus test" to determine whether or not banks should consider slowing the pace of their LBO financings. A "yes" answer to the following questions permits the LBO throttle to stay down. Does the bank understand complex capital structures? Is the bank willing to handle and capable of handling the instruments of modern finance such as swaps, caps, and synthetic assets? Does the bank have access to an appraiser of hard assets whose opinions are respected? Does the bank have access to an M&A (i.e., mergers and acquisitions) group whose opinions of going-concern values are respected? Does the bank have confidence in its legal and analytical personnel to offset the risk of fraudulent conveyance? Can top management and the board of directors live with the risk–return trade-offs of LBO transactions? And finally, is the bank capable of and comfortable with thoroughly investigating LBO management teams regarding their contingency plans for adverse external conditions?

Honest answers to these questions would seem to limit LBO players to only regional, superregional, and money-center banks. Of course, other banks can get a piece of the action through participations. In these situations, however, the down-stream banks (or upstream banks—remember Penn Square) should find agent banks that can pass the LBO litmus test.

LOAN PRICING AND TERMS OF LENDING[2]

Large business loans, which account for the bulk of all business loans, are made under two types of credit facilities: (1) lines of credit or "lines" and (2) loan commitments or "commitments." Lines, which are relatively informal arrangements, oblige banks upon the borrower's request (option) to quote a price on a fixed-rate loan for a particular amount and maturity (usually under one year) within the limits specified by the arrangement. Typically, lines are priced by marking up a reference or base rate, traditionally the prime rate, for the same maturity as the loan. For example, a 30-day loan would be priced off the rate on a 30-day CD. Such arrangements provide banks with full pricing flexibility. The size of the markups is used to regulate the dollar amount of loans outstanding as the borrower is offered an "all-in rate" (i.e., the base rate plus the markup) on a take-it-or-leave-it basis.

In contrast, loan commitments, unlike lines, require banks to lend up to the committed amount as long as the borrower meets the restrictions (called loan covenants) specified by the contract. The unused credit available under a commitment is subject to a fee. The most common type of loan commitment is a revolving one or "revolver." Under this form of committed facility, the borrower draws down funds up to a specified credit limit at a preestablished spread over the base rate. The loan can be repaid in part or in full at any time during the term of the commitment. From the borrower's perspective, revolvers are attractive because they reduce uncertainty about the price and availability of credit over the life of the agreement. From the bank's perspective, revolvers expose banks to interest-rate risks, liquidity risk, capital-adequacy risk, and credit risk. The use of revolvers by large banks for the period 1977:4 to 1984:3 is shown in Table 20-7.

Loans available under revolving arrangements typically are priced in one of two ways: (1) at a rate tied to the bank's prime rate with no set maturity or (2) at a rate linked to a money-market rate, such as the London interbank offer rate (called LIBOR) or a CD rate, with a *fixed* maturity (e.g., 30, 90, or 180 days) selected by the borrower (see Table 20-8). Regarding the money-market pricing scheme, some customers enter into agreements with banks that permit them to borrow domestic dollars from the bank's head office or Eurodollars from one of its foreign branches. This kind of

[2] This section draws on a Federal Reserve study by Brady [1985].

**TABLE 20-7 Commercial and Industrial Loans
Made to U.S. Residents by Selected Large Banks[a]
(Averages of Month-end Data)**

| | Loans Made under Revolving Loan Commitments | | |
| | | Percentage | |
Period	Dollar Amount (Billions)	OF All C&I Loans	Of All C&I Loans Made under Commitment
1977:4	19.7	19.3	24.7
1978:4	23.5	20.3	24.8
1979:4	31.0	24.3	27.1
1980:4	36.6	25.7	29.1
1981:4	46.3	28.8	32.6
1982:4	62.9	34.4	40.1
1983:4	62.5	34.0	41.2
1984:3	73.5	36.7	44.2

[a] Domestically booked loans of the approximately 114 respondents to the Board's monthly Commercial and Industrial Loan Commitments Survey that also file a Weekly Report of Condition.
Source: Brady [1985], Table 1, p. 2.

arrangement is called an *either/or facility*. According to Stigum and Branch [1983, p. 285], since around 1980, every large term loan negotiated by a major corporation with a money-market bank has contained an either/or option. In addition, Stigum and Branch claim that by 1980 line and loan agreements for major loans were being written without compensating-balance requirements. These deviations from the prime-rate and compensating-balance conventions are a reflection of the metamorphosis taking place in bank business lending.

Terms of Lending for C&I Loans

Information on the terms of lending at large commercial banks during the week of August 3–7, 1987, is shown in Table 20-8. The typical *short-term* C&I loan made during that week can be described (and contrasted with the typical short-term C&I loan made by "other banks") as follows:

	Large banks	Other banks
Average size	$1,307,000	$105,000
Weighted-average maturity	29 days	85 days
Weighted-average effective loan rate	7.98%	8.83%
Standard error for loan rate	.11%	.10%
Interquartile rate range	7.32%–8.57%	7.72%–9.65%
Most common base pricing rate	Fed funds	Prime
Dollar ratio of fixed to floating	70.9%	41.1%

In words, large banks, relative to other (smaller) banks, make larger short-term C&I loans; at lower, and primarily fixed, rates with the Fed funds rate (as opposed to the prime rate) as the most common base pricing rate; and for shorter maturities. These results, which are not unexpected, are interesting for the insights they give us about the competitiveness of the C&I loan market faced by large banks, and their borrowers. Specifically, C&I borrowers from large banks obtain more financing at lower and

TABLE 20-8   Terms of Lending at Commercial Banks: Survey of Loans Made August 3–7, 1987[a] (Commercial and Industrial Loans)[b]

Characteristic	Amount of Loans (Thousands of Dollars)	Average Size (Thousands of Dollars)	Weighted Average Maturity[c] Days	Loan Rate (%)			Loans Made Under Commitment (%)	Participation Loans (%)	Most Common Base Pricing Rate[g]
				Weighted Average Effective[d]	Standard Error[e]	Interquartile Range[f]			
Large Banks									
1 Overnight[h]	13,559,929	10,061	*	7.50	.07	7.25–7.72	76.0	3.6	Fed funds
2 One month and under	5,221,946	2,491	15	7.70	.10	7.19–7.93	83.1	6.0	Domestic
3 Fixed rate	4,516,988	4,488	14	7.57	.09	7.17–7.87	82.9	6.4	Domestic
4 Floating rate	704,958	647	19	8.52	.20	7.62–9.49	84.8	3.4	Domestic
5 Over one month and under a year	6,520,728	783	98	8.42	.11	7.59–9.11	82.7	17.2	Foreign
6 Fixed rate	4,210,278	2,724	66	8.32	.17	7.59–8.94	82.1	22.1	Foreign
7 Floating rate	2,310,450	341	157	8.58	.21	7.89–9.17	83.7	8.4	Prime
8 Demand[i]	6,782,199	531	*	8.71	.21	7.63–9.65	75.9	4.0	Prime
9 Fixed rate	462,720	1,734	*	7.61	.32	7.37–7.57	90.3	4.4	Domestic
10 Floating rate	6,319,479	505	*	8.79	.22	7.83–9.65	74.9	3.9	Prime
11 Total short term	**32,084,802**	**1,307**	**29**	**7.98**	**.11**	**7.32–8.57**	**78.5**	**6.8**	**Fed Funds**
12 Fixed rate (thousands of dollars)	22,740,014	5,468	16	7.67	.09	7.25–7.89	78.8	7.6	Fed funds
13 1–24	7,126	10	104	10.18	.16	9.38–11.02	32.0	5.1	Prime
14 25–49	8,051	33	91	9.92	.43	9.58–10.67	21.4	1.2	Prime
15 50–99	15,679	66	88	9.44	.22	9.04–10.11	39.6	2.0	Prime
16 100–499	124,586	222	62	8.80	.11	8.21–9.58	63.1	2.6	Prime
17 500–999	160,198	673	50	8.34	.12	7.65–8.65	83.7	3.0	Domestic
18 1000 and over	22,424,374	10,361	16	7.66	.09	7.25–7.86	78.9	7.7	Fed funds

(continues)

TABLE 20-8 (*Continued*)

Characteristic	Amount of Loans (Thousands of Dollars)	Average Size (Thousands of Dollars)	Weighted Average Maturity[c] Days	Loan Rate (%) Weighted Average Effective[d]	Standard Error[e]	Interquartile Range[f]	Loans Made Under Commitment (%)	Participation Loans (%)	Most Common Base Pricing Rate[g]
19 Floating rate (thousands of dollars)	9,344,787	458	124	8.72	.18	7.81–9.58	77.9	5.0	Prime
20 1–24	82,032	11	143	10.08	.12	9.20–10.75	83.0	.3	Prime
21 25–49	98,881	34	139	9.97	.13	9.11–10.75	82.0	.7	Prime
22 50–99	195,510	65	138	9.73	.07	9.11–10.20	83.2	1.1	Prime
23 100–499	1,020,245	209	145	9.45	.02	8.60–9.96	86.7	2.9	Prime
24 500–999	655,438	678	138	9.16	.08	8.57–9.66	84.8	6.7	Prime
25 1000 and over	7,292,681	5,421	119	8.52	.20	7.57–9.14	75.7	5.3	Prime
			(Months)						
26 Total long term	**2,752,198**	**1,450**	**52**	**8.28**	**.22**	**7.43–8.84**	**81.5**	**2.2**	**Domestic**
27 Fixed rate (thousands of dollars)	1,113,028	2.241	58	8.06	.29	7.43–8.57	87.9	.0	Foreign
28 1–99	7,666	27	49	11.54	.32	10.35–12.40	41.3	1.0	Other
29 100–499	13,900	255	52	10.65	.24	10.20–11.30	46.5	.0	Domestic
30 500–999	25,119	715	48	9.95	1.17	8.02–10.52	77.3	.0	Fed funds
31 1000 and over	1,066,343	8,876	59	7.96	.23	7.43–8.53	89.1	.0	Foreign
32 Floating rate (thousands of dollars)	1,639,170	1,169	47	8.42	.21	7.53–9.31	77.2	3.6	Domestic
33 1–99	24,517	34	40	10.19	.28	9.14–10.75	58.4	.2	Prime
34 100–499	77,910	226	47	9.59	.12	9.11–9.92	65.5	4.8	Prime
35 500–999	58,101	643	52	9.19	.22	8.57–9.73	77.7	.0	Prime
36 1000 and over	1,478,642	6,201	47	8.30	.23	7.44–8.84	78.1	3.8	Domestic

Loans made below Prime

Characteristic	Amount of Loans (Thousands of Dollars)	Average Size (Thousands of Dollars)	Days	Loans rate (%) Effective[d]	Nominal[k]	Prime rate[j]	Participation Loans (%)
37 Overnight[h]	12,854,344	11,398	*	7.44	7.17	8.25	3.8
38 One month and under	4,635,102	5,903	14	7.50	7.24	8.25	5.9

TABLE 20-8 (Continued)

39 Over one month and under a year	3,376,213	5,819	92	7.58	7.34	8.25	82.1	9.5
40 Demand[i]	2,280,917	4,426	*	7.50	7.27	8.25	40.0	1.5
41 Total short term	**23,146,576**	**7,694**	**19**	**7.47**	**7.22**	**8.25**	**75.9**	**4.8**
42 Fixed rate	19,910,195	8,559	12	7.46	7.20	8.25	79.4	4.9
43 Floating rate	3,236,381	4,745	115	7.56	7.32	8.25	54.2	4.6
			Months					
44 Total long term	**1,664,677**	**7,236**	**46**	**7.58**	**7.40**	**8.25**	**93.7**	**0.3**
45 Fixed rate	784,716	9,026	54	7.56	7.43	8.25	90.1	0.6
46 Floating rate	879,961	6,149	40	7.60	7.39	8.25	96.8	0.0

* Fewer than 10 sample loans

[a] The survey of terms of bank lending to business collects data on gross loan extensions made during the first full business week in the mid-month of each quarter by a sample of 340 commercial banks of all sizes. A subsample of 250 banks also report loans to farmers. The sample data are blown up to estimate the lending terms at all insured commercial banks during that week. The estimated terms of bank lending are not intended for use in collecting the terms of loans extended over the entire quarter or residing in the portfolios of those banks. Construction and land development loans include both unsecured loans and loans secured by real estate. Thus, some of the construction and land development loans would be reported on the statement of condition as real estate loans and the remainder as business loans. Mortgage loans, purchased loans, foreign loans, and loans of less than $1,000 are excluded from the survey.

For all insured banks total assets averaged $165 million. As of Dec. 31, 1985, assets of most of the large banks were at least $5.5 billion.

[b] Beginning with the August 1986 survey respondent banks provide information on the type of base rate used to price each commercial and industrial loan made during the survey week. This reporting change is reflected in the new column on the most common base pricing rate in Table 20-8 and footnote m from Table 20-9.

[c] Average maturities are weighted by loan size and exclude demand loans.

[d] Effective (compounded) annual interest rates are calculated from the stated rate and other terms of the loan and weighted by loan size.

[e] The chances are about two out of three that the average rate shown would differ by less than this amount from the average rate that would be found by a complete survey of lending at all banks.

[f] The interquartile range shows the interest rate range that encompasses the middle 50 percent of the total dollar amount of loans made.

[g] The most common base rate is that rate used to price the largest dollar volume of loans. Base pricing rates include the prime rate (sometimes referred to as a bank's "basic" or "reference" rate); the federal funds rate; domestic money market rates other than the federal funds rate; foreign money market rates; and other base rates not included in the foregoing classification.

[h] Overnight loans are loans that mature on the following business day.

[i] Demand loans have no stated date of maturity.

[j] Nominal (not compounded) annual interest rates are calculated from survey data on the stated rate and other terms of the loan and weighted by loan size.

[k] The prime rate reported by each bank is weighted by the volume of loans extended and then averaged.

[l] The proportion of loans made at rates below prime may vary substantially from the proportion of such loans outstanding in banks' portfolios.

[m] Among banks reporting loans to farmers (Table C), most "large banks" (survey strata 1 to 3) had over $600 million in total assets, and most "other banks" (survey strata 4 to 6) had total assets below $600 million.

The survey of terms of bank lending to farmers now includes loans secured by farm real estate. In addition, the categories describing the purpose to farm loans have now been expanded to include "purchase or improve farm real estate." In previous surveys, the purpose of such loans was reported as "other."

Source: *Federal Reserve Bulletin* [January 1988], Special Tables, pp. A70–75.

fixed rates, but for shorter periods, than customers with other banks. Of course, the underlying causes of these differences can most likely be traced to the size, creditworthiness, and greater number of alternatives (e.g., commercial paper) open to borrowers who take down loans that average $1.3 million. Since these borrowers provide the kind of foundations banks like for establishing strong customer relationships, they are the ones most likely to receive concessions from their banks (e.g., discounts from the prime rate, see the bottom half of Table 20-8).

For the typical *long-term* C&I loan, the description and contrast between large and other banks are as follows:

	Large Banks	Other Banks
Average size	$1,450,000	$83,000
Weighted-average maturity	52 months	52 months
Weighted-average effective loan rate	8.28%	9.80%
Standard error for loan rate	.22%	.14
Interquartile range	7.43%–8.84%	8.87%–10.53%
Most common base pricing rate	Domestic	Prime
Dollar ratio of fixed to floating	40.4%	38.3%
Dollar ratio of long to short term	8.6%	11.6%

In words, the story for long-term C&I loans is similar to the tale for short-term ones. The lone exception is the shift by large banks in the most common base pricing rate from the Fed funds rate to a "domestic" rate, where domestic refers to a domestic money-market rate (e.g., the negotiable CD rate) other than the federal funds rate (see note *g* to Table 20-8). Finally, as shown by the dollar ratio of long-term C&I loans to short-term C&I loans, the overwhelming majority of C&I loans tend to be short-term ones.

Terms of Lending for Loans to Farmers

Energy, agricultural, and LDC loans have been the trouble spots in the banking system during the 1980s. However, by the beginning of 1988 analysts and bank regulators were predicting that the farm-lending crisis had bottomed out. To gain some insight into the nature of farm lending, Table 20-9 presents the terms of lending on loans to farmers during the week of August 3–7, 1987. The data are presented for three groups of banks participating in the Federal Reserve's survey: (1) all banks, (2) large banks, and (3) other banks. Focusing on the purpose of the loan, we find that large banks make farm loans for two basic purposes: feeder livestock (42.5%) and other current operating expenses (32.5%). Other (smaller) banks make loans to farmers for the same purposes, only the percentages are different, namely 55.7 percent for current operating expenses and 21.6 percent for feeder livestock. These figures are for all sizes of loans. For large farm loans (i.e., those for $250,000 or more) slightly more than one-half of the dollar volume is made for feeder livestock. Obviously, only "city bankers" take seriously the adage: "Don't take anything as collateral that eats." In general, most small loans to farmers are made to cover current operating expenses such as seed, fertilizer, fuel, labor, and the like.

Let's compare the typical farm loan made by a large bank with the one made by a smaller bank, see the top of the next page. In words, community banks in agricultural

	Large Banks	Other Banks
Average size	$90,174	$13,987
Weighted-average maturity	5.1 months	9.4 months
Weighted-average effective loan rate	9.30%	11.11%
Standard error for loan rate	.55%	.12
Interquartile range	8.60%–10.20%	10.47%–11.91%
Proportion with floating rates	59.6%	53.6%
Proportion made under commitment	93.2%	39.1%

areas make lots of small loans to farmers for longer terms and at higher rates than large banks. Both groups of banks make primarily floating-rate loans. In contrast, large banks make most of their loans on a commitment basis, whereas other banks are less inclined to do so (i.e., 93% versus 39%).

Terms of Lending for Construction and Land Development Loans

To complete our analysis of the terms of lending, let's focus on Table 20-10 and the terms of lending for construction and land development loans. As classified by type of construction, these loans are made for three purposes: (1) single family, (2) multifamily, and (3) nonresidential. For large banks, almost 90 percent of their construction and land development loan dollars go for nonresidential purposes. In contrast, other (smaller) banks lend almost one-half of their construction and land development loan dollars for single-family purposes, although they still fund nonresidential projects to the tune of roughly 42 percent of loan volume. Since the figures in Table 20-10, as well as those in Tables 20-8 and 20-9, reflect dollar flows during the week of August 3–7, 1987, they are not necessarily representative of the average balance sheets for these banking groups.

Let's focus again on the two size groups as shown in Table 20-10 and contrast the typical construction and land development loan across these two groups.

	Large Banks	Other Banks
Average size	$1,512,000	$63,000
Weighted-average maturity	3 months	12 months
Weighted-average effective loan rate	9.14%	9.83%
Standard error for loan rate	.14%	.09
Interquartile range	8.73%–9.32%	9.11%–10.47%
Loans made under commitment	95.0%	66.9%
Participation loans	16.6%	13.8%

In words, we find a similar story to the other situations we have analyzed across the two banking groups. Specifically, the group of large banks makes larger loans (under commitment agreements) for a shorter time period at lower rates relative to other (smaller) banks. Finally, for both banking groups, construction and land development loans tend to be priced relative to the prime rate.

TABLE 20-9   Terms of Lending by Commercial Banks for Loans to Farmers[m]: Survey of Loans Made August 3–7, 1987[a]

Characteristic	All Sizes	Size Class of Loans (Thousands)					
		$1–9	$10–24	$25–49	$50–99	$100–249	$250 and Over
All Banks							
1 Amount of loans (thousands of dollars)	$972,091	$113,363	$107,665	$96,060	$140,093	$162,069	352,841
2 Number of loans	46,944	33,550	7,292	2,797	1,981	989	336
3 Weighted average maturity (months)[c]	8.0	7.0	6.9	7.3	15.3	8.6	5.4
4 Weighted average interest rate (percent)[d]	10.41	11.54	11.19	11.09	10.98	10.59	9.32
5 Standard error[e]	.57	.39	.26	.48	.41	.53	.79
6 Interquartile range[f]	9.50–11.33	10.77–12.31	10.34–12.13	10.36–12.13	10.52–11.83	10.11–11.07	8.60–10.38
By purpose of loan							
7 Feeder livestock	9.92	11.88	11.42	11.19	11.19	10.56	8.93
8 Other livestock	11.05	12.25	12.04	10.27	11.95	*	*
9 Other current operating expenses	10.82	11.40	11.19	11.21	10.63	10.83	10.08
10 Farm machinery and equipment	10.77	11.39	10.22	*	*	*	*
11 Farm real estate	10.88	11.59	11.76	*	*	*	*
12 Other	9.77	12.04	10.24	11.57	10.79	9.93	9.00
Percentage of amount of loans							
13 With floating rates	55.9	52.2	55.9	65.7	55.2	45.4	59.6
14 Made under commitment	59.9	46.9	50.6	51.8	47.2	52.3	77.7
By purpose of loan							
15 Feeder livestock	29.6	14.7	10.9	20.8	36.8	17.7	45.2
16 Other livestock	3.8	4.3	6.4	2.4	7.0	*	*
17 Other current operating expenses	46.8	68.4	69.2	57.5	30.7	54.4	32.9
18 Farm machinery and equipment	2.8	6.4	2.1	*	*	*	*
19 Farm real estate	2.6	1.2	3.2	*	*	*	*
20 Other	14.4	5.1	8.1	8.6	11.8	19.3	19.8
Large banks[m]							
1 Amount of loans (thousands of dollars)	$374,132	$8,197	$12,060	$16,781	$24,929	$43,127	$269,038
2 Number of loans	4,194	2,050	818	483	387	296	161
3 Weighted average maturity (months)[c]	5.1	5.3	6.2	6.4	6.5	7.8	4.7
4 Weighted average interest rate (percent)[d]	9.30	10.53	10.15	10.02	9.94	9.92	9.02
5 Standard error[e]	.55	.38	.16	.42	.35	.37	.74
6 Interquartile range[f]	8.60–10.20	10.00–10.83	9.58–10.74	9.50–10.52	9.24–10.47	9.14–10.52	8.60–9.84
By purpose of loan							
7 Feeder livestock	8.98	10.35	9.94	9.99	10.13	10.03	8.79
8 Other livestock	9.40	10.54	*	10.46	*	*	*

TABLE 20-9 (*Continued*)

9	Other current operating expenses	9.84	10.46	10.16	9.98	9.81	9.75
10	Farm machinery and equipment	10.28	11.09	*	*	*	*
11	Farm real estate	10.19	11.86	*	*	*	*
12	Other	9.05	10.47	10.18	10.08	9.87	8.73
	Percentage of amount of loans						
13	With floating rates	59.6	90.5	91.8	92.2	95.2	90.0
14	Made under commitment	93.2	82.4	85.3	84.7	91.8	91.7
	By purpose of loan						
15	Feeder livestock	42.5	9.7	15.2	19.3	22.2	27.2
16	Other livestock	3.0	1.4	*	7.5	*	*
17	Other current operating expenses	32.5	68.0	60.6	53.7	46.7	44.2
18	Farm machinery and equipment	.6	5.2	*	*	*	*
19	Farm real estate	.9	3.2	*	*	*	*
20	Other	20.5	12.6	16.3	14.8	22.6	19.7
	Other Banks[m]						
1	Amount of loans (thousands of dollars)	$597,959	$105,166	$95,604	$79,279	$115,165	$118,942
2	Number of loans	42,750	31,500	6,474	2,313	1,594	693
3	Weighted average maturity (months)[c]	9.4	7.1	7.0	7.4	16.6	8.8
4	Weighted average interest rate (percent)[d]	11.11	11.62	11.32	11.32	11.20	10.84
5	Standard error[c]	.12	.10	.20	.22	.19	.37
6	Interquartile range[f]	10.47–11.91	10.79–12.31	10.50–12.19	10.52–12.17	10.79–11.83	10.21–11.80
	By purpose of loan						
7	Feeder livestock	11.09	11.96	11.69	11.42	11.32	*
8	Other livestock	11.77	12.29	*	*	*	*
9	Other current operating expenses	11.18	11.47	11.31	11.44	10.93	*
10	Farm machinery and equipment	10.82	11.41	*	*	*	*
11	Farm real estate	10.99	*	*	*	*	*
12	Other	10.64	12.38	*	*	*	*
	Percentage of amount of loans						
13	With floating rates	53.6	49.2	51.3	60.0	46.5	29.2
14	Made under commitment	39.1	44.2	46.3	44.8	37.6	38.0
	By purpose of loan						
15	Feeder livestock	21.6	15.1	10.3	21.1	39.9	*
16	Other livestock	4.3	4.5	*	*	*	*
17	Other current operating expenses	55.7	68.4	70.3	58.3	27.2	*
18	Farm machinery and equipment	4.1	6.5	*	*	*	*
19	Farm real estate	3.6	*	*	*	*	*
20	Other	10.6	4.5	*	*	*	*

For notes see end of Table 20-8.

TABLE 20-10   Terms of Lending by Commercial Banks for Construction and Land Development Loans, Survey of Loans Made August 3–7, 1987

Characteristic	Amount of Loans (thousands of Dollars)	Average Size (thousands of Dollars)	Weighted Average Maturity (Months)^c	Weighted Average Effective^d	Loan Rate (%) Standard Error^e	Loan Rate (%) Interquartile Range^f	Loans Made Under Commitment (%)	Participation Loans (%)
All Banks								
1 Total	**3,679,913**	**236**	**5**	**9.30**	**.11**	**8.75–9.65**	**88.4**	**16.0**
2 Fixed rate (thousands of dollars)	1,944,077	327	3	9.23	.31	8.75–9.28	92.0	6.8
3 1–24	40,789	12	6	11.04	.25	10.47–12.13	41.6	36.8
4 25–49	40,700	34	18	11.12	.36	10.47–12.03	31.6	14.2
5 50–99	63,707	71	9	10.56	.50	10.47–10.97	12.7	11.3
6 100–499	36,819	175	9	10.13	.71	10.47–10.78	81.7	5.2
7 500 and over	1,762,062	11,236	2	9.08	.26	8.75–9.28	97.6	5.8
8 Floating rate (thousands of dollars)	1,735,836	180	8	9.38	.13	8.57–9.92	84.4	26.3
9 1–24	50,856	10	8	10.35	.12	9.66–10.75	84.3	1.6
10 25–49	52,673	36	7	9.85	.09	9.42–10.24	89.5	1.9
11 50–99	68,682	72	10	10.01	.10	9.65–10.75	78.9	3.6
12 100–499	306,440	200	13	9.55	.15	9.11–10.20	62.6	19.7
13 500 and over	1,257,185	3,256	7	9.25	.15	8.57–9.92	89.8	31.2
By type of construction								
14 Single family	621,561	63	9	9.75	.15	9.17–10.47	67.1	19.1
15 Multifamily	218,765	177	5	9.65	.12	9.21–10.34	89.8	6.0
16 Nonresidential	2,839,587	626	4	9.18	.11	8.73–9.32	93.0	16.1
Large Banks^m								
1 Total	**2,814,435**	**1,512**	**3**	**9.14**	**.14**	**8.73–9.32**	**95.0**	**16.6**
2 Fixed rate (thousands of dollars)	1,753,481	5,094	2	9.07	.36	8.75–9.28	97.5	5.9
3 1–24	1,510	11	9	10.20	.18	9.92–10.75	67.1	4.7
4 25–49	1,054	37	11	9.99	.51	9.92–10.75	54.8	.0
5 50–99	*	*	*	*	*	*	*	*
6 100–499	3,829	215	18	7.23	1.06	1.13–10.75	71.8	50.4
7 500 and over	1,746,234	11,832	2	9.08	.34	8.75–9.28	97.6	5.8

TABLE 20-10 (*Continued*)

8 Floating rate (thousands of dollars)	1,060,953	699	5	9.25	.18	8.57–9.79	91.0	34.4
9 1–24	5,701	11	10	9.80	.15	9.52–10.20	93.1	5.2
10 25–49	7,393	34	8	9.60	.09	9.11–9.92	88.1	5.9
11 50–99	14,718	73	8	9.71	.12	9.38–9.92	90.7	8.6
12 100–499	85,785	232	9	9.63	.13	9.31–9.92	76.8	7.5
13 500 and over	947,357	4,438	4	9.20	.23	8.51–9.69	92.3	37.6
By type of construction								
14 Single family	189,325	355	6	9.24	.20	8.12–9.65	97.1	14.7
15 Multifamily	148,590	642	4	9.67	.15	9.21–10.34	96.4	4.2
16 Nonresidential	2,476,519	2,257	3	9.10	.16	8.73–9.28	94.8	17.5
Other Banks[m]								
1 Total	**865,478**	**63**	**12**	**9.83**	**.09**	**9.11–10.47**	**66.9**	**13.8**
2 Fixed rate (thousands of dollars)	190,596	34	10	10.66	.21	10.47–10.97	41.4	14.6
3 1–24	39,280	12	6	11.07	.40	10.47–12.13	40.6	38.0
4 25–49	39,646	34	18	11.15	.18	10.47–12.03	30.9	14.6
5 50–99	62,853	71	9	10.58	.30	10.47–10.97	12.0	11.2
6 100–499	32,990	171	8	10.47	.22	10.47–10.78	82.9	.0
7 500 and over	*	*	*	*	*	*	*	*
8 Floating rate (thousands of dollars)	674,883	83	13	9.60	.20	9.11–10.20	74.1	13.6
9 1–24	45,155	9	8	10.42	.11	9.92–10.75	83.1	1.1
10 25–49	45,279	36	7	9.89	.13	9.42–10.61	89.8	1.3
11 50–99	53,965	71	10	10.09	.14	9.65–10.75	75.6	2.2
12 100–499	220,656	190	14	9.51	.29	8.84–10.20	57.1	24.5
13 500 and over	309,828	1,795	13	9.41	.20	8.87–10.20	82.2	11.5
By type of construction								
14 Single family	432,236	47	11	9.97	.16	9.58–10.65	53.9	21.1
15 Multifamily	70,175	70	8	9.60	.21	8.59–9.20	75.8	10.0
16 Nonresidential	363,068	106	14	9.71	.08	9.11–10.20	80.6	6.0

For notes see end of Table 20-8.
Note: 41.2 percent of construction and land development loans were priced relative to the prime rate.

EXHIBIT 20-1
The Costs of Credit Cards and an Economic Analysis of the Effects of an Interest-Rate Ceiling on the Demand for and Supply of Credit Card Funds

Rates and terms for standard MasterCard and Visa cards issued by the five banks with the largest U.S. market shares:

Bank	Market Share	Interest Rate	Annual Fee	Grace Period
Citibank	8.4%	19.8% [a]	$20.00	30 days
Bank of America	4.8	19.8	18.00	25 days
Chase Manhattan	4.1	17.5	20.00 [b]	25 days
First Chicago	3.6	19.8 [c]	20.00 [b]	25 days
Manufacturers Hanover Trust	2.9	17.8	15.00	25 days
AVERAGE (25 banks with low interest rates) [d]		14.8%	$17.76	22 days

[a] Lower rate (16.8%) available on some cards
[b] Waived if purchase volume exceeds $2,400 annually
[c] Variable rate (prime plus 9.4%) also available, currently 17.9%
[d] Includes savings institutions
Source: RAM Research, Bank Credit Card Observer

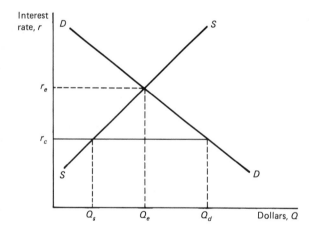

Consumer Credit and Credit Cards

Competition in the financial-services industry is most evident in the area of consumer lending. Although the majority of consumer credit (about 55%) is held outside commercial banks, they still have the largest share of the market (about 45%). Finance companies rank second as they hold about $1 out of every $4 of consumer credit outstanding. On a national level, 15 major players control one-third of consumer installment and revolving credit. These players can be grouped into four categories: (1) banks, (2) captive finance companies, (3) diversified financial-services firms, and (4) retailers. The industry leader is General Motors Acceptance Corporation (GMAC), with over $40 billion in consumer credit outstanding, mainly of course in automobile paper. The other leading players are Citicorp, Bank America, First Interstate, Security Pacific, and Chase Manhattan in the banking area; Ford Motor and General Electric (in addition to GMAC) in the area of captive finance companies; Prudential/Bache, American Express, Merrill Lynch, and Equitable Life Assurance in the diversified finance area; and Sears, J. C. Penney, and Montgomery Ward in the retailing area.

Over recent years for all commercial banks, consumer credit has averaged between 20 and 25 percent of total bank loans. This percentage, however, does vary with bank size. Focusing on Table 20-6, we see that banks *with* foreign offices had only 13.6 percent of their outstanding loans to individuals compared to 27.3 percent for banks *without* foreign offices. For both size groups, however, credit cards (and related plans) are an important credit facility, as they account for $1 out of every $3 of consumer credit for large banks and $1 out of every $4 of consumer credit for smaller banks. Although credit cards have been a rapidly growing area, they have been plagued by high operating expenses and heavy loan losses.

In 1987 and 1988, the U.S. Congress conducted extensive (and sometimes heated) debates about disclosure requirements for and interest rates on credit cards. One of the issues debated by Congress was the possibility of imposing an interest-rate ceiling on credit cards. Fortunately, rational minds prevailed and no ceiling has been imposed, as of this writing. Exhibit 20-1 presents some recent data on the costs of credit cards and an economic analysis of the effects of an interest-rate ceiling on the demand for and supply of credit card funds.

Focusing on the diagram in Exhibit 20-1, we find that without any rate ceiling the forces of supply and demand would clear the market at the equilibrium rate and quantity indicated by the coordinates $[r_e, Q_e]$. However, if an effective ceiling (r_c) is imposed (i.e., one below the equilibrium rate), then a distortion between supply and demand is created such that the quantity of credit demanded is greater than the quantity supplied. Thus, a ceiling would be self-defeating as it would hurt the groups it was designed to help because the least creditworthy consumers, those who can least afford to pay high interest rates, would presumably be rationed out of the market. Alternatively, suppliers could meet the demand (Q_d) by changing other terms of the credit card agreement to offset the lower rates of interest (e.g., by increasing the annual fee or reducing/eliminating the grace period, see the top half of Exhibit 20-1). Changing these other terms, however, would serve to increase the effective rate of interest, which again would not be the result Congress intended.

As we have seen, good intentions frequently have unintended evils. Market forces work best when they are unrestricted. However, with greater and clearer credit card disclosure, consumers should have a better chance of finding the lowest cost producers of credit card services.

FUNCTIONAL COST ANALYSIS OF BANK LENDING

A brief analysis of the commercial, consumer, and real-estate lending activities of commercial banks with respect to relative portfolio yield, loan-administration cost, and loan-loss experience (risk) is presented in this section. Evidence on these factors can be derived from the Functional Cost Analysis (FCA) studies conducted by the

Federal Reserve Banks (see Anderson [1979]). These data provide additional background for discussing loan-pricing decisions.

Functional Cost Analysis is a useful financial-management tool because it attempts to pinpoint the costs of various bank functions. Federal Reserve Banks have been conducting FCA surveys for almost three decades. FCA data enable bank managers to compare their costs for various bank functions with the average costs of banks of similar size and deposit structure. Like other financial-management tools, FCA has its shortcomings. The major drawback is the difficulty in allocating costs to the various bank functions, a technique called cost accounting. Thus, like other tools, FCA provides only benchmark figures for judging bank performance and operating efficiency.

A summary view of the functional costs and incomes of the four major bank lending activities is presented in Table 20-11. The gross yield, cost of funds, interest spread, operating expenses, net return, and loan-loss experience (all expressed as a percentage of funds used) are presented for (1) real-estate mortgage loans, (2) consumer installment loans, (3) commercial loans, and (4) credit-card loans. In addition, for comparative purposes, the data for bank investments in government securities are presented.

The important FCA message contained in Table 20-11 is that the administrative or operating expenses of the major bank lending functions vary considerably from one activity to another. The credit-card and installment-loan functions are much more expensive to administer than the mortgage-loan and commercial-loan functions. As a result, the gross yields on consumer-type loans must be much higher than those on other loans because of the higher administration costs. A more detailed breakdown of the income and costs of consumer loans for 1977 is[3]

Gross interest income	10.8%
Other income (e.g., fees)	0.5
TOTAL INCOME	11.3
Cost of making loans	1.8
Cost of collecting payments	1.4
Loan loss	0.4
Cost of funds	4.8
TOTAL COSTS	8.4
Net return	2.9%

Since the net return and spreads on installment loans in 1983 are similar to the 1977 figures, this function hasn't changed much in terms of operating expenses.

Looking at the credit-card function for banks with total deposits less than $200 million, we see that the gross yield or total income of 23.65 percent consisted of

Merchant discount	4.81%
Finance charge interest	15.17
Net interchange fees	1.71
Other income	1.96
TOTAL INCOME	23.65%

---

[3] These data are for 1977. See Anderson [1979], pp. 440–441.

TABLE 20-11   Functional Cost Analysis of Bank Funds-Using Activities, 1983[a]

Returns or Cost as a Percent of Funds Used	Real-Estate Mortgage Loans	Installment Loans (Mainly Consumer)	Securities (Taxable Basis)	Commercial and Other Loans	Credit-Card Loans[b]
Gross Yield	11.51%	15.21%	11.20%	12.44%	23.65%
Cost of funds (−)	8.06	8.01	7.97	7.93	7.95
Interest spread	3.45	7.20	3.23	4.51	15.70
Operating expense (−)	1.01	3.64	0.16	1.82	11.64
Net return (after loan) losses)	2.29%	2.98%	3.07%	1.64%	1.94%
Loan-loss experience	0.15%	0.58%	0.00%	1.05%	2.12%

[a] Figures are for reporting banks with deposits of $50 million to $200 million.
[b] For card banks. A bank is classified as a card bank if it administers its own card plan or is the primary regional agent of a national card plan. Such banks fully fund the credit-card outstandings and have records to report the number of accounts, account usage, and volume of credit losses.
  Source: Function Cost Analysis: 1983 Average Banks, Board of Governors of the Federal Reserve System.

The operating expenses allocated to the credit-card function consisted of the following items:

Officer salaries	1.48%
Employee salaries	2.06
Fringe benefits	.77
Subtotal	4.31%

Data services	.91%
Furniture and equipment	.42
Occupancy	.59
Publicity and advertising	.42
Credit-card activity and franchise fees	2.59
Other operating expense	2.39
TOTAL OPERATING EXPENSE	11.63%

For 54 banks with deposits over $200 million, operating expenses were almost 100 basis points higher at 12.60 percent. Some of this expense was offset by their higher gross yield of 24.22 percent.

CUSTOMER PROFITABILITY ANALYSIS

To measure the profitability of corporate customer and correspondent account relationships, many large banks employ a technique called customer profitability analysis (CPA).[4] CPA essentially is a more-detailed version of standard account analysis (SAA). SAA concentrates on three factors: (1) the revenue generated from a customer's account, (2) the expenses of servicing the account, and (3) the net profit or loss from the account—the difference between (1) and (2). A representative SAA form is shown

---

[4] This section is derived from Knight [1975]. Santomero [1985] stresses the importance of CPA in pricing business credit.

TABLE 20-12   A Sample Form for Standard Account Analysis

Account Analysis for:		
Month of:		
Earnings allowance		
Average Ledger Balance		$ _____
Less Average Uncollected Funds		$ _____
Average Collected Balance		$ _____
Less Legal Reserve of $(17\frac{1}{2}\%)$		$ _____
Average Balance Available for Investment		$ _____
Earnings Allowance (%)		
INVESTMENT VALUE		$ _____
EXPENSES		
Account Maintenance	$2.00	$ _____
Credits	7¢ each	$ _____
Debits	7¢ each	$ _____
Deposited items		
Not Encoded	3¢ each	$ _____
Encoded	2¢ each	$ _____
Returned Items	25¢ each	$ _____
Stop Payments	$2.00 each	$ _____
Wire Transfers	$1.50 each	$ _____
Coupon Envelopes		$ _____
Currency Transactions		$ _____
Coin Shipped		$ _____
Account Reconciliation		$ _____
Lockbox Services		$ _____
Float Overdrafts		$ _____
_____		$ _____
_____		$ _____
_____		$ _____
TOTAL EXPENSES		$ _____
NET PROFIT (OR LOSS)		$ _____

Source: Knight [1975], Table 1.

in Table 20-12. The focus of SAA tends to be on activity charges for which compensation balances are maintained (i.e., deposited items, account maintenance, wire transfers, etc.). The primary objective of SAA is to measure the adequacy of the customer's compensating-balance requirement. The technique mainly is used to analyze the accounts of nonborrowers with heavy activity charges (e.g., respondent banks).

In contrast, CPA attempts to measure the *total* profitability of a customer relationship by making allowances for other services such as loans, investment advising, federal-funds transactions, or data processing. For customers who use the non-deposit services of a bank, the profitability measure generated by SAA is meaningless and a CPA profit figure should be generated. A sample CPA form is shown in Table 20-13.

Lines 18, 19, 20, and 21 of Table 20-13 represent four alternative profitability measures of CPA. Line 18 is the ratio of net profits to allocated capital. This measure can be viewed as the banks pretax ROE on the customer level. Letting R = revenue, C = cost of funds, O = the costs of servicing the relationship, and K = allocated capital, the relevant formula is

$$\frac{\text{Net Profits}}{\text{Allocated Capital}} = \frac{R - C - O}{K} \qquad (20\text{-}1)$$

Line 19 measures customer profitability using the ratio of net profits to net funds

TABLE 20-13   A Sample Form for Customer Profitability Analysis

		Current Period		Last 12 Months
Account: XYZ Manufacturing		Date: April 11, 1988		
Affiliated Accounts: _____		Period: 12/31-6/30		
_____		Type of Loan: _____		
_____				

	Current Period		Last 12 Months
Sources and Uses of Funds			
1. Average Loan Balance:	$ ____		$ ____
2. Average Collected Balance:		$ ____	$ ____
a. Investable Balance (17.5% reserve):		$ ____	$ ____
3. Average Time Balance:		$ ____	$ ____
a. Investable Balance (3% reserve):		$ ____	$ ____
4. Total Loanable Funds (2a + 3a):	$ ____		$ ____
5. Bank Funds Used by Customer (1–4):	$ ____		$ ____
a. Allocated Capital (8% of 1):		$ ____	$ ____
b. Funds Transferred from Pool (5–5a):		$ ____	$ ____
Income			
6. Gross Interest Income on Loans:	$ ____		$ ____
7. Earnings on Deposits (xxx% of 4):	$ ____		$ ____
8. Fees Paid:			
a. Service Charge Fees:		$ ____	$ ____
b. Loan Commitments:		$ ____	$ ____
c. Data Processing:		$ ____	$ ____
d. Total (8a + 8b + 8c):	$ ____		$ ____
9. Total Income (6 + 7 + 8):	$ ____		$ ____
Expenses			
10. Activity Costs from Account Analysis:	$ ____		$ ____
11. Interest Accrued on Time Deposits:	$ ____		$ ____
12. Charge for Bank Funds Used:			
a. Allocated Capital (20% of 5a):		$ ____	$ ____
b. Pool Funds (xxx% of 5b):		$ ____	$ ____
c. Total (12a + 12b):	$ ____		$ ____
13. Loan Handling Expenses:	$ ____		$ ____
14. Cost of Fee Services:	$ ____		$ ____
15. Data Processing:	$ ____		$ ____
16. Total Expenses (10 + 11 + 12 + 13 + 14 + 15):	$ ____		$ ____
Net Income			
17. Net Income Before Taxes (9–16):	$ ____		$ ____
Profitability Measures			
18. Allocated Capital Index (17:5a):	____ %		____ %
19. Net Profits/Net Funds Used (17:5):	____ %		____ %
20. Net Profits/Gross Amount Borrowed (17:1):	____ %		____ %
21. Gross Profits/Net Funds Used [(17 + 12c):5]:	____ %	____ %	

Source: Knight [1975], Table 2.

used. Letting L = average borrowing by the customer and D = average funds provided by the customer, the profitability index is

$$\frac{\text{Net Profits}}{\text{Net Funds Used}} = \frac{R - C - O}{L - D} = \frac{R - O}{L - D} - \frac{C}{L - D} \tag{20-2}$$

The two terms on the RHS of Equation 20-2 provide a spread measure of the customer relationship. For example, if the gross profit index $[(R - O)/(L - D)]$ is 12 percent and the cost of funds is 10 percent, the net-profit ratio is 2 percent.

Line 20 is a measure of profitability applicable only to borrowers. It is defined as

$$\frac{\text{Net Profits}}{\text{Gross Amount Borrowed}} = \frac{R - C - O}{L} \tag{20-3}$$

Line 21 measures customer profitability using the ratio of gross profits to net funds used. It is defined as

$$\frac{\text{Gross Profits}}{\text{Net Funds Used}} = \frac{R - O}{L - D} \tag{20-4}$$

Formula 20-4, which also is the first term on the RHS of Equation 20-2, is not sensitive to the cost of funds as this term does not enter the equation.

Of the four profitability measures, only the return-on-capital approach (20-1) is applicable to all bank customers. It can be used to set minimum returns for the other ratios. The formulas with net funds used in the denominator (20-2 and 20-4) are not applicable to net depositors (i.e., those with $L - D < 0$) because profitable net depositors (i.e., those with $R - C - O > 0$) will show a negative profitability index. The profitability of borrowers who are not net users of funds can be analyzed by using Formula 20-3 and then comparing this result with the bank's cost of funds.

In today's environment with its volatile interest rates, banks must maintain a positive spread between their lending and borrowing rates adjusted for servicing costs. Since CPA focuses on these critical variables, it is an important tool of commercial-bank financial management.

THE LOAN POLICY OF A MAJOR SOUTHEASTERN BANK

It is critical that a bank have a written loan policy. This chapter concludes with a brief look at the loan policy of a major southeastern bank. The contents of the loan policy are presented in Table 20-14. The five major components of the bank's loan policy are described by the following headings: (1) general policies, (2) specific loan categories, (3) miscellaneous loan policies, (4) quality control, and (5) committees.

Loan Policy Summary

Like the investment policy presented in Chapter 16, a loan policy is an important and useful statement for a bank to have. In fact, it is *the* most important document in the asset-management area. By setting parameters, defining responsibilities, and establishing a system of checks and balances, the loan policy provides a framework for building an efficient loan-management program. A loan policy serves as an excellent introduction to some of the terminology and practical aspects of loan management.

TABLE 20-14 The Contents of the Loan Policy for a Major Southeastern Bank

General Policy

Management
Trade area
Balance loan portfolio
Portfolio administration
Loan to deposit ratio
Legal loan limit
Lending authority
Loan responsibility
Interest rates
Loan repayment
Collateral
Credit Information & Documentation
Delinquency ratios
Loan-loss reserves
Charge-offs
Extensions or renewals of past due installment loans
Consumer laws and regulations

Specific Loan Categories

Business development opportunities
Desirable loans by loan category:
1. Commercial loans
2. Agricultural loans
3. Mortgage loans
4. Installment and branch bank loans
5. VISA and revolving credit
6. Mortgage-banking subsidiary
7. Letters of credit
8. Loan commitments
9. Undesirable loans

Miscellaneous Loan Policies

Loans to executive officers, directors, 10 percent shareholders and companies they control
Employee loans
Mortgage-Banking subsidiary
Conflict of interest

Quality Control

1. Credit department
2. Loan review
3. Recovery department

Committees

Directors Loan Committee of the Board of Directors
Officers Loan Committee
Loan Review Committee

CHAPTER SUMMARY

Maintaining loan quality is critical to the success of a commercial bank. The numerous energy- and farm-bank failures of the 1980s and the thinly capitalized money-center banks bear witness to the havoc that poor quality energy, farm, and LDC loans, respectively, can cause. Measures of loan quality include net loan losses, provision for loan losses, loan-loss reserves, past due and nonaccrual loans, and examiner judgments of loan quality. This chapter has focused on some practical aspects of the management of credit risk in terms of lending practices and administration of the loan function. The keys to successful management of a loan portfolio focus on the ability of lenders to monitor and control ("discipline") the costs, loan losses, growth, and concentrations of their loan portfolios. In addition, they must provide the right kind of incentives for their loan "hunters" and their loan "skinners." A good loan policy provides a framework for setting parameters, defining responsibilities, and establishing a system of checks and balances for management of a bank's loan portfolio. Customer profitability analysis (CPA) is a technique for estimating the profitability of business accounts.

The major components of bank loan portfolios are commercial and industrial (C&I) loans, loans to individuals, and loans secured by real estate. Large banks concentrate their lending efforts on business credits, whereas small banks are retail shops specializing in consumer and/or farm lending. The growth rates, lending terms, and functional costs of producing these types of loans were analyzed and seen to differ across our two basic size groups, "big banks" versus "little banks." An important lending phenomenon of the 1980s, leveraged buyouts (LBOs), were analyzed. Similar to the REIT and LDC crises, some observers see LBO credits as a potential trouble spot for the banking system in the future. The combination of excessive growth and sloppy credit analysis, followed by an economic downturn, are the stuff of credit crises.

LIST OF KEY WORDS AND CONCEPTS

Accrual accounting versus cash accounting
Acquisition, development, and construction (ADC) loans
Agency costs and incentives
Allowance for loan losses (loan-loss reserve)
Accountants, appraisers, and attorneys (importance to LBOs)
Asset-based lending
Bank loan policy
Banks with (without) foreign offices
Base lending rates (prime, Fed funds, domestic, foreign)
Collateral
Commercial and industrial (C&I) loans
Consumer loans (loans to individuals or households)
Corporate restructurings
Credit card costs
Customer profitability analysis (CPA)
Delegated monitoring
Delinquency rates
Diversification
Either/or facility
Examiner classified assets (substandard, doubtful, and loss)

"Fortressed" balance sheet
Fraudulent conveyance
Functional cost analysis (FCA)
"Hunters" and "skinners"
Interest income
Interest-rate ceiling
Less-developed country (LDC)
Leveraged buyouts (LBOs)
Line of credit
Loan commitment ("revolver")
Loan participation
Loan portfolio "discipline"
Loans to farmers
Loans secured by real estate (single family, multifamily, nonresidential)
Monitoring codes and mechanisms
Net loan losses
Nonaccrual loan
Nonperforming loan
Past due loan
Provision for loan losses
Rate (floating versus fixed)
Repricing risk
Real estate investment trust (REIT)
Standard Industrial Classification (SIC) code
Terms of lending

REVIEW/DISCUSSION QUESTIONS

1. Who is J. Richard Fredericks, what does he do, and how does he attempt to do it? Be sure to talk about "fortressed" balance sheets and "discipline."
2. What are the keys to successful management of a bank loan portfolio? What role, if any, does a bank's loan policy play in this management? Where have the problem areas of bank lending been over the past two decades?
3. What kinds of loans do banks make and how does bank size affect loan composition, if at all? Describe the growth of bank loans by type of loan and bank size.
4. What are the various measures of bank loan quality and how do they differ from examiner judgments of loan quality?
5. What is the job of a "hunter"? A "skinner"? What problems can arise if the hunter is also the skinner? How would you structure these tasks if you were in charge?
6. How do terms of lending differ for "big banks" versus "little ones" across the following loan categories: (a) C&I loans, (b) loans to farmers, and (c) construction and land development loans.
7. What is an LBO and how does it compare/contrast with other forms of corporate restructurings? Are LBOs really new? What is asset-based lending and what are some of the pitfalls involved? Have banks been too eager to do LBOs? What combination of ingredients would lead to the triad of REIT/LDC/LBO syndrome?
8. Two Federal Reserve surveys were used in this chapter. Name and describe them, and discuss their importance to bankers. To regulators. Are the surveys important to anyone else?

PROBLEMS

1. JFS and Company has the following simplified balance sheet:

JFS	
$A = 200$	$D = 50$
	$E = 150$

If an LBO is arranged such that the firm's debt-to-asset ratio triples, without changing the firm's total assets, what will the post-LBO balance sheet look like? If your bank was asked to finance the deal, what would be your primary areas of concern? What would you do to protect against potential litigation based on "fraudulent conveyance"?

2. The CPA Bank has a target pretax ROE for each of its business customers of 15 percent and a target equity multiplier of 15 for the bank. If A&J Enterprise has $15 million in loans outstanding to the bank, determine the revenue the bank must earn for the relationship to be profitable under the following conditions: cost of funds is 10 percent, overhead expenses for the account amount to .015 of the sum of loan and deposit balances. A&J's DDA has an average balance of $500,000. Use the appropriate CPA formula given in the text to determine the required revenue. Assuming the loan has a 12-month maturity with a balloon payment of interest and principal, what are the nominal and effective loan rates charged by the bank?

3. Wage and price controls cause economic distortions. Using the standard supply and demand diagram, show what would happen to credit card flows if an effective rate ceiling was imposed on credit card lending. If banks decided to meet the excess demand created by the rate ceiling, what implicit pricing schemes could they use to make up for the loss in interest revenue? What do FCA data have to say about costs of the credit card function?

MATCHING QUIZ

Directions: Select the letter from the right-hand column that best matches the item in the left-hand column.

___ 1. J. Richard Fredericks	A. Examiner determined
___ 2. Lawrence E. Fox	B. Fed survey data on costs
___ 3. Robert A. Miller	C. Other bank common base rate
___ 4. Leveraged buyout	D. Large bank common base rate
___ 5. Corporate restructuring	E. Large bank domain
___ 6. C&I loans	F. Attempts to measure profitability
___ 7. Net loan losses	G. Balance sheet reserve account
___ 8. Nonaccrual status	H. Expense entry
___ 9. SIC codes	I. Tends to be well diversified
___ 10. REIT/LDC syndrome	J. Informal credit facility
___ 11. Prime rate	K. Formal credit facility
___ 12. Fed funds rate	L. Incentive/agency problem
___ 13. Commitment	M. Should be cautious after Penn Square
___ 14. Line of credit	
___ 15. Participation	N. Likes "fortressed" balance sheets
	O. Likes LBOs
___ 16. Nonresidential construction	
	P. Expresses concern about LBOs
___ 17. Single-family construction	
	Q. Uses up unused debt capacity
___ 18. CPA	
	R. Used for monitoring concentrations
___ 19. FCA	

___ 20. Loan policy	S. Costs, growth, and loan losses
___ 21. Provision for loan losses	T. Charge-offs minus recoveries
___ 22. Allowance for loan losses	U. Means cash accounting
___ 23. Substandard, doubtful, loss	V. Are LBOs next?
___ 24. Hunters/skinners	W. Community bank domain
___ 25. Feeder livestock	X. Farm loan collateral
___ 26. "Discipline" factors	Y. Important bank document
	Z. Spin-off

SELECTED REFERENCES

Altman, Edward I. [1985]. "Managing the Commercial Lending Process," in *Handbook for Banking Strategy*, R. C. Aspinwall and R. A. Eisenbeis, eds. New York: Wiley, pp. 473–510.

Anderson, Paul S. [1979]. "Costs and Profitability of Bank Functions," Federal Reserve Bank of Boston *New England Economic Review* (March/April), pp. 43–61.

Bailey, Jeff and G. Christian, Hill. [1985]. "Plowed Under," *The Wall Street Journal* (January 24), pp. 1, 20.

Bayer, Frank J. [1983]. *I Love Credit*. New York: Todd & Honeywell, Inc.

Behrens, Robert H. [1983]. *Commercial Problem Loans*. Boston: Bankers Publishing Company.

Behrens, Robert H. [1985]. *Commercial Loan Officer's Handbook*. Boston: Bankers Publishing Company.

Bloch, Ernest. [1986]. *Inside Investment Banking*. New York: Dow Jones-Irwin.

Blundell, William E. [1985]. "Out of Joint." *The Wall Street Journal* (February 2), pp. 1, 22.

Brady, Thomas F. [1985]. "Changes in Loan Pricing and Business Lending at Commercial Banks," *Federal Reserve Bulletin* (January), pp. 1–13.

Brealey, Richard, and Stewart, Myers. [1981]. *Principles of Corporate Finance*. New York: McGraw-Hill.

Cole, Robert H. [1984]. *Consumer and Commercial Credit Management*. Homewood Hills, IL: Irwin.

Fox, Lawrence E. [1987]. "Banks Are Not Too Eager," *The Journal of Commercial Bank Lending* (February), pp. 24–26.

Functional Cost Analysis: 1983 Average Banks. [1985]. New York: Federal Reserve Bank of New York.

Gill, Edward K. [1983]. *Commercial Lending Basics*. Reston, VA: Reston Publishing Company.

Guenther, Robert. [1985]. "Giving Up," *The Wall Street Journal* (February 7), pp. 1, 24.

Hale, Roger H. [1983]. *Credit Analysis: A Complete Guide*. New York: Wiley.

Hall, Robert D., and F. Blake Cloonen. [1984]. *Profitable Consumer Lending*. Boston: Bankers Publishing Company.

Hayes, Douglas A. [1977]. *Bank Lending Policies*. Ann Arbor: The University of Michigan.

Hoffman, Margaret A., and Gerald C. Fischer. [1984]. *Credit Department Management*. Philadelphia: Robert Morris Associates.

Knight, Robert E. [1975]. "Customer Profitability Analysis." Federal Reserve Bank of Philadelphia *Monthly Review* (April), pp. 11–20.

Miller, Robert A. [1987]. "Banks Are Too Eager," *The Journal of Commercial Bank Lending* (February), pp. 20–24.

Peterson, Richard L. [1985]. "Pricing Consumer Loans and Deposits." In Aspinwall and Eisenbeis, *op. cit.*, pp. 549–588.

Rosenblum, Harvey and Pavel, Christine. [1985]. "Banking Services in Transition: The Effects of Nonbank Competitors," in *Handbook for Banking Strategy*, R. C. Aspinwall and R. A. Eisenbeis, eds. New York: Wiley, pp. 203–266.

Simpson, Thomas D. [1988]. "Developments in the U.S. Financial System since the Mid-1970s," *Federal Reserve Bulletin* (January), pp. 1–13.

Sinkey, Joseph F., Jr. [1985]. "Regulatory Attitudes Toward Risk," in *Handbook for Banking Strategy*, R. C. Aspinwall and R. A. Eisenbeis, eds. New York: Wiley, pp. 347–380.

————. [1979]. *Problem and Failed Institutions in the Commercial Banking Industry*. Greenwich, CT: JAI Press.

Statistics on Banking. [1983]. Washington, DC: Federal Deposit Insurance Corporation.

Stigum, Marcia L., and Rene O. Branch. [1983]. *Managing Bank Assets and Liabilities*. Homewood Hills, IL: Dow Jones-Irwin.

Taylor, John Renford. [1983]. *Consumer Lending*. Washington, DC: American Bankers Association.

Villani, Kevin E. [1985]. "Pricing Mortgage Credit." In *Handbook for Banking Strategy*, R. C. Aspinwall and R. A. Eisenbeis, eds. New York: Wiley, pp. 607–660.

Wood, J. H. [1975]. *Commercial Bank Loan and Investment Behaviour*. New York: Wiley.

CHAPTER 21

Management of Off-Balance-Sheet Risk

WHY OFF-BALANCE-SHEET ACTIVITIES EXIST

The squeeze on bank earnings and market and regulatory demands for increased bank capital are the driving forces behind the surge in off-balance-sheet activities (OBSAs). Consider the action–reaction–interaction sequence of events in this area:

Action: The squeeze on earnings caused by greater competition, removal of interest-rate ceilings, and poor loan quality (especially for banks with energy, farm, or third-world debt).
Reaction: Banks attempt to offset the squeeze in earnings by engaging in OBSAs to increase fee income.
Action: Market forces signal a positive reaction to increases in bank equity and regulators require banks to increase their minimum capital ratios.
Reaction: Banks attempt to circumvent higher capital requirements by moving activities off the balance sheet.
Interaction: OBSAs enable banks to generate fee income and to circumvent capital requirements.
Reaction: Regulators propose risk-based capital requirements in an attempt to price the risk of OBSAs. Stay tuned to the financial news network for bankers's reactions to risk-based capital requirements.

These events, as we have noted in Chapter 14, can be captured neatly by our return-on-equity model: $ROE = ROA \times EM$, where ROE is net income over equity capital, ROA is net income over total assets, and EM, the equity multiplier, is total assets over equity capital. Suppose that a bank used to have the following ROE profile: $.20 = .01 \times 20$. If the factors described above squeeze ROA down to .0075, then ROE will drop to $.15 = .0075 \times 20$, other things equal. If on top of this "injury" the market and regulators jointly add the "insult" of a higher capital requirement, as reflected by a lower EM of 15, then ROE is further squeezed down to .1125 = .0075 × 15. Suppose now that through an aggressive OBSA program, the bank is *jointly* able to generate sufficient fee income to increase ROA from .0075 to .0090 and to minimize the adverse effects of the higher capital requirement. In this case, ROE rises to .1350 = .0090 × 15. In a nutshell, this is the tale of how OBSAs came to exist.

THE DOCUMENTATION OF OFF-BALANCE SHEET ACTIVITIES

As of September 30, 1987, the OBSAs shown in Table 21-1 totaled almost $3 trillion dollars. On that same day, bank capital stood at only $180 billion; that's an OBSA-to-capital ratio of 16.7. Since the banking industry's equity multiplier is of a similar magnitude, the banking system has at least as many assets off its balance sheet as on it. Moreover, since the OBSAs shown in Table 21-1 do not measure all of the banking system's unbooked activities, the OBSA–capital multiplier of 17 is under-estimated. The important point is that the banking system is bursting with OBSAs.

The five OBSAs shown in Table 21-1 are (1) standby letters of credit, (2) commercial letters of credit, (3) loan commitments, (4) foreign-exchange transactions, and (5) interest-rate swaps. Let's focus on each of these activities with respect to their conceptual, risk, and empirical aspects (also see Chapter 14).

Standby Letters of Credit

From 1980 through 1986, standby letters of credit (SLCs) grew at a compound annual rate of almost 24 percent. However, with only $170 billion in SLCs outstanding on September 30, 1987, they are less than 6 percent of the OBSAs reported in Table 21-1. Moreover, during the first nine months of 1987, SLCs declined at an annual rate of 1.6 percent. A longer view of the growth of SLCs, which highlights their rapid growth in the early 1980s, is shown in Figure 21-1. Since 1985, however, SLC growth has leveled off and even declined slightly. Simpson [1988] attributes this phenomenon to what we have called "regulatory interference." Specifically, since then, regulators have informally taken account of SLCs in conducting on-site examinations and reviewing applications for expansion. Additional pressures in this area included the deterioration of credit ratings at some large banks/BHCs and international agreement on capital standards led by the United States and the United Kingdom.

TABLE 21-1   The Growth of Bank Off-Balance-Sheet Activities, 1981–1987

Activity	$ Billions 1980	$ Billions 1986	Compound Annual Growth 1980 to 1986	$ Billions 1987–III[a]	Annual Growth from 1986
Letters of credit					
Standby	47	170	23.9%	168	−1.6%
Commercial	20	28	5.8%	30	9.6%
Loan commitments[b]	432	572	9.8%	595	5.4%
Foreign-exch. trans.	177	893	31.0%	1,558	110.0%
Interest-rate swaps[c]	186	367	97.3%	602	93.9%
Bank capital[d]	108	183	9.2%	180	−2.2%

[a] Data for 1987 are third-quarter preliminary. All other data are year-end.
[b] Data in column for 1980 are as of 1983 and the corresponding growth rate only covers the period 1983–1986.
[c] Data in column for 1980 are as of 1985 and the corresponding growth rate covers only one year.
[d] Bank capital is defined as the sum of perpetual preferred stock, common stock, surplus, undivided profits and capital reserves, cumulative foreign currency translation adjustments, and reserves for loan losses.
Source: Chessen [1987], Table 1, p. 4.

Billions of dollars

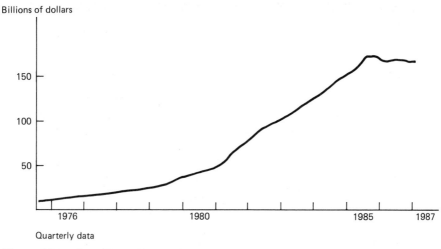

Quarterly data

Figure 21-1   Standby Letters of Credit at All Insured Commercial Banks

Source: Simpson [1988], Chart 8, p. 8.

What is an SLC? First, recall that a letter of credit is a document in which a bank vouches for someone's credit. In the case of a commercial letter of credit, a definite commitment to finance a transaction is agreed upon. In contrast, an SLC is a standby arrangement in which the bank pays or provides credit only if its customer defaults. In effect, an SLC is a financial guaranty, or form of insurance, waiting in the wings to back up the bank's customer. SLCs are used in both commercial and financial transactions. In the latter case, they provide guarantees for debt instruments such as commercial paper, notes, or bonds, and performance guarantees for construction contracts. Since banks tend to provide SLCs only for customers who are unlikely to default, the risk of these transactions would not appear to be great. In this case, why do the customers buy the insurance? For them, it is likely to be a positive NPV project because the cost savings (e.g., lower interest rate on a debt obligation) outweigh the fee paid to the bank for the SLC. In effect, the market perceives the bank's reputational capital as being substituted for that of the customer, which enhances the customer's access to financial markets.

Suppose that banks in their quest for greater fee income begin to write SLCs for riskier customers. In this situation, the bank's risk exposure would obviously increase. The higher fees charged such customers would have to compensate the bank for its greater risk exposure. Presumably the possibility of this situation getting out of hand is why the regulators have been exercising closer scrutiny of SLC underwritings. However, given the relatively small volume of SLCs outstanding and the apparent high credit standards applied to SLCs, the regulatory reaction could be an excessive one.

Commercial Letters of Credit

Compared to SLCs, commercial letters of credit are an even less important OBSA. As of September 30, 1987, these arrangements totaled only $30 billion, or only 1 percent of the OBSAs shown in Table 21-1. Moreover, from 1980 through 1986, they grew at less than 6 percent per year. The growth rate for the first nine months of 1987 was up slightly, however, to almost 10 percent. As instruments of bill and trade finance, banks have been writing commercial letters of credit for years. Again, unless banks begin underwriting riskier customers, the risk in this area would not appear to be great.

"Accepted" time drafts arising from commercial letters of credit are negotiable instruments that trade in the money market as "bankers acceptances."

Loan Commitments

Until 1983 data on loan commitments were not collected by bank regulators nor widely reported by banks in their financial statements. As of September 30, 1987, loan commitments totaled $595 billion for all banks, or roughly 20 percent of the OBSAs reported in Table 21-1. From 1983 through 1986, loan commitments grew at a compound annual rate of 9.8 percent. However, over the first nine months of 1987, the rate slowed to 5.4 percent.

A loan commitment is a formal arrangement or credit facility whereby a bank agrees to lend a customer a specified amount of money at an agreed-upon rate, usually at some spread over a base or reference rate such as the federal funds rate, the prime rate, or LIBOR. The customer, who pays a commitment fee for the service, may "take down" as much of the "committed facility" as needed up to the maximum specified in the agreement. Revolving underwriting or commitments are the most common type of loan commitment. These arrangements permit funds to be borrowed, repaid, and borrowed again for terms up to two or three years. For existing customers with long-term relationships, banks are able to track historical usage rates and by staying on top of current and expected future developments to generate fairly reliable usage rates for their outstanding loan commitments.

Foreign-Exchange Transactions

As of September 30, 1987, slightly more than one-half of the OBSAs reported in Table 21-1 were accounted for by foreign-exchange transactions, with a volume of almost $1.6 billion. From 1980 through 1986, these transactions grew at a compound rate of 31 percent. However, over the next nine months they exploded to an annual growth rate of 110 percent. This phenomenon was, in part, an attempt by the largest banks to recoup the heavy drain on earnings associated with the provision for loan losses allocated for third-world debt (e.g., mainly Brazil) during the second quarter of 1987. Moreover, these banks perceived the stock market crash of October 19, 1987, as an opportunity to make further gains in foreign-exchange transactions during the fourth quarter of 1987. They seized this opportunity and made a killing by registering a 230 percent increase in income from such transactions in the fourth quarter of 1987 compared to the fourth quarter of 1986 (see Hill and Quenther [1988]).

Profits in foreign-exchange trading come from two main sources: (1) trading profits generated by the bank trading for its own account and (2) fees generated by trading in currencies for its customers. Following the stock market crash and the continued adverse news on the U.S. trade deficit in the fourth quarter of 1987, the big banks bet that the dollar would decline. It did and their bets paid off. What if the dollar had not declined? Don't think about it! A spokesperson for Bankers Trust (one of the big winners and therefore presumably one of the big bettors), when asked about the downside risk, would not elaborate except to say the extraordinary profits were achieved while" … staying within … traditional risk policies."[1] Confirming this opinion, J. Richard Fredericks (recall he is the bank stock analyst from Montgomery

---

[1] Hill and Guenther [1988], p. 2.

Securities in San Francisco), when asked (on "Wall Street Week," February 12, 1988) about Bankers Trust's foreign-exchange (and LBO) profits in the fourth quarter of 1987, said he thought Bankers Trust had the "track record" to handle the risks involved in such deals.

Interest-Rate Swaps

The last OBSA in Table 21-1 is interest-rate swaps (see Chapters 14 and, especially, 17 for detailed treatment of swaps). These transactions were growing very rapidly in 1986 and the first nine months of 1987. Note that prior to 1985, data on swaps were not available. Accordingly, the track record on these activities is sparse. By September 30, 1987, interest-rate swaps for all commercial banks totaled $603 billion (notional value), or 20 percent of the OBSAs reported in Table 21-1, and 3.2 times the swaps outstanding in 1985. The notional value of a swap refers to the book value of the underlying debt and not to the stream of interest payments on the debt.

Recall that an interest-rate swap is simply an exchange of debt payments between two parties. Bankers participate in swaps by being one of the direct participants, or by acting as a third-party agent either in arranging swaps or as guarantors, or both. However they are involved, banks participate in swaps because they earn fees or reduce their borrowing costs, or both. Moreover, since the risks involved in interest-rate swaps are minimal, they do not appear to be a serious threat to bank capital or the safety and soundness of the banking system.

Bank Capital

Viewing bank capital as the ultimate cushion for absorbing losses, whether they arise from activities on or off the balance sheet, OBSAs need to be compared to this financial backstop. Current earnings and reserves are the immediate buffers for absorbing realized risks. From 1980 to 1986, bank capital (as defined in Table 21-1) grew at a compound annual rate of 9.2 percent. The decline in capital over the first nine months of 1987 was an aberration associated with the LDC debt crisis. Moreover, this decline will be cushioned by the high profits earned in the fourth quarter of 1987.

The critical point is that no reasonable amount of financial capital can offset imprudence and/or stupid management. If bank managers make bad decisions and/or bet the bank, the bank's shareholders, and perhaps uninsured creditors, will suffer, not to mention the deposit-insurance fund and taxpayers. Should bank regulators then be concerned about OBSAs and require banks to allocate capital for such activities? The next part of the book will deal with this issue in detail; for now suffice it to say that bank regulators should be *concerned* about anything banks do. However, they should be *most* concerned about who the managers are and their competencies, what policies they have in place, and what kinds of checks and balances they have available for monitoring risk-taking. If these things are in place, then, without jeopardizing financial stability, let market forces and the most efficient producers of financial services survive.

THE CONCENTRATION OF OBSAs IN LARGE BANKS

Off-balance-sheet activities are the domain of large banks. As of September 30, 1987, there were 35 banks with total assets greater than $10 billion. These 35 banks controlled the following dollar amounts and percentages of the OBSAs described in the previous section:

Standby letters of credit	$ 125.4 billion	74%
Commercial letters of credit	$ 20.0 billion	66%
Loan commitments	$ 367.2 billion	62%
Foreign-exchange transactions	$1,526.3 billion	98%
Interest-rate swaps	$ 571.3 billion	95%
TOTAL	$2,610.2 billion	88%

The full distribution of OBSAs by bank size is shown in Table 21-2. Focusing on the 135 banks with total assets greater than $3 billion, the following concentration is observed:

Standby letters of credit	$ 150.0 billion	89%
Commercial letters of credit	$ 26.2 billion	87%
Loan commitments	$ 486.7 billion	82%
Foreign-exchange transactions	$1,557.8 billion	100%
Interest-rate swaps	$ 594.8 billion	99%
TOTAL	$2,814.7 billion	95%

With 95 percent of OBSAs concentrated in less than 1 percent of the 13,850 reporting banks (i.e., .0097 = 135/13,850), there is no question of the dominance of regional, superregional, and money-center banks in the OBSA arena.

An alternative look at the OBSA data is provided by focusing on the average dollar amount of particular activities at banks with total assets less than $300 million. For these 12,981 banks, we observe the following averages: $315.8 thousand in SLCs, $77.0 thousand in commercial letters of credit, $2.1 million in loan commitments, $15.4 thousand in foreign exchange transactions, and $53.9 thousand in interest-rate swaps. Except for loan commitments, community banks are not in the OBSA ball game.

The Risk Exposure of the Major OBSAs Players

In Table 21-3, the risk exposures of the major players to each of the OBSA categories are highlighted. Risk exposure is measured by the dollar amount of each activity relative to the bank's capital plus reserves. In addition, the dollar volumes for December 31, 1986, and September 30, 1987, are shown, along with the nine-month percentage change. The rankings presented in Table 21-3 are based on the ratio of the particular OBSA to capital. The four banks with the greatest exposure across the five OBSA categories are:

OBSA Category	Bank	$ Billions	OBSA/Cap.
Standby letters of credit	Chemical Bank	7.7	2.3
Commercial letters of credit	Irving Trust	1.04	.8
Loan commitments	Mellon Bank	15.1	10.6
Foreign-exchange transactions	Bankers Trust	197.1	56.2
Interest-rate swaps	Chemical Bank	76.6	23.0

TABLE 21-2 Selected Off-Balance-Sheet Activities by Size of Bank as of September 30, 1987 (Preliminary Data; $ Billions)

Bank Size	Number of Banks	Standby Letters of Credit		Commercial Letters of Credit	
		Sum	% of Total	Sum	% of Total
Greater than $10 billion	35	$125.4	74%	$20.0	66%
$3 billion to $10 billion	100	24.6	15	6.2	21
$1 billion to $3 billion	207	9.3	6	2.0	7
$300 million to $1 billion	527	4.5	3	1.2	4
Less than $300 million	12,981	4.1	3	1.0	3
TOTAL	13,850	$167.9	100%	$30.3	100%

Bank Size	Loan Commitments		Foreign-Exchange Transactions		Interest-Rate Swaps	
	Sum	% of Total	Sum	% of Total	Sum	% of Total
Greater than $10 billion	$367.2	62%	$1526.3	98%	$571.3	95%
$3 billion to $10 billion	119.5	20	29.9	2	23.5	4
$1 billion to $3 billion	57.2	10	1.1	0	4.9	1
$300 million to $1 billion	24.6	4	0.1	0	2.7	0
Less than $300 million	26.9	5	0.2	0	0.7	0
TOTAL	$595.4	100%	$1557.8	100%	$603.1	100%

Source: Chessen [1987], Table 2, p. 5.

TABLE 21-3 Large Banks with the Highest Off-Balance-Sheet Activity to Capital Ratio[a][b] (Preliminary September 30, 1987 Data)

A. Standby Letters of Credit

Bank	SLCs/ Capital + Res.	SLCs ($ Billions)		Percentage Change in Dollar Volume from 12/86 to 9/87
		9/87	12/86	
Chemical Bank	2.32	$ 7.7	$ 7.5	2.7%
Bankers Trust	2.25	7.9	8.5	− 7.1
Marine Midland	2.00	2.7	2.6	3.8
Chase Manhattan	1.94	11.8	12.8	−7.8
Citibank	1.92	21.3	20.8	2.4
First Chicago	1.86	4.0	4.0	−0.0
Manufacturers Hanover	1.81	7.6	9.2	−17.4
Mellon Bank	1.79	2.6	2.8	−7.1
Security Pacific	1.75	5.1	5.0	2.0
Irving Trust	1.59	2.0	2.2	−9.1
TOTAL		72.7	75.4	−3.6

B. Commercial Letters of Credit[a]

Bank	CLCs/ Capital + Res.	CLCs ($ Billions)		Percentage Change in Dollar Volume from 12/86 to 9/87
		9/87	12/86	
Irving Trust	.81	$ 1.04	$ .81	28.4%
First Minneapolis	.48	.48	.33	50.0
National Westminster	.47	.37	.34	8.8
Manufacturers Hanover	.42	1.76	1.51	16.6
Chase Manhattan	.41	2.52	2.53	−0.4
Republic Nat. N.Y.	.41	.75	.60	25.0
Citibank	.35	3.93	3.76	4.5
Bank of America	.35	1.99	1.92	3.6
First Chicago	.32	.69	.83	−16.9
Chemical Bank	.32	1.07	1.11	−3.6
TOTAL		14.47	13.63	6.2

(*continues*)

TABLE 21-3 (*Continued*)

C. Loan Commitments[a]

Bank	Commitments/ Capital + Res.	Commitments ($ Billions)		Percentage Change in Dollar Volume from 12/86 to 9/87
		9/87	12/86	
Mellon Bank First Chicago	10.6	$ 15.1	$ 15.7	−3.8%
Security Pacific	9.0	19.3	21.1	−8.5
Bank of New England	8.3	24.3	24.7	−1.6
First Interstate CA	7.6	5.9	4.6	28.3
Chemical Bank	7.5	11.3	10.1	11.9
Bank of America	7.4	24.7	22.7	8.8
Texas Commerce	7.0	39.7	41.1	−3.4
Seattle-First	7.0	5.9	7.6	−22.4
NCNB	6.5	4.8	3.9	23.1
	6.1	6.0	5.8	3.4
TOTAL		$157.0	$157.3	−0.2

D. Foreign-Exchange Obligations[a]

Bank	Foreign Exchange/ Capital + Res.	Foreign Exchange ($ Billions)		Percentage Change in Dollar Volume from 12/86 to 9/87
		9/87	12/86	
Bankers Trust	56.2	$ 197.1	$ 78.6	150.8%
First Chicago	49.9	106.7	48.4	120.5
Chemical Bank	37.9	126.4	85.5	47.8
Morgan Guaranty	31.6	160.8	98.0	64.1
Citibank	30.3	337.2	214.2	57.4
Irving Trust	28.6	36.7	20.9	75.6
Chase Manhattan	27.7	169.5	104.2	62.7
Manufacturers Hanover	24.9	103.8	64.3	61.4
Bank of America	21.1	118.9	70.3	69.1
First Interstate CA	17.7	26.7	8.8	203.4
TOTAL		$1,383.8	$714.6	93.6

E. Interest-Rate Swaps[a]

Bank	Swaps/ Capital + Res.	Swaps ($ Billions)		Percentage Change in Dollar Volume from 12/86 to 9/87
		9/87	12/86	
Chemical Bank	23.0	$ 76.6	$ 35.5	115.8%
Bankers Trust	21.9	76.9	51.6	49.0
Manufacturers Hanover	14.7	61.3	38.0	61.3
Security Pacific	11.8	34.6	14.7	135.4
First Interstate CA	11.7	17.6	11.3	55.8
Morgan Guaranty	10.8	55.0	40.2	36.8
First Chicago	10.1	21.6	17.7	22.0
Citibank	9.5	105.2	66.1	59.2
Marine Midland	8.6	11.6	4.2	176.2
Chase Manhattan	7.4	45.5	21.9	107.7
Total		$505.9	$301.2	68.0

[a]Care must be taken not to interpret high ratios of SLCs to capital as necessarily indicative of greater risk-taking by banks. It is simply a way to measure volume relative to some standard. Whether or not capital is sufficient to cover unexpected losses in off-balance-sheet instruments—and all other unexpected balance sheet losses—depends on the individual institution and the quality of its assets and off-balance-sheet positions.

[b]Large banks are defined as those with assets greater than $10 billion. Capital is the sum of perpetual preferred stock, common stock, surplus, undivided profits and capital reserves, cumulative foreign currency translation adjustments, and reserves for loan losses.

Source: Chessen [1987], Table 3, pp. 6–8.

Focusing on all five of the OBSA categories in Table 23-3, we see that the money-center banks have the greatest risk exposure. Based on the ratio of OBSAs to capital, the rankings (as of September 30, 1987) are listed here:

Rank	Bank	OBSAs	Capital	OBSA/Capital
1	Bankers Trust	$ 281.9B	$ 3.5B	80.5
2	Chemical Bank	236.5	3.3	71.7
3	First Chicago	153.3	2.1	70.8
4	Citibank	467.7	11.1	42.1
5	Manufacturers	174.5	4.2	41.5
6	Chase Manhattan	226.8	6.1	37.2
7	Irving Trust	39.7	1.3	30.5
8	BankAmerica	160.6	5.6	28.7
9	Morgan Guaranty	215.8	11.9	18.1
10	First Interstate	55.6	4.6	12.1
11	Security Pacific	64.0	8.3	7.7
	TOTAL	$2,075.3B	$62.0	34.4

With more than $2 trillion dollars in OBSAs (which is a slight underestimate because not all of the banks made the top ten in each category in Table 21-3), these 11 money-center banks control two-thirds of the reported OBSAs. With an aggregate capital base of $62 billion, these banks have an average OBSA-to-capital ratio of 34.4. By comparing the rankings for all OBSAs with those in Panel D of Table 23-3 for foreign-exchange obligations, one can see that these two rankings are closely correlated.

Focusing on OBSAs for the regional banks represented in Table 23-3, we find that none of them, except for Marine Midland, make the top ten in the categories of foreign-exchange transactions, interest-rate swaps, or standby letters of credit. However, they do make their way into the rankings for loan commitments and commercial letters of credit as represented by such names as Bank of New England, NCNB, Texas Commerce, First Minneapolis, and Seattle-First. Thus, in terms of the rankings for greatest risk exposure, regional banks engage in the more traditional credit-related OBSAs compared to the money-center banks with their foreign-exchange trading and interest-rate swaps.

To further illustrate the role of OBSAs at regional banks and to show the schedule of commitments and contingencies collected by federal bank regulators, let's focus on Table 21-4, which shows Schedule RC-L for Wachovia Bank and Trust (WB&T) for December 31, 1987. By summing items 1–12 in Table 21-4, we see that WB&T had total OBSAs of almost $4.1 billion. With an equity capital base of $793 million, the bank had an OBSA-to-equity multiplier of 5.1, which is substantially below the money-center benchmark of 34-to-1. For WB&T, 97 percent of its OBSAs were concentrated in five activities, with loan commitments leading the way with $3.1 billion, or 77 percent of the total. Since the data for loan commitments shown in Table 21-4 measure only the unused portion of commitments that are fee paid or otherwise legally binding, they may understate the effective dollar amount of outstanding commitments because informal commitments are excluded. Nevertheless, since such commitments are not legally binding, the bank has a legal option out of such contingencies, at the expense of possible injury to the customer relationship. The complete breakdown of WB&T's

TABLE 21-4   Wachovia Bank and Trust Schedule RC-L Commitments and Contingencies December 31, 1987

	$ Thousands	Line
1. Commitments to make or purchase loans or to extend credit in the form of lease financing arrangements (report only the unused portions of commitments that are fee paid or otherwise legally binding)	3,127,215	1.
2. Futures and forward contracts (exclude contracts involving foreign exchange):		
a. Commitments to purchase	6,785	2.a.
b. Commitments to sell	78,035	2.b.
3. When-issued securities:		
a. Gross commitments to purchase	4,608	3.a.
b. Gross commitments to sell	1,688	3.b.
4. Standby contracts and other option arrangements:		
a. Obligations to purchase under option contracts	None	4.a.
b. Obligations to sell under option contracts	None	4.b.
5. Commitments to purchase foreign currencies and U.S. dollar exchange (spot and forward)	74,554	5.
6. Standby letters of credit and foreign office guarantees:		
a. Standby letters of credit and foreign office guarantees:		
(1) To U.S. addressees (domicile)	538,242	6.a.(1)
(2) To non-U.S. addressees (domicile)	25	6.a.(2)
b. Amount of standby letters of credit in items 6.a.(1) and 6.a.(2) conveyed to others through participations	7,078	6.b.
7. Commercial and similar letters of credit	111,747	7.
8. Participations in acceptances (as described in the instructions) conveyed to others by the reporting bank	None	8.
9. Participations in acceptances (as described in the instructions) acquired by the reporting (nonaccepting) bank	None	9.
10. Securities borrowed	None	10.
11. Securities lent	None	11.
12. Other significant commitments and contingencies (list below each component of this item over 25% of Schedule RC, item 28, "Total equity capital")	100,805	12.
None		
Memoranda		
1. Loans originated by the reporting bank that have been sold or participated to others during the calendar quarter ending with the report data (exclude the portions of such loans retained by the reporting bank; see instructions for other exclusions)	3,032	M.1.
2. Loans purchased by the reporting bank during the calendar quarter ending with the report data (see instructions for exclusions)	None	M.2.
3. Notional value of all outstanding interest rate swaps	44,400	M.3.

OBSA composition for December 31, 1987 follows:

Loan commitments	$3,127 million	(77%)
Standby letters of credit	538	(13%)
Commercial letters of credit	112	(3%)
Futures and forward contract (sell)	78	(2%)
Foreign-currency commitments	75	(2%)
All other contingencies	130	(3%)
TOTAL	$4,060 million	(100%)

What Are the Real Risks for the Major Players?

Over the past two decades, we have seen that big banks, such as Continental Illinois (1984), First Pennsylvania (1980), and Franklin National (1974), can fail. If mistakes can be made on the balance sheet, they can be made off the balance sheet also. The riskiness of particular activities and the size of the bet made on these activities determine the real risks faced by the major players. The activity with the greatest risk potential would appear to be foreign-exchange trading. Like betting on interest rates, betting on exchange-rate movements offers the prospect for large gains *and* large losses. As noted earlier, in the fourth quarter of 1987, the money-center banks were big winners in the foreign-exchange market. The real test for the riskiness of OBSAs will come when the foreign-exchange bets (or other bets) are wrong. Of course, if the sizes of the bets are prudent, then the damages should be manageable.

ASSET SECURITIZATION AND LOAN PARTICIPATIONS AS VEHICLES FOR GETTING ACTIVITIES OFF THE BALANCE SHEETS OF LARGE BANKS

The pressures for generating fee income and meeting capital requirements have led large banks to securitize (i.e., sell) assets, mainly loans, packaged as securities and to participate (i.e., share) loans with other banks. Although the two activities are quite similar in terms of their fee and capital implications, banks have been doing participations for years, whereas securitization is a recent phenomenon. Nevertheless, even though it's the new kid on the block, securitization is seen by some analysts and regulators as the banking innovation for the 1990s (see Rehm [1988]). Securitized assets and participated loans are attractive because they remove assets from a bank's balance sheet. However, under current banking laws, assets cannot be removed from the balance sheet, under either activity, if recourse is offered to the investors. Specifically, loan participations are without recourse to the originator because buy-backs are not permitted by banking laws. However, through standby letters of credit or other guarantees, the buyer may attempt to arrange legally to have indirect recourse to the originator. Through the same process, securitized assets may establish contingent claims on the originating bank.

Regarding the regulation of securitization, Owen J. Carney, director of the division of investment securities for the OCC, has stated: "The regulators are somewhat anxious about the whole process. Our policy is still evolving ... it's too complicated for a two-page banking circular."[2] The regulators are "anxious" about the possibility of "imprudent practices," which would bring closer supervision and more regulation.

[2] As quoted in the *American Banker* [February 8, 1988], p. 6.

Separation of the Traditional Bank Lending Function

The traditional bank lending function involves two components: (1) origination and (2) funding or loan warehousing. Until recently banks were fairly content to keep these two components together. Today, however, large banks are increasingly originating loans with the idea of selling them or offering participations. Why is this separation occurring and why is it likely to continue to occur? A bank with the expertise and reputation as an originator, but lacking the liquidity, capital, and/or cost structures to fund loans,[3] can specialize as an originator. In the case of large banks, the effective constraints are equity capital and cost, because (through liability management) they usually can buy all the liquidity they need in the marketplace, provided they maintain their creditworthiness. In contrast, smaller banks with higher capital ratios, less recognition, and slack loan demand usually have the capacity to provide funding. In addition, securitization offers small banks something they cannot buy in their local loan markets, the chance to diversify their loan portfolios.

Although the possibility of engaging in securitization and participations as originators is open to all banks, small banks lack the size and reputational capital needed to be effective players in these activities. Moreover, since the Penn Square fiasco in 1982, bankers are likely to be much more cautious about who the originators of loan participations are. Accordingly, the separation of the traditional lending function is occurring along the lines of big banks as originators and little banks (or securities investors) as buyers or funders. In addition, foreign banks, which on balance have less binding capital constraints, have been purchasing loans from large U.S. banks.

Large banks value the origination function because it enables them simultaneously to collect origination and servicing fees and to remove the originated assets from their balance sheets, which, assuming to recourse, eliminates credit and interest-rate risks and provides liquidity. Small banks welcome the opportunity to buy loans because it enables them to diversify their loan portfolios. In addition, they benefit by sharing the origination skills and reputational capital of the large banks, and depending on particular arrangements, by sharing the risks. In cases where the buyer has no recourse, the buyer faces agency and incentive problems associated with the originator (i.e., the buyer must watch out for lemons—caveat emptor). Accordingly, the buyer must have complete confidence in the originator's (1) ability to price credit and interest-rate risks (the problem of asymmetric information), (2) honesty, and (3) goals and objectives. If such confidence is lacking, then the buyer must attempt to duplicate the efforts (and therefore some of the costs) of the originator, or seek another originator. As of this writing, the market for securitized bank assets, excluding mortgages, is just developing. However, most of the paper issued has been of investment-grade quality as most loan sales have been made by banks with good credit ratings, with no incentives to sell "lemons." However, as the market expands, Penn Square–type originators may pop up.

Understanding the Process of Securitization[4]

The process of securitization involves five basic parties: (1) the loan originator (bank), (2) the loan purchase (an affiliated trust), (3) the loan packager (underwriter of the securities), (4) a guarantor (insurance company), and (5) investors (e.g., individuals or other banks) who buy the securities. The process, which is similar to the one for

---

[3] See Rose [1986] and [1987] for a discussion of these cost structures.

[4] This section draws on Johnson and Murphy [1987], pp. 30–33.

mortgage-backed securities (where GNMA, "Ginnie Mae," FNMA, "Fannie Mae" and FHLMC, "Freddie Mac," are the purchasers and packagers with the U.S. government or a private corporation the guarantor), is illustrated in Exhibit 21-1. When assets are securitized (i.e., made into securities), the ownership of the assets and the cash flows pass on to the investors, hence the name pass-through securities. Examples of assets banks have securitized include mortgages, car loans, computer leases, credit-card receivables, service-center receivables, and truck leases. Since pass-through securities are asset-backed claims, they are also known by the asset backing the security (e.g., mortgage-backed securities or certificates for automobile receivables [CARs]; see Exhibit 21-1).

The Market for Mortgage-Backed or Pass-Through Securities[5]

Although the markets for bank securitized assets are in their embryonic stages, the market for mortgage-backed or mortgage pass-through securities is well developed. As shown in Figure 21-2, mortgage pass-throughs were introduced in the mid-1970s and by mid-year 1987 had grown to roughly $600 billion. The years 1985 and 1986 were especially strong ones for mortgage-backed securities, as indicated by the steepness of the line for pass-throughs in those years.

It is critical to understand the importance of borrowers' preferences for fixed-rate mortgages and the process of securitization as explanations for the phenomenal growth of mortgage-backed securities. First, many borrowers want the certainty of a fixed mortgage payment; they do not want to bear the interest-rate risk of a variable-rate mortgage. And second, from 1966 through 1983, thrift institutions were burned (many beyond recognition) by interest-rate risk; accordingly, many thrifts do not want to bear interest-rate risk either. The solution: Make fixed-rate loans but get them off the balance sheet and into the hands of investors who are willing (and presumably

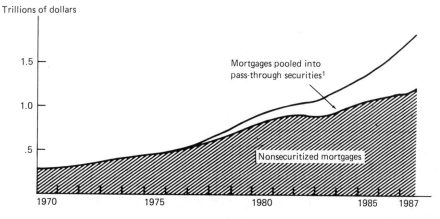

1. Pools include GNMA, FHLMC, and FNMA pass-throughs only.

Figure 21-2   Home Mortgage Debt Outstanding and the Growth of Mortgage-Backed Securities

Source: Simpson [1988], Chart 9, p. 11.

[5] This section draws on Simpson [1988], pp. 10–12.

EXHIBIT 21-1
The Process of Securitization

Step 1

Party:	The Originating bank
Function:	Originator and servicer
Cash flows/claims:	Loans (downstream)
	Loan principal + premiums if any (inflow)
	Interest + principal (passed through over time)
Example:	Marine Midland, automobile receivables

Step 2

Party:	Subsidiary or separate trust
Function:	Buys the loans from the bank and issues the securities
Cash flows/claims:	Loans (inflow)
	Loan principal + premiums (upstream outflow)
	Interest plus principal (passed through)
Example:	Salomon Brothers Affiliate and a separate trust

Step 3

Party:	Investment bankers
Function:	Underwrites and packages the securities and advises the trust
Cash flows/claims:	Collect fees and sells securities issued by the trust
Example	Salomon Brothers

Step 4

Party:	Guarantor
Function:	Wholly or partially insures securities
Cash flows:	Insurance fees (in) and services (out)
Example:	Companies specializing in financial guarantee insurance (e.g., Travelers Insurance Company)

Step 5

Party:	Investors
Function:	Buy securities
Cash flows/claims:	Cash outflow (principal) to buy securities
	Hold securities (claims)
	Interest + principal (cash inflow over time)
Example:	Certificates for Automobile Receivables (CARs) purchased by individuals, small banks, thrifts, and institutional investors

Note: The example shown here is the one mentioned by Johnson and Murphy [1987], p. 31.

more able) to bear interest-rate risk. How is this task accomplished? The process of securitization is the answer.

Most mortgage pass-throughs are federally related in that they are guaranteed or issued by GNMA, FNMA, or FHLMC. These agencies account for all but a small portion of mortgage-backed securities. The dominance of these agencies in the market can be attributed to three factors: (1) the standardization requirement for the underlying mortgages, (2) the size and hence the liquidity of the market, and (3) the federal safety net (guarantee) backing the mortgage pools. Given the guarantee feature of mortgage-backed securities, they are considered almost free of credit or default risk. Moreover, since the investors purchasing these securities are assumed willing to bear interest-rate risk, the primary risk they face is prepayment uncertainty. Specifically, the time for a debt issuer to refinance is when interest rates have fallen below the rates on outstanding debt. Accordingly, prepayments tend to rise as interest rates decline, reflecting the refinancing of existing mortgages and the greater activity in residential construction and trading of existing residences. Conversely, when interest rates are rising, prepayments tend to drop off. Nevertheless, since these relationships are not exact (i.e., completely predictable), mortgage-backed securities command an uncertainty premium (if you like a call premium) relative to Treasury and U.S. government securities. The more unpredictable (volatile) interest rates are, the larger is the prepayment or call premium, and vice versa.

As discussed in Chapter 9, mortgage-backed securities have led to the development of various derivative securities such as collateralized mortgage obligations (CMOs) and interest-only (IO) and principal-only (PO) obligations. These instruments present alternative ways of dealing with prepayment uncertainty. The complexities of administrating these innovative securities have made the development of markets for these instruments highly dependent on advances in computer and information technology, and, to some extent on research dealing with the pricing of complex options.

The Concept of Pass-Throughs Extended to Bank Loans

The primary motivation for the development of mortgage-backed securities was avoidance of interest-rate risk. Neither thrifts nor their customers wanted it. In contrast, banks have been motivated by the implicit tax on bank capital, by competitive pressures on bank profits, and by the desire to exploit their comparative advantage as originators (i.e., as assessors and underwriters of credit). As a result, the concept of the pass-through has been extended to various kinds of bank loans, but mainly to automobile loans and credit-card receivables. According to Simpson [1988], the amount of automobile and credit-card receivables outstanding at the beginning of 1988 was roughly $15 billion, mostly in the form of automobile receivables. The embryonic nature of this market is illustrated by comparing it to the $600 billion market for mortgage-backed securities.

Pass-throughs that are not collateralized or secured by "hard assets" are simply unsecured assets because the underlying loans are unsecured credits (e.g., credit-card receivables). In contrast, CARs (see Exhibit 21-1) are collateralized by hard (but movable) assets as the underlying collateral, namely automobiles. Both secured and unsecured pass-throughs have been enhanced or upgraded through the use of letters of credit, which in effect provides a guarantee. Depending on the structure of the guarantee, however, bank regulators may not permit the underlying asset to be removed from the bank's books, which of course defeats the purpose of securitizing the asset in the first place.

As shown in Exhibit 21-1, the process of securitization for bank loans closely follows the one for mortgages. Specifically, the loan originator usually handles the task of servicing the loan by collecting the principal and interest payments and passing them through to the ultimate investor. By removing assets from its balance sheet, the originating bank accomplishes its objectives of generating liquidity (by reducing funding requirements for the sold assets), eliminating the need for supporting capital, and generating fees, both origination and servicing. Once the supporting resources, both tangible and intangible, for originating loans are in place (e.g., loan officers, customer relationships, computer facilities, capital [dollar and reputational]), the marginal cost of producing additional loans for sale becomes quite low (i.e., economies of scale).

Barriers to Securitization

Can securitization be all things to all banks? Clearly, it can't. The three main barries to securitization focus on size, recourse, and risk. First, regarding the size barrier, Arnold [1986] estimates it takes a minimum pool of assets of $50 million to cost justify a private placement, and a pool of $100 million for a public offering. Legal and investment banking fees are the cost hurdles here. Since the U.S. banking system has roughly 12,000 banks whose total assets do not exceed $100 million, these banks are not capable, on an individual basis, of delivering such large pools of assets for sale. However, on a collective basis, via syndication or some other pooling method, community banks could combine resources to enter the business of securitization.

A second barrier to securitization focuses on the issue of recourse. In this context, recourse simply means that if any of the securitized assets default, then the buyer has "recourse" to the seller such that the seller is responsible for the losses. Clearly, if recourse is available, an asset is not effectively removed from a bank's balance sheet (i.e., it still must be backed by bank capital). Moreover, when recourse is available, bank regulators have ruled that securitized assets must remain on a bank's books. Given the "struggle model" view of bank regulation (i.e., the regulatory dialectic), we would expect innovative banks to attempt to circumvent recourse restrictions. Johnson and Murphy [1987] describe two examples of such innovative attempts. The first one, which the regulators did not allow, involved an attempt by Citibank in 1984 to arrange a "sale-and-guarantee agreement" whereby loan participations sold by Citibank were effectively issued with recourse. The deal involved the issuance of commercial paper (based on the participated loans) by the buyer of the loans (Chatsworth) with a third-party guarantee (by Travelers Insurance Company). The regulators were not sympathetic to this arrangement, as they saw it (i.e., loans with recourse) as simply another form of bank borrowing such as a repurchase agreement.

Another example of a recourse innovation, one which the regulators reluctantly approved, involved recourse to the holding company rather than to the bank. In 1985, Marine Midland and Valley National (Arizona) securitized some car loans which granted the guarantor recourse, not to the respective banks, but to the bank holding companies. Of course, unless one believes in "corporate separateness," the banks still were, to some degree, at risk.

A more recent innovation in the area of recourse focuses on something called a "spread account" or "overcollateralization." In this kind of arrangement, the difference between the interest rate on the securitized assets and the return on the underlying assets is placed in an "escrow" or spread account as a reserve against potential loan losses on the underlying assets. The account's size is dictated by the originator's historical loan-loss rate on the underlying assets. In this type of arrangement, the spread or reserve account represents the only recourse open to investors. If actual losses exceed those in the account, then the investors "eat" the excess as a loss. In contrast, if losses are less than those in the account, the originating bank receives the difference as a "bonus." Although both the OCC and the FDIC have supported the concept of a "spread account" (i.e., they permit assets securitized with spread-account arrangements to be removed from the bank's balance sheet), the Federal Reserve Board has balked at the idea. On balance, the Fed regards the process of securitization as a financing vehicle, and not as a sale of assets. Accordingly, even with a spread account, the Fed considers the bank's future earnings as potentially at risk.

The last aspect of securitization focuses on the risk associated with these transactions. As pools of loans, securitized assets, from the investor's perspective (e.g., a community bank) are safer than traditional loan sales or participations because they are diversified. Specifically, the pooled assets represent a number of borrowers rather than the one (or perhaps the two) found in traditional loan sales. Statistically, pooling results in both the overall risk being lower and the default rate of the pool being more predictable relative to individual loans.

The adverse side of pooling is the inability of the buyer to assess the quality of the underlying credits. Rather than one borrower to analyze, there may be hundreds of credits in the package. Moreover, if the buyer did have the time and expertise to analyze the credits, providing the documentation would be costly and defeat the purpose of engaging in securitization in the first place. Nevertheless, the buyer must watch out for "lemons." In this regard, market discipline is probably the buyer's best defense. Specifically, if an originator or packager of securitized assets gets a reputation for selling "lemons" (i.e., bad credits), its credibility in the marketplace will be tarnished. In the credit game, being a "scorned" player can be fatal because a bank's lifeblood, its liquidity, can dry up.

On the other side of the reputational coin, an originator's quest for maintaining its own quality standing in credit markets may lead it to drain the best credits from its portfolio, leaving only "trash" behind. Thus, originators' face a dilemma: Do they sell the (low-yielding) good credits and keep the (higher-yielding) trash, or do they sell the trash and keep the good stuff? If they chose the former, buyers do not have to worry about lemons; however, if they choose the latter, buyers must beware Obviously, neither of these extremes can prevail in an efficient market. Specifically, a bank that sells lemons will be discovered and not be able to market its securitized assets. Of course, if the lemons are marketed as "junk securities," then no deception is involved. In this case, however, regulators probably would not permit community banks and thrifts to buy such high-risk securities. In contrast, a bank that keeps too many lemons will find the relative quality of its loan portfolio souring, and its credit rating declining.

The solution to the originator's dilemma is to maintain a balance between the quality of its securitized assets and the quality of its own loan portfolio. In an efficient market, extreme behavior in either direction is likely to prove costly and to bring on greater regulatory intervention.

THE ACADEMIC VIEW OF OBSAs AND SECURITIZATION

During February 15–17, 1987, a conference at Northwestern University dealt with "Asset Securitization and Off-Balance-Sheet Risks of Depository Institutions." Although the conference was not limited to academics, the fact that selected papers from the conference were published in an academic journal, the *Journal of Banking and Finance* [September 1987], suggests the academic nature of the meetings. The focus of the conference was the rapidly changing banking practices associated with loan sales, asset securitization, and the rapid growth of contingent claims such as standby letters of credit, loan commitments, note-issuance facilities, interest-rate swaps, and the like. Since these activities are the focus of this chapter, it is appropriate to summarize the ideas and conclusions discussed at this conference. For this purpose, we rely on Greenbaum's "Foreword" to the conference's proceedings (pp. 355–357).

The conference opened with a discussion of the nature and extent of changes in banking practices. Three points worth noting are (1) the loss of market share by banking firms, especially money-center banks, to the capital markets (i.e., the shift from indirect finance to direct finance); (2) the rapid growth of off-balance-sheet activities and securitization; and (3) the relatively embryonic stage of bank asset securitization compared to housing-finance securitization in the thrift industry. Moreover, there was some debate about whether or not securitization is likely to become an important part of commercial banking in the future, since loan sales accomplish the same thing with fewer accounting and regulatory constraints. Nevertheless, since the "moral hazard" problem associated with loan sales can be resolved via the market discipline associated with securitization, the process (as we noted above) is likely to be an important banking technique in the 1990s.

Regarding the existence of securitization and contingencies (i.e., OBSAs), two views (not necessarily mutually exclusive) surfaced at the conference. In either case, however, the emphasis was on the explanatory power of the theory. One view emphasized these activities as being driven by changes in and the interaction between taxes and regulation. Together these forces have served to push assets off banks' balance sheets because they have raised banking's cost of funds relative to its competitors'. The other view is grounded in a technological explanation. Specifically, it stresses the importance of technological change in reducing (1) the costs of processing information associated with selling ("liquifying") assets and (2) informational asymmetries between borrowers and lenders. According to this approach, these changes give borrowers greater access to capital markets.

A more general view of the forces of change driving OBSAs and securitization is captured by our model of change based on TRICK. Specifically,

$$\text{TRICK} + \text{Rational Self-Interest} = \text{OBSAs} + \text{Securitization} \qquad (21\text{-}1)$$

Recall that TRICK stands for Technology, Reregulation, Interest-rate risk, Customers (competition for), and Kapital adequacy; and rational self-interest is manifested by managers of financial-services firms seeking out profitable opportunities. This framework, in conjunction with the ROE explanation given at the beginning of this chapter (and in Chapter 14), provides a comprehensive model for analyzing innovations in the financial-services industry. Clearly, OBSAs and the process of securitization are innovative reactions, driven by the forces of TRICK, designed to seek out profitable opportunities.

The issues of moral hazard and adverse selection associated with securitization also were debated at the conference. Don't be afraid of these terms. They are just fancy words for the "lemons problem" and the market-discipline issues we discussed above. In this regard, the issue of asset quality was seen as only one piece in the broader puzzle of the safety and soundness of depository institutions. The other pieces of the puzzle focused on the issues of leverage and capital requirements, including the proposal for risk-based capital requirements designed to price OBSAs.

Regarding the risks associated with OBSAs and securitization, there seemed to be agreement that, at this stage of their development, ignorance and uncertainty (on the part of bankers, regulators, auditors, and academics) prevail over understanding of the true risks associated with the activities. Under such circumstances, it usually is wise for all parties to proceed with caution.

Some of the other issues debated at the conference included why risk-neutral businesses hedge, establishing a rationale for loan commitments, the valuing of complex options as in the case of commercial real estate mortgages, and a discussion of the monetary-policy implications of changes in banking practices. For an academic view of these issues, the interested reader should see the conference papers as published in the *Journal of Banking and Finance* [September 1987].

Contingent-Commitment Banking

Academics in all disciplines, but especially those in finance and economics, have a bad habit of creating languages unto themselves and then communicating only with a small group of colleagues who know the language. Because most people do not understand the language of academics, their words tend to fall on deaf ears. The surprising part is that many academicians then wonder why they do not have more influence on business policies and practices. Every once in a while, however, like the proverbial blind squirrel who finds an acorn, an academic makes sense or coins a term that everyone can understand. Consider the term contingent-commitment banking, due to Kareken [1987], although the hyphenation is mine. In a nutshell, this term describes the focus of this chapter. If you are surprised, don't be. Just think about what the term means. Banking is the business of buying and selling credit. A commitment is a promise to do something in the future. A contingency means a dependency on another event, which implies uncertainty. Putting these definitions together, contingent-commitment banking involves the promise of an extension of credit on a conditional basis.

To dramatize the substantial changes occurring in commercial banking, Kareken [1987] notes that the business of banking is "... very much the business of making contingent promises or commitments; and even just a decade ago it was not" (p. 359). This chapter, like Kareken's paper, has attempted to explain the movement from traditional banking to contingent-commitment banking. In addition, we both look at the regulation of this new form of banking. From his analysis, Kareken draws two conclusions about the regulation of contingent-commitment banking. First, he argues that even if the last vestiges of traditional banking are removed, "... the Federal Reserve need not in the end be less effective as the U.S. monetary authority than it is at present" (p. 359). And second, he contends that neither higher capital standards nor risk-based capital requirements "... will make bank failures rarer than they otherwise would be" (p. 359).

CHAPTER SUMMARY

Commercial banking can be viewed as undergoing a metamorphosis much like that of a caterpillar into a butterfly. The slow-moving caterpillar reflects traditional banking. The dramatic and dynamic changes taking place in modern banking are the forces pushing the butterfly out of its (protective) cocoon. Although the butterfly of modern banking is not free yet, it is too late to attempt to reverse the process and return to the caterpillar days of traditional banking. However, until it is completely free, the butterfly is most vulnerable during this transitional stage.

The emergence of off-balance-sheet activities (OBSAs) and securitization capture two of the traits of modern banking. The forces of change as captured by TRICK can explain why banks are undertaking these nontraditional activities. Moreover, within the context of the return-on-equity model ($ROE = ROA \times EM$), the downward pressures on both ROA and EM reflect these forces of change in ways that get bankers attention and explain why they are moving assets off their balance sheets. The shift to contingent-commitment banking permits banks, other things equal, to increase ROA through the generation of fee income and, by removing assets from their balance sheets, to ease the increasing pressure being imposed by higher and higher capital requirements. The imposition of capital requirements on OBSAs would force banks to seek out alternative, and perhaps riskier, ways for circumventing higher capital requirements. The management of bank capital and dividends is the focus of the next section of this book.

LIST OF KEY WORDS AND CONCEPTS

Bank capital requirements
Commercial letter of credit
Contingent-commitment banking
Equity multiplier (EM)
Fee income (originating and servicing)
Foreign-exchange transactions
Funding (warehousing) loans
Guarantor
Interest-rate swaps
Lemons (problem of)
Loan commitments
Loan packager (underwriter)
Loan participations
Loan purchaser
Market discipline

Mortgage-backed security
Off-balance-sheet activity (OBSA)
Originating loans
Pass-through security
Recourse
Regulatory dialectic (struggle model)
Reputational capital
Return on assets (ROA)
Return on equity ($ROE = ROA \times EM$)
Securitization (the process of)
Spread account
Standby letter of credit (SLC)
Traditional lending function
TRICK

MATCHING QUIZ

Directions: Select the letter from the right-hand column that best matches the item in the left-hand column.

___ 1. Minimum for a private placement   A. Plagued by higher costs

___ 2. Minimum for a public offering   B. Kareken's term

___ 3. Insurance company role   C. Bankers Trust

___ 4. Role of investment banker   D. $50 million

___ 5. Role for small banks and thrifts   E. $100 million

___ 6. Recourse device

___ 7. Securitization

___ 8. Struggle model

___ 9. Domain of big banks

___ 10. Contingent-commitment banking

___ 11. Traditional lending function

___ 12. Standby letter of credit

___ 13. Foreign-exchange transactions

___ 14. Market discipline

___ 15. OBSA concentration

___ 16. OBSA leader

___ 17. Loan commitments

___ 18. Prudent rule

___ 19. Higher capital standards

___ 20. Loan warehousing

___ 21. Unsecured loans

___ 22. Secured loans

___ 23. Original pass-throughs

F. Forcing banks to go to OBSAs

G. Restrict the size of bet

H. OBSAs

I. Regional banks active here

J. In money-center banks

K. Combines origination and funding

L. Should catch "lemons"

M. Regulatory dialectic

N. Backs up commercial paper

O. Spread account

P. Buy securitized assets

Q. Guarantor

R. Underwrites and packages

S. Asset sales

T. Major OBSA for big banks

U. Credit-card receivable

V. Mortgages

X. CARs

REVIEW/DISCUSSION QUESTIONS

1. Use the ROE model and the TRICK framework to explan the existence of OBSAs and securitization, or contingent-commitment banking.
2. In terms of dollar volumes, growth, and risk considerations, what are the major bank off-balance-sheet activities, and where are they concentrated?
3. The traditional bank lending function has two components. What are they and what is happening to them?
4. What are the various steps in securitizing bank assets? Who are the major players in this process? What are the barriers to securitization?
5. What are the problems faced by both buyers and sellers of assets used for securitization? What role, if any, does "market discipline" play in this process? Regarding these problems, how do participations differ from securitizations?

6. What role does "recourse" play in loan participations and securitization? Explain what a "spread account" is and its role in the process of securitization. How have bank regulators reacted to this recourse technique?

7. Describe the market for mortgage-backed or pass-through securities. How does this market differ from the one for assets backed by bank loans? Distinguish between a secured and unsecured (securitized) bank asset.

8. Consider the following question (by Sanford Rose of the *American Banker*) and answer (by Lowell Bryan a Director of McKinsey & Company). For this and other interesting exchanges, see "The Future of Commercial Banking: A Roundtable Discussion," *Midland Corporate Finance Journal* [Fall, 1987], pp. 22–49.

> *Question*: Would you say that the principal reason why the banks should separate funding from origination is the excess capital tax?
>
> *Answer*: Well I think you get different value-added for different functions. If you look at where banks add value to the economy, their major contribution is in origination, the assessment and underwriting of credit. Commercial banks are the best credit risk underwriters in the financial-services industry (though you also have some horrible credit risk underwriters among the banks). Those are the unique, or proprietary, skills that banks have evolved; that is their fundamental comparative advantage.

Evaluate and discuss the issues related to this exchange.

PROBLEMS

1. For a number of years now, the OBSA Bank has been feeling the squeeze on its earnings due to removal of interest-rate ceilings on deposits and competition from other financial-services firms. In addition, because of higher capital requirements, the bank has had to slow down the growth of its assets. A consulting firm employed by OBSA has suggested a strategic plan based on a reduction in the bank's "burden." On the cost side, certain branches will be closed and early retirements encouraged. In addition, the latest technological developments will be employed as devices for cutting both managerial and staff labor costs. On the revenue side, the consultant has recommended an aggressive expansion into off-balance-sheet activities and asset sales via securitization to generate fee income. The consultant's fee is a performance-based one equal to 0.1 percent of the *improvement* in the bank's net income over the next year. Abbreviated financial statements for the beginning and the end of the relevant year are shown below. Use this information to determine the increase, if any, in OBSA's net income and the fee paid to the consultant.

Item (Millions of Dollars)	Period	
	t	*t* + 1
Interest income	834	917
Interest expense	559	615
Noninterest income	153	184
Noninterest expense	318	334
Taxes	22	30
Extraordinary items	0	0

Also attempt the following questions:

a. How much (in dollar terms) did the bank's burden improve over the year? What were the growth rates for the components of burden?

   b. At the beginning of the period (assumed to be one year) OBSA had total assets of $11.7 billion. If assets grew at a 10 percent rate during the year, what was the bank's return on average assets?

   c. Given a dividend payout ratio of 35 percent and an equity multiplier of 14.75 at the beginning of the year, determine the bank's return on average equity and its year-end EM. If OBSA's regulator demands a ratio of equity capital to assets of 6.5 percent, does the bank pass the test?

   d. Was OBSA able to increase its ROA and ROE without taking on any additional risk? What potential risks are behind off-balance-sheet activities and the securitization of assets? Discuss and debate. Should bank regulators slap capital requirements on these activities?

2. In case you didn't try this one in Chapter 9, here's a repeat of problem 11 from that chapter. You are the proud owner of a 30-year mortgage-backed security which has been stripped into interest-only (IO) and principal-only (PO) components. Originally issued in a fixed-rate market, rates suddenly and unexpectedly jump by 200 basis points. What would you expect the price movements on each component to be and why? [*Hint*: Think about what is likely to happen to prepayments under this scenario.]

SELECTED REFERENCES

Albert, Andrew. [1988]. "Chemical Raids Wall Street to Beef Up Unit that Securitizes and Sells Loans," *American Banker* (February 8), pp. 1, 14.

Arnold, Bruce R. [1986]. "Securitization of Loans." Speech presented at the Securitization of Loans Seminar, Federal Reserve Bank of New York (October 23).

Chessen, James. [1987]. "Third-Quarter Update: Bank Off-Balance Sheet Activity," *Regulatory Review* (November/December), pp. 1–8, FDIC.

"(The) Future of Commercial Banking: A Roundtable Discussion," *Midland Corporate Finance Journal* (Fall, 1987), pp. 22–49.

Hill, G. Christian, and Robert Guenther. [1988]. "Major Banks Found Post-Crash Turmoil To Yield Bonanza in Foreign Exchange," *The Wall Street Journal* (January 25), p. 2.

James, Christopher. (1987). "Off-Balance Sheet Banking," *Economic Review* (Number 4), Federal Reserve Bank of San Francisco, pp. 21–36.

Johnson, Sylvester and Amelia A. Murphy. (1987). "Going Off the Balance Sheet," *Economic Review* (September/October), Federal Reserve Bank of Atlanta, pp. 23–35.

Journal of Banking and Finance. [1987]. Selected Paper from the Conference on Asset Securitization and Off-Balance Sheet Risk of Depository Institutions (September), pp. 355–546.

Kareken, John H. [1987]. "The Emergence and Regulation of Contingent Commitment Banking," *Journal of Banking and Finance* (September), pp. 359–377.

Rehm, Barbara. [1988]. "Regulator Sees Pluses, Minuses in Asset Securitization Trend," *American Banker* (February 8), pp. 1, 6.

Rose, Sanford. [1987]. "Extending the Loan-Sales Revolution," *American Banker* (February 18), pp. 1, 6.

———. [1986]. "Rethinking Securitization," *American Banker* (November 4), pp. 1, 6.

Simpson, Thomas D. [1988]. "Developments in the U.S. Financial System since the Mid-1970s," *Federal Reserve Bulletin* (January), pp. 1–13.

Whittaker, J. Gregg. [1987]. "Interest-Rate Swaps: Risk and Regulation," *Economic Review* (March), Federal Reserve Bank of Kansas City, pp. 3–13.

PART VI

BANK CAPITAL STRUCTURE, MARKET VALUATION, AND FINANCING ISSUES

To complete our balance-sheet framework for commercial bank financial management, this part of the book focuses on the theory, regulation, and management of bank capital, both equity and long-term debt. Chapter 22 deals with the theory and regulation of bank capital. The notions of an optimal capital structure, risk-based capital requirements, and the determinants of the value of the banking firm are the theoretical and regulatory cornerstones of this chapter. In Chapter 23, we turn to some of the practical aspects of bank capital and dividend management by focusing on the market valuation of bank stock and financing issues. Such topics as the internal capital generation rate, dividend policy and payout, instruments for raising capital, long-term debt management, double leverage, capital planning, and the market valuation of bank stocks are analyzed.

Bank Capital Structure: Theory and Regulation

WHY IS BANK CAPITAL IMPORTANT?

Before we answer the question What is bank capital? which, thanks to regulatory and accounting veils, is not always an easy task, let's focus on why bank capital is important. The safety and stability of the financial system depends on the confidence depositors and other creditors have in banks and the banking system. Recall, that in Chapter 7, we established a function for modeling confidence in the banking system, which specified confidence as determined by four factors: (1) net worth (NW), (2) stability of earnings (SOE), (3) information quality (IQ), and (4) the market value of government guarantees (G).[1] In symbols, our confidence function is

$$\text{Confidence} = f(NW, SOE, IQ, G) \tag{22-1}$$

Each of these factors has a positive or direct effect on confidence (or perceived safety) in either individual banks or the banking system. Specifically, the more net worth a bank has, the safer it is perceived to be, other things equal. Second, the more stable a bank's earnings are, the safer it is perceived to be, other things equal. Third, the better the quality of information available about a bank's future earnings, the easier (i.e., less costly) it will be for interested parties to evaluate the situation. Accordingly, as information quality increases (e.g., regarding the market value of third-world debt held by money-center banks), confidence should increase, other things equal. And fourth, as the market value of government guarantees increases, confidence should increase, other things equal. Given the "too-big-to-fail doctrine," the perceived market value of the government guarantees may vary with the size of the bank (e.g., consider the government's treatment of Penn Square [1982] versus either Continental Illinois [1984] or First Pennsylvania [1980]).

Excluding the government guarantee, which is not subject to managerial decision, confidence in a bank (or any firm) depends on its net worth, the stability of its earnings, and the quality of information disclosed by management. If we assume that banks are subject to identical disclosure requirements, such that uniform information quality is assured for all data disclosed by banks, then net worth and stability or earnings are the determinants of confidence that are subject to some degree of managerial discretion. Furthermore, it is common to view bank capital or net worth as a buffer or cushion to absorb unexpected losses arising from credit, interest-rate,

---

[1] As noted in Chapter 7, this function is from Kane [1986].

liquidity, and operating risks. These risks, of course, are the major sources of instability in bank earnings. Thus, in a nutshell, bank capital is important because of the backstop role it plays in generating confidence about a bank's ability to handle uncertainty.

The Issue of Capital Adequacy

How much capital does a bank need to ensure the confidence of depositors, creditors, investors, and regulators? In the banking-and-finance literature, this question is known as the issue of bank capital adequacy. Anyone who knows the answer to this question can gain instant notoriety in the banking, financial, and regulatory communities. Since this chapter does not contain the answer to the question, your opportunity for fame (but not much fortune) still exists. However, a word of caution: Some of the best minds in banking and finance have been struggling with this issue for years, but with little success. Of course, we should not expect an easy answer to a complex issue. Nevertheless, in focusing on the issue of adequate bank capital, we can come up with the definitive (hedged) answer: "It depends on..." What it depends on, we turn to next.

Risk Considerations and the Importance of Interaction Effects

Just as each of us is unique from our fingerprints to our personalities, we can regard each bank as being unique. For our purposes, the uniqueness we want to focus on is a bank risk profile, and how this risk profile serves to determine the relative level of capital a bank needs. To illustrate, consider two banks: Bank A and Bank B. Assume that Bank B has more volatile earnings, inferior quality information, and a weaker government guarantee compared to Bank A. Which bank needs, on a relative basis, more capital? Clearly, Bank B does.

Next let's consider the interaction effects among the arguments of the confidence function shown in Equation 22-1. Suppose Bank A has achieved an optimal level of confidence in the marketplace, which corresponds to optimal values of NW, SOE, IQ, and G. Since NW or bank capital is our focal variable, we want to consider the interaction effects between it and the other three variables. On a one-to-one basis, as each of the other variables deteriorates, bank capital should increase to attempt to offset the adverse effects of the decline in the individual variable. In a dynamic situation with all factors changing simultaneously, the net effect on confidence would depend on the various interaction effects. It is unambiguously clear, however, that if a bank's earnings, information quality, or government guarantee decline (from an optimal equilibrium), bank capital should increase. In other words, as risk increases, bank capital, which is the cushion or buffer available to absorb losses, should increase.

Look Ma, No Risk!

At one time or another in our earliest bicycle-riding days, we might have yelled to our mothers: "Look Ma, no hands." What if a financial institution could yell to the marketplace (as its mother): "Look Ma, no risk!" In this situation, how much leverage (the finance term for capital adequacy) would the marketplace allow? Again, we are not concerned with the absolute amount of capital (or leverage), but with the relative amount. And again, we can answer unambiguously that, relative to a financial institution with risk exposure (say credit and interest rate), the firm without risk would be permitted a higher degree of financial leverage (i.e., a lower level of relative capital adequacy).

Hypothetical hogwash, you say. Well let me introduce you to "Sallie Mae," and tell you about her leverage. You may have heard about her three mortgage cousins: Ginnie Mae, Fannie Mae, and Freddy Mac. Sallie Mae is the nickname for the Student Loan Marketing Association, which was created by Uncle Sam in 1972. Sallie Mae operates a secondary market for qualifying student loans. With a portfolio of about $25 billion (as of early 1988), Sallie Mae is a major player in financial markets. What makes Sallie Mae unique is that she can say, with a straight face, "Look Ma, no risk!" Sallie Mae can speak with such verisimilitude because she has a portfolio that is free of both credit risk and interest-rate risk. (She is, however, still subject to operating risks, but we will ignore that little white lie.) The credit risk is absorbed by her uncle, Sam (the sugardaddy and creator of huge deficits), in the form of the federal guarantee behind student loans. (By the way, in 1987 student loan defaults cost U.S. taxpayers about $1.6 billion.) Regarding interest-rate risk, Sallie Mae runs, for the most part, an immunized portfolio because she borrows funds at the 91-day T-bill rate plus 30 or 40 basis points, and lends funds at the same T-bill rate plus 325 basis points (350 basis points for loans made prior to November 16, 1986). Sallie Mae lends by buying loans from originators of student loans (e.g., banks and thrifts). In the process, of course, she provides liquidity to the originators.[2]

Now that we know what Sallie Mae does, let's look at her leverage. At year-end 1987, she had an equity multiplier of about 33, which means $33 in assets for every $1 of equity capital. With an ROA of about 3/4 of one percent, Sallie Mae's 1987 ROE was almost 25 percent. Prior to the 1980s, when the credit and interest-rate risks of banking were not so obvious, some money-center banks had similar-sized equity multipliers and returns. Focusing on Sallie Mae's "capital adequacy," she has a capital-to-asset ratio of 3.0 percent. As of this writing, commercial banks must maintain a capital ratio of 6 percent, which increases to 8 percent (against risk-adjusted assets) by 1992. Since commercial banks cannot say, "Look Ma, no risk," they should be expected to have less leverage, or higher capital ratios, than a risk-free intermediary. In the final analysis, the amount of capital a bank should have depends on its risk profile.

WHAT IS BANK CAPITAL?

A firm's capital structure usually is defined in terms of its debt-to-asset or debt-to-equity ratio. Given the following balance sheet,

$$\text{Assets } (A) = \text{Debt } (D) + \text{Equity } (E) \qquad (22\text{-}2)$$

with $A = 100$, $D = 95$, and $E = 5$, the two ratios are $D/A = .95$ and $D/E = 19$. Now if someone were to suggest that we take 20 of the debt and call it equity, we would be justified in questioning the logic of such a move. This revised capital structure would have $D/A = .75$ and $D/E = 3$. Our gut reaction is to dismiss the revised capital structure as a figment of someone's imagination. After all, debt is debt and equity is equity. Isn't defining a portion of debt as equity like calling an orange an apple? If this is *Alice in Wonderland*, how can we expect to apply modern financial theory to it?

The Many Veils of Bank Bookkeeping

Most businesses keep at least two sets of books: one for the tax collector and one for the accountant/auditor. Banks, in addition, keep another set of books for the

---

[2] For two brief, but interesting, articles on Sallie Mae, see Novack [1988] and Strauss [1987]. The data presented in this paragraph and the next one are from these two sources.

regulator.[3] In finance, of course, the only books that count are those kept by the marketplace. Unfortunately, in the lower half of the real dual-banking system, where over 14,000 community-type banks reside, market-value books don't exist until a merger offer comes along. Moreover, even in the upper half of the real dual-banking system, because of banks' penchant for secrecy and because of the lack of active secondary markets for most of the assets held by banks, it is difficult to arrive at market values. Nevertheless, capital markets for banks with actively traded securities have been found to be at least weak-form efficient.

Setting aside the books kept by banks for the tax collector, there are three accounting standards that banks must adhere to:

1. book-value accounting
2. regulatory accounting
3. market-value accounting

The first two standards are referred to as GAAP and RAP, respectively, which stand for generally accepted accounting procedures and regulatory accounting procedures. In getting at market values, it is necessary to cut through the veils of GAAP and RAP. Although this double-veiled two-step is not as exciting as the dance of the seven veils, it can be just as revealing once the veils are removed.

The GAAP Veil on Bank Capital

Banking books are kept on a *book value* or *historical cost* basis. To measure bank capital or accounting net worth, one simply subtracts the book value of liabilities from the book value of assets—nothing more than the accounting identity rearranged as $NW = A - L$. This procedure is fine as long as the book and market values don't diverge too widely. When they do, however, one gets a distorted view of bank capital and its adequacy. To illustrate, consider the book value of bank capital for money-center banks at the height of the international debt crisis versus its market value, or the book value of S&L net worth during the height of the thrift crisis versus its market value. Devalued assets, whether in the form of underwater mortgages or questionable international loans, must be marked to market value if the accounting veil of book values is to be pierced.

The RAP Veil on Bank Capital

One of the worst elements of RAP is its treatment of bank capital. The crazy-quilt regulation of bank capital can be traced to two sources: (1) the notion that bank regulators are captives or pawns of the industry and (2) the tendency of the regulators to handle problems with stop-gap measures and patchwork methods. Both of these points are illustrated by the RAP treatment of bank capital. No rational lender would look at a would-be borrower's reserve for bad debts as part of the firm's capital, or at part of the firm's subordinated debt as the equivalent of equity capital. The banks love this double standard because they would not want to be scrutinized in the same way that they look at their customers' balance sheets. "Do as I say, not as I do," reflects the bankers' higher capital standards for their customers compared to themselves. One

[3] Some bankers have been known to keep another set of more private books. For example, C. Arnholt Smith kept some of USNB's records at his personal residence to hide them from the bank examiners and the Butcher brothers of Tennessee kept "portable" books that could be shuttled from one of their banks to another to hide bad loans from the FDIC.

explanation for this phenomenon is the dual argument that the regulators are in the industry's hip pocket and the regulator's penchant to protect its own turf and to tell Congress that everything is all right at any cost.

Under RAP, the notion of bank capital has become diluted and viewed as a blend of stockholders' equity, reserves for loan losses, and subordinated notes and debentures. On March 11, 1985, the OCC and FDIC adopted a common definition of bank capital for commercial banks.[4] This definition and the *minimum* standards for capital ratios are summarized in Table 22-1. The rules for the first time set the same capital requirements for all national and FDIC insured state nonmember banks, regardless of size. The Board of Governors of the Federal Reserve System adopted identical guidelines for state member banks and bank holding companies. The rules raised total capital levels in the banking system to 6 percent, and require that $5\frac{1}{2}$ percent be in primary capital.

The capital definitions and standards shown in Table 22-1 are in the process of being replaced by new definitions and standards. On January 27, 1988, the U.S. federal banking agencies announced their latest version of a plan for risk-based capital standards. Since the new RAP veils are a little more transparent than the old ones, some analysts see the plan as a step in the right direction.[5] This latest proposal is the response by U.S. bank regulators to an agreement for risk-based international capital standards established by the Bank for International Settlements on December 10, 1987. The accord, reached by the Basel Committee on Banking Regulations and Supervisory Practices, calls for international convergence of capital measurement and capital standards in 12 developed countries. The Basel Committee was comprised of representatives of the central banks and supervisory authorities of Belgium, Canada,

TABLE 22-1   Regulatory Definitions of Bank Capital and Minimum Capital Standards, 1985–1987

	Minimum Capital-to-Asset Ratio[a] Based Upon	
Bank Class[b]	Primary Capital	Total Capital[c]
Multinational	5.5%	6.0%
Regional	5.5%	6.0%
Community	5.5%	6.0%

[a] Definitions: *Primary capital* consists of shareholders' equity (including equity reserves), perpetual preferred stock, reserves for loan and lease losses, some mandatory convertible debt, minority interests in consolidated subsidiaries, and net worth certificates. *Total capital* consists of primary capital plus secondary capital, where *secondary capital* is defined to include only limited-life preferred stock and subordinated notes and debentures. Secondary capital is limited to 50 percent of primary capital.

[b] *Multinationals* are those institutions designated by their principal regulatory agency; typically the group includes the 17 largest BHCs. Regionals are all banks with over $1 billion in assets not designated as multinationals. *Community banks* include all other organizations.

[c] Three categories have been set up for evaluating total capital adequacy. In Category I, capital will be considered adequate if the institution's primary capital ratio is above the minimum guideline. In Category II, a bank will be considered as potentially undercapitalized and subject to extensive regulatory scrutiny. In Category III, the bank is considered to be undercapitalized and placed under continuing supervision (presumably this means classification as a problem bank). In applying these standards, an organization's consolidated financial statements are used.

[4] *Joint News Release,* OCC and FDIC. NR-85 20 [March 11, 1985].

[5] For a contrary view, see "Statement of the Shadow Financial Regulatory Committee on Regulatory Proposal for Risk-Related Capital Standard" [February 8, 1988]. Except for minor revisions, the capital guidelines shown in Table 22-2 and in the appendix (page 636) are the ones approved by the Fed on August 3, 1988.

France, Germany, Italy, Japan, Luxembourg, Netherlands, Sweden, Switzerland, United Kingdom, and the United States. Each country is responsible for constructing its own capital plan within the framework (and spirit) of the international agreement. The purpose of the international plan is to promote more equitable competition as well as increased safety for the international financial system. Both the Federal Reserve and the Bank of England have adopted conservative interpretations of the international agreement.

The new definitions of bank capital proposed by U.S. bank regulators recognize two types of capital: (1) core capital (Tier 1) defined as common stockholders' equity plus minority interest in consolidated subsidiaries minus goodwill and (2) "supplementary" capital defined as core capital plus portions of loan-loss reserves, perpetual and long-term preferred stock, and subordinated debt. The latter closely approximates the old definition of primary capital as defined in Table 22-1. The new 1988 capital standards and definitions are summarized in Table 22-2.

By year-end 1992, U.S. banks must have supplemental capital equal to a *minimum* of 8 percent of risk-adjusted assets. Moreover, a minimum of one-half of this total capital must be in the form of core capital (i.e., 4 percent of risk-adjusted assets must be in the form of core capital). A five-year transition period (1987 to 1992) is established for the new capital standards. By year-end 1990 through 1991, U.S. banks must meet an interim standard of 7.25 percent with a pure equity standard of approximately 3.25 percent.

To summarize, U.S. banks will be on a 6 percent capital standard for 1988 and 1989 (under the old definitions of capital and relative to total assets), and on a 7.25 percent standard for 1990–1991, followed by the 8 percent standard for year-end 1992 and beyond (under the new definitions and relative to risk-adjusted assets).

TABLE 22-2   Capital Standards for U.S. Commercial Banks and Bank Holding Companies (Established in 1988, Fully Effective in 1992)

Capital Definitions and Standards

Core Capital (Tier 1) consists of common stockholders' equity plus minority interest in consolidated subsidiaries less goodwill (existing goodwill is "grandfathered" for the transition period 1987 to 1992). By 1992, core capital must equal or exceed 4 percent of weighted-risk assets.

Supplementary Capital (Tier 2) consists of allowance for losses on loans and leases (general reserves only), perpetual and long-term preferred stock (original maturity 20 years or more), hybrid capital instruments (including perpetual debt and mandatory convertible securities), subordinated debt and intermediate-term preferred stock (average maturity of 7 years or more). The total of Tier 2 is limited to 100 percent of Tier 1 (amounts in excess of this limitation are permitted but do not qualify as capital). Within Tier 2, loan-loss reserves are limited by 1992 to 1.25 percent of weighted-risk assets, and subordinated debt and intermediate-term preferred stock (which are amortized for capital purposes as they approach maturity) are limited to 50 percent of Tier 1. The other components of Tier 2 have no limits, and amounts in excess of components with limitations are permitted but do not qualify as capital.

Deductions consist of investments in unconsolidated banking and finance subsidiaries, reciprocal holdings of bank-issued capital securities, and other deductions (such as other subsidiaries or joint ventures) as determined by supervisory authority with handling on a case-by-case basis or as a matter of policy after formal rulemaking.

Total capital (Tier 1 + Tier 2 − Deductions) must equal or exceed 8 percent of weighted-risk assets.

Risk weights and risk categories (see appendix to this chapter).

Notes: These definitions of qualifying capital are those for state member banks and bank holding companies as specified by the Board of Governors of the Federal Reserve System. The OCC and FDIC adopted similar standards for their banks. BHCs may count preferred stock as part of Tier 1 up to a maximum of 25% of core capital.

Source: "Risk-Based Capital," Office Correspondence, Division for Banking Supervision and Regulation, Board of Governors of the Federal Reserve System [draft copy dated January 25, 1988], Table 1, p. 124. The Fed gave its final approval for these standards on August 3, 1988.

For the purposes of determining risk-adjusted assets, bank assets will be classified into five asset-risk categories having weights of 0, .10, .20, .50, and 1.0, as perceived credit risk increases. These asset-risk categories, and the credit conversion factors for OBSAs, along with sample calculations are presented in the appendix to this chapter. Neither the concept nor the attempt to implement risk-based capital requirements are new. However, because of the recent surge and concern about off-balance-sheet activities (OBSAs, see Chapter 21), the requirement that banks allocate capital for these activities is new. For example, standby letters of credit (SLCs) are assigned to the risk class with a .50 weight, which means that for each $100 of SLCs a bank will need $2 of equity plus $2 of supplemental capital (see the appendix to this chapter for the complete list of conversion factors for OBSAs).

Letting $A1$ through $A5$ represent the five risk categories and letting E and T represent equity (core) capital and total (core + supplemental) capital, respectively, the *minimum* capital standards that U.S. commercial banks and bank holding companies must meet for December 31, 1992 are

$$T = .08[0(A1) + .10(A2) + .20(A3) + .50(A4) + 1.0(A5)] \tag{22-3}$$

and

$$E = .50T = .40[0(A1) + .20(A2) + .20(A3) + .50(A4) + 1.0(A5)] \tag{22-4}$$

Since the largest banks in the United States have relatively more risk assets, OBSAs, and goodwill on (or off) their balance sheets, the greatest burden of adjustment will be on these banks during the transition period 1987 to 1992. Moreover, as shown in Table 22-3, the money-center banks are at a considerable disadvantage vis-à-vis the superregional banks because of their risk exposure to the debt of less-developed countries (LDCs).

Market Values Cut the Veils

To cut the GAAP and RAP veils, all one has to do is to look at market values, if they are available. Using asterisks to indicate market values, Equation 22-2 can be rewritten as $A^* = D^* + E^*$. In the marketplace, only the residual value of the balance-sheet identity is observed, that is, $E^* = A^* - D^*$. The total equity value of the firm is equal to

$$\text{Equity Value} = \text{Price per Share} \times \text{Number of Shares Outstanding} \tag{22-5}$$

Let's illustrate this relationship for Citicorp as of December 31, 1986, when its stock price was $53 per share. With 150,577,830 shares of common stock outstanding, the market value of Citicorp's equity was almost $8 billion. In contrast, the book value of stockholders's equity was reported as almost $7.7 billion for a market-to-book ratio of 104 percent. With year-end 1986 total assets of $196 billion, the GAAP, RAP (using the 1985 definitions), and market value versions of Citicorp's capital ratios are

Market Value of Equity/Total Assets	= 4.07%
Book Value of Equity/Total Assets (GAAP)	= 3.92%
Primary Capital/Total Assets (RAP)	= 6.82%
Total Capital/Total Assets (RAP)	= 10.88%

The important point is that GAAP and RAP measures of capital ratios do not reflect the real worth of the relative buffer or cushion available for absorbing the realized risks of banking.

Critics of market-value accounting pooh-pooh it because market values are more volatile than book values. Although this criticism is certainly valid, one has to weigh

TABLE 22-3   LDC Exposure of the 25 Largest U.S. Bank Holding Companies

Rank (Best to Worst)				Ratios		
LDC Loans to Equity	LDC Loans to Primary Capital	Adjusted Reserve to NPA[a]	Name	LDC Loans to Equity (%)	LDC Loans to Primary Capital (%)	Adjusted Reserve to NPA (%)
1	1	NA	First Union Corp.	3.5	2.8	NA
2	2	1	Sun Trust	8.1	6.9	168.4
3	4	3	NCNB Corp.	16.6	13.3	97.5
4	5	2	NBD Bancorp	18.6	14.8	156.3
5	3	23	MCorp	19.4	12.3	26.8
6	6	5	Bank of New England	21.4	14.9	91.1
7	8	NA	PNC Financial	27.2	21.6	NA
8	7	9	First Bank System	31.2	20.2	66.6
9	11	14	Wells Fargo	49.5	49.5	55.4
10	10	18	Bank of Boston	69.1	45.7	42.6
11	9	17	Security Pacific	71.4	42.2	43.0
12	13	12	First Interstate	85.2	52.1	59.0
13	12	21	First Republic	91.0	50.7	35.0
14	15	4	J.P. Morgan	114.9	79.1	94.9
15	14	16	Mellon	137.5	67.7	48.7
16	16	15	Marine Midland	160.9	79.4	50.3
17	17	8	First Chicago	165.5	81.1	67.4
18	21	13	Continental Illinois	166.7	103.1	56.7
19	19	22	Chemical	171.2	100.0	27.3
20	18	6	Bankers Trust	177.6	96.9	78.4
21	22	7	Irving	211.6	118.6	71.3
22	20	20	Citicorp	220.7	102.0	40.6
23	23	11	Chase Manhattan	246.7	123.3	60.9
24	24	10	Bank America	348.9	138.1	64.7
25	25	19	Manufacturers Hanover	352.4	142.4	40.7

[a](Total Reserve minus LDC Reserve)/(Total NPA minus LDC NPA). NPA = Non-Performing Loans
Source: *Financial Institutions Credit Rating Handbook* [December 1987], Fixed Income Research, First Boston, p. 1.

the trade-off between volatility and removing the GAAP and RAP veils such that true worth is observed. What you see is what you get with market values! James G. Elhen, Jr., formerly with Goldman Sach & Company, put it this way[6]:

> In both banking and industry, the adequacy of capital is an elusive measure. Perhaps the only real determinant of adequacy is the aggregate consensus of the marketplace—that is leverage, or the inverse of the capital ratio, should be extended until the marketplace reacts adversely and reflects concern.

New Capital Standards and the Squeeze on Money-Center Banks

Based on year-end 1987 data, Citicorp's ratio of primary capital to total assets was 7.94 percent, and its ratio of equity capital to assets was 3.26 percent. Focusing on the new capital standards and using 1987 as the base year for comparison, let's consider how the risk-based capital requirements will affect Citicorp's capital ratios in 1990 and

[6] Federal Reserve Bank of Atlanta *Economic Review* [November 1983], p. 54.

1992. Goldman Sachs Investment Research has projected the following ratios for Citicorp:[7]

	1990	1992
Core capital ratio	4.10%	3.61%
Core + supplemental capital ratio	7.97%	6.98%

Given the 7.25 percent standard for 1990 and the 8 percent standard for 1992, Citicorp is projected to have a capital shortfall in 1992. Except for J.P. Morgan and Bankers Trust, the problem of a capital shortfall for money-center banks is the rule rather than the exception. In contrast, regional banks, except for those in the southwest, are being projected with capital ratios well above the minimum standards. Similar projections are expected for community banks, except for those with lingering energy- and farm-loan problems.

In general, the fewer risk assets (i.e., loans) and OBSAs a bank has and the less intangible capital (i.e., goodwill) it has, the easier its adjustment will be to the higher capital standards based on risk-adjusted assets. Accordingly, the money-center banks will face the most difficult adjustments over the transition period. In attempting to meet the new capital standards, any bank has essentially two paths it can follow: (1) increase its capital, either internally or externally, and/or (2) change the composition of its risk-adjusted assets, including its OBSAs. The second way can be viewed as a portfolio adjustment process in which a bank increases the composition of its assets and OBSAs away from the higher risk categories (i.e., $A4$ and $A5$ in Equations 22-3 and 22-4) toward the lower-risk ones (i.e., $A1$, $A2$, and $A3$). In previous chapters, we have shown that the volumes of loans and OBSAs vary directly with bank size.

Regarding increases in capital, let's first focus on what a bank can do to increase its core or equity capital, and then we will turn to the supplemental sources of capital. We begin by documenting the sources of increases in total equity capital for all insured commercial banks for the years 1981 through 1986. These data, which are shown in Table 22-4, also include a breakout for large banks, defined as institutions with

TABLE 22-4   Sources of Increases in Total Equity Capital. All Insured Commercial Banks, 1981–86 (Millions of Dollars, Except as Noted)

Item	1981	1982	1983	1984	1985	1986
Retained earnings[a]						
All banks	8,848	8,284	7,653	7,824	9,455	8,539
Large banks[a]	4,104	4,051	3,621	4,090	6,368	6,476
Net increase in equity capital						
All banks	11,163	9,374	10,739	14,958	14,720	16,502
Large banks	5,465	4,578	5,625	9,415	9,402	11,846
Percentage of net increase in equity capital from retained earnings						
All banks	79	88	71	52	64	52
Large banks	75	88	64	43	68	55

[a] Net income less cash dividends declared on preferred and common stock.
[b] Banks with fully consolidated assets of $billion or more at year end.
Source: Danker and McLaughlin [1987], Table 3, p. 540.

[7] "Bank-Track: Emerging Trends for Bank Stocks," *Investment Research* [December 1987], Special Third Issue, Goldman Sachs.

consolidated assets of $1 billion or more at year-end. Focusing on 1982, both all banks and large banks generated 88 percent of the increases in equity capital from retained earnings. However, by 1986 these figures were down to 52 percent for all banks and 55 percent for large banks. For the five-year period from 1981 to 1986, the addition to retained earnings at large banks grew at a compound annual rate of 9.5 percent, whereas the addition to retained earnings at all banks declined slightly at an annual rate of 0.7 percent. On a cyclical basis, both groups followed a similar pattern of additions to retained earnings declining from 1981 to 1983 and then rising over the next three years, except for all banks, which showed a decline from 1985 to 1986. Even more dramatically, by taking the difference between the all-banks and large-banks figures and computing the growth rate for that difference, we see that increases in retained earnings at "small banks" (i.e., those with assets less than $1 billion) have been *deteriorating* at a compound annual rate of 15.3 percent. The latter can be attributed to the decline in earnings at community banks located in energy and farm areas, which in turn has been caused by heavy loan losses and higher interest costs associated with the phase-out of Reg Q interest-rate ceilings over the period 1980 to 1986.

Focusing on the net increase in equity capital shown in Table 22-4, the increases in equity at all banks have been growing at a compound annual rate of 8.1 percent compared to 16.7 percent growth for large banks. To get a clearer picture of the net increase at small banks, we calculate the growth rate for the difference figure for these data. It reveals a deterioration in the growth of net increases in equity capital at small banks at an annual rate of 3.9 percent.

The important point to be gained from the data in Table 22-4, and the derivative calculations we have made is that large banks have been tapping external sources of equity capital more rapidly than smaller banks. This finding is not surprising since large banks have easier access to capital markets than small ones. If this is the case, then why are the largest banks projected as being squeezed by the new capital standards? The explanation is two fold. First, the money-center banks have riskier portfolios and a much higher volume of OBSAs, which, under risk-based capital requirements, will mean a larger relative volume of risk-adjusted assets. Keep in mind that the relevant ratio under the new standards is common equity capital (excluding preferred stock) to risk-adjusted assets. In this context, we can think of "numerator" and "denominator" effects. The money-center banks will face an adverse demoninator effect because of the definitional change from total assets to risk-adjusted assets.

The second point focuses on the numerator of the relevant ratio. The new capital standards exclude perpetual preferred stock from core capital and require that the intangible asset "goodwill" be deducted from common equity by year-end 1992. Since the money-center banks have more preferred stock outstanding and goodwill on their balance sheets, they are at a substantial disadvantage relative to other banks, but especially to their newest competitors—the superregionals.

In the final analysis, the money-center banks get hit twice by the new and higher capital standards: (1) in the numerator by the exclusion of preferred stock and the goodwill deduction and (2) in the denominator by the shift to risk-adjusted assets. Although the money-center banks must bear the brunt of the adjustment to the new capital standards, they also have the size, flexibility, and access to capital markets to be considered the best equipped to handle the adjustment. However, to avoid overextending themselves in the capital markets, and thereby risking potential dilution of earnings, the money-center banks will need to look for a combination of internal and external measures for adjusting to the new capital standards.

The external measures of adjustment refer to outside sources of capital, including common stock, preferred stock, subordinated debt, and various hybrid securities.

Although common equity can be used in unlimited amounts for meeting the new capital standards, the "supplemental" sources are restricted in terms of meeting the regulatory definition of total capital (core + supplemental). The major internal measures available to increase equity capital (i.e., retained earnings) include reducing the bank's "burden" (by better control of noninterest expenses and increased generation of fees and services charges), restricting the growth of activities with thin profit margins (i.e., adjusting portfolio mix to attempt to increase net interest income), selling bank assets and/or subsidiary businesses, tax avoidance, and changing the dividend payout ratio. The only way of generating supplemental capital internally is to increase loan-loss reserves, which means increasing the expense item provision for loan losses.

SMOOTHING BANK EARNINGS, CAPITAL MANIPULATIONS, AND THE 1987 LDC LOAN-LOSS PROVISIONS[8]

The income-smoothing hypothesis (applied to banks) suggests that bank managers may attempt to generate a smoothed earnings stream by increasing provision for loan losses when pretax and preprovision earnings are up, regardless of the economic conditions affecting the true quality of their loan portfolios. The 1987 earnings and capital manipulations engaged in by money-center and regional banks with LDC loan exposures seem to fit this scenario. The story begins with Brazil's decision in February 1987 to suspend payments on its international debt. This event provided the impetus for Citicorp's decision in May 1987 to bite the LDC-loan bullet by allocating $3 billion to its loan-loss reserve. Citicorp's decision proved to be a follow-the-leader move as all other banks with significant LDC exposures, both money-center and regional, followed the pied piper.

Although Citicorp's provision decision may have sent a signal to the marketplace regarding its future involvement and handling of LDC borrowers, the capital implications under the 1985 regulatory guidelines were unambiguous. Specifically, Citicorp (and the other banks/BHCs) reduced their second quarter earnings substantially as the "hits" were expensed, as provision for loan losses, through their income statements. Moreover, with earnings in the first quarter of 1987 up, one could argue that this was the appropriate time to do some income smoothing. Moreover, in terms of primary capital, the transaction was a wash, as the reduction in retained earnings was offset by the increase in the loan-loss reserve. Under 1985 capital guidelines, the entire loan-loss reserve was counted as part of primary capital (see Table 22-1). Under the new 1988 capital standards, core or equity capital would have been depleted by the entire amount of the reduction in retained earnings, and could have been only partially offset by the increase in supplemental capital via the loan-loss reserve. To the extent the new capital guidelines generate a more realistic picture of a bank's true capital adequacy, they are a step in the right direction.

UNDERSTANDING THE COMPONENTS OF BANK CAPITAL

Since the key component of bank capital is equity capital, let's begin with the items that make up this account. Equity capital consists of three components: (1) common stock, (2) surplus (i.e., the difference between the price at which the common stock

---

[8] See Greenawalt and Sinkey [1988] and Musumeci and Sinkey [1988] for some evidence on these issues.

sold and its par value, times the number of shares sold), and (3) retained earnings or undivided profits. To illustrate, consider the components of Wachovia Bank and Trust's equity capital as of December 31, 1987.

Common stock	$ 51,360,000
Surplus	78,587,000
Undivided profits	663,542,000
TOTAL EQUITY CAPITAL	$793,489,000

With 84 percent of its equity generated by retained earnings, WB&T has a figure substantially above that for other banks (i.e., most banks have a ratio of retained earnings to equity in the range of 45 to 65 percent). With total assets of $11,698 million, WB&T's ratio of equity capital to total assets is 6.81 percent, which puts it well above the 4 percent minimum to be required by year-end 1992.

For comparative purposes, let's consider the components of equity capital for Citicorp and its lead bank, Citibank, as of December 31, 1986. The data, which are in millions of dollars, are from Citicorp's 1986 annual report.

	Citicorp	Citibank	Bank/BHC
Preferred stock	$1,365	$ 0	0.0%
Common stock	602	751	124.7
Surplus	1,421	2,015	141.8
Retained earnings	6,059	5,243	86.5
Common stock in treasury	(387)	0	0.0
Shareholders' equity	$9,060	$8,009	88.4%

Compared to WB&T's equity accounts, Citicorp (but not Citibank) has two additional items: preferred stock and treasury stock. Preferred stock is simply capital stock to which preferences or special rights are attached, usually with respect to dividends and liquidation. Treasury stock refers to stock that a corporation has reacquired by purchase, gift, donation, inheritance, or other means. The value of treasury stock is treated as a deduction from equity capital.

For both Citicorp and Citibank, the ability of Citibank to generate retained earnings is crucial as 65 percent of Citibank's equity consists of retained earnings, and 86 percent of Citicorp's equity has been generated by Citibank. Given asset bases of $196 billion and $149 billion, the 1986 equity-to-assets ratios for Citicorp and Citibank were 4.6 percent and 5.5 percent, respectively. Following its $3 billion provision for LDC loan losses in the second quarter of 1987, Citicorp finished 1987 with an equity-to-asset ratio of 3.26 percent. Given Goldman Sachs's predictions for Citicorp's equity ratios (based on risk-adjusted assets) of 4.10 percent in 1990 and 3.61 percent in 1992, Citicorp/Citibank could be under some pressure to meet the 1992 minimum capital standards. Moreover, as mentioned above, the other money-center banks have the same potential problem. In contrast, the regional banks, as represented by WB&T, are not faced with this problem.

Core Capital = Common Equity − Goodwill

By December 31, 1992, banks with the intangible asset goodwill will be required to deduct the amount of this asset from equity capital in determining their ratios of core capital to risk-adjusted assets. Even more devastating, mainly to the money-center banks, than the deduction of goodwill is the regulatory definition of equity capital as simply common shareholder's equity, which means perpetual preferred stock is excluded from core capital (see Table 22-2). Similar to the relative proportions of riskier assets and OBSAs, money-center banks have relatively more preferred stock and goodwill on their balance sheets than regional banks.

Goodwill usually is listed as an "other asset" and, if it is material, described in a footnote to the account. For example, in its 1986 annual report, Citicorp reported (Note 6) goodwill, defined as the excess of purchase price over the estimated value of net assets acquired under the purchase method of accounting, of $977 million, up $272 million from the previous year. Citicorp is amortizing its goodwill using the straight-line method over the periods of expected benefits, which on a weighted-average basis approximates 16 years. Given Citicorp's shareholders' equity capital of $9,060 million, its core capital for year-end 1986 would have been $6,718 million (9,060 − 1,365 − 977), resulting in a core capital ratio of 3.42 percent compared to 4.62 percent without the goodwill deduction and including its preferred stock.

Supplementary Capital

The four components of supplementary capital are (1) loan-loss reserves, (2) perpetual and long-term preferred stock, (3) hybrid capital instruments (e.g., convertible securities), and (4) subordinated debt and limited-life preferred stock (see Table 22-2). Since the allowance or reserve for loan losses was analyzed in Chapter 20, our focus here is on the other three components of supplementary capital.

Let's continue with our example using Citicorp's capital structure. As noted above, Citicorp had, on December 31, 1986, almost $1.4 billion in preferred stock outstanding, consisting of three types: (1) adjustable-rate preferred ($540 million), (2) price-adjusted-rate preferred ($100 million), and (3) money-market cumulative preferred ($725 million). The issuance of $150 million in the third category accounted for the change in preferred stock during 1986. All of Citicorp's preferred series rank prior to common stock as to dividends and liquidation, and do not have general voting rights. Moreover, although Citicorp listed these preferred issues under "Shareholders' Equity," Note 11 (in the annual report) reveals all the series to be redeemable at Citicorp's option. Nevertheless, since these series do not have a stated maturity or sinking funds, they are considered "permanent." In contrast, Citicorp had $40 million in redeemable preferred stock outstanding on December 31, 1986. This series has a mandatory sinking fund and required retirements of $1 million per year running from 1990 through 2005 and of $3 million per year from 2006 to 2013.

Regarding "debt capital," Citicorp had $23.3 billion in this type of financing outstanding on December 31, 1986, consisting of $20.7 billion in long-term debt and $2.6 billion in subordinated capital notes. The maturity structure of Citicorp's long-term debt and its subordinated capital notes is shown in Table 22-5. The breakdown of the long-term debt reveals $15.7 billion (76%) issued by the parent company and $5 billion (24%) by subsidiaries. The subordinated capital notes shown in Table 22-5 are unsecured obligations. The ones with no stated maturities are obligations of Citicorp, whereas the ones with stated maturities are obligations of Citicorp subsidiaries, but they are unconditionally guaranteed on a subordinated basis by Citicorp. The combination of long-term debt (or debentures) and subordinated capital notes is referred to as "subordinated notes and debentures."

Aggregating the various kinds of acceptable capital under the 1985 RAP guidelines shown in Table 22-1, Citicorp reported "total capital" of $21.5 billion, or 10.9 percent of total assets on December 31, 1986. Using Citicorp's reported primary capital ratio as

TABLE 22-5   The Structure of Citicorp's Long-Term Debt and Subordinated Capital Notes, December 31, 1986

Long-Term Debt, Original Maturities of One Year or More[a]

In Millions of Dollars at Year End	Various Fixed-Rate Debt Obligations	Various Floating-Rate Debt Obligations	1986 Total	1985 Total
Parent Company				
Due in 1986	$ —	$ —	$ —	$ 3,032
Due in 1987	433	1,274	1,707	417
Due in 1988	735	568	1,303	1,431
Due in 1989	1,390	1,053	2,443	1,326
Due in 1990	1,135	59	1,194	1,015
Due in 1991	1,180	290	1,470	113
Due in 1992–1996	2,865	345	3,210	1,847
Due in 1997–2001	1,166	1,162	2,328	584
Due in 2002 and thereafter	780	1,262	2,042	1,523
	$ 9,684	$ 6,013	$15,697	$11,288
Subsidiaries				
Due in 1986	$ —	$ —	$ —	$ 1,329
Due in 1987	647	382	1,029	585
Due in 1988	886	85	971	672
Due in 1989	349	302	651	398
Due in 1990	354	407	761	425
Due in 1991	126	76	202	482
Due in 1992–1996	317	964	1,281	1,097
Due in 1997–2001	19	35	54	38
Due in 2002 and thereafter	15	34	49	2
	$ 2,713	$ 2,285	4,998	$ 5,028
TOTAL	$12,397	$ 8,298	$20,695	$16,316

[a] Maturity distribution is based upon contractual maturities or earlier dates at which debt is repayable at the option of the holder, due to required mandatory sinking fund payments or due to call notices issued.

Subordinated Capital Notes In Millions of Dollars at Year-End	1986	1985
Floating rate subordinated capital notes with no stated maturity	$ 500	$ —
Floating rate subordinated capital notes due 1996	1,050	1,050
$12\frac{1}{2}$% subordinated capital notes due 1996	349	349
Floating rate subordinated capital notes due 1997	500	500
$8\frac{3}{4}$% subordinated capital notes due 1998	249	—
TOTAL	$2,648	$1,899

Source: Citicorp Reports 1986, Notes 8 and 9, pp. 62–63.

a proxy for its core-plus-supplementary capital ratio,, the figure is 6.8 percent. As shown earlier, its core capital ratio would have been 3.4 percent. Although some analysts might argue that the new (1988) capital standards are flawed, they are a step in the direction of more closely approximating a ratio reflective of true underlying values.

Although Citicorp's capital structure is a complex one, it is representative of the kind of capital structure found in money-center or multinational banks. Moving down the ladder of complex capital structures, although superregional and regional

TABLE 22-6   The Effects of Bank Size on the Use of Debt Capital and Preferred Stock, December 31, 1985

	Subordinated Notes and Debentures			Preferred Stock		
		Percent of			Percent of	
	$Millions	Equity	Assets	$Millions	Equity	Assets
Banks with foreign offices	12,572	15.0	0.79	667	0.80	0.04
Banks without foreign offices and assets of:						
Less than $100 million	280	0.7	0.06	91	0.24	0.02
$100 mil. to $300 mil.	415	2.1	0.15	58	0.29	0.02
$300 million or more	1,392	5.1	0.34	176	0.64	0.04
TOTAL	2,087	2.4	0.18	326	0.38	0.03
All insured commercial banks	14,659	8.7	0.54	993	0.59	0.04

Notes: Moving down the left-hand column, the number of banks in each group is 272; 12,093; 1,542; 497; 14,132; and 14,404. The percentages were calculated from the dollar data as reported by the FDIC.
Source: FDIC, *Statistics on Banking* [1985], Table RC-2, p. 33.

BHCs/banks certainly make use of innovative capital instruments, they have, on balance, less complex capital structures. At the bottom of the ladder stand 13,000 or so community banks, whose capital structures are simple frameworks driven by retained earnings. The data in Table 22-6 illustrate how the use of capital instruments such as subordinated notes and debentures and preferred stock varies with bank size. The dominance of the 272 banks with foreign offices is clear-cut. Specifically, of the $14.6 billion in subordinated notes and debentures held by all insured commercial banks on December 31, 1985, the banks with foreign offices had issued 86 percent of the total (almost $12.6 billion). With respect to the issuance of preferred stock, the dominance is only slightly less, as the big banks issued $2 out of every $3 of the $993 million outstanding.

OPTIMAL BANK CAPITAL AND THE VALUE OF THE BANKING FIRM

In a perfect capital market without bankruptcy costs and taxes, Modigliani and Miller [1958] have shown that the value of the firm is independent of its financial structure. Relaxing one or more of the simplifying assumptions leads to an optimal capital structure. Consider first the situation in which interest on debt is tax-deductible but there are no bankruptcy costs. In this case, there is an incentive to substitute debt for equity in the firm's financial structure. In the absence of bankruptcy costs, the positive incentive for debt (in the form of tax savings) leads to a corner solution with all debt and no equity. In the case of no taxes but positive bankruptcy costs, the value of the firm is maximized when it is unlevered (that is, when it is a pure equity firm without any debt). Combining costly bankruptcy with the tax-deductibility of interest produces a situation in which bankruptcy costs provide a disincentive that offsets the tax-shield incentive to expand debt. Under these dual conditions, an optimal capital structure exists at which the value of the firm is maximized. These theorems of Modigliani and Miller are illustrated in Figure 22-1. Figure 22-1 (a) shows their pure case; Figure 22-1 (b) depicts the corner solution with all debt; Figure 22-1 (c) shows the unlevered firm with all equity and no debt; and Figure 22-1 (d) depicts the existence of an optimal capital structure $(D/A)^*$ which maximizes the value of the firm (V^*).

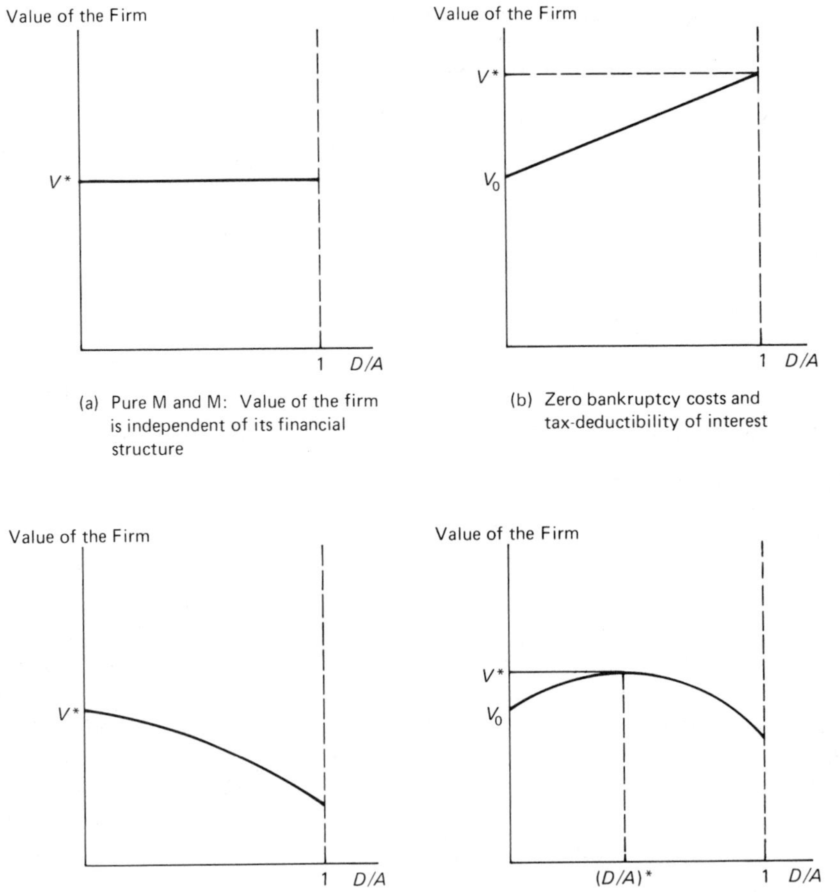

Value of the Firm

V^*

1   D/A

(a) Pure M and M: Value of the firm
     is independent of its financial
     structure

Value of the Firm

V^*

V_0

1   D/A

(b) Zero bankruptcy costs and
     tax-deductibility of interest

Value of the Firm

V^*

1   D/A

(c) Positive bankruptcy costs
     and no taxes

Value of the Firm

V^*

V_0

$(D/A)^*$ 1 D/A

(d) Combined effects of costly
     bankruptcy and tax savings on debt
     lead to an optimal capital structure

Note: D/A = debt-to-asset ratio

Figure 22-1   Financial Structure and the Value of the Firm

The Tax-Shield and Bankruptcy-Cost Concepts

To understand how financial structure affects the value of the firm, the concepts of tax shield and bankruptcy costs are critical. First, consider the concept of the *tax shield*. The important point is that the tax deductibility of interest expense increases the total income that a levered firm (relative to an unlevered or pure-equity firm) can pay out to both its stockholders and its bondholders. In this case, the value of the firm is equal to its value as a purely equity-financed firm plus the present value of the tax shield.

If this proposition is true, however, what stops firms from becoming purely debt-financed entities? Enter bankruptcy costs or, in general, the potential costs of financial distress. The standard argument goes like this. As a firm increases its use of debt, its risk of not being able to cover its fixed interest expenses increases. Thus, the highly levered firm may incur a cash-flow or debt-service problem that eventually could lead to bankruptcy. This greater leverage and greater potential for bankruptcy are not costless. The costs reflect the higher *ex ante* interest rates that creditors demand for holding the debt of highly levered firms, as compensation for the potential *ex post* bankruptcy costs (e.g., legal fees) they might have to pay if the firm fails. The costs of bankruptcy depend on the probability of the event occurring and the size of the associated costs if its does occur. Of course, the costs of financial distress need to be evaluated in present-value terms. Thus, the value of a levered firm can be expressed as its value as a pure-equity firm *plus* the present value of its tax shield *minus* the present value of the costs of bankruptcy. In symbols, this important proposition is

$$PV \text{ Firm} = [PV \text{ Pure-Equity Firm}] + [PV \text{ Tax Shield}] - [PV \text{ Bankruptcy Costs}] \quad (22\text{-}6)$$

Deposit Insurance and the Value of the Banking Firm[9]

The optimal capital structure for an uninsured bank is represented in Panel (d) of Figure 22-1. This section focuses upon the effects of having a governmental agency (the FDIC) guarantee a bank's debt. Like Buser, and Kane [1981a], we assume that the insurance coverage applies to all deposit balances and that there are no doubts about the ability or willingness of the FDIC to meet its insurance obligations. Neither of these assumptions takes us far from reality, as the widespread use of the deposit-assumption technique for handling failed banks and Treasury backing of the insurance fund are facts of life.

To illustrate the insight that Modigliani and Miller's framework has for analyzing the effects of deposit insurance on the value of the banking firm, we begin with the case where FDIC insurance is provided free of charge. This means that there are no fees, either explicit in the form of dollar premiums or implicit in the form of regulatory interference (e.g., capital regulation). In this case, the FDIC simply agrees to pay off all depositors in full in the event of bank failure without imposing any restraints on the bank. In Figure 22-1, which drawing would depict this situation? The correct answer is drawing (b). Free insurance, like zero bankruptcy costs, leads to the zero-equity corner solution. The preliminary insight suggested by this simple case is that perhaps deposit insurance is responsible for the decline in bank capital ratios. However, further analysis is required, so let us go on to the next step.

By combining drawings (b) and (d) of Figure 22-1 in drawing (a) of Figure 22-2, the value of the bank with free insurance (V_f) can be compared with its value without insurance (V). At any financial structure (as measured by the bank's deposit-to-asset ratio), the vertical distance between the two curves (V_f and V) reflects the value of free insurance to the bank. Merton [1977], Sharpe [1978], and others contend that the FDIC should charge an explicit insurance fee sufficient to exhaust this increase in value. If this "fair-value" pricing scheme were enforced, the V_f curve would collapse on the V curve as the value of the free insurance would be wiped out by the insurance premium. In this situation, with or without deposit insurance managers who attempt to maximize the value of the bank would operate at $(D/A)^*$ and the bank would be worth V^*.

If the FDIC were only in the insurance business (recall from Chapter 7 that we shouldn't judge a government agency by the words behind its initials), then, in a competitive market for deposit insurance, the neutral insurance contract described above might exist. However, a major part of FDIC's business is bank regulation. Thus, to avoid going out of business, the FDIC must price and administer its insurance contract so that it presents an insured bank with the opportunity to increase its value above the market-determined value V^* that it would have as an uninsured bank. The opportunity set of "acceptable" deposit-insurance contracts is represented by the shaded triangle in Figure 22-2(b). The boundaries of the set are defined by V_f, V^*, and $D/A = 1$. The latter assumes that the FDIC requires an insured bank to have some

---

[9] See Buser, Chen, and Kane [1981a].

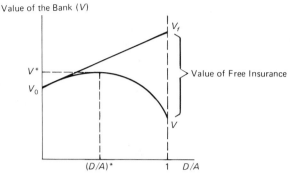

(a) Impact of "Free" Insurance on the Value of the Bank

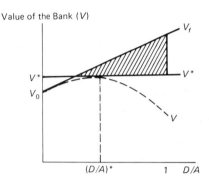

(b) The Opportunity Set of "Acceptable"
     Insurance Contracts

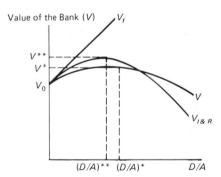

(c) The Impact of Costly Insurance and
     Regulatory Interference on the Value
     of an Insured Bank

**Figure 22-2   Deposit insurance
and the Value of the Banking Firm**

Adapted from Buser, Chen, and
Kane [1981a], Figures 2, 3, and 5,
pp. 55 and 58.

positive amount of equity capital. Excluding the three boundary lines, the area
inside the shaded triangle represents the set of *mutually acceptable* contracting
opportunities.

One of the major themes of this book is that to understand U.S. banking behavior
you must understand the concepts and uses of implicit and explicit interest. Similarly,
to understand deposit insurance and its impact on a bank's capital structure and
behavior, you must understand and distinguish between implicit and explicit deposit
insurance premiums. As explained in Chapter 7, the explicit deposit-insurance
premium is a constant set by law at 1/12 of 1 percent. The effective rate, until the
1980s, was about half of the nominal rate because of an annual rebate based upon the
FDIC's loss experience during the year. This explicit pricing structure encourages
moral-hazard behavior because no *explicit* penalty (in the form of higher insurance

premiums) exists for excessive risk-taking. Under this scheme, high-risk banks are subsidized by low-risk banks. To discourage moral-hazard behavior (i.e., excessive risk-taking) and to price its insurance more fairly, the FDIC uses regulatory interference to extract *implicit* insurance premiums from high-risk banks. Although this regulatory interference can take many forms, it mainly is manifested in the form of *capital regulation*. Capital regulation usually is administered by calling for an infusion of capital into the bank and/or by restricting the bank's growth opportunities.[10] The ultimate objective of capital regulation can be viewed as attempting to improve the bank's capital-to-asset ratio or, in terms of Figure 22-2, debt-to-asset ratio.

The impact of costly insurance and regulatory interference (i.e., explicit and implicit insurance premium) on the value of an insured bank is depicted in Panel (c) of Figure 22-2. The curve V_{I+R} ($I + R$ stands for *insurance* plus *regulation*) lies between the curves for free insurance (V_f) and no insurance (V) at "safe" levels of deposit debt (i.e., when capital is adequate). However, when deposit debt becomes excessive (i.e., when capital is inadequate), V_{I+R} falls below V. The vertical distance between V_f and V_{I+R} measures the varying value of implicit insurance premiums plus the fixed explicit premium. As a part of the insurance contract, an insured bank agrees to pay explicit premiums by subjecting itself to contingent regulatory interference. The vertical distance between V_{I+R} and V measures the net benefit to the bank of the insurance contract. The net benefit is positive when capital is perceived by examiners to be adequate, but negative when capital is perceived to be inadequate. The net benefit involves a trade-off between potential losses from costly bankruptcy without insurance and regulatory interference.

The optimal capital structure with implicit and explicit insurance premia occurs at $(D/A)^{**}$ (see Figure 22-2[c]). The corresponding value of the insured bank is V^{**}, which is greater than V^*. Since V^{**} is greater than V^*, a value-maximizing bank is willing to contract for deposit insurance.

Regulatory Interference and Capital Regulation

Regulatory interference is the process through which the banking authorities attempt to correct a perceived unsafe or unsound banking practice. The major instrument in this process is capital regulation. Other instruments include cease-and-desist orders, removal of bank officers and directors, and the threat of termination of deposit insurance. The concept and process of capital regulation are manifested in policy statements on capital by the banking authorities. For example, FDIC capital regulation requires banks to submit a "comprehensive capital plan" or "specific program for remedying the equity capital deficiency promptly." These plans or programs are costly for banks to prepare and implement. In addition, capital regulation takes the form of withholding approval on various types of applications (e.g., branching or holding-company expansion). These denials are costly because bank resources have been spent on the projects.

Capital regulation requires banks to divert resources to combat regulatory interference. The opportunity costs to banks of this diversion of resources represent one form of the implicit cost of deposit insurance. In the case of denials, both out-of-pocket and opportunity costs are incurred. Only in cases where the regulatory interference has become public knowledge or the market has diagnosed the bank's financial difficulties itself (e.g., Continental Illinois, First Pennsylvania, and Franklin National) is it

[10] Capital regulation for national banks and state-member bank is enforced by the OCC and the Fed, respectively. Thus, these banks pay their implicit insurance premiums indirectly. OCC and Fed bank-examination reports are passed on to the FDIC for further analysis. By law, the FDIC has the right to examine any insured bank.

likely to result in higher risk premiums demanded by uninsured creditors and/or in interruptions of asset and liability flows.

Variable-Rate Deposit Insurance

On the surface, it may appear that the FDIC does not have a risk-rated insurance premium. If we look at only the explicit insurance premium, this in fact is the case. However, once the total premium (i.e., explicit plus implicit price) is considered, the FDIC's effective pricing scheme is seen to be a variable-rate one. Implicit premiums in the form of regulatory interference make up the risk-rated variable component of the total premium. The critical factor in this pricing strategy is the concept of capital adequacy. Prior to the implementation of uniform capital standards in 1985, at least two standards for capital adequacy existed—one for giant banks and one for the rest of the industry. Capital standards determine the expected net value of deposit insurance to bank stockholders as a function of the bank's financial leverage.

Would the banking system be better off if the FDIC employed an *explicit* variable-rate scheme? Given the economic and financial preference for explicit pricing over implicit pricing, the answer is yes, in theory at least. The major merit to a risk-based pricing structure would be its fairness (i.e., low-risk banks would not be forced to subsidize high-risk banks). In the past, the FDIC has claimed that it agreed in principle with the concept of variable-rate deposit insurance but always rejected it as too difficult to implement. How would deposit insurance be priced by private insurers? You can bet it would be on the basis of risk. It is interesting to note that in the past the FDIC has had discussions with private insurers regarding this matter.

A COMPARISON OF RISK-BASED CAPITAL AND RISK-BASED DEPOSIT INSURANCE[11]

In 1986, the FDIC developed a proposal for risk-based deposit insurance based on two measures for assessing the risks of banking. The first measure is based on the CAMEL rating system that scores banks on a 1-to-5 basis with 4 and 5 ratings considered to be problem banks. Recall from Chapter 7 that CAMEL stands for capital adequacy (C), asset quality (A), management (M), earnings (E), and liquidity (L). The second measure is a risk index, I, developed by the FDIC from publicly available Call Report data (i.e., from the Report of Condition and the Report of Income and Dividends filed by banks). The estimated risk index is

$$I = .818 - .151X_1 + .211X_2 + .265X_3 + .177X_4 + .151X_5 - .347X_6$$

Where X_1 = percent of primary capital to total assets,
   X_2 = percent of loans more than 90 days past due to total assets
   X_3 = percent of nonaccruing loans to total assets
   X_4 = percent of renegotiated loans to total assets
   X_5 = percent of net loan charge-offs (annualized) to total assets
   X_6 = percent of net income (annualized) to total assets

Although the risk index has six variables, it is essentially a three-dimensional function centered on capital adequacy (X_1), loan quality (X_2 to X_5), and ROA profitability (X_6). The FDIC examination process has always had a heavy emphasis on loan quality,

[11] This section draws on a study by Avery and Belton [1987]. The section heading has the same title as their paper.

and with good reason because most problem and failed banks have had sour loan portfolios. To illustrate the calculations of the risk index consider the following mean profiles for groups of failed and nonfailed banks analyzed by Avery and Belton [1987, Table 3, p. 25]:

	Groups Means	
	Failed Banks	Nonfailed Banks
X_1	6.14	9.25
X_2	3.41	0.77
X_3	3.64	0.57
X_4	0.28	0.07
X_5	2.89	0.43
X_6	−2.94	0.90

Plugging these values into the risk-index formula, we get $I = 3.080$ for the average failed bank and $I = -.502$ for the average nonfailed bank.

The FDIC's proposed mapping from CAMEL and risk-index space to risk-based deposit insurance premiums would work like this: (1) banks having a positive score on the risk index (e.g., the average failed bank with a score of 3.080) *and* a CAMEL rating of 3, 4, or 5 would be classified as above-normal risk and pay an annual insurance premium of 1/6 of one percent, or twice the current rate; (2) all other insured banks (i.e., those with a negative score on the risk index [e.g., the average nonfailed bank with a score of −.502] or a CAMEL rating of 1 or 2) would be classified as normal risk and pay the standard premium of 1/12 of one percent.

The risk-based capital requirement being imposed on commercial banks by 1992 are captured by Equations 22-3 and 22-4 above. Avery and Belton [1987] have noted the major difference between the risk-based capital plan and the risk-based deposit insurance scheme. Specifically, the FDIC's plan is based on ex post measures of bank performance, such as earnings and loan quality, and examiner's judgments of asset quality and managerial skills via the CAMEL ratings. This performance-based method is derived from statistical models capable of distinguishing between failed and nonfailed banks or problem and nonproblem banks. In contrast, the approach of risk-based capital requirements focuses on the types of activities banks engage in both on and off their balance sheets, and argues that the riskier activities should be supported by higher levels of bank capital.[12]

In Tables 22-7 and 22-8, we show the estimated risk-based premiums and risk-based capital requirements, as calculated by Avery and Belton [1987]. Focusing on Table 22-7, the deposit-insurance fees are expressed as basis points of total domestic deposits. The benchmark premium here is 8.3 basis points which is equal to 1/12 of one percent, or the current FDIC flat premium paid by all banks. The first number in each cell of Table 22-7 is the average deposit-insurance premium for banks in the cell. To explain, consider row 9 in the table, which focuses on the 132 banks that failed in 1987 (through September 30). Forty-four of these banks (those in the first cell) had an estimated average insurance premium of 4.6 basis points and an average estimated probability of failure of 0.3 percent. In contrast, the 31 banks in the last cell had an estimated probability of failure of 35.6 percent and an average estimated insurance premium of 100 basis points, or 91.7 basis points above the current rate of 8.3 basis points. In row 10, note that 12,071 banks (89 percent of the 13,522 banks analyzed)

[12] For a more detailed discussion of the differences between risk-based capital and risk-based deposit insurance, see Avery and Belton [1987], pp. 23–25.

TABLE 22-7   Estimated Commercial Bank Risk-based Premiums—December 1985 (Basic Points of Total Domestic Deposits)

First number is the average premium for banks in the cell. Second number is average estimated probability of failure in percent. Third number is number of banks.

Asset Size Class ($ Millions)	Premium Size Class						
	(1) < 8.3	(2) 8.3–12.4	(3) 12.5–2.4	(4) 25–49	(5) 50–99	(6) 100	(7) All Banks
(1) < $10	2.4 .1 933.0	10.1 .6 29.0	17.2 1.2 23.0	32.1 2.3 16.0	61.6 4.5 9.0	100.0 34.5 25.0	6.3 1.1 1035.0
(2) $10–$25	2.6 .1 3135.0	10.0 .7 109.0	17.2 1.2 131.0	33.3 2.4 61.0	68.8 5.0 44.0	100.0 42.7 78.0	6.9 1.2 3558.0
(3) $25–$50	2.9 .1 3258.0	10.1 .7 112.0	17.1 1.2 105.0	35.0 2.5 47.0	70.4 5.1 26.0	100.0 33.6 54.0	5.9 .7 3602.0
(4) $50–$100	3.1 .2 2485.0	9.9 .7 116.0	16.8 1.2 72.0	33.9 2.4 29.0	74.3 5.4 19.0	100.0 35.6 36.0	5.9 .7 2757.0
(5) $100–$500	3.7 .2 1859.0	9.8 .6 85.0	16.4 1.1 65.0	32.9 2.3 28.0	71.7 5.2 7.0	100.0 71.1 16.0	5.7 .5 2060.0
(6) $500–$1000	4.3 .2 171.0	9.3 .6 14.0	17.3 1.2 9.0	29.4 2.1 3.0	69.7 5.0 3.0	100.0 54.8 2.0	7.5 .9 202.0
(7) < $1000	5.1 .3 230.0	9.8 .6 60.0	15.9 1.1 15.0	37.7 2.7 2.0	78.8 5.7 1.0	0.0 0.0 0.0	7.0 .4 308.0
(8) Banks failing in 1986	4.8 .3 17.0	10.8 .7 8.0	17.1 1.2 9.0	38.1 2.7 12.0	71.5 5.2 12.0	100.0 51.8 75.0	68.7 30.1 133.0
(9) Banks failing in 1987	4.6 .3 44.0	10.2 .7 11.0	16.9 1.2 20.0	32.2 2.3 17.0	69.8 5.1 9.0	100.0 35.6 31.0	37.3 9.3 132.0
(10) All banks	3.0 .1 12071.0	9.9 .7 525.0	16.9 1.2 420.0	33.6 2.4 186.0	69.8 5.0 109.0	100.0 37.4 211.0	6.2 .8 13522.0

Source: Board of Governors of the Federal Reserve System as reported by Avery and Belton [1987], Table 4, p. 27.

TABLE 22-8 Estimated Commercial Bank Risk-based Required Capital—December 1985 (Percent of Total Assets)

First number is the average capital ratio for banks in the cell. Second number is percent of banks that would have to raise capital. Third number is number of banks.

Asset Size Class ($ Millions)	Required Capital Class						
	(1) < 5.5	(2) 5.5–6.4	(3) 6.5–7.4	(4) 7.5–9.9	(5) 10.0–14.9	(6) 15.0	(7) All Banks
(1) < $10	4.6	6.0	7.0	8.5	11.8	15.0	6.1
	0.0	1.0	3.3	27.7	76.1	84.6	8.5
	529.0	198.0	119.0	130.0	46.0	13.0	1035.0
(2) $10–$25	4.7	5.9	7.0	8.5	11.6	15.0	5.9
	.1	.9	9.0	50.0	92.9	97.1	10.4
	1936.0	775.0	365.0	326.0	141.0	35.0	3558.0
(3) $25–$50	4.8	5.9	6.9	8.5	11.8	15.0	5.7
	.2	1.1	14.0	54.0	95.7	100.0	8.3
	2158.0	749.0	336.0	252.0	92.0	15.0	3602.0
(4) $50–$100	4.8	5.9	6.9	8.4	11.7	15.0	5.6
	.4	3.0	16.7	53.8	90.2	91.7	7.8
	1752.0	535.0	239.0	158.0	61.0	12.0	2757.0
(5) $100–$500	4.9	5.9	6.9	8.3	11.7	15.0	5.5
	.1	4.0	24.1	69.3	100.0	100.0	7.2
	1366.0	448.0	116.0	96.0	31.0	3.0	2060.0
(6) $500–$1000	4.9	5.9	6.9	8.7	10.9	15.0	5.5
	1.5	10.8	27.8	100.0	100.0	100.0	10.4
	137.0	37.0	18.0	6.0	3.0	1.0	202.0
(7) < $1000	5.0	5.9	6.8	8.6	10.2	0.0	5.4
	3.1	29.0	47.4	100.0	100.0	0.0	15.3
	191.0	93.0	19.0	4.0	1.0	0.0	308.0
(8) Banks failing in 1986	4.6	5.9	7.1	9.0	12.4	15.0	11.5
	0.0	33.3	53.3	86.4	98.1	100.0	86.5
	5.0	3.0	15.0	22.0	54.0	34.0	133.0
(9) Banks failing in 1987	5.0	6.0	6.8	8.8	12.1	15.0	9.2
	9.1	16.7	21.0	75.5	96.7	72.7	61.4
	11.0	12.0	19.0	49.0	30.0	11.0	132.0
(10) All banks	4.8	5.9	6.9	8.4	11.7	15.0	5.7
	.3	2.9	13.7	51.1	91.7	94.9	8.8
	8069.0	2815.0	1212.0	972.0	375.0	79.0	13522.0

Source: Board of Governors of the Federal Reserve System as reported by Avery and Belton [1987], Table 5, p. 29.

were estimated to have an average insurance premium of 3 basis points, well below the current level of 8.3 basis points. For these banks, the implication is that deposit insurance is overpriced.

In Table 22-8, estimated risk-based capital requirements, as calculated by Avery and Belton [1987], are presented. The structure of Table 22-8, which is similar to Table 22-7, shows in each cell (1) the average required capital level for the banks in the cell, (2) the percentage of banks that would be required to raise capital, and (3) the number of banks in the cell. The purpose of the table is to indicate how a risk-based capital system might work. Let's consider row 10 (all banks) to illustrate the results. If a capital ratio of less than 5.5 percent (3% is the lower bound) is required, then the 8,069 banks in that cell would have to meet an average ratio of 4.8 percent, and only 0.3 percent of all banks (40 or 41 banks) would need to raise capital. In contrast, for the fourth required class, the average required capital level would be 8.4 percent of total assets. Only 972 banks are observed in this cell, and 51.1 percent of all banks would have to raise capital to meet the standard.

To summarize, Avery and Belton conclude that risk-based deposit insurance and risk-based capital requirements have a common goal: the separation of banks according to risk. They suggest that the implementation of either type of system should contribute to the task of controlling bank risk exposure.

THE BANK EXAMINATION PROCESS, CAPITAL REGULATION, AND PROBLEM BANKS

The on-site bank examination is the basic weapon used to determine if a bank requires regulatory interference.[13] The degree of regulatory interference depends on the severity of the bank's problems. For minor problems, a meeting with the bank's management and/or board of directors may be all that is required. For severe problems, more drastic measures such as cease-and-desist orders, removal of bank officers, or actual financial assistance may be required. In February 1985, the FDIC proposed, but did not adopt, disclosing the identities of banks and employees cited in all enforcement actions. The FDIC claimed that such disclosure "...would facilitate the development of effective market discipline, thereby encouraging funds flows to the vast majority of banks that are prudently operated rather than to the marginal banks that tend to pay the highest rates."[14] Under securities laws, publicly traded companies must disclose only *final* enforcement actions.

To monitor potential claims on the deposit-insurance fund, the FDIC keeps a current record of banks that may require its financial assistance in the future. This log is referred to as the FDIC's problem-bank list. The list consists of three classes of problem banks referred to as

1. other problems (OP)
2. serious problems (SP)
3. potential payoff (PPO).

From 1970 to 1987, the average number of banks on the list has been around 500, roughly 3.4 percent of the population of insured commercial banks. Most of these

---

[13] To assist in scheduling bank examinations and to flag potential problem banks, the banking agencies employ computerized early-warning or surveillance systems to complement the bank-examination process. See Sinkey [1979] and Altman, Avery, Eisenbeis, and Sinkey [1981].

[14] See Langley [1985].

TABLE 22-9   Problem and Failed Commercial Banks, 1970–1987

| Year | Number of Banks | | | Failure Rate with Respect to Number of | |
	Failed	FDIC Problem List	All Insured	Problem Banks	All Insured Banks
1970	7	215	13,840	.0279	.00051
1971	6	239	13,939	.0251	.00043
1972	1	190	14,059	.0053	.00007
1973	6	155	14,298	.0387	.00042
1974	4	181	14,550	.0221	.00027
1975	13	347	14,714	.0343	.00088
1976	16	379	14,740	.0422	.00108
1977	6	368	14,741	.0163	.00041
1978	7	342	14,716	.0205	.00048
1979	10	287	14,688	.0195	.00068
1980	10	217[a]	14,758	.0147	.00068
1981	7	223	14,744	.0314	.00047
1982	34	340	14,451	.1000	.00235
1983	45	642	14,469	.0701	.00311
1984	79	848	14,503	.0932	.00545
1985	120	1,140	14,417	.1053	.00832
1986	145	1,484	14,500E	.0977	.01000
1987	203	1,575	14,500E	.1289	.01400

[a] FDIC classification procedures were revised slightly in 1980. In 1986 and 1987, the population of banks is estimated, as indicated by E, to be 14,500.
Source: FDIC, *Annual Reports and News Releases* [1970–1987].

troubled banks (roughly three out of four) fall into the least risky "other problem" category. Over this same time period, about 40 banks per year have failed, for an average failure rate of .0027. However, over the period 1985 through 1987, the number of FDIC problem and failed banks, which includes all insured commercial banks, has been historically high (see Table 22-9). Specifically, over this period, the average number of problem banks was about 1,400 per year and the average number of bank failures was 156 per year. Roughly, these figures imply one out of every ten banks was a problem institution over this period, and one out of every ten of the problem banks failed. Nevertheless, the problems and failures were isolated in the energy and agricultural sectors. For example, of the 203 banks closed in 1987, 54 were farm banks and 95 of the failures were located in three states: Texas (50), Oklahoma (31), and Louisiana (14). It is rare when a failed bank has not been on the FDIC's problem list for a number of months before its failure.

The Capital Ratio that Really Counts

In terms of measuring the risk that gets a bank placed on the FDIC's problem-bank list, Sinkey [1978] has shown that the capital ratio that best discriminates between problem and nonproblem banks is the FDIC's net capital ratio (NCR). This ratio is defined as

$$NCR = \frac{\text{Capital} + \text{Reserves} - \text{Classified Assets}}{\text{Average Assets}} \qquad (22\text{-}7)$$

where classified assets are those listed as "substandard," "doubtful," or "loss," based on bank examiners' perceptions of asset quality.[15] Based on 1973 and 1975 bank

[15] The weighted capital ratio (WCR) used in CAMEL is a refinement of the NCR. It places less weight on the least risky substandard classification. The WCR weighting scheme is similar to the one first suggested by me in 1976. The exact specification of NCR contains some other minor adjustments omitted from Equation 22-7. See Sinkey [1978].

The FDIC's Net Capital Ratio		
	Problem Banks	Nonproblem Banks
1973		
Mean	−2.3%	7.6%
(standard deviation)	(5.2)	(3.0)
Number of banks	143	163
1975		
Mean	−3.8%	7.9%
(standard deviation)	(6.4)	(3.2)
Number of banks	347	14,524

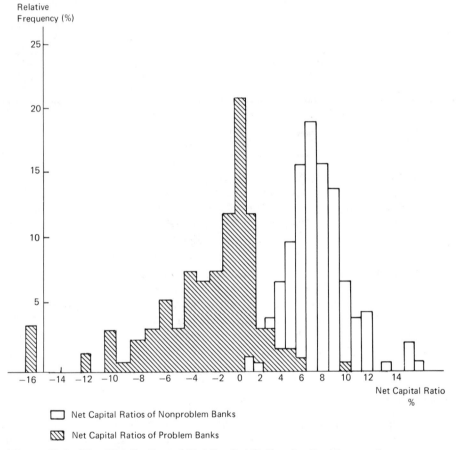

☐ Net Capital Ratios of Nonproblem Banks

▨ Net Capital Ratios of Problem Banks

Figure 22-3   The Distribution of Net Capital Ratios for Problem and Nonproblem Banks

Source: FDIC Bank Examination Data [1973].

examination data, NCR means and standard deviations for problem and nonproblem banks are presented, along with a frequency distribution based on the 1973 data, in Figure 22-3. The significant degree of separation between the groups explains why the rule

Classify as a problem bank if $NCR \leq 2.74\%$ (22-8)

was so accurate (95.4 percent accuracy) in reclassifying the sample of 143 problem banks and 163 nonproblem banks. Since the volume of classified assets was dominated by the substandard category, this led to the *de facto* definition of a problem bank as one with a large volume of substandard loans relative to its capital reserves. The results of these experiments reflect the importance of asset quality in determining a bank's capital adequacy. The deterioration in NCR from 1973 to 1975 for the problem-bank group reflects the greater vulnerability of troubled institutions to the recessionary phase of the business cycle.

CHAPTER SUMMARY

In a world of bankruptcy costs, taxes, and other imperfections, capital structure (leverage) is important because it affects value. In banking, capital or net worth plays an important role in the public's confidence in banks and the banking system. The term "capital adequacy" has been used to capture the overall soundness or risk exposure of individual banks. The notion of bank capital as a cushion or buffer (to absorb losses associated with credit and interest-rate risks) suggests an inverse relationship between the level of bank capital and risk exposure. The scheduled move, by 1992, to risk-based capital requirements reflects this basic idea. The inclusion of off-balance-sheet activities in the new risk-based capital formulas for "core" and "supplementary" capital reflects regulatory concern about the risks associated with contingent claims. Banks that can say, "Look Ma (to the marketplace and to regulators), no risk," are entitled to greater leverage. In contrast, banks with riskier portfolios and lots of OBSAs will be forced to hold more capital to support the greater potential risk exposure. Since money-center banks fit this description (e.g., with their heavy LDC debt exposure), they will have the most difficult time adjusting to the new capital standards, which rise to 8 percent of risk-adjusted assets by 1992 with one-half of this total required to be core or pure equity capital. As a result, the advantage over this transition period goes to the superregional and regional banks (outside the Southwest) in terms of having the capital to take advantage of future growth opportunities.

Risk-based capital requirements or risk-based deposit insurance are important ideas for constraining bank risk-taking. Whether or not either of the two, or both, can be successfully implemented remains to be seen. Current regulatory interference takes the form of capital regulation, cease-and-desist orders, and/or removal of bank officers as weapons for attempting to control problem and failed banks, whose numbers have soared in the 1980s mainly because of economic depressions in the energy and farm sectors. Although the heart of the process for identifying problem banks is grounded in the on-site bank examination process, the federal banking agencies have been attempting, since the early 1970s, to make increasing use of financial information to screen potential problem banks, or to price deposit insurance. The FDIC's risk index is an example of a model that could do either function, or both. Early-warning techniques and pricing risk are important because the ability of bank regulators to preserve bank charter values is critical to preserving the value of the FDIC's insurance fund. The inability to do this leads to bankruptcy, as evidenced by the defunct FSLIC.

On balance, both the theory and regulation of bank capital structure make for interesting, challenging, and thought-provoking study. In the next chapter, we turn to some of the practical aspects of the financial management of bank capital.

LIST OF KEY WORDS, CONCEPTS, AND ACRONYMS

Bank capital
Bank examination process
Bankruptcy costs
Capital adequacy
Capital notes and debentures
Capital structure (optimal)
Common equity capital
Confidence function $[=f(NW, SOE, IQ, G)]$
Core capital
Debt capital
Deposit insurance
Failed banks
Generally accepted accounting principles (GAAP)
Goodwill
Market value accounting
Money-center banks

Leverage
Loan-loss reserves
Net capital ratio
Preferred stock (perpetual versus limited life)
Problem banks (PPO, SP, OP)
Regulatory accounting principles (RAP)
Regulatory interference
Retained earnings
Risk-based capital requirements
Risk-based deposit insurance
Risk index
Sallie Mae (Look Ma, no risk!)
Superregional banks
Supplementary capital
Tax accounting principles (TAP)
Tax shield

MATCHING QUIZ

Directions: Select the letter from the right-hand column that best matches the item in the left-hand column.

___ 1. Core capital

___ 2. Supplementary capital

___ 3. Perpetual preferred stock

___ 4. Optimal capital structure

___ 5. Money-center banks

___ 6. Superregional banks

___ 7. Sallie Mae

___ 8. Confidence function

___ 9. GAAP

___ 10. RAP

___ 11. Goodwill

___ 12. Regulatory interference

A. 1,575

B. Cut the GAAP and RAP veils

C. Approximates core + supplementary

D. Preceded weighted capital ratio

E. 4 of 6 measure loan quality

F. Reflects the G in confidence

G. Trouble spots of the 1980s

H. Problem bank classes

I. Heart of problem identification

J. 1987 provision for loan losses

K. Common equity − goodwill

___ 13. Accounting manipulation

___ 14. On-site examinations

___ 15. Risk-adjusted assets

___ 16. PPO, SP, OP

___ 17. 10% problems, 10% failures

___ 18. Energy and farm sectors

___ 19. Deposit insurance

___ 20. Risk index

___ 21. Net capital ratio

___ 22. Primary capital

___ 23. Market values

___ 24. Standard for 1992

___ 25. Number of failures in 1987

___ 26. Problem banks at 12/31/87

L. Form of implicit pricing

M. Relects premium paid in mergers

N. Critical for financial stability

O. Excluded from core capital

P. Can exceed core but excess does not count for meeting standard

Q. Maximizes value of the firm

R. Have adjustment problem

S. Accounting standard

T. Regulatory standard

U. Have advantage in transition

V. Include OBSAs

W. Describes the mid-1980s

X. 8 percent with 4 percent in core

Y. Look Ma, no risk!

REVIEW/DISCUSSION QUESTIONS

1. Why is bank capital important? In an article in the *Journal of Political Economy*, Peltzman [1970] wrote about the substitution of deposit insurance for bank capital. Using the confidence function from Equation 22-1 in the text, describe the interaction between NW and G from the end of World War II until the early 1970s. What has happen since then, and especially in the 1980s?

2. By 1992, commercial banks and bank holding companies must meet new capital standards. What are they and how do they compare with the capital requirements established in 1985? What are the expected differential effects of the new capital standards on money-center banks? Regional and superregional banks? Community banks?

3. Describe the use of preferred stock and capital notes and debentures by U.S. commercial banks.

4. The term "capital adequacy" can be viewed as simply another way of describing leverage. What is the relationship between portfolio risks, such as credit risk and interest-rate risk, and leverage? Use this relationship to explain Sallie Mae's claim of "Look Ma, no risk!"

5. What has happened to the number of problem and failed banks in the 1980s? Describe the "why" and "where" of these difficulties and whether or not you think the problems have been systematic or unsystematic.

6. What effect does financial structure have on the value of the firm? Explain carefully, using the concepts of tax subsidies and bankruptcy costs in your answer. How does Ehlen's quote in the text relate to M&M's theory?

7. What insights can be gained by the application of M&M's model to the value of the banking firm? What are Buser, Chen, and Kane's conclusions regarding deposit insurance, capital regulation, and optimal bank capital? Carefully define and explain the significance of the following terms in your answer:
   a. charter value
   b. implicit insurance premium
   c. regulatory interference

8. Does the FDIC *really* have variable-rate deposit insurance? Who "collects" the implicit premiums from national and state-member banks?

9. What are the relationships among the bank-examination process, capital regulation, and problem banks? What do the symbols OP, SP, and PPO stand for?

10. Guttentag and Herring [1981] state: "The development of deposit insurance has eliminated the possibility of runs at most financial institutions, and converted potential runs into 'walks' at others. This has largely transformed the bankruptcy decision from a market-driven process to a deliberate, administrative process" (p. 1). Do you agree or disagree? If you agree, what are the important issues involved in the process?

11. How would you attempt to implement an explicit, variable-rate deposit-insurance pricing structure? How do risk-based capital requirements and the risk-based deposit insurance, as described in the text (and estimated by Avery and Belton [1987]), differ? How are they similar?

12. What are the many veils of bank bookkeeping and how effective is the "market-value knife" at cutting the veils for money-center banks? Regional and superregional banks? Community banks? Suppose you did an event study of the announcement effects of the proposed risk-based capital requirements on bank equity returns. On which of the three groups of banks could your test be applied, and what hypotheses would you test?

13. Regarding the definition of adequate bank capital, Maisel [1981], building on an earlier study by Sharpe [1978], has written:

   Capital is adequate either when it reduces the chances of future insolvency of an institution to some predetermined minimum level or, alternatively, when the premium paid by the bank to an insurer is "fair"; that is, when it fully covers the risks borne by the insurer. Such risks, in turn, depend upon the risk in the portfolio selected by the bank, on its capital, and on terms of the insurance with respect to when insolvency will be determined and what losses will be paid. (p. 20)

   Discuss and evaluate this statement.

PROBLEMS

1. The FDIC's risk index described in the text was estimated using a "probit model." Avery and Belton [1987], using a "logit model," reestimated the risk index (call it R here) as

$$R = -2.42 - .501X_1 + .428X_2 + .314X_3 + .269X_4 - .223X_5 - .331X_6$$
$$(3.07) \quad (4.89) \quad (5.16) \quad (4.31) \quad (1.07) \quad (1.60) \quad (2.68)$$

The Xs are the same ones as defined in the text and the figures in parentheses are t-statistics, indicating only X_4 and X_5 as statistically insignificant variables. The logistic form of the risk index implies that the probability of failure (PROB) for a given bank within a year is

$$PROB = 1/[1 - \exp(-R)]$$

where exp indicates the exponential operator. Using the group means for the Xs as supplied in the text, calculate the probability of failure for the average failed bank and the average nonfailed bank. Next, pick a bank you like (or dislike) and calculate its probability of failure. Only publicly available information is used in the risk index. Can you find the data, generate the six ratios, and calculate the probability of failure? Finally, which one of the variables in the R index has the "wrong" sign? If you are interested in learning more about probit, logit, and other classification techniques, see Altman, Avery, Eisenbeis, and Sinkey [1981].

2. Determine the capital-to-asset ratios for the following banks and give a brief description of each bank based on your findings.

Bank	ROE	ROA
A	.2000	.0150
B	−.1000	−.0010
C	.1500	.0075
D	.1500	.0065
E	.1500	.0100
F	.1750	.0109

3. The Debt Bank has the following capital structure:

Item	Amount ($ Millions)
Notes and debentures	11.5
Limited-Life preferred	0.0
Perpetual preferred	0.0
Common stock	51.4
Surplus	78.5
Undivided profits	405.2
Loan-loss reserves	66.7

If the bank's common stock is selling for $25 per share and there are 31,000,000 shares outstanding, calculate its capital position on the basis of (a) GAAP, (b) RAP using the 1992 capital standards, and (c) market values. What is the bank's market-to-book ratio? What does the bank's capital structure tell you about is sources of capital?

4. On February 12, 1988, J. Richard Fredericks, the San Francisco bank stock analyst with Montgomery Securities, appeared on PBS's "Wall Street Week with Louis Rukeyser." His recommended buy list included the following bank stocks and one "special situation":

J.P. Morgan (NYSE, 35)
Bankers Trust (NYSE, 34.75)

Fleet National (NYSE, NA)
Bank of New England (OTC, 26.5)
Core States (OTC, 39.125)
PNC (NYSE, 41.25)
SunTrust (NYSE, 22.25)
Barnett (NYSE, 34.5)
First Wachovia (NYSE, 38.5)
Banc One (NYSE, 25.25)
Wells Fargo (NYSE, 49.875)
Bancorp Hawaii (OTC, 55.25)
Sallie ("Look Ma, no risk!") Mae (NYSE, 77.5)

Assuming you bought one share of each of these stocks on February 12, 1988, find your holding-period return (excluding dividends) from then until the day you work this problem. The prices shown above represent your per share investment in each stock, and each price was the low one for that day. It is assumed you had pre- or inside information about Fredricks's list and your broker, God bless his/her little heart, got you in at the low price for the day. Moreover, since your broker had been churning your account for the past few years, and feeling a bit (but only a little bit) guilty about it, he/she gave you an early 1988 Valentine's Day present of free roundtrips in and out of the market for each of your one-share trades (i.e., you incur no transactions costs). Extra credit exercise: How would you do an event study to check for a "Fredericks's announcement effect" on the 13 stocks he recommended? More generally, do the recommendations made by guests on "Wall Street Week" generate abnormal returns for the shareholders of the recommended stocks?

5. Given the following pro forma information for the West Bank and The East Bank, determine their required risk-based capital, both core and supplementary, using the standards set for year-end 1992 (check the appendix for the appropriate weights and conversion factors). All dollars items are in thousands.

	The West Bank	The East Bank
Balance sheet items:		
Risk category 1	$ 5,000	$10,000
Risk category 2	15,000	20,000
Risk category 3	35,000	60,000
Risk category 4	15,000	20,000
Risk category 5	60,000	95,000
OBSAs:		
Standby letters of credit	50,000	100,000
Loan commitments (2-year maturity)	25,000	50,000
Commercial letters of credit	15,000	25,000

6. Complete the following table and write a 250- to 500-word essay about your findings.

Citicorp/Citibank Capital Structure, December 31, 1986	Citicorp		Citibank		Bank/BHC
Item	$mil	%	$mil	%	%
Domestic deposits					
Noninteresting bearing	12,666				85.0
Interest bearing	41,796				70.0
Foreign deposits					
Noninteresting bearing	3,791				99.0
Interest bearing	56,436				99.6
TOTAL DEPOSITS	114,689				87.1
Purchased funds and other borrowings	33,731				61.3
All other liabilities	15,261				85.1
Long-term debt	20,695				15.5
Subordinated capital notes	2,648				0
Redeemable preferred	40				0
Perpetual preferred	1,365				0
Common equity	7,695				104.1
TOTAL LIABILITIES AND EQUITY	196,124	100.0	144,808	100.0	73.8

Note: The components of "all other liabilities" include acceptances outstanding, accrued taxes and other expenses, and other liabilities.

CHAPTER 22

APPENDIX
The Federal Reserve's Risk-Based Capital Requirements

Overview

This appendix consists of six tables describing the Federal Reserve's proposal (dated January 25, 1988) for risk-based capital requirements. In Table 22-A1, the definitions of qualifying capital are presented. Table 22-A2 summarizes the risk weights and risk categories for state member banks and BHCs. The credit conversion factors for off-balance-sheet activities are shown in Table 22-A3. Examples of how to compute the risk-shaped capital requirements are shown in Tables 22-A4 and 22-A5. The appendix concludes with a description of the transitional and final arrangements for the initial, year-end 1990, and year-end 1992 capital standards. The OCC's announcement of a proposal for risk-based capital requirements, which were developed in conjunction with the Fed and FDIC, was made on March 1, 1988, and is entitled: "Capital: Risk-Based Capital Guidelines".

TABLE 22-A1 Definition of Qualifying Capital of State Member Banks and Bank Holding Companies

Components	Minimum Requirements and Limitations After Transition Period
Core Capital (Tier 1)	Must equal or exceed 4% of weighted-risk assets
Common stockholder's equity	No limit
Preferred stock (for BHCs only)	Limited to no more than 25% of Tier 1
Minority interest in consolidated subsidiaries	
Less: Goodwill[a]	
Supplementary Capital (Tier 2)	Total of Tier 2 is limited to 100% of Tier 1[b]
Allowance for losses on loans and leases (general reserves only)	No limit initially, by end of 1992, limited to 1.25%[b]
Perpetual and long-term preferred stock (original maturity 20 years or more)	No limit within Tier 2
Hybrid capital instruments (including perpetual debt and mandatory convertible securities)	No limit within Tier 2
Subordinated debt and intermediate-term preferred stock (average maturity of 7 years or more)	Subordinated debt and intermediate-term preferred stock are limited to 50% of Tier 1;[b] amortized for capital purposes as they approach maturity

TABLE 22-A1 (*Continued*)

Components	Minimum Requirements and Limitations After Transition Period
Revaluation reserves (equity and building)	Not formally included in supplementary capital or ratio calculation; regulators would encourage banks to disclose; would evaluate on case-by-case basis for international comparisons; and would take into account in making overall assessment of capital—would not cause regulatory accounting procedures to depart from GAAP
Deductions	
Investments in unconsolidated banking and finance subsidiaries	
Reciprocal holdings of bank-issued capital securities	
Other deductions (such as other subsidiaries or joint ventures) as determined by supervisory authority	On case-by-case basis or as matter of policy after formal rulemaking
Total Capital (Tier 1 + Tier 2 − Deductions)	Must equal or exceed 8% of weighted-risk assets

[a]Goodwill on books of bank holding companies before issuance of proposal would be "grandfathered" for transition period. All goodwill in banks would be deducted immediately as under current policies. All deductions are for capital adequacy purposes only; deductions would not affect accounting treatment.
[b]Amounts in excess of limitations are permitted but do not qualify as capital.

TABLE 22-A2   Summary of Risk Weights and Risk Categories for State Member Banks and Bank Holding Companies

Category 1: Zero percent

1. Cash (domestic and foreign).
2. Balances due from, and claims on, Federal Reserve Banks.
3. Securities (direct obligations) issued by the U.S. government or its agencies[a] with a remaining maturity of 90 days or less.

Category 2:10 percent

1. Securities issued by the U.S. government or its agencies[a] with remaining maturities of over 90 days and all other claims (loans and leases) on the U.S. government or its agencies.[a]
2. Securities and other claims guaranteed by the U.S. government or its agencies (including portions of claims guaranteed).
3. Portions of loans and other assets collateralized[b] by securities of the U.S. government or its agencies, or by cash on deposit in the lending institution.
4. Federal Reserve Bank stock.

Category 3:20 percent

1. All claims (long- and short-term) on domestic depository institutions.
2. Claims on foreign banks with an original maturity of one year or less.
3. Claims guaranteed by domestic depository institutions.
4. Local currency claims on foreign central governments to the extent the bank has local currency liabilities in the foreign country.
5. Cash items in the process of collection.
6. Securities and other claims on, or guaranteed by, U.S. government-*sponsored* agencies (including portions of claims guaranteed).[c]
7. Portions of loans and other assets collateralized[d] by securities of U.S. government-sponsored agencies.
8. General obligation claims on, and claims guaranteed by, U.S. state and local governments that are secured by the full faith and credit of the state or local taxing authority (including portions of claims guaranteed).

(continues)

TABLE 22-A2 (*Continued*)

Category 3:20 percent

---

9. Claims on official multinational lending institutions or regional development institutions in which the U.S. government is a shareholder or a contributing member.

Category 4:50 Percent

1. Public-purpose revenue bonds or similar obligations, including loans and leases, that are obligations of U.S. state or local governments, but for which the government entity is committed to repay the debt only out of revenues from the facilities financed.
2. Claims secured by mortgages on residential properties of one to four units, either owner-occupied or rented.

Category 5:100 Percent

1. All other claims on private obligors.
2. Claims on foreign banks with an original maturity exceeding one year.
3. Claims on foreign central governments that are not included in item 4 of Category 3.
4. Obligations issued by state or local governments (including industrial development authorities and similar entities) repayable solely by a private party or enterprise.
5. Premises, plant, and equipment; other fixed assets; and other real estate owned.
6. Investments in any unconsolidated subsidiaries, joint ventures, or associated companies—if not deducted from capital.
7. Instruments issued by other banking organizations that qualify as capital.
8. All other assets (including claims on commercial firms owned by the public sector).

---

[a] For the purpose of calculating the risk-based capital ratio, a U.S. Government agency is defined as an instrumentality of the U.S. Government whose obligations are fully and explicity guaranteed as to the timely repayment of principal and interest by the full faith and credit of the U.S. Government.

[b] Degree of collateralization is determined by the current market value.

[c] For the purpose of calculating the risk-based capital ratio, a U.S. government-*sponsored* agency is defined as an agency originally established or chartered to serve public purposes specified by the U.S. Congress but whose obligations are not *explicitly* guaranteed by the full faith and credit of the U.S. government.

[d] Degree of collateralization is determined by current market value.

TABLE 22-A3   Credit Conversion Factors for Off-Balance-Sheet Items

---

100 Percent Conversion Factor

1. Direct credit substitutes (general guarantees of indebtedness, including standby letters of credit serving as financial guarantees for loans and securities).
2. Acquisitions of risk participations in bankers acceptances and participations in direct credit substitutes (e.g., standby letters of credit).
3. Sale and repurchase agreements and asset sales with recourse, if not already included on the balance sheet.
4. Forward agreements (that is, contractual obligations) to purchase assets, including commitments with *certain* drawdown.

50 Percent Conversion Factor

1. Transaction-related contingencies (e.g., bid bonds, performance bonds, warranties, and standby letters of credit related to a particular transaction).
2. Unused commitments with an original maturity exceeding one year, including underwriting commitments and commercial credit lines.
3. Revolving underwriting facilities (RUFs), note issuance facilities (NIFs), and other similar arrangements.

20 Percent Conversion Factor

1. Commercial letters of credit.

Zero Percent Conversion Factor

1. Unused commitments which have an original maturity of one year or less or which are unconditionally cancellable at any time.

TABLE 22-A4

The following Table illustrates the calculation of risk-based capital ratio, as proposed in the Basel agreement. This example assumes a banking organization with $100,000 in total assets, $52,000 in certain off-balance-sheet credit equivalent amounts, and $7,000 in Tier 1 and Tier 2 capital as defined by the proposal.

Risk Category	On-Balance-Sheet and Credit Equivalent Amounts		Risk Weight		Weighted-Risk Assets and Off-Balance-Sheet Items
0 Percent	$ 5,000	×	0	=	0
10 Percent	10,000	×	0.10	=	$ 1,000
20 Percent	30,000	×	0.20	=	6,000
50 Percent	20,000	×	0.50	=	10,000
100 Percent	87,000	×	1.00	=	87,000
TOTAL	$152,000				$104,000

(including $100,000 in total assets and $52,000 in credit equivalent off-balance-sheet items, as derived in the example below)

Total Tier 1 and
Tier 2 Capital $7,000

Risk-based capital ratio (as proposed) $\dfrac{7,000}{\$104,000} = 6.7\%$

The following Table illustrates the calculation of the "credit equivalent" value of selected off-balance-sheet items by multiplying the principal amount by the appropriate "credit conversion factor." Each credit equivalent value would subsequently be assigned to one of the five risk categories (in the table above) depending on the identity of the obligor.

Off-Balance-Sheet Item	Principal Amount		Credit Conversion Factor		On-Balance-Sheet Credit Equivalent Amount[a]
Standby letter of credit (financial guarantee)	$40,000	×	1.00	=	$40,000
Commitment with original maturity of 3 years	20,000	×	0.50	=	10,000
Commercial letter of credit	10,000	×	0.20	=	2,000
TOTAL	$70,000				$52,000

[a] Assumes the item is assigned to Category 5 (100 percent risk weight) on the basis of the obligor.

TABLE 22-A5   Calculation of Credit Equivalent Amounts Interest Rate and Foreign Rate Related Transactions

Type of Contract (remaining maturity)	Notional Primary (Dollars) (1)	Potential Exposure			Current Exposure			Credit Equivalent Amount (Dollars)
			Potential Exposure Conversion Factor (2)	Potential Exposure (Dollars) (3)		Replacement Cost[a] (4)	Current Exposure (Dollars)[b] (5)	
		$\times$		$=$	$+$		$=$	
(1) 120-day forward foreign-exchange	5,000,000		.01	50,000		100,000	100,000	150,000
(2) 120-day forward foreign exchange	6,000,000		.01	60,000		−120,000	-0-	60,000
(3) 3-year single-currency fixed/floating interest rate swap	10,000,000		.005	50,000		200,000	200,000	250,000
(4) 3-year single-currency fixed/floating interest rate swap	10,000,000		.005	50,000		−250,000	-0-	50,000
(5) 7-year cross-currency floating/floating interest rate swap	20,000,000		.05	1,000,000		−1,300,000	-0-	1,000,000
TOTAL	$51,000,000							$1,510,000

[a] These numbers are purely for illustration.
[b] The larger of zero or a positive mark-to-market value.

TABLE 22-A6   The Scheduled Phase-In of Risk-Based Capital Requirements

	Transitional Arrangements		Final Arrangement
	Initial	Year-End 1990	Year-End 1992
1. Minimum standard of total capital to weighted-risk assets	None	7.25%	8.0%
2. Definition of Tier 1 capital	Common equity *plus* supplementary elements *less* goodwill.[a] (For bank holding companies, goodwill acquired before—will be grandfathered for transition period)	Common equity *plus* supplementary elements *less*: goodwill.[b] (For bank holding companies, goodwill acquired before—will be grandfathered for transition period)	Common equity *less* all goodwill
3. Minimum standard of Tier 1 capital to weighted-risk assets	None	3.625%	4.0%
4. Minimum standard of common stockholders' equity to weighted-risk assets	None	3.25%	4.0%
5. Limitations on supplementary capital elements			
a. General reserves	No limit within supplementary capital	1.5% of weighted risk assets	1.25% of weighted-risk assets
b. Subordinated debt and intermediate-term preferred stock	Combined maximum of 50% of Tier 1	Combined maximum of 50% of Tier 1	Combined maximum of 50% of Tier 1
c. Total qualifying supplementary capital	May not exceed Tier 1 capital	May not exceed Tier 1 capital	May not exceed Tier 1 capital
6. Definition total capital	Tier 1 *plus* Tier 2 *less*:	Tier 1 *plus* Tier 2 *less*:	Tier 1 *plus* Tier 2 *less*:
	—reciprocal holdings of banking organization capital instruments —investments in unconsolidated banking and finance subsidiaries	—reciprocal holdings of banking organization capital instruments —investments in unconsolidated banking and finance subsidiaries	—reciprocal holdings of banking organization capital instruments —investments in unconsolidated banking and finance subsidiaries

[a] Up to 25% of Tier 1 (before deduction of goodwill) may include supplementary elements.
[b] Up to 10% of Tier 1 (before deduction of goodwill) may include supplementary elements.
BHCs may count preferred stock as part of Tier 1 but it cannot count for more than 25% of Tier 1 total capital.

SELECTED REFERENCES

Altman, Edward I., Robert Avery, Robert A. Eisenbeis, and Joseph F. Sinkey, Jr. [1981]. *Application of Classification Techniques in Business, Banking, and Finance.* Greenwich, CT: JAI Press.

Avery, Robert B., and Terence M. Belton. [1987]. "A Comparison of Risk-Based Capital and Risk-Based Deposit Insurance," *Economic Review* Federal Reserve Bank of Cleveland (Quarter 4), pp. 20–30.

"Bank-Track: Emerging Trends for Bank Stocks." [1987] Investment Research, Goldman Sachs (December).

Battey, Phil. [1981]. "Fed Approves Definition of Capital." *American Banker* (December 3), pp. 1, 6, and 12.

Buser, Stephen A., Andrew H. Chen, and Edward J. Kane. [1981a]. "Federal Deposit Insurance, Regulatory Policy, and Optimal Bank Capital." *Journal of Finance* (Vol. XXXV, No. 1, March), pp. 51–60.

————. [1981b]. "Federal Deposit Insurance and Its Implications for the Management of Commercial Banks." The Ohio State University. Paper presented at the 1981 Eastern Finance Association Meetings.

"Capital: Risk-Based Capital Guidelines." [1988]. *News Release* 88-14, Comptroller of the Currency Administrator of National Banks, March 1. *Citicorp Reports 1986.* New York: Citicorp.

Danker, Deborah J., and Mary M. McLaughlin. [1986]. "The Profitability of United States-Chartered Insured Commercial Banks in 1986," *Federal Reserve Bulletin* (July), pp. 537–551.

Ehlen, James G., Jr. [1983]. "A Review of Bank Capital and Its Adequacy." Federal Reserve Bank of Atlanta *Economic Review* (November), pp. 54–60.

Financial Institutions Credit Rating Handbook. [1987]. Fixed Income Research, New York: First Boston (December).

Greenawalt, Mary B., and Joseph F. Sinkey, Jr. [1988]. "Bank Loan-Loss Provisions and the Income-Smoothing Hypothesis: An Empirical Analysis." Working Paper, The University of Georgia, forthcoming *Journal of Financial Services Research.*

Guttentag, Jack, and Richard Herring. [1981]. "The Insolvency of Financial Institutions: Assessment and Regulatory Disposition." University of Pennsylvania, The Wharton School, Working Paper No. 17-81.

Ingersall, Bruce. [1988]. "Fed Clears Minimum Capital Standards, Forcing Some Banks to Raise $15 Billion," *The Wall Street Journal* (August 4), p. 6.

Kane, Edward J. [1986]. "Competitive Financial Reregulation: An International Perspective." Paper presented at the 1986 Conference of the International Center for Monetary and Banking Studies (August). WPS 86-15, The Ohio State University.

Langley, Monica. [1985]. "FDIC Proposes Full Disclosure of Enforcement." *The Wall Street Journal* (February 12), p. 2.

Maisel, Sherman J. [1981]. *Risk and Capital Adequacy in Commercial Banks.* A National Bureau of Economic Research Monograph. Chicago: The University of Chicago Press.

Merton, Robert C. [1977]. "An Analytical Derivation of the Cost of Deposit Insurance Loan Guarantees: An Application of Modern Option Pricing Theory." *Journal of Banking and Finance* (Vol. 1, June), pp. 3–11.

————. [1978]. "On the Cost of Deposit Insurance When There Are Surveillance Costs." *Journal of Business* (Vol. 51, July), pp. 439–452.

Modigliani, Franco, and Merton Miller. [1958]. "The Cost of Capital, Corporation Finance, and the Theory of Investment." *American Economic Review* (Vol. 48, June), pp. 261–297.

————. [1963]. "Corporate Income Taxes and the Cost of Capital: A Correction." *American Economic Review* (Vol. 53, June), pp. 433–443.

Musumeci, James J., and Joseph F. Sinkey, Jr. [1988]. "The International Debt Crisis and Bank Security Returns Surrounding Citicorp's Loan-Loss Reserve Decision of May 19, 1987." Paper presented at the Conference on Bank Structure and Competition (May), Federal Reserve Bank of Chicago.

Nagle, Reid, and Bruce Petersen. [1985]. "Capitalization Problems in Perspective." In *Handbook for Banking Strategy*, R. C. Aspinwall and R. A. Eisenbeis, eds. New York: Wiley, pp. 293–316.

Nash, Nathaniel C. [1988]. "Banking Plan Seen Impeding Mergers," *The New York Times* (February 1), Section 1, pp. 1, 26.

Novack, Janet, [1988]. "Look Ma, no risk," *Forbes*, (January 25), pp. 52, 54.

Peltzman, Sam. [1970]. "Capital Investment in Commercial Banking and Its Relationship to Portfolio Regulation." *Journal of Political Economy*, (Vol. 78, No. 1), pp. 1–26.

Rehm, Barbara A. [1988]. "Fed Announces Plan to Enforce Risk-Based Capital Requirements," *American Banker* (January 28), pp. 1, 12.

"Risk-Based Capital." [1988]. Office Correspondence, Division of Banking Supervision and Regulation, Board of Governors of the Federal Reserve System, January 25.

Sharpe, William F. [1978]. "Bank Capital Adequacy, Deposit Insurance and Security Values." *Journal of Financial and Quantitative Analysis* (**13**, November), pp. 701–718.

Sinkey, Joseph F., Jr. [1985] "Regulatory Attitudes Toward Risk." In *Handbook for Banking Strategy*, R. C. Aspinwall and R. A. Eisenbeis, New York: Wiley, pp. 347–380.

———. [1979]. *Problem and Failed Institutions in the Commercial Banking Industry.* Greenwich, CT: JAI Press.

———. [1978]. "Identifying Problem Banks: How Do the Banking Authorities Measure a Bank's Risk Exposure?" *Journal of Money, Credit and Banking* (Vol. 10, No. 2), pp. 184–193.

"Statement of the Shadow Financial Regulatory Committee on Regulatory Proposal for Risk-Related Capital Standards." [1988]. Shadow Financial Regulatory Committee, Chicago, February 8.

Statistics on Banking, Washington, DC: FDIC (various issues).

Stignum, Marcia L., and Rene O. Branch, Jr. [1983]. *Managing Bank Assets and Liabilities.* Homewood Hills, IL: Dow Jones-Irwin.

Strauss, Michael. [1988]. "Maximizing Returns on Student Loans with Secondary Market Assistance." *Bank Administration* (November), pp. 44, 46, 50.

CHAPTER 23

Capital and Dividend Management

ACRONYM GUIDE TO KEY WORDS

EM = Equity multiplier (and its inverse, the ratio of
   equity to assets)
EPS = Earnings per share
P/E = Price-earnings ratio or multiple

MARKET VALUATION OF BANK STOCKS

During the 1980s, a bank's "capital adequacy," as reflected by its ratio of common equity to total assets, has been "discovered" as the "dominant tool" for the valuation of bank stocks. Specifically, the new rule in banking is: Core or equity capital has become one of the major determinants of the valuation of bank stocks. The investment researchers at Goldman Sachs, who claim to have discovered this new rule, put it this way[1]:

> While the bank stock market always cared about equity ratios, today it has become the supreme ratio. For once the regulatory view and the market are undeniably in sync. (p. 1)

Glory be, the FDIC (*Forever Demanding Increased Capital*) was right all along! Our study of capital and dividend management begins by looking at this new rule for the market valuation of bank stocks.

How Can This Be New?

Now wait a minute, you say. Isn't capital adequacy just another way of measuring leverage? Yes, it is. Then, how can the market for valuing bank stocks only have discovered such a fundamental financial relationship in the 1980s? To echo the words from a popular song of the 1960s: "The times, they are a changin'." Before we look at how the times have changed, let's focus on how the people at Goldman Sachs came up with this new valuation relationship for banks (actually bank holding companies).

---

[1] "Bank-Track, Emerging Trends for Bank Stocks: The Supremacy of Equity," *Investment Research*, Goldman Sachs [March 1988]. The analysts listed on this report are Robert Albertson, Charles Cranmer, Richard Goleniewski, and Janice Meehan. This section draws on their report.

Two Pictures Worth 1,000 Words Each

Figures 23-1 and 23-2 capture the essence of the new valuation rule. In both figures, we will be analyzing three fundamental variables. Moreover, these variables are not new to us. The two primary ones are (1) the ratio of common equity to total assets (the inverse of the equity multiplier, EM) and (2) the ratio of market value or price per share to earnings per share (EPS), the price-earnings (P/E) ratio or multiple. In both figures, the equity ratio is measured on the horizontal axis and the P/E ratio on the vertical axis. In this two-dimensional space, what would we expect the relationship between P/E and the inverse of EM to be? Since we are dealing with a risk-value relationship (risk is captured by the equity ratio or EM inverse and value by the P/E ratio), we would expect low values of the equity ratio to be associated with low values of the P/E ratio, and high values of the equity ratio to be associated with high P/E multiples. If the relationship is a linear one, a line fitted to the points will have a constant positive slope. Moreover, if the relationship is a "strong" one, the scatter of points (each point representing a pair of equity ratios and P/E ratios) will be tightly bunched around the fitted (regression) line.

Suppose now that we add a third dimension to our analysis, return on equity (ROE), and consider the following two ROE profiles of the familiar form $ROE = ROA \times EM$:

The Leverage Bank: $.20 = .005 \times 40$

The Equity Bank: $.20 = .010 \times 20$

As an investor, which bank would you (and the marketplace) value more highly? Being rational, you would select the earnings stream associated with The Equity Bank because its profitability comes with less financial risk, as reflected by its lower equity multiplier (20 versus 40), or higher ratio of equity capital to total assets (.05 versus .025). Suppose now that we want to incorporate the ROE element into our two-dimensional picture of the equity ratio and the P/E ratio. How can we do it without resorting to one of those (confusing) three-dimensional diagrams? By being innovative, as the Goldman Sachs researchers were, we can have each pair of $[EM^{-1}, P/E]$ points also represent a particular range of ROE, and identify banks within a particular range by a different symbol. On this basis, we would expect BHCs with high ROEs to be in the northeast quadrant and those with low ROEs to be in the southwest quadrant.

To recap, we are going to look at a scatter diagram in two-dimensional space with the coordinates of each point mapped with a symbol representing a particular range of ROE. Moreover, we should be comfortable with our expectation of a positive relationship between the two main variables, and with how and where we expect ROE to fit into the picture. Are you ready?

The Relationship for 1977

Figure 23-1 shows the scatter diagram for December 31, 1977. For this picture, the profitability ranges are ROE less than 12 percent, represented by the dots, and ROE greater than 12 percent, represented by the stars. Each star or dot is also labeled with letters identifying a particular BHC. Let's first focus on the overall picture. Clearly, our expectations are dashed. The 39 stars and dots (20 and 19, respectively) appear to be randomly distributed. As seen by the 1977 data for large BHCs, capital structure, as measured by the ratio of equity to assets, does not seem to matter as high P/E ratios are associated with both high leverage and low leverage. In addition, high P/E multiples are associated with both high and low ROE firms. However, using a P/E ratio of 7 as a cutoff, we have 13 BHCs with ROE less than 12 percent below the cutoff and

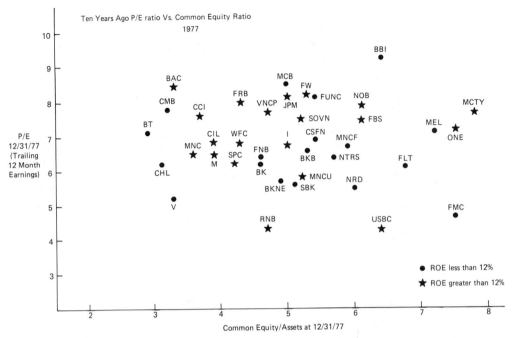

Figure 23-1   The Relationship between BHC P/E Ratios and Equity Ratios, December 31, 1977

Source: "Bank-Track," Investment Research, Goldman Sachs [March 1988], p. 2.

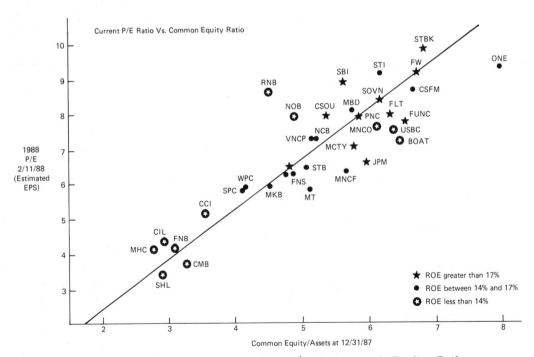

Figure 23-2 The Relationship between BHC P/E Ratios and Equity Ratios, February 11, 1988

Source: "Bank-Track," *Investment Research*, Goldman Sachs [March 1988], p. 3.

only 6 BHCs above it. In contrast, the 20 BHCs with ROE above 12 percent are more equally distributed with respect to the P/E cutoff with 11 above it and 9 below it. Nevertheless, nothing systematic emerges regarding the relationship between P/E and ROE. On balance, Figure 23-1 does not generate any rule for valuing BHC stocks.

The Relationship for 1988

Figure 23-2 is in stark contrast to Figure 23-1. Our expectations are not dashed in Figure 23-2; in fact, they are fulfilled as there is a strong positive relationship between the P/E ratios for BHCs and their ratios of common equity to total assets. Moreover, but not as strongly as the value–risk relationship, direct relationships between ROE and P/E value and between ROE and "capital adequacy" are observed. Specifically, BHCs with low ROEs tend to have low P/E ratios and low equity ratios; in contrast, BHCs with higher ROEs tend to have more adequate capital and higher P/E ratios.

Before getting into some of the more detailed aspects of Figure 23-2, let's consider its construction, which is only slightly different from Figure 23-1. First, Figure 23-2 uses a mixture of data from the period 1986 to 1988. Specifically, the equity ratio is measured as of December 31, 1987, ROE is measured for 1986 (to escape the distortions caused by the massive provision for LDC loan losses taken by most of the sample BHCs in 1987), and the P/E ratio is measured as of February 11, 1988, using projected EPS figures for 1988. In estimating 1988 earnings, the Goldman Sachs analysts excluded nonrecurring items and tax benefits that might distort core earnings, especially among the multinational BHCs. Regarding the breakdown of 1986 ROE figures, three ranges were used: (1) ROE less than 14 percent indicated by asterisks, (2) ROE between 14 percent and 17 percent indicated by dots, and (3) ROE greater than 17 percent indicated by stars. Because of mergers and acquisitions, there are three fewer observations in Figure 23-2 than in Figure 23-1. Except for these details in construction, the figures attempt to measure the same relationships at two different points in time. The findings, however, are dramatically different.

The regression line fitted to the data in Figure 23-2 reveals the expected positive relationship between risk and value. Although the report by Goldman Sachs described the regression line as "almost exactly one-for-one," this interpretation is a bit of an exaggeration, as revealed by the following data read from Figure 23-2[2]:

Equity Ratio	P/E Ratio
3%	3.85
4%	5.25
5%	6.65
6%	8.05
7%	9.45

Based on this approximation of the estimated relationship, an increase of 100 basis points in the equity ratio leads to an increase in the P/E ratio of 1,400 basis points. (Note that the equity ratio [horizontal axis] is measured in percent, whereas the P/E ratio [vertical axis] is not.) For our purposes, the exact relationship is not critically important; the important point is the positive relationship and the relatively tight fit around the regression line. In other words, the message for BHC managers is clear: An increase in your ratio of common equity to total assets is most likely to lead to an increase in the firm's P/E ratio, other things equal. Moreover, based on the estimated relationship for 1977, such a prescription could not have been made.

[2] Since the Goldman Sachs study did not report the estimated regression equation, it is not shown here.

Although there are some exceptions, as we move up the regression line from the southwest to the northeast, we tend to see asterisks, dots, and then stars. These symbols, of course, correspond to the ROE ranges described above. Let's focus on a few of the BHCs plotted in Figure 23-2 and concentrate on firms we have been following in various parts of this book. Specifically, let's look at Continental Illinois (CIL), Bankers Trust (BT), J. P. Morgan (JPM), First Wachovia (FW), and Banc One (One). Their profiles of $[P/E, EM^{-1}, ROE]$ are listed below[3]:

BHC	P/E	EM^{-1}	ROE
Continental Illinois (IL)	4.3	2.9%	8.5%
Bankers Trust (BT)	5.8	5.1%	16.3%
J. P. Morgan (JPM)	6.8	5.9%	19.9%
First Wachovia (FW)	9.1	6.7%	17.6%
Banc One (One)	9.3	7.9%	16.3%

The first three firms listed are money-center BHCs. Given their equity ratios and ROEs, we would expect the monotonic increase in the P/E ratios as observed. The interesting point, and the point the Goldman Sachs's rule is making, comes from observing the profiles for the two superregional BHCs, and comparing them to the money-center BHCs. First, consider the two superregionals. They illustrate a fundamental risk–return trade-off. Without knowing the P/E ratios, we can ask whether investors will value FW's higher risk–higher return profile more highly than One's lower risk–lower return profile, or vice versa? The market's answer on February 11, 1988, was to value Banc One slightly higher at 9.3 versus 9.1. Next, let's compare Bankers Trust and Banc One. They both had the same ROE for 1986 of 16.3 percent. However, their year-end 1987 equity ratios were substantially different at 5.1 percent and 7.9 percent. The higher equity ratio translated into a P/E ratio 60 percent higher for Banc One compared to Bankers Trust (i.e., 9.3 versus 5.8). These examples represent what the new rule for valuing bank stock has established.

Why Now and Not Earlier?

In answering this question, the Goldman Sachs report focused on a section entitled "Simply a Sign of the Times." In retrospect, the analysts suggested three reasons (signs) for the clustering around the equity ratio in 1988 but not in 1977: (1) the current focus on the "integrity" of a bank's balance sheet, which has been assaulted by LDC, energy, farm, and real estate lending problems (recall Fredericks's notion of a "fortressed balance sheet" as one supported by strong earnings and capital); (2) the importance of tangible equity capital for BHC expansion and the regulatory refocusing on equity or core capital as the key element in the new international capital guidelines; and (3) investor suspicion about ROA and ROE as performance measures because of adjustments being made to either the numerators (e.g., nonrecurring items) or the denominators of the ratios. The last point suggests that, today, bank balance sheets are more "believable."

To further highlight the signs of the time (and the change in those signs), let's consider the selected indicators of the performance of FDIC-insured commercial banks for 1981, 1986, and 1987, as shown in Table 23-1. The data for 1986 are included to illustrate the distorting effects of 1987 as an "outlier" year. Except for the buildup in bank capital, the signs are indeed adverse. Moreover, had we used 1987 data to

---

[3] The P/E ratios are read from Figure 23-2, whereas the ROEs and equity ratios are from "Bank Ratios and Rankings," Investment Research, Goldman Sachs [Fourth Quarter 1987], p. 3 and p. 11, respectively.

TABLE 23-1   Adverse Banking Trends: A Sign of the Times in the 1980s

Indicator	1981	1986	Change	1987
Return on assets	0.78%	0.64%	−0.14%	0.13%
Return on equity	13.08%	10.18%	−2.90%	2.56%
Equity capital to assets	5.83%	6.21%	0.38%	6.05%
Primary capital ratio	6.39%	7.22%	0.83%	7.69%
Nonperforming assets to assets	1.85%*	1.95%	0.10%	2.46%
Net charge-offs to loans	0.37%	0.99%	0.62%	0.89%
Asset growth rate	9.36%	7.62%	−1.74%	1.95%
Net operating income growth	7.60%	−16.20%	−23.80%	−84.53%
Number of unprofitable banks	741	2,784	2,043	2,366
Number of problem banks	196	1,457	1,261	1,559
Number of failed/assisted banks	7	144	137	201

Note: Since data on nonperforming loans were not available in 1981, the figure shown for 1981 is the one for 1982.
Source: "The FDIC Quarterly Banking Profile" [Fourth Quarter 1987], Table II, p. 3.

calculate the changes in the indicators, the situation would have looked even bleaker. Nevertheless, the outlook for the banking industry is improving since 1987 appears to have been a watershed year, as indicated by the turnaround in the farm debt crisis and the decisions by the money-center banks to come (almost) to grips with the LDC crisis. Still on the downside, however, the problems for energy banks have not abated. On March 17, 1988, the FDIC advanced $1 billion (for six months) to First Republic Bank Corp. of Dallas. In addition, the FDIC pledged to fully protect all depositors and general creditors of banks in the holding company. The FDIC guarantee however, did not extend to the bond and note holders of the holding company. FDIC Chairman Seidman made it clear that First Republic was not considered a mismanagement problem, as Continental Illinois was, but a problem due to the economy in Texas.[4] On July 29, 1988, First Republic was declared insolvent and acquired by NCNB Corp. Together the FDIC and NCNB injected over $1 billion into the 40 failed banks of First Republic.

The Supremacy of Equity: A Recapitulation

The Goldman Sachs Bank-Track investment report of March 1988 was titled "The Supremacy of Equity." The focus of the investment research was the recognition of a new relationship in which common equity was viewed as the dominant determinant of bank stock values. The clustering of bank stock P/E ratios around equity values, as shown in Figure 23-2, was the critical evidence for the new relationship, given the lack of clustering in Figure 23-1. The report concluded (p. 5):

> The most provocative conclusion might simply be to expect banks to issue new equity more readily than in the past! If bank managements accept the foregoing analysis and believe these two diagrams, the risk of dilution (of EPS) now appears secondary to the benefits of higher capital.

THE INTERNAL CAPITAL GENERATION RATE

A bank's or BHC's major source of equity capital is its earnings stream, a fact especially true for community banks without easy access to capital markets. In the previous section, we saw the importance of equity capital to the market valuation of bank

---

[4] As reported by the Associated Press in *The Atlanta Constitution* [March 18, 1988], Section C, p. 1.

stocks. In this section, we focus on how inadequate capital can limit a bank's growth opportunities. Consider the following situation. Suppose a bank has the simple balance sheet $100 = 90 + 10$ of the form $A = D + E$. If assets (A) and deposits (D) grow at 10 percent per period, then the bank's capital base (E) also must grow at 10 percent for its relative capital position not to deteriorate. That is, at 10 percent growth, the next period's balance sheet would be $110 = 99 + 11$. However, the bank's capital-to-asset and capital-to-deposit ratios would be unchanged from the previous period at 10 percent and 11.1 percent, respectively. If the bank does *not* pay out any of its earnings in the form of dividends, the bank's return on equity (ROE) must be 10 percent to maintain its relative capital position. If regulatory and market pressures restrict asset and deposit growth to the same growth rate as the capital base, then a positive payout ratio means that the bank must generate a higher ROE and/or seek external sources of capital. For example, with an ROE of 10 percent and payout ratio of 30 percent, the capital base expands only by 7 percent [i.e., $.07 = .10 (1 - .3)$] and growth would be restricted to 7 percent. Balance-sheet expansion at a 10 percent rate would require an ROE of 14.28 percent or a smaller ROE *plus* external capital.

An important concept and tool for the financial management of bank equity capital is the internal capital generation rate (g), which is equal to the product of a bank's ROE and its retention ratio (RR), that is,[5]

$$g = ROE \times RR \tag{23-1}$$

Recall that the retention ratio is simply one minus the payout ratio (i.e., $RR = 1 - PR$). Also recall from the ROE model that $ROE = ROA \times EM$ and that $ROA = PM \times AU$. Thus, the capital-generation rate can be expressed as

$$g = PM \times AU \times EM \times RR \tag{23-2}$$

In words, a bank's internal capital-generation rate depends upon its profitability (PM), asset utilization (AU), equity multiplier (EM), and retention ratio (RR). By increasing any one of these factors, other things equal, capital generation will improve.

From an internal perspective, the key to a bank's capital generation and hence its capital adequacy rests with the four key factors specified in Equation 23-2. Thus, if a bank wants to improve its capital position, it needs to get down to such basics as effective spread management, cost control, operating efficiency, and optimal financial and dividend policies.

The interaction between selected ROE and RR figures is summarized in the capital-generation matrix presented in Table 23-2. Each cell in the matrix represents a particular internal capital-generation rate determined by the product of the corresponding row and column elements. For example, giant BHCs tend to generate an ROE of roughly 15 percent and to pay out about 40 percent of their earnings in dividends (i.e., $RR = 1 - PR = .60$). Thus, they have capital-generation rates around 9 percent.

The capital-generation matrix is a useful tool for capital planning. For example, suppose that a bank anticipates (1) growth opportunities of 12 percent, (2) ROE of 15 percent, and (3) RR of 60 percent. The bank's internal capital-generation rate is 9 percent whereas its expected growth in assets and deposits is 12 percent. To prevent its capital ratios from deteriorating, the bank needs to plan for capital growth of

[5] Equation 23-1 is an approximation of the internal capital generation rate that understates the true rate. To be more accurate, g is equal to $(ROE \times RR)/(1 - ROE \times RR)$. The difference between the two formulas is the adjustment factor in the denominator. The approximation of g is accurate enough for our purposes and it is used in the examples in the text.

TABLE 23-2 The Capital-Generation Matrix[a]

Return on Equity (ROE)	Retention Ratio (RR)						
	.00	.20	.40	.50	.60	.80	1.00
.00	.00	.00	.00	.000	.00	.00	.00
.05	.00	.01	.02	.025	.03	.04	.05
.10	.00	.02	.04	.050	.06	.08	.10
.15	.00	.03	.06	.075	.09	.12	.15
.20	.00	.04	.08	.100	.12	.16	.20
.25	.00	.05	.10	.125	.15	.20	.25
.30	.00	.06	.12	.150	.18	.24	.30

[a]Each cell in the matrix represents an internal capital-generation rate (g), which is equal to **ROE × RR**. The blocked cell indicates the capital-generation rate available to the typical giant BHC. Such firms tend to return about 15 percent on equity and to pay out about 40 percent of their earnings in dividends (i.e., **RR = .60**). See footnote 5 for the exact specification of g; the product of **ROE** and **RR** is only an approximation of g.

12 percent. There are various combinations of ROE and RR that will generate an internal capital-generation rate of 12 percent. As depicted in Table 23-2, two such pairs are (.15 and .80) and (.20 and .60). If a combination of ROE and RR that generates a rate of 12 percent is not obtained, then the bank has two choices: (1) simply let its capital position deteriorate or (2) obtain *external* capital to maintain or cushion the decline in its capital position. Until the early 1980s, many banks/BHCs opted to let their capital positions deteriorate. However, since then, both market and regulatory pressures have joined forces to reward strong equity positions. As a result, bank capital positions began trending upward in the 1980s, as shown in Figure 23-3.

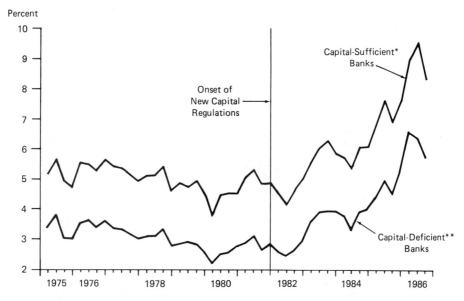

*Banks that met 1985 requirements in 1981.
**Banks that did not meet 1985 requirements in 1981.

Figure 23-3 Market Value Capital-to-Asset Ratios

Source: Keeley [1988], Chart 4, p. 15.

TABLE 23-3   Ratios of Net Income, Dividend Payout, and Retention Relative to Total Assets for Various Bank Size Classes, 1981–1986

Bank Asset Size	1981	1982	1983	1984	1985	1986
Less than $100 million						
Net income/assets (%)	1.14	1.07	.96	.81	.70	.53
Payout/assets (%)	.35	.39	.38	.39	.41	.38
Retention/assets (%)	.79	.68	.58	.42	.29	.15
Number of banks	12,353	12,081	11,811	11,554	11,332	11,011
$100 million to $1 billion						
Net income/assets (%)	.91	.84	.84	.88	.84	.71
Payout/assets (%)	.39	.40	.42	.43	.85	.43
Retention/assets (%)	.52	.44	.42	.45	.39	.28
Number of banks	1,651	1,813	2,012	2,135	2,259	2,398
Over $1 billion (excluding money-center banks)						
Net income/assets (%)	.66	.60	.54	.53	.78	.75
Payout/assets (%)	.30	.29	.29	.27	.29	.34
Retention/assets (%)	.36	.31	.25	.26	.49	.41
Number of banks	195	220	243	263	290	321
Money-center banks						
Net income/assets (%)	.53	.53	.54	.52	.45	.46
Payout/assets (%)	.22	.23	.27	.24	.25	.21
Retention/assets (%)	.31	.30	.27	.28	.20	.25
Number of banks	9	9	9	9	9	9

Source: Danker and McLaughlin [1987], Table A.1, pp. 547–550.

THE DIVIDEND PAYOUT RATIO

Since $g = ROE \times RR$ and since $RR = 1 - PR$, where PR is the dividend payout ratio, we can identically express g as $ROE \times [1 - PR]$. For firms that pay dividends, the "golden rule" is: Don't cut the dividend. Even in the face of adverse earnings, dividend-paying firms tend to hold the line. Consider the banking industry; from 1940 until 1986 the average payout ratio has been roughly 44 percent. However, in 1987 when net income declined by almost $10 billion to $3.7 billion, commercial banks paid cash dividends on capital stock of $10.6 billion for a payout ratio of 286 percent.

Since the dividend–payout ratio can be unstable because of the variability in bank earnings, an alternative measure of payout is to compare cash dividends to total assets. This measure of payout is shown in Table 23-3 for four size classes of banks for the years 1981 through 1986. In addition, ratios of net income to total assets (ROA) and retention to total assets are shown in the table. These data can be summarized by observing the following six-year averages calculated from the table:

Asset Size Class	ROA	= Payout/Assets	+ Retention/Assets
Less than $100 million	.87%	.38%	.49%
$100 million to $1 billion	.84%	.42%	.42%
Greater than $1 billion (no MCs)	.64%	.30%	.34%
Money-center banks	.50%	.24%	.26%

What we observe are three phenomena. First, as bank size increases, average ROA for the period 1981 through 1986 declined. Second, as bank size increases, payout (relative to total assets) first rises then declines. And third, as bank size increases, retention (relative to total assets) declines steadily. Competition and access to capital markets offer potential explanations for these phenomena. Specifically, the greater competitiveness of loan and deposit markets for larger banks means fewer dollars relative to total assets (lower ROA) for distribution between payout and retention (relative to total assets). However, because of their greater access to capital markets, larger banks are able to reduce their profitability/retention disadvantage by raising external capital.

EXTERNAL SOURCES OF CAPITAL

When regulatory or market forces require a bank/BHC to increase its capital beyond its internal capital-generation rate, the organization must turn to external sources of capital. Although both equity and debt capital are available for such purposes, under the new capital guidelines established for 1992, common equity has been assigned a more critical role. Accordingly, preferred stock and subordinated notes and debentures will count less in the eyes of the regulators in terms of meeting capital standards. For healthy banks, additional capital frequently is needed to permit growth opportunities to be realized without unduly extending the bank's capital cushion or unduly increasing the internal retention of earnings. For problem banks, additional capital is required to replenish the erosion of the bank's capital account due to loan or security losses.

If a bank has a choice between equity capital or debt capital to augment its capital position, the advantages and disadvantages of each must be weighed carefully. Debt capital (in the form of long-term subordinated debt) is desirable because the interest payments associated with the debt are a tax-deductible expense and because it does not have the potentially diluting effects on earnings and control of an equity issue. The disadvantage of a debt issue are its fixed interest payments, its lack of "permanency" (there is uncertainty about whether or not the debt can be rolled over at maturity), and the fact that only a portion of it may actually count in measuring the bank's capital adequacy. Equity capital is desirable because all of it counts in measuring a bank's capital adequacy, because it is permanent, and because the dividend payments are not a fixed expense. The disadvantages of an equity issue are its high cost relative to debt and its potential dilutive effects. The "high" cost of equity relates to the bankruptcy-cost potential created by the use of less expensive debt.

An alternative to either debt or equity capital is preferred stock, which is a hybrid of the two forms. Preferred stock is safer than equity capital but riskier than debt from the investor's perspective.[6] From the issuer's perspective, it provides flexibility but lacks the tax deductibility associated with interest on debt.

From a regulatory perspective (under 1985 guidelines), permanent or perpetual preferred stock counted as primary capital, whereas limited-life or sinking-fund preferred was part of secondary or other capital.[7] In contrast, under the originally proposed 1992 capital guidelines, preferred stock, provided it had a maturity of seven

---

[6] For corporate investors, dividends received are subject to an 85 percent exclusion, which reduces the marginal corporate tax rate from 34% to 5.1%. For individuals, dividends are subject to double taxation.

[7] Other forms of preferred stock include convertible preferred, adjustable-rate preferred, and convertible-exchangeable preferred. The latter can be converted into subordinated debt after a period of years. See Nagle and Petersen [1985].

years or longer, would count only as part of supplementary or Tier 2 capital. Under the final guidelines, however, BHCs may count preferred stock as part of core or Tier 1 capital up to a maximum of 25%.

The exclusion of perpetual preferred stock from core or equity capital would have been a severe blow to the banking industry, especially to the largest banks/BHCs, who have been heavy users of this source of capital. To illustrate, in 1978 all insured commercial banks had only $114 million in perpetual preferred stock outstanding; by year-end 1986, this figure had risen to $1.4 billion, a compound annual growth rate of 37 percent. As a percent of equity capital (defined to include perpetual preferred stock), perpetual preferred rose from 0.47 percent of equity in 1978 to 0.78 percent in 1986. Industry figures on limited-life preferred, which were not available until 1984, show less extensive use. For example, the amounts outstanding for all insured commercial banks in 1984, 1985, and 1986 were $122 million, $15 million, and $81 million, respectively.[8]

Other sources of external capital for banks/BHCs include debt/equity swaps and mandatory convertible securities. Debt/equity swaps for banks were devised in 1982 by Salomon Brothers. These transactions involve the swapping of new shares of common stock (equity) for outstanding discounted bonds (debt). However, since the amount of debt outstanding is limited, these swaps cannot generate much equity. Another instrument developed in 1982 was mandatory convertibles. Typically, this instrument is a 12-year floating-rate note pegged to LIBOR which, at the option of the issuer, is convertible into equity at or before maturity. In addition, the investor has the option of receiving cash if the issuer can sell the issue. The beauty of these transactions, as described by an official of Chase Manhattan Bank, is: "Because we're issuing common stock as a payment of interest, we get a tax deduction, there's no dilution, and it's counted as primary (core) capital."[9]

Access to Capital Markets and Capital Financing

In finance theory, the assumption of equal access to capital markets is frequently invoked. In the real world of banking capital markets, equal access is a fiction, as numerous community banks simply do not have the opportunity to tap domestic capital markets and obviously do not have access to foreign capital markets. To illustrate, consider the $1.4 billion in perpetual preferred stock outstanding at year-end 1986. Of this total, $1 billion (71%) was issued by the 263 banks with foreign offices and another $200 million (14%) was issued by the 545 banks without foreign offices but with assets greater than $300 million. The remaining $200 million was issued by the 13,385 banks without foreign offices and with total assets less than $300 million. Regarding subordinated notes and debentures, a similar tale can be told. The corresponding percentages across the three groups for the $16.9 billion outstanding at year-end 1986 was (1) 86 percent by banks with foreign offices, (2) 10 percent by banks without foreign offices but with assets greater than $300 million, and (3) 4 percent by the myraid of remaining small banks.[10]

The story with respect to common stock (including surplus) is not quite as bleak. Of the $93.5 billion outstanding at year-end 1986, the 263 banks with foreign offices had issued $43.6 billion (47%) compared to $16.4 billion (18%) for the 552 banks without

---

[8] These data are from the FDIC's *Statistics on Banking* (various years).

[9] As reported by Miller [1986], p. 18. Other information in this paragraph is derived from this source.

[10] FDIC, *Statistics on Banking* [1986], Table RC-2, p. 32. The figures in the next paragraph are from this source also.

TABLE 23-4 Capital Financing by Commercial Banks and BHCs, 1970–1985

| Year | Total Amount Raised (Millions) | Percentage Composition | | |
		Capital Notes and Debentures	Preferred Stock	Common Stock
1970	229.5	54.9%	0.0%	45.1%
1971	1,669.5	92.5	0.1	7.4
1972	2,636.8	91.6	0.3	8.2
1973	1,110.9	92.1	0.0	7.9
1974	1,340.0	96.6	0.7	2.6
1975	1,561.6	92.6	5.0	2.4
1976	2,481.2	85.9	0.0	14.1
1977	2,791.8	80.9	12.7	6.3
1978	1,618.7	65.8	9.1	26.5
1979	2,451.3	92.9	2.2	4.9
1980	1,509.4	64.0	22.8	13.2
1981	1,443.5	42.3	2.5	55.1
1982	5,506.1	58.5	34.7	6.8
1983	9,945.8	67.6	25.2	7.2
1984	12,763.1	81.7	5.8	12.5
1985	20,596.8	77.5	13.1	9.4

Sources: Irving Trust for the years 1970 to 1983, and Miller [1986], p. 18, for 1984 and 1985. Miller's figures include capital raised by thrift institutions.

foreign offices but with assets greater than $300 million. The balance of $33.5 billion (35%) was issued by the 13,385 banks without foreign offices and with total assets less than $300 million. Within this group of small banks, $21 billion was issued by banks with total assets less than $100 million, leaving $12 billion for banks with assets greater than $100 million but less than $300 million.

The amount of external capital raised by commercial banks and BHCs for the years 1970 to 1985 is shown in Table 23-4. A number of trends in bank capital financing are obvious from these data. First, banks and BHCs have been raising larger and larger amounts of capital in the 1980s, as indicated by the 14-fold increase from 1980 to 1985. Second, the major kinds of capital raised in the 1980s, except for 1981, have been subordinated notes and debentures and preferred stock. And third, from our previous discussion, we know that these instruments are mainly issued by large banks/BHCs.

Who are the investment bankers that commercial banks (and thrift institutions) seek out when they want to raise capital? In 1985 the leading underwriters of capital for banks and S&Ls were these[11]:

Manager	$ Millions	% Total	Issues
Salomon Brothers	5,580	27.1	72
First Boston	3,302	16.0	59
Shearson Lehman Brothers	2,925	14.2	43
Merrill Lynch Capital Markets	2,660	12.9	39
Goldman Sachs	2,109	10.2	22
Drexel Burnham Lambert	1,274	6.2	25
Six-firm totals	17,850	84.6	260
Industry totals	20,597	100.0	369

[11] These data, and those in the next paragraph, are from Miller [1986], pp. 19–20.

Of the 369 issues brought to market in 1985, the six leading firms accounted for 70 percent of the activity. Moreover, these 260 issues accounted for 85 percent of the dollar volume of capital raised. Accordingly, the remaining 109 issues totaled only $2.7 billion for an average issue size of roughly $25 million.

Regarding initial public offerings (IPOs) by banks and S&Ls in 1985, the leading managers were the following:

Manager	$ Millions	% Total	Issues
Merrill Lynch Capital Markets	193	22.4	7
Salomon Brothers	179	20.8	3
First Boston	144	16.6	2
Drexel Burnham Lambert	135	15.7	4
Four-firm totals	651	75.5	16
Industry totals	862	100.0	46

With 16 IPOs accounting for 75 percent of new issue volume in 1985, the remaining 30 IPOs totaled only $211 million for an average issue size of only $7 million.

BANK HOLDING COMPANY CAPITAL AND LEVERAGE

One of the major functions of a BHC is to generate external capital for its rapidly growing affiliates, either bank or nonbank subsidiaries. A common practice is for the parent company to issue long-term debt and to channel it to subsidiaries either as equity or debt capital. When parent debt is downstreamed as equity, the transaction is referred to as "double leverage."[12] The fact that the subsidiary uses the equity to boost its assets explains the term *double leverage*. The parent company uses the dividends paid by the equity investment in its subsidiaries to service its debt. If these subsidiaries encounter financial difficulties, then the ability of the parent to service the debt could be in danger. Moreover, if the subsidiary is a bank, regulatory pressure to maintain adequate bank capital may impede the flow of dividends to the parent. In contrast, since the nonbank subsidiaries of bank holding companies are less heavily regulated, they are less likely to encounter this kind of regulatory interference.

Holding Company Financial Statements and Double Leverage

To illustrate the concept of double leverage, we need to look at the relationships among parent, subsidiary, and consolidated financial statements, as depicted in Table 23-5. In this illustration, the parent company is assumed to have two *wholly owned* subsidiaries: a bank subsidiary and a nonbank subsidiary. The balance sheet for the consolidated holding company is obtained by summing up each of the accounts (i.e., assets, liabilities, and equity) across the parent *and* all of the subsidiaries and then eliminating all intercompany relationships. The only intercompany relationships in this example are the parent's investments in the wholly owned subsidiaries. If these relationships were ignored, the consolidated balance sheet would be $120 = 111 + 9$ instead of $114 = 111 + 3$.

---

[12] See Boczar and Talley [1981] and Harris [1987] for discussions of the concept of double leverage.

TABLE 23-5 An Illustration of Double Leverage and the Relationships among BHC Financial Statements ($ Billions)

Before

Parent company

Investment in Subsidiaries	6	Liabilities	10
Other Assets	7	Equity	3
	13		13

Nonbank subsidiary				Bank subsidiary			
Assets	7	Liabilities	6	Assets	100	Liabilities	95
			1			Equity	5
	7		7		100		100

Consolidated holding company

Assets		Liabilities:	
Parent	7	Parent	10
Nonbank sub	7	Nonbank sub	6
Bank sub	100	Bank sub	95
			111
		Equity:	
		Parent	3
	114		114

After

Parent company

Investment in Subsidiaries	7	Liabilities	11
Other Assets	7	Equity	3
	14		14

Nonbank subsidiary				Bank subsidiary			
Assets	7	Liabilities	6	Assets	101	Liabilities	95
		Equity	1			Equity	6
	7		7		101		101

Consolidated holding company

Assets:		Liabilities:	
Parent	7	Parent	11
Nonbank sub	7	Nonbank sub	6
Bank sub	101	Bank sub	95
			112
		Equity:	
		Parent	3
	115		115

After the double-leverage transaction, in which parent debt is downstreamed as equity in the bank subsidiary, the consolidated balance sheet reads $115 = 112 + 3$. Using the debt-to-equity ratio to measure leverage, the double-leverage operation has the following effects:

	Debt/Equity	
	Before	After
Parent	$10/3 = 3.3$	$11/3 = 3.6$
Bank	$95/5 = 19.0$	$95/6 = 15.8$
Consolidated HC	$111/3 = 37.0$	$112/3 = 37.3$

As a result of the transaction, the leverage of the bank has been reduced, whereas the leverage of the parent and the consolidated holding company have increased.

The Significance and Measurement of Double Leverage

Prior to the establishment of uniform capital guidelines for both banks and BHCs in 1988 (effective in 1992), BHCs could attempt to have their cake and eat it too by using double leverage. Specifically, they could attempt to leverage holding company ROE by issuing debt capital and simultaneously using the funds to meet regulatory requirements for adequate bank capital in their bank subsidiaries. The regulatory penchant for focusing on the adequacy of bank capital, but not to the total exclusion of BHC capital adequacy, encouraged such behavior. After having induced such behavior by BHCs, bank regulators are now concerned that many banks have too much double leverage.

There are two primary measures of double leverage.[13] The first one is an absolute measure defined as the parent's investments in subsidiaries minus the parent's equity. Given the example in Table 23-5, the measures of double leverage are $3 billion (before) and $4 billion (after). This measure represents the dollar amount of the parent company's investments in subsidiaries that has been debt financed. The second measure is a relative one called the *double leverage ratio* (DLR). It is constructed as the ratio of the parent's investments in subsidiaries to the parent's equity. In Table 23-5, the DLRs are 2.0 (before) and 2.3 (after). As a relative measure, DLRs are useful in making comparisons across BHCs.

Double-Leverage Activity by Large BHCs

During the decade of the 1970s, the 50 largest BHCs increased their absolute double leverage on an aggregate basis almost tenfold from $572 million in 1970 to $5,087 million in 1979. The DLR for these 50 companies increased from 104.86 percent to 114.37 percent over the same period. Double-leverage ratios for the 50-firm sample described above and for selected companies in the sample are presented in Table 23-6. The selected BHCs include Citicorp, BankAmerica, J. P. Morgan, First Pennsylvania, and Wachovia. The aggregate data in Table 23-6 reveal that extensive use of

TABLE 23-6 Double-Leverage Ratios for Selected Bank Holding Companies, 1970–1979

Year	50 Large BHCs[a]	Citicorp	BankAmerica	J.P. Morgan	First Pennsylvania	Wachovia
1970	104.86	115.63	98.74	99.53	99.68	100.02
1971	104.91	107.70	98.08	99.16	101.59	99.97
1972	106.83	115.66	97.38	98.33	100.66	99.48
1973	110.07	115.64	103.76	107.83	116.51	99.07
1974	112.95	121.35	109.57	106.21	118.53	98.87
1975	113.72	131.94	111.70	102.89	119.27	98.59
1976	113.89	129.27	116.96	100.58	119.06	97.26
1977	114.23	139.27	117.96	99.85	119.31	97.11
1978	113.55	142.77	117.86	106.76	107.07	98.33
1979	114.37	152.13	114.60	105.87	113.92	97.92
Average	110.94	127.14	108.66	102.70	111.56	98.66

[a] Based upon aggregate data. From 1970 through 1974, the number of BHCs in the sample was not 50 but 31, 36, 41, 45, and 49, respectively. All figures are expressed as percentages.
Source: Boczar and Talley [1981], Figure 1, p. 54 and Figure 2, p. 56. Figures given in the text are from the source. Reprinted by permission.

[13] See Boczar and Talley [1981], p. 53.

double leverage occurred from 1972 through 1974. This leverage primarily was used to accommodate the growth of lead banks and to finance the acquisition of both bank and nonbank subsidiaries. The aggregate data, of course, mask the diversity of individual companies' approaches to double leverage. The data for the five selected companies reveal this diversity. For example, Citicorp has made extensive use of double leverage to finance its aggressive worldwide expansion. In contrast, J. P. Morgan and Wachovia have adopted "conservative" strategies, whereas BankAmerica and First Pennsylvania have been more reflective of the typical large BHCs use of double leverage. On balance, there is substantial variation in the use of double leverage by large BHCs.

For a more up-to-date picture of double-leverage activity by money-center BHCs, the following 1986 data are insightful[14]:

Bank Holding Company	Equity Invested in Subsidiaries	Total Equity	Double-Leverage Ratio
Citicorp	$16,648	$9,060	184%
Manufacturers Hanover	5,416	3,776	144
Bankers Trust	3,544	2,721	130
Chase Manhattan	6,245	4,883	128
Chemcial	3,544	3,120	114
J. P. Morgan	4,724	5,130	92

Compared to the decade of the 1970s, Citicorp has continued its aggressive use of double leverage, whereas J. P. Morgan has shown a posture even more conservative than the one it had in the 1970s.

The Major Risk of Double Leverage

Is double leverage all return and no risk? Can it keep stockholders and regulators satisfied without affecting a BHC's risk exposure? Of course it can't! Leverage is a double-edged sword that works for the BHC when times are good but cuts against the company when times are bad. The primary risk of double leverage focuses on *interest coverage* of the parent company's debt. Interest coverage is concerned with the funds (usually earnings before interest and taxes) that are available to meet interest payments. The major cash flow to the parent is dividends from its subsidiaries, especially those from the lead bank. If the lead bank experiences a cash-flow problem, the parent company might have difficulty servicing its debt. Furthermore, bank dividends are subject to statutory limitations and regulatory control. For example, without prior approval of the OCC, the maximum dividend that a national bank can pay in a given year is equal to its current year's earnings plus the additions to retained earnings for the two previous years.

To measure the risk inherent in double leverage, analysts focus on a number of factors. In general, the parent's liquidity and cash-flow position are the main concern. More specifically, such factors as the parent's dependency on bank dividends, the probability that bank dividends might be reduced, the double-leverage ratio, and the

---

[14] These data are from Harris [1987], p. 50. The figure for equity invested in subsidiaries includes intangibles to reflect the price paid in excess of book value for holding company subsidiaries.

payback period associated with double leverage are considered.[15] Over recent years the potential risk of some double leverage has been realized to the extent that several holding companies have had trouble servicing their debt.

STOCK REPURCHASES AND CAPITAL REGULATION

Given the banking agencies' penchant for capital regulation, stock repurchases by banks/BHCs are anathema to them. From a financial-management perspective, the effect of stock repurchases on the value of the firm is not unambiguous. On the one hand, the repurchase should, other things equal, improve the company's EPS and its ROE because fewer shares are outstanding and because the equity multiplier is larger, respectively. On the other hand, the repurchase will change the firm's capital structure and its perceived risk exposure. Thus, like any financial decision, a stock repurchase involves a risk–return trade-off. In terms of the constant-growth model, a stock repurchase would be expected to increase D_1, k, and g and thus the effect upon value $P_0 = D_1/(k - g)$, would depend upon the changes in D_1 and g relative to the change in k. Manager's expectations regarding these changes should determine the appropriate action.[16]

Citicorp has been one of the most active BHCs in the capital markets, both in issuing stock and repurchasing it. During October of 1977, Citicorp announced that it would repurchase on the open market 3 million shares of its 128 million in outstanding common shares, less than 2 percent of its total dollar capital. By January 19, 1978, the repurchase plan was completed. Since Citicorp shares were trading in the low 20s over this period, (the 1977 high was $33\frac{1}{2}$), the repurchases cost roughly $65 million, approximately 10 weeks of the company's earnings. Citicorp's rationale for the repurchase scheme was to enhance its "... ability to access capital markets in the future." That is, repurchases decrease the number of shares outstanding, thereby increasing earnings per share and reducing *total* dividend costs. Other things equal the lower total cash dividends will over time gradually replenish the reduced common stock via increased transfers of net income to retained earnings. In addition, Citicorp was counting on debt conversion, exercise of stock options, and a projected 10–15 percent annual earnings growth to augment its capital base.

In a letter dated December 16, 1977, the Comptroller of the Currency, John G. Heimann, criticized Citicorp for shrinking its capital base. Heimann wrote, "Since one of the major functions of equity capital is to provide a cushion against unforeseen occurrences, any reduction in equity capital, be it to the bank or its inseparable partner—the holding company—is of concern to me." In addition, Heimann expressed concern about (1) the *timing* of the reduction; (2) the fact that Citicorp "... does not appear to be overcapitalized"; and (3) Citicorp's earnings projections ("... it is always possible [they] will not be realized."). Heimann's letter is an example

---

[15] The double-leverage payback period is defined as the dollar amount of double leverage divided by the holding company's annual consolidated earnings. It measures the time it would take to pay off the double-leveraged debt using after-tax earnings. See Boczar and Talley [1981], p. 57. The consolidated income-expense statement for a holding company is calculated in a manner similar to the derivation of the consolidated balance sheet, that is, we add up each income or expense item and then adjust for any within company flows. The idea is to eliminate all "inside" income and expenses and consider only the "outside" flows.

[16] Schall and Haley [1977, p. 624] report that managers are often overly optimistic regarding the effect of stock repurchases. Some evidence indicates that the share prices of companies that have repurchased stock do not outperform the market.

of the kind of jawboning that goes on in capital regulation. The effectiveness of this weapon on giant banks is indicated by Citicorp's response to it. Chairman Walter B. Wriston wrote in reply, "Your letter of December 16 is duly noted."[17]

ODE TO BANK CAPITAL

The pecking order of capital regulation goes from Senators and Congressmen to bank regulators and then to bankers. The Heimann–Wriston exchange is an example of what happens on the second level of pecking.[18] On the first level, politicians peck on the regulators. To illustrate, Senator William Proxmire once charged former Comptroller James Smith with failing to exert pressure on large banks to increase their capital. He told Smith, "I'm not asking you to apply it (capital regulation) ruthlessly. Apply it in a namby-pamby way. Play the violin and sing while you're doing it. Just do it."

On March 11, 1977, I was testifying before the Committee on Banking, Housing, and Urban Affairs of the United States Senate, a committee that at the time was chaired by Senator William Proxmire of Wisconsin. The hearings focused on the condition of the banking system and how effectively the banking agencies had carried out their statutory responsibility to assure a "safe and sound" banking system. I concluded my

Figure 23-4   Ode to Bank Capital

Source: Sinkey [1979] p. 43. Reprinted by permission

[17] Personal communication from Robert R. Dince, who was a Deputy Comptroller at the time.

[18] The Heimann–Wriston exchange and the "Ode to Bank Capital" are from Sinkey [1979].

statement on a lighthearted note with my "Ode to Bank Capital":

Oh bank capital, oh bank capital.
Our regulators' stricken hero,
Please don't, please don't
Please don't go to zero.

Senator Proxmire, showing a lack of appreciation for my Odgen Nashism and, more important, an apparent misunderstanding of *how markets work*, responded: "If it [bank capital] does [go to zero], that is just something that will happen because of the markets and we can't do anything about it."[19] There is, of course, no need to "do anything about it." In an efficient market, risk-averse investors would not permit bank capital to go to zero (technically infinite financial leverage), or even to approach zero, without demanding compensation for the increased riskiness. As a bank's capital decreases below the industry or market norm, the risk premiums demanded by investors increase, forcing the bank to reduce its leverage (i.e., increase its capital) *or* to pay for its increased risk exposure. The market's signal for greater riskiness is a higher required rate of return and reduced value. In the case of Continental Illinois, the market's signal was more immediate in the form of a liquidity crisis that eventually led to a bailout and nationalization of the bank.

BANKING, INVESTMENT BANKING, AND CAPITAL PLANNING

One of the most important steps in the life cycle of a bank or BHC is the formation of an effective investment-banking relationship.[20] Frequently, community banks have not established such relationships. The value of an investment-banking relationship to the community bank is that it eases some of the burden of raising capital and of worrying about the appeal of the bank's stock. Since it is difficult for a bank's CEO to be market-maker *and* the manager of the bank, Nadler [May, 1981] strongly recommends that an outside investments firm be found to be the market-maker for the community bank's stock. Given the limited access that small banks have to capital markets, strong investment-banking relationships are all the more important for such institutions.

For banks that are looking to establish investment-banking relationships or that are reviewing existing relationships, Cates [1974] has suggested two basic guidelines. First, consider the range and content of investment-banking services that are needed. And second, follow a formal selection procedure in selecting an investment-banking firm (or firms) so as to establish a "presence" as a client. Cates, who has had experience on both sides of the bargaining table, regards the selection process to be of overriding importance. He recommends a "team" approach in terms of the bank's screening, selecting, and doing business with an investment firm.

Once an investment-banking relationship has been established, the bank team has professionals available who can help them with the capital-planning process. Developing or improving a bank's stock appeal is an important step in long-range capital planning. Since capital regulation is a fact of banking life, it is important that bankers develop capital-planning programs and tap the resources of investment bankers in their endeavors.

[19] Unedited transcript, Committee on Banking, Housing and Urban Affairs, March 11, 1977, lines 1–3, p. 150, inserts mine.
[20] Both Cates [1974] and Nadler [May 1981] stress the importance of this relationship.

CHAPTER SUMMARY

Capital and dividend decisions are important financial-management functions. In a highly regulated industry that stresses capital regulation, as banking does, these decisions take on added significance. If a bank's capital is judged to be inadequate, either by regulators or by the market, its growth opportunities will be limited. Judging the demands of regulators, shareholders, security analysts, and depositors makes the management and planning of a bank's capital-adequacy position a delicate task, one that is complicated by the uncertainty about what actually constitutes adequate capital. On balance, the adequacy of a bank's capital position is determined by a complex interaction of its liquidity, profitability, and quality of management.

Because it enables a bank to acquire assets and liabilities to support its operations over time, capital is the most basic resource of a bank. The basic capital problem a bank faces is to generate enough capital to take advantage of its profitable growth opportunities. Without access to external capital, a bank's asset growth cannot exceed its internal capital-generation rate, if it wishes to maintain its capital-to-asset ratio. This chapter has focused on this basic problem. By introducing and analyzing such concepts as the internal capital-generation rate, the interaction of liquidity and capital management, the dividend-payout ratio, external sources of funds (e.g., double leverage), and investment-banking relationships, the fundamental issues of capital management and planning have been addressed. Based on investment research by Goldman Sachs, the regulatory view and the market appear to be in agreement on the supremacy of equity capital as the key determinant of bank stock values.

LIST OF KEY WORDS AND CONCEPTS

Access to capital markets	Investment bankers
Capital regulation	Merrill Lynch Capital Markets
Common stock	Ode to Bank Capital
Dividend-payout ratio	Preferred stock
Double leverage	Price-earnings ratio (P/E)
Earnings per share (EPS)	Retention ratio (RR)
Equity multiplier (EM)	Return on equity (ROE)
Equity-to-asset ratio (EM^{-1})	Salomon Brothers
External equity (sources)	Stock repurchases
Financial statements (parent,	Subordinated notes and debentures
subsidiary, consolidated)	Supremacy of equity
Goldman Sachs	Two pictures worth 1,000 words
Initial public offering (IPO)	(each)
Internal capital generation rate	
($g = ROE \times RR$)	

REVIEW/DISCUSSION QUESTIONS

1. Investment researchers at Goldman Sachs claim to have found a "rule" for valuing bank stocks. What is the rule? Explain in detail how they found it. Why wasn't this relationship found in earlier data? What are some of the signs of the time that banking has changed?

2. What is the internal capital generation rate and what are its determinants? How do these factors relate to the capital problem faced by banks?

3. What is the potential problem in measuring dividend payout as the ratio of dividends per share (DPS) to earnings per share (EPS)? How can this problem be remedied? Using this alternative measurement, how do net income, payout, and retention ratios vary with bank size?

4. What are the external sources of capital available to banks? Do all banks have equal access to these sources? Which firms are the heaviest users of external capital? Who assists bankers in tapping capital markets?

5. What is double leverage, who uses it, and what are the risks involved?

6. How are the consolidated financial statements for a bank holding company constructed?

7. Is there a conflict between stock repurchases and capital regulation? Do stock repurchases increase the value of the firm? What is the pecking order in the capital-regulation process?

8. What are the relationships between (a) a bank's liquidity, profitability, and quality of management and (b) its capital adequacy? Would your answer differ based on the size of the bank? If so, how?

9. According to bank stock analysts at Goldman Sachs, bank balance sheets are more "believable" than bank income-expense statements. In contrast, consider what another analyst has to say (as reported by Kreuzer [1987], p. 46):

> Balance sheets reflect less and less the true condition of a bank today, but nonetheless net interest income is still a major contributor to profitability. Understanding the quality that underlies that stream of income is of paramount importance to an analyst. Difficult to get at—but of paramount importance.

Evaluate and discuss both positions, and include in your analysis Frederick's notion of a "fortressed balance sheet."

MATCHING QUIZ

Directions: Select the letter from the right-hand column that best matches the item in the left-hand column.

___ 1. The picture in 1977	A. Proxmire misunderstood
___ 2. The picture in 1988	B. Interest coverage
___ 3. Double-leverage leader	C. No relationship revealed
___ 4. IPO leader in 1985	D. Supremacy-of-equity rule
___ 5. Leading underwriter in 1985	E. Citicorp
___ 6. Dividend-payout ratio	F. Internal capital generation rate
___ 7. Price-earnings ratio	G. Subject to manipulation
___ 8. Perpetual preferred stock	H. LDC/energy/farm debt crises

___ 9. Access to capital markets

___ 10. Return on equity

___ 11. A sign of the times

___ 12. Retention ratio

___ 13. Debt-earn-back test

___ 14. $ROE \times EM$

___ 15. The inverse of EM

___ 16. Initial public offering

___ 17. Subordinated notes and debentures

___ 18. Underwriting process

___ 19. Risk of double leverage

___ 20. Ode to Bank Capital

___ 21. Goldman Sachs

I. Debt capital

J. Merrill Lynch Capital Markets

K. Salomon Brothers

L. Discovered equity rules

M. P/E

N. Developed by Citicorp

O. Not a part of core capital

P. Not equal in banking

Q. $ROA \times EM$

R. g/ROE

S. IPO

T. Investment bankers job

U. Equity ratio

PROBLEMS

1. The Leverage Bank currently has an equity multiplier (EM) of 25; in contrast, The Equity Bank has an EM of 14.28. Using Figure 23-2, determine the P/E ratios for each bank. If The Leverage Bank is able to reduce its EM to 20, what will the change in its P/E ratio be, assuming the relationship in Figure 23-2 holds? If The Equity Bank falls on hard times and its EM soars to 30, what will its P/E multiple be? Explain how your analysis would change if you used Figure 23-1 instead of Figure 23-2.

2. Calculate the internal capital generation rate for each of the following banks and describe each bank's situation.

Bank	PM	AU	EM	Payout Ratio
A	.07	.10	15	.30
B	.00	.11	25	.40
C	.10	.10	20	.45
D	.08	.12	16	.35
E	.05	.10	30	.50

3. Determine the present value of the bank that has the following characteristics: $k = .20$, $g = .12$, $EPS_0 = \$5$, and $RR = .6$.

4. Determine the dollar amount of double leverage and the DLR for the following BHC on a before and after basis.

Parent Company (Before)			
Investment in subs.	7	Liabilities	11
Other assets	8	Equity	4
	15		15

Parent Company (After)			
Investment in subs.	9	Liabilities	13
Other assets	8	Equity	4
	17		17

SELECTED REFERENCES

Albertson, Robert, Charles Cranmer, Richard Goleniewski, and Janice Meehan. [1988]. "Bank-Track Emerging Trends for Bank Stocks: The Supremacy of Equity," *Investment Research* (March), Goldman Sachs.

————, Charles Cranmer, Richard Goleniewski, and Janice Meehan. [1987]. "Bank Ratios and Rankings," *Investment Research* (Fourth Quarter), Goldman Sachs.

Boczar, Gregory E. [1981]. "External Sources of Bank Holding Company Equity." *The Magazine of Bank Administration* (February), pp. 41–44.

Boczar, Gregory E., and Samuel H. Talley. [1981]. "Bank Holding Company Leverage." *The Magazine of Bank Administration* (May), pp. 53–57.

Brealey, Richard, and Stewart Myers. [1981]. *Principles of Corporate Finance.* New York: McGraw-Hill.

Cates, David C. [1974]. "Bank Capital Management." *The Bankers Magazine* (Winter), pp. 11–12.

Danker, Deborah J., and Mary M. McLaughlin. [1987]. "The Profitability of U.S.-Chartered Insured Commercial Banks in 1986," *Federal Reserve Bulletin* (July), pp. 537–551.

Dyl, Edward A. [1978]. "The Marginal Cost of Funds Controversy." *Journal of Bank Research* (Autumn), pp. 191–192.

Gupta, Manak C., and David A. Walker. [1975]. "Dividend Disbursal Practice in Commercial Banking." *Journal of Financial and Quantitative Analysis* (September), pp. 515–529.

Harris, Timothy J. [1987]. "Bank Double Leverage," *Bankers Monthly* (November), pp. 49–52.

Howard, Donald S., and Gail M. Hoffman. [1980]. *Evolving Concepts of Bank Capital Management.* New York: Citicorp.

Keeley, Michael C. [1988]. "Bank Capital Regulation in the 1980s: Effective or Ineffective?" *Economic Review*, Federal Reserve Bank of San Francisco (Winter, No. 1), pp. 3–20.

Keen, Howard, Jr. [1978]. "Bank Dividend Cuts: Recent Experience and the Traditional View." *Business Review*, Federal Reserve Bank of Philadelphia, (November/December), pp. 5–13.

Kelly, Charles W. [1974]. *Valuing Your Money Inventory.* New York: Citicorp.

Kennedy, William F. [1980]. *Determinants of Large Bank Dividend Policy.* Ann Arbor: UMI Research Press.

Kreuzer, Terese. [1987]. "Who Owns the Big Banks?" *Bankers Monthly* (August), pp. 43–46.

Miller, Merton H., and Franco Modigliani. [1961]. "Dividend Policy Growth and the Valuation of Shares." *Journal of Business* (October), pp. 411–433.

Miller, Richard B. [1986]. "Raising Bank Capital," *Bankers Monthly Magazine* (January 15), pp. 17–21.

Modigliani, Franco, and Merton H. Miller. [1958]. "The Cost of Capital, Corporation Finance, and the Theory of Investment." *American Economic Review* (June), pp. 261–297.

Nadler, Paul S. [1981]. "How Attractive Is Your Stock?" *Bankers Monthly Magazine* (May 15), pp. 10–12.

————. [1981]. "Managing the Bank Capital Position." *Bankers Monthly Magazine* (April 15), pp. 6–10.

————. [1980]. "Community Banks in Capital Squeezes." *Bankers Monthly Magazine* (March 15), pp. 5–9.

Nagle, Reid, and Bruce Peterson. [1978]. "Capitalization Problems in Perspective." In *Handbook for Banking Strategy*, R. C. Aspinwall and R. A. Eisenbeis, eds. New York: Wiley, pp. 317–346.

Odgen, William S. [1981]. "Debt Management: A Key to Capital Planning." *The Magazine of Bank Administration* (March), pp. 24–31.

Quarterly Banking Profile. [1987]. Fourth quarter, FDIC.

Schall, Lawrence, and Charles W. Haley. [1977]. *Introduction to Financial Management*. New York: McGraw-Hill.

Sinkey, Joseph F., Jr. [1979]. *Problem and Failed Institutions in the Commercial Banking Industry*. Greenwich, CT: JAI Press.

Spong, Kenneth, Larry Meeker, and Forest Myers. [1980]. "The Paradox of Record Bank Earnings and Declining Capital." *The Magazine of Bank Administration* (October), pp. 22–27.

Statistics on Banking. (various issues). FDIC.

Terry, Ronald, and Z. Christopher Mercer. [1978]. "Capital Planning and Capital Adequacy." In *The Bankers' Handbook*, W. H. Baughn and C. E. Walker, eds. Homewood, IL: Dow Jones-Irwin, pp. 454–466.

Watson, Ronald D. [1977]. "The Marginal Cost of Funds Concept in Banking." *Journal of Bank Research* (Autumn), pp. 136–147.

Watson, Ronald D. [1974]. "Insuring Some Progress in the Bank Capital Hassle." *Business Review*, Federal Reserve Bank of Philadelphia (July–August), pp. 3–18.

Vojta, George J. [1973]. *Bank Capital Adequacy*. New York: Citicorp.

PART VII

SPECIAL BANKING TOPICS

Internationalization and the removal of geographic barriers to domestic expansion are two of the dynamic forces of change at work in the U.S. financial system. This section of the book focuses on these two topics. In Chapter 24, international banking is analyzed, with special emphasis on the international debt crisis and the various opportunities for private financial markets to develop innovations (e.g., debt-equity swaps) to assist in restructuring third-world debt. The appendix to Chapter 24 deals with the relationships among exchanges rates, interest rates, and inflation.

The removal of geographic barriers to domestic expansion has prompted a wave of mergers and acquisitions in the U.S. financial-services industry. Moreover, the 1980s have witnessed a new phenomenon in banking, the hostile takeover. Such takeovers, of course, have been common in nonbanking circles. These activities, and other types of corporate restructurings, are covered in Chapter 25.

The key word for this part of the book is *restructuring*. In Chapter 24, the focus is on the *restructuring* of the debt held by less-developed countries; in Chapter 25, the focus is on the corporate *restructuring* of the firms that make up the financial-services industry.

International Banking, The International Debt Crisis, and Opportunities for Financial Innovation

International banking will continue to increase in importance, but it will also become even more complex. The quality of people will be a decisive factor.

> Wilfried Guth
> Deutsche Bank, Frankfurt

The heyday of overseas banking already has passed the U.S. institutions and the international financial role played by American banks is likely to be diminished still further in coming years.

> Arturo Porzecanski
> Morgan Guaranty Trust Company

A rolling loan gathers no loss.

> International banker's rule

Countries don't go bankrupt.

> Walter Wriston
> Citicorp

Countries don't go bankrupt, but bankers who lend to them do.[1]

> Christine Bogdanowicz-Bindert
> Shearson Lehman Brothers

INTRODUCTION: NECESSITY AS THE MOTHER OF INNOVATION

Necessity, as the adage goes, is the mother of invention. In banking and finance, we are more concerned with the profitable application of inventions, or innovations, rather than inventions. In efficient markets, opportunities for innovations are unrestricted. The international debt crisis has created an opportunity for a new vision of

---

[1] The epigram sources are Guth [1981], p. 27, and Porzecanski [1981], p. 5. The last two quotes are from Mayer [1987], p. 1, and the source for the middle one is unknown.

commercial financing for less-developed countries (LDCs). Among other things, this chapter focuses on these two key issues: the international debt crisis and the opportunities for creative financing to attempt to provide viable alternatives to the problems of third-world debt. As background for analyzing these two issues, we present an introduction to international banking. The internationalization or globalization of financial institutions and markets is one of the most interesting and topical areas of banking and finance. Moreover, with the anticipated advances in technology and financial innovations, this area is likely to remain an interesting and topical one for many years to come.

The analytical framework of this chapter is based on the assumption that the fundamental principles of financial management guiding a bank's international operations are no different from those applied to its domestic operations. The analysis certainly is more complex because of the need to consider cross-border and cross-currency risks (i.e., "country risk"), but the basic analytical tools employed are the same. In this regard, we focus on the financial management of the complex risk-return relationships of international banking and finance. We begin by defining international banking, and then by looking at the importance of international banking to the U.S. commercial-banking system.

DEFINITION AND IMPORTANCE OF INTERNATIONAL BANKING

Let's define international banking as engaging in financial activities that involve cross-border and cross-currency risks. The activities, whether on or off the balance sheet, are, for the most part, the same whether we are dealing with domestic or international banking. Specifically, the activities are accepting deposits and making loans on the balance sheet and arranging contingent commitments off the balance sheet. Domestic banking is less complicated than international or cross-currency/cross-border banking because there is only one currency and one political regime or government to handle. Imagine if you will how much more complicated (and risky) U.S. banking would be if we had to deal with 50 independent political states each with its own currency. The principles of banking and risk management would not be any different, but dealing with the risks of 50 different currencies and 50 different sovereignties would complicate the analyses. Nevertheless, as the Western European model shows, the task can be managed quite easily.

Country Risk Is the Name of the Game

Regarding country risk and the international debt crisis, Walter Wriston, the former chairman of Citicorp, once quipped: "Countries don't go bankrupt." To wit, one sage retorted: "But bankers who lend to them do." Touché! For the record, as of this writing, we have not seen a U.S. money-center or regional bank go bankrupt because of the international debt crisis. Some of the banks may be insolvent on a market-value basis, but no offical bankruptcies have been declared. Moreover, the numerous U.S. commerical banks that have failed in the 1980s had, for the most, no significant activity in international banking. Of course, Continental Illinois was an exception. However, although Continental's liquidity crisis began in the international money market, the bank's mismanagement began with its domestic lending portfolio (remember Penn Square). Nevertheless, the worldwide decline in energy and farm prices was a major cause of financial difficulties in the energy and farm belts of the United States, not to mention the havoc it caused in LDCs. On balance, a bank does not have to be directly engaged in international banking for its operations to be affected by the international economy.

In international banking, "country risk" is the focus of risk management. Whenever a financial institution transacts across a national border or in a foreign currency, exposure to transfer and or convertibility risks, known jointly as "country risk," exists. Even though foreign borrowers may be willing and able to repay their debts, exchange controls may prevent loans from being repaid because of the inability of borrowers to obtain and/or to transfer currency. Alternatively, borrowers, including countries, may exhibit an unwillingness to repay their debts and take a position that their loans should be restructured or renegotiated.

Country risk is manifested in the form of nonperforming assets. If a U.S. bank is not paid within 90 days, for whatever reason, the loan or asset must be placed on a cash basis, and interest previously accrued but not paid must be deducted from current earnings. Since nonaccrual loans adversely affect bank earnings, they can also adversely affect a bank's equity capital, other things equal. In a nutshell, country risk can reduce shareholder wealth.

U.S. Commercial Banks with Foreign Offices

As of year-end 1986, only 263 U.S. commercial banks, less than 2 percent of the population, had foreign offices. However, these 263 banks controlled 58 percent of the assets and 53 percent of the deposits held by all insured commercial banks. The consolidated assets of banks with foreign offices totaled $1.7 trillion consisting of $1.3 trillion in domestic offices and $400 billion (23%) in foreign offices. In contrast, on December 31, 1978, these figures were $848 billion in consolidated assets consisting of $608 in domestic offices and $240 billion (28%) in foreign offices. Over the eight-year period from year-end 1978 to year-end 1986, assets in domestic offices grew at a compound annual rate of almost 10 percent compared to only 6.6 percent growth in foreign offices. On the deposit side, funds in domestic offices grew at a compound annual rate of 9.5 percent compared to 4.5 percent deposit growth in foreign offices.[2]

These data tend to support Porzecanski's claim that the "heyday of overseas banking has passed." Actually, the go-go era for international (and domestic banking) slowed down considerably during the mid-1970s as the 1974 credit crunch, the REIT crisis, and failures of the Bankhaus Herstatt of Germany and Franklin National Bank of New York demonstrated that not all the growth was safe and sound. Following this setback, international banking activity picked up again, only to be flattened by the international debt crisis of 1982 (and 1983, and 1984, and so on), and by Continental Ilinois's liquidity crisis and bailout in 1984.

Off-Balance-Sheet Activities

As we have seen in previous chapters, the 1980s have witnessed a tremendous growth in off-balance-sheet activities (OBSAs). Moreover, these activities mainly have been the domain of large banks. We add a third point here that many OBSAs, such as foreign-exchange transactions, international money transfers, documentary letters of credit, Euronote issuance facilities, Eurocommercial paper, and so on, are international banking activities. Thus, although, as documented above, on-balance-sheet activities in the international arena have been growing more slowly than domestic on-balance-sheet activities, OBSAs, many of which are international in character, have been growing faster than on-balance-sheet activities. The important point is that in modern

---

[2] The figures in this paragraph are from FDIC. *Statistics on Banking* [1982] and [1986], Washington D. C.

commercial banking, and this is especially true when dealing with multinational banks, one has to look not only at activities on the balance sheet but also at the myriad of off-balance-sheet arrangements.

THE INTERNATIONAL BANKING ACTIVITIES OF U.S. MONEY-CENTER BANKS

International or global banking is obviously not important to the day-to-day operations of the numerous community banks in the United States. When these banks need international banking services for their customers, they can go to their correspondent banks, either regional or money-center types. The major U.S. players in global banking are the money-center banks such as Citibank, Bank of America, and Chase Manhattan. As of December 31, 1986, these three organizations ranked 17th, 29th, and 40th in total deposits on a worldwide scale, based on a listing compiled by the *American Banker* [July 30, 1987, p. 48]. The top seven spots on this list were occupied by Japanese banks led by Dai-Ichi Kangyo Bank Ltd. of Tokyo with $186 billion in deposits up $61 billion (49%) from the previous year. In contrast, the deposit gains by the three largest U.S. banks during 1986 were $8.5 billion, −$12 billion, and $2.1 billion, respectively.

Of the major U.S. players in international banking, Citicorp/Citibank is the most aggressive. For example, based on cross-border and foreign-currency outstandings, Citicorp had $48 billion or 24 percent of its year-end 1986 assets in this category. The bulk of these assets were held by two groups of countries: (1) developed countries with $25.4 billion in outstandings and (2) non-oil developing countries with $18.2 billion. Although the latter, of course, represents the major threat to Citicorp's future earnings stream, it does not include $1.5 billion in *restructured* loans to Mexico. Total cross-border and foreign-currency outstandings to Mexico totaled $2.77 billion at year-end 1986, which was dwarfed by the $4.56 billion owed by Brazil.[3]

At year-end 1987, Citicorp had total assets of $204 billion funded, in part, by total deposits of almost $120 billion. Fifty-three percent of this deposit base ($64 billion) was generated by deposits from foreign or overseas offices with almost 93 percent ($60 billion) of these overseas deposits in the form of interest-bearing balances.

The distribution of Citicorp's net income for the years 1984 through 1986 is shown in Table 24-1. Focusing on the most recent year and the top half of the table, we see that Citicorp derived 54 percent of its $1 billion in net income from North America, followed by 24 percent from Central and South America. In the lower half of the table a breakdown of Citicorp's net income based on economic classifications designated by the Organization of Economic Cooperation and Development (OECD) is presented. The classification "total OECD" includes most of the industrialized nations of the world, whereas "total NIC" stands for "newly industrialized countries," which includes the countries of Mexico, Brazil, and Argentina. And, of course, LDC stands for less-developed countries. Using these three categories, the distribution of Citicorp's net income for 1986 was 69 percent from the OECD group, 27 percent from the NIC group, and 4 percent from the LDC group. The effects of LDC risk on Citicorp's net earnings stream is reflected by the decline in net income from LDCs, which was $124 billion in 1984 before dropping to $37 billion in 1986.

---

[3] These cross-border and foreign-currency outstandings are presented on a regulatory basis, and include all loans, deposits at interest with banks, acceptances, other interest-bearing investments, and other monetary assets. Adjustments are made to include the excess of local currency outstandings over local currency liabilities, if any, for each country included in a category and to allow for external guarantees and collateral. The data and definitions are from *Citicorp Reports 1986*, pp. 22–23.

TABLE 24-1   Geographic Distribution of Citicorp's Net Income, 1984–1986

Net Income In Millions of Dollars

	1986		1985		1984	
North America	$ 568	54%	$463	46%	$367	41%
Caribbean, Central and South America	257	24	245	25	177	20
Europe, Middle East and Africa	99	9	191	19	208	23
Asia/Pacific	134	13	99	10	138	16
TOTAL	$1,058	100%	$998	100%	$890	100%

Net Income OECD Classification In Millions of Dollars

	1986		1985		1984	
Total OECD[a]	$ 732	69%	$646	65%	$540	61%
Total NIC[a]	289	27	244	24	226	25
Total LDC/Other[a]	37	4	108	11	124	14
TOTAL	$1,058	100%	$998	100%	$890	100%

[a]OECD indicates industrialized countries, NIC stands for newly industrialized countries, and LDC for less-developed countries. See the text discussion for additional details.
Source: Citicorp Report 1986, p. 50.

The money-center banks with the greatest exposure to the debt of developing countries relative to their 1987 capital positions were Manufacturers Hanover (352%), BankAmerica (349%), Chase Manhattan (247%), Citicorp (221%), and Irving Bank (212%). These exposures are based on the outstanding debt of five countries: Brazil ($109 billion), Mexico ($100 billion), Argentina ($53 billion), Venezuela ($34 billion), and Philippines ($28 billion). Twenty-one percent of this $324 billion in third-world debt is owed to U.S. banks, most of it to U.S. money-center banks.[4]

To summarize, the dominant U.S. players in multinational banking are, not surprisingly, the money-center banks. Although Citicorp is the biggest U.S. player in the international arena, it pales in relationship to the role of the Japanese banks, which occupied the top seven spots in the 1986 listing of the world's largest banks. Nevertheless, because of its relatively strong capital position, Citicorp is not the U.S. money-center bank with the greatest risk exposure to the current trouble spot of international banking—third-world debt.

VALUE MAXIMIZATION, DOMESTIC REGULATION, AND THE EXPANSION OF INTERNATIONAL BANKING

The concepts of value maximization and the regulatory dialectic provide logical explanations for the expansion by U.S. banks into international banking. First, the banks and BHCs engaged in international activities are publicly held corporations with actively traded securities. The directors and managers of these organizations must answer, in theory at least, to their shareholders. Moreover, rational shareholders are interested in maximizing their expected returns given their risk preferences. The basic determinants of value are cash flow (i.e., dividends), risk, and growth (i.e.,

---

[4] The figures in this paragraph are those reported on PBS's *Wall Street Week* (February 12, 1988).

capital gains or price appreciation). The constant-growth model compactly summarizes these determinants of value in the following equation:

$$P_0 = D_1/(k - g) \tag{24-1}$$

where P_0 = the price or present value of a share of common stock, D_1 = the expected dividend per share in the next period, k = the capitalization rate, and g = the expected dividend growth rate in subsequent years.

The essence of financial management is to make risk–return decisions such that the value of the firm is maximized. Thus, even without domestic banking restrictions, value-maximizing banks and BHCs would be looking for profitable growth opportunities in the form of new markets and products. The international market was, and still is, a logical place to look for those opportunities. This natural quest for profitable growth opportunities in international markets was stimulated further because of restrictions placed on domestic banking activities (i.e., interest rate, geographic, and product specialization). To circumvent these restrictions, large BHCs and banks poured resources into the unregulated international market. The 31 percent compound annual growth rate in total assets experienced by the foreign branches of U.S. banks over the period 1966–1975 attests to the opportunities that were available.

The expected returns, risk, and growth opportunities of international banking need to be analyzed to determine their impact on the value of the bank. The existence of country risk is the critical factor that separates international banking from its domestic counterpart. Couched in terms of modern portfolio theory, a bank's country risk can be divided into a systematic (nondiversifiable) component and an unsystematic (diversifiable) component. By holding a diversified portfolio of international assets and liabilities, unsystematic country risk can be reduced. Thus, systematic country risk is the relevant concern for international bankers. The critical problem for managers, stockholders, and regulators is to measure this risk and to assign an appropriate risk premium for the additional exposures.

In terms of our valuation formula, the perceived risk of international operations must be compensated for with an appropriate expected return. This return could take the form of expected cash flows that permit higher dividend payments, or greater price appreciation. However, actual returns may fall short of expected ones because of loan defaults, payment interruptions, refinancing losses, or rescheduling losses. Recent cases of multilateral debt rescheduling requested by national governments from international banks represent the kind of event that can cause actual returns to be less than expected ones and thereby increase the bank's return variance (i.e., its risk).

THE DELIVERY SYSTEMS OF INTERNATIONAL BANKING

The alternative organizational forms that banks can employ to deliver international banking services are:

1. *Correspondent-Bank Relationships.* This approach is the least costly way of providing international services for customers. Basically, it is a defensive position designed to provide a full menu of banking services without substantial investment. However the opportunity for expansion is limited with this approach.
2. *International Department.* As the base for home operations, this department is a prerequisite for expansion into international banking. The size of the

department will determine the required investment and personnel require-ments. A general package of services for multinational customers is the basic objective here. This vehicle provides some flexibility, direct control over opera-tions, and the opportunity to exert pressure on correspondents for better service. Because of the broad range of services provided by international depart-ments and because of their special operations, accounting, and personnel re-quirements, they are frequently referred to as "a bank within a bank."

3. *Participations.* This vehicle offers an opportunity for loan expansion without extensive foreign investment or travel. Loan participations usually are organized by money-center banks, but not guaranteed by them. Participations enable new banks in the international market to "get their feet wet" (e.g., in terms of evaluating international loans) and to get known in the marketplace.

4. *Representative Offices.* This form of delivery system focuses on establishing contacts and providing information to the home office. Representative offices, whether foreign or domestic, are not permitted to gather deposits or make loans. A representative office can serve as a test vehicle for a future overseas branch without incurring the costs of establishing a full-service branch.

5. *Overseas Branches.* This approach permits a high degree of flexibility and control regarding the provision of international services, access to the Eurocur-rency markets, and ability to attract new business. The investment costs are, of course, substantial, especially if a worldwide network is desired. Foreign taxes usually must be paid.

6. *Edge Act and Agreement Corporations.* These subsidiaries are in effect out-of-state international departments. They carry out the function of an international branch within the United States. Edge and agreement corporations are permitted to engage only in foreign banking and investment activities. Edge Act corpora-tions are chartered by the Fed, whereas "agreement corporations" are state-chartered companies that agree to operate under the same Fed regulations that apply to Edges. As a result of the International Banking Act of 1978, Edge Act banks were permitted to establish branches. Recently, some banks have been establishing networks of Edge offices as a means of preparing for geographic deregulation in the United States.

7. *Foreign Affiliates.* These entities may be either majority owned or minority owned. They have the potential to provide a variety of financial services and joint ventures. To illustrate, in 1965 Mellon National Bank of Pittsburgh made a major foray into international banking by purchasing a substantial equity interest in the Bank of London and South America (BOLSA). BOLSA offered Mellon an oppor-tunity to gain access to (1) the London money and foreign-exchange markets, (2) markets in Spain, Portugal, and Latin America, and (3) an experienced group of international bankers and operational procedures.[5]

8. *International Banking Facilities (IBFs).* On December 3, 1981, the Fed granted U.S. banks the right to carry on their Eurocurrency business at home by establishing "free-trade" zones for international banking within the United States. Access to the IBFs is limited to individual non-U.S. residents, foreign corporations, foreign banks, and foreign subsidiaries of U.S. corporations. IBFs are not required to have offices separate from domestic facilities, but they must have a separate set of books. Deposits in IBFs were not subject to Reg Q interest-rate ceilings, but they do count in determining FDIC deposit-insurance

---

[5] See Lees [1974], pp. 76–77.

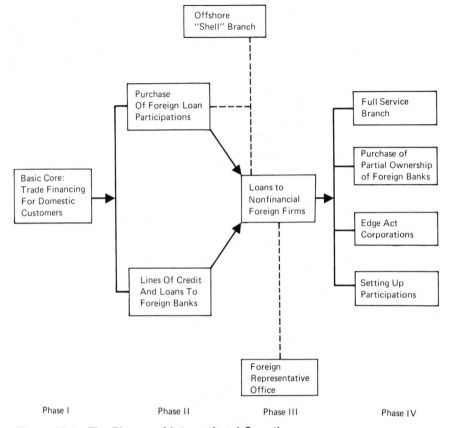

Figure 24-1   The Phases of International Growth

Phase I   Trade Financing for Local Exporters and Importers
Phase II   Loans to Foreign Banks and Loan Participations
Phase III   Direct Loans to Foreign Nonfinancial Firms
Phase IV   Subsidiary Establishment and Loan Syndication
Source: Baer and Garlow [1977], Chart 2, p. 130.

accessments. IBFs are not permitted to accept deposits from or make loans to U.S. residents and they cannot be used to finance activities in the United States. Deposits in IBFs are required to stay on the books for at least two days and the deposit instruments are not permitted to be negotiable. To encourage the establishment of IBFs, some states such as California, Florida, Georgia, and New York have passed laws making IBF deposits exempt from state and local income taxes. However, banks still are subject to federal income tax on earnings attributed to IBFs. The effect of IBFs on the Eurocurrency market mainly has been a distributional one, shifting some deposits into U.S. free-trade zones.

In terms of claims on unrelated parties, recent data show the dominant international delivery system to be foreign branches. These offices, which number around 2,500, generate about 57 percent of the total claims, followed by main offices (including IBFs) and foreign subsidiaries with 28 and 13 percent of total claims.[6]

The way in which a bank's international operations might develop is depicted in Figure 24-1. This schematic, which is from Baer and Garlow [1977], views the pattern

---

[6] Board of Governors of the Federal Reserve System.

of growth as consisting of four phases. Alternatively, we could view the phases as various stages in the life cycle of a bank's international delivery system. In Phase I, the basic core of international operations is established in terms of providing trade financing for local exporters and importers. In Phase II, the bank moves into making loans to foreign banks and into loan participations. In Phase III, loans to nonfinancial foreign firms are started as offshore facilities are established and market contracts made. In Phase IV, the bank moves into establishing subsidiaries and organizing foreign loan syndications. In this phase, the bank's international department takes on a stature similar to that of the international division of a money-center bank.

INTERNATIONAL BANKING MARKETS

International banking markets perform a financial-intermediation function similar to domestic banking markets. That is, the banks in these markets gather deposits from surplus-spending units and lend them to deficit-spending units. The basic difference between international or external banking and domestic or internal banking is that international banking occurs across national boundaries, whereas domestic banking occurs within a country. For example, a U.S. bank may gather deposits in its London branch and lend them in Japan through its Tokyo branch. Thus, foreign-exchange risk and foreign-country risk, which are not relevant for domestic banking, are important considerations in international banking.

The Eurocurrency Market

Multinational banks operate mainly in the international money market or the "Euro-currency" market. A Eurocurrency is a claim in that currency held by a non-resident of the currency's country of origin. The Eurodollar is the major Eurocurrency. In general, a Eurodollar is a U.S. dollar claim arising from a dollar-denominated deposit, note or bond held by a nonresident of the U.S. The major instruments of international banking are Eurodollar deposits and loans. A Eurodollar deposit is a dollar-denominated deposit located in a bank or branch outside the United States. A Eurodollar loan is a dollar-denominated loan made by a bank or branch located outside the United States. The essence of international banking or Eurobanking is to bid for Eurodollar CDs or time deposits of $100,000 or more and to make Eurodollar loans with the proceeds.

To facilitate the expansion of their assets, multinational banks frequently engage in interest-arbitrage transactions. That is, they borrow funds in one foreign currency and country and make loans in another currency and country. For example, a bank might gather "petrodollar" deposits in the Middle East and loan them to developing nations in Africa or Asia. The existence of these arbitrage situations is due to substantially different interest rates across countries. The objective of these arbitrage transactions is to maximize the interest-rate spreads, given the bank's risk preferences.

The process of credit expansion in Eurocurrency markets may involve the redepositing of the original deposit in a series of banks before a loan to a nonbank customer actually is made. Of course, until the loan is made, credit expansion has not occurred. To estimate the size of the Eurocurrency market in terms of credit-generating capacity, interbank deposits must be netted out. The size of the (net) Eurocurrency market is estimated to be about $1 trillion. The interbank redepositing of funds takes place in the interbank market. Funds in this market trade on the basis of the receiving bank's size, reputation, and creditworthiness, similar to the domestic market for federal funds and large CDs. The spread in the interbank market is narrow, around .25 percent, commensurate with the risk. However, high-risk institutions, like the now defunct Herstatt and Franklin National banks, have to pay larger risk premiums or go without interbank funding.

The base or anchor rate in the Eurocurrency market is the London interbank offer rate (LIBO rate or LIBOR). LIBOR represents the rate at which leading multinational banks in London are willing to lend to each other. The flow of funds from an initial deposit to a loan, on the basis of markup pricing, is illustrated by the following example:

Transaction	Price (Rate)	Premium
Initial Eurodollar deposit	15.000% (LIBOR)	—
First interbank deposit[a]	15.125%	.125%
Second interbank deposit[a]	15.375%	.250%
Third interbank deposit[a]	15.875%	.500%
Eurodollar loan	18.000%	2.125%

[a] The interbank deposits also are called *bank placements*.

The markups or premiums on interbank deposits or placements are relatively small because the costs and risks are minimal. In contrast, Eurodollar loans are more costly to administer and typically more risky; thus, they require a larger markup. These loans are made on a floating-rate basis with adjustments made every three to six months depending upon the maturity of the underlying liability instrument (time deposit).

The use of LIBOR-plus pricing in the Eurocurrency markets is functionally equivalent to the use of prime rate-plus pricing in the U.S. domestic market. In addition to markup pricing, the use of commitment fees is an integral part of Eurocurrency pricing arrangements. These fees, which are subject to competitive pressures, typically range in size from .25 to .5 percent with payment required at the time the commitment is made. The U.S. banking practice of compensating balances is not employed in Eurocurrency markets, or in domestic European banking markets.

Because of the unrestricted nature of the Eurocurrency market, competition is intense for both loans and deposits. Relative to domestic markets international markets are more efficient, as evidenced by the higher deposit rates and lower loan rates observed. As a result, profit margins and spreads are thinner. The size of a particular segment of the Eurocurrency market (e.g. Eurodollars) can be viewed as being determined by the interest spread that multinational banks are willing to accept.

Like the foreign-exchange market, the Eurocurrency market is not restricted to a particular location; it is a mechanism for transferring funds that knows no boundaries. The diversity of international-banking markets for the foreign branches of U.S. banks is summarized in Table 24-2. These data represent the geographic distribution of U.S. foreign branch assets for the period 1973 to 1984. These assets are divided fairly equally among three general areas including the United Kingdom (e.g., London), Caribbean Basin (e.g., Bahamas), and other locations (e.g., Continental Europe, Africa, and Asia).

The wholesale nature of international banking is illustrated by the data presented in Table 24-3. These figures measure the 1980 and 1986 foreign-loan composition of U.S. banks with foreign offices. In 1986 over 50 percent of these loans were commercial and industrial ones, which is substantially higher than the comparable figure of 37 percent for the domestic loan portfolio of these banks. The difference between the two figures approximates the percentage of consumer loans in the domestic loan portfolio. Loans to foreign governments and loans to banks in foreign coun-

**TABLE 24-2   The Geographic Distribution of
U.S. Foreign Branch Assets, 1973–1984**

Year	United Kingdom U.S. $ Millions	Percent	Caribbean Basin U.S. $ Millions	Percent	Other Locations U.S. $ Millions	Percent	Total U.S. Foreign Branches U.S. $ Millions	Percent
1973	61,732	50	25,297	21	38,837	29	121,886	100
1974	69,804	46	34,424	23	47,677	31	151,905	100
1975	74,883	42	48,915	28	52,695	30	176,493	100
1976	81,466	37	70,603	32	67,351	31	219,420	100
1977	90,933	35	83,953	32	84,011	33	258,897	100
1978	106,593	35	99,402	32	100,800	33	306,795	100
1979	130,873	35	120,890	33	112,402	32	364,165	100
1980	144,717	36	123,837	31	132,581	33	401,135	100
1981	157,229	34	149,108	32	156,510	34	462,847	100
1982	161,067	34	145,156	31	163,209	35	469,432	100
1983	158,732	33	151,532	32	166,275	35	476,539	100
1984	144,385	32	146,811	32	161,009	36	452,205	100

Sources: Hoffman [1980], Table 1, p. 23 for years 1973 to 1979 and *Federal Reserve Bulletin* [January 1982] and [February 1985].

tries totaled almost $65 billion at the end of 1986 and together they accounted for roughly 29 percent of foreign loans. These three categories accounted for almost 79 percent of the loan portfolio in foreign offices.

To summarize, the Eurocurrency market has a number of important characteristics. First, it is basically a wholesale market. Large CDs are the basic liability instrument with loan participations frequently used to facilitate denomination intermediation into large loans. Second, the international domestic money markets are competing sectors in the global market for financial assets and liabilities. Third, the Eurocurrency market is an unregulated one that is not subject to restrictions such as reserve requirements

**TABLE 24-3   Loan Composition of U.S. Banks with
Foreign Offices, 1980 and 1986**

Loan Category	1980 $ Millions	1980 Percent of Total Gross Loans	1986 $ Millions	1986 Percent of Total Gross Loans
Commercial and industrial loans	$109,401	58.65%	114,151	50.33%
Loans to foreign governments	26,980	14.46	35,784	15.78
Loans to banks in foreign countries	26,751	14.34	29,069	12.81
Loans to other financial institutions	7,088	3.80	N/A	N/A
Real estate loans	6,741	3.61	17,274	7.61
All other loans	9,581	5.14	30,547	13.47
Total gross loans	$186,542	100.00%	226,825	100.00%
Less unearned income	1,678	0.90	2,123	0.93
Less allowance for possible loan losses	235	0.13	N/A	N/A
Net loans	$184,629	98.97%	224,702	99.07%

Source: FDIC, *Annual Report* [1980], Table 110C, pp. 260–261. FDIC, *Statistics on Banking* [1986], Table RC-5, p. 36.

or deposit-insurance fees. This fact makes the international-banking sector particularly attractive to U.S. banks because they are more heavily regulated than other banks. Fourth, the Eurocurrency market is more competitive than domestic financial markets. As a result, profit margins and interest spreads are thinner because deposit rates must be higher and loan rates lower to compete with domestic financial institutions. And, fifth, the risk analysis required in Eurocurrency markets is more complex because of foreign-exchange risk and foreign-country risk,[7] factors which are not critical in domestic financial markets. However, in Eurocurrency markets, it is possible to separate these risks. On balance, Eurocurrency markets link the various currencies and countries of the world into a global financial market.

The Foreign-Exchange Market

The Eurocurrency market should not be confused with the foreign-exchange market. In the foreign-exchange market, one currency is traded for another; in the Eurocurrency market, international-banking activities take place (i.e., gathering deposits and making loans, usually in Eurodollars). Like the Eurocurrency market, the foreign-exchange market has no central marketplace and transactions are made by telephone or telex. The foreign-exchange market exists because of trade between countries with *different* currencies. That is, exporters prefer not to hold foreign currencies. They want to be paid in their *national* currency. Current quotations for the major exchange rates are available in daily publications such as the *Wall Street Journal* or from major financial institutions. The quoted rates are wholesale ones for amounts of $1 million or more as traded among major banks. Retail transactions typically provide fewer units of foreign currency per dollar.

The foreign-exchange market is dominated by giant commercial banks, domestic and foreign. To provide foreign-exchange services to their customers, these banks take a position (i.e., hold inventories) in the major currencies of the world. Some U.S. banks do this by keeping deposits with foreign banks. In addition to providing for customers' foreign currency needs in either the *spot* or *forward* markets,[8] banks also trade for their own account in the foreign-exchange market.

The importance of foreign-exchange income to the major U.S. banks is reflected by the fact that it accounts for anywhere from 10 percent to 60 percent of the overseas operating income of these banks. For 1986, Citicorp's foreign-exchange income was $412 million, or 39 percent of its net income of $1,058 million. Foreign-exchange income consists of two components: (1) trading profits or losses and (2) translation gains or losses. The latter refers to gains or losses on all monetary items on the balance sheet as a result of adjustments for exchange-rate movements.[9] The total gain or loss due to revaluation of the balance sheet is entered on the income-expense statement as a gain or a loss. The sum of the translation gain or loss plus the trading profits or losses equals total foreign-exchange income. The variability of foreign exchange income is a good indicator of the risk involved in foreign-exchange operations. In general, the net international income of the largest U.S. BHCs is highly volatile. In some cases, however, this volatility moves in the opposite direction of total net income and the overall effect is a stabilizing one. For example, in 1983 Citicorp's

---

[7] These risks are discussed later in the chapter.

[8] Transactions in the spot market are for immediate delivery (i.e., usually within two business days) whereas transactions in the forward market are for future delivery at an exchange rate established when the forward contract is signed. The forward market provides a mechanism for hedging against foreign-exchange risk. The concept is identical to using the futures market to hedge against interest-rate risk.

[9] The Financial Accounting Standards Board requires these adjustments as a result of its 1976 ruling, FASB-8.

total net income went down by 14 percent but its net international income went up by 42 percent.

Coordinated Use of the Eurocurrency and Foreign-Exchange Markets

Interest-arbitrage transactions in the Eurocurrency market can be protected against foreign-exchange risk through the use of the forward exchange market. The idea is to hedge the exchange risk by using forward exchange contracts to insure the profitability of the arbitrage transaction. In this context, exchange gains or losses should not be treated as exchange-trading gains or losses, but as adjustments to the interest earnings of the arbitrage transactions.[10] For example, if a Eurodollar loan that nets 1 percent has a corresponding exchange loss on the forward contract of 0.4 percent of the loan, then the net profitability of the arbitrage transaction is 0.6 percent. Forward exchange contracts can be used to hedge both Eurocurrency interest-arbitrage transactions and spot foreign-exchange transactions. This approach provides protection against unfavorable movements in exchange rates; but, at the same time, it eliminates the possibility of windfall profits due to favorable movements in exchange rates.

The Eurobond Market

The Eurobond market is the international market for long-term debt; it is *not* the long-term segment of the Eurocurrency market. Eurobonds are similar to domestically issued bonds except that they are not subject to the legal restrictions of the countries in whose currencies the bonds are denominated, provided the bonds are sold mainly to nonresidents. The most popular currency for Eurobonds is the U.S. dollar. Eurobonds are placed simultaneously in various countries through syndicates of investment or merchant bankers. In terms of dollar-equivalent volume, the Eurobond market is about one-tenth the size of the Eurocurrency market. Compared to the Eurocurrency and foreign-exchange markets, the Eurobond market is of minor importance to international commercial banking.

THE INTERNATIONAL DEBT CRISIS

Since Mexico started the ball rolling in 1982, rarely has a week gone by without some news about the international debt crisis. Five years later, on February 20, 1987, Brazil announced the unilateral suspension of interest payments on its public-sector and private-sector debt held by foreign banks. This event presumably precipitated the massive loan-loss provisions by U.S. money-center and regional banks in the second quarter of 1987. The LDC debt crisis has been around for a number of years now, and it is unlikely to go away in the near future. Let's take a look at how this mess got started.

Closing the Barn Door Before the LDC Horse Got Out[11]

The international debt crisis (i.e., the LDC debt crisis) was precipitated by some horrendously bad banking practices. The tale woven by the former lending officer and presented in Exhibit 24-1 gives one indication of how bad the practice was out in the

[10] See Johnson and Lewis [1975], p. 83.

[11] This section draws on the work of Makin [1984], Chapter 7, pp. 129–53.

EXHIBIT 24-1
LDC Lending: An Insider's View[a]

It is 1978. Thanks to the venal, repressive regime of President Ferdinand Marcos of the Philippines, I am safely and happily roosting in one of Manila's best hotels, the Peninsula. I am about to set in motion a peculiar and idiosyncratic process that will result in a $10 million loan to a Philippine construction company, a bedfellow of the Marcos clan—a loan that will soon go sour. I am unaware that any of this is going to happen as I enter the lobby of the Peninsula on my way to dinner, still trying to digest the live octopus that a Taiwanese bank served me last night, and attempting to remember exactly what it was they wanted and why they had gone to so much trouble.

International banking is an interesting business anyway, but what makes it rather more interesting in this case—both to me and to the hapless Ohioans whose money I am selling—is that I am 25 years old, with one and a half years of banking experience. I joined the bank as a "credit analyst" on the strength of an MA in English. Because I happened to be fluent in French, I was promoted 11 months later to loan officer and assigned to the French-speaking Arab countries of North Africa, where I made my first international calls. This is my third extended trip, and my territory has quickly expanded. I have visited 28 countries in six months.

I am far from alone in my youth and inexperience. The world of international banking is now full of aggressive, bright, but hopelessly inexperienced lenders in the mid-twenties. They travel the world like itinerant brushmen, *filling loan quotas*, peddling financial wares, and living high on the hog. Their bosses are often bright but hopelessly inexperienced 29-year-old vice presidents with wardrobes from Brooks Brothers, MBAs from Wharton or Stanford, and so little credit training they would have trouble with a simple retail installment loan. *Their* bosses, sitting on the senior loan committee, are pragmatic, nuts-and-bolts bankers whose grasp of local banking is often profound, the product of 20 or 30 years of experience. But the senior bankers are fish out of water when it comes to international lending. Many of them never wanted to lend overseas in the first place, but were forced into it by the internationalization of American commerce; as their local clientele expanded into foreign trade, they had no choice but to follow them or lose the business to the money-center banks. So they uneasily supervise their underlings, who are the hustlers of the world financial system, the tireless pitchmen who drum up the sort of loans to Poland, Mexico, and Brazil that have threatened the stability of the system they want to promote.

"And now for the rest of the story ..."[b]

The loan was eventually made after being partially guaranteed by the

EXHIBIT 24-1 (*Continued*)

Philippines' largest bank. However, after 18 months the loan was on nonaccrual status and it was rescheduled. By the summer of 1983, the bank had received only a fraction of the debt and the guarantee was never called. Since October 1983, the Philippines had declared a moratorium on its external debt of $25 billion until 1985. In 1980, the banker changed jobs and moved to a West Coast bank at twice the salary. He quit shortly after that and turned from banking to writing.

[a] S.C. Gwynne, "Adventures in the Loan Trade," *Harper's* [September, 1983], pp. 22–26.

[b] Makin [1984], p. 149.

field. In this section, we focus on risk management and lending philosophy at the corporate level.

The key message of portfolio theory is diversification. The ultimate way to reduce risk is to find projects whose returns are unrelated or, ideally, move in opposite directions. The latter is illustrated by the situations of undertakers and life insurance companies; their returns move in opposite directions. International lending to LDCs was frequently in the form of "umbrella loans" to the governments of the countries. With the funds dispersed by the government over a wide range of projects, the country's loan portfolio presumably was diversified. The banks, however, had lost control over the creditworthiness of the borrowers within the country. Thus, they were running the risk of getting diversified, but risky, loans *within* the countries. Once the return is negative it is small consolation to know that it is also stable. Another form of diversification that the banks tried to achieve is that they were lending across countries such as oil exporters (e.g., Mexico and Venezuela) and oil importers (e.g., Brazil and Argentina). Unfortunately, since all of these countries were still in the LDC portfolio, there were certain risks that were not diversifiable (e.g., the propensity for these governments to be wasteful intermediaries and to resort to the inflation tax to reduce the burden of internal debt).

The terms of LDC loans were dominated in dollars at floating interest rates without any collateral. Since governments never go bankrupt because they have the power to tax, there presumably was no need for collateral. The first two terms were designed to protect against foreign inflation and domestic inflation, respectively. These terms were stacked against both the borrower *and* the lender; neither could win. The banks were making these loans without any control over their quality and *before* they had the funding (i.e., liability management). With LIBOR plus pricing, they simply bought OPEC dollars in the Eurocurrency market at the going rate of interest, marked them up, and sent them along to the borrower. When U.S. inflation and interest rates took off in 1980 and 1981, LDC lenders were rolled into higher and higher interest rates that they could never repay without massive reschedulings.

The cute phrase, "a rolling loan gathers no loss," is true only in accounting terms. In terms of market values, a rolling loan gathers tremendous loss. Consider the following demonstration of this momentum.[12] Let's take a nice round number like $100 billion

---

[12] The example in this paragraph is similar to Makin's [1984], pp. 150–151.

TABLE 24-4   Major South American LDC Exposure Ranking

	12/31/86 Major South American LDC Exposure		12/31/86 Major South American LDC Cross-Border Exposure ($ Millions)
	To Primary Capital	To Stockholders' Equity	
Manufacturers Hanover	139%	199%	$ 7,505
Bank America	88 E	181 E	7,301 E
Chase Manhattan	96	150	6,420
Chemical	94	133	4,162
Irving	89	135	1,416
Marine Midland	88	116	1,592
Citicorp	77	115	10,400
J.P. Morgan	71	88	4,509
Bankers Trust	70 E	121 E	3,300 E
Continental Illinois	63	78	1,596
First Chicago	63	91	2,140
Republic Bcp. (Texas)	52	65	788
Mellon Bank Corp.	46 E	63 E	1,148 E
Wells Fargo	43	66	1,534
Bank of Boston	41	53	950
Bank of New York	38	52	574
First Interstate	38	46	1,283
Security Pacific	34 E	48 E	1,403 E
Norwest	25	32	422

E = Estimated

12/21/86 Amounts Owed to U.S. Banks by South American Nations ($ Billions)			
Argentina	$ 8.5	Jamaica	$ .2
Bolivia	.1	Mexico	23.7
Brazil	22.4	Nicaragua	.7
Chile	6.5	Paraguay	.1
Colombia	2.1	Peru	1.3
Costa Rica	.4	Trinidad and Tobago	.2
Dominican Republic	.4	Uruguay	.9
El Salvador	.1	Venezuela	9.1
Guatemala	.1	Other	.3
Honduras	.2		

Source: Fixed Income Research, First Boston [December 1987].

and, to simplify the mathematics, a 10 percent rate of interest. The annual interest payment alone on this loan is $10 billion. Now with a rolling loan, the lender gives the borrower $10 billion to make the interest payment. The total debt, however, has escalated to $110 billion. Next year's interest payment then is $11 billion. If it is rolled, the total debt increases to $121 billion. After a decade of this charade, the total debt has ballooned to $100(1.10)^{13} or $259.37 billion. The magic of compound interest has doomed the borrower and the lender has been pouring good money after bad. To see the impossibility of the borrower's situation, think of an LDC economy trying to maintain its creditworthiness in the face of triple-digit inflation, a strong dollar, and political and social unrest. Is it any wonder that the IMF has tried to impose austerity programs on troubled LDC borrowers? Part of the solution to the LDC problem is that

[13] Regarding prudent judgments, when Walter Wriston, former head of Citicorp, was asked what went wrong with international lending, he replied: "... we have *imprudent* moments." See Makin [1984], p. 153.

the governments of both the lender and borrower countries must keep their economic houses in order. For now the competition for LDC borrowers has been replaced by cooperation to keep the stack of debtor cards from falling down. The IMF and various central banks (i.e., the U.S. taxpayers) have a safety net in place to catch the debris if there is a collapse.

Country Risk: A More Detailed Look

The political, economic, legal, and social turmoil in countries such as Mexico, Brazil, Argentina, Poland, Iran, Afghanistan, El Salvador, and the Falkland Islands are examples of country risk. Country risk is the principal factor that distinguishes international lending from domestic lending. International bankers, regulators, and others are concerned about country risk because of the potential *claim* on bank earnings and capital that such risk entails. The critical steps are to *measure* and *analyze* a bank's exposure to particular countries, especially the developing ones. The first step involves estimating the bank's *effective* exposure, defined as the sum of credits (loans) and commitments adjusted for any loan guarantees.

Once a bank's effective exposure has been quantified, it usually is compared to the bank's capital base. A benchmark capital-exposure ratio of 25 percent is regarded as a country-risk flag by the U.S. banking authorities. This standard is not absolute, however, because the effective exposure also depends on the stability of the country to which the bank is exposed. For example, a 25 percent exposure to a developed country like West Germany or Japan is less serious than the same exposure to less-developed countries. Symptoms of country risk come in the form of nonperforming loans, loan losses, and debt rescheduling. The major South American LDC exposures faced by U.S. banks are shown in Table 24-4. These data, which are for December 31, 1986, show the money-center banks as having the greatest exposure. Moreover, as noted earlier, although Citicorp has the greatest dollar exposure, its exposure relative to its stronger capital position is less severe. The capital exposure of the 10 money-center banking companies to the debt of Argentina, Brazil, Mexico, and Venezuela at year-end 1986 is shown in Table 24-5. This group of banks held 80 percent, 80 percent, 56 percent, and 75 percent, respectively, of the total loans made by U.S. banks to these four countries.

INNOVATIONS IN COMMERCIAL FINANCING FOR LDCs[14]

In 1987 the major U.S. banking companies appeared to accept the reality of the LDC debt crisis.[15] Now that they have finally passed through the "denial stage," it is time to get down to some hard bargaining.[16] Not the "zero-sum" renegotiating that has been going on since 1982 but "positive-sum" restructuring that can benefit both the LDCs and the banks. Although some positive-sum solutions have been proposed since the

[14] This section draws, in part, on Lessard [1987], who discusses the alternatives available for developing "positive-sum" ways out of the LDC crisis.

[15] For an alternative view on this issue entitled "Banks Didn't Bite the Foreign Loan Bullet," see Harris [1988].

[16] I have in mind here Elizabeth Kübler-Ross's five stages of death and dying, which are denial, anger, bargaining, depression, and acceptance. This model has such wide applicability in explaining human behavior that I have generalized it to "the five stages of anything." For example, on the next exam you blow, see how your emotions are likely to run the gamut through these five stages. Try it, you'll like it, if it's not *your* exam.

TABLE 24-5   Major Banking Companies' Cross-Border Loans to South American LDCs Ranked by Percent of Primary Capital, December 31, 1986

Argentina	% Primary Capital	$Billions	Brazil	%Primary Capital	$ Billions
Manufact. Hanover	27%	$1.4	Manufact. Hanover	43%	$2.3
Bank of Boston	15	.4	Chase Manhattan	41	2.7
Irving	15	.3	Bank America	37	2.7
Continental Ill.	15	.4	Marine Midland	36	.6
J.P. Morgan	14	.9	Citicorp	36	4.6
Chase Manhattan	14	1.0	Chemical	33	1.5
Citicorp	10	1.4	J.P. Morgan	30	1.9
Chemical	9	.4	Irving	25	.4
Bankers Trust	9	.2	First Chicago	22	.7
First Chicago	8	.3	Continental Ill.	19	.5

This group of banking companies' exposure represents 80% of Argentina's $8.5 billion in loans from U.S. banks.

This group of banking companies' exposure represents 80% of Brazil's $22.4 billion in loans from U.S. banks.

Mexico	%Primary Capital	$ Billions	Venezuela	% Primary Capital	$ Billions
Manufact. Hanover	35%	$1.9	Irving	26%	$ .4
Bank America	34	2.5	Manufact. Hanover	19	1.0
Chemical	32	1.4	Bank America	17	1.3
Bankers Trust	28	1.3	Chase	16	1.1
First Chicago	27	.9	Chemical	16	.7
Chase	25	1.6	Continental Ill.	11	.3
Irving	22	.4	J.P. Morgan	9	.6
Citicorp	21	2.9	Bankers Trust	9	.2
Interfirst	20	.2	Citicorp	7	1.0
First City	19	.2	First Chicago	7	.2

This group of banking companies' exposure represents 56% of Mexico's $24 billion in loans from U.S. banks.

This group of banking companies' exposure represents 75% of Venezuela's $9.1 billion in loans from U.S. banks.

Source: Fixed Income Research, First Boston [December 1987].

money-center banks bit the LDC bullet in the second quarter of 1987, most of the bargaining has been in the form of restructuring original "general obligation" financings. These restructurings mainly have been one-way, zero-sum games in which the banks always come up with the short end of the LDC stick. Specifically, reducing interest rates and forgiving principal repayments rarely benefit lenders.

The viable alternatives, which are beginning to play a more prominent role in the restructuring of international claims, include such innovative transactions as debt for debt, debt for equity, and debt for commodities. These kinds of exchanges offer the possibility of gains to both LDCs and the lending banks. Lessard [1987] has cast the LDC restructuring problem in terms of the traditional constrained-optimization dilemma of financial economics. He writes: "In general, it is possible to define an efficient financing mix that maximizes the value of the commitments a country is able to make subject to the constraints on both its ability and willingness to pay under different circumstances" (p. 7). The current financing mix of LDC debt is dominated by general obligation, floating-rate debt. This monolithic structure has not solved, and

TABLE 24-6 The Capitalization of Mexico

Capital Structure	Current (1987)	Proposed
LIBOR-linked general obligations	$100 billion	$50 billion
Private borrowings	30	15
Private, portfolio equity	10	25
Direct investment	10	20
Oil-linked general obligations	0	30
Debt forgiveness	0	10
TOTAL	$150 billion	$150 billion

Source: Lessard [1987], adapted from his Figure 1, p. 18. The data are meant to be only rough approximations.

probably will not solve, the LDC debt crisis. The two fundamental problems with general obligation financing are (1) vulnerability to external shocks (e.g., declines in oil/commodity prices) and (2) failure to generate incentives and market discipline within LDC economic systems (e.g., uncontrolled monetary growth and hyperinflation). Innovative financing structures are a step in the right direction because they tend to reduce this vulnerability and create the right kind of incentives. Examples of such innovations include equity-for-debt swaps, commodity-linked debt financing, project or stand-alone finance, alternative quasi-equity arrangements (such as production sharing), interest-rate and currency swaps, and futures and options. To the extent that these innovative deals are successful in regaining LDC access to world financial markets and making the international financial system safer, they represent "positive-sum" transactions that benefit both parties.

To illustrate the kind of "efficient financing mix" Lessard [1987, p. 18] has in mind, consider his example for the recapitalization of Mexico, as depicted in Table 24-6. Mexico's 1987 capital structure can be approximated by data shown on the left-hand side of the table; on the right-hand side is Lessard's proposal for remedying Mexico's debt crisis. Although the numbers shown in the table are only rough approximations, they capture the flavor of Lessard's idea of an efficient financing mix. Since throughout 1987 Mexican general obligation debt traded for about 50 cents on the dollar (see Table 24-7 for these and other market prices on developing country debt), financial markets can be viewed as not considering the current Mexican capital structure as a viable one. Excluding the debt forgiveness, the only *new* component in the capital structure is the oil-linked general obligation, although existing components are, of course, rearranged. What does this new component do for Mexico? It links Mexican debt-serving capacity to its comparative advantage in the world economy—oil. Although there are various ways in which such oil-linked debt might be packaged, Lessard gives "oil-participation notes," a type of cumulative participating security, as an example. If oil prices do not behave nicely, the Mexican government cannot be blamed for mismanaging the economy. Lenders/investors would base their expected returns on expectations of future oil prices.

In general, Lessard views the problem of restructuring LDC debt on the basis of country characteristics as linked to five critical dimensions: (1) concentration of export revenues, (2) extent of dependence on external financing, (3) private versus public mix in financing, (4) the degree of development of domestic capital markets, and (5) the current level of direct foreign investments. Continuing with the Mexican example, Lessard rates Mexico as "moderate," "very high," "high," "moderate," and "moderate" across these five categories. An optimal set of country characteristics would consist of diversified export revenues, limited dependence on external

**TABLE 24-7 Market Prices For Developing
Country Debt (as a percentage of face)**

Country	Jan 87	Feb 87	Mar 87	Apr 87	May 87	Jun 87
Argentina	62–65	62–65	62–64	58–60	58–60	57.5–58.5
Brazil	74–76.5	73.5–75.5	68–70	63–66	62–65	61–63
Chile	65–68	66–69	66–69	67–70	67–70	68–70
Colombia	—	86–89	86–89	86–89	85–88	85–88
Ecuador	63–65.5	62–64.5	62–64	52–56	52–55	51–54
Mexico	54–57	56.5–58.5	57–59	56–59	57–60	57–59
Peru	16–19	16–19	16–19	15–18	14–18	14–17
Philippines	72–76	72–76	72–76	70–73	70–72.5	69.5–72
Poland	41–43.5	41–43.5	41–43.5	43–45.5	43–45.5	43–45
Romania	86–89	86–89	86-89	86–89	86–89	86–89
Venezuela	72–74	72–74	72–74	72–74	72–74	71–73
Yugoslavia	77–81	77–81	77–81	77–81	77–80	75–77

Country	Jul 87	Aug 87	Sep 87	Oct 87	Nov 87	Dec 87
Argentina	46–49	45–47	38–41	34–38	33–37	35–38
Brazil	58–61	52–54	41–44	35–40	37–41	$45–47\frac{1}{2}$
Chile	67.5–69.5	64–66	56–59	50–53	50–53	60–63
Colombia	81–83	80–82	80–82	75–80	72–76	67–72
Ecuador	45–47	41–43	32–35	31–34	31–34	34–38
Mexico	55–57	51–53	46–49	46–49	48–52	51–54
Peru	10–12	7–10	0–7	2–7	2–7	2–7
Philippines	68.5–71	65–67	65–66	57–60	55–60	49–52
Poland	42–44	42–44	42–44	41–43	39–42	41–43
Romania	86–89	86–89	86–89	86–89	84–87	81–83
Venezuela	70–72	65–67	55–58	50–54	49–53	49–52
Yugoslavia	73–75	72–74	65–67	57–62	55–60	53–55

Source: Shearson Lehman Brothers.

financing, a balanced mix of private and public financing, well-developed capital markets, and a high level of direct foreign investment.[17]

Future Financing Needs of Third-World Countries

Over the next decade, the expected financing needs of LDCs are conservatively estimated to be $20 billion per year. Since major banks throughout the world are most likely to be unwilling and/or unable to fund these needs, innovative financing arrangements are a must. Where and how will these funds be generated and what are the political and social consequences of not generating them? Although the latter question goes beyond the dimensions of this book, the former does not. The "how" in the form of innovative financing arrangements we have already discussed. The answer to "where" is the world capital markets. Since LDC financing needs amount to less than 10 percent of current net fundings provided by OECD institutions and markets, the task is a feasible one. The stumbling block, however, is the current lack of creditworthiness among LDCs whose debt is trading at a discount (see Table 24-7). If the proposed new financing arrangements are seen by the marketplace as viable, they could provide the impetus for establishing what Lessard [1987] calls "credible commitments" by LDCs to meet the terms of their obligations. Countries that can establish credibility in financial markets should be able to generate the funds they need. In this regard, the Mexican oil-linked securities shown in the proposal in Table 24-6 are an example of a credible commitment.

---

[17] The dimensions and ratings in this paragraph are from Lessard [1987], p. 19 and Figure 2, p. 20.

Recapitulation

In our analysis of asset-liability management (ALM) in Chapter 13, we noted the importance of rate, volume, and mix to the efficient management of a bank's portfolio of earnings assets. The crux of the LDC debt problem is that the current vector of [rate, volume, mix] is all wrong. Without monetary discipline, LIBOR-linked financing is self-defeating. Without market credibility, volume will be insufficient to stimulate economic growth.[18] And, perhaps most important, without the right mix of capital, including innovative financing arrangements, the whole vector could collapse. It is in the best interests of the lending banks of the world, and the world itself, to see to it that LDCs get the right (optimal) financing vector of rate, volume, and mix.

CHAPTER SUMMARY

The major U.S. banks, as exemplified by Citicorp and its competitors, are multinational corporations that depend heavily on international markets for gathering deposits and making loans. The quest for maximization of shareholder wealth and restrictive domestic regulations jointly explain the rapid expansion and development of international activities by U.S. banks. The important international banking markets are the Eurocurrency market and the foreign-exchange market. Alternative delivery systems such as foreign branches, representative offices, and Edge Act corporations can be employed to reach these markets.

Financial managers and bank regulators mainly are concerned about country risk and how it may jeopardize expected returns from international loans. The major source of country risk in bank loan portfolios arises from credits to LDCs. A bank's exposure to a particular country is measured by the sum of its credits and commitments adjusted for loan guarantees. Modern portfolio theory and supervisory approaches to foreign lending suggest that diversification is the key to managing the riskiness of bank portfolios. Nevertheless, in a portfolio of LDC loans, it is difficult to diversify away the risks associated with governments' role as a wasteful intermediary and their ability to use the inflation tax. Once a portfolio's return is negative, its variability tends to become less crucial. Prudent credit standards and lending terms were lacking in most LDC lending agreements.

Viable (positive-sum) solutions to the LDC debt crisis must focus on the rate, volume, and mix of the capital structures in these countries. The floating-rate general obligation debt contract has been the wrong instrument at the wrong time for LDCs. Innovative financing arrangements such as debt-equity swaps and debt contracts linked to the ability of countries to service their debt offer hope for the future. However, the transition from the traditional mode of financing to the more innovative one will not be easy as long as zero-sum-game mentality prevails.

The complicated world of international banking and finance can be made more understandable by focusing on four key propositions: (1) the Fisher effect, (2) the expectations theory, (3) the theory of interest-rate parity, and (4) the law of one price. As explained in the appendix to this chapter, these theorems link together differences in exchange rates, interest rates, and inflation rates.

---

[18] In 1985, the U.S. Treasury initiated the so-called Baker Plan to promote structural changes in the economic policies of LDCs aimed at generating economic growth and balance-of-payments equilibrium. The plan, which was endorsed by the World Bank and the International Monetary Fund (IMF), also called for a reduction in inflation and increased lending by private banks on a worldwide basis. As of this writing, the Baker plan would have to be described as less than successful.

LIST OF KEY WORDS AND CONCEPTS

Bank capital exposure (to LDC debt)
Constrained optimization problem
Country risk
Delivery systems of international
  banking
Eurobond market
Eurocurrency market
Floating-rate loan (LIBOR-linked
  versus oil- or commodity-linked)
Foreign-exchange market
General obligation financing
Innovations in commercial financing
  for LDCs
International banking

International debt crisis
Less-developed country (LDC)
Market value of LDC debt
Money-center bank
Newly industrialized country (NIC)
Off-balance-sheet activities (OBSAs)
Optimal financing mix
Organization for Economic
  Cooperation and Development
  (OECD)
U.S. commercial banks with foreign
  offices
Vector of [rate, volume, mix]

MATCHING QUIZ

Directions: Select the letter from the right-hand column that best matches the item in the left-hand column.

_H_ 1. "Countries don't go bankrupt."

___ 2. Banks with foreign offices

___ 3. Country risk

___ 4. 90 days past due

___ 5. OBSAs

___ 6. Japanese banks

___ 7. Citicorp/Citibank

_B_ 8. Dai-Ichi Kangyo Bank

___ 9. BankAmerica

___ 10. Manufacturers Hanover

___ 11. Constrained optimization

___ 12. Value max and reg dialectic

___ 13. Correspondent relationship

___ 14. International department

A. LDC financing needs

B. World's largest bank (1986)

C. Largest U.S. banking company

D. Prerequisite for international
    banking

E. Most LDC debt linked to this

F. Explain world expansion

G. Greatest LDC capital exposure

H. Walter Wriston

I. Provides access to international
    banking

J. Top Eurocurrency

K. Considers ability to pay

L. Where currencies are traded

M. Created in 1981

___ 15. IBFs   N. S. C. Gwynne

___ 16. Eurodollars   O. Credit control lacking

___ 17. LIBOR   P. 1985 Treasury LDC plan

___ 18. Foreign-exchange market   Q. 2% of banks but 58% of assets

___ 19. Insider view of LDC lending   R. Requires cash accounting

___ 20. Umbrella loans   S. Many are foreign related

___ 21. Baker Plan   T. Dominate world banking system

___ 22. Need $20 billion per year   U. Lost $12B in deposits in 1986

___ 23. Efficient financing mix   V. Cross-border/cross-currency risks

___ 24. LDC [rate, volume, mix]   W. Lessard's LDC framework

___ 25. Oil-linked GOs   X. Innovative instrument for Mexico

___ 26. Brazil   Y. Owes $109 billion

                                                         Z. Wrong time and place

REVIEW/DISCUSSION QUESTIONS

1. How do domestic and international banking differ? Who are the major U.S. players in international banking and what is the major risk they face? Who are the major players in global banking?
2. What role do OBSAs play in international banking? How have the domestic and foreign components of U.S. bank balance sheets been growing lately?
3. Use the concepts of value maximization and the regulatory dialectic to explain the expansion of U.S. banks into international banking.
4. What are the various delivery systems of international banking?
5. Briefly but carefully distinguish among the Eurocurrency market, the foreign-exchange market, and the Eurobond market. What is a Eurodollar? What is the base or anchor rate in the Eurocurrency market? Describe how loans and deposits are priced in this market.
6. Discuss the origins, current situation, and prospects for the international or LDC debt crisis.
7. Lessard views the LDC debt crisis in the context of a constrained-optimization problem. Explain what this means and describe and discuss some of his proposed solutions for the debt crisis. What criteria does Lessard suggest for characterizing debtor countries?
8. What is the supervisory approach to foreign lending? How would a portfolio theorist view this framework?
9. Discuss and debate the epigrams presented at the beginning of this chapter.

10. Do rich nations have an obligation to help poor nations overcome poverty and develop? Are U.S. banks doing their part to help LDCs develop? Is it possible for a financial manager to attempt to maximize value and be altruistic at the same time? Are lenders' "imprudent moments" a form of altruism?

PROBLEM

1. Based on the data presented in Table 24-7, Shearson Lehman Brothers calculates a Developing Country Debt Index as a weighted average of the outstanding commercial bank debt to the countries listed in the table. Given the following information, complete the last column below by determining the market value of the outstanding debt during 1987.

Month	Index	Face Amount of Indexed Debt ($B)	Market Value
January	66.7	279.4	
February	66.3	279.4	
March	64.8	279.4	
April	62.7	281.8	
May	62.6	281.8	
June	61.7	281.8	
July	58.7	281.8	
August	54.6	281.8	
September	47.9	281.8	
October	44.6	281.8	
November	45.3	281.8	
December	48.1	281.8	

Given these market values, why might banks be reluctant to write off any LDC debt? Focusing on the prices in Table 24-7, what would your write-off strategy be comparing Peru versus Romania? What events happened in 1987 that might explain the drop in the index from 66.7 to 48.1? If during the first two months of 1988, the index had values of 47.3 and 45.3 on a face amount of 284.4, what was the market value of the outstanding debt? Determine the change in the value of the debt from January 1986 to February 1988, if the index was 73.3 in January 1986 with a face amount of 274.8.

CHAPTER 24

APPENDIX
Exchange Rates, Interest Rates, and Inflation

The various relationships among exchange rates, interest rates, and inflation rates across countries make international banking and finance a complex area.[1] Application of the Fisher effect, the expectations theory, and the concept of parity to international financial management can establish some basic relationships to reduce the degree of this complexity.

The Fisher Effect

Since the nominal or money rate of interest equals the real rate of interest plus the expected rate of inflation (i.e., the Fisher effect), differences in nominal interest rates across countries can be traced to one or both of these components. In a perfect international capital market, real rates would be the same across countries and differences in nominal interest rates could be explained by differences in the expected rates of inflation. Given the unrestricted nature of the Eurocurrency markets, real rates of interest are more likely to be equal in these markets than they are in domestic financial markets. In the absence of taxes, market imperfections, and government regulations, differences in interest rates across countries can be attributed to differences in expected rates of inflation.

The Expectations Theory

In the pure-expectations theory of the term structure of interest rates, a one-to-one correspondence between expected short-term spot rates and forward rates of interest is established. The expectations theory applied to the foreign-exchange market provides a similar linkage between the spot market and the forward market. That is, on average, the forward exchange rate is equal to the expected spot exchange rate. Alternatively, the difference between the forward rate (F) and the spot rate (S) equals the expected change in the spot rate. Expressed as a percentage change, the relationship is[2]

$$(F_{t+1} - S_t)/S_t = [E(S_{t+1}) - S_t]S_t \tag{24-A1}$$

---

[1] For an excellent and more detailed discussion of these relationships, see Brealey and Myers [1980], pp. 685–708. This appendix draws on their exposition.

[2] The LHS of Equation 24-A1 is called the *foreign-exchange agio* or simply the *exchange agio*. Agio refers to the premium or discount paid for the exchange of one currency for another.

Multiplying by S_t and adding S_t to both sides of Equation 24-A1, the basic expectations-theory relationship for the foreign-exchange market is

$$F_{t+1} = E(S_{t+1}) \tag{24-A2}$$

If the one-to-one correspondence depicted in Equation 24-A2 holds, then international bankers (and others) can ensure their interest-arbitrage transactions and foreign-exchange commitments in the forward market at a "fair" price. To the extent that nonexpectational elements (e.g., risk, transactions costs) distort the one-to-one correspondence, the forward rate can be either above or below the expected spot rate. In this case, the price of the forward contract includes either a premium or a discount on the price of the "insurance."

The Theory of Interest-Rate Parity

The fundamental principle of this theory is that a foreign rate of interest covered for exchange risk should be equal to the domestic interest rate. In the unrestricted Eurocurrency market, interest-rate parity tends to be the rule rather than the exception. In contrast, in restricted domestic markets, the existence of taxes and government regulations leads to differences in interest rates between countries even after coverage for exchange risk. Arbitrage fails to eliminate the existence of "covered" interest-rate differentials between countries because the potential profits are taxed away or because the actual capital flows are restricted.

In technical terms, the interest-rate-parity theory requires that the interest rate-foreign exchange relationship between two countries results in the equality of the interest agio and the exchange agio (see footnote 2). *Interest agio* is simply the interest-rate differential between two countries as an equilibrium condition; interest-rate parity guarantees that any gains arising from interest-rate differentials will be wiped out by losses from coverage against exchange risk in the forward market.

To illustrate the interest-rate-parity concept, consider the following example for country A and country B. The one-year interest rate in A is 8 percent; in B, it is 10 percent. The spot exchange rate is two of A's dollars for one of B's dollars (i.e., $S_{A/B} = 2$). The one-year forward exchange rate is $F_{A/B} = 1.9636$. Will a bank in country A be better off investing one million dollars in A or B? A loan in country A will produce a gross return of 80,000 (= 1,000,000 × .08) in A-dollars. A loan in country B will produce a return of 50,000 (= 500,000 × .10) in B-dollars. With the principal (500,000) and interest (50,000) of the loan in B covered by the forward contract at $F_{A/B} = 1.9636$, the value of the proceeds in A-dollars is 1,080,000 (=550,000 × 1.936), which equals the proceeds from the loan in A.

The agio equilibrium condition for interest-rate parity is

$$\text{Interest Agio} = \text{Exchange Agio} \tag{24-A3}$$

In symbols, the condition is

$$\frac{(r_A - r_B)}{(1 + r_B)} = \frac{(F_{A/B} - S_{A/B})}{S_{A/B}} \tag{24-A3'}$$

Using the data from the example, the agio values are

$$\frac{(.08 - .10)}{1.10} = \frac{(1.9636 - 2.0)}{1.9636}$$

$$-.018 = -.018$$

In words, the interest-rate advantage of investing in country B is offset by the forward discount in the exchange rate. If the flow of funds is from country B to country A, then the interest-rate *disadvantage* would be made up by the forward *premium* in the exchange rate. In this situation, the agio condition is

$$\frac{(.10 - .08)}{1.08} = \frac{(.50926 - .5000)}{.5000}$$

$$.0185 = .0185$$

The Law of One-price

Suppose that you could buy ATMs in Tokyo for $40,000 each and sell them to United States bankers for $50,000 each. If no one else recognized this profitable opportunity, you could get rich quick. Unfortunately, other shrewd businesspersons will recognize this opportunity and bid up the price of ATMs in Tokyo and perhaps cut the price of the ATMs they sell in the United States. In equilibrium, arbitrage will ensure that the dollar prices of ATMs in Japan and in the United States will be equal. If the dollar/yen exchange rate is .005 (i.e., 200 yen = $1), the original disequilibrium ATM situation can be expressed as

Yen Price of *ATM* × $ Price of Yen = $ Price of *ATM*

8 Million Yen × .005 = $50,000

$40,000 < $50,000

If the equilibrium ATM price is $45,000 and the exchange rate is fixed, the price of an ATM in Japan will be 9 million yen. This equilibrium process is referred to as the *law of one price*. In general, it states

$$\frac{\text{Foreign Currency}}{\text{Price of Product}} \times \frac{\text{Price of Foreign}}{\text{Currency}} = \frac{\text{Domestic Price}}{\text{of Product}} \tag{24-A4}$$

Or alternatively,

$$\text{Price of Foreign Currency} = \frac{\text{Domestic Price of Product}}{\text{Foreign Currency Price of Product}} \tag{24-A4'}$$

Applied to the price level in a country, the law of one price is known as the *theory of purchasing-power parity.*

By definition, the price of foreign currency (i.e., the exchange rate) is equal to the ratio of domestic to foreign product prices. From the previous example, in equilibrium, the ratio of domestic ATM prices is .005 = 45.000/9,000,000. Suppose now that 10 percent inflation is expected in the United States but only 5 percent inflation is expected in Japan. In equilibrium, the expected exchange rate will be .005238 = 49,500/9,450,000. In words, the dollar is expected to depreciate against the yen because of the higher expected rate of United States inflation. The important implication of the law of one price is that the expected change in the spot exchange rate is linked to the expected difference in inflation rates. Using previous notation and the following symbols, I = inflation rate, $ = dollar, and Y = yen, this equilibrium condition can be expressed as

$$\frac{E(I_\$ - I_Y)}{1 + I_Y} = \frac{E(S_{\$/Y}) - S_{\$/Y}}{S_{\$/Y}} \tag{24-A5}$$

Using data from the previous example, an illustration is

$$\frac{(.10 - .05)}{1.05} = \frac{(.005238 - .005)}{.005}$$

$$.0476 = .0476$$

The important empirical implication of Equation 24-A5 is that the best estimate of the expected change in the spot exchange rate is the expected differential in the inflation rates.

Recapitulation

Four fundamental financial or economic concepts have been applied in this appendix: (1) the Fisher effect, (2) the expectations theory, (3) interest-rate parity, and (4) the law of one price (purchasing-power parity). These models provide a basic foundation for understanding the relationships among exchange rates, interest rates, and inflation. Once these basic principles are mastered, the complexity of international banking and finance becomes much more manageable.

SELECTED REFERENCES

Baughn, William H., and Donald R. Mandich, eds. [1983]. *International Banking Handbook.* Homewood Hills, IL: Dow Jones-Irwin.

Beazer, William F. [1977]. "Mathematical Modelling of Bank Asset and Liability Management." *Euromoney* (April), pp. 64–68.

Brealey, Richard, and Stewart Myers. [1981]. *Principles of Corporate Finance.* New York: McGraw-Hill.

Citicorp Reports 1986. New York: Citicorp.

Crane, Dwight B., and Samuel L. Hayes, III. [1983]. "The Evolution of International Banking Competition and its Implications for Regulation." *Journal of Bank Research* (Spring), pp. 39–48.

Dod, David P. [1981]. "Bank Lending to Developing Countries." *Federal Reserve Bulletin* (September), pp. 647–656.

Donaldson, T. H. [1979]. *International Lending by Commercial Banks.* New York: Wiley.

Dufey, Gunter, and Ian H. Giddy. [1978a]. *The International Money Market.* Englewood Cliffs, NJ: Prentice-Hall.

———. [1978b]. "The Unique Risk of Eurodollars." *Journal of Commercial Bank Lending* (June), pp. 50–61.

Economic Report of the President. [1981]. Washington, DC: United States Government Printing Office.

Federal Reserve Bulletin. [1982]. Washington, D.C.: Board of Governors of the Federal Reserve System (January).

Fisk, Charles, and Frank Rimlinger. [1979]. "Nonparametric Estimates of LDC Repayment Prospects." *Journal of Finance* (March), pp. 429–438.

Foreign Bank Competitive Analysis. [1984]. New York: Citicorp (February).

Gray, Jean M., and H. Peter Gray. [1981]. "The Multinational Bank: A Financial MNC?" *Journal of Banking and Finance* (March), pp. 33–64).

Guth, Wilfried. [1981]. "International Banking: The Next Phase." *The Banker* (October), pp. 27–34.

Gwynne, S. C. [1983]. "Adventures in the Loan Trade." *Harper's* (September), pp. 22–26.

Harris, Timothy J. [1988]. "Banks Didn't Bite the Foreign Loan Bullet," *Bankers Monthly* (February), pp. 42–47.

Hoffman, Stuart G. [1980]. "U.S. Banks Expand Offshore Banking in Caribbean Basin." Federal Reserve Bank of Atlanta *Economic Review* (July/August), pp. 22–25.

Johnson, Howard G., and J. James Lewis. [1975]. "Keep Control of Foreign-Exchange Operations." *The Bankers Magazine* (Spring), pp. 79–83.

Kammert, James L. [1981]. *International Commercial Banking Management.* New York: AMACOM.

Key, Sydney J. [1985]. "The Internationalization of United States Banking." In *Handbook for Banking Strategy,* R. C. Aspinwall and R. A. Eisenbeis, eds. New York: Wiley, pp. 267–292.

Korth, Christopher M. [1980]. "The Evolving Role of United States Banks in International Finance." *The Bankers Magazine* (July–August), pp. 68–73.

———— [1979]. "Developing a Country-Risk Analysis System." *Journal of Commercial Bank Lending* (December), pp. 53–68.

Lees, Francis A. [1974]. *International Banking and Finance.* London: The Macmillan Press Ltd.

Lessard, Donald R. [1987]. "Recapitalizing Third-World Debt: Toward a New Vision of Commercial Financing for Less-Developed Countries," *Midland Corporate Finance Journal* (Fall), pp. 6–21.

Lewis, M. K. and K. T. Davis. [1987]. *Domestic and International Banking.* Cambridge, MA: MIT press.

Makin, John H. [1984]. *The Global Debt Crisis.* New York: Basic Books.

Mathis, F. John, ed. [1978]. *Offshore Lending by United States Commercial Banks.* Washington, D C and Philadelphia: Bankers' Association for Foreign Trade and Robert Morris Associates.

Mayer, Martin. [1987]. "Under the Mexican Hat," *American Banker* (December 31), pp. 1, 11.

"New Supervisory Approach to Foreign Lending." [1978]. Federal Reserve Bank of New York *Quarterly Review* (Spring), pp. 1–6.

Norton, Robert E. [1984]. "The Best of the Big Banks." *Fortune* (August 20), pp. 193–196, 216–219.

" 'Paper' International Earnings Spur Bank Expansion at Home." [1984]. *Savings Institutions* (June), pp. 39–42.

Porzecanski, Arturo C. [1981]. "The International Financial Role of United States Commercial Banks: Past and Future." *Journal of Banking and Finance* (March), pp. 5–16.

Quinn, Melanie R. [1982]. "A Selected Bibiliography on the Topic of International Banking Supervision and Risk." Washington D C: Comptroller of the Currency, Staff Paper 1982-2.

Riley, Willian H. [1980]. "How Regional Banks Approach Country Exposure and Country Risk." *Journal of Commercial Bank Lending* (March), pp. 33–44.

Robinson, Stuart W., Jr. [1972]. *Multinational Banking.* Netherlands: A. W. Sijthoff International Publishing Company.

Sargen, Nicholas. [1977]. "Economic Indicators and Country-Risk Appraisal." *Economic Review,* Federal Bank of San Francisco (Fall), pp. 19–35.

Shearson Lehman Brothers Developing Country Index. [1988]. New York: Shearson Lehman Brothers

Sinkey, Joseph F., Jr. [1985]. "Regulatory Attitudes Toward Risk." In *Handbook for Banking Strategy,* R. C. Aspinwall and R. A. Eisenbeis, eds. New York: Wiley, pp. 347–380.

Smith, Allerton G., Patricia A. Phillips, and Robert K. Citrone. [1987]. *Financial Institutions Credit Rating Handbook* (December). Fixed Income Research, First Boston.

"Special Report: International Banking—Europe's Innovations in Management and Technology." [1980]. *ABA Banking Journal* (January), pp. 76–78.

Statistics on Banking, FDIC, Washington, D. C. (various issues).

Sterling, Jay. [1980]. "How Big is the International Lending Market?" *The Banker* (January), pp. 77–87.

Steuber, Ursel. [1976]. *International Banking.* Netherlands: A. W. Sijthoff International Publishing Company.

Wallich, Henry C, [1982]. "A Regulator's View of the Rescheduling Problem." Board of Governors of the Federal Reserve System (February 9).

———— [1981a]. "International Lending and the Role of Bank Supervisory Cooperation." Board of Governors of the Federal Reserve System (September 24).

———— [1981b]. "LDC Debt—To Worry Or Not To Worry." Board of Governors of the Federal Reserve System (June 2).

———— [1980a]. "American Banks Abroad in 1985." Board of Governors of the Federal Reserve System (March 11).

———— [1980b]. "The Future Role of The Commercial Banks." Board of Governors of the Federal Reserve System (January 24).

Walter, Ingo. [1981]. "Country Risk, Portfolio Decisions, and Regulation in International Bank Lending." *Journal of Banking and Finance* (March), pp. 77–92.

Zenoff, David B. [1985]. *International Banking: Management and Strategies.* London: Euromoney Publications.

Bank Mergers, Restructuring, and Corporate Control in the Financial-Services Industry

INTRODUCTION

One of the interesting and controversial questions in corporate finance is: Do takeovers create value? With the proliferation of antitakeover measures, one might assume a takeover was a fate worse than (corporate) death. However, the laissez-faire approach to financial economics contends (and the evidence suggests) that takeovers are good for the economy because they guarantee that a firm's assets are *controlled* by managers who can use them most productively (i.e., maximize their value). The issue here is one of *corporate control*. Given the objective of maximization of shareholder wealth, who can argue against takeovers? Obviously, those who do not believe in the objective and the accompanying view of a corporation as "a bundle of contracts" will be the first to attack it. These critics favor a more subjective or "soft" view of the corporation based on values like loyalty and commitment rather than the "hard" values (prices) found in the stock market.[1]

This chapter focuses on the mergers, restructurings, and the battles for corporate control taking place in banking, and within the financial-services industry (FSI). We begin by looking at the merger and restructuring activities going on in banking. Then we present some theoretical underpinnings to provide a foundation for understanding the issues of corporate control and restructuring activity.

TAKEOVERS, CORPORATE CONTROL, AND RESTRUCTURING ACTIVITIES[2]

Corporate-control transactions, or simply control transactions, are activities that fundamentally restructure an organization. The key words are *control* and *restructuring*. Takeovers, mergers, and leveraged buyouts are the transactions that make financial

---

[1] See Helm and Dobrzynski [1988] for a *Business Week* view of these issues, and an interesting profile of Professor Mike Jensen, formerly of The University of Rochester and now at The Harvard Business School. See footnote 2 and the references at the end of the chapter for some academic readings.

[2] See Jensen [1986]; Copeland and Weston [1988], Chapter 19; Ross and Westerfield [1988], Chapter 26, and the four papers in the "Symposium on Takeovers," Varian [1988] for a detailed discussion of these issues. Beatty, Santomero, and Smirlock [1987], Neely [1987], and Matthews [1988] focus on bank mergers and acquisitions. Also see Stern [1987], "The Future of Commercial Banking: A Roundtable Discussion," [1987].

news headlines. Closely associated with these transactions, but less well known, are such activities as divestitures, spinoffs, and stock repurchases. These control transactions affect firms fundamentally in terms of their expansion, contraction, corporate control, and ownership structure. The emotional and colorful terms used in fighting takeovers, and referred to as antitakeover measures, are "shark repellents," "poison pills," "greenmail," and "golden parachutes."

TRICK and Interstate Banking

In this chapter, we are primarily concerned with bank mergers and acquisitions (M&A). "Merger mania" and other such terms have been used to describe the tremendous amount of merger activity during the 1980s. Banking and the financial-services industry have not been immune to this mania. Interstate banking is where the geographic action is in the FSI. From our TRICK framework, the T, R, and K components are the driving forces behind interstate banking and bank merger activity. Technology, as reflected by the T component, has made geographic barriers obsolete. Reregulation, the R component, has opened the door to regional interstate banking, and nationwide banking. As of this writing, 15 states permit interstate banking on a nationwide basis, either reciprocal (e.g., New York) or nonreciprocal (e.g., Texas). And capital adequacy, the K component, will determine which banks will be able to expand. This factor is especially critical in light of the risk-based capital requirements proposed for 1992, which are seen as handicapping the money-center banks relative to the regionals and superregionals.

Merger Activity in Banking

During the 1950s, the average number of combinations in banking (both commercial and savings, with "combinations" broadly defined as absorptions, consolidations, and mergers)[3] was 150 per year. During the 1960s and the 1970s, the figures dropped slightly to 145 and 143, respectively. However, during the 1980s, the figure rose to over 400 per annum. Focusing on mergers for banks and thrifts and excluding the other forms of combinations, the following data for 1986 and 1987 are informative[4]: In 1986, 302 bank mergers were consummated with an aggregate price of $16.7 billion to acquire an aggregate equity of $9.9 billion and aggregate earnings of $1 billion. These figures generate an average price-to-equity ratio of 1.7 and an average price-to-earnings ratio of 16.7. The ratios for 1987 were 1.8, up slightly from 1986, and 14.2, down slightly from 1986. However, the number of deals in 1987 was down to 229 with an aggregate price of $17.1 billion to acquire $9.6 billion in equity and $1.2 billion in earnings. Almost one-half of the value ($8.3 billion) generated by these mergers occurred in the three months preceding the stock market crash of October 19, 1987. The last three months of 1987 generated only $2.1 billion in aggregate merger prices. The stock market crash put an abrupt halt to what had been nine months of numerous high-priced bank and thrift merger deals. Among the ten largest deals in 1987, the highest premium paid for a bank was the three-times book value paid by National Westminster Bank PLC, London for First Jersey National Corp., Jersey City, N.J. By geographic region, the 229 mergers of 1987 were distributed as follows: 64 in the Midwest, 51 in the Southeast, 36 in the Midatlantic states, 34 in the West, 23 in the

---

[3] These figures are calculated from the list of combinations in Beatty, Santomero, and Smirlock [1987], Table 1, p. 1.

[4] These data are from Matthews [1988].

Southwest, and 21 in New England. Merger activity among thrifts was most active in the northeast, and especially in New England.

Two of the ten largest bank mergers in 1987 involved acquisitions by foreign banking companies of U.S. banking companies. The National Westminster deal mentioned above was the sixth largest deal with a value of $820 million. The sixth largest deal of 1987, worth $800 million, was the acquisition by Hongkong and Shanghai Banking Corporation of Marine Midland Bank of Buffalo.

The Deal Makers

Expanding our M&A horizon beyond the banking and thrift industries to the FSI, in 1987 Salomon Brothers announced or completed 26 transactions in the FSI with a total value of approximately $11.7 billion. The deals, which ranged in size from $16 million to $3.4 billion, are shown in Table 25-1. Other major players in FSI deal-making include Goldman Sachs, First Boston, and Merrill Lynch Capital Markets. For example, Goldman Sachs was involved in the largest banking deal of 1987, the $1.34 billion pending acquisition of Fidelcor (Philadelphia) by First Fidelity Bancorp (Newark). Merrill Lynch completed the $505 million deal in which Sovran Financial Corp. of Norfolk, V., acquired Commerce Union Corp. of Nashville, which was the tenth largest banking deal of 1987.

The first nine months of 1987 were extremely active with bank M&A activity. The five leading investment bankers serving as advisors to banks in M&A transactions over this period were

Investment Banker	$ Millions	Number of Deals
J. P. Morgan Securities	4,133.5	4
Morgan Stanley	2,665.1	4
Goldman Sachs	2,196.7	3
Salomon Brothers	744.6	3
Merrill Lynch Capital Markets	467.0	2
Five-firm total	$10,206.9	16

These M&A transactions, as reported by O'Rourke [1988, p. 20], include only 100 percent takeover deals, and both completed and pending transactions.

Hostile Takeovers in Banking?

Is nothing sacred? In the "club" that banking once was, a "hostile takeover" would have been totally unacceptable behavior. Banking was much too civilized for such activity. However, since the club has fallen by the wayside and since *the* rule of the FSI merger game is "gobble or be gobbled," hostile takeovers have made their way into banking. A list of significant hostile takeover attempts in banking for the period 1981 through 1987 is shown in Table 25-2. The item at the top of the list, Bank of New York's bid for Irving Trust, was closed on October 5, 1988. Next to First Interstate's abortive attempt to acquire BankAmerica for a $3.2 billion package of common stock, preferred stock, and convertible notes, Bank of New York's bid ranks as the second largest hostile takeover attempt in U.S. banking history with a $1.4 billion offer of common stock and cash. Bank of New York's successful takeover of Irving could have important implications for the future of bank-merger activity, and in particular for the future of hostile takeovers in banking.

TABLE 25-1   M&A Activity in the FSI by Salomon Brothers in 1987

Client	Transaction
• Fleet/Norstar Financial Group, Inc.	Merger of Fleet Financial Group, Inc. and Norstar Bancorp Inc.
• Texas Commerce Bancshares, Inc.	Acquisition by Chemical New York Corporation
• The E.F. Hutton Group Inc.	Acquisition by Shearson Lehman Brothers Holdings Inc.[a]
• The Hongkong and Shanghai Banking Corporation	Acquisition of the remaining outstanding common stock of Marine Midland Banks, Inc.
• BankAmerica Corporation	Defense against unsolicited offer by First Interstate Bancorp
• The Bank of Nova Scotia	Acquisition of The McLeod Young Weir Corporation[a]
• The Home Group,, Inc.	Acquistion of Carteret Bancorp Inc.[a]
• H.F. Ahmanson & Company	Acquisition of The Bowery Savings Bank[a]
• GLENFED, Inc.	Acquisition of Guarantee Financial Corporation of California
• PNC Financial Corp	Acquisition of The Central Bancorporation, Inc.[a]
• PNC Financial Corp	Acquisition of Citizens Fidelity Corporation
• Alexander & Alexander Services Inc.	Sale of Sphere Drake Insurance Group Public Limited Company to Sphere Drake Acquisitions (U.K.) Limited
• Chemical New York Corporation	Acquisition of Chemical's Factoring Business by The Citizens and Southern Corporation
• U.S. Bancorp	Acquisition of Peoples Bancorporation
• U.S. Bancorp	Acquisition of Old National Bancorporation
• BankAmerica Corporation	Sale of The Charles Schwab Corporation to CL Acquisition Corporation
• Butcher and Company Incorporated	Sale of substantial minority interest to S. D. Fürst von Thurn und Taxis
• The Union Central Life Insurance Company	Acquisition of 52% of Manhattan National Corporation
• Avco Financial Services, Inc.	Acquisition of Avco's credit card operations by a subsidiary of Household International, Inc.
• Equitable Investment Corporation	Sale of Equitable Relocation Management Corporation to Travelers Mortgage Services, Inc.
• AT&T Credit Corporation	Acquisition of The Inventory Finance Division of The CIT Group Holdings, Inc.
• Santa Fe Southern Pacific Corporation	Sale of Bankers Leasing and Financial Corporation to Citicorp[a]
• National Machine Tool Finance Corporation	Acquisition by The Summit Bancorporation
• Freedom Federal Savings Bank	Acquisition by a subsidiary of Household International, Inc.[a]
• Orbanco Financial Services Corporation	Acquisition by Security Pacific Corporation
• Pacific First Financial Corporation	Sale of California mortgage servicing operations to Commonwealth Mortgage Company of America, L.P.

[a] Transaction pending at the time of this writing.
Source: Salomon Brothers

TABLE 25-2 Significant Hostile Takeover Attempts in Banking 1981–1987

Date	Bidder	Target	Offer	Outcome
1987	Bank of New York ($22.1 B)	Irving Trust ($24.2 B)	$1.4 B common stock & cash	Deal finally closed in October 1988. First hostile takeover of a major U.S. bank.
1987	Marshall & Illsley ($5.3 B)	Marine Corp ($4.3 B)	$560 MM common stock or cash	M&I intended to eliminate dilution through savings from in-market consolidation. Marine Corp accepted a lower $525 MM stock-for-stock bid from out-of-state white knight Banc One.
1987	Wilmington Trust ($2.8 B)	Delaware Trust ($1.1 B)	$190 MM common stock	Wilmington intended to eliminate dilution through savings from in-market consolidation. Delaware Trust accepted a comparably priced stock-for-stock bid from out-of-state white knight Meridian Bancorp.
1986	First Interstate ($52.5 B)	BankAmerica Corp ($107.2 B)	$3.2 B common & pref stock & conv notes	First Interstate withdrew bid following BankAmerica's sale of strategic assets and proposals to issue new capital.
1986	Fleet Financial Group ($10.0 B)	The Conifer Group ($3.9 B)	$540 MM common stock	Conifer accepted a higher $656 MM stock-for-stock bid from in-state white knight Bank of New England.
1985	Comerica ($9.5 B)	Michigan National ($6.8 B)	$350 MM common stock	Marine Midland, acting as white knight, made a stake-out equity infusion into Michigan National. Additional capital restructuring was undertaken to frustrate the proposed acquisition.
1985	Meridian Bancorp ($5.7 B)	Commonwealth ($1.3 B)	$113 MM common stock	Commonwealth accepted a higher $119 MM bid from Mellon Bank.
1984	Midlantic Banks ($6.4 B)	Statewide Bancorp ($0.8 B)	$70 MM stock or cash	Marine Midland, acting as white knight, made a stake-out equity infusion into Statewide.
1983	Norstar Bancorp ($3.6 B)	Security New York ($1.6 B)	$95 MM common stock & cash	Norstar acquired Security New York.
1983	Barnett Banks ($6.9 B)	Florida Coast ($0.6 B)	$75 MM cash	Barnett acquired Florida Coast.
1982	Huntington Bancshares ($3.6 B)	Union Commerce ($1.5 B)	$96 MM common stock & cash	Huntington Bancshares acquired Union Commerce following a tender offer. Subsequent asset quality and personnel problems made earning out dilution substantially more difficult than Huntington had anticipated.
1981	Southeast Banking Corp ($5.8 B)	Florida National Banks ($2.5 B)	$240 MM cash	Florida National struck a deferred merger agreement with Chemical New York.

Source: O'Rourke [1988], p. 18.

Regarding First Interstate's attempt to acquire BankAmerica, the fifth item in Table 25-1, which lists M&A activity by Salomon Brothers in 1987, is, "Defense against unsolicited offer (i.e., hostile takeover) by First Interstate Bankcorp." The client, of course, was BankAmerica. Thus, investment bankers, such as Salomon Brothers, work both sides of the merger street. On the one hand, they put deals together; and, on the other hand, they work to stop hostile deals from taking place. Since BankAmerica has been floundering on the financial seas for most of the 1980s, one has to wonder what its shareholders thought about the transfer of wealth to Salomon Brothers (and other expenses) to prevent the takeover. Recall that takeover evidence suggests takeovers are good for the economy because they entrust a company's assets to those who can manage them most efficiently. In the process, of course, they benefit the shareholders of the acquired firm (e.g., BankAmerica if the deal had been consummated).

Regarding BankAmerica's shareholders, it is interesting to note that as of March 31, 1987, the third, fifth, and sixth largest shareholders of BankAmerica were Citicorp with 3,133,495 shares, Wells Fargo Bank with 2,442,179, and Bankers Trust with 1,490,683.[5] Although some of these shares are likely to be "custodial" ones, others are not. Thus, as one money manager noted: "Banks do, in fact, vote the shares of other banks."[6] Wonder how Citicorp, Wells Fargo, and Bankers Trust voted on First Interstate's hostile takeover attempt of BankAmerica? Suppose Citicorp and/or Bankers Trust have their eyes on BankAmerica as a future takeover target. Would they want First Interstate to be in control? What if Wells Fargo wanted to keep First Interstate out of northern California? Intriguing questions. In searching for these and other answers, Kreuzer [1987] found some of the major holders of bank stocks unwilling to be interviewed, even off the record.

A COST-BENEFIT FRAMEWORK FOR ANALYZING BANK MERGERS AND ACQUISITIONS

According to Myers, "Mergers are tricky; the benefits and costs of proposed deals are not always obvious."[7] This section presents a framework for analyzing bank mergers and acquisitions. The focal point of the analysis is a cost-benefit rule that emphasizes determining values and premiums. This kind of analysis is important for both acquirers (bidders) and acquirees (targets).

The *benefit* of a bank merger can be stated as the difference between (1) the total present value of the merged banks and (2) the sum of their present values if they do not merge. This definition of benefit emphasizes the economic value of the bank merger with the value-estimation process being similar to a capital-budgeting problem in financial management. Letting V represent present value, the benefit, B, is

$$B = V_{Bank\ 1\&2} - V_{Bank\ 1} - V_{Bank\ 2} \qquad (25\text{-}1)$$

The fact that $V_{Bank\ 1\&2}$ is greater than the sum of $V_{Bank\ 1} + V_{Bank\ 2}$ is, of course, what makes mergers potentially worthwhile. The aspects of a proposed merger that make this *synergy* possible are explained later in the chapter.

[5] For these and other interesting facts about "Who Owns the Big Banks?", see Kreuzer [1987].

[6] *Ibid.*, p. 44. A bank holding company is permitted to own up to 5 percent of the stock of another bank under the Federal Reserve Board's Regulation Y, and with the Board's permission a BHC may go over this 5 percent limit.

[7] Myers [1976], p. 633. The framework developed in this chapter is based on Myers' work, pp. 633–645. Also see Brealey and Myers [1981], pp. 657–684.

Given Equation 25-1, the *cost* of the merger can be defined as the difference between the amount paid for Bank 2 and its value as a separate bank. Letting $P_{Bank\ 2}$ represent the payment to the owners of Bank 2, the cost of the merger, C, is

$$C = P_{Bank\ 2} - V_{Bank\ 2} \qquad (25\text{-}2)$$

Estimating C critically depends on how merger benefits are shared between the owners of Bank 1 and Bank 2 and upon how the merger is financed (e.g., cash or common stock or some combination of the two). From the point of view of the acquired firm, Bank 2, the cost represents the "premium" paid for the bank (i.e., rearranging Equation 25-2, $P_{Bank\ 2} = V_{Bank\ 2} + C$ and C is the premium). The managers of Bank 2 will, of course, want to maximize the premium, while the managers of Bank 1 will want to minimize the premium (i.e., the cost). The give-and-take of the negotiation process will determine the size of C.

Combining Equations 25-1 and 25-2, Bank 1 should merge with Bank 2 if the benefit exceeds the cost, that is,

$$B - C = (V_{Bank\ 1\&2} - V_{Bank\ 1} - V_{Bank\ 2}) - (P_{Bank\ 2} - V_{Bank\ 2}) > 0 \qquad (25\text{-}3)$$

Rearranging terms, the net gain $(B - C)$ also can be expressed as

$$B - C = V_{Bank\ 1\&2} - V_{Bank\ 1} - P_{Bank\ 2} > 0 \qquad (25\text{-}4)$$

In words, the net gain from the merger of Bank 1 with Bank 2 will be positive if the present value of the resulting entity, Bank 1&2, is greater than the present value of Bank 1 plus the price paid for Bank 2, where the price of Bank 2 is its present value plus the purchase premium. The net gain $(B - C)$ can be regarded as the net present value (NPV) of the merger. It is obvious from Equation 25-4 that the stockholders of Bank 1 gain when the strictly positive condition holds (i.e., $B - C > 0$).

A Numerical Example

The four inputs required to conduct the cost-benefit analysis just described are

1. $V_{Bank\ 1\&2} = $ *The Synergistic Present Value of the Combined Banks*
2. $V_{Bank\ 1} = $ *The Present Value of Bank 1*
3. $V_{Bank\ 2} = $ *The Present Value of Bank 2*
4. $C = $ *The Purchase Premium of Cost of the Merger*

Given these values, it is a simple matter to plug the figures into Equation 25-4 and crank out the answer. The "art" of the analysis lies in coming up with estimates of the four inputs. If all bank stocks were traded in efficient markets, the market values of the acquiring and acquired banks would be equal to their present values and half of the problem would be solved. However, the purchase premium and value of the resulting consolidated bank still would be unknown.

The process of the merger cost-benefit analysis can be illustrated mechanically using the constant-growth model as the value-determining mechanism. Although this approach is a simplistic representation of the real world, it provides some interesting insights. Later in this chapter more realism is introduced. The example is summarized in Table 25-3. In this hypothetical situation, Bank 1 sees Bank 2 as a desirable merger partner because it is a low-risk bank (as reflected by $k = .10$) with growth opportunities ($g = .05$ is judged to be low). The acquisition of Bank 2 is expected to result in a $1.00 increase in the dividend paid by Bank 1&2 and an increase of .01 in its growth rate. The synergistic effect or benefit of the merger (from Equation 25-1) is $20 million ($= 100 - 50 - 30$). Given that $V_{Bank\ 2} = $ $30 million, and assuming a cash

708 Part VII Special Banking Topics

TABLE 25-3 A Hypothetical Merger Cost-Benefit Analysis Using the Constant-Growth Model

Variable	Bank 1	Bank 2	Bank 1&2
Expected dividend (D_1)	$2.00	$1.50	$3.00
Capitalization rate (k)	.12	.10	.12
Growth rate (g)	.08	.05	.09
Share price $(P_0 = D_1/(k - g))$	$50	$30	$100
Number of shares outstanding (N)	1,000,000	1,000,000	1,000,000[a]
Total market value $(V = P_0 \times N)$	$50,000,000	$30,000,000	$100,000,000

Cost-Benefit Analysis[b]

$$B - C = (V_{Bank\ 1\&2} - V_{Bank\ 1} - V_{Bank\ 2}) - (P_{Bank\ 2} - V_{Bank\ 2}) > 0$$
$$= (100 - 50 - 30) - (P_{Bank\ 2} - 30) < 0$$
$$= 20 - P_{Bank\ 2} + 30 < 0$$
$$= 50 - P_{Bank\ 2} < 0$$

$\therefore$ Breakeven purchase price = 50
Breakeven cost or purchase premium = 50 − 30 = 20

[a] Assumes a cash transaction.
[b] Millions of dollars.

transaction, the breakeven purchase price to be paid by Bank 1 is $50 million. Alternatively, the breakeven cost of the merger (from Equation 25-2) is $20 million (i.e., this is the maximum premium that Bank 1 should be willing to pay for Bank 2). If it is assumed that the benefits of the mergers are shared equally by the owners of both banks, then the purchase price would be $40 million, with a cost or premium of $10 million.

The example in Table 25-1 assumes that the merger is a cash transaction. Suppose, however, that the owners of Bank 2 would prefer not to be faced with the payment of a capital-gains tax.[8] If the same effective purchase price was negotiated, then a stock exchange of four shares of Bank 1 for every five shares of Bank 2 would be transacted.[9] Thus, immediately after the exchange of stock, but before the synergy occurred, a shareholder with 100 shares of Bank 2 would find the value of his holdings increasing from $3,000 (= $30 × 100) to $4,000 (= $50 × 80). However, after the synergistic benefits are realized, the value of the investor's 80 shares of Bank 1&2 will be $4,480 (= $56 × 80).[10] If the market values of Bank 1 and Bank 2 *before* the merger are estimated correctly, then, because of the exchange of stock, part of the benefits generated by the merger will accrue to Bank 2's shareholders as they now own 44.4 percent (= 800,000/1,8000,000) of Bank 1&2. The true cost of the merger, therefore, cannot be determined from Equation 25-2. The relevant formula when the acquisition is financed by common stock is

$$C = \theta V_{Bank\ 1\&2} - V_{Bank\ 2} \tag{25-5}$$

where θ (theta) is the proportion of Bank 1&2 owned by Bank 2's shareholders. With $\theta = .444$ the cost of the merger is $14.4 million, that is,

$$C = .444(100) - 30 = 14.4$$

[8] This assumes, of course, that they purchased their shares for less than $40 per share.

[9] Note that $40 million in cash is equal to 800,000 shares valued at $50 per share.

[10] The per-share value of $56 is determined as follows. With 1.8 million shares outstanding after the exchange and with total expected dividend payments constant at $3 million, the expected per share dividend is $1.67. Other things equal, $P_0 = 1.67/(.12 - .09) = 55.67$ or approximately $56. Total value is unchanged at $100 million (≈$56 × 1.8 million).

Note that this is $4.4 million greater than the cost of the merger when it is a cash acquisition. The implication is that Bank 1's shareholders should be indifferent between an offering of $14.4 million in cash and a stock offering worth $10 million before the merger announcement. From Equation 25-5, it is clear that the larger the benefits generated by the merger, the greater is the cost of the 800,000-share offer.

In the case of an acquisition financed by common stock, the focal point of the cost-benefit calculation essentially is an attempt to estimate the market value of the acquired bank's shares *after* the merger is consummated and announced. When this occurs, the price of Bank 2's stock rises to roughly $56, a capital gain of $26 over the initial price of $30. Of course, this assumes that the market evaluates the benefits of the merger the same way that Bank 1 has (i.e., total benefits of $20 million). After the market has reacted to the merger, the cost of the acquisition is easy to determine:

$$C = \$55.67(800,000) - \$30,000,000$$
$$= \$44,536,000 - \$30,000,000$$
$$= \$14,536,000$$

This figure is approximately equal to the one of $14.4 million discussed above.

Estimating the Cost of a Bank Merger: Further Considerations

Two basic points have been established: (1) the cost of a merger is the difference between the price paid for the acquired bank and its value as a separate entity, and (2) the cost calculation is a relatively simple one when the merger is a cash transaction. However, suppose that the true or intrinsic value of the acquired bank is different from its market price or value around the time of the merger. Such a situation could arise because rumors of the impending merger drive the market price of the stock above its intrinsic or present value. In this case, Equation 25-2 would become

$$C = (P_{Bank\ 2} - MP_{Bank\ 2}) + (MP_{Bank} - V_{Bank\ 2}) \tag{25-6}$$

where *MP* stands for *market price*. The first term on the RHS of Equation 25-6 represents the premium paid over the market value of Bank 2, while the second term represents the difference between the market and intrinsic values. When $MP_{Bank\ 2} = V_{Bank\ 2}$, Equation 25-6 reduces to Equation 25-2. Suppose now, continuing with the example of the previous section, that rumors of the proposed merger force the price of Bank 2's stock to $35 per share from $30 per share. Using Equation 25-6, the cost of the merger, assuming a cash transaction, is $15 million, that is,

$$C = (45 - 35) + (35 - 30)$$
$$= 15$$

This cost is $5 million higher than the "rumorless" cost. Thus, a merger rumor is good news for the seller but bad news for the buyer.

Cash Versus Stock Financing

In a cash transaction, the payment to the owners of the acquired bank is independent of whether or not the merger is a synergistic one. In other words, since they receive their money up front, their reward does not depend on the success of the merger. Thus, in a cash transaction, the cost of the merger can be estimated using Equation 25-2, which does not include the benefits of the merger. In contrast, if common-stock financing is employed, the cost of the merger is determined by Equation 25-2, which includes the benefits, since they are shared with the owners of the acquired bank. Moreover, the greater the merger benefits are, the greater is the cost of stock financing, other things equal. One factor in favor of stock financing is that it lessens the effect of over- or underevaluation of the acquired bank. For example, suppose that Bank 1 was too generous with its 4-for-5 exchange with Bank 2. The market then will penalize the resulting bank and Bank 2's shareholders will have to absorb some of the penalty. In the opposite situation, that of underevaluation of Bank 2, the benefits will be spread over all the shareholders, much to the chagrin of Bank 1's shareholders but to the joy of Bank 2's shareholders. Thus, from the acquiring bank's point of view, a cash (stock) transaction is favored if the acquired bank is undervalued (overvalued). The opposite is true from the acquired bank's perspective.

ALTERNATIVE VALUATION METHODS

The cost-benefit analysis presented here has a present-value formation. While this is the conceptually correct method for determining value, in practice estimating future cash flows and the appropriate discount or capitalization rate are difficult tasks. As a result, bankers have developed "rules of thumb" designed to determine the "premium" that should be offered for a potential merger candidate's stock. The premium usually is expressed as a percentage of some base such as book value or earnings per share. The purpose of this section is to present, discuss, and illustrate the alternative methods for developing bank-merger terms.[11]

The Book-Value Approach

The book-value approach to determining merger premiums and exchange ratios has intuitive appeal because value commonly is thought of in book-value terms. Thus, for example, if Bank 1 has a book value of $100 and Bank 2 has a book value of $50 per share, then one share of Bank 1 would exchange for two shares of Bank 2, assuming no premium. If the shareholders of Bank 2 require a 100 percent premium on book value, the exchange ratio would be 1-for-1. The formula for determining book-to-book premiums is

$$\text{Premium} = \frac{B_{Bank\ 1}(ER) - B_{Bank\ 2}}{B_{Bank\ 2}} \qquad (25\text{-}7)$$

where

$B_{Bank\ 1}$ = book value per share of Bank 1 (the acquiring bank)

ER = the exchange ratio of Bank 1 for Bank 2

$B_{Bank\ 2}$ = the book value per share of Bank 2 (the acquired bank)

The numerator of the formula is simply the difference between book value received, $B_{Bank\ 1}(ER)$ and book value sold, $B_{Bank\ 2}$. To illustrate, using the previous data, the premium is

$$\frac{100(1) - 50}{50} = 1.0 \text{ or } 100\%$$

[11] The first three techniques presented in this section are those suggested by Darnell [1973].

Alternatively, given the premium (P), the exchange ratio is given by

$$ER = \frac{B_{Bank\ 2}(1 + P)}{B_{Bank\ 1}} \tag{25-8}$$

By definition, the book values used in Equations 25-7 and 25-8 are the differences between the banks' total assets and total liabilities divided by the number of shares outstanding. In practice, however, it is common to use *adjusted* book values to account for asset quality, loan-loss reserves, the maturity risk of fixed-rate assets, potential contingent liabilities, and other factors. From the balance-sheet identity $K = A - L$, where K represents unadjusted book value, and using asterisks $(*)$ to denote adjusted figures, adjusted book value is defined as $K^* = A^* - L^*$. To illustrate, suppose that Bank 2's unadjusted book value is $50 = 600 - 550$ ($ millions). However, if the bank has poor asset quality estimated at 10 and contingent liabilities also estimated to be 10, then $K^* = 590 - 560 = 30$. With 1,000,000 shares outstanding, the adjusted book value is $30 per share compared to the unadjusted figure of $50 per share. Adjusted book values are important because they represent lower bounds in the valuation process.

Koch and Baker [1983], in a survey of BHC acquisition activity in the Sixth Federal Reserve District, found that the price paid for an acquisition generally was substantially above the adjusted book value of the bank being acquired. They found the ratio of purchase price to book value ranged from 95.7 percent to 244 percent, with an average of 156.75 percent. Rounding this premium off to 1.5 times book and assuming book values of 100 and 50 (as above), then the exchange ratio (using Equation 25-8) would be $ER = 50(1 + 1.5)/100 = 125/100 = 1.25$. That is, 1.25 shares of Bank 1 are traded for each share of Bank 2.

The book-value approach is the most widely used method of calculating merger premiums. It focuses on the bid price of the acquiring bank relative to book value of the acquired bank. The advantages of the approach are (1) book values that are easily understood and calculated (like the payback period in capital-budgeting analysis), (2) book values are stable compared to market values, and (3) book values are isolated from the capriciousness of the stock market. The major disadvantage of the book-value approach is that it does not consider market value, which is the price that investors mainly should be concerned about. Since market value reflects the so-called going-concern value of a bank, it is perferred to book value, which is a liquidation or "dead-concern" concept.

Market-to-Book Premiums

Since investors should be concerned about market value, which is a reflection of a stock's present value, a natural approach is to look at market-to-book premiums. In this approach, the market price of the acquiring bank is substituted for its book value. Letting MP represent market price, Equation 25-7 becomes

$$Premium = \frac{MP_{Bank\ 1}(ER) - B_{Bank\ 2}}{B_{Bank\ 2}} \tag{25-9}$$

To illustrate, if $MP_{Bank\ 1} = \$80$ and $ER = 1$, then, continuing with the previous example, the premium is

$$P = \frac{80(1) - 50}{50} = .60 \text{ or } 60\%$$

In this approach, the ER formula is

$$ER = \frac{B_{Bank\ 2}(1 + P)}{MP_{Bank\ 1}} \tag{25-10}$$

Terry and Sexton [1975] claim that market-to-book premiums in the range of 150 to 200 percent are normal.

The difficulty with using market value is that only several hundred banks or BHCs have shares that are actively traded, which leaves roughly 14,000 banks whose stocks are traded in thin markets. Unless the acquiring bank is actively traded on at least a regional exchange, the market-to-book approach probably is unreliable. Since the prices of inactively traded shares tend to be biased upward, it is difficult to trade a substantial number of shares without a major price movement.

The EPS Approach

A third approach is to focus upon income-to-income premiums. This technique compares EPS received with EPS sold. The premium formula for this approach is

$$\text{Premium} = \frac{EPS_{Bank\ 1}(ER) - EPS_{Bank\ 2}}{EPS_{Bank\ 2}} \tag{25-11}$$

For example, with $EPS_{Bank\ 2} = \$4.00$, $EPS_{Bank\ 2} = \$2.00$, and $ER = \frac{1}{2}$, the premium is zero. The ER formula for this approach is

$$ER = \frac{EPS_{Bank\ 2}(1 + P)}{EPS_{Bank\ 1}} \tag{25-12}$$

Bank stock specialists who favor the EPS approach contend that the relative sizes of the banks' income streams are important in determining their value for exchange purposes. However, the earnings approach, which requires uniform accounting practices across banks, considers neither the *timing* nor the *riskiness* of the income stream. In addition, current EPS may not be a good indicator of a bank's future earning power.

Terry and Sexton [1975] have suggested using a weighted average of either historical or forecasted EPS in place of current earnings. The historical approach should be a better indication of past performance while the pro forma approach should be a better indicator of future performance. To illustrate the historical approach, consider the following weighting scheme and historical EPS data:

Period	Weight	Bank 1's EPS	Bank 2's EPS
t	.500	$5.00	$1.00
t − 1	.200	4.00	2.00
t − 2	.125	3.00	3.00
t − 3	.100	2.00	4.00
t − 4	.075	1.00	5.00
	1.000		

Bank 1's weighted average EPS is $3.95 while Bank 2's is $2.04. Given a premium of 100 precent, the exchange rate using the weighted averages is approximately 1.0 (i.e., 4.08/3.95). In contrast, if current earnings are used (i.e., period *t* EPSs), the ER is 0.4

(i.e., 2/5). On a *pro forma* basis, consider the following example:

Period	Weight	Bank 1's EPS	Bank 2's EPS
t + 1	.500	$5.25	$1.50
t + 2	.200	5.50	2.00
t + 3	.125	5.75	2.50
t + 4	.100	6.00	3.00
t + 5	.075	6.25	3.50
	1.000		

With a premium of 100 percent, the ER using the weighted averages, which are $5.52 for Bank 1 and $2.02 for Bank 2, is .73 (i.e., 4.04/5.52) while the ER using current EPSs is still 0.4. If the income-to-income approach is used, a weighted-average scheme is preferred; however, the basic criticisms of the EPS approach are not eliminated.

The Price-Earnings Approach

Price-earnings or P/E ratios reflect the value that a bank's earnings (EPS) command in the marketplace. This approach requires, of course, that the shares be traded in efficient markets, otherwise the P/E ratios will be unreliable. The premium formula in this situation is[12]

$$\text{Premium} = \frac{(MP/EPS)_{Bank\,1}(ER) - (MP/EPS)_{Bank\,2}}{(MP/EPS)_{Bank\,2}} \quad (25\text{-}13)$$

Solving for ER, the exchange ratio is given by

$$ER = \frac{(MP/EPS)_{Bank\,2}(1 + P)}{(MP/EPS)_{Bank\,1}} \quad (25\text{-}14)$$

If Bank 1 has a P/E ratio of 12.5 and Bank 2 has one of 7.5, then with a 1-for-1 ER the premium is 67 percent. If the premium is 100 percent, then ER would be 1.2 or six shares of Bank 1 for every five shares of Bank 2.

The Market-Value Approach

This approach focuses on relative market values or prices for determining premiums and exchange ratios. By deleting the EPSs from Equations 25-13 and 25-14, the premium and ER formulas are established. Like the P/E approach, this method requires that both the acquiring and the acquired banks have actively traded stocks.

The Core-Deposits Approach

This approach focuses on paying premiums for "core deposits" defined as demand deposits (excluding public funds), savings deposits, and fixed-rated time deposits. Banks with a substantial base of core deposits are desirable merger partners because of the relatively low cost of their funds. However, with the reduction of core deposits as Reg Q was phased out, such banks have become harder to find. This structural change in deposit composition tends to make interstate banking less attractive and therefore may reduce the demand for merger partners.

---

[12] The P/E ratio is written as *MP/EPS* in Equations 25-13 and 25-14, since *MP* was used for market price in Equations 25-9 and 25-10.

THE NATURE OF THE ACQUISITION PREMIUM

The acquisition premium is the difference between the acquisition cost and the appraised or fair market value of the acquired net worth, where net worth, of course, is simply the difference between the market value of *booked* assets and the market value of *booked* liabilities. (Since a "booked" item is simply one that appears on the balance sheet, an "unbooked" item does not appear on the balance sheet.) For example, if the acquisition cost is $10 million and the market value of net worth is estimated to be $7 million, the difference of $3 million is the acquisition premium. It represents the price paid for the unbooked intangible assets. If part (or all) of the acquisition premium can be allocated to specific, identifiable intangible assets, the premium is allocated based on the fair market value of those assets. The balance of the the premium, if any, is considered to be goodwill. Continuing with the previous example, if two-thirds of the premium of $3 million can be assigned to specific intangible assets (e.g., core deposits), then the premium is so allocated with the balance of $1 million going to goodwill. For tax purposes, the allocation of the premium between identifiable intangible assets and goodwill is crucial because the former is amortizable for tax purposes, and therefore affects cash flow, whereas the latter is not amortizable for tax purposes.

Intangible Assets and the Separability Issue

Intangible assets are defined as nonphysical assets that either involve rights, often ill-defined, against outsiders in general or represent anticipated future benefits that may not attach to a specific physical asset.[13] The words "ill-defined" and "may not attach" clearly indicate that some intangible assets may *not* be identifiable. Intangible assets are classified as either *identifiable* or *unidentifiable*. The financial assets held by a bank are intangible assets that are easily identified (e.g., loans and securities). Unidentifiable intangible assets are in the nature of goodwill/going-concern value and for banks include such factors as the quality of management, customer relations, market presence, charter value, the deposit-insurance guarantee, trade name, reputation, and so on. In the aggregate, these factors are, in essence, what the buyer receives for the acquisition premium. In banking, where entry and exit are tightly controlled, a bank's charter, which gives it the right to do business as a bank (i.e., to both accept demand deposits and make commercial loans), is by far its most important intangible asset. Moreover, today (and since 1933) it is virtually impossible to obtain a bank charter without simultaneously being accepted for deposit insurance.[14] Thus, the bank charter and deposit-insurance guarantee are inextricably interwoven into the fabric of U.S. banking. Since it is impossible to separate the two, they will be referred to together as the "charter-insurance contract" with "charter-insurance value" used to indicate the present value of the contract. The charter-insurance contract is a *perpetual* agreement that is terminated either by the issuer through a declaration of insolvency or by the issuer through merger with another bank.

With the charter-insurance contract as its foundation, a bank can build its market presence, establish customer relations, and hope to build a trade name and reputation associated with the commercial-banking industry. Since commercial banks are the

---

[13] Egginton [1982], p. 28.

[14] National banks are required to join the Federal Reserve System and all Fed member banks must be insured by the FDIC. Moreover, most states will *not* grant a charter without the FDIC's prior approval of insurance for the proposed bank.

kingpins of the financial-services industry in the United States, the charter-insurance contract represents a unique and scarce resource. Although the reregulated and more competitive environment of the financial-services industry in the 1980s has diminished some of the *monopoly power* of the charter-insurance contract, it still is a fundamental ingredient of the package of intangible assets held by an established bank. If this is true, then why should an institution that already has a charter-insurance contract want to acquire another one? The critical linkage is that the contract at the "retail level" (i.e., consumers and small businesses) is tied to a *local* geographic market. There are two ways to get into such markets: (1) by *de novo* entry or (2) by acquisition of an existing bank. The latter, of course, is more desirable from the potential entrant's perspective because it eliminates a competitor and starts the entrant at the asset and liability values of the acquired bank. In contrast, a *de novo* entrant starts from scratch and faces an additional competitor. (The Justice Department is assigned the task of protecting consumer interests from anticompetitive behavior in such markets.)

Studies of local banking markets indicate that such markets are more monopolistic than competitive.[15] The highly valued charter-insurance contract is due to the monopoly power found in these markets. Moreover, since monopoly power means control over price and the power to earn "excess" or "abnormal" profits, it represents a dominant market position. As Horngren [1984] states: "Goodwill is fundamentally the price paid for 'excess' or 'abnormal' earning power" (p. 555). Moreover, he notes that goodwill is originally generated internally and gives as an example: "... a happy combination of advertising, research, management talent, and timing [that] may give a particular company a dominant market position for which another company is willing to pay dearly. This ability to command a premium price for the *total business* is goodwill" (p. 555, emphasis added). For a bank, the *total business* is built on the foundation of the charter-insurance contract with customer relationships, reputation, and so on, providing the finishing touches.

To focus on the separability issue more closely, consider the following T-account or simple balance sheet, which lists both booked and unbooked assets for a hypothetical bank.

	Bank T-account	
	Tangible (real) assets Identifiable intangible (financial) assets	Liabilities
	- - - - - - - - - - - - - - - -	

Goodwill/
Going-concern
value (*en masse*)
	Unidentifiable intangible
	  assets:
	  Charter-insurance contract
	  Customer relationships
	  Reputation
	  Market presence
	  Trade name
	  etc.
		Net worth

The dashed line separates the booked assets from the unbooked ones. Unidentifiable intangible assets *en masse* account for the goodwill/going-concern value of the bank, where "going concern" (i.e., established business) refers to the ability of a

---

[15] See Heggestad [1979] for a summary of the literature.

TABLE 25-4   Purchase Accounting Versus Pooling-of-Interests Accounting

Pooling of Interests Criteria	Purchase vs. Pooling-of-Interests

Conditions for Pooling of Interest Method—(*All must be met or it is a "Purchase"*)
A. Combining Companies Criteria:
  1. Subsidiaries or divisions of another corporation (if within two years before the plan of combination is initiated) are not allowed.
  2. Each of the combining companies is *independent* of the other combining companies.
    a. Thus no more than 10 percent of any company can be held as intercorporate investments prior to the initiation of the plan of combination.
B. Combining of Interests Criteria:
  1. The combination must be completed within one year after the plan is initiated.
  2. After the date the plan of combination is initiated, the issuing corporation issues *voting common stock* in exchange for at least 90 percent of the *voting common stock* of another combining company.
  3. Ratio of interest or predecessor owners must remain the same.
  4. "Voting rights" must remain the same, thus no "voting trusts" are allowed.
  5. "Contingent buyouts" not allowed (e.g., based on future earnings of either parent or sub, etc.).
C. Absence of "Planned Transactions" Criteria:
  1. No future "buyout" agreements allowed (for example, through treasury stock, to dissident shareholders).
  2. The combined corporation cannot guarantee loans on stock issued in the combination, thus allowing some previous stock owners to get cash (in effect "sell") from their stock.
  3. The combined corporation does not intend to plan or dispose of a significant part of the assets of the combining companies within two years after combination, except for disposals of duplicated facilities.
	The fundamental differences between the pooling and purchase methods are:
	1. In a "purchase," the net income of a newly acquired subsidiary will be included in consolidated net income *from the date of acquisition.* In a "pooling," net income of the subsidiary for the *entire year* is added to consolidated net income regardless of the date of "pooling."
	2. In a "purchase", only retained earnings from the date of acquisition are included in consolidated retained earnings. In a "pooling" *all* acquired retained earnings of the subsidiary are added to consolidated retained earnings.
	3. In a "purchase," net book values of a newly acquired company are adjusted to acquisition date fair values. In a "pooling" net book values of the "pooled" companies remain the same.
	4. In a "purchase," any difference between the amount paid for the subsidiary and the fair value of assets acquired would result in positive and negative goodwill which should be amortized over a period not to exceed 40 years. In a "pooling" no consolidated goodwill is created.
	5. In a "purchase" where newly issued stock was exchanged for a newly purchased company, the shareholders' equity would be increased by the *fair market value* of the stock issued. In a pooling when new stock is issued for a newly acquired "pooled corporation," the shareholders' equity is increased by the total *net book value* of the newly pooled corporation.

Source: Koch and Baker [1983], p. 17.

business to generate earnings without interruption because of a change in ownership. Because of the perpetual nature of the charter-insurance contract and because the contract is the heart of the bank's goodwill/going-concern value, the *en masse* package of unidentifiable intangible assets must be regarded as having an indefinite life. Moreover, to attempt to dismantle the package would be self-destructive because the parts are so interwoven that only the main thread—the charter-insurance contract—would be likely to survive.

Focusing on the T-account, it is easy to see why depository institutions that have been technically insolvent have still traded for positive values in the marketplace.

That is, unbooked values have accounted for the difference. In particular, the deposit-insurance guarantee has been exploited. When the market value of an insured institution's net assets declines, the value of the charter-insurance contract takes on added value. Understanding the nature of unidentifiable intangible assets is the key to understanding the nature of the acquisition premium.

ACCOUNTING METHODS: PURCHASE VERSUS POOLING OF INTERESTS

The revaluation of assets, the recognition of intangibles, and the treatment of goodwill (discussed in the previous section) are considerations that arise from the use of "purchase accounting." There are two distinct methods used to account for business combinations: (1) pooling of interests, which does *not* revalue assets or liabilities and (2) purchase accounting, which does.[16] These two methods, however, are not alternatives and management is not free to select one over the other. Business combinations that do not meet the criteria for pooling-of-interest accounting must use the purchase method. The criteria for pooling of interests and the differences between purchase and pooling of interest are described in Table 25-4. Looking at acquisitions in the Sixth Federal Reserve District, Koch and Baker [1983] found that of the 139 combinations analyzed, 54 percent used pooling of interest and 46 used purchase accounting. They discovered that most of the acquisitions using the pooling method involved the establishment of a one-bank holding company (OBHC) through the purchase of a bank. The popularity of the OBHC (see Chapter 8) is linked to the pooling method because it permits a transfer of ownership from the bank to the holding company without the stockholders incurring any tax liability. Recall that tax considerations have been a major factor in the establishment of BHCs.

In a nutshell, the accounting criteria for pooling are (1) independence, (2) continuity of interest, and (3) absence of planned transactions. The advantages of pooling include simple accounting, stock-for-stock exchanges, and regulatory considerations. The disadvantages are possible difficulty of achievement, dilution, and the retention of historical values. The advantages of the purchase method are greater flexibility in negotiations, avoidance of ownership dilution, and the opportunity to revalue assets. The disadvantages are difficult accounting, the effects on future earnings, and the controversial handling of goodwill and other intangibles.

The effects of pooling versus purchase with respect to capital adequacy (as measured by the capital-to-asset ratio), EPS, ROA, and ROE are illustrated by the following example:[17]

	Buyer	Seller
Total assets	$1,000 M	$100 M
Total equity	$ 50 M	$ 8 M
Net income	$ 10 M	$ 1.2 M
Shares outstanding	5 M	
Earnings per share	$2.00	
Stock price	$10/share	

---

[16] The accounting standards have been spelled out in Accounting Principles Board (APB) Opinions No. 16 and No. 17 established in October 1970. In 1973, the APB was succeeded by the Financial Accounting Standards Board (FASB). The latest FASB pronouncement in this area is Statement No. 72, "Accounting for Certain Acquisitions of Banking or Thrift Institutions" [February 1983].

[17] *Planning Bank Mergers and Acquisitions*, Ernst & Whinney [1984], pp. 5–11.

The effects of pooling versus purchase on the relevant financials are:

| | | Buyer combined | |
	Buyer	Pooling	Purchase
Capital/assets	5%	5.3%	4.6%
EPS	$2.00	$1.75	$1.85
ROA	1%	1.02%	.85%
ROE	20%	19.2%	18.5%

The pooling transaction is based on an exchange of shares of 1.75 times book whereas the purchase transaction is based upon the buyer paying $14 per share for the selling corporation with the same exchange ratio (i.e., 1.75 times book). To get the financial statements for the buyer combined under the pooling method, simply add or pool the respective numbers together (i.e., Total Assets = $1,100, Capital = $58, Net Income = $11.2, and Share Outstanding = 6.4 = 5 + 1.75 × .8).[18] For the purchase transaction, the accounting is more complicated. In this example, it works out as total assets = $1,088, capital = $50, net income = $9.25, and shares outstanding = 5. The lower asset total is due to the revaluation to market values. The $12 million "hit" is amortized against earnings over a 16-year period. Thus, net income is reduced by $12/16 = $.75 million, hence the figure of $9.25 million. In the purchase transaction, the stock price stays as $10 per share whereas in the pooling method the dilution drops it to $9.06 = $58/6.4.

ALTERNATIVE ACQUISITION STRUCTURES

The BHC is the dominant organizational form in U.S. commercial banking. Therefore, not surprisingly, most bank mergers and acquisitions are made by BHCs or their subsidiaries. There are four basic alternative legal structures used to put deals together. First, a bank, either in the form of a BHC subsidiary or an independent organization, may acquire another bank, called the "target." The ruling federal agency in the case of an acquisition by a bank (as opposed to a BHC) is the agency with jurisdiction over the surviving or acquiring bank. The Fed has jurisdiction over all acquisitions made by a holding company. When a bank subsidiary acquires a target, it is called a *merger into a subsidiary bank*. If the holding company acquires the target, it is called a *direct acquisition*, which is the second major type of transaction. A third structure is one called a "phantom" or "triangular" bank merger. In this arrangement, a new phantom bank is chartered solely for the purpose of acquiring the target organization. Since there are three entities involved (i.e., the holding company, the phantom, and the target), the name "triangular" also is used. In this form, it is called a *forward* triangular merger because it is also possible to do a *reverse* triangular merger. The latter structure has the target bank acquiring the phantom organization, which maintains the charter of the target bank. The final major structural form is the merger or acquisition of two holding companies directly, with the target company disappearing and its subsidiaries becoming subsidiaries of the acquiring company. With the advent of regional interstate banking this type of transaction has become increasingly popular, a topic which we turn to next.

---

[18] These figures and the ones that follow are in millions.

REGIONAL INTERSTATE BANKING, NATIONWIDE BANKING, AND THE MERGER OF EQUALS

Regional interstate banking began, especially in the Southeast, through mergers of equals rather than by acquisitions. A merger of equals involves the *pooling* of bank assets, with little or no premium paid to the shareholders of the acquired bank/BHC. In an acquisition, the buyer usually decides management structure and other critical factors. To get such control, however, usually requires a premium of roughly 50 percent of the acquired bank's market value. Such acquisitions can be very costly in terms of cash, debt, or securities. Hence, in banking, large buyouts have been rare. Instead, regional banks have focused on avoiding high premiums by going the merger-of-equals route. Until recently mergers of equals have been rare because of potential antitrust problems in local markets within states. However, with the advent of regional reciprocity, wider geographic markets have been opened up.

The first merger agreement under the Southeast's interstate banking law was announced in July 1984 between Trust Company of Georgia, headquartered in Atlanta, and Sun Banks Inc. of Orlando, Florida. The merger, described as "a marriage of opposites," was billed as a "50–50 partnership" or merger of equals.[19] The merger was a surprise because of the different images and reputations of the companies. Trust Company was noted as a conservatively managed but highly profitable bank with strong ties to the Coca-Cola Company. In contrast, Sun Banks was an aggressive growth bank almost twice the size of Trust Company. Even more surprising was that the deal came down with Trust Company calling the shots. The new organization, which is headquartered in Atlanta and headed by Robert Strickland, the Chairman and CEO of Trust Company, is called SunTrust Banks Inc. Although the premerger organizations were clearly opposites, as partners they blend well with Trust Company supplying capital strength and quality management and Sun Banks providing access to some of the fastest growing banking markets in the United States. A profile of the banks and their markets at the time of the merger is shown in Table 25-5. The exchange ratio in the deal was one share of SunTrust for each share of Trust Company and 1.1 shares of SunTrust for each share of Sun Banks.

In another major consolidation in the Southeast, Citizens and Southern Georgia Corporation (C&S) acquired Landmark Banking Corporation of Florida in 1985. This combination, however, was not a merger of equals, as 19.7 million new common shares of C&S were exchanged for all 21.3 million common shares of Landmark. The exchange ratio was one share of Landmark for .9249 share of C&S. The pooling-of-interest method was used in this transaction. The financials on the deal, as of December 31, 1984, were as follows:

	C&S	Landmark	Combined
Assets	$8.0 billion	$3.8 billion	$11.8 billion
Loans	$5.1 billion	$2.2 billion	$7.2 billion
Deposits	$5.7 billion	$3.1 billion	$8.8 billion
Equity	$441 million	$224 million	$665 million
Net Income	$72.4 million	$34 million	$102.2 million
ROE	.1642	.1517	.1544
ROA	.0090	.0089	.0087
EM	18.14	16.96	17.74

---

[19] See Mantius [1984].

TABLE 25-5   The SunTrust Merger of Equals

	Sun Banks	Trust Company of Georgia
The Banks at a Glance (as of March 31, 1984)		
First quarter		
Net income	$19.2 million	$20.9 million
Return on assets	.87 percent	1.74 percent
Return on equity	14.9 percent	24.86 percent
Assets	$9.2 billion	$4.8 billion
Loans	$4.9 billion	$2.7 billion
Deposits	$7.7 billion	$3.7 billion
Capital as percent of assets	6.36 percent	8.26 percent[a]
Equity as percent of assets	5.8 percent	7.0 percent
Shares outstanding	22,010,000	29,945,000
Branch offices	297	169
Employees	9,000	5,000

Comparing the Banking Markets	Florida	Georgia
Deposits		
Banks	$62 billion	$31 billion
S&Ls	$62 billion	$14 billion
Credit Unions	$3 billion	$2.5 billion
Total	$127 billion	$47.5 billion
Number of Institutions		
Banks	287	385
With Billion-Plus Deposits	10	4
S&Ls	135	71
With Billion-Plus Deposits	16	3
Automated Teller Machines	2,500	750

[a] Excludes Coca-Cola Co. stock with a market value of $110 million.
Sources: Sun Banks and Trust Company of Georgia; Speer & Associates Inc.

The acquisition was expected to dilute C&S's earnings by about 10 percent in 1985 and to be a drag on earnings for the next five years. C&S's chief financial officer stated: "A 10 percent initial dilution for a market of this size and quality is acceptable. It is not a significant problem for us. Five years is the time frame we are projecting to earn it back."[20]

In addition to the new regional interstate banking activity, big combinations have taken place within states. For example, North Carolina's third- and fourth-largest BHCs merged in 1985 to become the second-largest BHC in the state with almost $10 billion in total assets. The merger called for First Union Corp. of Charlotte to exchange 1.54 shares for each share of Northwestern Financial Corp. of North Wilkesboro. The exchange rate represents a premium of roughly one-third of Northwestern's market value and twice its book value. On the day of the merger announcement, March 4, 1985, the ratio of market values declined from .84 to .70 as Northwestern's price shot up by 8 points to 55 following a brief suspension of trading earlier in the day. First Union's price was down $\frac{3}{4}$ on the day of the announcement.

Regional interstate banking has by no means been restricted to the southeastern part of the United States; it has been a nationwide phenomenon in the mid and late 1980s. Moreover, some of the deals have been coast-to-coast transactions between

[20] See Mantius [1985].

superregionals. For example, in 1987 Security Pacific of Los Angeles and Fleet Financial of Providence, R.Is., worked out a deal giving them greater presence in their home regions. Three emerging superregionals making substantial gains in size and geographic coverage in 1987 were Sovran Financial of Virginia, Banc One of Ohio, and PNC Financial Corporation of Pennsylvania. Finally, regarding nationwide banking, a number of states already permit nationwide entry without reciprocity including Alaska, Arizona, Maine, Nevada, Texas, and Utah. States permitting national entry only with reciprocity include California (in 1991), Kentucky, Louisiana, Michigan, New Jersey, New York, Ohio, Pennsylvania (in 1990), Rhode Island, Washington, and West Virginia.

CHAPTER SUMMARY

Technological developments, geographic deregulation, and the financial difficulties of energy and farm banks, and thrifts, have made the FSI fertile breeding ground for the merger mania of the 1980s. Moreover, until the stock market crash of October 19, 1987, merger activity in banking proceeded at a record pace in 1987. The once club-like atmosphere of banking has even been shaken by hostile takeovers. The laissez-faire approach to financial economics contends (and the evidence suggests) that takeovers are good for the economy because they assure that a firm's assets are controlled by managers who can use them most efficiently. The ability of financial-services firms, especially banks and thrifts, to expand and acquire other firms in the future will greatly depend on the strength of their capital positions, especially in light of the new and more stringent risk-based capital requirements scheduled for banks by 1992.

This chapter has focused on the mergers, restructuring, and battles for corporate control in banking. Along with some of the deals and deal makers of the 1980s, a framework for analyzing bank mergers and acquisitions has been presented. The basic condition for determining the net gain from a merger is to compare the synergistic value of the combined banks ($V_{Bank\ 1\&2}$) to the sum of the value of the acquiring bank ($V_{Bank\ 1}$) plus the price paid for the acquired bank ($P_{Bank\ 2}$). As expressed in Equation 25-4, the condition for a cash sale is

$$B - C = V_{Bank\ 1\&2} - V_{Bank\ 1} - P_{Bank\ 2} > 0$$

In a stock transaction, $P_{Bank\ 2}$ is replaced by $\theta V_{Bank\ 1\&2}$ (see Equation 25-5, p. 708). While the net-present-value approach is the conceptually correct method for evaluating bank mergers, in practice, rules of thumb have been developed because of the difficulty (or perhaps because of lack of skill or laziness) in estimating future cash flows and an appropriate discount rate. These rules of thumb are expressed in the various formulas for exchange ratios and premiums, which are based on such measures as book values, earnings per share, price-earnings ratios, and market values. Examples of the alternative valuation methods were presented and empirical findings regarding the prices of bank mergers and acquisitions were summarized.

LIST OF KEY WORDS AND CONCEPTS

Book-value approach
Cash versus stock financing (of merger)

Charter-deposit insurance contract
Core deposits
Corporate control and restructuring

EPS approach
Goodwill/going-concern value
Hostile takeovers
Intangible assets (identifiable versus
    unidentifiable)
Interstate banking
Investment bankers (M&A activity)
Laissez-faire
Market-to-book premiums
Merger of equals

Merger premium
Mergers and acquisitions (M&A)
Net gain or benefit (from merger)
Pooling-of-interest accounting
Price-earnings approach
Purchase accounting
Regional interstate banking
Separability issue
Takeovers

MATCHING QUIZ

Directions: Select the letter from the right-hand column that best matches the item in the left-hand column.

___ 1. National Westminster

___ 2. Laissez-faire

___ 3. Takeovers

___ 4. Hostile takeovers

___ 5. "Soft" view of corp.

___ 6. "Hard." view of corp.

___ 7. Corporate control

___ 8. Antitakeover measure

___ 9. Technology and deregulation

___ 10. Risk-based capital (1992)

___ 11. Big FSI deal maker

___ 12. Leading deal maker in 1987
       bank M&A

___ 13. First Interstate

___ 14. Bank of New York

___ 15. Handle takeovers and
       antitakeovers

___ 16. Cost-benefit rule

A. J. P. Morgan Securities

B. Deposit guarantee

C. Price of unbooked assets

D. Crude valuation model

E. Low cost funds

F. Potential M&A constraint

G. Often quoted M&A price

H. $2 + 2 = 5$

I. Hostile bidder for Irving

J. Hostile bidder for BoA

K. Investment bankers

L. Do they create value?

M. Freedom of choice/action

N. Even in banking

O. Loyalty/commitment

P. Bundle of contracts

Q. Takeover issue

___ 17. Synergy   R. New York

___ 18. Adjusted book value   S. Texas

___ 19. Price-to-book ratio   T. Assets revalued

___ 20. Core deposits   U. Second best price

___ 21. Constant-growth model   V. Poison pill

___ 22. Acquisition premium   W. Driving bank merger mania

___ 23. Intangible asset   X. Salomon Brothers

___ 24. Purchase method   Y. Paid three times book

___ 25. Reciprocal nationwide state   Z. Present-value rule

___ 26. Nonreciprocal nationwide
        state

REVIEW/DISCUSSION QUESTIONS

1. Do you have a "hard" or a "soft" view of what a corporation should be? How is this view likely to affect your opinion of takeovers? Why do laissez-faire financial economists favor takeovers? How are takeovers, corporate control, and restructuring related?

2. What does M&A stand for? Who are the M&A deal makers in banking and in the FSI? How do investment bankers attempt to prevent takeovers?

3. On April 21, 1987, the U.S. Supreme Court upheld an Indiana statute blocking hostile takeovers. Other states have enacted or attempted to enact similar laws. Should hostile takeovers be banned? Where do you stand? How does your position relate to your answer to the first question?

4. Why have hostile takeovers been rare in banking until the 1980s? Describe some of the deals and update Table 25-2.

5. Trace the etymology of the word *synergy* and explain its meaning in a merger context. In what elementary sense is the concept of *synergy* counterintuitive?

6. Why isn't an NPV framework widely used in analyzing bank mergers?

7. Use the constant-growth model to explain how the managers of acquiring and acquired banks might arrive at different present values for the acquired bank.

8. What are the interrelationships among TRICK, interstate banking, and consolidation of the depository-institutions industry?

9. Why do merger premiums exist? What, in effect, are the premiums paid for? Why don't these values normally appear on the balance sheet?

10. Explain the concepts of the charter insurance contract and charter insurance value.

11. Briefly explain the four alternative legal structures used to put mergers and acquisitions together.

PROBLEMS

1. Given the following chart and information, write a brief "event-study" report regarding Bank of New York's bid for Irving Bank.[1] On September 25, 1987, Bank of New York offered $80 per share, or $1.4 billion for Irving Bank. On November 20, 1987, Bank of New York revised its offer downward to $68 per share, or $1.2 billion. Play Paul Harvey and determine "the rest of the story" of this hostile-takeover attempt.

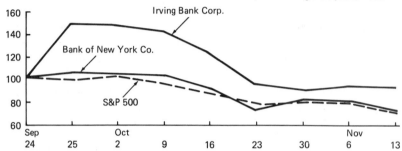

Sagging Prices Prompt Reduction in Irving Bid

Sept. 24 closing share prices = 100

2. Bank X, which is valued at $50 million, wants to merge with Bank Y. The managers of Bank X predict a synergistic value of $75 million for the resulting bank; what is the maximum cash price they should be willing to pay for Bank Y? What is the maximum price if stock financing is used and the shareholders of Bank Y end up with 10 percent of the shares of the new bank?

3. Given the following information determine the number of shares that you, as the buyer, would be willing to exchange for Bank A and Bank B in separate transactions.[2]

	Buyer	Bank A	Bank B
Deposits (000,000)	$750.9	$24.5	$21.7
Equity (000,000)	$62.3	$1.4	$2.1
Net operating income (000)	$7,125	$208	$223
Shares outstanding (000)	3,000	50	39
EPS	$2.37	$4.16	$5.72
Market price per share	$32	N.A.	N.A.
Book value per share	$20.77	$28.00	$53.85

4. Big Bank and Little Bank have the following financial characteristics:

	Big Bank	Little Bank
Total assets	$10,000 B	$100 M
Total equity	$550 M	$7 M
Net income	82.5 M	$1.2 M
Shares outstanding	12.2 M	.7 M
EPS	$6.76	$1.71
Stock price	$45/share	$10/share

---

[1] Chart courtesy of the *American Banker* [November 23, 1987], p. 1.

[2] These data are slightly adjusted figures from Terry and Sexton [1975], Table 2, p. 89.

Assuming an exchange ratio 1.5 times book, calculate the combined financials for a pooling and a purchase transaction ($15 paid per share) of Little Bank by Big Bank. In the purchase transaction, assume that a $20 million "hit" must be absorbed and that it is amortized against earnings over a ten-year period. Also compare the individual and combined financials with respect to ROE, ROA, and EM.

SELECTED REFERENCES

Beatty, Randolph P., Anthony M. Santomero, and Michael Smirlock. [1987]. *Bank Merger Premiums: Analysis and Evidence.* New York: Salomon Brothers Center/New York University.

Benston, George J., Gerald Hanweck, and David B. Humphrey. [1981]. "Scale Economies in Banking: Restructuring and Reassessment." Research Papers in Banking and Financial Economics (November). Board of Governors of the Federal Reserve System, Division of Research and Statistics, Washington, D.C.

Brealey, Richard, and Stewart Myers. [1981]. *Principles of Corporate Finance.* New York: McGraw-Hill, pp. 657–684.

Born, Jeffery A., Robert A. Eisenbeis, and Robert S. Harris. [1988]. "The Benefits of Geographical and Product Expansion in the Financial Services Industry." *Journal of Financial Services Research* (January), pp. 161–182.

Bullington, Robert A., and Arnold E. Jensen. [1981]. "Pricing a Bank." *The Bankers Magazine* (May–June), pp. 94–98.

Chaut, Robert, and Matthew A. Troxell. [1982]. "Some Effects of Purchase Accounting." *American Banker* (January 7).

Copeland, Thomas, and J. Fred Weston. [1988]. *Financial Theory and Corporate Policy.* Reading, MA: Addison-Wesley.

Darnell, Jerome C. [1973]. "Bank Mergers: Prices Paid to Marriage Partners." *Business Review*, Federal Reserve Bank of Philadelphia (July), pp. 16–25.

———. [1971]. "Merger Guidelines from the Phillipsburg National Bank Case." *The Magazine of Bank Administration* (June), pp. 30–33.

Egginton, Don A. [1982]. *Accounting for the Banker.* London: Longman Group Limited.

Garino, David P. [1981]. "Banks Grab Footholds Out of State, Betting that Restrictions Will End." *The Wall Street Journal* (February 2), Section 2, p. 35.

Heggestad, Arnold A. [1985]. "Fundamentals of Mergers and Acquisitions." In *Handbook for Banking Strategy*, R. C. Aspinwall and R. A. Eisenbeis, eds. New York: Wiley, pp. 703–724.

———. [1979]. "Market Structure, Competition, and Performance in Financial Industries: A Survey of Banking Studies." In *Issues in Financial Regulation*, Franklin R. Edwards, ed. New York: McGraw-Hill, pp. 449–490.

Helm, Leslie, and Judith H. Dobrzynski. [1988]. "Meet Mike Jensen, The Professor of Merger Mania." *Business Week* (February 8), pp. 66–67.

Jensen, Michael C. [1987]. "The Takeover Controversy: Analysis and Evidence." *Midland Corporate Finance Journal* (September), pp. 6–32.

Horngren, Charles. [1984]. *Introduction to Financial Accounting.* Englewood Cliffs, NJ: Prentice-Hall.

"Interstate Banking: Mergers and Acquisitions in the Southeast under Regional Reciprocity." [1984], New York: First Boston Research (March 21).

Koch, Donald L., and Robert M. Baker. [1983]. "Purchase Accounting and the Quality of Bank Earnings." Federal Reserve Bank of Atlanta *Economic Review* (April), pp. 14–22.

Koltveit, James M. [1983]. *Accounting for Banks.* New York: Matthew Bender.

Kreuzer, Teresa. [1987]. "Who Owns the Big Banks?" *Bankers Monthly* (August), pp. 43–46.

Mantius, Peter. [1985]. "Merger to Dilute C&S Profits." *The Atlanta Journal Constitution* (February 27), pp. 1-C, 3-C.

————. [1984]. "A Marriage of Opposites." *The Atlanta Journal Constitution* (July 8), pp. 1-E, 6-E.

Martin, Michael J. [1975]. "Bank Holding Company Acquisitions of Mortgage Banking Firms." *Mergers & Acquisitions* (Fall), pp. 19–26.

Matthews, Gordon. [1988]. "Despite the Crash, 1987 Was a Year for Mergers." *American Banker* (January 12), pp. 1, 14.

Meeks, G. [1977]. *Disappointing Marriage: A Study of the Gains from Merger.* London: Cambridge University Press.

Myers, Stewart C. [1976]. "Introduction: A Framework for Evaluating Mergers." In *Modern Developments in Financial Management*, Stewart C. Myers, ed. New York: Praeger, pp. 633–645.

Neely, Walter P. [1987]. "Banking Acquisitions: Acquirer and Target Shareholder Returns." *Financial Management* (Winter), pp. 66–74.

O'Rourke, Daniel. [198]. "Bank Versus Bank: The Hostile Takeover (and How to Fight It)," *Bank Administration* (January), pp. 16–19.

Planning Bank Mergers and Acquisitions. [1984]. Visual Aid Supplement. New York: Ernst & Whinney.

Poulos, Nick. [1981]. "Top Atlanta Banks 'Well-Positioned'." *The Atlanta Constitution*, (January 30), p. 14-D.

Pound, John, and Gregg Jarrel. [1987]. "Hostile Takeovers and the Regulatory Dilemma: Twenty-Five Years of Debate." *Midland Corporate Finance Journal* (Summer), pp. 224–38.

Rappaport, Alfred. [1979]. "Do You Know the Value of Your Company?" *Merger & Acquisitions* (Spring), pp. 12–17.

Roll, Richard. [1986]. "The Hubris Hypothesis of Corporate Takeover," *Journal of Business* (April), pp. 197–216.

Ross, Stephen A., and Randolph W. Westerfield. [1988]. *Corporate Finance.* St. Louis: Times Mirror/Mosby Publishing.

Stern, Joel. [1987]. "The Future of Commercial Banking: A Roundtable Discussion," *Midland Corporate Finance Journal* (Fall), pp. 22–49.

Terry, Ronald, and Merrill C. Sexton. [1975]. "Valuation of Banks in Acquisition." *The Bankers Magazine* (Summer), pp. 86–89.

Varian, Hal R. [1988]. "Symposium on Mergers," *Journal of Economic Perspectives* (Winter), pp. 3–82.

PART VIII

EPILOGUE

An epilogue is a concluding section to round off the design of a literary work. Most textbooks stop abruptly with a "special topics" section, which leaves the student hanging—to twist slowly in the academic winds. To remedy this shortcoming, I present this epilogue. Its purpose is to bring it all together by showing you where you have been and what the major concepts are for the financial management of commercial banks in the financial-services industry. Whether or not you read the entire book, I recommend you begin *and* end your study of commercial banking with this epilogue.

Overview and Summary of Commercial Bank Financial Management in the Financial-Services Industry

A COMPACT VIEW OF THE CONTENTS

The typical contents section of a textbook extends for too many pages to give a compact overview of its subject matter. To remedy this, Table 26-1 presents a compact summary of the contents of this book. Excluding this epilogue, the book has seven parts consisting of 25 chapters. The purpose of this final word is to attempt to bring it all together by briefly summarizing each chapter, and by highlighting the key ideas or concepts in each chapter.

PART ONE. INTRODUCTION TO BANKING AND THE FINANCIAL-SERVICES INDUSTRY

Chapter 1. Banking in the FSI

We began by asking the question: *Are banks special?* In today's environment of the *financial-services industry* (FSI), we are hard-pressed to put on our sweater and slippers, and sing to commercial banks, à la PBS's Mr. Rogers, "You are special." Too many *players* are doing what banks do (and in many cases doing it well) for anyone beyond the mental age of Mr. Roger's typical viewer to believe the *specialness argument*. Accordingly, the landscape of the FSI is dotted with many players, who, like this epilogue, are coming together. Although it is unlikely the players will ever be completely homogenized, we can think of them as falling under the generic term of *financial-services firm* (FSF). Nevertheless, we can expect the separation of commercial and investment banking, as called for by the *Glass-Steagall Act* of 1933, to continue to be dismantled. In the process, we will most likely continue to see a blurring of the distinction between banking and commerce.

The driving forces of change in the FSI are captured by *TRICK* and summarized in our *model of change*:

$$\text{TRICK} + \text{Rational Self-Interest} = \text{Financial Innovation} \tag{26-1}$$

TABLE 26-1   Contents of Commercial Bank Financial Management in the Financial-Services Industry

The components of TRICK are T = Technology, R = Reregulation, I = Interest-rate risk, C = Customers/Competition, and K = Kapital adequacy. Rational self-interest is manifested in terms of pursuit of profitable opportunities. A financial innovation is the profitable application of some invention. The combination of TRICK plus rational self-interest, in a laissez-faire environment, generates financial innovation. Since the end of World War II and especially in the 1980s, the various innovations in the FSI have lead to its "-ization" in terms of institutional*ization*, global*ization*, and securit*ization*.

Key Concepts in Chapter 1

      Financial-services firm (FSF)
      Financial-services industry (FSI)
      Glass–Steagall Act
      Model of charge: TRICK + Rational Self-Interest = Innovation
      Specialness argument

Chapter 2. The Banks of Banking: Consumer, Corporate, and Investment

Armed with the knowledge that banks are not quite as *special* as some people would have us believe, we focus on the question: *What is a bank?* We begin with the *etymology* of the word *bank* and then move to three basic ways of viewing a bank: (1) as a *balance sheet* or *portfolio*, (2) as a *regulated firm*, (3) as a *deliverer of financial services*. The combination of the first two ideas suggests that banks face a special constrained-optimization problem. This theme is carried throughout the book by persistent emphasis on the balance sheet or portfolio aspects of banks as regulated firms. The last notion, which generates the subtitle for the chapter, emphasizes the three basic segments or markets in which major banks operate: *consumer*, *corporate*, and *investment*. The players in the FSI face different market opportunities and different regulatory constraints. The latter has led the more regulated players to call for a "level-playing field."

Key Concepts in Chapter 2

> Balance-sheet or portfolio concept
> Deliverer of financial services (consumer, corporate, and investment)
> Regulated firm (regulation is what makes banks "special")

PART THREE. BANKING THEORY AND FINANCIAL MANAGEMENT

Chapter 3. The Fundamentals of Financial Management

Rather than rehash the basic concepts and ideas taught in the first course in finance, this chapter focuses on modern finance in the real world with particular emphasis on its application to banks and the other players in the FSI. The *economic model of the firm*, as opposed to the accounting one, and the concept of *economic value added* (EVA) are stressed. These notions are viewed in the context of *efficient markets* in which "lead steers" dominate the market, and therefore *corporate communications* should attempt to reach the *lead steers*. Coverage of the stock market crash of October 19, 1987, is included. Value maximization and *alternative managerial motives* are addressed and the *economics of executive compensation* is introduced. The chapter concludes with a look at the six fundamental building blocks of finance as captured in the *hexagram of financial management*. Specifically, the six key ideas are (1) valuation rules (NPV and value additivity), (2) efficient-market theory, (3) portfolio theory, (4) capital asset pricing theory, (5) option pricing theory, and (6) agency theory.

Key Concepts in Chapter 3

> Corporate-communications
> Economic model of the firm
> Economic value added (EVA)
> Efficient markets
> Executive compensation
> Hexagram of financial management
> Lead steers

Chapter 4. Banking and Finance Theory and Models of the Banking Firm

The fundamental question addressed here is: Why do financial intermediaries, such as banks, exist? In a world of *perfect and complete markets*, financial intermediaries would not exist. From this abstraction, we can focus on *market imperfections* and *incompleteness* as reasons for why financial intermediaries exist. The chapter begins with a look at the *consumption-savings decision* and how *financial markets* help to smooth spending patterns. Banking in the theory of finance and *models of the banking firm* are highlighted, including a new approach of viewing banks as *delegated monitors*.

Key Concepts in Chapter 4

Banking in the theory of finance
Delegated monitoring
Financial markets (role of)
Market imperfections and incompleteness
Models of the banking firm
Perfect capital market (assumptions)

PART THREE. FINANCIAL INNOVATION AND THE ENVIRONMENT OF THE FSI

Chapter 5. Financial Innovation and the Institutions, Markets, and Instruments of the FSI

The *process of financial innovation* as captured by our *model of change* (Equation 26-1 on page 729) is applied in this chapter to explain the innovative developments in the institutions, markets, and instruments of the FSI. Some *preliminary distinctions* in the diffusion of financial innovations focus on (1) invention versus innovation, (2) induced versus autonomous innovation, and (3) market-induced versus regulatory-induced innovations. Given this foundation, the various institutions, markets, and instruments of the FSI are described.

Key Concepts in Chapter 5

Financial institutions
Financial instruments
Financial markets
Induced innovation (market versus regulatory)
Invention
Innovation
Model of change: TRICK + Rational Self-Interest = Innovation
Process (diffusion) of financial innovation

Chapter 6. Bank Technological Innovation, the Payments System, and Information Processing

The most persistent force of change in the FSI is *technology*. This chapter begins with a look at the importance of *technology in banking*. On most report cards, banking does not receive a very high grade (e.g., C-) for innovative technology. The sage's comment is: "Another hole in the wall, the ATM." This chapter builds on the process of financial innovation established in the previous chapter and applies it to technology in banking and the *diffusion of electronic banking*. The evolution of money and the development of *payments systems* is the focal point of the diffusion process. The basic components and issues of electronic banking are analyzed including *automated clearing houses* (ACHs), *automated teller machines* (ATMs), and *point-of-sale systems* (POS). In addition, *telephone/home banking* and *videotex* are explored.

Key Concepts in Chapter 6

> Automated clearing houses (ACHs)
> Automated teller machines (ATMs)
> Diffusion of electronic banking
> Payments systems
> Point-of-sale systems (POS)
> Technology in banking

Chapter 7. The Theory, Objectives, and Agencies of Bank Regulation

The regulatory objectives of *safety*, *stability*, and a *competitive financial structure* are conflicting ones. Beginning with the Fed's shift to a monetary aggregates target in 1978, we have witnessed a series of events designed to make the financial system more competitive (e.g., *DIDMCA* of 1982, the *Garn–St Germain* Act of 1982, and the *Competitive Equality Banking* Act of 1987). The combination of *reregulation* and the other forces of change as captured by TRICK have made the financial system more competitive, at the expense of reduced safety and stability. Three layers of *financial-services competition* are captured by modeling the *confidence function*, the *convenience function*, and the *competition for regulatory services*. The regulatory players (agencies) engaged in this competition are the Fed, the OCC, the FDIC, the SEC, and the various state banking agencies. The competition among regulators and regulatees is best captured by the notion of the *regulatory dialectic* or *struggle model*. Within this context, the concepts of *economies of scope* and *structural arbitrage* are explained. The details of bank reregulation in the 1980s are presented in the appendix of this chapter.

Key Concepts in Chapter 7

> Agencies of bank regulation (e.g., Fed, OCC, FDIC.)
> Confidence function
> Convenience function
> Competition for regulatory services
> Deposit insurance
> Economies of scope
> Financial-services competition (layers)
> Objectives of bank regulation (e.g., safety versus competition)
> Regulatory dialectic (struggle model)
> Reregulation (concept and acts, e.g., DIDMCA)
> Structural arbitrage

Chapter 8. Regulatory Restrictions, Financial Innovation, and Deposit Insurance

The *bank holding company* (BHC), the payment of *implicit interest*, and exploitation of *deposit-insurance subsidies* have been, and still are, three practices common to banking. This chapter focuses on how these phenomena were induced, in part, by *regulatory restrictions*. As such, each of these developments can be viewed as attempts to circumvent regulatory restrictions, or as regulatory-induced innovations. In the process, the details of (1) the BHC movement and BHC regulation are explored, (2) the payment of implicit interest analyzed, and (3) the background, issues, and reform of deposit insurance discussed. The FDIC's innovative use of *warrants* in bailing out failed banks is analyzed and discussed in the appendix to the chapter.

Key Concepts in Chapter 8

> Bank holding company (organizational structure and regulation of)
> Deposit insurance
> Implicit interest
> Regulatory restrictions (e.g., geographic)
> Warrants (and FDIC bailouts)

Chapter 9. Interest Rates, Asset Prices, and the Interest-Rate Environment: Theories, Conventions, and Innovations

This chapter focuses on the theories, conventions, and innovations related to the pricing of *fixed-income securities* and the study of *interest rates*. The major theories presented are the *term* and *risk structures* of interest rates, *duration* analysis, the *Fisher effect*, and an overall theory of *interest-rate determination*. The pricing conventions associated with T-bills and CDs are described. The concepts of a *yield curve* and the *interest-rate cycle*, and their relevancy for the management of financial institutions, are highlighted. The developments of duration analysis and *derivative securities* are the two innovations stressed in this chapter.

Key Concepts in Chapter 9

> Default-risk structure of interest rates
> Derivative securities
> Duration
> Fisher effect
> Fixed-income securities
> Interest-rate theory and cycle
> Pure-expectations theory (PET)
> Term structure of interest rates
> Yield curve

PART FOUR. THE BIG PICTURE: PERFORMANCE AND COST ANALYSES, STRATEGIC PLANNING, AND ASSET-LIABILITY MANAGEMENT

Chapter 10. The Return-on-Equity Model: Performance and Decomposition Analysis

This chapter focuses on the *return-on-equity (ROE) model*, an accounting framework, for analyzing bank/BHC (or any firm's) performance. Although market prices and returns (e.g., *price-earnings* or P/E ratios) are better gauges of overall performance, such data simply are not available for over 14,000 banking firms. Moreover, since stock price data do not permit analysts to investigate the causes of good or bad performance, a need for such an analytical framework exists. ROE *decomposition analysis* is presented as such a method. The basic model is

$$ROE = ROA \times EM = PM \times AU \times EM \qquad (26\text{-}2)$$

where ROA = return on assets, EM = equity multiplier, PM = profit margin, and AU = asset utilization. This preliminary analysis permits you to attribute ROE performance to profit margin, asset efficiency, or leverage, or some combination of the three. To determine more precise attributes of good or bad performance requires the more detailed decomposition analysis described in the chapter. In the process of doing this "Sherlock Holmes" work, one gets a firm understanding of the how to get to a bank's bottom line, and what determines it. Using both individual and industry data, the concepts and components of ROE decomposition analysis are illustrated with numerous examples for various types of banks. The chapter contains two appendices. In Appendix A, detailed financial data for insured commercial banks for the years 1981 through 1987 are presented; in Appendix B, the student gets to apply the ROE framework to the case of Continental Illinois.

Key Concepts in Chapter 10

> Decomposition analysis
> Equity multiplier (leverage)
> Performance measurement
> Ratio analysis
> Return on assets (ROA)
> ROE model

Chapter 11. Bank Costs: Functions, Economies, Controls, and Analysis

One of the key characteristics of high-performance banks is the ability to *control expenses*. This chapter focuses on bank *operating costs* in terms of functional relationships, economies of scale and scope, empirical evidence, and control measures. Both theoretical and practical aspects of banking costs are studied. Regarding public policy, the existing evidence suggests the removal of geographic restrictions will not lead to a *natural monopoly* in banking (i.e., *economies of scale* are exhausted quickly in banking). The evidence regarding product restrictions and *economies of scope* is less clear. On balance, shareholders will benefit the most from managers who focus on the scope and efficiency of production processes and cost functions, rather than on the size of the organization, other things equal. The Tax Reform Act of 1986 and its effects on commercial banks is covered in the appendix to this chapter.

Key Concepts in Chapter 11

> Average total cost
> Cost complementarities, dispersion, and functions
> Economies of scale
> Economies of scope
> Factors of production and input prices
> Functional cost analysis (FCA)
> Production functions and returns to scale
> Ray average cost
> Technological change (shift parameter)

Chapter 12. Bank Strategic Planning in the Financial-Services Industry

Where is the bank today? Where is the bank going? And how is the bank going to get there? Strategic planners must ask and answer these three questions. For banks/BHCs in the financial-services industry, this chapter focuses on the issues surrounding these three questions for money-center, regional, and community banks. The thrust of strategic planning is *allowing for alternative futures*. Analysis of the components of TRICK provides a framework for strategic planning. The starting point is making reasonable *assumptions* regarding each of the *components of TRICK*. The planning process is designed to highlight an organization's *strengths, weaknesses, opportunities*, and *threats*, or *SWOT analysis*. Financial innovation provides one way to SWOT the components of TRICK. Banc One of Columbus, Ohio, and Citicorp are regarded by many analysts as examples of innovative banking companies. Most bankers regard providing a competitive return on equity and assets as the number one objective of strategic planning.

Key Concepts in Chapter 12

> Chief executive officer
> Financial-services industry (FSI)
> Innovation
> Railroad syndrome
> ROE and ROA
> Strategic planning
> SWOT analysis
> TRICK

Chapter 13. Asset-Liability Management (ALM)

Asset-liability management (ALM) can be viewed as the first step in implementing a bank's strategic plan. ALM, which has a *short-term horizon* of less than one year, is designed to allow for alternative *liquidity* and *interest-rate* scenarios over the short run. This chapter focuses on ALM from a balance-sheet perspective, including the management of off-balance-sheet activities. From this vantage, ALM is the key plan driving a bank's financial performance. Following an overview and historical perspective on ALM, the amount of repricing control ALM managers actually have is shown to be limited. The focal variable of ALM is net interest margin (NIM), the difference between interest income and interest expense adjusted by earning assets. The decomposition of NIM is an important analytical device. *Net interest income* (NII) has the enormous task of having to cover a bank's provision for loan losses, its "burden," its taxes, its dividend payment, and its internal capital generation. Day-to-day ALM usually focuses on a bank's *dollar gap*, defined as the difference between its *rate-sensitive assets* (RSA) and its *rate-sensitive liabilities* (RSL), measured over various relevant time horizons such as one, three, or six months. The principal concern of this daily/weekly ALM routine is the *sensitivity* of the bank's net interest income to changes in interest rates, given its GAP position. The key formula is

$$\Delta NII = \Delta r \times GAP \tag{26-3}$$

where *NII* is the change in NII and *r* captures the change in the relevant interest rates. Given a bank's gap position, which can be positive, negative, or zero, the product of *r* and *GAP* determines the change in net interest income. Combinations of interest-rate changes and GAP positions, such as a negative GAP when interest rates are rising, that produce negative changes in net interest income are to be avoided. Various methods and practices of ALM are covered in the chapter.

Key Concepts in Chapter 13

>   Asset-liability management (ALM)
>   Asset-liability-management committee (ALCO)
>   "Burden" (= noninterest income − noninterest expense)
>   Dollar GAP (= *RSA* − *RSL*)
>   GAP management
>   Net interest income (NII)
>   Net interest margin (NIM)
>   Rate-sensitive asset (RSA)
>   Rate-sensitive liability (RSL)
>   Rate, volume, and mix (effects of)

PART FIVE. MANAGEMENT OF BANK PORTFOLIO RISKS: LIQUIDITY, INTEREST RATE, CREDIT, AND OFF-BALANCE SHEET

Chapter 14. An Overview of Bank Risk Management

Risk management is the heart of bank financial management. This chapter provides an overview of this topic as an introduction to the financial management of the key risks in banking: liquidity, credit, interest rate, and off-balance sheet. Two key concepts in the chapter are the notions of *risk* and *portfolio*. A bank's balance sheet (portfolio) generates a combination of risks reflected by its liquidity, interest-rate sensitivity, asset quality, and contingent claims. The focal descriptive device is a *comprehensive framework* that catalogs the critical risks faced by bank holding companies and their subsidiaries. A simple graphical analysis is used to illustrate bank portfolio allocation and the technique of risk management.

Key Concepts in Chapter 14

>   Balance sheet (portfolio)
>   Bank holding company (BHC)
>   Credit risk
>   Etymology (of risk and portfolio)
>   Interest-rate risk
>   Liquidity risk
>   Off-balance-sheet activities (definition, types, and risk of)
>   Portfolio allocation
>   Risk and risk management
>   Subsidiary risk

Chapter 15. Management of Liquidity Risk: Stored Liquidity Versus Liability Management

Until Continental Illinois' *liquidity crisis* in the spring of 1984, many banks, especially the largest ones, had taken *liquidity* as a nonrisk under the mistaken assumption that liquidity could always be purchased in the marketplace. Needless to say, Continental's experience changed that outlook. This chapter focuses on liquidity risk and its management. The basic distinction, as the subtitle of the chapter indicates, is between *liquidity stored in the balance sheet* versus liquidity purchased in the marketplace, or *liability management*. The trade-offs, functions, and measurement of bank liquidity, whether stored or purchased, are emphasized. In addition, the theory and practice of liability management are highlighted.

Key Concepts in Chapter 15

> Continental Illinois
> Core deposits
> Customer relationships
> Deposit interest costs
> Large-liability dependence (LLD)
> Liability management (LM and its three faces)
> Liquidity and liquidity crisis
> Regulatory restrictions
> Stored liquidity
> Too-big-to-fail doctrine
> Unexpected change
> Volatile liabilities

Chapter 16. Characteristics and Risk Management of the Investment Portfolio

The traditional role of a bank's investment portfolio is to generate income and to provide a liquidity reserve. In addition, prior to the *Tax Reform Act of 1986*, the *municipal bond* component of a bank's investment portfolio provided an important vehicle for *tax sheltering income*. This chapter focuses on the characteristics and risk management of bank investments, defined as securities issued by the U.S. Treasury, by agencies of the Federal government, and by state and local governments. Since many banks do not actively manage their investments, a distinction between *active* and *passive* investment management is made. Evidence of active investment management and the *market structures of active investment management* (i.e., brokered trading, dealer trading, and market making) are presented. Following a description of the investment portfolio of insured commercial banks, the risk–return characteristics of bank investment securities are analyzed. The portfolio of municipal securities is analyzed based on the Tax Reform Act of 1986 with emphasis on calculating *tax-equivalent yields*. The chapter concludes with a look at a suggested bank *investment policy*.

Key Concepts in Chapter 16

> Active versus passive investment management
> Brokered trading
> Dealer trading
> Investment policy
> Interaction between interest-rate risk and liquidity risk
> Market making
> Market structures of active investment management
> Municipal obligations
> Portfolio composition (and bank size)

Tax-equivalent yield
Tax Reform Act of 1986
Trading-account activities
Unanticipated inflation

Chapter 17. Managing Interest-Rate Risk: Duration, Futures, Swaps, and Options

This chapter focuses on four techniques for managing interest-rate risk: (1) duration analysis, (2) interest-rate swaps, (3) interest-rate or financial futures, and (4) financial options. Since the business of banking involves "betting" on interest-rate movements, these techniques can be used to hedge such bets. The concepts of *hedging* and speculating are introduced followed by the distinction between a microhedge and a macrohedge. A *macrohedge* is designed to protect ("immunize") a bank's entire balance sheet (as measured by its net worth) from unexpected changes in interest rates. In contrast, a *microhedge* protects only a particular asset within the portfolio. *Duration analysis* is presented as a tool for managing interest-rate risk and for predicting interest-sensitive cash flows. Defined as the *effective time until repricing*, duration is a more precise measure of maturity or interest-rate risk. *Swap finance* and the market for interest-rate swaps are analyzed, followed by discussions of the use of *financial futures* and *options* in managing interest-rate risk. Appendix A shows the duration linkage between a change in value and a change in interest rates.

Key Concepts in Chapter 18

Duration
Financial futures
Financial options
Hedging versus speculating
Interest-rate risk
Macrohedge versus microhedge
Pure-discount (zero-coupon) securities
Swap finance and interest-rate swaps

Chapter 18. Management of Credit Risk I: Concepts, Models, and Credit Analysis

In Chapter 1, we began with the question: Are banks special? In this chapter, we begin with the question: Are bank loans special? Our answer in this chapter is: Yes, bank loans are special. *Delegated monitoring* and the *bank–customer relationship* are seen as reasons for this specialness. *Agency theory* and delegated monitoring are used to model the credit decision-making process. Lenders have to grapple with the problems of *asymmetric information* and borrower *dishonesty*. A model of the *credit-risk function* is presented and the *five Cs* of creditworthiness analyzed. Sources of *loan repayment* (*cash flow* is the name of the game) are analyzed and the usefulness of *accounting ratios* and *classification models* studied.

Key Concepts in Chapter 18

Accounting ratios
Agency theory
Asymmetric information
Bank–customer relationship

Classification models (credit scoring)
Credit risk and analysis
Delegated monitoring
Five Cs of creditworthiness
Sources of loan repayment (e.g., cash flow)

Chapter 19. Management of Credit Risk II:
The Diversification and Pricing of Risk

The *raison d'être* of portfolio theory is *diversification*. This chapter begins with a look at how two big unit banks in the 1980s failed to diversify and price risk properly. As a result, they both failed, although one, Continental Illinois, was bailed out. This chapter focuses on the diversification and *pricing of risk*. *Loan-pricing models* and analysis of *contagion effects* provide the theoretical foundations for this chapter. Three approaches are stressed: (1) default-risk premiums, (2) credit rationing, and (3) bank equity returns in capital markets. From a practical perspective, lenders who practice *variable-rate pricing* must consider the *interaction* between interest-rate risk and credit risk. The role of the *prime rate* and other banking conventions are discussed, and a *risk-management approach* to loan pricing is presented.

Key Concepts in Chapter 19

Adverse selection
Capital-market models and equity returns
Compensating balances
Contagion effects
Credit rationing
Customer relationship
Default risk and default-risk premium
Diversification
Pricing risk
Prime rate
Risk-management approach to loan pricing
Variable-rate pricing

Chapter 20. Management of Credit Risk III:
Lending Practice and Loan Administration

A bank's loan portfolio is the driving force behind its financial performance. Discipline and quality are the key factors here: discipline in the area of *loan growth* and quality in terms of borrower creditworthiness. These two factors tend to go hand-in-hand with poor loan quality, frequently following a period of excessive loan growth. In banking, *loan quality* is the key to the performance game. The concept of *delegated monitoring* is used to analyze the keys to successful management of the loan portfolio, with the emphasis on loan quality. Following a description of the various kinds of loans banks make, alternative measures of bank loan quality are presented and analyzed. The problems of incentives, discipline, monitoring, and concentrations of credit are addressed next. The special case of *leveraged buyouts* (LBOs) are examined as a possible successor to previous acronym-related lending problems in banking (e.g., REIT and LDC lending problems). *Loan pricing* and *terms of lending* for various loan categories are analyzed. Functional cost analysis (FCA) and customer profitability loan categories are analyzed. Functional cost analysis (FCA) and customer profitability analysis precede the presentation of the *loan policy* of a major southeastern bank.

Key Concepts in Chapter 20

Commercial and industrial (C&I) loans
Credit concentrations
Customer profitability analysis (CPA)
Delegated monitoring
Functional cost analysis (FCA)
"Hunters" versus "skinners"
Leveraged buyouts (LBOs)
Loan policy
Loan pricing
Loan quality (importance and measurement)
Repricing risk
Terms of lending

Chapter 21. Management of Off-Balance-Sheet Activities and Securitization

Two factors explain the surge in bank *off-balance-sheet activities* (OBSAs): (1) the squeeze on bank earnings and (2) market and regulatory demands for increased (and risk-based) capital. The ROE model ($ROE = ROA \times EM$) neatly captures these forces. With both ROA and EM being squeezed downward, banks have turned to OBSAs to generate *fees* to increase ROA without putting upward pressure on EM, where EM is the reciprocal of the equity-to-asset ratio. This chapter focuses on the management of OBSAs and the *process of securitization.* Following the documentation of OBSAs, including standby and commercial letters of credit, loan commitments, foreign-exchange transactions, and interest-rate swaps, the concentration of OBSAs in large banks is observed. Next, *securitization* (the selling of loans) is analyzed in terms of the separation of the traditional bank lending function into *origination* versus *funding* or *loan warehousing.* The chapter concludes with a look at OBSAs and securitization as *contingent-commitment banking.*

Key Concepts in Chapter 21

Contingent-commitment banking
Fee income
Foreign-exchange transactions
Interest-rate swaps
Letter of credit (standby versus commercial)
Loan commitment
Loan function (origination versus funding)
Off-balance-sheet activities (OBSAs)
Pass-through securities
Recourse
ROE model ($ROE = ROA \times EM$)
Securitization

PART SIX. BANK CAPITAL STRUCTURE, MARKET VALUATION, AND FINANCING ISSUES

Chapter 22. Bank Capital Structure: Theory and Regulation

Bank capital (or net worth) plays a critical role in the amount of *confidence* the public has in a financial institution. Such confidence is crucial to the safety and stability of the financial system. In addition to bank capital, confidence also is a function of the stability of the bank's earnings, the quality and costliness of information available about the bank, and the market value of government guarantees associated with the bank. This chapter focuses on the theory and regulation of bank capital. The issue of *capital adequacy* captures the essence of the chapter. *Risk considerations* and the importance of *interaction effects* are stressed in the analysis of this issue. The example of "Sallie Mae" (Look Ma, no risk!) is used to illustrate these points. The problem of *defining bank capital* and the many *veils of bank bookkeeping* (GAAP, RAP, and market values) are explored. The new *risk-based capital standards*, scheduled for 1992, are presented and analyzed, especially in terms of the expected squeeze on money-center banks. *Optimal bank capital* and the *value of the banking firm* are analyzed within the framework of deposit insurance. *Regulatory interference*, as a form of implicit pricing, plays a crucial role in the case of "free deposit insurance." The on-site *bank examination process* provides an important vehicle for the *implicit pricing* of deposit insurance. The chapter includes a comparison of risk-based capital and risk-based deposit insurance. The details of the new risk-based capital requirements are presented in the appendix to the chapter.

Key Concepts in Chapter 22

>   Bank examination process
>   Capital adequacy
>   Equity capital
>   GAAP versus RAP versus market values
>   Goodwill
>   Implicit pricing
>   Measurement of bank capital
>   Optimal bank capital
>   Perpetual preferred stock
>   Problem and failed banks
>   Regulatory interference
>   Risk-based capital requirements
>   Risk-based deposit insurance
>   Value of the banking firm

Chapter 23. Capital and Dividend Management

This chapter begins by looking at a "new rule" for the *market valuation* of bank stocks. Specifically, investment researchers at Goldman Sachs have found a strong linear relationship between bank *P/E ratios* and *ratios of equity capital to total assets*. The rule is said to be a new one because the relationship was not found until 1988. After the theoretical and empirical foundations of this relationship are explored, we turn to the importance of *internal capital generation* to banks. The internal capital generation rate, g, can be approximated by the product of a bank's ROE and its retention ratio (RR), that is, $g = ROE \times RR$. If a bank's managers want to grow at a rate faster than g *and* maintain their *capital adequacy*, they must find *external sources of capital. Access to capital markets* and bank *capital financing* are explored next, including a close look at holding company financial statements and the phenomenon of *double leverage*, defined as holding company debt downstreamed as bank equity. The chapter concludes with stock repurchases, and the importance of investment bankers to the process of bank capital planning.

Key Concepts in Chapter 23

Access to capital markets
Capital adequacy
Dividend-payout ratio
Double leverage
Equity capital ratio
External sources of bank capital
Goldman Sachs rule for valuing bank stocks
Internal capital generation rate ($g = ROE \times RR$)
Price-earnings or P/E ratio
Retention ratio (RR)
Return on equity (ROE)

PART SEVEN. SPECIAL BANKING TOPICS

Chapter 24. International Banking, the International Debt Crisis, and Opportunities for Financial Innovation

This chapter focuses on the third "-ization" to be covered in this book. With institutionalization and securitization out of the way, only globalization or internationalization remains. Advances in *technology* have made the transmission of either people or *information* across international boundaries an every-day occurrence. For U.S. money-center banks some of these transmissions have not been profitable ones, as witnessed by the *international debt crisis* of the 1980s. This chapter focuses on the development of international banking, the ensuing debt crisis, and the *opportunities for financial innovation* presented by the crisis. Technology, regulation, and the quest for value maximization have been the driving forces behind the expansion of U.S. banks into international banking. Of the more than 14,000 commercial banks in the United States, *international banking*, defined as engaging in activities that involve cross-border and cross-currency risks, is dominated by the dozen or so *money-center banks*. Nevertheless, in the rankings of the world's largest banks in the 1980s, U.S. banks have paled in relationship to the Japanese banks. Following a discussion of the *delivery systems* and *markets* of international banking, the international debt crisis is explored. The key concept for international risk management is *country risk*. The *floating-rate general obligation debt contract* has been the wrong instrument at the wrong time for less-developed countries (LDCs). *Innovative commercial financing*, such as *debt-equity swaps* and debt contracts linked to the ability of countries to service their debt, offers hope for the future for both the lenders and the borrowers in this crisis. These restructurings can be viewed as *positive-sum games* instead of zero-sum games. The chapter concludes with a look at country-risk management from a regulatory perspective. The appendix to the chapter focuses on some basic relationships among exchange rates, interest rates, and inflation.

Key Concepts in Chapter 24

> Bank capital exposure (to LDC debt)
> Constrained-optimization problem
> Country risk
> Delivery systems of international banking
> Eurocurrency market
> Floating-rate loan (LIBOR-linked versus oil- or commodity-linked)
> Foreign-exchange market
> General obligation financing
> Innovations in commercial financings for LDCs
> International banking
> Less developed countries (LDCs)
> Optimal financing mix (for LDCs)
> U.S. commercial banks with foreign offices

Chapter 25. Bank Mergers, Restructuring, and Corporate Control in the Financial-Services Industry

The laissez-faire approach to financial economics contends (and the evidence suggests) that *takeovers* are good for the economy because they guarantee that a firm's assets are *controlled* by managers who can use them most productively. This chapter focuses on the mergers, restructurings, and battles for corporate control taking place in banking, and within the FSI. The chapter begins with a review of the merger activity in banking preceding the stock market crash of October 19, 1987. The first nine months of 1987 saw *bank merger activity* proceed at a record pace. The once club-like atmosphere of banking has even been shaken by *hostile takeovers* in the 1980s (e.g., First Interstate's attempt to takeover BankAmerica and Bank of New York's bid for Irving Trust). A *cost-benefit framework* for analyzing bank mergers and acquisitions is presented. Following a discussion of alternative *valuation methods*, the existence and nature of bank *merger premiums* are analyzed, including a discussion of the difference between purchase and pooling-of-interest accounting. The chapter concludes with analyses of regional interstate banking, the merger of equals, and the process of planning for bank mergers and acquisitions.

Key Concepts in Chapter 25

> Core-deposit intangible
> Goodwill/going-concern value
> Hostile takeovers
> Intangible assets
> Interstate banking
> Investment bankers (M&A activity)
> Merger of equals
> Merger premium
> Mergers and acquisitions (M&A)
> Pooling-of-interest accounting
> Purchase accounting

PART EIGHT. EPILOGUE

Chapter 26. Overview and Summary of Commercial Bank Financial Management in the Financial-Services Industry

This chapter represents an attempt to put the book in perspective by bringing it all together in a compact setting. Since this chapter is intended as both an introductory overview and a summary, it should be read at the beginning *and* at the end of your course. The summaries and lists of key concepts for each chapter are intended to whet your appetite for knowledge in your overview reading, and to tie it all together in your summary reading.

Acronym Glossary and Index

ABA American Bankers Association. The major bank trade association in the United States with headquarters in Washington, D.C. [p. 33]

ACH Automated clearinghouse. An automated system used by banks for clearing checks drawn on each other. ACHs are very efficient at handling recurring transactions such as pre-authorized deposits or payments. [pp. 129–134]

ALCO Asset liability management committee. The bank committee that handles the task of asset-liability management, viewed by some analysts as the most important committee in a bank. [pp. 361–362]

ALM Asset-liability management. The coordinated management of a bank's assets and liabilities. Focus is on gap or duration position relative to unexpected changes in interest rates. Volatility of net interest income or net interest margin is a performance measure of ALM. [pp. 360–382]

ATC Average total cost. Defined as total cost divided by total output, this is the basic concept used to check for economies of scale. If ATC declines as output increases, economies of scale exist. [pp. 310–311]

ATM Automated teller machine. Device that enables customers to perform routine banking transactions without the aid of a human teller. Most popular EFT component. [pp. 135–139]

AU Asset utilization. Total income divided by total or average assets. Measures income per dollar of assets. Since $ROA = PM \times AU$, $AU = ROA/PM$. [pp. 268–270]

BHC Bank holding company. Any organization that owns one or more banks. The dominant organizational form in United States banking in terms of dollars of assets and deposits controlled. [pp. 181–197]

BOPEC The Fed's BHC rating system. B stands for bank subsidiaries, O for other or nonbank subsidiaries, P for the parent company, E for consolidated earnings, and C for consolidated capital. [pp. 195–197]

C&I Commercial and industrial loans. Bank business loans—for banks in nonrural areas, the major loan category. [pp. 539–541]

CAMEL Bank regulatory rating system. C stands for capital, A for asset quality, M for management, E for earnings, and L for liquidity. [pp. 196–197]

CAPM Capital asset pricing model. Model for pricing systematic risk. Beta measures a stock's volatility relative to the market portfolio which has a beta of 1. Aggressive stocks have betas greater than 1 and defensive stocks have betas less than 1. [pp. 62–63]

CARS Certificates for automobile receivables. Securitized credits based on automobile loans. [pp. 589–591]

CD Certificate of deposit. A bank deposit liability that comes in various forms. Wholesale, large, or jumbo CDs are the primary instrument of liability management (LM). These instruments have a minimum size of $100,000 and typically trade in blocks of $1 million. Retail or consumer CDs are characterized by longer maturities and smaller denominations, e.g., a three-year, $5,000 CD. [pp. 236–237, 420–421]

CEO Chief executive officer. Leading corporate officer. In strategic planning, the person responsible for the corporation's vision of where it is going and how it is going to get there. [pp. 330–331]

CPA Customer profitability analysis. Technique for measuring the profitability of a bank's corporate customers. [pp. 567–570]

CSBS Conference of State Bank Supervisors. Organization that coordinates the various state banking agencies. With both federal and state chartering and regulation of banks, the United States is said to have a dual banking system. [pp. 165–166]

DIDMCA Depository Institutions Deregulation and Monetary Control Act. A major deregulation *and* control act passed in 1980; among other things, it permitted NOW accounts but slapped reserve requirements on all depository institutions. [p. 171]

DINB Deposit Insurance National Bank. A device used by the FDIC (under Section 11 of the FDI Act) to take care of the emergency banking needs of communities by organizing (chartering) and operating (for up to two years) a limited-service facility known as a DINB. [pp. 201–202]

DSU Deficit spending unit. In either direct or indirect finance, the unit that needs funds and therefore borrows. [pp. 33–35, 72–78]

EFT Electronic funds transfer. Modern method for transferring funds that is based not on paper devices, but on electronic impulses or images. [pp. 126–129]

EFTS Electronic funds transfer system. Systems for transferring funds automatically through electronic devices such as ATMs, ACHs, and POSs. [pp. 129–146]

EM Equity multiplier. The ratio of total assets to total equity. Since $ROE = ROA \times EM$, $EM = ROE/ROA = ROE/[PM \times AU]$. [pp. 266–271]

EPS Earnings per share. Net income divided by number of shares outstanding. An accounting measure of performance. Looks at value or stock price as the product of P/E ratio and EPS. [p. 46]

EVA Economic value added. Measures economic value as the return on capital minus the cost of capital times average total capital. $EVA = [r - k]K$. [pp. 51–52]

FCA Functional cost analysis. Method for analyzing the functional costs of banks based on survey data collected by the Fed. [pp. 320–321]

FDIC Federal Deposit Insurance Corporation. Federal agency that insures deposits in commerical and savings banks and supervises commercial banks that are not members of the Federal Reserve System (called insured nonmember banks) and savings banks. [pp. 162–163, 199–208]

FED Federal Reserve System. The central bank in the United States and the chief regulator of bank holding companies (BHCs) and state member banks. [pp. 164–165]

FHLBB Federal Home Loan Bank Board. Federal regulator of savings and loan associations and parent of the FSLIC. [p. 162]

Five Cs or 5 Cs Character, Capacity, Collateral, Capital, and Conditions. Framework for analyzing the creditworthiness of a borrower. Character captures the willingness to repay whereas capacity, collateral, and capital focus on the financial ability to repay. The conditions factor focuses on the effects of external events and the borrowers vulnerability to such shocks (e.g., energy, farm, and real estate recessions). [pp. 495–496]

FSF Financial-services firm. A firm that provides financial services. Generic term for the basic business unit in the financial-services industry. [pp. 4, 16–17]

FSI Financial-services industry. Generic term to capture the fusion of once segmented industries such as commerical banking, investment banking, insurance, and real estate. [pp. 3–18, 95–117]

FSLIC Federal Savings and Loan Insurance Corporation. Federal agency that insures deposits in savings and loan associations (S&Ls). As of this writing, it is bankrupt and may have to be merged with the FDIC. [pp. 162, 199]

g the internal capital generation rate. The rate at which a firm can grow through internal capital generation and not require external capital to preserve its capital structure. The rate, g, can be approximated by the product of the firm's return on equity (ROE) and its retention ratio (RR). [pp. 29, 285]

GAP Dollar or ratio measure of the relationship between rate-sensitive assets (RSA) and rate-sensitive liabilities (RSL) calculated over a particular maturity or duration horizon. A measure of interest-rate sensitivity for depository institutions. *Dollar GAP = RSA − RSL* and *gap ratio = RSA/RSL.* [pp. 369–372, 375–379]

IO Industrial organization, as in "IO model." A model of industrial organization described by a structure–conduct–performance linkage. Popular with Fed economists. [pp. 154–155]

IO Interest only. A derivative or stripped debt instrument in which the investor receives interest payments only. The other part of this type of security is the PO or principal only. [pp. 227–228]

IOS Investment opportunity set. Conceptual device to reflect the investment opportunities available to a firm or industry. In the financial-services industry, the heavily regulated players such as banks and thrifts faced more restricted IOSs relative to the less regulated players. [pp. 75–77]

LBO Leveraged buyout. A transaction in which a group of investors uses leverage (debt) to buy out the existing owners of a company. LBOs are a form of activity under the general heading of "corporate restructuring." [pp. 550–553]

LDC Less-developed countries. Countries that have not reached economic and financial maturity. Important to large banks/BHCs because of the billions of dollars lent to these countries. These loans today are valued at less than their book values. Although the "MBA" countries of Mexico, Brazil, and Argentina are examples of LDCs, LDCs are not restricted to South America. [pp. 671–672, 683–691]

LIBOR London Interbank Offer Rate. International money-market rate at which multinational banks lend large blocks of Eurodollars to each other. [pp. 679–680]

LLD Large-liability dependence. A measure of the extent to which a bank depends on "hot money" or large liabilities to fund its balance sheet. This is meaningful only for larger institutions since smaller ones have few large liabilities. [p. 430]

LM Liability management. The process by which bankers attempt to develop nontraditional borrowing arrangements and to use them profitably, especially to meet loan demand. LM-1 is reserve position management and focuses on temporary changes in the composition of the balance sheet, whereas LM-2 is a generalized or loan-position strategy designed to expand the balance sheet. [pp. 421–429]

MBHC Multibank holding company. An organization that owns two or more banks. [pp. 183–189]

M&M Modigliani and Miller. The "candy boys" are famous finance theorists noted for, among other things, their contribution to understanding the capital structure of the firm. Buser, Chen, and Kane have applied their approach to the insured banking firm and in the process generated insights about optimal bank capital and deposit insurance. [pp. 79–80, 617–622]

NBSS National Bank Surveillance System. The surveillance system used by the Office of the Comptroller of the Currency (OCC) to monitor national banks. [pp. 152, 167]

NII Net interest income. The difference between interest income and interest expense. The "spread" that must cover a bank's loan losses, "burden," securities losses, taxes, dividends, and its internal capital generation. [pp. 29, 277, 365–369]

NIM Net interest margin. Net interest income divided by earning assets, the focal variable of asset-liability management. [pp. 29, 277, 365–369]

NPV Net present value. The difference between a project's present value of future cash flows and its cost. To maximize the value of the firm, managers should accept only positive NPV projects. [pp. 57–59, 75–78]

OBHC One-bank holding company. An organization that owns only one bank. [pp. 184–191]

OBSA Off-balance sheet activity. A product or service that does not appear on a bank's balance sheet but generates a contingent claim on it. Examples include loan commitments, letters of credit, and interest-rate swaps. [pp. 577–596]

OCC Office of the Comptroller of the Currency. This is the Federal charterer and regulator of national banks. A national bank must join the Federal Reserve System and therefore must be insured by the FDIC. [pp. 30–31]

P/E Price-earnings ratio. Ratio of market price to earnings per share or EPS. Benchmark measure of the relative value of a firm's earnings in the marketplace. [pp. 645–649]

PET Pure-expectations theory. Theory of the term structure of interest rates based solely on expectations of future short-term rates. Serves as the foundation for most of the other theories of the term structure. [pp. 245–247]

PM Profit margin. Ratio of net income to total income. Since $ROA = PM \times AU$, $PM = ROA/AU$. [pp. 268–273]

PO Principal only. A derivative or stripped security in which the investor buys only the principal portion of the debt instrument. See also IO. [pp. 226–227]

POS Point of sale. A point-of-sale system is an EFT device used to automatically transfer funds between a customer's account and a merchant's account. Designed to be used with a "debit card." [pp. 139–141]

RAC Ray average cost. Concept used to capture the notion of average cost for a multiproduct firm such as a bank. [pp. 312–313]

REIT Real estate investment trust. An organization that channels funds into real estate and real estate-related activities, especially construction. In the mid-1970s large banks/BHCs encountered financial difficulties because of loans made to REITs and because of their association as advisors to REITs. [p. 550]

ROA Return on assets. Defined as net income divided by total or average assets. Measures profitability per dollar of assets and is considered one of the best (accounting) measures of overall firm performance. Since $ROE = ROA \times EM$, $ROA = ROE/EM$. [pp. 266–270]

ROE Return on equity. Defined as net income divided by total or average equity. Measures profitability from the shareholder's point of view. Can be decomposed into a performance measure and a leverage factor, that is, $ROE = ROA \times EM$. [pp. 266–273]

RP Repo/Repurchase agreement. A security/asset sold under agreement to repurchase. Repos and purchases of federal funds are the major instruments of short-term liability management. [pp. 427–428]

RR Retention ratio. The fraction of EPS allocated to retained earnings. Equals 1 minus the payout ratio or DPS/EPS. Since $g = ROE \times RR$, $RR = g/ROE$. [pp. 650–652]

RSA Rate-sensitive asset. An asset that reprices within some designated time period such as one, two, or three months, as opposed to a fixed-rate asset. Contrast a variable-rate commercial loan tied to the prime rate with a fixed-rate mortgage. The commercial loan reprices any time the prime rate changes, whereas the mortgage reprices only if it is sold, refinanced, or matures. [pp. 369–370]

RSL Rate-sensitive liability. A liability that reprices within some designated time period. Short-term or variable-rate liabilities are rate sensitive debt instruments whereas fixed-rate notes, debentures, and bonds are less sensitive. [pp. 369–370]

S&L Savings and loan association (also abbreviated as SLA). Depository institution with a penchant to borrow short and lend long. These "thrift institutions" are insured by the FSLIC. [pp. 108–110]

SEC Securities and Exchange Commission. Federal agency designated to protect the interest of shareholders. Over the past decade SEC-mandated disclosure requirements have made bank financial statements more open and less of a mystery. [pp. 60–62, 155–156]

SLC Standby letter of credit. A guarantee arrangement in which a bank provides credit only if its customer defaults; the bank is "standing by" or "waiting in the wings" contingent upon the default. SLCs are off-balance sheet activities that generate contingent claims on banks. [pp. 579, 582–585]

SSU Surplus-spending unit. Economic units that provide funds, either directly or indirectly, to deficit-spending ones. [pp. 32–35, 72–78]

SWOT Strengths, Weaknesses, Opportunities, and Threats. SWOT analysis is an important part of the process of strategic planning. [pp. 233–239]

TE Tax-equivalent. Process of converting tax-free rates or data for comparison with taxable rates or data, as in NIM(TE) or tax-equivalent net interest margin. The adjustment is made by dividing the tax-free figure by $[1 - t]$, where t is the marginal tax rate. For example, given a tax-free rate of 8% and a tax rate of .25, the tax-equivalent yield is $.08/[1 - .25] = .08/.75 = .1067 = 10.67\%$. [pp. 453–454]

TRICK Technology, Reregulation, Interest-rate risk, Customers, and Kapital adequacy. The driving forces of change in the financial-services industry. TRICK plus rational self-interest leads to financial innovation. [pp. 7–11, 334–338]

Author Index

Burns, A. F., 178
Buser, Stephen A., 69, 85, 92, 93, 163, 178, 220, 223, 439, 489, 512, 619–62
Buynak, Thomas M., 327
Byars, Lloyd, 356

Campbell, Tim S., 85, 86, 92
Caproni, Albert, III, 327
Carrington, Tim, 306
Cates, David C., 375, 387, 662, 666
Chan, Yuk-Shee, 24, 42, 86, 92
Chance, Don, 387
Chase, Samuel B., Jr., 222
Chault, Robert, 725
Chen, Andrew H., 69, 85, 92, 163, 178, 220, 223, 439, 489, 512, 620, 642
Chessen, James, 402, 578, 583–584, 599
Chesser, Delton L., 505–506, 512
Chew, Donald H., Jr., 46, 263, 306
Christophe, Cleveland A., 109, 119
Citrone, Robert K., 699
Clark, Lindley H., Jr., 534
Cloonen, F. Blake, 575
Cocheo, Steve, 356
Cohen, Allen M., 128, 149
Cohen, Kalman J., 84, 92, 387
Coldwell, Philip E., 191, 195, 222
Cole, David W., 267, 306
Cole, Robert H., 575
Coleman, Alan, 232
Collins, Mitchell C., 86, 92
Compton, Eric N., 149
Conover, C. T., 30, 179
Cook, Timothy A., 119
Copeland, Thomas, 725
Cordell, David M., 387
Corrigan, E. Gerald, 3–5, 14, 20, 129, 149, 491, 512
Cramer, Robert H., 258, 459
Crane, Dwight B., 459, 698
Cranmer, Charles 644, 666
Cravens, David, 357
Crosse, Howard, 439
Culbertson, John M., 258
Cunningham, Scott, 340–342, 357

Daly, George G., 84, 92
Danker, Deborah J., 273, 275–276, 290–296, 306, 642, 652, 666
Darnell, Jerome C., 710, 725
Davis, K. T., 699
Debussey, Fred, 222
Dentzer, Susan, 114, 119
Devinney, Timothy M., 85, 92
Diamond, Douglas W., 85, 88, 92, 489, 512

Diller, Stanley, 439
Dince, R. R., 156, 179, 180, 661
Dingler, Melinda, 356
Dobrzynski, Judith H., 701, 725
Dod, David P., 698
Donaldson, T. H., 698
Drucker, Peter F., 330, 357
Dufey, Gunter, 698
Dunahee, Michael H., 345–346, 357
Durand, David, 505, 507, 512
Dybvig, Phillip H., 85, 92
Dyl, Edward A., 666

Eastwood, Clint, 360
Edgeworth, Francis Y., 84, 92
Edwards, Franklin R., 53, 69, 82, 84, 92, 149
Egginton, Don A., 714, 725
Ehlen, James G., Jr., 642
Eisemann, Peter C., 222
Eisenbeis, Robert A., 184, 222, 306, 494, 503, 505, 512, 626, 641, 725
Elliot, John C., 137, 149
Epperson, James F., 258
Fabozzi, Frank J., 486
Fama, Eugene F., 72, 78, 85, 92, 488, 512
Fannin, William, 357
Fellows, James A., 92
Fischer, Gerald C., 222, 524, 534, 575
Fisher, Irving, 70, 72, 92, 122, 141, 237–238
Fisher, Jack Clark, 258
Fisher, John, 150
Fisk, Charles, 698
Flannery, Mark J., 70, 387, 400, 516, 518, 534
Flax, Steven, 357
Ford, William F., 115, 119, 280, 306
Fox, Lawrence E., 552, 575
Francis, Darryl R., 222, 231
Francis, Jack Clark, 387
Frank, Allan Dodds, 179
Frankenstein, Doctor, and Igor, 206
Frieder, Larry A., 357
Friedman, Milton, 154, 206, 439
Frydman, Halina, 500–501, 512

Galai, Dan, 213, 224
Galbraith, J. K., 206
Garbade, Kenneth D., 258, 459
Garino, David P., 439, 725
Garlow, David, 678
Gart, Alan, 150
Gibson, W. E., 179
Giddy, Ian H., 698
Gigot, Paul A., 115, 119, 299, 306

Subject Index